Microsoft

SQL Server 2022
Administration Inside Out

Randolph West
William Assaf
Elizabeth Noble
Meagan Longoria
Joey D'Antoni
Louis Davidson

With contributions from:
William Carter
Josh Smith
Melody Zacharias

SQL Server 2022 Administration Inside Out
Published with the authorization of Microsoft Corporation by: Pearson Education, Inc.
Copyright © 2023 by Pearson Education.

ISBN-13: 978-0-13-789988-3
ISBN-10: 0-13-789988-2

Library of Congress Control Number: 2023930547

1 2023

Trademarks

Warning and Disclaimer

Special Sales

Editor-in-Chief: Brett Bartow
Executive Editor: Loretta Yates
Associate Editor: Charvi Arora
Development Editor: Kate Shoup
Technical Reviewers: William Carter, Louis Davidson, Meagan Longoria, Elizabeth Noble, Josh Smith
Managing Editor: Sandra Schroeder
Senior Project Editor: Tracey Croom
Copy Editor: Rebecca Rider
Indexer: Rachel Kuhn
Proofreaders: Audrey Doyle, James Fraleigh
Editorial Assistant : Cindy Teeters
Cover Designer: Twist Creative, Seattle
Compositor : Jeff Lytle, Happenstance Type-O-Rama
Graphics: Jeff Wilson, Happenstance Type-O-Rama

Pearson's Commitment to Diversity, Equity, and Inclusion

Pearson is dedicated to creating bias-free content that reflects the diversity of all learners. We embrace the many dimensions of diversity, including but not limited to race, ethnicity, gender, socioeconomic status, ability, age, sexual orientation, and religious or political beliefs.

Education is a powerful force for equity and change in our world. It has the potential to deliver opportunities that improve lives and enable economic mobility. As we work with authors to create content for every product and service, we acknowledge our responsibility to demonstrate inclusivity and incorporate diverse scholarship so that everyone can achieve their potential through learning. As the world's leading learning company, we have a duty to help drive change and live up to our purpose to help more people create a better life for themselves and to create a better world.

Our ambition is to purposefully contribute to a world where:

- Everyone has an equitable and lifelong opportunity to succeed through learning.

- Our educational products and services are inclusive and represent the rich diversity of learners.

- Our educational content accurately reflects the histories and experiences of the learners we serve.

- Our educational content prompts deeper discussions with learners and motivates them to expand their own learning (and worldview).

While we work hard to present unbiased content, we want to hear from you about any concerns or needs with this Pearson product so that we can investigate and address them.

- Please contact us with concerns about any potential bias at *https://www.pearson.com /report-bias.html*.

Dedications

To Marinus (as always), to the friends we've lost along the way, and to the friends we make by saying "yes" to new opportunities.

—Randolph West

The previous book in this series was published in March 2020, at the advent of a historic disruption: social, political, economic, and educational. I dedicate this book to all those who have been made unsafe and further marginalized by the COVID-19 pandemic.

—William Assaf

To Mind, Danny, Eve, Mom, and Dad, for your encouragement and support.

—Elizabeth Noble

I dedicate this book to my dad, who passed away in 2022. He was always supportive of my educational and professional goals.

—Meagan Longoria

I would like to thank my other authors and my family for helping this work go so smoothly.

—Joey D'Antoni

To all my friends at CBN who provided me with training, inspiration, practice, and until recently, servers to test code on for so many years.

—Louis Davidson

To all those who need someone to believe in them. Know that there are two, Me and You, because as Henry Ford said, "Whether you think you can or you can't, you're right!"

—Melody Zacharias

In memory of Ruby Jean Carter. You were the embodiment of love, patience, and strength.

—William Carter

For data professionals everywhere always looking to learn and grow.

—Josh Smith

Contents at a glance

Table of Contents

Part I: Introduction

Part III: SQL Server management

Chapter 11   Implement high availability and disaster recovery 487

Part V: Performance

About the Authors

Randolph West *(they/them)* lives in Calgary, Alberta, Canada, with a husband and two dogs. After being a consultant for millennia, Randolph now writes full-time at Microsoft Docs, still yelling at the screen. Occasional voice actor. Occasional blogger at *bornsql.ca*. Not to be trusted around chocolate. Yes, this is a short bio.

William Assaf *(he/him)* is a senior content developer for Microsoft, writing Learn content for SQL Server, Azure SQL Database, Azure Synapse Analytics, and more. A long-time Baton Rougean, William and his adventure buddy Christine moved to Seattle during the pandemic. They love their new home but are still New Orleans Saints fans. Before joining Microsoft, William was a Data Platform MVP, SQL Saturday and SQL community organizer, and a long-time DBA and data consultant. As a consultant for 13 years, he worked with clients across the U.S. on SQL Server and Azure SQL platform optimization, management, data integration, disaster recovery, and high availability, and led a multi-city team of senior consulting SQL DBAs. William has written for Microsoft SQL certification exams since 2011 and was the team lead author of the 2017 and 2019 editions of *SQL Server Administration Inside Out* by Microsoft Press.

Elizabeth Noble is a Director of Database Development, the author of *Pro T-SQL 2019*, and a Microsoft Data Platform MVP. Ze has spoken at several SQL Saturdays across the United States and at PASS Summit. Most of zir topics focus on DevOps, collaboration with other IT departments, and automated database deployments. Zir passion is to help others improve the quality and speed of deploying database changes through automation. When ze is not trying to automate all things, ze can be found spending time with zir dogs, playing disc golf, or paddleboarding (if the weather is right).

Meagan Longoria is a Microsoft Data Platform MVP living in Denver, Colorado. She is an experienced consultant and trainer who has worked with the Microsoft Data Platform for over 15 years. She enjoys creating solutions in Azure, SQL Server, and Power BI that make data useful for decision makers and make the lives of information workers a little bit easier. Meagan enjoys sharing her knowledge with the technical community by speaking at conferences, blogging (*DataSavvy.me*), and sharing tips and helpful links on Twitter (*@mmarie*).

Joseph D'Antoni is a Principal Consultant at Denny Cherry & Associates Consulting. He is recognized as a VMWare vExpert and a Microsoft Data Platform MVP, and has over 20 years of experience working in both Fortune 500 and smaller firms. He has worked extensively on database platforms and cloud technologies and has specific expertise in performance tuning, infrastructure, and disaster recovery.

Louis Davidson has over 20 years as a data architect and technical writer. Recently he joined Redgate as the editor of the Simple Talk website after 20-plus years working for a nonprofit, where he was the lead SQL Server architect and programmer. Louis has been the principal author on many technical books about SQL Server, including six editions of a book on database design. Louis' blog, located at *simple-talk.com* for many years, provides information about technical issues and upcoming presentations, including previewing the thought process that goes into writing presentations, books, and blogs.

Melody Zacharias is a Microsoft MVP for the data platform and Microsoft Regional Director. She has co-written several books on data, including *SQL Server 2019 Administration Inside Out* by Microsoft Press. She speaks at conferences on data, technology, women in Tech, professional development, and more. You can find her on her blog at *sqlmelody.com*, on Twitter *@SQLMelody*, and as */melodyzacharias* on LinkedIn.

William F. Carter *(he/him)* is a technologist and Microsoft SQL Server consultant with 25 years of experience dating back to SQL Server 6.5. Bill is passionate about helping individuals and organizations use technology and data to drive change and bring about successful outcomes. When not managing data and architecting solutions, he loves to model and 3D print props for the local high school's theater department. You can connect with him on LinkedIn at *www.linkedin.com/in/william-f-carter/*.

Josh Smith has held several titles over the last 20 years, including Stage Manager, Art Director, Teacher, Case Manager, and—for the last 10 years—Database Administrator. They currently infrequently write at *accitentionaldba.com* and post more often but with much less focus on Twitter as *@sqldeployhelmet*. They are team pineapple on pizza, have a completely reasonable fear of spiders, and are the current president of the Inland Northwest Data Professionals Association in Spokane, Washington.

Acknowledgments

Randolph West

It may take a village to raise a child, but it takes a small country to write a book. Five books in, and I still don't understand how it comes together at the end. Thank you to Loretta and Charvi at Microsoft Press, and to William Assaf, for long and thoughtful conversations. My co-authors and technical editors, obviously. To Marinus, thank you for begrudgingly letting me do another book even though I still don't sit at the desk you bought me. Thanks to Trixie for the slower walks, our new puppy Tilley for keeping me on my toes, and Apple for making a quiet laptop.

A lot of us wouldn't be here without the tireless efforts of medical professionals during the global pandemic. Join me in thanking your healthcare friends when you get a chance. Thank your teachers. Thank your first responders. Thank the people who keep the lights on and the water flowing. Hug a queer person.

I would like to extend a special acknowledgment to Melody Zacharias, who has been a major contributor to the Microsoft Data Platform community for a number of years. Melody selflessly introduced me to the community in Canada and even included me as one of the authors in her *Let Them Finish* book. She has helped so many people in our community and also deserves a special mention in the production of this book.

William Assaf

Becoming an empty nester has allowed me to spend more time than ever with my best friend and adventure buddy. Thanks, Christine, for tolerating endless nights of writing, rewriting, and editing this book instead of hiking, exploring, or snuggling.

I'd like to thank Loretta Yates, our intrepid and tactful editor throughout our Microsoft Press experience. I'd also like to thank the mentors and managers and colleagues in my professional career heretofore, who affected my trajectory, and to whom I remain grateful for technical and nontechnical lessons learned. I'd like to thank Connie Murla, David Alexander, Darren Schumaker, Ashagre Bishaw, Charles Sanders, Todd Howard, Chris Kimmel, Richard Caronna, Mike Huguet, Mike Carter, Jason Prell, James Sampson, Jason Roth, and finally Patrick Leblanc, a fellow Baton Rouge native, whose friendship has repeatedly challenged me and furthered my career. I'd also like to thank my father, a rare stamped mechanical and electrical engineer (and a HAM), and both my older brothers who are brilliant software engineers, for letting me play games on their 386s all summer long. I'd finally like to thank the STEM educators, nonprofit volunteers, and organizers in my hometown of Baton Rouge, Louisiana. They are doing the hard work of developing our future coworkers and coauthors among my home state's perpetually underfunded, underappreciated, and underestimated public school youth.

Elizabeth Noble

I would like to thank Randolph West and William Assaf for inviting me to collaborate on this book. I also want to thank the entire team that made this book possible. You all were kind, supportive, and encouraging. I'd also like to thank my many mentors (mostly unofficial) including Phil Pledger, Mike Lawell, Ed Watson, and Rob Volk. You each have provided encouragement and guidance over the years. Rie Merritt, thank you for welcoming me to my second user group meeting. If it weren't for you, I would not have come back to my third meeting or have met this wonderful community. I want to thank my family for giving me the time and space to work on this book. To Mom, thank you for being my cheerleader. To Dad, thank you for nudging me every so often to see how the book was going. Also, in memory of Khari, my forever companion, thank you for making sure that I remembered to take care of myself.

Meagan Longoria

First, I'd like to thank the co-authors and co-editors who collaborated on this book. It was a pleasure to work with them and learn from them. I would also like to thank my coworkers at Denny Cherry & Associates Consulting for their technical advice and support. I also want to acknowledge my laptop bag for safely carrying my computer through many states and a couple of countries while I worked on this book. I think everyone should consider a nice laptop bag. Finally, I'd like to thank my dog Izzy for being understanding when dinner was a little late due to writing or editing, and for reminding me to take breaks to go on walks. Life is better with a dog.

Joey D'Antoni

I would like to thank my wife Kelly, and my coworkers at Denny Cherry & Associates Consulting, for helping me and giving me time to work on this project. Also, thanks to the team at Microsoft for answering dumb questions when I had them.

Louis Davidson

I would like to acknowledge the rest of the team on this book for their wonderful work that makes tech editing the chapters I worked on some of the easiest technical book work I have ever participated in.

Melody Zacharias

I really want to thank William Assaf and Randolph West for their push/encouragement to do another book with them. It is always a pleasure to work with some of the best professionals in the industry. There have been a few who are special in the community who made this possible: Argenis Fernandez who introduced me to #SQLFamily, John Morehouse who mentored and encouraged me to do my first presentation, Dave Kawula for encouraging me to write my first book, and Rie Merritt for keeping me going and inspired to inspire others year after year. I would not be doing this if not for your encouragement. Thank you all for each experience that changed my life for the better. No family is perfect, but my #SQLFamily is an amazingly supportive and inclusive family, and I am so proud to be a member. Thank you to Marsha Pierce and Rob Ludeman, for bringing me into the Pure Family, and for letting me share my crazy obsession with SQL Server with Pure. Most of all, thank you to my family for understanding when I go back into my office after dinner and on weekends to work on this book and all the presentations and other community work I do. Thank you for accepting me as I am.

William Carter

I want to thank my children, Kadence and Kayla, for inspiring me to continue to grow and embrace change. I'd like to thank my mom and dad and my personal village of family, friends, and teachers who instilled in me the passion and perseverance to pursue my dreams. Finally, I want to thank Joel Whittington, Fred Seals, and William Assaf, three of my mentors who I respect and admire a great deal. Each of you directly impacted my professional and personal growth, sharing your wisdom and humor along the way.

Josh Smith

I'd like to thank those in the SQL Server community who have taken the time to provide me with opportunities to learn and grow in my career, including the authors of this book for taking a chance and inviting me to join the other technical editors. I am eternally grateful for the patience of my family throughout the last 10 years, but over this past summer in particular, as we've attempted to do ALL THE THINGS at the same time. Sara, hopefully by the time I am showing you this in print, we've finished unpacking.

Foreword

The world of data is getting more complicated. As threats and technologies evolve, businesses may fall behind.

As a consultant before joining Microsoft, I walked into an industrial plant where the sysadmins did not know what SQL Server backup was. To them, a file system backup or virtual machine (VM) storage snapshot was enough. (It is not enough.) I worked with a small regional bank that thought a 3 TB+ SQL Server transaction log file was just the cost of doing business. I helped a healthcare broker that was being actively probed via SQL injection attacks. In each case, the seeds of business-crippling disaster were planted, waiting to sprout.

As a reader of this book, you likely know the basics of what is necessary to secure your data platform from disaster, whether it is malicious actors or natural disaster. (If not, we have you covered there too.)

As the latest team brought together to write this *Microsoft SQL Server Administration Inside Out* series book, we have always tried to present to you a complete, practical, field-tested picture of administration tasks, including wisdom and tips collected from our own experience as administrators and architects. Just as the authors of this book have brought a collective effort to guide and advise, it has never been more important to organize collective effort across the entire IT department.

In terms of the basics of cybersecurity, Microsoft's own Digital Defense Report makes it clear. The primary protections companies can take are to "patch systems regularly and keep software up to date, and to use MFA" (Microsoft Digital Defense Report, October 2021, *https://go.microsoft.com /fwlink/p/?LinkID=2173952*).

Patching is just the basics. What else?

- Led by Microsoft's Zero Trust model, enable the use of integrated, multifactor, password-less authentication wherever possible, including to our SQL Server instances and Azure SQL platforms.

- Use multifactor authentication (MFA) everywhere possible, including for access to your Active Directory–authenticated resources on desktops, mobile devices, and collaboration applications.

- Immediately replicate database backups to offsite, heterogenous systems to protect them from ransomware encryption attacks.

- Separate day-to-day accounts from administrative accounts to ensure that commonly entered user credentials don't have all the keys to the kingdom.

- Protect from software supply-chain attacks by using secure admin workstations (SAWs) and privileged administrative workstations (PAWs). (See "Protecting high-risk environments with secure admin workstations," May 2018, at *https://www.microsoft.com/insidetrack /protecting-high-risk-environments-with-secure-admin-workstations*.)

- Secure network connections by default, and in this new era of widespread fully remote work, consider the security of VPN and virtualized networking software and hardware. Microsoft's Zero Trust model has led the company to move away internally from a ubiquitous, always-connected global VPN to mitigate the impact of a single compromised device.

- "Antimalware and detection and response technologies should be deployed across the ecosystem [...] from virtual machines and containers to machine learning (ML) algorithms, databases, and applications." (Microsoft Digital Defense Report, October 2021.)

As data platform professionals, we need modern tools and skills to secure data from attack and recover data in case attacks are successful. Disaster recovery checklists around the world are not only being triggered by annual "100-year" flood events, but by cybercrime and malicious activity, such as ransomware attacks. The landscape of digital security affects the entire enterprise, and your database platform is the crown jewel for attackers.

When it comes to your Microsoft data platform, in the cloud, on-premises, hybrid, as a service, or otherwise, we want to provide you with the tools to administer with confidence. Chapter 10, "Develop, deploy, and manage data recovery," dives deep into a disaster recovery scenario and the runbook every SQL Server administrator should have ready. New features of Microsoft SQL Server 2022 make it easier than ever to span a durable, secured data infrastructure across hybrid environments, including a new feature to sync bidirectionally between on-premises SQL Server instances and Azure SQL managed instances (see Chapter 18, "Provision Azure SQL Managed Instance"). Not only is what used to be a one-way ticket into Azure SQL Managed Instance now reversible, but failover and failback from SQL Server 2022 to Azure SQL Managed Instance is now possible.

In addition to covering all the new features coming with SQL Server 2022, this book contains more than four years of new features that roll out to Azure SQL platforms outside of the year-numbered SQL Server product. We'll be sure to point out the new capabilities of Azure SQL Managed Instance, for example, that have arrived in the November 2022 feature wave in conjunction with SQL Server 2022. Many new features simplify our job of securing the data estate, such as the introduction of Windows Authentication to Azure SQL Managed Instance using Azure Active Directory and Kerberos, an important feature that arrived in August 2022.

Like Azure's infrastructure approach, the authors of this book aim to make it easier for businesses to protect their technology platform and avoid preventable disasters. We want to make it *less likely* that you will leave your data estate vulnerable due to ignorance. We draw from 100+ years of combined experience across this author team, which consists of Microsoft employees, Data Platform MVPs, consultants, entrepreneurs, leaders, on-call DBAs, data architects, and day-to-day SQL Server administrators. We want to inform you of low-hanging fruit to be picked, and of practical, easy wins. We hope this approach gives you—and your data—more confidence and reassurance.

—William Assaf, Database Docs, Microsoft

Introduction

Who this book is for

Data platform administration was never the narrow niche skillset that employers or recruiters might have suspected. The job description continues to broaden, with support for new operating systems and platforms: cloud-based and serverless in addition to on-premises, hybrid environments, even on-premises to cloud failover. We wrote this book for data professionals who are unafraid to add these new skillsets and features to their utility belt, and to give courage and confidence to those who are still hesitant. Data platform administrators should read this book to become more prepared and so they are aware of features when talking to their colleagues in application development, data analytics, and system administration.

How this book is organized

This book gives you a comprehensive look at the various features you will use. It is structured in a logical approach to all aspects of Microsoft SQL Server and Azure SQL administration, whether you are architecting, implementing, developing, or supporting development.

Part I: Introduction

Chapter 1, "Get started with SQL Server tools," gives you a tour of modern tooling for SQL Server administrators, from the installation media and all tooling, including SQL Server Management Studio and Azure Data Studio, to performance and reliability monitoring tools, tools for writing PowerShell, and more.

Chapter 2, "Introduction to database server components," introduces the working vocabulary and concepts of database administration, starting with hardware-level topics such as memory, processors, storage, and networking. We then move into high availability basics (much more on those later), security, and hardware and OS virtualization.

Chapter 3, "Design and implement an on-premises database infrastructure," introduces the architecture and configuration of SQL Server, including deep dives into transaction log virtual log files (VLFs), data files, in-memory online transaction processing (OLTP), accelerated database recovery (ADR), and other new features of SQL Server 2022. We also spend time with tempdb and its optimal configuration and server-level configuration options. Finally, we introduce you to Kubernetes.

Part II: Deployment

Chapter 4, "Install and configure SQL Server instances and features," reviews installation of SQL Server for Windows platforms when SQL Server Setup is needed to install SQL Server. We discuss volume settings and layout for a SQL Server instance, editions, Smart Setup and unattended setup configuration, and setup logging. Look here also for post-installation check-lists and configuration guidance, and for configuration and guidance for other features including SSIS, SSAS, and SSRS, as well as PolyBase.

Chapter 5, "Install and configure SQL Server on Linux," reviews configuration of SQL Server on Linux instances, including feature differences between Windows and Linux. We'll provide guidance and caveats on Linux distributions, Linux-specific monitoring and storage considerations, and tooling for setup and administration.

Chapter 6, "Provision and configure SQL Server databases," reviews creation and configuration of SQL Server databases on any SQL Server platform, including strategies for migrating and moving databases. Database options and properties are discussed, as are database collations.

Chapter 7, "Understand table features," completes the drill down from instances to databases to tables, covering table design, data types, keys, and constraints. The use of IDENTITY and sequences, computed columns and other column properties, as well as special table types, are discussed. We review special types of tables including temporal tables, introduce memory-optimized tables (more on these in Chapter 14), and graph tables. We review FILESTREAM and FileTable for storing blobs, table partitioning for storing and switching large amounts of data, and strategies for tracking data changes. Finally, we dive deep into PolyBase, the powerful SQL Server feature for virtualization of third-party or non-relational data sources.

Part III: SQL Server management

Chapter 8, "Maintain and monitor SQL Server," covers the care and feeding of SQL Server instances on both Windows and Linux, including monitoring for database corruption, monitoring index activity and fragmentation, and maintaining and monitoring indexes and index statistics. We dive into Extended Events, the superior alternative to traces, and cover Resource Governor, used for insulating your critical workloads. We review monitoring and data collection strategies based in Windows, Linux, and Azure, as well as the SQL Assessment API. Finally, we discuss the current Microsoft servicing model for SQL Server.

Chapter 9, "Automate SQL Server administration," introduces automating activities for SQL Server, including maintenance plans, but also custom solutions involving PowerShell, including the latest features available in PowerShell. We also review built-in tools and features needed to automate tasks to your SQL Server, including database mail, SQL Server Agent jobs, proxies, SQL Server Agent alerts, event forwarding, and Policy-Based Management.

Chapter 10, "Develop, deploy, and manage data recovery," covers the fundamentals of SQL Server database backups in preparation for disaster recovery scenarios, including a backup and recovery strategy appropriate for your environment. We use a memorable narrative to explain various factors, features, and failures in a fictional disaster recovery scenario. We discuss how backups and restores in a hybrid environment, Azure SQL Database recovery, and geo-replication are important assets for the modern DBA.

Chapter 11, "Implement high availability and disaster recovery," goes beyond backups and into strategies for disaster recovery, from log shipping to availability groups, as well as monitoring and troubleshooting availability groups. We compare HA and DR strategies and dive into proper architecture for maximizing SQL Server uptime.

Part IV: Security

Chapter 12, "Administer instance and database security and permissions," begins with the basics of authentication: the configuration, management, and troubleshooting of logins and users. Then, we dive into permissions, including how to grant and revoke server and database-level permissions and role membership, with a focus on moving security from server to server.

Chapter 13, "Protect data through classification, encryption, and auditing," takes the security responsibilities of the SQL Server DBA past the basics of authentication and permissions and discusses advanced topics including the various features and techniques for encryption, such as transparent data encryption (TDE) and Always Encrypted, as well as protecting data in motion with TLS. We cover modern strategies for row-level security and protection of sensitive data. We discuss security measures to be taken for SQL Server instances and Azure SQL databases as well as the SQL Server Audit feature.

Part V: Performance

Chapter 14: "Performance tune SQL Server," dives deep into isolation and concurrency options, including read committed snapshot isolation (RCSI), and why your developers shouldn't be using NOLOCK. We discuss various strategies for memory-optimized data, including delayed durability. We review graphical execution plans analysis, the important Query Store feature, and automatic plan correction. We also review important performance-related dynamic management objects (DMOs) and new SQL Server 2022 performance features in the intelligent query processing family, including degree of parallelism (DOP) feedback, cardinality estimation (CE) feedback, and enhancements to memory grant feedback.

Chapter 15: "Understand and design indexes," tackles performance from the angle of indexes, including their creation, monitoring, and tuning. We review all the various forms of indexes at our disposal, past rowstore clustered and nonclustered indexes and into other types of indexes including columnstore and memory-optimized hashes. We review statistics and statistics options, including how they work on a variety of index and table types, such as the new XML compression feature in SQL Server 2022.

Part VI: Cloud

Chapter 16, "Design and implement hybrid and Azure database infrastructure," discusses the infrastructure options for Azure-based SQL Server databases, including platform as a service (PaaS) options of Azure SQL Database, Azure SQL Managed Instance, and infrastructure as a service (IaaS) options of Azure VMs running SQL Server instances. We discuss the resource scalability options for Azure SQL Database, which have dramatically expanded recently. We discuss management and governance in the Azure SQL data platform using the Azure portal and PowerShell.

Chapter 17, "Provision Azure SQL Database," covers the cloud-first database service without peer in the marketplace. This platform powers many web-based applications and services, scalable from a basic $5/month plan, to 128-vCore powerhouses, to hyperscale hardware. You will learn about the Azure SQL Database platform, compatibility, security, and availability. You will also learn how to create servers, databases, and elastic pools, and how to perform important management tasks for your databases.

Chapter 18, "Provision Azure SQL Managed Instance," details the powerful Azure SQL Managed Instance offering, including provisioning, managing, and scaling the instance. We review the service objectives, limitations and advantages, and security features of the managed instance.

Chapter 19, "Migrate to SQL Server solutions in Azure," covers various strategies for Azure migrations, including the Microsoft tools provided for testing and migrating SQL Server workloads. We review differences and limitations for on-premises feature migration strategies to Azure platforms, including how to migrate SSIS packages to the integration runtime. Finally, we review post-migration steps, best practices for security and resiliency during migration, and the common causes for migration failures.

Conventions

This book uses special text and design conventions to make it easier for you to find the information you need.

Text conventions

The following conventions are used in this book:

- **Boldface type** is used to indicate text that you should type where directed.

- For your convenience, this book uses abbreviated menu commands. For example, "Select Tools > Track Changes > Highlight Changes" means you should select the Tools menu, point to Track Changes, and then select the Highlight Changes command.

- Elements with the Code typeface are meant to be entered on a command line or inside a dialog box. For example, "type cd \Windows to change to the Windows subdirectory" means that you should be entering cd \Windows with your keyboard or text input device.

- The first letters of the names of menus, dialog boxes, dialog box elements, and commands are capitalized—for example, the Save As dialog box.

- *Italicized type* indicates new terms.

Book features

In addition to the text conventions, this book contains sidebars to provide additional context, tips, or suggestions.

Inside OUT

These are the book's signature tips. In these tips, you'll get the straight scoop on what's going on with the software or service—inside information about why a feature works the way it does. You'll also find field-tested advice and guidance as well as details that give you the edge on deploying and managing like a pro.

READER AIDS

Reader aids are exactly that—Notes, Tips, and Cautions provide additional information on completing a task or specific items to watch out for.

Errata, updates, and book support

We've made every effort to ensure the accuracy of this book and its companion content. You can access updates to this book in the form of a list of submitted errata and their related corrections at:

www.MicrosoftPressStore.com/SQLServer2022InsideOut/downloads

If you discover an error that is not already listed, please submit it to us at the same page.

For additional book support and information, please visit:

MicrosoftPressStore.com/Support

Please note that product support for Microsoft software and hardware is not offered through the preceding addresses. For help with Microsoft software or hardware, go to *support.microsoft.com*.

Get started with SQL Server tools

This chapter provides information about where to find many of the Microsoft tools used to manage and work with the Microsoft SQL Server platform. It also walks you through the installation, configuration, and basic utility of each tool, including an overview of the two main tools for working with SQL Server: SQL Server Management Studio (SSMS) and Azure Data Studio (ADS).

NOTE

Although SQL Server 2022 also runs on Linux, some of the administration tools that work with the Windows Server version do not work with the Linux version. We note the specific cases for which platform-specific tools are available.

SQL Server setup

You can install SQL Server 2022 natively on Windows and Linux. All SQL Server containers rely on SQL Server on Linux images from Ubuntu or Red Hat. These images can be deployed to desktop machines using Docker or Kubernetes whether you are running Windows, macOS, or Linux for development purposes. For production support, you can only deploy those containers to a Linux machine running Docker or Kubernetes with full support.

The following section covers installing SQL Server natively on Microsoft Windows.

➤ For more details on how to set up and configure SQL Server, read Chapter 4, "Install and configure SQL Server instances and features."

1

Install SQL Server with the Installation Center

The SQL Server Installation Center is the application you use to install and add features to an instance of SQL Server. If you are installing SQL Server manually, this is the application that opens when you run the Setup.exe file for SQL Server. As illustrated in Figure 1-1, it can also serve as a launch point for downloading the installation packages for Data Migration Assistant (which replaced the SQL Server Upgrade Advisor), SQL Server Management Tools, SQL Server Reporting Services, and SQL Server Data Tools.

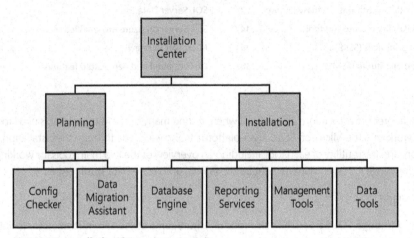

Figure 1-1 Installation Center components.

It might seem a bit confusing, but on the Installation tab, the installers for SQL Server Reporting Services, SQL Server Management Tools, and SQL Server Data Tools are merely links that redirect to a download location on a Microsoft website for each of these components' installation files. You also can download and install the tools independently without using Installation Center. These links are available as a sort of backward-compatibility option. Prior to SQL Server 2017, these installers were included in the Installation Center.

NOTE

As a best practice, you should install SQL Server Management Studio and Data Tools only on client machines, not the production instance. This ensures a smaller installation and administration footprint on the server. It is therefore uncommon to use the Installation Center on client machines.

Inside OUT

How do you install SQL Server 2022 on Linux?

SQL Server is fully supported on Red Hat Enterprise Linux (RHEL), SUSE Linux Enterprise Server (SLES), and Ubuntu, using the built-in package manager for each distribution.

The main SQL Server installation feature is the Database Engine. You can install the command line tools, SQL Server Agent, Full-Text Search, and SQL Server Integration Services (SSIS) as optional packages.

For more information about installing SQL Server on Linux, see Chapter 5, "Install and configure SQL Server on Linux," or visit Microsoft Docs at *https://learn.microsoft.com/sql/linux /sql-server-linux-setup*.

Plan before an upgrade or installation

When you first start the SQL Server Installation Center, it opens with the Planning tab preselected. This tab has two tools that you might find useful before installing or upgrading a SQL Server instance to SQL Server 2022: Configuration Checker and Data Migration Assistant.

Configuration Checker

The Configuration Checker tool checks for conditions that might prevent a successful SQL Server 2022 installation. When you choose **Configuration Checker**, a wizard runs on the local server. There is no option to choose an alternate computer location. The wizard returns an HTML report listing all installation requirement rules (facets) and the results of each test. Most of these rules are universal to all Windows configurations, and you can easily remedy most of them.

- **AclPermissionsFacet.** Checks if the SQL Server registry keys are consistent. Certain registry keys are required to install SQL Server and some registry key values must match. If these matching values are not present and consistent, SQL Server will not be successfully installed or upgraded.

- **FacetDomainControllerCheck.** We recommend that you do not install SQL Server 2022 on a domain controller, for two reasons. First, it can compromise the security of both Active Directory and the SQL Server instance. Second, it can cause resource contention between the two services. Microsoft also recommends against installing SQL Server on a domain controller. For more information, see *https://learn.microsoft.com/sql/sql-server/ install/security-considerations-for-a-sql-server-installation#Install_DC*.

- **IsDotNetInstalled.** This rule determines if the Microsoft .NET Framework 4.7.2 or newer is installed on the system.

- **MediaPathLength.** The path for the location from which SQL Server 2022 is being installed must be fewer than 260 characters in length.

- **RebootRequiredCheck.** No installation reboots can be pending.

- **SetupCompatibilityCheck.** No subsequent incompatible versions of SQL Server can be installed on the computer.

- **ThreadHasAdminPrivilegeCheck.** The account running SQL Server must have administrative rights on the computer.

- **WmiServiceStateCheck.** This checks whether the Windows Management Instrumentation (WMI) service is started and running on the computer.

NOTE

The minimum version of Windows Server for SQL Server 2022 is Windows Server 2016.

Data Migration Assistant (DMA)

There is a link on the Planning tab in the Installation Center to download the Data Migration Assistant installation package.

NOTE

The Data Migration Assistant is now continually updated by Microsoft. You can download the most recent version from *https://www.microsoft.com/download/details.aspx?id=53595*.

This application is really two tools in one, which you can use to create two project types:

- An assessment of upgrade or migration readiness

- A migration of data between versions of SQL Server and/or Azure SQL Database

For the assessment project type, the source server can be either a SQL Server instance or Amazon Web Services (AWS) Relational Database Service (RDS) for SQL Server instance. For the migration project type, the source server must be a SQL Server instance. The following target server choices accommodate both assessment and migration:

- Azure SQL Database

- Azure SQL Managed Instance

- SQL Server on Azure Virtual Machines

- SQL Server

Assessment

The assessment project type of the Data Migration Assistant detects database-specific compatibility issues between origin and destination SQL Server versions during pre-upgrade discovery. It is common between versions for there to be deprecation and feature differences, and this is especially true if the target server type is an Azure SQL Database. If not addressed, some of these items might affect database functionality during or after upgrade. The tool neatly outlines all findings and makes recommendations.

The assessment project type examines the following aspects of upgrading or migrating SQL Server:

- **Feature parity.** The assessment project provides a comprehensive set of recommendations, alternative approaches available in Azure, and mitigating steps.

- **Compatibility issues.** The assessment project provides partially supported or unsupported features that would block migration. Compatibility issues are categorized as breaking changes, behavior changes, or deprecated features.

NOTE

You can find a list of T-SQL differences between SQL Server and Azure SQL Database at *https://learn.microsoft.com/azure/sql-database/sql-database-transact-sql-information*.

Migration

Using the migration project type of the Data Migration Assistant, an administrator can move a database's schema, data, and other objects such as database roles from a source server to a destination server. The wizard associated with this feature works by providing a user with the option to select a source and destination server and to choose one or more databases for migration.

The Migration Scope setting allows you to choose what to migrate. You can choose between the database schema only, the data only, or both the schema and data.

Move to SQL Server

For SQL Server migrations, there must be a backup location that is accessible by both the source and the destination server—generally a UNC path, such as \\server01\folder\subfolder\. If this is a network location, the service running the source SQL Server instance must have write permissions for the directory. In addition, the service account running the destination SQL Server instance must have read permissions to the same network location.

If this poses a challenge, there is a **Copy The Database Backups To A Different Location That The Target Server Can Read And Restore From** check box that you can select to break up the process into steps and utilize the (hopefully) elevated permissions of the administrator running the wizard.

When you select this option, the security privileges of the account of the individual running the Data Migration Assistant are used to perform the copy of the file from the backup location to the restore location. The user must have access to each of these locations with the needed read and write permissions for this step to succeed.

The wizard also gives the user the option to specify the location to restore the data files and log files on the destination server.

As a final step, the wizard presents the user with a list of logins for migration consideration, with conflicting login names or logins that already exist identified. Where possible, the wizard attempts to map orphaned logins and align login security IDs (SIDs).

Move to Azure SQL Database

The Data Migration Assistant tool performs an Azure SQL Database migration in two phases:

1. **Schema.** First, it generates a script of the database schema (you can save this script before deployment for archival and testing purposes), which you deploy to the destination database.

2. **Data.** If you choose to move the data, another step is added after the creation of the tables on the destination database. This gives you the opportunity to verify that all tables exist in the destination database after the initial schema migration. Data migration uses Bulk Copy Program (BCP) under the hood. Any trusted constraints from the source database should be trusted in the database after data is copied, but it is a best practice to validate that constraints did not become untrusted in the copy process.

The schema migration is required; the data migration is optional.

Install or upgrade SQL Server

When it comes to administration and development tools used to work with SQL Server, the other important tab in the Installation Center is the Installation tab. This tab contains a link to install the Database Engine (the SQL Server service). A few of the utilities discussed in this chapter are installed as options only during a full Database Engine installation and cannot be downloaded and installed independently.

During an in-place upgrade of an existing SQL Server instance, you can neither add nor remove components. The process will simply upgrade existing components.

CAUTION

An in-place upgrade to SQL Server 2022 will uninstall SQL Server Reporting Services if it is installed.

If you have multiple versions installed on the same server (instance stacking), several shared components will be upgraded automatically, including SQL Server Browser and SQL Server VSS Writer.

➤ You can read more about multiple instances and versions of SQL Server at *https://learn.microsoft.com/sql/sql-server/install/work-with-multiple-versions-and-instances-of-sql-server*.

Tools and services installed with the Database Engine

SQL Server 2022 provides optional tools and services that you can select during the installation process. We look at some of them in the sections that follow. (Note that this list is not exhaustive and that some of these components might not be available in SQL Server 2022 on Linux.)

Inside OUT

What feature improvements should you know about outside of the Database Engine?

SQL Server Analysis Service (SSAS) 2022 introduces Horizontal Fusion, a query execution plan optimization that reduces the number of queries required against a data source to return results. It also supports parallel execution plans for DirectQuery, which takes advantage of the scalability that large data sources may be able to provide. You can find more improvements by visiting *https://learn.microsoft.com/analysis-services/what-s-new-in-sql-server-analysis-services*.

Additionally, SQL Server Reporting Services (SSRS) 2022 includes an updated web portal, security enhancements, browser performance improvements, accessibility fixes, and enhanced Windows Narrator support. For more information about improvements and deprecated features, see *https://learn.microsoft.com/sql/reporting-services/what-s-new-in-sql-server-reporting-services-ssrs*.

➤ For more in-depth information about configuring features, see Chapter 4.

Machine Learning Services

Starting with SQL Server 2016, Microsoft has created an extensibility framework for executing external code on SQL Server. Machine Learning Services now support the following external languages:

- R (introduced in SQL Server 2016)

- Python (introduced in SQL Server 2017)

- Java (introduced in SQL Server 2019)

Machine Learning Services is available for both Windows and Linux.

A Database Engine instance is required for Machine Learning Services in SQL Server 2022. Support for the previously available standalone Machine Learning Server, which supported R and Python, ended on July 1, 2022.

Beginning with SQL Server 2022, runtimes for R, Python, and Java are no longer installed with SQL Setup. You must run the SQL Setup Wizard to install Machine Learning Services and Language Extensions. Then you must install your desired R, Python, or Java runtime(s) and packages.

> **NOTE**
>
> **After installing your desired runtime(s), be sure to enable the external scripting feature using the following TSQL command:**
>
> ```
> EXEC sp_configure  'external scripts enabled';
> ```
>
> **Then restart the SQL Server service.**

➤ **There are separate Microsoft Docs articles for installing Machine Learning Services on SQL Server 2019 and prior and for SQL Server 2022. For installation on SQL Server 2022 on Windows, see** *https://learn.microsoft.com/sql/machine-learning/install/sql-machine-learning-services-windows-install-sql-2022*. **For information about installing Machine Learning Services for SQL Server 2022 on Linux, see** *https://learn.microsoft.com/sql/linux/sql-server-linux-setup-machine-learning-sql-2022*.

Data Quality Services

Standardizing, cleaning, and enhancing data is critical to validity when performing analytical research. SQL Server Data Quality Services allows for both homegrown knowledgebase datasets and cloud-based reference data services by third-party providers.

Data Quality Services is a product that facilitates important data quality tasks, including the following:

- Knowledgebase-driven correction

- De-duplication

- Additional metadata enrichment

Data Quality Services has two parts: the Data Quality Server and the Data Quality Client. Data Quality Server has a dependency on the Database Engine. Apart from that, you can install these two components on the same computer or on different computers. The tools are completely independent, and you can install them in any order. (In other words, it doesn't matter which one you install first.)

To be functional, the Data Quality Client tool needs only to be able to connect to a Data Quality Server. In addition, there are certain operations the Data Quality Client can perform that require an installation of Microsoft Excel local to the client installation. It is commonplace to have the Data Quality Client on one or more workstations, but not the computer running SQL Server.

Data Quality Server

To install Data Quality Server, you must first select its check box during SQL Server 2022 setup. This copies an installer file to a drive you specify. After you install SQL Server 2022, you can install Data Quality Server. To start, in your Windows **Start** menu, expand **Microsoft SQL Server 2022**, and then select **SQL Server 2022 Data Quality Server Installer**. This runs the DQSInstaller.exe file. The installation asks you to type and confirm a database master key password. It then creates three new databases into the SQL Server instance chosen as the host server: DQS_Main, DQS_Projects, and DQS_Staging_Data.

Data Quality Client

The Data Quality Client is an application used in conjunction with master data management (not to be confused with Master Data Services), data warehousing, or just plain data cleaning. It is typically used by a data steward who has a deep understanding of the business and domain knowledge about the data itself. You can use this tool to create knowledgebases surrounding data element rules, conversions, and mappings to help manage and align data elements. You can also use it to create and run data quality projects and to perform administrative tasks.

To sign into a Data Quality Server using the Data Quality Client tool, you must be either a member of the sysadmin server role or of one of these three roles in the DQS_Main database:

- dqs_administrator

- dqs_kb_editor

- dqs_kb_operator

Command line interface

You can use and administer SQL Server from a command line. This is especially relevant with Linux as a supported operating system (OS) for SQL Server. Utilities such as SQLCMD and BCP run on Windows, Linux, and macOS, with some minor differences.

SQLCMD

The SQLCMD utility is used to run T-SQL statements, stored procedures, or script files, using an ODBC connection to a SQL Server instance.

Inside OUT

What does ODBC mean?

ODBC stands for Open Database Connectivity, which is an open-standard application programming interface (API) for communicating from any supported OS to any supported Database Engine.

Although some people might consider the SQLCMD utility "old school" because it has been around since SQL Server 2005, it is still very popular because of its utility in automating scripts. You can invoke SQLCMD from any of the following:

- Windows, Linux, or macOS command line

- Windows, Linux, or macOS script files

- SQL Server Agent job step

- Using PowerShell with the command line

NOTE

Both SQL Server Management Studio and Azure Data Studio can invoke SQLCMD mode, which makes possible some very useful functionality. Although it's technically part of SQLCMD, it is not strictly a command line tool. You can read more about it at *https://learn.microsoft.com/sql/relational-databases/scripting/edit-sqlcmd-scripts-with-query-editor*.

Inside OUT

What is mssql-cli?

mssql-cli is an interactive command line utility for querying SQL Server that runs on Windows, macOS, and Linux. It offers significant improvements over SQLCMD; however, it is not installed with SQL Server by default.

Features of mssql-cli include:

- IntelliSense for T-SQL

- Syntax highlighting

- Multi-line editing

- Support for configuration files

mssql-cli is installed on Windows and macOS using pip (a package manager for Python packages). On Linux, the Microsoft repository must be registered before using a package manager to install mssql-cli.

You can read more about mssql-cli at *https://learn.microsoft.com/sql/tools/mssql-cli*.

BCP

If you think SQLCMD is "old school," hold on to your hat. The Bulk Copy Program (BCP), introduced in 1992 with the release of the very first edition of SQL Server, makes SQLCMD look like the new kid on the block.

It is quite a testament that to this day, BCP is still a practical way to work with SQL Server to insert or export large quantities of data. It uses minimal logging techniques and bulk data flows to its advantage.

If this reminds you of SQL Server Integration Services, be aware that BCP is not nearly as powerful. You use BCP to move data between data files (text, comma-delimited, or other formats) and a SQL Server table.

You can use BCP to import files into SQL Server tables or to export data from SQL Server tables into data files. BCP requires the use of a format file to designate the structure of the receiving table and the data types allowed in each column. Fortunately, BCP helps you to create this format file quite easily.

There are a few things about BCP that you must understand and do for the tool to perform optimally:

- Put the database into the simple or bulk-logged recovery model.

- Drop any non-clustered indexes on the destination table.

- Insert sorted data and use the `sorted_data` option if a clustered index exists.

- Run BCP on the same machine as the SQL Server.

- Place source and destination files on separate physical drives.

- Manually grow SQL data files in advance if growth is expected.

- Take advantage of instant file initialization.

- Use `sp_tableoption` to set table lock on bulk load (TABLOCK) to ON.

➤ For more information, go to *https://learn.microsoft.com/sql/tools/bcp-utility*.

CHAPTER 1

Inside OUT

How do you download the most recent command line tools?

The versions of SQLCMD and BCP installed with SQL Server 2022 on Windows are updated through a separate package called Line Utilities for SQL Server, available at *https://learn .microsoft.com/sql/tools/sqlcmd-utility.*

For features like Always Encrypted and Azure Active Directory authentication, SQLCMD requires a minimum of version 13.1. It is entirely possible (and likely) to have more than one version of SQLCMD installed on a server, so be sure to check that you are using the correct version by running sqlcmd -?.

Separate installers for Linux and macOS versions of these command line tools are available and regularly updated.

SQL Server PowerShell Provider

If you love to use a command line or if you have begun to use PowerShell to help manage and maintain your SQL Servers, Microsoft offers the PowerShell Provider for SQL Server. It can be installed with Windows PowerShell and PowerShell 7.

NOTE

There are two PowerShell modules for SQL Server: SQLPS and SQLServer. SQLPS is an older module included in SQL Server for backward compatibility but is no longer updated. You should use the SqlServer module, which is installed separately via the PowerShell Gallery and is regularly updated. SqlServer also provides functionality to run SQLCMD scripts by using the invoke-sqlcmd cmdlet.

The SQL Server PowerShell Provider uses SQL Server Management Objects (SMO), which are included when you install the SqlServer PowerShell module. These objects were designed by Microsoft to provide for the management of SQL Server programmatically. There are many ways that developers and administrators can use PowerShell to automate their work in SQL Server, especially when dealing with multiple server environments.

➤ To learn more about automation in SQL Server using PowerShell, see Chapter 8, "Maintain and monitor SQL Server."

SQL Server Configuration Manager

SQL Server Configuration Manager is a tool that uses the Microsoft Management Console as a shell. To launch SQL Server Configuration Manager, locate **SQL Server 2022 Configuration Manager** on the Windows **Start** menu under **Apps** or search for SQLServerManager16.msc.

NOTE

SQL Server on Linux has its own set of configuration tools, which you can read about in Chapter 5.

Administrators use SQL Server Configuration Manager to manage SQL Server services. These services include the Database Engine, the SQL Server Agent, SQL Server Integration Services, the PolyBase Engine, and others. SQL Server Configuration Manager provides a graphical user interface (GUI) to perform the following tasks associated with SQL Server–related services:

- Start or stop a service

- Alter the start mode (manual, automatic, disabled)

- Change startup parameters, including trace flags

- Create server aliases

- Change the service Log On As accounts

- Manage client protocols, including TCP/IP default port, keep alive, and interval settings

- Manage FILESTREAM behavior

Inside OUT

Can you manage SQL Server services from Windows Services Manager?

Although you can perform most of these same tasks using the default Windows Services Manager (Control Panel > Administrative Tools > Services), we do not recommend doing so.

Windows Services Manager (services.msc) does not provide all the various configuration options found in SQL Server Configuration Manager. More importantly, it omits adjusting important registry settings that need to be changed, which will compromise the stability of your SQL Server environment.

You must always change SQL Server services using SQL Server Configuration Manager. This is especially true for managing SQL Server service accounts.

Performance and reliability monitoring tools

The Database Engine Tuning Advisor, Extended Events, and Profiler tools are installed with the Database Engine and do not require additional installation steps. This section explores each of these tools in more detail.

Database Engine Tuning Advisor

Among the many administrative tools Microsoft provides to work with SQL Server is the Database Engine Tuning Advisor. You can start it either from the **Start** menu or from within SQL Server Management Studio (SSMS) by selecting **Tools > Database Engine Tuning Advisor**. Using this tool, you can analyze a server-side trace captured by SQL Server Profiler. It analyzes every statement that passes through the SQL Server and presents various options for possible performance improvement.

> NOTE
>
> The Database Engine Tuning Advisor is not supported on Azure SQL Database or Azure SQL Managed Instance.

The suggestions made by the Database Engine Tuning Advisor focus solely on indexing, statistics, and partitioning strategies. The Database Engine Tuning Advisor simplifies the implementation of any administrator-approved changes it suggests. You need to scrutinize these changes to ensure that they will not negatively affect the instance.

> CAUTION
>
> You should not run the Database Engine Tuning Advisor directly on a production server because it can leave behind hypothetical indexes and statistics that can persist without a DBA's knowledge. These will require additional resources to maintain. Use the is_hypothetical column in the sys.indexes system view to find hypothetical indexes for manual removal.

Extended Events

Technically, the Extended Events GUI (client only) is installed with and is a built-in part of SSMS, but we discuss it here with the other performance-specific tools for categorical reasons.

> ➤ You can read more about how Extended Events are supported in Azure SQL Database, with some differences, at *https://learn.microsoft.com/azure/sql-database/sql-database-xevent-db-diff-from-svr*.

SQL Server Extended Events (or XEvents) is an event-handling system created to replace SQL Server Profiler. Think of it as the "new and improved" version of Profiler. It is more lightweight, full-featured, and flexible, all at once. Extended Events offer a way to monitor what's happening in SQL Server with much less overhead than an equivalent trace run through the SQL Profiler. This is because Extended Events are asynchronous.

You access Extended Events through SSMS by connecting to a SQL Server instance, navigating to the **Management** folder, and expanding the **Extended Events** node to display **Sessions**. Right-click **Sessions**; then, on the shortcut menu that opens, select **New Session Wizard**. You can use this wizard to schedule events to run at server startup or immediately after the event has been created.

NOTE

SQL Server Management Studio provides a simple Extended Events viewer called XEvent Profiler. It is meant to replace the standalone Profiler tool for monitoring activity in real time on a SQL Server instance.

Scripting Extended Events sessions via T-SQL can be a much quicker and more consistent way to create a library of Extended Event sessions for reuse in multiple environments. This gives you the flexibility to start and stop them as needed, even as a job in SQL Server Agent.

➤ **For more information on using Extended Events, see Chapter 8.**

Scenarios for use

You can use Extended Events in a wide range of scenarios. There are more than 1,700 events available in SQL Server 2022. Here are some of the most common uses for Extended Events:

- Troubleshooting

- Diagnosing slowness

- Diagnosing deadlocks

- Diagnosing recompiles

- Debugging

- Login auditing

- Baselining

By scripting out an event session and using automation, you have a stock set of sessions that you can use to troubleshoot depending on the problem. You can deploy these solutions on any server that needs a closer examination into performance issues.

You can also use Extended Event trace to provide a baseline from which you can track code improvements or degradation over time.

Management Data Warehouse

The Management Data Warehouse (MDW), introduced in SQL Server 2008, collects data about the performance of a SQL Server instance and feeds the information back to an administrator in a Visual Analytic–style format.

MDW has not seen significant new feature development since it was released. It has not been broadly adopted and has mostly been supplanted by Query Store and other third-party monitoring tools.

MDW has its own relational database containing tables that are the recipient (target) of specific Extended Events collection activities. Upon installation, MDW provides three reports: Server Active History, Query Statistics History, and System Disk Usage. You can create additional reports and add them to the MDW collection. Using this three-report configuration makes it possible for a database administrator to do basic performance baselining and to plan for growth. It also allows for proactive tuning activities.

> ➤ For more information on configuring a Management Data Warehouse, see *https://learn .microsoft.com/sql/relational-databases/data-collection/configure-the-management-data -warehouse-sql-server-management-studio*.

SQL Server Reporting Services (SSRS)

Starting with SQL Server 2017, SQL Server Reporting Services (SSRS) is a separate download outside the SQL Server installer. You can use SSRS to create reports on a variety of data sources. It includes a complete set of tools for creating, managing, scheduling, and delivering reports. The reports can include charts, maps, data matrixes, and more.

SSRS provides a web portal interface to manage and organize reports and other items. Internet Information Services (IIS) is not required to use SSRS.

Installation

You must download SSRS separately, either by following the stub on the main Installation Center screen or by going to *https://learn.microsoft.com/sql/reporting-services/install-windows/ install-reporting-services*.

Completing the installation of SSRS results in the following:

- Installation of the Report Server Service, which consists of the following:

  - Report Server Web Service

  - Web portal (for viewing and managing reports and report security)

  - Report Server Configuration Manager

- Configuration of the Report Service and web portal URLs

- The establishment of the service accounts needed for SSRS to operate

➤ **You can read more about configuring SSRS in Chapter 4.**

After the installation is complete, using administrative rights, browse to the following directories to verify that the installation was successful and that the service is running:

- *localhost/Reports*

- *localhost/ReportServer*

If you are running a named instance of SQL Server, you need to use the Web Portal URL tab in the Report Server Configuration Manager dialog box to determine the exact path of both the web service URL and the web portal URL, as illustrated in Figure 1-2.

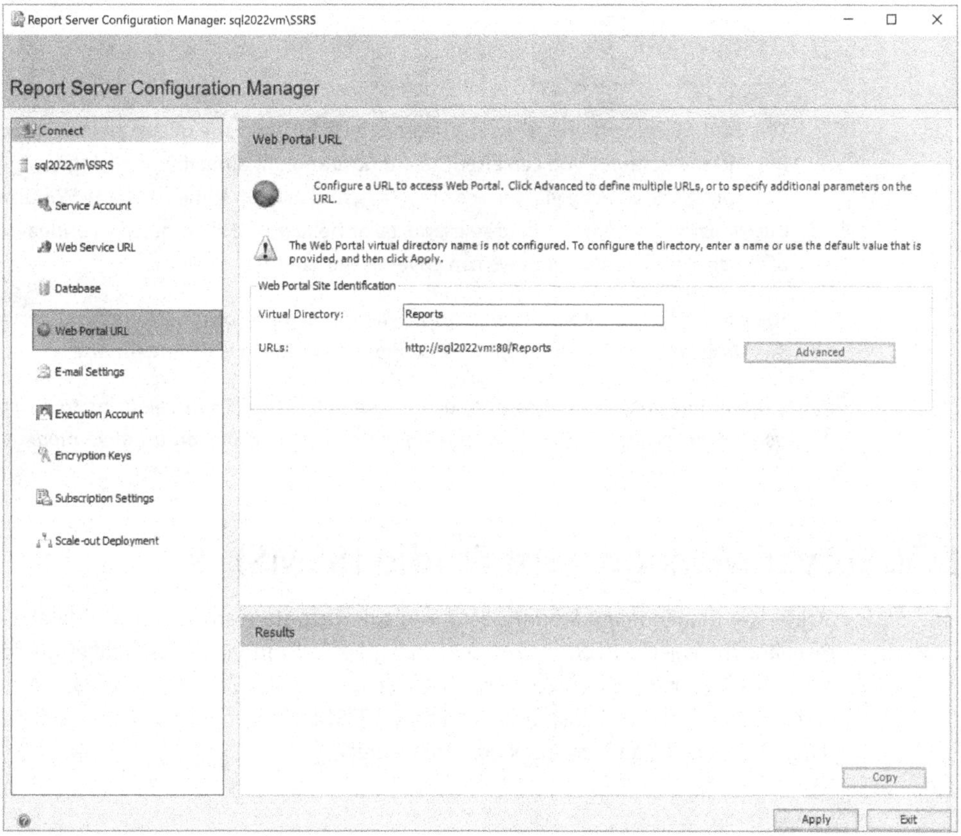

Figure 1-2 Web Portal URL setting in Report Server Configuration Manager.

Report Server Configuration Manager

The Report Server Configuration Manager simplifies the customization of the behavior of features and capabilities offered by SSRS. You can use it to perform the following tasks and more:

- Create or select existing Report Server databases.

- Define the URLs used to access the Report Server and Report Manager.

- Configure the Report Server service account.

- Modify the connection string used by the Report Server.

- Set up email distribution capability.

- Integrate with a Power BI service.

Inside OUT

How do you configure SSRS?

The Configuration Manager in SSRS comes with no shortage of customization options. Beyond the defaults, you can alter the configuration of almost any setting using the GUI, through SSMS, directly via web.config files, and even in some cases the Windows Registry. Customizing accounts, IP addresses, ports, or behaviors can be quite an endeavor, the scope of which is far beyond what we can cover in this chapter.

You can find more information at *https://learn.microsoft.com/sql/reporting-services /install-windows/reporting-services-configuration-manager-native-mode*.

To configure an SSL certificate to secure your SSRS installation, see *https://learn.microsoft .com/sql/reporting-services/security/configure-ssl-connections-on-a-native-mode-report-server*.

SQL Server Management Studio (SSMS)

SQL Server Management Studio (SSMS) is the *de facto* standard SQL Server database development and management tool. It provides a rich graphical interface and simplifies the configuration, administration, and development tasks associated with managing SQL Server and Azure SQL Database environments. SSMS also contains a robust T-SQL script editor, and comes stocked with many templates, samples, and script-generating features.

Inside OUT

Does SSMS support other operating systems?

SSMS is a Windows-only application. It does not work in Linux or macOS environments. Instead, you can use the free cross-platform Azure Data Studio to connect to SQL Server, Azure SQL Database, and Azure Synapse Analytics (formerly Azure SQL Data Warehouse) from Windows, Linux, and macOS.

For more information about Azure Data Studio, read the section "Azure Data Studio" later in this chapter.

Releases and versions

Since the release of SQL Server 2016, SSMS has been a freestanding toolset that you can download and install independent of the Database Engine.

Install SQL Server Management Studio

As of this writing, the latest major version of SQL Server Management Studio (SSMS) is 19.*x*. It can be installed alongside previous major versions of SSMS, including those bundled with earlier versions of SQL Server.

CAUTION

We recommend that you do not install SSMS on a computer running a production instance of SQL Server. Instead, install SSMS on a workstation and connect that to the production instance through a secure connection. Aside from reducing the temptation to use Remote Desktop to connect to a production instance, it has the added benefit of limiting the attack surface area.

To install SSMS, first download the latest version of the product here: *http://aka.ms/ssms*. After you download the executable file, install it. There's not much more to it than that. The installation finishes with a Setup Completed message. In some cases, you may be prompted to restart your computer.

At this point, you can start the application by opening your **Start** menu and browsing to **Microsoft SQL Server Tools 19 > Microsoft SQL Server Management Studio 19**. For ease of access, you might want to pin the program to your Start menu or copy the icon to your desktop.

Azure Data Studio (ADS) is installed with SSMS by default. If you have ADS installed on the same computer, you can invoke ADS features, such as queries or notebooks, from inside SQL Server Management Studio.

> ➤ Read about integration between SSMS and ADS in the "Azure Data Studio" section later in this chapter.

Inside OUT

Can you prevent ADS from being installed with SSMS?

While ADS is installed by default when you install SSMS, there is currently an option to prevent this installation. To do so, run the SSMS installer from the command line and use the `DoNotInstallAzureDataStudio` option. For example, if you have navigated to the folder where the SSMS installer is located, you would use the following command:

```
SSMS-Setup-ENU.exe /Passive DoNotInstallAzureDataStudio=1
```

Upgrade SQL Server Management Studio

SSMS will notify you if an update is available. You can also manually check whether one is available. To do so, select **Tools** > **Check For Updates**. The different versions of the SSMS components—the installed version and the latest available version—will display. If any updates are available, you can select the **Update** button to open a webpage from which you can download and install the latest recommended version.

Now that the tools used to manage SQL Server are completely independent of the Database Engine, upgrading SSMS is easy. It is also much safer to upgrade; there is no longer any concern about accidentally affecting your production environment because you upgraded your SSMS toolset.

Features of SQL Server Management Studio

The power of SSMS is in the many ways in which you can use it to interact with one or more SQL Server instances. This section highlights some useful features.

Object Explorer and Object Explorer Details

Object Explorer is the default SSMS view, providing both a hierarchical and tabular view of each instance of SQL Server and the child objects within those instances (including databases, tables, views, stored procedures, functions, and so on).

NOTE

Object Explorer uses its own connection to the database server, and can block certain database-level activities, just like any other SSMS query.

Object Explorer presents two panes (see Figure 1-3): the Object Explorer pane (left) and the Object Explorer Details pane (right). The Object Explorer pane is strictly hierarchical, whereas the

Object Explorer Details pane is both hierarchical and tabular. As such, the latter provides additional functionality over its companion pane; for example, object search and the selection and scripting of multiple noncontiguous objects. To display the Object Explorer Details pane, choose **View** > **Object Explorer Details** or press **F7**.

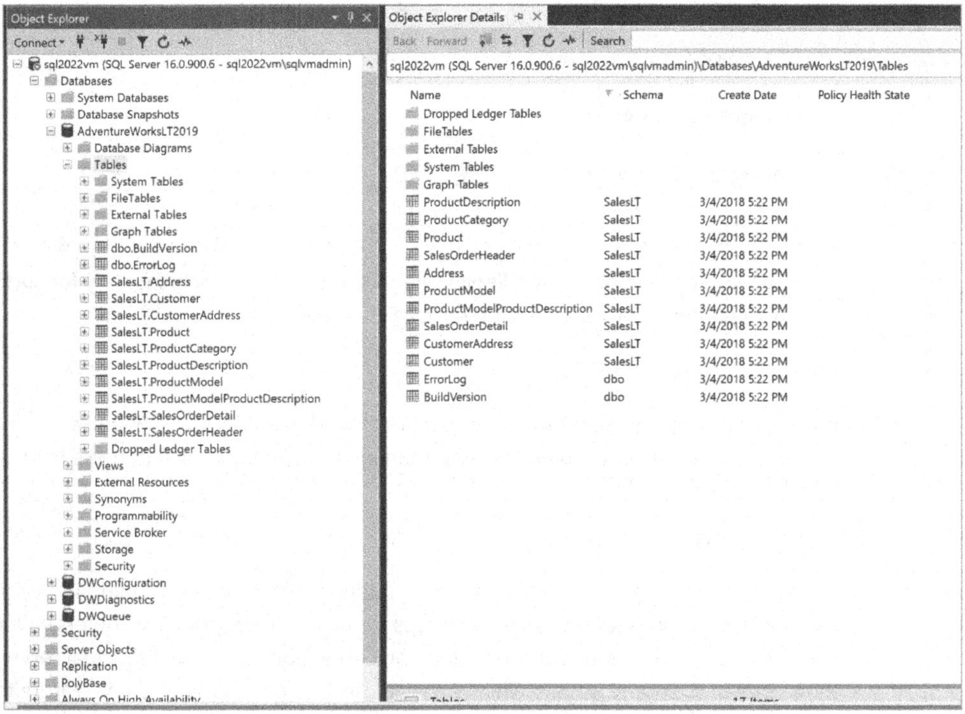

Figure 1-3 The Object Explorer view in SQL Server Management Studio.

Server Registration

The Server Registration feature within SSMS can both save time and make it easier to manage a complex environment by saving a list of commonly accessed instances. Registering connections in advance for future reuse provides the following benefits:

- Preservation of connection information

- Creation of groups of servers

- Aliasing of servers with more meaningful names

- Ability to add detailed descriptions to both servers and server groups

- Import and export of registered server groups for sharing between machines or teammates

To access the Server Registration feature within SSMS, select **View > Registered Servers** or press **Ctrl+Alt+G**.

You can use SSMS to register and manage four different types of servers and services:

- Database Engine
- Analysis Services
- Reporting Services
- Integration Services

NOTE

Server Registration for SQL Server Integration Services is included only for backward compatibility for versions prior to SQL Server 2012.

Database Engine

When you use the Server Registration feature to work with Database Engines, two nodes appear: Local Server Groups and Central Management Servers. Each of these has some very useful features.

Local Server Groups node

The Local Server Groups node allows for the addition of either freestanding individual server registrations or the creation of server groups. Think of server groups as folders within the Local Server Groups node. Each of these folders can contain one or more individual servers. Figure 1-4 shows one of the many ways in which you can use the Local Server Groups feature to organize and save frequently used Database Engine connections.

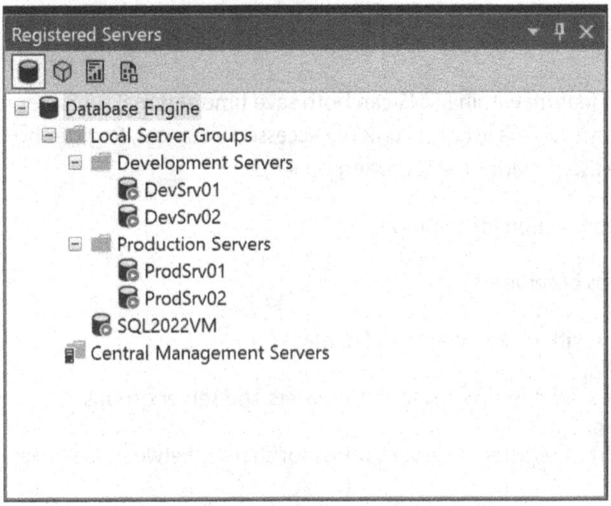

Figure 1-4 Local Server Groups.

From the Local Server Groups node, you can access the following tools:

- **Export Registered Server Wizard.** To access the Export Registered Servers Wizard, right-click the **Local Server Groups** folder node or any folder or server nested within this node. Then, on the shortcut menu, select **Tasks > Export**. From there, you have quite a bit of freedom. You can choose to export from any level within the tree structure as well as whether to include usernames and passwords. In the preceding case, if you want to export only the Development Servers node and any servers within it, you can do so by choosing within this wizard where to save the created file and then build out an XML document with the extension .regsrvr.

- **Importing Registered Servers.** To access the Import Registered Servers Wizard, right-click the **Local Server Groups** folder node or any folder or server nested within this node. Then, on the shortcut menu, select **Tasks > Import**. This opens the Import Registered Servers dialog box, which you can use to select a previously created .regsrvr file, as demonstrated in Figure 1-5.

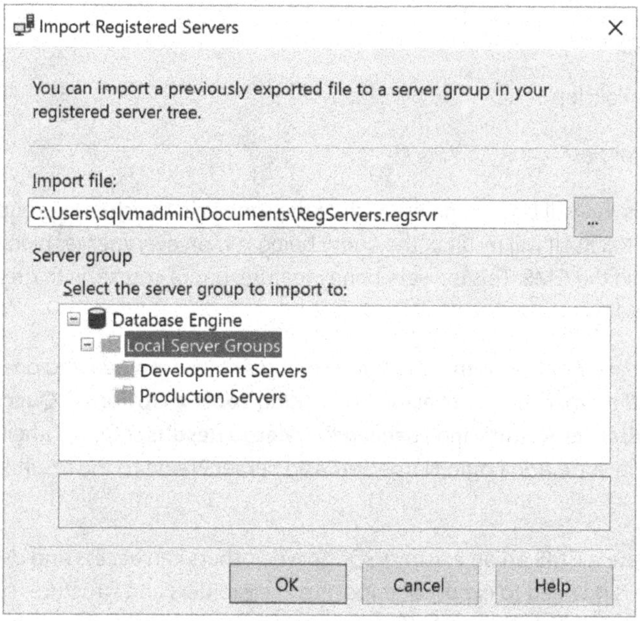

Figure 1-5 Importing registered servers.

From here you can choose the folder in which you would like the imported object or object tree to reside. If you select a folder that already contains the same structures you are attempting to import, a message will appear asking you to approve an update/overwrite to the existing object structure.

Central Management Servers node

As mentioned, the second node available in the Database Engine feature is Central Management Servers. At first glance, this might appear to be almost the same thing as the Local Server Groups node. It allows you to add servers and create folders with descriptive names to which you can add servers. However, the Centralize Management Servers node includes some very significant differences.

First, when using this feature, you must choose a SQL Server instance to play the role of a Central Management Server (CMS). You can alias the server with a new name, but the server itself must exist. After you have chosen a server to play this role and have created a CMS, you can create new server groups or individual server registrations using the same methods explained in the "Local Server Groups node" section.

Here is where things become interesting. If you right-click any level (a server, a group, or the CMS itself), you are presented with multiple options:

- New Query

- Object Explorer

- Evaluate Policies

- Import Policies

Anything that is run will be run against each of the servers in the chosen group's tree. Running a query on the CMS itself will result in the query being run on every server hierarchically present in all trees within the CMS. This is a very handy feature, but of course, with great power comes great responsibility!

The default behavior of CMS is that multiple server results are merged into one result set. You can change and customize this behavior by choosing **Tools** > **Options** > **Query Results** > **SQL Server** > **Multiserver Results** and enabling the **Merge Results** setting. Other behavior options available here include Add Login Name and Add Server Name to the result set from a CMS query.

When you create a CMS on an existing SQL Server, others can access and use the structure setup, so there is no need to export or import to keep folders and structures synchronized. This is great for team collaboration and efficiency.

Filtering objects

In the default Object Explorer view, SSMS lists items within each category in alphabetical order, starting with the schema name. There are several main groups, or tree categories, that are common across all versions of SQL Server. These include the following:

- **Databases.** This provides a full list of databases (including system databases) on the SQL Server instance. Database snapshots also appear here.

- **Security.** This contains a diverse list of object types, including logins, server roles, credentials, cryptographic providers, and audits.

- **Server Objects.** These include backup devices, endpoints, linked servers, and server-level triggers.

- **Replication.** This provides information about publishers and subscriptions.

- **Always On High Availability.** This includes Failover Clustering and Availability Groups.

- **Management.** This category covers diverse features and tools, including Policy Management, Data Collection, Resource Governor, Extended Events, Maintenance Plans, Database Mail, DTC (Distributed Transaction Coordinator), and SQL Server error logs.

- **SQL Server Agent.** Includes jobs, alerts, operators, proxies, and error logs of its own.

- **Integration Services Catalogs.** This contains the SQL Server Integration Services package catalog, depending on the SQL Server version.

By default, SSMS lists all objects alphabetically beneath each tree category. When working with databases that have a large quantity of objects, this can become quite aggravating, as the user may be subject to long list load times and must expend energy scrolling and watching the screen very closely for the object in question.

Fortunately, SSMS has a filtering feature. You can apply filters to many object categories, such as user databases, tables, views, stored procedures, table-valued functions, user-defined functions, and even database users.

You can independently configure filter settings in either the Object Explorer pane or the Object Explorer Details pane. The available filters change based on the type of item selected (databases, tables, stored procedures, etc.). Table 1-1 lists the available filtering options for tables.

TABLE 1-1   SQL Server Management Studio filters and options

Filter	Options
Name	Contains Equals Does Not Contain
Schema	Contains Equals Does Not Contain
Owner	Equals Does Not Equal
Durability Type	Equals Does Not Equal
Is Memory Optimized	Equals
Creation Date	Equals Less Than Less Than or Equal More Than More Than or Equal Between Not Between

After you have selected a filter, the suffix *(filtered)* appears in the Object Explorer or Object Explorer Details tree above your filtered list.

To clear an applied filter and display all objects in a tree again, right-click a filtered category and choose **Filter** > **Remove Filter**.

Multi-Select

In the Object Explorer pane, you can select only one object at a time. The Object Explorer Details pane, however, provides a multi-select feature that enables you to work on multiple objects (tables, views, jobs, and so on) at the same time.

Following the standard in the Windows environment, the **Shift** key allows for the selection of contiguous objects, whereas the **Ctrl** key allows for the selection of objects one by one. You can initiate actions on multiple objects using the GUI or you can choose to script multiple objects at once. Scripting each object into its own file or merging all object scripting into one larger file are both available options. Merging object scripting is helpful for both creating and deleting multiple objects at once.

Inside OUT

What are some of the changes released with SQL Server Management Studio (SSMS) v19?

SSMS v19 provides user-interface improvements for data classification as well as the Query Tuning Assistant. It also improves support for ledger tables so you can see columns that have been dropped. However, this version of SSMS does not contain the Stretch Database Wizard or any references to the SQL Server Native Client (SQLNCLI or SNAC), as those features are deprecated.

Additional tools in SQL Server Management Studio

SSMS provides time-saving tools and techniques to make you more productive. This section provides just a few highlights.

IntelliSense tools

IntelliSense is a ubiquitous Microsoft technology found in many of its products to help with code completion. IntelliSense effectively reduces the amount of typing you do by offering shortcuts and autocompleting keywords and object names. This also makes your code more accurate.

Additionally, SSMS comes with snippets to help you code more easily. *Snippets* are preconfigured code fragments that you can quickly drop into (using the Insert Snippet command) or around (using the Surround With command) an existing block of code. You also can create your own snippets—you build them using XML—but that is beyond the scope of this discussion.

> **NOTE**
>
> You can manage code snippets from the Tools menu, via the Code Snippets Manager option.

Let's look at some use cases for snippets.

One of the options in SQL Server 2012 and later versions is to include a snippet for an IF statement. After testing a block of code, you can quickly add the IF statement (including the BEGIN/END statements) by highlighting your code and choosing a snippet.

There are three ways to access snippets:

- Use a keyboard shortcut, such as **Ctrl+K** followed by **Ctrl+S** (**Surround With**), and **Ctrl+K** followed by **Ctrl+X** (**Insert Snippets**).

- Right-click and choose an option from the context menu that opens.

- Choose **Edit** > **IntelliSense** and select a snippets option—for example, **Surround With**. (See Figure 1-6.)

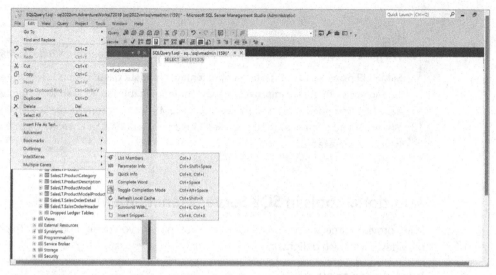

Figure 1-6 Accessing the Surround With snippet from the Edit menu.

When you choose **Surround With**, a snippet surrounds the highlighted code with the snippet template code. You can even insert "placeholder" text for replacing later.

There are only a few stock Surround With snippet options, but there are many Insert Snippet options. You can find these by choosing **Edit** > **IntelliSense** > **Insert Snippet**. You can also double-click the **Function** folder to see the available snippets and use them the same way you do the Surround With snippets (except that the code is placed at the current location of the cursor within a block of code rather than around selected code).

Inside OUT

Did someone say keyboard shortcuts?

SQL Server Management Studio offers a large range of keyboard shortcuts for increasing productivity. By far the most popular is **F5**, which runs a query; you can also use **Ctrl+E** to do that.

You can show and hide the results pane of a query by using **Ctrl+R**. Accessing the Code Snippets Manager is as easy as **Ctrl+K** followed by **Ctrl+B**. Do you want to include the Actual Query Plan in a query? Use **Ctrl+M**. **Ctrl+F5** parses a query before you run it to ensure that the syntax is correct.

You can find the full list of SSMS keyboard shortcuts at *https://learn.microsoft.com/sql /ssms/sql-server-management-studio-keyboard-shortcuts.*

Guided upgrades using the Query Tuning Assistant

SSMS 18.0 introduced the Query Tuning Assistant (QTA), which works with the Query Store to help guide SQL Server upgrades from SQL Server 2016 and SQL Server 2017 to SQL Server 2019 and above. Note that the QTA does not support Azure SQL Database, Azure SQL Managed Instance, or Azure SQL Analytics.

> ➤ The QTA is covered in more detail in Chapter 14, "Performance tune SQL Server." You
> can also read the official documentation at *https://learn.microsoft.com/sql/relational
> -databases/performance/upgrade-dbcompat-using-qta.*

Customize menus and shortcuts

SSMS is based on the Visual Studio integrated development environment (IDE), which means that it is customizable and extensible. Adding extensions is beyond the scope of this book, but the next few sections describe how to customize elements such as the toolbars and keyboard shortcuts.

Customize toolbars

By default, SSMS displays only the standard toolbar at the top. However, there are many other toolbars available for use. To access these options, on the toolbar, select **Tools > Customize**. This opens the **Customize** dialog box, which has two tabs:

- **Toolbars.** On this tab, you can select the toolbars that are useful in your work environment. Among the many choices are toolbars for working with database diagrams, Extended Events, and XML.

- **S.** You can use this tab to set up a custom toolbar or to edit the drop-down menus and functionality of an existing toolbar.

Tool options

You also can customize the appearance of your SSMS interface. Select **Tools > Options** to adjust the color, font, keyboard hotkeys, length of strings in results, location of results, scripting preferences, international settings, theme, autorecovery timeframe, and more.

One very handy option in the **Options** dialog box is **Keyboard > Query Shortcuts**. SSMS comes with several shortcuts already turned on (see Figure 1-7), but you can use this setting to tailor them to your needs. Many long-time DBAs make heavy use of this setting to reduce the number of keystrokes required to carry out common procedures.

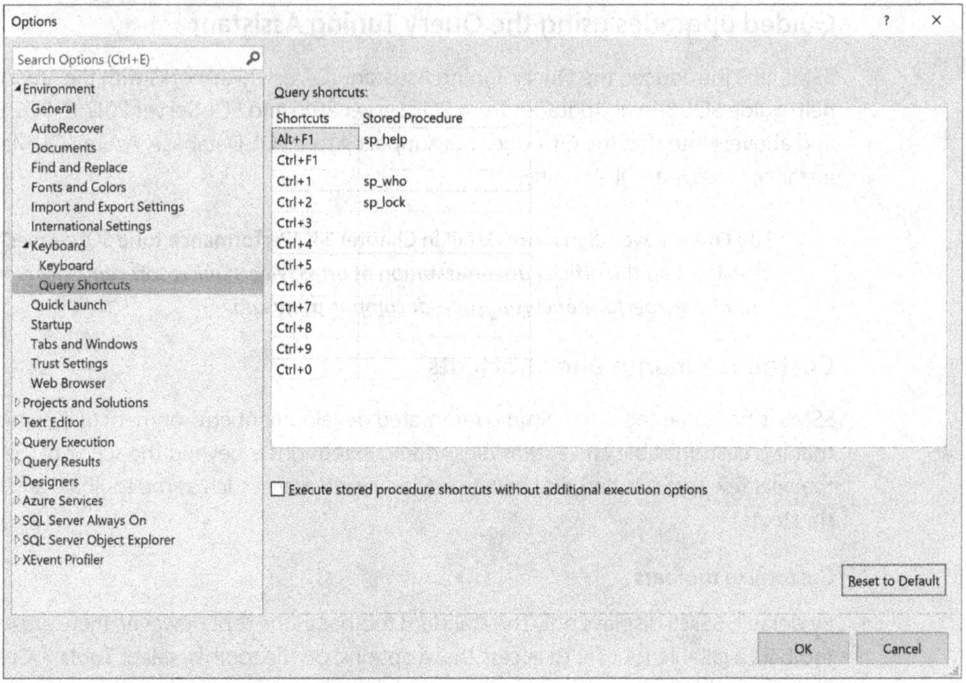

Figure 1-7 Managing query shortcuts.

Using shortcuts in SSMS, you can highlight text and then activate the keyboard shortcut to run the associated stored procedure, supplying a parameter of the highlighted text. For instance, to see the name, created date, and a list of columns and associated data types in a view, you can use the sp_help system procedure. As you can see in Figure 1-7, this procedure is called by the keyboard shortcut **Alt+F1**. This shortcut is not modifiable, but several others are.

If you populate a query window with the name of a view, and then use the keyboard shortcut **Alt+F1**, you will see results like the ones shown in Figure 1-8.

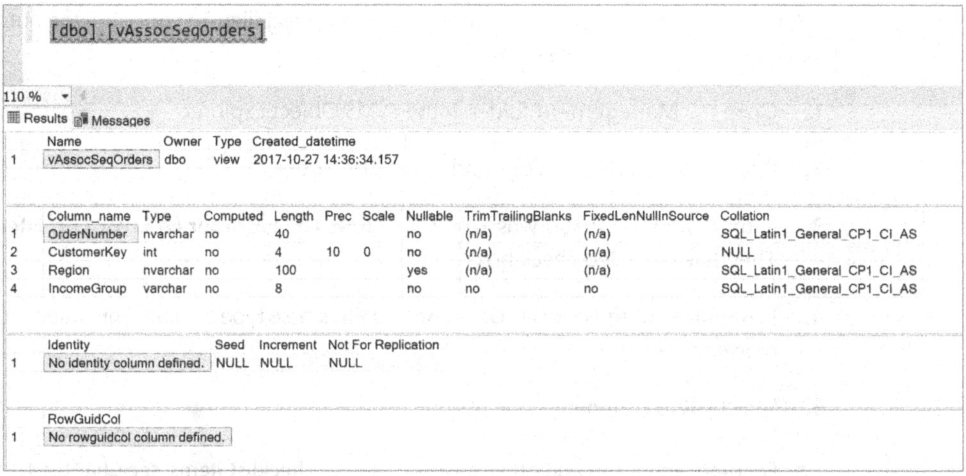

```
[dbo].[vAssocSeqOrders]
```

110 %

Results   Messages

	Name	Owner	Type	Created_datetime
1	vAssocSeqOrders	dbo	view	2017-10-27 14:36:34.157

	Column_name	Type	Computed	Length	Prec	Scale	Nullable	TrimTrailingBlanks	FixedLenNullInSource	Collation
1	OrderNumber	nvarchar	no	40			no	(n/a)	(n/a)	SQL_Latin1_General_CP1_CI_AS
2	CustomerKey	int	no	4	10	0	no	(n/a)	(n/a)	NULL
3	Region	nvarchar	no	100			yes	(n/a)	(n/a)	SQL_Latin1_General_CP1_CI_AS
4	IncomeGroup	varchar	no	8			no	no	no	SQL_Latin1_General_CP1_CI_AS

	Identity	Seed	Increment	Not For Replication
1	No identity column defined.	NULL	NULL	NULL

	RowGuidCol
1	No rowguidcol column defined.

Figure 1-8 Using query shortcuts in SSMS.

Error logs

Each SQL Server instance maintains a distinct set of relevant SQL Server Error Log messages that are accessible in two places:

- The **Management > Error Logs** node

- The context menu that appears when you right-click an instance in the Registered Servers window

These log files contain information about the SQL Server instance when coming online, what configuration settings were applied (or failed to execute), when backups occurred, when corruption is detected, when I/O is taking too long, partial stack dumps, and lots of other useful data. It's a great place to go to when troubleshooting stability or performance problems and to look for things that might cause trouble in the future.

To keep the log information to a reasonable and searchable size, the information is kept in a series of files rather than in one single file. It is possible to close one file and start a new, blank file. Unfortunately, however, the default settings for cycling the log are not very useful.

NOTE

It is not currently possible to change the number of error log files in SQL Server on Linux.

By default, SQL Server keeps the six most-recent error log files. To configure the number of log files to maintain, follow these steps:

1. Open the **Management** folder in the SSMS Object Explorer.

2. Right-click **SQL Server Logs** and select **Configure**.

3. In the dialog box that opens, select the **Limit The Number Of Error Log Files Before They Are Recycled** check box.

4. In the **Maximum Number Of Error Log Files** box, type a value. This value must be between 6 and 99.

5. Select **OK** to continue.

➤ For more about this and other post-installation checklist items, see Chapter 4.

Every time the SQL Server service is restarted, it cycles the log file. This creates a brand-new, empty log file and moves the previous log file down one spot in the list. Any log file older in sequence than the maximum specified number of files to keep is deleted.

You also can choose to manually cycle the log file by using the sp_cycle_errorlog command. Or you can automate this process by using a SQL Server Agent job. When working with SQL Server instances that are quite large and remain online for a long time, this can prevent any single log file from becoming overly large and unwieldy.

No matter which method you use, the resulting action is the same: The current file is closed, and a new, blank file is opened. If this causes the file count to exceed the maximum number of files, the oldest file is deleted.

Activity Monitor

Activity Monitor provides information about what is currently running on the SQL Server and how that code might be affecting the instance. It lets you easily view common hardware-specific performance metrics and a list of recently used queries (with metrics, code, and execution plans). You can sort all the grids, and even filter some of them. Out of the box, this is the place to begin if you need to do rudimentary troubleshooting and baselining.

To open the Activity Monitor window, right-click the SQL Server instance in the **Object Explorer** pane and select **Activity Monitor** from the context menu that appears.

The Activity Monitor window consists of six distinct parts:

- **Overview.** This displays a basic version of what you might already be familiar with viewing in the Task Manager window, but with a SQL Server flair in the form of four distinct graphs (discussed in the next section).

- **Processes.** By default, this displays all non-system processes with open connections to the SQL Server instance. However, you can also select a process and right-click to view the associated SQL script or live execution plan, among other options.

- **Resource Waits.** This displays the wait events of active, open connections.

- **Data File I/O.** This displays the difference between two interval readings of the storage subsystem.

- **Recent Expensive Queries.** This displays information about the most expensive queries from the past 30 seconds.

- **Active Expensive Queries.** This displays a more detailed view of the most expensive queries running at that moment, based on the column you have selected to sort on.

You can expand each of these parts to show more information, with the Overview section expanded by default. If you want to sort or filter the results, select the column header of any of the columns in each section.

The next several sections discuss these Activity Monitor Window components in more detail.

Overview

Four graphs in the Overview relay the most basic overview of the instance. The % Processor Time graph is an average combined value for all logical processors assigned to the instance (see the section "Allocate CPU cores with an affinity mask" in Chapter 3, "Design and implement an on-premises database infrastructure"). The other three graphs are Waiting Tasks (an instance-level value), Database I/O (all databases, measured in MB/sec) and Batch Requests/sec (all databases).

Each graph displays information in near-real time, refreshing every 10 seconds by default. You can configure the refresh interval by right-clicking any of the graphs and choosing an option from the context menu that appears. The refresh interval can be as short as 1 second to as long as 1 hour. The graph settings are adjusted as a unified set; all four graphs use the same interval setting, so changing one interval changes them all. Likewise, selecting Pause on any of the graphs pauses the entire set.

Processes

The Processes section of Activity Monitor displays all non-system processes (also known as tasks) with open connections to the SQL Server instance, regardless of whether the process is actively running a query. It provides the following types of important metadata:

- **Session ID.** The session process identifier (SPID) of the current process

- **User Process.** Displays a 1 if this is a user process and a 0 if it is a system process (this list is filtered to show only user processes by default)

- **Login.** The login name of the user running this process

- **Database.** The name of the database

- **Task State.** Populated from the list of possible tasks in the task_state column of the sys.dm_os_tasks dynamic management view

- **Command.** Populated from the list of command types in the command column of the sys.dm_exec_requests dynamic management view

- **Application.** The name of the application

- **Wait Time (ms).** The amount of time this task has been waiting, in milliseconds

- **Wait Type.** The current wait type for this task

- **Wait Resource.** The resource for which this task is waiting

- **Blocked By.** If this task is being blocked by another process, this shows the SPID of the blocking process

- **Head Blocker.** If there is a chain of blocking processes, this is the SPID of the process at the start of the blocking chain

- **Memory Use (KB).** How much memory this process is using

- **Host Name.** The host name of the machine that made this connection

- **Workload Group.** The name of the Resource Governor workload group that this process belongs to (you can read more about the Resource Governor in Chapter 3)

Each column allows you to filter to specific values. For example, right-click any row in the **Processes** pane to see the detailed T-SQL query being run (last T-SQL command batch), trace the process in SQL Profiler, or kill the process.

Resource Waits

The Resource Waits section of the Activity Monitor displays the wait events of active, open connections, sorted by default by the cumulative wait time (in seconds).

This can be very useful when you're trying to determine the root cause of a performance issue. Having a baseline for these counters when things are good is very useful later, when you're trying to gauge whether a problem you're experiencing is new or normal.

Understanding the meaning of certain wait times can help you diagnose the root cause of slowness, be it storage, memory pressure, CPU, network latency, or a client struggling to receive and display a result set. Following are the wait statistics provided by this section:

- Wait Category

- Wait Time (ms/sec)

- Recent Wait Time (ms/sec)

- Average Waiter Count

- Cumulative Wait Time (sec)

   ➤ **You can read more about Resource Waits at** *https://learn.microsoft.com/sql/relational -databases/system-dynamic-management-views/sys-dm-os-wait-stats-transact-sql* **or by referring to the "Understand wait types and wait statistics" section in Chapter 8.**

Data File I/O

The Data File I/O section of the Activity Monitor displays the difference between two readings taken from the metadata stored in the `sys.dm_io_virtual_file_stats` dynamic management view. For this reason, when you first expand this section, you might not see results for a short while. The server needs at least two readings, so, for example, if your interval is 10 seconds, you'll wait 10 seconds before data appears.

The information displayed shows each of the data files for all of the databases on the SQL Server, the file location and name, megabytes per second read (MB/sec read), megabytes per second written (MB/sec written), and average response time in milliseconds (ms).

Generally, average response times of 5 milliseconds or less allow for acceptable performance, the occasional outlying peak notwithstanding.

Recent Expensive Queries

The Activity Monitor's Recent Expensive Queries section displays information about the most expensive queries that have run on the SQL Server instance in the past 30 seconds. It includes both queries in flight and queries that have finished.

To see the full query text or the execution plan currently in use, right-click any of the queries listed. Here are the fields returned in this pane:

- Query

- Executions/min

- CPU (ms/sec)

- Physical Reads/sec

- Logical Writes/sec

- Logical Reads/sec

- Average Duration (ms)

- Plan Count

- Database

Active Expensive Queries

If you're trying to determine what is running at this precise moment that might be causing performance issues, the Active Expensive Queries part of the Activity Monitor is the place to look. It is more granular than the aggregated "past 30 seconds" view provided in the Recent Expensive Queries section. In addition, the list of queries in this part shows some very interesting details that are available at only a granular level:

- Session ID

- Database

- Elapsed Time

- Row Count

- Memory Allocated

Again, you can see the full query text and the execution plan by right-clicking, but here you get an additional feature: Show Live Execution Plan. This might differ if a query is running long.

Inside OUT

Does Activity Monitor use considerable resources?

Activity Monitor does use resources, as there is overhead associated with any monitoring tool. When you expand any of the detail areas in Activity Monitor, it must query the system metadata in real time to populate the columns and/or graphs on the screen. When you collapse the area, these queries stop.

After you have finished viewing a section, we recommend that you collapse that section or close the Activity Monitor tab to avoid unnecessary "observer overhead."

SQL Server Agent

SQL Server Agent is a service on both Windows and Linux that you can use to schedule automated tasks, called jobs, as illustrated in Figure 1-9. These jobs mostly run routine maintenance (backups, index defragmentation, statistics updates, and integrity checks), but you can also use them to periodically run custom code.

Figure 1-9 The SQL Server Agent tree view.

> **NOTE**
>
> You can filter SQL Server Agent nodes. This was described earlier in this chapter in the section "Filtering objects" in the discussion of Object Explorer.

Windows Server has built-in functionality for job notifications to email the status of a job to a person or group using the Database Mail feature. The setup provides a few straightforward configuration options that apply to notifications that are sent: Success, Failure, and Completion.

> ➤ For more information on configuring Database Mail, and on configuring SQL Agent to use Database Mail, see Chapter 9, "Automate SQL Server administration."

Job Activity Monitor

Job Activity Monitor provides a snapshot view of all jobs on a server. Using this feature, you can quickly see many attributes of the jobs scheduled on a SQL Server instance, and you can use many of these attributes to narrow the list of jobs displayed. Table 1-2 lists the attributes.

TABLE 1-2 Job activity attributes

Job activity attribute	Values	Can use to filter?
Name		X
Enabled	No Yes	X
Status	Between Retries Executing	X
Last Run Outcome	Idle Not Idle Performing Completed Action Suspended Waiting for Step to Finish Waiting for Worker Thread	X
Last Run		X
Next Run		X
Category		X
Runnable	Yes No	X
Scheduled	Yes No	X
Category ID		

Notify operators with alerts

You can configure alerts to notify you when a specific event occurs. Unlike jobs that run on a schedule, alert notifications can be sent in reaction to a scenario that has been set off. Examples include emailing the DBA team when a data or log file experiences auto growth, or when Target Server Memory drops below a certain threshold on a virtual machine.

SQL Server Agent's alerting feature gives administrators the ability to create three different types of alerts:

- **Event alerts.** These are raised by SQL Server's Error and Severity mechanism. You can specify this for all databases or for a single database. You can use an error number or a severity level to set off an alert. Text within the system message can be parsed to only alert in specific scenarios.

- **Performance condition alerts.** These alerts use the entire library of SQL Server Performance Monitor counters. Any counter object can be chosen, the sub counter object specified, the counter instance noted (if applicable), and a threshold (falls below, becomes equal to, or rises above) provided at which an alert should fire. Figure 1-10 shows the configuration of a performance condition alert definition to notify an administrator if the Page Life Expectancy metric on a SQL Server instance drops below 5 minutes.

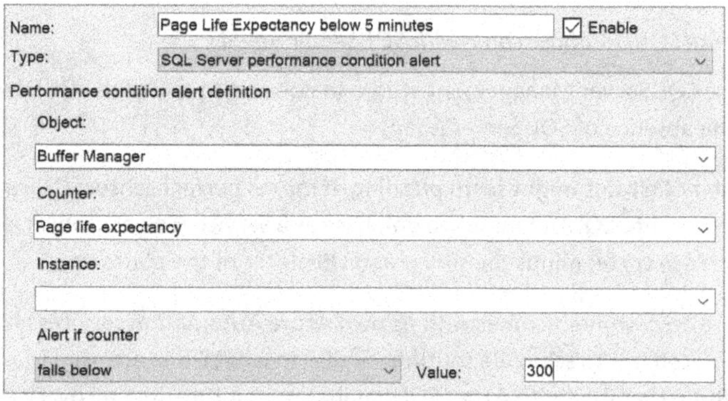

CHAPTER 1

Figure 1-10 Creating a performance condition alert.

- **Windows Management Instrumentation (WMI) alerts.** A WMI alert uses the Windows Management Instrumentation Event Provider to allow for more complicated actions upon the detection of an event that sets off an alert. One example is to use the alerting system to detect a deadlock and then save the XML deadlock graph information to a table for later analysis. Another is to detect any DDL or system configuration changes that occur and to document them for later review. Because the WMI Provider has access to many server event classes and properties, this feature is quite versatile. It does come with several catches, however:

  - It requires Service Broker to be enabled in the msdb database of the instance.

  - If your code queries objects within a particular database on the server, Service Broker must be enabled on that database also.

  - It is not very GUI-friendly and requires a bit more programming know-how than the other alert options.

  - It is not supported on SQL Server on Linux or Docker containers.

➤ You can read more about creating WMI alerts in Chapter 8, as well as at *https://learn .microsoft.com/sql/ssms/agent/create-a-wmi-event-alert.*

A response to an alert can be to run a job, notify a list of operators, or both.

Operators

Operators are users or groups designated as points of contact to receive notifications from the SQL Server Agent. They are most commonly defined with email addresses, but there are additional delivery methods available.

Inside OUT

Does Azure SQL Database come with SQL Server Agent?

If you use SQL Server Management Studio to connect to an Azure SQL Database, you might notice the absence of SQL Server Agent.

Although at first this might seem puzzling, it makes perfect sense. SQL Server Agent is an OS service. Azure SQL Database is a database as a service (DBaaS), which is essentially a sole database (*à la carte*) minus the server and OS pieces of the platform.

The Azure environment comes with its own Azure Automation services and elastic jobs, which you can use to schedule routines similar to what DBAs are used to with SQL Server Agent. But remember, with Azure SQL databases, point-in-time recovery is included automatically.

Another option is to use Azure SQL Managed Instance, which is covered in Chapter 18, "Provision Azure SQL Managed Instance."

Azure Data Studio

Azure Data Studio (ADS) is an exciting addition to the administration and development toolkit for the database platform, including SQL Server, Azure SQL Database, Azure Synapse Analytics (formerly Azure SQL Data Warehouse), and PostgreSQL.

Think of ADS as more of a developer-focused tool compared to SSMS. While ADS performs many of the same tasks as SSMS, it is more focused on development than administration, and can run cross-platform on Windows, macOS, and Linux.

Often, but not always, when ADS is missing native features required for database administration, there is an extension built by Microsoft or by a partner that fills that need.

While ADS is installed along with SSMS by default, you can install it separately. If a version you have installed is newer than the version being installed/upgraded with SSMS, the newer version will not be overwritten.

➤ You can download the latest version of Azure Data Studio from *https://aka.ms/azuredatastudio*.

Inside OUT

Is Azure Data Studio open-source software?

Azure Data Studio—like Visual Studio Code, which it is based on—is an open-source software (OSS) project based on the Electron shell and on Node.js, a JavaScript runtime. It is free for use, and anyone can contribute to the project.

For more information about the project, and to contribute your own code, see *https://github.com/microsoft/azuredatastudio*.

User interface

Azure Data Studio is based on the same shell as Visual Studio Code. Thus, it shares a similar development environment and is fully extensible. In other words, you can easily install third-party plugins and extensions to improve your workflow, or even write your own and contribute them to the main product codebase. Many of the extensions for Visual Studio Code will run on Azure Data Studio.

The main interface for Azure Data Studio is made up of viewlets and tiles, similar in concept to the docked windows in SSMS. These elements present information to monitor and administer your database environment. (See Figure 1-11.)

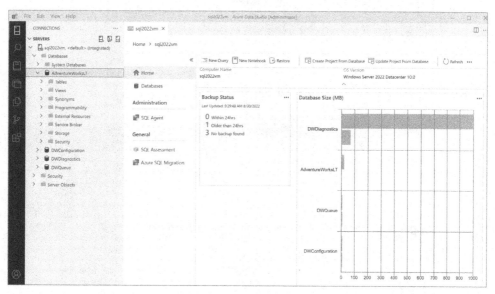

Figure 1-11 The Azure Data Studio user interface.

The Interface is fully customizable, with a dashboard that shows:

- Insights, performance metrics, and telemetry

- Recent connections

- An Object Explorer (like SSMS; see Figure 1-12)

- A query window for code

- A results grid that can be exported to CSV, Excel, JSON, and XML

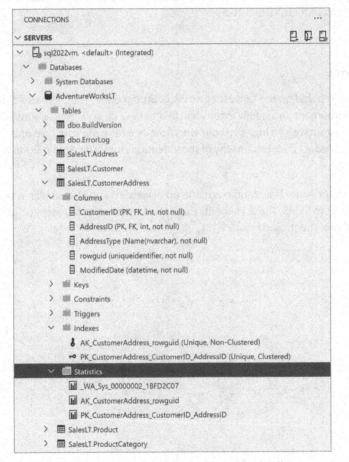

Figure 1-12 The Object Explorer view in Azure Data Studio.

NOTE

Whereas SSMS uses dialog boxes that pop up in the center of the application interface, the Azure Data Studio dialog boxes, or flyouts, appear from the right of the user interface until the necessary action is performed. This takes some getting used to for people who are more familiar with the SSMS interface.

Highlighted features in Azure Data Studio

Azure Data Studio includes many of the same core features for administering and developing on a SQL Server that you would expect to find in SSMS. These include:

- Managing registered servers

- Viewing server and database reports

- Writing queries

- Managing security

- Generating scripts

- Viewing and analyzing query plans

- Performing tasks such as database consistency checks

- Maintaining indexes and statistics

- Running backups and restores

Certain dialog boxes in SSMS can be run from inside Azure Data Studio (and vice versa), as long as the latest versions of both applications are installed on the same Windows computer. This allows an integrated experience through the seamless use of different features across both applications from within the tool of your choice.

For example, you can select a database, right-click, and choose **Generate Scripts** to open the familiar Generate Scripts wizard from SSMS. (See Figure 1-13 and Figure 1-14.)

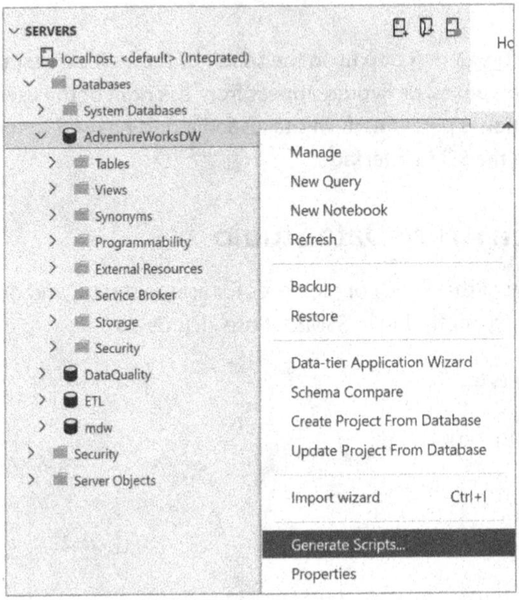

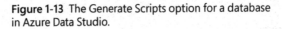

∨ SERVERS

∨ 🖥 localhost, <default> (Integrated)

   ∨ 📁 Databases

      > 📁 System Databases

      ∨ 🗄 AdventureWorksDW

         > 📁 Tables

         > 📁 Views

         > 📁 Synonyms

         > 📁 Programmability

         > 📁 External Resources

         > 📁 Service Broker

         > 📁 Storage

         > 📁 Security

      > 🗄 DataQuality

      > 🗄 ETL

      > 🗄 mdw

   > 📁 Security

   > 📁 Server Objects

Menu:
- Manage
- New Query
- New Notebook
- Refresh
- Backup
- Restore
- Data-tier Application Wizard
- Schema Compare
- Create Project From Database
- Update Project From Database
- Import wizard   Ctrl+I
- Generate Scripts...
- Properties

Figure 1-13 The Generate Scripts option for a database in Azure Data Studio.

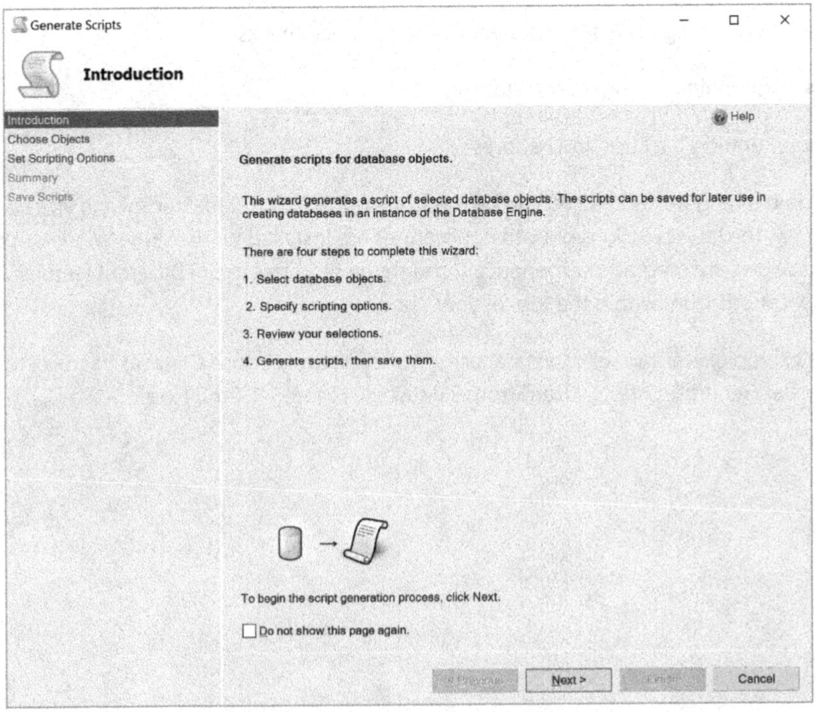

Generate Scripts   — ☐ ✕

Introduction

Introduction
Choose Objects
Set Scripting Options
Summary
Save Scripts

🔘 Help

Generate scripts for database objects.

This wizard generates a script of selected database objects. The scripts can be saved for later use in creating databases in an instance of the Database Engine.

There are four steps to complete this wizard:

1. Select database objects.

  2. Specify scripting options.

3. Review your selections.

4. Generate scripts, then save them.

To begin the script generation process, click Next.

☐ Do not show this page again.

      < Previous   Next >   Finish   Cancel

Figure 1-14 The SSMS Generate Scripts wizard, opened from ADS.

Since the release of SQL Server 2019, many significant features have been added to Azure Data Studio. For example:

- Support for Always Encrypted and Always Encrypted with secure enclaves was added.

- The SQL Assessment API extension was published.

- The SQL Database Projects extension was published with schema compare functionality.

- The SQL Server Import extension became generally available.

- Support was added for KQL in notebooks.

- The Table Designer UI was added.

- The Query Plan Viewer was added.

- The Azure Arc extension was updated.

- The Azure SQL Migration extension became generally available.

- Object Explorer was updated to add support for SQL ledger objects.

Inside OUT

What is KQL?

KQL is the abbreviated name for Kusto Query Language. KQL is the open-source language used to query tables in Azure Data Explorer, including logs collected from Azure resources such as SQL Server and Azure SQL Database that are stored in a Log Analytics workspace.

You can learn more about Kusto queries and how Kusto compares to SQL at *https://learn .microsoft.com/azure/data-explorer/kusto/query*.

Extend the features of Azure Data Studio

Azure Data Studio allows for additional features that are not part of the base product, directly from the interface, on the **Extensions** pane. To access the **Extensions** pane, select **View > Extensions**, or press **Shift+Ctrl+X** (Windows and Linux) or **Shift+Cmd+X** (macOS).

Extensions recommended by Microsoft are identified by a white star on a blue background at the top left of the extension item. (See Figure 1-15.)

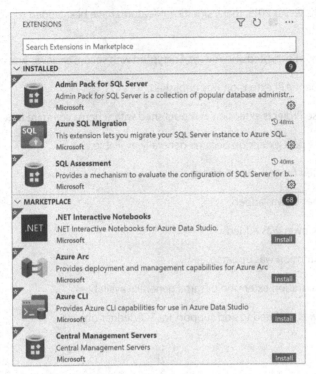

Figure 1-15 The Extensions Marketplace.

To install an extension, select its **Install** button. When the extension is installed, you may be prompted to reload the application; select the **Reload** button, and Azure Data Studio will reopen with the extension enabled.

NOTE

Some extensions may need to be installed manually. You do this by choosing **File > Install Extension from VSIX Package.** Take care when trusting third-party extensions installed in this manner.

Access the command line

One extremely useful feature in Azure Data Studio (and Visual Studio Code) is the built-in command line interface. This terminal allows you to interact with the underlying OS from within the application using familiar terminal types like PowerShell or the command prompt, or other terminal types like Git Bash. This improves productivity because you don't need to switch away from the Azure Data Studio interface to manipulate files or execute external scripts.

To access the terminal, choose **View** > **Terminal** or use **Ctrl**+` (backtick) on Windows and Linux or **Cmd**+` on macOS.

Notebooks in Azure Data Studio

One of the fundamental ways in which Azure Data Studio is helpful to data professionals is through its support of notebooks, based on Project Jupyter (pronounced *Jupiter*).

Notebooks already support many languages, including R, Python, and PowerShell, which makes them a natural addition to the data scientist's toolkit. But their use has expanded to data analysts and big data developers as well.

Inside OUT

What is Project Jupyter?

Much like this book, technical documentation and code is traditionally static. It appears in fixed type, sometimes with diagrams, to assist you in understanding a topic. Any code included in that documentation must usually be typed in by hand or copied and pasted into an execution environment to be run. In contrast, web pages make documentation and code easier to work with due to their interactive nature.

Project Jupyter uses web technology to address the problem of static code by presenting notebooks as interactive web applications. Code can now be executed from within the documentation, which itself is written in Markdown format. Find out more about Project Jupyter at *https://jupyter.org/*.

Notebooks as runbooks

One particularly interesting feature for data professionals is SQL kernel support. This enables you to create powerful interactive and shareable notebooks with SQL Server and PostgreSQL as supported environments.

In this book, we refer to these notebooks as *SQL notebooks*. As of version 1.16.0 (released in March 2020), SQL notebooks support creating and saving charts.

The structure of SQL notebooks makes them an ideal format for runbooks. A *runbook* is a set of standardized written procedures for completing repetitive tasks. SQL notebooks allow you to mix cells containing text explanations for steps in a task with the cells containing SQL to be run to execute a task. The results of an executed SQL script can be saved in the notebook as well. This is helpful for showing expected results of a task.

Using the Markdown language, you can convert existing scripts and documentation into SQL notebooks. Because these documents are plain text files that render as web pages, they can be treated like source code and checked into a source control system. This gives you a lot more control over versioning, especially around runbooks.

> ➤ See Chapter 10, "Develop, deploy, and manage data recovery," for a practical use case for runbooks.

Inside OUT

What is Markdown?

Markdown (commonly written in lowercase as *markdown*) is a plain text markup language created by John Gruber and Aaron Swartz in 2004. It was originally designed to output HTML pages. Markdown differs from other markup languages such as RTF, HTML, and PDF formats because its syntax makes the documents easier for humans to read.

Markdown has been adopted by many organizations, including GitHub (a Microsoft subsidiary), and is the language in which Jupyter notebooks are written. Microsoft Docs are also composed in Markdown and are open source on GitHub.

SQL Server Data Tools

SQL Server Data Tools (SSDT) provides developers with a set of tools for working with SQL Server, as well as SQL Server Integration Services (SSIS), Reporting Services (SSRS), and Analysis Services (SSAS).

SQL Server Data Tools is a built-in workload within Visual Studio 2022 or later. In contrast, the SSIS, SSRS, and SSAS project templates must be downloaded from within Visual Studio using Extension Manager. You will need to use the built-in workload to work with database projects.

NOTE

Despite having similar names, Visual Studio is an entirely different product from Visual Studio Code. SSDT is not supported in Visual Studio Code.

SQL Server Integration Services

SQL Server Integration Services (SSIS) is a versatile platform for importing, transforming, and exporting data. Frequently used for extract, transform, load (ETL) processes, SSIS can integrate with many external systems using standard tasks, interfaces, and protocols.

SSIS manages these solutions using packages, which you create and modify using a GUI. Packages feature a control flow and data flow in their design, so you can include both orchestration and data manipulation logic.

SSIS packages can be executed in SSIS on a Windows or Linux server running SQL Server. In Azure, Azure Data Factory can execute SSIS packages on a Windows server in Azure running an

Azure-SSIS Integration Runtime. Regardless of the service being used to execute an SSIS package, these packages are built using the SSIS project template in Visual Studio.

SSIS contains other functionality in addition to SSIS packages. This includes the SSISDB Upgrade Wizard, the Import and Export Wizard, and the Data Profiling Task and Viewer. These features are discussed next.

SQL Server Integration Services Package Upgrade Wizard

The SQL Server Integration Services Package Upgrade Wizard is a tool that you can use to upgrade SSIS packages created in versions earlier than SQL Server 2022. Although you most commonly access this tool from SQL Server Data Tools, you can also find and launch it from SSMS and from the Windows command prompt. Part of the upgrade wizard in all these scenarios involves the automated backup of the original packages.

To launch this wizard from SQL Server Data Tools:

1. Open an Integration Services Project.

2. Right-click **SSIS Packages**.

3. Select **Upgrade All Packages**.

To launch it from SSMS:

1. Connect to Integration Services.

2. Expand **Stored Packages**.

3. Right-click the **File System** or **MSDB** node.

4. Select **Upgrade Packages**.

To launch it from the Windows command prompt:

1. Navigate to the Microsoft SQL Server\160\DTS\Binn folder.

2. Locate and run the **SSISUpgrade.exe** file.

SQL Server Import and Export Wizard

The Import and Export Wizard simplifies the act of copying of data from a source to a destination. It uses SQL Server Integration Services to copy data by creating a package in memory. You can choose to save the package the wizard creates for future reuse. The variety of source and destination platforms supported by the wizard is generous. In some cases, you might need to download and install additional drivers and providers from a vendor or from a Microsoft Feature Pack. Table 1-3 lists examples of compatible data sources.

TABLE 1-3   Data sources in the Import and Export Wizard

Type	Details
Enterprise databases	SQL Server, Oracle, DB2
Text files	CSV or any other delimiter
Excel/Access	May require Access Runtime
Azure	Azure Storage
Open source	PostgreSQL, MySQL
Others	ODBC, .NET Framework, OLEDB

You can launch the Import and Export Wizard from the following places:

- The Start menu

- The command prompt

- SQL Server Management Studio

- SQL Server Data Tools

Data Profiling Task and Viewer

You can use the Data Profiling Task within SQL Server Integration Services to clarify data patterns (normal versus abnormal) and identify data quality issues before they reach a particular destination (usually a data warehouse). This tool provides visibility into the data quality by calculating and documenting the following metadata and statistical metrics:

- **Column Length Distribution Profile.** Reports the distinct lengths of strings in a selected column and the percent of total rows in the table that each string length represents. This helps you identify invalid values.

- **Column Null Ratio Profile.** Reports the percentage of null values in a selected column. This helps you identify unexpectedly high ratios of missing values.

- **Column Pattern Profile.** Reports a set of regular expressions that cover the specified percentage of values in a selected column. This helps you identify values that are invalid or not in the correct format.

- **Column Statistics Profile.** Reports minimum, maximum, average, and standard deviation for a selected numeric column, or minimum and maximum for a selected datetime column. This helps you identify values that may be outside of the expected range.

- **Column Value Distribution Profile.** Reports the distinct values in a selected column and the percentage of rows in a table that the value represents. This helps you identify unexpected values, especially when you know the number of distinct values expected.

The Data Profiling Task creates an XML output file. You can view this file by using the Data Profile Viewer, which is a standalone application and does not require Visual Studio or SQL Server Integration Services to run.

Figure 1-16 presents an example of the Data Profile Viewer. It displays the XML created by a Data Profile Task, pointed at Microsoft's WideWorldImporters sample database and analyzing the Sales.Customers table.

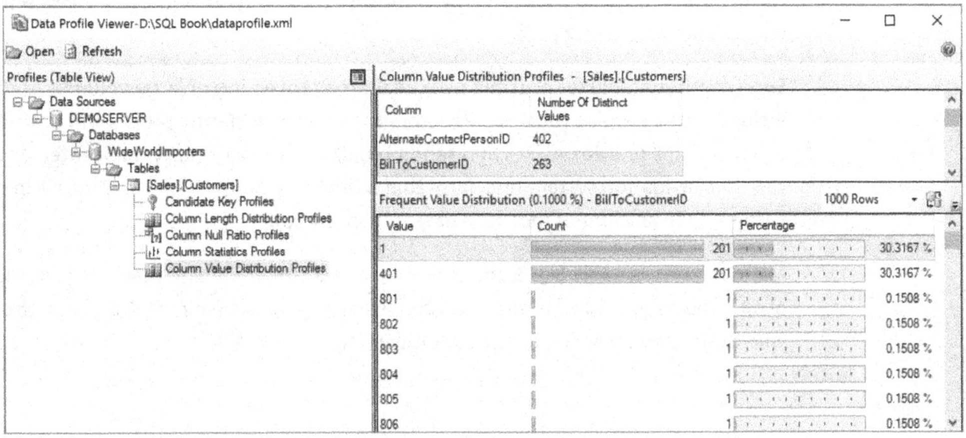

Figure 1-16 The Data Profile Viewer, showing column distribution.

SQL Server on Azure Arc–enabled servers

Azure Arc is a bridge that allows you to build applications and services with the flexibility to run across datacenters, at the edge, and in multi-cloud environments. You can manage your instances of SQL Server from Azure with SQL Server on Azure Arc–enabled servers.

Beginning with SQL Server 2022, you can now install the Azure Arc agent with the Azure extension for SQL Server when you install SQL Server on Windows. When you install the Azure Arc agent with the SQL Server extension, you can automatically enable the instance for Azure Arc. This will register the SQL Server instance as a resource in Azure so you can attach additional Azure management services to it.

There are some limitations to this new and evolving product. For example, Azure Arc–enabled servers do not currently support SQL Server failover cluster instances (FCIs).

➤ Find out more about SQL Server on Azure Arc–enabled servers at *https://learn.microsoft .com/sql/sql-server/azure-arc/overview*.

Inside OUT

What does "the edge" mean regarding databases?

Whereas cloud computing means that data is processed on servers in a private or public cloud such as Azure, edge computing means that data is processed in remote locations of a network. This processing occurs either on an IoT device or a local server. If data needs to be further aggregated or processed by a central server, only the important data is transmitted, which minimizes latency.

Edge computing makes possible near–real time processing of large volumes of data. This includes use cases like retail stores across the country instantly processing payments from wireless point-of-sale devices and sending data back to a primary datacenter. Another use case is an irrigation system on a farm that adjusts the amount of water it uses in real time based on the amount of moisture detected in the soil.

Microsoft offers Azure SQL Edge to support data streaming and machine learning as part of an edge computing solution. You can read more about Azure SQL Edge at *https://learn .microsoft.com/azure/azure-sql-edge/overview*.

Microsoft Purview

Microsoft Purview is a unified data-governance service that helps you manage your on-prem-ises, multi-cloud, and software-as-a-service (SaaS) data. It allows you to map and classify data across your organization with automated data discovery, data sensitivity classifications, and data lineage.

The data catalog functionality of Microsoft Purview helps you find trusted data sources by browsing and searching your data assets. Data Estate Insights gives you an overview of your data estate to help you discover what kinds of data you have and where. Data Sharing allows you to securely share data internally or with other organizations.

➤ Learn more about Microsoft Purview at *https://learn.microsoft.com/azure/purview/overview*.

Azure SQL and SQL Server databases can be registered as data sources and scanned by Micro-soft Purview. To enable this functionality on a SQL Server in a private network, you need to install the Azure Extension for SQL Server (the same extension used with Azure Arc). You'll also need a self-hosted integration runtime to perform the scan.

➤ Find out more about connecting to and managing on-premises SQL Server instances in Microsoft Purview at *https://learn.microsoft.com/azure/purview/register-scan-on-premises -sql-server*.

Discontinued and deprecated features

Every new version of SQL Server introduces some exciting new features while deprecating or even discontinuing features from earlier versions of SQL Server. Deprecated features may be removed from a future version of the product, so you should not use them for new development. Discontinued features have already been removed and might block upgrades to the latest database compatibility level or migrations to Azure SQL Database.

Several chapters in this book reference features that have been deprecated or discontinued. But the easiest way to stay up to date is to check the Microsoft documentation. As of this writing, three features were deprecated between SQL Server 2019 and SQL Server 2022: Distributed Replay, Machine Learning Server, and Stretch Database. SQL Server Big Data Clusters was also retired.

You can also access the list of deprecated features by using the following T-SQL query. It returns a list of more than 250 features that are deprecated, along with a count of the number of occurrences on your SQL Server instance. This sample script helps you identify and resolve specific occurrences of deprecated feature use in your instance.

```
SELECT object_name, counter_name, instance_name, cntr_value, cntr_type
FROM sys.dm_os_performance_counters
WHERE object_name = 'SQLServer:Deprecated Features';
```

In addition to the deprecated features, three features were discontinued: SQL Server Big Data Clusters, SQL Server PolyBase scale-out groups, and installation of Machine Learning Services packages.

➤ **For more discontinued features, see** *https://learn.microsoft.com/sql/database-engine /discontinued-database-engine-functionality-in-sql-server.*

Introduction to database server components

One of the best ways to develop a better understanding of SQL Server is to understand the infrastructure that supports the database. Having a better grasp of hardware, networking, availability options, security, and virtualization enables you to design, implement, and provision solutions that benefit your organization. Learning these concepts enables you to make good decisions to help create a stable environment for your databases. These decisions can affect anything from performance to uptime.

SQL Server runs on Windows and Linux, as well as in Linux containers. Microsoft has crafted the Database Engine to work the same way on other platforms as it does on Windows. The saying "it's just SQL Server" applies, but here we highlight places where there are differences.

We first discuss hardware. No matter which configuration you end up using, there are four basic components in a database infrastructure:

- Memory

- Processor

- Permanent storage

- Network

We then introduce high availability (HA) offerings, including new functionality for availability groups introduced in SQL Server 2022. When considering strategies for SQL Server HA and disaster recovery (DR), you design according to the organization's requirements for business continuity in terms of a Recovery Point Objective (RPO) and Recovery Time Objective (RTO).

We next provide an overview of security, including Active Directory, service principal names, federation and claims, and Kerberos. We cover ways to access the Database Engine, either on-premises or in Azure. As data theft has become more prevalent, you need to consider the security of the database itself, the underlying OS and hardware (physical or virtual), the network, and database backups.

Finally, we look at the similarities and differences between virtual machines (VMs) and containers, and when you should use them. Whether running on physical or virtual hardware, databases perform better when as much of the data as possible can be cached in memory and backed by fast, persistent storage that is redundant, with low latency and high random input/output operations per second (IOPS).

Memory

SQL Server is designed to use as much memory as it needs, and as much as you give it. By default, the upper limit of memory that SQL Server can access is limited only by the physical random-access memory (RAM) available to the server or to the edition of SQL Server you're running (whichever is lower). SQL Server on Linux has additional memory limits to avoid out-of-memory (OOM) errors.

Understand the working set

The physical memory made available to SQL Server by the operating system (OS) is called the *working set*. This working set is broken up into several sections by the SQL Server Memory Manager. The two largest and most important sections are the buffer pool and the procedure cache, also known as the *plan cache*.

In the strictest sense, *working set* applies only to physical memory. However, as you will soon see, the buffer pool extension blurs the lines because it uses non-volatile storage.

We look deeper into default memory settings in Chapter 3, "Design and implement an on-premises database infrastructure," in the "Configuration settings" section.

Cache data in the buffer pool

For best performance, SQL Server caches data in memory, because it is orders of magnitude faster to access data directly from memory than from traditional storage.

The buffer pool is an in-memory cache of 8 KB data pages that are copies of pages in the database file. Initially, the copy in the buffer pool is identical. Any changes to data are first applied to this buffer pool copy (and the transaction log) and then asynchronously applied to the data file.

When you run a query, the Database Engine requests the data page it needs from the buffer manager. (See Figure 2-1.) If the data is not already in the buffer pool, a page fault occurs. (This is an OS feature that informs the application that the page isn't in memory.) The buffer manager fetches the data from the storage subsystem and writes it to the buffer pool. When the data is in the buffer pool, the query continues.

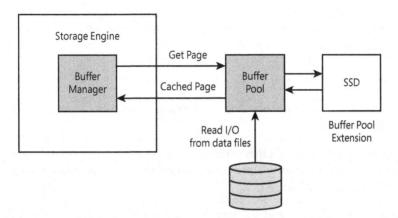

Figure 2-1 The buffer pool and the buffer pool extension.

The buffer pool is usually the largest consumer of the working set because it's where your data is. If the amount of data requested for a query exceeds the capacity of the buffer pool, the data pages spill to a drive, using either the buffer pool extension or a portion of tempdb.

The buffer pool extension uses non-volatile storage to extend the size of the buffer pool. It effectively increases the database working set, forming a bridge between the storage layer where the data files are located and the buffer pool in physical memory.

For performance reasons, this non-volatile storage should be solid-state storage, directly attached to the server.

> ➤ To learn how to turn on the buffer pool extension, read the section "Configuration settings" in Chapter 3. To learn more about tempdb, read the section "Data files and filegroups," also in Chapter 3.

Cached plans in the procedure cache

The procedure cache is usually smaller than the buffer pool. When you run a query, Query Optimizer compiles a query plan to explain to the Database Engine exactly how to run the query. To save time, it keeps a copy of that query plan so it won't need to compile the plan each time the query runs. It is not quite as simple as this, of course—plans can be removed, and trivial plans are not cached, for instance—but it's enough to give you a basic understanding.

The procedure cache is split into various cache stores by the Memory Manager. This is also where you can see if there are single-use query plans that are consuming memory.

> ➤ For more information about cached execution plans, read Chapter 14, "Performance tune SQL Server" or visit *https://blogs.msdn.microsoft.com/blogdoezequiel/2014/07/30 /too-many-single-use-plans-now-what/*.

Lock pages in memory

When you turn on the lock pages in memory (LPIM) policy, Windows cannot trim (reduce) SQL Server's working set.

Locking pages in memory ensures that Windows memory pressure cannot take resources away from SQL Server or push SQL Server memory into the Windows Server system page file, which dramatically reduces performance.

Under normal circumstances, Windows doesn't "steal" memory from SQL Server flippantly; it is done in response to memory pressure on the Windows Server. Indeed, all applications can have their memory affected by pressure from Windows.

However, without the ability to relieve pressure from other applications' or a virtual host's memory demands, LPIM can prevent Windows from deploying enough memory to remain stable. Because of this, LPIM cannot be the only method used to protect SQL Server's memory allocation.

NOTE

The Linux kernel is far stricter with memory management and forcibly terminates processes that use too much memory. With SQL Server on Linux, a dedicated setting called `memory.memorylimitmb` limits the amount of physical memory SQL Server can see. (By default, this is 80 percent of physical memory.) Chapter 5, "Install and configure SQL Server on Linux," covers this in more detail.

The controversy of the topic is stability versus performance, in which the latter was especially apparent on systems with limited memory resources and older operating systems. On larger servers with operating systems since Windows Server 2008, there is a lesser need for this policy to insulate SQL Server from memory pressure.

The prevailing wisdom is that the LPIM policy should be turned off by default for SQL Server unless all the following conditions apply:

- The server is virtual. See "Avoid overcommitting more memory than you have" later in this chapter.

- Physical RAM exceeds 16 GB (the OS needs a working set of its own).

- Max Server Memory has been set appropriately (SQL Server can't use everything it sees).

- The Memory\Available Mbytes performance counter is monitored regularly (to keep some memory free).

Use caution when enabling the LPIM policy, as it can adversely affect performance when starting SQL Server.

> ➤ You can read more about enabling LPIM at *https://learn.microsoft.com/troubleshoot/sql /admin/non-yielding-error-lock-pages-disable*.

Editions and memory limits

Since SQL Server 2016 Service Pack 1, many Enterprise edition features have found their way into the lower editions. Ostensibly, this was done to enable software developers to have far more code that works across all editions of the product.

Although some features are still limited by edition (high availability, for instance), features such as columnstore and In-Memory OLTP are turned on in every edition, including Express. Enterprise edition can use all available physical RAM for these features, though other editions are artificially limited.

> ## Inside OUT
>
> *What are some considerations for using In-Memory OLTP?*
>
> When implementing In-Memory OLTP, you should begin with an overhead of at least double the amount of data for a memory-optimized object. For example, if a memory-optimized table is 5 GB, start with at least 10 GB of RAM available for the exclusive use of that table. You should monitor performance to determine if you need to adjust the amount of RAM available for In-Memory OLTP objects. Keep this in mind before turning on this feature in Standard edition of SQL Server.
>
> Take care, too, when using memory-optimized table-valued functions (TVFs) in Standard edition, because each new object requires resources. Too many TVFs could starve the working set and cause SQL Server to crash.
>
> You can learn more here: *https://learn.microsoft.com/sql/relational-databases/in-memory -oltp/estimate-memory-requirements-for-memory-optimized-tables*.

Central processing unit

The central processing unit (CPU), often called the "brain" of a computer, is the most important part of a system. CPU speed is measured in hertz (Hz), or cycles per second, with the speed of modern processors measured in GHz, or billions of cycles per second. Modern systems can have more than one CPU, and each CPU can in turn have more than one CPU core (which might themselves be split up into virtual cores, or vCores).

For a typical SQL Server transactional workload, single-core speed matters. It is better to have fewer cores with higher clock speeds than more cores with lower speeds. That way, queries requiring fewer resources will complete faster. This is useful on non-Enterprise editions, especially when considering licensing.

Simultaneous multithreading

Some CPU manufacturers have split their physical cores into virtual cores to try to eke out even more performance using a feature called *simultaneous multithreading* (*SMT*). You can expect between 15 and 30 percent real-world performance improvement by enabling SMT, depending on the type of SQL Server workload. Intel calls this *Hyper-Threading*, so when you buy a single Intel Xeon CPU with 20 physical cores, the OS will see 40 virtual cores because of SMT.

➤ To learn more about SQL Server and SMT, see David Klee's article "SQL Server and CPU Hyper-Threading in virtual environments" at *https://www.davidklee.net/2020/04/10 /sql-server-and-cpu-hyper-threading-in-virtual-environments/*.

SMT becomes especially murky with virtualization because the guest OS might not have any insight into the physical versus logical core configuration.

NOTE

Think of SMT as an increase in overall CPU capacity as opposed to a performance boost. Performance depends on the type of workload the CPU is processing, and in some cases, SMT may be detrimental. Always test your workload against different hardware configurations.

Security vulnerabilities in modern CPUs

In recent years, security vulnerabilities (known as *speculative execution* vulnerabilities; see the upcoming Inside OUT box) were discovered in CPUs that implement SMT. There are two Microsoft Knowledge Base articles that go into more detail:

●   *https://support.microsoft.com/help/4073225/*

●   *https://support.microsoft.com/help/4457951/*

For Intel CPUs, our advice is to disable SMT (Hyper-Threading) for both physical and virtual environments for all CPUs prior to 2019, which is when the Whiskey Lake architecture became available. On AMD CPUs, we recommend disabling SMT for virtual environments. If any VMs are running untrusted code on the same host as your production servers, your risk increases.

➤ For more information about allocating virtual CPUs, see "Understand virtualization and containers" later in this chapter.

Inside OUT

How do speculative execution vulnerabilities affect you?

Modern microprocessors (including CPUs) use a type of circuit called a *branch predictor*, which tries to guess the result of an instruction before it happens. This improves overall performance in the execution pipeline if that result occurs. This is known as *speculative execution*.

When the instruction has a different result from the predicted outcome, the branch containing the incorrectly predicted value may reveal private information to attackers observing the instructions as they occur before these results are discarded.

Because this is a hardware issue, affected CPU vendors have issued firmware patches to work around this class of vulnerability, but cannot completely defend against it without seriously affecting performance. For full protection, newer CPUs released since 2019 are required.

Unfortunately, it is not practical to replace every CPU manufactured before this date. In these cases, you must ensure that you have patched your operating system fully. Additionally, you must check that any firmware released for your CPUs (called *microcode*) has been applied, even if it does affect performance. This is especially true for CPUs used in VM hosts, where SMT should be disabled.

Ultimately, the type of threats you might expect to face in your environment will dictate whether you decide to disable SMT or patch against it.

Non-uniform memory access

CPUs are the fastest component of a system, so they spend a lot of time waiting for data to come to them. In the past, all CPUs shared one bank of RAM on a motherboard, using a shared bus. This caused performance problems as more CPUs were added because only one CPU could access the RAM at a time.

Multi-channel memory architecture tries to resolve this by increasing the number of channels between CPUs and RAM to reduce contention during concurrent access.

A more practical solution is for each CPU to have its own local physical RAM, situated close to each CPU socket. This configuration is called *non-uniform memory access* (*NUMA*). The advantages of NUMA are that each CPU can access its own RAM, making processing much faster. If a CPU needs more RAM than it has in its local set, however, it must request memory from one of the other CPUs in the system (called *foreign memory access*), which carries a performance penalty.

SQL Server is NUMA-aware. In other words, if the OS recognizes a NUMA configuration at the hardware layer, where more than one CPU is plugged in, and if each CPU has its own set of physical RAM (see Figure 2-2), SQL Server will split its internal structures and service threads across each NUMA node.

Since the release of SQL Server 2014 Service Pack 2, the Database Engine automatically configures NUMA nodes at an instance level, using what it calls *soft-NUMA*. If more than eight CPU cores are detected (including SMT cores), soft-NUMA nodes are created automatically in memory.

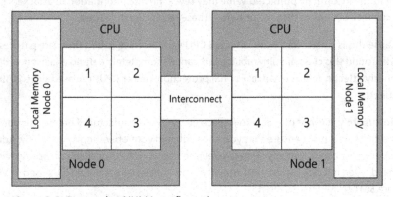

Figure 2-2 Two-socket NUMA configuration.

Inside OUT

What is the relationship between core counts and editions?

SQL Server Standard edition has an artificial limit of four sockets or 24 CPU physical cores that it can use, whichever is lower. For instance, if a system contains two 16-core CPUs, for a total of 32 cores, Standard edition will need to be licensed for all 32 cores, even though it won't use eight of them.

Additionally, the NUMA distribution will be unbalanced because SQL Server will use the first 16 cores on the first CPU and eight from the second CPU unless you configure the SQL Server CPU usage using the affinity settings. (For information on how to do this, see the section "Configuration settings" in Chapter 3.)

Be careful when choosing the hardware and edition for your SQL Server installation. If you plan to install several VMs on one system, a better option would be Enterprise edition, licensed for all physical cores on the server. This would automatically cover all SQL Server VMs and containers that you install on that hardware.

Disable power saving everywhere

Modern systems can use power-saving settings to reduce the amount of electricity consumed by a server. Although this is good for the environment, it is bad for query performance, because the CPU core speed might be reduced to save energy.

For all operating systems running SQL Server, turn on High Performance at the OS level, and double-check that High Performance is set at the BIOS level, as well. Note that for dedicated VM hosts, making this change at the BIOS level will require downtime.

Data storage

When data is not in memory, it is at rest, and must be persisted (saved) somewhere. Storage technology has evolved rapidly over the past decade, so we no longer think of storage as a mechanical hard drive containing one or more spinning metal disks with a magnetic surface.

NOTE

Old habits die hard, and colloquially you may still refer to a non-volatile storage subsystem as "the disk," even if it might take another form. We refer to it as a "drive."

Irrespective of the underlying mechanism, a SQL Server storage subsystem should have low latency, so that when the Database Engine accesses the drive to perform reads and writes, those reads and writes should complete as quickly as possible. The following list presents some commonly used terms with respect to storage devices.

- **Drive.** The physical storage device. This might be a mechanical drive, a solid-state drive with the same form factor as a mechanical drive, or a card that plugs directly into the motherboard.

- **Volume.** A logical representation of storage, as viewed by the OS. This might be one drive, part of a drive, or a logical section of a storage array. On Microsoft Windows, a volume usually gets its own drive letter or mount point.

- **Latency.** The time it takes for data to be read from a drive (seconds per read) and written (seconds per write) to a drive. Latency is usually measured in milliseconds.

CHAPTER 2

- **IOPS.** Short for *input/output operations per second*. IOPS is the number of reads and writes per second. A storage device might have differing performance depending on whether the IOPS are sequential or random. IOPS are directly related to latency by means of the queue depth.

- **Queue depth.** The number of outstanding read and write requests in a storage device's request queue. The deeper the queue depth, the faster the drive.

SQL Server performance is directly related to storage performance. The move toward virtualization and shared storage arrays has placed more emphasis on random data access patterns. Low latency and high random IOPS benefit the average SQL Server workload. The next two chapters go into more detail about the preferred storage configuration for SQL Server.

Types of storage

Non-volatile storage can be split up into three categories: mechanical, solid-state, and persistent memory.

Mechanical hard drives

Traditional spinning disks have an inherent latency, called *seek time*, due to their shape and physical nature. The read/write head is mounted on an arm that scans the surface of the disk as it spins, seeking a particular area at which to perform the I/O operation. If the data on the spinning disk is fragmented, it can take longer to access, because the head must skip around to find data or free space.

The standard interfaces for mechanical drives are Serial ATA (SATA) and Serial Attached SCSI (SAS).

As spinning disks increase in capacity, the tracks between data become narrower, which decreases performance and increases the likelihood of mechanical failure or data corruption. The rotational energy in the disk itself pushes the physical limits, so there is also a limit to the speed of the motor. In other words, mechanical disks grow bigger but slower and more prone to failure.

Solid-state drives

Solid-state technology, which uses flash memory, eliminates seek time entirely because the path to each cell where the data is stored is almost instantaneous. This is what makes solid-state storage so much faster than mechanical storage.

Solid-state storage devices can take many different forms. The most common in consumer devices is a 2.5-inch enclosure with a SATA interface. This is also common with mechanical laptop drives, which facilitate a drop-in replacement of mechanical storage by solid state storage.

In server architecture, however, flash memory can take several forms. For local storage, the Peripheral Component Interconnect Express (PCIe) interface is used to plug directly into the motherboard. An example of this is Non-Volatile Memory Express (NVMe).

As technology evolves, performance will only improve as capacity grows. Solid-state storage is not perfect, though; data can be written to a particular cell only a certain number of times before it fails. You might have experienced this yourself with USB thumb drives, which tend to fail after heavy usage. Algorithms to balance writes across cells, a process called *wear-leveling*, help extend the lifespan of solid-state devices.

Another problem with flash memory is write-amplification. On a mechanical drive, if a file is overwritten, the previous file is marked for deletion but is not actually deleted from the disk surface. When the drive needs to write to that area again, it overwrites the location without removing what was there before.

Solid-state drives must erase the location in question before writing the new data. This has a performance impact. Compounding this performance impact, the size of the cells might also require a larger area to be erased than the file itself (if it is a small file). Various techniques exist to mitigate write amplification, but this reduces the lifespan of flash memory.

The performance problems with mechanical disks, and the lifespan problems with both mechanical and solid-state drives, can be mitigated by combining them into drive arrays. These reduce the risk of failure (by balancing the load) and increase performance.

Persistent memory

Persistent memory allows data to remain in RAM without needing to be persisted to traditional storage. It is provided in the same form factor as RAM, which in turn is split evenly between traditional RAM and solid-state components, with a backup power requirement.

Frequently accessed data is retained in the RAM portion as usual. If there is a loss of main power, data in that RAM is immediately copied to the solid-state component while on backup power. When the main power supply returns, the contents of the solid-state component are copied back into RAM when it is safe to do so. This improves performance because SQL Server is optimized to use this technology. We cover this in more detail in the section "Persistent memory enlightenment."

➤ See more about persistent memory at *https://docs.pmem.io/*.

NOTE

Persistent memory is limited by the capacity of the motherboard, processor, and each memory module. At the time of this writing, persistent memory modules are available in sizes up to 512 GB.

Configure the storage layer

Non-volatile storage can stand alone, in the form of direct-attached storage (DAS), or be combined in many ways to provide redundancy or consolidation—perhaps even offering different levels of performance to better manage costs. For example, archive data might not need to be stored on the fastest available storage if it is infrequently accessed.

Direct-attached storage

DAS is plugged directly into the system that is accessing it. Also called *local storage*, it can comprise independent mechanical hard drives, solid-state drives, tape drives for backups, CD and DVD-ROM drives, or even enclosures containing storage arrays.

DAS has a lower latency than a storage area network (SAN) or network-attached storage (NAS), both discussed in more detail later in the chapter, because there is no network to traverse between the system and the storage. DAS cannot be shared with other systems, however, unless the local file system is shared across the network using a protocol such as Server Message Block (SMB) 3.0.

For SQL Server, DAS comprising flash (solid-state) storage is preferred for tempdb. DAS is also supported and recommended in failover cluster instances. You can use DAS for the buffer pool extension, too.

> ➤ To see how best to configure tempdb, see the section "Configuration settings" in Chapter 3.

Storage arrays and RAID

Combining drives in an enclosure with a controller to access each drive, without any thought to redundancy or performance, is called JBOD (colloquially, "just a bunch of disks"). These drives might be accessed individually or combined into a single volume.

When done correctly, combining drives into an array can increase overall performance and/or lower the risk of data loss should one or more of the drives in the array fail. This is called *redundant array of independent disks (RAID)*.

RAID offers several levels of configuration, which trade redundancy for performance. More redundancy means less raw capacity for the array, but it can also reduce the potential for data loss.

Striping without parity (RAID 0) uses multiple drives to improve raw read/write performance, but with zero redundancy. If one drive fails, there is a significant chance of catastrophic data loss across the entire array. JBOD configurations that span across drives fall under this RAID level.

Mirroring (RAID 1) uses two drives that are written to simultaneously. Although there is a slight write penalty because both drives must save their data at the same time, and one might take longer than the other, read performance is nearly double that of a single drive because both drives can be read in parallel (with a small overhead caused by the RAID controller selecting the drive and fetching the data). Usable space is 50 percent of raw capacity, and one drive in the pair can be lost and still have all data recoverable.

Striping with parity (RAID 5) requires an odd number of three or more drives. For every single write, one of the drives is randomly used for parity (a checksum validation). There is a larger write penalty because all drives must save their data, and parity must be calculated and persisted. But if a single drive is lost from the array, the other drives can rebuild the contents of the lost drive based on the parity—although it can take some time to rebuild the array. Usable space is calculated as the number of drives minus one. If there are three drives in the array, the usable space is the sum of two of those drives, with the space from the third used for parity (which is evenly distributed over the array). Only one drive in the array can be lost and still have full data recovery.

Combinations of the base RAID configurations are used to provide more redundancy and performance, including:

- **RAID 1+0.** With RAID 1+0, also called RAID 10, two drives are configured in a mirror (RAID 1) for redundancy, and then each mirror is striped together (RAID 0) for performance reasons.

- **RAID 0+1.** With RAID 0+1, the drives are striped first (RAID 0), and then mirrored across the entire RAID 0 set (RAID 1).

  Usable space for RAID 0+1 and 1+0 is 50 percent of the raw capacity. To ensure full recovery from failure in a RAID 1+0 or 0+1 configuration, an entire side of the mirror can be lost, or only one drive from each side of the mirror can be lost.

- **RAID 5+0.** With RAID 5+0, also called RAID 50, three or more drives are configured in a RAID 5 set, which is then striped (with no parity) with at least one other RAID 5 set of the same configuration. Usable space is $(x - 1) / y$, where x is the number of drives in each nested RAID 5 set and y is the number of RAID 5 sets in this array. If there are nine drives, six of them are usable. Only one drive from each RAID 5 set can be lost with full recovery possible. If more than one drive in any of the RAID 5 sets is lost, the entire 5+0 array is lost.

SQL Server requires the best possible performance from a storage layer. In terms of RAID configurations, RAID 1+0 offers the best performance and redundancy.

NOTE

RAID is not an alternative to backups because it does not protect against other types of data loss. RAID does not interact with the SQL Server transaction log, and transaction log backups are typically required for an enterprise disaster recovery solution. A common backup medium is digital tape, due to its low cost and high capacity, but more organizations are using cloud storage options, such as Microsoft Azure Archive Storage and Amazon Glacier, for long-term, cost-effective backup storage solutions. Be sure your SQL Server backups are copied securely off-premises, and then tested regularly by restoring those database backups and running DBCC CHECKDB on them. We discuss backups in detail in Chapter 11, "Implement high availability and disaster recovery."

Centralized storage with a storage-area network

A storage-area network (SAN) is a network of storage arrays that can contain tens, hundreds, or even thousands of drives (mechanical or solid-state) in a central location, with one or more RAID configurations, providing block-level access to storage. This reduces wasted space and allows for easier management across multiple systems, especially for virtualized environments.

Block-level means the OS can read or write blocks of any size and any alignment. This offers the OS a lot of flexibility in making use of the storage.

You can carve the total storage capacity of the SAN into logical unit numbers (LUNs), and each LUN can be assigned to a physical or virtual server. You can move these LUNs around and resize them as required, which makes management much easier than attaching physical storage to a server.

The disadvantage of a SAN is that you might be at the mercy of misconfiguration or a slow network. For instance, the RAID might be set to a level that has poor write performance, or the blocks of the storage might not be aligned appropriately. Storage administrators who do not understand specialized workloads like SQL Server might choose a performance model that satisfies the rest of the organization to reduce administration overhead, but that penalizes you.

Inside OUT

What is the difference between Fibre Channel and iSCSI?

Storage arrays might use Fibre Channel (FC) or Internet Small Computer Systems Interface (iSCSI) to connect systems to their storage.

FC can support data transfer at a higher rate than iSCSI, which makes it better for systems that require lower latency, but it comes at a higher cost for specialized equipment.

iSCSI uses standard TCP/IP, which makes it potentially cheaper because it can run on existing network equipment. You can improve iSCSI throughput by isolating the storage to its own dedicated network.

Network-attached storage

Network-attached storage (NAS) is usually a specialized hardware appliance connected to the network, typically containing an array of several drives, providing file-level access to storage.

Unlike the SAN's block-level support, NAS storage is configured on the appliance itself, and uses file-sharing protocols such as Server Message Block (SMB), Common Internet File System (CIFS), and Network File System (NFS) to share the storage over the network.

NAS appliances are common because they provide access to shared storage at a much lower monetary cost than a SAN. When using these appliances, however, you should keep in mind security considerations regarding file-sharing protocols.

Storage Spaces

Windows Server 2012 and later versions support Storage Spaces, which offer a way to manage local storage in a more scalable and flexible manner than RAID.

Instead of creating a RAID set at the storage layer, Windows Server can create a virtual drive at the OS level. It might use a combination of RAID levels, and you can decide to combine different physical drives to create performance tiers.

For example, a server might contain 16 drives—eight spinning disks and eight solid-state disks. You can use Storage Spaces to create a single volume with all 16 drives, keeping the active files on the solid-state portion, increasing performance dramatically.

Azure Premium SSD v2, which became generally available in October 2022, is poised to replace Storage Spaces in Azure. For more information, visit *https://aka.ms/premiumv2doc*.

SMB 3.0 file share

SQL Server supports storage located on a network file share that uses the SMB 3.0 protocol or higher because it is now fast and stable enough to support the storage requirements of the Database Engine (performance and resilience). This means you can build a failover cluster instance (discussed in more detail later in the chapter) without shared storage such as a SAN.

Network performance is critically important, though, so we recommend a dedicated and isolated network for the SMB file share, using network interface cards (NICs) that support remote direct memory access (RDMA). This enables the SMB Direct feature in Windows Server to create a low-latency, high-throughput connection using the SMB protocol.

SMB 3.0 might be a feasible option for smaller networks with limited storage capacity and a NAS or in the case of a failover cluster instance without shared storage. For more information, read Chapter 11.

Persistent memory enlightenment

Instead of having to go through the slower channels of the file system and underlying non-volatile storage layer, SQL Server 2022 can access more efficient persistent memory (PMEM) operations directly—a feature called *enlightenment*. This feature is available on both Windows Server and Linux.

> ➤ For more information about persistent memory support on Windows Server, visit *https:// blogs.msdn.microsoft.com/sqlserverstorageengine/2016/12/02/transaction-commit-latency -acceleration-using-storage-class-memory-in-windows-server-2016sql-server-2016-sp1/*.

The hybrid buffer pool

SQL Server 2022 can leverage the hybrid buffer pool, which uses persistent memory enlightenment to automatically bypass RAM, and lets you access *clean* data pages directly from any database files stored on a PMEM device. Data files are automatically mapped upon SQL Server startup; when a database is created, attached, or restored; or when the hybrid buffer pool is enabled. You enable this feature at the instance level; if you don't need to use it on individual user databases, you can disable it at the database level.

The PMEM device must be formatted with a file system that supports Direct Access Mode (DAX)—namely XFS, ext4, or NTFS. Data file sizes should be in multiples of 2 MB, and if you are on Windows, a 2-MB allocation size is recommended for NTFS. You should also enable the LPIM option on Windows.

NOTE

As mentioned, the abbreviation for Direct Access Mode is DAX. This should not be confused with Data Analysis Expressions in SQL Server Analysis Services.

➤ For configuring DAX for SQL Server on Linux, visit *https://learn.microsoft.com/sql/linux /sql-server-linux-configure-pmem*.

CAUTION

You should not use the hybrid buffer pool on an instance with less than 16 GB RAM.

This feature is considered hybrid because dirty pages must be copied to the regular buffer pool in RAM before making their way back to the PMEM device and marked clean during a regular checkpoint operation.

➤ For more information about hybrid buffer pools, visit Microsoft Docs at *https://learn.microsoft .com/sql/database-engine/configure-windows/hybrid-buffer-pool*.

Connect to SQL Server over the network

We have covered a fair amount about networking while discussing the storage layer, but there is far more to it. This section looks at what is involved when accessing the Database Engine over a network, and briefly discusses virtual local area networks (VLANs).

Unless a SQL Server instance and the application accessing it are entirely self-contained on the same server, database access is performed over one or more network interfaces. This adds complexity with authentication, given that attackers might be scanning and modifying network packets in flight.

SQL Server 2022 requires strict rules with respect to network security. This means older versions of the connectors or protocols used by software developers might not work as expected.

Transport Layer Security (TLS) and its forerunner Secure Sockets Layer (SSL)—together known as TLS/SSL or just SSL—are methods that allow network traffic between two points to be encrypted. Where possible, you should use newer libraries that support TLS encryption. If you cannot use TLS to encrypt application traffic, you should use IPSec, which is configured at the OS level.

CAUTION

Ensure that all TCP/IP traffic to and from the SQL Server is encrypted. On Windows Server, you should use the highest version of TLS available to you, with TLS v1.3 support introduced with SQL Server 2022. However, this isn't required when using the Shared Memory Protocol with applications located on the same server as the SQL Server instance.

➤ For more information about encryption in SQL Server, including the new TLS v1.3, see Chapter 13, "Protect data through classification, encryption, and auditing."

Protocols and ports

Connections to SQL Server are made over the Transmission Control Protocol (TCP), with port 1433 as the default port for a default instance. Some of this is covered in Chapter 1, "Get started with SQL Server tools," and again in Chapter 13. Any named instances are assigned random ports by the SQL Server Configuration Manager, and the SQL Browser service coordinates any connections to named instances. It is possible to assign static TCP ports to named instances by using the Configuration Manager.

You can use SQL Server Configuration Manager to change the default port after SQL Server is installed. We do not recommend changing the port for security reasons, however, because it provides no security advantage to a port scanner—although some network administration policies still require it.

Networking is also the foundation of cloud computing. Aside from the fact that the Azure cloud is accessed over the Internet (itself a network of networks), the entire Azure infrastructure is a virtual fabric of innumerable components tied together through networking. This fabric underlies both infrastructure-as-a-service (VMs with Windows or Linux running SQL Server) and platform-as-a-service (Azure SQL Database and Azure SQL Managed Instance) offerings.

Added complexity with Virtual Local Area Networks

A VLAN gives network administrators the ability to logically group machines together even if they are not physically connected through the same network switch. This enables servers to share their resources with one another over the same physical LAN, without interacting with other devices on the same network.

CHAPTER 2

VLANs work at a very low level (the data link layer, or OSI Layer 2), and are configured on a network switch. A port on the switch might be dedicated to a particular VLAN, and all traffic to and from that port is mapped to a particular VLAN by the switch.

High-availability concepts

With each new version of Windows Server, terminology and definitions tend to change or adapt according to the new features available. With SQL Server on Linux, it is even more important to get our heads around what it means when we discuss high availability (HA).

At its most basic, HA means that a service offering of some kind (for example, SQL Server, a web server, an application, or a file share) will survive an outage of some kind, or at least fail predictably to a standby state, with minimal loss of data and minimal downtime.

Everything can fail. An outage might be caused by a failed hard drive, which could in turn be a result of excessive heat, cold, or moisture, or a datacenter alarm that is so loud that its vibrational frequency damages the internal components and causes a head crash.

Other things can go wrong, too, as noted in the following list:

- A failed NIC
- A failed RAID controller
- A power surge or brownout causing a failed power supply
- A broken or damaged network cable
- A broken or damaged power cable
- Moisture on the motherboard
- Dust on the motherboard
- Overheating caused by a failed fan
- A faulty keyboard that misinterprets keystrokes
- Failure due to bit rot
- Failure due to a bug in SQL Server
- Failure due to poorly written code in a file system driver that causes drive corruption
- Capacitors failing on the motherboard
- Insects or rodents electrocuting themselves on components (this also smells really bad)

- Failure caused by a fire-suppression system that uses water instead of gas

- Misconfiguration of a network router causing an entire geographical region to be inaccessible

- Failure due to an expired SSL or TLS certificate

- Human error, such as running a `DELETE` or `UPDATE` statement without a `WHERE` clause

- Domain Name System (DNS) error

The list is not exhaustive (and most of the time, the problem is DNS). The bottom line is, it's incredibly important to *not* make assumptions about hardware, software, and network stability.

Why redundancy matters

Armed with the knowledge that everything can fail, you should build in redundancy where possible. The sad reality is that these decisions are governed by budget constraints. The amount of money available is inversely proportional to the amount of acceptable data loss and length of downtime. For business-critical systems, however, uptime is paramount, and a highly available solution will be more cost effective than being down, considering the cost-per-minute to the organization.

It is nearly impossible to guarantee zero downtime with zero data loss. There is always a trade-off. The business needs to define that trade-off, based on resources (equipment, people, money), and the technical solution is in turn developed around that trade-off. This strategy is driven by two values called the Recovery Point Objective and Recovery Time Objective, which are defined in a Service-Level Agreement (SLA).

Recovery Point Objective

A good way to think about the concept of a Recovery Point Objective (RPO) is to ask two questions:

- "How much data are you prepared to lose?"

- "When a failure occurs, how much data will be lost between the last transaction log backup and the failure?"

The answers are measured in seconds or minutes.

> **NOTE**
>
> **If your organization differentiates archive data from current data, this should form part of the discussion around RPO, specifically as it relates to the maximum allowed age of your data. You may not need to bring archived data online immediately after a disaster as long as it is made available at some specified time in the future.**

Recovery Time Objective

The Recovery Time Objective (RTO) is defined as how much time is available to bring the environment up to a known and usable state after a failure. There might be different values for HA and disaster recovery (DR) scenarios. This value is usually measured in hours.

Disaster recovery

HA is not DR. They are often grouped under the same heading (HA/DR), mainly because there are shared technology solutions for both. But HA is about keeping the service running, whereas DR is what happens when the infrastructure fails. DR is like insurance: You don't think you need it until it's too late. As for HA, it costs more money the shorter the RPO.

> **NOTE**
>
> **A disaster is any failure or event that causes an unplanned outage.**

Clustering

Clustering is the connecting of computers (nodes) in a set of two or more nodes that work together and present themselves to the network as one computer.

In most cluster configurations, only one node can be active in a cluster. To ensure that this happens, a *quorum* instructs the cluster as to which node should be active. It also steps in if there is a communication failure between the nodes.

Each node has a vote in a quorum. However, if there is an even number of nodes, to ensure a simple majority, an additional witness must be included in a quorum to allow for a majority vote to take place. You can see more about this process in the "Resolve cluster partitioning with quorum" section later in this chapter.

Inside OUT

What is "Always On"?

Always On is not the name of a specific technology; rather, it's a marketing term for a group of features. Two separate technologies fall under the Always On label; these are addressed later in this chapter. Two important things to remember: Always On does not mean availability groups, and there is a space between *Always* and *On*.

Windows Server Failover Clustering

As the article titled "Failover Clustering Overview" (*https://learn.microsoft.com/windows-server /failover-clustering/failover-clustering-overview*) describes it:

> *A failover cluster is a group of independent computers that work together to increase the availability and scalability of clustered roles. [...] If one or more of the cluster nodes fail, other nodes begin to provide service (a process known as failover). In addition, the clustered roles are proactively monitored to verify that they are working properly. If they are not working, they are restarted or moved to another node.*

The terminology here matters. *Windows Server Failover Clustering* (WSFC) is the name of the technology that underpins a *failover cluster instance* (*FCI*). An FCI is created when two or more Windows Server Failover Clustering nodes (computers) are connected in a Windows Server Failover Clustering resource group and masquerade as a single machine behind a network end-point called a *virtual network name* (*VNN*). A SQL Server service that is installed on an FCI is said to be *cluster aware*.

Linux failover clustering with Pacemaker

Instead of relying on Windows Server Failover Clustering, SQL Server on a Linux cluster can use any cluster resource manager. When SQL Server 2017 was released, Microsoft recommended using Pacemaker because it ships with several Linux distributions, including Red Hat and Ubuntu. This advice still holds true for SQL Server 2022.

➤ You can read more about the Pacemaker recommendation *https://learn.microsoft.com/sql /linux/sql-server-linux-business-continuity-dr*.

Inside OUT

What happens when a Linux node fails?

If something goes wrong in a cluster, and a node is in an unknown state after a set time-out period, that node must be isolated from the cluster and restarted or reset. On Linux clusters, this is called *node fencing*, following the STONITH principle ("Shoot the Other Node in the Head"). If a node fails, STONITH will provide an effective, if drastic, manner of resetting or powering-off a failed Linux node.

CHAPTER 2

Resolve cluster partitioning with quorum

Most clustering technologies use the quorum model to prevent a phenomenon called *partitioning*, or "split brain." If there is an even number of nodes, and half of these nodes go offline from the view of the other half of the cluster, or vice versa, you end up with two halves thinking that the cluster is still up and running, each with a primary node (split brain).

Depending on connectivity to each half of the cluster, an application continues writing to one half of the cluster while another application writes to the other half. A best-case resolution for this scenario requires rolling back to a point in time before the event occurred, which would cause the loss of any data written after the event.

To prevent this, each node in a cluster shares its health with the other nodes using a periodic heartbeat. If more than half do not respond in a timely fashion, the cluster is considered to have failed. Quorum works by having a simple majority vote on what constitutes "enough nodes."

In Windows Server Failover Clustering, there are four types of majority vote: Node, Node and File Share, Node and Disk, and Disk Only. In the latter three types, a separate witness that does not participate directly in the cluster is used. This witness is given voting rights when there is an even number of nodes in a cluster, and therefore a simple majority (more than half) would not be possible. The witness is ideally housed in a site separate from the cluster nodes, so that it can be a reliable witness of the cluster's health to all nodes. If a separate site is not available, the witness should be housed in whatever site currently hosts the primary node, requiring some automation to move the witness for planned and unplanned failovers.

Always On FCIs

You can think of a SQL Server FCI as two or more nodes with shared storage—usually a SAN, because it is most likely to be accessed over the network.

On Windows Server, SQL Server can take advantage of Windows Server Failover Clustering to provide HA (the idea being minimal downtime) at the server-instance level by creating an FCI of two or more nodes. From the network's perspective (application, end users, and so on), the FCI is presented as a single instance of SQL Server running on a single computer, and all connections point at the VNN.

When the FCI starts, one of the nodes assumes ownership and brings its SQL Server instance online. If a failure occurs on the first node (or there is a planned failover due to maintenance), there are at least a few seconds of downtime during which the first node cleans up as best it can, and then the second node brings its SQL Server instance online. Client connections are redirected to the new node after the services are up and running.

Inside OUT

How long does the FCI failover take?

During a planned failover, any dirty pages in the buffer pool must be written to the drive; thus, the downtime could be longer than expected on a server with a large buffer pool. You can read more about checkpoints in Chapter 3 and Chapter 4, "Install and configure SQL Server instances and features." You can also consider using SQL Server's accelerated database recovery (ADR) feature to improve failover times, also discussed in Chapter 3.

On Linux, the principle is very similar. A cluster resource manager such as Pacemaker manages the cluster. When a failover occurs, the same process is followed from SQL Server's perspective, in which the first node is brought down, and the second node is brought up to take its place as the owner. The cluster has a virtual IP address, just as on Windows. However, you must manually add the VNN to the DNS server.

> ➤ You can read more about setting up a Linux cluster in Chapter 10, "Develop, deploy, and manage data recovery."

FCIs are supported on SQL Server Standard edition but are limited to two nodes.

The versatility of log shipping

SQL Server transaction log shipping is an extremely flexible technology that provides a relatively inexpensive and easily managed HA and DR solution. The principle is as follows: A primary database is in either the full or bulk logged recovery model, and transaction log backups are taken regularly every few minutes. These transaction log backup files are transferred to a shared network location, where one or more secondary servers restore the transaction log backups to a standby database.

If you use the built-in Log Shipping Wizard in SQL Server Management Studio, on the **Restore** tab, select **Database State When Restoring Backups**, and then select **No Recovery Mode** or **Standby Mode**. (For more information, see *https://learn.microsoft.com/sql/database-engine /log-shipping/configure-log-shipping-sql-server*.)

If you are building your own log shipping solution, remember to use the RESTORE feature with NORECOVERY, or RESTORE with STANDBY.

If a failover occurs, the tail of the log on the primary server is backed up in the same way if available (guaranteeing zero data loss of committed transactions), transferred to the shared location, and restored after the latest regular transaction logs. The database is then put into RECOVERY _PENDING state, which is where crash recovery takes place, rolling back incomplete transactions and rolling forward complete transactions.

➤ **You can read more about crash recovery in Chapter 3.**

As soon as the application is pointed to the new server, the environment is back up again with zero data loss (if the tail of the log was copied across) or minimal data loss (if only the latest shipped transaction log was restored).

Log shipping works on all editions of SQL Server, on Windows and Linux. Because Express edition does not include the SQL Server Agent, Express can only be a witness, and you must manage the process through a separate scheduling mechanism. You can even create your own solution for any edition of SQL Server—for instance, using Azure Storage and AzCopy.exe.

Always On availability groups

As mentioned, availability groups are generally what people mean when they incorrectly say, "Always On." (Similarly, they are not "database availability groups," or "DAGs.") In shorthand, you can refer to these as availability groups (AGs).

You can think of an AG as multiple copies of the same database, with each copy associated with its own storage. Data is written to one of the databases and then copied to the other databases in the AG, synchronously or asynchronously. Having multiple instances in the AG also provides redundancy in case a server becomes unavailable, as well as automatic data corruption correction and the potential for readable secondary replicas.

Inside OUT

What was database mirroring?

AGs replace database mirroring. Database mirroring worked at the database level by maintaining two copies of a single database across two separate SQL Server instances, keeping them synchronized with a steady stream of active transaction log records. This feature is now in maintenance mode. Unlike a deprecated feature, it will not be removed from the product in a future version. However, it is no longer supported on Windows and has not been made available for Linux.

AGs give you the ability to keep a discrete set of databases highly available across one or more nodes in a cluster. They work at the database level as opposed to an entire server-instance level, the way FCIs do. Unlike the cluster-aware version of SQL Server when it is installed as part of an FCI, SQL Server on an AG is installed as a standalone instance.

An AG operates at the database level only. On Windows Server, this is through Windows Server failover clustering; on Linux it is through a cluster resource manager like Pacemaker. As shown in Figure 2-3, the AG is a set of one or more databases in a group (an availability replica) that is replicated (using log shipping) from a primary replica. There can be only one primary replica and a maximum of eight secondary replicas, using synchronous or asynchronous data synchronization.

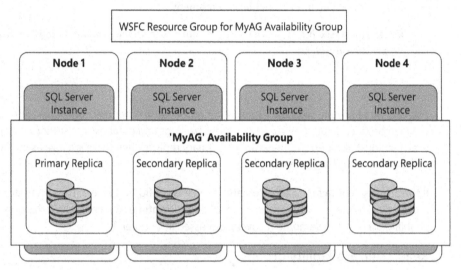

Figure 2-3 A Windows Server Failover Clustering cluster with four nodes.

Let's take a closer look at synchronous and asynchronous data synchronization:

- **Synchronous data synchronization.** The log is hardened (transactions are committed to the transaction log) on every secondary replica before the transaction is committed on the primary replica. This guarantees zero data loss, but with a potential performance impact on a highly transactional workload if network latency is high. You can have two synchronous-commit replicas per AG.

- **Asynchronous data synchronization.** The transaction is considered committed as soon as it is hardened in the transaction log on the primary replica. If something were to happen before the logs are hardened on all the secondary replicas, there is a chance of data loss, and the recovery point would be the most recently committed transaction that successfully made it to all of the secondary replicas. With delayed durability enabled, this can result in faster performance, but with a higher risk of data loss.

CHAPTER 2

Inside OUT

What is delayed durability?

Delayed durability (also known as *lazy commit*) is a storage-optimization feature that returns a successful commit before transaction logs are persisted to the storage layer. Although this can improve performance, the risk of data loss is higher because the transaction logs are saved only when the logs are flushed to a drive asynchronously. There is even a risk of data loss when the SQL Server service is shut down. As such, you should avoid delayed durability in a production environment.

To learn more, see *https://learn.microsoft.com/sql/relational-databases/logs/control-transaction-durability*.

You can use read-only secondary replicas for reports and other read-only operations to reduce the load on the primary replica. This includes backups and database consistency checks; however, you must also perform these on the primary replica when there is a low-usage period or planned maintenance window.

If the primary replica fails, and automatic failover is configured, one of the secondary replicas is promoted to the primary with a few seconds of downtime. You can reduce this downtime by enabling accelerated database recovery, discussed in Chapter 3.

Read-scale availability groups

SQL Server 2017 introduced a new architecture that allows for multiple read-only secondary replicas, but does not offer HA: read-scale AGs. The major difference is that a read-scale AG does not have a cluster resource manager. Automated failover is not possible, but manual failover is.

This allows for simpler setup and reduced contention on business-critical workloads by using read-only routing or connecting directly to a readable secondary replica without relying on a clustering infrastructure on Windows or Linux. Many environments may not choose to configure automatic failover anyway, and to instead automate the failover of SQL Server and other layers of the application infrastructure with external automation.

➤ For more information, see *https://learn.microsoft.com/sql/database-engine/availability-groups/windows/read-scale-availability-groups*.

Distributed availability groups

Instead of having an AG on one cluster, a distributed AG can span two separate AGs, on two separate clusters (Windows Server Failover Clustering or Linux, where each cluster can run on a different OS). These clusters can be geographically separated. You can configure a distributed AG provided that the two AGs can communicate with each other. This allows a more flexible DR scenario, and it makes possible multi-site replicas in geographically diverse areas.

Each AG in a distributed AG can contain the maximum number of replicas, and you can mix major versions of SQL Server in the same distributed AG.

The main difference from a normal AG is that the configuration is stored in SQL Server, not the underlying cluster. With a distributed AG, only one AG can perform data modification at any time, even though both AGs have a primary replica.

Contained availability groups

One of the common challenges of managing AGs, including automatic failovers, relates to managing server-level objects, like logins and SQL Server Agent jobs. It is easy to set these up when the AG is created, but managing these changes over time can be tedious.

With the introduction of contained AGs in SQL Server 2022, you can manage items that have historically only been available at the server level within the contained AG. Each contained AG will have its own master and msdb system database that are synchronized between replicas, synchronizing system security and SQL Agent information automatically.

> ➤ You can find additional information about contained AGs in Chapter 11.

Basic availability groups

SQL Server Standard edition supports a single-database HA solution, with a limit of two replicas. The secondary replica does not allow backups or read access. Although these limits can be frustrating, they do make it possible to offer another kind of HA offering with Standard edition: basic AGs.

Basic AGs support and replace the use cases for existing legacy database mirroring solutions and for scenarios requiring simple two-node synchronization in Standard edition.

NOTE

You cannot upgrade a basic AG to a regular AG.

> ➤ For more information, see *https://learn.microsoft.com/sql/database-engine/availability -groups/windows/basic-availability-groups-always-on-availability-groups*.

Availability groups on SQL Server on Linux

SQL Server on Linux supports AGs, though with a different underlying infrastructure, using third-party cluster managers like Pacemaker instead of the Windows Server Failover Cluster Manager. There are different settings and configuration options with a cluster manager not designed by Microsoft.

Some features are not fully supported for SQL Server on Linux, including the Microsoft Distributed Transaction Coordinator (MSDTC). Some of the automation around failover is different in SQL Server on Linux.

One extra feature with SQL Server on Linux is the ability to add an additional configuration-only replica to provide a third vote for the cluster. This behaves differently from a WSFC-based cluster witness.

➤ Read more about AGs on Linux at *https://learn.microsoft.com/sql/linux/sql-server-linux -availability-group-overview*. For a complete walkthrough of AGs in SQL Server on Linux, see "Configure availability groups in SQL Server on Linux" in Chapter 11.

Query Store on replicas

Query Store has one feature within SQL Server that has made managing and resolving performance issues much easier since its introduction in SQL Server 2016. However, prior to SQL Server 2022, you could only collect Query Store data from the primary replica in an AG. Using the secondary node for heavy read activity is an important use case, but until SQL Server 2022, the read-only workloads could not benefit from the Query Store.

SQL Server 2022 introduces the ability to collect Query Store information from all secondary replicas. This information is asynchronously written back to Query Store on the primary replica, where all query information can be analyzed together. Chapter 11 covers Query Store on replicas in more depth.

Secure SQL Server

Security is covered in more depth in Chapter 12, "Administer instance and database security and permissions," and in Chapter 13. So, what follows is a basic overview of server access security, not a discussion about permissions within SQL Server.

When connecting to SQL Server on Windows or Linux, or connecting to Azure SQL, security is required to keep everyone out except the people who need access to the database.

Active Directory (AD), using Integrated Authentication, is the primary method for connecting to SQL Server on a Windows domain. When you sign into an AD domain, you are provided a token that contains your privileges and permissions. This is different from SQL Server authentication, however, which is managed directly on the SQL Server instance and requires a username and password to travel over the network.

Integrated Authentication and Active Directory

AD covers several different identity services, but the most important is Active Directory Domain Services (AD DS), which manages your network credentials (your user account) and what you can do on the network (access rights). Having a network-wide directory of users and permissions facilitates easier management of accounts, computers, servers, services, devices, file sharing, and so on.

In this type of environment, SQL Server would be managed as just another service on the network, and the AD DS would control who has access to that SQL Server instance. This is much easier than having to manage individual user access per server, which is time consuming, difficult to troubleshoot, and prone to human error.

New in SQL Server 2022 for both Windows and Linux, authentication via Azure Active Directory (Azure AD) is supported for on-premises instances. This provides for additional implementation of single sign-on (SSO) and multifactor authentication (MFA) for accessing SQL Server resources using various supported applications including SQL Server Management Studio and Azure Data Studio. Currently, configuring Azure AD integration with SQL Server is not part of SQL Setup and is configured post-installation by registering the instance with the Azure extension for SQL Server.

➤ For more information, see *https://learn.microsoft.com/sql/relational-databases/security /authentication-access/azure-ad-authentication-sql-server-overview#connect-sql-server -to-azure-with-azure-ad.*

Inside OUT

Is AD supported on Linux?

Yes! SQL Server on Linux supports AD authentication using domain credentials and Kerberos. For more, read *https://learn.microsoft.com/sql/linux/sql-server-linux-active-directory -auth-overview.*

Authenticate with Kerberos

Kerberos is the default authentication protocol used in a Windows AD domain; it is the replacement of NT LAN Manager (NTLM).

Kerberos ensures that authentication occurs in a secure manner, even if the network itself might not be secure, because passwords and weak hashes are not transferred over the wire. Kerberos works by exchanging encrypted tickets verified by a ticket granting server (TGS)—usually the domain controller.

A service account that runs SQL Server on a particular server under an AD service account must register its name with the TGS so that client computers can connect to that service over the network. This is called a *service principal name* (*SPN*).

CAUTION

NTLM is the authentication protocol on standalone Windows systems and is used on older operating systems and domains. You can also use NTLM as a fallback on AD domains for backward compatibility.

The NTLM token created during the sign-in process consists of the domain name, the username, and a one-way hash of the user's password. Unfortunately, this hash is considered cryptographically weak and can be cracked (decrypted) in a few seconds by modern cracking tools. It is incumbent on you to use Kerberos where possible.

Understand the service principal name

When a client logs into a Windows domain, it is issued a ticket by the TGS, as shown in Figure 2-4. This ticket is called a *ticket granting ticket* (*TGT*), but it's easier to think of it as the client's credentials. When the client wants to communicate with another node on the network such as SQL Server, this node, or "principal," must have an SPN registered with the TGS.

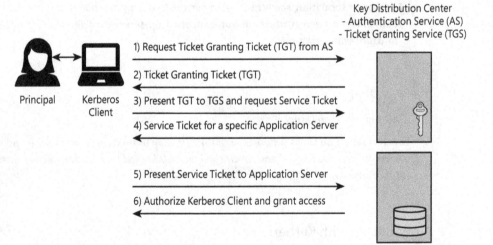

Figure 2-4 How Kerberos authentication works.

The client uses this SPN to request access. After a verification step, the TGS sends a ticket and session key to both the SQL Server and the client, respectively. When the client uses the ticket and session key on the SQL Server, the connection is authenticated by the SQL Server using its own copy of the session key.

For SQL Server to use Kerberos authentication instead of the older NTLM, the Windows domain account that runs the SQL Server service must register the SPN with the domain controller. Otherwise, the authentication will fall back to NTLM, which is far less secure. The easiest way to achieve this is to grant the service account the *Write ServicePrincipalName* permission in AD DS. To configure an SPN manually, you must use the Setspn.exe tool, which is built into Windows.

NOTE

You can also manage SPNs using the dbatools PowerShell module, available from *https://dbatools.io*.

Access other servers and services with delegation

Kerberos delegation enables an application such as SQL Server to reuse end-user credentials to access a different server. This is intended to solve the so-called *double-hop issue*, in which the TGS verifies only the first hop, namely the connection between the client and the registered server. In normal circumstances, any additional connections (the second hop) would require reauthentication.

Delegation impersonates the client by sending the client's TGT on the client's behalf. This in turn causes the TGS to send tickets and session keys to the original server and the new server, allowing authentication. Because the original connection is still authenticated using the same TGT, the client now has access to the second server.

For delegation to work, the service account for the first server must be trusted for delegation, and the second server must be in the same AD forest or between forests with the appropriate trust relationship.

Azure Active Directory

Azure Active Directory (Azure AD) is concerned with identity management for Internet-based and on-premises services, which use HTTP and HTTPS to access websites and web services without the hierarchy associated with on-premises AD.

You can employ Azure AD for user and application authentication—for example, to connect to Azure SQL services or Microsoft Office 365. There are no organizational units or group policy objects. You cannot join a machine to an Azure AD domain, and there is no NTLM or Kerberos authentication. Instead, protocols like OAuth, OpenID Connect (based on OAuth 2.0), SAML, and WS-Federation are used.

You can authenticate (prove who you are), which then provides authorization (permission, or claims) to access certain services, and these services might not be controlled by the service that authenticated you. Think back to network credentials. On an on-premises AD, your user credentials know who you are (your authentication) and what you can do (your authorization).

Protocols like OpenID Connect blur these lines by extending an authorization protocol (what you can do) into an authentication protocol (who you are). This works in a similar manner to Kerberos, whereby an authorization server allows access to certain Internet services and applications, although permissions are granted with claims.

CHAPTER 2

Assert your identity with claims

Claims are a set of "assertions of information about the subject that has been authenticated" (*https://learn.microsoft.com/azure/active-directory/develop/access-tokens#claims-in -access-tokens*).

Think of your user credentials as a security token that indicates who you are, based on how you were authenticated. This depends on the service you originally connected to (i.e., Facebook, LinkedIn, Google, Office 365, or Twitter).

Inside that user object is a series of properties, or attributes, usually in the form of key-value pairs. The specific attributes, or claims, depend on the authentication service used.

Authentication services like Azure AD might restrict the amount of information permissible in a user object to provide the service or application just enough information about you to prove who you are, and to give you access to the service you're requesting, without sharing too much about you or the originating authentication service.

Federation and single sign-on

Federation is a fancy word that means an independent collection of websites or services that can share information between them using claims. An authentication service enables you to sign in with one entity (LinkedIn, GitHub, or Microsoft) and then use that identity for other services controlled by other entities.

This is what makes claims extremely useful. If you use a third-party authentication service, that third party will make certain information available in the form of claims (key-value pairs in your security token) that another service to which you're connecting can access without needing to sign in again, and without that service having access into the third-party service.

For example, suppose you use LinkedIn to sign into a blogging service so you can leave a comment on a post. The blogging service does not have access to your LinkedIn profile, but the claims it provides might include a URL to your profile image, a string containing your full name, and a second URL back to your profile. This way, the blogging service does not know anything about your LinkedIn account, including your employment history, because that information is not in the claims necessary to leave a blog post comment.

Log into Azure SQL Database

Azure SQL Database uses three levels of security to allow access to a database. First is the firewall, which is a set of rules based on origin IP address or ranges and allows connections to only TCP port 1433.

The second level is authentication (proving who you are). You can either connect by using SQL Authentication, with a username and password (like connecting to a contained database on an on-premises SQL Server instance), or Azure AD authentication.

Microsoft recommends using Azure AD whenever possible because it does the following (according to *https://learn.microsoft.com/azure/sql-database/sql-database-aad-authentication*):

- Centralizes user identities and offers password rotation in a single place

- Eliminates the storage of passwords by enabling integrated Windows authentication and other forms of authentication supported by Azure AD

- Offers token (claims-based) authentication for applications connecting to Azure SQL Database

The third level is authorization (what you can do). This is managed inside the Azure SQL database using role memberships and object-level permissions, and works in a similar way to an on-premises SQL Server instance.

➤ You can read more about SQL Server security in Chapters 12 and 13.

Kerberos for Azure SQL Managed Instance

Windows Authentication for Azure AD principals, which is in preview as of this writing, enables you to connect traditional on-premises applications to an Azure SQL Managed Instance. You can set up your existing Azure AD tenant as a Kerberos realm. Then, on the AD domain, you create an incoming trust for that Azure AD realm. When a client sends a Kerberos ticket to the Azure SQL Managed Instance, the ticket is exchanged by this feature for an Azure AD token. This allows authentication for Azure AD without providing access to the internal domain.

Understand virtualization and containers

Hardware abstraction has been around for many years. In fact, Windows NT was designed to be hardware independent. We can take this concept even further by abstracting through virtualization and containers.

- **Virtualization.** Abstracts the entire physical layer behind what's called a *hypervisor*, or virtual machine manager (VMM), so that physical hardware on a host system can be logically shared between different VMs, or guests, running their own operating systems.

- **Containers.** Abstract away not just the hardware, but the entire operating system as well. Because it does not need to include and maintain a separate OS, a container has a much smaller resource footprint—often dedicated to a single application or service with access to the subset of hardware it needs.

A virtual consumer (a guest OS or container) accesses resources in the same way as a physical machine. As a rule, it has no knowledge that it is virtualized.

CHAPTER 2

Inside OUT

What is the cloud?

You can think of the cloud as a massive, virtualized environment. Millions of servers are sitting in datacenters all over the world, running tens or hundreds of virtual consumers (VMs and containers) on each server. The service fabric (the software that controls and manages the environment) is what differentiates each cloud vendor.

Going virtual

The move to virtualization and containers has come about because in many organizations, physical hardware is not being used to its full potential, and systems might spend hundreds of hours per year sitting idle. By consolidating an infrastructure, you can share resources more easily, reducing the amount of waste and increasing the usefulness of hardware.

Certain workloads and applications are not designed to share resources, however, and misconfiguration of shared resources by system administrators might not take these specialized workloads into account. SQL Server is an excellent example of this, because it is designed to use all the physical RAM in a server by default.

If resources are allocated incorrectly from the host level, contention between the virtual consumers takes place. This phenomenon is known as the *noisy neighbor*, in which one consumer monopolizes resources on the host, which negatively affects the other consumers. With some effort on the part of the network administrators, this problem can be alleviated.

The benefits far outweigh the downsides, of course. You can move consumers from one host to another in the case of resource contention or hardware failure. Some orchestrator software can even do this without even shutting down the consumer.

It is also much easier to take snapshots of virtualized file systems than physical machines, which you can use to clone VMs, for instance. This reduces deployment costs and time when deploying new servers, by "spinning up" a VM template and configuring the OS and the application software that was already installed on that virtual hard drive.

Expanding on the concept of VM templates, you can also get these same benefits using containers. With containers, you can spin up a new container, which includes all the software needed to run an application, based on an image in much the same way.

NOTE

A *container* is an image that is composed from a plain text configuration file. Docker containers, for example, are composed using a Dockerfile.

Over time, the benefits become more apparent. New processors with low core counts are becoming more difficult to find. Virtualization makes it possible for you to move physical workloads to virtual consumers (now or later) that have the appropriate virtual core count, and gives you the freedom to use existing licenses, thereby reducing cost.

> ➤ David Klee writes more about this in the article "Point Counterpoint: Why Virtualize a SQL Server?" available at *http://www.davidklee.net/2017/07/12/point-counterpoint-why -virtualize-a-sql-server.*

While there are several OS-level virtualization technologies in use today (including Windows containers), we focus on Docker containers specifically. As for VM hypervisors, there are two main players in this space: Microsoft Hyper-V and VMware.

Provision resources for virtual consumers

Setting up VMs or containers requires an understanding of their anticipated workloads. Fortunately, as long as resources are allocated appropriately, a virtual consumer can run almost as quickly as a physical server on the same hardware, but with all of the benefits that virtualization offers. It makes sense, then, to overprovision resources for many general workloads.

Avoid overcommitting more memory than you have

Suppose you have 10 VMs filling various roles—such as Active Directory domain controllers, DNS servers, file servers, and print servers (the plumbing of a Windows-based network, with a low RAM footprint)—all on a single host with 64 GB of physical RAM.

Each VM might require 16 GB of RAM to perform properly. However, in practice, you have determined that 90 percent of the time, each VM can function with 4 to 8 GB RAM, leaving 8 to 12 GB of RAM unused per VM. You could thus overcommit each VM with 16 GB of RAM (for a total of 160 GB), but still see acceptable performance, without having a particular guest swapping memory to the drive because of low RAM, 90 percent of the time.

For the remaining 10 percent of the time, for which paging unavoidably takes place, you might decide that the performance impact is not sufficient to warrant increasing the physical RAM on the host. You are therefore able to run 10 virtualized servers on far less hardware than they would have required as physical servers.

CAUTION

Because SQL Server uses all the memory it is configured to use (limited by edition), it is not good practice to overcommit memory for VMs running SQL Server. It is critical that the amount of RAM assigned to a SQL Server VM is available for exclusive use by the VM, and that the Max Server Memory setting is configured correctly (see Chapter 3). This is especially critical if you use the LPIM policy.

CHAPTER 2

Provision virtual storage

In the same way that you can overcommit memory, you can overcommit storage. This is called *thin provisioning*, in which the consumer is configured to assume that there is a lot more space available than is physically on the host. When a VM begins writing to a drive, the actual space used is increased on the host until it reaches the provisioned limit.

This practice is common with general workloads, for which space requirements grow predictably. An OS like Windows Server might be installed on a guest with 127 GB of visible space, but there might be only 250 GB of actual space on the drive shared across 10 VMs.

For specialized workloads like SQL Server, thin provisioning is not a good idea. Depending on the performance of the storage layer and on the data access patterns of the workload, it is possible that the guest will be slow due to drive fragmentation (especially with storage built on mechanical hard drives), or even run out of storage space. This can occur for any number of reasons, including long-running transactions, infrequent transaction log backups, or a growing tempdb.

It is therefore a better idea to use thick provisioning of storage for specialized workloads. That way, the guest is guaranteed the storage it is promised by the hypervisor, and there is one less thing to worry about when SQL Server runs out of space at 3 a.m. on a Sunday morning.

NOTE

Most of the original use-cases around containers were web and application server workloads, so early implementations did not include options for persisting data across container restarts. This is why container storage was originally considered to be *ephemeral*. Now that containers can be used for SQL Server, persistent storage is available using either bind points or named volumes.

When processors are no longer processors

Virtualizing CPUs is challenging, because as discussed earlier in this chapter, CPUs work by having a certain number of clock cycles per second. For logical processors (the physical CPU core plus any logical cores if SMT is enabled), each core shares time slices, or time slots, with each VM. Every time the CPU clock ticks over, that time slot might be used by the hypervisor or any one of the guests.

Just as it is not recommended to overprovision RAM and storage for SQL Server, you should not overprovision CPU cores. If there are four quad-core CPUs in the host (four CPU sockets populated with a quad-core CPU in each socket), there are 16 cores available for use by the VMs, or 32 when accounting for SMT.

Inside OUT

How is CPU virtualization affected by SMT (Hyper-Threading)?

Even though it is possible to assign as many virtual CPUs (vCPUs) as there are logical cores, we recommend that you limit the number of vCPUs to the number of physical cores available (in other words, excluding SMT) for two reasons:

First, the number of execution resources on the CPU itself is limited to the number of physical cores. Second, CPUs manufactured before 2019 may be susceptible to security vulnerabilities (discussed previously in the "Security vulnerabilities in modern CPUs" section). In this case, you may want to disable SMT altogether, or just patch your OS and CPU microcode if the risks are acceptable.

Virtual CPU

A virtual CPU (vCPU) maps to a logical core, but in practice, the time slots are shared evenly over each core in the physical CPU. A vCPU is more powerful than a single core because the load is parallelized across each core.

One of the risks of mixing different types of workloads on a single host is that a business-critical workload like SQL Server might require all the vCPUs to run a large, parallelized query. If there are other guests using those vCPUs during that specific time slot and the CPU is overcommitted, those guests will need to wait.

There are certain algorithms in hypervisors that allow vCPUs to cut in line and take over a time slot. However, this results in a lag for the other guests, causing performance issues. For example, suppose a file server has two virtual processors assigned to it. Further assume that on the same host, a SQL Server has eight virtual processors assigned to it. It is possible for the VM with fewer virtual logical processors to "steal" time slots because it has a lower number allocated to it.

There are several ways to deal with this, but the easiest solution is to keep like with like. That is, any guests on the same host should have the same number of vCPUs assigned to them, running similar workloads. That way, the time slots are more evenly distributed, and it becomes easier to troubleshoot processor performance. It might also be practical to reduce the number of vCPUs allocated to a SQL Server instance so that the time slots are better distributed.

CAUTION

A VM running SQL Server might benefit from fewer vCPUs. If too many cores are allocated to the VM, it could cause performance issues due to foreign memory access because SQL Server might be unaware of the underlying NUMA configuration. Remember to size your VM CPU core allocation as a multiple of a NUMA node size.

The network is virtual, too

Before, certain hardware devices, such as NICs, routers, firewalls, and switches, might have been used to perform discrete tasks. But now, these tasks can be accomplished exclusively through a software layer using virtual network devices.

Several VMs might share one or more physical NICs on a physical host, but because it's all virtualized, a VM might have several virtual NICs mapped to that one physical NIC.

This enables several things that previously might have been cumbersome and costly to implement. For example, software developers can now test against myriad configurations for their applications without having to build a physical lab environment using all different combinations.

With the general trend of consolidating VMs and containers, virtual networking facilitates combining and consolidating network devices and services into the same environment as these virtual consumers, lowering the cost of administration and reducing the need to purchase separate hardware. You can replace a virtualized network device almost immediately if something goes wrong, vastly reducing downtime.

Design and implement an on-premises database infrastructure

This chapter covers the architecture of an on-premises database infrastructure, including the differences between data and transaction log files, and how certain features work to ensure durability and consistency even during unexpected events.

We cover what certain important configuration settings mean, both from a performance and best-practice perspective. We also go into detail about the different kinds of data compression and file system settings that are most appropriate for your environment.

The sample scripts in this chapter, and all scripts for this book, are available for download at *https://www.MicrosoftPressStore.com/SQLServer2022InsideOut/downloads.*

Introduction to SQL Server database architecture

The easiest way to observe the implementation of a SQL Server database is by its files. Every SQL Server database has at least two main kinds of files:

- **Data.** The data itself is stored in one or more filegroups. Each filegroup in turn comprises one or more physical data files.

- **Transaction log.** This is where all data modifications are saved until committed or rolled back and then hardened to a data file. There is usually only one transaction log file per database.

NOTE

There are several other file types used by SQL Server, including logs, trace files, and memory-optimized filegroups, which we discuss later in this chapter.

Data files and filegroups

When you create a user database without specifying any overriding settings, SQL Server uses the *model* database as a template. This provides your new database with its default configuration, including ownership, compatibility level, file growth settings, recovery model (full, bulk-logged, simple), and physical file settings.

By default, each new database has one *transaction log file* and one data *filegroup*. This data filegroup is known as the *primary filegroup*, comprising a single data file by default. It is known as the primary data file, which has the file extension .mdf. (See Figure 3-1.)

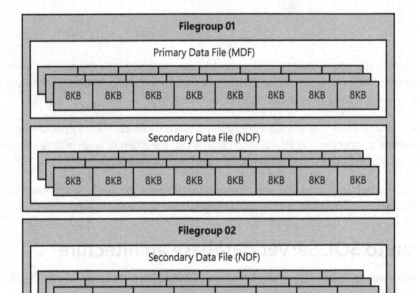

Figure 3-1 The data files as they make up one or more filegroups in a database.

NOTE

The file extensions used for SQL Server data and transaction log files are listed by convention only and are not required.

You can have more than one file in a filegroup, which can provide better performance through parallel reads and writes (but please test this scenario before adding too many files). Secondary data files generally have the file extension .ndf.

For large databases (more than 100 GB), you can separate your data into multiple filegroups based on a business rule (one per year, for instance). The real benefit comes with adding new filegroups and splitting your logical data storage across those filegroups. This makes it possible for you to do things like piecemeal backups and online restores at a filegroup level in Enterprise edition. Only offline filegroup restore is available in Standard edition.

Inside OUT

How do I manage partial recovery using filegroups?

When designing your database, we recommend that you avoid using the primary filegroup for user data. Should a disaster occur, you can restore your primary filegroup and most current data immediately (using partial restore), which brings the database online much more quickly than having to restore everything from a single filegroup.

You can also age-out data into a filegroup that is set to read-only and store it on slower storage than the current data, to manage storage costs better.

If you use table partitioning (see the "Partition tables" section later in the chapter), splitting partitions across filegroups makes even more sense.

Group data pages with extents

SQL Server data pages are 8 KB in size. Eight of these contiguous pages is called an *extent*, which is 64 KB in size.

There are two types of extents in a SQL Server data file:

- **Uniform extent.** All eight 8-KB pages per extent are assigned to a single object.

- **Mixed extent (rare).** Each page in the extent is assigned to its own separate object (one 8-KB page per object).

Mixed extents were originally created to reduce storage requirements for database objects, back when mechanical hard drives were much smaller and more expensive. As storage becomes faster and cheaper, and SQL Server more complex, contention (a hotspot) can occur at the beginning of a data file, especially if a lot of small objects are being created and deleted.

Mixed extents are turned off by default for tempdb and user databases, and are turned on by default for system databases. If you want, you can configure mixed extents on a user database by using the following command:

```
ALTER DATABASE <dbname> SET MIXED_PAGE_ALLOCATION ON;
```

CHAPTER 3

Contents and types of data pages

All data pages begin with a header of 96 bytes, followed by a body containing the data itself. At the end of the page is a slot array, which fills up in reverse order, beginning with the first row, as illustrated in Figure 3-2. It instructs the Database Engine where a particular row begins on that particular page. Note that the slot array does not need to be in any particular order after the first row.

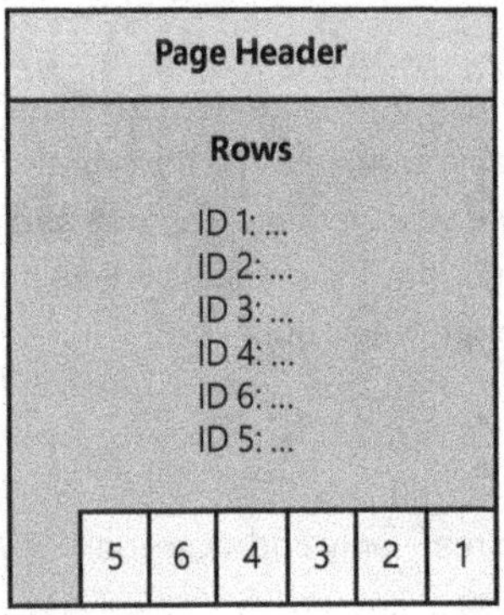

Page Header
Rows
ID 1: ...
ID 2: ...
ID 3: ...
ID 4: ...
ID 6: ...
ID 5: ...

| 5 | 6 | 4 | 3 | 2 | 1 |

Figure 3-2 A typical 8-KB data page, showing the header, the data, and the slot array.

At certain points in the data file, there are system-specific data pages (also 8 KB in size). These help SQL Server recognize and manage the different data within each file.

Several types of pages can be found in a data file:

- **Data.** Regular data from a heap or a clustered index at the leaf level (the data itself; what you would see when querying a table).

- **Index.** Non-clustered index data at the leaf and non-leaf level, as well as clustered indexes at the non-leaf level.

- **Text/image.** Sometimes referred to as *large object (LOB) data types*. These include text, ntext, image, nvarchar(max), varchar(max), varbinary(max), Common Language Runtime (CLR) data types, xml, and sql_variant where it exceeds 8 KB. Overflow data can also be stored here (data that has been moved *off-page* by the Database Engine), with a pointer from the original page.

- **Global Allocation Map (GAM).** Keeps track of all free extents in a data file. There is one GAM page for every GAM interval (64,000 extents, or roughly 4 GB).

- **Shared Global Allocation Map (SGAM).** Keeps track of all extents that can be mixed extents. It has the same interval as the GAM.

- **Page Free Space (PFS).** Keeps track of free space inside heap and large object pages. There is one PFS page for every PFS interval (8,088 pages, or roughly 64 MB).

- **Index Allocation Map (IAM).** Keeps track of which extents in a GAM interval belong to a particular allocation unit. (An *allocation unit* is a bucket of pages that belong to a partition, which in turn belongs to a table.) It has the same interval as the GAM. There is at least one IAM for every allocation unit. If more than one IAM belongs to an allocation unit, it forms an IAM chain.

- **Bulk Changed Map (BCM).** Keeps track of extents modified by bulk-logged operations since the last full backup. It is used by transaction log backups in the bulk-logged recovery model to see which extents should be backed up.

- **Differential Changed Map (DCM).** Sometimes called a *differential bitmap*. Keeps track of extents that were modified since the last full or differential backup. Used for differential backups.

- **Boot page.** Contains information about the database. There is only one boot page per database.

- **File header page.** Contains information about the file. There is only one per data file.

➤ To find out more about the internals of a data page, visit *https://learn.microsoft.com/sql /relational-databases/pages-and-extents-architecture-guide* and read Paul Randal's post, "Inside the Storage Engine: Anatomy of a page," at *https://www.sqlskills.com/blogs/paul /inside-the-storage-engine-anatomy-of-a-page*.

CHAPTER 3

Inside OUT

What about memory-optimized objects?

Even memory-optimized objects rely on the storage subsystem and require significant IOPS. (For more about storage, refer to Chapter 2, "Introduction to database server components.) For example, the transaction log must still be written to, though in a highly efficient manner.

Memory-optimized objects do not map to 8-KB data pages on disk the same way regular objects do. They use their own filegroup called the memory-optimized filegroup and they are implemented in a similar fashion as the FILESTREAM filegroup, in that all objects are stored in folders on the underlying file system.

All data files and delta file pairs for memory-optimized objects are stored in this memory-optimized filegroup. The file pairs record changes to the tables and are used during recovery (including when the SQL Server is restarted) to repopulate the objects in memory (if using the default SCHEMA_AND_DATA durability). You can remove the memory-optimized filegroup only by dropping a database.

You must provide four times the drive space that your memory-optimized tables require. We therefore recommend a minimum of four storage containers for this filegroup, spread across physical drives. For more information, visit *https://learn.microsoft.com/sql/relational-databases/in-memory-oltp/the-memory-optimized-filegroup*.

Verify data pages by using a checksum

By default, when a data page is read into the buffer pool, a checksum is automatically calculated over the entire 8-KB page and compared to the checksum stored in the page header on the drive. This is how SQL Server keeps track of page-level corruption—by detecting when the contents of a data page do not match the results the Database Engine expects. This corruption can happen through storage failures, physical memory corruption, or SQL Server bugs. If the checksum stored on the drive does not match the checksum in memory, corruption has occurred. A record of this suspect page is stored in the msdb database, and you will see an error message when that page is accessed.

The same checksum is performed when writing to a drive. If the checksum on the drive does not match the checksum in the data page in the buffer pool, page-level corruption has occurred.

Although the PAGE_VERIFY property on new databases is set to CHECKSUM by default, it might be necessary to check databases that have been upgraded from previous versions of SQL Server, especially those created prior to SQL Server 2005 (compatibility level 90).

You can look at the checksum verification status on all databases by using the following query:

```
SELECT name, page_verify_option_desc
FROM sys.databases;
```

You can reduce the likelihood of data page corruption by using error-correcting code (ECC) memory. Data page corruption on the drive is detected by using DBCC CHECKDB and other operations.

➤ For information on how to proactively detect corruption, review the sections on database corruption in Chapter 8, "Maintain and monitor SQL Server."

Record changes in the transaction log

The transaction log is the most important component of a SQL Server database because it is where all units of work (transactions) performed on a database are recorded, before the data can be written (flushed) to the drive. The transaction log file usually has the file extension .ldf.

NOTE

Although it is possible to use more than one file to store the transaction logs for a database, we do not recommend this because there is no performance or maintenance benefit to using multiple files. To understand why and where it might be appropriate to have more than one, see the section "Inside the transaction log file" later in the chapter.

A successful transaction is said to be *committed*. An unsuccessful and completely reversed transaction is said to be *rolled back*.

In Chapter 2, we saw that when SQL Server needs an 8-KB data page from the data file, it usually (if the page doesn't already exist in the buffer pool) copies it from the drive and stores a copy of it in memory in an area called the *buffer pool* while that page is required. When a transaction needs to modify that page, it works directly on the copy of the page in the buffer pool. If the page is subsequently modified, a log record of the modification is created in the log buffer (also in memory), and that log record is then written to the drive. This process happens synchronously—a transaction is not considered complete by the Database Engine until it is written into the transaction log.

SQL Server uses a technique called *write-ahead logging* (*WAL*), which ensures that no changes are written to the data file before the necessary log record is written to the drive in a permanent form (in this case, non-volatile storage).

However, you can use *delayed durability* (also known as *lazy commit*), which does not save every change to the transaction log as it happens. Instead, it waits until the log cache grows to a certain size (or `sp_flushlog` runs) before flushing it to the drive.

CAUTION

If you turn on delayed durability for your database, the performance benefit has a downside of potential data loss if the underlying storage layer experiences a failure before the log can be saved. Indeed, `sp_flushlog` should also be run before shutting down SQL Server for all databases with delayed durability enabled.

➤ You can read more about log persistence and how it affects durability of transactions in Chapter 14, "Performance tune SQL Server," and at *https://learn.microsoft.com/sql /relational-databases/logs/control-transaction-durability*.

A transaction's outcome is unknown until a commit or rollback occurs. An error might occur during a transaction, or the operator might decide to roll back the transaction manually because the results were not as expected. In the case of a rollback, changes to the modified data pages must be undone. SQL Server will use the saved log records to undo the changes for an incomplete transaction.

Only when the transaction log file is written to can the modified 8-KB page be saved in the data file, though the page might be modified several times in the buffer pool before it is flushed to the drive using a checkpoint operation.

Our guidance, therefore, is to use the fastest storage possible for the transaction log file(s), because of the low-latency requirements.

Flush data to the storage subsystem with checkpoints

Recall from Chapter 2 that any changes to data are written to the database file asynchronously for performance reasons. This process is controlled by a *database checkpoint*. As its name implies, this is a database-level setting that can be changed under certain conditions by modifying the recovery interval or running the CHECKPOINT command in the database context.

The checkpoint process takes all the modified pages in the buffer pool, as well as transaction log information that is in memory, and writes it to the storage subsystem. This reduces the time it takes to recover a database because only the changes made after the latest checkpoint need to be rolled forward in the Redo phase (see the "Restart with recovery" section later in the chapter).

Inside the transaction log file

A transaction log file is split into logical segments, called *virtual log files* (*VLFs*). These segments are dynamically allocated when the transaction log file is created and whenever the file grows. The size of each VLF is not fixed, and is based on an internal algorithm, which depends on the version of SQL Server, the current file size, and file growth settings. Each VLF has a header containing a *minimum log sequence number* and information indicating whether the VLF is active.

Every transaction is uniquely identified by a log sequence number (LSN). Each LSN is ordered, so a later LSN will be greater than an earlier LSN. The LSN is also used by database backups and restores.

➤ **For more information see Chapter 8, and Chapter 10, "Develop, deploy, and manage data recovery."**

Figure 3-3 illustrates how the transaction log is circular. When a VLF is first allocated by creation or file growth, it is marked inactive in the VLF header. Transactions can be recorded only in active portions of the log file, so the Database Engine looks for inactive VLFs sequentially. Then, as it needs them, the Database Engine marks them as active to allow transactions to be recorded.

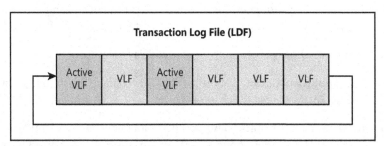

Figure 3-3 The transaction log file, showing active and inactive VLFs.

The operation to make a VLF inactive is called *log truncation*, but this operation does not affect the size of the physical transaction log file. It just means that an active VLF has been marked inactive and can be reused.

There are several reasons why log truncation can be delayed. After the transactions that use an active VLF are committed or rolled back, what happens next depends on several factors:

- **The recovery model**

  - **Simple.** An automatic checkpoint is queued after the recovery interval timeout is reached or if the log becomes 70 percent full.

  - **Full or bulk-logged.** A transaction log backup must take place after a transaction is committed. A checkpoint is queued if the log backup is successful.

- **Other processes that can delay log truncation:**

  - **Active backup or restore.** The transaction log cannot be truncated if it is being used by a backup or restore operation.

  - **Active transaction.** If another transaction is using an active VLF, it cannot be truncated.

  - **Availability group replica.** Availability group changes must be synchronized before the log can be truncated. This occurs in high-performance mode or if the mirror is behind the principal database.

  - **Replication.** Transactions that have not yet been delivered to the distribution database can delay log truncation.

CHAPTER 3

- **Oldest page.** If a database is configured to use indirect checkpoints, the oldest page in the database might be older than the log sequence number (LSN), which can delay truncation.

- **Database snapshot creation.** This is usually brief, but creating snapshots (manually or through database consistency checks, for instance) can delay truncation.

- **Log scan.** Usually brief, but this, too, can delay a log truncation.

- **Checkpoint operation.** See the section "Flush data to the storage subsystem with checkpoints" earlier in the chapter.

- **In-Memory OLTP checkpoint.** A checkpoint for In-Memory OLTP needs to be performed for memory-optimized tables. An automatic checkpoint is created when the transaction log is larger than 1.5 GB since the last checkpoint.

➤ To learn more, read "Factors that can delay log truncation" at *https://learn.microsoft.com /sql/relational-databases/logs/the-transaction-log-sql-server#FactorsThatDelayTruncation.*

After the checkpoint is issued and the dependencies on the transaction log (as just listed) are removed, the log is truncated by marking those VLFs as inactive.

The log is accessed sequentially in this manner until it gets to the end of the file. At this point, the log wraps around to the beginning, and the Database Engine looks for an inactive VLF from the start of the file to mark active. If there are no inactive VLFs available, the log file must create new VLFs by growing according to the auto growth settings.

If the log file cannot grow, it will stop all operations on the database until VLFs can be reclaimed or created.

Inside OUT

What do I do if I run out of space in the transaction log file?

If a transaction log runs out of space because no inactive VLFs are available, you first must take a transaction log backup (if the database is in the full or bulk-logged recovery model). Failing that, you can grow the transaction log file. If there is insufficient space on the drive to grow the transaction log file, you can assign a second log file to the database on a different drive.

In many cases, a transaction log file runs out of space because the database is in the full or bulk-logged recovery model, and transaction log backups are not being created regularly. We recommend that you allow transaction log files to grow automatically, with a fixed auto growth size, and to generate regular transaction log backups.

CHAPTER 3

If you find yourself running out of space on a regular basis due to long-running transactions (or unfettered log growth in simple recovery), consider using shorter transactions and enabling accelerated database recovery. For more on accelerated database recovery, see "A faster recovery with accelerated database recovery" later in this chapter.

The Minimum Recovery LSN

When a checkpoint occurs, a log record is written to the transaction log stating that a checkpoint has commenced. After this, the Minimum Recovery LSN (MinLSN) must be recorded. The MinLSN is the minimum of either the LSN at the start of the checkpoint, the LSN of the oldest active transaction, or the LSN of the oldest replication transaction that hasn't been delivered to the transactional replication distribution database. In other words, the MinLSN "...is the log sequence number of the oldest log record that is required for a successful database-wide rollback" (*https://learn.microsoft.com/sql/relational-databases/sql-server-transaction-log -architecture-and-management-guide*).

> ➤ To learn more about the distribution database, read about replication in Chapter 11, "Implement high availability and disaster recovery."

This way, crash recovery knows to start recovery only at the MinLSN and can skip over any older LSNs in the transaction log (if they exist). This process minimizes the number of records to be processed at database startup, after a restore.

The checkpoint also records the list of active transactions that have made changes to the database. If the database is in the simple recovery model, the unused portion of the transaction log before the MinLSN is marked for reuse. All dirty data pages and information about the transaction log are written to the storage subsystem, the end of the checkpoint is recorded in the log, and (importantly) the LSN from the start of the checkpoint is written to the boot page of the database.

NOTE

In the full and bulk-logged recovery models, a successful transaction log backup issues a checkpoint implicitly.

Types of database checkpoints

Checkpoints can be activated in a number of different scenarios. The most common is the automatic checkpoint, which is governed by the recovery interval setting (see the Inside OUT sidebar that follows to see how to modify this setting) and by default takes place approximately once every minute for active databases (those databases in which a change has occurred at all).

CHAPTER 3

NOTE

Infrequently accessed databases with no transactions do not require a frequent checkpoint, because nothing has changed in the buffer pool.

Other checkpoint events include the following:

- Database backups (including transaction log backups)

- Database shutdowns

- Adding or removing files on a database

- SQL Server instance shutdown

- Minimally logged operations (for example, in a database in the simple or bulk-logged recovery model)

- Explicit use of the CHECKPOINT command

Inside OUT

How do you set the recovery interval?

The recovery interval "...defines an upper limit on the time recovering a database should take. The SQL Server Database Engine uses the value specified for this option to determine approximately how often to issue automatic checkpoints on a given database" (*https:// learn.microsoft.com/sql/database-engine/configure-windows/configure-the-recovery -interval-server-configuration-option*). You can also visit that page to learn how to configure this setting.

We recommend that you do not increase this value unless you have a very specific need. A longer recovery interval can increase database recovery time, which can affect your Recovery Time Objective (RTO).

Try to keep your transactions as short as possible. This will also improve recovery time if you have a crash and have to apply changes from the transaction log. Consider using accelerated database recovery, which you can read about in the "A faster recovery with accelerated database recovery" section later in this chapter.

You can read more about coding efficient transactions at *https://learn.microsoft.com/sql /relational-databases/sql-server-transaction-locking-and-row-versioning-guide.*

Four types of checkpoints can occur:

- **Automatic.** Issued internally by the Database Engine to meet the value of the recovery interval setting at the instance level. On SQL Server 2016 and higher, the default is 1 minute.

- **Indirect.** Issued to meet a user-specified target recovery time at the database level if the TARGET_RECOVERY_TIME has been set.

- **Manual.** Issued when the CHECKPOINT command is run.

- **Internal.** Issued internally by various operations, such as backup and snapshot creation, to ensure consistency between the log and the drive image.

➤ For more information about checkpoints, visit *https://learn.microsoft.com/sql/relational -databases/logs/database-checkpoints-sql-server*.

Restart with recovery

Whenever SQL Server starts, recovery (also referred to as *crash recovery* or *restart recovery*) takes place on every single database (on at least one thread per database, to ensure that it completes as quickly as possible) because SQL Server does not know for certain whether each database was shut down cleanly.

The transaction log is read from the latest checkpoint in the active portion of the log, or the LSN it gets from the boot page of the database (see the "The Minimum Recovery LSN" section earlier in the chapter), and scans all active VLFs looking for work to do.

All committed transactions are rolled forward (Redo portion) and then all uncommitted transactions are rolled back (Undo portion). This process ensures that the data that was written to the transaction log, but did not yet make it into the data files, is played back into the data files. The total number of rolled forward and rolled back transactions are recorded for each database with a respective entry in the SQL Server Error Log file.

SQL Server Enterprise edition brings the database online immediately after the Redo portion is complete. Other editions must wait for the Undo portion to complete before the database is brought online.

➤ See Chapter 8 for more information about database corruption and recovery.

The reason we cover this in such depth in this introductory chapter is to help you to understand why drive performance is paramount when creating and allocating database files.

When a transaction log file is created or file growth occurs, the portion of the drive must be stamped with a known starting value. (The file system literally writes the binary value 0xC0 in

CHAPTER 3

every byte in that file segment.) This is commonly called *zeroing out* because the binary value was 0x00 prior to SQL Server 2016.

As you can imagine, this can be time consuming for larger files, so you need to take care when setting file growth options—especially with transaction log files. You should measure the performance of the underlying storage layer and choose a fixed growth size that balances performance with reduced VLF count. Instant file initialization does not apply to the initial allocation of transaction log files during restore or recovery. A large transaction log file could impact the duration.

> ## Inside OUT
>
> **How can you verify that instant file initialization (IFI) is enabled?**
>
> IFI is granted to a SQL Server service account via the **Perform Volume Maintenance Tasks permission in Local Security Policy on the Windows server. But it's straightforward to verify whether IFI is in place for the SQL Server service, via the** `sys.dm_server_services` **dynamic management view:**
>
> ```
> SELECT servicename, instant_file_initialization_enabled
> FROM sys.dm_server_services
> WHERE filename LIKE '%sqlservr.exe%';
> ```

MinLSN and the active log

As mentioned, each VLF contains a header that includes an LSN and an indicator as to whether that VLF is active. The portion of the transaction log from the VLF containing the MinLSN to the VLF containing the latest log record is considered the active.

All records in the active log are required to perform a full recovery if something goes wrong. The active log must therefore include all log records for uncommitted transactions, too, which is why long-running transactions can be problematic. Replicated transactions that have not yet been delivered to the distribution database can also affect the MinLSN.

Any type of transaction that does not allow the MinLSN to increase during the normal course of events affects the overall health and performance of the database environment, because the transaction log file might grow uncontrollably.

When VLFs cannot be made inactive until a long-running transaction is committed or rolled back, or if a VLF is in use by other processes (including database mirroring, availability groups, and transactional replication, for example), the log file is forced to grow. Any log backups that include these long-running transaction records will also be large. The recovery phase can therefore take longer because there is a much larger volume of active transactions to process.

> ➤ You can read more about transaction log file architecture at *https://learn.microsoft.com/sql /relational-databases/sql-server-transaction-log-architecture-and-management-guide*.

A faster recovery with accelerated database recovery

SQL Server 2019 introduced accelerated database recovery (ADR), which can be enabled at the database level. If you are using Azure SQL Database, ADR is enabled by default. At a high level, ADR trades extra space in the data file for reduced space in the transaction log, and for improved performance during manual transaction rollbacks and crash recovery—especially in environments where long-running transactions are common.

It is made up of four components:

- **Persisted version store (PVS).** This works in a similar way to read committed snapshot isolation (RCSI), recording a previously committed version of a row until a transaction is committed. The main difference is that the PVS is stored in the user database and not in tempdb, which allows database-specific changes to be recorded in isolation from other instance-level operations.

- **Logical revert.** If a long-running transaction is aborted, the versioned rows created by the PVS can be safely ignored by concurrent transactions. Additionally, upon rollback, the previous version of the row is immediately made available by releasing all locks.

- **Secondary log stream (sLog).** The sLog is a low-volume in-memory log stream that records non-versioned operations (including lock acquisitions). It is persisted to the transaction log file during a checkpoint operation and is aggressively truncated when transactions are committed.

- **Cleaner.** This asynchronous process periodically cleans page versions that are no longer required. SQL Server 2022 introduces a multi-threaded version cleanup—beneficial when you have a small number of large databases on a given server. Beyond multi-threading the version cleaner process consumes less memory and capacity.

SQL Server 2022 also introduces user transaction cleanup, which clears pages in the version store that could not be cleaned up due to table-level locks blocking the cleanup the process. Beyond these changes, the ADR process has been better optimized to consume fewer resources.

Where ADR shines is in the Redo and Undo phases of crash recovery. In the first part of the Redo phase, the sLog is processed first. Because it contains only uncommitted transactions since the last checkpoint, it is processed extremely quickly. The second part of the Redo phase begins from the last checkpoint in the transaction log, as opposed to the oldest committed transaction.

In the Undo phase, ADR completes almost instantly by first undoing non-versioned operations recorded by the sLog, and then performing a logical revert on row-level versions in the PVS and releasing all locks.

CHAPTER 3

Customers using this feature may notice faster rollbacks, a significant reduction in transaction log usage for long-running transactions, faster SQL Server startup times, and a small increase in the size of the data file for each database where this is enabled (on account of the storage required for the PVS). As with all features of SQL Server, we recommend that you do testing before enabling this on all production databases.

Partition tables

SQL Server allows you to break up the storage of a table or index into logical units, or *partitions*, for easier management and maintenance while still treating it as a single table. All tables in SQL Server are already partitioned if you look deep enough into the internals. It just so happens that there is one logical partition per table by default.

> Chapter 7, "Understand table features," goes into more detail about table partitioning.

This concept is called *horizontal partitioning*. Suppose a database table is growing extremely large, and adding new rows is time consuming. You might decide to split the table into groups of rows, based on a partitioning key (typically a date column), with each group in its own partition. You can then store these in different filegroups to improve read and write performance.

Breaking up a table into logical partitions can also result in a query optimization called *partition elimination*, by which only the partition that contains the data you need is queried. However, it was not designed primarily as a performance feature. Partitioning tables will not automatically result in better query performance; in fact, performance might be worse due to other factors, specifically around statistics.

Even so, there are some major advantages to table partitioning, which benefit large datasets, specifically around rolling windows and moving data in and out of the table. This process is called *partition switching*, by which you can switch data into and out of a table almost instantly.

Assume you need to load data into a table every month and then make it available for querying. With table partitioning, you put the data you want to insert into a separate table in the same database, which has the same structure and clustered index as the main table. Then, a switch operation moves that data into the partitioned table almost instantly because no data movement is needed.

This makes it very easy to manage large groups of data or data that ages out at regular intervals (sliding windows), because partitions can be switched out nearly immediately.

Inside OUT

Should you use partitioned tables or partitioned views?

Because table partitioning is available in all editions of SQL Server, you might find it an attractive option for smaller databases. However, it might be more prudent to use partitioned views instead.

Partitioned views use a database view that is a union query against a group of underlying tables. Instead of querying a partitioned table directly, you would query the view.

Using key constraints on the primary key for each base table still allows the query optimizer to use a tactic like "partition" elimination (base table elimination). Performance-wise, moving data in and out of the partitioned view would be almost instantaneous because you need to update only the view itself to add or remove a particular base table.

Compress data

SQL Server supports several types of data compression to reduce the amount of drive space required for data and backups, as a trade-off against higher CPU utilization.

➤ You can read more about data compression *https://learn.microsoft.com/sql/relational-databases/data-compression/data-compression*.

In general, the amount of CPU overhead required to perform compression and decompression depends on the type of data involved, and in the case of data compression, the type of queries running against the database, as well. Even though the higher CPU load might be offset by the savings in I/O, we always recommend testing before implementing this feature.

Table and index compression

SQL Server includes several options for compressing data stored in tables and indexes. We discuss compressing *rowstore* data in this section. You can read more about *columnstore* indexes in Chapter 15, "Understand and design indexes."

NOTE

SQL Server 2019 introduced a new collation type, UTF-8, which may improve storage of Latin-based strings. See Chapter 7 for more information.

Row compression

You turn on row compression at the table or index level, or on the individual partition level for partitioned objects. Each column in a row is evaluated according to the type of data and contents of that column, as follows:

- Numeric data types (such as integer, decimal, floating point, datetime, money, and their derived types) are stored as variable-length strings at the physical layer.

- Fixed-length character data types are stored as variable-length strings, where the blank trailing characters are not stored.

- Variable-length data types, including large objects, are not affected by row compression.

- Bit columns consume more space due to associated metadata.

Row compression can be useful for tables with fixed-length character data types and where numeric types are overprovisioned (e.g., a bigint column that contains mostly int values). Unicode compression alone can save between 15 and 50 percent, depending on your locale and collation.

➤ You can read more about row compression at *https://learn.microsoft.com/sql/relational -databases/data-compression/row-compression-implementation*.

Page compression

You enable page compression at the table or index level, but it operates on all data pages associated with that table, including indexes, table partitions, and index partitions. Leaf-level pages (look ahead to Figure 3-4) are compressed using three steps:

1. Row compression

2. Prefix compression

3. Dictionary compression

Non-leaf-level pages are compressed using row compression only. This is for performance reasons.

Inside OUT

What is the difference between leaf-level and non-leaf-level pages?

Clustered and non-clustered rowstore indexes in SQL Server are stored in a structure known as a *B+ tree*. The tree has a root node, which fans out to child nodes, with the data itself at the leaf level.

Any nodes that appear between the root and leaf levels are called *intermediate*, or *non-leaf-level* nodes. Data in the leaf level is accessed (through a seek or a scan operation) by using page identifiers in the root and intermediate levels, which contain pointers to the respective starting key values in the leaf level. When the leaf level is reached, the slot array at the end of each page contains a pointer to the exact row.

Figure 3-4 presents an example of a clustered index.

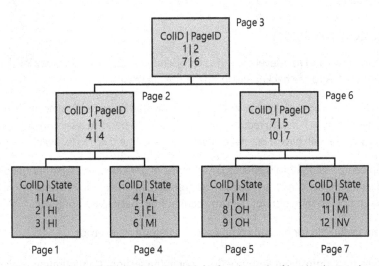

Figure 3-4 A small clustered index with leaf and non-leaf levels, clustered on ColID.

> ➤ You can read more about indexes in Chapter 7, Chapter 14, and Chapter 15. To learn more about index structures, visit *https://learn.microsoft.com/sql/relational-databases/sql-server-index-design-guide*.

Prefix compression works per column, by searching for a common prefix in each column—for example, the values AAAB and AAAC. In this case, the values of AAA would be moved to the header. A row is created just below the page header, called the *compression information* (*CI*) structure, containing a single row of each column with its own prefix. If any of a single column's rows on the page match the prefix, its value is replaced by a reference to that column's prefix.

Dictionary compression then searches across the entire page, looking for repeating values (irrespective of the column), and stores these in the CI structure. When a match is found, the column value in that row is replaced with a reference to the compressed value.

If a data page is not full, it will be compressed using only row compression. If the size of the compressed page along with the size of the CI structure is not significantly smaller than the uncompressed page, no page compression will be performed on that page.

Compress and decompress Transact-SQL functions

While page and row compression act on most data types, they do not work well on binary large object (BLOB) data types, such as videos, images, and text documents. With the ability to store JSON documents in SQL Server 2016, Microsoft introduced the COMPRESS and DECOMPRESS T-SQL functions, which use standard gzip compression to compress the data itself.

In SQL Server 2022, there is a dedicated method for compressing off-row XML data for both columns and indexes. XML compression is defined as part of the CREATE TABLE and CREATE INDEX statements.

Backup compression

Whereas page-level and row-level compression operate at the table and index level, backup compression applies to the backup file for the entire database.

Compressed backups are usually smaller than uncompressed backups. This means fewer I/O operations are involved, which in turn reduces the time it takes to perform a backup or restore. For larger databases, this can have a dramatic effect on how long it takes to recover from a disaster.

The backup compression ratio is affected by the type of data involved, whether the database is encrypted, and whether the data is already compressed. In other words, a database using page and/or row compression might not gain any benefit from backup compression.

The CPU can be limited for backup compression in Resource Governor.

> ➤ You can read more about Resource Governor in the section "Configuration settings" later in this chapter, and in more detail in Chapter 8.

In most cases, we recommend turning on backup compression, keeping in mind that you might need to monitor CPU utilization.

Intel QuickAssist Technology

SQL Server 2022 introduces support for Intel QuickAssist Technology (Intel QAT) data compression with SQL Server backups. This can potentially double your backup speed and reduces storage capacity by approximately 5 percent. The Intel QAT backup compression requires that you install Intel QAT drivers on the server.

> ➤ You can read more about integrated acceleration and offloading at *https://learn.microsoft .com/sql/relational-databases/integrated-acceleration/use-integrated-acceleration-and -offloading.*

Manage the temporary database

tempdb is the working area of every database on the instance, and there is only one tempdb per instance. SQL Server uses this temporary database for several things that are mostly invisible to you, including temporary tables, table variables, triggers, cursors, sorting, version data for snapshot isolation and read-committed snapshot isolation, index creation, user-defined functions, and many more.

Additionally, when performing queries with operations that don't fit in memory (the buffer pool and the buffer pool extension), these operations spill to the drive, requiring the use of tempdb.

Storage options for tempdb

Every time SQL Server restarts, tempdb is cleared out. If tempdb's data and log files don't exist, they are re-created. If the files are configured at a size that is different from their last active size, they will automatically be resized as they are re-created at startup. Like the database file structure described earlier, there is usually one tempdb transaction log file and one or more data files in a single filegroup.

Performance is critical for tempdb—even more than with other databases—to the point that the current recommendation is to use your fastest storage for tempdb before using it for user database transaction log files.

Where possible, use solid-state storage for tempdb. If you have a failover cluster instance, have tempdb on local storage on each node.

Starting with SQL Server 2019, tempdb can store certain metadata in memory-optimized tables for increased performance.

Inside OUT

How does memory-optimized metadata make tempdb faster?

SQL Server 2019 introduced a feature where the system tables used for managing the metadata for temporary objects can be converted to in-memory tables, reducing contention on this metadata. This means temporary objects can be created, modified, and destroyed much more quickly due to better concurrency.

You can enable this feature at the instance level by using the following command and restarting SQL Server:

```
ALTER SERVER CONFIGURATION SET MEMORY_OPTIMIZED TEMPDB_METADATA = ON;
```

To read more about this feature, including the limitations around transactions and column-store indexes, visit *https://learn.microsoft.com/sql/relational-databases/databases/tempdb -database#memory-optimized-tempdb-metadata*.

CHAPTER 3

SQL Server 2022 introduces performance enhancements to two internal page types: Global Allocation Map (GAM) and Shared Global Allocation Map (SGAM) pages, in both user databases and tempdb. These enhancements benefit tempdb-heavy workloads. Workloads that may benefit include, for example, busy databases with read-committed snapshot isolation or applications that make heavy use of temporary tables.

Recommended number of files

As with every database, only one transaction log file should exist for tempdb.

For physical and virtual servers, the default number of tempdb data files recommended by SQL Server Setup should match the number of logical processor cores, up to a maximum of eight, keeping in mind that your logical core count includes symmetrical multithreading (for example, Hyper-Threading). Adding more tempdb data files than the number of logical processor cores rarely results in improved performance. In fact, adding too many tempdb data files could severely harm SQL Server performance.

➤ You can read more about processors in Chapter 2.

Increasing the number of files to eight (and possibly more, based on other factors) reduces tempdb contention when allocating temporary objects, as processes seek out allocation pages in the buffer pool. If the instance has more than eight logical processors allocated, you can test to see whether adding more files helps performance. This is very much dependent on the workload.

You can allocate the tempdb data files together on the same volume (see the "Types of storage" section in Chapter 2), provided the underlying storage layer can meet the low-latency demands of tempdb on your instance. If you plan to share the storage with other database files, keep latency and IOPS in mind.

Inside OUT

Do you need Trace Flags 1118 and 1117 for tempdb?

On versions prior to SQL Server 2016, Trace Flag 1118 turned off mixed extents at the instance level, which reduced contention when creating and deleting many temporary objects. Trace Flag 1117 ensured that all files allocated to any database grew at the same rate. Because trace flags are instance-wide, it meant that all databases were affected by these trace flags, even though they mainly benefited tempdb.

Since SQL Server 2016, these trace flags have no effect. Instead, uniform extents are turned on by default for tempdb (MIXED_PAGE_ALLOCATION was mentioned previously in this chapter), as is the setting to autogrow all files at the same time.

Configuration settings

SQL Server has scores of settings that you can tune to your workload. There are also best prac-tices regarding the appropriate settings (such as file growth, memory settings, and parallelism). We cover some of these in this section.

➤ Chapter 6, "Provision and configure SQL Server databases," contains additional configura-tion settings for provisioning databases.

Manage system usage with Resource Governor

Using Resource Governor, you can specify limits on resource consumption at the application-session level. You can configure these in real time, which allows for flexibility in managing work-loads without affecting other workloads on the system.

➤ You can find out more about Resource Governor in Chapter 8.

A resource pool represents the *physical resources* of an instance, which means you can think of a resource pool itself as a mini SQL Server instance. This allows a DBA to determine quality of service for various workloads on the server.

To make the best use of Resource Governor, it is helpful to logically group similar workloads together into a *workload group* so you can manage them under a specific resource pool. For example, suppose a reporting application has a negative impact on database performance due to resource contention at certain times of the day. By classifying it into a specific workload group, you can limit the amount of memory or disk I/O that the reporting application can use, reducing its effect on, say, a month-end process that needs to run at the same time.

This is done via *classification*, which looks at the incoming application session's characteristics. That incoming session will be categorized into a workload group based on your criteria. This facilitates fine-grained resource usage that reduces the impact of certain workloads on other, more critical workloads.

> ### CAUTION
>
> Classification offers a lot of flexibility and control because Resource Governor supports user-defined functions (UDFs). Resource Governor uses a scalar UDF that allows you to employ system functions, tables, and even other UDFs to classify sessions. This means a poorly written classifier function can render the system nearly unusable. Always test classifier functions and optimize them for performance. If you need to troubleshoot a classifier function, use the dedicated administrator connection (DAC) because it is not subject to classification.

CHAPTER 3

Configure the operating system page file

Operating systems use a portion of the storage subsystem for a page file (also known as a *swap file*, or *swap partition* on Linux) for virtual memory for all applications, including SQL Server, when available memory is not sufficient for the current working set. It does this by offloading (paging out) segments of RAM to the drive. Because storage is slower than memory (see Chapter 2), data that has been paged out is also slower when working from the system page file.

The page file also captures a system memory dump for crash forensic analysis, a factor that dictates its size on modern operating systems with large amounts of memory. Therefore, the general recommendation for the system page file is that it should be at least the same size as the server's amount of physical memory.

Another general recommendation is that the page file should be managed by the operating system (OS). For Windows Server, this should be set to System Managed. Since Windows Server 2012, that guideline has functioned well, but in servers with large amounts of memory, it can result in a very large page file. So, be aware of that if the page file is located on your OS volume. This is also why the page file is best moved to its own volume, away from the OS volume.

On a dedicated SQL Server instance, you can set the page file to a fixed size, relative to the max server memory assigned to SQL Server. In principle, the database instance will use as much RAM as you allow it, to that max server memory limit, so Windows will preferably not need to page SQL Server out of RAM. On Linux, the swap partition can be left at the default size or reduced to 80 percent of the physical RAM, whichever is lower.

> ### NOTE
> If the Lock Pages in Memory policy is enabled, SQL Server will not be forced to page out of memory, and you can set the page file to a smaller size. This can free up valuable space on the OS drive, which can be beneficial to the OS.

➤ For more about *Lock Pages in Memory*, see the section by the same name in this chapter.

Take advantage of logical processors with parallelism

SQL Server is designed to process data in parallel streams, which can be more efficient than single-threaded operations. For more information about multithreading, refer to the section "Central processing unit" in Chapter 2.

➤ You can find out more about parallel query plans in Chapter 14.

In SQL Server, parallelism makes it possible for portions of a query (or an entire query) to run on more than one logical processor at a time. This has certain performance advantages for larger queries, because the workload can be split more evenly across resources. There is an implicit overhead with running queries in parallel, however, because a controller thread must manage the results from each logical processor and then combine them when each thread is completed.

The SQL Server Query Optimizer uses a *cost-based optimizer* when coming up with query plans. This means it makes certain assumptions about the performance of the storage, CPU, and memory, and how they relate to different query plan operators. Each operation has a cost associated with it.

SQL Server will consider creating parallel plan operations, governed by two parallelism settings: Cost Threshold for Parallelism and Max Degree of Parallelism. These two settings can make a large difference to the performance of a SQL Server instance if it is using default settings.

Query plan costs are recorded in a unitless measure. In other words, the cost bears no relation to resources such as drive latency, IOPS, number of seconds, memory usage, or CPU power. Query tuning can be difficult if you don't keep this in mind. What matters is the *magnitude* of this measure.

Cost threshold for parallelism

This is the minimum cost a query plan can incur before the optimizer will even *consider* parallel query plans. If the cost of a query plan exceeds this value, the query optimizer will take parallelism into account when coming up with a query plan. This does not necessarily mean that every plan with a higher cost is run across parallel processor cores, but the chances are increased.

The default setting for cost threshold for parallelism is 5. Any query plan with a cost of 5 or higher will be considered for parallelism. While parallelism is helpful for queries that process large volumes of data, the overhead of using parallelism is less efficient for relatively small queries and can hurt overall server throughput. Given how much faster and more powerful modern server processors are than when this setting was first created, many queries will run just fine on a single core—again, because of the overhead associated with parallel plans. You should change this value on your server. Consider starting with a value of 35 and testing by increasing in increments of 5 to determine the most beneficial setting for your workload.

Inside OUT

Why doesn't Microsoft change the defaults?

Microsoft is reticent to change default values because of its strong support of backward compatibility. Many applications in use today are no longer supported by their original creators and might depend on default settings in Microsoft products. Besides, if it is a best practice to change the default settings when setting up a new instance of SQL Server, it does not make much of a difference either way.

NOTE

Certain query operations can force some or all of a query plan to run serially, even if the plan cost exceeds the cost threshold for parallelism. Paul White's article "Forcing a Parallel Query Execution Plan" describes a few of these. You can read Paul's article at *https://www.sql.kiwi/2011/12/forcing-a-parallel-query-execution-plan.html.*

It might be possible to write a custom process to tune the cost threshold for parallelism setting automatically, using information from the Query Store, but this would be an incredibly complex task and would not be supported in many independent software vendor applications. Because the Query Store works at the database level, it helps identify the average cost of queries per database, and find an appropriate setting for the cost threshold relative to your specific workload.

➤ See more about the Query Store in the "Leverage the Query Store feature" section in Chapter 14.

SQL Server 2022 introduces feedback for degree of parallelism, which automatically adjusts the max degree of parallelism (MAXDOP) for individual queries where the degree of parallelism has caused performance issues. This enhancement does require the Query Store to be enabled.

Cost threshold for parallelism is an advanced server setting; you can change it by using the command sp_configure 'cost threshold for parallelism'. You can also change it in SQL Server Management Studio by using the **Cost Threshold For Parallelism** setting, which can be found in the **Advanced** page of the **Server Properties** dialog box.

Max degree of parallelism

SQL Server uses the MAXDOP value to select the maximum number of schedulers to run a parallel query plan when the cost threshold for parallelism is reached.

Starting with SQL Server 2019, the setup process introduced an automatic recommendation for MAXDOP based on the number of processors available at setup. This option can also be configured at the individual database level, both in Azure SQL and SQL Server.

The problem with this default setting for most workloads is twofold:

- Parallel queries can consume all resources, preventing smaller queries from running or forcing them to run slowly while they find time in the CPU scheduler.

- If all logical processors are allocated to a plan, it can result in foreign memory access, which, as we explain in Chapter 2 in the "Non-uniform memory access" section, carries a performance penalty.

Specialized workloads can have different requirements for MAXDOP. For standard or online transaction processing (OLTP) workloads, to make better use of modern server resources, the MAXDOP setting must take NUMA nodes into account:

- **Single NUMA node.** With up to eight logical processors on a single node, the recommended value should be set to 0 or the number of cores. With more than eight logical processors, the recommended value should be set to 8.

- **Multiple NUMA nodes.** With up to 16 logical processors on a single node, the recommended value should be set to 0 or the number of cores. With more than 16 logical processors, the recommended value should be set to 16.

➤ For more recommendations about MAXDOP, see *https://support.microsoft.com/help/2806535*.

MAXDOP is an advanced server setting. You can change it by using the `sp_configure 'max degree of parallelism'` command. You can also change it in SQL Server Management Studio by using the **Max Degree Of Parallelism** setting in the **Advanced** page of the **Server Properties** dialog box.

SQL Server memory settings

Since SQL Server 2012, the artificial memory limits imposed by the license for lower editions (Standard, Web, and Express) apply to the buffer pool only (see *https://learn.microsoft.com/sql /sql-server/editions-and-components-of-sql-server-2022*).Edition-specific memory limits are not the same thing as the *max server memory* configuration option, though. The max server memory setting controls all of SQL Server's memory allocation, which includes (but is not limited to) the buffer pool, compile memory, caches, memory grants, and CLR (Common Language Runtime, or .NET) memory.

Additionally, limits to columnstore and memory-optimized object memory are calculated over and above the buffer pool limit on non-Enterprise editions, which gives you a greater opportunity to use available physical memory.

This makes memory management for non-Enterprise editions more complicated, but certainly more flexible, especially taking columnstore and memory-optimized objects into account.

Max Server Memory

As noted in Chapter 2, SQL Server uses as much memory as you allow it. Therefore, you want to limit the amount of memory that each SQL Server instance can control on the server, ensuring that you leave enough system memory for the following:

- The OS itself (see the algorithm in the next section)

- Other SQL Server instances installed on the server

- Other SQL Server features installed on the server—for example, SQL Server Reporting Services, SQL Server Analysis Services, or SQL Server Integration Services

- Remote desktop sessions and locally run administrative applications like SQL Server Management Studio (SSMS) and Azure Data Studio

- Antimalware programs

- System monitoring or remote management applications

- Any additional applications that might be installed and running on the server (including web browsers)

CAUTION

If you connect to your SQL Server instance via a remote desktop session, make sure you have a secure VPN connection in place.

Because of feedback, and some SQL Server operations taking place outside the main process memory for SQL Server, Microsoft has introduced new guidance around setting Max Server Memory for SQL Server. To learn more about configuring this setting, visit *https://learn.microsoft.com/sql/database-engine/configure-windows/server-memory-server-configuration-options#max_server_memory*.

OS reservation

Microsoft recommends subtracting the number of potential memory thread allocations that are outside of the control of the Max Server Memory setting. To get this number, multiply the stack size (which on most modern servers will be 2048 KB) by the *max worker threads* (discussed in further detail in the upcoming section "Max worker threads") configuration option on your SQL Server. You should then subtract an additional 25 percent for other allocations outside of that main memory, like backup buffers, allocations from linked server calls, and columnstore indexes. The remaining number should be used to initially set max memory for your database server. This guidance has been incorporated into the max memory recommendation in the SQL Server installation process.

Performance Monitor to the rescue

Ultimately, the best way to see if the correct value is assigned to Max Server Memory is to monitor the Memory\Available MBytes value in Performance Monitor. This way, you can ensure that Windows Server has enough working sets of its own and adjust the setting downward if this value drops below 300 MB.

➤ Performance Monitor is covered in more detail in Chapter 8.

Max Server Memory is an advanced server setting. You can change it by using the command `sp_configure 'max server memory'`. You can also change it in SQL Server Management

Studio by way of the **Max Server Memory** setting in the **Server Properties** section of the **Memory** node.

Max worker threads

Every process on SQL Server requires a *thread*, or time on a logical processor, including network access, database checkpoints, and user activity. Threads are managed internally by the SQL Server scheduler, one for each logical processor, and only one thread is processed at a time by each scheduler on its respective logical processor. These threads consume memory, which is why it's generally a good idea to let SQL Server manage the maximum number of threads allowed automatically.

While this setting should rarely be changed from the default of 0, changing this value might help performance. In most cases the availability of worker threads is not the performance problem; rather, long-running code holding onto those threads is the root cause. A default of 0 means that SQL Server will dynamically assign a value when starting, depending on the number of logical processors and other resources.

To check whether your server is currently under CPU pressure, run the following query, which returns one row per CPU core:

```
SELECT AVG(runnable_tasks_count)
FROM sys.dm_os_schedulers
WHERE status = 'VISIBLE ONLINE';
```

> ➤ Glenn Berry provides a history in one-minute increments using this same dynamic management view (DMV) at *https://sqlserverperformance.wordpress.com/2010/04/20/a-dmv-a-day -%e2%80%93-day-21/*.

If the number of tasks is consistently high (in the double digits), your server is under CPU pressure. You can mitigate this in several other ways that you should consider before increasing the number of max worker threads. Also, be aware that in some scenarios, lowering the number of max worker threads can improve performance.

> ➤ You can read more about setting max worker threads at *https://learn.microsoft.com /sql/database-engine/configure-windows/configure-the-max-worker-threads-server -configuration-option*.

Lock Pages in Memory

The Lock Pages in Memory policy prevents Windows from taking memory away from applications such as SQL Server in low-memory conditions, but it can cause instability if you use it incorrectly. You can mitigate the danger of OS instability by carefully aligning max server memory capacity for any installed SQL Server features (discussed earlier) and reducing the competition for memory resources from other applications.

CHAPTER 3

When reducing memory pressure in virtualized systems, it is also important to avoid over-allocating memory to guests on the virtual host. Meanwhile, locking pages in memory can still prevent the paging of SQL Server memory to the drive due to memory pressure, which is a significant performance hit.

➤ For a more in-depth explanation of the Lock Pages in Memory policy, see Chapter 2.

Optimize for ad hoc workloads

Ad hoc queries are defined, in this context, as queries that are run only once. Applications and reports typically run the same queries many times, and SQL Server recognizes them and caches them over time.

By default, SQL Server caches the runtime plan for a query after the first time it runs, with the expectation of using it again and saving the compilation cost for future runs. For ad hoc queries though, these cached plans will never be reused, yet will remain in cache.

When you set **Optimize for Ad Hoc Workloads** to **true**, a plan will not be cached until it is recognized to have been called twice. In other words, it will cache the full plan on the second execution. The third and all ensuing times it is run would then benefit from the cached runtime plan.

If you wish to enable this option, bear in mind that it can affect troubleshooting performance issues with single-use queries. Therefore, it is recommended that you set this option to true only after testing.

NOTE

Enabling forced parameterization at the database level can force query plans to be parameterized even if they are considered unique by the query optimizer, which can then reduce the number of unique plans. Provided you test this scenario, you can get better performance using this feature than with Optimize for Ad Hoc Workloads.

This is an advanced server setting. You can change it by using the `sp_configure 'optimize for ad hoc workloads'` command. You can also change it in SQL Server Management Studio by using the **Optimize for Ad Hoc Workloads** setting in the **Advanced** page of the **Server Properties** dialog box.

Allocate CPU cores with an affinity mask

It is possible to assign only certain logical processors to SQL Server. This might be necessary on systems that are used for instance stacking (more than one SQL Server instance installed on the same OS) or when workloads are shared between SQL Server and other software.

SQL Server on Linux does not support the installation of multiple instances on the same server. Virtual consumers (virtual machines or containers) are probably a better way of allocating these resources, but there might be legitimate or legacy reasons for setting core affinity.

Suppose you have a dual-socket NUMA server, with both CPUs populated by 16-core processors. Excluding simultaneous multithreading (SMT), this is a total of 32 cores. However, SQL Server Standard edition is limited to 24 cores or four sockets, whichever is lower.

When it starts, SQL Server will allocate all 16 cores from the first NUMA node and 8 from the second NUMA node. It will write an entry to the Error Log stating this, and that's where it ends. Unless you know about the core limit, you will be stuck with unbalanced CPU core and memory access, resulting in unpredictable performance.

One way to solve this without using a VM or container is to limit 12 cores from each CPU to SQL Server using an affinity mask (see Figure 3-5). This way, the cores are allocated evenly. When combined with a reasonable MAXDOP setting of 8, foreign memory access is not a concern.

NOTE

I/O affinity allows you to assign specific CPU cores to I/O operations, which may be beneficial on enterprise-level hardware with more than 16 CPU cores. You can read more at *https://support.microsoft.com/help/298402.*

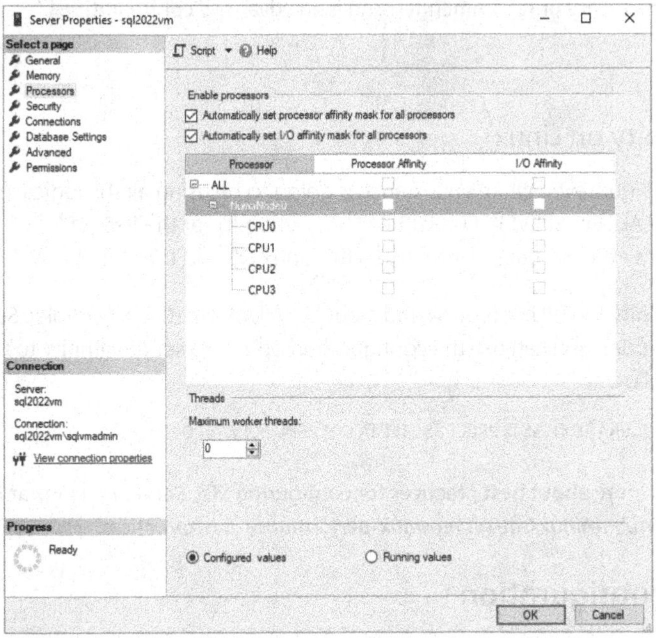

Figure 3-5 Set the affinity mask in SQL Server Management Studio.

By setting an affinity mask, you instruct SQL Server to use only specific cores. The remaining unused cores are marked as offline to SQL Server. When SQL Server starts, it will assign a scheduler to each online core.

CAUTION

Affinity masking is not a legitimate way to circumvent licensing limitations with SQL Server Standard edition. If you have more cores than the maximum usable by a certain edition, all logical cores on that machine must be licensed.

Inside OUT

How do you balance schedulers across processors if you limit affinity?

When no affinity is set, SQL Server doesn't assign schedulers to specific cores. With affinity set, it is possible that an external process (that is, a process outside SQL Server) is also bound to a particular core. This can result in queries being blocked by that external process or SQL Server becoming CPU bound by a lack of scheduler flexibility.

To avoid this unexpected behavior, enable Trace Flag 8002, which lets SQL Server decide which of the available cores the scheduler can use. This behavior seems intuitive but is necessary when SQL Server runs with processor affinities. Keep in mind that affinity masking is not typically necessary or recommended and is an advanced configuration.

Configure affinity on Linux

For SQL Server on Linux, even when an instance is going to be using all the logical processors, you should use the ALTER SERVER CONFIGURATION option to set the PROCESS AFFINITY value. This value maintains efficient behavior between the Linux OS and the SQL Server Scheduler.

You can set the affinity by CPU or NUMA node, but the NUMA method is simpler. Suppose you have four NUMA nodes. You can use the configuration option to set the affinity to use all the NUMA nodes as follows:

```
ALTER SERVER CONFIGURATION SET PROCESS AFFINITY NUMANODE = 0 TO 3;
```

➤ You can read more about best practices for configuring SQL Server on Linux at *https://learn .microsoft.com/sql/linux/sql-server-linux-performance-best-practices*.

File system configuration

This section primarily deals with the default file system on Windows Server. Any references to other file systems, including Linux file systems, are noted separately.

The NT File System (NTFS) was created for the first version of Windows NT, bringing with it more granular security than the older File Allocation Table (FAT)–based file system, as well as a journaling file system. (Think of it as a transaction log for your file system.) You can configure several settings that deal with NTFS in some way to improve your SQL Server implementation and performance.

Instant file initialization

As stated, transaction log files need to be zeroed out at the file system for recovery to work properly. However, data files are different, and with their 8-KB page size and allocation rules, the underlying file might contain sections of unused space.

With instant file initialization (IFI), a feature enabled by the Perform Volume Maintenance Tasks Active Directory policy, data files can be instantly resized without zeroing-out the underlying file. This adds a major performance boost.

Inside OUT

Does instant file initialization (IFI) benefit transaction log files, too?

With one exception, IFI does not benefit transaction log files, so keep this in mind when growing or shrinking transaction log files. The exception is that starting in SQL Server 2022, and included in Azure SQL Database at the time of this writing, IFI can benefit growth events of transaction log files that are less than or equal to 64 MB. This applies to manual file growth initiated by you, as well as autogrowth events initiated by SQL Server. This should be a big performance improvement if your transaction log files unexpectedly grow. Of course, you should try to avoid autogrowth events altogether.

Otherwise, without IFI, all activity in a database will stop until the file growth or shrink operations complete on the transaction log file.

CHAPTER 3

The trade-off is a tiny, perhaps insignificant security risk: data that was previously used in drive allocation currently dedicated to a database's data file now might not be fully erased before use. Because you can examine the underlying bytes in data pages using built-in tools in SQL Server, individual pages of data that have not yet been overwritten inside the new allocation could be visible to a malicious administrator.

CAUTION

It is important to control access to SQL Server's data files and backups. When a database is in use by SQL Server, only the SQL Server service account and the local administrator have access. However, if the database is detached or backed up, there is an opportunity to view that deleted data on the detached file or backup file that was created with instant file initialization turned on.

Because this is a possible security risk, the Perform Volume Maintenance Tasks policy is not granted to the SQL Server service by default, and a summary of this warning is displayed during SQL Server setup.

Without IFI, you might find that the SQL Server wait type PREEMPTIVE_OS_WRITEFILEGATHER is prevalent during times of data-file growth. This wait type occurs when a file is being zero-initialized; thus, it can be a sign that your SQL Server is wasting time that could be skipped with the benefit of IFI. Keep in mind that PREEMPTIVE_OS_WRITEFILEGATHER is also generated by transaction log files, which do not benefit from IFI.

Note that SQL Server Setup takes a slightly different approach to granting this privilege than SQL Server administrators might take. SQL Server assigns access control lists (ACLs) to automatically created security groups, not to the service accounts that you select on the Server Configuration Setup page. Instead of granting the privilege to the named SQL Server service account directly, SQL Server grants the privilege to the per-service security identifier (SID) for the SQL Server database service—for example, the NT SERVICE\MSSQLSERVER principal. This means that SQL Server service will maintain the ability to use IFI even if its service account changes.

You can determine whether the SQL Server Database Engine service has been granted access to IFI by using the sys.dm_server_services dynamic management view via the following query:

```
SELECT servicename, instant_file_initialization_enabled
FROM sys.dm_server_services
WHERE filename LIKE '%sqlservr.exe%';
```

If IFI was not configured during SQL Server setup, and you want to do so later, open the Windows **Start** menu. Then, in the Search box, type **Local Security Policy**. In the pane on the left of the window that appears, expand **Local Policies** (see Figure 3-6); then select **User Rights Assignment**. Finally, locate the **Perform Volume Maintenance Tasks** policy and add the SQL Server service account to the list of objects with that privilege.

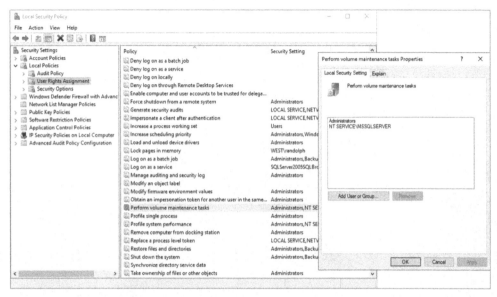

Figure 3-6 Turning on instant file initialization (IFI) through the Local Security Policy setup page.

NTFS allocation unit size

SQL Server performs best with an allocation unit size of 64 KB. Depending on the type of storage, the default allocation unit on NTFS might be 512 bytes, 4,096 bytes (also known as Advanced Format 4K sector size), or some other multiple of 512 bytes.

Because SQL Server deals with 64-KB extents (see the section "Group data pages with extents" earlier in the chapter), it performs best with an allocation unit size of 64 KB, to align the extents with the allocation units. This applies to the Resilient File System (ReFS) on Windows Server, and XFS and ext4 file systems on Linux.

> NOTE
>
> We cover aligned storage in more detail in Chapter 4 in the section "Important SQL Server volume settings."

Install and configure SQL Server instances and features

This chapter reviews the process of installing and configuring a Microsoft SQL Server instance as well as creating and migrating databases. We pay special attention to new features introduced in SQL Server 2022 as well as other recent features you might not have noticed in earlier editions of SQL Server. We also discuss how to deploy SQL Server using containers and Kubernetes.

We present a post-installation checklist for you to use to verify your installation. When necessary, we also direct you to other sources of information and details for critical steps elsewhere in this book.

The content in this chapter related to SQL Server Setup mainly applies to SQL Server installations on Windows operating systems. Provisioning is vastly simplified for Azure SQL Database, Azure SQL Managed Instance, SQL Server on Linux, SQL Server in Linux containers, and Azure virtual machine (VM) images with pre-installed SQL Server from the Azure Marketplace. Even so, many recommended settings in this chapter apply for server-based platforms of SQL Server, such as in Linux containers or SQL Server on Linux. They are, after all, still very much the same SQL Server products that have always existed on Windows.

This chapter focuses on server-level setup and settings. Chapter 6, "Provision and configure SQL Server databases," covers the initial creation and configuration of databases inside the SQL Server instance.

➤ For more on SQL Server on Linux, see Chapter 5, "Install and configure SQL Server on Linux."

➤ For more on Azure SQL Database, see Chapter 17, "Provision Azure SQL Database."

➤ For more on Azure SQL Managed Instance, see Chapter 18, "Provision Azure SQL Managed Instance."

➤ For more on database migrations to SQL Server platforms in Azure, see Chapter 19, "Migrate to SQL Server solutions in Azure."

CHAPTER 4

What to do before installing SQL Server

Before running SQL Server Setup on your Windows Server, there are several factors and settings to consider—some of which you *cannot* easily change after installation. For example, choosing between the default instance and a named instance or choosing an instance collation are not decisions you can easily reverse after installation. (More about the server-level collation option later in this chapter, in the "Instance collation" section.)

However, many mistakes made in installation can be resolved afterward—albeit likely with some tedium and outages. For example, skipping the initial default data and log directories may land all your databases on the operating system (OS) volume. They can be moved to the appropriate volumes later, but it's best to get it right the first time.

CAUTION

Do not install SQL Server on the same server as a domain controller. In some scenarios, it is not supported, and can even cause SQL Server Setup to fail.

SQL Server 2022 has most of the same hardware and software requirements as SQL Server 2019. There are some differences, however. For example, SQL Server 2022 requires .NET Framework 4.7.2, which you can download from *https://dotnet.microsoft.com/download/dotnet-framework/net472*.

In addition, we recommend you acquire the following before starting SQL Server Setup:

- Active Directory (AD) service accounts for the SQL Server service, SQL Agent service, and other features if needed

- The latest download of cumulative updates to bring the instance up to the latest patch level

- A licensing decision around the number of processors and the edition to buy

- A secure enterprise digital location for various passwords you will generate, backups of certificates, and keys

- A decision as to whether to install the default or a named instance

- A plan for where SQL Server files will go, with each volume formatted to the 64-KB disk unit allocation size (discussed in the next section)

Inside OUT

What are SQL Server service accounts?

SQL Server service accounts are the accounts used to handle the communication of services between the OS and SQL Server. Using AD accounts on Windows for these accounts is a best practice. These can be updated and set up after installation in SQL Server Configuration Manager if needed.

If possible, it is recommended to use managed service accounts (MSAs) or group managed service accounts (gMSAs). These are specially provisioned Windows accounts whose passwords are self-managed by Windows. This means privileged service account secrets no longer need to be secured and managed, providing greater security. For more information, visit *https://learn.microsoft.com/windows-server/security/group-managed-service-accounts /group-managed-service-accounts-overview.*

Decide on volume usage

For many good reasons, various types of SQL Server files should be placed on separate volumes. Although you can move user and system database data and log files to other locations after installation, it's best to plan your volumes before installation.

The examples in this chapter assume your Windows OS installation is on the C: volume of your server. You should have many other volumes for SQL Server files, and we'll review a sample layout soon. One of the basic guiding principles for a SQL Server installation is that anywhere you see "C:\," you should change it to another volume. This helps minimize SQL Server's footprint on the OS volume (especially if you install multiple SQL Server instances), and can have potential disaster recovery implications in terms of volume-level backups and restores.

Inside OUT

What if you are tight on space on the OS volume after installing SQL Server?

There are some easy ways and some tricky ways to minimize the footprint of a SQL Server installation on the OS volume of your server (typically the C: volume, as it is for this example). In general, SQL Server Setup and cumulative updates delete temporary files involved in their installation, but not log files or configuration files, which should have a minimal footprint. Apart from log files, we recommend that you not delete any files installed by SQL Server Setup or cumulative updates. Instead, let's look at some proactive steps to move these files off the C: volume.

Some parts of SQL Server Setup install on the OS volume (typically, and in this and future examples, the Windows C: volume). These files, which are staging areas for SQL Server Setup, are created on the OS volume in a C:\Program Files\Microsoft SQL Server\160\Setup Bootstrap\ subfolder structure, where 160 is specific to the internal version number (16.0) of SQL Server 2022. This folder is used for future cumulative updates or feature changes.

If you're extremely tight on space before installing SQL Server, you will also find that the root binaries installation directory is, by default, C:\Program Files\Microsoft SQL Server\. When you're using the SQL Server Setup user interface, there is no option to change this. You will, however, find this installation directory folder path listed as the INSTANCEDIR parameter in the config file that is generated by SQL Server Setup. How to use the config file to install SQL Server is further covered in the section "Automate SQL Server Setup with configuration files" later in this chapter.

If this is the first SQL Server instance you are installing on a server, you will have the opportunity to change the location of shared features files, the data root directory for the instance (which contains the system databases), and default database locations for user database files and their backups. If this is not the first SQL Server 2022 instance installation on this server, the shared features directory locations (for Program Files and Program Files x86) will already be set for you, and you cannot change them.

You should place as much of the installation as possible on other volumes, not the OS volume. Keep in mind that a full-featured installation of SQL Server 2022 can consume more than 14 GB.

Inside Out

What can you do with the D: volume on an Azure VM?

For Microsoft Azure Windows VMs, do not set the installation directories for any settings on the "Temporary Storage" D: volume. In a Linux VM, the same applies to /dev/sdb1.

The D: volume is the temporary storage volume on an Azure VM. The temporary storage volume is a high-speed disk that is locally present on the machine hosting the Azure VM, so it has better performance and lower latency than the default C: volume. The temporary storage volume contains only the Windows page file by default and is wiped upon server restart, resize, or host migration.

The only possible long-term use for the temporary storage volume is for tempdb files, which can exist on this drive if certain other considerations are taken. Otherwise, do not store any non-temporary files in the temporary storage.

For more details on using the D: volume for tempdb files, see "Locate tempdb files on the VM" in Chapter 16, "Design and implement hybrid and Azure database infrastructure."

The following sample scenario is a good starting point for a volume layout for your SQL Server installation (the volume letters don't matter):

- **Volume C.** The OS. Some SQL Server files must be installed here.

- **Volume E.** SQL Server installation files, log files, SQL Server database data files.

- **Volume F.** SQL Server database log files.

- **Volume G.** SQL Server tempdb data files and log files. (Alternatively, use the D: Temporary Storage volume on Azure Windows VMs.)

- **Volume H.** SQL Server backups (if written locally).

Here are some more advanced volume decisions:

- Use additional volumes for your largest data files (larger than 2 TB) for storage manageability:

  - For the most active databases

  - For FILESTREAM filegroups

  - For database replication snapshot files

  - For the Windows page file, especially for servers with large amounts of memory

Inside OUT

Why separate SQL Server files onto different volumes?

There are good reasons to separate your SQL Server files into various volumes, and not all of them are related to performance. You should still separate your files onto different volumes even if you exclusively use a storage area network (SAN).

More discrete storage I/O on a physical server with dedicated drives means better performance. But even in a SAN, separating files onto different volumes is also done for stability. Think of the volumes as bulkheads on a submarine. If a volume fills and has no available space, files cannot be allocated additional space. On the OS volume, running out of free space would result in Windows Server stability issues—user profile and remote desktop problems at least—and affect other applications.

Important SQL Server volume settings

There are some settings to consider for volumes that host SQL Server data and log files, and this guidance applies specifically to these volumes. For other volumes—for example, those that contain the OS, application files, or backup files—the default Windows settings are acceptable unless otherwise specified.

When adding these volumes to Windows, there are important volume configuration settings that you must examine or discuss with your storage administrator:

- When creating new drives, opt for GUID Partition Table (GPT) over Master Boot Record (MBR) disk types for new SQL Server installations. GPT is a newer disk-partitioning scheme than MBR, and GPT disks support files and volumes larger than 2 TB. In contrast, the older MBR disk type is capped at 2 TB.

- The appropriate file unit allocation size for SQL Server volumes is 64 KB, with few exceptions. Setting this to 64 KB for each volume can have a significant impact on storage efficiency and performance. The Windows default is 4 KB, which is not optimal for SQL Server data and log files.

  To check the file unit allocation size for an NT File System (NTFS) volume, run the following from the Administrator: Command Prompt, repeating for each volume:

  ```
  fsutil fsinfo ntfsinfo d:
  ```

  The file unit allocation size is returned with the Bytes Per Cluster; thus, the desired 64 KB would be displayed as 65,536 (bytes). If formatted as the default, this will display 4096. Correcting the file unit allocation size requires formatting the drive, so it is important to check this setting before installation.

  If you notice this on an existing SQL Server instance, your likely solution is to create a new volume with the proper file unit allocation size and then move files to the new volume during an outage. Do *not* format or re-create the partition on volumes with existing data; you will lose the data when it is reformatted.

  Modern storage devices are currently in a transition between disks that use a Bytes per Physical Sector size of 512 bytes (the old standard) and "4K Native" disks that have both a Bytes per Sector size and a Bytes per Physical Sector size of 4 KB. Usually, a DBA will not notice or even be aware of this difference. When configuring availability groups or log shipping between servers on different storage systems with mixed Bytes per Physical Sector modes, however, this can result in very poor performance, with the transaction logs unable to truncate, and the error message "There have been *nnn* misaligned log IOs which required falling back to synchronous IO." You may encounter this with hybrid availability groups spanning on-premises and Azure VM–based SQL Server instances, for example.

  This cannot be resolved via reformatting, but can potentially be resolved via hardware-level storage or firmware settings. To avoid this, all storage that hosts the transaction log files of SQL Servers in an availability group or log shipping relationship should have the same Bytes per Physical Sector.

A workaround is to apply Trace Flag 1800 as a startup flag on the SQL Server instances that use storage without having a Bytes per Physical Sector setting of 4K. TF1800 overrides disk default behavior and writes the transaction log in 4-KB sectors, resolving the issue. TF1800 must be enabled on the on-premises SQL Server instances in the case of using the older on-premises and Azure VM availability group.

Check the Bytes per Physical Sector setting of a volume by using the same `fsutil` command noted in the previous code sample.

- A hardware-level concept related to file unit allocation size called *disk starting offset* deals with how Windows, storage, disk controllers, and cache segments align their boundaries. Aligning disk starting offset was far more important before Windows Server 2008. Since then, the default partition offset of 1,024 KB has been sufficient to align with the underlying disk's stripe unit size, which is a vendor-determined value and rarely a concern for DBAs. Still, it should be verified upon first use of a new storage system or upon the migration of disks to a new storage system. This can be verified in consultation with the drive vendor's information.

  To access the disk starting offset information, run the following from the Administrator: Command Prompt:

  ```
  wmic partition get BlockSize, StartingOffset, Name, Index
  ```

  A 1,024-KB starting offset is a Windows default, which is displayed as 1048576 (bytes) for Disk #0 Partition #0.

  Like the file unit allocation size, the only way to change a disk partition's starting offset is destructive: You must re-create the partition and reformat the volume to align with the vendor-supplied offset.

SQL Server editions

The following are brief descriptions of all the editions in the SQL Server family, including past editions that you might recognize. It's important to use the appropriate licenses for SQL Server, even in preproduction systems.

> **NOTE**
>
> This book is not intended to be a reference for licensing or sales-related documentation; still, editions are a key piece of knowledge for SQL Server administrators to understand what features may or may not be available.

- **Enterprise.** Appropriate for production environments; not appropriate for preproduction environments such as user acceptance testing (UAT), quality assurance (QA), testing, development, or a sandbox. For these environments, you should instead use the free

CHAPTER 4

Developer edition. You'll have a far easier time in a licensing audit if your preproduction environment installations are Developer edition.

- **Developer.** Appropriate for all preproduction environments, especially those under a production Enterprise edition. Not allowed for production environments. This edition has the same features and capacity as Enterprise edition and is free.

- **Standard.** Appropriate for production environments. Lacks the scale and compliance features of Enterprise edition required in some regulatory environments. Limited to the lesser of 4 sockets or 24 cores and 128 GB of buffer pool memory, whereas Enterprise edition is limited only by the OS for compute and memory.

- **Web.** Appropriate for production environments but limited to low-cost server environments for web hosting.

- **Express.** Not appropriate for most production environments or preproduction environments. Appropriate only for environments in which data size is small, is not expected to grow, and can be backed up with external tools or scripts (because Express edition has no SQL Server Agent to automate backups). The free Express edition is ideal for production proofs-of-concept, lightweight applications, and student projects. It lacks some critical features and is severely limited on compute (lesser of 1 socket or 4 cores), available buffer pool memory (1,410 MB), and individual database size (10-GB capacity).

- **Express with Advanced Services.** Like Express edition in all caveats and limitations, this edition includes some additional features, including R integration and full-text search.

- **Evaluation.** Functionally the same as Enterprise edition, and free with a 180-day shutdown timer. Evaluation edition isn't supported. This edition can be upgraded to any edition except for Express. Do not use this edition if you plan for a clustered installation, because an upgrade in that case is not supported.

It's worth noting that the hardware limitations of SQL Server editions have not changed since SQL Server 2016.

NOTE

When you run the SQL Server 2022 Setup, you can choose to install several features outside the core database features. Installing SQL Server features on multiple Windows servers requires multiple licenses per server, even if you intend to install each SQL Server instance's features only once.

There is an exception to this rule, however: If you have licensed all physical cores on a host server for SQL Server Enterprise edition, and purchased Software Assurance, you can install any number or combination of SQL Server instances and their standalone features on virtual guests.

Change SQL Server editions and versions

Upgrading editions in-place is supported by a feature of the SQL Server 2022 installer. You can upgrade in the following order: Express, Web, Standard, and Enterprise.

You cannot downgrade a SQL Server version or licensed edition. This type of change requires a fresh installation and migration. For example, you cannot downgrade in-place from SQL Server 2022 Enterprise edition to Standard edition.

In-place upgrades for major versions (from 2019 to 2022, for example) is supported but not recommended. Instead, we strongly recommend that you perform a fresh installation of the newer version and then migrate from old to new instances. This method offers major advantages in terms of duration of the planned outage, rollback capability, and robust testing in parallel.

Although in-place upgrades to SQL Server 2022 are not recommended, upgrades are supported for versions as old as SQL Server 2012 SP4. You can even migrate databases using detach and reattach, from older versions of SQL Server to SQL Server 2022, as long as the source database compatibility level is 90 or higher. Databases with a compatibility of 90 (SQL Server 2005) will be automatically upgraded to compatibility level 100. Databases already at compatibility level 100 will not change.

A supported upgrade also assumes that the OS and previous version of SQL Server are not 32-bit installations. Beginning with SQL Server 2016, SQL Server is available only for 64-bit platforms. For more information on upgrades to SQL Server 2022, visit *https://learn.microsoft.com/sql /database-engine/install-windows/supported-version-and-edition-upgrades-2022*.

Install a new instance

In this section, you learn how to begin a new SQL Server 2022 instance installation, upgrade an existing installation, or add features to an existing instance.

The instructions in this chapter are the same for the first installation or any subsequent installations, whether it is for the default or any named instances of SQL Server 2022. As opposed to an exhaustive step-by-step instruction list for installations, we've opted to cover the important decision points and the information you need and to highlight new features from SQL Server 2022.

Even though you can change *almost* all of the decisions you make in SQL Server Setup after installation, those changes potentially require an outage or server restart. Making the proper decisions at installation time is the best way to ensure the least administrative effort. Some security and service account decisions should be changed only via the SQL Server Configuration Manager application, not through the Services console (services.msc). This guidance will be repeated elsewhere for emphasis.

We begin by going through the typical interactive installation. Later in this chapter, we will go over some of the command-line installation methods that you can use to automate the installation of a SQL Server instance.

Plan for multiple SQL Server instances

You can install as many as 50 SQL Server instances on a Windows Server, although we obviously do not recommend this. In a Windows failover cluster, the maximum number of SQL Server instances is reduced by half if you're using shared cluster drives.

Only one of the SQL Server instances on a server can be the default instance. All, or all but one, of the SQL Server instances on a SQL Server will be named instances. The default instance is reachable by connecting to the name of the Windows Server, whereas named instances require an instance name. The SQL Browser service is required to handle traffic for named instances on the SQL Server.

For example, you can reach the default instance of a SQL Server by connecting to `servername`. All named instances have a unique instance name, such as `servername\instancename`.

NOTE

If the Browser service is not turned on, this does not mean you cannot reach the instance, but that you will need to know the specific port on which it is listening. You reach the instance using `servername,portnumber` in place of the instance name.

Inside OUT

What is different about SQL Server on an Azure VM?

The Azure Marketplace provides VM images that are pre-installed with SQL Server, with a wide selection of edition and compute options, so you usually won't install SQL Server yourself. However, the default configuration might require some tweaking.

When it comes to licensing, there are two types of SQL Server licensing agreements for Azure VMs. SQL Server VM images in the Azure Marketplace contain the SQL Server licensing costs as an all-in-one billing package.

Alternatively, if you'd like to leverage your existing Enterprise licensing agreement using the Azure Hybrid Benefit, there are three options:

- Choose bring-your-own-license (BYOL) VM images using the same process, then later associate your existing Enterprise license agreements. The image names you're looking for here are prefixed with BYOL.

- Manually upload an .iso file to the VM and install SQL Server 2022 as you would on any other Windows Server.
- Upload an image of an on-premises VM to provision the new Azure VM.

You cannot change from the built-in licensing model to the BYOL licensing model after the VM has been provisioned. You need to make this decision before creating your Azure VM.

Install SQL Server on Windows

The rest of this chapter is dedicated to installations of SQL Server that are not part of a premade Azure Marketplace VM and apply to the installation of SQL Server on any Windows Server.

While logged in as a local Windows administrator, begin by mounting the installation .iso to the Windows server. These days, this rarely involves inserting a physical disc or USB flash drive, although you can use them if necessary.

Launch SQL Server Setup

You should not run SQL Server Setup with the installation media mounted over a remote network connection, a shared remote desktop drive, or any other high-latency connection. For a faster SQL Server Setup experience, unpack the contents of the .iso file to a physical folder local to the server.

Start setup.exe on the SQL Server Setup media, running the program as a Windows user with administrator privileges. If AutoPlay is not turned off (it usually is), setup.exe will start when you first mount the media or double-click to open the .iso. Instead, as a best practice, right-click **setup.exe** and select **Run As Administrator** on the shortcut menu that appears.

We'll review here a few items (not all) in the SQL Server Installation Center worth noting before you begin an installation.

In the pane on the left, select **Planning** to open a long list of links to Microsoft documentation websites. Most helpful here might be a standalone version of the System Configuration Checker, which you run during SQL Server Setup later, but it could save you a few steps if you review it now. A link to download the Data Migration Assistant (DMA) is also present, which is a helpful Microsoft-provided tool for upgrading from prior versions of SQL Server.

On the **Maintenance** page, you will find the following:

- The **Edition Upgrade Wizard** is relatively painless. This is only for promoting your existing installation's edition, as discussed earlier.

- The **Repair** feature is not commonly used except in the case of an instance with a corrupted installation. You might also need to repair an instance of SQL Server when the executables, .dll files, or Windows Registry entries have become corrupted or damaged by disk corruption, antimalware, malware, or malicious activity. A failed SQL Server in-place upgrade or cumulative update installation might also require a repair, which could be better than starting from scratch.

- Removing a node from an existing SQL Server failover cluster is an option in the **Maintenance** page. Adding a node to an existing SQL Server failover cluster is an option in the **Installation** page.

- The **Advanced** page features a link to perform an installation based on a configuration file. We will discuss how to easily generate and use a configuration file later in this chapter, in the section "Automate SQL Server Setup with configuration files." If you are tasked with installing multiple SQL Servers with mostly common settings, consider this time-saving method. There are also links to wizards for advanced failover cluster installations.

> ➤ We discuss failover cluster instances (FCIs) in Chapter 11, "Implement high availability and disaster recovery."

Windows Update in the SQL Server Setup

Since SQL Server 2012, the SQL Server installer has had the ability to patch itself within the Setup wizard. The **Product Updates** page is presented after the **License Terms** page, and, after you accept it, it is downloaded from Windows Update (or Windows Server Update Services) and installed along with other SQL Server Setup files.

This is recommended, so a SQL Server 2022 Setup with Internet connectivity is the easiest way to carry out the installation. This also could be described as a way to "slipstream" updates, including hotfixes and cumulative updates, into the SQL Server installation process, eliminating these efforts post-installation.

For servers without Internet access, there are two setup.exe parameters that support downloading these files to an accessible location and making them available to Setup. When starting setup.exe from Windows PowerShell or the command line (you can read more about this in the next section), you set the /UpdateEnabled parameter to FALSE to turn off the download from Windows Update. The /UpdateSource parameter can then be provided as an installation location of .exe files. Note that the /UpdateSource parameter is a folder location, not a file. You will find more on these two parameters later in the "Install by using a configuration file" section.

Regardless, after installation is complete, and before the SQL Server enters further use, verify that the latest SQL Server patches have been applied. For SQL Server 2022, see the official build versions at *https://support.microsoft.com/help/4518398*.

Install SQL Server stand-alone installation

Although what follows in this chapter is not a step-by-step walk-through, we do cover key new features and decision points of the **New SQL Server Stand-Alone Installation** option of the SQL Server Installation Center.

Inside OUT

Where are the installers for SQL Server Management Studio and SQL Server Data Tools?

SQL Server Management Studio, SQL Server Data Tools (for Visual Studio 2015 and higher), and SQL Server Reporting Services are no longer installed with SQL Server's traditional setup media. These products are now updated regularly (as often as monthly) and available for download.

You should keep up-to-date versions of SQL Server Management Studio (SSMS) on administrator workstations and laptops.

Avoid installing SSMS locally on the SQL Server if possible. In fact, avoid the need to use Remote Desktop Connection to manage and administer the SQL Server altogether. For all SQL Server platforms, try to use SSMS, Azure Data Studio, PowerShell, and other tools to do as much of your work on SQL Server remotely as possible.

PolyBase Services

Immediately after the instance configuration is a new configuration for the port range of Poly-Base services. This is where you choose a range of ports to use for this service. If you plan to use PolyBase, the ports typically used are TCP ports between 16450 and 16460, of which there must be at least six ports. These should be allowed through the firewall if needed. This option was added to SQL Server Setup in SQL Server 2022.

Grant Perform Volume Maintenance Tasks

On the same **Server Configuration** page on which service accounts are set, notice the **Grant Perform Volume Maintenance Task privilege to the SQL Server Database Engine Service** check box. Selecting this check box automates what used to be a standard post-installation checklist step for SQL DBAs beginning with Windows Server 2003.

The reason to grant this permission to use instant file initialization is to speed the allocation of large database data files, which could dramatically reduce the Recovery Time Objective (RTO) capacity for disaster recovery. This can mean the difference between hours and minutes when restoring a very large database. It can also have a positive impact when creating databases with large initial sizes, or in large autogrowth events—for example, with multiple data files in the tempdb (more on this next). It is recommended that you allow SQL Server Setup to turn on this setting.

Inside OUT

How can you verify that instant file initialization is enabled?

IFI is granted to a SQL Server service account via the **Perform Volume Maintenance Tasks** permission in Local Security Policy on the Windows server. But it's straightforward to verify whether IFI is in place for the SQL Server service, via the `sys.dm_server_services` dynamic management view:

```
SELECT servicename, instant_file_initialization_enabled
FROM sys.dm_server_services
WHERE filename LIKE '%sqlservr.exe%';
```

➤ For more information on instant file initialization, see Chapter 3, "Design and implement an on-premises database infrastructure."

Instance collation

The **Collation** tab on the **Server Configuration** page allows you to choose a collation for the Database Engine. The collation determines how character data is stored, sorted, and compared. For more information, see the section on collation in Chapter 7, "Understand table features."

Initially, the instance collation provided in SQL Setup is the default collation for the server's regional settings, but you might need to change this collation based on vendor or developer specifications.

While changing the collation of a database is easy, the instance collation is important to get right at the time of SQL Server installation, as changing the instance collation is quite difficult.

The server collation you set here acts as the collation for all system databases as well as the default for any newly created user databases. For new application development, you may choose to take advantage of UTF-8 collations as the server default, introduced in SQL Server 2019.

Inside OUT

How do you change the server collation after installing SQL Server?

This is one of those things you want to get right at the time of installation. To change the collation of the SQL Server instance, reference this lengthy and difficult Microsoft guide, at *https:// learn.microsoft.com/sql/relational-databases/collations/set-or-change-the-server-collation.*

In the case of Azure SQL Managed Instance, you cannot change the server-level collation after it is created. For more information, visit *https://learn.microsoft.com/sql/relational -databases/collations/set-or-change-the-server-collation#setting-the-server-collation -in-managed-instance.*

Mixed Mode authentication

SQL Server supports two modes of authentication: Windows Authentication and SQL Authentication. Windows Authentication is preferable to SQL Authentication, and in multiple places in this book we will emphasize this.

> ➤ You can read more on this topic in Chapter 12, "Administer instance and database security and permissions," but it is important to note this decision point here.

Ideally, all authentication is made via Windows Authentication, through types of server principals called *logins* that reference Windows accounts—ideally, AD domain accounts or, starting with SQL Server 2022, Azure Active Directory (Azure AD) principals. These are created by your existing enterprise security team, which manages password policy, password resets, password expiration, and so on.

A redundant security model for connecting to SQL Server also exists within each instance: SQL Server Authenticated logins. Logins are maintained at the SQL Server level, are subject to local policy password complexity requirements, are reset/unlocked by SQL DBAs, have their own password change policy, and so forth.

Enabling Mixed Mode (SQL and Windows Authentication Mode) activates SQL Authenticated logins. Be aware that SQL Authentication is not on by default, and isn't the recommended method of connection. The recommended Windows Authentication cannot be turned off. When possible, applications and users should use Windows Authentication.

Enabling Mixed Mode also activates the *sa* account, which is a special built-in SQL Server Authentication that is a member of the server sysadmin role. Setup will ask for a strong password to be provided at this time.

CHAPTER 4

➤ You can learn more about the sa account and server roles in Chapter 12.

If you find you have an actual need to enable SQL Server Authentication, but didn't do this during SQL Server Setup, you can do it later by connecting to the SQL Server instance via Object Explorer in SQL Server Management Studio. To do so, right-click the server name and select **Properties** from the shortcut menu. Then, select the **Security** page and change to **Mixed Mode**. You must perform a SQL Server service restart to effect this change.

Default settings for the tempdb database

Starting with SQL Server 2016, SQL Server Setup provides a more realistic default configuration for the number and size of tempdb data files. This has been a common to-do list for all post-installation checklists for DBAs since the early days of SQL Server.

The TempDB database page in SQL Server Setup provides not only the ability to specify the number and location of the tempdb's data and log files, but also their initial size and auto-growth rates. The best number of tempdb data files is almost certainly greater than one and less than or equal to the number of logical processor cores, including hyper-threading for local machines. For example, with 16 logical processors, SQL Server Setup will default the installation to have eight tempdb data files.

Adding too many tempdb data files can degrade SQL Server performance—perhaps severely. For example, with 20 logical processors, SQL Server Setup will still default the installation to have 8 tempdb data files. If you add 20 tempdb data files, SQL Server may struggle to respond.

➤ For more information on the best number of tempdb data files, see Chapter 3.

Specifying tempdb's initial size to a larger, normal operating size is important and can improve performance after a SQL Server restart when the tempdb data files are reset to their initial size. Setup accommodates an individual tempdb data file initial size up to 256 GB. For data file initial sizes larger than 1 GB, you will be warned that SQL Server Setup can take a long time to complete if instant file initialization is not turned on.

Since SQL Server 2016, all tempdb files autogrow at the same time, keeping file sizes the same over time, which is critical to the way multiple tempdb data files are used. This is superior to the old way of ensuring tempdb data files stay the same size: using the server-level setting via server Trace Flag 1117, which applied the data file growth behavior to all databases. Trace Flag 1117 is no longer necessary.

Also note the naming convention for the second tempdb data file and beyond: *tempdb_mssql_n .ndf*. A SQL Server uninstallation will automatically clean up tempdb data files with this naming convention. For this reason, we recommend that you follow this naming convention for tempdb data files.

➤ The tempdb system database is discussed in detail in Chapter 3.

Default settings for MAXDOP

New in SQL Server 2019 were defaults for the configuration of the server-wide **Maximum Degree of Parallelism (MAXDOP)** setting on the **Database Engine Configuration** page under the new **MaxDOP** tab.

In the same way that new tempdb defaults since SQL Server 2016 are dependent on the detected processors, a suggested default MAXDOP is also configured based on the number of logical processors. For many servers with 16 or fewer virtual processor cores, the default is the same as the number of cores, effectively the same as a MAXDOP setting of 0, which allows for unlimited parallelism.

For example, with 8 logical processors, SQL Server Setup will default the installation to use a MAXDOP of 8. With over 16 logical processors, SQL Server Setup may default to half the number of logical processors—at most 16. For example, with 20 logical processors, SQL Server Setup will default the installation to use a MAXDOP of 10.

➤ For more recommendations about MAXDOP, visit Microsoft Support at *https://support .microsoft.com/help/2806535*. See also the section on "Max degree of parallelism" in Chapter 3.

You can always reconfigure the MAXDOP after installation without a restart, though not without potential disruption. Although changing the server-wide (or database-level) MAXDOP setting takes effect immediately, it is definitely not advisable to do so during normal production operating hours, because it can lead to widespread plan recompilation and a heavy CPU spike. This server-wide MAXDOP setting can be overridden at the database, query, or Resource Governor group level. The **MaxDOP** tab in the **Database Engine Configuration** tab has a recommended MAXDOP setting of 8 for a server with eight virtual cores. This is effectively the same as a MAXDOP of 0, but offers the administrator an option to potentially change the MAXDOP at the time of installation.

NOTE

Some applications recommend disabling parallelism on their databases. Consult your vendor's specifications and recommendations documentation. MAXDOP can be set at the server level now, then configured and overridden at each database level after SQL Server Setup is complete using a database scoped configuration.

➤ For much more information on performance tuning, parallelism, and the MAXDOP setting, see Chapter 14, "Performance tune SQL Server."

CHAPTER 4

Default settings for Maximum Server Memory

New in SQL Server 2019 were defaults for the configuration of the instance-level **Max Server Memory** option, a common post-installation checklist item, under the **Memory** tab of the **Database Engine Configuration** page. SQL Server Setup makes a guess based on total server memory for an appropriate option. In previous versions of SQL Server, it was important to remember to change the Max Server Memory setting after installation was complete; otherwise, SQL Server memory would be uncapped and have access to all memory on the server.

You can configure this Max Server Memory option intelligently at the time of installation. It's important to note (and there's a check box to accept this guess) that SQL Server Setup assumes this SQL Server instance will run alone on this server. If you expect to host other applications on this server, or to run memory-heavy features of SQL Server on the same server such as SSAS or SSRS, you should further reduce the Max Server Memory setting for the SQL Server instance.

➤ Chapter 3 discussed the Max Server Memory setting, in the "Configuration settings" section.

Let's use an example of the new Max Server Memory recommendation for a Windows Server with one SQL Server instance and 16 GB of memory. SQL Server Setup recommends a Max Server Memory setting of 12672 MB. The Min Server Memory setting, which establishes a floor for memory allocation, is set to 0. It is generally unnecessary to change this setting from the default. You might find this setting useful for situations in which the total system memory is insufficient and many applications, including SQL Server instances, are present. The Min Server Memory setting is not immediately allocated to the SQL Server instance upon startup; instead, it does not allow memory below this level to be freed for other applications. Figure 4-1 shows the Memory tab of the Database Engine Configuration page, with the Min Server Memory and Max Server Memory settings visible.

After installation, server memory settings are accessible via SQL Server Management Studio, in Object Explorer, and on the Server Properties page.

You should ensure that SQL Server leaves enough memory for the OS and other applications. Keep in mind that SQL Server will slowly consume more memory over time and may take hours or days, depending on your business cycle, for the SQL Server instance to consume the maximum amount of memory made available. Lowering this setting after installation and during operation does not return SQL Server memory back to the OS immediately; rather, it does so over time during SQL Server activity. Increasing this setting will not immediately show the effect of a change in memory use.

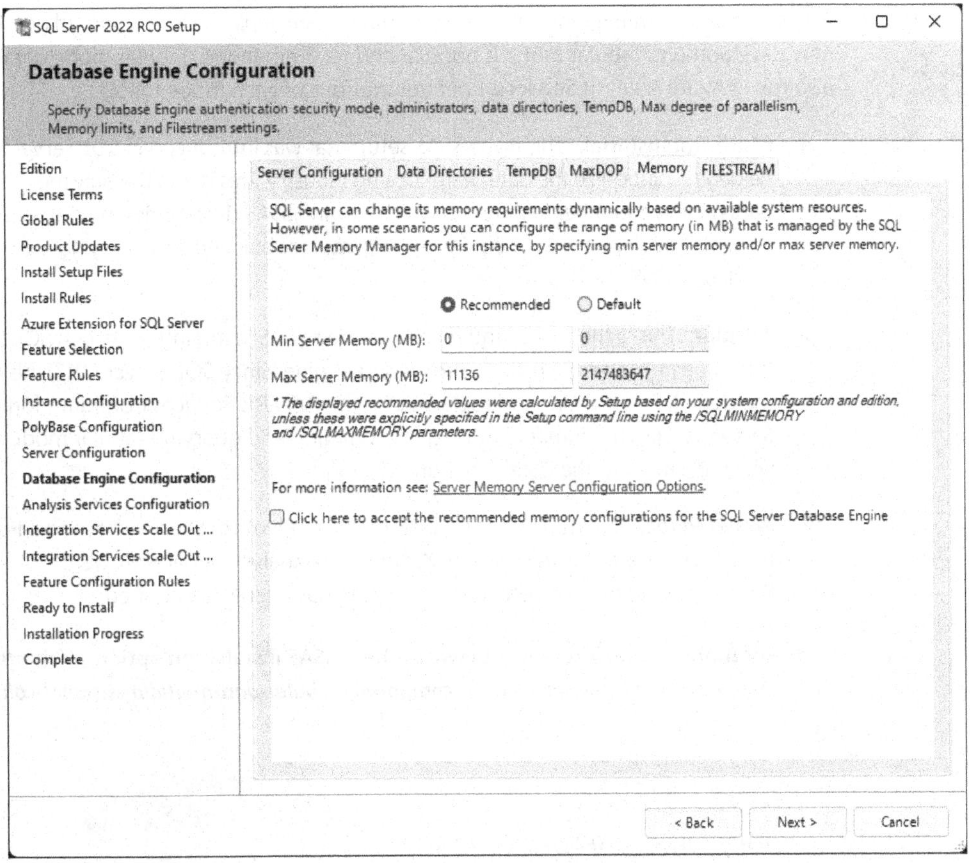

Figure 4-1 This figure displays the minimum and maximum server default memory settings for the SQL Server setup.

Install common features

Aside from the SQL Server service itself, other features of the product might be common to your installations. For example, SQL Server Analysis Services, SQL Server Integration Services, and SQL Server Reporting Services are part of the license and are provided at no additional cost. This section covers the installation of these features using SQL Server Setup. Later, this chapter covers the post-installation steps necessary to use them.

Install SQL Server Analysis Services

Installing SQL Server Analysis Services (SSAS) requires you to decide ahead of time which mode to install. Each instance of SSAS can be in only one mode, which means that with a single license, you can run either Multidimensional mode, the newer Tabular mode (introduced in SQL Server 2012), or Power Pivot mode.

Ask your business intelligence (BI) decision makers which platform you should use. For most new development, Tabular mode is popular and recommended. Tabular mode databases can also run in Azure Analysis Services. Brief descriptions of each mode follow:

- **Multidimensional.** This is the SSAS setup that was introduced in SQL Server 2000 and helped revolutionize the data-warehousing industry. This is also the only mode to support data mining and other features on which existing SSAS data models predating SQL Server 2012 may be dependent. The primary language for building and querying multidimensional models is MDX.

- **Tabular.** This is the newer and recommended SSAS setup introduced in SQL Server 2012, using the in-memory VertiPaq processing engine. Since SQL Server 2017, this has been the default installation mode selected on the Analysis Services Configuration page of SQL Server Setup. The primary language for building and querying tabular models is DAX, which is similar to the Excel function language.

- **Power Pivot.** This mode installs SSAS in Power Pivot for SharePoint mode. Power Pivot workbooks use both DAX and MDX. Note that Analysis Services Power Pivot for Share-Point support for Microsoft SharePoint 2019 has been discontinued.

➤ For more on the differences between these SSAS installation options, visit *https://learn .microsoft.com/analysis-services/comparing-tabular-and-multidimensional-solutions-ssas.*

Inside OUT

What if you choose the wrong SSAS mode?

If you choose one SSAS mode at installation, but your BI developers want another mode, the supported option is to uninstall and reinstall the SSAS feature. However, changing the SSAS mode from Multidimensional to Tabular, or vice versa, after installation is not supported, and administrators are specifically warned not to do this.

Packages developed for each mode are not supported for the other. If no databases have been deployed to the SSAS server instance, changing the DeploymentMode property in the MSMDSRV.ini file should make it possible to change an existing instance. But again, this is not a supported change. The file is located in %Programfiles%\Microsoft SQL Server\ MSAS15.instancename\OLAP\Config\.

Install SQL Server Integration Services

The SQL Server Integration Services (SSIS) instance is installed once per server per version, not once per instance like other features. Starting in SQL Server 2017, however, a new Integration

CHAPTER 4

Services Scale Out Configuration became available. We discuss this new feature further in the next section.

A 64-bit version of SSIS is installed on 64-bit operating systems. If you worry about connecting to 32-bit servers, data sources, or application installations (such as Microsoft Office), you don't need to. Those connections are not dependent on the 32-bit/64-bit installation and are handled at the package or connection-string level. Unlike other features, you can install SSIS on a 32-bit OS; however, we do not recommend this.

Installations of different versions of SSIS are installed side by side on a server. Specifically, SSIS 16.0 is compatible with prior versions.

Apart from configuring the service account, you need not do any additional configuration when installing SSIS during SQL Server Setup. The default virtual service account is NT Service\MsDtsServer160.

Inside OUT

Should you install SSIS alone on a server?

A standalone installation of SSIS without a matching Database Engine instance is possible but not recommended. For the modern Project Deployment model of SSIS, the storage and logging of packages will still be dependent on a SQL Server Database Engine, and the execution of packages on a schedule still requires a SQL Agent service.

So, the SSIS workload is not best isolated in this way. A dedicated installation including the SQL Server Database Engine and SQL Server Agent is a better configuration to isolate SSIS package runtime workloads from other database workloads. Both options carry the same licensing cost.

CHAPTER 4

Install SQL Server Integration Services Scale Out configuration

Since SQL Server 2017, SSIS supports a Scale Out configuration, by which you can run a package on the same or multiple SQL Server instances. This also allows for high availability of SSIS, and a similar architecture allows for integration and "lift and shift" code deployments from on-premises SSIS to the Azure Integration Runtime.

➤ Additional information on integration runtimes can be found in Chapter 19.

The master node talks to worker nodes in an SSIS Scale Out system, with the communication over a port (8391 by default) and secured via a new Secure Sockets Layer (SSL) certificate. The SQL Server installer can automatically create a 10-year self-signed certificate and endpoint for communication when the master node is set up.

When adding another SSIS installation as a Scale Out Worker, start the new SSIS Manage Scale Out window via SQL Server Management Studio. To do so, right-click the catalog you have created and select **Manage Scale Out**. At the bottom of the page, select the + button to add a new Scale Out Worker node.

Next, you provide the server name on which to connect. If using a named instance, provide only the server name of the node; do not include the instance name. A dialog box confirms the steps taken to add the Scale Out Worker node, including copying and installing certificates between the Worker node and Master node, updating the endpoint and HttpsCertThumbprint of the worker, and restarting the Worker node's Scale Out service.

After the worker node is added, refresh the **Worker Manager** page. Then select the new Worker node entry, which will be red. Finally, turn on the Worker node by selecting **Enable Worker**.

You also can copy and install the certificates manually between servers. You will find them in %Program Files%\Microsoft SQL Server\160\DTS\Binn\.

➤ **For more information on certificates between servers, visit** *https://learn.microsoft.com /sql/integration-services/scale-out/deal-with-certificates-in-ssis-scale-out*. **For a Microsoft-provided walk-through of setting this up, visit** *https://learn.microsoft.com/sql /integration-services/scale-out/walkthrough-set-up-integration-services-scale-out*.

One major security difference with Scale Out is that even though the SSIS service account doesn't run packages or need permission to do very much, the Scale Out Master and Worker service accounts *do* run packages. The SSIS service account is different from the Scale Out Master and Scale Out Worker service accounts.

The Worker and Master nodes do not appear in SQL Server Configuration Manager (as of SQL Server 2019) but do appear in the Services console (services.msc). By default, these services run under virtual accounts NT Service\SSISScaleOutMaster160 and NT Service\SSISScaleOutWorker160, but you might want to change these to a Windows-authenticated domain service account that will be used to run packages across the Scale Out.

Install SQL Server Reporting Services

Starting with SQL Server 2017, SQL Server Reporting Services (SSRS) is no longer found in the SQL Server Setup media; it is instead available as a simplified, unified installer and a small download. SSRS is now a 95+MB download named SQLServerReportingServices.exe but still needs a SQL Server Database Engine instance as part of the license to host the two Report Server databases. Note that SSRS isn't free, and that the separate installer isn't a licensing change— although SQL Server Express with Advanced Services offers some limited SSRS support.

➤ For more information on the limitations of SSRS with SQL Server Express license, see *https://learn.microsoft.com/sql/reporting-services/reporting-services-features-supported-by-the-editions-of-sql-server-2016*.

To install SSRS, you need to provide a license key upon installation in a production environment. You can choose a free edition to install (Evaluation, Developer, or Express), but you should note that Developer edition is not allowed in a production environment.

The "native mode" of SSRS Is now the only mode since SQL Server 2017. If you are familiar with Reporting Services Report Manager from the past, accessible via the URL *servername/Reports*, that is the "native mode" installation of Reporting Services.

Report Server Configuration Manager is in a new location, in its own Program Files menu: Microsoft SQL Server Reporting Services. After installation, start the Report Server Configuration Manager (typically installed in a path like \Program Files (x86)\Microsoft SQL Server\160\Tools\Binn\RSConfigTool.exe). The Report Server Configuration Manager application itself is largely unchanged since SQL Server 2008.

The default SSRS service account is the virtual service account called NT SERVICE\SQLServer ReportingServices. It is a second-best option, however. We recommend that you instead create a new domain service account to be used only for this service—for example, Domain\svc_ServerName_SSRS or something with a similar naming convention. You will need to use a domain account if you choose to configure Report Server email with Report Server service account (NTLM) authentication.

If you choose to change the SSRS service account later, you must use the Reporting Services Configuration Manager tool. As with other SQL Server services, you should never use the Services console (services.msc) to change service accounts.

After installation, you will need to follow up on other changes and necessary administrative actions—for example, configuring the SSRS Execution Account and email settings or backing up the encryption key using Reporting Services Configuration Manager.

SSRS can also integrate with Microsoft Power BI dashboards. A page in the Report Server Configuration Manager supports the registration of this installation of SSRS with a Power BI account. You will be prompted to sign into Azure AD. The account you provide must be a member of the Azure tenant where you intend to integrate with Power BI. The account should also be a member of the system administrator in SSRS, via Report Manager, and a member of the sysadmin role in the SQL Server that hosts the Report Server database.

CHAPTER 4

Inside OUT

Where is SSRS SharePoint Integrated mode?

Starting with SQL Server 2017, SharePoint Integrated mode has been removed. The simplified "native" mode is the only installation available. This matches the moves that Microsoft has made in other areas that step away from the SharePoint on-premises product in favor of SharePoint Online features and development.

Instead, you can integrate SSRS native mode with on-premises SharePoint sites via embedded SSRS reports, including SSRS reports stored in the Power BI Report Server.

Similarly, there is no future support for SSRS integration with SharePoint Online.

Install machine learning features

The Machine Learning Services feature makes it possible for developers to integrate with the R and Python language extensions using standard Transact-SQL (T-SQL) statements.

Data scientists can take advantage of this feature to build advanced analytics, data forecasting, and algorithms for machine learning. Data engineers can leverage these languages to integrate predictive analytic and machine learning. The scripts you create can be executed in-database without having to move data. You can prepare, clean, train, evaluate, perform feature engineering, and deploy machine learning models where the data resides. This eliminates the transfer of data across the network to another server.

Machine Learning Services is not a standalone feature. It requires a Database Engine instance. Also, it is now only available in the Instance Features section, and is no longer available in the Shared Features section.

Beginning with SQL Server 2022, runtimes for R, Python, and Java are no longer installed with SQL Setup. You must run the SQL Setup Wizard to install Machine Learning Services and Language Extensions. Then you must install your desired R, Python, or Java runtime(s) and packages.

You can install and use your open-source package and framework of choice, such as PyTorch, TensorFlow, and others. Machine Learning Services use an extensibility framework to run Python and R scripts.

NOTE

After installing your desired runtime(s), be sure to enable the external scripting feature using the following T-SQL command:

```
EXEC sp_configure  'external scripts enabled';
```

Then restart the SQL Server service.

> ➤ Note that there are separate Microsoft Docs articles for installation of Machine Learning Services on SQL Server 2019 and prior, and for SQL Server 2022. For installation on SQL Server 2022 on Windows, visit *https://learn.microsoft.com/sql/machine-learning/install /sql-machine-learning-services-windows-install-sql-2022*. For information about installing Machine Learning Services for SQL Server 2022 on Linux, see *https://learn.microsoft.com /sql/linux/sql-server-linux-setup-machine-learning-sql-2022*.

Availability groups are supported for Machine Learning Services, to ensure business continuity by configuring packages on each node, and failover cluster instances are supported from SQL Server 2019 onward.

You can execute Python and R scripts on a SQL Server instance with the stored procedure `sp_execute_external_script`.

You can find more details on each framework for this evolving feature in these Microsoft Docs articles:

- **Extensibility framework.** *https://learn.microsoft.com/sql/machine-learning/concepts /extensibility-framework*

- **Python extension.** *https://learn.microsoft.com/sql/machine-learning/concepts /extension-python*

- **R extension.** *https://learn.microsoft.com/sql/machine-learning/concepts/extension-r*

Install PolyBase Query Service for External Data

The PolyBase connector is a much-marketed feature for allowing native connectors for external data sources—even non-Microsoft or non–relational database platforms like Oracle, Teradata, and MongoDB.

Using PolyBase EXTERNAL tables, we can use SQL data types and T-SQL queries to seamlessly query data sources in-place in what Microsoft calls *data virtualization.* This eliminates the need for complex heterogeneous data movement and reduces the need for developers to have knowledge of other external query languages.

The PolyBase Query Engine feature is specifically designed for read and write queries on non-Microsoft database platforms like Oracle and DB2, but also for Azure Blob Storage files, MongoDB, and more. This is a superior alternative to linked servers to the same external data sources, because PolyBase allows "push down" computation for these external sources, reducing the amount of data transferred and increasing the performance of analytical-scale queries.

Install Azure extension for SQL Server

A new feature for SQL Server 2022 is extensibility for Azure features. This is in large part where the connections are initially set up for the features that make up the most Azure-connected version of SQL Server to date. Let's look at the most common ones available so you understand what you are setting up.

Azure Arc–enabled servers

Azure Arc–enabled SQL Server instances are on-premises but still managed by Azure. This extends the services of Azure to the datacenter or wherever it is needed.

Azure Arc–enabled servers are supported only for the following operating systems:

- Windows Server 2012 R2 and higher

- Ubuntu 16.04 and 18.04 (x64)

- Red Hat Enterprise Linux (RHEL) 7 (x64)

- SUSE Linux Enterprise Server (SLES) 15 (x64)

NOTE

SQL Server instances on Azure Arc–enabled servers are not currently supported in Linux containers.

To perform all the actions needed to connect an Azure Arc–enabled server to Azure, you need an account with all of the following privileges:

- Microsoft.HybridCompute/machines/extensions/read

- Microsoft.HybridCompute/machines/extensions/write

- Microsoft.HybridCompute/machines/extensions/delete

- Microsoft.HybridCompute/machines/read

- Microsoft.HybridCompute/machines/write

- Microsoft.GuestConfiguration/guestConfigurationAssignments/read

- Microsoft.Authorization/roleAssignments/write

- Microsoft.Authorization/roleAssignments/read

To enable the services so that Azure Arc recognizes your instance, you need to register it for the services you want to take advantage of. There are a few steps to follow, both in Azure and on the server itself, for existing instances. Detailed instructions on how to do this can be found at *https://learn.microsoft.com/sql/sql-server/azure-arc/overview*.

Inside OUT

What are Azure Arc–enabled servers?

Azure Arc–enabled servers are servers that are managed by Azure but reside outside of Azure. These can reside on a private network, corporate network, or other public cloud. The experience is designed to be like how you would manage an Azure VM.

Azure Arc–enabled servers unlock additional features and advantages, including unified cloud manageability, but also, for example, the ability to use Azure AD–integrated authentication in on-premises SQL Servers. Azure Arc is a continuously evolving and developing technology, with new announcements arriving regularly.

Microsoft Defender for Cloud

Microsoft Defender for Cloud is a Cloud Security Posture Management (CSPM) and Cloud Workload Protection Platform (CWPP) that can be run in Azure but has been extended to on-premises and third-party clouds for multi-cloud opportunities with Azure Arc. The purpose of Defender is to assess, secure, and defend from threats. It does this by:

- Continuously assessing your security posture so you can identify opportunities, track vulnerabilities, and report

- Securing resources and checking best practices to provide cloud recommendations

- Defending from, detecting, alerting on, and resolving threats in real-time so you can prevent security events from happening

➤ For more detailed steps on setting up Microsoft Defender for Cloud, see the Microsoft Cloud Guide tutorial at *https://mslearn.cloudguides.com/guides/Protect%20your%20 multi-cloud%20environment%20with%20Microsoft%20Defender%20for%20Cloud*.

Microsoft Defender is only supported for SQL Server on Windows machines and must have one of the RBAC roles assigned to it, as described in the next paragraph.

➤ Details on how to install Defender on your Azure Arc–enabled server for SQL Server can be found at *https://learn.microsoft.com/sql/sql-server/azure-arc/configure-advanced -data-security*.

Microsoft Defender for Cloud uses Azure role-based access control (RBAC)—a built-in set of roles assigned to users, groups, and services in Azure—to assess, manage, and access resources. Users require the Assignments role with write permissions, such as a User Access Administrator or Owner. You can access information related to a resource when you are assigned the role of Owner, Contributor, or Reader for the subscription or the resource's resource group.

CHAPTER 4

Other built-in roles are specific to Microsoft Defender for Cloud:

- Security Reader users have viewing rights, which lets them view recommendations, alerts, security policies, and security states, but not make changes.

- Security Admin users have the same rights as Security Reader users but can also update the security policy, dismiss alerts and recommendations, and apply recommendations.

➤ **For detailed instructions on how to assign roles in the Azure portal, see "Assign Azure roles using the Azure portal" at** *https://learn.microsoft.com/azure/role-based-access-control /role-assignments-portal.*

➤ **Find instructions for assigning administrator roles in Azure AD at** *https://learn.microsoft.com /azure/active-directory/roles/manage-roles-portal.*

Azure AD Authentication

New with SQL Server 2022, you can authenticate SQL Server with Azure AD using the following methods:

- Azure AD Password

- Azure AD Integrated

- Azure AD Universal with Multi-Factor Authentication

- Azure AD access token

Azure AD support makes hybrid integrations with Azure Synapse Analytics, Azure SQL Managed Instance, Azure Arc, and other services easier. If your Windows Server AD is federated with Azure AD, users can use those credentials to sign into SQL Server. However, Azure AD authentication does not support service accounts or other complex architectures of AD.

Azure AD support requires that both SQL Server and the host server (Windows or Linux) be registered with Azure Arc.

➤ **For more details on Azure AD, see Chapter 12.**

Microsoft Purview

Microsoft Purview is a data-governance tool designed to support organizations in finding, understanding, governing, and consuming data stores. Microsoft Purview has been a cloud-first feature for some time, and has come to SQL Server on-premises with SQL Server 2022.

As with many other Azure hybrid features, SQL Server must be registered with Azure Arc to use Microsoft Purview. In addition, you will need to create a Microsoft Purview account and enable Azure AD.

➤ For information on creating a Microsoft Purview account, see *https://learn.microsoft.com /azure/purview/create-catalog-portal.*

CAUTION

Take care when assigning permissions for Microsoft Purview. There are inherent risks with the various admin roles, and these should be shared among different people in your organization. To prevent policies from being modified, you can use Azure Resource Manager (ARM) locking. More details on setting up Purview for an Azure Arc server are available at *https://learn .microsoft.com/azure/purview/how-to-data-owner-policies-arc-sql-server#configuration.*

Azure extension for SQL Server

To connect SQL Server to Azure Arc and take advantage of Microsoft Defender, Azure AD, and Microsoft Purview, you must install the Azure extension for SQL Server during SQL Server Setup on the Azure Extension for SQL Server page (see Figure 4-2). You can use your existing Azure credentials or an Azure Service Principal, and then complete the required fields such as Azure Research Group, Azure Region, and Azure Tenant ID. If you are not interested in connecting your SQL Server instance to Azure Arc, simply deselect the Azure Extension for SQL Server check box.

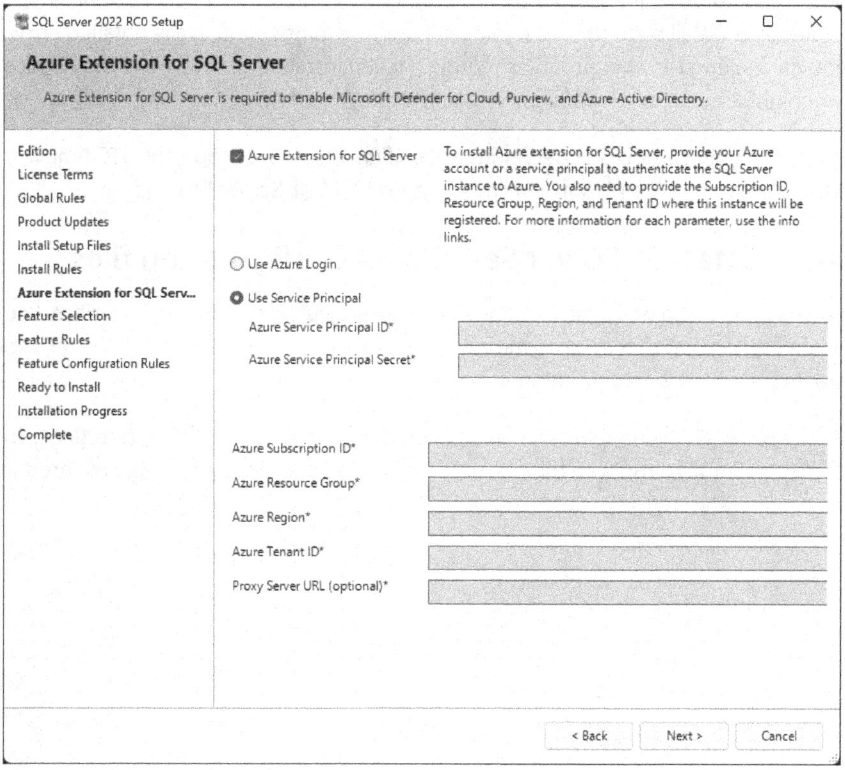

Figure 4-2 The Azure Extension for SQL Server page displays a number of required fields to enable Azure Arc features.

CHAPTER 4

Log SQL Server Setup

SQL Server Setup generates many logging files for diagnostic and troubleshooting purposes. These logs should be the first place you go if you have an issue with Setup.

First, a System Configuration Check Report .htm file is generated each time you run Setup. You can view this report in SQL Server Setup near the start of the installation steps.

A new timestamp-named folder of log files is generated for each launch of SQL Server Setup. After you proceed past the **Ready to Install** page, and regardless of whether Setup was a complete success, it generates a number of log files in the following folder:

```
%programfiles%\Microsoft SQL Server\150\Setup Bootstrap\Log\YYYYMMDD_HHMMSS\
```

However, when you run Setup using the /Q or /QS parameters for unattended installation, the log file is written to the Windows %temp% folder.

A log summary file of the installation is created that uses the following naming convention:

```
Summary_instancename_YYYYMMDD_HHMMSS.txt
```

Setup generates similar files for the Component and Global Rules portions of Setup, as well as a file called Detail.txt in the same folder. These files might contain the detailed error messages you are looking for when troubleshooting a failed installation. The Windows Application Event log might also contain helpful information in that situation.

You'll also find the new SQL Server instance's first error log encoded at UTC time in this folder, showing the log from startup, similar to the normal SQL Server Error Log.

Automate SQL Server Setup with configuration files

Let's dig more into what you can do with setup.exe outside of the user interface. You can use configuration files to automate the selection process when installing SQL Server, which helps to create a consistent configuration.

Values provided in configuration files can prepopulate or override Setup settings. They also can configure Setup to run with the normal user interface or silently without any interface.

Start SQL Server Setup from the command line

You can start setup.exe from either Windows PowerShell or the command prompt, providing repeatability and standardization of parameter options. You also can use it to prefill sections of the Setup wizard or to change the default behavior of Setup.

For the purposes of the installer, ensure you always use the Administrator level for these two shells. The title on each application window should be preceded by *Administrator:*—for example, Administrator: Windows PowerShell.

Sometimes you also might find it necessary to start Setup from the command line or Windows PowerShell because of a workaround for a specific problem or to automate and standardize future SQL Server installations. To start Windows PowerShell or the command prompt as Administrator, in the **Start** menu, search for the desired application, right-click it, and then select **Run As Administrator** on the shortcut menu that opens.

From the location of the SQL Server Setup installation files—for example, the mounted .iso file—execute the following command with PowerShell or the Windows Prompt:

```
.\setup.exe /ConfigurationFile=c:\install\SQL2019_basic.INI
```

This sample script, and all scripts for this book, are available for download at *https://www. MicrosoftPressStore.com/SQLServer2022InsideOut/downloads*. The preceding code sample uses a configuration file to pre-select installation choices—for example, features to be installed. Let's talk more about configuration files.

Generate a configuration file

Writing a configuration file by hand is not necessary, and can be tedious. Instead of going through that effort, you can let SQL Server Setup create a configuration file for you.

Work your way through the normal SQL Server Setup user interface, completing everything as you normally would, but pause when you get to the **Ready to Install** page. Near the bottom of this page is a path (see Figure 4-3). At that location, you'll find a generated configuration file, ready for future use and modification if needed.

For example, the first modification you need to make to the .ini file is to accept the SQL Server license terms via the IACCEPTSQLSERVERLICENSETERMS parameter, which isn't automatically provided in the automatically generated .ini file. Unless you modify an .ini file to provide this, it isn't possible to run the installer without user interaction.

CHAPTER 4

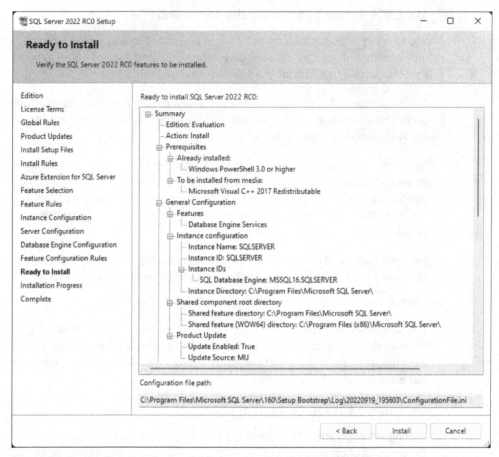

Figure 4-3 The Ready to Install page displays a summary of the installation steps as well as the path to the configuration file that has been prepared.

Install by using a configuration file

Now that you have a configuration file generated using the previous walk-through, you can take the next step to automate or standardize your installation.

You can start setup.exe from a command prompt with a configuration file by using the /CONFIGURATIONFILE parameter of setup.exe. Or you can launch SQL Server Setup with a configuration file by navigating to the **Advanced** page of the SQL Server Installation Center that starts with setup.exe in Windows. Once there, select the **Install Based On A Configuration File** check box. A message appears, asking you to browse to the .ini file. After you select the appropriate file, setup.exe will start with those options.

One thing to keep in mind is that configuration files generated by setup.exe do not and should not store the passwords you provided for any service accounts. If you do want to configure service account credentials in your configuration file, for security reasons, do not store the service account passwords in plain text in a configuration file. Instead, store passwords separately and securely, and provide them when you run setup.exe.

Each service's account parameters are available in a setup.exe runtime parameter, which is listed in Table 4-1.

Table 4-1 Common setup.exe parameters and their purposes

Service	Parameter name	Description
SQL Server Database Engine	/SQLSVCPASSWORD	Password for the SQL Server Database Engine Services service account. This is the service account for sqlservr.exe. It is required if a domain account is used for the service.
SQL Server Agent	/AGTSVCPASSWORD	Password for the SQL Server Agent service account. This is the service account for sqlagent.exe. It is required if a domain account is used for the service.
sa password	/SAPWD	Password for the sa account. It is required when /SECURITYMODE=SQL is used, which enables Mixed Mode authentication.
Integration Services	/ISSVCPASSWORD	Password for the Integration Services service. It is required if a domain account is used for the service.
Reporting Services (Native)	/RSSVCPASSWORD	Password for the Reporting Services service. It is required if a domain account is used for the service.
Analysis Services	/ASSVCPASSWORD	Password for the Analysis Services service account. It is required if a domain account is used for the service.
PolyBase	/PBDMSSVCPASSWORD	Password for the PolyBase service account.
Full-Text filter launcher service	/FTSVCPASSWORD	Password for the Full-Text filter launcher service.

CHAPTER 4

For example, in the snippet that follows, the PROD_ConfigurationFile_Install.INI provides the account name of the SQL Server Database Engine service account, but the password is provided when setup.exe runs in the command prompt or PowerShell:

```
setup.exe /SQLSVCPASSWORD="securepwd" /ConfigurationFile="d:\SQL\PROD_Install.INI"
```

You can provide further parameters like passwords when you run Setup. Parameter settings provided override any settings in the configuration file, just as the configuration file's settings override any defaults in the Setup operation. Table 4-2 lists and describes the parameters.

Table 4-2   Common setup.exe parameters of which you should be aware

Parameter usage	Parameter	Description
Unattended installations	/Q	Specifies Quiet Mode with no user interface and user interactivity allowed.
Unattended installations	/QS	Specifies Quiet Mode with user interface but no user interactivity allowed. Will fail if all needed information or parameters are not provided.
Accept license terms	/IACCEPTSQLSERVERLICENSETERMS	Must provide in any configuration file looking to avoid prompts for installation.
R open license terms	/IACCEPTROPENLICENSETERMS	Must provide for any unattended installation involving the R language option for Machine Learning Services.
Python open license terms	/IACCEPTPYTHONLICENSETERMS	Must provide for any unattended installation involving the Python language option for Machine Learning Services.
Instant file initialization	/SQLSVCINSTANTFILEINIT	Set to true to grant Perform Volume Maintenance Task privilege to the Database Engine service account (recommended).
Windows accounts to provision as members of the sysadmin role	/SQLSYSADMINACCOUNTS	Must provide groups or service accounts to specify as the initial members of the sysadmin role.
Provision the user running SQL Server Setup as a member of the sysadmin role	/ADDCURRENTUSERASSQLADMIN	If desired, specify the current local Windows Server user running SQL Server Setup as an initial member of the sysadmin role. Not desired if using a personal named account; use a group instead.
tempdb data file count	/SQLTEMPDBFILECOUNT	Set to the number of desired tempdb data files to be installed initially.
Enable TCP/IP	/TCPENABLED="1"	Disabled by default and used in many installations. Enable TCP/IP here to save yourself a step in Configuration Manager later on.

By default, the /UpdateEnabled parameter is enabled and doesn't need to be specified, and SQL Server will include updates found via Windows Update. If you choose to disable this behavior by providing /UpdateEnabled=False, you can also specify /UpdateSource as the location of the cumulative update or other SQL patch file executables to be included in the installation.

SQL Server on Azure virtual machines

Azure options are continuously evolving, making it hard to comprehensively cover them in any one book. SQL Server 2022 is touted as the most Azure-connected version to date. It is Microsoft's way of bringing you hybrid flexibility from ground to cloud, so it is worthwhile covering some of those intersections here.

At the time of writing, there are three options:

- **Azure VMs.** VMs hosted in Azure. They function very similarly to VMs in your on-premises environment, except they are hosted in Azure. You have the same responsibilities for protection and management, but with the utilities and services of Azure at your disposal.

- **SQL Server on Azure VMs.** Azure VMs with a preset configuration of SQL Server you choose based on your desired workload. The default workload environment is production, but there are options for dev/test as well. You can choose between different performance tiers; some focus on CPU-intensive workloads, while others focus on memory-optimized workloads, with variations in between. These tiers provide a wide selection of virtual hardware to run enterprise applications, relational databases, analytics, in-memory workloads, and intensive batch processing.

- **Azure Arc VMs.** VMs that can be created in one of your non-Azure environments. Typically, this is on-premises, but it could also be another cloud provider, public or private.

Post-installation server configuration

After you install SQL Server, there are several changes to make or confirm on the OS and in settings for SQL Server.

Post-installation checklist

You should run through the following checklist on your new SQL Server instance. The order of these items isn't necessarily specific. Many deal with SQL Server and/or Windows configuration settings. You want to evaluate whether these are appropriate for your environment, but you should consider and apply them to most SQL Server installations.

- Check your SQL Server patch level version and apply patches if necessary.

- Review maximum server memory settings for other features.

CHAPTER 4

- Review the surface area configuration facet.

- Set up SQL Agent.

- Turn on TCP/IP if needed.

- Verify server power options.

- Configure antivirus exclusions for SQL Server processes and files.

- Evaluate whether Lock Pages in Memory is necessary.

- Review the size and location of the Windows page file.

- Set up scheduled backups, index maintenance, log retention maintenance, and integrity checks.

- Back up service master and database master keys.

- Increase SQL Agent and SQL Error Log retention from the defaults.

- Suppress successful backup messages.

- Increase default SQL Agent history retention.

Let's look at each of these in more detail in the following subsections.

Check your SQL Server patch level version and apply patches if necessary

After you install SQL Server, check the version number against the latest cumulative updates list—especially if you did not opt to or could not use Windows Update during SQL Server Setup. You can view the version number in SQL Server Management Studio's Object Explorer or via a T-SQL query on either of the following built-in functions:

```
SELECT @@VERSION;
SELECT SERVERPROPERTY('ProductVersion');
SELECT SERVERPROPERTY('Edition');
```

While you're at it, double-check that you installed the right edition of SQL Server, too!

> **NOTE**
>
> Take the opportunity before your SQL Server enters production to patch it. For information about the latest cumulative updates for SQL Server, visit *https://learn.microsoft.com /troubleshoot/sql/general/determine-version-edition-update-level#sql-server-complete -version-list-tables*, and select your version or build.

Review maximum server memory settings for other features

Other features of SQL Server have their own maximum server memory settings. As you will notice by their default settings, for servers on which both the Database Engine and SSAS and/or SSRS are installed, competition for and exhaustion of memory is possible. It is recommended that you protect the Database Engine by lowering the potential memory impact of other applications.

Limit SSAS memory

SQL Server Analysis Services (SSAS) has not just one maximum server memory limit, but five, and you can enforce limits by hard values in bytes or by a percentage of total physical memory of the server.

You change these memory settings via SSMS by connecting to the SSAS instance in Object Explorer. To start, right-click the server and select **Properties** on the shortcut menu. Some of the memory settings described here are identical for Multidimensional and Tabular installations, whereas others are for Tabular mode only:

- **LowMemoryLimit.** A value that serves as a floor for memory, but also the level at which SSAS begins to release memory for infrequently used or low-priority objects in its cache. Below this level, no memory maintenance is performed by SSAS. The default value is 65, or 65 percent of total server physical memory (or technically the virtual address space, but SSAS, among other features, is no longer supported on 32-bit systems, so this is not a concern).

- **TotalMemoryLimit.** A value that serves as a threshold for SSAS to begin to release memory for higher priority requests. This is not a hard limit. The default is 80 percent of total server memory.

- **HardMemoryLimit.** A hard memory limit that leads to more aggressive pruning of memory from cache and potentially to the rejection of new requests. By default, this is displayed as 0, and is effectively the midway point between the `TotalMemoryLimit` and the server physical memory. The `TotalMemoryLimit` must always be less than the `HardMemoryLimit`.

- **VertiPaqMemoryLimit.** For SSAS installations in Tabular mode only, a value that serves as a memory limit for the VertiPaq processing engine. The default is 60, or 60 percent of server physical memory. Above this percentage, and only if `VertiPaqPagingPolicy` is turned on (it is by default), SSAS begins to page data to the hard drive using the OS page file. Paging to a drive can help prevent out-of-memory errors when the `HardMemoryLimit` is met.

- **QueryMemoryLimit.** A value that can limit the amount of memory used by individual DAX queries, preventing any one query from dominating memory. For any individual query, this setting can be overridden by a new XMLA property, `DbpropMsmdRequest MemoryLimit`, specified for the query connection. This setting can be specified as a percentage (values <=100) or as a number of bytes greater than 100. The default setting of 0 implies no limit to the memory of individual queries.

Figure 4-4 shows the General page of the Analysis Server Properties dialog box, as started in Object Explorer in SSMS, and the locations of the preceding memory configuration properties with their defaults in SQL Server 2019 for a Tabular mode installation of SSAS. Note that the Show Advanced (All) Properties check box is checked.

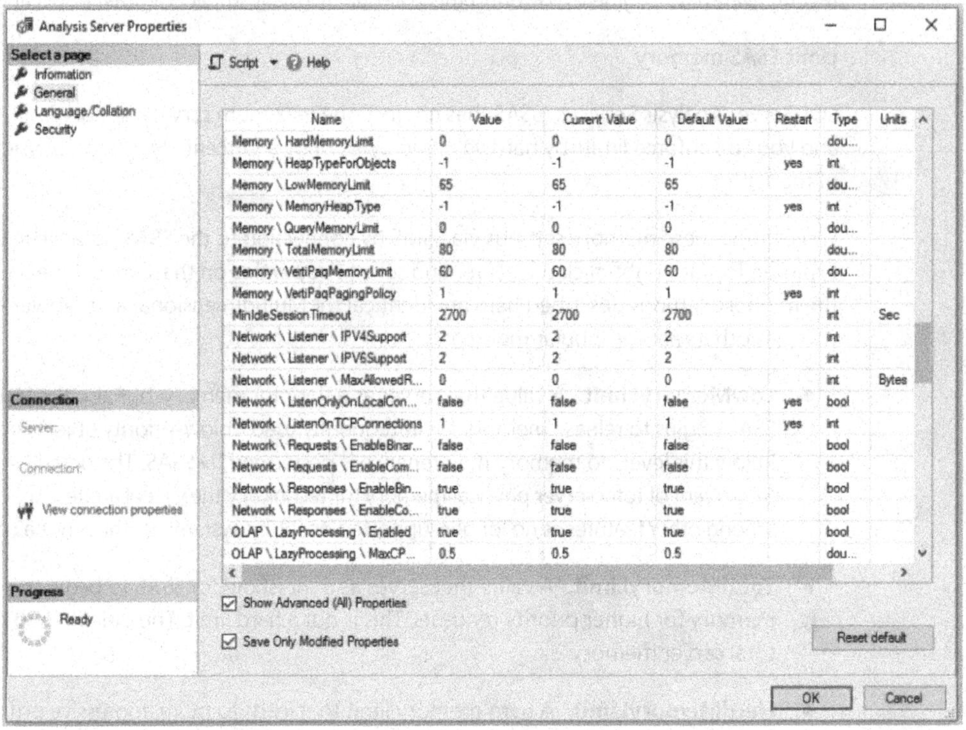

Figure 4-4 The General page in the Analysis Server Properties dialog box showing the default settings.

Limit SSRS memory

Four options are available for limiting SQL Server Reporting Services (SSRS) memory: MemorySafety Margin, MemoryThreshold, WorkingSetMaximum, and WorkingSetMinimum. All four are based on numbers contained in tags within a config file, so be sure to make a backup of it before editing. You can configure memory settings only in the RSReportServer.config file, which is a text file stored at %ProgramFiles%\Microsoft SQL Server Reporting Services\SSRS\ReportServer.

NOTE

This location has changed from previous versions, but the config file name has not.

Two of the settings are in the config file by default; two more are available to administrators to use in advanced scenarios. Let's look at each one:

- **MemorySafetyMargin.** The percentage of `WorkingSetMaximum` that SSRS will use before taking steps to reduce background task memory use and prioritize requests coming from the web service, attempting to protect user requests. User requests could still be denied.

- **MemoryThreshold.** The percentage of `WorkSetMaximum` at which SSRS will deny new requests, slow down existing requests, and page memory to a hard drive until memory conditions improve.

Two more settings are given values automatically upon service startup, but you can override them in the config file. Two older memory settings from SQL Server 2005 with which SQL DBAs might be familiar are `MemoryLimit` and `MaximumMemoryLimit`, but these two values have been ignored since SQL Server 2008.

- **WorkingSetMaximum.** By default, this is the server's total physical memory. This setting does not appear by default in the config file, but you can override it to reduce the amount of memory of which SSRS will be aware. This value is expressed in kilobytes of memory.

- **WorkingSetMinimum.** By default, this value is 60 percent of `WorkingSetMaximum`. If SSRS needs memory below this value, it will use memory and not release it due to memory pressure. This setting does not appear by default in the config file, but you can override it to increase the variability of SQL SSRS's memory use.

These four settings can appear in the rsreportserver.config file. As demonstrated here, you could override the default settings to 4 GB maximum and 2 GB minimum (each expressed in KB):

```
<MemorySafetyMargin>80</MemorySafetyMargin>
<MemoryThreshold>90</MemoryThreshold>
<WorkingSetMaximum>4194304</WorkingSetMaximum>
<WorkingSetMinimum>2097152</WorkingSetMinimum>
```

Limit Machine Learning Server memory

Like SSAS and SSRS, the Machine Learning Server has a config file at %ProgramFiles%\Microsoft SQL Server\MSSQL15.instancename\MSSQL\Binn\rlauncher.config.

By default, Machine Learning Server is similar to 20 percent of total server memory. You can override this by adding a tag to the config file to provide a value for `MEMORY_LIMIT_PERCENT`. This value is not in the config file by default.

CHAPTER 4

Remember to make a backup of this config file before editing. The following is an example of the contents of the rlauncher.config file, with the default memory limit changed to 25 percent:

```
RHOME=C:\PROGRA~2\MICROS~1\MSSQL1~4.SQL\R_SERV~2
MPI_HOME=C:\Program Files\Microsoft MPI
INSTANCE_NAME=SQL2K22
TRACE_LEVEL=1
JOB_CLEANUP_ON_EXIT=1
USER_POOL_SIZE=0
WORKING_DIRECTORY=C:\Program Files\Microsoft SQL
Server\MSSQL16.SQL2K22\MSSQL\ExtensibilityData
PKG_MGMT_MODE=0
MEMORY_LIMIT_PERCENT=25
```

Review the surface area configuration

If you are a veteran SQL Server DBA, you will remember when the SQL Server Surface Area Configuration was a separate application. Now, surface area settings are a facet, accessed via the Facets dialog box in SSMS starting with SQL Server 2008.

To view surface area configuration settings in SSMS, open Object Explorer, connect to the SQL Server, right-click the server, and select **Facets** on the shortcut menu. (The Facets window sometimes takes a moment to load.) Then, in the dialog box that opens, change the value in the list box to **Surface Area Configuration**.

Most of these options should remain off unless needed because they present a specific potential for misuse by an administrator or unauthorized user. In typical installations of SQL Server 2022, however, you should consider enabling three of these options:

- **Database Mail.** This should be enabled on most instances to allow SQL Server to, at the very least, send out a message in case of a high-severity incident or job failure, and to allow developers to send custom email messages using the system procedure sp_send _dbmail. You also can turn this setting on or off via the Database Mail XPs option in sp _configure. (More about this setting in Chapter 9, "Automate SQL Server administration.")

- **Remote Dedicated Admin Connection.** This could be particularly useful for bypassing a malfunctioning login trigger or Resource Governor. You also can turn this setting on or off via the remote admin connections option in sp_configure. (More on this setting in Chapter 13: "Protect data through classification, encryption, and auditing.")

- **CLR Integration.** Turn on if you need to use SSIS or to write CLR objects. You also can turn this setting on or off via the clr_enabled option in sp_configure.

You should turn on other options in the Surface Area Configuration only if they are specifically required by an application and you are aware of the potential security concerns.

Set up SQL Agent

There are several post-installation tasks to set up in SQL Agent before SQL Server can begin to help you automate, monitor, and back up your new instance.

> ➤ Chapter 8, "Maintain and monitor SQL Server," and Chapter 9 cover SQL Agent and monitoring topics in detail.

You will likely want to do the following:

1. Change the SQL Agent service from Manual to Automatic startup.

2. Set up a Database Mail account and profile (see Chapter 9) to send email notifications for alerts or job status notifications.

3. Set up an operator for a distribution group of IT professionals in your organization who would respond to a SQL Server issue.

4. Configure SQL Server Agent to use Database Mail, including a fail-safe operator.

5. Set up SQL Server Alerts for desired errors and high severity (Severity 21+) errors.

At the very least, these steps are put in place so that SQL Server can send out a call for help. Even if you have centralized monitoring solutions in place, the most rare and severe of errors should be important enough to warrant an email.

You can choose to configure many Windows Management Instrumentation (WMI) conditions, Performance Monitor counter conditions, and SQL Server Error messages by number or severity in SQL Server Alerts. However, do not overcommit your inboxes, and do not set an inbox rule to Mark As Read and file away emails from SQL Server. By careful selection of emails, you can assure yourself and your team that emails from SQL Server will be actionable concerns that rarely arrive.

> ➤ For much more information on maintaining and monitoring SQL Server, see Chapter 8.

Turn on TCP/IP if needed

Depending on the edition you have installed, the common network protocol TCP/IP is off by default. The only protocol that *is* on is Shared Memory, which allows only local connections. You will likely not end up using Shared Memory alone to connect to the SQL Server for common business applications that use multiple servers for database, web, and application tiers.

NOTE

It is possible to enable TCP/IP by default at the time of installation if using a configuration file for SQL Server Setup, but this option does not appear in the UI for SQL Server Setup. It must be changed after installation is complete.

When you connect to SQL Server using SSMS while local to the server, you connect to the Shared_Memory endpoint whenever you provide the name of the server, the server\instance, localhost, dot character (.), (local), .\instance, or (local)\instance.

TCP/IP, however, is ubiquitous in many SQL Server features and functionality. Many applications will need to use TCP/IP to connect to the SQL Server remotely. Many SQL Server features require TCP/IP to be enabled, including the Remote Dedicated Admin Connection (DAC), the availability groups listener, and Kerberos authentication.

To configure TCP/IP, open the SQL Server Configuration Manager application locally on the server. Then, in the left pane, select **SQL Server Network Configuration**. Browse to the protocols for your newly installed instance of SQL Server. The default instance of SQL Server, here and in many places, will appear as **MSSQLSERVER**.

You can also enable TCP/IP for a SQL Server instance with PowerShell:

```
Import-Module SqlServer
$wmi = new-object('Microsoft.SqlServer.Management.Smo.Wmi.ManagedComputer')
#Path to the local server
$path = "ManagedComputer[@Name='$env:COMPUTERNAME']/"
$path = $path+"ServerInstance[@Name='SQL2K22']/ServerProtocol[@Name='Tcp']"
#Enable the TCP protocol on the local server, on the named instance SQL2K22
$TCPIP = $wmi.GetSmoObject($path)
$TCPIP.IsEnabled = $true
$TCPIP.Alter()
$TCPIP.IsEnabled
#Restart SQL Server Database Engine service to apply the change
```

After turning on TCP/IP, regardless of what method you use, you need to restart the SQL Server Database Engine service for it to take effect.

NOTE

Turning on Named Pipes is not required or used unless an application specifically needs it.

Verify server power options

The Windows Server Power Options setting should be set to High Performance for any server hosting a SQL Server instance.

In other power plans, Windows might not operate the processor at maximum frequency during normal or even busy periods of SQL Server activity. This applies to physical or virtual Windows servers.

Review this setting and ensure that the group policy will not change it back to Balanced or another setting. Also ensure that group preferences are configured with High Performance selected for new SQL Servers. Finally, you may also need to check that the BIOS is also configured for High Performance.

Configure antivirus exclusions for SQL Server processes and files

Configure any antivirus software installed on the SQL Server to ignore scanning files with exten-sions used by your SQL Server data and log files. Typically, these will be MDF, LDF, and NDF files.

Also, configure any antivirus programs to ignore folders containing SQL Server files. These could include:

- Full-text catalog files

- Backup files

- Replication snapshot files

- SQL Server trace (TRC) files

- SQL Audit files

- Analysis Services database

- Log and backup files

- FILESTREAM and FileTable folders

- SSRS temp files and log files

Processes might also be affected, so set antivirus programs to ignore the programs for all instances of the SQL Server Database Engine service, Reporting Services service, Analysis Ser-vices service, and R Server (RTerm.exe and BxlServer.exe).

In SQL Server FCIs and availability groups, configure antivirus software to exclude the MSCS folder on the quorum drive if in use, the MSDTC directory on the MSDTC share, and the Win-dows\Cluster folder on each cluster node, if they exist.

CHAPTER 4

Inside OUT

What if you suspect antivirus or antimalware software is interfering with SQL Server?

This is one of the more challenging troubleshooting exercises: a strange error message, DLL error, or file accessibility issue. It is critical to configure antivirus to exclude SQL Server files and folders from on-access scans, exclusive-lock scans, and more.

If you notice, for example, random databases failing to recover upon SQL Server startup, or error messages like "File activation failure" or "Unable to open the physical file," sqlservr.exe may not be able to gain exclusive access to the files because they are being scanned by another application. Use the Windows Sysinternals Process Explorer application to search for handles, including your SQL Server files, and potentially catch that other application accessing the file. Download the Sysinternals Process Explorer at *https://aka.ms /processexplorer.*

Antivirus applications may also interfere with service packs and cumulative updates if those files, even if they are signed by Microsoft, have not been pre-approved for execution in the production environment. Communicate with the teams that control antivirus, antiransomware, or antimalware solutions in your enterprise.

Optimize for ad hoc workloads

The server-level setting Optimize for Ad Hoc Workloads doesn't have the most intuitive name. We are not optimizing ad hoc queries; we are optimizing SQL Server memory usage to prevent ad hoc queries from consuming unnecessary cache.

➤ For more about the Optimize for Ad Hoc Workloads setting, see Chapter 3.

For the unlikely scenario in which a large number of queries are executed only two times, setting this option to **True** would be a net negative for performance. Enabling this setting can also affect performance tuning for single-use queries.

➤ For more about cached execution plans, read Chapter 14.

Evaluate whether Lock Pages in Memory is necessary

Consider using the Lock Pages in Memory policy for environments in which instances of SQL Server are expected to experience memory pressure due to other applications, server limitations, or overallocated virtualized systems. This is an in-depth topic to be carefully considered.

➤ For more about the Lock Pages in Memory setting, see Chapter 2, "Introduction to database server components."

➤ For more about the Windows page file, see Chapter 3.

Inside OUT

How can you tell if the Lock Pages in Memory policy is in effect?

Starting with SQL Server 2016 SP1, you can check whether the Lock Pages in Memory policy has been granted to the Database Engine using the following query:

```
SELECT sql_memory_model_desc
FROM sys.dm_os_sys_info;
--CONVENTIONAL = Lock pages in memory privilege is not granted
--LOCK_PAGES = Lock pages in memory privilege is granted
--LARGE_PAGES = Lock pages in memory privilege is granted in Enterprise mode
--   with Trace Flag 834 ON
```

Review the size and location of the Windows page file

The page file is used to page out system memory. It can also capture a system memory dump for crash forensic analysis, a factor that dictates its size on modern operating systems with large amounts of memory. Therefore, the general recommendation for the system page file is that it should be at least the same size as the server's amount of physical memory. This is also why the page file is best moved to its own volume, away from the OS volume, so that it does not unexpectedly grow and create space issues.

➤ For more guidance on the operating system page file, see the section "Configure the operating system page file" in Chapter 3.

Set up scheduled backups, index maintenance, log retention maintenance, and integrity checks

Backups are a critical part of disaster recovery. They should begin as soon as possible after installation, and before users or applications begin to use the SQL Server.

Generate database backups, at least of the master and msdb system databases, right away. You should also back up other SQL Server Setup–created databases, including ReportServer, ReportServerTempDB, and SSISDB, as soon as possible.

➤ For more information on backups, index maintenance, and monitoring, see Chapter 11.

As soon as your new SQL Server instance has databases in use, regularly perform selective index maintenance and integrity checks that consider the current fragmentation levels of indexes rather than performing index maintenance on entire databases. In many cases, statistics maintenance may be more effective in the shorter term.

➤ For more information on automating maintenance, see Chapter 9.

Back up service master and database master keys

You should back up service master keys and any database master keys as they are created, securely storing their information.

➤ For more information on service master and database master keys, see Chapter 13.

To back up the instance service master key, use the following command:

```
BACKUP SERVICE MASTER KEY TO FILE = 'localfilepath_or_UNC'
ENCRYPTION BY PASSWORD = 'complexpassword'
```

As soon as database master keys come into existence in each user database—for example, as you implement features like transparent data encryption (TDE) or column data encryption, back up individual database master keys as follows:

```
BACKUP MASTER KEY TO FILE = 'localfilepath_or_UNC' ENCRYPTION BY PASSWORD =
'complexpassword'
```

If you implement TDE, Always Encrypted, native backup encryption, column encryption, or any other native or external solutions that generate certificates, keys, and/or passwords, develop a secure storage and retrieval method inside your enterprise. Failure to back up master and data-base master keys could compromise future disaster recovery attempts!

Increase SQL Agent and SQL error log retention from the defaults

By default, SQL Server maintains the current SQL Server Error Log plus six more historical error logs. Logs are cycled each time the SQL Server service is started.

One fun weekend of server troubleshooting or maintenance where the SQL Server service is restarted many times could wipe out a significant amount of your error history. This could make the task of troubleshooting periodic or business cycle–related errors difficult or impossible.

You need visibility into errors that occur only during a monthly processing, monthly patch day, or periodic reporting, for example. Follow these steps:

1.   In SQL Server Management Studio, in Object Explorer, connect to the SQL Server instance.

2.   Expand the **Management** folder, right-click **SQL Server Logs**, and select **Configure** in the shortcut menu.

3.   Select the **Limit the Number of Error Logs Before They Are Recycled** check box.

4.   For the **Maximum Number of Error Log Files** setting, type a value larger than 6. You might find that a value between 25 and 50 will result in more useful log history contained for multiple business cycles.

On SQL Server instances that generate a large amount of log noise, consider other options to reduce the clutter of the SQL Server Error Log, including Trace Flag 3226 to suppress the logging of successful backup operations. (Much more on this in the next section.)

You may also choose to configure a SQL Agent Job to manually cycle the SQL Server Error Log using sp_cycle_errorlog so that no one log file contains so much data it becomes unwieldly for scan and analysis. Consider scheduling sp_cycle_errorlog to execute weekly, and keep 50 SQL Agent error jobs, leaving at most 50 weeks of history.

Suppress successful backup messages

By default, SQL Server writes an event to the SQL Server error log upon a successful database backup, whether it be FULL, DIFFERENTIAL, or TRANSACTION LOG.

On instances with many databases, and with many databases in the full recovery model with regular transaction log backups, the amount of log activity generated by just their successful frequent log backups could flood the log with clutter, lowering log history retention.

NOTE

You can review successful backup history by querying the msdb system database. It has a series of tables dedicated to storing the backup history for all databases, including msdb .dbo.backupset and msdb.dbo.backupmediafamily. The built-in "Backup and Restore Events" report in SQL Server Management Studio provides access to this data, as well.

➤ For more on backups, see Chapter 10, "Develop, deploy, and manage data recovery."

SQL Server Trace Flag 3226 controls an option at the instance level to suppress successful backup notifications.

There are many trace flags available to administrators to alter default behavior—many more options than there are user interfaces to accommodate them in SQL Server Management Studio. Take care when turning them on and understand that many trace flags are intended only for temporary use when aiding troubleshooting. Because Trace Flag 3226 is intended to be a permanent setting, simply enabling the trace flag by using DBCC TRACEON is not sufficient, as the trace flag will no longer be active following a SQL Server service restart. Instead, add the trace flag as a startup parameter to the Database Engine service by using SQL Server Configuration Manager. In the **Properties** of the SQL Server service, go to the **Startup Parameters** tab, and use the syntax -T*flagnumber*. This field is essentially adding parameters that are passed to the sqlserver.exe executable. For example, enter **-T3226**, then select **Add**. The change will not take effect until the SQL Server Database Engine service is restarted.

➤ For more information on SQL Server Configuration Manager, refer to Chapter 1, "Get started with SQL Server tools."

Increase default SQL Agent history retention

Similarly, you might find that the SQL Server Agent history is not sufficient to cover an adequate amount of job history, especially if you have frequent job runs.

You can use SSMS to change the job history settings for SQL Server Agent. In Object Explorer, connect to the SQL Server instance. Then right-click **SQL Server Agent**, select **Properties** from the shortcut menu, and select the **History** page.

This page is not intuitive and can be confusing. The first option, **Limit Size of Job History Log**, is a rolling job history retention setting. Consider adding zeros to increase the maximum log history size in rows from the default of 1,000 to 10,000 or more, and increasing the maximum job history per job in rows from the default of 100 to 2,000 or more. This data is stored in the msdb system database and will cause that database to grow larger over time. Consider pre-allocating some additional file space to the msdb data file now.

Heads up: The second option on the **History** page, **Remove Agent History**, along with its corresponding **Older Than** text box, is *not* a rolling job history retention setting. Rather, it is an immediate and manual job history pruning. Select this second check box and select **OK**. When you return to the **History** page, you will find the second check box is cleared. Behind the scenes, SQL Server Management Studio immediately ran the `msdb.dbo.sp_purge_jobhistory` stored procedure to remove the job history once.

Post-installation configuration of other features

SQL Server Database Engine installation is now complete, but three other features require post-installation configuration: SSIS, SSRS, and SSAS. You will need to perform the steps detailed in this section before use if these features are installed.

SSISDB initial configuration and setup

Among the best features added by SQL Server 2012 were massive improvements to SSIS—specifically a new server-integrated deployment, built-in performance data collector, environment variables, and more developer quality-of-life improvements. For these reasons, you should use the new Project Deployment Model and built-in SSISDB for all new development.

When the Integration Services Catalog is created, a new user database called SSISDB is also created. You should back it up and treat it as an important production database.

You must create the SSISDB catalog soon after installation and before an SSIS development can take place. You will need to create the catalog only once. Because this involves potential surface area configuration changes and the creation of a new strong encryption password, a SQL DBA, not an SSIS developer, should perform this step and should store the password securely alongside others generated at the time of installation.

To create the catalog, in Object Explorer, connect to your instance, right-click **Integration Services Catalog**, and select **Create Catalog** in the shortcut menu that appears. In the single-page setup window, select the **Enable CLR Integration** check box, decide whether SSIS packages should be allowed to be run at SQL Server Startup (we recommend this due to the maintenance and cleanup performed then), and provide an encryption password for the SSISDB database.

The encryption password is for the SSISDB database master key. After you create it, you should back up the SSISDB database master key and securely store the SSISDB database password where it can be retrieved along with other disaster-recovery information for this server.

➤ For more on database master keys, see Chapter 13.

The SSISDB database will contain SSIS packages and their connection strings. The SSISDB encryption would not allow these sensitive contents—a treasure trove of connections to other servers—to be decrypted by a malicious user who gains access to the database files or backups. This SSISDB password will be required if the database is restored to a new server, so you should store it in a secure location within your enterprise.

NOTE

If you receive an error when creating the SSSIDB catalog that reads "The catalog backup file 'C:\Program Files\Microsoft SQL Server\150\DTS\Binn\SSISDBBackup.bak' could not be accessed" or similar, it is probably because SSIS was not actually installed. Most likely, the 6-MB template database backup was not copied from the SQL Server media, probably because the SSIS feature was not a selected feature. To rectify this, you can run SQL Server Setup again or copy the SSISDBBackup.bak file from another SQL Server installation of the same version.

SQL Server Reporting Services initial configuration and setup

There are still tasks to perform upon first installation of an SSRS native-mode installation from the downloaded installer file, SQLServerReportingServices.exe.

➤ Get the latest installer and see what's new in SSRS at *https://learn.microsoft.com/sql /reporting-services/what-s-new-in-sql-server-reporting-services-ssrs.*

At the end of the Microsoft SQL Server 2022 Reporting Services installer wizard, on the Setup Completed screen, select the **Configure Report Server** button to open the Reporting Services Configuration Manager application. Then connect to the newly installed SSRS instance and review the following options, from top to bottom:

- **Service Account.** You can change the SSRS service account here. Remember that you should use only the Reporting Services Configuration Manager tool to make this change, never services.msc.

- **Web Service URL.** The web service URL is not for user interaction; rather, it is for Report Manager and custom applications to programmatically connect to the SSRS instance.

  By default, a web service on TCP Port 80 is created called ReportServer. For named instances, the web service will be called ReportServer_*instancename*. The URL for the webservice would then be:

  servername/ReportServer

  or:

  servername/ReportServer_*instancename*

  To accept defaults, at the bottom of the application window, select **Apply**.

  You can optionally configure an SSL certificate for a specific URL for the Web Portal in the **Advanced** section here. Choose an identity and an HTTPS certificate that's been loaded to the server, and the Reporting Services Configuration Manager will make the necessary changes.

CHAPTER 4

➤ For more information on configuring SSL connections for the SSRS Web Service and Web Portal, visit *https://learn.microsoft.com/sql/reporting-services/security/configure-ssl -connections-on-a-native-mode-report-server*.

● **Database.** Each SSRS instance requires a pair of databases running on a SQL Server instance. Executing the SSRS installer alone does not configure the databases for SSRS; you need to configure them via Reporting Services Configuration Manager. The database names by default are ReportServer and ReportServerTempDB, or, for a named instance, ReportServer$*InstanceName* and ReportServer$*InstanceName*TempDB. Both of these databases are important, and you should create a backup schedule for each. The ReportServerTempDB is not a completely transient database like the SQL Server instance's tempdb system database.

The databases for SSRS can be hosted on an on-premises SQL Server instance or Azure VM–hosted SQL Server instance or, since SQL Server 2019, an Azure SQL Managed Instance.

To set the databases for a new instance of SSRS, in the **Database** page of the Reporting Services Configuration Manager, select **Change Database**, and then follow the Report Server Database Configuration Wizard.

● **Web Portal URL.** The web portal URL is the user-friendly website that hosts links to reports and provides administrative features to the SSRS instance. This is the link to share with users if you will be using the SSRS portal. By default, the URL for the web portal is *servername*/Reports for the default instance, or *servername*/Reports_*InstanceName* for named instances. You can change the name from the default if desired. To proceed, at the bottom of the application window, select **Apply**.

● **Email Settings.** You use these email settings to send reports to user subscribers via email. SSRS uses its own email settings and does not inherit from the SQL Server instance's Database Mail settings. This setting is optional if you do not intend to send reports to subscribers via email.

SSRS can authenticate to an SMTP server using anonymous (No Authentication), Basic, or NT LAN Manager (NTLM) authentication, which uses the SSRS service account to authenticate to the SMTP server.

Modern email systems likely require at least TLS 1.2. For example, with Office 365, TLS 1.0 and 1.1 have been deprecated since 2020. Older versions of Windows and SQL Server may need to be patched to support TLS 1.2.

➤ If you suspect the TLS 1.2 requirement is preventing SSRS from sending emails, review *https://support.microsoft.com/topic/kb3135244-tls-1-2-support-for-microsoft-sql-server -e4472ef8-90a9-13c1-e4d8-44aad198cdbe*.

SQL Server 2022 introduces support for TLS 1.3 as well. Leverage this when you can, including with SMTP connections.

NOTE

Enterprise SMTP servers usually have an allow list of IP addresses. You will need to add this server's IP to this list to relay email.

- **Execution Account.** You can optionally provide this domain account to be used when reports are configured to run unattended on a schedule or to connect to remote servers for external images. This credential must be a domain account.

    To follow the principle of least privilege, the execution account should not be the same as the SSRS service account. Further, this account should have minimal read-only access to any data sources that will require it. You also can give it EXECUTE permissions to stored procedures that serve as data sources for reports, but you should never give it additional SQL Server permissions or let it be a member of any server roles, including sysadmin.

- **Encryption Keys.** Immediately after installation, and after the two SSRS databases have been created, you should back up this instance's encryption keys. These are used to encrypt sensitive information such as connection strings in the two databases. If the databases are restored to another server and this key is not available from the source server, credentials in connection strings will not be usable, and you will need to provide them again for the reports to run successfully on a new server.

    If you can no longer locate the backup of a key, back it up again. Alternatively, rotate the key by using the **Change** operation on this page and then back it up.

    To restore the original key to a new server to which the databases have been moved, use the Restore operation on this page.

NOTE

SSRS key encryption is different from TDE, which was first supported for SSRS databases in SQL Server 2019. SSRS encryption keys are used inside tables to secure connection strings, while TDE is used to secure database files from being restored or attached to other SQL Servers.

- **Subscription Settings.** Use this page to specify a credential to reach file shares to which report subscriptions can be written. Reports can be dropped in this file share location in PDF, Microsoft Excel, or other formats for consumption. Multiple subscriptions can employ this file share credential, which can be used on this page in a central location. This account should be different from the SSRS execution account, to follow the principle of least privilege.

- **Scale-Out Deployment.** Visit this page on multiple SSRS instances to join them together. By using the same SSRS databases for multiple SSRS instances, multiple front ends can provide processing for heavy reporting workloads, including heavy subscription workloads. The server names can optionally be used in a network load balancer such as Network Load Balancing (NLB), or you can distribute workload to each SSRS instance from different applications.

Upon first installation, the **Scale-Out Deployment** page will show that the instance is "joined" to a single server scale-out. Each scale-out instance of SSRS must use the same settings on the **Database** page of the Reporting Services Configuration Manager. Connect to each instance in the scale-out and visit this page by opening it on each SSRS instance to view the status, add servers to the scale-out, or remove servers.

➤ For more detail on scale-out deployments of SSRS, visit *https://learn.microsoft.com/sql /reporting-services/install-windows/configure-a-native-mode-report-server-scale-out -deployment.*

- **Power BI Integration.** Use this page to associate the SSRS instance to a Microsoft Power BI account—specifically to an account in Azure AD. The administrator joining the Power BI instance to the SSRS instance must be:

  - A member of the Azure AD

  - A member of the system administrator role of the SSRS instance

  - A sysadmin on the SQL Server instance that hosts the SSRS databases

➤ For the latest information on Power BI/SSRS integration and the latest Azure authentication features, visit *https://learn.microsoft.com/sql/reporting-services/install-windows /power-bi-report-server-integration-configuration-manager.*

SQL Server Analysis Services initial configuration and setup

No additional steps are required after setup to begin using a new SSAS instance.

You can initiate manual backups of SSAS databases in Object Explorer in SQL Server Management Studio as well as restore SSAS databases. Because of the nature of SSAS databases, their size, and how they are populated, they are not typically backed up on a schedule, but you can do so by passing an XMLA command via a SQL Server Agent job step by typing **SQL Server Analysis Services**.

When installing SSAS, a security group should have been chosen to grant permissions to SSAS server administrators, granting a team full access to the server.

If you need to add a different group to the administrator role of the SSAS instance, open SQL Server Management Studio. Then, in Object Explorer, connect to the Analysis Services instance. Right-click the server and select **Properties** on the shortcut menu. Then, on the **Security** page, add Windows-authenticated accounts or groups to the administrator role.

Azure Synapse Link for SQL Server

This feature replicates operational data into a dedicated SQL pool in Azure Synapse Analytics, directly from SQL Server 2022.

Azure Synapse Analytics is an enterprise analytics service in the Azure cloud running on both serverless and dedicated resource models. Azure Synapse Analytics is a combination of broad technologies, including relational data warehousing, serverless data pools for nonrelational data, built-in machine learning, and other big data technologies.

Far outside the scope of this book, Azure Synapse Analytics accelerates insights into data for logs, time series data, and data integrations. The built-in streaming and deep integrations with Power BI, Cosmos DB APIs, and Azure Machine Learning (AzureML), as well as other analytics tools and pipelines, provide convenient access to cloud resources for all kinds of workloads.

Azure Synapse Link connection

The Azure Synapse Link connection initially does a bulk upload, and then a continuous incremental upload of change feed data on a regular basis. The link between the SQL Server 2022 database and the dedicated SQL pool is mapped and can be changed. This ensures the ability to create, manage, monitor, and delete link connections or add and delete tables to the connection. To access corporate data inside a firewall, it is recommended to use a self-hosted integration runtime (IR).

> ➤ For step-by-step details on how to create a self-hosted IR, read the documentation here: *https://learn.microsoft.com/azure/data-factory/create-self-hosted-integration-runtime ?tabs=synapse-analytics.*

NOTE

Self-hosted IRs created for Azure Synapse workspaces currently cannot be shared across Azure data factories or between other Synapse workspaces, unlike other self-hosted integration runtimes.

Azure Synapse Link landing zone

The landing zone is an intermediate staging location required to hold the data as it comes in from the SQL Server and before it is loaded into the Synapse dedicated SQL pool.

You must provide an Azure Data Lake Storage (ADLS) Gen2 account to be used as a landing zone, and this landing zone cannot be used for anything else. It must be different from the account created with the Azure Synapse Analytics workspace. An unexpired shared access signature (SAS) token for the ADLS Gen2 account is also crucial, because without it, the data will fail to replicate.

CHAPTER 4

Ensure your database in SQL Server 2022 has a master key created by running the following command:

```
CREATE MASTER KEY ENCRYPTION BY PASSWORD = '<a new password>'
```

➤ For current detailed steps on how to set up your own Azure Synapse link for SQL Server 2022, see *https://learn.microsoft.com/azure/synapse-analytics/synapse-link/connect -synapse-link-sql-server-2022#create-your-target-synapse-dedicated-sql-pool.*

The Synapse Link feature is also available for data in Microsoft Dataverse for the Power Platform, Cosmos DB APIs, and Azure SQL Database.

➤ For all the known limits and issues outstanding with Synapse Link, review the list here: *https://learn.microsoft.com/azure/synapse-analytics/synapse-link/synapse-link-for-sql -known-issues.*

NOTE

The Azure Synapse Link for SQL Server 2022 is in preview at the time of this writing and important details may change.

Container orchestration with Kubernetes

SQL Server in Linux containers is almost identical to SQL Server on Windows or Linux. As noted in Chapter 2, the Database Engine is just the same.

This section discusses how to deploy SQL Server in containers on Kubernetes, a container orchestration system initially developed by Google. Processes like fault tolerance, workload schedule, and even networking are all provided by the management layer of Kubernetes.

Once the orchestration is set up, you can configure and manage the databases inside the containers like any other SQL Server instances. One reason Kubernetes (also known as K8s, because there are eight letters between the K and the s) has become a staple in modern datacenters is its flexibility in container orchestration and management. It provides enterprise-level infrastructure functionality to the container development process favored by most DevOps organizations, making it, as Google describes it, the "operating system for the data center."

Let's use the analogy of an actual orchestra, comprising a conductor, instrument sections, musicians, their instruments, and their sheet music. While no analogy is perfect, this might help you picture things more easily. At the bottom are your musical instruments. Each instrument needs to be played by a musician, guided by their sheet music. Groups of musicians play together in a section. Finally, the conductor oversees the entire performance. In our analogy, Kubernetes is the conductor, containers are the instruments, clusters are the instrument families (like the string section or the brass section), and musicians are the pods with their sheet music.

Inside OUT

What is the difference between a Kubernetes cluster, a node, and a pod?

Kubernetes clusters consist of two types of nodes: *masters* and *workers*. The master nodes run cluster operations and schedule work, while the worker nodes run the container workloads. While the lowest unit of deployment is a container, it is important to note that containers are always deployed into higher-level pods. Pods provide location affinity within the cluster, meaning dependent workloads are deployed together.

Kubernetes relies on a software-defined infrastructure (the sheet music in our analogy). When you deploy your containers, you use a YAML (a recursive acronym standing for *YAML Ain't Markup Language*) file that defines:

- The container image you are using

- Any storage you are persisting

- The container CPU and memory configuration of the pod

- The networking configuration

- Other metadata about the deployment

The deployment manifest is converted from YAML to JSON by kubectl and then deployed to the Kubernetes API, where it is parsed and then deployed into a key-value store (called etcd) that stores the cluster metadata. The objects in the manifest are deployed in their respective pods, services, and storage. The cluster controller (part of the *control plane*) ensures that the manifest is running and is in a healthy application state, and redeploys the manifest in the event of node failure or an unhealthy application state. The cluster will always attempt to maintain the desired state of the configuration, as defined in the deployed manifests.

Inside OUT

What is the Kubernetes control plane?

The Kubernetes control plane is a set of processes and pods that control cluster management. These services record all the Kubernetes objects in the system and execute the desired state configuration for all objects within the cluster.

CHAPTER 4

Kubernetes support for SQL Server

Microsoft introduced support for Kubernetes after the release of SQL Server 2017 (see Figure 4-5). Early releases of Kubernetes lacked support for persisted storage, which is an obvious problem for database containers. The implementation uses a Kubernetes service to act as a persisted front-end name and IP address for the container. In this scenario, if the pod fails, the service stays running, and a new copy of the pod is launched and then pointed at the persisted storage. This is nearly analogous to the architecture of a SQL Server failover cluster instance (FCI).

➤ Refer to Chapter 2 for a more in-depth discussion on FCIs.

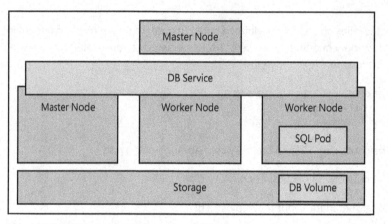

Figure 4-5 SQL Server on Kubernetes architecture.

The SQL Server Kubernetes deployment provides for just a single container per SQL Server pod. Services provide load balancing and persistent IP addressing, while *persistent volume claims* ensure that storage is persisted across container failures or node movement. By defining a persistent volume claim, you align a specific disk volume to your pod deployment to persist data files.

Recent releases of both Kubernetes and Windows Server allow Kubernetes to support both Windows nodes and Windows containers, but SQL Server currently only supports containers on Linux. Kubernetes is also much more broadly used on Linux, so community support will be much more prevalent on that platform.

➤ To learn more about Kubernetes, read *The Kubernetes Book* (2022) by Nigel Poulton and *Kubernetes: Up and Running* (2022) by Brendan Burns et al.

Inside OUT

What is OpenShift?

Many organizations deploy open-source software with a support agreement in place. Some common examples of this are Red Hat Enterprise Linux (RHEL) and Percona for MySQL databases. Red Hat has also introduced its own Kubernetes offering called OpenShift. While OpenShift is mainly core Kubernetes components, it also introduces some additional tooling into the space for licensed customers—specifically a project called Istio, which offers a service mesh management layer across Kubernetes clusters.

➤ You can find out more about RHEL in Chapter 5.

Deploy SQL Server in containers

As mentioned, SQL Server runs on Windows, on Linux, and in containers. When originally released with SQL Server 2017, container support was touted for use in development. After all, there was limited support in the container world for persisted storage at the time, and SQL Server lacked support for an enterprise orchestration framework like Kubernetes.

While database containers still make for a fantastic development environment, the support in SQL Server for availability groups and AD authentication means that container deployment is quickly becoming an option for production workloads as well.

➤ You can read more about availability groups in Chapter 11.

Get started with SQL Server in a Docker container

One of the biggest attractions of running SQL Server in a container is that your choice of OS does not matter. While the container images of SQL Server use Linux as their base, your host machine can run Windows, Linux, or macOS.

While containers can run on almost all host operating systems, SQL Server in containers is only supported for production on Linux hosts running Intel or AMD 64-bit CPU architecture.

NOTE

SQL Server containers do not run on Apple silicon. While SQL Server can run on Apple silicon using the Rosetta 2 emulator and a compatible container host, it is not a supported configuration.

First, you will need to install Docker Desktop on your workstation.

➤ Download Docker Desktop from *https://www.docker.com/products/docker-desktop*.

CHAPTER 4

After you have Docker installed, you can deploy a SQL Server container with the following steps:

1. Pull a copy of the container image from the Microsoft Container Registry (MCR) to your local environment. To do so, run this command from either a bash shell on Linux or macOS, or an elevated PowerShell prompt on Windows:

```
sudo docker pull mcr.microsoft.com/mssql/server:2022-latest
```

➤ You can find out more about the bash shell in Chapter 5 and about PowerShell in Chapter 9.

2. Use the following command to deploy the container. Note that the backslash in this command is a way to split a single bash command across multiple lines:

```
sudo docker run -e 'ACCEPT_EULA=Y' -e 'MSSQL_SA_PASSWORD=<YourStrong!Passw0rd>' \
   -p 1433:1433 --name sql2022 \
   -v /users/randolph/mssql:/mssql \
   -d mcr.microsoft.com/mssql/server:2022-latest
```

CAUTION

There is currently no secure way to obfuscate the SA password in a Docker deployment. Microsoft recommends that you change your SA password after you have deployed your container. Do not store the SA password in any saved configuration files. Be careful not to accidentally commit passwords in configuration files to source control.

You may be curious what these parameters (also called *switches* in Linux) mean:

- The docker pull command downloads the container image to your local container repository.

- The docker run command is where the deployment takes place.

- The -e switch allows for an environmental variable to be passed into the deployment. (Chapter 5 covers environment variables.) In this case, you are accepting the End-User License Agreement (EULA) for SQL Server, and providing a strong password for the SA account.

- The -p (or --publish; note the double-dash before the parameter) switch publishes the container's public and private port for your container. To run multiple SQL Server containers simultaneously, specify a TCP port other than 1433 for the subsequent containers that are deployed.

- The --name switch (note the double-dash before the parameter) specifies the name of your container. This is not required, but if it is not specified, the system will generate a name.

- The -v switch is probably the most important in terms of database use. It allows a persistent volume to be mounted from your local machine to your container. In this case, the local directory /users/randolph/mssql will appear in the container as /mssql. Use this directory to store database backups or data files to be mounted to the container.

- The -d switch refers to the container image you are deploying. In this case you are deploying a SQL Server 2022 container from the MCR.

➤ These are only a few of the command-line parameters that you might need. The full list is documented here: *https://docs.docker.com/engine/reference/commandline/run/*.

NOTE

Docker on macOS does not support persistent volumes. Microsoft recommends that you use separate data container volumes to persist data files that are stored in /var/opt /mssql/data. You can read the background on this issue at *https://github.com/microsoft /mssql-docker/issues/12*, and you can learn more about data container volumes at *https://docs.docker.com/storage/volumes/*.

Inside OUT

Can you use containers in development?

Yes. Development is one of the main uses for containers. Given the ease of deploying SQL Server in a container, you can envision a process where a software vendor builds orchestration to perform automated regression tests against every cumulative update (CU) of a release of SQL Server, or across multiple releases. This is just one excellent use case for databases in containers.

After the container is deployed, execute the docker ps command (which lists all the running containers) to confirm that your container is running. (In some environments you may need to run sudo docker ps.) Also, you can connect to your container using SQL Server tools like SSMS or Azure Data Studio, or sqlcmd, by connecting to localhost. This is possible because when you deployed the container, you configured it to run on TCP port 1433, which is the default SQL Server port.

```
randolph@charon        docker ps
CONTAINER ID     IMAGE                                          COMMAND
CREATED          STATUS            PORTS                        NAMES
24a2a3bda258     mcr.microsoft.com/mssql/server:2019-latest     "/opt/mssql/bin/perm…"
4 minutes ago    Up 4 minutes      0.0.0.0:1433→1433/tcp        sql2019
randolph@charon        sqlcmd -Usa -S localhost
Password:
1>
```

Figure 4-6 A screenshot of docker ps output and the sqlcmd connection.

NOTE

If you use a custom TCP port (or deploy multiple SQL Server containers) you can connect to `localhost` followed by the port number, separated with a comma. For example, `localhost,1455`.

You can also connect into your container with an interactive shell and execute `sqlcmd`. The first command will launch the bash shell within your container:

```
sudo docker exec -it sql1 "/bin/bash"
```

After launching the interactive bash shell within your container, you then call `sqlcmd` using the full path, since it is not in the path by default:

```
/opt/mssql-tools/bin/sqlcmd -S localhost -U SA -P '<YourNewStrong!Passw0rd>'
```

Once your SQL Server container is deployed, you can execute T-SQL just like it was any other SQL Server.

Get started with SQL Server on Kubernetes

Although running SQL Server in a single Docker container is relatively easy, running SQL Server on a Kubernetes infrastructure is more challenging.

Kubernetes as part of Docker Desktop

You can install Kubernetes with Docker Desktop. However, as mentioned, persistent volumes are not supported on Intel-based macOS. If you are using Docker on Windows and you are running Windows 10 or Windows 11 Professional, you can configure Kubernetes after enabling Hyper-V.

➤ You can find the instructions for deploying Docker with Kubernetes at *https://docs.docker.com/desktop/kubernetes.*

Kubernetes using minikube

Another commonly used option for development and testing of Kubernetes is minikube, which runs across Windows, Linux, and macOS. minikube is an open-source project that allows for a deployment to your local workstation.

➤ Configuring minikube is part of the main Kubernetes documentation, available at *https://kubernetes.io/docs/tutorials/hello-minikube.*

Kubernetes using the Azure Kubernetes Service

If you need to simulate a production environment, we recommend deploying using Azure Kubernetes Service (AKS). (See Figure 4-7.) AKS is a managed service that allows you to quickly deploy a Kubernetes cluster of 1 node or up to 100 nodes.

➤ Configuring AKS is part of the main Azure documentation, available at *https://learn.microsoft
.com/azure/aks/learn/quick-kubernetes-deploy-cli*.

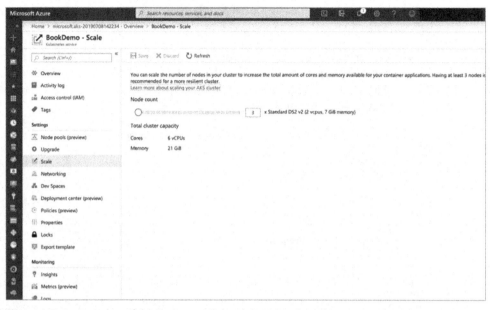

Figure 4-7 A screenshot of the Azure portal showing AKS scale options.

AKS offers the benefit of hosting a highly available control plane for the cluster in Azure, as
well as deploying the latest release of Kubernetes without installing software, worrying about
dependencies, or finding hardware to build on. The other benefit of AKS is that the service itself
is free. You are charged only for the underlying VM compute costs. Storage in AKS is provided
by using either Azure Managed Disks or the Azure File service that acts as a file share.

Deploy SQL Server on Kubernetes

Once you have a Kubernetes cluster or simulated cluster like minikube, you can start deploying
SQL Server. First, you will need to create a secret in Kubernetes to store your SA password:

```
kubectl create secret generic mssql --from-literal=MSSQL_SA_PASSWORD="<password>"
```

If kubectl (the Kubernetes command-line tool) is not installed on the machine where you are
managing your cluster, you will need to install it to manage your deployment.

➤ Instructions for installing kubectl are available at *https://kubernetes.io/docs/tasks/tools
/install-kubectl*.

Next, you will create a persistent volume claim (PVC). As mentioned, containers were originally
designed to be ephemeral and not persist data across restarts or failures. A PVC will ask the

cluster to provide a mapping to a persistent volume (PV). A PV can be statically or dynamically provisioned.

- A statically provisioned PV is defined by the cluster administrator. A PVC will be matched to that PV based on size and access mode.

- A dynamically provisioned PV is provisioned from a cluster-defined storage class. A PV asks the storage class to provision the volume from the underlying storage subsystem of the cluster. This can be a cloud provider's persistent volume such as Azure Managed Disks, or even an on-premises SAN.

If you are using Azure Kubernetes Services, save the following code to a file called pvc.yaml:

```
kind: StorageClass
apiVersion: storage.k8s.io/v1
metadata:
    name: azure-disk
provisioner: kubernetes.io/azure-disk
parameters:
  storageaccounttype: Standard_LRS
  kind: Managed
---
kind: PersistentVolumeClaim
apiVersion: v1
metadata:
  name: mssql-data
  annotations:
    volume.beta.kubernetes.io/storage-class: azure-disk
spec:
  accessModes:
  - ReadWriteOnce
  resources:
    requests:
      storage: 8Gi
```

This code defines the Azure storage class, and then an 8-GB volume. This code example uses Azure Storage, which is how you would implement on AKS. You will use slightly different code if you are using storage local to your cluster, like you do when using minikube or Docker:

```
kind: PersistentVolumeClaim
apiVersion: v1
metadata:
  name: mssql-data-claim
spec:
  accessModes:
  - ReadWriteOnce
  resources:
  requests:
   storage: 8Gi
```

Just like in the Azure example, save this file to pvc.yaml and then deploy using this `kubectl` apply command:

```
kubectl apply -f C:\scripts\pvc.yaml
```

CAUTION

`ReadWriteOnce` **is one of three access modes available for persistent volumes. It is the only option that allows both writes and single-node mounting. You will corrupt your databases if a volume is mounted by multiple writers.**

The next step is to deploy the SQL Server service and the pod itself. In the following code, you specify the load balancer service as well as the container running SQL Server. Kubernetes can use extensive metadata to describe and categorize your environment, as you will note from the metadata and label fields in the following YAML. Much like in the Docker script earlier, you define a port, passing in the SA password you defined in the secret and accepting the EULA. Finally, in the last section, you define the load balancer, which gives you a persistent IP address for your SQL instance.

```yaml
apiVersion: apps/v1
kind: Deployment
metadata:
  name: mssql-deployment
spec:
  replicas: 1
  template:
    metadata:
      labels:
        app: mssql
    spec:
      terminationGracePeriodSeconds: 10
      containers:
      - name: mssql
        image: mcr.microsoft.com/mssql/server:2022-latest
        ports:
        - containerPort: 1433
        env:
        - name: MSSQL_PID
          value: "Developer"
        - name: ACCEPT_EULA
          value: "Y"
        - name: MSSQL_SA_PASSWORD
          valueFrom:
            secretKeyRef:
              name: mssql
              key: MSSQL_SA_PASSWORD
        volumeMounts:
        - name: mssqldb
```

CHAPTER 4

```
            mountPath: /var/opt/mssql
        volumes:
        - name: mssqldb
          persistentVolumeClaim:
            claimName: mssql-data
---
apiVersion: v1
kind: Service
metadata:
  name: mssql-deployment
spec:
  selector:
    app: mssql
  ports:
    - protocol: TCP
      port: 1433
      targetPort: 1433
  type: LoadBalancer
```

You can save this YAML as sql.yaml. Then, using the same `kubectl apply -f` command, you can deploy it from where you manage Kubernetes.

Congratulations, you now have SQL Server running on Kubernetes. You can run the `kubectl get pods` and `kubectl get services` commands as shown in Figure 4-8 to see your deployment.


```
 randolph@charon  kubectl get services
NAME               TYPE           CLUSTER-IP     EXTERNAL-IP     PORT(S)          AGE
kubernetes         Cluster-IP     10.0.0.1       <none>          443/TCP          83m
mssql-deployment   LoadBalancer   10.0.149.78    52.183.90.238   1433:32495/TCP   31m
 randolph@charon  kubectl get pods
NAME                                READY   STATUS    RESTARTS   AGE
mssql-deployment-5bc9cc6d54-m9zlr   1/1     Running   0          31m
 randolph@charon 
```

Figure 4-8 A screenshot showing the load balancer and SQL Server pod in a Kubernetes deployment. © 2023 The Linux Foundation

If you review the output of the `kubectl get services` command, you will see the external IP address of your SQL Server service. You can now use any SQL Server client tool to connect to that address with the SA password you created in the secret.

CAUTION

This configuration exposes port 1433 to the Internet and should only be used for demonstration purposes. To secure your cluster for production usage, review AKS networking best practices at *https://learn.microsoft.com/azure/aks/best-practices*.

Review cluster health

Kubernetes provides a built-in dashboard for monitoring the overall health of your cluster and its resource use. If you are using AKS, you can view this by running the `az aks browse` command with the resource group and cluster names. Depending on the configuration and version of your cluster, you may need to create a cluster role binding to view the dashboard, as shown in Figure 4-9.

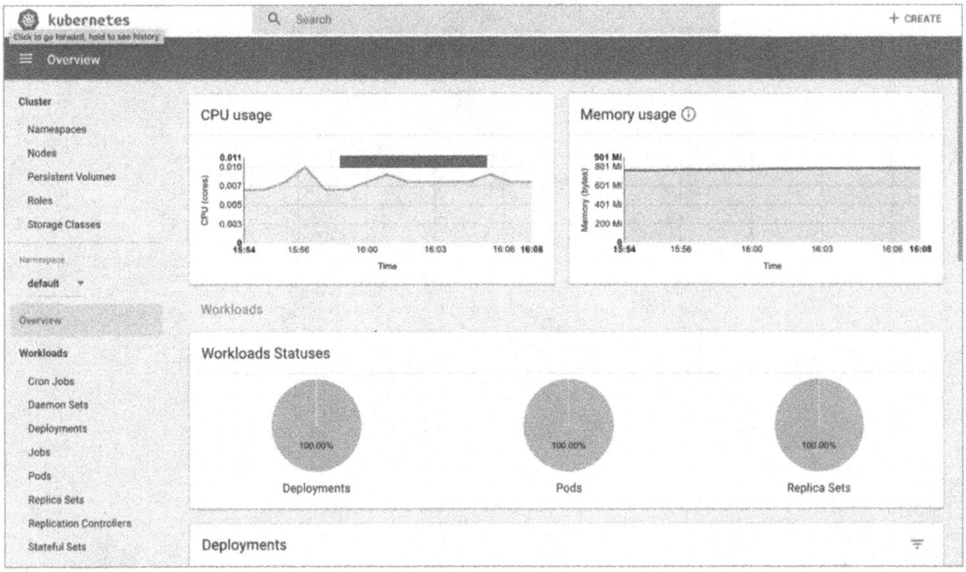

Figure 4-9 A screenshot of the Kubernetes web dashboard.

> ➤ If you are not using AKS, you can find instructions on installing and configuring a dashboard for your cluster at *https://kubernetes.io/docs/tasks/access-application-cluster/web-ui-dashboard*.

Kubernetes deployments move all your infrastructure into scripts. For some automation-focused administrators, this may be the holy grail that they have been waiting for. But it is important to manage these scripts just as you would your application code. They should be version-controlled in a source control system like Azure DevOps or GitHub. If you are hosting your own repositories, you should ensure they are backed up and highly available.

CHAPTER 4

Install and configure SQL Server on Linux

Since SQL Server 2017, you can install SQL Server on multiple platforms: Windows, Linux, and in containers. Chapter 4, "Install and configure SQL Server instances and features," discussed installing SQL Server on containers and in a Kubernetes environment, as well as performing setup and configuration on Windows Server.

This chapter covers Linux distributions, the basic differences between Windows and Linux, how to install SQL Server on the supported distributions of Linux, and the main differences in SQL Server on Windows and Linux. It is a shorter chapter because the differences are minimal.

What is Linux?

Linux, sometimes referred to as GNU/Linux, is an operating system (OS) including a *kernel*, *system libraries*, and a *package manager*. A Linux *distribution* (or *distro* for short) is a software collection composed of the Linux kernel, system libraries and tools, and numerous software packages (the equivalent of installer files on Windows), maintained by commercial and non-commercial organizations from all over the world.

Inside OUT

Why is it sometimes called GNU/Linux?

As mentioned in Chapter 2, "Introduction to database server components," a *kernel* is a low-level interface that manages computer hardware such as CPU, RAM, storage, and network devices. An operating system is software that provides an interface between the kernel and the applications that need to use it.

The Linux kernel was originally created by and named after a Finnish computer science student named Linus Torvalds, in 1991. When Torvalds made the kernel available for free online, it was then combined with an existing operating system called GNU (a recursive acronym that stands for "GNU's not Unix!") that was lacking its own kernel.

Even though many GNU packages are still included in the myriad Linux distributions under active development today, the name *GNU/Linux* is not widely used. Many distribution maintainers and software vendors, even the authors of this book, usually just say "Linux" to refer to the kernel and operating system.

There are several hundred distributions in active development worldwide, with many of the same software packages available in each one, so it can be confusing trying to pick a distribution. Microsoft supports SQL Server on three distributions, which makes your decision easier.

Like Windows Server Core, Linux distributions may offer a server-only configuration with a smaller package footprint and a command-line user interface. You can also install a desktop user interface through a *window manager* package, which is similar to the Windows desktop. To install SQL Server on Linux, you can use whichever server or desktop configuration you prefer. However, the desktop environment uses more system resources.

Inside OUT

Why use Linux?

For those of you who prefer Linux, you can run SQL Server natively in your existing environment without needing to run Windows. On the other hand, if you prefer Windows, you can continue using SQL Server on Windows without concerning yourself with Linux.

You can use SQL Server in containers for development and testing, but they are only supported on Linux and Kubernetes. Those container images are based on the Ubuntu distribution. We cover containers in Chapter 2, and deploying to Kubernetes in Chapter 4.

Differences between Windows and Linux

Windows is a *proprietary* OS created and maintained by Microsoft. Linux is an *open-source* OS created and maintained by a loose collection of volunteers, as well as various commercial and noncommercial organizations.

The main difference between Windows and Linux is philosophical. Because Linux is open source, if there is a feature you want to change or add, the end-user license lets you modify the source code yourself and recompile it. With a proprietary OS, the license does not permit modification, so you must submit a feature request and hope that enough people think it is a worthwhile addition.

On a technical level, Linux has a different directory structure, file system, and user interface from Windows. Applications written for one OS do not run natively on the other without some form of code modification or recompilation. For example, you cannot simply copy the sqlservr.exe file from Windows to Linux and run it. We cover this in more detail in the section "Caveats of SQL Server on Linux" later in this chapter.

NOTE

Code written in certain languages with their own runtime engines (for example .NET, Python, and Java) may run on both Windows and Linux if they access resources that are common to each OS.

Active Directory Domain Services authentication

Unlike with Windows, Active Directory Domain Services (AD DS) is not built into Linux and must be installed separately. SQL Server can then use Active Directory on both operating systems, which is recommended for centralized security and management. This allows you to extend your current Active Directory (AD) to access SQL Server instances on Linux as an extension of your Windows network.

➤ Setting up Kerberos authentication on Linux (which AD uses) is outside of the scope of this book, but you can learn how here: *https://learn.microsoft.com/sql/linux/sql-server-linux -active-directory-authentication.*

NOTE

SQL Server 2022 introduces Azure Active Directory (Azure AD) authentication powered by Azure Arc, which is not the same as Active Directory Domain Services (AD DS). To use Azure Arc with SQL Server on Linux, you need the Azure extension for SQL Server on Linux, just as you would on Windows.

➤ You can read more about Azure Arc in Chapter 4, and at *https://learn.microsoft.com/sql /sql-server/azure-arc/overview.*

File systems and directory structures

Windows Server supports NTFS and ReFS. Several file systems are supported on Linux and might differ between distribution and edition, but will usually be ext4. SQL Server is supported on both ext4 and XFS, because these two file systems provide similar features to NTFS, including journaling, large partitions, and fine-grained access control.

NOTE

A journaling file system keeps track of changes that are not yet committed. It helps prevent corruption in the case of a disaster—for example, after a power failure or system crash.

On Windows, individual volumes are addressed by a letter followed by a colon. For example, the default volume for a Windows OS is C: and all files beneath the root directory (C:\) are addressable through that drive letter. Files are stored logically in folders, and these folders and subfolders (also called *directories* and *subdirectories*) are located beneath the root directory on each drive and separated by a backslash (\).

On Linux, the directory structure is based off a root directory, called / (a single forward slash). While files are also stored in directories and subdirectories, everything, including individual drives, are addressed as subdirectories beneath the root directory separated by a slash (/).

NOTE

On Linux, the forward slash character (/) is just referred to as a slash. This differentiates it from a backslash (\).

Package managers

Every Linux distribution comes with a package manager to install, manage, update, and delete packages using online repositories. For practical purposes, this is the major difference between distributions when installing software.

When a package manager installs an application (the package), it connects to a central repository controlled by the distribution maintainer. You can also register a third-party repository to install packages outside of that distribution, provided the repository provides packages in the appropriate format.

Package managers use information from repositories to ensure that packages are compatible with one another, which makes it much easier to keep your system stable and up to date. This built-in dependency resolution means that you install only what you need. If a package is dependent on one or more other packages that are not installed, the package manager will automatically install those dependencies.

Inside OUT

How do you navigate around Linux?

On Windows, you typically employ a combination of the mouse and keyboard to navigate around the OS using the Start menu and File Explorer, and in SQL Server with Configuration Manager and Management Studio. You can also use the command prompt, or the new Windows Terminal, to run commands from a command-line interface (CLI).

On Linux, you interact with the OS (and SQL Server) using the CLI. This is known as a *shell*, the most common of which is called *bash* (Bourne again shell). Other common shells are *ksh* (Korn shell) and *zsh* (Z shell). In this book, all Linux script samples will run on bash.

NOTE

PowerShell runs on both Windows and Linux. You should familiarize yourself with PowerShell to give yourself an advantage managing SQL Server on both operating systems. You can learn more about this in Chapter 9, "Automate SQL Server administration."

Run commands with elevated privileges

Many commands for installing, configuring, and administering Linux require administrative privileges, just like on Windows. The commands are preceded by the sudo keyword, which stands for *superuser do*. This is less risky than logging in as the superuser account (*root*). You will be prompted for the root password when you run sudo for the first time after a fixed period (usually 15 minutes).

NOTE

Some Linux distributions do not allow you to log in directly as the root account for added security. We recommend using the sudo command as a best practice.

Linux distributions supported by SQL Server

As noted, several hundred choices make it difficult to decide on which Linux distribution you should install. For SQL Server, however, the choice is a lot easier because it is supported only on the following three commercial distributions:

- **Red Hat Enterprise Linux (RHEL).** Maintained by Red Hat, Inc., RHEL uses the RPM package manager through the command yum (which stands for *Yellowdog Updater, Modified*).

- **SUSE Linux Enterprise Server (SLES).** Maintained by SUSE Group, SLES uses the ZYpp package manager through the command zypper (which stands for *Zen/YaST Packages Patches Patterns Products*).

- **Ubuntu Server (Ubuntu).** Maintained by Canonical Ltd., Ubuntu uses the APT package manager through the command apt-get or aptitude (which stands for *Advanced Package engine*).

NOTE

Although Docker is included in the list of supported Linux distributions, this is not entirely accurate. Docker is just one of several OS-level virtualization engines on which you can deploy SQL Server containers. However, SQL Server containers are only supported for a production environment on Linux and Kubernetes. You can read more about Linux containers in Chapter 2, and about Kubernetes deployments in Chapter 4.

Having a vendor and support agreement behind an open-source implementation can be comforting and beneficial to organizations that have limited experience with a new technology stack. This support is especially valuable for SQL Server administrators starting out with Linux who are more familiar with Windows Server.

Considerations for installing SQL Server on Linux

As discussed in previous chapters, SQL Server has several considerations for CPU, RAM, and storage. In the vast majority of cases, you will apply the same principles as you would on Windows, with some minor caveats.

➤ We cover CPU and RAM configuration in Chapters 2, 3, and 4. The next section adds Linux-specific configuration using `mssql-conf`.

Configure OS settings

Microsoft recommends the following OS settings for a dedicated SQL Server instance to run optimally on Linux.

CAUTION

Some configuration settings do not persist between reboots, so you will have to create an init.d script, which runs at boot time. Refer to your distribution's documentation for details on how to configure the options that follow.

Configure high performance

Aside from the computer's BIOS, where high performance should be enabled (in other words, power saving should be disabled), you can also modify CPU settings at the Linux kernel level:

- Set the CPU frequency governor to 100% using the `cpupower` command.

- Use the `performance` option with the `x86_energy_perf_policy` command.

- Set the `min_perf_pct` setting to 100%.

- Set `C-States` to C1 only.

These CPU settings are functionally equivalent to enabling High Performance on Windows.

➤ You can read more about CPU C-States and power-saving modes at *https://www.hardwaresecrets .com/everything-you-need-to-know-about-the-cpu-c-states-power-saving-modes*.

Configure NUMA nodes

For computers with more than one NUMA node, use the `sysctl` command to disable auto-NUMA balancing, setting `kernel.numa_balancing` to 0. You do this because SQL Server handles NUMA internally.

Configure virtual address space

Chapter 2 discussed the working set, or memory provided by the OS for use by a process—in this case, SQL Server. The working set resides in a virtual address space, which in turn is mapped to physical memory by internal OS structures. The default setting for the number of memory map areas in virtual memory might not be sufficient for SQL Server on Linux, so you should use the `sysctl` command to change `vm.max_map_count` to the upper limit of 262144 (262,144).

Configure Transparent Hugepages

Certain Linux distributions, including Red Hat, provide improved performance on systems by increasing the size of memory blocks transparently to the underlying process. This is beneficial for applications with contiguous memory access patterns and works to SQL Server's advantage. Transparent Hugepages (THP) is already enabled on Linux by default, so you should leave this on for a dedicated SQL Server instance.

Set up the file system

As mentioned in Chapter 3, "Design and implement an on-premises database infrastructure," SQL Server on Linux requires either the ext4 or XFS file system. If the file system supports it, use a 64-KB block size to match the size of an extent. Otherwise, use the largest size that it supports. (For example, ext4 may only support a block size of 4 KB.) With newer storage subsystems and SANs, this block size is less important than it used to be.

By default, SQL Server places the data and log files in /var/opt/mssql/data. Notice that this path starts with a single forward slash, which is the root directory on a Linux system. This path then includes var, which is a default directory created for the OS to write data during normal operation. (*var* stands for *variable*.) Then, opt (which stands for *optional*) is for optional packages that are not included in a default installation of Linux. The next directory is mssql, which stands for *Microsoft SQL*.

> ### NOTE
> You can use *symbolic* or *hard links* to redirect the default data path to a different physical location (for instance, another drive), but we recommend using the `mssql-conf` tool to change the location instead, like you would on Windows.

A good practice is to keep transaction log files and tempdb on your fastest available storage. Additionally, you should mount volumes using the `noatime` attribute, which prevents tracking

CHAPTER 5

the last accessed time for that volume, thereby improving performance. This is managed in the file system table configuration file known as *fstab*. Refer to the fstab documentation for more information.

Recommended disk settings

For optimal settings at the physical disk level, you can set the disk read-ahead to 4096 bytes using the `blockdev` command. Additionally, there are several settings you can configure using the `sysctl` command:

- Set `kernel.sched_min_granularity_ns` to 10000000 (10,000,000).

- Set `kernel.sched_wakeup_granularity_ns` to 15000000 (15,000,000).

- Set `vm.dirty_ratio` to 40.

- Set `vm.dirty_background_ratio` to 10.

- Set `vm.swappiness` to 10.

CAUTION

Some `sysctl` settings may be overridden by modules that load later in the boot process. You can read more about this at *https://linux.die.net/man/8/sysctl*.

Inside OUT

How do you edit files on Linux?

You edit files on Linux from the command line. While there are many text editors available, not all of them are installed by default.

The default file editor that will nearly always be available is *vi* (visual editor). It is extremely powerful, but that means it is also complex. Opening files is a matter of running vi from the command line followed by the name of the file you want to create or modify. To save and quit from a vi session, however, you must type `:wq` and then press Enter. The colon instructs vi that you want to perform a command: The w writes (saves) the file, and q quits the session.

If you're new to Linux, you might find that the vi editor is quite different from what you're used to. In that case, you might want to replace it with *nano*, which you can install using your distribution's package manager. On Red Hat, you can install nano using the following command:

```
yum install nano
```

Install SQL Server on Linux

To integrate better with Linux, SQL Server leverages the package manager concept, meaning you only install the components you need, starting with the Database Engine package. This can drastically reduce the amount of time it takes to install SQL Server compared to Windows. For instance, on an Internet-connected machine with a high-speed connection, you can download, install, and configure SQL Server 2022 in under 5 minutes.

Table 5-1 shows which packages are available for SQL Server on Linux. The command-line tools include `sqlcmd` and `bcp`, which work the same as their Windows counterparts.

Table 5-1   SQL Server packages for Linux

Component	Package name
SQL Server Database Engine	`mssql-server`
Full-Text Search	`mssql-server-fts`
SQL Server Integration Services	`mssql-server-is`
PolyBase	`mssql-server-polybase`
SQL Server Agent (included in Database Engine)	`mssql-server-agent`
SQL Server command-line tools	`mssql-tools`
SQL Server 2022 Language Extensions	`mssql-server-extensibility`

> **NOTE**
>
> SQL Server Agent is installed with the Database Engine but is not enabled by default. To enable SQL Server Agent, use `mssql-conf` and set `sqlagent.enabled` to `true`. You can read more about `mssql-conf` in the section "Use mssql-conf to set up and configure SQL Server" later in this chapter.

Inside OUT

Can you install named instances on SQL Server on Linux?

No, you can only install a single instance of SQL Server on Linux on a machine. Named instances are not supported. Installing more than one instance (known as *instance stacking*) is also not supported on Linux.

If you need to install more than one SQL Server instance on the same machine, we recommend either creating individual virtual machines (VMs) per SQL Server install or using SQL Server in Linux containers. In general, maintenance is much easier when SQL Server is installed on separate virtual consumers (VMs or containers), because that has a lower impact on other software.

CHAPTER 5

You can find more information about virtual consumers in Chapter 2, and additional information about SQL Server in containers in Chapter 3. Chapter 4 discusses deploying containers in Kubernetes.

Installation requirements

The minimum system requirements for SQL Server on Linux are as follows:

- **CPU.** 2 GHz (x64-compatible), with two physical cores

- **Memory.** 3.25 GB RAM

- **Storage.** 6 GB (formatted with either ext4 or XFS)

NOTE

While SQL Server Express edition is artificially limited to 1,410 MB for the buffer pool, it can use additional memory for columnstore and memory-optimized objects. You can read more about edition scale limits at *https://learn.microsoft.com/sql/linux/sql-server -linux-editions-and-components-2022*.

Download and install packages

You can install SQL Server on a computer that is connected to the Internet or on an offline computer. In the latter case you must download the packages you need and copy them to the offline machine.

➤ A walk-through for installing SQL Server on each distribution is available at *https://learn .microsoft.com/sql/linux/sql-server-linux-overview*.

Download the third-party repository configuration file

You must download SQL Server packages directly from Microsoft because they are not available from the official distribution repositories. You must add the Microsoft package repository to the list of approved repositories on your computer, depending on which version of the Linux distribution you have installed.

NOTE

When you add a third-party repository, you must first import that repository's public keys to ensure that any files you are downloading are verified. Read more about public key encryption in Chapter 13, "Protect data through classification, encryption, and auditing."

The following sample bash command loads the package repository configuration for SQL Server 2022 for RHEL 8.x into the repository on your machine. In this example, the trailing space and backslash at the end of the first line are a bash convention to indicate that the command spans more than one line:

```
sudo curl -o /etc/yum.repos.d/mssql-server.repo \
https://packages.microsoft.com/config/rhel/8/mssql-server-2022.repo
```

Download the package

Once the package manager is configured to accept packages from Microsoft and the list of available packages is refreshed, you can install SQL Server immediately or download the packages for offline installation on another computer. For RHEL, the following command will download the package locally (as well as any dependencies):

```
sudo yum localinstall mssql-server_2022.x86_64.rpm
```

Install the package

Depending on the distribution and package manager, you will install the SQL Server Database Engine package using one of the following methods:

- **RHEL.** `sudo yum install -y mssql-server`

- **SLES.** `sudo zypper install -y mssql-server`

- **Ubuntu.** `sudo apt-get install -y mssql-server`

Each `install` command has a `-y` switch, which forces any prompts to agree to the question in the affirmative. This is useful for agreeing to install dependencies without prompting for each one—for example, in unattended installs (see the next section). If you want to confirm every prompt manually, you can remove the `-y` switch.

Perform an unattended installation

You can also install SQL Server on Linux using a shell script, which is recommended for production deployments and deployments across multiple servers, to ensure a consistent experience. The script should include all the steps you need to register the Microsoft package repository, download the requisite packages, and perform the post-installation configuration.

See the "Configure SQL Server on Linux" section later in this chapter for more information about post-installation steps. You can also get a sample bash script from Microsoft Docs, depending on the distribution you have chosen, from the following locations:

- **RHEL.** *https://learn.microsoft.com/sql/linux/sample-unattended-install-redhat*

- **SLES.** *https://learn.microsoft.com/sql/linux/sample-unattended-install-suse*

- **Ubuntu.** *https://learn.microsoft.com/sql/linux/sample-unattended-install-ubuntu*

CHAPTER 5

Update packages

With the Microsoft SQL Server package repository as an approved third-party option, the distribution's package manager will update SQL Server components (including cumulative updates) at the same time as other OS updates. This is functionally equivalent to the Windows Update feature titled "Receive updates for other Microsoft products."

To update the packages on your Linux OS, including any updates of SQL Server components you have installed, use the following commands:

- **RHEL.** `sudo yum update`

- **SLES.** `sudo zypper update`

- **Ubuntu.** `sudo apt-get update`

  NOTE

  On Red Hat Enterprise Linux, you must use `subscription-manager` to register your computer with the Red Hat Network (RHN) before updates will work.

Configure SQL Server on Linux

After you install the SQL Server Database Engine package, you need to configure SQL Server for the first time. This differs from the way SQL Server on Windows works (unless you perform an unattended install), because you can follow SQL Server Setup and configure the settings as you go, whereas on Linux, you configure SQL Server after it is installed.

Inside OUT

How do you configure the Linux firewall to allow access to SQL Server?

With both Linux and Windows, you need to open TCP port 1433 (and TCP port 1434 for the Dedicated Admin Connection) to allow access to your SQL Server instance from other machines on your network.

Each Linux distribution might have a different firewall package installed as the default, but on RHEL, the `firewalld` package can be configured with the following commands:

```
sudo firewall-cmd --zone=public --add-port=1433/tcp --permanent
sudo firewall-cmd --zone=public --add-port=1434/tcp --permanent
sudo firewall-cmd -- reload
```

The firewall configuration must be reloaded after it has been modified to take effect.

➤ You can read more about TCP ports in Chapter 13.

Use mssql-conf to set up and configure SQL Server

Windows uses the SQL Server Configuration Manager to configure SQL Server at the OS level. Linux does not have its own registry, so SQL Server's configuration is stored in a plain text file and accessed when the SQL Server service starts up.

You will initially interact with SQL Server through the CLI—most likely the bash shell. To configure SQL Server after installing the Database Engine package, you must run mssql-conf from the command line.

Inside OUT

Is there another way to configure SQL Server on Linux?

mssql-conf is the preferred method for setting up SQL Server on Linux. However, you can also use environment variables for initial (first-run) setup and to set up a SQL Server container on Linux, because containers generally do not use mssql-conf. We cover the container scenario in Chapter 4.

For initial configuration, you can use the following variables:

- **ACCEPT_EULA.** Required to use SQL Server. Can be set to any value.
- **MSSQL_PID.** The product ID, which can be Evaluation, Developer, Express, Web, Standard, Enterprise, or a product key.
- **MSSQL_SA_PASSWORD.** Must follow password complexity rules.
- **MSSQL_TCP_PORT.** Usually TCP port 1433.

➤ You can view a complete list of these environment variables at *https://learn.microsoft.com /sql/linux/sql-server-linux-configure-environment-variables*.

NOTE

The mssql-conf tool is written in Python, as are several other command-line tools for working with SQL Server. When you install SQL Server on Linux, you may notice that one of the dependencies installed is the Python package.

Configuration settings

The executable package for mssql-conf is in the /opt/mssql/bin path. You can see that /opt is a directory off the root directory where optional packages are stored, and mssql stands for Microsoft SQL. The bin directory stands for binaries, which are functionally the same as executable files on Windows.

CHAPTER 5

> **NOTE**
>
> **To execute a binary file on Linux and other Unix-like operating systems, you must either provide the full path to the binary or, if you have navigated to the directory already, you must prefix the binary with ./ (a period and a slash).**

mssql-conf uses a configuration file (called mssql.conf), which is a plain text file located at /var/opt/mssql/mssql.conf. Remember that /var is where files are written to, which is a convenient way to remember the difference between /opt and /var/opt.

The mssql-conf tool has two phases: first-run (initial) setup, and configuration, both of which we cover next.

> **NOTE**
>
> **Once your SQL Server instance has been set up the first time, you can connect to it from any computer running SQL Server Management Studio, Azure Data Studio, sqlcmd, or mssql-conf—indeed, any tool that can connect to SQL Server.**

First-run setup

From bash, run the following command to enter the configuration tool to configure SQL Server 2022 on Linux:

```
sudo /opt/mssql/bin/mssql-conf setup
```

You are presented with a numbered list. If you make an error, you can quit the tool and run it again.

Choose the correct edition

SQL Server on Linux might not ask you to enter a license key. When you set up SQL Server for the first time, you are prompted for the edition you will be using. The following editions are available (this list is copied from the mssql-conf setup prompt):

1. Evaluation (free, no production use rights, 180-day limit)

2. Developer (free, no production use rights)

3. Express (free)

4. Web (PAID)

5. Standard (PAID)

6. Enterprise (PAID)—CPU Core utilization restricted to 20 physical/40 hyperthreaded

7. Enterprise Core (PAID)—CPU Core utilization up to Operating System Maximum

8. I bought a license through a retail sales channel and have a product key to enter.

Make your selection based on the edition you want to install and move on to the next prompt. You are shown the path to the license agreement, and then prompted to accept that agreement.

The Evaluation, Developer, and Express editions are free and do not require a paid license, but you will still be prompted to agree to the license terms. A good guideline for choosing a license is that if you plan to process production data under any circumstances (including if you want to test your database backups), you cannot use the Evaluation or Developer edition, and must purchase a paid license. Alternatively, you can use the artificially limited Express edition.

Choose the language

Now you are prompted to choose a default language for the SQL Server instance. You can choose from among 11 different options: English, German, Spanish, French, Italian, Japanese, Korean, Portuguese, Russian, Simplified Chinese, or Traditional Chinese.

Choose a SQL Server system administrator password

Your system administrator (SA) password should be a strong password. Microsoft's guidance is to choose an alphanumeric password with a minimum length of eight uppercase and lowercase characters, including letters, digits, and symbols. If you plan to use AD authentication, you can disable this account later.

> ## NOTE
>
> **Our password recommendation is similar, but you should increase the minimum length to 15 characters. You can generate and save the password using a password manager, so there is no need to pick a memorable password. You should not use the sa account directly unless it is an emergency or you are setting up the instance.**

After you choose a password, you will be prompted to confirm it. Once that's done, the SQL Server service will restart, taking these settings into account.

Configure the SQL Server instance

The configuration settings for SQL Server are managed using the same `mssql-conf` tool, replacing the SQL Server Configuration Manager on Windows.

CHAPTER 5

Inside OUT

How do you manage the SQL Server service on Linux?

Like Windows, Linux has services, called *daemons*. You can start, stop, and restart the SQL Server service using the following commands:

- **Stop SQL Server** `systemctl stop mssql-server`
- **Start SQL Server** `systemctl start mssql-server`
- **Restart SQL Server** `systemctl restart mssql-server`

Remember to restart the SQL Server service after you have changed the configuration.

There is a wide range of settings that you can use to customize your SQL Server instance. This is a brief overview of what is available (taken from *https://learn.microsoft.com/sql/linux/sql-server-linux-configure-mssql-conf*):

- **Agent.** Enables SQL Server Agent. Although SQL Server Agent is installed along with the Database Engine, you still need to enable it.

- **Collation.** Sets a new collation for SQL Server on Linux.

- **Customer Feedback.** Specifies whether SQL Server sends feedback to Microsoft. This option cannot be disabled on free editions.

  ➤ You can read more about the collection of usage and diagnostic data at *https://learn.microsoft.com/sql/sql-server/usage-and-diagnostic-data-configuration-for-sql-server-tools*.

- **Database Mail Profile.** Sets the default database mail profile for SQL Server on Linux.

- **Default Data Directory.** Sets the default directory for new SQL Server database data files (.mdf). As noted in Chapter 3, we recommend moving this to a dedicated volume.

- **Default Log Directory.** Changes the default directory for new SQL Server database log (.ldf) files. As noted in Chapter 3, we recommend moving this to a dedicated volume.

- **Default Master Database Directory.** Changes the default directory for the master database and log files. As noted in Chapter 3, we recommend moving this to a dedicated volume.

- **Default Master Database File Name.** Changes the name of master database files. We do not recommend changing this in the normal course of business, but it is useful in a disaster recovery scenario when restoring a master database.

- **Default Dump Directory.** Changes the default directory for new memory dumps and other troubleshooting files. You can set the dump file type using the Dump Type option (see below).

- **Default Error Log Directory.** Changes the default directory for new SQL Server ERROR-LOG, Default Profiler Trace, System Health Session XE, and Hekaton (Memory-Optimized) Session XE files.

- **Default Backup Directory.** Changes the default directory for new backup files. We recommend moving this to a dedicated volume separate from the data and log files to ensure business continuity should a drive failure occur.

- **Dump Type.** Sets the type of memory dump file to collect in the event of a crash or exception in a SQL Server process. Each size setting (Mini, Miniplus, Filtered, and Full) provides a different level of detail in a memory dump for troubleshooting purposes. You can set the path for the dump directory using the Default Dump Directory option (see above).

- **High Availability.** Enables availability groups.

➤ See Chapter 11, "Implement high availability and disaster recovery," for more information about availability groups on Linux.

- **Local Audit Directory.** Sets a directory to add local audit files.

- **Locale.** Sets the locale for SQL Server to use, in the form of a language code identifier (LCID).

- **Memory Limit.** Sets the memory limit for SQL Server. Avoid going over the default of 80 percent of the maximum physical memory available on the server; Linux will terminate the SQL Server instance without warning if it detects high resource utilization.

➤ You can read more about the aptly named out-of-memory (OOM) killer at *https://lwn.net /Articles/317814*.

- **TCP Port.** Changes the port on which SQL Server listens for connections. Do so only if you have a specific business case. We do not recommend changing it for security reasons because a network sniffing tool will detect the new port almost instantly.

- **TLS.** Configures Transport Layer Security (TLS). This is used to enforce encryption and to configure the path to the certificate and private key. You can also set TLS versions here, but Microsoft recommends only using TLS 1.2 (and higher when available). We cover TLS in more depth in Chapter 13. If you use Kerberos authentication to connect your SQL Server instance to AD, the Kerberos keytab file is also configured here.

- **Trace Flags.** Sets the trace flags that the service is going to use. We recommend enabling at least Trace Flag 3226, which disables messages in the error log for successful database backups.

CHAPTER 5

Caveats of SQL Server on Linux

SQL Server on Linux is implemented using a thin translation layer called the SQL Platform Abstraction Layer (SQLPAL), which maps Windows system calls to Linux system calls. This allows the exact same code for the Database Engine to be used on both operating systems. So, the Linux version does not have internal awareness that it is running on a different platform, and as far as SQL Server is concerned, it is running inside Windows.

➤ You can read the introduction from the SQL Server team on how SQLPAL came about at *https://cloudblogs.microsoft.com/sqlserver/2016/12/16/sql-server-on-linux-how-introduction/*.

This platform abstraction is both hugely powerful and limiting. It is powerful because now SQL Server runs on Windows, Linux, in containers, and on ARM64 devices with Azure SQL Edge. But it is limiting because only enough Windows system calls have been translated to the underlying OS to get these to work. Certain features are not available due to this limitation, including access to the Windows Registry. Only a very small stub of the Registry is included to support the required Windows system calls (including the Windows Data Protection API).

➤ You can find out more about Azure SQL Edge at *https://azure.microsoft.com/products/azure-sql/edge/*.

We covered the lack of a Registry to explain why mssql-conf replaces SQL Server Configuration Manager in the previous section, but several other features of SQL Server, which are dependent on Windows features, have not been implemented.

Missing SQL Server features on Linux

The list of features not available for SQL Server 2022 on Linux has shrunk since SQL Server 2017 was released. Microsoft has stated that new features will be enabled over time. If you need any of the following features, you must use SQL Server on Windows.

- SQL Server Analysis Services (SSAS)

- SQL Server Reporting Services (SSRS) (however, the SSRS databases can be hosted on a Linux instance)

- Master Data Services (MDS)

- Data Quality Services (DQS)

- FILESTREAM and FileTable (requires NTFS or ReFS)

- Extended stored procedures

- Volume Shadow Copy Service (VSS) snapshots

- Buffer Pool Extension

- SQL Server Agent Alerts

A few other features are available, but with limitations:

- **Database Mirroring.** This feature is in maintenance mode. We recommend that you use another high availability solution such as log shipping or availability groups. We cover availability groups on Linux and Windows in Chapter 11.

- **SQL Server Integration Services (SSIS).** There is a component that lets you run SSIS packages, but the feature is quite limited otherwise. Another side effect is that the designer for Maintenance Plans in SQL Server Management Studio does not work.

- **SQL Server Browser Service.** Linux does not allow more than one instance, so this is not a significant gap.

NOTE

Stretch Database was never supported on Linux, and with SQL Server 2022 it has been deprecated.

➤ To stay up to date on unsupported features on Linux, visit *https://learn.microsoft.com/sql /linux/sql-server-linux-editions-and-components-2022#unsupported-features-and-services*.

CHAPTER 5

CHAPTER 6

Provision and configure SQL Server databases

This chapter reviews various strategies for creating new databases and adding existing databases to a SQL Server. It covers considerations for database migrations, including key points to remember when moving databases from instance to instance and various strategies for moving databases. It also reviews the creation of new user databases and discusses important database properties to be aware of throughout the application development lifecycle.

All scripts for this book are available for download at *https://www.MicrosoftPressStore.com /SQLServer2022InsideOut/downloads*.

Add databases to a SQL Server instance

Chapter 3, "Design and implement an on-premises database infrastructure," discussed several database configurations, including the physical configuration of files and storage.

Although many of the same database settings are available and should be considered for Azure SQL Database, the remainder of this chapter refers to SQL Server databases on both Windows and Linux as well as on Azure SQL Managed Instance. For information on Azure SQL Databases, see Chapter 17, "Provision Azure SQL Database."

> **NOTE**
> If you are tasked with moving or upgrading databases, you must understand how to create new databases. Later in this chapter, we'll discuss tools to assist with upgrading database-compatibility levels and other important considerations for database migrations.

Inside OUT

If SQL Server installed databases on my instance, does that make them system databases?

Just because a database is shipped and installed by Microsoft as part of a SQL Server feature, it doesn't mean it counts as a system database.

CHAPTER 6

In SQL Server Management Studio (SSMS), in Object Explorer, you'll see at least four system databases, and perhaps additional databases for SQL Server Reporting Services (SSRS) and SQL Server Integration Services (SSIS) if you have installed these features.

Only the four standard system databases placed in the system subfolder of Object Explorer are considered system databases in various features inside SQL Server, namely master, model, msdb, and tempdb.

The distribution database, for the replication feature, will also appear in the systems subfolder if present. The ReportServer, ReportServerTempDB, and SSISDB databases are Microsoft-installed user databases.

In maintenance plans or catalog views such as sys.databases, you will see these SSRS and SSIS databases treated as user, not system, databases. This is an important distinction for disaster recovery planning, configuration, and policy enforcement.

Create a database

This section reviews the basics of database settings and configuration. As a database administrator (DBA), you might not regularly create databases from scratch, but you should be familiar with most of the settings and design decisions that go into database creation, including the addition of database files and the required tools and/or syntax to set and validate your settings.

Manage default settings

It is important to understand the role of the model database when creating new databases, regardless of the method of creation. The model database and its entire contents and configuration options are copied when creating most new databases, including tempdb upon service restart. For this reason, you should never store any data (even for testing) in the model database. Similarly, do not grow the model database from its default size, because this will cause all future databases to be that size or larger. Even if you specify a smaller size than the model database, the files created will be the size of the model database.

The location of the model database's files is not, however, used as a default for new databases. Instead, the default location for database files is at the server level.

You can view these default storage locations, which we recommend you change and must be valid, in the **Server Properties** window in SSMS, on the **Database Settings** page. There you will find the default locations for data, log, and backup files, which are stored in the Windows Registry. On the **Database Settings** page, you'll also see the **Recovery Interval** setting, which is **0** by default, meaning that SQL Server can manage the frequency of internal automatic checkpoints. This typically results in an internal checkpoint frequency of 1 minute.

NOTE

The Recovery Interval setting is not the same as the TARGET_RECOVERY_TIME setting at the database level. We'll discuss TARGET_RECOVERY_TIME for individual databases later in this chapter, in the section "Indirect checkpoints." Just be aware that changing the instance-level recovery interval setting is not the same as changing the TARGET_RECOVERY_TIME in each database.

Also on the **Database Settings** page of **Server Properties** are the **Default Index Fill Factor** and **Default Backup Compression** settings. These are server-level defaults applied to each database. However, you cannot configure them separately for each database. You can change fill factor with each index operation or choose a different backup compression option each time you perform a backup.

Inside OUT

Can default data and log file locations cause future cumulative updates to fail?

Portions of cumulative updates reference the default file locations. Patches will fail if these default database locations change to an invalid path, if the complete subfolder path does not exist, or if SQL Server loses permissions to access the locations. You might see errors such as "Operating system error 3 (The system cannot find the path specified.)" in the detailed log of the cumulative update. You will need to restart the cumulative update after correcting the problem with the default locations.

The following settings are inherited by new databases from the model database unless they are overridden at the time of creation:

- Initial data and log file size

- Data and log file autogrowth setting

- Data and log file maximum size

- Recovery model

- Target recovery time (overrides the system default recovery interval)

- All database-scoped configurations, including the database-level settings for legacy cardinality estimation, MaxDOP, parameter sniffing, and Query Optimizer fixes

- All automatic settings, including auto close, auto shrink, and auto create/update statistics (discussed later in this chapter)

➤ View the full list at *https://learn.microsoft.com/sql/relational-databases/databases/model-database*.

CHAPTER 6

Inside OUT

Can your SSMS connections to the model database block CREATE DATABASE statements?

User connections, including query windows in SSMS with the model database context, can block the creation of user databases. Close or disconnect any SSMS query windows that use the model database context. If you are configuring the model database by using Transact-SQL (T-SQL) commands, you might inadvertently leave SSMS query windows open. Create database statements need to reference the model database.

You might see the error, "Could not obtain exclusive lock on database 'model.' Retry the operation later. CREATE DATABASE failed. Some file names listed could not be created. Check related errors. (Microsoft SQL Server, Error: 1807)." For applications like SharePoint that create databases, this could lead to application errors.

Own the databases you create

The login that runs the CREATE DATABASE statement will become the owner of any database you create, even if the account you are using is not a member of the sysadmin group. Any principal that can create a database becomes the owner of that database, even if, for example, they have only membership to the dbcreator built-in server role.

Ideally, databases are not owned by named individual accounts. You might decide to change each database to a service account specific to that database's dependent applications. You must do this after the database is created.

➤ For more information on best practices with respect to database ownership and how to change the database owner, see Chapter 12, "Administer instance and database security and permissions."

NOTE

If your server is an Azure Arc–enabled server, you can change the database to use an Azure Active Directory (Azure AD) group using the AUTHORIZATION statement. For step-by-step instructions, visit *https://learn.microsoft.com/sql/t-sql/statements/alter-authorization -transact-sql*. You can read more about installing Azure Arc–enabled servers in Chapter 4, "Install and configure SQL Server instances and features."

Create additional database files

Every SQL Server database needs at least one data file and one log file. You can use additional data files to maximize storage capacity, management, and performance. However, there is no performance advantage to be gained with more than one transaction log file for a database. SQL Server does not write to them randomly, but sequentially.

➤ We discuss physical database architecture in detail in Chapter 3.

The only scenario in which a second transaction log file could be needed is if the first fills up its volume. If no space can be created on the volume to allow for additional transaction log file data to be written, the database cannot accept new transactions and will refuse new application requests. In this scenario, one possible troubleshooting method is to temporarily add a second transaction log file on another volume to create the space to allow the database transactions to resume accepting transactions. The end resolution involves clearing the primary transaction log file, performing a one-time-only shrink operation to return it to its original size, and removing the second transaction log file. There is no other performance or stability benefit to having a second transaction log file.

Use SQL Server Management Studio to create a new database

You can create and configure database files, specifically their initial sizes, in SSMS. To begin, in Object Explorer, right-click **Databases** and select **New Database** in the shortcut menu to open the **New Database** dialog box.

After you have configured the new database's settings, but before you select **OK**, you can script the T-SQL for the CREATE DATABASE statement.

Here are a few suggestions when creating a new database:

- Pre-grow your database and log file sizes to an expected size. This avoids autogrowth events as you initially populate your database. You can greatly speed up this process by using the Perform Volume Maintenance Task policy for the SQL Server service account so that instant file initialization is possible.

  ➤ Chapter 3 covers instant file initialization.

- Consider the simple recovery model for your database until it enters production use. Then, the full or bulk-logged recovery models might be more appropriate.

  ➤ For more information on database backups and the appropriate recovery model, see Chapter 10, "Develop, deploy, and manage data recovery."

- Review the logical and physical file names of your database and the locations. The default locations for the data and log files are server-level settings, but you can override them here. You also can move the files later (covered later in this chapter).

- As soon as the database is created, follow up with your backup strategy to ensure that it is covered as appropriate with its role. This may involve adding it to an existing maintenance plan, SQL Server Agent job, or third-party backup application.

CHAPTER 6

Deploy a database via SQL Server Data Tools

You can also deploy developed databases to a SQL Server instance using a database project in SQL Server Data Tools (SSDT). SSDT provides a professional and mature environment for teams across your enterprise to develop databases, check them into source control, generate change scripts for incremental deployments, and reduce object scripting errors.

SSDT can generate incremental change scripts using the Data Compare feature or deploy databases directly. It also has the option to drop or re-create databases for each deployment, although this is turned off by default.

You might find it easiest to create the new database by using SSMS and then deploy incremental changes to it with SSDT.

Move existing databases

There are several strategies for moving or copying a SQL Server database from one instance to another. You should consider each as it relates to necessary changes to application connection strings, DNS, storage, and security environments. This section reviews a few options for migration.

Restore a database backup

Restoring a backup is an easily understandable way to copy data from one instance to another. You can also carry out this method in a way that minimizes outages.

Let's compare two simplified migration processes. The following is a sample migration checklist using only a full backup/restore:

1. Begin the application outage.

2. Perform a full backup of the database on the old instance.

3. Copy the database backup file to the new server.

4. Restore the full backup on the new instance.

5. Resolve any SQL-authenticated login issues or any other changes necessary before directing database queries to the new instance.

   ➤ This is covered in more detail in Chapter 12, in the section, "Perform common security administration tasks."

6. Change the connection strings in applications and/or DNS and/or aliases.

7. End the application outage.

➤ **For more information on types of database backups and database restores, see Chapter 10.**

In the preceding scenario, the application outage must last the entire span of the backup, copy, and restore, which for large databases could be quite lengthy—even with native SQL Server backup compression reducing the file size. Ultimately, however, doing it with the downtime is faster and less complex.

Instead, consider the following strategy:

1. Perform a full backup of the database on the old instance.

2. Copy the database backup file to the new server.

3. Restore the full backup using the `WITH NORECOVERY` option on the new instance.

4. Begin the application outage.

5. Take a differential backup and then a log backup of the database on the old instance.

6. Copy the differential backup file and the log backup file to the new server.

7. Restore the differential backup file `WITH NORECOVERY` on the new instance.

8. Restore the transaction log backup `WITH RECOVERY` on the new instance.

9. Resolve any SQL-authenticated login issues or any other changes necessary before directing database queries to the new instance.

10. Change the connection strings in applications, DNS, and/or aliases.

11. End the application outage.

In this scenario, the application outage spans only the duration of the differential and transaction logs' backup/copy/restore operations, which for large databases should be a tiny fraction of the overall size of the database.

This scenario does require more preparation and scripting in advance, as well as coordination with the usual backup system responsible for transaction log backups. By taking a manual transaction log backup, you can create a split transaction log backup chain for another system. You'll want to account for this in your planning.

Attach detached database files

Detaching, copying, and attaching database files also accomplishes the goal of placing the database on a new instance. It is relatively straightforward to disassociate (detach) the files from the old SQL Server, copy the files to the new instance, and then attach the files to the new SQL Server. This is largely limited by the data-transfer speed of copying the files. You might also consider moving the SAN drives to the new server to decrease the time spent waiting for files to copy.

Attaching copied database files can be faster than restoring a full database backup; however, it cannot minimize the outage by taking advantage of transaction log backups (see earlier).

Copying the full set of database files (remember, these might contain many more files than just the .mdf and .ldf files, including secondary data files and FILESTREAM containers) is not faster than restoring a transaction log backup during the application outage, and is not a true recovery method. Because database backup files can also be compressed natively by SQL Server, the data-transfer duration between old and new servers will be reduced by using the backup/restore strategy.

Move data with BACPAC files

A BACPAC file is an XML format file that contains the database schema and row data, allowing for the migration of databases, ideally at the start of a development/migration phase (although not for large databases). SSMS can both generate and import BACPAC files, and the Azure portal can import them when moving an on-premises SQL Server to Azure SQL Database.

NOTE

Some features of SQL Server change how the engine stores information in database files. Databases that contain these features cannot be moved to editions of SQL Server that do not support them. To check if the database you are moving has any of these features, and to find out what they are, query sys.dm_dm_persisted_sku_features.

Upgrade database compatibility levels

SQL Server databases upgraded from an older version to a newer version will retain the prior compatibility level. Compatibility level is a database-level setting.

For example, restoring or attaching a database from SQL Server 2012 to SQL Server 2022 will result in the database assuming the SQL Server 2012 (110) compatibility mode. This is not necessarily a problem, but it does have consequences with respect to how you can use features or whether you can leverage improvements to performance. You will have to manually promote the database to SQL Server 2022 compatibility level 160.

Inside OUT

Are there any Microsoft-provided tools to assist with a database migration and/or upgrade?

To assist upgrade projects and aid consumption of Azure services, Microsoft has developed tools for the evaluation and even the migration of data.

The Data Migration Assistant (DMA) is important for legacy upgrades of databases from older versions. A clean assessment from DMA is needed and highly recommended for a Microsoft-supported upgrade of an old database. The DMA can help identify T-SQL code, features, or options not supported in a newer version, and can suggest the necessary remediation. The target of a DMA-supported migration can be any of the three Azure SQL platforms or an on-premises SQL Server installation.

The Azure Database Migration Service (DMS) is a managed service to handle the upgrade and migrations of SQL Server databases to Azure. It relies on the DMA's assessment and recommendations, but can help you take the next step of moving the data to an Azure platform—especially when a simple backup and restore is not possible, as with Azure SQL Database.

We'll discuss Azure Database Migration Service in more detail in Chapter 18, "Provision Azure SQL Managed Instance," and Chapter 19, "Migrate to SQL Server solutions in Azure."

You can view the compatibility level of a database in SSMS. To do so, right-click a database in Object Explorer and select **Properties**. Then, on the **Options** page, notice the current setting in the **Compatibility Level** list box. You can also view this setting for all databases in the system catalog via sys.databases, in the compatibility_level column.

You can change the compatibility level setting by choosing a new value from the **Compatibility Level** list box. Alternatively, you can use the ALTER DATABASE command to change the COMPATIBILITY_LEVEL setting.

SQL Server provides database compatibility modes for backward compatibility with database-level features, including improvements to the Query Optimizer, additional fields in dynamic management objects, syntax improvements, and other database-level objects.

Inside OUT

Are there any new breaking code changes to SQL Server?

Since SQL Server 2005 and database compatibility level 90, there have been very few changes to allowed syntax that would cause working T-SQL code to break in a newer version of SQL Server. As a rare example, the FASTFIRSTROW syntax stopped working in compatibility level 110. T-SQL code that works as far back as compatibility level 90 will almost certainly execute in SQL Server 2022 and compatibility level 160, though performance could vary. As mentioned, it is strongly recommended to use the Microsoft Data Migration Assistant (DMA) tool on SQL Server 2008 and later versions to assess a database.

CHAPTER 6

For example, some recent syntax additions, such as the STRING_SPLIT() and OPENJSON func-tions, added in SQL Server 2016, do not work when run on a database in a prior compatibility level. Some syntax improvements, such as DATEFROMPARTS() and AT TIME ZONE, will work in any database in any database compatibility mode in SQL Server 2017 or later.

SQL Server 2022 supports compatibility levels down to SQL Server 2008 (internal version 100). Any database attached or restored that was on compatibility level 90 will be upgraded to ver-sion 100. This minimum has been the same since SQL Server 2016. Any attempt to set a database compatibility level lower than 100 will fail.

Changing the database compatibility level does not require a service restart, but we strongly recommend that you *not* perform this operation during normal operating hours. Promoting the database compatibility level should be thoroughly tested in preproduction environments. Even though syntax errors are unlikely in the newer compatibility level, other changes to the Query Optimizer engine from version to version could result in performance changes that must be evaluated prior to rollout to a production system. At the very least, the compatibility level change could cause widespread cached plan invalidation and an immediate CPU spike due to plan compilation.

> ➤ For more information on the differences between compatibility levels in SQL Server ver-sions, see "Differences between compatibility levels" at *https://learn.microsoft.com/sql /t-sql/statements/alter-database-transact-sql-compatibility-level#differences-between -compatibility-levels.*

Inside OUT

When should you keep a database in a prior compatibility mode?

It is a common forget to promote the database compatibility level to the new SQL Server version level after a database upgrade. You will miss out on new database features, but there can be good—albeit temporary—reasons to keep a database in a prior compatibility mode. Changes from version to version in SQL Server are additive and rarely regressive.

The most common reason to run a database in a prior compatibility mode is not technical; rather, the administrator might be limited by vendor support or software certification.

One notable exception relates to a feature introduced in SQL Server 2014: Improvements to the cardinality estimator resulted in the same or better performance for most situations, but poor query performance in rare situations. In the case of a query whose performance regressed when executed in compatibility level 120 or higher, forcing the legacy cardinality estimator back into use is the most realistic near-term solution. Changing the database's compatibility mode down to SQL Server 2012 (110) would accomplish this, but three more appropriate options are available, listed here in order of preference:

- The `LEGACY_CARDINALITY_ESTIMATION` database-scoped configuration option, introduced in SQL Server 2016, can force the old cardinality estimation model into use only for that database. It has the same effect on the database at Trace Flag 9481.
- Trace Flag 9481 will force a database in SQL Server 2014 compatibility mode to use the legacy cardinality estimation model from SQL Server 2012 and earlier.
- You can modify an individual query to use the legacy cardinality estimator with `OPTION (USE HINT ('FORCE_LEGACY_CARDINALITY_ESTIMATION'));`, which has been available since SQL Server 2016 with Service Pack 1.

NOTE

You can upgrade the SSISDB database, which contains the SSIS Catalog, independently of other databases by using the SSISDB Upgrade Wizard. This makes it easier to move your SSIS packages and environments from instance to instance by restoring or attaching a database from a previous version to a SQL Server 2022 instance. For more information, visit *https://learn.microsoft.com/sql/integration-services/install-windows/upgrade-integration-services-packages-using-the-ssis-package-upgrade-wizard*.

Other considerations for migrating databases

As an administrator, you'll need to move a database from one instance to another—perhaps to refresh a preproduction environment, to move to a new SQL Server instance, or to promote a database into production for the first time.

In addition to database compatibility levels and SQL Server database version and compatibility modes, when copying a database into a new environment, you'll need to keep the following in mind:

- SQL Server edition
- SQL logins
- Encryption
- Database settings

Let's look at each of these in more detail.

SQL Server edition

Editions generally progress upward in terms of cost and feature set, beginning with Express, Web, Standard, and finally Enterprise edition. (Developer edition is the same as Enterprise edition, except you can use it in a production environment.) Moving a database instance up from Express, Web, or Standard edition expands the features available for use in the database.

The concern for DBAs is when database instances need to move *down* from Enterprise, Standard, or Web edition. Many features that were historically exclusive to Enterprise edition were included in Standard edition for the first time in SQL Server 2016 with Service Pack 1, expanding what we could do with Standard edition as developers and administrators.

You will encounter errors related to higher-edition features when restoring or attaching to an instance that does not support that edition. There are fewer of these all the time, and many are in the realm of capacity or tuning more than in core features. This is important because you cannot turn off the use of higher-edition features on the lower-edition instance; you must disable the use of these features before restoring or attaching the database to a lower-edition instance.

You can avoid this problem by using a dynamic management view that lists all edition-specific features in use. Keep in mind that some features are supported in all editions but are limited. For example, memory-optimized databases are supported even in the Express edition, but with only a small amount of allocated memory.

To view all edition-specific features in use in each database, run the following query:

```
SELECT feature_name
FROM sys.dm_db_persisted_sku_features;
```

This DMV may return no records if no edition-sensitive features are in use in the current database context. However, if, for example, you create a partitioning function for horizontal table partitioning, the DMV will immediately return a row for the feature name "Partitioning." While table partitioning is supported in all editions of SQL Server, certain performance benefits of table partitioning are supported only in the Enterprise edition—for example, partitioned table parallelism and distributed partitioned views. Thus, the performance of your partitioned tables may vary from edition to edition.

> ➤ For more information on the data returned by sys.dm_db_persisted_sku_features, visit *https://learn.microsoft.com/sql/relational-databases/system-dynamic-management-views /sys-dm-db-persisted-sku-features-transact-sql*. For more information on features by edition, visit *https://learn.microsoft.com/sql/sql-server/editions-and-components-of-sql-server-2019*.

SQL logins

SQL-authenticated logins and their associated database users are connected via security identifier (SID), not by name. When moving a database from one instance to another, the SIDs in the

SQL logins on the old instance might be different from the SIDs in the SQL logins on the new instance, even if their names match. After migration to the new instance, SQL-authenticated logins will be unable to access databases where their database users have become "orphaned," and you must repair this. This does not affect Windows Authenticated logins for domain accounts.

This condition must be repaired before applications and end users can access the database in its new location. Refer to the "Orphaned SIDs" section in Chapter 12.

The database owner should be included in the security objects to be accounted for on the new server. Ensure that the owner of the database, listed either in the **Database Properties** window or the owner_sid column in the sys.databases catalog view, is still a valid principal on the new instance.

For databases with partial containment, contained logins for each type will be restored or attached along with the database. This should not be a concern.

Transparent data encryption

Transparent data encryption (TDE) settings will follow the database as it is moved from one instance to another, but the certificate and its security method will not. For example, the server certificate created to encrypt the database key, and the private key and its password, are not backed up along with the database. This is, after all, the entire purpose of TDE—to prevent a database from being attached or restored to a server that lacks the proper certificate.

These objects must be moved to the new instance along with the database *before* any attempt to restore or attach the database. They must also be backed up and securely stored with the rest of your enterprise security credentials, certificates, and sensitive data.

> ### NOTE
>
> **Restoring an unencrypted database over an encrypted database is allowed. When might you inadvertently do this? If you restore a backup from the database before it is encrypted, you will end up with an unencrypted database. You must then reapply TDE.**

➤ For more information on TDE, see Chapter 13, "Protect data through classification, encryption, and auditing."

Database configuration settings

You should review database-specific settings at the time of migration. You can review them with a quick glance of the sys.databases catalog view or from the database **Properties** window in SSMS.

The following is not a complete list of database settings; we cover these and many more later in the chapter. You should pay special attention to these settings when restoring, deploying, or attaching a database to a new instance:

- **Read only.** If the database was put in READ_ONLY mode before the migration to prevent data movement, be sure to change this setting back to READ_WRITE.

- **Recovery model.** Different servers might have different backup and recovery methods. In a typical environment, the full recovery model is appropriate for production environments when the data loss tolerance of the database is smaller than the frequency of full backups, or when point-in-time recovery is appropriate. If you are copying a database from a production environment to a development environment, you will likely want to change the recovery model from Full to Simple. If you are copying a database from a testing environment to a production environment for the first time, you will likely want to change the recovery model from Simple to Full.

NOTE

After changing a database recovery model from Simple to Full, immediately take a full backup of the database to start the transaction log recovery chain. Then, you can start taking transaction log backups at regular intervals.

> For more information about database backups and the appropriate recovery model, see Chapter 10.

- **Page verify option.** For all databases, this setting should be CHECKSUM. The legacy TORN_PAGE_DETECTION option is a sign that this database has been moved over the years up from a pre-SQL Server 2005 version but this setting has never changed. Since SQL Server 2005, CHECKSUM has been the superior and default setting, but it requires an administrator to manually change. Always take a full database backup before changing this setting.

    Unfortunately, just changing this setting is not sufficient. Checksums are not immediately created when you change the page verify option to CHECKSUM, so the data pages are not protected right away. To apply the checksums manually, rebuild all indexes in the database.

> For more information about the important page verify option in each database, see the section "Set the database's page verify option" in Chapter 8, "Maintain and monitor SQL Server."

- **Trustworthy.** It is not recommended to ever enable this setting unless doing so is necessary because of an inflexible architecture requirement. Using this setting to mark a database as trustworthy could allow malicious activity on one database to affect other databases, even if specific permissions have not been granted. It is crucial not only to ensure this setting is disabled, but also to understand cross-database permission chains in a multitenant or web-hosted shared SQL Server environment.

If this setting was enabled on a previous system and was required because of external assemblies, cross-database queries, and/or Service Broker, you will need to turn it on again on the new server (assuming it's still needed).

If your application security model depends on the Trustworthy setting, you must remember to enable it after restoring or attaching the database. When restoring a database, Trustworthy is set to off no matter the value when it is backed up.

NOTE

The Trustworthy setting tells SQL Server that the contents of the database should be trusted. It allows certain operations like cross-database access and common language runtime (CLR) assemblies to access data outside the server. It is not recommended unless there are no other options available, as it is not a secure method of communication between servers.

➤ **For more on object ownership, see Chapter 12.**

Database-scoped configurations

Database-scoped configurations were introduced in SQL Server 2016 and Azure SQL Database v12. They represent a container for a set of configuration options available at the database level. In earlier versions, these settings were available only at the server or individual query level, such as Max Degree of Parallelism (MaxDOP).

➤ **For more information on parallelism and MaxDOP, see Chapter 14, "Performance tune SQL Server."**

You should evaluate these options for each database after it is copied to a new instance to determine whether the settings are appropriate. The desired MaxDOP, for example, could change if the number of logical processors differs from the original system.

You can view each of these database-scoped configurations in SSMS. In Object Explorer, right-click a database and select **Properties** in the shortcut menu. In the **Database Properties** window, in the pane on the left, select **Options**. On the **Options** page, a **Database-Scoped Configurations** heading appears at the top of the **Other Options** list.

The current database context is important for determining which database's properties will be applied to a query that references objects in multiple databases. This means the same query, run in two different database contexts, will have different execution plans—potentially because of differences in each database's MaxDOP setting, for example. If there is a discrepancy between levels, such as the server level or query level, the more granular level overrides higher levels.

CHAPTER 6

Among the new features introduced in SQL Server 2022 are two new and related database-scoped configurations you should know about:

- **Degree of Parallelism Feedback (DOP_FEEDBACK).** This is a Query Store–dependent feature that automatically adjusts the degree of parallelism for repeated queries. (See the next section for more information about Query Store.) It compares the runtime statistics with previous plans after each execution. If the new plan is not the same or better, the feedback is cleared.

- **ASYNC_STATS_UPDATE_WAIT_AT_LOW_PRIORITY.** This option enables you to avoid concurrency issues with the Auto Update Statistics Asynchronously setting.

Database properties and options

This section reviews some commonly changed and managed database settings. There are quite a few settings on the **Options** page in the **Database Properties** window, many involving rarely changed defaults or ANSI-standard deviations for legacy support.

You can view each of these settings in SSMS via Object Explorer. To do so, right-click a database and select **Properties** in the shortcut menu. Then, in the **Database Properties** window, in the pane on the left, select **Options**. You also can review database settings for all databases in the sys.databases catalog view.

The subsections that follow discuss the settings that you need to consider when creating and managing SQL Server databases.

Collation

Collations exist at three levels in a SQL Server instance:

- Database

- Instance

- tempdb

By default, the collation of the tempdb database matches the collation of the instance and should differ only in otherwise unavoidable circumstances. Ideally, the collations in all user databases match the collation at the instance level and for tempdb, but there are scenarios in which an individual database might need to operate in a different collation.

Often, databases differ from the server-level collation to enforce case sensitivity. But you can also enforce language usage differences (such as kana or accent sensitivity) and sort order differences at the database level.

The default collation for the server is decided at installation and is preselected for you based on your operating system's regionalization settings. You can (and should) override this during installation. Some applications require a case-sensitive collation.

Although the server-level collation is very difficult to change (see Chapter 4), databases can change collation. You should change a database's collation only before code is developed for the database, or only after extensive testing of existing code.

Unmatched collations in databases could cause performance issues when querying across those databases, so you should try to avoid collation differences between databases that will be shared by common applications. For example, if you write a query that includes a table in a database that's set to the collation SQL_Latin1_General_CP1_CI_AS (which is case insensitive and accent sensitive) and a join to a table in a database that's set to SQL_Latin1_General_CP1_CS_AS (which is case sensitive and accent sensitive), you will receive the following error:

```
Cannot resolve the collation conflict between "SQL_Latin1_General_CP1_CI_AS" and "SQL_
Latin1_General_CP1_CS_AS" in the equal to operation.
```

Short of changing either database to match the other, you will need to modify your code to use the COLLATE statement when referencing columns in each query. The following sample succeeds in joining two sample database tables together, despite the mismatched database collations:

```
SELECT * FROM CS_AS.sales.sales s1
INNER JOIN CI_AS.sales.sales s2
ON s1.[salestext] COLLATE SQL_Latin1_General_CP1_CI_AS = s2.[salestext];
```

NOTE

In contained databases, collation is defined at two different levels: the database and the catalog. You cannot change the catalog collation from Latin1_General_100_CI_AS_WS_KS_SC. Database metadata and variables are always in the catalog's collation. The COLLATE DATABASE_DEFAULT syntax can also be a very useful tool if you know the collation before execution.

Inside OUT

How do you take advantage of the new UTF-8 support?

SQL Server 2019 introduced support for UTF-8 collations, such as Latin1_General_100_CI_AS_SC_UTF8. Now you can choose an instance-level UTF-8 collation or configure databases or individual tables with UTF-8 collations.

UTF-8 is the most popular character-encoding set for XML, HTML, and the World Wide Web. More than 90 percent of web pages are encoded with UTF-8. Until SQL Server 2019, nvarchar and nchar data types supported only UTF-16, while varchar and char support encoding via a code page, such as Windows Latin 1, Code Page 1252. You may be familiar with these options if you worked with flat files in SSIS development.

Choosing a UTF-8 collation allows for a wider variety of character values inside the `varchar` and `char` data types, at a fraction of the storage compared to UTF-16 in `nvarchar` or `nchar` in most cases.

➤ For more about UTF-8 in SQL Server 2019, see Chapter 7, "Understand table features."

Recovery model

The full recovery model is appropriate for production environments in which the database's data-loss tolerance is smaller than the frequency of full backups or when point-in-time recovery is necessary. As mentioned earlier in this chapter, if you are copying a database from a production environment to a development environment, you will likely want to change the recovery model from Full to Simple. If you are copying a database from a testing environment to a production environment for the first time, you will likely want to change the recovery model from Simple to Full, then immediately take a full backup to begin the recovery chain.

➤ For more information on database backups and the appropriate recovery model, see Chapter 10.

Compatibility level

SQL Server provides database compatibility levels for backward compatibility to database-level features, including improvements to the Query Optimizer, additional fields in dynamic management objects, syntax improvements, and other database-level objects.

Compatibility level is a database-level setting. Databases upgraded from an older version to a newer version will retain a prior compatibility level. You must manually promote a database's compatibility level when restoring up to a new version of SQL Server.

NOTE

As mentioned, reverting the database's compatibility level to SQL Server 2012 (110) was a common tactic when databases were first upgraded to SQL Server 2014 because of changes to the cardinality estimator. There are multiple more nuanced and less drastic methods for dealing with the new cardinality estimator, however. Refer to the section "Upgrade database compatibility levels" earlier in this chapter for more information.

Containment type

Partially contained databases represent a fundamental change in the relationship between server and database. They are an architectural decision that you make when applications are intended to be portable between multiple SQL Server instances or when security should be entirely limited to the database context, not in the traditional server login/database user sense.

➤ For more information about the security implications of contained databases, see Chapter 12.

Azure SQL databases are themselves a type of contained database. They can move from host to host in the Azure platform-as-a-service (PaaS) environment, transparent to administrators and users. You can design databases that can be moved between SQL Server instances in a similar fashion, should the application architecture call for such capability.

Changing the containment type from None to Partial converts the database to a partially contained database and should not be taken lightly. We do not advise changing a database that has already been developed without the partial containment setting, because there are differences with how temporary objects behave and how collations are enforced. Some database features, including change data capture (CDC), change tracking, replication, and some parts of Service Broker, are not supported in partially contained databases. You should carefully review, while logged in as a member of the sysadmin server role or the db_owner database role, the system dynamic management view sys.dm_db_uncontained_entities for an inventory of objects that are not contained.

Auto close

You should enable this setting only in very specific and resource-exhausted environments. When this feature is enabled, it can cause performance degradation on busy databases because of the increased overhead of opening and closing the database after each connection. AUTO_CLOSE also flushes the procedure cache after each connection. When active, it unravels the very purpose of application connection pooling—for example, rendering certain application architectures useless and increasing the number of login events. You should never enable this setting as part of performance tuning or a troubleshooting exercise on a busy environment.

Auto create statistics

When you enable this setting, the Query Optimizer automatically creates statistics needed for runtime plans, even for read-only databases. (Statistics are stored in tempdb for read-only databases.) Some applications, such as SharePoint, handle the creation of statistics programmatically; due to the dynamic nature of its tables and queries, SharePoint handles statistics creation and updates by itself. Unless a sophisticated, complex application like SharePoint insists otherwise, you *should* enable this setting. You can identify auto-created statistics in the database; they use a naming convention similar to _WA_Sys_<*column_number*>_<*hexadecimal*>.

Inside OUT

What are statistics?

SQL Server uses statistics to describe the distribution and nature of data in tables. The Query Optimizer needs the auto create statistics setting to be enabled so it can create single-column statistics when compiling queries. These statistics help the Query Optimizer create optimal runtime plans. Without relevant and up-to-date statistics, the Query Optimizer might not choose the best way to execute queries.

CHAPTER 6

➤ For much more about statistics objects, see Chapter 15, "Understand and design indexes."

Auto create incremental statistics

Introduced in SQL Server 2014, this setting allows for the creation of statistics that take advantage of table partitioning, reducing the overhead of statistics creation. This setting has no impact on nonpartitioned tables. You should enable this setting because it can reduce the cost of creating and updating statistics.

Once enabled, this setting will have an effect only on newly created statistics. To affect existing statistics objects on tables with partitions, you should update the statistics objects to include the INCREMENTAL = ON parameter, as shown here:

```
UPDATE STATISTICS [Purchasing].[SupplierTransactions]
[CX_Purchasing_SupplierTransactions] WITH RESAMPLE, INCREMENTAL = ON;
```

When INCREMENTAL = ON, the statistics are re-created as per partition statistics. When OFF, the statistics tree is dropped and SQL Server recomputes the statistics. This is why you need to change the setting. You should also, when applicable, update any manual scripts you have implemented to update statistics to use the ON PARTITIONS parameter, as demonstrated here:

```
UPDATE STATISTICS [Purchasing].[SupplierTransactions]
[CX_Purchasing_SupplierTransactions] WITH RESAMPLE ON PARTITIONS (1);
```

To determine whether statistics were created incrementally, you can check the value of the is_incremental column in the sys.stats catalog view.

Auto shrink

You should *never* enable this setting. It will automatically return any free space of more than 25 percent of the data file or transaction log to the file system. You should shrink a database only as a manual, one-time operation to reduce file size after unplanned or unusual file growth. This setting will result in unnecessary fragmentation and overhead. After completion, it may result in frequent rapid log autogrowth events as the database resizes itself again.

Auto update statistics

When this setting is enabled, statistics will be updated periodically. The Query Optimizer considers statistics to be out of date when a ratio of data modifications to rows in the table has been reached. The Query Optimizer checks for and updates the out-of-date statistic before running a query plan and therefore has some overhead, though the performance benefit of updated statistics usually outweighs this cost. This is especially true when the updated statistics result in a better optimization plan. Because the Query Optimizer updates the statistics first and then runs the plan, the update is described as synchronous.

Auto update statistics asynchronously

This setting changes the behavior of the auto update statistics setting in one important way: Query runs will continue even if the Query Optimizer has identified an out-of-date statistics object. The statistics will be updated afterward.

NOTE

Enabling the Auto Update Statistics setting is a prerequisite for the Auto Update Statistics Asynchronously setting to have any effect. There is no warning or enforcement in SSMS for this.

Inside OUT

Should you enable Auto Update Statistics and Auto Update Statistics Asynchronously in SQL Server 2022?

Yes! (Again, unless the application specifically recommends not to, such as SharePoint.)

Starting with database compatibility level 130, the ratio of data modifications to rows in the table that helps identify out-of-date statistics has been aggressively lowered, causing statistics to be automatically updated more frequently. This is especially evident in large tables in which many rows are regularly updated. In SQL Server 2014 and earlier, this more aggressive behavior was not on by default, but could be enabled via Trace Flag 2371, starting with SQL Server 2008 R2 with Service Pack 1.

Since SQL Server 2016, it is more important than in previous versions to enable Auto Update Statistics Asynchronously, which can reduce the overhead involved in automatic statistics maintenance and provide for more consistent query performance.

Allow snapshot isolation

This setting allows for the use of snapshot isolation (SI) mode at the query level. When you enable this setting, the row versioning process begins in tempdb, though this setting does little more than allow for this mechanism to be used in this database. To begin to use SI mode in the database, you must change code—for example, to include SET TRANSACTION ISOLATION LEVEL SNAPSHOT.

➤ For much more on snapshot isolation, see Chapter 14.

Read committed snapshot isolation (RCSI)

Enabling the read committed snapshot isolation (RCSI) setting changes the default isolation mode of the database from READ COMMITTED to READ COMMITTED SNAPSHOT (RCSI). While RCSI can be beneficial and is the enterprise, scalable solution for concurrency issues, you should not enable this setting during regular business hours; instead, do it during a maintenance window. Ideally, however, this setting is on and accounted for during development.

When RCSI is enabled, the snapshot uses optimistic concurrency control, withholding any locks that would prevent other transactions from updating rows. If a snapshot transaction attempts to commit an update to a row that was changed after the transaction began, the transaction is rolled back and an error is raised.

Enabling RCSI will have an immediate impact to the use of the local database, and potentially the tempdb database as well, in the form of rising IO_COMPLETION and WAIT_XTP_RECOVERY wait types, so you need to perform proper load testing. This setting, however, potentially results in a major performance improvement and this is the core of enterprise-level concurrency.

Multiple factors could determine whether snapshot versions are contained in the user database or in tempdb. When RCSI is enabled, long-running transactions can also prevent the cleanup of the persistent version store (PVS) when the accelerated database recovery (ADR) feature is enabled. This isn't typically a problem, but you should understand and monitor for a growing PVS when ADR is enabled.

➤ SQL Server 2022 introduced performance improvements for ADR and its PVS cleanup process. For more information, see *https://learn.microsoft.com/sql/relational-databases /accelerated-database-recovery-troubleshoot.*

➤ For much more about RCSI, see Chapter 14.

Page verify option

For all databases, this setting should be CHECKSUM. The presence of the legacy TORN_PAGE _DETECTION or NONE option is a sign that this database has been restored up from a pre-SQL Server 2005 version, but this setting has never changed. Since SQL Server 2005, CHECKSUM has been the superior and default setting. Always take a full database backup before changing this setting.

Unfortunately, just changing this setting is not sufficient to apply checksums to each data page. Checksums are not immediately created when you change the page verify option to CHECKSUM, so the data pages are not protected right away. To apply the checksums manually, rebuild all indexes in the database.

For more information about the important page verify option setting in each database, see the section "Set the database's page verify option" in Chapter 8.

Trustworthy

It is not recommended to ever enable this setting unless it is made necessary because of an inflexible architecture requirement. Using this setting to mark a database as trustworthy could allow malicious activity on one database to affect other databases, even if specific permissions have not been granted. Before enabling this setting, you should understand the implications of cross-database ownership chains in a multitenant or web-hosted shared SQL Server environment.

➤ For more on object ownership, see Chapter 12.

Database Read-Only

You can set an older database, or a database intended for nonchanging archival, to READ_ONLY mode to prevent changes. Any member of the server sysadmin role or the database db_owner role can revert this to READ_WRITE, so you should not consider this setting a security measure.

Query Store

Introduced in SQL Server 2016, the Query Store is a built-in data gathering and reporting mechanism for measuring and tracking cached runtime plans. It is highly recommended, as it provides historical data for queries, not just for cached plans.

Though extremely useful, Query Store is not active by default in older versions of SQL Server. With the introduction of SQL Server 2022, Query Store is enabled by default in new databases. Shortly after the release of SQL Server 2022, the Query Store will be enabled by default in new databases in Azure SQL Database and Azure SQL Managed Instance. You should turn it on as soon as possible if you intend to use it to aid performance tuning and troubleshooting cached runtime plans.

➤ For more information on the Query Store, as well as retrieving cached query plans, see Chapter 14.

Inside OUT

How can you best use the Query Store to help with a database compatibility level upgrade?

Consider using the Query Tuning Assistant (QTA) tool, which has been part of SSMS since version 18. The QTA leverages the Query Store to evaluate workloads before and after a compatibility level change and to identify regressed queries.

The QTA also works hard to generate the best possible plan from various Query Optimizer models. Unlike the Database Engine Tuning Advisor (DTA), the QTA does not and cannot generate workloads; it only observes workloads. For more information on the QTA, other tools, and strategies for migrating a SQL Server database to Azure, see Chapter 19.

CHAPTER 6

Indirect checkpoints

If your database was created in SQL Server 2016 or later, it is already configured to use indirect checkpoints, as it has been the default setting for all new databases since then—even if you created the database in a previous compatibility level.

By default, in databases created in SQL Server 2016 or higher, this setting is 60 seconds. In databases created in SQL Server 2012 or 2014, this option was available, but set to 0, which indicates that legacy automatic checkpoints are in use.

Databases created on prior versions of SQL Server, however, will continue to use the classic automatic checkpoint, which has been in place since the 1990s (SQL Server 7.0) with only minor tweaks.

Inside OUT

What is a checkpoint?

A *checkpoint* is the process by which SQL Server writes to the drive both data and transaction log pages modified in memory, also known as *dirty* pages.

You can issue checkpoints manually by using the CHECKPOINT command, but doing so is rarely necessary, and is usually limited to troubleshooting, because checkpoints are issued automatically in the background for you.

Before SQL Server 2016 and since SQL Server 7.0, all databases use *automatic* checkpoints by default. The rate at which dirty pages are committed to memory has increased with versions, as disk I/O and memory capacities of servers have increased. The aim of automatic checkpoints was to ensure that all dirty pages were managed within a goal defined in the recovery interval server configuration option. By default, this was 0, which meant automatic checkpoints were in effect. The effective timing of a checkpoint tended to be around 60 seconds, but was highly variable, and was generally unrelated to the number of pages dirtied by transactions between checkpoints.

An *indirect* checkpoint follows a new strategy of taking care of dirty pages that is far more scalable and can improve performance, especially on modern systems with a large amount of memory. Indirect checkpoints manage dirty pages in memory differently; instead of scanning memory, they proactively gather lists of dirty pages. Indirect checkpoints then manage the list of dirty pages and continuously commit them from memory to the drive, on a pace to not exceed an upper bound of recovery time. This upper bound is defined in the TARGET_RECOVERY_TIME database configuration option.

So, even though the recovery time goal hasn't really changed, the method by which it is achieved has. Indirect checkpoints are significantly faster than automatic checkpoints, especially as servers are configured with more and more memory. You might notice an improvement specifically in the performance of backups.

You can configure a database created on an older version of SQL Server to use indirect checkpoints instead of automatic checkpoints with a single command: TARGET_RECOVERY_TIME. The value will be 0 for databases still using automatic checkpoint. The master database will also have a TARGET_RECOVERY_TIME of 0 by default. Consider setting TARGET_RECOVERY_TIME to 60 seconds to match the default for all databases created in SQL Server 2016 or higher, as shown here:

```
ALTER DATABASE [database_name] SET TARGET_RECOVERY_TIME = 60 SECONDS;
```

You can check this setting for each database in the TARGET_RECOVERY_TIME_IN_SECONDS column of the sys.databases catalog view.

> ### NOTE
>
> As of SQL Server 2016, a specific performance degradation involving nonyielding schedulers or excessive spinlocks can arise due to the TARGET_RECOVERY_TIME setting being applied to the tempdb by default. It is not common, however. It is identifiable and resolvable with analysis and a custom solution to disable indirect checkpoints on the tempdb, as detailed in this blog post from the SQL Server Tiger Team at *https://learn .microsoft.com/archive/blogs/sql_server_team/indirect-checkpoint-and-tempdb-the-good -the-bad-and-the-non-yielding-scheduler*.

➤ For more on the differences between the different checkpoint types and on the interaction between the database TARGET_RECOVERY_TIME setting and the server's recovery interval setting, see *https://learn.microsoft.com/sql/relational-databases/logs/database-checkpoints -sql-server*.

Accelerated database recovery (ADR)

New in SQL Server 2019, accelerated database recovery (ADR) does not appear in the SSMS Database Properties page as of this writing, nor is it enabled by default. There are trade-offs to be aware of that we'll discuss later, but this is a powerful, much-desired feature of SQL Server that is available in both Enterprise and Standard editions.

You can enable ADR with the following T-SQL statement:

```
ALTER DATABASE [database_name] SET ACCELERATED_DATABASE_RECOVERY = ON;
```

> ### NOTE
>
> ADR is enabled by default in Azure SQL Database and Azure SQL Managed Instance, and cannot be disabled.

Enabling ADR requires exclusive access to the database and could be blocked by other connections to the database, which might require the closure of other connections. You can see the status of this setting in the catalog view sys.databases, in the new column `is_accelerated_database_recovery_on`.

ADR represents a significant overhaul of the SQL Server recovery process. It is a reworking of the machinery that the Database Engine uses to recover each database on:

- SQL Server instance startup, especially after an unexpected shutdown

- Rollback of a long-running transaction

- Availability group failover

ADR results in much faster recovery times in these scenarios, including near-instant recovery for many operations. ADR accomplishes this by way of a new progressive log management pattern inside the transaction log that eliminates the need for the transaction log to ever be scanned from the beginning of the oldest active transaction. Instead, it can be processed at recovery from only the last successful checkpoint. With ADR, the transaction log is aggressively truncated, even in the presence of active long-running transactions, which prevents it from growing out of control.

The trade-offs include an increase in storage requirements for each user database with ADR enabled. This could require a sudden increase of 10 percent or more space in the user database file, so administrators should be aware of this impact.

You should monitor and consider the growth of the persistent version store (PVS) for ADR. The PVS is a local version store to retain previous state information for transactions, especially long-running transactions. The presence of snapshot isolation queries and/or enabling the RCSI database setting can increase retention of versions in the PVS.

> ➤ Microsoft has provided a variety of troubleshooting scenarios and monitoring solutions, including using the `sys.dm_tran_persistent_version_store_stats` DMV. For more information, see *https://learn.microsoft.com/sql/relational-databases/accelerated-database -recovery-troubleshoot*.

SQL Server 2022 brings several improvements to ADR and the PVR cleanup process, including lower memory usage for tracking pages that require cleanup and the ability to clean locked pages.

NOTE

Database mirroring, the maintenance mode ancestor to availability groups, is not supported for databases with ADR enabled.

Move and remove databases

Earlier in this chapter, we discussed database migrations from older to newer servers and the considerations involved. This section reviews the steps and options for moving databases inside a SQL Server instance and the various methods and stages of removing databases from use.

Move user and system databases

This section discusses moving the physical location of database files, the most common reasons for this being either because of improper initial locations or the addition of new storage volumes to a server. Relocating system and user databases involves similar processes, with the master database being an exception. Let's look at each scenario.

Locate SQL Server files

As discussed in the checklist earlier in this chapter, you can review the location of all database files by querying the sys.master_files catalog view. If you did not specify the intended location for the data files while you were on the Data Directories page of the Database Engine Configuration step of SQL Server Setup, you will generally find your system database files on the OS volume at %programfiles%\Microsoft SQL Server*instance*\MSSQL\Data.

> NOTE
>
> In the sys.master_files catalog view, the physical name of each file, the logical name (specified when you create/add a file to a database), and the name of the database may not match in some situations. It is possible, through restore operations, to accidentally create multiple databases with the same logical file names. Before moving database files around, consider setting the values in sys.master_files as reference, and be sure you understand the difference between the database names, logical file names, and physical file locations.

Ideally, there should be no data or log files on the OS volume, even system database files. You can, however, move these after SQL Server Setup is complete.

When you're planning to move your database data or log files on Windows, prepare their new file path location by granting FULL CONTROL permissions to the per-SID name for the SQL Server instance. (This is not necessarily the SQL Server service account.) For the default instance, this will be NT SERVICE\MSSQLSERVER; for named instances, it will be NT SERVICE\ MSSQL$*instancename*.

Moving database data or log files on Linux only requires that the mssql account has access to the new file path.

Inside OUT

Where does SQL Server keep track of the locations of database files?

The location of the master database is stored separately from all others, and can be modified in SQL Server Configuration Manager.

All other database file locations are stored in the master database. When the SQL Server process is started, three pieces of location information are provided to the service:

- The location of the master database data file
- The location of the master database log file
- The location of the SQL Server error log

You can find this information in the startup parameters of the SQL Server service in the SQL Server Configuration Manager application.

Move databases within instances

Earlier in this chapter, we discussed reasons for moving user database files. Let's review the differences between various ways to move a database within the same SQL Server instance.

The OFFLINE option is one way to quickly remove a database from usability:

```
ALTER DATABASE [database_name] SET OFFLINE;
```

Because this requires exclusive access to the database, you can use the ROLLBACK IMMEDIATE syntax to end all other user sessions:

```
ALTER DATABASE [database_name] SET OFFLINE WITH ROLLBACK IMMEDIATE;
```

It is also the most easily reversed:

```
ALTER DATABASE [database_name] SET ONLINE;
```

You should set maintenance activities to ignore databases that are offline because they cannot be accessed, maintained, or backed up. While the database is offline, the data and log files remain in place in their location on the drive and can be moved. The database is still listed with its files in sys.master_files.

Taking a database offline is an excellent intermediate administrative step before you DETACH or DROP a database—for example, a database that is not believed to be used anymore. Should a user report that they can no longer access the database, the administrator can simply bring the database back online, which is an immediate action.

You can separate a database's files from the SQL Server by using DETACH. The data and log files remain in place in their location on the drive and can be moved. But detaching a database removes it from sys.master_files.

To reattach the database, in SSMS, in Object Explorer, follow the Attach steps. It is not as immediate an action and requires more administrative intervention than taking the database offline.

When reattaching the database, you must locate at least the primary data file for the database. The Attach process will then attempt to reassociate all the database files to SQL Server control, in their same locations. If their locations have changed, you must provide a list of all database files and their new locations.

NOTE

If you are detaching or restoring a database to attach or copy it to another server, do not forget to follow up by also moving logins and then reassociating orphaned database users with their logins. For more information, review Chapter 12.

Inside OUT

When moving user database files on the same instance, why should you use offline/online instead of detach/attach?

There are a few reasons you need to take a user database offline instead of detaching, moving, and reattaching the files.

While the database is offline, database information remains queryable in sys.master_files and other system catalog views. You can still reference the locations of database files after taking the database offline to ensure that everything is moved. Also, it is not possible to detach a database when the database is the source of a database snapshot or part of a replication publication. Taking a database offline is the only method possible in these scenarios.

Note that you cannot detach or take system databases offline to move them. A service restart is necessary to move system databases, including the master database.

Finally, a DROP DATABASE command, issued when you use the Delete feature in Object Explorer, removes the database from the SQL Server and deletes the database files on the drive. An exception to this behavior is if the destination database is offline. Deleting an offline database and detaching a database are therefore similar actions.

Dropping a database does not by default remove its backup and restore history from the msdb database, though there is a check box at the bottom of the SSMS Drop Database dialog box that you can select for this action. The stored procedure `msdb.dbo.sp_delete_database_backuphistory` is run to remove this history.

For databases with a long backup history that has not been maintained by a log history retention policy, the step to delete this history can take a long time and could cause SSMS to stop responding. Instead, delete old backup and restore history incrementally by using `msdb.dbo.sp_delete_backuphistory` and/or run multiple instances of the `msdb.dbo.sp_delete_database_backuphistory` stored procedure in separate SSMS query windows.

> ➤ **For more information on this and related stored procedures, visit** *https://learn.microsoft.com/sql/relational-databases/system-stored-procedures/sp-delete-database-backuphistory-transact-sql.*

> ➤ **For more information on backup and restore history, see Chapter 8.**

Move user database files

You can move user databases without a SQL Server instance restart and without disrupting other databases by taking the database offline, updating the locations and/or metadata, moving them, and then bringing the database online again.

Use the following steps to move user database files:

1. Take a manual full backup of the soon-to-be-affected databases.

2. During a maintenance outage for the database and any dependent applications, take the user database offline. Then run a T-SQL script to alter the location of each database file. Here's an example of the T-SQL statements required:

```
ALTER DATABASE [database_name] SET OFFLINE WITH ROLLBACK IMMEDIATE
ALTER DATABASE [database_name] MODIFY FILE ( NAME = logical_data_file_name,
FILENAME = 'location\physical_data_file_name.mdf' );
ALTER DATABASE [database_name] MODIFY FILE ( NAME = logical_log_file_name,
FILENAME = 'location\physical_log_file_name.ldf' );
ALTER DATABASE [database_name] SET ONLINE;
```

3. While the database is offline, physically copy the database files to their new location. (You will delete the old copies when you've confirmed the new configuration.) When the file operation is complete, bring the database back online.

4. Verify that the data files have been moved by querying sys.master_files. The `physical_name` column should reflect the new location correctly.

5. Delete the files in the original location to reclaim the space. To be safe and for rollback reasons, back up the database and the master database before the deletion.

6. Perform a manual backup of the master database.

Move system database files, except for master

You cannot move system database files while the SQL Server instance is online; thus, you must stop the SQL Server service.

1. Take a manual full backup of the soon-to-be-affected databases.

2. For model, msdb, and tempdb, run a T-SQL script (like the script for moving user databases provided previously). SQL Server will not use the new locations of the system databases until the next time the service is restarted. You cannot set the system databases to offline.

3. During a maintenance outage for the SQL Server instance, stop the SQL Server instance. Then copy the database files to their new location. (You will delete the old copies when you've confirmed the new configuration.) The only exception here is that the tempdb data and log files do not need to be moved—they will be re-created automatically by SQL Server upon service start.

4. When the file operation is complete, start the SQL Server service again.

5. Verify that the data files have been moved by querying sys.master_files. Look for the physical_name column to reflect the new location correctly.

6. Delete the files in the original location to reclaim the space.

7. Perform a manual backup of the master database.

If you encounter problems starting SQL Server after moving system databases to another volume—for example, if the SQL Server service account starts and then stops—do the following:

1. Verify that the SQL Server service account and SQL Server Agent service account have permissions to the new file location.

    ➤ Review the list of File System Permissions Granted to SQL Server service accounts at *https:// learn.microsoft.com/sql/database-engine/configure-windows/configure-windows-service -accounts-and-permissions#Reviewing_ACLs.*

2. Check the Windows Application Event Log and System Event Log for errors.

3. If you cannot resolve the issue, start SQL Server with Trace Flag 3608, which does not start the SQL Server fully, only the master database.

4. If necessary, move all other database files, including the other system databases, back to their original location by using T-SQL commands issued through SSMS.

> **NOTE**
>
> For more information on moving system database files, visit *https://learn.microsoft.com /sql/relational-databases/databases/move-system-databases*.

Move master database files

Moving the master database files is not difficult, but it is a more complicated process than moving the other system databases. Instead of issuing an ALTER DATABASE ... ALTER FILE statement, you must edit the parameters passed to the SQL Server service in SQL Server Configuration Manager.

1. Open SQL Server Configuration Manager and select **SQL Server Services** on the left.

2. Right-click the **SQL Server** service and choose **Properties**.

3. The **Startup Parameters** page contains three entries with three files in their current paths. Edit the two parameters beginning with -d and -1 (lowercase L). The -e parameter is the location of the SQL Server Error Log; you might want to move that, as well.

4. After editing the master database data file (-d) and the master database log file (-1) locations, select **OK**. Keep in mind that the SQL Server service will not look for the files in their new location until the service is restarted. (If you have other startup parameters in this box, do *not* modify them now.)

5. Stop the SQL Server service. Then copy the master database data and log files to their new location. (You will delete the old copies when you've confirmed the new configuration.)

6. When the file operation is complete, restart the SQL Server service.

7. Verify that the data files have been moved by querying sys.master_files, a dynamic management view that returns all files for all databases. Look for the physical_name column to correctly reflect the new location.

8. After you have verified that SQL Server is recognizing the database files in their new locations, delete the files in the original location to reclaim the space.

Inside OUT

Anything else you should move if moving the system databases?

If you plan to move all system databases to a different volume and get rid of the old file paths, you also will need to move the SQL Server Agent Error Log, or the SQL Server Agent will not be able to start. You can do this in SSMS. In Object Explorer, connect to the SQL

Server instance, and expand the SQL Server Agent folder. Then right-click **Error Logs** and select **Configure** in the shortcut menu. Finally, provide a new Error Log file location for the SQLAGENT.OUT file.

Verify that the SQL Server Agent per-SID name for the SQL Server Agent service has FULL CONTROL permissions to the new folder. The per-service SID account will be NT Service\ SQLSERVERAGENT for default instances or NT Service\SQLAgent$*instancename* for named instances.

When you later restart the SQL Server service and the SQL Server Agent service, the Agent error log will be written to the new location.

Single-user mode

By default, all databases are in MULTI_USER mode. Sometimes, it is necessary to gain exclusive access to a database with a single connection, typically in SQLCMD or in an SSMS query window.

For example, when performing a restore, the connection must have exclusive access to the database. By default, the restore will wait until it gains exclusive access. You could attempt to discontinue all connections, but there is a much easier way: Setting a database to SINGLE_USER mode removes all other connections but your own.

Setting a database to SINGLE_USER mode also requires exclusive access. If other users are connected to the database, running the following statement will be unsuccessful:

```
ALTER DATABASE [database_name] SET SINGLE_USER;
```

It is then necessary to provide further syntax to decide how to treat other connections to the database.

- **WITH NO_WAIT.** The ALTER DATABASE command will fail if it cannot gain exclusive access to the database. Note that without this statement or other WITH commands below, the ALTER DATABASE command will wait indefinitely.

- **WITH ROLLBACK IMMEDIATE.** Roll back all conflicting requests, killing other SSMS Query window connections, for example.

- **WITH ROLLBACK AFTER *n* SECONDS.** Delays the effect of WITH ROLLBACK IMMEDIATE by *n* SECONDS. (This is not particularly more graceful to competing user connections, just delayed.)

For example:

```
ALTER DATABASE [database_name] SET SINGLE_USER WITH ROLLBACK IMMEDIATE;
```

Instead of issuing a WITH ROLLBACK, you might choose to identify other sessions connected to the destination database—for example, by using the following:

```
SELECT * FROM sys.dm_exec_sessions
WHERE db_name(database_id) = 'database_name';
```

and then evaluate the appropriate strategy for dealing with any requests coming from that session, including communication with that user and the closing of unused connections to that database in dialog boxes, SSMS query windows, or user applications.

After you have completed the activities requiring exclusive access, set the database back to MULTI_USER mode:

```
ALTER DATABASE [database_name] SET MULTI_USER;
```

You need to gain exclusive access to databases before a restore or to take a database offline. This script to change the database to SINGLE_USER and back to MULTI_USER is a common step wrapped around a database restore. This is done to avoid users gaining access while the script is being run and then it is set to MULTI_USER again after the work is done.

➤ **For more information on database restores, see Chapter 10.**

CHAPTER 6

CHAPTER 7

Understand table features

A key aspect of relational databases is how data is stored in tables. It is important to understand both how tables should look to the user and how they are structured internally.

This chapter covers fundamentals including data types, keys, and constraints. It also covers special table types, including temporal tables and graph tables. At times, organizations choose to store binary large objects (BLOBs) within relational tables. This chapter covers the implications of storing this type of data within SQL Server, as well as other important table-related concepts including vertical and horizontal partitioning and change-tracking methods. Finally, it covers how PolyBase can help you use connectors to interact with data sources outside of SQL Server.

A proper relational database design requires considerations beyond the SQL Server features included in this chapter. Mapping application requirements, normalization, and organization-specific requirements are not covered in this book. There are many texts available to teach you those elements of relational database design, starting perhaps with the theory writings of relational model innovators C. J. Date and E. F. Codd.

All scripts for this book are available at *https://www.microsoftpressstore.com /SQLServer2022InsideOut/downloads*.

Review table structures

This section reviews information that is relevant when creating tables. First, it looks at system data types, emphasizing the data design decisions surrounding their use. Next, it briefly discusses primary and foreign key concepts. Then, it covers constraints, their impact on table design, and how they can help meet data integrity requirements. The section ends with user-defined data types and computed columns.

CHAPTER 7

> NOTE
>
> Beyond coverage of primary keys and unique constraints, indexing is not covered in this chapter, although table design is not complete without considering it. For guidance on indexing, read Chapter 14, "Performance tune SQL Server," and Chapter 15, "Understand and design indexes."

General-purpose data types

Selecting the appropriate data type when designing relational databases is crucial. You can change a column's data type after the fact, but doing so can be an expensive operation. A poorly chosen data type can result in suboptimal performance or might allow for unexpected values to be stored in the column. Therefore, proper data type choice becomes a decision point about performance, data integrity, and even application security.

The intent of this section is not to provide exhaustive coverage of each system data type available in SQL Server; rather, it's to provide the information and guidance necessary to make solid table design decisions.

Alphanumeric types

Alphanumeric types (also known as *strings*) are commonly discussed in terms of fixed versus variable length, and with Unicode versus without Unicode support. The char and nchar data types are fixed length, and varchar and nvarchar are variable length. The difference is how each is encoded. The nchar and nvarchar data types are always encoded as 16-bit Unicode, using UTF-16. In contrast, char and varchar use 8-bit data types that store data in ASCII or, starting in SQL Server 2019, UTF-8. More information about these new collations and their purpose is included later in this section.

As a database designer, you must understand that the (*n*) in a [var]char(*n*) column definition indicates the number of bytes allocated for the column, not the number of characters that can be stored. The same is true for n[var]char(*n*) columns, though the size indicates the number of byte-pairs that can be stored. This is important because:

- [var]char columns can store strings from double-byte character sets, and can use UTF-8 collations, which may require 2 or 4 bytes to store one character. The following subsection includes full coverage of UTF-8 collations.

- n[var]char columns can store characters in the Unicode supplementary character range, which may require 4 bytes.

> NOTE
>
> You might be tempted to use an ASCII varchar data type to save space. However, you may need Unicode support more often than you think, and it often starts with people's names. Additionally, users expect to store emojis and other Unicode character data in columns. Finally, increasing internationalization of applications is also best supported by using Unicode string data types.

Collation

With string data, collation becomes an important consideration. This is determined using the code page, which is one element of the collation. Collation also determines how data is compared and sorted, such as whether casing and accented letters are considered to be different.

> **NOTE**
>
> If the full range of Unicode characters must be supported in a column, the collation should be set to a supplementary characters collation. These collations' names end in _SC and have been available since SQL Server 2012. The most frequently used characters have Unicode point values between 0x20 and 0xFFFF (point values below 0x20 are control characters). Thus, without using supplementary characters, 65,515 characters can be represented. Those include accented letters for most languages, many symbols, characters for Asian and Cyrillic languages, and many more.

➤ For more information about Unicode supplementary characters, see *https://learn.microsoft.com /sql/relational-databases/collations/collation-and-unicode-support#Supplementary_Characters*.

SQL Server 2019 introduced a new family of collations that support UTF-8. These collations apply only to the char and varchar data types and store the string data using UTF-8 encoding. They effectively turn these two data types into Unicode data types, including support for supplementary characters. When you define a column or conversion to use a UTF-8 collation, the encoding is automatically updated.

Among other things, collation determines how the high-order bits in each character's byte(s) are interpreted. Collation supports internationalization by allowing different character representations for characters whose integer values are greater than 127, up to 255.

Inside OUT

Should you expect space savings when using UTF-8 collations?

Answering this question requires at least a cursory understanding of how character data is encoded in UTF-8. The number of bytes required to encode characters varies from 1 to 4. The characters at the lowest code points (0–127) require only 1 byte, just like other collations. This is designed to maintain compatibility with ASCII. These 128 characters are the most common characters in Latin script, including uppercase and lowercase letters, digits, and many punctuation marks. However, code points 128–2,047 already require 2 bytes in UTF-8, while only requiring 1 byte in the non-UTF-8 collations. That code point range includes Latin accented characters, some additional punctuation marks, such as the inverted exclamation point (¡), and symbols (such as currency symbols). UTF-8 requires more storage space than UTF-16 for characters in the code point range 2,048–65,535. An extra script file in the book's downloads illustrates some of these caveats.

Thus, whether you should expect space savings is quite nuanced and depends on how many characters in the average varchar column will require more than 1 byte to be encoded (when compared to varchar using collations other than UTF-8) or more than 2 bytes (when compared to nchar or nvarchar). For an internationalized application, this might be difficult to forecast.

We do not suggest switching collations to UTF-8 for the purpose of saving storage space. UTF-8 collations are designed to support internationalization of existing applications and databases without incurring massive changes and associated test requirements. For new application or database development where internationalization is expected, using UTF-16 encoding (with the nchar and nvarchar data types) is highly recommended.

➤ For complete details about collation and Unicode support, visit *https://learn.microsoft.com /sql/relational-databases/collations/collation-and-unicode-support*.

CAUTION

You define the column width by the number of bytes, never by the number of characters that can be stored. If you decide that UTF-8 is the right encoding to use for an existing database, you need to ensure that the column width in bytes can accommodate the potentially larger size of the existing column values once converted to UTF-8. During the collation conversion, SQL Server will silently truncate any values that do not fit.

Before converting, you can determine if any strings will require more bytes than the column width supports using a Transact-SQL (T-SQL) statement like the one that follows, where val is a varchar(8) column in a table called CollationTest:

```
-- If COUNT > 0, then there are rows whose data size will be larger than the
-- current column width supports
SELECT COUNT(*)
FROM dbo.CollationTest
WHERE DATALENGTH(
    CAST(CAST(val AS VARCHAR(32))
        COLLATE Latin1_General_100_CS_AS_SC_UTF8 AS VARCHAR(32))) > 8;
```

This WHERE clause is used to determine which values will no longer fit in the width of the column (8 bytes), after altering the column to use a collation from the UTF-8 family of collations, where a single character might take up four times as much space (8 * 4 = 32). Quadrupling the byte count of the source column is not necessary; any value larger than the source column width will do.

Two CASTs are required:

- The inner CAST converts val from varchar(8) to varchar(32) to simulate the UTF-8 column width.

- The outer CAST converts val at the UTF-8 collation. This needs to be varchar(32) to analyze the converted UTF-8 records in the column val.

Large value data

No discussion of alphanumeric types would be complete without an examination of varchar(max) and nvarchar(max). By specifying max instead of a value between 1 and 8,000 bytes (for varchar) or between 1 and 4,000 byte-pairs (for nvarchar), the storage limit increases to 2 GB. If the column's value exceeds 8,000 bytes, the data is not stored in the table's storage structure. Large value data is stored out of row, though for each such column, 24 bytes of overhead is stored in the row. Of those 24 bytes, the first 16 bytes are used to store metadata, and the last 8 bytes contain the pointer to the row in the row-overflow page.

NOTE

The details of storing large value data also apply to the varbinary(max) and xml data types, both of which are discussed later in this chapter.

SQL Server has a row size limit of 8,060 bytes. Even if you do not use [n]varchar(max) columns, some data may be stored out of row or "off-row." Any data that is stored off-row will incur some overhead when it is read. The flip side is that when a T-SQL statement does not reference a column whose data is stored off-row, there is a performance benefit. If your table's usage patterns indicate that large value type columns are not frequently included in statements, you can optimize performance by storing the data off-row, even if the row size is less than 8,000 bytes. The following T-SQL statement enables the large_value_types_out_of_row option for the PurchaseOrders table in the WideWorldImporters sample database:

```
DECLARE @TableName NVARCHAR(776) = N'Purchasing.PurchaseOrders';
-- Turn the option on
EXEC sp_tableoption @TableNamePattern = @TableName
    , @OptionName = 'large value types out of row'
    , @OptionValue = 1;
GO
-- Verify the option setting
SELECT [name], large_value_types_out_of_row
FROM sys.tables
WHERE object_id = OBJECT_ID(@TableName);
```

After this is run, the values are not immediately migrated to out of row storage. This is true for any table, regardless of whether there is data populated. For example, the preceding table has no values in any of the varchar(max) columns; only when an existing data row is updated will the values be stored out of row. You could force such updates to happen by executing an

UPDATE statement that sets the column value to any value or even itself, although this operation will be quite expensive on large tables. We don't recommend this unless you have determined that the immediate benefit of forcing those values to be stored off-row exceeds the cost of the update operation.

In the T-SQL CREATE statement (but not in an ALTER statement), you can opt to store the data for large value type columns in a separate filegroup. In the CREATE TABLE statement, use the TEXTIMAGE_ON clause to specify the name of the filegroup where large object (LOB) data should be stored. If you want to change the TEXTIMAGE_ON setting, you will need to create a new table and copy the data in the table.

➤ If you need to store more than 2 GB in a single column, consider using the FILESTREAM feature, discussed in the "Store large binary objects" section later in this chapter.

Numeric types

When considering numeric types in computer systems, it is important to understand the nature of your data. One of the most important concepts to understand is the difference between exact and approximate numeric types.

Approximate numeric types store values using a floating-point structure. In SQL Server, the number of bits in the mantissa is limited to 24 or 53, resulting in a respective precision of 7 or 15 digits. Due to the nature of the structure and the limited number of bits, these types cannot accurately store all numbers in the supported range. On the other hand, although exact types store numbers without losing precision, this comes at a loss of range. For approximate floating-point types, the range is very large and useful for scientific-like numbers and operations, where a small loss of precision might not matter. Math with these values is implemented in hardware, so performance is far better than anything other than integers. For exact types, the range is limited, but sufficient for operations requiring precision, such as those involving monetary values.

SQL Server provides real and float as approximate data types, although their implementation is closely related. The real data type is lower precision than the float data type. It is possible to specify the number of bits for the mantissa when defining float, but SQL Server will always use either 24 bits or 53 bits; any other value you specify is rounded up to either 24 or 53. The real data type is the same as specifying float(24), or in effect any number of mantissa bits between 1 and 24.

➤ For more information about floating-point values, see Randolph West's blog post on how these values are implemented, at *https://bornsql.ca/blog/how-sql-server-stores-data-types-floating-points*.

NOTE

The sample scripts for this chapter include an extra file that illustrates important caveats when converting from approximate floating-point numbers to exact types.

Exact numeric types include `tinyint`, `smallint`, `int`, and `bigint`, which are all whole numbers of varying byte sizes and therefore range. SQL Server does not support unsigned integers.

Some exact numeric types support decimal-point numbers. Foremost among these is the `decimal` data type. In SQL Server, another name for `decimal` is `numeric`. The `decimal` data type supports a precision of up to 38 digits, before or after the decimal point. The number of digits determines the storage size. In addition, you can specify the scale, which determines the number of digits to the right of the decimal point.

Other exact numeric types that support decimal point numbers are `money` and `smallmoney`. They have the same range as `int` and `bigint`, but with the decimal point shifted four places to the left. Because of this, any math calculations will be treated like integers and can be done in registers in the CPU. This enables them to perform calculations faster than non-integer numbers. These data types can store monetary data with a precision of up to four digits to the right of the decimal point—in other words, to the ten-thousandth.

Choosing between `decimal` and `money` or `smallmoney` is primarily determined by your need for range and precision. For monetary values, and if your multiplications and divisions will always return the desired result when using only four significant digits to the right of the decimal point, `smallmoney` and `money` may be good choices because they are more efficient in terms of storage space. For higher precision and larger scale, `decimal` is the right choice. In addition, `decimal` may be a better choice if the operations performed on the data create precision issues due to intermediate steps in math using only four digits.

Inside OUT

When should you use a numeric data type instead of a character data type?

You can store any numeric value, such as an amount or an identifier consisting only of digits, in an alphanumeric column or in a numeric data type column. Generally, you should choose a numeric data type if the values will be used in some type of calculation or when magnitude matters—for example, to calculate a discount on a monetary value. Another example for which numeric data types are used is in quantities because you might need to adjust the quantity by adding or subtracting additional units. On the other hand, a US ZIP code is best stored as an alphanumeric value because leading zeros must be preserved. The same can be true in an employee ID number or any other values that are not used in mathematical functions.

In addition to considering whether you need to use the value in calculations, you also need to consider the differences in how values are sorted. In a numeric column sorted in ascending order, the value 12 will come before 100. But in an alphanumeric column, 100 will come before 12. Either one can produce the desired answer based on your use case.

Date and time types

Date and time data types available in SQL Server 2022 include the aged datetime and smalldatetime types. Although these are not technically deprecated, we strongly caution against using them for new development due to issues surrounding precision, available date range, and lack of control over the precision and storage size. Additionally, these data types are not aligned with the SQL standard, lowering portability of the data between platforms. Their immediate replacement is datetime2, which in no case consumes more than 8 bytes of storage space (the same as datetime), but addresses precision, increases the date range, and can store dates in less than 8 bytes in return for lower precision. As a matter of detail, specifying datetime2(3) provides the same precision as datetime, but does so while requiring 1 fewer byte.

NOTE

All date and time data types discussed here are available in all currently supported versions of SQL Server. They are by no means new data types, but, unfortunately, are too frequently left unused for fear of backward-compatibility problems.

This does not mean, however, that all date and time-of-day values should be stored in datetime2. There are three additional data types that you should consider for storing date or time values:

- **date.** If you need to store only a date without time or time zone information, this is your best choice. The date data type stores only a date and supports the same date range as datetime2. It stores the date in only 3 bytes, making it much more efficient than datetime (fixed at 8 bytes) and datetime2 (minimally 6 bytes). An example of such a case is a date of birth. A date of birth is commonly stored to calculate someone's age, which is not generally treated as dependent on the time zone or on the time. Assume a person is born at 11 p.m. Central European Summer Time. If they moved to Southeast Asia, they would not celebrate their birthday a day later, even though the actual point in time of their birth was the next day in Southeast Asia. (That being said, some applications, such as one used in a neonatal facility, might need to store a more precise "time of birth," so make sure you understand the requirements before choosing your data type.)

- **datetimeoffset.** This data type provides the same precision and range as datetime2 but includes an offset value in hours and minutes to indicate the difference from UTC. This data type neither tracks nor understands actual time zones or daylight saving time (DST). It would be up to the application to track the time zone where the value originated to allow the application or recent versions of SQL Server to perform correct date arithmetic. (See the following note for more information.)

NOTE

Before SQL Server 2016, SQL Server had no understanding of time zones or DST. SQL Server 2016 and Azure SQL Database introduced the AT TIME ZONE function, which converts between time zones and applies or reverts a DST offset. The rules SQL Server applies are based on the Windows functionality for time zones and DST. These rules are explained and illustrated with examples at *https://learn.microsoft.com/sql/t-sql/queries /at-time-zone-transact-sql*.

With SQL Server on Linux, AT TIME ZONE returns the same results as executing the function on a Windows host.

- **time.** This data type stores a time-of-day value consisting of hours, minutes, seconds, and fractional seconds, with a precision up to 100 nanoseconds. The exact fractional second precision and storage size is user defined by specifying a precision between 0 and 7. The time data type is a good choice when storing only a time-of-day value that is not time-zone sensitive, such as for a reminder. A reminder set for 11 a.m. might need to be activated at 11 a.m. regardless of time zone and date.

NOTE

The time data type can store no more than 23 hours, 59 minutes, 59 seconds, and 0.9999999 fractions of a second. This can make this data type unsuitable for storing elapsed time if there is a chance that elapsed time will be 24 hours or more. We typically suggest storing elapsed time in an integer value that holds the number of time units that have passed, based on the minimum precision you desire. Any fields that could exceed 2.1 billion in the lifetime of the application should use the bigint data type.

Inside OUT

How do you correctly retrieve the current system date and time?

In addition to continued use of the datetime data type despite the availability of the better datetime2 type, we also observe the common use of the lower-precision functions CURRENT_TIMESTAMP, GETDATE(), and GETUTCDATE(). Although these functions continue to work, they return values of the datetime type.

There are replacement functions available in SYSDATETIME(), SYSDATETIMEOFFSET(), and SYSUTCDATETIME(). Although their names don't make it immediately clear, SYSDATETIME() and SYSUTCDATETIME() return the improved datetime2(7) type. SYSDATETIMEOFFSET() also returns a value of type datetimeoffset(7). SYSDATETIME() and SYSUTCDATETIME() are functionally equivalent to GETDATE() and GETUTCDATE(), respectively. SYSDATETIMEOFFSET() does not have a functional equivalent and is thus the only option if you need to include the time zone offset on the server other than using the AT TIME ZONE function.

> Even if you cannot modify the schema of your database to change all `datetime` columns to `datetime2` (or `datetimeoffset`), you might benefit in the long term from adopting the improved functions now. Even though the range of valid dates for `datetime` is much smaller on the lower end than for `datetime2` and `datetimeoffset`, the upper end is the same (December 31, 9999). Discarding the future possibility of time-travel to before the year 1753, none of the improved functions will return a `datetime2` or `datetimeoffset` value that cannot be cast to `datetime`.

➤ For detailed technical comparisons between the available date and time data types, visit *https://learn.microsoft.com/sql/t-sql/functions/date-and-time-data-types-and-functions -transact-sql*.

Binary types

Some data cannot be efficiently represented as an alphanumeric string. For example, data that has been encrypted by the application should be stored as a binary value. The same might also apply to storing contents of binary file formats, such as PDF files.

SQL Server provides the `binary` data type to store fixed-length binary values, and `varbinary` to store variable-length binary values. (The `image` data type has been deprecated for almost two decades, and you should not use it.) For both data types, you specify the number of bytes that will be stored, up to 8,000. If you need to store more than 8,000 bytes, you can specify `varbinary(max)`. This will allow up to 2 GB to be stored, although if the value exceeds 8,000 bytes, those bytes are not stored in the data row. As with [*n*]`varchar`, `varbinary` values may be stored out of row if the total row size would exceed 8,000 bytes.

NOTE

When storing binary values that are on average larger than 1 MB, you should review whether using FILESTREAM is not a better choice. FILESTREAM is discussed in the "Understand FILESTREAM" section later in this chapter.

➤ Refer to the section "Large value data" earlier in this chapter for details on how `varbinary(max)` data is stored and access can be optimized.

Specialized data types

In addition to the data types that are designed to store traditional numeric, alphanumeric, and date and time values, SQL Server provides more specialized data types. These data types are more specific to certain use cases than the general-purpose data types.

Some specialized data types have SQL common language runtime (CLR) functions that make working with them significantly easier. For example, the hierarchyid data type has a ToString() function that converts the stored binary value into a human-readable format. These SQL CLR function names are case-sensitive, regardless of the case sensitivity of the instance or database.

Spatial data types: geometry and geography

The spatial data types provide a way to work with flat (planar) or ellipsoidal (round-earth) coordinates. The geometry data type is for a flat coordinate system, whereas the geography data type is for round-earth coordinates. In addition, both data types also support elevation, or Z, values. Both data types are CLR types that are available in every database, regardless of whether the SQL CLR feature is enabled.

SQL Server provides several methods to work with the values of these data types, including finding intersections, calculating surface area and distance, and many more. SQL Server supports methods defined by the Open Geospatial Consortium (OGC) as well as extended methods designed by Microsoft. The methods defined by the OGC are identified by their ST prefix.

Generally, you create a geometry or geography value by using the static STGeomFromText method. You can use this method to define points, lines, and polygons (closed shapes). The code example that follows creates two geometric points, one with coordinates (0, 0) and the second with coordinates (10, 10). Then, it calculates and outputs the distance between both points:

```
-- Define the variables
DECLARE @point1 GEOMETRY, @point2 GEOMETRY, @distance FLOAT;
-- Initialize the geometric points
SET @point1 = geometry::STGeomFromText('POINT(0  0)', 0);
SET @point2 = geometry::STGeomFromText('POINT(10 -10)', 0);
-- Calculate the distance
SET @distance = @point1.STDistance(@point2);
SELECT @distance;
```

The result in the output is approximately 14.14. (See Figure 7-1; note that no units are defined here.) The second argument in the STGeomFromText method is the spatial reference ID (SRID), which is relevant only for the geography data type. Still, it is a required parameter for the function, and you should specify 0 for geometry data.

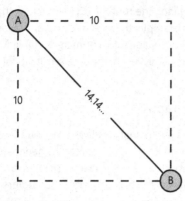

Figure 7-1 The geometry defined in the sample script.

Using spatial data types in a database is valuable when you use the Database Engine to perform spatial queries. You have probably experienced the results of spatial queries in many applications—for example, when searching for nearby pizza restaurants on Bing Maps. Application code can certainly also perform those spatial queries; however, it would require the database to return all pizza restaurants along with their coordinates. By performing the spatial query in the database, the size of the data returned to the application is significantly reduced. SQL Server supports indexing spatial data such that spatial queries can perform optimally.

➤ **For a complete reference on the geometry and geography data types, the methods they support, and spatial reference identifiers, visit** *https://learn.microsoft.com/sql/t-sql/spatial -geometry/spatial-types-geometry-transact-sql* **and** *https://learn.microsoft.com/sql/t-sql /spatial-geography/spatial-types-geography.*

NOTE

For an example of the geography **data type, refer to the WideWorldImporters sample database. The** Application.StateProvinces **table includes a** Border **column of type** geography. **To visually see the** geography **data type at work, run a** SELECT **statement on all rows in the table using SQL Server Management Studio (SSMS). In addition to the row results, SSMS will display a Spatial results tab on which a map of the globe will be drawn.**

The XML data type

The xml data type is designed to store XML documents or snippets. But support for XML goes beyond just storing XML data. The XML data type can enforce an XML schema, in which case the column is referred to as *typed*. XML data can also be queried using XQuery syntax. SQL Server further supports XML by formatting relational data output as XML or retrieving XML data in a relational structure.

A relational database is generally used to store highly structured data, by which we mean data that has a known schema. And even though schemas can change, at any given time every row in a table will have the same columns. Yet, for some scenarios, this strict schema is not appropriate. It might be necessary to accommodate storing data where different rows have different attributes. Sometimes, you can meet this requirement by adding additional nullable sparse columns.

A column set is a feature by which you can manage a group of sparse columns as XML data. Column sets come with significant limitations. Defining many sparse columns becomes onerous because a substantial number of columns can introduce challenges in working with the table. There, just storing the data as plain XML in an xml data type can alleviate the column sprawl. Additionally, if data is frequently used in XML format, it might be more efficient to store the data in that format in the database.

➤ You can read more about sparse columns in the "Sparse columns" section later in this chapter. For detailed guidance on the use of column sets, see *https://learn.microsoft.com/sql /relational-databases/tables/use-column-sets*.

Although XML data could be stored in (n)varchar columns, using the specialized data type allows SQL Server to provide functionality for validating, querying, indexing, and modifying the XML data.

NOTE

SQL Server 2022 introduces XML compression, which can dramatically reduce the amount of storage required for XML data and XML indexes.

➤ Refer to the section "Large value data" earlier in this chapter for details on how xml data is stored and access can be optimized.

Inside OUT

How can you work with JSON in SQL Server just like XML?

SQL Server 2016 introduced support for JSON, though it is not a distinct data type like XML. JSON support includes parsing, querying, modifying, and transforming JSON stored in varchar columns using functions. The brief sample that follows illustrates how to check if a value is valid JSON, using the ISJSON() function, and extracting a scalar value, using the JSON_VALUE() function.

```
DECLARE @SomeJSON nvarchar(50) = '{ "test": "passed" }';
SELECT ISJSON(@SomeJSON) IsValid, JSON_VALUE(@SomeJSON, '$.test') [Status];
```

The output from this code has two columns. The first column has the value 1 because the variable holds valid JSON data, and the second contains the value passed.

> For an additional example, examine the columns CustomFields and OtherLanguages in the Application.People table in the WideWorldImporters sample database. OtherLanguages is a computed column, which extracts some JSON data from the CustomFields column using the JSON_QUERY() function.

➤ For complete information on handling JSON-formatted data in SQL Server and Azure SQL Database, refer to *https://learn.microsoft.com/sql/relational-databases/json/json-data -sql-server*.

The rowversion data type

This data type generates a database-wide unique binary value upon each modification of row data. This binary value increments with each INSERT or UPDATE statement that affects the row, even if no other row data is modified. A common function of this data type is as a row change indicator for use with applications that use optimistic concurrency or as a database-wide change indicator.

NOTE

The rowversion **data type was previously known as** timestamp. rowversion **is the recommended name to use;** timestamp **is deprecated. Unfortunately, SSMS does not support the use of** rowversion **in the table designer or when scripting a table; it continues to use** timestamp.

The name timestamp is the same as the SQL ISO standard timestamp, but it does not work according to the ISO standard. Contrary to what the timestamp name might imply, the data in a rowversion column does not map to a moment in time.

When designing tables with rowversion, keep the following restrictions in mind:

- A table can have only a single rowversion column. Considering the context of rowversion, this restriction is perfectly sensible, and we've included it here only for completeness.

- You cannot specify a value for the rowversion column in INSERT or UPDATE statements. However, unlike with identity or computed columns, you must specify a column list in INSERT statements for tables with a rowversion column. Note that specifying the column list is recommended anyway.

- Although the Database Engine will not generate duplicate rowversion values within a database, rowversion values are not unique across databases or instances.

Duplicate rowversion values can exist in a single database if a new table is created by using the SELECT INTO syntax. The new table's rowversion values will be the same as those of the source table. This behavior might be desired when, for example, modifying a table's schema by creating a new table and copying all the data into it. In other instances, this behavior might not be desired. In those cases, you should not include the rowversion column in the SELECT INTO statement. You should then alter the new table to add a rowversion column. This behavior and workaround are illustrated in an extra sample script file in the accompanying downloads for this book.

Implement optimistic concurrency

Including a rowversion column in a table is an excellent way to implement a row change indicator to achieve *optimistic concurrency*. With optimistic concurrency, a client reads data with the intent of updating it. Unlike with *pessimistic concurrency*, however, a lock is not maintained. Instead, in the same transaction as the UPDATE statement, the client will verify that the rowversion was not changed by another process. If it wasn't, the update proceeds. But if the rowversion no longer matches what the client originally read, the update will fail. The client application can then retrieve the current values and present the user with a notification and suitable options, depending on the application needs. Many object-relational mappers (ORMs), including Entity Framework, support using a rowversion column type to implement optimistic concurrency.

Inside OUT

Can you implement optimistic concurrency without rowversion?

There are other ways to implement optimistic concurrency. A client application can track the value of each individual column in the updated row, then verify that only the columns affected by its own UPDATE statement have not been modified. Specifically, client A reads a row of data and intends to change only the Name column. Client B reads the same row of data and updates the Address column. When client A attempts to update the Name, it finds that the Name column's value is unchanged and will proceed with the update.

This approach is suitable in some scenarios, but it has some drawbacks. First, each client needs to maintain additional state information—namely, the original value of each column. In a web application, the amount of state information to maintain can grow very large and consume a lot of memory. In a web farm scenario, maintaining such state information might require shared state configuration because the web client might not communicate with the same web server on the POST that it did on the GET.

Perhaps more importantly, the data row can be inconsistent after the second update. If each client updates a column in the same row, the row's data might not reflect a valid business scenario. Certainly, the row's values would not reflect what each client believes it would be.

Alternatively, you can use read committed snapshot isolation (RCSI) to enable optimistic concurrency at the database level, which is discussed in more detail in Chapter 6, "Provision and configure SQL Server databases."

The uniqueidentifier data type

The `uniqueidentifier` data type stores a 16-byte value known as a *globally unique identifier* (*GUID*). SQL Server can generate GUIDs using one of two functions: `NEWID()` and `NEWSEQUENTIALID()`. `NEWSEQUENTIALID()` generates a GUID that is greater than a previously generated GUID by this function *since the last restart of the server*. You can use `NEWSEQUENTIALID()` only in a default constraint for a column; it is more suitable for use as a clustered primary key than `NEWID()`. Unlike `NEWID()`, which generates random values, the increasing nature of the GUIDs generated by `NEWSEQUENTIALID()` means that data and index pages will fill completely.

> ### NOTE
>
> Although GUIDs generated using `NEWID()` were originally generated by incorporating a system's network interface card (NIC) MAC address, this has not been the case for many years, because it might have been possible to identify the system on which it was created. All GUIDs in SQL Server use a pseudorandom value, according to the UUID version 4 standard. The chance of collision is extremely low.
>
> However, the `NEWSEQUENTIALID()` function *is* dependent on the MAC address of the machine's network interface. This means that the starting point of the sequence generated by `NEWSEQUENTIALID()` could change when the machine's network interface changes. A NIC change can occur with regularity on virtualized and PaaS platforms. With `NEWSEQUENTIALID()`, you will eventually experience fragmentation because the sequential GUIDs will have a smaller value than the previous sequence after a restart.

> ➤ The `uniqueidentifier` data type plays an important role in some replication techniques. For more information, see Chapter 11, "Implement high availability and disaster recovery."

The hierarchyid data type

The `hierarchyid` data type enables an application to store and query hierarchical data in a tree structure. A tree structure means that a row will have zero or one parent and zero or more children. There is a single root element denoted by a single forward slash (/). `hierarchyid` values are stored as a binary format but are commonly represented in their string format. Each element at the same level in the hierarchy (referred to as a *sibling*) has a unique numeric value (which might include a decimal point). In the string representation of a `hierarchyid` value, each level is separated by a forward slash. The string representation always begins with a slash (to denote the root element) and ends with a slash.

For example, as illustrated in Figure 7-2, a `hierarchyid` whose string representation is /1/10/ is a descendant of the /1/ element, which itself is a descendant of the implicit root element /. It must be noted, however, that SQL Server does not enforce the existence of a row with the ancestor element. This means it is possible to create an element /3/1/ without its ancestor /3/ being a value in a row. Implicitly, it is a child of /3/, even if no row with `hierarchyid` value /3/ exists. Similarly, the row with `hierarchyid` element /1/ can be deleted if another row has `hierarchyid` value /1/10/. If you don't want this, the application or database will need to include logic to enforce the existence of an ancestor when inserting and to prevent the deletion of an ancestor.

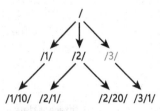

Figure 7-2 hierarchyid values. The value /3/ is in gray to indicate it is implicit.

Perhaps surprisingly, SQL Server does not enforce uniqueness of the hierarchyid values unless you define a unique index or constraint on the hierarchyid column. It is, therefore, possible for the /3/1/ element to be defined twice. This is likely not the desired situation, so we recommend that you ensure uniqueness of the hierarchyid values.

Using the hierarchyid data type is appropriate if the tree is most commonly queried to find descendants, such as children, children-of-children, and more. This is because hierarchyid processes rows depth-first if it is indexed. You can create a breadth-first index by adding a computed column to the table (which uses the .GetLevel() method on the hierarchyid column) and then creating an index on the computed column followed by the hierarchyid column. You cannot, however, use a computed column in a clustered index, so this solution will still be less efficient compared to creating a clustered index on the hierarchyid value alone.

A hierarchyid method worth mentioning is .GetAncestor(). This method returns the hierarchyid value of the current node's parent. Conversely, .IsDescendantOf() determines whether a node is a descendant, direct or otherwise, of the hierarchyid provided as the function's parameter.

➤ **For a complete overview of the** hierarchyid **data type, refer to** *https://learn.microsoft .com/sql/relational-databases/hierarchical-data-sql-server.*

The sql_variant data type

The sql_variant data type enables a single column to store data of diverse types. You can also use this type as a parameter or a variable. In addition to storing the actual value, each sql_variant instance also stores metadata about the value, including its system data type, maximum size, scale and precision, and collation. Using sql_variant can be indicative of a poor database design, and you should use it judiciously. Client libraries that do not know how to handle that data might convert it to nvarchar(4000), with potential consequences for data that doesn't convert well to character data.

In queries, you can retrieve the base type of the stored value and the base types' properties using the `SQL_VARIANT_PROPERTY()` function. For example, using `SQL_VARIANT_PROPERTY (<columnname>, 'BaseType')`, you can retrieve the sysname of the underlying type. Other values that can be provided as the property parameter value of the function are `Precision`, `Scale`, `TotalBytes`, `Collation`, and `MaxLength`. If a particular property doesn't apply to the underlying data type, the way `precision` doesn't apply to `varchar`, the function returns `NULL`.

Data type precedence

When using a T-SQL operator that combines values that might be of different data types, how does the Database Engine handle the difference? The answer is that the data type with the lower precedence is converted to the data type with the higher precedence, assuming the conversion is possible. If it's not, then an error is returned.

In the following code sample, the string variable `@TheirString` (a varchar) is first converted to `datetime2` because `datetime2` takes precedence over `varchar`. Then the comparison is executed.

```
DECLARE @MyDate datetime2(0) = '2022-12-22T20:05:00';
DECLARE @TheirString varchar(10) = '2022-12-20';
SELECT DATEDIFF(MINUTE, @TheirString, @MyDate);
```

➤ For a complete list of data types in precedence order, visit *https://learn.microsoft.com /sql/t-sql/data-types/data-type-precedence-transact-sql*.

Constraints

Constraints define rules to which your data must adhere, and those rules are enforced by the Database Engine. This makes constraints a very powerful mechanism for guaranteeing data integrity. This section provides details on *primary* and *foreign keys*, which are used to establish relationships, and *unique*, *check*, and *default* constraints.

Primary keys, foreign keys, and relationships

Proper relational database design calls for a process called *normalization*. Through normalization, logical entities are broken into multiple related tables. Primary keys are created for entities, and foreign keys establish relationships between entities. A detailed discussion of normalization is beyond the scope of this book.

Without intending to wax poetic, keys are the nervous system of a relational database. They establish the relationships between the multiple tables created through normalization. A relational database system uses both *primary keys* and *foreign keys*. In a single table, the primary key values must be unique because those values can be used as foreign key values in the related table. The foreign key values can also be unique in the related table, in which case the established relationship is a one-to-one relationship. This is discussed in the "Vertical partitions" section later in the chapter.

NOTE

This chapter does not include coverage of indexes, even though a primary key and a unique constraint are always associated with an index. Frequently, foreign key columns are also indexed, as their values are often used to query the table. For information on indexing, see Chapter 15.

A table can have exactly one primary key. This primary key can consist of multiple columns, in which case it's referred to as a *compound primary key*. A simple primary key only has one column. In no case can a nullable column be (part of) the primary key. If additional columns' values should be unique, you can apply a unique index or constraint. (See the next sections for coverage on additional constraint types.)

NOTE

In most cases, SQL Server does not require that tables have a primary key. Some features, such as FILESTREAM and certain types of replication, might require tables to have a primary key. In general, though, you should default to designing tables with primary keys unless there is an overriding reason not to.

Foreign keys are intended to establish *referential integrity*. Referential integrity allows values found in the foreign key column(s) to exist in either the primary key, unique constraint, or unique index column(s). By default, foreign keys in SQL Server have referential integrity enforced. It is possible to establish a foreign key without referential integrity enforced, or to alter the foreign key to turn referential integrity off and on. This functionality is useful during import operations or certain types of database maintenance.

This applies to check constraints, too, which are discussed later in this section. The same is also true for primary keys if they are not enabled. However, during normal operations, foreign keys should have referential integrity enabled to protect the integrity of your data. Otherwise, establishing the relationship is useful only for documentary purposes, which can be helpful, but less so than knowing the foreign key references are always correct.

NOTE

If a foreign key is a composite key in which one or more columns allow NULL, a row with a NULL value in just one of the foreign key columns will pass the integrity check, even if the other columns contain values that do not exist in the parent table. This is because foreign key constraints fail only on a `false` result, not NULL or `true`.

To provide referential integrity, we recommend prohibiting NULL values in some columns of a composite foreign key and allowing them in others. It's certainly acceptable to have NULL values in all columns of the composite foreign keys; this indicates that the relationship is optional. In that case, create a check constraint (covered later in this section) to ensure either all foreign key columns are NULL or none are.

One table can have multiple foreign keys.

When defining a foreign key, you can specify how to handle an operation in the parent row that would invalidate the relationship. Cascading specifically means that the same operation will be run on the child row(s) as was run on the parent. Thus, if the primary key value is updated, the foreign key values will be updated, and if the parent row is deleted, the foreign key values will be deleted. Alternatively, on updates or deletes in the parent table, no action can be taken (the default, which would cause the update or delete statement to fail if referential integrity is enforced), the foreign key value can be set to NULL (effectively creating an orphaned row), or the foreign key value can be set to its default constraint's specification (effectively mapping the child row to another parent).

Unique constraints

A *unique constraint* enforces unique values in one column or selected columns. Unlike a primary key, the unique constraint allows the column(s) to be nullable, though NULL values in a constraint are treated as one value in SQL Server, not an unknown value. This means it is possible to have many rows with a NULL value if you are using a compound key. Otherwise, there will only be one NULL value.

> ➤ Refer to Chapter 15 for guidance on unique filtered indexes, which can be used to work around this limitation.

Like primary and foreign keys, referential integrity is enabled by default for unique constraints. It is possible to disable the unique index, which will also disable the unique constraint.

SQL Server 2022 enables you to allow resumable add table constraints. The following sample adds a unique constraint to the column CountryName in the Application.Countries table in the WideWorldImporters sample database with a resumable add table constraint.

```
ALTER TABLE [Application].Countries WITH CHECK
    ADD CONSTRAINT UC_CountryName_Resume UNIQUE (CountryName)
    WITH (ONLINE = ON, RESUMABLE = ON, MAX_DURATION = 60);
```

When creating any type of unique constraint or index, the name must be distinct. The following could also be added to the table as well (which would create the exact same duplicate physical structure, which is not of any value):

```
ALTER TABLE [Application].Countries WITH CHECK
    ADD CONSTRAINT UC_CountryName_Resume2 UNIQUE (CountryName)
    WITH (ONLINE = ON, RESUMABLE = ON, MAX_DURATION = 60);
```

Check constraints

A *check constraint* enforces rules that can be expressed by using a Boolean expression. For example, in the Sales.Invoices table in the sample WideWorldImporters database, there is a check constraint defined that requires the ReturnedDeliveryData column to either be NULL or contain valid JSON, as shown below.

```
ALTER TABLE Sales.Invoices WITH CHECK
    ADD CONSTRAINT CK_Sales_Invoices_ReturnedDeliveryData_Must_Be_Valid_JSON
    CHECK ((ISJSON(ReturnedDeliveryData)<>(0)));
```

Check constraints can reference more than one column. A frequently encountered requirement is that when one column contains a specific value, another column cannot be NULL.

Using constraints with compound conditions also provides an opportunity to provide check constraints in the face of changing requirements. If a new business rule requires that a nullable column must now contain a value, but no suitable default can be provided for the existing rows, you should consider creating a check constraint that verifies whether an incrementing ID column or date column is larger than the value it held when the rule took effect. For example, consider the table Sales.Invoices in the previous sample, which has a nullable column Comments. If effective September 1, 2022, every new and modified invoice must have a value in the Comments column, the table could be altered using the following script:

```
ALTER TABLE Sales.Invoices WITH CHECK
    ADD CONSTRAINT CH_Comments CHECK (LastEditedWhen < '2022-09-01'
    OR Comments IS NOT NULL);
```

A problem that you cannot solve by using a constraint is when a column must contain unique values if a value is provided. In other words, the column should allow multiple rows with NULL, but otherwise should be unique. The solution then is to use a filtered unique index.

➤ Read about filtered unique indexes in Chapter 15.

Default constraints

The fourth and final constraint type is the *default constraint*. A default constraint specifies the value that will be used as the default value when an INSERT statement does not specify a value for the column.

Default constraints are useful in a number of scenarios, most notably when adding a new non-nullable column to a table with existing data. This scenario is demonstrated in the following code sample, which adds a PrimaryLanguage column to the Application.People table in WideWorldImporters.

```
ALTER TABLE [Application].People
    ADD PrimaryLanguage nvarchar(50) NOT NULL
        CONSTRAINT DF_Application_People_PrimaryLanguage DEFAULT 'English';
```

Sequence objects

A *sequence* is a database object that generates numeric values in a specified order. Unlike the new SQL Server 2022 function GENERATE_SERIES() (which returns a table of numeric values), sequences are used when you want to retrieve the next available value.

How the sequence is generated depends on its start value, increment value, and minimum and maximum values. A sequence can be ascending, which is the case when the increment value is positive. When the increment value is negative, the values provided by the sequence are descending. A sequence object has some similarities to a column with an identity specification, but there are important distinctions:

- You can define a sequence to cycle, meaning when the numbers in the sequence are exhausted, the next use will return a previously generated number. Which number will be returned when the sequence cycles is determined by the increment. If it is an ascending sequence, the minimum value is returned; if it is a descending sequence, the maximum value is returned.

- A sequence is not bound to just one table. You can use numbers generated by the sequence in any table in the database or outside of a table.

- Sequence numbers can be generated without inserting a new row in a table.

- Values generated from a sequence can be updated or overridden without extra work.

Sequences are used when the application wants to have a numeric sequence generated one at a time—for example, before inserting one or more rows. Consider the common case of a parent-child relationship. Even though most developer tools expect to work with identity columns, knowing the value of a new parent row's primary key value and using it as the foreign key value in the child rows can have benefits for the application—for example, making the value modifiable—because the identity column values cannot be updated.

A sequence is especially useful when a single incrementing range is desired across multiple tables. More creative uses for a sequence include using it with a small range—say, 5—to automatically place new rows in one of five buckets.

To create a sequence, use the CREATE SEQUENCE command. When creating the sequence, you specify a data type that can hold an integer value; the start, increment, minimum, and maximum values; and whether the numbers should cycle when the minimum or maximum value is reached. However, all these are optional. If no data type is specified, the type will be bigint.

Ideally, you should match the data type of the sequence to the data type of the column that will be holding the value. If no increment is specified, it will be 1. If no minimum or maximum value is specified, the minimum and maximum value of the underlying data type will be used. By default, a sequence does not cycle.

The sample script that follows creates a sequence called MySequence of type int. The values start at 1001 and increment by 1 until 1003 is reached, after which 1001 will be generated again. The script demonstrates the cycling of the values using a WHILE loop.

```
-- Define the sequence
CREATE SEQUENCE dbo.MySequence AS int
    START WITH 1001
    INCREMENT BY 1
    MINVALUE 1001
    MAXVALUE 1003
    CYCLE;
-- Declare a loop counter
DECLARE @i int = 1;
-- Execute 4 times
WHILE (@i <= 4)
BEGIN
    -- Retrieve the next value from the sequence
    SELECT NEXT VALUE FOR dbo.MySequence AS NextValue;
    -- Increment the loop counter
    SET @i = @i + 1;
END;
```

The output of the script will be 1001, 1002, 1003, and 1001. The sequence is used by calling NEXT VALUE FOR. You can use NEXT VALUE FOR as a default constraint or as a function parameter unless it's a table-valued function. There are quite a few more places where NEXT VALUE FOR cannot be used, including subqueries, views, user-defined functions, and conditional expressions.

> ➤ For a full listing of limitations, visit *https://learn.microsoft.com/sql/t-sql/functions /next-value-for-transact-sql#limitations-and-restrictions*.

NOTE

Sequences are cached by default. When using caching, the current value is saved in memory; this might cause values to be skipped from the sequence on a server restart. You can turn off caching by specifying the NO CACHE clause in the CREATE or ALTER SEQUENCE statement. Doing this will allow the sequence values to be persisted at the cost of additional calls to disk. You can control the size of the cache by using the CACHE clause and specifying an integer constant.

CHAPTER 7

Inside OUT

Considerations with NEXT VALUE FOR

Using NEXT VALUE FOR multiple times for the same sequence in the same statement will result in only one value per row being used. For example, in the following T-SQL snippet, the first and the second column of the new row will have the same value:

```
INSERT INTO dbo.SomeTable VALUES (NEXT VALUE FOR dbo.MySequence,
    NEXT VALUE FOR dbo.MySequence, 'More data...');
```

This might not be the desired scenario. One solution is to use two separate sequences, although there is no guarantee they will return different numbers, even if their start values are different. Another solution is to define the sequence object's increment as 2 and, for one of the columns, add 1 to the sequence value, as in the following snippet:

```
INSERT INTO dbo.SomeTable VALUES (NEXT VALUE FOR dbo.MySequence,
    NEXT VALUE FOR dbo.MySequence + 1, 'More data...');
```

If you must guarantee that the values are different, you should place a CHECK CONSTRAINT on the table. However, we recommend evaluating the need for having two columns in the same table with autogenerated numeric values.

NEXT VALUE FOR generates and returns a single value at a time. If multiple values should be generated at once, the application can use the sp_sequence_get_range stored procedure. This procedure allocates as many numbers from the sequence as specified and returns metadata about the generated numbers. The actual values that are generated are not returned. The sample script that follows uses the MySequence sequence to generate five numbers. The metadata is captured in variables and later output. Note that the data type of most output parameters is sql_variant. The underlying type of those parameters is the data type of the sequence.

```
-- Declare variables to hold the metadata
DECLARE @FirstVal sql_variant, @LastVal sql_variant,
    @Increment sql_variant, @CycleCount int,
    @MinVal sql_variant, @MaxVal sql_variant;
-- Generate 5 numbers and capture all metadata
EXEC sp_sequence_get_range dbo.MySequence
    , @range_size = 5
    , @range_first_value = @FirstVal OUTPUT
    , @range_last_value = @LastVal OUTPUT
    , @range_cycle_count = @CycleCount OUTPUT
    , @sequence_increment = @Increment OUTPUT
    , @sequence_min_value = @MinVal OUTPUT
    , @sequence_max_value = @MaxVal OUTPUT;
-- Output the values of the output parameters
SELECT @FirstVal AS FirstVal, @LastVal AS LastVal
    , @CycleCount AS CycleCount, @Increment AS Increment
    , @MinVal AS MinVal, @MaxVal AS MaxVal;
```

The output of this sample script will vary with each run. Because of the specific way in which the MySequence object was defined, however, every three cycles, the output will repeat.

NOTE

Although the only required output parameter is `@range_first_value`, if the application intends to use any value but the first, the application should consume all the metadata that is returned as part of the optional output parameters. Without it, the application might infer the incorrect value. By fetching the values, you know you have the value you expect. It is up to the application to calculate the actual numbers generated by using the first value, last value, increment, minimum and maximum value, and cycle count output parameters.

CAUTION

You might receive error 11732 when using sequences. This error indicates that the limit of the sequence has been reached and the sequence does not cycle. If this error occurs when using the `sp_sequence_get_range` stored procedure, no values are returned; that is, the sequence is not affected at all.

User-defined data types and user-defined types

SQL Server supports defining new data types. Two variations exist:

- **User-defined data types (UDTs).** These alias existing data types.

- **User-defined types.** These are .NET Framework types.

An effective and common use for UDT is creating table types. As the name implies, a table type defines a table structure as a type that can then be used as a function or stored procedure parameter. Such a parameter enables the easy passing of multiple values or rows to the function or procedure.

We should warn against the liberal use of either variant of custom data types. They can make a database schema significantly more difficult to understand and troubleshoot. Alias types add little value because they do not create new behavior, but on the other hand, some architects find the "self-documenting" aspect attractive. SQL CLR user-defined types enable SQL Server to expose new behavior, but they might come with a significant security risk if they are used improperly.

➤ More details about the security of CLR user-defined types can be found at *https://learn .microsoft.com/sql/relational-databases/clr-integration/common-language-runtime -integration-overview.*

User-defined data types

Alias data types are merely a new name for an existing system data type including the same length and precision as the original data type, optionally a default nullability specification. Specifying a default value or a validation rule for the alias is deprecated functionality.

For example, if you want to ensure that a customer name was always defined as an nvarchar column with a maximum length of 100 characters, you might use the CREATE TYPE statement as shown here:

```
CREATE TYPE CustomerNameType FROM nvarchar(100);
GO
```

After creating this UDT, in any place where you would ordinarily specify nvarchar(100), you can use CustomerNameType instead. This can be in a table's column definition, as the return type of a scalar function, or as a parameter to a stored procedure.

The following abbreviated CREATE TABLE statement, which is based on the WideWorldImporters sample Customers table, illustrates how CustomerNameType replaces nvarchar(100):

```
CREATE TABLE Sales.Customers (
    CustomerID INT NOT NULL,
    CustomerName CustomerNameType, -- can override nullability of the type here
...
```

UDTs can adversely affect data quality, as there are no additional methods of providing data protection.

CLR user-defined types

You develop user-defined types in a .NET language such as C#, and you must compile them into a .NET assembly. This .NET assembly is then registered in the database where the type will be used. A database can use these types only if SQL CLR is enabled.

Use caution when enabling CLR and granting permissions to assemblies, especially for trust-worthy databases. Depending on the permissions granted, an assembly may be able to acquire sysadmin privileges, gain access to system resources, access user data, or any combination of the above.

Sparse columns

Sparse columns store NULL values in an optimized manner, reducing space requirements for storing NULL values at the expense of overhead to retrieve non-NULL values. As discussed in the earlier section "The XML data type," a potential workaround for saving storage space for tables with many columns that allow NULL and have many NULL values is using sparse columns. Tables with sparse columns can have up to 30,000 columns. Sparse columns exist at the storage layer and are not counted as part of the maximum number of columns a table can have. Microsoft suggests that a space savings of at least 20 percent should be achieved before the overhead is worth it.

➤ The Microsoft Docs at *https://learn.microsoft.com/sql/relational-databases/tables/use -sparse-columns* define the space savings by data type when using sparse columns.

NOTE

Not all data types can be defined as sparse columns. Specifically, you cannot define geography and geometry, image, text and ntext, rowversion, and UDTs as sparse columns.

Sparse columns are defined in CREATE or ALTER TABLE statements by using the SPARSE keyword. The sample script that follows creates a table, OrderDetails, with two sparse columns, ReturnedDate and ReturnedReason. Sparse columns are useful here because we might expect most products to *not* be returned and for the ReturnedDate and ReturnedReason columns to be retrieved only occasionally.

```
CREATE TABLE dbo.OrderDetails (
    OrderId int NOT NULL,
    OrderDetailId int NOT NULL,
    ProductId int NOT NULL,
    Quantity int NOT NULL,
    ReturnedDate date SPARSE NULL,
    ReturnedReason varchar(50) SPARSE NULL);
```

NOTE

For brevity, the CREATE TABLE script in the preceding example does not define primary keys, foreign keys, or columns that you might typically expect in an order details table.

Computed columns

Typically, columns store persisted data. Derived data—that is, data that is the result of a calculation—is not ordinarily stored. Instead, the application derives it every time it's needed. In some circumstances, storing derived data in the database can be beneficial. SQL Server supports storing derived data using computed columns and indexed views.

Computed columns are defined in a table as the result of an expression of other columns in the table, function calls, and perhaps constants. Computed column values can either be calculated when accessed (the default) or persisted, depending on the need.

Using computed columns is always a trade-off. You use a computed column when you determine that there is some benefit to the Database Engine being aware of the derived data. You might find this beneficial because the database could be the central source of the computation instead of having to spread it out across multiple systems. Another trade-off is found when you persist computed columns; you trade storage space for compute efficiency.

If the expression that calculates the computed column's value is deterministic, that column can be persisted and indexed. An expression is deterministic if the expression will always return the same result for the same inputs. An example of a deterministic expression is `OrderQuantity + 1`. Given the same value for `OrderQuantity`, the result will always be the same. An example of a nondeterministic expression is one that uses the `SYSDATETIME()` function; the expression returns a different result each time it is executed.

➤ **For a complete discussion of indexing computed columns, visit** *https://learn.microsoft.com /sql/relational-databases/indexes/indexes-on-computed-columns.*

The WideWorldImporters sample database contains two computed columns in the `Sales .Invoices` table. One of these is `ConfirmedDeliveryTime`. It is derived by examining the contents of the JSON value stored in the `ReturnedDeliveryData` column and converting it to a `datetime2` value. The `datetime2` value is not persisted in this case. This means each time `ConfirmedDeliveryTime` is queried, the expression is evaluated. If the column was persisted, the expression would be evaluated only when the row is created or updated.

When defining a computed column, instead of specifying a data type, you specify the AS clause followed by an expression. Using the `Sales.OrderLines` table in the same sample database, you can create a computed column to calculate the order line's extended price. The following sample SQL statement illustrates how:

```
ALTER TABLE Sales.OrderLines
    ADD ExtendedPrice AS (Quantity * UnitPrice) PERSISTED;
```

This statement creates a new column in the table called `ExtendedPrice`. Its value is computed using the expression `Quantity * UnitPrice`. The column is persisted because we expect to be querying this value frequently. The type of the computed column is determined by SQL Server based on the result of the expression. In this case, the data type is set to `decimal(29,2)`. If the determined data type is not suitable for your needs, you can apply a cast in the expression to a more appropriate data type.

Special table types

As data storage needs have become more specialized, SQL Server has gained extended functionality to support these scenarios in the form of special table types. These table types support scenarios that would otherwise require significant effort by the database developer to implement. This section discusses temporal tables, memory-optimized tables, external tables, and graph tables. We discuss another special table type, `FileTable`, in the next section.

➤ External tables and PolyBase are discussed later in this chapter, in the section "Benefits of PolyBase for external data sources and external tables."

System-versioned temporal tables

System-versioned temporal tables, or *temporal tables* for short, are designed to keep not only current values of rows, but also historic values. In addition to the current table, there is a companion history table with the same schema structure. The history table stores the historic rows. SQL Server can create the history table at the time the current table is created, and you can opt to specify the history table's name or let SQL Server create an anonymous history table. Alternatively, you might use an existing table as the history table, in which case the Database Engine will validate that the schema matches that of the current table. Creating a history table by hand can be complex, but specifying a history table that was previously used and was disconnected for some reason is a valuable option.

When a table is designed to be a temporal table, it must have two explicitly defined columns of type datetime2, which are used to indicate the validity period of the row. The datetime2 columns can have any precision between 0 and 7. You define the name of these columns and add the GENERATED ALWAYS AS ROW START|END clause. In addition to that clause, two more clauses are required in the table declaration: PERIOD FOR SYSTEM_TIME (start_time_col, end_time_col) and WITH (SYSTEM_VERSIONING = ON).

NOTE

Temporal tables should be used when users need to query the data and see changes over time. Later sections in this chapter cover change tracking and change data capture and compare these features to temporal tables and how they can be used for ETL type processes.

Create a system-versioned temporal table

The simple CREATE TABLE statement that follows illustrates the use of these clauses to create a system-versioned temporal table with an anonymous history table:

```
CREATE TABLE dbo.Products (
    -- Clustered primary key is required
    ProductId int NOT NULL PRIMARY KEY CLUSTERED
  , ProductName varchar(50) NOT NULL
  , CategoryId int NOT NULL
  , SalesPrice money NOT NULL
  , SysStartTime datetime2 GENERATED ALWAYS AS ROW START NOT NULL
  , SysEndTime datetime2 GENERATED ALWAYS AS ROW END NOT NULL
  -- PERIOD FOR SYSTEM_TIME to indicate columns storing validity start and end
  , PERIOD FOR SYSTEM_TIME (SysStartTime, SysEndTime))
-- SYSTEM_VERSIONING clause without HISTORY_TABLE option creates
-- an anonymous history table, meaning the name will be auto-generated
WITH (SYSTEM_VERSIONING = ON);
```

NOTE

The row's start and end validity column values are managed by SQL Server. The values in those columns are in the UTC time zone. Neither validity period column will ever be NULL and the end time will always be 9999-12-31 in the base table.

An existing table can also be altered to become a temporal table. This is a two-stage process, in which you first alter the table to include the two required datetime2 columns and then alter the table to turn on system versioning while optionally specifying a history table name. The history of all columns in the table will be captured, so if the table is very volatile, and if it includes columns that you don't care to track, this feature may not be useful.

When creating a new table or altering an existing one, you can apply the optional HIDDEN property to the columns for the validity period to exclude the columns from a standard SELECT statement. This might be useful to ensure backward compatibility with existing applications that query the table.

Understand data movement in temporal tables

The Database Engine manages the movement of data from the current table to the history table. The following list details the data movements that take place with each Data Manipulation Language (DML) operation:

- **INSERT and BULK INSERT.** A new row is added to the current table. The row's validity start time is set to the transaction's start time. The validity end time is set to the datetime2 type's maximum value—December 31, 9999—at a fractional second, or a whole second when using datetime2(0). There is no change in the history table.

- **UPDATE.** A new row is added to the history table with the old values. The validity end time of the history row is set to the transaction's start time. In the current table, the row is updated with the new values and the validity start time is updated to the transaction's start time. If the same row is updated multiple times in the same transaction, multiple history rows with the same validity start and end time will be inserted. Those rows will not be retrieved using typical queries; only the current version of non-deleted rows will be returned. For instance, if only one column is changed, the entire row will be duplicated in the history structure.

- **DELETE.** A new row is added to the history table containing the values from the current table. The validity end period of the history row is set to the transaction's start time. The row is removed from the current table.

MERGE statements need no special consideration. A MERGE operation behaves as if separate INSERT, UPDATE, and DELETE statements are executed, as determined necessary by the MATCH clauses. Those statements add rows to the history table, as just described.

Query temporal tables

Querying a temporal table is no different from querying another table if your query only needs to return current data. This makes it possible to modify an existing database and alter tables into temporal tables without requiring application modifications.

NOTE

Recall that when using the HIDDEN property on the period columns, existing applications won't be exposed to those columns. You must explicitly include hidden columns if you want to query them.

When designing queries that need to return historical data or even a mix of current and historical data, you use the FOR SYSTEM_TIME clause in the FROM clause of the SELECT statement. There are five subclauses used with FOR SYSTEM_TIME that help you define the time frame for which you want to retrieve rows. The following list describes these subclauses. It also provides a sample T-SQL statement for each one that you can run on the WideWorldImporters sample database to see its effects.

NOTE

The IsCurrent column in the output indicates whether the retrieved row is the current row or a history row. This is accomplished by checking whether the ValidTo column contains the maximum datetime2 value. Due to the nature of the WideWorldImporters sample data, you might need to scroll through several hundred rows before encountering a value of 0 for IsCurrent, which indicates that it is a history row.

- **ALL.** The result set is essentially the union between the current and the history tables. Multiple rows can be returned for the same primary key in the current table. This will be the case for any row that has one or more history entries, as shown here:

```
SELECT PersonID, FullName,
    CASE WHEN ValidTo = '9999-12-31 23:59:59.9999999' THEN 1
        ELSE 0 END AS IsCurrent
FROM Application.People FOR SYSTEM_TIME ALL
WHERE PeriodId = 11
ORDER BY ValidFrom;
```

- **AS OF.** This returns rows that were valid at the single point in time in the UTC time zone. Rows that have been deleted from the current table or that didn't exist yet will not be included:

```
/* AS OF sub-clause returns all rows that were valid at one point in time.
 * Recall the SYSTEM_TIME is UTC.
 * Showing an example here of how to convert a local time to UTC:
 * Local time is March 13, 2022 12:00 AM (midnight) US Pacific Time
 * (the start of the day).
```

```
* March 13 is not in daylight saving time, so the offset is -8 hours.
* Thus, records we're looking for were active on March 13, 2022 8 AM UTC.
* Calling the AT TIME ZONE function twice gives the desired time in UTC.
*/
DECLARE @AsOfTime datetime2(7) = CONVERT(datetime2(7), '2022-03-13T00:00:00', 126)
    AT TIME ZONE 'Pacific Standard Time' AT TIME ZONE 'UTC';
SELECT PersonID, FullName
    , CASE WHEN ValidTo = '9999-12-31 23:59:59.9999999' THEN 1
          ELSE 0 END 'IsCurrent'
FROM [Application].People FOR SYSTEM_TIME AS OF @AsOfTime
ORDER BY ValidFrom;
```

- **FROM ... TO.** This returns all rows that were active between the specified lower bound and upper bound. In other words, if the row's validity start time is before the upper bound or its validity end time is after the lower bound, the row will be included in the result set. Rows that became active exactly on the upper bound or that closed exactly on the lower bound are not included. This clause might return multiple rows for the same primary key value:

```
SELECT PersonID, FullName,
    CASE WHEN ValidTo = '9999-12-31 23:59:59.9999999' THEN 1
          ELSE 0 END AS IsCurrent
-- SYSTEM_TIME uses UTC so provide date range in UTC as well
FROM Application.People FOR SYSTEM_TIME FROM '2022-03-13' TO '2022-04-23'
ORDER BY ValidFrom;
```

- **BETWEEN ... AND.** This is like FROM ... TO, but rows that opened exactly on the upper bound are included:

```
SELECT PersonID, FullName,
    CASE WHEN ValidTo = '9999-12-31 23:59:59.9999999' THEN 1
          ELSE 0 END AS IsCurrent
FROM Application.People FOR SYSTEM_TIME BETWEEN '2022-03-13' AND '2022-04-23'
ORDER BY ValidFrom;
```

- **CONTAINED IN (,).** This returns rows that were active exclusively between the lower and the upper bound. If a row was valid earlier than the lower bound or valid past the upper bound, it is not included. A row that was opened exactly on the lower bound or closed exactly on the upper bound will be included. If the upper bound is earlier than the maximum value for datetime2, only history rows will be included:

```
DECLARE @now datetime2(7) = SYSUTCDATETIME();
SELECT PersonID, FullName,
    CASE WHEN ValidTo = '9999-12-31 23:59:59.9999999' THEN 1
          ELSE 0 END AS IsCurrent
FROM Application.People FOR SYSTEM_TIME CONTAINED IN ('2022-03-13', @now)
ORDER BY ValidFrom;
```

NOTE

In the sample statement for the CONTAINED IN subclause, the variable @now is declared and initialized with the current UTC time. This is necessary because the FOR SYSTEM_TIME clause does not support functions as arguments.

Manage temporal tables

Altering a temporal table will generally cause its associated history table to be altered in the same way. This applies when adding, altering, or removing columns. However, there are a few operations that require you to disable system versioning. These include adding an identity, rowguidcol, or computed column; adding a sparse column in most cases; and adding a column set.

CAUTION

If you add a new column that does not allow NULL to a temporal table, the default value you're required to specify will be used to fill the new column in both the current table and the history table. While it's hard to imagine another solution that Microsoft could have implemented, one might argue that the history table doesn't reflect the truth at the time its records were active.

To drop a temporal table, you must disable system versioning and then drop both the current table and the history table using two separate DROP TABLE statements.

Inside OUT

How do you design temporal tables to use the least amount of space?

Introduced in SQL Server 2017, you can use HISTORY_RETENTION_PERIOD with SYSTEM _VERSIONING when defining or altering system-versioned temporal tables. By default, HISTORY_RETENTION_PERIOD is set to INFINITE, meaning SQL Server will not automatically purge history data. By defining a finite period, such as 6 MONTHS, SQL Server will automatically purge history records with a valid end time older than the finite period. Two conditions must hold true, however. First, the temporal history retention flag must be enabled for the database (which it is by default). And second, the history table must have a clustered or columnstore index. For a rowstore clustered index, the first column in the index must be the column corresponding to the end of the validity period. If these conditions hold true, a background task is created to clean up the aged data.

In addition to using automatic retention, which controls the growth of the history table, you can also consider vertically partitioning the temporal table. Vertical partitioning is discussed in more detail in the "Vertical partitions" section later in this chapter. Splitting the table vertically into two tables, and only making one table system versioned, results in significant space savings, because the history is kept only for the columns in the system-versioned table. This does come at the expense of potentially frequent JOINs between both tables. This approach is also not suitable if you are system-versioning tables for compliance requirements for which all row data must be available in exactly the form it was at any given point.

Besides reducing the history kept by setting a retention period and using vertical partitioning to avoid keeping history for columns that do not require it, you might also consider horizontal partitioning or a custom cleanup script to manage the history data. These options are described in detail at *https://learn.microsoft.com/sql/relational-databases /tables/manage-retention-of-historical-data-in-system-versioned-temporal-tables.*

Memory-optimized tables

A traditional disk-based table's data is loaded in memory as needed. The Database Engine handles loading data from durable storage to memory and removing the data from memory again. Many factors play a role in when data is loaded or released from memory. Data in memory-optimized tables is kept in memory at all times. This data is durable by default because it is persisted to disk (though the format of the data is different from that of disk-based tables). A *schema-only, non-durable* option is available, which does not retain data between service restarts and certain other operations.

The benefits of keeping all data from specific tables in memory is blazing-fast performance, which often can be improved by another order of magnitude by applying a columnstore index to the memory-optimized table. (Columnstore indexes are covered in Chapter 15.) This of course requires the server to have sufficient memory to hold the memory-optimized tables' data in memory while still leaving enough room for other operations. If the system runs out of memory (OOM), errors will occur, and you'll need to take specific steps to recover.

➤ To avoid OOM issues, monitor memory usage. The Microsoft Docs at *https://learn.microsoft .com/sql/relational-databases/in-memory-oltp/monitor-and-troubleshoot-memory-usage #bkmk_Monitoring* describe how to monitor and troubleshoot memory usage for memory-optimized tables.

➤ Guidance for resolving various OOM issues is available at *https://learn.microsoft.com/sql /relational-databases/in-memory-oltp/resolve-out-of-memory-issues.*

Memory-optimized tables are available in all editions of SQL Server and in Azure SQL Database's Premium and Business Critical tiers. However, memory limitations present in the Express and Standard editions of SQL Server do apply to memory-optimized tables.

NOTE

Over time, many limitations of memory-optimized tables that were present in earlier versions of SQL Server have been eliminated.

➤ This chapter discusses only the setup and configuration of memory-optimized tables, along with caveats. You can find a complete discussion of the purpose and use of memory-optimized tables in Chapter 15.

Database preparation for memory-optimized tables

Before creating memory-optimized tables, you must prepare the database. The database compatibility level must be at least 130. For SQL Server, you need to create a memory-optimized filegroup. There is no such requirement for Azure SQL Database—or, more accurately, the filegroup is intrinsically present.

CAUTION

You cannot remove a memory-optimized filegroup without dropping the database.

Microsoft provides a T-SQL script to ensure that these settings are correct and that a memory-optimized filegroup is created. You can even run the script in Azure SQL Database to ensure that the database supports memory-optimized tables.

➤ Rather than reprinting this script here, we refer you to the SQL Server samples GitHub page at *https://raw.githubusercontent.com/microsoft/sql-server-samples/main/samples/features /in-memory-database/in-memory-oltp/t-sql-scripts/enable-in-memory-oltp.sql*.

The script first checks to ensure that the instance or database supports memory-optimized tables, using the SERVERPROPERTY(N'IsXTPSupported') function call. On SQL Server, the script will create a memory-optimized filegroup and container if none already exist. The script also checks and sets the database-compatibility level.

After these actions are complete, you are ready to create one or more memory-optimized tables. The WITH (MEMORY_OPTIMIZED = ON) is the key clause of the CREATE TABLE statement that makes your table a memory-optimized table. Memory-optimized tables support indexing, but you must create and delete them using an ALTER TABLE ... ADD/DROP INDEX statement instead of a CREATE/DROP INDEX statement.

Natively compiled stored procedures and user-defined functions

You can access memory-optimized tables via interpreted T-SQL statements and stored procedures. However, you can achieve significant additional performance gains if you use *natively compiled stored procedures*. These stored procedures are compiled to machine code the first time they are run rather than evaluated every time they run.

NOTE

Natively compiled stored procedures can access only memory-optimized tables. Traditional interpreted stored procedures and ad hoc queries can reference both disk-based tables and memory-optimized tables in the same statement—for example, to join a memory-optimized table with a disk-based table.

To create a natively compiled stored procedure, use the WITH NATIVE_COMPILATION clause of the CREATE PROCEDURE statement. Natively compiled stored procedure objects require the use of the SCHEMABINDING option. The BEGIN ATOMIC statement is also required; it replaces BEGIN TRANSACTION for natively compiled procedures and functions. This statement either begins a new transaction or creates a save point in an existing transaction on the session. When creating a save point in an existing transaction, only the changes made by the stored procedure would be rolled back if the stored procedure were to fail.

The BEGIN ATOMIC statement has two required options:

- **TRANSACTION_ISOLATION.** You must set this value to one of the three supported isolation levels: snapshot, repeatable read, or serializable.

- **LANGUAGE.** This is a name value from the sys.syslanguages system compatibility view. For example, for United States English, it is us_english, and for Dutch it is Nederlands.

The BEGIN ATOMIC statement is also where delayed durability can be specified (DELAYED _DURABILITY = ON). With delayed durability, the Database Engine reports to the client that the transaction committed before the log record has been committed to a drive. This creates a risk of data loss should the service or server shut down before the asynchronous log write is completed. You should take the same care to use delayed durability with BEGIN ATOMIC as with BEGIN TRANSACTION. To use delayed durability, it must not be disabled at the database level. Schema-only memory-optimized tables do not use transaction logging, so when modifying data in those tables, there is no benefit in specifying delayed durability.

➤ **For more information on delayed durability, see Chapter 14.**

The following short sample script creates a memory-optimized table and natively compiled stored procedure in a database that has been prepared previously.

```
CREATE TABLE dbo.UserDetails (
    UserId    int NOT NULL,
    DetailId  int NOT NULL,
    Detail    nvarchar(50) NOT NULL,
    CONSTRAINT PK_UserDetails PRIMARY KEY NONCLUSTERED (UserId, DetailId)
) WITH (MEMORY_OPTIMIZED = ON, DURABILITY = SCHEMA_AND_DATA);
GO
CREATE PROCEDURE dbo.GetUserName
    @userId int
```

```
WITH NATIVE_COMPILATION, SCHEMABINDING
AS
BEGIN ATOMIC
    WITH (TRANSACTION ISOLATION LEVEL = SNAPSHOT,
          LANGUAGE = N'us_english')
    SELECT Detail
    FROM dbo.UserDetails
    WHERE UserId = @userId
        -- Assume this refers to the name
        AND DetailId = 1;
END;
GO
```

NOTE

Several T-SQL statements and constructs are not supported with memory-optimized tables and natively compiled stored procedures. A full list of these unsupported constructs is available in Microsoft Docs at *https://learn.microsoft.com/sql/relational -databases/in-memory-oltp/transact-sql-constructs-not-supported-by-in-memory-oltp*.

Caveats to memory-optimized tables

To put it plainly, you should probably not convert all of your tables to memory-optimized tables. There are several caveats you must consider before adopting memory-optimized tables and when deciding which tables to turn into memory-optimized tables. This section discusses these caveats.

Memory-optimized tables support only three transaction isolation levels: snapshot, repeatable read, and serializable. If your application needs other isolation levels, you will not be able to implement memory-optimized tables. Refer to Chapter 14 for complete details about transaction isolation levels.

CAUTION

Changing the database's read-commit snapshot property will cause schema-only memory-optimized tables to be truncated. Although database designers are aware that schema-only memory-optimized tables are not persisted and might load initial data into such tables when the SQL Server service starts, they might not know to reload data after a database property change.

Because all memory-optimized table data is kept in memory, you would correctly expect additional memory requirements. When planning for memory size, however, you should consider that the memory requirement of a memory-optimized table can be more than twice the size of the data in the table. This is due to processing overhead requirements, including the row versions that are kept.

➤ To review specific guidance on planning for memory size, refer to *https://learn.microsoft* *.com/sql/relational-databases/in-memory-oltp/estimate-memory-requirements-for* *-memory-optimized-tables.*

When persisted memory-optimized tables are used, upon service start, the Database Engine will load all data from the drive to memory. Indexes of memory-optimized tables are not persisted, and they are rebuilt entirely upon service start as the index operations are not logged. The service is not available while these operations take place. With large tables, this can lead to significantly longer service start times. Even though you might carefully plan your service or server restarts for a maintenance window, an unplanned failover on a failover cluster instance (FCI) will also take that amount of time. This might be detrimental to meeting your Service-Level Agreement (SLA), which might have been the entire reason to configure an FCI in the first place. If the performance of memory-optimized tables is needed in combination with a high-availability configuration, you might consider availability groups instead. Because the Database Engine service is running on the secondary, there is no delay caused by having to read the data from a drive and rebuilding indexes.

➤ Read about FCI and availability groups in Chapter 11.

One way to reduce database startup time due to memory-optimized tables is to ensure that checkpoints are taken frequently. This is because checkpoints cause the updated rows in the memory-optimized table to be committed to the data file. Any data that is not committed to the drive must be read from the transaction log. For large tables, this benefit is likely small.

Another contributor to delays, though after service start, is when natively compiled stored procedures are run for the first time. This can take about as long as running a traditional stored procedure because the compiled version of the stored procedure is not saved. Any time a natively compiled stored procedure is run subsequently, the compiled version will be faster.

Memory-optimized tables use an optimistic concurrency model. While memory-optimized tables don't use locks, latches, or spinlocks, they are subject to isolation level errors and update conflicts. This means a client application might experience unexpected conflicts (which are shown as errors that are truly just messages to the client that their data is being used in an incompatible manner). You should design the application to handle those. Ironically, one of the greatest benefits of memory-optimized tables is optimistic concurrency, but it also causes one of the largest drawbacks, in that applications must be designed to correctly handle the errors generated.

Not unlike when faster drive storage is used for SQL Server, when adopting memory-optimized tables, you might find that the CPU usage is much higher. This is because much less time is spent waiting for I/O operations to complete. This is exactly why you implemented memory-optimized tables: CPU utilization is higher because data is being processed faster! However, you might inadvertently reduce the number of concurrent requests that can be served, especially if one instance runs multiple databases. If this is a concern, consider using Resource Governor to manage the relative CPU usage for specific workloads.

Graph tables

Introduced in SQL Server 2017 and extended in SQL Server 2019, graph functionality provides schema extensions to store directed graph data—that is, nodes and edges—in the relational database. Fitting graph data in a relational database is challenging, and this feature attempts to resolve these challenges. The graph features in SQL Server are useful in some common scenarios, particularly when trying to integrate graph structures with relational ones, but are currently not a complete replacement for dedicated graph databases that support advanced scenarios.

Graph data is often associated with networks, such as social networks, and hierarchies. More generally, graphs are data structures that consist of nodes and edges. The nodes represent entities and the edges represent the connections between those entities. Nodes are also referred to as *vertices*, and edges as *relationships*.

Some use cases lend themselves particularly well to being stored in a graph model. For example:

- **Highly interconnected data.** A commonly used example of highly interconnected data is that of social networks. Social network data expresses relationships among people, organizations, posts, pictures, events, and more. In such a data model, each entity can be connected to any other entity, creating lots of many-to-many relationships. In a relational database, this requires the creation of a table for each many-to-many relationship. Querying such relationships requires two or more JOIN clauses, which can quickly create lengthy SELECT statements. Such statements can be difficult to digest and are potentially error prone. Graph databases offer support for flexible definitions of relationships and query syntax that is less verbose.

- **Hierarchical data.** A single node in a graph can have many parents in addition to many children. You may also find it conceptually easier to build even a simple tree, where a node has only one parent, using nodes and edges.

- **Many-to-many relationships that can be extended at any time during the data life cycle.** Relational databases have strict requirements for the definition of tables and relationships. For a data model that is required to evolve quickly to support new relationships, adding new relationships is easy enough in a relational database, but a graph lets you use the same table/edge for multiple relationships. This strict schema requirement can get in the way of meeting evolving requirements in a timely fashion.

You can effectively implement these use cases by employing a graph database. While these features are evolving and regularly being improved, SQL Server's graph features do not (yet) provide a solution that is on par with dedicated graph databases. The "Graph table shortcomings" section later in the chapter discusses some of the limitations of the current implementation.

Define graph tables

In SQL Server, you store graph data in two table types: *node* and *edge* tables. These table types are still stored internally as relational structures, but the Database Engine has additional capabilities to manage and query the data that is stored within them.

The T-SQL CREATE TABLE syntax has two clauses: AS NODE and AS EDGE. The following T-SQL script creates a People node table and a Relationships edge table. You can run this script in any existing or new database; there are no specific requirements of the database:

```
CREATE TABLE dbo.People (
    PersonId int NOT NULL PRIMARY KEY CLUSTERED,
    FirstName nvarchar(50) NOT NULL,
    LastName nvarchar(50) NOT NULL
) AS NODE;
CREATE TABLE dbo.Relationships (
    RelationshipType nvarchar(50) NOT NULL,
    -- Two people can only be related once
    CONSTRAINT UX_Relationship UNIQUE ($from_id, $to_id),
    CONSTRAINT EC_People_ConnectsTo_People CONNECTION (dbo.People TO dbo.People)
) AS EDGE;
```

In the sample script, both the node and the edge table contain user-defined columns. Edge tables are not required to have user-defined columns, but node tables must have at least one. In the case of edge tables, which model relationships, simply modeling the relationship without additional attributes can be all you need. In the case of node tables, which model entities, there is no value in a node without properties, as the nodes exist to compare properties to one another. Designing a node table is comparable to designing a relational table; you would still consider normalization and other concepts.

The sample script also defines an *edge constraint*, a feature introduced in SQL Server 2019. Edge constraints restrict which node types can be associated using a particular edge. In this case, a Relationships edge is defined between two nodes of type People.

The edge constraint may be repeated multiple times in a single-edge table definition, but the entries in the table must comply with all constraints. Alternatively, multiple edge constraint clauses may be defined within the same edge constraint, in which case any of the constraint clauses must be satisfied.

NOTE

Edge constraints and edge constraint clauses are not the same thing. An edge constraint is used to enforce integrity on an edge table. An edge constraint can have one or more edge constraint clauses, and an edge constraint clause is used to define relationships between nodes.

The next script defines a second node table, `Animals`; removes the existing edge constraint; and finally creates a new edge constraint with two clauses, allowing a relationship to exist between two `People` rows or between a `People` row and an `Animals` row.

```
CREATE TABLE dbo.Animals (
    AnimalId int NOT NULL PRIMARY KEY CLUSTERED,
    AnimalName nvarchar(50) NOT NULL
) AS NODE;
-- Drop and re-create the constraint, because an edge constraint cannot be altered
ALTER TABLE Relationships
    DROP CONSTRAINT EC_Relationship;
ALTER TABLE Relationships
    ADD CONSTRAINT EC_Relationship CONNECTION (dbo.People TO dbo.People,
        dbo.People TO dbo.Animals);
```

NOTE

Edge constraints not only enforce the type(s) of node that can be connected using the edge, they also enforce referential integrity between the nodes and the edge. SQL Server supports cascading deletes of edges when a node is deleted. Specify ON DELETE CASCADE in the CONSTRAINT clause to enable cascading of the delete operation, or ON DELETE NO ACTION (the default) if deleting the node should fail.

In addition to user-defined columns, both table types also have one or more columns that are added to the table implicitly to support graph operations. Node tables have two system-generated implicit (also called *pseudo*) columns, $graph_id and $node_id:

- **graph_id_<hex_string_1>.** This is a `bigint` column, which stores the internally generated graph ID for the row. This column is internal and cannot be explicitly queried. However, information about this column will be accessible in sys.columns.

- **$node_id_<hex_string_2>.** This returns a computed `nvarchar` value that includes the internally generated `bigint` value and schema information. This column can be queried but you should avoid explicitly querying this column. Instead, you should use the NODE _ID_FROM_PARTS() query to access the JSON.

In addition to optional user-defined columns, edge tables have three implicit columns:

- **$edge_id_<hex_string_3>.** This is a system-managed value, comparable to the $node_id column in a node table.

- **$from_id_<hex_string_4>.** This references a node ID from any node table in the graph that meets the edge constraints. This is the source node in the directed graph.

- **$to_id_<hex_string_5>.** This references a node ID from any node table in the graph that meets the edge constraints. This is the target node in the directed graph.

Inside OUT

When should you choose graph tables over relational tables?

There is nothing inherent to a graph database that makes it possible for you to solve a problem that you cannot also solve using a relational database. The relational database concept has been around for nearly five decades, and relational database management systems are as popular as ever.

However, the use cases described earlier, and queries described momentarily, are examples of data models and operations that might be better addressed by a graph structure. This is because the Database Engine has specific optimizations to address some of the types of queries that are often run against such models.

In addition, a graph table can still contain foreign keys referring to relational tables, and a relational table can contain a foreign key referring to a graph table.

Work with graph data

DML statements generally work the same in graph tables as they do in relational tables. Some operations are not supported. An edge table does not support updating either the $frHi, om_id, or $to_id column value. Thus, to update a relationship, the existing edge row must be deleted and a new one inserted. User-defined columns of edge tables do support update operations.

When querying graph data, you can write your own table joins to join nodes to edges to nodes, though this approach offers none of the benefits of graph tables. Instead, we recommend using the MATCH comparison operator in the WHERE clause. The MATCH operator uses a style of expression referred to as *ASCII art* to indicate how nodes and edges should be traversed. You might be surprised to find that the node and edge tables are specified using old-style join syntax first. The MATCH subclause then performs the actual equi-joins necessary to traverse the graph.

The brief examples that follow are intended to provide an introduction only. They build on the creation of the People and Relationship tables shown in the previous example. First, a few rows of sample data are inserted. Then, the sample data is queried using the MATCH subclause:

```
-- Insert a few sample people
-- $node_id is implicit and skipped
INSERT INTO dbo.People VALUES
    (1, 'Karina', 'Jakobsen'),
    (2, 'David', 'Hamilton'),
    (3, 'James', 'Hamilton'),
    (4, 'Stella', 'Rosenhain');
-- Insert a few sample relationships
```

```
-- The first sub-select retrieves the $node_id of the from_node
-- The second sub-select retrieves the $node_id of the to_node
INSERT INTO dbo.Relationships VALUES
    ((SELECT $node_id FROM People WHERE PersonId = 1),
     (SELECT $node_id FROM People WHERE PersonId = 2),
     'spouse'),
    ((SELECT $node_id FROM People WHERE PersonId = 2),
     (SELECT $node_id FROM People WHERE PersonId = 3),
     'father'),
    ((SELECT $node_id FROM People WHERE PersonId = 4),
     (SELECT $node_id FROM People WHERE PersonId = 2),
     'mother'));
-- Simple graph query
SELECT P1.FirstName + ' is the ' + R.RelationshipType +
    ' of ' + P2.FirstName + '.'
FROM dbo.People P1, dbo.People P2, dbo.Relationships R
WHERE MATCH(P1-I->P2);
```

The arrow used in the MATCH subclause means that a node in the People table should be related to another node in the People table using the Relations edge. As with self-referencing many-to-many relationships, the People table needs to be present in the FROM clause twice to allow the second People node to be different from the first. Otherwise, the query would retrieve only edges in which people are related to themselves. (There are no such relationships in our sample.)

The true power of the MATCH subclause is evident when traversing the graph between three or more nodes. One such example would be finding restaurants your friends have liked in the city where your friends live and where you intend to travel.

➤ **For a more comprehensive sample graph database, refer to** *https://learn.microsoft.com/sql /relational-databases/graphs/sql-graph-sample.*

SQL Server 2019 introduced support for the shortest path algorithm. With this support, it is now possible for the MATCH clause to traverse an arbitrary number of nodes to find a related node. Several T-SQL syntax elements are required, including a SHORTEST_PATH function as well as FOR PATH and WITHIN GROUP (GRAPH PATH) clauses. The following sample retrieves all the direct descendants of one of the people in the same table:

```
-- Construct Stella Rosenhain's direct descendants' family tree
-- In our example data, two rows will be returned
SELECT P1.FirstName
       , STRING_AGG(P2.FirstName, '->') WITHIN GROUP (GRAPH PATH) AS Descendants
FROM dbo.People P1
    , dbo.People FOR PATH P2
    , dbo.Relationships FOR PATH related_to1
WHERE (MATCH(SHORTEST_PATH(P1(-(related_to1)->P2)+)))
    -- Stella Rosenhain
    AND P1.PersonId = 4);
```

CHAPTER 7

Running the preceding query shows that David is the direct descendant of Stella. The query also returns a record showing that James is David's descendant. However, Karina is not returned in the query because she is not a descendant of Stella. A more complex example is included in the accompanying files for this book.

Graph table shortcomings

Since the first graph features were released with SQL Server 2017, additional investments have been made to overcome the limitations found in that release. Most notably, the SHORTEST_PATH function enables both the shortest path graph analytic function and transitive closures (the ability to recursively traverse edges). Still, many limitations compared to native graph databases remain.

The following list contains two notable syntax limitations starting in SQL Server 2019 and a brief description of their significance for implementing a graph. Hopefully, this will provide the information you need to make an informed decision about using SQL Server for graph data.

- **Need to explicitly define edges as tables.** Graphs model pairwise relations between entities (the nodes). Flexibility can be key in maximizing the benefits of graph models. Even though the nodes and their properties are often well understood, new relationships can be modeled as new needs arise or additional possibilities emerge. The need to make schema modifications to support new types of edges reduces flexibility. Some of this can be addressed by defining one or a few edge tables and storing the edge properties as XML or JSON. This approach, too, has drawbacks in terms of performance and ease of writing queries against the data.

- **Limited polymorphism.** *Polymorphism* is the ability to find a node of any type connected to a specified starting node. In SQL Server, a workaround for graph models with few node and edge types is to query all known node and edge types and combine the result sets by using a UNION clause. For large graph models, this solution becomes impractical.

Store large binary objects

Large objects (LOBs), including XML and binary large objects (BLOBs), can be used to store files. However, storing LOBs—and more specifically BLOBs—in a relational database has been known to cause debate. Before SQL Server offered the FILESTREAM feature as a specialized way for the Database Engine to manage BLOBs, database designers had two options, neither of which would likely meet all your requirements:

- Store the BLOB, such as an image, video, or document file, in a varbinary column. Downsides of this approach include rapid growth of the data file, frequent page splits, and pollution of the buffer pool. Benefits include transactional integrity and integrated backup and recovery of the BLOB data.

- Have the application store the BLOB in the file system and use an nvarchar column to store a local server or UNC path to the file. Downsides of this approach include requiring the application to manage data integrity (avoiding missing files or files without associated database records) and lack of integrated security (the mechanism to secure the BLOBs is an entirely different model than that for protecting the database). There are some benefits, though, primarily around performance and ease of programming for the client to work with the BLOBs (using traditional file I/O APIs provided by the OS).

The FILESTREAM feature is designed to provide the best of both worlds. FILESTREAM is not a data type, but an extension to varbinary(max), which changes how data is stored as well as providing additional capabilities.

This section discusses FILESTREAM and an extension of FILESTREAM called FileTable. FileTable lets you access varbinary data via the built-in OS file manager.

Understand FILESTREAM

There are three requirements to take advantage of FILESTREAM:

- The instance must be configured to allow at least one of several levels of FILESTREAM.

- Your database needs at least one FILESTREAM filegroup.

- Any table containing a FILESTREAM column requires a unique, non-NULL rowguid.

A FILESTREAM filegroup refers to a location on an NT File System (NTFS) or Resilient File System (ReFS) volume under the control of the Database Engine. The Database Engine uses this location to store binary data and log files for the binary data.

When a FILESTREAM filegroup is available in the database, FILESTREAM can be used as a modifier on varbinary(max) column declarations. When creating a table with a FILESTREAM column, you can specify on which filegroup the FILESTREAM data will be stored. When multiple FILESTREAM database files are added to a single filegroup, they will be used in round-robin fashion, as long as they don't exceed their maximum size.

In general, FILESTREAM's performance benefits kick in when the average BLOB size is 1 MB or larger. For smaller BLOB sizes, storing the BLOBs in the database file using a varbinary(max) column is better for performance. You might determine, however, that the ease of programming against file I/O APIs in the client application is an overriding factor and decide to use FILESTREAM even with smaller BLOBs.

If any of your BLOBs exceed 2 GB in size, you will need to use FILESTREAM. The varbinary(max) data type supports a maximum BLOB size of 2 GB. Another reason for choosing FILESTREAM is the ability to integrate BLOBs with SQL Server Semantic Search. To be clear, varbinary(max) columns can also be integrated with Semantic Search, but BLOBs stored in traditional file systems cannot. Semantic Search in SQL Server supports extracting and indexing statistically relevant keywords or phrases, which in turn enables the identification of similar or related documents. Among other things, Semantic Search can be used to suggest tags for an article or identify résumés based on a job description.

➤ More information about Semantic Search is available at *https://learn.microsoft.com/sql /relational-databases/search/semantic-search-sql-server*.

Inside OUT

How do you move data from a varbinary(max) column to FILESTREAM?

Unfortunately, moving from varbinary(max) columns to FILESTREAM is not as easy as modifying the column to add the FILESTREAM modifier. Attempting to modify the column in that way will result in an error. Instead, you can use the following three-step process after creating a FILESTREAM filegroup:

1. Create a new varbinary(max) FILESTREAM column in the table, or in another table if you want to use vertical partitioning.

2. Copy the data from the existing varbinary(max) column to the new FILESTREAM column. This operation can cause a significant amount of database activity, depending on the number of rows and the size of the BLOBs.

3. Drop the varbinary(max) column. Optionally, you can then rename the FILESTREAM column to the name of the dropped column. Until you have (optionally) deployed a modified application that uses the I/O APIs with FILESTREAM to achieve better performance, the existing application's T-SQL statements will continue to work on the FILESTREAM column.

In addition to being aware that this operation can potentially cause significant database activity, you also need to ensure that sufficient storage space is available to hold both copies of the data. (If you are moving the BLOBs to different storage hardware, this might be less of a concern.) After completing the process, you should consider whether shrinking the data file is appropriate.

Finally, while these operations take place, consider placing a lock on the table. Otherwise, transactions may modify the data in the varbinary(max) or add new rows. In step 3, that data could be lost.

Even though FILESTREAM BLOBs are stored in the file system, they are managed by the Database Engine. This includes transactional consistency and point-in-time restores. Thus, when a BLOB is deleted, the file on the drive backing that BLOB is not immediately deleted. Similarly, when a BLOB is updated, an entirely new file is written, and the previous version is kept on the drive. When the deleted file or previous file version is no longer needed, the Database Engine will eventually delete the file using a garbage-collection process. You are already aware of the importance of generating transaction log backups with databases in the full recovery model. This way, the transaction log can be truncated and stop growing. When using FILESTREAM, this mantra applies doubly: The number of files will keep growing until they are deleted by the garbage collector.

CAUTION

You should never modify the contents of a FILESTREAM folder (a *data container*) manually. Doing so can lead to FILESTREAM data corruption.

FileTable

FileTable makes it possible to access BLOBs managed by the Database Engine using traditional file share semantics. Applications that can read and write from a file share can access BLOBs managed by the SQL Server Database Engine as if they were on a regular Server Message Block (SMB) file share.

Although clients can use file I/O APIs to work with FILESTREAM, obtaining a handle to the BLOB requires the use of specific client libraries and application modifications. There might be applications that cannot be modified to work with FILESTREAM but for which having BLOBs managed by the relational engine would have significant advantages. It was for this purpose that FileTable, which is a special table type, was developed.

NOTE

FileTable is not currently available on SQL Server on Linux due to its reliance on Windows APIs.

A FileTable has a fixed schema, so you can neither add user-defined columns nor remove columns. The only control provided is the ability to define indexes, even unique ones, on some FileTable columns.

The fixed schema has a FILESTREAM column that stores the actual file data in addition to many metadata columns, and the non-NULL unique rowguid column required of any table containing FILESTREAM data. FileTable can organize data hierarchically, meaning folders and subfolders are supported concepts.

➤ For a detailed discussion of the FileTable schema, visit *https://learn.microsoft.com/sql /relational-databases/blob/filetable-schema*.

Table partitions

Table partitioning occurs when you design a table that stores data from a single logical entity in physically separate structures. In other words, rather than storing all the entity's data in a single physical data structure, the data is split into multiple physical data structures, but the user continues to treat it as a single unit, as normal.

Table partitioning has multiple purposes, some of which relate to performance, either when querying or when loading data. (We discuss this later in detail.) As shown in Figure 7-3, there are two types of partitioning: horizontal partitioning and vertical partitioning. This section discusses each of these separately, including common use cases and recommendations.

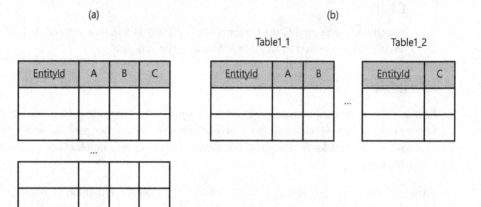

Figure 7-3 (a) Horizontal partitioning splits a table's data rows. (b) Vertical partitioning splits a table's columns.

As illustrated in Figure 7-3, horizontal and vertical partitioning are distinctly different. Horizontal partitioning splits the data rows, and each partition has the same schema. Vertical partitioning splits the entity's columns across multiple tables.

Figure 7-3 shows a table partitioned in only two partitions, but you can partition tables into many partitions. You can also mix horizontal and vertical partitioning.

NOTE

In SQL Server, *partitioning* usually refers to horizontal partitioning, only because it is the name of a feature. This book discusses both horizontal and vertical partitioning; as such, we always explicitly declare which partitioning type is being discussed.

Horizontally partitioned tables and indexes

In a large-scale database, in which a single table can grow to hundreds of gigabytes or more, some operations become more difficult. For example, adding new rows can take an excessive amount of time and might also cause SELECT queries on the table to fail due to lock escalation. Similar concerns exist with respect to removing data and index maintenance.

Horizontal partitioning can address these concerns. However, it is not a silver bullet that will make all performance problems in large tables disappear. On the contrary, when applied incorrectly, horizontal partitioning can have a *negative* effect on your database workload. This

section builds on the brief discussion of partitioning found in Chapter 3, "Design and implement an on-premises database infrastructure."

NOTE

Support for horizontal partitioning in SQL Server was limited to SQL Server Enterprise edition until the release of SQL Server 2016 with Service Pack 1. Since then, all editions support horizontal table and index partitioning.

About horizontal partitions

SQL Server's partitioning feature supports horizontal partitioning with a partition function, which determines in which partition of the table a given row will be stored. Each partition can be stored in its own filegroup in the same database.

When partitioning a table, the rows of the table are not all stored in the same physical place. So, when designing partitions, you must decide on a partition key, which is the column that will be used to assign a row to exactly one partition. From a logical viewpoint, however, all rows belong to the same table.

A query without a WHERE clause returns all rows, regardless of which partition they are stored in. This means the Database Engine must do more work to retrieve rows from different partitions. Your goal when partitioning for query performance should be to write queries that eliminate partitions. You can accomplish this by including the *partition key* in the WHERE clause.

Additional benefits of horizontal partitioning include the ability to set specific filegroups to read-only. By mapping partitions containing older data to read-only filegroups, you can be assured that this data is unchangeable without affecting your ability to insert new rows. In addition, you can exclude read-only filegroups from regular backups. Finally, during a restore, filegroups containing the most recent data could be restored first, allowing new transactions to be recorded faster than if the entire database needed to be restored.

NOTE

Restoring selected files or filegroups while keeping the database available is called an *online restore*, which is still supported only in the Enterprise edition.

Index partitioning

In addition to horizontal table partitioning, SQL Server also supports *index partitioning*. A partitioned index is said to be aligned with the table if the table and the index are partitioned in the same number of partitions using the same column and boundary values.

When a partitioned index is aligned, you can direct index maintenance operations to a specific partition. This can significantly speed up the maintenance operation because you can rebuild or reorganize a partition rather than the entire index. On the other hand, if the entire index needs to be rebuilt, SQL Server will attempt to do so in a parallel fashion. Rebuilding multiple indexes simultaneously creates memory pressure. Because of this, we recommend that you *not* use partitioning on a system with less than 16 GB of RAM.

> **NOTE**
> Achieving an aligned index is typically done by using the same partition function and scheme as the table. However, it is not strictly necessary to create an aligned partitioned index. If you choose to use a different function or scheme, you must remember to modify the function for the index simultaneously with the table's partition function. Therefore, we recommend that you use one partition function for both the partition schema and the aligned partitioned index.

You might benefit from creating a partitioned index without partitioning the table. You can still use this nonaligned index to improve query efficiency if only one or a few of the index partitions need to be used. In this case, you must also use the index's partition key in the WHERE clause to gain the performance benefit of eliminating partitions.

Define partitions and partition a table

We now demonstrate how to create a horizontally partitioned table using the SQL Server feature. Three database objects are involved in defining partitions and partitioning a table:

- A partition function, which defines the number of partitions and the boundary values

- A partition scheme, which defines on which filegroup each partition is placed

- The table to be partitioned

> **NOTE**
> For brevity, the following script does not show the creation of the database with the filegroups and files necessary to support the partition scheme. The sample script included with the book downloads does include the CREATE DATABASE statement, as well as a CREATE TABLE statement followed by an INSERT statement and SELECT statements from DMVs to review the table's partition statistics.

```
-- Create a partition function for February 1, 2019, through January 1, 2020
CREATE PARTITION FUNCTION MonthPartitioningFx (datetime2)
    -- Store the boundary values in the right partition
    AS RANGE RIGHT
   -- Each month is defined by its first day (the boundary value)
    FOR VALUES ('20190201', '20190301', '20190401',
        '20190501', '20190601', '20190701', '20190801',
        '20190901', '20191001', '20191101', '20191201', '20200101');
-- Create a partition scheme using the partition function
-- Place each trimester on its own partition
-- The most recent of the 13 months goes in the latest partition
CREATE PARTITION SCHEME MonthPartitioningScheme
```

```
AS PARTITION MonthPartitioningFx
TO (FILEGROUP2, FILEGROUP2, FILEGROUP2, FILEGROUP2,
    FILEGROUP3, FILEGROUP3, FILEGROUP3, FILEGROUP3,
    FILEGROUP4, FILEGROUP4, FILEGROUP4, FILEGROUP4, FILEGROUP4);
```

If you visualize the table data as being sorted by the partition key in ascending order, the left partition is the partition on top. When defining a partition function, you indicate whether the boundary value—in this example, the first day of each month—will be stored in the partition on the left (the default) or the partition on the right (as specified in the sample).

Figure 7-4 shows the relationship between the partition function and the partition scheme. In the sample, the partition function created 13 partitions using 12 boundary values. The partition scheme then directed these 13 partitions to three filegroups by specifying each filegroup four times and the last filegroup five times (because it will hold the last partition).

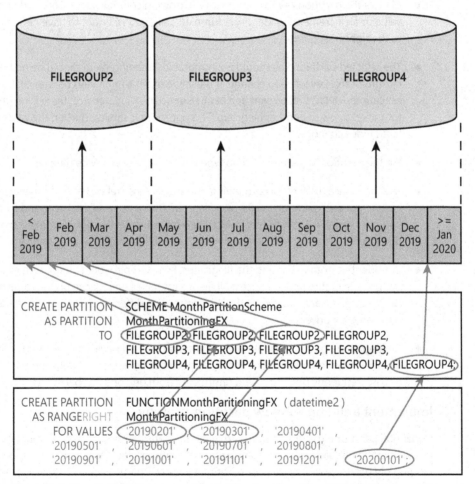

Figure 7-4 The relationship between the partition function, the partition scheme, and the filegroups on which the partitions will be stored.

Horizontal partition design guidelines

When designing horizontal partitions, keep these guidelines in mind, with the understanding that your mileage may vary:

- The number of parallel operations that can be run per query depends on the number of processor cores in the system. Using more partitions than processor cores limits the number of partitions that will be processed in parallel. So, even though SQL Server now supports up to 15,000 partitions, on a system with 12 processor cores, at most 12 partitions will be processed in parallel. You may choose to use fewer partitions than the number of available processor cores to set aside capacity for other queries. There is also the option to disable parallel partition processing or to change the number of processors that a single query can use. Be advised that changing the number of processors per query is a server configuration.

- Choose the partition key to accommodate growing column values. This could be a date value or an incrementing identity column. Usually, you will want to have new rows added to the rightmost partition.

- The selected partition key should be immutable, meaning there should be no business reason for this key value to change. If the value of a partition key changes, SQL Server will execute the UPDATE statement as a DELETE and INSERT statement; there is no provision to "move" a row to another filegroup. This approach is similar to when the value of a clustered index changes.

- For the partition key, a narrow data type is preferable over a wide data type.

- To achieve most benefits of partitioning, specifically those related to performance, you will need to put each partition into its own filegroup. This is not a requirement, and some or all partitions can share a single filegroup. For example, the next section discusses a sliding window partition strategy, in which partitioning is beneficial even if all are in the same filegroup.

- Consider the storage backing the filegroups. For example, your storage system might not provide higher performance if all filegroups have been placed on the same physical drives. Be aware that even if the drive letters are different, they may still all be on the same physical drive.

- Tables that are good candidates for partitioning are tables with many—as in millions or billions—rows for which data is mostly added as opposed to updated, and on which queries are frequently run that would return data from one or a few partitions.

Implement a sliding window partition strategy

Horizontal partitioning is often applied to relational data warehouses. A common data warehouse operation is loading a significant amount of data to a fact table while simultaneously purging old data. The sliding window partition strategy is particularly well-suited for tables for which data is regularly added and removed. For example, data in a fact table can be purged after 13 months. Perhaps each time data is loaded into the data warehouse, rows older than 13 months are removed while new rows are added. This is a sliding window in that the fact table always contains the most recent 13 months of data.

To set up a sliding window, you need a partition function and scheme as well as the fact table. You should also set up a stored procedure that modifies the partition function to accommodate the new boundary values. Finally, you will need a staging table with the same columns and clustered index as the partitioned table.

NOTE

The next example assumes that data is loaded in the data warehouse only once every month. This is not particularly realistic, but the example still works when data is loaded more frequently, even in real time. Only the first load operation for a new month will need to modify the partition function.

Figure 7-5 illustrates what happens on March 1, 2020, when data is loaded for the month of February 2020. The fact table is partitioned into 13 partitions, one for each month. An automated process, which is not depicted here, modifies the partition function to accommodate the new date range by splitting the rightmost partition, holding the most recent data, in two. Then, the partition holding the oldest month's data is switched out to a staging table and the new data is switched in from a staging table. Finally, the leftmost partition, which held the oldest data but is now empty, is merged with the second leftmost partition.

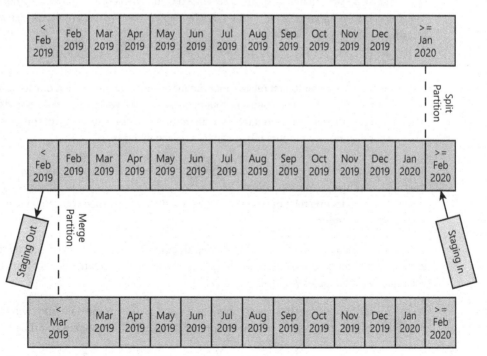

Figure 7-5 An overview of the sliding window partition strategy.

NOTE

Implementing a sliding window partition strategy is not without pitfalls. To fully automate it, job auditing is required to ensure that the process that modifies the partition function operates successfully. Additional complexity is introduced if the switched-out, old data is to be archived rather than purged. Archiving a partition usually involves moving the specific partition to a new table.

You can optimize the process of switching the old partition out and the new partition in by using a memory-optimized table as the staging table.

NOTE

In addition, you can use the SQL Server partition feature for the history table, as described here: *https://learn.microsoft.com/sql/relational-databases/tables/manage-retention-of -historical-data-in-system-versioned-temporal-tables#using-table-partitioning-approach*.

Vertical partitions

Vertical partitioning makes sense when a single table would ordinarily contain many columns, some of which might contain large values that are infrequently queried. In some cases, indexes with included columns will not do enough to alleviate the issues. You may be able to improve performance by storing the infrequently accessed columns in another table. Another problem that you can solve by vertical partitioning is when you run into a maximum row size limit or maximum column count limit.

NOTE

We encourage you to first review your database design to ensure that one logical entity really needs such wide columns or that many attributes. Perhaps the table could be normalized into multiple related tables. If all those columns are needed, splitting the entity vertically into two or more tables can be a reasonable tactic.

An entity that is vertically partitioned into multiple tables can usually be identified by the fact that the tables have a common name prefix or suffix and share the same primary key values. A conceptual one-to-one relationship exists between the tables, which you can enforce by using a foreign key constraint.

Unlike with horizontal partitioning, SQL Server does not have a feature that directly supports vertical partitioning. As the database designer, you will need to create the necessary schema to vertically partition tables yourself.

Be careful not to abuse vertical partitioning as a strategy. Every time data from two tables is needed in a single result set, a join operation will be required. These joins could be expensive operations—or are at least more expensive than reading data from a single page—and might nullify other performance benefits if you run them frequently.

There are a few special cases for using vertical partitioning. One relates to the FileTable feature. FileTables, as noted earlier in this chapter, have a fixed schema. You might, however, need to store additional metadata about the files. Because you are unable to extend the schema, you will need to create a new table that uses the same primary key as the FileTable. Using INSERT and DELETE triggers, you can guarantee data integrity by ensuring that for every row in the FileTable, there is a matching row in your extended metadata table.

A second special case is related to temporal tables, also discussed earlier in this chapter. If there is no requirement to capture the history of all columns in the temporal table, splitting the logical entity into two vertical partitions (or perhaps more if additional considerations apply) can reduce the amount of space consumed by unneeded historical data.

Capture modifications to data

SQL Server supports several methods for capturing row data that has been modified, including temporal tables (discussed earlier in this chapter). This section discusses *change tracking* and *change data capture*, and provides recommendations on their use. Although these features allow applications to detect when data has changed, temporal tables operate very differently and serve different purposes.

NOTE

The SQL Server auditing feature is not covered in this section. Auditing may also meet your needs, especially if you need to track the execution of SELECT and DDL statements or include the principal that executed the statements.

➤ Auditing is a security feature, and is discussed in Chapter 13, "Protect data through classification, encryption, and auditing."

Use change tracking

Change tracking only tracks whether a row has changed. If you need to also track the data that has changed, see the next section, "Use change data capture." Change tracking is mostly useful for synchronizing copies of data with occasionally offline clients or for extract, transform, load (ETL) operations. For example, an application that facilitates offline editing of data will need to perform a two-way synchronization when reconnected. One approach to implementing this requirement is to copy the data to the client. If there is concern about loading all the data on the client, however, you can also load a subset of the data. When the client goes offline, the application reads and updates data using the offline copy. When the client re-establishes connectivity to the server, changes can be merged efficiently. The application is responsible for detecting and managing conflicting changes where the client has changed rows that it needs to integrate into the live data.

Configuring change tracking is a two-step process: First, you enable change tracking for the database. Then, you enable change tracking for the table(s) you want to track.

NOTE

Change tracking and memory-optimized tables are mutually exclusive. A database can-not have both at the same time.

Before performing these steps, you can set up snapshot isolation for the database. Snapshot isolation is not required for proper operation of change tracking, but it is very helpful for accu-rately querying the changes. Another very useful strategy is to copy the changes either using a database snapshot or in a snapshot isolation level transaction. This technique ensures that the data your copy process sees is not changing. Because data can change as you are querying it, using the snapshot isolation level inside an explicit transaction enables you to see consistent results until you commit the transaction.

> ➤ For an end-to-end example of how an application can use change tracking to accomplish two-way data synchronization with an occasionally offline data store, see *https://learn .microsoft.com/sql/relational-databases/track-changes/work-with-change-tracking -sql-server.*

The following sample script enables snapshot isolation on the WideWorldImporters sample database. Then, it enables change tracking on the WideWorldImporters sample database and on two tables: `Sales.Orders` and `Sales.OrderLines`. Only on the `Sales.Orders` table is col-umn tracking activated, so change tracking will include which columns were included in UPDATE statements (whether or not the values were actually changed). Next, change tracking is disabled for `Sales.OrderLines`. Finally, the `sys.change_tracking_tables` catalog view is queried to retrieve a list of tables with change tracking enabled.

```
USE master;
GO
-- Enable snapshot isolation for the database, if desired
ALTER DATABASE WideWorldImporters
    SET ALLOW_SNAPSHOT_ISOLATION ON;
-- Enable change tracking for the database
ALTER DATABASE WideWorldImporters
    SET CHANGE_TRACKING = ON
    (CHANGE_RETENTION = 5 DAYS, AUTO_CLEANUP = ON);
USE WideWorldImporters;
GO
-- Enable change tracking for Orders
ALTER TABLE Sales.Orders
    ENABLE CHANGE_TRACKING
```

```
      -- and track which columns were included in the statements
WITH (TRACK_COLUMNS_UPDATED = ON);
-- Enable change tracking for OrderLines
ALTER TABLE Sales.OrderLines
    ENABLE CHANGE_TRACKING;
-- Disable change tracking for OrderLines
ALTER TABLE Sales.OrderLines
    DISABLE CHANGE_TRACKING;
-- Query the current state of change tracking in the database
SELECT *
FROM sys.change_tracking_tables;
```

A major benefit compared to implementing a custom solution is that change tracking does not make any schema changes to the user tables such as triggers, or require additional user tables to store the captured changes. In addition, change tracking is available in all editions of SQL Server and in Azure SQL Database. Autocleanup ensures that the database does not grow unchecked.

NOTE

We recommend enabling autocleanup and setting a retention period of sufficiently long duration to ensure that data synchronization has taken place. Applications can check whether they have waited too long to synchronize; that is, applications can find out whether cleanup has already removed tracking information since the application last synchronized.

Although change tracking can track which rows have changed and optionally which columns were included in an UPDATE statement's SET clause, it cannot indicate what the old values were or how often the row has been changed. If your use case does not require this, change tracking provides a lightweight option for tracking. If your use case does require one or both, consider using change data capture instead, discussed next.

Use change data capture

Change data capture varies in some important ways from change tracking. First and foremost, change data capture captures the historical values of the data. This requires a significantly higher amount of storage than change tracking. Unlike change tracking, change data capture uses an asynchronous process to write the change data. This means the client need not wait for the change data to be committed before the database returns the result of the DML operation, as it uses the log to do this asynchronously.

NOTE

Because change data capture relies on the SQL Server Agent, it is not available in Azure SQL Database, although it is available in Azure SQL Managed Instance. Starting with SQL Server 2016 with Service Pack 1, change data capture is available in Standard edition.

NOTE

Since SQL Server 2017 CU 15, change data capture and memory-optimized tables can be used in the same database. Previously, a database could not have both at the same time.

The following script enables change data capture on a database using the `sys.sp_cdc_enable_db` stored procedure. Then, the script enables change data capture for the `Sales.Invoices` table. The script assumes that a user-defined database role cdc_reader has been created. Members of this role will be able to query the captured data changes.

```
USE WideWorldImporters;
GO
EXEC sys.sp_cdc_enable_db;
EXEC sys.sp_cdc_enable_table
    @source_schema = 'Sales',
    @source_name = 'Invoices',
    @role_name = 'cdc_reader';
```

NOTE

If you run the preceding script while SQL Server Agent is stopped, the cdc_reader database role will be created as well as the SQL Server Agent jobs. If you try to run it again, you will get an error that the specific capture instance already exists.

After executing these statements, data changes to the `Sales.Invoices` table will be tracked, complete with before and after data.

➤ Additional optional settings for change data capture include which columns to track and on which filegroup to store the change table. For more information, visit *https://learn.microsoft .com/sql/relational-databases/track-changes/enable-and-disable-change-data-capture -sql-server*.

Inside OUT

How can application developers best use change tracking and change data capture?

There are two important considerations to effectively use these SQL Server features in client applications:

- An application should identify itself by using a source ID when synchronizing data. By providing a source ID, the client can avoid obtaining the same data again. A client specifies its own source ID by using the `WITH CHANGE_TRACKING_CONTEXT` clause at the start of statements.

- An application should perform the request for changed data in a snapshot isolation-level transaction. This will prevent another application from updating data between the check for updated data and when data updates are sent. The snapshot isolation level must be enabled at the database level, as described in the previous section.

Query change tracking and change data capture

When change tracking or change data capture is enabled, SQL Server offers functions for querying the tracking and capture information. These functions are demonstrated here using the WideWorldImporters sample as modified in the preceding two sections.

Query change tracking

The following code sample updates a row in the Sales.Orders table, which has change tracking enabled. The next statement in the sample then demonstrates how to query the information gathered by change tracking.

```
-- Modify a row in the Orders table,
-- which has change tracking enabled
UPDATE Sales.Orders
    SET Comments = 'I am a new comment!'
    WHERE OrderID = 1;
DECLARE @OrderCommentsColumnId int =
    COLUMNPROPERTY(OBJECT_ID('Sales.Orders'), N'Comments', 'ColumnId'),
    @DeliveryInstructionsColumnId int =
    COLUMNPROPERTY(OBJECT_ID('Sales.Orders'), N'DeliveryInstructions', 'ColumnId');
-- Query all changes to Sales.Orders
SELECT *
    -- Determine if the Comments column was included in the UPDATE
    , CHANGE_TRACKING_IS_COLUMN_IN_MASK(@OrderCommentsColumnId,
        CT.SYS_CHANGE_COLUMNS) CommentsChanged
    -- Determine if the DeliveryInstructions column was included
    , CHANGE_TRACKING_IS_COLUMN_IN_MASK(@DeliveryInstructionsColumnId,
        CT.SYS_CHANGE_COLUMNS) DeliveryInstructionsChanged
FROM CHANGETABLE(CHANGES Sales.Orders, 0) as CT
ORDER BY SYS_CHANGE_VERSION;
```

The output includes the values of the primary key—in this case the values of the single column OrderID—and a SYS_CHANGE_OPERATION column indicating that an UPDATE statement was executed using the value U. Because you enabled column tracking for the Orders table, there is a non-NULL value for the SYS_CHANGE_COLUMNS column in the output.

For each column for which you'd like to determine whether it was included in the UPDATE statement, use the CHANGE_TRACKING_IS_COLUMN_IN_MASK function. It uses the column as the position in the SYS_CHANGE_COLUMNS bitmask to indicate if the value is changed. In the sample, two output columns are added that determine if the Comments and DeliveryInstructions columns were included in the UPDATE statement. A value of 1 indicates yes, and 0 indicates no.

Query change data capture

The following code sample updates a row in the Sales.Invoices table that has change data capture enabled. Then the change data capture table is queried with the option all update old, which causes the single UPDATE statement to have two rows in the output, one containing the old image and the other row containing the updated data.

```
-- Modify a row in the Invoices table,
-- which has change data capture enabled
UPDATE Sales.Invoices
    SET Comments = 'I am a new invoice comment again'
    WHERE InvoiceID = 1;
DECLARE @from_lsn binary(10) = sys.fn_cdc_get_min_lsn('Sales_Invoices'),
    @to_lsn binary(10) = sys.fn_cdc_get_max_lsn();
-- Each capture instance will have unique function names
-- By default, the capture instance name is schema_table
-- Note: there may be a slight delay before output is returned
SELECT *
FROM cdc.fn_cdc_get_all_changes_Sales_Invoices(@from_lsn, @to_lsn,
    N'all update old');
```

NOTE

There are many more change data capture functions and stored procedures available. These are covered at *https://learn.microsoft.com/sql/relational-databases/system -functions/change-data-capture-functions-transact-sql* and *https://learn.microsoft .com/sql/relational-databases/system-stored-procedures/change-data-capture-stored -procedures-transact-sql.*

Compare change tracking, change data capture, and temporal tables

This section compares three features that have common use cases. Table 7-1 should prove help-ful when you're deciding which change tracking feature is appropriate for your needs.

Table 7-1   A comparison of features and uses of change tracking, change data capture, and temporal tables.

	Change tracking	Change data capture	Temporal tables
Requires user schema modification	No	No	Yes
Available in Azure SQL Database	Yes	No	Yes
Edition support	Any	Enterprise and Standard	Any
Provides historical data	No	Yes	Yes
Tracks DML type	Yes	Yes	No
Has autocleanup	Yes	Yes	Yes
Time of change indicator	LSN	LSN	datetime2

Benefits of PolyBase for external data sources and external tables

PolyBase is a feature that allows SQL Server to query and interact with data sources outside of SQL Server. This concept is called *data virtualization*. In data virtualization, data that is external to the SQL Server is made to behave like internal SQL Server data. When working with data virtualization, you'll become intimately familiar with the CREATE DATABASE SCOPED CREDENTIAL and CREATE EXTERNAL DATA SOURCE T-SQL syntax.

While PolyBase is the SQL Server feature for data virtualization, the feature name isn't necessarily uniform across SQL platforms. For example, Azure Synapse Analytics and Azure SQL Manage Instance have data virtualization (the latter introduced in September 2022), but do not use the PolyBase feature name. There are four key scenarios that best use PolyBase in SQL Server:

- Parallelized import of data into SQL Server

- Joining multiple data sources in a single query

- Eliminating data latency and reducing the need for multiple copies of data

- Archiving data to alternate storage

Unified data platform features

PolyBase enables database administrators to create a unified data platform for data analytics and applications. Through the use of PolyBase, SQL Server can interact with different file types and databases using T-SQL. Supported external data sources include Oracle, MongoDB, Teradata, Generic ODBC, Azure Storage, and SQL Server.

Some recent version-specific changes to PolyBase include:

- Starting with SQL Server 2019, PolyBase is available on Linux as well as Windows.

- Starting in SQL Server 2022, PolyBase offers functionality to allow connections to S3-compatible object storage, including the ability to interact with Apache Parquet file and Delta table formats. Hadoop external data sources are retired in SQL Server 2022.

- Comma-separated values (CSV) files are also supported in Azure Storage in SQL Server 2022.

- PolyBase scale-out groups are deprecated in SQL Server 2019 and retired in SQL Server 2022.

- While it isn't called PolyBase, Azure SQL Managed Instance supports some data virtualization features. Azure SQL Managed Instance even has some features that PolyBase doesn't, like the ability to authenticate to Azure Blob Storage with a managed identity.

NOTE

The external provider capabilities of PolyBase are tricky. The details of CREATE EXTERNAL DATA SOURCE change with every major version of SQL Server. Azure SQL platforms have different capabilities as well. For example, Cloudera CDH and Hortonworks HDP support in SQL Server 2019 was removed from SQL Server 2022. In Microsoft Learn Docs, pay special attention to the version selector (top-left) for the CREATE EXTERNAL DATA SOURCE reference article at *https://learn.microsoft.com/sql/t-sql/statements/create-external-data-source-transact-sql*. Each version of SQL Server contains different LOCATION argument options, for example.

Microsoft provides how-to guides for each of the many different types of external data sources—for example, how to configure PolyBase to access external data in Oracle.

Pushdown computation

Pushdown computation is supported for numerous data sources, including generic ODBC, Oracle, SQL Server, Teradata, MongoDB, and Azure Blob Storage.

The purpose of pushdown computation is to allow specific computations to be performed on the external data source. This distributes some of the workload of the query to the remote data source, reducing the amount of data that needs to be transmitted and therefore improving query performance. The computations include joins, aggregations, expressions, and operators.

➤ For more information about what computations work with pushdown, visit *https://learn.microsoft.com/sql/relational-databases/polybase/polybase-pushdown-computation#enable-pushdown-computation*.

INSIDE OUT

How can you tell if pushdown computation occurred in a PolyBase query?

There is only certain T-SQL syntax supported for translation to the external data source's ODBC commands, and there are some limitations that would prevent pushdown from otherwise occurring.

The methods for determining whether pushdown has occurred may vary by SQL Server version. Before SQL Server 2019, Trace Flag 6408 was required to surface certain key indicators of pushdown. Starting with SQL Server 2019, the read_command column of sys.dm_exec_external_work will contain the remote query, with the limitation that it only contains the first 4,000 characters of the remote query.

Microsoft provides a detailed walk-through for detecting PolyBase pushdown for joins, aggregations, and filters here: *https://learn.microsoft.com/sql/relational-databases/polybase/polybase-how-to-tell-pushdown-computation*.

Install and configure PolyBase

This section looks at the installation of PolyBase and the application of PolyBase concepts.

Installation

When installing PolyBase on a Windows machine, keep these points top of mind:

- PolyBase can be installed on only one instance per server.

- To use PolyBase, you need to be assigned the sysadmin role or Control Server permission.

- In SQL Server 2019 and after, you must enable PolyBase using `sp_configure` after installation. This is an important step to remember in both Windows and Linux.

- If the Windows firewall service is running during installation, the necessary firewall rules
  will be set up automatically. Other firewalls external to your SQL Server instance may still
  require changes.

For step-by-step instructions on how to install PolyBase, see the Microsoft documentation for
your specific version of SQL Server:

- On Windows, see *https://learn.microsoft.com/sql/relational-databases/polybase/
  polybase-installation*.

- On Linux (Red Hat, Ubuntu, or SUSE), see *https://learn.microsoft.com/sql/relational
  -databases/polybase/polybase-linux-setup*.

NOTE

**Decide on the service account for PolyBase in advance. The only way to change the ser-
vice account for the PolyBase Engine Service and Data Movement Service is to uninstall
and reinstall PolyBase.**

With the installation complete, you accomplish the next steps via T-SQL syntax:

1. Create the database master key, if it doesn't already exist, with `CREATE MASTER KEY`.

2. Create a database scoped credential for the data source with `CREATE DATABASE SCOPED
    CREDENTIAL`.

3. Configure the external data source with `CREATE EXTERNAL DATA SOURCE`.

4. Create external tables, with `CREATE EXTERNAL TABLE`.

For additional details, follow the steps at *https://learn.microsoft.com/sql/relational-databases
/polybase/polybase-configure-sql-server*. These steps are also covered in this chapter.

Configure and enable

A master key is a symmetric key used to protect other keys and certificates in the database. It is encrypted with both an algorithm and password. A master key is necessary to protect the credentials of the external tables. Details on how to create and update a master key, and the instructions to set it up, can be found in this chapter in the section "External tables."

Inside OUT

How many master keys can a database have?

Each database can only have one master key. Before creating a new master key, query the `sys.symmetric_keys` table in the desired database to confirm there is not a master key already present.

If you try to create a master key on a database that already has a master key, you will receive the following error:

```
There is already a master key in the database. Please drop it before
performing this statement.
```

However, you can have multiple passwords for the same master key. If you already have a master key created, and you want a specific password for use with PolyBase, you can issue the following command:

```
ALTER MASTER KEY ADD ENCRYPTION BY PASSWORD  = '<strong password here>';
```

Starting in SQL Server 2019, you need to enable PolyBase globally using `sp_configure`. Once complete, you must run `RECONFIGURE`, and then restart the SQL Server service. Both PolyBase services will have to be started manually as they are turned off during this process and do not restart automatically.

This can be done with these commands:

```
exec sp_configure @configname = 'polybase enabled', @configvalue = 1;
RECONFIGURE [ WITH OVERRIDE ] ;
```

➤ For more details on this command, visit *https://learn.microsoft.com/sql/database-engine /configure-windows/polybase-connectivity-configuration-transact-sql*.

NOTE

If you are unsure if PolyBase is installed, you can check its SERVERPROPERTY with this command:

```
SELECT SERVERPROPERTY ('IsPolyBaseInstalled') AS IsPolyBaseInstalled;
```

It returns 1 if it is installed and 0 if it is not.

Shared access signatures

As the name suggests, a *shared access signature* (*SAS*) is a way to share an object in your storage account with others without exposing your account key. This gives you granular control over the access you grant, at the account, service, or user level.

- You can set a start time and expiry time.

- Azure Blob Storage containers, file shares, queues, and tables are all resources that accept SAS policies.

- You can set an optional IP address or range from which access will be accepted.

- You can restrict access from HTTPS clients by specifying the accepted protocol.

An SAS is used to allow clients to read, write, or delete data in your Azure Storage account without access to your account key. This is typically necessary when a client wants to upload large amounts of data or high-volume transactions to your storage account, and creating a service to scale and match demand is too difficult or expensive.

The SAS is a signed Uniform Resource Identifier (URI) that points to resources and includes a token containing a set of query parameters that indicate how the resource can be accessed. Azure Storage checks both the storage piece and the provided token piece of the SAS URI to verify the request. If for any reason the SAS is not valid, it receives an error code 403 (Forbidden), and access is denied.

There are three different types of SAS:

- User delegation shared access signatures rely on Azure AD credentials.

- The service SAS delegates access via the storage account key to a resource in a single storage service (blob, queue, table, or file service).

- The account-level SAS delegates access via the storage account key to resources in one or more storage services within a storage account. This also includes the option to apply access to services such as Get/Set Service Properties and Get Service Stats.

  ➤ For details on all the parameters that can be set with shared access signatures, see *https:// learn.microsoft.com/azure/storage/common/storage-dotnet-shared-access-signature -part-1#shared-access-signature-parameters.*

You can create an ad hoc SAS either as an account SAS or a service SAS, and the start time, expiry time, and permissions are all specified in the SAS URI, the SECRET that is used to eventually create the CREDENTIAL in SQL Server.

You can also create policies to use for many shared access signatures. You may find that using the free Azure Storage Explorer application makes creating stored access policies and shared access signatures easy. You can download it here: *https://aka.ms/storageexplorer*. You can also create policies and shared access signatures in PowerShell.

Inside OUT

Are there any risks to using or storing a SAS URI?

Yes. Anyone who has the SAS URI can access your storage account. It belongs in the SECRET of a CREATE CREDENTIAL T-SQL statement and shouldn't be stored anywhere it could be discovered—including in source control or unsecured documentation.

If a SAS expires (an expiration date must be provided), applications relying on the SAS could break. In SQL Server, you should generate a new SAS and ALTER the credential to use it.

To mitigate against SAS expiration, we recommended that you:

- Always use HTTPS to create or distribute a SAS.
- Use storage access policies.
- Set the expiration on an account SAS far in the future and regularly monitor and rotate the SAS as necessary.
- Set the expiration on an ad hoc SAS shorter to reduce the risk if compromised.
- Ensure clients renew with enough time to avoid disruption.
- Ensure you use the principle of least privilege when creating SAS URIs to reduce risk. Consider multiple shared access signatures with narrowly defined permissions.

Data uploaded with a SAS is not validated in any way, so a middle tier that performs rule valida-tion, authentication, and auditing may still be the better option. Regardless of what you choose, monitor your storage for spikes in authentication failures.

➤ Examples of how to create account and service SAS can be found at *https://learn.microsoft .com/azure/storage/common/storage-dotnet-shared-access-signature-part-1#sas-examples*.

Port requirements for Hadoop

If you plan to access Hadoop with PolyBase in SQL Server 2016 through SQL Server 2019, there are some additional requirements. These relate to which cluster components and ports need to be open for PolyBase to interact correctly with a Hadoop external data source. The ports for the following cluster components must be open:

- HDFS ports

    - NameNode

    - DataNode

- Resource manager

    - Job submission

    - Job history

Table 7-2 shows the default ports for these components. These ports are dependent on the version of Hadoop. In addition, the ports may be different if Hadoop is using a custom configuration.

Table 7-2   Port requirements for Hadoop access with PolyBase.

Hadoop cluster component	Default port
NameNode	8020
DataNode (Data transfer, non-privilege IPC port)	50010
DataNode (Data transfer, privilege IPC port)	1019
Resource Manager Job Submission (Hortonworks 1.3)	50300
Resource Manager Job Submission (Cloudera 4.3)	8021
Resource Manager Job Submission (Hortonworks 2.0 on Windows, Cloudera 5.x on Linux)	8032
Resource Manager Job Submission (Hortonworks 2.x, 3.0 on Linux, Hortonworks 2.1–3 on Windows)	8050
Resource Manager Job History	10020

Database scoped credential

Database scoped credentials are used to access non-public blob storage accounts from SQL Server or Azure Synapse with PolyBase. SQL Server with PolyBase also requires database scoped credentials for several types of connectors for PolyBase, including S3-compliant object storage, ODBC generic types, and Azure Blob Storage.

➤ Find the syntax to create scoped credentials at *https://learn.microsoft.com/sql/t-sql /statements/create-database-scoped-credential-transact-sql.*

Inside OUT

Can I just use system credentials for my scoped credentials?

System credentials start with ##. Database scoped credentials cannot start with the pound sign (#). This means system credentials are not eligible to be scoped credentials.

NOTE

If your SAS key value begins with a question mark (?), be sure to remove the leading ? because it will not be recognized. Ensure you have already set up a master key. The master key will be used to protect these credentials. If you do not yet have a master key, the instructions to set it up can be found later in this chapter in the section, "External tables."

External data sources

External data sources are used to establish connectivity to systems outside of SQL Server for data virtualization or loading data using PolyBase. The most common use cases are loading data with bulk INSERT or OPENROWSET activities, or accessing data that would otherwise not be available in SQL Server because it resides on another system—even a non-relational storage system.

The details of the CREATE EXTERNAL DATA SOURCE T-SQL syntax have changed with every major version of SQL Server. In Microsoft Docs, pay special attention to the version selector (top-left) in the CREATE EXTERNAL DATA SOURCE reference article: *https://learn.microsoft.com /sql/t-sql/statements/create-external-data-source-transact-sql.*

The following example shows how to load data from a CSV file in an Azure Blob Storage location that has been configured as an external data source. This requires a database scoped credential using a shared access signature.

```
-- Create the External Data Source
-- Remove the ? from the beginning of the SAS token
-- Do not put a trailing /, file name, or shared access signature parameters at the end
of the LOCATION URL when configuring an external data source for bulk operations.
CREATE DATABASE SCOPED CREDENTIAL AccessPurchaseOrder
WITH
    IDENTITY = 'SHARED ACCESS SIGNATURE'
, SECRET = '******srt=sco&sp=rwac&se=2022-02-01T00:55:34Z&st=2023-12-
29T16:55:34Z***************'
;
CREATE EXTERNAL DATA SOURCE ExternalPurchaseOrder
WITH
(LOCATION   = 'https://newinvoices.blob.core.windows.net/week3'
,CREDENTIAL = AccessPurchaseOrder, TYPE = BLOB_STORAGE)
```

```
;
--Insert into
BULK INSERT Sales.Orders
FROM 'order-2022-11-04.csv'
WITH (DATA_SOURCE = ' ExternalPurchaseOrder');
```

NOTE

Ensure you have at least read permission on the object that is being loaded, and that the expiration period of the SAS is valid (all dates are in UTC time). A credential is not needed if the Azure Blob Storage account has public access.

Creating the external data source can be tricky. Your external data source may require some specifics of the connection string to be provided via the CONNECTION_OPTIONS parameter of the CREATE EXTERNAL DATABASE statement.

➤ **Microsoft recently documented the details of potentially required third-party provider parameters in an article for** CREATE EXTERNAL DATA SOURCE CONNECTION_OPTIONS, **at** *https://learn.microsoft.com/sql/t-sql/statements/create-external-data-source-connection -options.*

External file format

The external file format is required before you can create the external table, but only for some external data source types. As suggested, the file format specifies the layout of the data to be referenced by the external table. Hadoop, Azure Blob Storage, and Azure Data Lake Storage all need an external file format object defined for PolyBase. Delimited text files, Parquet, and both RCFile and ORC Hive files are supported.

Here's an example:

```
CREATE EXTERNAL FILE FORMAT skipHeader_CSV
WITH (FORMAT_TYPE = DELIMITEDTEXT,
    FORMAT_OPTIONS(
        FIELD_TERMINATOR = ',',
        STRING_DELIMITER = '"',
        FIRST_ROW = 2,
        USE_TYPE_DEFAULT = True)
);
```

➤ **Syntax for this command can be found at** *https://learn.microsoft.com/sql/t-sql/statements /create-external-file-format-transact-sql.*

Starting with SQL Server 2022, you can also query data directly from the folder of Delta tables in Azure Blob Storage. Creating an external file format is required, but simpler:

```
CREATE EXTERNAL FILE FORMAT deltaTable1 WITH (FORMAT_TYPE = DELTA);
```

Inside OUT

Can any format be used as an external file?

Delimited text files, RCFile, Apache Parquet, and ORC Hive files are supported but have some limitations. ORC offers better compression and performance than the RCFile. Delimited text has some limitations on the field terminators, string delimiters, and date formats.

External tables

External tables are used to read specific external data and to import data into SQL Server. You don't have to create an external table. You can use OPENROWSET to query data on some external data sources, but external tables provide strong data typing and easy joins to traditional SQL Server tables using T-SQL queries. External tables are an important part of the promise PolyBase brings as a single plane of data, inside SQL Server, for your entire data estate.

No actual data is moved to SQL Server during the creation of an external table; only the meta-data and basic statistics about the folder and file are stored. The intent of the external table is to be the link connecting the external data to SQL Server to create the data virtualization. The external table looks much like a regular SQL Server table in format and has a similar syntax, as you see here with this external Oracle table.

```
-- Create a Master Key
   CREATE MASTER KEY ENCRYPTION BY PASSWORD = 'password';
   CREATE DATABASE SCOPED CREDENTIAL credential_name
   WITH IDENTITY = 'username', Secret = 'password';
-- LOCATION: Location string for data
   CREATE EXTERNAL DATA SOURCE external_data_source_name
   WITH ( LOCATION = 'oracle://<server address>[:<port>]',
   CREDENTIAL = credential_name)
--Create table
   CREATE EXTERNAL TABLE customers(
   [O_ORDERKEY] DECIMAL(38) NOT NULL,
   [O_CUSTKEY] DECIMAL(38) NOT NULL,
   [O_ORDERSTATUS] CHAR COLLATE Latin1_General_BIN NOT NULL,
   [O_TOTALPRICE] DECIMAL(15,2) NOT NULL,
   [O_ORDERDATE] DATETIME2(0) NOT NULL,
   [O_ORDERPRIORITY] CHAR(15) COLLATE Latin1_General_BIN NOT NULL,
   [O_CLERK] CHAR(15) COLLATE Latin1_General_BIN NOT NULL,
   [O_SHIPPRIORITY] DECIMAL(38) NOT NULL,
   [O_COMMENT] VARCHAR(79) COLLATE Latin1_General_BIN NOT NULL
   )
   WITH ( LOCATION='customer', DATA_SOURCE= external_data_source_name   );
```

NOTE

Schema drift can affect external tables. If the external source changes, it is not automagically changed in the external table definition. Any change to the external source will need to be reflected in the external table definition.

In ad hoc query scenarios, such as querying Hadoop data, PolyBase stores the rows retrieved from the external data source in a temporary table. After the query completes, PolyBase removes and deletes the temporary table. No permanent data is stored in SQL tables.

In an import scenario, such as SELECT INTO from an external table, PolyBase stores rows returned as permanent data in the SQL table. The new table is created during query execution when PolyBase retrieves the external data.

PolyBase can push some of the query computation to improve query performance. This action is called *predicate pushdown*. It is used by specifying the Hadoop resource manager location option when creating the external data source and enabling pushdown using these parameters:

```
PUSHDOWN                 = [ON | OFF]
, RESOURCE_MANAGER_LOCATION = '<resource_manager>[:<port>]'
```

With some third-party data providers, instead of using the PUSHDOWN keyword, you may need to specify pushdown-related keywords in the CONNECTION_OPTIONS argument of CREATE EXTERNAL DATA SOURCE.

You can create many external tables that reference the same or different external data sources.

NOTE

Elastic query also uses external tables, but the same table cannot be used for both elastic queries and PolyBase. Although they have the same name, they are not the same.

Statistics

Statistics on external tables are created the same as other tables.

Syntax for CREATE STATISTICS can be found at *https://learn.microsoft.com/sql/t-sql/statements /create-statistics-transact-sql*.

Catalog views

There are catalog views for the installation and running of PolyBase.

- **sys.external_data_sources.** Used to identify external data sources and to give visibility into related metadata. This includes the source, type, and name of the remote database, and in the case of Hadoop, the resource manager's IP and port. This can be very helpful.

CHAPTER 7

- **sys.external_file_formats.** Used to obtain details on the external file format for the sources. Along with the file format type, it includes details about the delimiters, general format, encoding, and compression.

- **sys.external_tables.** Contains a row for each external table in the current database. It details information needed about the tables, such as ID links to preceding tables. Many of the columns provide details about external tables over the shard map manager; this is a special database that maintains global mapping information about all shards (databases) in a shard set. The metadata allows an application to connect to the correct database based upon the value of the sharding key. Every shard in the set contains maps that track the local shard data (known as *shardlets*).

Dynamic management views

Several dynamic management views can be used with PolyBase to troubleshoot issues, such as finding long-running queries, and to monitor nodes in a PolyBase group.

➤ A list of relevant views can be found at *https://learn.microsoft.com/sql/relational-databases/polybase/polybase-troubleshooting#dynamic-management-views*.

More PolyBase examples, architectures including S3 and URL queries

S3-compatible object storage is a new feature of SQL Server 2022, providing both backup and restores to S3-compatible storage and for use with PolyBase. SQL Server 2022 enables you to connect to external data stored in any S3-compatible object storage. These functions allow you to connect to various files stored in S3 storage, including Parquet files. You can read from these files and, if you grant the correct permissions to the S3 user, write to them.

Many developers like to use S3-compatible object storage, and the relative low cost makes it a desirable solution to store files. However, challenges can arise when trying to access these files within a relational database. If you would like to write files directly to S3-compatible storage without using SSIS, PolyBase may be a good solution. To set this connection up, you need to create several objects, including a database scoped credential, external data source, external file format, and external table.

➤ For more information and details on the permissions and limitations of this new feature of SQL Server 2022, see *https://learn.microsoft.com/sql/relational-databases/polybase/polybase-configure-s3-compatible*.

The following code walks you through how to set this up.

```
-- Create database scoped credential
IF NOT EXISTS(SELECT * FROM sys.credentials WHERE name = 'sqlserver2022parquets3')
BEGIN
```

```
CREATE DATABASE SCOPED CREDENTIAL sqlserver2022parquets3 --PolyBaseS3
WITH IDENTITY = 'S3 Access Key',
 SECRET = '######';
END
-- Create external source
-- Can use URL not just IP address
CREATE EXTERNAL DATA SOURCE sqlserver2022parquetdc
WITH
(
    LOCATION = 's3://sqlserver2022parquet.s3.us-east-1.amazonaws.com/',
    CREDENTIAL = sqlserver2022parquets3
);
-- Create external file format
CREATE EXTERNAL FILE FORMAT ParquetFileFormat WITH (FORMAT_TYPE = PARQUET);
GO
-- Create external table
-- Location below specifies folder and filename
CREATE EXTERNAL TABLE Warehouse.ColdRoomTemperaturesParquet (
    [ColdRoomTemperatureID] [bigint] ,
    [ColdRoomSensorNumber] [int] ,
    [RecordedWhen] [datetime2](7) ,
    [Temperature] [decimal](10, 2) ,
    [ValidFrom] [datetime2](7) ,
    [ValidTo] [datetime2](7)  )
WITH (LOCATION = '/output/ColdRoomTemperatures.parquet',
DATA_SOURCE = sqlserver2022parquetdc,
FILE_FORMAT = ParquetFileFormat);
GO
-- Query data directly from S3 storage with OPENROWSET
SELECT   TOP 1 *
FROM     OPENROWSET
         (   BULK 'output/ColdRoomTemperatures.parquet',
             FORMAT       = 'PARQUET',
             DATA_SOURCE  = 'sqlserver2022parquetdc'
         ) AS [cc];
-- Can query the external table directly as well
SELECT   TOP 1 *
FROM Warehouse.ColdRoomTemperaturesParquet;
```

Inside OUT

How do you set up S3-compatible object storage?

Over the past several years, the use of S3-compatible object storage has become increasingly popular among developers. However, one of the challenges has been how to integrate S3-compatible object storage with SQL Server. For those of us accustomed to working with SQL Server, this becomes even trickier, as we are not always familiar with how to set up S3-compatible object storage. This can make it increasingly difficult to get a proof-of-concept set up and tested.

> If you want to set up your own S3-compatible object storage with the new capabilities of SQL Server 2022, you can with MinIO using their free GNU AGPL v3 edition. Anthony Nocentino has written detailed instructions on how you can get MinIO set up correctly. You can find more details at *https://www.nocentino.com/posts/2022-06-10-setting-up-minio -for-sqlserver-object-storage*.

PolyBase examples with a generic ODBC driver

While PolyBase allowed connections to Oracle, Teradata, and MongoDB in prior versions of SQL Server, SQL Server 2022 introduces the ability to connect using ODBC generic types. By installing the appropriate driver and setting up the external database objects, you can connect to other relational databases, including MySQL or SAP as examples. (This feature is supported only by SQL Server on Windows at the time of this book's writing.)

The following sample code contains an example of a generic ODBC connector for MySQL:

```
-- Create database scoped credential
IF NOT EXISTS(SELECT * FROM sys.credentials WHERE name = 'sqlserver2022mysql')
BEGIN
 CREATE DATABASE SCOPED CREDENTIAL sqlserver2022mysql
 WITH IDENTITY = 'sqlzelda',
 SECRET = '<Strong Password>';
END
-- Create external source
CREATE EXTERNAL DATA SOURCE sqlserver2022mysqldc
WITH ( LOCATION = 'odbc://localhost:3306',
CONNECTION_OPTIONS = 'Driver={MySQL ODBC 8.0 ANSI Driver};
ServerNode = localhost:3306',
--PUSHDOWN = ON,
CREDENTIAL = sqlserver2022mysql );
-- Create external table
-- Location below specifies folder and filename
CREATE EXTERNAL TABLE Warehouse.ColdRoomTemperatureMySQL
(
    ColdRoomTemperatureID INT NOT NULL,
    ColdRoomSensorNumber INT NOT NULL,
    Temperature DECIMAL(10, 2) NOT NULL--,
)
 WITH
 (
    LOCATION='coldroom.coldroomtemperatures',
    DATA_SOURCE = sqlserver2022mysqldc
 );
GO
-- Add index to external table
CREATE STATISTICS stx_coldroomsensornumber
ON Warehouse.ColdRoomTemperatureMySQL (ColdRoomSensorNumber)
```

```
WITH FULLSCAN;
-- Can query the external table directly as well
SELECT TOP 1 ColdRoomTemperatureID
```

Here, FROM [Warehouse].[ColdRoomTemperatureMySQL] is the external table virtualizing data through the generic ODBC connector. To re-create this example, you need to download the MySQL ODBC 8.0 ANSI driver, though you can use any data provider's ODBC driver to use this feature.

Azure bulk operations examples

In addition to being able to access Azure Blob Storage, PolyBase will also allow you to access CSV files and Delta tables. When connecting to Azure Blob Storage, you will be able to query, import, and export data. You can access these files by querying external tables or opening the files directly using OPENROWSET. For example:

```
CREATE DATABASE SCOPED CREDENTIAL AzureBlob
WITH  IDENTITY = 'SHARED ACCESS SIGNATURE',
SECRET = 'sv=2018-03-28&ss=bfqt&srt=sco&sp=rwdlacup
&se=2099-08-19T23:56:04Z&st=2022-08-19T15:56:04Z&spr=https&sig=ZWHPwhateverD';
CREATE EXTERNAL DATA SOURCE AzureBlob_ForBulk
WITH  ( LOCATION = 'https://container.blob.core.windows.net/subfolder' , --No trailing /
CREDENTIAL = AzureBlob, TYPE = BLOB_STORAGE);
```

Maintain and monitor SQL Server

Previous chapters covered the importance and logistics of database backups, but what else do you need to do on a regular basis to maintain a healthy SQL Server?

This chapter lays the foundation for the *what* and *why* of Microsoft SQL Server monitoring, based on dynamic management objects (DMOs), Database Consistency Checker (DBCC) commands, Extended Events (which replace Profiler/trace), and other tools provided by Microsoft.

Beyond simply setting up these tools, this chapter reviews what to look for on SQL Server instances on Windows and Linux, as well as SQL monitoring solutions in the Azure portal.

There is a lot for a DBA to be concerned with to monitor your databases—corrupt data files, lack of use of indexes and stats, properly sized data files, and baselined performance metrics, just to start. This chapter covers these topics and more.

All sample scripts in this book are available for download at *https://MicrosoftPressStore.com /SQLServer2022InsideOut/downloads*.

Detect, prevent, and respond to database corruption

After database backups, the second most important task concerning database integrity is proper configuration to prevent—and monitoring to mitigate—database corruption. A very large part of this is a proactive schedule of detection for rare cases when corruption occurs despite your best efforts. This isn't a complicated topic and mostly revolves around configuring one setting and regularly running one command.

Set the database's page verify option

For all databases, the page verify option should be CHECKSUM. Since SQL Server 2005, CHECKSUM has been the superior and default setting, but it requires a manual change after a database is restored up to a new SQL Server version.

If you still have databases whose page verify option is not CHECKSUM, you should change this setting immediately. The legacy NONE or TORN_PAGE_DETECTION options for this setting are a clear sign that this database has been moved over the years from a pre–SQL Server 2005 version. This setting is never automatically changed; you must change this setting after restoring the database up to a new version of SQL Server.

WARNING

Before making the change to the CHECKSUM **page verify option, take a full backup!**

Inside OUT

Is enabling the CHECKSUM page verify option as easy as changing the setting in the database?

Unfortunately, no. Changing the page verify option to CHECKSUM is a quick change, but the checksums are not immediately created and so do not begin to protect the data pages immediately.

A checksum must be generated and stored for each page, so to truly verify that no corruption exists, it is recommended that you rebuild every index on every table after changing the page verify option to CHECKSUM. This obviously can be time consuming and could create a lot of transaction log activity, but it is necessary.

If corruption is found with the newly enabled CHECKSUM setting, the database can drop into a SUSPECT state, in which it becomes inaccessible. It is entirely possible that changing a database from NONE or TORN_PAGE_DETECTION to CHECKSUM could result in the discovery of existing, even long-present database corruption.

You should periodically run CHECKDB on all databases. This is a time-consuming but crucial process. You should run DBCC CHECKDB at least as often as your backup retention plan. Consider DBCC CHECKDB nearly as important as regular database backups.

The only reliable solution to database corruption is restoring from a known good backup.

For example, if you keep local backups around for one month, you should ensure that you perform a successful DBCC CHECKDB at least once per month, but more often is recommended. This ensures you will at least have a recovery point for uncorrupted, unchanged data, and a starting point for corrupted data fixes.

The DBCC CHECKDB command covers other more granular database integrity check tasks, including DBCC CHECKALLOC, DBCC CHECKTABLE, and DBCC CHECKCATALOG, all of which are important, and in only rare cases need to be run separately to split up the workload.

Running DBCC CHECKDB with no other parameters or syntax performs an integrity test on the current database context. Without specifying a database, however, no other additional options can be provided.

On large databases, DBCC CHECKDB is a resource-intensive operation (CPU, memory, and I/O), can take hours, and affects other user queries because of that resource consumption. DBCC CHECKDB may take hours to complete and tie up CPU resources, so it should be run only outside of business hours. To mitigate this, consider specifying the MAXDOP option (more on that in a moment). You can evaluate the progress of a DBCC CHECKDB operation (as well as backup and restore operations) by referencing the value in sys.dm_exec_requests.percent_complete for the executing session.

Here are some parameters worth noting:

- **NOINDEX.** This can reduce the duration of the integrity check by skipping checks on nonclustered rowstore and columnstore indexes. It is not recommended.

  Example usage:

  ```
  DBCC CHECKDB (databasename, NOINDEX);
  ```

- **REPAIR_REBUILD.** This ensures you have no data loss. However, there are some limitations to its potential benefit. You should run this only after considering other options, including a backup and restore, because although it might have some success, it is unlikely to result in a complete repair. It can also be very time consuming, involving the rebuilding of indexes based on attempted repair data.

  ➤ Review the DBCC CHECKDB documentation at *https://learn.microsoft.com/sql/t-sql/database-console-commands/dbcc-checkdb-transact-sql*.

  Example usage:

  ```
  DBCC CHECKDB (databasename) WITH REPAIR_REBUILD;
  ```

- **REPAIR_ALLOW_DATA_LOSS.** You should run this only as a last resort to achieve a partial database recovery, because it can force a database to resolve errors by simply deallocating pages, potentially creating gaps in rows or columns. You must run this in SINGLE_USER mode, and you should run it in EMERGENCY mode. Review the DBCC CHECKDB documentation for a number of caveats, and do not execute this command casually.

  Example usage (last resort only, not recommended!):

  ```
  ALTER DATABASE WorldWideImporters SET EMERGENCY, SINGLE_USER;
  DBCC CHECKDB('WideWorldImporters', REPAIR_ALLOW_DATA_LOSS);
  ALTER DATABASE WorldWideImporters SET MULTI_USER;
  ```

> **NOTE**
>
> A complete review of EMERGENCY mode and REPAIR_ALLOW_DATA_LOSS is detailed in this blog post by Microsoft's original DBCC CHECKDB engineer, Paul Randal: *http://sqlskills.com/blogs/paul/checkdb-from-every-angle-emergency-mode-repair-the-very-very-last-resort*.

- **WITH NO_INFOMSGS.** This suppresses informational status messages and returns only errors.

  Example usage:

  ```
  DBCC CHECKDB (databasename) WITH NO_INFOMSGS;
  ```

- **WITH ESTIMATEONLY.** This estimates the amount of space required in tempdb for the CHECKDB operation.

  Example usage:

  ```
  DBCC CHECKDB (databasename) WITH ESTIMATEONLY;
  ```

- **WITH MAXDOP = n.** Similar to limiting the maximum degree of parallelism in other areas of SQL Server, this option limits the CHECKDB operation's parallelism, possibly extending duration but potentially reducing the CPU utilization. SQL Server Enterprise edition supports parallel execution of the DBCC CHECKDB command, up to the server's MAXDOP setting. Therefore, in Enterprise edition, consider MAXDOP = 1 to run the command single-threaded, or, overriding the other limitations on maximum degree of parallelism with MAXDOP = 0, allowing the CHECKDB unlimited parallelism to potentially finish sooner. Outside of Enterprise and Developer editions of SQL Server, objects are not checked in parallel.

  Example usage, combined with the aforementioned NO_INFOMSGS command to show multiple parameters:

  ```
  DBCC CHECKDB (databasename) WITH NO_INFOMSGS, MAXDOP = 0;
  ```

> You can see all the syntax options for CHECKDB, and those options that can be used together, at *https://learn.microsoft.com/sql/t-sql/database-console-commands/dbcc-checkdb-transact-sql#syntax*.

> For more information on automating DBCC CHECKDB, see Chapter 9, "Automate SQL Server administration."

Inside OUT

How do you tell when a DBCC CHECKDB was last run on a database?

SQL Server writes each execution of DBCC CHECKDB to the SQL Server Error Log, but also records it internally. You can retrieve the latest good known execution date of DBCC CHECKDB by using the SELECT DATABASEPROPERTYEX command.

For example:

```
SELECT DATABASEPROPERTYEX ('dbname' , 'LastGoodCheckDbTime');
```

Repair database data file corruption

Of course, the only real remedy to data corruption after it has happened is to restore from a backup that predates the corruption. The well-documented DBCC CHECKDB option for REPAIR _ALLOW_DATA_LOSS, discussed previously, should be a last resort.

It is possible to repair missing pages in clustered indexes by piecing together missing columns in nonclustered indexes. If you are fortunate enough that corruption is only in nonclustered indexes, you can simply rebuild those indexes to recover from corruption. However, in many cases, clustered index or system pages are corrupt, meaning the only option is to restore the database. It is also possible to recover from data corruption, admittedly a lucky endeavor that this author has benefited from, by identifying the objects reported by DBCC CHECKDB and performing index rebuild operations on them.

Finally, availability groups provide a built-in data-corruption detection and automatic repair capability by using uncorrupted data on one replica to replace inaccessible data on another.

> ➤ For more information on this feature of availability groups, see Chapter 11, "Implement high availability and disaster recovery."

Recover from database transaction log file corruption

In addition to following guidance in the previous chapter on the importance of backups, you can reconstitute a corrupted or lost database transaction log file by using the code that follows. A lost transaction log file could result in the loss of uncommitted data (or in the case of delayed durability tables, the loss of data that hasn't been made durable in the log yet), but in the event of a disaster recovery involving the loss of the .ldf file with an intact .mdf file, this could be a valuable step.

It is possible to rebuild a blank transaction log file in a new file location for a database by using the following command:

```
ALTER DATABASE DemoDb SET EMERGENCY, SINGLE_USER;
ALTER DATABASE DemoDb REBUILD LOG
ON (NAME= DemoDb_Log, FILENAME = 'F:\DATA\DemoDb_new.ldf');
ALTER DATABASE DemoDb SET MULTI_USER;
```

NOTE

Rebuilding a blank transaction log file using ALTER DATABASE ... REBUILD LOG **is not supported for databases containing a** MEMORY_OPTIMIZED_DATA **filegroup.**

Database corruption in Azure SQL Database

Like many other administrative concerns with a platform as a service (PaaS) database, integrity checks for Azure SQL Database are automated. Microsoft takes data integrity in its PaaS database offering very seriously and provides strong assurances of assistance and recovery for this product. Albeit rare, Azure engineering teams respond 24×7 globally to data-corruption reports. The Azure SQL Database engineering team details its response promises at *https://azure.microsoft.com/blog/data-integrity-in-azure-sql-database/*.

NOTE

While Azure SQL Managed Instance has many PaaS-like qualities, automated integrity checks are not one of them. You should set up maintenance plans to execute DBCC CHECKDB, **index maintenance, and other maintenance topics discussed in this chapter for Azure SQL Managed Instance.**

➤ We discuss Azure SQL Managed Instance in detail in Chapter 18, "Provision Azure SQL Managed Instance."

Maintain indexes and statistics

Index fragmentation occurs when insert, update, and delete activity occurs within tables, and there is not enough free space for that data, causing data to be split across pages. It can also happen when index pages get out of order, resulting in inefficient scans. Index fragmentation is caused by improper organization of rowstore data within the file that SQL Server maintains. Removing fragmentation is really about minimizing the number of pages that must be involved when queries read or write those data pages. Reducing fragmentation in database objects is vastly different from reducing fragmentation at the drive level, and has little in common with the Windows Disk Defragmenter application. Although this doesn't translate to page locations on disk, and has even less relevance on storage area networks (SANs), it does translate to the activity of I/O systems when retrieving data.

In performance terms, the higher the amount of fragmentation (easily measurable in dynamic management views, as discussed later), the more activity is required for accessing the same amount of data.

The causes of index fragmentation are writes. Our data would stay nice and tidy if applications would stop writing to it! Updates and deletes will inevitably have a significant effect on clustered and nonclustered index fragmentation, plus the effect that inserts can have on fragmentation because of clustered index design.

Inside OUT

Can heaps be fragmented?

A *heap* (a table without a clustered index) doesn't suffer from fragmentation. (How can unordered pages be out of order?) Rather, heaps suffer from wasted space within the heap structure. This is thanks to the use of forwarding pointers, a mechanism for keeping data associated, but is realistically far worse for performance than fragmentation.

Forwarding pointers are followed from pointer to pointer as the table is scanned, until finally arriving at the page where the data is now stored. Deletes and updates leave wasted space, where the data will no longer fit on the same page, in a heap that cannot be reclaimed even with an index rebuild operation.

To reclaim wasted space within a heap, you must execute an ALTER TABLE statement with the REBUILD option or, ironically, create a clustered index on the table, and then, to make it a heap again, drop the clustered index. The latter process can be very costly if you have nonclustered indexes on the table, as they will all be rebuilt twice in the process.

The information in this section is largely unchanged from previous versions of SQL Server and applies to SQL Server instances, databases in Azure SQL Database, Azure SQL Managed Instance, and even dedicated SQL pools in Azure Synapse Analytics (formerly known as Azure SQL Data Warehouse).

Change the fill factor when beneficial

Each rowstore index on disk-based objects has a numeric property called a *fill factor* that specifies the percentage of space to be filled with rowstore data in each leaf-level data page of the index when it is created or rebuilt. The instance-wide default fill factor is 100 percent, which is represented by the setting value 0, and means that each leaf-level data page will be filled with as much data as possible. A fill factor setting of 80 (percent) means that 20 percent of leaf-level data pages will be intentionally left empty when data is inserted. You can adjust this fill factor percentage for each index to manage the efficiency of data pages.

A non-default fill factor may help reduce the number of page splits, which occur when the Database Engine attempts to add a new row of data or update an existing row with more data to a page that does not have enough space to add a new row. In this case, the Database Engine will clear out space for the new row by moving a proportion of the old rows to a new page. A page split can be a time-consuming and resource-consuming operation, with many page splits possible during writes, and will lead to index fragmentation.

However, setting a non-default fill factor will also increase the number of pages needed to store the same data and increase the number of reads needed for query operations. For example, a fill factor of 50 will roughly double the space on the drive that it initially takes to store and therefore access the data when compared to the default fill factor of 0.

In most instances, data is read far more often than it is written and inserted, updated, and deleted upon occasion. Indexes will therefore benefit from a high or default fill factor—usually more than 80—because it is almost always more important to keep the number of reads to a manageable level than to minimize the resources needed to perform a page split. You can deal with index fragmentation by using the REBUILD or REORGANIZE commands, as discussed in the next section.

If the key value for an index is constantly increasing, such as an autoincrementing IDENTITY or SEQUENCE-populated field as the first key of a clustered index, the data is added to the end of a data page and any gaps would not need to be filled. In the case of a table for which data is always inserted sequentially and never updated, changing the fill factor from the default may offer no advantage. Even after fine-tuning a fill factor, the benefit of reducing page splits might not be noticeable to write performance. The design of your database may affect your choice of fill factor—for example, if your clustered index key is a GUID, you may choose to lower the fill factor.

You can set a fill factor when an index is first created, or you can change it by using the ALTER INDEX ... REBUILD syntax, as discussed in the next section.

> **NOTE**
>
> The OPTIMIZE_FOR_SEQUENTIAL_KEY feature, introduced in SQL Server 2019, can further benefit IDENTITY and SEQUENCE-populated columns. For more on this recommended new feature, see Chapter 15, "Understand and design indexes."

Track page splits

If you intend to fine-tune the fill factor for important tables to maximize the performance/storage space ratio, you can measure page splits in two ways: with a query on a DMV (discussed here), and with an Extended Event session (covered later in this chapter).

You can use the performance counter DMV to measure page splits in aggregate on Windows Server, as shown here:

```
SELECT * FROM sys.dm_os_performance_counters WHERE counter_name ='Page Splits/sec';
```

The `cntr_value` increments whenever a page split is detected. This is a bit misleading because to calculate the page splits per second, you must sample the incrementing value twice and divide by the time difference between the samples. When viewing this metric in Performance Monitor, the calculation is done for you.

You can also track `page_split` events alongside statement execution by adding the page `_split` event to sessions such as the Transact-SQL (T-SQL) template in the Extended Events wizard. You'll see an example of this later in this chapter, in the section "Use Extended Events to detect page splits."

> ➤ **Extended Events and the `sys.dm_os_performance_counters` DMV are discussed in more detail later in this chapter in the section "Query performance metrics with DMVs." This section also includes a sample session script to track `page_split` events.**

Monitor index fragmentation

You can find the extent to which an index is fragmented by interrogating the `sys.dm_db _index_physical_stats` dynamic management function (DMF).

Unlike most DMVs, this function can have a significant impact on server performance because it can tax I/O. To query this DMF, you must be a member of the sysadmin server role or the db_ddladmin or db_owner database roles. Alternatively, you can grant the VIEW DATABASE STATE or VIEW SERVER STATE permissions. The `sys.dm_db_index_physical_stats` DMF is often joined to catalog views like sys.indexes or sys.objects, which require the user to have some permissions to the tables in addition to VIEW DATABASE STATE or VIEW SERVER STATE.

> ➤ **For more information, visit** *https://learn.microsoft.com/sql/relational-databases/system -dynamic-management-views/sys-dm-db-index-physical-stats-transact-sql#permissions* **and** *https://learn.microsoft.com/sql/relational-databases/security/metadata-visibility -configuration.*

Keep this in mind when scripting this operation for automated index maintenance. (We talk more about automating index maintenance in Chapter 9.)

Some of the following samples can be executed against the WideWorldImporters sample database. You can download then restore the WideWorldImporters-Full.bak file from this location: *https://go.microsoft.com/fwlink/?LinkID=800630*. For example, to find the fragmentation level of all indexes on the Sales.Orders table in the WideWorldImporters sample database, you can use a query such as the following:

```
USE WideWorldImporters;
SELECT
DB = db_name(s.database_id)
, [schema_name] = sc.name
, [table_name] = o.name
, index_name = i.name
, s.index_type_desc
, s.partition_number -- if the object is partitioned
```

```
, avg_fragmentation_pct = s.avg_fragmentation_in_percent
, s.page_count -- pages in object partition
FROM sys.indexes AS i
CROSS APPLY sys.dm_db_index_physical_stats
(DB_ID(),i.object_id,i.index_id, NULL, NULL) AS s
INNER JOIN sys.objects AS o ON o.object_id = s.object_id
INNER JOIN sys.schemas AS sc ON o.schema_id = sc.schema_id
WHERE i.is_disabled = 0
AND o.object_id = OBJECT_ID('Sales.Orders');
```

The `sys.dm_db_index_physical_stats` DMF accepts five parameters: `database_id`, `object_id`, `index_id`, `partition_id`, and `mode`. The `mode` parameter defaults to `LIMITED`, the fastest method, but you can set it to `Sampled` or `Detailed`. These additional modes are rarely necessary, but they provide more data, as well as more precise data. Some result set columns will be `NULL` in `LIMITED` mode. For the purposes of determining fragmentation, the default mode of `LIMITED` (used when the parameter value of `NULL` is provided or the literal `LIMITED`) suffices.

The five parameters of the `sys.dm_db_index_physical_stats` DMF are all nullable. For example, if you run the following script, you will see fragmentation statistics for all databases, objects, indexes, and partitions:

```
SELECT * FROM sys.dm_db_index_physical_stats(NULL,NULL,NULL,NULL,NULL);
```

We recommend against executing this in a production environment during operational hours because, again, it can have a significant impact on server resources, resulting in a noticeable drop in performance.

Maintain indexes

After your automated script has identified the objects most in need of maintenance with the aid of `sys.dm_db_index_physical_stats`, it should proceed with steps to remove fragmentation in a timely fashion during a maintenance window. The commands to remove fragmentation are `ALTER INDEX` and `ALTER TABLE`, with `REBUILD` and `REORGANIZE` options. We explain the differences later, but briefly, rebuild is more thorough and potentially disruptive, whereas reorganize is less thorough, not disruptive, but often sufficient.

You must implement index maintenance for both rowstore and columnstore indexes; we cover strategies for both in this section.

Ideally, your automated index maintenance script runs as often as possible during regularly scheduled maintenance windows and for a limited amount of time. For example, if your business environment allows for a maintenance window each night between 1 a.m. and 4 a.m., try to run index maintenance each night in that window. If possible, modify your script to avoid starting new work after 4 a.m. or using the `RESUMABLE PAUSE` feature at 4 a.m. (More on the latter strategy in the upcoming section "Rebuild indexes.") In databases with very large tables, index maintenance may require more time than you have within in a single maintenance window. Try to use the limited amount of time in each maintenance window with the greatest effect. Given ample time, this approach tends to work best to reduce fragmentation rather than, for example, a single very long maintenance period during a weekend. This feature also allows your active transaction log pages to be cleared with a log backup during the paused phases of an index rebuild.

➤ For more on maintenance plans and automating index maintenance, including the typical "care and feeding" of a SQL Server, see Chapter 9.

Inside OUT

Can you cancel an index maintenance operation?

If index maintenance runs long and begins to disrupt other activities, be careful when stopping or killing the process and forcing a rollback. Killing the session or cancelling the request of a long-running index rebuild is no quick remedy, but a painful rollback can be avoided in two ways:

- If you started the index maintenance operation with the RESUMABLE option, introduced in SQL Server 2017, issue a PAUSE command. (More on the RESUMABLE option later in this chapter.)

- Accelerated database recovery (ADR) can prevent a lengthy rollback after the operation is killed.

Without ADR, the rollback of a large, long-running index REBUILD step could take a very long time and continue blocking, even after a SQL Server service restart. Even when an ONLINE index REBUILD operation is killed, its rollback is not an ONLINE operation!

Instead, consider the following measures to prevent this scenario from happening:

- In your index maintenance loop that performs index maintenance, rebuild or reorganize an index as granularly as possible. Avoid using the ALL keyword to process all indexes on a table. Perform index maintenance on individual index partitions if possible.

- In your index maintenance script, write code to check the time. If your index maintenance is outside of an allowed time window, don't begin a new index maintenance operation, or use the PAUSE option, explained next.

- Specify ONLINE = ON, RESUMABLE = ON when beginning the REBUILD operation. If an index maintenance step overruns a maintenance window, you can issue a PAUSE, saving you the time of a lengthy and disruptive rollback. You could also specify a MAX_DURATION option when starting index rebuild; that way, the operation will automatically pause itself if it exceeds the duration. The rebuild can then be resumed later on. (The RESUMABLE option is covered in more detail in the next section.)

- Enable the new accelerated database recovery (ADR) option in each database.

➤ For more on enabling the accelerated database recovery option, see Chapter 6, "Provision and configure SQL Server databases."

Rebuild indexes

Performing an INDEX REBUILD operation on a rowstore index (clustered or nonclustered) physically re-creates the index B-tree leaf level. The goal of moving the pages is to make storage more efficient and to match the logical order provided by the index key. A rebuild operation is destructive to the index object and blocks other queries attempting to access the pages unless you provide the ONLINE option. Because the rebuild operation destroys and re-creates the index, it must update the index statistics afterward, eliminating the need to perform a subsequent UPDATE STATISTICS operation as part of regular maintenance.

Long-term table locks are held during the rebuild operation. One major advantage of SQL Server Enterprise edition remains the ability to specify the ONLINE option, which allows for rebuild operations that are significantly less disruptive to other queries, though not completely. This makes index maintenance feasible on SQL Servers with round-the-clock activity.

Consider using ONLINE with index rebuild operations whenever short maintenance windows are insufficient for rebuilding fragmented indexes offline. An online index rebuild, however, might take longer than an offline rebuild. There are also scenarios for which an online rebuild is not possible, including deprecated data types image, text, and ntext, or the xml data type. Since SQL Server 2012, it has been possible to perform ONLINE index rebuilds on the max lengths of the data types varchar, nvarchar, and varbinary.

For the syntax to rebuild the FK_Sales_Orders_CustomerID nonclustered index on the Sales.Orders table with the ONLINE functionality in Enterprise edition, see the following code sample:

```
ALTER INDEX FK_Sales_Orders_CustomerID
ON Sales.Orders
REBUILD WITH (ONLINE=ON);
```

It's important to note that if you perform any kind of index maintenance on the clustered index of a rowstore table, it does not affect the nonclustered indexes. Nonclustered index fragmentation will not change if you rebuild the clustered index.

Instead of rebuilding each index on a table individually, you can rebuild all indexes on a table by replacing the name of the index with the keyword ALL. For example, to rebuild all indexes on the Sales.OrderLines table, do the following:

```
ALTER INDEX ALL ON [Sales].[OrderLines] REBUILD;
```

This is usually overkill and inefficient, however, because not all indexes may have the same level of fragmentation or need for maintenance. Remember, we should perform index maintenance as granularly as possible.

For memory-optimized tables, we recommend a manual routine maintenance step using the ALTER TABLE ... ALTER INDEX ... REBUILD syntax. This is not to reduce fragmentation in the in-memory data; rather, it is to examine the number of buckets in a memory-optimized table's hash indexes. For more information on rebuilding hash indexes and bucket counts, see Chapter 15.

NOTE

You can change the data compression option for indexes with the rebuild operation using the DATA_COMPRESSION **option. For more detail on data compression, see Chapter 3, "Design and implement an on-premises database infrastructure."**

Aside from ONLINE, there are other options that you might want to consider for rebuild operations. Let's look at them:

- **SORT_IN_TEMPDB.** Use this when you want to create or rebuild an index using tempdb for sorting the index data, potentially increasing performance by distributing the I/O activity across multiple drives. This also means that these sorting worktables are written to the tempdb database transaction log instead of the user database transaction log, potentially reducing the impact on the user database log file, and allowing for the user database transaction log to be backed up during the operation.

- **MAXDOP.** Use this to mitigate some of the impact of index maintenance by preventing the operation from using parallel processors. This can cause the operation to run longer, but to have less impact on performance.

- **WAIT_AT_LOW_PRIORITY.** First introduced in SQL Server 2014, this is the first of a set of parameters that you can use to instruct the ONLINE index maintenance operation to try not to block other operations. This feature is known as Managed Lock Priority, and this syntax is not usable outside of online index operations and partition-switching operations. (SQL Server 2022 also introduced the ability to use WAIT_AT_LOW_PRIORITY for DBCC SHRINKDATABASE and DBCC SHRINKFILE operations.) Here is the full syntax:

```
ALTER INDEX PK_Sales_OrderLines on [Sales].[OrderLines]
REBUILD WITH (ONLINE=ON (WAIT_AT_LOW_PRIORITY (MAX_DURATION = 5 MINUTES,
ABORT_AFTER_WAIT = SELF)));
```

The parameters for MAX_DURATION and ABORT_AFTER_WAIT instruct the statement on how to proceed if it begins to be blocked by another operation. The online index operation will wait, allowing other operations to proceed.

The ABORT_AFTER_WAIT parameter provides an action at the end of the MAX_DURATION wait:

- SELF instructs the statement to terminate its own process, ending the online rebuild step.

- BLOCKERS instructs the statement to terminate the other process that is being blocked, terminating what is potentially a user transaction. Use with caution.

- NONE instructs the statement to continue to wait. When combined with MAX_DURATION = 0, it is essentially the same behavior as not specifying WAIT_AT_LOW_PRIORITY.

CHAPTER 8

- **RESUMABLE.** Introduced in SQL Server 2017, this feature makes it possible to initiate an online index creation or rebuild that can be paused and resumed later, even after a server shutdown. You can also specify a MAX_DURATION in minutes when starting an index rebuild operation, which will pause the operation if it exceeds the specified duration. You cannot specify the ALL keyword for a resumable operation. The SORT_IN_TEMPDB=ON option is not compatible with the RESUMABLE option.

NOTE

Starting with SQL Server 2019, the RESUMABLE **syntax can also be used when creating an index. An** ALTER INDEX **and** CREATE INDEX **statement can be similarly paused and resumed.**

To leverage resumable index maintenance operations, you can see a list of resumable and paused index operations in a new DMV, sys.index_resumable_operations, where the state_desc field will reflect RUNNING (and pausable) or PAUSED (and resumable).

Here is a sample scenario of a paused/resumed index maintenance operation on a large table in the sample WideWorldImporters database:

```
ALTER INDEX PK_Sales_OrderLines on [Sales].[OrderLines]
REBUILD WITH (ONLINE = ON, RESUMABLE = ON);
```

From another session, show that the index rebuild is RUNNING with the RESUMABLE option:

```
SELECT object_name = object_name (object_id), *
FROM sys.index_resumable_operations;
```

From a third session, run the following to pause the operation:

```
ALTER INDEX PK_Sales_OrderLines on [Sales].[OrderLines] PAUSE;
```

You can then show that the index rebuild is paused:

```
SELECT object_name = object_name (object_id), * FROM sys.index_resumable_operations;
```

This sample is on a relatively small table, and may not allow you to execute the pause before the index rebuild is completed. This will result in a disconnection of the session of the original index maintenance, and a severe error message. In the SQL Server Error Log, the event is not a severe error message, but an informative note that "An ALTER INDEX 'PAUSE' was executed for...."

To resume the index maintenance operation, you have two options:

- Reissue the same index maintenance operation, which will warn you it'll just resume instead.

  ```
  ALTER INDEX PK_Sales_OrderLines on [Sales].[OrderLines] REBUILD
  WITH (ONLINE = ON, RESUMABLE = ON);
  ```

- Issue a RESUME to the same index.

```
ALTER INDEX PK_Sales_OrderLines on [Sales].[OrderLines] RESUME;
```

Inside OUT

Are all CREATE and ALTER INDEX operations resumable now?

These operations are not resumable by default, only with those operations that were started with the syntax RESUMABLE = ON. The default of this parameter is RESUMABLE=OFF, so index operations are not resumable by default.

Be aware of this beneficial new feature for both index CREATE and ALTER operations, and prepare to take advantage of it from now on. For very large tables, you should consider using the RESUMABLE feature to pause index maintenance during normal utilization.

It is possible for a RESUMABLE rebuild operation to be blocked by uncommitted transactions and unable to be paused. In this case, you will see the ALTER INDEX ... PAUSE statement is blocked by the ALTER INDEX ... REBUILD statement. Long-running transactions can be a problem for many reasons, with this among them.

The RESUMABLE syntax also supports a MAX_DURATION syntax, which has a different meaning than the MAX_DURATION syntax used in the ABORT_AFTER_WAIT. The MAX_ DURATION option could be very useful to you, automatically pausing an online index operation after a specified amount of time. For example, this allows for the index operation to be resumed during the next maintenance window. The MAX_DURATION > 0 option allows the operation to run indefinitely, and is not a required parameter for RESUMABLE=ON. Here's an example:

```
ALTER INDEX PK_Sales_OrderLines on [Sales].[OrderLines]
REBUILD WITH (ONLINE=ON, RESUMABLE=ON, MAX_DURATION = 60 MINUTES);
```

Reorganize indexes

Performing a REORGANIZE operation on an index uses fewer system resources and is much less disruptive than performing a full rebuild, while still accomplishing the goal of reducing fragmentation. It physically reorders the leaf-level pages of the index to match the logical order. It also compacts pages to match the fill factor on the index, though it does not allow the fill factor to be changed. This operation is always performed online, so long-term table locks (except for schema locks) are not held, and queries or modifications to the underlying table or index data will not be blocked by the schema lock during the REORGANIZE transaction.

Because the REORGANIZE operation is not destructive, it does not automatically update the statistics for the index afterward as a rebuild operation does. Thus, you should always follow a REORGANIZE step with an UPDATE STATISTICS step.

➤ **For more on statistics objects and their impact on performance, see Chapter 15.**

The following example presents the syntax to reorganize the PK_Sales_OrderLines index on the Sales.OrderLines table:

```
ALTER INDEX PK_Sales_OrderLines on [Sales].[OrderLines] REORGANIZE;
```

None of the options available to rebuild that we covered in the previous section are available to the REORGANIZE command. The only additional option that is specific to REORGANIZE is the LOB_COMPACTION option. It compresses large object (LOB) data, which affects only LOB data types: image, text, ntext, varchar(max), nvarchar(max), varbinary(max), and xml. By default, this option is enabled, but you can disable it for non-heap tables to potentially skip some activity, though we do not recommend it. For heap tables, LOB data is always compacted.

Update index statistics

SQL Server uses statistics to describe the distribution and nature of the data in tables. The Query Optimizer needs the auto create setting enabled (it is enabled by default) so it can create single-column statistics when compiling queries. These statistics help the Query Optimizer create the most optimal query plans at runtime. The auto update statistics option prompts statistics to be updated automatically when accessed by a T-SQL query. This only occurs when the table is discovered to have passed a threshold of rows changed. Without relevant and up-to-date statistics, the Query Optimizer might not choose the best way to run queries.

An update of index statistics should accompany INDEX REORGANIZE steps to ensure that statistics on the table are current, but not INDEX REBUILD steps. Remember that the INDEX REBUILD command also updates the index statistics.

The basic syntax to update the statistics for an individual table is as follows:

```
UPDATE STATISTICS [Sales].[Invoices];
```

The only command option to be aware of concerns the depth to which the statistics are scanned before being recalculated. By default, SQL Server samples a statistically significant number of rows in the table. This sampling is done with a parallel process starting with database compatibility level 150. This is fast and adequate for most workloads. You can optionally choose to scan the entire table by specifying the FULLSCAN option, or a sample of the table based on a percentage of rows or a fixed number of rows using the SAMPLE option, but these options are typically reserved for cases of unusual data skew where the default sampling may not provide adequate coverage for your column or index.

You can manually verify that indexes are being kept up to date by the Query Optimizer when auto_create_stats is enabled. The sys.dm_db_stats_properties DMF accepts an object _id and stats_id, which is functionally the same as the index_id, if the statistics object corresponds to an index. The sys.dm_db_stats_properties DMF returns information such as the modification_counter of rows changed since the last statistics update, and the last _updated date, which is NULL if the statistics object has never been updated since it was created.

Not all statistics are associated with an index, such as statistics that are automatically created. There will generally be more statistics objects than index objects. This function works in SQL Server and Azure SQL Database. You can easily tell if a statistics object (which you can gather from querying sys.stats) is automatically created by its naming convention, WA_Sys_<column_ name>_<object_id_hex>, or by looking at the user_created and auto_created columns in the same view.

➤ For more on statistics objects and their impact on performance, see Chapter 15.

Inside OUT

Do you need to update statistics regularly even if auto_create_stats is enabled for the database?

Yes, you should still maintain statistics health by updating them regularly. Updating statistics regularly, if your maintenance window time allows, will definitely not hurt, and will likely help by reducing the number of statistics updates that happen automatically during regular business hours.

When auto_update_stats is on, statistics are updated periodically based on (and during) actual usage. Statistics are considered out of date by the Query Optimizer when a ratio of data modifications to rows in the table has been reached. The Query Optimizer will check for and update the out-of-date statistic before running a query plan. Therefore, the auto _update_stats option has some small runtime overhead, though the performance benefit of updated statistics usually outweighs this cost. We also highly recommend enabling the auto_update_stats_async option because it helps minimize this runtime overhead by updating the statistics after running the query, instead of before.

You should also enable the auto_update_stats and auto_update_ stats_async options, as discussed in Chapter 4, "Install and configure SQL Server instances and features," and Chapter 14, "Performance tune SQL Server," on all user databases, unless the application specifically requests that it be disabled, such as with Microsoft SharePoint.

Reorganize columnstore indexes

You must also maintain columnstore indexes, but these use different internal objects to measure the fragmentation of the internal columnstore structure. Columnstore indexes need only the REORGANIZE operation. For more on designing columnstore indexes, see Chapter 15.

You can review the current structure of the groups of columnstore indexes by using the DMV `sys.dm_db_column_store_row_group_physical_stats`. This returns one row per row group of the columnstore structure. The state of a row group, and the current count of row groups by their states, provides some insight into the health of the columnstore index. Most row group states should be COMPRESSED. Row groups in the OPEN and CLOSED states are part of the delta store and are awaiting compression. These delta store row groups are served up alongside compressed data seamlessly when queries use columnstore data.

The number of deleted rows in a rowgroup is also an indication that the index needs maintenance. As the ratio of deleted rows to total rows in a row group that is in the COMPRESSED state increases, the performance of the columnstore index will be reduced. If delete_rows is larger than or greater than the total rows in a rowgroup, a REORGANIZE step will be beneficial.

Performing a REBUILD operation on a columnstore index is essentially the same as performing a drop/re-create and is not necessary. However, if you want to force the rebuild process, using the WITH (ONLINE = ON) syntax is supported starting with SQL Server 2019 for rebuilding (and creating) columnstore indexes. A REORGANIZE step for a columnstore index, just as for a non-clustered index, is an online operation that has minimal impact to concurrent queries.

You can also use the REORGANIZE WITH (COMPRESS_ALL_ROW_GROUPS=ON) option to force all delta store row groups to be compressed into a single compressed row group. This can be useful when you observe many compressed row groups with fewer than 100,000 rows.

Without COMPRESS_ALL_ROW_GROUPS, only compressed row groups will be compressed and combined. Typically, compressed row groups should contain up to one million rows each, but SQL might align rows in compressed row groups that align with how the rows were inserted, especially if they were inserted in bulk operations.

➤ We talk more about automating index maintenance in Chapter 9.

Manage database file sizes

It is important to understand the distinction between the size of a database data or log files, which act simply as reservations for SQL Server to work in, and the data within those reservations. Note that this section does not apply to Azure SQL Database, because this level of file management is not available and is automatically managed.

In SQL Server Management Studio (SSMS), you can right-click a database, select **Reports**, and choose **Disk Usage** to view the Disk Usage report for a database. It contains information about how much data is in the database's files.

Alternatively, the following query uses the FILEPROPERTY function to reveal how much data there is inside a file reservation. We again use the undocumented but well-understood `sp_msforeachdb` stored procedure to iterate through each of the databases, accessing the sys.database_files catalog view.

```
DECLARE @FILEPROPERTY TABLE
( DatabaseName sysname
,DatabaseFileName nvarchar(500)
,FileLocation nvarchar(500)
,FileId int
,[type_desc] varchar(50)
,FileSizeMB decimal(19,2)
,SpaceUsedMB decimal(19,2)
,AvailableMB decimal(19,2)
,FreePercent decimal(19,2) );
INSERT INTO @FILEPROPERTY
exec sp_MSforeachdb 'USE [?];
SELECT
 Database_Name                = d.name
, Database_Logical_File_Name  = df.name
, File_Location               = df.physical_name
, df.File_ID
, df.type_desc
, FileSize_MB = CAST(size/128.0 as Decimal(19,2))
, SpaceUsed_MB = CAST(CAST(FILEPROPERTY(df.name, "SpaceUsed") AS int)/128.0 AS
decimal(19,2))
, Available_MB = CAST(size/128.0 - CAST(FILEPROPERTY(df.name, "SpaceUsed") AS int)/128.0
AS decimal(19,2))
, FreePercent = CAST(((((size/128.0) - (CAST(FILEPROPERTY(df.name, "SpaceUsed") AS
int)*8/1024.0)) / (size*8/1024.0) ) * 100. AS decimal(19,2))
 FROM sys.database_files as df
 CROSS APPLY sys.databases as d
 WHERE d.database_id = DB_ID();'
SELECT * FROM @FILEPROPERTY
WHERE SpaceUsedMB is not null
ORDER BY FreePercent asc; --Find files with least amount of free space at top
```

Run this on a database in your environment to see how much data there is within database files. You might find that some data or log files are near full, whereas others have a large amount of space. Why would this be?

Files that have a large amount of free space might have grown in the past but have since been emptied out. If a transaction log in the full recovery model has grown for a long time without having a transaction log backup, the .ldf file will have grown unchecked. Later, when a transaction log backup is taken, causing the log to truncate, it will be nearly empty, but the size of the .ldf file itself will not have changed. It isn't until you perform a shrink operation that the .ldf file will give its unused space back to the operating system (OS). In most cases, you should never shrink a data file, and certainly not on a schedule. The two main exceptions are if you mistakenly oversize a file or you applied data compression to a number of large database objects. In these cases, shrinking files as a one-time corrective action may be appropriate.

You should manually grow your database and log files to a size that is well ahead of the database's growth pattern. You might fret over the best autogrowth rate, but ideally, autogrowth events are best avoided altogether by proactive file management.

Autogrowth events can be disruptive to user activity, causing all transactions to wait while the database file asks the OS for more space and grows. Depending on the performance of the I/O system, this could take seconds, during which activity on the database must wait. Depending on the autogrowth setting and the size of the write transactions, multiple autogrowth events could be suffered sequentially.

> **Growth of database data files is also greatly sped up by instant file initialization, which is covered in Chapter 3.**

Understand and find autogrowth events

You should change autogrowth rates for database data and log files from the initial (and far too small) default settings, but, more importantly, you should maintain enough free space in your data and log files so that autogrowth events do not occur. As a proactive DBA, you should monitor the space in database files and grow the files ahead of time, manually and outside of peak business hours.

You can view recent autogrowth events in a database via a report in SSMS or a T-SQL script (see the code example that follows). In SSMS, in Object Explorer, right-click the database name. Then, on the shortcut menu that opens, select **Reports**, select **Standard Reports**, and then select **Disk Usage**. An expandable/collapsible region of the report contains data/log files auto-grow/autoshrink events.

The autogrowth report in SSMS reads data from the SQL Server instance's default trace, which captures autogrowth events. This data is not captured by the default Extended Events session, called system_health, but you could capture autogrowth events with the sqlserver.database_file_size_change event in an Extended Event session.

To view and analyze autogrowth events more quickly, and for all databases simultaneously, you can query the SQL Server instance's default trace yourself. The default trace files are limited to 20 MB, and there are at most five rollover files, yielding 100 MB of history. The amount of time this covers depends on server activity. The following sample code query uses the fn_trace_gettable() function to open the default trace file in its current location:

```
SELECT
DB = g.DatabaseName
, Logical_File_Name = mf.name
, Physical_File_Loc = mf.physical_name
, mf.type
-- The size in MB (converted from the number of 8-KB pages) the file increased.
, EventGrowth_MB = convert(decimal(19,2),g.IntegerData*8/1024.)
, g.StartTime --Time of the autogrowth event
```

```
-- Length of time (in seconds) necessary to extend the file.
, EventDuration_s = convert(decimal(19,2),g.Duration/1000./1000.)
, Current_Auto_Growth_Set = CASE
WHEN mf.is_percent_growth = 1
 THEN CONVERT(char(2), mf.growth) + '%'
 ELSE CONVERT(varchar(30), mf.growth*8./1024.) + 'MB'
END
, Current_File_Size_MB = CONVERT(decimal(19,2),mf.size*8./1024.)
, d.recovery_model_desc
FROM fn_trace_gettable(
(select substring((SELECT path
FROM sys.traces WHERE is_default =1), 0, charindex('\log_',
(SELECT path FROM sys.traces WHERE is_default =1),0)+4)
+ '.trc'), DEFAULT) AS [g]
INNER JOIN sys.master_files mf
ON mf.database_id = g.DatabaseID
AND g.FileName = mf.name
INNER JOIN sys.databases d
ON d.database_id = g.DatabaseID
ORDER BY StartTime desc;
```

Understanding autogrowth events helps explain what happens to database files when they don't have enough space. They must grow, or transactions cannot be accepted. What about the opposite scenario, where a database file has "too much" space? We cover that next.

Shrink database files

We need to be as clear as possible about this: Shrinking database files is not something that you should do regularly or casually. If you find yourself every morning shrinking a database file that grew overnight, stop. Think. Isn't it just going to grow again tonight?

One of the main concerns with shrinking a file is that it indiscriminately returns free pages to the OS, helping to create fragmentation. Aside from potentially ensuring autogrowth events in the future, shrinking a file creates the need for further index maintenance to alleviate the fragmentation. A shrink step can be time consuming, can block other user activity, and is not part of a healthy complete maintenance plan.

Database data and logs under normal circumstances—and in the case of the full recovery model with regular transaction log backups—grow to the size they need to be because of actual usage. Frequent autogrowth events and shrink operations are bad for performance and create fragmentation.

To increase concurrency of shrink operations, by allowing DBCC SHRINKDATABASE and DBCC SHRINKFILE to patiently wait for locks, SQL Server 2022 introduces the WAIT_AT_LOW_PRIORITY syntax. This same keyword has similar application for online index maintenance commands and behaves similarly. When you specify WAIT_AT_LOW_PRIORITY, the shrink operation waits until it can claim the shared schema (Sch-S) and shared metadata (Sch-M) locks it needs. Other queries won't be blocked until the shrink can actually proceed, resulting in less potential for blocked queries. The WAIT_AT_LOW_PRIORITY option is less configurable for the two shrink commands, and is hard-coded to a 1-minute timeout. If after 1 minute the shrink operation cannot obtain the necessary locks to proceed, it will be cancelled.

Shrink data files

Try to proactively grow database files to avoid autogrowth events altogether. You should shrink a data file only as a one-time event to solve one of three scenarios:

- A drive volume is out of space and, in an emergency break-fix scenario, you reclaim unused space from a database data or log file.

- A database transaction log grew to a much larger size than is normally needed because of an adverse condition and should be reduced back to its normal operating size. An adverse condition could be a transaction log backup that stopped working for a timespan, a large uncommitted transaction, or a replication availability group issue that prevented the transaction log from truncating.

- For the rare situation in which a database had a large amount of data deleted from the file, an amount of data that is unlikely ever to exist in the database again, a one-shrink file operation might be appropriate.

Shrink transaction log files

For the case in which a transaction log file should be reduced in size, the best way to reclaim the space and re-create the file with optimal virtual log file (VLF) alignment is to first create a transaction log backup to truncate the log file as much as possible. If transaction log backups have not recently been generated on a schedule, it may be necessary to create another transaction log backup to fully clear out the log file. Once empty, shrink the log file to reclaim all unused space, then immediately grow the log file back to its expected size in increments of no more than 8,000 MB at a time. This allows SQL Server to create the underlying VLF structures in the most efficient way possible.

> ➤ For more information on VLFs in your database log files, see Chapter 3.

The following sample script of this process assumes a transaction log backup has already been generated to truncate the database transaction log and that the database log file is mostly empty. It also grows the transaction log file backup to 9 GB (9,216 MB or 9,437,184 KB). Note the intermediate step of growing the file first to 8,000 MB, then to its intended size.

```
USE [WideWorldImporters];
--TRUNCATEONLY returns all free space to the OS
DBCC SHRINKFILE (N'WWI_Log' , 0, TRUNCATEONLY);
GO
USE [master];
ALTER DATABASE [WideWorldImporters]
```

```
MODIFY FILE ( NAME = N'WWI_Log', SIZE = 8192000KB );
ALTER DATABASE [WideWorldImporters]
MODIFY FILE ( NAME = N'WWI_Log', SIZE = 9437184KB );
GO
```

CAUTION

You should never enable the autoshrink database setting. It automatically returns any free space of more than 25 percent of the data file or transaction log. You should shrink a database only as a one-time operation to reduce file size after unplanned or unusual file growth. This setting could result in unnecessary fragmentation, overhead, and frequent rapid log autogrowth events. This setting was originally intended, and might only be appropriate, for tiny local and/or embedded databases.

Monitor activity with DMOs

SQL Server provides a suite of internal dynamic management objects (DMOs) in the form of views (DMVs) and functions (DMFs). It is important for you as a DBA to have a working knowledge of these objects because they unlock the analysis of SQL Server outside of built-in reporting capabilities and third-party tools. In fact, third-party tools that monitor SQL Server almost certainly use these very dynamic management objects.

DMO queries are discussed in several other places in this book:

- Chapter 14 discusses reviewing, aggregating, and analyzing cached execution plan statistics, including the Query Store feature introduced in SQL Server 2016.

- Chapter 14 also discusses reporting from DMOs and querying performance monitor metrics within SQL Server DMOs.

- Chapter 15 covers index usage statistics and missing index statistics.

- Chapter 11 details high availability and disaster recovery features like automatic seeding.

- The section "Monitor index fragmentation" earlier in this chapter talked about using a DMF to query index fragmentation.

Observe sessions and requests

Any connection to a SQL Server instance is a session and is reported live in the DMV sys.dm_exec_sessions. Any actively running query on a SQL Server instance is a request and is reported live in the DMV sys.dm_exec_requests. Together, these two DMVs provide a thorough and far more detailed replacement for the sp_who or sp_who2 system stored procedures, as well as the deprecated sys.sysprocesses system view, with which longtime DBAs might be more familiar. With DMVs, you can do so much more than replace sp_who.

By adding a handful of other DMOs, we can turn this query into a wealth of live information, including:

- Complete connection source information

- The actual runtime statement currently being run (like DBCC INPUTBUFFER, but not limited to 254 characters)

- The actual plan XML (provided with a blue hyperlink in the SSMS results grid)

- Request duration

- Cumulative resource consumption

- The current and most recent wait types experienced

Sure, it might not be as easy to type in as sp_who2, but it provides much more data, which you can easily query and filter. Save this as a go-to script in your personal DBA tool belt. If you are unfamiliar with any of the data being returned, take some time to dive into the result set and explore the information it provides; it will be an excellent hands-on learning resource. You might choose to add more filters to the WHERE clause specific to your environment. Let's take a look:

```
SELECT
 when_observed = sysdatetime()
, s.session_id, r.request_id
, session_status = s.[status] -- running, sleeping, dormant, preconnect
, request_status = r.[status] -- running, runnable, suspended, sleeping, background
, blocked_by = r.blocking_session_id
, database_name = db_name(r.database_id)
, s.login_time, r.start_time
, query_text = CASE
WHEN r.statement_start_offset = 0
 and r.statement_end_offset= 0 THEN left(est.text, 4000)
ELSE SUBSTRING (est.[text], r.statement_start_offset/2 + 1,
CASE WHEN r.statement_end_offset = -1
    THEN LEN (CONVERT(nvarchar(max), est.[text]))
    ELSE r.statement_end_offset/2 - r.statement_start_offset/2 + 1
END
) END --the actual query text is stored as nvarchar,
--so we must divide by 2 for the character offsets
, qp.query_plan
, cacheobjtype = LEFT (p.cacheobjtype + ' (' + p.objtype + ')', 35)
, est.objectid
, s.login_name, s.client_interface_name
, endpoint_name = e.name, protocol = e.protocol_desc
, s.host_name, s.program_name
, cpu_time_s = r.cpu_time, tot_time_s = r.total_elapsed_time
, wait_time_s = r.wait_time, r.wait_type, r.wait_resource, r.last_wait_type
, r.reads, r.writes, r.logical_reads --accumulated request statistics
```

```
FROM sys.dm_exec_sessions as s
LEFT OUTER JOIN sys.dm_exec_requests as r on r.session_id = s.session_id
LEFT OUTER JOIN sys.endpoints as e ON e.endpoint_id = s.endpoint_id
LEFT OUTER JOIN sys.dm_exec_cached_plans as p ON p.plan_handle = r.plan_handle
OUTER APPLY sys.dm_exec_query_plan (r.plan_handle) as qp
OUTER APPLY sys.dm_exec_sql_text (r.sql_handle) as est
LEFT OUTER JOIN sys.dm_exec_query_stats as stat on stat.plan_handle = r.plan_handle
AND r.statement_start_offset = stat.statement_start_offset
AND r.statement_end_offset = stat.statement_end_offset
WHERE 1=1 --Veteran trick that makes for easier commenting of filters
AND s.session_id >= 50 --retrieve only user spids
AND s.session_id <> @@SPID --ignore this session
ORDER BY r.blocking_session_id desc, s.session_id asc;
```

Notice that the preceding script returned `wait_type` and `last_wait_type`. Let's dive into these important performance signals now.

Understand wait types and wait statistics

Wait statistics in SQL Server are an important source of information and can be a key resource for finding bottlenecks in performance at the aggregate level and at the individual query level. A *wait* is a signal recorded by SQL Server indicating what SQL Server is waiting on when attempting to finish processing a query. This section provides insights into this broad and important topic. However, entire books, training sessions, and software packages have been developed to address wait type analysis.

Wait statistics can be queried and provide value to SQL Server instances as well as databases in Azure SQL Database and Azure SQL Managed Instance, though there are some waits specific to the Azure SQL Database platform (which we'll review). Like many DMOs, membership in the sysadmin server role is not required, only the permission VIEW SERVER STATE, or in the case of Azure SQL Database, VIEW DATABASE STATE.

You saw in the query in the previous section the ability to see the current and most recent wait type for a session. Let's dive into how to observe wait types in the aggregate, accumulated at the server level or at the session level. Waits can occur when a request is in the runnable or suspended state. SQL Server can track many different wait types for a single query, many of which are of negligible duration or are benign in nature. There are quite a few waits that can be ignored or that indicate idle activity, as opposed to waits that indicate resource constraints and blocking. There are more than 1,000 distinct wait types in SQL Server 2022 and even more in Azure SQL Database. Some are better documented and understood than others. We review some that you should know about later in this section.

> ➤ You can see the complete list of wait types at *https://learn.microsoft.com/sql/relational-databases/system-dynamic-management-views/sys-dm-os-wait-stats-transact-sql#WaitTypes.*

Monitor wait type aggregates

To view accumulated waits for a session, which live only until the close or reset of the session, use the sys.dm_exec_session_wait_stats DMV.

In sys.dm_exec_sessions, you can see the current wait type and most recent wait type, but this isn't always that interesting or informative. Potentially more interesting would be to see all the accumulated wait stats for an ongoing session. This code sample shows how the DMV returns one row per session, per wait type experienced, for user sessions:

```
SELECT * FROM sys.dm_exec_session_wait_stats
ORDER BY wait_time_ms DESC;
```

There is a distinction between the two time measurements in this query and others. The value from signal_wait_time_ms indicates the amount of time the thread waited on CPU activity, correlated with time spent in the runnable state. The wait_time_ms value indicates the accumulated time in milliseconds for the wait type, including the signal_wait_time_ms, and so includes time the request spent in the runnable and suspended states. Typically, wait_time_ms is the wait measurement that we aggregate. The waiting_tasks_count is also informative, indicating the number of times this wait_type was encountered. By dividing wait_time_ms by waiting_tasks_count, you can get an average number of milliseconds (ms) each task encountered this wait.

You can view aggregate wait types at the instance level with the sys.dm_os_wait_stats DMV. This is the same as sys.dm_exec_session_wait_stats, but without the session_id, which includes all activity in the SQL Server instance without any granularity to database, query, time frame, and so on. This can be useful for getting the "big picture," but it is limited over long spans of time because the wait_time_ms counter accumulates, as illustrated here:

```
SELECT TOP (25)
 wait_type
, wait_time_s = wait_time_ms / 1000.
, Pct = 100. * wait_time_ms/nullif(sum(wait_time_ms) OVER(),0)
, avg_ms_per_wait = wait_time_ms / nullif(waiting_tasks_count,0)
FROM sys.dm_os_wait_stats as wt ORDER BY Pct DESC;
```

Eventually, the wait_time_ms numbers will be so large for certain wait types that trends or changes in wait type accumulations rates will be mathematically difficult to see. You want to use the wait stats to keep a close eye on server performance as it trends and changes over time, so you need to capture these accumulated wait statistics in chunks of time, such as one day or one week.

```
--Script to set up capturing these statistics over time
CREATE TABLE dbo.usr_sys_dm_os_wait_stats
(   id int NOT NULL IDENTITY(1,1)
,   datecapture datetimeoffset(0) NOT NULL
,   wait_type nvarchar(512) NOT NULL
```

```
,   wait_time_s decimal(19,1) NOT NULL
,   Pct decimal(9,1) NOT NULL
,   avg_ms_per_wait decimal(19,1) NOT NULL
,   CONSTRAINT PK_sys_dm_os_wait_stats PRIMARY KEY CLUSTERED (id)
);
--This part of the script should be in a SQL Agent job, run regularly
INSERT INTO
Dbo.usr_sys_dm_os_wait_stats
(datecapture, wait_type, wait_time_s, Pct, avg_ms_per_wait)
SELECT
datecapture = SYSDATETIMEOFFSET()
, wait_type
, wait_time_s = convert(decimal(19,1), round( wait_time_ms / 1000.0,1))
, Pct = wait_time_ms/ nullif(sum(wait_time_ms) OVER(),0)
, avg_ms_per_wait = wait_time_ms / nullif(waiting_tasks_count,0)
FROM usr_sys.dm_os_wait_stats wt
WHERE wait_time_ms > 0
ORDER BY wait_time_s;
```

Using the metrics returned in the preceding code, you can calculate the difference between always-ascending wait times and counts to determine the counts between intervals. You can customize the schedule for this data to be captured in tables, building your own internal wait stats reporting table.

The sys.dm_os_wait_stats DMV is reset—and all accumulated metrics are lost—upon restart of the SQL Server service, but you can also clear them manually. Understandably, this would clear the statistics for the whole SQL Server instance. Here is a sample script of how you can capture wait statistics at any interval:

```
DBCC SQLPERF ('sys.dm_os_wait_stats', CLEAR);
```

You can also view statistics for a query currently running in the DMV sys.dm_os_waiting _tasks, which contains more data than simply the wait_type; it also shows the blocking resource address in the resource_description field. This data is also available in sys.dm _exec_requests.

> ➤ For a complete breakdown of the information that can be contained in the resource _description field, see *http://learn.microsoft.com/sql/relational-databases/system -dynamic-management-views/sys-dm-os-waiting-tasks-transact-sql.*

The query storage also tracks aggregated wait statistics for queries that it tracks. The waits tracked by the Query Store are not as detailed as the DMVs, but they do give you a quick idea of what a query is waiting on.

> ➤ For more information on reviewing waits in the Query Store, see Chapter 14.

CHAPTER 8

Understand wait resources

What if you observe a query wait occurring live, and want to figure out what data the query is actually waiting on?

SQL Server 2019 delivered some new tools to explore the archaeology involved in identifying the root of waits. While an exhaustive look at the different wait resource types—some more cryptic than others—is best documented in Microsoft's online resources, let's review the tools provided.

The undocumented DBCC PAGE command (and its accompanying Trace Flag 3604) were used for years to review the information contained in a page, based on a specific page number. Whether trying to see the data at the source of waits or trying to peek at corrupted pages reported by DBCC CHECKDB, the DBCC PAGE command didn't return any visible data without first enabling Trace Flag 3604. Now, for some cases, we have the pair of new functions, sys.dm_db_page_info and sys.fn_PageResCracker. Both can be used only when the sys.dm_exec_requests.wait_resource value begins with PAGE. So, the new tools leave out other common wait_resource types like KEY.

The DMVs in SQL Server 2019 and SQL Server 2022 are preferable to using DBCC PAGE because they are fully documented and supported. They can be combined with sys.dm_exec_requests —the hub DMV for all things active in SQL Server—to return potentially useful information about the object in contention when PAGE blocking is present:

```
SELECT r.request_id, pi.database_id, pi.file_id, pi.page_id, pi.object_id,
pi.page_type_desc, pi.index_id, pi.page_level, rows_in_page = pi.slot_count
FROM sys.dm_exec_requests AS r
CROSS APPLY sys.fn_PageResCracker (r.page_resource) AS prc
CROSS APPLY sys.dm_db_page_info(r.database_id, prc.file_id, prc.page_id, 'DETAILED') AS
pi;
```

Benign wait types

Many of the waits in SQL Server do not affect the performance of user workload. These waits are commonly referred to as *benign waits* and are frequently excluded from queries analyzing wait stats. The following code contains a starter list of wait types that you can mostly ignore when querying the sys.dm_os_wait_stats DMV for aggregate wait statistics. You can append the following sample list WHERE clause.

```
SELECT * FROM sys.dm_os_wait_stats
WHERE
    wt.wait_type NOT LIKE '%SLEEP%' --can be safely ignored, sleeping
AND wt.wait_type NOT LIKE 'BROKER%' -- internal process
AND wt.wait_type NOT LIKE '%XTP_WAIT%' -- for memory-optimized tables
AND wt.wait_type NOT LIKE '%SQLTRACE%' -- internal process
AND wt.wait_type NOT LIKE 'QDS%' -- asynchronous Query Store data
AND wt.wait_type NOT IN ( -- common benign wait types
'CHECKPOINT_QUEUE'
```

```
,'CLR_AUTO_EVENT','CLR_MANUAL_EVENT' ,'CLR_SEMAPHORE'
,'DBMIRROR_DBM_MUTEX','DBMIRROR_EVENTS_QUEUE','DBMIRRORING_CMD'
,'DIRTY_PAGE_POLL'
,'DISPATCHER_QUEUE_SEMAPHORE'
,'FT_IFTS_SCHEDULER_IDLE_WAIT','FT_IFTSHC_MUTEX'
,'HADR_FILESTREAM_IOMGR_IOCOMPLETION'
,'KSOURCE_WAKEUP'
,'LOGMGR_QUEUE'
,'ONDEMAND_TASK_QUEUE'
,'REQUEST_FOR_DEADLOCK_SEARCH'
,'XE_DISPATCHER_WAIT','XE_TIMER_EVENT'
--Ignorable HADR waits
, 'HADR_WORK_QUEUE'
,'HADR_TIMER_TASK'
,'HADR_CLUSAPI_CALL');
```

Through your own research into your workload, and in future versions of SQL Server, as more wait types are added, you can grow this list so that important and actionable wait types rise to the top of your queries. A prevalence of these wait types shouldn't be a concern; they're unlikely to be generated by or negatively affect user requests.

Wait types to be aware of

This section shouldn't be the start and end of your understanding of or research into wait types. Many of them have multiple avenues to explore in your SQL Server instance, or at the very least, names that are misleading to the DBA considering their origin. There are some, or groups of some, that you should understand, because they indicate a condition worth investigating. Many wait types are always present in all applications but become problematic when they appear in large frequency and/or with large cumulative waits. *Large* here is of course relative to your workload and your server.

Different instance workloads will have a different profile of wait types. Just because a wait type is at the top of the aggregate sys.dm_os_wait_stats list, it doesn't mean that is the main or only performance problem with a SQL Server instance. It is likely that all SQL Server instances, even finely tuned instances, will show these wait types near the top of the aggregate waits list. You should track and trend these wait stats, perhaps using the script example in the previous section.

Important waits include the following, provided in alphabetical order:

- **ASYNC_NETWORK_IO.** This wait type is associated with the retrieval of data to a client (including SQL Server Management Studio and Azure Data Studio), and the wait while the remote client receives and finally acknowledges the data received. This wait almost certainly has very little to do with network speed, network interfaces, switches, or firewalls. Any client, including your workstation or even SSMS running locally on the server, can incur small amounts of ASYNC_NETWORK_IO as data is retrieved to be processed. Transactional and snapshot replication distribution will incur ASYNC_NETWORK_IO. You will see a large amount of ASYNC_NETWORK_IO generated by reporting applications such as Tableau,

SSRS, SQL Server Profiler, and Microsoft Office products. The next time a rudimentary Access database application tries to load the entire contents of the Sales.OrderLines table, you'll likely see ASYNC_NETWORK_IO.

Reducing ASYNC_NETWORK_IO, like many of the waits we discuss in this chapter, has little to do with hardware purchases or upgrades; rather, it's more to do with poorly designed queries and applications. The solution, therefore, would be an application change. Try suggesting to developers or client applications incurring large amounts of ASYNC_NETWORK_IO that they eliminate redundant queries, use server-side filtering as opposed to client-side filtering, use server-side data paging as opposed to client-side data paging, or use client-side caching.

- **CXPACKET.** A common and often-overreacted-to wait type, CXPACKET is a parallelism wait. In a vacuum, execution plans that are created with parallelism run faster. But at scale, with many execution plans running in parallel, the server's resources might take longer to process the requests. This wait is measured in part as CXPACKET waits.

  When the CXPACKET wait is the predominant wait type experienced over time by your SQL Server, you should consider turning both the Maximum Degree of Parallelism (MAXDOP) and Cost Threshold for Parallelism (CTFP) dials when performance tuning. Make these changes in small, measured gestures, and don't overreact to performance problems with a small number of queries. Use the Query Store to benchmark and trend the performance of high-value and high-cost queries as you change configuration settings.

  If large queries are already a problem for performance and multiple large queries regularly run simultaneously, raising the CTFP might not solve the problem. In addition to the obvious solutions of query tuning and index changes, including the creation of column-store indexes, use MAXDOP as well to limit parallelization for very large queries.

  Until SQL Server 2016, MAXDOP was either a setting at the server level, a setting enforced at the query level, or a setting enforced to sessions selectively via Resource Governor (more on this toward the end of this chapter in the section "Protect important workloads with Resource Governor"). Since SQL Server 2016, the MAXDOP setting has been available as a database-scoped configuration. You can also use the MAXDOP query hint in any statement to override the database or server-level MAXDOP setting.

Inside OUT

What about the new CXCONSUMER wait type?

First introduced in SQL Server 2017 CU3 (and included in SQL Server 2016 with Service Pack 2), the CXCONSUMER wait type eats into the previous activity that would incur CXPACKET waits. So, since SQL Server 2017 CU3, and including SQL Server 2022, you'll see a mix of both wait types.

Before the introduction of CXCONSUMER, CXPACKET was incurred by both threads that consume and produce data as part of an execution plan. However, the producer threads were most problematic, most affected by the maximum degree of parallelism (MAXDOP) and cost threshold for parallelism, and most affected by out-of-date statistics. You have more control over the problematic producer threads. These are still reported by CXPACKET. The consumer threads are now reported by CXCONSUMER.

On the other hand, the consumer threads in parallelism aren't easily influenceable by query tuners, so reporting these as CXCONSUMER waits helps you focus on the more correctable waits reported by CXPACKET. In some cases, optimizing your parallelism settings may reduce the incurrence of this wait stat.

- **IO_COMPLETION.** This wait type is associated with synchronous read and write operations that are not related to row data pages, such as reading log blocks or virtual log file (VLF) information from the transaction log, or reading or writing merge join operator results, spools, and buffers to disk. It is difficult to associate this wait type with a single activity or event, but a spike in IO_COMPLETION could be an indication that these same events are now waiting on the I/O system to complete.

- **LCK_M_*.** Lock waits have to do with blocking and concurrency (or lack thereof). (Chapter 14 looks at isolation levels and concurrency.) When a request is writing and another request in READ COMMITTED or higher isolation is trying to lock that same row data, one of the 60+ different LCK_M_* wait types will be the reported wait type of the blocked request. For example, LCK_M_IS means that the thread wants to acquire an Intent Shared lock, but some other thread has it locked in an incompatible manner.

  In the aggregate, this doesn't mean you should reduce the isolation level of your transactions. Whereas READ UNCOMMITTED is not a good solution, read committed snapshot isolation (RCSI) and snapshot isolation are good solutions; see Chapter 14 for more details. Rather, you should optimize execution plans for efficient access, for example, by reducing scans as well as avoiding long-running multistep transactions. Also, avoid index rebuild operations without the ONLINE option. (See the "Rebuild indexes" section earlier in this chapter for more information.)

  The wait_resource provided in sys.dm_exec_requests, or resource_description in sys.dm_os_waiting_tasks, provide a map to the exact location of the lock contention inside the database.

➤ For a complete breakdown of the information that can be contained in the resource _description field in your version of SQL Server, visit *https://learn.microsoft.com/sql /relational-databases/system-dynamic-management-views/sys-dm-os-waiting-tasks -transact-sql.*

- **MEMORYCLERK_XE.** The MEMORYCLERK_XE wait type could spike if you have allowed Extended Events session targets to consume too much memory. We discuss Extended Events later in this chapter, but you should watch out for the maximum buffer size allowed to the ring_buffer session target, among other in-memory targets.

- **OLEDB.** This self-explanatory wait type describes waits associated with long-running external communication via the OLE DB provider, which is commonly used by SQL Server Integration Services (SSIS) packages, Microsoft Office applications (including querying Excel files), linked servers using the OLE DB provider, and third-party tools. It could also be generated by internal commands like DBCC CHECKDB. When you observe this wait occurring in SQL Server, in most cases, it's driven by long-running linked server queries.

Inside OUT

What design changes could avoid OLEDB wait types?

You reduce OLEDB wait types by reducing execution time for queries executing via the OLE DB provider, or by better integrating data flows by avoiding flat files, data manipulation via Access or Excel, or the use of linked servers. For connections to non–SQL Server database platforms, instead of flat file extract/imports to send data, consider PolyBase to connect directly and write T-SQL queries on Oracle data sources, for example.

- **PAGELATCH_* and PAGEIOLATCH_*.** These two wait types are presented together not because they are similar in nature—they are not—but because they are often confused. To be clear, PAGELATCH has to do with contention over pages in memory, whereas PAGEIOLATCH relates to contention over pages in the I/O system (on the drive).

  PAGELATCH_* contention deals with pages in memory, which can rise because of the overuse of temporary objects in memory, potentially with rapid access to the same temporary objects. This can also be experienced when reading in data from an index in memory or reading from a heap in memory.

  A rise in PAGEIOLATCH_* could be due to the performance of the storage system (keeping in mind that the performance of drive systems does not always respond linearly to increases in activity). Aside from throwing (a lot of!) money at faster drives, a more economical solution is to modify queries and/or indexes and reduce the footprint of memory-intensive operations, especially operations involving index and table scans.

  PAGEIOLATCH_* contention has to do with a far more limiting and troubling performance condition: the overuse of reading from the slowest subsystem of all, the physical drives. PAGEIOLATCH_SH deals with reading data from a drive into memory so that the data can be accessed. Keep in mind that this doesn't necessarily translate to a request's row count, especially if index or table scans are required in the execution plan. PAGEIOLATCH_EX and

PAGEIOLATCH_UP are waits associated with reading data from a drive into memory so that the data can be written to.

Inside OUT

How can SQL Server help alleviate high durations for the PAGELATCH_* category of wait types?

If long PAGELATCH_* waits are encountered in tempdb system tables, a feature of SQL Server 2019 and newer may improve performance: the new memory-optimized tempdb metadata server option. This moves system tables containing tempdb metadata into non-durable memory-optimized tables, eliminating latches on tables that become "hot spots" because of rapid inserts and updates. SQL Server 2022 adds new improvements to address this contention. For more on this topic, see the topic "Storage options for tempdb" in Chapter 3.

SQL Server 2019 also introduced an index option to specifically address one of the common causes of PAGELATCH_EX waits. These can be related to inserts that are happening rapidly and/or page splits related to inserts. The index option OPTIMIZE_FOR_SEQUENTIAL_KEY is specifically for tables with clustered keys on IDENTITY or SEQUENCE that have high write volumes, creating "hot spots" for sequential inserts. If you observe high amounts of PAGELATCH_EX, it may be because of contention for individual pages in memory due to sequential inserts. This index option in SQL Server 2019 improves performance for tables that have a sequential key.

- **RESOURCE_SEMAPHORE.** This wait type is accumulated when a request is waiting on memory to be allocated before it can start. Although this could be an indication of memory pressure caused by insufficient memory available to process the queries being executed, it is more likely caused by poor query design and poor indexing, resulting in inefficient execution plans. Aside from throwing money at more system memory, a more economical solution is to tune queries and reduce the footprint of memory-intensive operations. The memory grant feedback features that are part of Intelligent Query Processing help address these waits by improving memory grants for subsequent executions of a query.

- **SOS_SCHEDULER_YIELD.** Another flavor of CPU pressure, and in some ways the opposite of the CXPACKET wait type, is the SOS_SCHEDULER_YIELD wait type. The SOS_SCHEDULER_YIELD is an indicator of CPU pressure, indicating that SQL Server had to share time with, or yield to, other CPU tasks, which can be normal and expected on busy servers. Whereas CXPACKET is SQL Server complaining about too many threads in parallel, SOS_SCHEDULER_YIELD is the acknowledgement that there were more runnable tasks for the available threads. In either case, first take a strategy of reducing CPU-intensive queries and rescheduling or optimizing CPU-intense maintenance operations. This is more economical than simply adding CPU capacity.

- **WAIT_XTP_RECOVERY.** This wait type can occur when a database with memory-opti-mized tables is in recovery at startup and is expected. As with all wait types on perfor-mance-sensitive production SQL Server instances, you should baseline and measure it, but be aware this is not usually a sign of any problem.

- **WRITELOG.** The WRITELOG wait type is likely to appear on any SQL Server instance, includ-ing availability group primary and secondary replicas, when there is heavy write activity. The WRITELOG wait is time spent flushing the transaction log to a drive and is due to physical I/O subsystem performance. On systems with heavy writes, this wait type is expected.

  You could consider re-creating the heavy-write tables as memory-optimized tables to increase the performance of writes. Memory-optimized tables optionally allow for delayed durability, which would resolve a bottleneck writing to the transaction log by using a memory buffer. For more information, see Chapter 14.

- **XE_FILE_TARGET_TVF and XE_LIVE_TARGET_TVF.** These waits are associated with writing Extended Events sessions to their targets. A sudden spike in these waits would indicate that too much is being captured by an Extended Events session. Usually these aren't a problem, because the asynchronous nature of Extended Events has a much lower impact than traces.

Monitor with the SQL Assessment API

The SQL Assessment API is a code-delivered method for programmatically evaluating SQL Server instance and database configuration. First introduced with SQL Server Management Objects (SMO) and the SqlServer PowerShell module in 2019, calls to the API can be used to evaluate alignment with best practices, and then can be scheduled to monitor regularly for variance.

You can use this API to assess SQL Servers starting with SQL Server 2012, for SQL Server on Win-dows and Linux. The assessment is performed by comparing SQL Server configuration to rules, stored as JSON files. Microsoft has provided a standard array of rules.

> ➤ Review the default JSON configuration file at *https://learn.microsoft.com/sql/tools/sql -assessment-api/sql-assessment-api-overview*.

Use this standard JSON file as a template to assess your own best practices if you like. The assessment configuration files are organized into the following:

- **Probes.** These usually contain a T-SQL query—for example, to return data from DMOs (discussed earlier in this chapter). You can also write probes against your own user tables to query for code-driven states or statuses that can be provided by applications, ETL packages, or custom error-handling.

- **Checks.** These compare desired values with the actual values returned by probes. They include logical conditions and thresholds. Here, like with any SQL Server monitoring tool, you might want to change numeric thresholds to suit your SQL environment.

Inside OUT

What do you need to know about SMO?

SMO is a framework for developers to interface with SQL Server programmatically, bypassing T-SQL and PowerShell commands. While custom development of SMO applications is far beyond the scope of this book, the use of SMO to interact with the new SQL Assessment API is relatively easy and should not require assistance from developers.

SMO used to be installed via the SQL Server Feature Pack, in the SharedManagementObjects.msi file. Starting with SQL Server 2017, the NuGet package is how the binaries are distributed. More details follow.

Get started with the SQL Assessment API

To begin evaluating default or custom rules against your SQL Server, you must verify the presence of .NET Framework 4.0 and the latest versions of SMO and the Sql Server PowerShell module.

If you want to try this out on a server with an installation of SQL Server 2022 and the latest PowerShell Sql Server module, this sample PowerShell script should work:

```
$InstanceName='sql2022' #This should be the name of your instance
Get-SqlInstance -ServerInstance $InstanceName | Invoke-SqlAssessment | Out-GridView
```

For servers with installations of SQL Server, SMO should already be present on the Windows Server. For your local administration machine or a centralized server from which you'll monitor your SQL Server environment, you'll need to install SMO and the latest PowerShell Sql Server module.

While a developer might use Visual Studio's Package Manager, you do not need to install Visual Studio to install the SMO NuGet package. Instead, you can use the cross-platform nuget.exe command line utility. You can also install and use the command line interface tool dotnet.exe if desired.

➤ More information about the various options is available at *https://learn.microsoft.com /nuget/install-nuget-client-tools*.

After you download nuget.exe, follow these steps:

1. Open a PowerShell window with Administrator permissions and navigate to the folder where you saved nuget.exe. Note that when calling an executable from a PowerShell window, you need to preface the executable with ./ (dot slash), which is a security mechanism carried over from UNIX systems. The command to download and install SMO via nuget.exe should take just a few seconds to complete:

```
nuget install Microsoft.SqlServer.SqlManagementObjects
```

Optionally, specify an installation location for the installation:

```
nuget install Microsoft.SqlServer.SqlManagementObjects -OutputDirectory "c:\nuget\
packages"
```

SMO is maintained and distributed via a NuGet package at *https://nuget.org/packages/Microsoft.SqlServer.SqlManagementObjects*.

In the installation directory, you'll find several new folders. These version numbers are the latest at the time of writing and will likely be higher by the time you read this book.

- System.Data.SqlClient.4.6.0

- Microsoft.SqlServer.SqlManagementObjects.150.18147.0

2. With SMO in place, the second step to using the SQL Assessment API is to install the SqlServer PowerShell module. If you don't already have the latest version of this module installed, launch a PowerShell console as an administrator, launch Visual Studio Code as an administrator, or use your favorite PowerShell scripting environment. The following command will download and install the latest version, even if you have a previous version installed:

```
Install-Module -Name SqlServer -AllowClobber -Force
```

The AllowClobber parameter instructs Install-Module to overwrite cmdlet aliases already in place. Without AllowClobber, the installation will fail if it finds that the new module contains commands with the same name as existing commands.

➤ For more information on installing and using the SqlServer PowerShell module, including how to install without Internet connectivity, see Chapter 9.

3. With SMO and the SqlServer PowerShell module installed, you are ready to compare SQL Server health with the default rule set by a PowerShell command—for example, as we demonstrated at the start of this section:

```
Get-SqlInstance -ServerInstance . | Invoke-SqlAssessment | Out-GridView
```

Here, the period is shorthand for localhost, so this command executes an assessment against the API of the local default instance of SQL Server. To run the assessment against a remote SQL Server instance using Windows Authentication:

```
Get-SqlInstance -ServerInstance servername | Invoke-SqlAssessment | `
Out-GridView
```

Or, for a named instance:

```
Get-SqlInstance -ServerInstance servername\instancename | `
Invoke-SqlAssessment | Out-GridView
```

Out-GridView (which is part of the default Windows PowerShell cmdlets) pops open a new window to make it easier to review multiple findings than reading what could be many pages of results in a scrolling PowerShell console. You can output the data any way you like using common PowerShell cmdlets.

➤ For more sample syntax on assessing SQL Server instances via the `Invoke-SqlAssessment` cmdlet, visit *https://learn.microsoft.com/powershell/module/sqlserver/invoke-sqlassessment.*

The output of `Invoke-SqlAssessment` includes a helpful link to Microsoft documentation on every finding, the severity of each finding, the name of the check that resulted in a finding, an ID for the check for more granular review, and a helpful message. Again, all of this is provided by Microsoft's default ruleset, on which you can base your own custom checks and probes with custom severity and messages.

To use your own customized configuration file, you can use the `-Configuration` parameter:

```
Get-SqlInstance -ServerInstance servername | Invoke-SqlAssessment `
-Configuration "C:\toolbox\sqlassessment_api_config.json" | Out-GridView
```

Use Extended Events

The Extended Events feature is the best way to "look live" at SQL Server activity, replacing deprecated traces. Even though the default Extended Event sessions are not yet complete replacements for the default system trace (we give an example a bit later), consider Extended Events for all new activity related to troubleshooting and diagnostic data collection. The messaging around Extended Events is that it is the replacement for traces for a decade.

NOTE

The XEvent UI in SSMS is easier than ever to use, so if you haven't switched to using Extended Events to do what you used to use traces for, the time is now!

We'll assume you don't have a lot of experience creating your own Extended Events sessions. Let's become familiar with some of the most basic terminology for Extended Events:

- **Sessions.** A set of data collection instructions that can be started and stopped; the new equivalent of a "trace."

- **Events.** Items selected from an event library. Events are what you may remember "tracing" with SQL Server Profiler. These are predetermined, detectable operations during runtime. Events you'll most commonly want to look for include `sql_statement_completed` and `sql_batch_completed`—for example, for catching an application's T-SQL code.

  Examples: `sql_batch_starting`, `login`, `error_reported`, `sort_warning`, `table_scan`

- **Actions.** The headers of the columns of Extended Events data that describe an event, such as when the event happened, who and what called the event, its duration, the number of writes and reads, CPU time, and so on. In this way, actions are additional data captured when an event is recorded. In SSMS, Global Fields is the name for actions, which allow additional information to be captured for any event—for example, `database_name` or `database_id`.

Examples: `sql_text`, `batch_text`, `timestamp`, `session_id`, `client_hostname`

- **Predicates.** Filter conditions created on actions to limit the data captured. You can filter on any action or field returned by an event you have added to the session.

  Examples: `database_id > 4`, `database_name = 'WideWorldImporters'`, `is_system = 0`

- **Targets.** Where the data should be sent. You can watch detailed and "live" Extended Events data captured asynchronously in memory for any session. A session, however, can also have multiple targets, such as a `ring_buffer` (an in-memory buffer), an `event_file` (an .xel file on the server), or a histogram (an in-memory counter with grouping by actions). A session can have only one of each target.

  ➤ For more information about the different targets see the section "Understand the variety of Extended Events targets" later in this chapter.

SQL Server installs with three Extended Events sessions ready to view. Two of these, `system_health` and `telemetry_xevents`, start by default; the third, `AlwaysOn_Health`, starts when needed. These sessions provide a basic coverage for system health, though they are not an exact replacement for the system default trace. (The default trace captures query activity happening against the server for troubleshooting purposes.) Do not stop or delete these sessions, which should start automatically.

NOTE

If the `system_health`, `telemetry_xevents`, and/or `AlwaysOn_Health` sessions are accidentally dropped from the server, you can find the scripts to re-create them for your instance in this file: *instancepath*\MSSQL\Install\u_tables.sql. Here's an example: E:\Program Files\Microsoft SQL Server\MSSQL16.MSSQLSERVER\MSSQL\Install\u_tables.sql.

You'll see the well-documented definitions of the two Extended Event sessions toward the bottom of the file. If you just want to see the script that created the definitions for the built-in Extended Events sessions, you can script them via SSMS by right-clicking the session, selecting **Script Session As** in the shortcut menu, choosing **Create To**, and specifying a destination for the script.

NOTE

Used to using SQL Server Profiler? The XEvent Profiler delivers an improved "tracing" experience that mimics the legacy SQL Server Profiler trace templates. Extended Events sessions provide a modern, asynchronous, and far more versatile replacement for SQL Server traces, which are, in fact, deprecated. For troubleshooting, debugging, performance tuning, and event gathering, Extended Events provide a faster and more configurable solution than traces.

View Extended Events data

The XEvent Profiler in SSMS is the perfect place to view Extended Events data. Since SQL Server Management Studio 17.3, the XEvent Profiler tool has been built in. You'll find the XEvent Profiler in the SSMS Object Explorer window, in the SQL Server Agent menu. Figure 8-1 shows an example of the XE Profiler TSQL session.

Figure 8-1 The XE Profiler T-SQL live events display in SSMS, similar to the deprecated Profiler T-SQL trace template.

NOTE

Though not a full replacement for SSMS, Azure Data Studio also has capabilities for managing Extended Event sessions, via the SQL Server Profiler extension that can be quickly downloaded and added. Search for the "SQL Server Profiler" extension or add the "Admin Pack for SQL Server" extension via the Extensions Marketplace in Azure Data Studio.

An Extended Events session can generate simultaneous output to multiple destinations, only one of which closely resembles the .trc files of old.

You can create other targets for a session on the **Data Storage** page of the **New Session** dialog box in SSMS. To view data collected by the target, expand the session, right-click the package, and select **View Target Data** in the shortcut menu. (See Figure 8-2.)

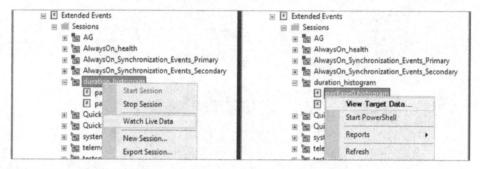

Figure 8-2 A side-by-side look at the difference between Watch Live Data on an Extended Events session and View Target Data on an Extended Events session target.

When viewing target data, you can right-click to re-sort, copy the data to the clipboard, and export most of the target data to .csv files for analysis in other software.

Unlike Watch Live Data, View Target Data does not refresh automatically. However, for some targets, you can configure SSMS to poll the target automatically by right-clicking the **View Target Data** window, selecting **Refresh Interval** in the shortcut menu, and choosing a refresh interval (between 5 seconds and 1 hour).

NOTE

Currently, there is no built-in way in SSMS to write Extended Events session data directly to a SQL Server table. However, the Watch Live Data interface provides easy point-and-click analysis, grouping, and filtering of live session data. We review the target types next. Take some time to explore the other available target types; they can easily and quickly reproduce your analysis of trace data written to SQL Server tables.

The section that follows presents a breakdown of the possible targets. Many of these do some of the heavy lifting that you might have done previously by writing or exporting SQL trace data to a table and then performing your own aggregations, counts, or data analysis. Remember: You don't need to pick just one target type to collect data for your session.

Understand the variety of Extended Events targets

As mentioned, you can always watch detailed and "live" Extended Events data captured asynchronously in memory for any session through SSMS. You do this by right-clicking a session and selecting **Watch Live Data** from the shortcut menu. You'll see asynchronously delivered detailed data, and you can customize the columns you see, apply filters on the data, and even create groups and on-the-fly aggregations, all by right-clicking inside the Live Data window.

The Live Data window, however, isn't a target. The data isn't saved anywhere outside the SSMS window, and you can't look back at data you missed before launching Watch Live Data. You can create a session without a target, and Watch Live Data is all you'll get, but often that is all you need for a quick observation.

Here is a summary of the Extended Event targets available to be created. Remember, you can create more than one target per session.

- **Event File target (.xel).** Writes the event data to a physical file on a drive asynchronously. You can then open and analyze it later, much like deprecated trace files, or merge it with other .xel files to assist analysis. (In SSMS, select the **File** menu, select **Open**, and then select **Merge Extended Events Files**.)

    If you are using Azure SQL Database or Managed Instance and you would like to persist Extended Event data, you can only use the Event File target to Azure Blob Storage. You also need to create a credential using a shared access signature (SAS).

    ➤ The instructions for connecting your Azure SQL Database and Blob Storage for Extended Events can be found at *https://learn.microsoft.com/azure/azure-sql/database/xevent-code-event-file*.

    When you view the event file data in SSMS (right-click the event file and select **View Target Data**), the data does not refresh live. Data continues to be written to the file behind the scenes while the session is running. So, to view the latest data, you must close the .xel file and open it again.

    By default, .xel files are written to the *instancepath*\MSSQL\Log folder.

- **Histogram target.** Counts the number of times an event has occurred and bucketizes an action, storing the data in memory. For example, you can capture a histogram of `sql_statement_completed` broken down by the number of observed events by client-hostname action, or by the duration field.

    When configuring the histogram type target, you must choose a number of buckets (or slots, in the T-SQL syntax) that is greater than the number of unique values you expect for the action or field. If you're bucketizing by a numeric value such as duration, be sure to provide a number of buckets larger than the largest duration you could capture over time. If the histogram runs out of buckets for new values for your action or field, it will not capture data for them.

You can provide any number of histogram buckets, but the histogram target will round the number up to the nearest power of 2. Thus, if you provide a value of 10 buckets, you'll see 16 buckets.

- **Pair matching or Pairing target.** Used to match events, such as the start and end of a SQL Server batch execution, and find occasions when an event in a pair occurs without the other, such as `sql_statement_starting` and `sql_statement_completed`. Select a start and an end from the list of actions you've selected.

- **Ring_buffer target.** Provides a fast, in-memory first in, first out (FIFO) asynchronous memory buffer to collect rapidly occurring events. Stored in a memory buffer, the data is never written to a drive, allowing for robust data collection without performance overhead. The customizable dataset is provided in XML format and must be queried. Because this data is in-memory, you should be careful how high you configure the Maximum Buffer Memory size, and never set the size to 0 (unlimited).

- **Service Broker target.** Used to send messages to a target service of a customizable message type.

Although the aforementioned targets are high-performing asynchronous targets, there are two synchronous targets:

- **Event Tracing for Windows (ETW) target.** Used to gather SQL Server data, to be combined with Windows event log data, for troubleshooting and debugging Windows applications.

- **Event counter target.** Counts the number of events in an Extended Events session. You use this to provide data for trending and later aggregate analysis. The resulting dataset has one row per event with a count. This data is stored in memory, so although it's synchronous, you shouldn't expect any noticeable performance impact.

NOTE

Be aware when using synchronous targets that the resource demand of synchronous targets might be more noticeable.

Further, there are two session options that can affect the performance impact of an Extended Event session. The defaults are reasonably safe and are unlikely to result in noticeable performance overhead, so they don't typically need to be changed. You might, however, want to change them if the event you're trying to observe is rare, temporary, and outweighs your performance overhead concerns.

- **EVENT_RETENTION_MODE.** Determines whether, under pressure, the Extended Event session can miss a captured event. The default, ALLOW_SINGLE_EVENT_LOSS, here can let target(s) miss a single event when memory buffers used to stream the data to the target(s) are full.

  You instead specify ALLOW_MULTIPLE_EVENT_LOSS, which further minimizes the potential for performance impact on the monitored server by allowing more events to be missed.

  Or you could specify NO_EVENT_LOSS, which does not allow events to be missed, even if memory buffers are full. All events are retained and presented to the target. While not the same as using a synchronous target, it can result in the same effect: Performance of the SQL Server could suffer under the weight of the Extended Event session. Using this option is not recommended.

- **MAX_DISPATCH_LATENCY.** Determines the upper limit for when events are sent from the memory buffer to the target. By default, events are buffered in memory for up to 30 seconds before being sent to the targets. You could change this value to 1 to force data out of memory buffers faster, reducing the benefit of the memory buffers. A value of INFINITE or 0 allows for the retention of events until memory buffers are full or until the session closes.

Let's look at querying Extended Events session data in T-SQL with a couple of practical common examples.

Use Extended Events to capture deadlocks

We've talked about viewing data in SSMS, so let's review querying Extended Events data via T-SQL. Let's query one of the default Extended Events sessions, system_health, for deadlocks.

Back before SQL Server 2008, it was not possible to see a deadlock. You had to see it coming—to enable one or more trace flags before the deadlock, which allowed deadlocks to be captured to the SQL Server Error Log. With the system_health Extended Events session, a recent history of event data is captured, included deadlock graphs. This data is captured to both a ring_buffer target with a rolling 4-MB buffer, and to an .xel file with a total of 20 MB in rollover files. Either target will contain the most recent occurrences of the xml_deadlock_report event, and although the ring_buffer is faster to read from, the .xel file by default contains more history. Further, the .xel file isn't subject to the limitations of the 4-MB ring_buffer target or the potential for missed rows.

The T-SQL code sample that follows demonstrates the retrieval of the .xel file target as XML:

```
DECLARE @XELFile nvarchar(256), @XELFiles nvarchar(256)
        , @XELPath nvarchar(256);
--Get the folder path where the system_health .xel files are
SELECT    @XELFile =      CAST(t.target_data as XML)
        .value('EventFileTarget[1]/File[1]/@name', 'NVARCHAR(256)')
FROM sys.dm_xe_session_targets t
```

```
        INNER JOIN sys.dm_xe_sessions s
          ON s.address = t.event_session_address
WHERE s.name = 'system_health' AND t.target_name = 'event_file';
--Provide wildcard path search for all currently retained .xel files
SELECT @XELPath =
      LEFT(@XELFile, Len(@XELFile)-CHARINDEX('\',REVERSE(@XELFile)))
SELECT @XELFiles = @XELPath + '\system_health_*.xel';
--Query the .xel files for deadlock reports
SELECT DeadlockGraph = CAST(event_data AS XML)
      , DeadlockID = Row_Number() OVER(ORDER BY file_name, file_offset)
FROM sys.fn_xe_file_target_read_file(@XELFiles, null, null, null) AS F
WHERE event_data like '<event name="xml_deadlock_report%';
```

Inside OUT

How can you test your deadlock capture strategy?

Here's a quick, two-connection script to produce a deadlock. To use it, first open two query connections in SSMS to a testing database. You should then be able to use the default system_health Extended Events session to view the details of the deadlock. If your server has not recorded any deadlocks, this query will not have results.

Run this script in connection 1:

```
CREATE TABLE dbo.dead (col1 INT);
INSERT INTO dbo.dead SELECT 1;
CREATE TABLE dbo.lock (col1 INT);
INSERT INTO dbo.lock SELECT 1;
BEGIN TRAN t1;
UPDATE dbo.dead WITH (TABLOCK) SET col1 = 2;
```

Run this script in connection 2:

```
BEGIN TRAN t2;
UPDATE dbo.lock WITH (TABLOCK) SET col1 = 3;
UPDATE dbo.dead WITH (TABLOCK) SET col1 = 3;
COMMIT TRAN t2;
```

Now, back in connection 1:

```
UPDATE dbo.lock WITH (TABLOCK) SET col1 = 4;
COMMIT TRAN t1;
```

Within a moment, one of your sessions is closed as the victim of a deadlock.

This example returns one row per captured xml_deadlock_report event and includes an XML document, which in SSMS Grid results will appear as a blue hyperlink. Select the hyperlink to open the XML document, which will contain complete details of all elements of the deadlock. If you want to see a deadlock graph, save this file as an .xdl file, and then open it in SSMS.

Use Extended Events to detect autogrowth events

The SQL Server default trace captures historical database data and log file autogrowth events, but the default Extended Events sessions shipped with SQL Server do not. The Extended Events that capture autogrowth events are database_file_size_change and databases_log_file _size_changed. Both events capture autogrowths and manual file growths run by ALTER DATABASE ... MODIFY FILE statements, and include an event field called is_automatic to differentiate them. Additionally, you can identify the query statement sql_text that prompted the autogrowth event.

The following is a sample T-SQL script to create a startup session that captures autogrowth events to an .xel event file (which is written to F:\Data—you should change this to an appropriate directory on your system) and also a histogram target that counts the number of autogrowth instances per database:

```
CREATE EVENT SESSION [autogrowths] ON SERVER
ADD EVENT sqlserver.database_file_size_change(
 ACTION(package0.collect_system_time,sqlserver.database_id
,sqlserver.database_name,sqlserver.sql_text)),
ADD EVENT sqlserver.databases_log_file_size_changed(
 ACTION(package0.collect_system_time,sqlserver.database_id
,sqlserver.database_name,sqlserver.sql_text))
ADD TARGET package0.event_file(
--.xel file target
SET filename=N'F:\DATA\autogrowths.xel'),
ADD TARGET package0.histogram(
--Histogram target, counting events per database_name
SET filtering_event_name=N'sqlserver.database_file_size_change'
,source=N'database_name',source_type=(0))
--Start session at server startup
WITH (STARTUP_STATE=ON);
GO
--Start the session now
ALTER EVENT SESSION [autogrowths]
ON SERVER STATE = START;
```

➤ Refer to the section "Understand and find autogrowth events" earlier in this chapter for more information, including how to prevent autogrowth events.

Use Extended Events to detect page splits

As discussed, detecting page splits can be useful. You might choose to monitor page splits when load testing a table design with its intended workload, or when finding insert statements that cause the most fragmentation.

The following sample T-SQL script creates a startup session that captures autogrowth events to an .xel event file, and also a histogram target that counts the number of page splits per database:

```
CREATE EVENT SESSION [page_splits] ON SERVER
ADD EVENT sqlserver.page_split(
 ACTION(sqlserver.database_name,sqlserver.sql_text))
ADD TARGET package0.event_file(
SET filename=N'page_splits', max_file_size=(100)),
ADD TARGET package0.histogram(
SET filtering_event_name=N'sqlserver.page_split'
,source=N'database_id',source_type=(0))
--Start session at server startup
WITH (STARTUP_STATE=ON);
GO
--Start the session now
 ALTER EVENT SESSION [page_splits] ON SERVER STATE = START;
```

➤ Refer to the section "Track page splits" earlier in this chapter for more information, including how to prevent page splits.

Secure Extended Events

You can also think of Extended Events as a diagnostic tool for developers. Given knowledge of your own data classification and regulatory requirements, you should consider granting the necessary permissions to developers, even if temporarily.

There are certain sensitive events that you cannot capture with a trace or Extended Event session. For example, the T-SQL statement CREATE LOGIN for a SQL-authenticated login will not capture the value of the password.

To access Extended Events in SQL Server, a developer needs the ALTER ANY EVENT SESSION permission. This grants that person access to create Extended Events sessions by using T-SQL commands, but not to view server metadata in the New Extended Events Session Wizard in SSMS. For that, you need one further commonly granted developer permission: VIEW SERVER STATE.

In Azure SQL Database, Extended Events have the same capability, but for developers to view Extended Events sessions, you must grant them an ownership-level permission, CONTROL DATABASE. However, we do not recommend this for developers or non-administrators in production environments.

➤ For more about object permissions, see Chapter 12, "Administer instance and database security and permissions."

Capture performance metrics with DMOs and data collectors

For years, server administrators have used the Windows Performance Monitor (perfmon.exe) application to visually track and collect performance information about server resources, application memory usage, disk response times, and so on. In addition to the live Performance Monitor graph, you can also configure Data Collector Sets in Performance Monitor to gather the same metrics over time.

SQL Server has many metrics made visible through DMVs as well. This book has neither the scope nor the space to investigate and explain every available performance metric, or even every useful one. Instead, this section reviews the tools and covers a sampling of important performance metrics.

These metrics exist at the OS or instance level, so this chapter does not review granular data for individual databases, workloads, or queries. However, identifying performance with isolated workloads in near-production systems is possible. Like aggregate wait statistics, there is significant value in trending these Performance Monitor metrics on server workloads, monitoring peak behavior metrics, and for immediate troubleshooting and problem diagnosis.

Query performance metrics with DMVs

Beyond the Windows Performance Monitor and Linux metrics, this chapter has already mentioned a DMV that exposes most of the performance metrics within SQL Server: sys.dm_os _performance_counters. It behaves the same in Windows and Linux, thanks to the magic of the SQL Platform Abstraction Layer (SQLPAL), which helps SQL Server look and act much the same way on both Windows and Linux.

There are some advantages to this DMV in that you can combine it with other DMVs that report on system resource activity (check out sys.dm_os_sys_info, for example), and you can fine-tune the query for ease of monitoring and custom data collecting. However, sys.dm_os_ performance_counters does not currently have access to metrics outside the SQL Server instance categories—even the most basic operating system metrics, like % Processor Time.

The following code sample uses sys.dm_os_performance_counters to return the operating system's total memory, the instance's current target server memory, total server memory, and page life expectancy:

```
SELECT Time_Observed = SYSDATETIMEOFFSET()
, OS_Memory_GB = MAX(convert(decimal(19,3), os.physical_memory_kb/1024./1024.))
, OS_Available_Memory_GB = max(convert(decimal(19,3),
sm.available_physical_memory_kb/1024./1024.))
, SQL_Target_Server_Mem_GB = max(CASE counter_name
WHEN 'Target Server Memory (KB)' THEN convert(decimal(19,3), cntr_value/1024./1024.)
END)
, SQL_Total_Server_Mem_GB = max(CASE counter_name
WHEN 'Total Server Memory (KB)' THEN convert(decimal(19,3), cntr_value/1024./1024.)
```

```
END)
, PLE_s = MAX(CASE counter_name WHEN 'Page life expectancy' THEN cntr_value END)
FROM sys.dm_os_performance_counters as pc
CROSS JOIN sys.dm_os_sys_info as os
CROSS JOIN sys.dm_os_sys_memory as sm;
```

NOTE

In servers with multiple SQL Server instances, sys.dm_os_performance_counters displays only metrics for the instance on which it is run. You cannot access performance metrics for other instances on the same server via this DMV.

Some queries against sys.dm_os_performance_counters are not as straightforward. For example, although Performance Monitor returns the Buffer Cache Hit Ratio as a single value, querying this same memory metric via the DMV requires creating the ratio from two metrics. This code sample divides two metrics to provide the Buffer Cache Hit Ratio:

```
SELECT Time_Observed = SYSDATETIMEOFFSET(),
Buffer_Cache_Hit_Ratio = convertDECIMAL (9,1)t, 100 *
(SELECT cntr_value = convert(decimal (9,1), cntr_value)
FROM sys.dm_os_performance_counters as pc
WHERE pc.COUNTER_NAME = 'Buffer cache hit ratio'
AND pc.OBJECT_NAME like '%:Buffer Manager%')
/
(SELECT cntr_value = convert(decimal (9,1), cntr_value)
FROM sys.dm_os_performance_counters as pc
WHERE pc.COUNTER_NAME = 'Buffer cache hit ratio base'
AND pc.OBJECT_NAME like '%:Buffer Manager%'));
```

Finally, some counters returned by sys.dm_os_performance_counters are continually incrementing integers. Let's return to our earlier example of finding page splits, where we demonstrated how to find the accumulating value. The counter name Page Splits/sec is misleading when accessed via the DMV, because it is an incrementing number. To calculate the rate of page splits per second, you need two samples to calculate the difference between the first and second values. This strategy is appropriate only for single-value counters for the entire server or instance. For counters that return one value per database, you would need to use a temporary table to calculate the rate for each database between the two samples. You could also capture these values to a table at regular intervals to enable reporting over time.

```
DECLARE @page_splits_Start_ms bigint, @page_splits_Start bigint
, @page_splits_End_ms bigint, @page_splits_End bigint;
SELECT @page_splits_Start_ms = ms_ticks
, @page_splits_Start = cntr_value
FROM sys.dm_os_sys_info CROSS APPLY
sys.dm_os_performance_counters
WHERE counter_name ='Page Splits/sec'
AND object_name LIKE '%SQL%Access Methods%'; --Find the object that contains page splits
```

```
WAITFOR DELAY '00:00:05'; --Duration between samples 5s

SELECT @page_splits_End_ms = MAX(ms_ticks),
@page_splits_End = MAX(cntr_value)
FROM sys.dm_os_sys_info CROSS APPLY
sys.dm_os_performance_counters
WHERE counter_name ='Page Splits/sec'
AND object_name LIKE '%SQL%Access Methods%'; --Find the object that contains page splits
SELECT Time_Observed = SYSDATETIMEOFFSET(),
Page_Splits_per_s = convert(decimal(19,3),
(@page_splits_End - @page_splits_Start)*1.
/ NULLIF(@page_splits_End_ms - @page_splits_Start_ms,0));
```

You can gain access to some OS metrics via the DMV sys.dm_os_ring_buffers, including metrics on CPU utilization and memory. This DMV returns thousands of XML documents, generated
every second, loaded with information on SQL exceptions, memory, schedulers, connectivity, and
more. It is worth noting that the sys.dm_os_ring_buffers DMV is one of several OS-level views
that are documented but not supported.

> **For more information, visit** *https://learn.microsoft.com/sql/relational-databases/system
-dynamic-management-views/sql-server-operating-system-related-dynamic-management
-views-transact-sql.*

In the code sample that follows, we pull the SQL Server instance's CPU utilization and the server
idle CPU percentage for the past few hours. The remaining CPU percentage can be chalked up
to other applications or services running on the server, including other SQL Server instances.

```
DECLARE @ts_now bigint = (SELECT cpu_ticks/(cpu_ticks/ms_ticks) FROM sys.dm_os_sys_info
WITH (NOLOCK));

SELECT TOP(256) SQLProcessUtilization AS [SQL Server Process CPU Utilization],
SystemIdle AS [System Idle Process],
100 - SystemIdle - SQLProcessUtilization AS [Other Process CPU Utilization],
DATEADD(ms, -1 * (@ts_now - [timestamp]), GETDATE()) AS [Event Time]
FROM (SELECT record.value('(./Record/@id)[1]', 'int') AS record_id,
record.value('(./Record/SchedulerMonitorEvent/SystemHealth/SystemIdle)[1]', 'int')
AS [SystemIdle],
record.value('(./Record/SchedulerMonitorEvent/SystemHealth/ProcessUtilization)[1]',
'int')
AS [SQLProcessUtilization], [timestamp]
FROM (SELECT [timestamp], CONVERT(xml, record) AS [record]
FROM sys.dm_os_ring_buffers WITH (NOLOCK)
WHERE ring_buffer_type = N'RING_BUFFER_SCHEDULER_MONITOR'
AND record LIKE N'%<SystemHealth>%') AS x) AS y
ORDER BY record_id DESC;
```

Now you should have a grasp on using most of the DMVs for gathering performance metrics to
capture various types of data streams coming out of SQL Server.

Inside OUT

Does the ring buffer incur overhead with all this data it is capturing to memory?

There is some background overhead for ring-buffer data collection, but compared to other data collection methods, it is far more efficient. SQL Server instances always have this diagnostic activity present, constantly and by design, so the ring buffer won't be at fault for sudden or even gradual performance degradation.

Only appropriate on resource-limited servers and/or instances with extremely high frequency transaction activity, it's possible to disable the ring buffer by using trace flags. This can result in a small performance gain, but you should test and measure it against the loss of diagnostic data on which your own administrative queries or third-party products rely.

➤ For more information on using trace flags to disable ring-buffer data collection, visit *https://support.microsoft.com/help/920093*.

Capture performance metrics with Performance Monitor

To get a complete, graphical picture of server resource utilization, it's necessary to use a server resource tool. Performance Monitor is more than just a pretty graph; it is a suite of data collection tools that can persist outside your user profile.

To open Performance Monitor, type **performance** in the Windows **Start** menu and select the **Performance Monitor** icon, or press the **Windows+R** key combination and type **perfmon**. You can configure the live Performance Monitor graph, available in the Monitoring Tools folder, to show a live picture of server performance. To do so, right-click the (mostly empty) chart to access properties, add counters, clear the graph, and so on.

Choosing **Properties** in that same shortcut menu opens the **Performance Monitor Properties** dialog box. Under **General**, you can configure the sample rate and duration of the graph. You can also display up to 1,000 sample points on the graph live. This can be 1,000 1-second sample points for a total of 16 minutes and 40 seconds, or more time if you continue to decrease the sample frequency. For example, you can display 5,000 5-second sample points, for more than 83 minutes of duration in the graph.

A Data Collector Set allows you to collect data from one or more Performance Monitor counters, and to run that collection non-interactively. This data is stored in log files and is how administrators most commonly use Performance Monitor. You can access the collected Performance Monitor data by navigating to the Reports folder; the User Defined folder contains a new report with the graph created by the Data Collector. Figure 8-3 shows that more than 15 days of data performance was collected in the Data Collector, which we're viewing in the Memory folder, selecting the most recent report that was generated when we stopped the Memory Data Collector Set.

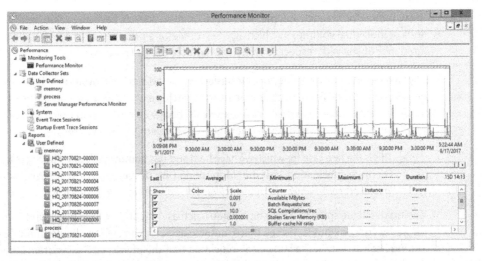

Figure 8-3 The Windows Performance Monitor application.

Monitor key performance metrics

This section contains some Performance Monitor metrics to look at when assessing the health and performance of your SQL Server. Although we don't have the space in this book to provide a deep dive into each metric, its causes, and its indicators, you should take time to investigate and research metrics on your server that appear outside with the guidelines provided here.

We don't provide many hard numbers in this section—things like "Metric X should always be lower than Y." You should track trends, measure metrics at peak activity, and investigate how metrics respond to server, query, and configuration changes. What might be normal for an instance with a read-heavy workload might be problematic for an instance with a high-volume write workload, and vice versa.

The following subsections review common performance monitoring metrics, including where to find them in Windows Performance Monitor and in SQL Server DMOs if available. When one of these sections contains a DMV entry, it means the corresponding metric is available in Windows and Linux. When not available via DMVs, you can find these same OS-level metrics in Linux using tools detailed in the next section, "Monitor key performance metrics in Linux."

Average Disk seconds per Read or Write

Performance Monitor: PhysicalDisk:Avg. Disk sec/Read and PhysicalDisk:Avg. Disk sec/Write

DMO: `sys.dm_io_virtual_file_stats` offers similar metrics for each data and log file. Typically, this data is used in conjunction with the Performance Monitor data to confirm or deny behavior.

View this metric on each volume. The _Total metric doesn't have any value here; you should look at individual volumes in which SQL Server files are present. This metric has the clearest guidance of any with respect to what is acceptable or not for a server.

Try to measure this value during your busiest workload, and also during backups. You want to see the average disk seconds per read and write operation (considering that a single query could have thousands or millions of operations) below 20 milliseconds, or .02 seconds. Below 10 milliseconds is optimal and very achievable with modern storage systems.

> ➤ This is the rare case for which we have hard and fast numbers specified by Microsoft to rely on. For more information, visit the "Monitoring Disk Usage" blog post at *https://social.technet .microsoft.com/wiki/contents/articles/3214.monitoring-disk-usage.aspx*.

Seeing this value spike to a very high value (such as .1 second or 100 milliseconds) isn't a major cause for concern, but if you see these metrics sustaining an average higher than .02 seconds during peak activity, it is a fairly clear indication that the physical I/O subsystem is being stressed beyond its capacity. Low, healthy measurements for this number don't provide any insight into the quality or efficiency of queries and execution plans, only the response from the disk subsystem. The Avg. Disk sec/Transfer counter is simply a combination of both read and write activity, unrelated to Avg. Disk Transfers/sec.

Page Life Expectancy (PLE)

Performance Monitor: MSSQL$InstanceName:Buffer Manager/Page Life Expectancy (s)

DMV: sys.dm_os_performance_counters
WHERE object_name like '%Buffer Manager%'
AND counter_name = 'Page life expectancy'

Page Life Expectancy (PLE) is a measure of time (in seconds) that indicates the age of data in memory. PLE is one of the most direct indicators of memory pressure, though it doesn't provide a complete picture of memory utilization in SQL Server. In general, you want pages of data in memory to grow to a ripe old age; when they do, it means there is ample memory available to SQL Server to store data to serve reads without going back to the storage layer.

A dated, oft-quoted metric of 300 seconds isn't applicable to many SQL Server instances. While 300 seconds might be appropriate for a server with 4 GB of memory, it's far too low for a server with 64 GB of memory. Instead, you should monitor this value over time. Does PLE bottom out and stay there during certain operations or scheduled tasks? If so, your SQL Server performance might benefit from more memory during those operations. Does PLE grow steadily throughout production hours? If so, the data in memory is likely to be sufficient for the observed workload.

Page Reads

Performance Monitor: MSSQL$InstanceName:Buffer Manager/Page reads/sec

DMV: sys.dm_os_performance_counters
WHERE object_name like '%Buffer Manager%'
AND counter_name = 'Page reads/sec'

This is an average of the number of page read operations completed recently. The title is a bit misleading—these aren't page reads out of the buffer; rather, they are out of physical pages on the drive, which is slower than data pages coming out of memory.

You should make the effort to lower this number by optimizing queries and indexing, improving efficiency of cache storage, and, of course, as a last resort, increasing the amount of server memory. Although every workload is different, a value less than 90 is a broad, overly simple guideline. High numbers indicate inefficient query and index design in read-write workloads or memory constraints in read-heavy workloads.

Memory Pages

Performance Monitor: Memory:Pages/sec

DMV: Not available.

Similar to `Buffer Manager\Page Reads/sec`, this is a way to measure data coming from a drive as opposed to coming out of memory. This metric is a recent average of the number of pages pulled from a drive into memory, which will be high after SQL Server startup. Although every workload is different, a value of less than 50 is a broad guideline. Sustained high or climbing levels during typical production usage indicate inefficient query and index design in read-write workloads, or memory constraints in read-heavy workloads. Spikes during database backup and restore operations, bulk copies, and data extracts are expected.

Batch Requests

Performance Monitor: MSSQL$InstanceName:SQL Statistics\Batch Requests/sec

DMV: `sys.dm_os_performance_counters WHERE object_name like '%SQL Statistics%' AND counter_name = 'Batch Requests/sec'`

This is a measure of aggregate SQL Server user activity, indicating the recent average of the number of batch requests. Any command issued to the SQL Server contains at least one batch request. Higher sustained numbers are good; they mean your SQL Server instance is sustaining more traffic. Should this number trend downward during peak business hours, it means your SQL Server instance is being outstripped by increasing user activity.

Page Faults

Performance Monitor: Memory\Page Faults/sec

DMV: Not available.

A memory page fault occurs when an application seeks a data page in memory, only to find it isn't there because of memory churn. A soft page fault indicates the page was moved or otherwise unavailable; a hard page fault indicates the data page was not in memory and must be retrieved from the drive. The Page Faults/sec metric captures both.

Page faults are a symptom, the cause being memory churn, so you might see an accompanying drop in Page Life Expectancy (PLE). Spikes in page faults, or an upward trend, indicate the amount of server memory was insufficient to serve requests from all applications, not just SQL Server.

Available Memory

Performance Monitor: Memory\Available Bytes or Memory\Available KBytes or Memory\Available MBytes

DMV: `SELECT available_physical_memory_kb FROM sys.dm_os_sys_memory`

Available memory is operating system memory currently unallocated to any application. Server memory above and beyond the SQL Server instance(s) total `MAX_SERVER_MEMORY` setting, minus memory in use by other SQL Server features and services or other applications, is available. This will roughly match what shows as available memory in the Windows Task Manager.

Total Server Memory

Performance Monitor: MSSQL$InstanceName:Memory Manager\Total Server Memory (KB)

DMV: `sys.dm_os_performance_counters`
`WHERE object_name like '%Memory Manager%'`
`AND counter_name = 'Total Server Memory (KB)'`

This is the actual amount of memory that SQL Server is using. It is often contrasted with the next metric (Target Server Memory). This number might be far larger than what Windows Task Manager shows allocated to the SQL Server Windows NT 64 Bit background application, which shows only a portion of the memory that sqlserver.exe controls. The Total Server Memory metric is correct.

Target Server Memory

Performance Monitor: MSSQL$InstanceName:Memory Manager\Target Server Memory (KB)

DMV: `sys.dm_os_performance_counters`
`WHERE object_name like '%Memory Manager%'`
`AND counter_name = 'Target Server Memory (KB)'`

This is the amount of memory to which SQL Server *wants* to have access and is currently working toward consuming. If the difference between Target Server Memory and Total Server Memory is larger than the value for Available Memory, SQL Server wants more memory than the Windows Server can currently acquire. SQL Server will eventually consume all memory available to it under the Max Server Memory setting, but it might take time.

Monitor key performance metrics in Linux

While monitoring SQL Server on Linux is identical to SQL Server on Windows in most ways, there are some exceptions, especially when the monitoring source is coming from outside the SQLPAL.

As stated, you'll find that the DMOs perform the same for SQL Server instances on Windows and in Linux. It's in the OS layer that the differences in metrics available, and especially the tools used to collect them, are stark. This section reviews a sampling of tools you can use for Linux-specific OS monitoring, keeping in mind that there is a wealth of monitoring solutions on various Linux distributions.

> ➤ For more about SQL Server on Linux, see Chapter 5, "Install and configure SQL Server on Linux."

View performance counters in Linux

The dynamic management view sys.dm_os_performance_counters behaves the same and delivers identical output on Windows and Linux. For example, the Performance Monitor metrics in the previous section listed as available in the DMV are also available in SQL Server on Linux.

The top command, built into Linux and with near-identical output on all distributions, launches a live full-console display of CPU and memory utilization and process metrics, not dissimilar from Windows Task Manager. The screen is data rich and starkly black and white, however, so consider the more graphical command htop. Though not present by default on all Linux distributions, it can be quickly downloaded and easily installed. This command's output (see Figure 8-4) shows much of the same useful data with a more pleasant format and with color highlights.

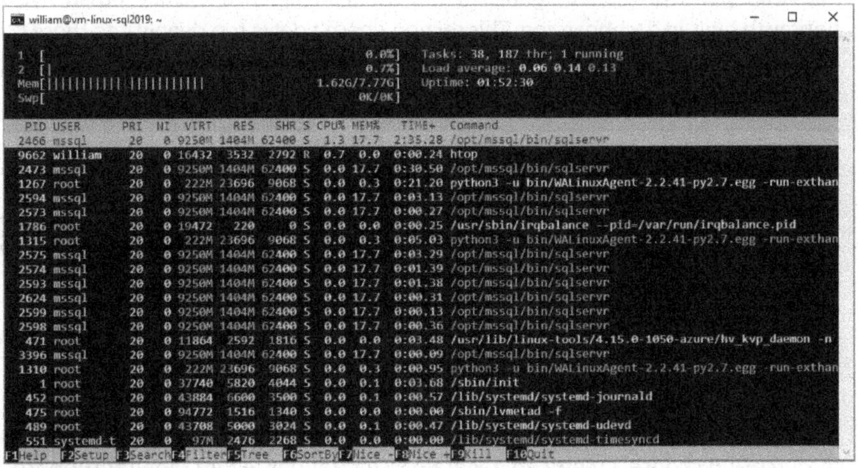

Figure 8-4 The htop command's live, updating look at the Linux server's CPU, memory, and process utilization.

Another built-in Linux tool is vmstat, which includes extended information on process memory, like runnable/sleeping processes, memory availability, swap memory use, memory I/O activity, system interrupts, and CPU utilization percentages. While vmstat returns a snapshot of the data, the syntax vmstat n appends fresh data to the console once every *n* seconds.

For querying items in SQL Server on Linux not available in sys.dm_os_performance_counters, such as Avg Disk sec/read and Avg Disk sec/write for each volume, different Linux tools are needed.

The iostat tool is available to install via the syststat performance monitoring tools, using the package manager on your operating system. Source code for iostat is available at *https://github.com/sysstat/sysstat*.

For example:

```
user@instance:~$ iostat -x
```

Using the -x parameter to return extended statistics yields basic host information, a current CPU activity utilization breakdown, and a variety of live measurements for devices, including logical disk volumes. The measures r_await and w_await are the average durations in milliseconds for read and write requests.

Other alternative packages include dtrace and nmon, the latter of which includes a simple bash-based GUI.

Monitor key performance metrics in Azure portal

The Azure portal provides a significant amount of intelligence to cloud-based SQL operations with built-in dashboarding. This section doesn't delve too deeply into those continuously improving standard features, but it does spend a little time talking about the sophisticated custom dashboarding and monitoring via Kusto and Azure Log Analytics.

View data in Azure Monitor

The Azure platform's built-in metrics tool, Azure Monitor—accessible via the Azure portal—automatically tracks several basic key performance and usage metrics in any Azure SQL Database. Azure Monitor Logs is one half of the data platform that supports Azure Monitor. The other is Azure Monitor Metrics, which stores numeric data in a time-series database. Some of these metrics are configured for you as part of the service (like metrics) while others require you to configure them (for example, SQL Diagnostics).

You query this data via the Azure Monitor Metrics pane, where you can drill down to an Azure resource and choose a metric to generate visualizations. Azure Monitor supports pinning generated visualizations to Azure portal dashboards, allowing you to create and monitor key database metrics at a glance.

When using Azure Monitor Metrics for an Azure SQL Database, for example, you can add metrics for DTU usage, or for percentages of the measures that make up a DTU. In the example in Figure 8-5, the Azure Monitor Metrics pane displays both DTU used and the average Log IO percentage on the same graph.

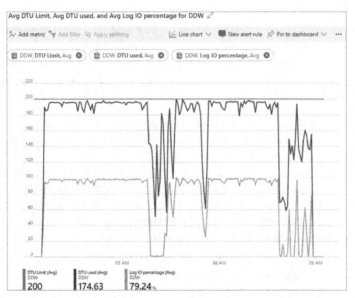

Figure 8-5 The Azure Monitor Metrics pane for an Azure SQL Database.

You can do more complicated charting via Azure Monitor by adding more metrics, which allows for visualization of multiple dimensions of interrelated data simultaneously, such as service request count per hour versus database CPU or DTU utilization.

You use filtering or splitting to further break down metrics with more than one value—for example, disk metrics. You can either filter on specific LUNs when viewing Data Disk Read Bytes/sec, for example, or you can split the data into different graph series, one for each LUN. If this sounds familiar, filtering and splitting using the Azure portal is not dissimilar from the same in Windows Performance Monitor. For example, this is similar to the selection of volumes when adding the Physical Disk\Avg. Disk sec/Read counter.

Leverage Azure Monitor logs

Azure Monitor is built on the Azure Log Analytics platform, using the same data storage and query mechanisms. Azure Log Analytics is itself a separate platform built to aggregate and query big data of varying schemas in near-real time. Azure Monitor log data is stored in a Log Analytics workspace, but is distinctly under the Azure Monitor product name, which also includes Application Insights.

Many Microsoft Azure resource types natively support syncing varying diagnostic and metric information to Azure Log Analytics. Azure SQL Database natively supports the export of information to Log Analytics via the Diagnostic Settings pane for the respective database in the Azure portal. Diagnostic settings support streaming basic metrics, as well as varying types of logs to log analytics.

Contrary to Azure Monitor, Log Analytics supports the ingesting of information from on-premises servers as well via the Azure Log Analytics agent. You might be familiar with the System Center Operations Manager (SCOM) monitoring tool, the Microsoft Monitoring Agent (MMA). The Azure Monitor agent is the evolution and replacement of the MMA and enables you to attach to an Azure Monitor or send data to a Log Analytics workspace.

Once your Log Analytics workspace is receiving data, you can query the workspace via the Logs pane in the Log Analytics workspace resource using the Kusto Query Language (KQL).

The following sample query gathers all DTU consumption metrics for Azure SQL Databases sending their logs to the Log Analytics workspace. It displays the 80th percentile of DTU consumption per time grain—in this case every 60 minutes. The intent is to normalize spikes of DTU usage and help to visualize sustained increase in DTU percentage that may be indicative of inefficient queries or a degradation between deployments.

```
AzureMetrics
| where MetricName == 'dtu_consumption_percent'
| summarize percentile(Average, 80) by bin(TimeGenerated, 1h)
| render timechart
```

➤ For more on KQL, see *https://learn.microsoft.com/azure/data-explorer/kusto/query/*.

Figure 8-6 visualizes the results of this query, which will work with any Log Analytics workspaces that have SQL databases sending log data.

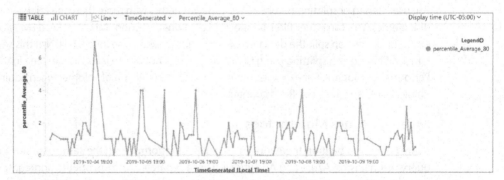

Figure 8-6 A Log Analytics query using Kusto and its charted result of average DTU utilization over time.

NOTE

As with Azure Monitor, results of Log Analytics queries can be pinned to a Microsoft Azure portal dashboard by using the Pin to Dashboard button in the header bar.

As mentioned, the preceding query extrapolates the 80th percentile of average DTU usage as a percent of quota, denoted by 'dtu_consumption_percent', in 1-hour increments. While useful, variances in usage patterns of the databases can lead to numerous peaks and valleys in the data rendered. This can make it hard to visually spot when the analyzed data is indicating a regression in performance—that is, a spike in DTU consumption.

As an alternative, the following query, visualized in Figure 8-7, applies a finite impulse response (series_fir()) to produce a 12-hour moving average of the analyzed data. This type of function is often used in signal processing, which a log stream resembles. This second example is a minor demonstration of the power and ease of drawing meaningful metrics out of the log data stream coming from Azure SQL resources, a more sophisticated look that should be more useful and readable at larger time scales.

```
AzureMetrics
| where MetricName == 'dtu_consumption_percent'
| make-series 80thPercentile=percentile(Average, 80)
 on TimeGenerated in range(ago(7d), now(), 60m)
| extend 80thPercentile=series_fir(80thPercentile, repeat(1, 12), true, true)
| mv-expand 80thPercentile, TimeGenerated
| project todouble(80thPercentile), todatetime(TimeGenerated)
| render timechart with (xcolumn=TimeGenerated)
```

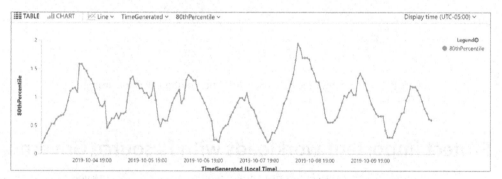

Figure 8-7 A Log Analytics query graph shows the output of a Kusto Query Language query.

➤ For more on series_fir(), see *https://learn.microsoft.com/azure/data-explorer/kusto /query/series-firfunction.*

Create Microsoft Log Analytics solutions

Perhaps the most important takeaway from Log Analytics is the ability to add or create solution packages. These can encapsulate queries, dashboards, and drill down reports of information.

Added via the Azure Marketplace, the Azure SQL Analytics solution and SQL Health Check solution attach to a Log Analytics workspace and can provide near-immediate feedback across your environment, scaling to the hundreds of thousands of databases if necessary.

Figure 8-8 is a sample live display from a production Azure SQL Analytics solution backed by a Log Analytics workspace. It shows at-a-glance information from production Azure SQL databases regarding database tuning recommendations, resource utilization, wait types and duration, as well as health check outcomes for metrics like timeouts and deadlocks.

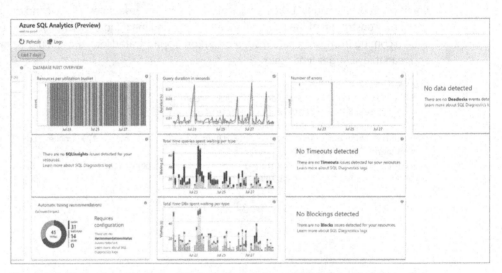

Figure 8-8 Output from the Azure SQL Analytics solution available from the Microsoft Azure Marketplace.

Protect important workloads with Resource Governor

Resource Governor, an Enterprise edition feature, is the only feature you can use to identify connections as they connect, and to limit the resources they can consume.

You can identify connections from virtually any connection property—basically, anything you can get from a system function, including the login name (SUSER_SNAME() or ORIGINAL_LOGIN()), hostname (HOST_NAME()), application name (APP_NAME()), and time functions (SYSDATETIME()).

➤ You can learn more about building a classifier function at *https://learn.microsoft.com/sql /relational-databases/resource-governor/resource-governor-classifier-function*.

After you've identified and classified the connection properties, you can limit properties at the individual session level or limit the resources of a resource pool. You can override the MAXDOP setting for these sessions, lower their priority, or cap the CPU, memory, or drive I/O that individual sessions can consume.

For example, you can limit all read-heavy queries coming from an SSRS server, or long-running reports coming from a third-party reporting application, or dashboard/search queries based on their application name or login. Then, you can limit these queries as a set, capping them to 25 percent of the process, disk I/O, or SQL Server memory. SQL Server will enforce these limitations and potentially slow down the identified queries; meanwhile, important read-write workloads continue to operate with the remaining 75 percent of the server's resources.

Be aware that using Resource Governor to limit long-running SELECT statements, for example, does not alleviate concurrency issues caused by locking. In fact, limiting long-running queries could alleviate memory or CPU contention but exacerbate existing locking problems.

➤ **See Chapter 14 for strategies to overcome concurrency issues, keeping in mind that using the** READ UNCOMMITTED **isolation level is a risky, clumsy strategy to solving concurrency issues in your applications.**

When enabled, Resource Governor is transparent to connecting applications. No code changes are required in the queries to implement Resource Governor, only a working knowledge of the connection properties you will use to identify queries, such as those returned by APP_NAME(), HOST_NAME(), or SUSER_SNAME().

CAUTION

The value returned by APP_NAME(), or that appears in the sys.dm_exec_sessions .program_name column, is specified in the application connection string. Filtering by this value should not be used as a security method, as connection strings can be changed to specify any string. If you're a paranoid DBA, it may also be something to watch for, if savvy users or tricky developers realize they can change their application connection strings and get more resources for their queries!

By default, sessions are split between two workload groups: workload group 1, named *internal* for system queries internal to the Database Engine, and workload group 2, named *default* for all other user queries. You can find the current groups in the DMV sys.resource_governor _workload_groups. While these groups still appear in SQL Server editions other than Enterprise (or Developer or Evaluation), Resource Governor is an Enterprise-only feature.

CHAPTER 8

Configure the Resource Governor classifier function

Before configuring Resource Governor to classify workloads arriving at your SQL Server, you must create a classifier function in the master database that operates at the creation of every new session. You can write the classifier function however you like, but keep in mind that it will be run for each new connection, so it should be as efficient and simple as possible.

The classifier function must return a sysname data type value. (The sysname built-in user-defined data type is equivalent to nvarchar(128) NOT NULL.) The classifier function return value must be the name of a Resource Governor workload group to which a new connection is to be assigned. Though sysname defaults to a NOT NULL data type, the function can return a NULL value, meaning that the session is assigned to the default group.

A workload group is simply a container of sessions. Remember, when configuring Resource Governor defensively (as is most common), it is the default workload group that you want to protect; it contains "all other" sessions, including high–business value connections that perform application-critical functions, writes, and so on.

The sample code that follows defines a classifier function that returns GovGroupReports for all queries coming from two known-fictional reporting servers. You can see in the comments other sample connection identifying functions, with many more options possible.

```
CREATE FUNCTION dbo.fnCLASSIFIER() RETURNS sysname
WITH SCHEMABINDING AS
BEGIN
-- Note that any request that you do not assign a @grp_name value for returns NULL,
-- and is classified into the 'default' group.
DECLARE @grp_name sysname
IF (
--Use built-in functions for connection string properties
 HOST_NAME() IN ('reportserver1','reportserver2')
--OR APP_NAME() IN ('some application') --further samples you can use
--AND SUSER_SNAME() IN ('whateveruser') --further samples you can use
)
 BEGIN
     SET @grp_name = 'GovGroupReports';
   END
RETURN @grp_name
END;
```

Be mindful when querying other user resources, such as tables in a user database; this can cause a noticeable delay in connection creation. If you must have the classifier function query a table, store the table in the master database, and keep the table small and the query efficient.

After creating the function, which can have any name, you must register it as the classifier function for this instance's Resource Governor feature. The function is still not active yet for new logins; you must set up workload groups and resource pools first, then enable your changes.

Configure Resource Governor resource pools and workload groups

Configuring resource pools (limitations that many sessions share) and workload groups (limitations for individual sessions) is the next step. You should take an iterative, gradual approach to configuring the Resource Governor, and avoid making large changes or large initial limitations to the affected groups.

If you have a preproduction environment to test the impact of Resource Governor on workloads with realistic production scale, you should consider performance load testing to make sure the chosen settings will not cause application issues due to throttling resources.

The sample code that follows can be an instructional template to creating an initial pool and group. If you seek to divide your sessions up further, multiple groups can belong to the same pool, and multiple pools can be limited differently. Commented-out examples of other common uses for Resource Governor are included. In this example, we create a pool that limits all covered sessions to 50 percent of the instance's memory, and a group that limits any single query to 30 percent of the instance's memory, and forces the sessions into MAXDOP = 1, overriding any server, database, or query-level setting:

```
CREATE RESOURCE POOL GovPoolMAXDOP1;
CREATE WORKLOAD GROUP GovGroupReports;
GO
ALTER RESOURCE POOL GovPoolMAXDOP1
WITH (-- MIN_CPU_PERCENT = value
     --,MAX_CPU_PERCENT = value
     --,MIN_MEMORY_PERCENT = value
 MAX_MEMORY_PERCENT = 50
);
GO
ALTER WORKLOAD GROUP GovGroupReports
WITH (
     --IMPORTANCE = { LOW | MEDIUM | HIGH }
     --,REQUEST_MAX_CPU_TIME_SEC = value
     --,REQUEST_MEMORY_GRANT_TIMEOUT_SEC = value
     --,GROUP_MAX_REQUESTS = value
        REQUEST_MAX_MEMORY_GRANT_PERCENT = 30
        , MAX_DOP = 1
)
USING GovPoolMAXDOP1;
```

➤ For complete documentation of the possible ways to limit groups and pools, visit *https:// learn.microsoft.com/sql/t-sql/statements/alter-workload-group-transact-sql* and *https://learn .microsoft.com/sql/t-sql/statements/alter-resource-pool-transact-sql*.

With the workload groups and resource pools in place, you are ready to tell Resource Governor to start using your changes:

```
-- Register the classifier function with Resource Governor
ALTER RESOURCE GOVERNOR WITH (CLASSIFIER_FUNCTION= dbo.fnCLASSIFIER);
```

After you have configured the classifier function, groups, and pools, you can enable Resource Governor by using the following query, placing its functionality into memory. New sessions will begin being sorted by the classifier function and new sessions will appear in their groups. You should also issue the RECONFIGURE command to apply changes made:

```
-- Start or reconfigure Resource Governor
ALTER RESOURCE GOVERNOR RECONFIGURE;
```

If anything goes awry, you can disable Resource Governor with the following command, and re-enable it with the same command as above.

```
--Disable Resource Governor
ALTER RESOURCE GOVERNOR DISABLE;
```

After you disable Resource Governor, existing sessions will continue to operate under the Resource Governor's rules, but new queries will not be sorted into your workload groups, only into the default. Sessions will behave with the default settings when disabled.

After you configure it and turn it on, you can query the status of Resource Governor and the name of the classifier function by using the following sample script:

```
SELECT rgc.is_enabled, o.name
FROM sys.resource_governor_configuration AS rgc
LEFT OUTER JOIN master.sys.objects AS o
ON rgc.classifier_function_id = o.object_id
        INNER JOIN master.sys.schemas AS s
        ON o.schema_id = s.schema_id;
```

Monitor resource pools and workload groups

The group_id columns in both sys.dm_exec_requests and sys.dm_exec_sessions define the Resource Governor group of which the request or session is a part. Groups are members of pools.

You can query the groups and pools via the sys.resource_governor_workload_groups and sys.resource_governor_resource_pools DMVs. Use the following sample query to observe the number of sessions that have been sorted into groups, noting that group_id = 1 is the internal group, group_id = 2 is the default group, and other groups are defined by you, the administrator:

```
SELECT
 rgg.group_id, rgp.pool_id
, Pool_Name = rgp.name, Group_Name = rgg.name
, session_count= ISNULL(count(s.session_id) ,0)
FROM sys.dm_resource_governor_workload_groups AS rgg
LEFT OUTER JOIN sys.dm_resource_governor_resource_pools AS rgp
```

```
ON rgg.pool_id = rgp.pool_id
LEFT OUTER JOIN sys.dm_exec_sessions AS s
ON s.group_id = rgg.group_id
GROUP BY rgg.group_id, rgp.pool_id, rgg.name, rgp.name
ORDER BY rgg.name, rgp.name;
```

While only Enterprise edition lets you modify the Resource Governor, all editions have the same code, so executing this query on another editions (even Express) will return an internal pool.

> ➤ You can reference a (dated) troubleshooting guide for a list of error numbers and their meanings that might be raised by Resource Governor, at *https://learn.microsoft.com /previous-versions/sql/sql-server-2008-r2/cc627395(v=sql.105)*. Unfortunately, there does not appear to be a more up-to-date version of this reference material.

Understand the SQL Server servicing model

Database administrators and CIOs alike must adjust their normal comfort levels with new SQL Server editions. No longer can IT leadership say, "Wait until the first service pack," before moving, because as of SQL Server 2017, there are no more service packs, only cumulative updates!

This section outlines the current processes for SQL Server on-premises versions. Note that Azure SQL Database and Managed Instance keeps your database engine up to date very soon after new versions are deployed.

Inside OUT

How do you patch SSRS?

Starting with SQL Server 2017, SSRS is no longer patched with SQL Server CUs. Instead, you upgrade SSRS by downloading and running the same SSRS installer again. Note that your patching procedures for SQL Server need to include this second and separate step to keep all related SQL Server software up to date.

Updated servicing model

Microsoft has adopted a new model for its product life cycles. In the past, its service model included service packs (SPs), cumulative updates (CUs), and general distribution releases (GDRs). However, beginning with SQL Server 2017 and continuing with SQL Server 2022, the following changes are in effect:

- SPs are longer be released.

- CUs are released approximately every month for the first 12 months of general release, and then every two months for the remaining four years of the five-year duration of the mainstream support period. In October 2018, this cadence was increased from quarterly to every two months for SQL Server 2017 and all future releases.

- Critical updates via GDR patches (which contain critical security-only fixes) do not have their own path for updates between CUs.

NOTE

For example, on February 14, 2023, Microsoft released an important security update for all supported versions of SQL Server to patch a remote code execution vulnerability. The authors of this book strongly recommend that you apply this update as soon as possible. For more information on the February 2023 GDR release for each version of SQL Server, visit *https://aka.ms/sqlbuilds*.

- Slipstream media is no longer provided for SQL Server (after SQL 2017 CU 11) for those who still used slipstream media for new instance installs. Instead, Microsoft recommends leveraging the existing SQL Server Setup, which provides automatic download and installation of the latest CUs or downloading CUs manually for offline installations.

➤ **For more information on offline installations of SQL Server on Windows Servers, see Chapter 4.**

Microsoft has maintained in recent years that there is no need to wait for an SP, because the general availability (GA) release has been extensively tested by both internal Microsoft QA and external preview customers. For those dealing with stubborn or reactionary clients or leadership, a possible alternative under the new model could be to target an arbitrary CU, such as CU 2.

Inside OUT

Do you need to patch SQL Server on Linux and container images after creation?

No, Linux `mssql-server` packages and the "latest" tagged container images are always updated, and install with the latest CU baked in. This is the default behavior. You can optionally install a non-current version.

You can review past SQL Server on Linux versions here: *https://learn.microsoft.com/sql /linux/sql-server-linux-release-notes-2022*.

You can review container images available at Docker Hub, at *https://hub.docker.com /_/microsoft-mssql-server*. (Note the underscore in the URL.)

Plan for the product support life cycle

As we were writing this book, SQL Server 2012 reached the end of extended support. Unless paying a hefty ransom for continuing support of these products is an option for you, databases on these old versions must be migrated as soon as possible. Similarly, Windows Server 2012 and

2012 R2 are reaching their end-of-support dates, in October 2023. No more security patches, even critical, will be released publicly, putting their use in violation of any sensible policy for secure software policy and a red flag on any security audit.

In your planning for long-term use of a particular version of SQL Server, you should keep in mind the following life cycle:

- **0 to 5 years: mainstream support period.** Security and functional issues are addressed through CUs. Security issues only might also be addressed through GDRs.

- **6 to 10 years: extended support.** Only critical functional issues will be addressed. Security issues might still be addressed through GDRs.

- **11 to 16 years: premium assurance.** The extended support level can be lengthened with optional payments or by migrating your workload to an Azure service. Either way, you will be paying for the privilege of maintaining an old version of SQL Server.

CHAPTER 8

Automate SQL Server administration

In the previous chapter, you learned about various tasks needed to maintain and monitor SQL Server. Managing these tasks can be time consuming and overwhelming, especially if you try to do them manually.

This chapter reviews common ways of automating Microsoft SQL Server instance administration, starting with an exploration of the tools that enable them.

NOTE

If you are unfamiliar with automating common administration tasks, this is an opportunity to grow and become a more seasoned DBA.

This chapter varies little for SQL Server instances on Windows and Linux except in the case of PowerShell. In some cases, you might have to run these commands from a Windows server. Where there are exceptions for Linux, we point them out.

Little in this chapter applies to Microsoft Azure SQL Database because many of the administration tasks are already automated, including most performance tuning and backup tasks. No initial configuration is needed. If you need more control, many of the features available in Azure SQL Database are being released through Azure SQL Managed Instance. As the Azure SQL platform as a service (PaaS) offering has matured, it has become a powerful cloud-based and complementary platform to SQL Server, neither fully replacing nor overlapping with the feature set or purpose of on-premises SQL Server instances.

Technically, the Azure elastic jobs feature is the automation framework for Azure SQL Database. However, it has been in preview for years. The Microsoft eventual road map for a generally available elastic jobs announcement or alternative solution is not public. Elastic jobs are nevertheless deployed in many Azure production environments. Read more about the current status of this preview feature at *https://learn.microsoft.com/azure/azure-sql/database/job-automation-overview*.

If you are not comfortable with preview features handling automation tasks for your Azure SQL Database, consider:

- Azure Data Factory for data movement and T-SQL commands

- Azure Automation for PowerShell

- Azure Logic Apps for low-code workflows with triggers

- ➤ **For more information about automation in Azure SQL database platforms, see Chapter 17, "Provision Azure SQL Database," and Chapter 18, "Provision Azure SQL Managed Instance."**

Sample scripts in this chapter, and all scripts for this book, are all available for download at *https://www.MicrosoftPressStore.com/SQLServer2022InsideOut/downloads*.

Foundations of SQL Server automated administration

Since automation implies a mostly hands-off approach to repeatable tasks, DBAs need to understand two foundational automation tools:

- **Database Mail.** Allows SQL Server to send emails to notify you of the outcome of SQL Server Agent jobs, server performance and error alerts, or custom notifications with Transact-SQL (T-SQL) calls to the dbo.sp_send_dbmail stored procedure (located in the msdb database).

  ## NOTE
  There are many ways (and products to buy) to be notified of an error or job failure in your SQL Server instance. Database mail is a built-in, easy, foundational notification feature to accomplish many notification tasks, as well as a platform for developing custom email-based reporting and notifications.

- **SQL Server Agent.** The automation engine available in all editions of SQL Server except for Express. You can use SQL Server Agent to automate most maintenance tasks in SQL Server. It's also available in Azure SQL Managed Instance, but not in Azure SQL Database. Let's review these two key tools, both of which are fully supported on Windows and Linux.

Database Mail

Database Mail uses Simple Mail Transfer Protocol (SMTP) to send email. Email is handled asynchronously outside the SQL Server process, isolating both the process and any potential performance impact to the SQL Server instance. By design, this process is run outside SQL Server using a separate executable DatabaseMail.exe, which is started asynchronously using Service Broker.

Set up Database Mail

To begin sending automated emails, you must configure Database Mail. Then, configure SQL Server Agent to use the Database Mail profile you create.

In SQL SSMS, start the Database Mail Configuration Wizard by locating it in the **Management** folder of the server node you are configuring and selecting **Configure Database Mail**. You'll need to set up a profile and then an associated account.

The wizard turns on the Database Mail feature in the Surface Area facet of the SQL Server instance. You need to do this only once. Database Mail is among a select few Surface Area facets that you should turn on for most SQL Server instances. To view surface area configuration settings in SSMS, open Object Explorer, connect to the SQL Server, right-click the server, and select **Facets** on the shortcut menu. (The Facets window sometimes takes a moment to load.) Then, in the dialog box that opens, change the value in the list box to **Surface Area Configuration**. Choose **Database Mail** and set the property value to **True**.

A Database Mail profile can be public or private. In the case of a private profile, only sysadmins and specific associated server principals are given access (users or roles in databases). A public profile allows any principal that is a member of the built-in database role DatabaseMailUsersRole in the msdb database.

Ideally, all Database Mail profiles are private. That way, by default only members of the sysadmin role are allowed access, and only those credentials that will be used to send emails will be given access. If you would like to grant additional database principals to access private database mail profiles, you can use the stored procedure msdb.dbo.sysmail_add_principalprofile_sp. This is crucial in a multitenant environment, or an environment that allows access to external developers or vendors, but even in internal environments, it could provide protection against malicious use to send emails.

When creating a Database Mail profile, you have the option to specify whether the profile will be the default—even if there is only one Database Mail profile created. If you choose a Database Mail profile to be the default, it will be used as the global profile for outgoing mail and will be used to send mail if a profile is not specified with the dbo.sp_send_dbmail stored procedure.

You can configure a Database Mail profile to use almost any SMTP configuration, including nonstandard ports and Secure Sockets Layer (SSL). You also can configure it with Windows Authentication (common for SMTP servers in the same domain), basic authentication (common for web authentication), or no authentication (common for anonymous relay in the local network, usually with an IP allow list).

> ➤ For more on SSL and TLS, refer to Chapter 13, "Protect data through classification, encryption, and auditing."

CHAPTER 9

You can configure Database Mail to use any SMTP server that it can reach, including web-based SMTP servers. You can even use Outlook web mail or another web-based email account if you're configuring for testing purposes or have no other viable internal SMTP options. An internal SMTP server with Windows Authentication using a service account is preferred, though, because it gives you more control over your own environment.

Inside OUT

What if you have multifactor authentication (MFA) set up for Outlook web mail?

To send emails using SMTP for Outlook while you have MFA enabled, you will need to set up an app password. For step-by-step instructions, see *https://support.microsoft.com/account -billing/using-app-passwords-with-apps-that-don-t-support-two-step-verification-5896ed9b -4263-e681-128a-a6f2979a7944.*

NOTE

For Azure infrastructure-as-a-service (IaaS) environments without an internal SMTP presence, Twilio SendGrid is a common and supported SMTP solution. For more information, visit *https://docs.sendgrid.com/for-developers/partners/microsoft-azure-2021.*

After you configure your account's SMTP settings (you'll need to test them later), the Database Mail account will have several options that you can adjust:

- **Account Retry Attempts.** Defaults to **1**. You should probably leave this as is to avoid excessive retries that could lock out an account or trigger spam detection.

- **Account Retry Delay (seconds).** Defaults to **60**. Again, you should leave this as is, for the same reasons as for Account Retry Attempts.

- **Maximum File Size (Bytes).** Defaults to roughly **1** MB. You should change this only if necessary.

- **Prohibited Attachment File Extensions.** Specifies which file extensions cannot be sent. It is commonly set if third-party or multitenant development occurs on the SQL Server instance. This is a comma-delimited list that, by default, is "exe,dll,vbs,js."

- **Database Mail Executable Minimum Lifetime (seconds).** Defaults to **600 Seconds** (10 minutes), which is a counter that starts after an email message is sent. If no other messages are sent in that time frame, the Database Mail executable stops. If stopped, the Database Mail process is started again any time a new email is sent. You'll see messages indicating "Database Mail process is started" and "Database Mail process is shutting down" in the Database Mail log when this happens.

- **Logging Level.** Defaults to **Extended**, which includes basic start/stop and error messages that should be kept in the Database Mail log. Change this to **Verbose** if you are troubleshooting Database Mail and need more information, or to **Normal** to suppress informational messages and see errors only.

After you've set up a Database Mail profile and account, you can send a test email via SSMS. Right-click **Database Mail** and select **Send Test E-Mail** on the shortcut menu that opens. Or you can send a plain-and-simple test email via T-SQL by using the following code:

```
exec msdb.dbo.sp_send_dbmail
@recipients ='yournamehere@domain.com',
@subject ='test';
```

This code does not specify a @profile parameter, so the command will use the default profile for the current user, the default private profile if it exists, or the global (default public) profile. If you do not have a default Database Mail profile set up, you will get the following error:

```
Msg 14636, Level 16, State 1, Procedure msdb.dbo.sp_send_dbmail, Line 112 [Batch Start
Line 0]
No global profile is configured. Specify a profile name in the @profile_name parameter.
```

This is all that is necessary for developers and applications to send emails using Database Mail.

> In case you have issues with setting up or sending emails, we cover troubleshooting later in this chapter in the "Troubleshoot Database Mail" section.

To allow SQL Server Agent to send emails based on job outcomes and alerts, you need to create an operator in SQL Server Agent, and then configure SQL Server Agent's alert system to use a Database Mail profile. We look at SQL Server Agent and its initial configuration in depth later in this chapter.

Inside OUT

What about Database Mail on Linux?

SQL Server on Linux requires the Database Mail profile to be set using mssql-conf or an environment variable. We recommend using mssql-conf with the following command (where default is the name of the profile you created):

```
sudo /opt/mssql/bin/mssql-conf set sqlagent.databasemailprofile default
```

For step-by-step instructions, visit *https://learn.microsoft.com/sql/linux/sql-server-linux-db-mail-sql-agent*.

Allow anonymous relay for anonymous authentication

If you're using anonymous authentication internally with Microsoft Exchange, verify that the internal SMTP anonymous relay has a dedicated receive connector that allows for anonymous relay. By design, a receive connector just for anonymous relay should allow only a small list of internal hosts—your SQL Server instance(s) among them.

Maintain email history in the msdb database

The email messages attempted and sent by Database Mail are recorded and queued in a table in the msdb database named dbo.sysmail_mailitems. As you might suspect, data in the msdb tables for Database Mail will grow, potentially to an unmanageable size. This can cause queries to the msdb's Database Mail tables to run for a long time. There is no automated process in place to maintain a retention policy for these tables, though there is a stored procedure to delete older messages, as well as a lengthy reference article in place to guide you through creating a set of archive tables and a SQL Server Agent job to maintain data over time. You can find both of these at *https://learn.microsoft.com/sql/relational-databases/database-mail /create-a-sql-server-agent-job-to-archive-database-mail-messages-and-event-logs*.

Troubleshoot Database Mail

We've already mentioned the Database Mail log. Now let's go over the other diagnostics available for Database Mail.

➤ Find out more about reading the Database Mail log at *https://learn.microsoft.com/sql /relational-databases/database-mail/database-mail-log-and-audits*.

Read email logs in the msdb database

If the SMTP Server or the Database Mail process becomes unavailable, the messages are queued in a table in the msdb database named dbo.sysmail_mailitems. This msdb database contains metadata tables for the Database Mail feature, including dbo.sysmail_allitems, which tracks all outbound email activity. Look for items for which the sent_status doesn't equal sent for signs of messages that weren't successfully sent; for example:

```
--Find recent unsent emails
SELECT m.send_request_date, m.recipients, m.copy_recipients, m.blind_copy_recipients
, m.[subject], m.send_request_user, m.sent_status
FROM msdb.dbo.sysmail_allitems AS m
WHERE
-- Only show recent day(s)
m.send_request_date > dateadd(day, -3, sysdatetime())
-- Possible values are sent (successful), unsent (in process),
-- retrying (failed but retrying), failed (no longer retrying)
AND m.sent_status <> 'sent'
ORDER BY m.send_request_date DESC;
```

There is also a view provided in msdb, dbo.sysmail_unsentitems, that filters on (sent _status = 'unsent' OR sent_status = 'retrying'). There are four possible values for sent_status in dbo.sysmail_allitems: sent, unsent, retrying, and failed.

➤ You can find more information about these and other sysmail views, including failed items and sent items, at *https://learn.microsoft.com/sql/relational-databases/system-catalog -views/sysmail-allitems-transact-sql.*

Inside OUT

How do you monitor SQL Server Reporting Services report subscription emails?

SQL Server Reporting Services (SSRS) uses an entirely different process, SMTP configuration, and authentication to send report subscriptions via email. To monitor these, the default location for log messages in the log files starting with SSRS in SQL Server 2016 is the following subfolder:

%programfiles%\Microsoft SQL Server Reporting Services\SSRS\LogFiles

Enable Service Broker on the msdb database

After restoring the msdb database or setting up Database Mail for the first time, the Service Broker feature might not be turned on for the msdb database. You can check the is_broker _enabled field in the system catalog view sys.databases; if it is 0, this is the case, and you must remedy it. Otherwise, if you try to send email and the Service Broker is disabled, you will receive the following self-explanatory error message:

```
Msg 14650, Level 16, State 1, Procedure msdb.dbo.sp_send_dbmail, Line 73 [Batch Start
Line 18] Service Broker message delivery is not enabled in this database. Use the ALTER
DATABASE statement to enable Service Broker message delivery.
```

To turn on Service Broker for the msdb database, you must stop the SQL Server Agent service and close any connections active to the msdb database before running the following code:

```
ALTER DATABASE msdb SET ENABLE_BROKER;
```

Identify SMTP server authentication

Authentication with the SMTP server is likely the problem if you observe errors in the Database Mail log after attempting to send email, such as:

```
Cannot send mails to mail server. (Mailbox unavailable. The server response was: 5.7.1
Unable to relay...
```

or:

```
Cannot send mails to mail server. (Mailbox unavailable. The server response was: 5.7.1
Service unavailable...
```

CHAPTER 9

SQL Server Agent

SQL Server Agent is the native automation platform for internal task automation, maintenance, log and file retention, and even backups. SQL Server Agent is like Windows Task Scheduler (and cron on Linux), but it has several advantages for automating SQL Server tasks, including integration with SQL Server security, authentication, logging, and native T-SQL programming.

On Windows, SQL Server Agent can accomplish many of the same tasks as Windows Task Scheduler, including running operating system (CmdExec) and PowerShell commands. (CmdExec and PowerShell tasks are not available on Linux.) Metadata, configuration, and history data for the SQL Server Agent are kept in the msdb database.

Inside OUT

How do you enable SQL Server Agent?

On Windows Server, SQL Server Agent is a service that is managed through SQL Server Configuration Manager.

On Linux, SQL Server Agent is managed using the mssql-conf command line utility. You can read more in Chapter 5, "Install and configure SQL Server on Linux."

Configure SQL Server Agent jobs

A job contains a series of steps. Each job step is of a type that allows for different actions to take place, such as the aforementioned T-SQL, CmdExec, or PowerShell tasks.

A job can be automatically started based on a number of conditions, including the following:

- A predefined schedule or schedules

- In response to an alert

- As a result of running the dbo.sp_start_job stored procedure in the msdb database

- When SQL Server Agent starts

- When the host computer is idle

You can script jobs in their entirety through SSMS, providing script-level recoverability, migration to other servers, and source control possibility for SQL Server Agent jobs. Jobs are backed up and restored via the msdb database or scripted for backup and migration.

In SSMS, in Object Explorer, expand **SQL Server Agent**, then expand the **Jobs** folder. Next, right-click any job, select **Properties**, and navigate to the **Steps** page. Here you will see that job steps do not necessarily need to run linearly. You can set a job to default to start at any job step. Additionally, when starting a job, you can manually change the start step for the job.

Each job step reports back whether it succeeded or failed, and you can configure it to move to another step or fail based on the job step outcome. These step completion actions are defined on the **Advanced** page of the **Job Step Properties** dialog box. However, for future ease of management, we recommend that you create job steps that are designed and run in a consistent pattern. Using a standard process will help others more easily understand and support these SQL Server Agent jobs. This embraces another key aspect of database automation: creating processes that can be easily managed.

You can assign jobs to categories. In fact, many system-generated jobs (such as replication) are assigned to categories. You can access settings to create your own categories in SSMS by right-clicking the **Jobs** folder under **SQL Server Agent** and selecting **Manage Categories** on the shortcut menu.

In T-SQL, you can run this script to add a new category:

```
EXEC msdb.dbo.sp_add_category @class=N'JOB', @type=N'LOCAL', @name=N'Health Check';
```

This should aid your efforts to report on, maintain, redeploy, and migrate jobs in the future.

Understand job step security

A critical step that many developers and administrators skip is the use of credentials and proxies in SQL Server Agent job steps. SQL Server Agent jobs, by default, run steps in the security context of the SQL Agent service account. This may be acceptable for some local usage such as indexing, but using a proxy to run a job step instead of the SQL Server Agent service account or another named user is the most secure approach. Proxies make it possible for administrators to set job steps to run under a specific credential rather than giving the SQL Server Agent service account access to everything that each job needs.

Proxies are used for all job step types except one. It is not possible to run a T-SQL script job step using a proxy. A T-SQL step will run in the security context of the owner of the job if the owner is not a sysadmin. If the owner of the job is a member of the sysadmin server role, the job will run as the SQL Server Agent service account.

For all other job step types, there is a proxy. You can select the job step to run as a proxy on the **Job Step Properties** page. SQL Server Agent checks for access to the subsystem each time the job step is run to verify that the security has not changed.

A subsystem can be one of the following items:

- Operating system (CmdExec)

- Replication agent (Snapshot, Log Reader, Distribution, Merge, or Queue Reader)

- Analysis Services query or Analysis Services command

- SSIS package execution

- PowerShell script

- Microsoft ActiveX script (discontinued as of SQL Server 2016; replaced with PowerShell script)

You can associate each proxy with one or more subsystems, but to reduce your attack surface, you should create many proxies for different job step security requirements and subsystems.

Without a proxy specified, jobs must be owned by a member of the sysadmin role to run job steps other than the T-SQL step type. This is because the T-SQL step type allows you to specify an account under **Run as** so that the code will run under a different user's permissions. These job steps will then run as the SQL Server Agent service account. This isn't ideal, for two reasons:

- The SQL Server Agent service account should not have local administrator privileges on the server. This reduces the risk to the operating system (OS) from potential misuse for SQL Server Agent jobs. Service accounts are discussed in Chapter 4, "Install and configure SQL Server instances and features," and Chapter 12, "Administer instance and database security and permissions."

- The SQL Server Agent service account must be a member of the sysadmin server role, so it has far too many privileges inside SQL Server than necessary to safely run SQL Agent jobs.

The owner of the job must also have permission to use any subsystem that the job's steps use. This is important because job steps often need to access other servers, and proxies give you the ability to assign pinpoint rights to those other resources. You will not be able to create or modify a job step for a subsystem if the job owner is not listed as a principal who has access to the proxy. Sysadmins automatically have access to all proxies.

Proxies map to credentials on the SQL Server; you'll find a subfolder for credentials in the **Security** folder on the **Server** level in Object Explorer in SSMS. Each proxy is linked to a credential in SQL Server. The credential stores the account's username and password, which means that if it changes, the proxy and SQL Server Agent job steps that depend on it will not be able to authenticate and will fail. Therefore, you should use service accounts, not individuals' named accounts, in credentials that will be used by proxies. Credential account passwords shouldn't be widely known, and the accounts should not regularly be used interactively by administrators to avoid accidentally becoming locked out.

NOTE

You should keep a script for recovering locked service accounts in a safe place.

You can create a credential for a local Windows account or a domain account. You also can create credentials for accounts on Extensible Key Management (EKM) modules, including the Azure Key Vault service. The Windows account of the credential must have **Log on as a batch job** permission on the server. As a local administrator, you can grant this permission in the **Local Security Policy** dialog box.

➤ You can read more about Azure Key Vault and EKM modules in Chapter 13.

Secure permissions to interact with jobs

To set up a SQL Server Agent job in SSMS, your login must be a member of the sysadmin server role or one of the SQL Server Agent database roles in the msdb database. The SQLAgentOperatorRole, SQLAgentReaderRole, and SQLAgentUserRole have permission to create jobs, start jobs, view jobs, view a job's history, and edit job properties, though mostly only for jobs they own.

➤ For granular details on the limitations and overlapping of each role, visit *https://learn .microsoft.com/sql/ssms/agent/sql-server-agent-fixed-database-roles*.

The SQLAgentUserRole is the least privileged of the three roles, but the other two roles are members of the SQLAgentUserRole. Typically, membership to these roles is limited to service accounts and third-party developers. Grant permission on proxies to custom database roles, individuals, or service accounts. Do not grant permissions directly to the SQLAgentUserRole database role, including the ability to use proxies.

Schedule and monitor jobs

A job can be run based on one or more schedules assigned to it. You give schedules a name upon creation and can assign them to multiple jobs. This can be especially useful for uncommon or esoteric job schedules, or to centralize management of jobs that should run simultaneously. To view and select schedules from other jobs, select the **Pick** button on the **Schedules** tab of the **Job Properties** dialog box. You will see only the job schedules to which you have access.

There are four schedule types:

- Start automatically when SQL Server Agent starts

- Start whenever the CPUs become idle

- Recurring

- One time (for running a schedule manually—for instance, during testing or a one-off index rebuild)

Jobs run asynchronously when they are started manually or by SQL Server Agent. A dialog box with a spinning progress icon appears, but you can close it, and the job will continue to run until completion. You can monitor the progress of jobs in SSMS by viewing the Job Activity Monitor, and you can observe the job's current request in `sys.dm_exec_requests`.

NOTE

Using the SQL Server Agent extension, you can also view and manage SQL Agent jobs in Azure Data Studio. For more information, visit *https://learn.microsoft.com/sql/azure -data-studio/sql-server-agent-extension.*

You can use T-SQL to query the status of jobs with the undocumented stored procedure `master.dbo.xp_sqlagent_enum_jobs`, which you can join to `msdb.dbo.sysjobs`, as shown here:

```
--Jobs still running
DECLARE @xp_sqlagent_enum_jobs TABLE (
id int not null IDENTITY(1,1) PRIMARY KEY,
Job_ID uniqueidentifier not null,
Last_Run_Date int not null,
Last_Run_Time int not null,
Next_Run_Date int not null,
Next_Run_Time int not null,
Next_Run_Schedule_ID int not null,
Requested_To_Run int not null,
Request_Source int not null,
Request_Source_ID varchar(100) null,
Running int not null,
Current_Step int not null,
Current_Retry_Attempt int not null,
[State] int not null);

INSERT INTO @xp_sqlagent_enum_jobs
EXEC master.dbo.xp_sqlagent_enum_jobs 1, '';

SELECT j.name
, state_desc = CASE ej.state
WHEN 0 THEN 'not idle or suspended'
WHEN 1 THEN 'Executing'
WHEN 2 THEN 'Waiting for thread'
WHEN 3 THEN 'Between retries'
WHEN 4 THEN 'Idle'
WHEN 5 THEN 'Suspended'
WHEN 7 THEN 'Performing completion actions'
END
, *
 FROM msdb.dbo.sysjobs j
 LEFT OUTER JOIN @xp_sqlagent_enum_jobs ej
 ON j.job_id = ej.Job_ID
ORDER BY j.name;
```

Configure and view job history

Every time a job is run, a record is maintained in the msdb database in the dbo.sysjobhistory table. To review the job's history, right-click it in SSMS and select **Job History** on the shortcut menu. History is stored for each job step. You can expand a given job to view the output for each step, including any errors.

With jobs that run frequently (for example, transaction log backup jobs), a large amount of job history will be created and stored in msdb. It is initially defaulted to two very low and likely unrealistic row caps: 1,000 rows of history for all jobs, and 100 rows of history at most for one job. If a job runs once per hour, it loses visibility into history after just four days—likely an unrealistic window for troubleshooting and diagnostic information.

In SSMS, in Object Explorer, right-click **SQL Server Agent**, select **Properties**, and select the **History** page. As shown in Figure 9-1, this page is not intuitive. The first option, **Limit** *size of* *job history* **log**, is a rolling job history retention setting. You might find it a good start to simply add a 0 to each value, increasing the maximum log history size in rows from the default of 1,000 to 10,000 or more, and also increase the maximum job history per job in rows from the default of 100 to 1,000 or more. These settings would store just over 41 days of history for a job that runs hourly, if this were the only job on the server. You might find these numbers also insufficient on a SQL Server instance with many frequently running jobs, so you should increase these settings until you have a comfortable job run history retention.

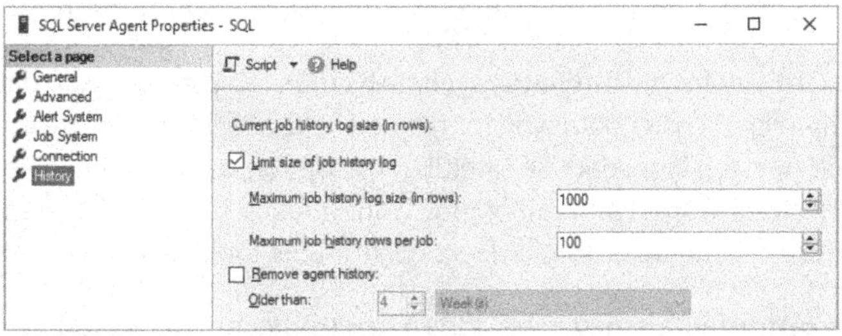

Figure 9-1 The two options to retain SQL Agent job history.

The job history log can be useful, but it has two limitations of which you should be aware:

- The message text in the Job History viewer is truncated after 1,024 characters. To view the full results of the output, you must query the dbo.sysjobhistory table. The message column in that table is considerably larger at 8,000 characters.

- The history of SQL Server Integration Services (SSIS) package execution in the SQL Server Agent job history is extremely limited—reduced to details around the fact that the package started, completed, and/or errored, without additional details. More verbose detail appears in the thorough history available in the SSISDB. To access and view this history, open the **Integration Services Catalogs** menu in SSMS and select the project or packages that failed.

CHAPTER 9

Inside OUT

Where should you deploy SSIS packages?

Using the Project Deployment model for SSIS packages provides superior built-in logging and trending when running a package.

The Project Deployment model and the SSISDB database, both originally released in SQL Server 2012, combined with further integration with SQL Server Agent, make for a far superior option for SSIS development than the old Package Deployment model.

You can still deploy legacy Package Deployment model packages to msdb, but we do not recommend this for new development.

You can also configure additional logging for each job step to capture the full step output and, more commonly, the error text. The following options are available on the **Advanced** page of the **Job Step Properties** dialog box:

- **Output file.** You can send step output to an Output file and Append output to existing file. Be wary of keeping the **Append output to existing file** option turned on long term—the output file can grow to a significant size in a short amount of time. If your history file becomes too large, this may cause the SQL Server Agent to crash.

- **Log to table.** This writes to the dbo.sysjobstepslogs table in the msdb database. This table has an nvarchar(max) data type for the Log field, allowing for more output data to be captured per step if needed. Be careful of this option, as well—the table can grow to a significant size in a short amount of time. You should schedule the stored procedure sp_delete_jobsteplog to remove old records from the table over time.

- **Include step output in history.** This adds a row to the job history log to include the output of the job step. This should contain valuable information, and, unlike with the other two options, job history is automatically maintained over time by SQL Server Agent.

Administer SQL Server Agent operators

An *operator* is an alias in SQL Server Agent that allows you to set up a name and email address(es) to receive messages. Usually, an operator should not be pointed to an individual (although you can create a semicolon-delimited list of email address); instead, it should be pointed to a distribution group (even if that group initially contains only one person). In most situations, you will create an operator to notify SQL Server first responders in your environment. You should maintain your environment's list of DBA personnel in distribution lists, and not inside the operator lists of each SQL Server instance.

NOTE

The pager email name is deprecated along with the on-duty schedule, so don't use these. Alerting using Net Send is also deprecated and has been removed from the user interface.

To set up an operator, in SSMS, in Object Explorer, expand the **SQL Server Agent** folder, right-click **Operator**, and select **New Operator** on the shortcut menu.

NOTE

If you have a big team and an on-call rotation, you could set up a scheduled process in a SQL Server Agent job to update an "on call rotation" distribution list email address to resource(s) currently "on call." Use the sp_update_operator **stored procedure to update the email address for an operator on a schedule.**

Configure alerts

Alerts are created to set conditions and, when met, prompt email notifications or the kickoff of SQL Server Agent jobs in response. Alerts are versatile and can look for SQL Server events in the Error Log for performance conditions that you would view in the Performance Monitor application or for Windows Management Instrumentation (WMI) queries.

As recommended in the "Set up SQL Agent" section of Chapter 4, you should set up alerts for high-severity SQL Server errors. However, do not overcommit your personal inbox with alerts, and do not set an inbox rule to Mark As Read and file away emails from SQL Server. By careful selection of emails, you can assure yourself and your team that emails from SQL Server will be actionable concerns that rarely arrive.

With a large number of SQL Server instances under your purview, email alerts for even severe issues can become too numerous and frequent. This is especially true if you receive individual alerts from each server! Look into gathering and queuing actionable errors in a system that provides for aggregation, dashboarding, and team assignment. There are third-party log-collection and log-management software applications that perform the task of log aggregation and centralized alerting.

You might also configure the **Delay between responses** setting for each alert to prevent an unchecked flooding of emails arriving from a repeating error. Consider a delay of up to 5 minutes between responses, as your environment and Service-Level Agreement (SLA) deem appropriate.

You can specify only a single error message or severity per alert. Consider scripting the mass creation of a standard batch of alerts, to be created consistently on all your SQL Server instances. We include a script in the accompanying downloads for this book as an example that includes the alerts we will examine in just a moment.

CHAPTER 9

First, we review the three types of alerts you can set up:

- SQL Server event alert

- Performance condition alert

- WMI event alert

NOTE

On Linux, you can only set up a SQL Server event alert, but as we'll show, it is possible to query performance counters using a dynamic management view.

SQL Server event

You should set up alerts on actual error messages that are important enough for you to receive emails. SQL Server generates a lot of informational-only events, such as successful backup messages, for which you would not want to receive messages.

You can set up alerts based on the actual error number (samples follow shortly) or any error of a certain severity (1 to 25). You can optionally filter the alert to a single database or for a specific message text.

It is common practice to set up alerts for severity 16 through 19 and 21 through 25 because these tend to be actionable errors. Severities 21 and above are severe and unrecoverable errors.

The most common severity 20 errors are nuisance authentication-related and transient (the user tried, experienced an error, tried again, and succeeded). An alert for severity 20 might send out many unactionable alerts to the SQL Server DBA team. You will still see severity 20 issues in the SQL Server Error Log and should make note of them as they appear, especially if they do so in large numbers, given that this can be a sign of greater authentication or domain issues or malicious intrusion attempts. The goal of alerts is to send out actionable errors or performance conditions worth investigating.

NOTE

Every SQL Server error message includes a severity, but that doesn't mean you want to be alerted to them. For example, basic syntax, CHECK constraint, and FOREIGN KEY constraint errors that you might make while writing queries in SSMS or Azure Data Studio will surface as severity 15 or 16 errors, which aren't worth alerting.

You might also want to configure alerts to send out error messages for the following SQL Server error numbers that are not already covered in severities 16 through 19 and 21 through 25. These errors are rare, but immediately actionable:

- **825 (severity 10).** A dreaded "read-retry" error, which occurs when a file read succeeds after failing *n* number of times. This is often a harbinger of a database-integrity failure and should prompt immediate action.

- **854, 855, 856 (severity 10).** Uncorrectable hardware memory corruption detected via the operating system's memory diagnostics. This may indicate a potentially immediate threat to system stability due to memory.

- **3624 (severity 20).** An internal SQL Server error called an *assertion failure*. This is typically a software bug, though it could indicate internal data corruption. Errors at this severity are often addressed via a SQL Server cumulative update or patch.

Performance conditions

On Windows, you can set up performance condition alerts for any performance counter in the SQLServer category—the same set of alerts you would see in Windows Performance Monitor with the prefix SQLServer or MSSQL$*instancename*. For example, if you want to receive an email when the SQL Server's page life expectancy (PLE) drops below a certain value, you select it in the same way you would in Performance Monitor: Choose the **Buffer Manager** object, the **Page Life Expectancy** counter, the **Falls Below** comparison operator, and a comparison value. In the case of PLE, this is measured in seconds.

Inside OUT

How do you query performance counters using DMVs?

As discussed in Chapter 8, "Maintain and monitor SQL Server," you can query most performance counters from SQLServer or MSSQL$*instancename* objects via the sys.dm_os _performance_counters dynamic management view (DMV) on both Windows and Linux. There is one caveat, however: In some cases, the calculation is not as straightforward. For example, consider the Buffer Cache Hit Ratio (BCHR) metric, one piece of the puzzle when looking at memory utilization. Calculating the actual BCHR as it appears in Performance Monitor requires division of two simultaneous counter values:

```
DECLARE @object_name SYSNAME = CASE
    WHEN CHARINDEX('\', @@SERVERNAME) = 0
    THEN 'SQLServer'
    ELSE 'MSSQL$' + SUBSTRING(@@SERVERNAME, CHARINDEX('\', @@SERVERNAME) + 1, 100)
    END + ':Buffer Manager'
SELECT [BufferCacheHitRatio] = (bchr * 1.0 / bchrb) * 100.0
FROM (
    SELECT bchr = cntr_value
    FROM sys.dm_os_performance_counters
    WHERE counter_name = 'Buffer cache hit ratio'
    AND object_name = @object_name
    ) AS r
CROSS APPLY (
    SELECT bchrb = cntr_value
    FROM sys.dm_os_performance_counters
    WHERE counter_name = 'Buffer cache hit ratio base'
    AND object_name = @object_name
    ) AS rb;
```

CHAPTER 9

NOTE

SQL Server samples the data periodically, so there might be a few seconds' delay between when you receive the alert and when the threshold was reached.

WMI event alert conditions

The third option for SQL Server Agent alerts allows for custom WMI queries to be run (for SQL Server on Windows only). WMI queries can gather alerts on a variety of Data Definition Language (DDL) events in SQL Server, such as CREATE, ALTER, and DROP. While WMI queries follow the basic syntax of T-SQL queries, the FROM of the WMI query will be a WMI object, not an object in a SQL Server database.

➤ You can see an example of a WMI event alert at *https://learn.microsoft.com/sql/relational -databases/wmi-provider-server-events/sample-creating-a-sql-server-agent-alert-with-the -wmi-provider.*

➤ You can reference the WMI provider classes and properties at *https://learn.microsoft.com /sql/relational-databases/wmi-provider-server-events/wmi-provider-for-server-events-classes -and-properties.*

This type of alert is not as straightforward as the other types. In general, you might find better results, more flexibility, and less complexity by using Extended Events, SQL Server Agent jobs, SQL Server Audit, and/or third-party monitoring tools than by using WMI alert queries.

➤ You can read more about Extended Events in Chapter 8.

Setting up an email recipient for a WMI event alert does not send over any useful or actionable information in the email aside from the alert's name. This does little more than let you know that a WMI event occurred (observed asynchronously, so there might be some delay).

To view the information regarding the event—for example, the T-SQL command associated with the event—you must enable token replacement. To do so, open the **SQL Server Agent Properties** dialog box. Then, at the bottom of the **Alert System** page, select the **Token Replacement** check box. This allows for the tokenization (replacement at runtime) of WMI commands in a T-SQL job step.

➤ For more on the tokens that you can use in a T-SQL job step, visit *https://learn.microsoft .com/sql/ssms/agent/use-tokens-in-job-steps.*

We have prepared a sample WMI event alert to capture the CREATE DATABASE DDL event in the accompanying downloads for this book.

SQL Server Agent job considerations when using availability groups

If you are running SQL Server Agent jobs in an availability group environment, you will still need to configure maintenance plans on each SQL Server instance. You must cover databases that are writeable when the instance is the primary replica, databases not included in availability groups, as well as the system databases master and msdb. You should ensure that your maintenance plans, regardless of platform, are consistently updated on all replicas and also are aware of their local replica role so that maintenance plans do not need to be turned on, turned off, or reconfigured when a failover occurs.

The SQL Server Agent must be enabled, and your SQL Server Agent jobs must exist on all replicas of the availability group and be replica-aware. (The script should know if it is running on the primary replica for a database.) You will need multiple versions of any custom maintenance task in order to separate scripts for databases in each availability group, and one more for databases not in an availability group (including any system databases that you intend to maintain with custom scripts).

To avoid having SQL Server Agent jobs generate an error when their local replica is not the primary replica for a database, you can add a T-SQL step to the start of the job to detect and raise a failure. The goal of the first step is to prevent subsequent job steps from running and failing against secondary replica databases, which will not be writeable. Name the first step "Am I Primary?" or something similar, and then add the following script:

```
--add as step 1 on every AG-aware job
IF NOT EXISTS (
SELECT @@SERVERNAME, *
    FROM sys.dm_hadr_availability_replica_states rs
    INNER JOIN sys.availability_databases_cluster dc
    on rs.group_id = dc.group_id
    WHERE is_local = 1
    and role_desc = 'PRIMARY'
--Any databases in the same Availability Group
    and dc.database_name in (N'databasename1', N'databasename2'))
BEGIN
    print 'local SQL instance is not primary, skipping';
    throw 50000, 'Do not continue', 1;
END;
```

This code causes step 1 to fail when it is not run on a primary replica for the specified database(s). If you run the preceding code referencing a database that is not in an availability group, the script will also cause step 1 to fail. In the Advanced settings of the "Am I Primary?" job step, the **On Success Action** setting should be **Go to The Next Step**, as usual, but the **On Failure Action** setting should be **Quit the Job Reporting Success**, which would not register as a job failure. Instead of a green check mark or a red X next to the job, SQL Server Job History displays a yellow triangle. This prevents subsequent job steps from running and failing against secondary replica databases, which will not be writeable.

CHAPTER 9

> **NOTE**
>
> The previous script is not appropriate for maintenance plan jobs. Any change to the
> maintenance plan will re-create the job and overwrite the new "Am I Primary?" task you
> added. Instead, take advantage of the availability group–aware backup priority settings
> in the Back Up Database task. We look at this in more detail in the next section.

➤ For more about availability groups, see Chapter 11, "Implement high availability and disaster recovery."

Maintain SQL Server

This section reviews what you should be doing as a day-to-day database administrator of a SQL Server instance, how to accomplish these tasks, and the built-in tools that SQL Server provides to help you. SQL Server editions above Express edition (because Express has no SQL Server Agent) ship fully featured and ready for you to configure to perform basic maintenance.

> **NOTE**
>
> This section provides ways to accomplish all major maintenance objectives using tools
> built into SQL Server. However, that doesn't mean you shouldn't use third-party tools.

For the most part, the tasks in this section are built into Azure SQL Database and Azure SQL Managed Instance. In some cases, maintenance tasks are completely automated (especially in the case of disaster recovery) or partially automated (in the case of index maintenance). This section focuses on SQL Server instances because the fast evolution of Azure SQL reduces the hands-on maintenance required by DBAs on the PaaS platform.

➤ For more information on Azure SQL Database and Azure SQL Managed Instance, see Chapter 17 and Chapter 18.

Basic care and feeding of SQL Server

You can carry out the regular proactive maintenance of a SQL Server instance by using one or more of the following strategies:

- SQL Server maintenance plans, including the option to use a Maintenance Plan Wizard

- Custom scripting using DMVs and T-SQL or PowerShell commands

- Third-party tools

Each has advantages and disadvantages, and each requires different compromises between ease of setup, customizability, cost, and maintainability.

You can run these strategies via SQL Server Agent jobs. You can configure each one to provide customized activity logging, retention, and the ability to view history in different ways.

Regardless of the strategy or strategies you adopt, whether with built-in or third-party tools, you should accomplish the following as a *bare minimum* on a regular schedule, tailored to meet your SLA and recovery objectives agreed with your organization:

- Back up system and user databases.

    - Full backups for all databases.

    - Transaction log backups for databases not in the simple recovery model.

    - To save space and reduce time to recover using transaction log restores, differential backups between less frequent full backups. Differential backups can also be used for databases in the simple recovery model.

- Implement a retention policy for database backups, if backups are stored locally, by deleting backups after a business-approved amount of time. In the case of tape backups, have a rotation policy instead.

- Implement a retention policy for various SQL Server event logs and history.

    - SSMS maintenance plan log text files can be deleted after a certain amount of time using the Maintenance Cleanup task.

    - Prune the history of backup and restore operations in msdb.

    - Prune the Database Mail log.

    - SQL Server Error Log files are already maintained by SQL Server to a configurable number of log files. (The default is six, which should be increased.)

    - SQL Server Agent job history is also maintained automatically by settings in the SQL Server Agent properties.

- Maintain index and heap health in SQL Server.

    - There are different strategies to reduce fragmentation in clustered and nonclustered indexes.

    - Columnstore indexes also require maintenance via REORGANIZE steps, especially if there is update or delete activity in the table, and fragmentation is measured differently.

    - Monitor heap structures (tables without a clustered index) for excessive forwarding pointers.

- Update statistics.

  - This should accompany INDEX REORGANIZE steps, but not INDEX REBUILD steps. Remember that the INDEX REBUILD command also updates index statistics.

- Check database integrity via DBCC CHECKDB.

- Maintain copies of backed up data in secure off-premises facilities.

  - Storage area network (SAN) replication or another file-level backup system can accomplish this, as can integration with Azure Storage for easy cloud-based backup.

  - Remember that your data-loss tolerance isn't defined by how often you take backups, but by how often those backups get securely off-premises and tested!

What will vary is how often these tasks need to run on each server and database, and what type of backups you need. This section of the chapter walks you through the process of creating tools to manage the previous tasks by writing T-SQL scripts scheduled using SQL Server Agent, using the Maintenance Plan Designer, and using the Maintenance Plan Wizard.

Even though we don't make recommendations regarding third-party tools, we do want to note that many third-party tools do not provide an end-to-end solution for maintaining secure offsite backups (the final item in the previous list), which typically involves coordination with the storage administrators and/or cloud hosting such as Azure Storage. SQL Server Managed Backup to Azure is a full-featured SQL Server backup solution (though not free, it is relatively inexpensive). It is the Microsoft-recommended backup solution for SQL Server instances running on Azure virtual machines (VMs).

If you want to maintain direct control of backing up off-premises, you can use BACKUP ... TO URL statements to write backups directly to Azure Storage, often to complement local backup storage. (Scripting this yourself is free, of course, but Azure Storage is not.) To meet your Recovery Time Objective (RTO) goals, or in the event of an external network failure, you should also maintain local backups within your network for a time. Remember to take regulatory data-retention guidelines into account.

> ➤ For more details about backups, schedules, T-SQL command parameters, and backup strategy, refer to Chapter 10, "Develop, deploy, and manage data recovery."

Use SQL Server maintenance plans

SQL Server maintenance plans are a free, low-cost, low-complexity, visually built option to implement SQL Server maintenance and disaster recovery. The drag-and-drop tasks built into the maintenance plan design surface have some distinct shortcomings that we'll review. You will see differences when creating maintenance plans in SSMS from version to version of SQL Server.

NOTE

Maintenance plans are not supported for SQL Server on Linux, but that doesn't prevent you from targeting a Linux instance from SQL Server on Windows.

The Maintenance Plan Wizard is a step-by-step tour through most of the steps necessary for SQL Server. This wizard guides you through an easy process of creating a maintenance plan with most of the basics, which you can then review with the maintenance plan design surface in SSMS. To begin with a fresh slate, open the **Management** folder in Object Explorer, right-click on **Maintenance Plans**, and select **New Maintenance Plan**. This prepopulates objects for you in the designer, with which we recommend you become familiar.

The Maintenance Plan designer has three main elements: the subplans list, the design surface, and the maintenance plan tasks toolbox. When you open a maintenance plan, the first two elements will be obvious, but the toolbox might not be docked. To display the toolbox and pin it to the side of SSMS, open the **View** menu and select **Toolbox** or press **Ctrl+Alt+X**.

If you have any experience with SSIS, the interface of a maintenance plan will feel very familiar. Behind the scenes, maintenance plans create and store SSIS packages internally.

The tasks in a maintenance plan and the choices in the Maintenance Plan Wizard translate directly to the options you're already familiar with in SQL Server Agent jobs or the options for backups and index maintenance T-SQL commands. For example, the **Run As** option on the first screen of the wizard and in the **Subplan** properties of the designer provides a list of proxies, just as a SQL Server Agent job step does. Instead of using the SQL Server Agent service account, ideally you should choose an SSIS proxy (under the **Management** node) that has access to the SSIS Package Execution subsystem.

NOTE

You may see an explanation screen as the first screen of many wizards in SSMS, and you can choose not to show these explanations in the future.

Cover databases with the maintenance plan

When you select the maintenance tasks that you want the wizard to configure, you'll be able to select the databases you want to run the tasks against. The options are:

- All databases

- System databases

- All user databases

- Specify a list of databases

You also have the option to ignore databases for which the status is not online, which we also recommend.

To isolate the configuration, maintenance, and logging from one another, it is common to create two maintenance plans: one for system databases (master, model, and msdb) and at least one for all user databases, depending on business requirements. The system plan just handles system database backups, and the user plan handles everything else. This ensures that if there are any issues with ongoing changes to the maintenance plan for user databases, crucial system database backups are unaffected.

Inside OUT

Will a SQL Server maintenance plan automatically detect a new database created on SQL Server?

Yes, a maintenance plan can accomplish this if you configure it correctly. This could be invaluable when applications are configured to procedurally create new databases, such as SharePoint.

You should try to configure maintenance plan tasks to use either the **All Databases** or **All User Databases** setting (assuming you have another task that covers system databases). When you select either of these, new databases are automatically included in the maintenance plan. This makes your job as an administrator easier. If you choose a specific fixed list of databases using the **These Databases** option and list, new databases will be ignored, and you will need to remember to add the databases to the maintenance plan.

If you have a database that you don't use anymore, and you no longer want to cover it with a maintenance plan, consider taking the database offline. Then use the option in many maintenance plan tasks to ignore databases where the status is not online.

There is one caveat regarding transaction log backup tasks using either of the two **All** options for databases. After you create a new database in the full recovery model, the backup task that creates transaction log backups in the maintenance plan will attempt to take a transaction log backup, and will fail. This is because a database must first have a full database backup taken before a transaction log backup will succeed. When you create a new database, take a manual full backup, or your maintenance plan will show errors until a full backup is performed. Other databases' transaction log backups will continue to run as usual, even if one or more databases fail.

Maintenance plan tasks

On the first page of the Maintenance Plan Wizard, you have the option to run each task with separate schedules or with a single schedule for the entire plan. We recommend you choose the **Separate Schedules For Each Task** option, or if you're building the maintenance plan in the designer, break activities into multiple subplans, each with its own schedules. This is because some tasks such as index maintenance or database-integrity checks can take a long time to run, and you do not want your backups in serial with those, and then delayed and inconsistently occurring. To work the maintenance plan into your after-hours windows, you will want more scheduling flexibility than a single start time for all tasks to run serially.

The **Select Maintenance Tasks** page of the Maintenance Plan Wizard features a list of all built-in maintenance tasks. In the graphical designer, you have one additional tool to run custom T-SQL scripts named the **Execute T-SQL Statement Task**. You can use this to run your custom maintenance scripting or other administrative scripts. We review this later in this section.

> NOTE
>
> The Maintenance Plan Wizard can create only one copy of each available task. To create two different tasks of the types we'll be looking at in a moment—for example, one for system databases and one for user databases—you will need to use the Maintenance Plan designer in SSMS.

The following sections present the available tasks that you can select from, along with descriptions of what they do.

Check Database Integrity task

The Check Database Integrity task runs DBCC CHECKDB to check for database corruption—a necessary task that you should run periodically. You should run DBCC CHECKDB at least as often as your backup retention plan. For example, if you keep local backups around for one month, you should perform a successful DBCC CHECKDB no fewer than one time per month—and more often, if possible. On large databases, this task could take hours.

> ➤ For more about data corruption and checking database integrity, see Chapter 8.

The options available in the maintenance plan task match the common parameters you would use in the DBCC CHECKDB command. The **Physical Only** check box uses the PHYSICAL_ONLY parameter of DBCC CHECKDB, which limits DBCC CHECKDB to checking physical structures, torn pages, checksum failures, and common hardware failures. It is less comprehensive as a result. However, using PHYSICAL_ONLY can take significantly less time to complete while still detecting the signs of common storage hardware failure.

> NOTE
>
> A common practice when using the PHYSICAL_ONLY option of DBCC CHECKDB or the Check Database Integrity maintenance plan task is to maintain a system in which production databases are restored on a matching nonproduction system, and running a time-consuming full integrity check (without the PHYSICAL_ONLY parameter) to catch any corruption issues. However, there is no substitute for running a full DBCC CHECKDB on your production system.

Shrink Database task

There is no sound reason to ever perform a Shrink Database task on a schedule. A Shrink Database task removes free space from a file and returns it to the OS, causing the file to experience an autogrowth event the next time data is written to it. Do not ever include the Shrink Database task in the maintenance plan.

> ## Inside OUT
>
> **When should you shrink your database?**
>
> If you have deleted a significant portion of data from your database, you can perform a one-off shrink of the database to reclaim drive space, provided that the immediate next step is to rebuild all indexes in that database. A shrink database (or shrink file) task heavily fragments the database, and rebuilding the indexes will remove this fragmentation.

Reorganize Index task

A Reorganize Index task runs an `ALTER INDEX ... REORGANIZE` statement, which reduces index fragmentation but does not update statistics. By default, this task does not reorganize all indexes. If you need to reorganize all indexes on a scheduled basis, you will need to remove the default values on this task. On large databases, this could take hours, but will have less overhead, less query disruption, and finish faster than a Rebuild Index task (discussed next).

Because Reorganize Index is an online operation and reads only one 8-KB data page at a time, it will not take long-term table locks and might block other user queries for only a very short amount of time. Online index operations will consume server resources and generate large amounts of logged transactions.

If you use this task in your maintenance plan, remember to add an Update Statistics task to run immediately after it.

> ➤ The "Rebuild Index task" section covers a method to maintain indexes that are above a certain fragmentation percentage.

Rebuild Index task

More thorough than a Reorganize Index step at removing index fragmentation, this task runs an `ALTER INDEX ... REBUILD` statement and does update statistics. The options available in the **Rebuild Index** dialog box correspond to the options for the `ALTER INDEX ... REBUILD` syntax.

NOTE

At the time of this writing, maintenance plans currently do not support RESUMABLE index rebuilds, which might be necessary for you on very large tables. See Chapter 8 for more information on ALTER INDEX ... REORGANIZE and REBUILD.

With Enterprise edition, you can perform a Rebuild Index step as an online operation, which is not likely to block other user queries like an offline rebuild does. Not all indexes and data types can have an online rebuild performed, so the **Maintenance Plan** dialog box for the Rebuild Index task will ask you what you want to happen.

Rebuilding indexes without the ONLINE option will block other user queries attempting to use that index, and will consume additional server resources. On large tables, this could take hours to finish, and even more without the ONLINE option due to the overhead of managing blocking.

Inside OUT

Do you need to maintain memory-optimized table indexes?

Memory-optimized table indexes do not accumulate fragmentation on-disk and do not need regular maintenance for fragmentation. However, you should routinely monitor the number of distinct values in hash index keys, and adjust the number of buckets in a hash index over time with the ALTER TABLE ... ALTER INDEX ... REBUILD syntax.

Memory-optimized tables are ignored by maintenance plans in SSMS.

Maintain indexes above a certain fragmentation percentage

You can intelligently limit index maintenance to certain thresholds, starting with the options to select between **Fast** (LIMITED), **Sampled**, and **Detailed**. This corresponds to the parameters provided to the structural statistics dynamic management function (DMF), sys.dm_db_index _physical_stats.

NOTE

This task does not operate on columnstore indexes. See Chapter 15, "Understand and design indexes," for more information on maintaining columnstore indexes.

You can configure the Reorganize Index and Rebuild Index tasks to maintain only indexes filtered by percentage of fragmentation and page count, both from sys.dm_db_index_physical _stats, and/or actual index usage (based on the sys.dm_db_index_usage_stats DMF).

The fragmentation threshold is 15 percent by default in the Reorganize Index task, and 30 percent in the Rebuild Index task, but these values are only a guideline.

Other options added to the Reorganize Index and Rebuild Index tasks match the options for the ALTER INDEX ... REORGANIZE, and REBUILD T-SQL commands, covered in detail in Chapter 8.

Update Statistics task

The Update Statistics task runs an UPDATE STATISTICS statement, rebuilding index statistics, which we discuss in Chapter 15. Do not follow an Index Rebuild task with an Update Statistics task for the same objects, because this is redundant work. Updating statistics is an online operation, so it will not block other user queries, but it will consume server resources unnecessarily. This task should finish faster than either a REORGANIZE or REBUILD step. On larger databases, or databases with flash storage, this task can replace more frequent Rebuild Index or Reorganize Index tasks.

Inside OUT

How does auto_create_stats *affect the Update Statistics task in a maintenance plan?*

You should maintain the health of Update Statistics with regularity, even if not in a maintenance plan. When auto_update_stats is enabled, statistics are updated periodically based on usage. Statistics are considered out of date by the Query Optimizer when a ratio of data modifications to rows in the table has been reached. The Query Optimizer checks for and updates the out-of-date statistic before running a query plan. Therefore, auto_update _stats has some small runtime overhead, though the performance benefit of updated statistics usually outweighs this cost. We also recommend enabling auto_update_stats _async, which helps minimize this runtime overhead by updating the statistics after the query is run, instead of before.

Enable these for all user databases unless the application specifically requests that it be disabled, such as is the case with Microsoft SharePoint.

You can also manually identify the date on which any statistics object was last updated by using the sys.dm_db_stats_properties DMF. In your databases, you might see that there are statistics that are quite old. This means they might not have been accessed in a way that prompts the auto_update_stats update and have not had an INDEX REBUILD, which would also update the statistics.

Regularly updating both column and index statistics for a database, if your maintenance window time allows, will almost certainly help. By doing so, you can reduce the number of statistics updates that happen automatically during transactions in regular business hours.

History Cleanup task

This task deletes older rows in msdb tables that contain database backup and restore history, prunes the SQL Server Agent log file, and removes older maintenance plan log records. These are accomplished by running three stored procedures in the msdb database: `dbo.sp_delete_backuphistory`, `dbo.sp_purge_jobhistory`, and `dbo.sp_maintplan_delete_log`, respectively. You should run this task to prevent excessively old data from being retained, according to your environmental data-retention requirements. This will save space and prevent large table sizes from degrading the performance of maintenance tasks. This step should finish quickly and not disrupt user queries. This step does not delete backup files or maintenance plan log files; that is the job of the Maintenance Cleanup task, discussed next.

Maintenance Cleanup task

The Maintenance Cleanup task deletes files from folders and is commonly used to delete old database backup files, using the system stored procedure `master.dbo.xp_delete_file`. You also can use it to clean up the .txt files that maintenance plans write their history to in the SQL Server instance's Log folder. You can configure the task to look for and delete any extension by folder directory, and then specify that subdirectories be included. The date filter uses the Date Modified file attribute (not the Date Created attribute). While this may not be an issue in many cases, it can prevent files from being cleaned up if you are appending data to these files. Combined with the option to create a subdirectory for each database, this means you can create and remove backup files in the folder structure for each database.

> ### NOTE
>
> In the case of maintenance plans, by default, logs are kept in a table, `msdb.dbo.sysmaintplan_log`, as well as in text files in the SQL Server instance default Log folder. Deleting one does not delete the other. You should maintain a retention policy on both sources of the maintenance plan run history.

The Maintenance Cleanup task deletes files only from folders, and thus isn't an option to enforce a retention policy for backups to URL in Azure Storage.

Inside OUT

How do you delete old backups in Azure Storage?

You should use the stored procedure `sp_delete_backup` to clean up file snapshot–based backups created in Azure Storage, which are continuous chains of backups starting from a single full database backup.

To clean up old backups taken to Blob storage using the BACKUP ... TO URL syntax, you should not try to delete the base blob of the backup using Microsoft Azure Storage Explorer or the Azure Storage viewer in SSMS, for example. Aside from the files, there are pointers to the file-snapshots in a file-snapshot backup set that must be deleted as well.

Note also that SQL Server Managed Backup to Azure has its own retention plan, which is currently limited to a maximum of 30 days.

Execute SQL Server Agent Job task

Using this task, you can orchestrate the asynchronous start of another SQL Server Agent job during the maintenance plan, perhaps to start another middle-of-the-night process as soon as possible after maintenance is complete.

Back Up Database (Full, Differential, Transaction Log) task

With this task, you can take a backup of any kind of the specified databases. The options in the **Maintenance Plan** dialog box for the backup are similar to the SSMS **Database Backup** dialog box, plus some minor extra options, including an option to ignore replica priority in an availability group database.

NOTE

The standard extensions for backup files are .bak (full), .dif (differential), and .trn (log), but these are just conventions. You can provide any file extension (or none at all) for your backup types, as long as you are consistent across your entire SQL Server environment with backup file extensions.

The Back Up Database task affords you multiple strategies for backups, including backing up to disk or to Azure Storage via URL as well as to the deprecated tape backup support.

Backing up to URL writes files directly to Azure Storage natively, without the need to install any software or network connections. This was a fairly limited feature before SQL Server 2016, but now can be accomplished via a shared access signature (SAS) credential for secure access to Azure Blob Storage.

> ➤ A step-by-step walk-through is available at *https://learn.microsoft.com/sql/relational -databases/tutorial-use-azure-blob-storage-service-with-sql-server-2016*. Note that this process hasn't changed much since SQL Server 2016.

You can configure disk backups to append multiple database backups multiple times to the same file or files, or create a backup file and a subdirectory for each database per backup. This is generally recommended both for ease of accessing files and for using tools to remove out-of-date files as needed. For backups to disk, we recommend that each database has a subdirectory in the folder location to separate the backup files of databases with potentially different retention plans or recovery strategies. The maintenance plan backup will automatically create subdirectories for new databases, and when performing backups, append a timestamp and a unique string to backup names in the following format:

databasename_backup_yyyy_mm_dd_hhmmss_uniquenumber.bak|dif|trn

We recommend that you select the options for **Verify Backup Integrity**, **CHECKSUM**, and **Compress Backup** for all database types, for all databases.

> ## NOTE
> **If you are backing up your databases to a compressed location, you can still enable database backup compression. While there may be an additional resource cost of compressing the backups, this can save time if you are copying all your backups to a different or central location.**

This is supported even for backups to URL. Keep in mind that the Verify Backup step performs a RESTORE VERIFYONLY statement to examine the backup file and verify that it was valid, complete, and should be restorable. *Should be* is key, because the only way to truly test whether the backup was valid is to test a restore. The RESTORE VERIFYONLY does not actually restore the database backup, but could give you an early heads-up on a potential drive or backup issue, and is always recommended when time permits. The Verify Backup step could significantly increase the duration of the backup, scaling with the size of the database backup, but is time well worth spending in your regular maintenance window.

Execute T-SQL Statement task (not available in the wizard)

This task can run T-SQL statements against any SQL Server connection, with a configurable time-out. A simple text box accepts T-SQL statements. Because of its simplicity, we recommend that instead of pasting lengthy commands, you reference a stored procedure. This would be easier to maintain and potentially keep in source control by developing the stored procedure in other tools. You may find it useful to keep this and other stored procedures in a database specifically dedicated to database administration tasks.

Maintenance plan report options

By default, maintenance plans create a report in two places to record the history for each time a subplan runs. Logs are kept in a table, msdb.dbo.sysmaintplan_log, as well as in .txt files in the SQL Server instance default Log folder. You can also choose the **Email Report** option in the Maintenance Plan Wizard, which adds a Notify Operator task.

Build maintenance plans using the Maintenance Plan designer in SSMS

Due to the nature of wizards, there are some inherent issues with configuring a robust maintenance solution that covers all the needs of your databases with the Maintenance Plan Wizard.
Fortunately, the SSMS Maintenance Plan designer gives you the ability to set up your task run
order and precedence constraints as well as to maintain multiple subplan schedules within a
maintenance plan. Figure 9-2 displays a sample maintenance plan.

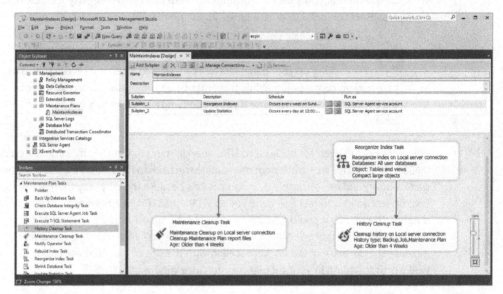

Figure 9-2 A sample maintenance plan for user databases has been created, with multiple subplans,
each running on a different schedule.

In Figure 9-2 , a sample maintenance plan for user databases has been created, with multiple
subplans, each running on a different schedule. Subplan_1 runs every week on Sunday and
starts with the Reorganize Index Task. Subplan_2 runs the Update Statistics Task every day.
Looking at Subplan_1, the first task is a Reorganize Index Task. Both the Maintenance Cleanup
Task and History Output Task run after the Reorganize Index Task.

When you save the maintenance plan, each of the subplans in the maintenance plan will become
a SQL Server Agent job with the naming convention *maintenance plan name.subplan name*.

NOTE

**When you save a maintenance plan, the job(s) it creates might be owned by your personal
login to the SQL Server. Be aware that if your account becomes disabled or locked out, this
will prevent the SQL Server Agent job from running. To avoid this, it would be better to
have all maintenance plans owned by an account that is not tied to a specific user.**

At the top of the Maintenance Plan designer window is where the subplans are listed. Initially, there will be just one plan, called Subplan_1. You should break down the tasks that will be accomplished in the subplan by the schedules they will follow, and name them accordingly. You can add subplans and manage their schedules in the Maintenance Plan designer window. Note that you should not make changes to the SQL Server Agent jobs after they've been created; otherwise, the next time you edit the maintenance plan, your changes will most likely be overwritten.

The large gray area beneath the subplan list is the design surface for maintenance plans—a graphical, drag-and-drop interface. To add tasks to a subplan, you can drag a task from the toolbox to the design surface. To serialize the running of multiple tasks, select one, and then select the green arrow beneath the box, dragging it to the task that should follow. You can create a long string of sequential activities or a wide set of parallel-running activities, similar to designing SSIS packages.

NOTE

Each Maintenance Plan task has a View T-SQL button that shows you the exact T-SQL that will be run to perform the maintenance tasks. You can use this to learn the commands for maintenance tasks so you can make your own customized plans, which we talk about in the next section.

When not to use SQL Server maintenance plans

Personal preference, of course, is a fine enough reason not to use built-in maintenance plans. You can write your own, as long as your library of scripts or third-party tools accomplishes the necessary maintenance tasks with consistency, configurability, and good logging for review.

For SQL Server instances with manageable maintenance windows, maintenance plans will meet your needs if the schedules are set up appropriately. You can create a variety of maintenance plans to cover databases with various levels of importance or availability based on business requirements (with the caveat of not being able to detect new databases). For very large databases or databases with 24×7 availability requirements, more granularity for maintenance operations will likely be necessary.

Not every business has the luxury of having all night and/or all weekend to perform maintenance outside of business hours. When you become familiar with the T-SQL commands and their various options, you can be creative to overcome tight scheduling, crowded maintenance windows, very large databases, or other maintenance plan complications.

After reviewing the capabilities of the Back Up Database and Rebuild Index tasks, you should consider maintenance plans more full-featured and capable of handling the bulk of maintenance, even on larger databases with tight schedules. Ultimately, the success of maintenance plans or custom scripts depends on your understanding of the various options available for the seven core maintenance tasks listed earlier in this chapter and elsewhere in this book.

Back up availability groups using a secondary replica

This section may look out of place here, but rest assured it makes sense. We have been looking at single-instance SQL Server maintenance tasks up to now, but automation applies to availability groups as well. Even maintenance plans can be used successfully with availability groups.

> ➤ You can read more about availability groups in Chapter 2, "Introduction to database server components," and Chapter 11.

One of the many useful features in availability groups is the ability to utilize read-only secondary replicas for remote backups. Performing backups on a secondary replica, including a geographically separated replica, introduces complexity but has a big advantage. Backups do not take locks and will never block a user query, but they will incur significant CPU, memory, and I/O overhead. Backups can slow database response, so on servers with large databases and/or busy 24×7 utilization, it might be helpful, and in some cases necessary, to find alternative strategies to backups. Taking database backups on secondary replicas is one of the alternatives to move the resource expense of backups off the primary replica.

Understand backup priority values

In SSMS, in Object Explorer, expand the **Always On High Availability** node for the instance of the primary replica, and then the **Availability Groups** node. Right-click the availability group you want to view, select **Properties**, and look at the **Backup Preferences** page. It's important to understand the priority values and how they interact with various backup tasks.

The default option is **Prefer Secondary**, which specifies that backups occur on the secondary replica first or, if it is not available, on the primary replica. You then can provide priority values (0 to 100, where 100 is highest) to decide which of the multiple secondary replicas should be the preferred backup location. The values apply to both full and transaction log backups.

Other self-explanatory options include **Primary**, **Secondary Only**, and **Any Replica**, which uses the priority values to decide which replica is preferred for the backups. When failing over to another replica, you will need to review and script the changes to the backup priority. Your planned failover scripts should include the reassignment of backup priority values.

This Backup Preferences page affects only backup systems or scripts that are aware of the backup preferences. For example, in SSMS, in Object Explorer, right-click a database, select **Tasks** on the shortcut menu, and then **Backup**. The dialog box that opens takes a backup of a database but does not include any availability groups–aware settings. On the other hand, the Back Up Database task in SQL Server maintenance plans is aware of availability group backup priority value settings.

You are limited to taking full copy-only database backups and transaction log backups on readable secondary replica databases. When including databases in an availability group, the maintenance plan Back Up Database task will warn you if you are attempting to configure a full database backup without a copy-only check or differential backup, or if you select the **For availability databases, ignore Replica Priority for Backup and Backup on Primary Settings** check box. If this is misconfigured, it is possible to create a maintenance plan that will run but not create backups of databases in an availability group.

> ➤ For more information on using replica backup priorities, visit *https://learn.microsoft.com /sql/database-engine/availability-groups/windows/active-secondaries-backup-on-secondary -replicas-always-on-availability-groups* and *https://learn.microsoft.com/sql/database-engine /availability-groups/windows/configure-backup-on-availability-replicas-sql-server.*

Use replica backup priority in your backup schedules

If you attempt to configure a full database backup without copy-only or a differential backup on a secondary node, you will see the warning in the Back Up Database task, "This backup type is not supported on a secondary replica and this task will fail if the task runs on a secondary replica." If you select the **Ignore Replica Priority** check box, the warning will read, "Note: Ignoring the backup priority and availability group settings may result in simultaneous parallel backups if the maintenance plan is cloned on all replicas."

Maintenance plans should run on a schedule on all availability group replicas. The priority values for backups can cause a backup not to be taken on a primary or nonpreferred secondary replica, but the maintenance plan backup task will start and complete as usual. The maintenance plans will use the backup priority values and do not need to be configured when different replicas in the availability group become primary.

You can still take a manual backup of any type of the databases and bypass the availability group backup preferences. In fact, your backup strategy might include intentionally taking full backups in more than one node of a geographically dispersed availability group.

If you are not using SQL Server maintenance plans or scripting to take backups, be aware that not all third-party backup solutions are aware of availability group backup preferences or even availability groups in general. Maintenance plans in SSMS are aware of these backup preferences, and your custom scripting can be, too, via the scalar function `sys.fn_hadr_backup _is_preferred_replica`. This function returns a 0 or 1, based on whether the current SQL Server instance is operating as the preferred backup.

Inside OUT

How do you prevent a broken chain when taking backups on secondary replicas?

Taking backups of the same database on multiple servers could lead to some parts of a backup recovery chain being stored on different servers. If your FULL backups were stored on Server A, and your DIFF and LOG backups were stored on Server B, you would have to combine backups from both Server A and Server B to do a point-in-time restore. While that is possible, it

CHAPTER 9

may cost precious time in the case of disaster recovery. The solution to this is rather obvious: Always ensure that backups are copied securely to the same location, from one datacenter or secured site to another, which is likely where your availability group replicas are.

Just as you would copy your backups of a standalone SQL Server instance to another location, you must copy your backups of availability group databases off-premises, ideally to each other. You can accomplish this with two strategies.

Copy the backups taken on the secondary node to the primary regularly, and make sure you maintain a chain of transaction log backups together with their root full and/or differential backups, regardless of where the backups were taken. You should keep a complete chain intact in multiple locations.

Strategies for administering multiple SQL Servers

There are options for creating orchestration in SQL Server to allow for a multiplication and standardization of SQL Server DBA effort across multiple servers. The potential to set up SQL Server Agent jobs that are run simultaneously on multiple servers is powerful, especially for custom-developed scripts to gather and report information back to a central SQL Server.

➤ You should be aware of the Registered Servers and Central Management Server SSMS features discussed in Chapter 1, "Get started with SQL Server tools."

Master/Target servers for SQL Agent jobs

Master/Target (MSX/TSX) servers are built into SQL Server Agent to help DBAs who want to manage identical jobs across multiple SQL Server instances. This feature has been in the product since SQL Server 7.0, but many DBAs are unaware of the convenience that it can deliver. There is no doubt that the feature is useful and works seamlessly with technologies it could not have foreseen, including availability groups (more on that later).

You can designate one SQL Server as a Master server (MSX), set up multiserver jobs on that server, and configure each instance to have its SQL Server Agent jobs remotely managed into a Target server (TSX). The MSX cannot be a TSX of itself, so using a separate production server to orchestrate multiserver administration of SQL Server Agent jobs is necessary. The MSX should be a production environment server that does not host performance-sensitive production workloads.

Other considerations for the MSX include the following:

- Of the servers you have available, choose the most recent version of SQL Server for the MSX. You can communicate with a TSX within two versions of the MSX. For instance, if you have a SQL Server 2022 MSX, the TSX can be running SQL Server 2017, SQL Server 2019, or SQL Server 2022.

- Each TSX can have only one MSX.

- Before changing the name of a TSX, first defect it from the MSX and then reenlist it. However, we recommend modifying a TSX name using DNS instead.

- Do not use a built-in account for the SQL Server Agent service account on all servers; instead, use a domain service account, as recommended earlier in this chapter in the "Understand job step security" section.

- While Azure SQL Managed Instance has many of the features of SQL Agent, multiserver administration is not supported.

Create an MSX/TSX with SSMS

In SSMS, in Object Explorer, right-click **SQL Server Agent**, select **Multi Server Administration**, and then select **Make This A Master** to launch the Master Server Wizard. The wizard first sets up a special operator just for running multiserver jobs; this operator is created for you and named MSXOperator. You can specify only one operator to run multiserver jobs, so think carefully about who should be notified about these jobs. Specify the email address. As always with operators, it's best not to use an individual's email addresses, but to use an email distribution group, instead.

Next, the wizard presents locally registered and Central Management–registered servers so you can select them as targets for the MSX. Select the target servers from the list or, at the bottom, select **Add Connection** and add servers not registered in your list.

When you are finished with the wizard, the labels in Object Explorer will be different for both master and target SQL Server Agents. Similarly, on the MSX, under **SQL Server Agent** in Object Explorer, you will see two new subfolders under Jobs: **Local Jobs** and **Multi-Server Jobs**.

By default, SSL encryption is used between the servers, but you can change this through a registry setting. You should not need to change it, however, because encrypted communication between the servers is recommended, even on your internal networks. You will need to install an SSL certificate on the server before using it through the wizard.

> ➤ If you cannot use SSL but need to secure the connection between a TSX and an MSX, see *https://learn.microsoft.com/sql/ssms/agent/set-encryption-options-on-target-servers* for the exact entries.

Although we do not recommend it, you can disable the encryption of an MSX/TSX by changing the registry set to not use encryption. The registry key HKEY_LOCAL_MACHINE\SOFTWARE\Microsoft \Microsoft SQL Server\instance\SQLServerAgent\MSxEncryptChannelOptions is by default 2, which means all communication is encrypted. Changing this to 0 on all servers removes encryption.

Manage multiserver (MSX/TSX) administration

To manage SQL Server Agent jobs in a multiserver environment, set up the job the same way you would any other job on the MSX. Then, navigate to the targets page on the job, which outside of a multiserver environment has no use. From there, select the **Target Multiple Servers** option button; then select the servers on which the job should run. In the background, code is run to send the jobs to the TSX.

Any jobs with steps that use proxies will need the proxy accounts to have access to the TSX, and a proxy by that same name on the TSX. Otherwise, the job will not find a proxy on the TSX. By default, matching proxy names from MSX to TSX isn't allowed, because of the potential for malicious action. This must be enabled via the registry on the TSX.

> ➤ For more information, visit *https://learn.microsoft.com/sql/ssms/agent/troubleshoot -multiserver-jobs-that-use-proxies.*

On a TSX, jobs appear in the SQL Server Agent, in the Jobs folder, but you can't edit them.

Sometimes, synchronizing job definitions to the TSX will not be queued up and will not post to a server. In this case, issue the following command, but be aware that this will delete and re-create any jobs specified for the target server, therefore cancelling those jobs on the TSX:

```
EXEC msdb.dbo.sp_resync_targetserver '<Target Server Name>';
```

Most other issues with multiserver jobs are solved by defecting the TSX and then adding it again.

Manage multiserver administration in availability groups

MSX/TSX works with availability groups and can be quite useful for ensuring that jobs stay synchronized across servers. MSX/TSX data is stored in system tables in the msdb database, which cannot be part of an availability group.

While SQL Server 2022 allows you to set up the MSX feature in a contained availability group, it is not recommended due to the additional complexity in managing SQL Server Agent jobs. Thus, you should not have the MSX on a SQL Server instance in the availability group, because this would limit your ability to failover and use SQL Server Agent Multiserver Administration. You would lose your ability to orchestrate jobs across the target servers if one of the nodes in your availability group was unreachable, compromising your failover state. Instead, consider other high-availability solutions for the MSX.

Using MSX/TSX for availability group SQL Server Agents doesn't change the need to set up the "Am I Primary?" logic in step 1 of any job that should run only on a SQL Server instance that currently hosts the primary replica.

> ➤ For a code sample, refer to the section "SQL Server Agent job considerations when using availability groups" earlier in this chapter.

SQL Server Agent event forwarding

Event forwarding occurs when one central Windows server receives the SQL Server events of many. The server that is the destination of many other servers' forwarded events might handle a heavy workload, especially network traffic. The destination server should be a production-environment server that does not host performance-sensitive production workloads. You can refer to this server as the *alerts management server*.

Event forwarding allows the Windows Event Viewer to be a single-pane view of events on many instances of SQL Server. Further, it allows for alerts on the alerts management server to prompt a response to the originating server, via SQL Server Agent alerts. Forwarded errors arrive in the Windows Application Event Log, not the SQL Server Error Log. Because of this, the SQL Server Agent service account needs to be a local Windows administrator.

Typically, this setup is the same server as your MSX/TSX server; in fact, the features work together. If your MSX and alerts management server are on separate SQL Server instances, you will not have the ability to run a job to respond to specific events.

Set up event forwarding

You configure event forwarding in the SQL Server Agent Properties dialog box. In SSMS, open the **SQL Server Agent Properties** dialog box and choose the **Advanced** page. In the **SQL Server Event Forwarding** section, select the **Forward Events to a Different Server** check box. In the text box, type the name of the alerts management server. Be aware that the alerts management server that receives forwarded events must be the SQL Server default instance of a server. (In other words, it cannot be a named instance.)

You can also choose whether to send all events or only unhandled alerts that have not been handled by local alerts on each SQL Server instance. You can then specify a minimum error severity to be forwarded. Choose a severity level that matches your needs, keeping in mind the caveat of nuisance severity errors.

> ➤ For information about alerts and error severity, refer to the section "Foundations of SQL Server automated administration" earlier in this chapter.

Policy-based management

Policy-based management (PBM) is a powerful tool for enforcing rules for configuration settings, options for databases and servers, security principals, table design, even database object naming conventions. As of this writing, this feature does not yet apply to Azure SQL Database.

PBM is structured around policies. Policies contain a single condition, which is a Boolean expression. The condition expression is evaluated against properties and settings of destination objects, such as the server itself, a database, a table, or an index.

For example, you might set up a condition around the `AdHocRemoteQueries` server-level setting.

SQL Server has a large list of facet properties built into it, such as `AdHocRemoveQueriesEnabled` in the Surface Area Configuration facet. (As discussed in Chapter 4, this facet contains a number of security-sensitive features, many—but not all—of which we recommend you disable unless needed.) To check that this Surface Area Configuration option is always turned off, create an expression that checks whether `AdHocRemoveQueriesEnabled` can be evaluated to `Enabled = False`.

Policies can contain only one condition, but you can configure many different expressions, any one of which could initiate the policy. You can, for example, create a PBM policy called "Configuration Settings," a PBM condition called "Settings That Should be Disabled," and a list of expressions, each of which evaluates a different Surface Area Configuration option.

To access a list of PBM facets, right-click the server name in **Object Explorer** and select **Facets**. This opens the SSMS **View Facets** dialog box; select **Export Current State as Policy** to ease the implementation of many configuration options into policy. You can apply the resulting settings to the local server as a policy right away, or export them as .xml, which then can be imported as a new policy.

PBM is built into SSMS, accessible via the **Policy Management** subfolder in the **Management** folder. To export a policy, in SSMS, in Object Explorer, in the **Policy Management** folder, right-click a policy, choose **Export Policy**, and follow the prompts. To import a policy, right-click on the **Policies** folder, choose **Import Policy**, and follow the prompts.

Evaluate policies and gather compliance data

After you create a policy, you have multiple options for when to evaluate it: on demand (manually); on a schedule; and continuously, which either logs or blocks policy violations.

SQL Server maintains a history of all policy evaluations in a policy history log, which is available within SSMS. To access it, expand the **Management** folder for the instance, right-click **Policy Management**, and select **View History** on the shortcut menu.

In the **System Policies** subfolder, you'll find 14 prebuilt policies for checking the health of availability groups, and two more for the SQL Server Managed Backup feature, first introduced in SQL Server 2014. The SQL Server Managed Backup policies begin with `SmartAdmin`.

For example, after creating a policy, you can configure it with On Demand Evaluation Mode (see the code examples at the end of this section), and then test it by enabling the `AdHocRemoteQueries` setting in the Surface Area Configuration facet. You can also enable it using T-SQL with the following command:

```
EXEC sp_configure 'Ad Hoc Distributed Queries', 1;
GO
RECONFIGURE;
GO
```

A message will immediately appear in the SQL Server Error Log stating, "Policy 'Keep AdHoc RemoteQueries Disabled' has been violated by target 'SQLSERVER:\SQL*servername**instancename*'," accompanied by a severity 16 error 34053 message.

The on-demand Evaluate mode gives the administrator an immediate report of all policy compliance. From the **Evaluate Policies** window—which you access by expanding **Policy Management**, right-clicking **Policies**, and choosing **Evaluate**—you can view any number of policies. Should any expressions fail, the policy will display a red X beside it. In this example, evaluating the policy with the AdHocRemoteQueries facet enabled displays an error message and provides you with the ability to apply the change to bring the servers in line with policy.

In the **Target Details** pane of the **Evaluate Policies** window, you can select **Details** to start an analysis of all expression evaluations in the condition.

You can have the policies run automatically by either defining a schedule or having the policy evaluated in response to an action. To select either of these options, go to **Policy Management**, expand the list, and choose **Policies**. To set up an evaluation method for a specific policy, right-click the policy and select **Properties**. Then, in the **Evaluation Mode** drop-down near the bottom of the window, select **On Schedule**. You will get the option to set up the schedule in the same window. The scheduled Evaluate mode generates only SQL Server Error Log activity.

The other option in the drop-down is **On Demand**. This option makes it possible for you to create a policy that prevents developers or other administrations from making DDL changes that violate condition expressions. Not all facet expressions allow for the On Change: Prevent Evaluation mode.

This is accomplished by rolling back the transaction that contains the violating action. As with all rollbacks, this transaction could contain other statements and could cause a database change deployment to fail in a manner that could complicate your change process. In many cases, it may be preferable to have rules automated so that the developers can quickly see if their changes don't meet coding standards. Not only can this save time in the development and QA process, but it removes the burden of enforcing these changes from the DBA. Administrators and database developers should be aware of the potential impact to database deployments. You should limit the use of the On Change: Prevent Evaluation mode to security-related or stability-related properties in both production and QA environments, such as the following:

- **Server security.** @CrossDBOwnershipChainingEnabled

  Enforce the evaluation of this to False unless this is part of application security design.

- **Server security.** @PublicServerRoleIsGrantedPermissions

  Enforce the evaluation of this setting to False in any circumstance.

- **Login.** @PasswordPolicyEnforced

  Enforce the evaluation of this setting to True for all logins.

CHAPTER 9

- **Certificate.** `@ExpirationDate`

  Enforce that this date is not within a certain time frame in the future (six months), in every database (sample code to follow).

- **Database.** `@AutoShrink`

  Enforce the evaluation of this setting to `False` in all databases.

- **Database.** `@AutoClose`

  Enforce the evaluation of this setting to `False` in all databases.

Samples

You can script policies to T-SQL for application to multiple servers, though be wary of applying policies for production systems to development systems, and vice versa. You can use a T-SQL script to create the two aforementioned samples. This script is available in the accompanying downloads for this book.

The first part of the script creates a sample policy to keep the Surface Area Configuration option `AdHocRemoteQueries` turned off (it will be evaluated on demand). The result sets returned by these queries contain only the integer IDs of new policy objects that have been created.

The second part of the script verifies whether any non-system certificates have an expiration in the next six months and, if so, fail the policy. The policy will also ignore any certificates with ## in the name. These are built into SQL Server, are for internal use only, are generated when SQL Server is installed, and cannot be modified. Also keep in mind that certificates used for transparent data encryption (TDE) will continue to work just fine after expiration, so there's no cause for concern if they show up in this list.

The result sets returned by these queries contain only the integer IDs of new policy objects that have been created.

Use PowerShell to automate SQL Server administration

SQL Server has supported close integration with PowerShell for over a decade. PowerShell is a robust shell scripting language that you can use to perform many administrative tasks. It was first released in 2006, has been integrated with SQL Server since 2008, and was made open source and cross-platform in 2016.

The goal of this section is not to list every possible interaction of PowerShell with SQL Server, Azure, or availability groups, but to provide instructional, realistic samples that will help you to learn the PowerShell language and add it to your DBA toolbox. All the scripts in this section are available in the accompanying downloads for this book.

➤ We review several useful PowerShell scripts for Azure SQL Database interaction in Chapter 17.

IT professionals in all walks of life are learning PowerShell to ease their administrative tasks with various technologies, not just SQL Server on Windows and Linux, but Active Directory, Machine Learning, Azure, Office 365, SharePoint, Exchange, and even Office products like Microsoft Excel. There is very little in the Microsoft stack for which PowerShell cannot help. Developers have created third-party downloadable modules, available for download in the PowerShell Gallery (*https://powershellgallery.com*), to further enhance PowerShell's ability to interact even with non-Microsoft platforms such as Amazon Web Services, Slack, Internet of Things (IoT) devices, Linux, and more.

Inside OUT

How do you make better use of PowerShell?

If you'd like to adopt more PowerShell for administration in your database, you'll need more than the samples in this chapter, though we selected these because we feel they are good learning examples.

Consider adding the open-source suite of PowerShell cmdlets, dbatools, which is available to download from the PowerShell Gallery or directly from *https://dbatools.io*. This suite has furthered the development of helpful PowerShell cmdlets for automating high availability, security migrations, backups, and more. You can read more in Chrissy LeMaire et al., *Learn dbatools in a Month of Lunches* (Manning Publications, 2022).

There are even scenarios for which PowerShell fills feature gaps in configuration panels and UI, necessitating some basic literacy for PowerShell on the part of the modern system administrator, DBA, or developer. PowerShell is especially useful when building code to automate the failover of Windows Server failover clusters or for interacting with DNS. You also can use PowerShell remoting to manage multiple Windows servers and SQL Server instances from a single command prompt.

PowerShell is a full-featured shell where you can still manage the file system and launch applications you're familiar with as a Windows or Linux user—for example, `ping`, `ipconfig`, `ifconfig`, `telnet`, `net start`, `regedit`, `notepad`, `sqlcmd`, and even `shutdown`.

NOTE

You should get into the habit of using the PowerShell console window directly, as well as in Visual Studio Code or Azure Data Studio with PowerShell extensions.

You can also start a PowerShell console from within SSMS; simply right-click most folders and select **Launch PowerShell** on the shortcut menu.

CHAPTER 9

➤ Follow the instructions in "Install the PowerShell SQLServer module" later in this section before using this feature.

You might find the Visual Studio Code or Azure Data Studio environments more conducive to authoring multiline PowerShell scripts, especially if you have any prior familiarity with Visual Studio or Visual Studio Code.

PowerShell basics

Cmdlets for PowerShell follow a pattern of *verb-noun*. This helps provide ease and consistency when trying to find cmdlets to run your desired task.

For database administration tasks, we will become familiar with cmdlets and using SQL Server Management Objects (SMO). PowerShell for SQL Server is installed separately from SQL Server Setup or the SSMS installation and can be installed from the PowerShell Gallery. While this functionality is available in SSMS 17.0 going forward, you should use the most current release of SSMS available. At the time of writing this book, SSMS 19.0 is the most current version. We will demonstrate how to install and check the current version of the SQLServer module.

For each cmdlet, there is a built-in way to receive a description of the cmdlet and see all the parameters along with descriptions and examples (if provided by the author). Let's try it on Invoke-Sqlcmd, a cmdlet that runs a T-SQL query using statements supported by the sqlcmd command.

First, run the cmdlet Update-Help. This command updates the extensive and helpful local help files for PowerShell and installed modules.

NOTE

The Visual Studio Code shortcuts for running scripts are different from SSMS, and you need to be aware of the following:

- In SSMS, pressing F5 runs the entire script if no text is highlighted, or just the highlighted text if any is selected. Pressing Ctrl+E does the same by default.
- In Visual Studio Code, pressing F5 saves and then runs the entire script file, regardless of whether any code is highlighted. Pressing F8 runs only highlighted code.

Install the PowerShell SQLServer module

You must be running at least Windows PowerShell 5.0 on Windows to download modules from the PowerShell Gallery. On Linux you need PowerShell 7. (Note that PowerShell 7 also runs on Windows and macOS.) To determine the version of PowerShell on your system, run the following code in the PowerShell window:

```
$PSVersionTable
```

The PSVersion value contains the current installed version of PowerShell.

Inside OUT

How do you install Windows PowerShell and PowerShell 7?

The latest version of Windows PowerShell, version 5.1, ships in every supported version of Windows. Windows 10 and higher and Windows Server 2016 and higher already have PowerShell 5.0 or 5.1 installed. To upgrade your version of PowerShell to 5.1, you should install the latest version of Windows Management Framework 5.1, which includes PowerShell.

Visit *https://learn.microsoft.com/powershell/scripting/install/installing-windows-powershell* for links to the current download by OS to upgrade your Windows PowerShell. Note that installing this package will require you to reboot your server or workstation.

To install the newer PowerShell 7 for Windows, Linux, and macOS, visit *https://learn.microsoft .com/powershell*. While the SQLServer PowerShell module will install correctly on PowerShell 7 on macOS and Linux, some of the cmdlets may not work as expected due to underlying OS dependencies.

There are many PowerShell modules available that can be useful for managing SQL Server. However, before installing these modules, you should confirm that the modules come from a trusted source. You should also test PowerShell, including modules, in a lower environment so you can confirm that PowerShell will not negatively affect your environment. In addition, you may want to discuss the use of PowerShell and any specific modules with your internal security team.

To install the latest version of the SQLServer module, use the following code on an Internet-connected device, running the PowerShell console or Visual Studio Code in administrator mode:

```
Install-Module -Name SQLServer -Force -AllowClobber
```

In the preceding script, we used a few handy parameters. Let's review them:

- **-Name.** Specifies the unique name of the module you want.

- **-Force.** Prevents you from having to answer Yes to confirm you want to download.

- **-AllowClobber.** Allows this module to overwrite cmdlet aliases already in place. Without AllowClobber, the installation will fail if it finds that the new module contains commands with the same name as existing commands.

To find the current installed versions of the SQLServer PowerShell module, as well as other SQL modules (including SQLPS), use the following:

```
Get-Module -ListAvailable -Name "sql*" | Select-Object Name, Version, RootModule
```

To access the help information for any cmdlet, use the `Get-Help` cmdlet. Here are some examples:

```
#Basic Reference
Get-Help Invoke-SqlCmd
#See actual examples of code use
Get-Help Invoke-SqlCmd - Examples
#All cmdlets that match a wildcard search
Get-Help -Name "*Backup*database*"
```

Note that the # character begins a single-line comment in PowerShell code. Alternatively, you can use <# and #> to enclose and declare a multiline comment block.

Offline installation

To install the module on a server or workstation that is not Internet-connected or cannot reach the PowerShell Gallery, go to a workstation that can reach the PowerShell Gallery and has at least Windows PowerShell 5.0 or PowerShell 7. Then, use the following command to download the module, making sure to choose a folder that exists on your machine.

```
Save-Module -Name SQLServer -LiteralPath "C:\temp\"
```

Next, copy the entire C:*temp*\SqlServer\ folder to the machine that cannot reach the Power-Shell Gallery to a path that is in the list of `PSModule` paths. The potential paths for modules list is stored in a `PSModulePath` environment variable, which you can view in Windows System Properties, or more easily with this PowerShell script:

```
$env:PSModulePath.replace(";","`n"")
```

The default folder for the module downloaded from the gallery would likely be C:\Program Files\WindowsPowerShell\Modules on Windows, or /usr/local/share/powershell/Modules on Linux. Verify that this path is available or choose another `PSModule` folder, and then copy the downloaded SQLServer folder there. The following script adds the `SQLServer` module, and then shows a list of all available modules on your workstation:

```
Import-Module SQLServer
Get-Module
```

> **NOTE**
>
> When writing code for readability, we recommend you use the actual cmdlet names. With PowerShell, there are many shorthand and shortcuts possible, but you should try to write easy-to-read code that is approachable and maintainable for the next administrator.

Use PowerShell with SQL Server

PowerShell can interact with SQL Server instances all the way back to SQL Server 2000 (with some limitations in earlier versions). This book is not a good medium to demonstrate the full capability that PowerShell can bring to your regular DBA tasks, nor should it try to detail all the possibilities. Nonetheless, here are some selected, representative, but simple examples.

Backup-SqlDatabase

Let's learn about some more basics and syntax of PowerShell via the `Backup-SqlDatabase` cmdlet. With this PowerShell cmdlet, you have access to the same parameters as the T-SQL command BACKUP DATABASE.

Again, use PowerShell's built-in help files to see full syntax and examples, many of which will be familiar to you if you have a good understanding of the BACKUP DATABASE options.

```
Get-Help Backup-SqlDatabase -Examples
```

Here is an example of how to back up all databases on a local SQL Server instance, providing the backup path, and including a subfolder with the database's name. If you are using a Windows computer, the default execution policy is `RemoteSigned`. If you would like to verify your execution policy before running the following script, you can run `Get-ExecutionPolicy`. If your policy is not set to `RemoteSigned`, you can run the following: `Set-ExecutionPolicy -ExecutionPolicy RemoteSigned -Scope LocalMachine`. The script also adds the current date and time to the name of the backup file:

```
#Backup all databases (except for tempdb)
$instanceName = "localhost" #set instance to back up
$path = "F:\Backup"
Get-SqlDatabase -ServerInstance $instanceName | `
    Where-Object { $_.Name -ne 'tempdb' } | `
    ForEach-Object {
    Backup-SqlDatabase -DatabaseObject $_ `
    -BackupAction "Database" `
    -CompressionOption On `
    -BackupFile "$($path)\$($_.Name)\$($_.Name)_$(`
        Get-Date -Format "yyyyMMdd")_$(`
        Get-Date -Format "HHmmss_FFFF").bak" `
    -Script #The -Script generates T-SQL, but does not execute
}
```

Here are some notes about this script:

- Adding the `-Script` parameter to this and many other cmdlets outputs only the T-SQL code, split by G0 batch separators; it does not actually perform the operation.

- The back tick, or grave accent (`` ` ``) symbol (below the tilde on most standard keyboards), is a line extension operator. Adding the `` ` `` character to the end of a line gives you the ability to display long commands, such as in the previous example, over multiple lines.

- The pipe character (|) is an important concept in PowerShell to grasp. It passes the output of one cmdlet to the next. In the previous script, the list of databases is passed as an array from `Get-SQLDatabase` to `Where-Object`, which filters the array and passes it to `ForEach-Object`, which loops through each value in the array.

Remove-Item

Let's learn some more about common PowerShell syntax parameters. You can use the Remove-Item cmdlet to write your own retention policy to delete old files, including backup files, stored locally. Remember to coordinate the removal of old local backups with your off-premises strategy that keeps backups safely in a different location.

In this script, we use the Get-ChildItem cmdlet to Recurse through a subfolder, ignore folders, and select only files that are more than $RetentionDays old and have a file extension in a list we provide:

```
$path = "F:\Backup\"
$RetentionDays = 1
$BackupFileExtensions = ".bak", ".trn", ".dif"
Get-ChildItem -Path $path -Recurse | `
    Where-Object { !$_.PSIsContainer `
        -and $_.CreationTime -lt (get-date).AddDays(-$RetentionDays) `
        -and ($_.Extension -In $BackupFileExtensions) `
        } | Remove-Item -WhatIf
```

Here are some notes about this script:

- The $RetentionDays parameter is a positive value, but a negative is added to it as part of the AddDays() method to subtract the number of retention days from the current date (specified with get-date).

- The Get-ChildItem cmdlet gathers a list of objects from the provided path, including files and folders. The -Recurse parameter of Get-ChildItem causes the cmdlet to include subfolders.

- The $_ syntax is used to accept the data from the object before the previous pipe character (|). In this example, the objects discovered by Get-ChildItem are passed to the Where-Object, which filters the objects and passes that data to Remove-Item.

- Adding the -WhatIf parameter to this and many other cmdlets does not actually perform the operation, but provides a verbose summary of the action, instead. For example, rather than deleting old backup files, this PowerShell script returns something similar to the following sample:

```
What if: Performing the operation "Remove File" on target "F:\Backup\backup_
test_202202010200.bak".
```

Invoke-Sqlcmd

The Invoke-Sqlcmd cmdlet can run T-SQL commands, including on remote SQL Server instances and Azure SQL databases. Invoke-Sqlcmd can run batch file scripts that used to be run by sqlcmd. Use Invoke-Sqlcmd when no cmdlet exists to return the same data for which you're already looking. In this script, we connect to a database in Azure SQL Database and run a query to see current sessions:

```
$instanceName = "azure-databasename.database.windows.net"
Invoke-Sqlcmd -Database master -ServerInstance $instanceName `
-Query "select * from sys.dm_exec_sessions" | `
Format-Table | Out-File -FilePath "C:\Temp\Sessions.txt" -Append
```

NOTE

If you see the error message "Could not load file or assembly 'Microsoft.SqlServer .BatchParser'," find step-by-step instructions to resolve it at *https://social.technet.microsoft .com/wiki/contents/articles/35832.sql-server-troubleshooting-could-not-load-file-or -assembly-microsoft-sqlserver-batchparser.aspx*.

Here are some notes about this script:

- The Invoke-SqlCmd cmdlet uses Windows Authentication by default. Notice that we passed no authentication information at all. You can also provide the UserName and Password parameters to the Invoke-SqlCmd to connect via SQL Authentication to SQL Server instances, though this is not recommended unless you are on a secure connection. There is also the option to connect to Azure SQL Database or Azure SQL Managed Instance using an access token or a service principal.

- The | Format-Table cmdlet has a big impact on the readability of script output. Without Format-Table, the script returns a long list of column names and row values. The Format-Table output does not include all columns by default, but returns a wide line of column headers and row values, similar to how SSMS returns results in Text mode.

- The | Out-File cmdlet dumps the output to a text file instead of to the PowerShell console, creating the script if needed. The -Append parameter adds the text to the bottom of an existing file.

- The Out-File can be handy for archival purposes, but for viewing live rowsets—especially SQL Server command results—try using the Out-GridView cmdlet instead (Windows-only). It provides a full-featured grid dialog box with re-sortable and filterable columns, and so on. Out-GridView is used instead in the following sample:

```
$instanceName = "localhost"
Invoke-Sqlcmd -Database master -ServerInstance $instanceName `
-Query "select * from sys.dm_exec_sessions" | `
Out-GridView
```

Inside OUT

What happened to my cursor in Visual Studio Code when running PowerShell?

Unlike SSMS, running a script in PowerShell moves the cursor to the PowerShell terminal pane (which is not actually a Results window, but a live terminal window) by default. This means you need to move your cursor back up to the script pane after each run to continue to edit your PowerShell code.

You can change this behavior in Visual Studio Code. Open the **File** menu, select **Preferences**, and choose **Settings**, or press **Ctrl+,** (comma), to open the Visual Studio Code User Settings dialog box. Then, on the right side, provide the following code to override the **Default Setting** option:

```
"powershell.integratedConsole.focusConsoleOnExecute": false
```

If you have installed the PowerShell extension in Azure Data Studio, you can update this value by going to **Settings > Extensions > PowerShell Configuration**, and deselecting the **Integrated Console: Focus Console On Execute** check box.

No restart is necessary. Now the cursor will remain in the scripting pane after running a PowerShell command.

Use PowerShell with availability groups

You can script the creation and administration of availability groups and automate them with PowerShell instead of using SSMS commands or wizards. If you work in an environment in which creating, managing, or failing over availability groups is a repeated process, you should invest time in automating and standardizing these activities with PowerShell.

Following are some code samples to help you along the way, starting with the very beginning. Suppose a new group of servers has been created for availability groups, and you need to add the Failover Clustering feature to each server. This could be time consuming and click-heavy in a remote desktop session to each server. Instead, consider the following script in which we quickly deploy the failover clustering feature and tools on four servers (you can parameterize the computer names as you require):

```
Invoke-Command -Script {Install-WindowsFeature -Name "Failover-Clustering" } `
  -ComputerName SQLDEV11, SQLDEV12, SQLDEV14, SQLDEV15
Invoke-Command -Script {Install-WindowsFeature -Name "RSAT-Clustering-Mgmt" } `
  -ComputerName SQLDEV11, SQLDEV12, SQLDEV14, SQLDEV15
Invoke-Command -Script {Install-WindowsFeature -Name "RSAT-Clustering-PowerShell" } `
  -ComputerName SQLDEV11, SQLDEV12, SQLDEV14, SQLDEV15
```

➤ For more about enabling and configuring availability groups, see Chapter 11.

Inside OUT

Why is Invoke- not working correctly across remote machines?

You should verify that the same module and versions are installed on any machines to which you will be issuing commands remotely. You can also install the modules via `Invoke-Command`, as well:

```
#Local server
  Install-Module -Name SQLServer -Force -AllowClobber
    Import-Module -Name SQLServer
#Remote Server
Invoke-Command -scriptblock {
    Install-Module -Name SQLServer -Force -AllowClobber
    Import-Module -Name SQLServer
 } -ComputerName "SQLSERVER-1"
```

Let's fast-forward to an in-place availability group, with two replicas set to asynchronous synchronization. A planned failover is coming up, and you need to automate the script as much as possible. Start with the sample script in the accompanying downloads, which accomplishes these goals:

- Sets asynchronous replicas to synchronous and waits so we can perform a planned failover with no data loss

- Performs availability group failover

- Sets replicas back to asynchronous

Here are a few notes about the script:

- We need to do some character trickery to pass in a named instance in the SMO path for the availability group, providing %5C for the backslash (\) in the replica name, SQLSERVER-0\SQL2022. The need here is rare, albeit frustrating.

- We see another control structure, `Do ... Until`. In this case, we're waiting until the `RollupSynchronizationState` of the availability group has changed from `Synchronizing` to `Synchronized`, indicating that the synchronization has changed from asynchronous to synchronous.

- After the replica is set to synchronous, the failover can occur without data loss, without being forced. In an emergency, in which the primary server SQLSERVER-0 is offline, we could skip the steps where we change the synchronization and proceed straight to the most important cmdlet in the script: `Switch-SqlAvailabilityGroup`. Except in a forced failover, for which data loss is possible, we must specify the `-AllowDataLoss` and `-Force` parameters.

- You must run this entire script from the primary node, as it is currently written. A hint of how you could customize the script to be run from anywhere lies in the `Invoke-Command` cmdlet, where we connect to the original secondary replica (now the primary replica) and set the synchronization from asynchronous back to synchronous.

Develop, deploy, and manage data recovery

The first and foremost responsibility of a production DBA is to ensure that a database can be recovered in the event of a disaster. This chapter outlines the fundamentals of data recovery and SQL Server recovery models. Then, it covers backup devices in SQL Server before discussing the different types of backups. Next, it shows you how to create and verify database backups, and how to restore databases from those backups. This chapter ends with a discussion of defining a recovery strategy based on a fictitious scenario.

NOTE

As discussed in Chapter 2, "Introduction to database server components," a disaster is any unplanned event caused by, but not limited to, natural disaster, hardware or software failure, malicious activity, or human error. Quite a few adverse events and disasters are caused by human error.

This chapter does not provide any guidance for fixing a corrupt database; Microsoft recommends restoring from a last-known good database backup if you experience corruption. Instead, as mentioned, this chapter focuses on database backups and restores. The next chapter, Chapter 11, "Implement high availability and disaster recovery," covers how to achieve high availability and use SQL Server disaster recovery features to keep your environment running even in the face of disaster. After reading this chapter and the one that follows, you will understand how to achieve close to zero data loss with minimal downtime.

➤ You can read more about data corruption in Chapter 8, "Maintain and monitor SQL Server."

You don't design a backup strategy; you design a *recovery* strategy. You must allow for potential downtime and data loss, within acceptable limits. These are defined by the business requirements for getting an environment back up and running after a disaster.

Technical solutions such as those for high availability (HA) and disaster recovery (DR) are available in Microsoft SQL Server to support these organizational requirements. In other words,

CHAPTER 10

business requirements define the approach you will take in your organization to plan for and survive a disaster.

We should also point out that this is only a small but important part of a larger business continuity plan (BCP). A BCP is designed to enable ongoing business operations while the DR plan is executed. A BCP defines the critical business functions and processes that might be supported by your SQL Server environment and how these functions will continue after disaster strikes.

➤ The US federal government provides guidance and tools for developing a BCP at *https:// www.ready.gov/business-continuity-plan*.

NOTE

This chapter makes several references to Chapter 3, "Design and implement an on-premises database infrastructure"—particularly in the context of transaction log files, virtual log files (VLFs), and log sequence numbers (LSNs). If you have not yet read that chapter, we highly recommend that you do so before reading any further here.

This chapter includes recovery strategies for hybrid and cloud environments, but the sections on backup devices, types of backups, and creating and restoring backups apply to on-premises environments only. For SQL Server virtual machines in Azure, see Chapter 16, "Design and implement hybrid and Azure database infrastructure."

There is an old saying among seasoned DBAs that a DBA is only as good as their last backup and will only keep their job if they tested it. This should serve as a reminder that backups are important, but just as important (if not more so) is testing those backups.

Prepare for data recovery

Designing a recovery strategy that achieves zero data loss with zero downtime is incredibly expensive and almost impossible. Ultimately, recovery is a balance between budget, acceptable downtime, and acceptable data loss.

NOTE

Emotions run high when systems are down, so it is incumbent on all organizations to define possible outcomes at the outset and how to deal with them. Meanwhile, runbooks and practice help keep heads cool when dealing with a stressful outage.

The governance of these requirements is outlined in a *Service-Level Agreement* (*SLA*). An SLA is a business document that specifies measurable commitments you make to the business related to availability and recovery objectives in case of a failure. Included in the SLA is the *Recovery Point Objective* (*RPO*) and *Recovery Time Objective* (*RTO*). The RPO expresses the amount of work that may be lost, in units of time such as minutes, when the service is returned to normal operation. The RTO expresses the amount of time that the service may be unavailable in case of a failure or disaster. The SLA might also include consequences and penalties (financial or otherwise) if you do not meet these timelines. Although you use technical solutions to satisfy these requirements, it is important to remember that your recovery strategy should be the best fit for the organization's business needs.

➤ **For more information about achieving HA, read Chapter 11.**

A disaster recovery scenario

Let's paint a picture of a disaster recovery scenario. This scenario spirals out of control pretty fast, so buckle up.

Imagine it's 4:57 p.m. on a beautiful, sunny Friday afternoon. Just as you are about to head home for the weekend, disaster strikes: The electricity goes out for the entire city block where your office is located, and the uninterruptible power supply (UPS) in the server room has been removed for repairs. You haven't rehearsed this scenario, because no one ever thought the UPS would be removed for maintenance for an extended period.

Your transaction log backups run every 15 minutes, because that's what the RPO stipulates. Also, you have a batch script in the Windows Task Scheduler that copies your files remotely, so your logs have been copied safely offsite. Or have they?

Suddenly you have a sinking feeling in the pit of your stomach about a warning you saw in your email this morning while you were on the phone with a colleague, which you accidentally deleted, and which, thanks to that annoying muscle-memory habit you have of emptying deleted items whenever you see them, is gone forever.

Your phone squawks to inform you it has 2 percent battery remaining. Your laptop has some charge, but not much, because you were planning to charge it when you got home. Still, you crack open your laptop to check whether you can somehow undelete that email. Oh, right, your Internet is down.

Your phone rings. It's the vice president of marketing, who is away this week at a conference. He wants to check the sales figures for a report the board is putting together for an important meeting this evening. The pressure is on! As the VP—who, by the way, doesn't care about power failures because the company spent thousands of dollars on that UPS—asks when he can access those figures, your phone dies.

You decide to charge your phone off the laptop. That way, you can also use the tethered cellular connection to log into the DR site. But the signal in this area is weak, so you must move to the window on the other side of the office. As you stand up to move, your laptop decides that it's time to install operating system updates, because it's now after 5 p.m. Eventually, though, the laptop cancels the updates, because there's no Internet access.

You move to the new location, where the signal is stronger. After an agonizing few minutes, your phone finally starts. Finally! You connect to your offsite datacenter through a Remote Desktop Protocol (RDP) session. It takes three attempts, though, because you had forgotten that RDP to this server works only with the administrator user account.

The SQL Server instance has its own service account, so you must download and use psexec to run SQL Server Management Studio (SSMS) as that service account in interactive mode. First, though, you must change a registry entry to allow that user to use interactive login. You check the backup folder. The latest log file is from 4:30 p.m. Great.

That means the 4:45 p.m. backup didn't copy over. Oh, it's because the drive is full. That must have been what the email warning was about.

After clearing out some files that another colleague had put on the drive temporarily, you write the script you've been meaning to write to restore the database because you didn't have time to set up log shipping.

You export the backup directory listing to a text file and begin looking for the latest full backup, differential backup, and transaction log backup files. But now you see that the last differential backup doesn't make sense, because the size is all wrong.

You remember that one of your developers made a full backup of the production database on Monday evening, but didn't use the COPY_ONLY option, and you don't have access to that file. The latest differential file is useless. You must start from Sunday's full backup file, and then use Monday afternoon's differential backup and all transaction log files since then. That's more than 400 files to restore.

Eventually, with a bit of luck and text manipulation, you begin running the restore script. One particular log file takes a very long time. In your panicked state, you wonder whether it has somehow become stuck. After a minute or two of clicking around, you realize SQL Server had to grow the transaction log of the restored database because it was replaying that annoying index rebuild script that failed on Tuesday morning and needed to roll back.

Finally, at 6:33 p.m., your offsite database is up and running with the latest database backups, up to and including the one from 4:30 p.m. Just then, the lights come back on in the office. The power failure that affected the block where your office is has been resolved.

You need to do a full DBCC CHECKDB of the production server as soon as it starts, but it takes hours because the server is five years old and was installed with ECC RAM (which is useful but causes longer bootup times). This will push you out of the two-hour RTO that you and your boss agreed to, so you go with a failover approach.

You update the connection settings in the application to point to the offsite datacenter. Just then, your phone dies once more, but at least the office has power to charge everything again.

You send the VP an email to say the reports should be working. Your cellular data bill is coming out of the expenses for his trip, you tell yourself as you pack up to go home.

As you walk to the bus stop, it occurs to you that the files you cleared out to free up drive space probably included the full database backup created by the developer from Monday night, and that you might have saved some time by checking them first.

Define acceptable data loss: RPO

When disaster strikes, you might lose a single byte in a single row in a single 8-KB data page due to memory or drive corruption. How do you recover from that corruption? Worse, what happens if you lose an entire volume or drive, the storage array, or even the entire building?

The RPO should answer the question, "How much data are you prepared to lose?" The RPO is usually measured in seconds or minutes. Your job is to deliver a technical implementation that meets this objective, perhaps by ensuring there is less time between the last known good backup and the moment of the point of failure. To achieve this, you must consider whether your backups are being done correctly, regularly, and copied offsite securely and in a timely manner.

In the nightmarish scenario we just laid out, the organization decided that losing 15 minutes' worth of data was acceptable, but ultimately data changes over 27 minutes were lost. This is because the drive on the server at the DR site was full, and the most recent backup did not copy over. To satisfy a 15-minute window, the transaction log backups would need to be created more frequently, as would the offsite copy. Ideally, backups are copied offsite immediately after they are taken.

If the organization requires zero data loss, the budget must significantly increase to ensure that whatever unplanned event occurs, SQL Server's memory and transaction log remains online, and that all backups are working and being securely copied offsite as soon as possible.

Inside OUT

Why is the RPO measured in time, and not drive usage?

Transactions vary in size, but time is constant.

Chapter 3 looked at how every transaction is assigned an LSN to keep track of things in the active portion of the transaction log. Each new LSN is greater than the previous one. (This is where the word *sequence* comes into play.)

The RPO refers to the most recent point in time in the transaction log history to which you will restore the database, based on the most recently committed LSN at that specific moment in time, or the latest LSN in the log backup, whichever satisfies the organization's RPO.

Define acceptable downtime: RTO

Time is money. Every minute an organization is unable to work has a cost, and lost productivity adds up quickly. The RTO is the amount of time by which you need to have everything up and running again after a disaster. You might orchestrate a failover to your DR site in another building, or a manual failover using log shipping. The RTO is usually measured in hours.

In our disaster scenario, the RTO was two hours. Our intrepid but woefully unprepared and accident-prone DBA barely made it. A few factors acted against the plan (if it could be called a plan).

For an organization to require zero downtime, the budget is exponentially increased. This is where a combination of HA and DR technologies combine to support the requirements.

NOTE

Different types of adverse events may have different RPOs and RTOs. A failure of a single drive in the enterprise SAN shouldn't come with any data loss or downtime. A power failure in a branch office might result in downtime, but no data loss. The loss of an entire facility due to an unforeseen natural disaster may require the organization to accept both data loss and downtime.

Different applications may have different RTOs as well. The e-commerce system might have a dramatically smaller RTO than the business travel expense tracking system. Regardless, application leadership should be aware of the RTO and RPO their budget is buying.

Establish and use a runbook

When panic sets in, you need a clear set of instructions to follow, just like our deer-in-the-headlights DBA in our fictional scenario. This set of instructions is called a *runbook*.

The runbook is one of many documents that make up a DR plan. It is part of the BCP. It covers the steps necessary for someone (including your future self) to bring the databases and supporting services back online after a disaster. In an eventuality in which you or your team members become incapacitated, the document should be accessible and understandable to another DBA who has appropriate access, but doesn't have intimate knowledge of the environment.

From our example scenario, issues like the RDP user account not being able to log in to SSMS, downloading the requisite tools, knowing to skip an out-of-band differential backup, and so on would not be immediately obvious to many people. Even the most experienced DBA in a panic will struggle with thinking clearly.

The level of detail in a runbook is defined by the complexity of the systems that need recovery and the time available to bring them back again. Your organization might be satisfied with a simple Microsoft Excel spreadsheet containing configurations for a few business-critical systems. Or it might need something more in-depth, complete with screenshots, links to vendor documentation and downloads, and expected outcomes at each step. In either case, the run-book should be updated as the system changes and stored in a version control system (which itself should be backed up properly). It is not unreasonable to have a paper copy, too, as you may not have access to all drives in the case of multiple outages or if you have to walk someone else through the process over the phone in the remote DR location.

The rest of this chapter describes how SQL Server provides backup and restore features to help you develop a recovery strategy that is most appropriate for your environment, so that when your organization wants to produce a BCP, you have sufficient knowledge to guide an appropri-ate and achievable technical response.

Most important, you must be able to rehearse a DR plan. The runbook won't be perfect, and rehearsing scenarios will help you produce better documentation. That way, when disaster does strike, even the most panicked individual will be able to figure things out. Many organizations schedule regular walk-throughs and practice scenarios for DR. Some even perform a failover from one datacenter to another each month to rehearse their failover automation. When it is important to your business, you must train for it like an athlete. Financial organizations might check backups daily, perform system checks monthly, conduct walk-throughs of the DR plan quarterly, and perform full system failover annually.

Ransomware attacks

Ransomware is a kind of malware designed to deny a user or organization access to files on their computer by encrypting them and demanding a ransom payment to unencrypt them. Unfortunately, not only do businesses have no guarantee the criminals will unencrypt the files after the ransom is paid, but those same criminals might do it again, or the files might not be usable or not in a fully usable state.

While organization leadership might feel that it will never happen to them, the reality is it can and does happen to everyone. In a 2020 survey of 600 US companies, 68 percent said they had experienced a ransomware attack and paid the ransom. Another 10 percent said they were infected but did not pay any money, while only 22 percent were never infected at all.

> ➤ For more information about this survey, visit *https://www.statista.com/statistics/701282 /ransomware-experience-of-companies*.

Microsoft issues an annual Digital Defense Report. It is an interesting if not unnerving read. One of the things to learn from the report is that novel or zero-day vulnerabilities are not required to successfully attack your infrastructure. "Most methods still rely on unpatched edge applications, lateral movement via connected drives, and weak credentials on available services" (Microsoft Digital Defense Report 2021, October 2021, *https://query.prod.cms.rt.microsoft.com/cms/api/ am/binary/RWMFli*). The report also emphasizes that prompt patching is still a critical activ-ity: "Identification and rapid exploitation of unpatched vulnerabilities has become a key tactic.

Rapid deployment of security updates is key to defense" (Microsoft Digital Defense Report 2022, November 2022, *https://query.prod.cms.rt.microsoft.com/cms/api/am/binary/RE5bUvv*).

Obviously, cybersecurity is not just a data platform topic, but databases are a prize target for ransomware and data exfiltration attacks. As noted in the report, "Maintaining a strong baseline of IT security hygiene through prioritized patching, enabling anti-tamper features, using attack surface management tools like RiskIQ to get an outside-in view of an attack surface, and enabling multifactor authentication across the full enterprise have become baseline fundamentals to proactively defend against many sophisticated actors" (Microsoft Digital Defense Report 2022, November 2022, *https://query.prod.cms.rt.microsoft.com/cms/api/am/binary/RE5bUvv*). RiskIQ's suite of cybersecurity tools was acquired by Microsoft in 2021, and is now called Microsoft Defender Threat Intelligence and Microsoft Defender External Attack Surface Management.

Perpetrators are referred to as *bad actors*. They also get inside systems in similar ways to malware and viruses: by using social engineering techniques or bribery via unwitting or coerced insider threats. (We discuss password hashing in Chapter 13, "Protect data through classification, encryption, and auditing.")

Once a bad actor gains access to an organization's network, they begin encrypting data, which causes applications to crash and go offline. A ransom is requested, often in a cryptocurrency that is impossible to trace; when the ransom is paid, the data is unencrypted . . . maybe.

Many organizations protect their assets by categorizing their risks and by having security teams assess the threats and methodologies attackers use. They manage cybersecurity with a focus on detection-based defenses like firewalls and antimalware software. But the reality is, there is no perfect ransomware protection, only resilient recovery. The best response to a ransomware attack is a solid strategy to restore your data with very little downtime.

How do you restore if your data has been encrypted? This is where resilient backups—ones that a bad actor with administrative credentials cannot corrupt—is critical. A trusted immutable backup is needed. It is the key item to your recovery, and what all software and hardware vendors have in common.

NOTE

An immutable backup is a way of protecting data that ensures the data is fixed, unchangeable, and can never be deleted, encrypted, or modified.

Any backup is only a good backup if it is usable. You must be able to restore it and make sure it is not corrupt. Some software vendors do this automatically, but you should not rely on them. If you are a DBA, your first and most important responsibility is to be able to restore a database, with no data loss, within the RTO window.

Immutable copies do not just protect against ransomware attacks. They also protect against accidental deletion and other human errors. Before ransomware attacks became a widespread issue, organizations would restore less than 10 percent of their backed-up production data over the course of a year. That is now changing, making it even more vital to ensure data is valid, correct, and accessible.

> ➤ See the section "Availability and security of backup media" later in this chapter for more information.

Understand different types of backups

There are three different backup types:

- Full

- Differential

- Transaction log

To recover a database, you need at least a full database backup. Differential backups are optional. They only include the data pages that have changed since the last full backup. Differential backups can reduce the amount of time required to restore a database. Transaction log backups are incremental backups that enable point-in-time restores. We talk more about each of these backup types in the subsections that follow.

In Enterprise edition, you can also create file-level and filegroup-level backups (known as partial backups) to allow a more controlled procedure when restoring. This is especially useful for very large databases (VLDBs).

> ➤ You can read more about the files that make up a SQL Server database in Chapter 3.

A key part of understanding backups and their ability to restore is understanding recovery models. After these introductory paragraphs, we discuss recovery models first. The backup types, along with partial database backups and backup options, are covered afterward.

CHAPTER 10

Inside OUT

How large is a VLDB?

Opinions differ as to what constitutes a VLDB, based on individual experience and available hardware resources (such as memory and drive space).

For the purposes of this chapter, any database that exceeds 100 GB is considered a VLDB. Although modern solid-state storage arrays do mitigate many of the challenges facing databases of this size, they are not cost-effective for all environments. You can read more about solid-state storage, and storage arrays, in Chapter 2.

Regardless of the type of backup, it will always contain the active portion of the transaction log, including relevant LSNs. This ensures full transactional consistency when the backup is restored.

Every SQL Server native backup also contains a header and a payload. The *header* describes the backup device, what type of backup it is, backup start and stop information (including LSN information), and information about the database files. The *payload* is the content of the data or transaction log files in the backup. If transparent data encryption (TDE) or backup encryption was enabled, the payload is encrypted.

➤ **You can read more about TDE in Chapter 13.**

An overview of SQL Server recovery models

A key part of understanding backups and their ability to restore is grasping recovery models. In SQL Server, a database's recovery model determines how the transaction log is maintained, which affects your options for backups and restores. SQL Server supports three recovery models:

- **Full.** With this model, transactions are logged and kept at least until the transaction log has been backed up. This model allows a full point-in-time recovery. In this model, full, transaction log, and differential can be created. (We talk more about these three types of backups shortly.) The transaction log must be regularly backed up to avoid continuous growth. All database changes are fully logged and can be replayed.

- **Bulk-logged.** This model reduces the amount of transaction log used for certain bulk operations. SQL Server only logs what the Database Engine needs to undo the bulk operation, but the bulk operation cannot be replayed. Non-bulk operations are logged and maintained as in the full recovery model. This model can allow a point-in-time recovery only if no bulk-logged operations are in that portion of the transaction log backup. Full, transaction log, and differential backups can be created. Here too, the transaction log must be backed up to avoid continuous growth.

- **Simple.** Transactions are logged only until they are committed to the data file(s) on disk. Only full and differential backups can be created.

These models provide a high level of control over the types of backups, and thus restore options, available to your databases. We talk more about each of these models in the subsections that follow.

NOTE

These are called *recovery models*. If you see the term *recovery mode*, it is incorrect.

You can change the recovery model of a database in SSMS in Object Explorer, or by using the following Transact-SQL (T-SQL) statement and choosing the appropriate option in the square brackets:

```
ALTER DATABASE <dbname> SET RECOVERY [ FULL | BULK_LOGGED | SIMPLE ];
```

Full recovery model

For databases that require point-in-time recovery—which is the case for most business-critical systems—we recommend the full recovery model. The recovery model for new databases is based on the recovery model for the model database. By default, the model database is in the full recovery model.

In this recovery model, after the first full backup takes place, the virtual log files in the transaction log remain active and are not cleared until a transaction log backup writes these log records to a log backup. Only then will the log be truncated (cleared). Keep in mind that a truncated log file does not return unused space to the operating system.

Assuming you implement a process to ensure that these backups are securely copied offsite as soon as they are created, and that you regularly test these backups, you can use them to restore your database in the event of a disaster. Provided the right circumstances are in play, you might even be able to create a tail-log backup to achieve zero data loss if that data has been committed and made durable.

➤ Tail-log backups are defined in the "Transaction log backups" section later in this chapter.

➤ You can read more about durability, including delayed durability, in Chapter 2.

Bulk-logged recovery model

With the bulk-logged recovery model, typical commands are logged as they are in the full recovery model, but bulk operations are minimally logged. This reduces the size of the transaction log records and subsequent log backups. The downside is that this model eliminates the option of replaying certain operations from a transaction log backup, including BULK INSERT, INSERT ... SELECT, SELECT ... INTO (all using the TABLOCK hint), and BCP operations. Certain indexing operations are also minimally logged. This affects your ability to restore a database to a point in time if that time is included in a transaction log backup that includes bulk-logged operations.

➤ For more details, see *https://learn.microsoft.com/sql/relational-databases/logs/the-transaction-log-sql-server#MinimallyLogged*.

NOTE

Minimal logging is not supported for memory-optimized tables.

There is a way to achieve near-point-in-time recovery. This allows a more flexible recovery strategy than the simple recovery model (more on this in the next section), without generating large transaction logs for bulk operations. For example, suppose you want to use the bulk-logged recovery model to perform minimally logged operations, without breaking the log backup chain. Here's how it works:

> **NOTE**
> Your database must be in the full recovery model before the bulk-logged operation is performed.

1. You create a transaction log backup. (Again, we talk about these momentarily.)

2. You switch to the bulk-logged recovery model and perform the bulk-logged operations.

3. You immediately switch the database back to the full recovery model.

4. You back up the log again.

This process ensures that the backup chain remains unbroken and allows point-in-time recovery to any point before or after the bulk-logged operation. The Microsoft Docs on this subject note that the bulk-logged recovery model is intended specifically for this scenario to temporarily replace the full recovery model during bulk operations.

Simple recovery model

Databases in the simple recovery model can be restored only to the point in time when the backups were completed. Point-in-time recovery is not supported. After a transaction in the simple recovery model is committed or rolled back, a checkpoint is implicitly issued, which truncates (clears) the log.

Databases that use the simple recovery model can use full and differential backups. This recovery model is better suited to development databases, databases that change infrequently, and databases that can be rebuilt from other sources.

Full backups

A full database backup is a transactionally consistent copy of the entire database. The payload of this type of backup includes every 8-KB data page in every database file in all filegroups, FILESTREAM and memory-optimized files, and the portion of the transaction log that is necessary to roll forward or roll back transactions that overlapped with the backup window.

➤ You can read more about the active portion of the transaction log in Chapter 3.

You can perform full backups on databases in all recovery models, and you can compress them. Since SQL Server 2016, you can also compress databases encrypted with TDE.

With a minimal amount of T-SQL code, you can perform a full backup to a backup disk target. For example, you can use the following code to back up the WideWorldImporters sample database on a default instance with a machine called SERVER to a local drive (the drive path must exist):

```
BACKUP DATABASE WideWorldImporters
TO DISK = N'C:\SQLData\Backup\SERVER_WWI_FULL_20221218_210912.BAK';
GO
```

Transaction log backups

Transaction log backups are incremental backups of a database. In the full recovery model, all transactions are fully logged. This means you can bring a database back to a point in time on or before that transaction log backup was created, provided the restore is successful. These backups allow for a recovery to any moment in time in the sequence (in other words, the *backup chain*—more on that in a moment).

In a transaction log backup, the active portion of the transaction log is backed up. Transaction log backups apply only to databases in the full and bulk-logged recovery models. Databases in the full recovery model can be restored to a point in time, whereas databases in the bulk-logged recovery model can be restored to a point in time if the transaction log does not contain bulk-logged operations. The transaction log does not contain the information necessary to replay bulk operations in the bulk-logged recovery model.

Inside OUT

What is a tail-log backup?

A tail-log, or tail-of-the-log, backup is fundamentally the same thing as an ordinary transaction log backup. The difference is in the circumstances in which you would perform this kind of log backup.

When performing a tail-log backup, you might need to use the NO_TRUNCATE clause on the BACKUP statement if the database is damaged. The NO_TRUNCATE clause allows the transaction log to be backed up, even if only the transaction log file is accessible and undamaged. Thus, even if the database is inaccessible or damaged, the committed transactions can be backed up.

CHAPTER 10

In a disaster scenario, the automation for performing transaction log backups might be offline, or your backup drive might not be available. Any time you need to manually perform a transaction log backup to ensure the remaining transactions in the log are safely stored somewhere after a failure has occurred, it is considered a tail-log backup. Performing a tail-log backup that you can restore properly later is how you can achieve zero data loss following some adverse events.

➤ You can read more about tail-log backups at *https://learn.microsoft.com/sql /relational-databases/backup-restore/back-up-the-transaction-log-when-the -database-is-damaged-sql-server.*

Differential backups

A differential backup is a convenience feature to reduce the number of transaction log backups (and time) required to restore a database to a point in time. A differential backup is always based on the last full database backup that wasn't taken with the COPY_ONLY option. Differential backups contain all changed extents, FILESTREAM files, and memory-optimized data files since the last full backup. They cannot be restored on their own. To restore a database using a differential backup, you need that differential backup's base full backup.

In many cases, a differential backup is much smaller than a full backup. This allows for a more flexible backup schedule. You can take a full backup less frequently and take the differential backups more regularly, taking up less space than full backups would.

Think back to Chapter 3, where we looked at extents. As a reminder, an *extent* is a 64-KB segment in the data file comprising a group of eight physically contiguous 8-KB data pages. After a default full backup completes (without the copy-only option, which we cover later), the differential bitmap is cleared. All subsequent changes in the database, at the extent level, are recorded in the differential bitmap. When the differential backup runs, it looks at the differential bitmap and backs up only the extents that have been modified since the full backup, along with the active portion of the transaction log. This is quite different from a transaction log backup, which records every change in the database, even if the change is made repeatedly to the same rows in the same tables. Thus, a differential backup is not the same thing as an incremental backup.

Even though you cannot restore a database to a point in time (or LSN) that occurs within the differential backup itself, differential backups can vastly reduce the number of transaction log files required to effect those same changes.

Differential backups apply to databases in the full, bulk-logged, and simple recovery models.

CAUTION

If a full backup is taken out-of-band without the COPY_ONLY option, this will affect subsequent differential backups. In that case, you will be restricted to using transaction log backups exclusively to restore the backup chain. If you want to create a full backup of a database without affecting the differential backup schedule, always use the COPY_ONLY option. The copy-only backup mechanism is covered later in this chapter.

Inside OUT

What do you do if your differential backup is larger than your full backup?

Differential backups grow larger as the number of changed extents in the database increases. So, a differential backup could end up being larger than a full backup over time.

This is possible in situations in which every extent is modified in some way—for example, if all the indexes in the database are rebuilt. In this case, the differential backup will be the same size as a full backup. When it then adds the active portion of the log, you end up with a differential backup that is larger than the full backup.

SQL Server 2017 and later versions provide a column called modified_extent_page_count in the dynamic management view (DMV) sys.dm_db_file_space_usage to let you know how large a differential backup will be. A good rule of thumb is to take a full backup if the differential backup approaches 80 percent of the size of a full backup.

➤ You can read more about differential backups at *https://learn.microsoft.com/sql/relational-databases/backup-restore/differential-backups-sql-server*.

The backup chain

A backup chain starts with a full backup, followed by a series of differential and/or transaction-log backups. You can combine these into a recovery sequence to restore a database to a particular point in time after the full backup or to the time of the latest backup, whichever is required. Databases in the full recovery model can be restored to a point in time because transactions are fully logged in that recovery model.

NOTE

You can also restore a database in the bulk-logged recovery model to a point in time, provided the transaction log backup does not contain bulk-logged operations up to that point in time.

CHAPTER 10

Figure 10-1 illustrates a backup chain that starts with a full backup, which contains the most recent LSN of the active portion of the transaction log at the time that backup finished, followed by multiple transaction log backups and differential backups based on that full backup.

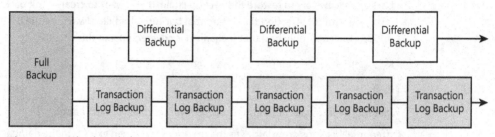

Figure 10-1 A backup chain.

You can use a combination of the most recent differential backup (which must be based on that same full backup) and any additional transaction log backups to produce a point-in-time recovery. If you do not have a differential backup, or if the point in time you want to restore to is before the end of the differential backup, you must use transaction log backups. Either option will work, provided the LSNs required in the sequence are contained in each of those backups.

Until you run the very first full backup on a database using the full or bulk-logged recovery model, the database is *pseudo-simple*—that is, it behaves as though it is in the simple recovery model. Active portions of the log are cleared whenever a database checkpoint is issued, and the transaction log remains at a reasonably stable size unless a large transaction causes it to grow. This may seem unexpected, but there's no need to keep a transaction log that can't be restored.

Remember: A database restore always begins with a full backup (piecemeal restores are an uncommon exception and discussed later in this chapter). Until there is a full backup, there's no need for historic transactions to be kept. Conversely, once the first full backup is created, less-experienced DBAs can be taken by surprise by the sudden and seemingly uncontrolled growth of the transaction log.

We recommend that you configure appropriate maintenance plans (including transaction log backups and monitoring) immediately after you create a new database. It is also a good idea to continue taking log backups even while a full backup is in progress. These log backups will ensure the backup chain is preserved even if the full backup fails or is cancelled.

NOTE

Backup chains can survive database migrations and upgrades, as long as the LSNs remain intact. This is what makes certain HA features possible in SQL Server.

Inside OUT

How long can the backup chain be?

Provided you have an unbroken backup chain for which the LSNs are all intact, you can potentially have many thousands of log backups stretching back over months or even years. You can apply these backups, along with the full backup on which they are based (and assuming the files are intact), to restore the database to a current point in time, even if the database was moved or upgraded during that time. However, this can be extremely time consuming and will negatively affect the RTO—especially if the backups need to be retrieved from slow storage (including tape). Legend has it that some organizations were forced to close down as a result of missing the RTO. It is a far better practice to perform regular full backups (and differential database backups if they are useful) along with transaction log backups so that the dependency chain is shorter.

➤ You can read more about designing an appropriate backup schedule in the "Create and verify backups" section later in this chapter. For more on maintenance plans, read Chapter 9, "Automate SQL Server administration."

Fix a broken backup chain with differential backups

A backup chain is broken when a database is switched from the full recovery model to the bulk-logged or simple recovery model for any reason (such as shrinking the transaction log file during an emergency to reclaim storage space). A backup chain can also be broken if a full database backup is taken "out-of-band" and is then discarded or becomes unavailable when a restore is required.

After you switch back to the full recovery model, you can restart the log backup chain—without having to perform a full database backup—by taking a differential backup. As long as you use this or a more recent differential backup in a later recovery, along with the accompanying transaction log backups, the backup chain will be repaired.

If you keep the database in the bulk-logged recovery model, you can restore the backup chain by taking a differential backup after bulk-logged operations. Combined with the transaction log backups taken after the differential backup, you can restore the database back to a point in time after the bulk-logged operation, or to a point in time before the transaction log backup containing a bulk-logged operation.

File and filegroup backups

You can take a more granular approach by backing up individual data files and filegroups, which use the full or differential options, as well. These options are available in the SSMS user

CHAPTER 10

interface; alternatively, you can use the official documentation to create appropriate T-SQL statements.

CAUTION

If a single file in a filegroup is offline (for instance, during a restore), the entire filegroup is also offline. This affects backups.

Partial backups

Because read-only filegroups do not change, it does not make sense to include them in ongoing backup processes. Primarily used for VLDBs that contain read-only filegroups, partial backups exclude those read-only filegroups, as required.

Partial backups contain the primary filegroup, any read-write filegroups, and one or more optional read-only filegroups. Partial backups can also contain a single file from a filegroup, but be aware that a filegroup cannot be brought online until all the files are available.

➤ To read more about partial backups, visit *https://learn.microsoft.com/sql/relational -databases/backup-restore/partial-backups-sql-server*.

File backups

You can use file backups to restore individual files if they become corrupt. This makes restoring easier, because for VLDBs, it takes much less time to restore a single file than the entire data-base. Unfortunately, file backups increase complexity due to increased administration of the additional file backups over and above the full, differential, and transaction log backups. This overhead extends to recovery script maintenance.

➤ To read more about file backups, visit *https://learn.microsoft.com/sql/relational-databases /backup-restore/full-file-backups-sql-server*.

Additional backup options and considerations

This section includes several options and special considerations for creating backups in SQL Server.

Database snapshots

A database snapshot is a read-only static view of a database at the point in time the snapshot was created. A database snapshot isn't a backup and shouldn't be considered as such, but it can play a role in disaster recovery when used tactically.

You could, for example, take a database snapshot immediately before making a major change. The snapshot can serve as a read-only copy of the database before the major change, as well as a point to revert to if the major change has unexpected consequences.

To create a database snapshot, you create a special database snapshot file, commonly with the extension .ss. For example, to create a database snapshot of the WideWorldImporters database at the iso date and time November 2, 2022, at 10:45 a.m.:

```
CREATE DATABASE WideWorldImporters_202211021045 ON
( NAME = WideWorldImporters, FILENAME =
'C:\Program Files\Microsoft SQL Server\MSSQL16.MSSQLSERVER\MSSQL\Data\WideWorldImporters
_data_202211021045.ss' )
AS SNAPSHOT OF WideWorldImporters;
```

The WideWorldImporters_202211021045 database can now be connected to and read from as a read-only copy of the database at a point in time.

Before reverting to the snapshot, you must remove any other database snapshots for the database. To revert the entire WideWorldImporters to the database snapshot, the T-SQL command is simple:

```
RESTORE DATABASE WideWorldImporters FROM
DATABASE_SNAPSHOT = ' WideWorldImporters_202211021045';
```

You can use database snapshots to ease administration when testing new functionality to reduce the time required to restore to a point in time, but they carry the same risks as regular database files. Snapshots are not guaranteed backups, and you should not use them to replace native SQL Server backups.

Database snapshots are unrelated to other features or concepts that share the same vocabulary, such as snapshot backups, snapshot isolation of transactions, or snapshot replication. For more on database snapshots, see *https://learn.microsoft.com/sql/relational-databases/databases /database-snapshots-sql-server*.

Backup encryption

Since SQL Server 2014, it has been possible to encrypt database backups using an asymmetric key pair. This is different from the encryption provided for backups with TDE enabled. The key difference is that to restore an encrypted backup, you need the asymmetric key, not the database master key (DMK) or the certificate encrypted by the DMK.

➤ Chapter 13 discusses DMKs in more detail.

Like any asymmetric encryption process, you need a cipher (the encryption algorithm) and an asymmetric key or certificate. Supported ciphers are Advanced Encryption Standard (AES), with key sizes of 128, 192, and 256 bits, and 3DES (also known as Triple DES). As discussed in depth in Chapter 13, AES is a safer and faster cipher than 3DES. You must back up and store the key or certificate in a secure location.

➤ For more about security and encryption, see Chapter 13.

As noted in Chapter 3, you can also compress backups. This is recommended unless the database itself is already compressed, in which case you should first evaluate whether your case will benefit from backup compression. SQL Server 2016 introduced support for backup compression of databases encrypted with TDE.

Inside OUT

Anything to watch out for with backup encryption?

Some unpatched versions of SQL Server 2017 and SQL Server 2016 contained flaws that could corrupt backups of databases encrypted with TDE when they were compressed. These flaws were fixed in cumulative updates in May 2018. For more information on this phenomenon, visit *https://support.microsoft.com/topic/kb4101502-fix-tde-enabled-database-backup -with-compression-causes-database-corruption-in-sql-server-d6df5614-9b20-4e0f-37d7 -eceda1eabe29*.

We recommend that you follow Microsoft's guidance and evaluate and apply cumulative updates as they are released for just this reason. This is also a cautionary tale for regularly, if not automatically, testing your backups to ensure they can be restored successfully.

NOTE

The MAXTRANSFERSIZE data transfer option with the BACKUP statement specifies the largest possible size of transfers between SQL Server and the backup media (in bytes). Backup compression for a database encrypted with TDE does not kick in unless the BACKUP statement contains a MAXTRANSFERSIZE value greater than 65,536. If MAXTRANSFERSIZE is not specified or is set to its minimum value of 65,536 bytes (64 KB), the backup will not be compressed. Valid values for MAXTRANSFERSIZE are multiples of 64 KB, up to 4 MB.

Backup checksums

SQL Server can perform optional checksum verifications on database backups. By default, backups do not perform a checksum. You can change this behavior either by Trace Flag 3023 or in the backup job or T-SQL script that takes backups. We recommend you enable backup checksum where possible, ideally using the trace flag, so it is the default behavior.

Without backup checksum enabled, no validation is performed on data pages or log blocks. This means any logical corruption will also be backed up without showing any of the errors you might see with a DBCC CHECKDB operation. This is to allow for scenarios in which you want to back up a corrupt database before attempting to fix the corruption. Alternatively, you can create the backup with checksum enabled but add the CONTINUE_AFTER_ERROR option.

➤ To read more about recovering from corruption, see Chapter 8.

With backup checksum enabled, a checksum is calculated over the entire backup file. Additionally, the page checksum on every 8-KB data page (for both page verification types of checksum or torn-page detection) and the log block checksum from the active portion of the log will be validated.

CAUTION

Physical corruption, in which the data cannot be read from the drive, including corruption in memory-optimized filegroups, will cause the backup to fail.

The backup checksum can significantly increase the time for a backup to run, but adds some peace of mind, short of running a recommended DBCC CHECKDB on a restored database.

Copy-only backup

When a full backup runs with the default settings, a reserved data page known as the *differential bitmap* (discussed previously in this chapter) is cleared. Any differential backups that are created on the database after that will be based off that full backup.

You can change the default behavior by using the COPY_ONLY option, which does not clear the differential bitmap. Copy-only backups are useful for creating out-of-band backups without affecting the differential backup schedule. In other words, only differential backups are affected by the lack of the COPY_ONLY option. Transaction log backups, and thus the backup chain, are not affected.

Memory-optimized tables

Standard backups include memory-optimized tables. During the backup process, a checksum is performed on the data and delta file pairs to check for corruption. Any corruption detected in a memory-optimized filegroup will cause a backup to fail, requiring you to restore from the last known good backup.

Remember: The storage requirements for a memory-optimized table can be much larger than its usage in memory, which will affect the size of your backups.

➤ To learn more about how to back up memory-optimized files, visit *https://learn.microsoft .com/sql/relational-databases/in-memory-oltp/backing-up-a-database-with-memory -optimized-tables.*

System database backups

The SQL Server system databases contain important information about your system, and some of these should be backed up as well.

A system database that does not need to be backed up is tempdb. This tempdb database is re-created every time your SQL Server instance restarts and cannot be backed up or restored.

The model database typically does not contain data or database objects; this system database serves only as a template. It should be backed up for consistency.

The master system database holds all the instance-level information and should be backed up on regular intervals. You should also take a full backup of the master database immediately before and after any significant changes, such as the installation of a cumulative update.

Another system database that should be backed up is msdb. This system database is used by the SQL Server Agent for job control. This database also contains the backup and restore history tables.

In addition to these four system databases (master, msdb, model, and tempdb) that are present on every SQL Server instance, you might also have a distribution system database. This database exists if you have configured replication, and should also be backed up regularly, on the same schedule as full backups for replicated databases.

> ➤ Microsoft provides additional guidance for backing up replicated databases at *https://learn .microsoft.com/sql/relational-databases/replication/administration/back-up-and-restore -replicated-databases.*

Back up non-database items

Successfully restoring data may require more than just the backup files. For example, restoring a database with TDE enabled will require the original certificate used to set up encryption. If you're restoring to a different server, you must restore the certificate, including its private key, before attempting to restore the database.

Items you should consider backing up in addition to the database include the following:

- Certificates

- Logins

- SSIS packages not stored in the SSISDB, but in the file system

- Flat files, configuration files, or other custom-developed files necessary for jobs and business applications

Availability and security of backup media

Your backups must be safeguarded from corruption or deletion and from the disasters you're trying to defend against. This means backup files should be available in multiple locations, including both on-premises and offsite. It's not wise to keep backups only on-premises because a disaster or ransomware attack might affect your entire site. However, it's advisable to keep one backup copy locally, because that copy is easier and quicker to access.

Inside OUT

What is a good resilient copy policy for database backups?

Consider the 3-2-2-1-0 rule for your database backups, and other parts of your business continuity plan:

- Three different copies of your data (3)
- On two different media (2)
- With two offsite copies (2)
- One of which is air-gapped or immutable (1)
- With no errors after recovery (0)

The devices that store your backups must be secured with appropriate access controls, physical and virtual. Authorized individuals, and *only* authorized individuals, must be able to access the backups to implement the data recovery plan. The backups contain the same sensitive information as your databases. Unauthorized access may lead to a security breach. (Unfortunately, attackers know organizations sometimes neglect to protect backups as well as data stores.) However, you must also plan for the eventuality that a disaster renders your identity and access management (IAM) infrastructure unavailable.

Similar considerations apply for backups to Azure Storage. You must verify that access to the storage account is limited to authorized individuals. Azure provides mechanisms for securing storage accounts, which are outside the scope of this text.

➤ For information on the many options for securing Azure Storage accounts, see *https://learn .microsoft.com/azure/storage/blobs/security-recommendations*. Additional best practices for using shared access signatures are available at *https://learn.microsoft.com/azure/storage /common/storage-sas-overview#best-practices-when-using-sas*.

Understand backup devices

SQL Server writes database backups to physical backup devices. These storage media might be virtualized, but for the purposes of this section, they are considered physical. They include disk, tape, and URL. (Tape backup is now deprecated, and we will not cover it in detail.)

CAUTION

The option to back up SQL Server databases to tape will be removed from a future version of SQL Server. When creating a recovery strategy, use disk or URL. You should change any existing recovery strategies that involve tape to use another media type.

CHAPTER 10

Back up to disk

SQL Server backups are most commonly stored directly on a local volume or network path, referred to as the *backup disk*. A backup disk contains one or more backup files, and each file contains one or more database backups.

A database backup might also be split across multiple files. To back up VLDBs in less time, striping the backup across multiple files can be a valuable strategy. Be careful, however, because you must have all files in the set to successfully restore.

Back up to URL

Since SQL Server 2012 (with Service Pack 1 and Cumulative Update 2), you can back up your SQL Server database directly to Azure Blob Storage. This is made possible by using an Azure Storage account URL as a destination.

SQL Server 2016 added the ability to back up to Azure block blobs. This is now the preferred blob type when backing up to Azure Storage. When striping a backup on up to 64 blobs, block blobs support much larger backups and enable higher throughput than page blobs.

NOTE

Backing up to URL is especially useful for hybrid scenarios and for Azure SQL Managed Instance.

To back up a database to a block blob, you must provide a token for a shared access signature (SAS) for a standard Azure Storage account. (Premium storage accounts are not supported.) You can create a SAS using the Azure portal, PowerShell, the Azure Storage Explorer application, or other means. Before creating the SAS, you should define a matching stored access policy for the blob container that will store the backup files. This policy allows the SAS to be changed or revoked.

A SAS *token* represents the SAS. It is a query string that contains several elements that refer to the SAS. When creating a SAS token, you must specify the permissions that will be allowed using the SAS token. Read, write, delete, and list permissions are minimally required. The SAS token you obtain will begin with a question mark (?), but that question mark must be removed before SQL Server can successfully use the SAS token. (Readers versed in web technologies will understand that the question mark is the beginning of a URL query string and not part of the content.)

NOTE

A SAS must have an expiration date. Make sure the expiration date is sufficiently far in the future so your backups don't start failing unexpectedly. Regardless of the expiration date of the SAS token, it's a good idea to rotate the secret on a regular schedule. As with other certificates in your environment, mark your calendars in advance of the expiration date you choose.

The SAS token must be used to create a credential. The credential's name is the URL to the Azure Storage container. After the credential is created, backing up the database to Azure Storage only requires specifying the TO URL clause, as illustrated in the upcoming sample.

The following sample creates a credential using a SAS token and backs up the SSIO2022 database to the SSIO2022 Azure Storage account. The sample uses the WITH FORMAT option to overwrite an existing backup at the same URL. Your use case may require you to keep historic backups, in which case you should probably generate the backup file name by including the date and time of the backup. If you keep historic backups, you must create a scheme to remove outdated backup files; the RETAINDAYS and EXPIREDATE options are not supported with the TO URL clause.

```
CREATE CREDENTIAL [https://ssio2022.blob.core.windows.net/onprembackup]
    WITH IDENTITY = 'SHARED ACCESS SIGNATURE',
    -- Remember to remove the leading ? from the token
    SECRET = 'sv=2022-03-28&ss=…';
BACKUP DATABASE SamplesTest
    TO URL = 'https://ssio2022.blob.core.windows.net/onprembackup/db.bak'
    -- WITH FORMAT to overwrite the existing file
    WITH FORMAT;
```

➤ Extensive guidance on backup to URL is available at *https://learn.microsoft.com/sql /relational-databases/backup-restore/sql-server-backup-to-url*.

For security reasons, the container holding your SQL Server database backups should be configured as Private. We recommend that you configure the storage account to require secure transfer, meaning only HTTPS connections are allowed. Secure transfer is required by default on all new Azure Storage accounts. You can further secure the SAS token by restricting the IP addresses that can connect to the Azure Storage service using the token. If you choose to do so, you must remember to obtain a new token and update the database credential when your organization's outbound IP addresses change.

CHAPTER 10

NOTE

Did you know that SSMS 18 and later support connecting to Azure Storage? While Azure Storage Explorer is a great tool for managing Azure Storage accounts, the option to connect to an Azure Storage account used for SQL Server backups directly from within SSMS can be a time-saver. You can access this functionality from the Back Up Database dialog box.

Backup and media sets

As noted, SQL Server backups are written to media types (devices)—namely tape, disk (which includes locally connected volumes, solid-state drives, and UNC network paths), and Azure Blob Storage. Each of these types has specific properties, including format and block size.

Media set

A *media set* is an ordered collection of a fixed type and number of devices (see Figure 10-2). For example, if you are using a backup disk, your media set will comprise a fixed number of one or more files.

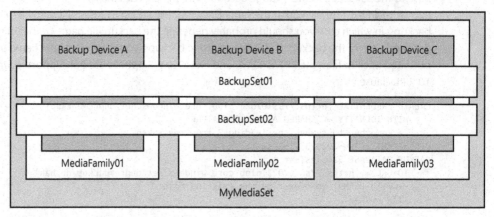

Figure 10-2 A media set, containing three media families spread over three devices.

A backup will always contain at least one media set. With tape backup now deprecated, media sets with multiple devices are less common. Other factors to consider:

- **Backup window.** The backup window might be too short to allow the backup to finish unless it's striped across multiple files or URLs.

- **Backup to URL.** The recommended block blobs in Azure Storage can hold 200 GB per blob at most. If your backup is larger than 200 GB, you'll need to use multiple block blobs. Better backup performance may also be achieved using multiple block blobs, assuming your Internet upload speed is sufficient. We should note that concerns surrounding the integrity of striped backups are less acute in Azure Storage because you can, and should, configure the storage account with automatic redundancy, if not geo-redundancy.

SQL Server Enterprise edition supports mirroring media sets. A mirrored media set writes another copy of the backup. This feature provides you with a redundant copy of your backup on the same type of media. When the mirrored media sets are appropriately segmented on different storage hardware, this redundant copy increases the reliability of the backup, because an error in one backup set might not affect the mirrored copy.

➤ To read more about mirrored backup media sets, see *https://learn.microsoft.com/sql /relational-databases/backup-restore/mirrored-backup-media-sets-sql-server*.

Media family

In each media set, all backup devices used in that media set make up the *media family*. The number of devices in that set is the number of media families. If a media set uses three backup devices that are not mirrored, there are three media families in that media set.

Backup set

A successful backup added to a media set is called a *backup set*. Information about successful backups is stored in the header of the backup set.

You can reuse an existing backup set by adding new backups for a database to the end of that media. This grows the media by appending the backup. However, we do not recommend this practice, because the integrity of previous backups relies on the consistency of that media. An errant INIT option in the backup command could even accidentally overwrite existing backups in the backup set.

Inside OUT

What media set, media family, and backup set should you use?

For typical SQL Server instances, we recommend that you back up your databases to multiple, individual, clearly named, self-contained files. Only one backup should be stored in each file. If you are using a third-party solution (free or paid), make sure they follow a strong naming convention, as well.

In other words, the filename itself should contain the server and instance name, the database name, the type of backup (full, differential, or transaction log), as well as the date and time of the backup. This makes locating, managing, and restoring backups much easier because every file is a separate backup set, media family, and media set.

For example, a full backup of the WideWorldImporters sample database on the default instance of a SQL Server called SERVER, taken on February 9th, 2023, at 10:53:44 p.m., might have the following filename: SERVER_WideWorldImporters_FULL_20230209_225344.BAK. To avoid issues with filenames during daylight saving time (DST) changeover, we recommend specifying the time in UTC or with time zone offset.

Similarly, differential and transaction log backups should follow the naming convention but use a different file extension. The file extension does not actually matter, but a common practice is .dif for differential backups and .trn for transaction log backups.

Back up to S3-compatible storage

New in SQL Server 2022 is Simple Storage Service (S3)–compatible object storage integration. This feature extends existing `BACKUP TO URL` and `RESTORE FROM URL` functionality to S3 URLs using a REST API. URLs pointing to S3-compatible resources are prefixed with s3:// to denote that the S3 API is being used.

> ➤ An introduction to the S3 protocol and how it is used at Microsoft can be found at *https://learn.microsoft.com/sql/relational-databases/backup-restore/sql-server-backup-and-restore-with-s3-compatible-object-storage.*

Requirements for S3-compatible storage

URLs beginning with the s3:// prefix assume that the underlying protocol is HTTPS, which means SQL Server will require a TLS certificate. Additionally, you will need credentials (an Access Key ID and Secret Key ID) to access the S3-compatible endpoint. You cannot back up to S3-compatible storage unless a bucket has been created on the S3-compatible storage account. Creating a bucket is not possible from within SQL Server.

Control backup size and speed

Your backup will use multiple parts—a maximum of 10,000 parts per URL, ranging in size from 5 MB to 20 MB, with a default of 10 MB. You can adjust this size using `MAXTRANSFERSIZE`. If a maximum of 10,000 parts at 20 MB per part is not sufficient, you can stripe your backup across multiple URLs, to a maximum of 64.

NOTE

You must enable backup compression if you back up to S3-compatible storage and modify the `MAXTRANSFERSIZE` setting.

If a backup to S3-compatible storage fails, any temporary files created during the backup process will not be automatically removed. You must remove them manually.

> ➤ For more information about backing up to S3-compatible storage, visit *https://learn.microsoft.com/sql/relational-databases/backup-restore/sql-server-backup-to-url-s3-compatible-object-storage.*

Create and verify backups

You should completely automate your SQL Server backups, whether you use the built-in SSMS Maintenance Plan Wizard or a third-party solution (free or paid). Always ensure that backups are successful by observing that the backup files exist and that the backup task does not error out. Additionally, you must regularly test backups by restoring them, which you should also do with an automated process.

For example, the dbatools.io library of SQL Server administration cmdlets includes `Test-DbaLastBackup`, which automatically restores, runs a `DBCC CHECKDB`, and drops a database. Consider this tool or similar automation solutions. For more information, see *https://docs.dbatools.io/Test-DbaLastBackup.html*.

➤ **You can read more about maintenance plans in Chapter 9.**

SQL Server Agent is an excellent resource for automating backups, and many third-party solutions use it, too—as does the Maintenance Plan Wizard.

Create backups

You can design a backup solution to satisfy a recovery strategy by using all or a combination of the available backup types. This chapter already covered the backup types and code samples.

Inside OUT

How frequently should you run backups?

Business requirements and database size will dictate how long your maintenance window is and what needs to be backed up in that window. You might have a critical database small enough that it can be fully backed up daily and therefore has no need for differential backups. Larger databases might require a weekly schedule, augmented by daily differential backups.

A database in the full recovery model should have transaction log backups occurring as a factor of the RPO. Transaction logs should be backed up and securely copied offsite at a more frequent interval than your RPO. Assuming your RPO is 5 minutes, you should back up your transaction log so it takes less than 5 minutes to back it up and copy it offsite. For example, you can back up the log every 3 minutes, which gives you 2 minutes to get the backup offsite. This is to accommodate the implicit delay between when a backup ends and when the backup has been copied offsite. In the case of a disaster, there is a higher chance that the files are copied offsite with a smaller copy interval. A backup is realistically not available to meet the RPO until it is copied offsite successfully.

Databases that can be rebuilt using existing processes might not need to be backed up at all. Such databases should use the simple recovery model.

The buffer pool (see Chapter 2) is not used for database backups. The *backup buffer* is a portion of memory outside the buffer pool, big enough to read pages from the data file and write those pages to the backup file. The backup buffer is usually between 16 MB and 32 MB in size.

Memory pressure can reduce the backup and restore buffer sizes, causing backups and restores to take longer.

CAUTION

It is possible to increase the number of backup buffers (using the BUFFERCOUNT option) as well as the transfer size of each block to the backup media (using the MAXTRANSFERSIZE option) to improve throughput. However, we recommend this cautiously, and only in circumstances where the defaults calculated by SQL Server prove problematic. Allocating too many buffers or increasing the transfer size too much might cause out-of-memory exceptions during the backup operation, which will cause the backup to fail. While this is not a situation that would require a server restart, it does diminish the automation you set up for backups. You can read more about this possible issue at *https://blogs.msdn.microsoft.com /sqlserverfaq/2010/05/06/incorrect-buffercount-data-transfer-option-can-lead-to-oom -condition*.

Verify backups

After you create a backup, we highly recommend that you immediately verify that the backup was successful. Although rare, corruption is always possible. Most of the time, it is caused by the storage layer (including device drivers, network drivers, and filter drivers), but it can also occur in non-ECC RAM or as the result of a bug in SQL Server itself.

NOTE

A *filter driver* is software that intercepts all drive reads and writes. This class of software includes defragmentation tools and security products like antivirus software. This is a good opportunity to remind you to exclude SQL Server files (data, logs, and backups) from antivirus scanners, and to note that defragmenting solid-state storage is a bad idea because it will dramatically reduce the lifespan of the drive.

➤ See KB309422 for more information on which antivirus exclusions to add for SQL Server, available at *http://support.microsoft.com/help/309422*.

There are two ways to verify a backup. You can probably guess that the most complete way is to restore it and use DBCC CHECKDB to perform a full consistency check on the restored database.

The other, quicker method is to use RESTORE VERIFYONLY. If you backed up your database using the checksum option (which is enabled by default on compressed backups), the restore will verify the backup checksum as well as the data page and log block checksums as it reads through the backup media. The convenience with RESTORE VERIFYONLY is that you do not need to allocate drive space to restore the data and log files, because the restore will read directly from the backup itself.

Inside OUT

Why should you perform a DBCC CHECKDB if you have backup checksums enabled?

Although backup checksums are verified by RESTORE VERIFYONLY, it is possible for corruption to occur after a page is verified, as it is being written to the drive or while it is copied offsite. A successful RESTORE VERIFYONLY is not a clean bill of health for the backup.

You can build an automated process on another server with a lot of cheaper drive space to restore all databases after they have been backed up and perform a DBCC CHECKDB on them. This also gives you an excellent idea of whether you can meet your RTO as databases grow. A successful DBCC CHECKDB is the *only* way to know that a database is free of corruption.

Restore a database

To restore a database, you generally start with a full backup (piecemeal restore is covered in a later section).

If you plan to use differential and/or transaction log backups, you must use the NORECOVERY keyword for all but the last of the backup files you will restore.

- You restore a database in the simple recovery model by using a full backup to begin, plus the most recent differential backup based on the full backup if it is available.

- You can restore a database in the bulk-logged recovery model by using a full backup, along with the most recent differential backup based on that full backup, if available. Should you want to restore to a specific point in time for a bulk-logged database, this might be possible if no bulk-logged operations exist in the transaction log backups you use.

- You can restore a database in the full recovery model to a point in time using a full backup, plus any transaction log backups that form part of the backup chain. You can use a more recent differential backup (based on that full backup) to bypass a number of those transaction log backups, where appropriate.

CAUTION

Differential and transaction log backups rely on a corresponding full backup. If the full backup is not available, the differential and transaction log backups are useless. All transaction log backups must be available at least to the point in time to which you're trying to restore.

CHAPTER 10

Each transaction log backup is replayed against the database being recovered, using the NORECOVERY option, as though those transactions are happening in real time. Each file is restored in sequential order up to the required point in time or until the last transaction log backup is reached, whichever comes first.

NOTE

When restoring a chain of transaction log backups, especially the first one in the sequence after a full or differential backup, it's possible for the LSN of the transaction log backup to be earlier than the latest LSN of the full or differential backup that was restored. In most cases, you can ignore the error message that appears, because the next transaction log file in the restore sequence will usually contain the required LSN.

After the entire chain has been restored (indicated by the WITH RECOVERY option), only then does the recovery kick in (covered in some detail in Chapter 3). All transactions that are committed will be rolled forward, and any in-flight transactions will be rolled back.

Some examples of restoring a database are included in the section that follows.

Restore a database using a full backup

You can perform a database restore through SSMS, Azure Data Studio, or by using a T-SQL statement. In this example, only a full backup file is available to restore a database. The full backup comes from a different server, where the path of the original database is different, so the database's files must be relocated (moved) on the new server with the MOVE option.

To see the progress of the restore, you can set the statistics to display to the output window with the STATS option. The default is to write progress for every 5 percent complete. No statistics will be output until the files have been created on the file system.

```
RESTORE DATABASE WideWorldImporters
FROM DISK = N'C:\SQLData\Backup\SERVER_WideWorldImporters_FULL_20220918_210912.BAK'
WITH MOVE N'WideWorldImporters' TO N'C:\SQLData\WWI.mdf',
MOVE N'WideWorldImporters_log' TO N'C:\SQLData\WWI.ldf',
STATS = 5,
RECOVERY;
GO
```

The RECOVERY option (the default) at the end brings the database online immediately after the full backup has been restored. This prevents any further backups from being applied. If you want to restore a differential backup after this full backup, you must use the NORECOVERY option. Later, bring the database online only after restoring subsequent differential or transaction log backups. This is covered in the next section.

Restore a database with differential and log backups

Restoring using full, differential, and transaction log backups is more complicated, but you can still perform it through SSMS's graphical wizard, Azure Data Studio, or by using a series of T-SQL statements.

For this scenario, we recommend creating your own automated scripts. For example, after every transaction log backup, you can use the information in the msdb database to build a script to restore the entire database to that point in time and then save the script in the same folder as the backup file(s).

> ### NOTE
>
> **When restoring a database using more than one backup type (full, plus differential and/or transaction log), each** `RESTORE` **statement that will be followed by another restore file must include a** `WITH NORECOVERY` **option. This prevents recovery from running until needed. You can either use the** `WITH RECOVERY` **option on the final file to run recovery and bring the database online or you can add an extra line to the end of the script as in the following example.**

You restore a database by using the RESTORE command. Full and differential restores use the RESTORE DATABASE option by convention. You can also restore transaction logs by using the RESTORE DATABASE option, but you might prefer to use RESTORE LOG, instead, for clarity:

```
-- First, restore the full backup
RESTORE DATABASE WideWorldImporters
FROM DISK = N'C:\SQLData\Backup\SERVER_WideWorldImporters_FULL_20220918_210912.BAK'
WITH
MOVE N'WideWorldImporters' TO N'C:\SQLData\WWI.mdf',
MOVE N'WideWorldImporters_log' TO N'C:\SQLData\WWI.ldf',
NORECOVERY;
GO
-- Second, restore the most recent differential backup
RESTORE DATABASE WideWorldImporters
FROM DISK = N'C:\SQLData\Backup\SERVER_WideWorldImporters_DIFF_20220926_120100.BAK'
WITH NORECOVERY;
GO
-- Finally, restore all transaction log backups after the differential
RESTORE LOG WideWorldImporters
FROM DISK = N'C:\SQLData\Backup\SERVER_WideWorldImporters_LOG_20220926_121500.BAK'
WITH NORECOVERY;
GO
RESTORE LOG WideWorldImporters
FROM DISK = N'C:\SQLData\Backup\SERVER_WideWorldImporters_LOG_20220926_123000.BAK'
WITH NORECOVERY;
GO
-- Bring the database online
RESTORE LOG WideWorldImporters WITH RECOVERY;
GO
```

Remember: Specify `WITH RECOVERY` in the final transaction log file restore, or in a separate command as in the previous example.

The `RECOVERY` option instructs SQL Server to run recovery on the database, which might include an upgrade step if the new instance has a newer version of SQL Server on it. When recovery is complete, the database is brought online.

Restore a database to a point in time

If configured properly, it is possible to restore a database to the exact moment in time (or more precisely, to the exact LSN) before a disaster occurred. A point-in-time restore requires an LSN or timestamp (meaning any specific date and time value) to let the `RESTORE` command know when to stop restoring. You can even restore to a specific mark in the transaction log backup, which you specify at transaction-creation time by explicitly naming a transaction. This requires knowing in advance that this transaction might be the cause for a point-in-time restore, which is rarely the case in a disaster scenario.

> ### NOTE
>
> **Some scenarios where you might suspect in advance that a point-in-time recovery is required include performing a schema upgrade, perhaps as part of an application release.**

> ➤ To see more about marking transactions, go to *https://learn.microsoft.com/sql/t-sql /statements/restore-statements-transact-sql*.

> ### CAUTION
>
> **The timestamp used for a point-in-time restore comes from the transaction log itself and refers to the local date and time on the SQL Server instance when the transaction started. Remember to take time zones and daylight saving time into consideration when restoring a database to a point in time.**

Depending on the cause of the disaster, you might want to investigate the current state of the database to determine the best recovery approach. You might need to close connections to the database and set the database to single user mode. In single user mode, you have time to find out what happened (without making modifications), take a tail-log backup when possible and necessary, and recover the database to the moment before disaster struck.

In some cases, you might opt to leave the database active but restore it to a new database and reload changes from the restored version. The feasibility of this depends on the database schema, the number of changes that have been made since the adverse event, and the RTO.

A point-in-time restore works only when restoring transaction log backups, not full or differential backups. The point in time must be after the full backup from which you begin the restore process. This fact may make it valuable to keep several full backups prior to the most recent one. Some errors, such as human error or database corruption, may not always be detected before a new full backup is taken.

Inside OUT

How can you tell when the unplanned event took place?

To find out when a disaster occurred that isn't immediately apparent, you can query the active portion of the transaction log if it is available, using an undocumented system function that reads from the active VLF(s), as demonstrated here:

```
SELECT * FROM sys.fn_dblog(NULL, NULL);
```

This displays all transactions that have not yet been flushed by a checkpoint operation. The NULL parameters are the start and end LSN, but of course, if you knew those, you wouldn't be searching the log in the first place.

Using a standard WHERE clause, you can trace back to the point immediately before the event took place. For example, if you know a user deleted a row from a table, you could write a query looking for all delete operations:

```
SELECT * FROM sys.fn_dblog(NULL, NULL)
WHERE operation LIKE '%delete%';
```

To get this to work, SQL Server should still be running, and the transaction log should still be available (although this technique does work on offline transaction log files using sys.fn_dump_dblog).

To see more from Paul Randal about reading from the transaction log, visit *https://www .sqlskills.com/blogs/paul/using-fn_dblog-fn_dump_dblog-and-restoring-with-stopbeforemark -to-an-lsn/.*

The process is the same as in the previous example, except for the final transaction log file, for which the point in time is specified by using the STOPAT or STOPBEFOREMARK options. Let's look at each option:

- **STOPAT.** A timestamp. You must know this value from the time an unexpected event occurred. If it's unclear when the event occurred, you might need to explore the transaction log.

- **STOPBEFOREMARK or STOPATMARK.** A log sequence number or transaction name. You must know the LSN value from exploring the active portion of the transaction log (see the preceding Inside OUT).

Assuming you have followed the same sequence as shown in the previous example, the final transaction log restore might look like this:

```
-- Restore point in time using timestamp
RESTORE LOG WideWorldImporters
FROM DISK = N'C:\SQLData\Backup\SERVER_WideWorldImporters_LOG_20170926_123000.BAK'
WITH STOPAT = 'Sep 26, 2017 12:28 AM',
RECOVERY;
GO
-- Or restore point in time using LSN
-- Assume that this LSN is where the bad thing happened
RESTORE LOG WideWorldImporters
FROM DISK = N'C:\SQLData\Backup\SERVER_WideWorldImporters_LOG_20170926_123000.BAK'
WITH STOPBEFOREMARK = 'lsn:0x0000029f:00300212:0002',
RECOVERY;
GO
```

➤ To read more about database recovery, including syntax and examples, visit *https://learn .microsoft.com/sql/t-sql/statements/restore-statements-transact-sql*.

Restore a database piecemeal

Partial database backups deal with file and filegroup backups to ease the manageability of your VLDB. This is an advanced topic with much detail to be discovered in your environment.

Partial recovery is useful for bringing a database online as quickly as possible to allow the organization to continue working. You can then restore any secondary filegroups later, during a planned maintenance window.

Piecemeal restores begin with something called the *partial-restore sequence*. In this sequence, the primary filegroup is restored and recovered first. If the database is under the simple recovery model, all read/write filegroups are then restored.

➤ To learn more about the SQL Server recovery process, read Chapter 3.

While this is taking place, the database is offline until restore and recovery is complete. Any unrestored files or filegroups remain offline, but you can bring them online later by restoring them.

Regardless of the database's recovery model, the RESTORE command must include the PARTIAL option when doing a piecemeal restore, but only at the beginning of the sequence. Because transactions might span more than just the recovered filegroups, these transactions can become deferred, meaning that any transaction that needs to roll back cannot do so while a filegroup is offline. The transactions are deferred until the filegroup can be brought online again, and any data involved in that deferred transaction is locked in the meantime.

Restore a database piecemeal under the simple recovery model

To initialize a partial recovery of a database under the simple recovery model, you must begin with a full database or a partial backup. The restore will bring the primary filegroup and all read/write secondary filegroups online. You can then bring the database online. If any read-only filegroups were damaged or corrupted and you need to restore them, you will do those last.

Restore a database piecemeal under the full recovery model

As with the simple recovery model, you must begin with a full database or partial backup (which must include the primary filegroup). When possible, you should also have a tail-log backup to help restore the database to the most recent point in time.

It is possible to restore and recover only the most important read-write filegroups first, then restore additional read-write filegroups, before finally restoring any read-only filegroups. Depending on the design of the database and applications, the organization may resume critical operations sooner than if the entire database needed to be restored.

Point-in-time restore is provided under the following conditions:

- The first RESTORE DATABASE command must include the PARTIAL option.

- For a point-in-time restore against read-write filegroups, you need an unbroken log backup chain, and you must specify the time in the RESTORE statement.

➤ To see more about piecemeal restores, including code examples, visit *https://learn.microsoft .com/sql/relational-databases/backup-restore/piecemeal-restores-sql-server*.

NOTE

If you skip a FILESTREAM filegroup during partial recovery, you can never again recover it unless the entire database is restored in full.

Define a recovery strategy

Consider our scenario from the beginning of the chapter, in which anything and everything that could go wrong did go wrong. This section highlights certain issues that could have been addressed by an appropriate recovery plan. You can then implement this recovery plan, step by step, using your runbook. We also discuss recovery strategies around hybrid environments, and briefly discuss Azure SQL Database.

NOTE

The word *strategy* means there is a long-term goal. Your recovery strategy must adapt to environmental changes. A runbook is a living document; it requires incremental improvements as you test it.

CHAPTER 10

A sample recovery strategy for our DR scenario

Several avoidable problems occurred in the fictional DR story at the beginning of the chapter:

- There was no redundant power system in place.

- There was no redundant Internet connection (outside of a personal cellular device).

- There was no runbook to guide the accident-prone DBA.

- The security on the DR server did not follow recommended best practices.

- Sending the backups offsite failed.

The following subsections discuss some key considerations for your recovery strategy beyond taking backups.

Keep the lights on

In your runbook, ensure your UPS collection and backup generators can run all necessary equipment for long enough to keep emergency lights on, laptops charging, network equipment live, and servers running (including a monitor) so that your DBA can log in to the SQL Server instance long enough to run a tail-log backup if necessary. If the RTO allows it, you might be able to proactively shut down gracefully rather than attempting to keep less critical systems running with limited power. A graceful shutdown before a looming sudden shutdown is a smart idea.

It might sound like a small detail, but you should even have a list of diesel suppliers in your runbook, especially if your generators must keep running for several hours. Clean power is also important. Generators cause power fluctuations, which can damage sensitive electronic equipment. A power conditioner should be installed with your generator, and you must make sure it works correctly.

In our scenario, the backup power failed. There was no sufficient way to ensure electricity would continue to flow after the building lost power, which had several knock-on effects, including the inability to charge laptops and cellphone batteries.

Redundant Internet connection

If your backups are being copied securely offsite or you have a hybrid environment in which systems are connected across datacenters using virtual private networks (VPNs), make sure these routes can stay connected if one of the links goes down. In our scenario, the DBA had no option but to use a low-quality cellular connection. While cellular modems can be a part of your recovery strategy, they can be fickle, and fail under sudden public demand. It's also difficult to connect servers this way.

Know where the runbook is

The runbook itself should be printed out and stored in a secure but easily accessible location (for example, a fireproof safe or lockbox). Don't forget to have an electronic copy available, as well, stored with a cloud provider of your choice and kept up to date.

Make sure your offsite backups are secure and tamper-proof

Security of the offsite location for backups is critical, and no one should have access to that site unless they are required to do a recovery. In our sample scenario, our DBA accidentally deleted an email alert indicating that the offsite storage for backups was almost full. This alert is a good one to have, but it was not acted on appropriately. Also, the cause of the alert was an avoidable situation because the colleague who used up the free space should not have been able to access critical organization resources.

Remote, offsite backups ideally aren't accessible via network shares. Air-gapped backups are protected from ransomware attacks running rampant in your network. Copying offsite backups into your network should be through just-in-time access or other temporary means.

Regularly check and test your backups

Automate your backups and post-backup steps to verify backup success. Use maintenance plans (see Chapter 9) or established third-party backup tools such as dbatools.io or Ola Hallengren's Maintenance Solution (available from *https://ola.hallengren.com*).

Verify that you have a process to check that your backups are taking place and test that process often. For example, if SQL Server Agent is crashing, your notifications might not fire. Test the backups, as well, by having a machine that restores backups continuously and by running DBCC CHECKDB where possible. If you can afford it, have log shipping configured so that all backups are restored as soon as they come into offsite storage. Ensure that the backup files are being securely copied offsite as soon as they can be.

If you're unable to continuously restore databases, run random spot checks of your backups by picking a date and time in the backup history and restoring the backup. Aside from testing the databases themselves, this is a good rehearsal for when something goes wrong. Use the runbook for these exercises to ensure it is, and remains, up to date. Remember to run DBCC CHECKDB on any database you restore.

You might find as databases grow that the SLA becomes out of date and that the RTO is no longer achievable. Running these tests will alert you to this situation long before it becomes a problem and will allow you to tweak how you perform backups in the future. For example, you might discover that it is much quicker to spin up an Azure virtual machine (VM) with SQL Server and restore the business-critical databases stored in Azure Blob Storage than to struggle with VPN connections and failed hardware on-premises.

CHAPTER 10

Our DBA assumed the backups were taking place every 15 minutes and being copied offsite immediately afterward. This was not the case, and instead of losing 15 minutes of data, the organization lost as much as 27 minutes' worth.

Check the security of your disaster recovery site

Your DR site might have outdated security access controls, whether physical or virtual. Be sure you stay up to date, especially when people leave the company. You don't want to be in the position of having to call someone who left your organization two years ago to ask for a firewall password—especially not at 3 a.m. on a Sunday (as is this author's experience). If you must use a remote desktop connection to access a server, protect it by using a VPN.

Prepare tools and credentials

Check that you have already downloaded additional tools and documented how to use them. Unless they pose a security risk, have them available on the recovery systems in advance.

Keep all passwords and keys (symmetric and asymmetric) in a password manager as well as printed and stored in a secure location with the runbook where practical. Make sure all digital certificates are backed up securely.

Automate restore scripts

In case the msdb database is inaccessible, and you cannot generate a restore script from a database backup history, be sure you have a tool that generates a restore script based on files in a folder in your offsite storage. Many tools do this, including the `Restore-DbaDatabase` command in the free dbatools (available from *https://dbatools.io*). This is also when self-evident backup file naming and extensions help you to create the recovery chain.

Practice your disaster recovery plan

In concert with your HA strategy, which involves automated and manual failovers (see Chapter 11 for more on this), you should perform regular drills to test your runbook. You can also have people in your organization who are unfamiliar with the environment look through the runbook. They can provide valuable information regarding assumptions you might have made.

The cadence is up to your organization, but a full DR scenario should be tested at least once a year. Any changes you need to make to the runbook should be made immediately. If the recovery fails, add notes of how it failed and what you did to resolve the failure. All this information is extremely valuable.

Recovery strategies for hybrid and cloud environments

Many organizations use a combination of on-premises infrastructure and services in remote locations, including Azure services, third-party datacenters, and other cloud vendors.

Recover data in hybrid and cloud environments

The strategy for recovering data in a hybrid environment is very similar to an on-premises strategy, except that you must take network connection, latency, and bandwidth into account. When designing a recovery strategy for a hybrid environment, pick a DR site that is central, but geo-replicated.

It is prudent to use virtualization technologies that allow for VM and file system snapshots to ensure that your virtual servers are backed up regularly. These VM backups can be spun up in case of a disaster more quickly than rebuilding physical servers. You can augment these with appropriate native SQL Server backups that are tested properly.

If you already use Azure Storage for your backups, this reduces the network bandwidth and latency issues if you can restore your organization's databases to Azure VMs or databases in Azure SQL Database.

Remember that after failing over to a DR site, you must fail back to your on-premises site when it is up and running again. Based on the magnitude of the disaster, you may need to keep the DR site as the new primary, in which case you must set up a new DR site.

Recovering a database in Azure SQL Database

Chapter 17, "Provision Azure SQL Database," offers an in-depth look at managing Azure SQL Database, including preparing for DR. There are three options to consider when restoring a point-in-time backup, which play into your runbook:

- **Database replacement.** You can replace an existing database using a database backup. This requires you to verify the service tier and performance level of the restored database. To replace your existing database, rename the existing one and restore to the old name.

- **Data recovery.** If you need to recover data from a previous point in time, you can restore the database to a new database. Azure SQL Database lets you specify the point in time within the backup retention period to which you wish to restore.

- **Deleted database.** If you deleted a database and you are still within the recovery window, you can restore that deleted database to the time just before it was deleted.

The geo-restore feature can restore a full backup to any server in any Azure region from a geo-redundant backup. Databases on the basic performance tier can take up to 12 hours to geo-restore. This estimated recovery time should factor into your RTO. With Azure SQL Database, you're also giving up control over the RPO. When properly implemented, as discussed in Chapter 17, Azure SQL Database supports an RPO of as little as 5 seconds.

> ➤ To read more about recovering a database in Azure SQL Database, including associated costs, read Chapter 17, or visit *https://learn.microsoft.com/azure/sql-database/sql-database-recovery-using-backups*.

CHAPTER 10

Implement high availability and disaster recovery

Two main goals for any database administrator are to ensure databases remain available to the business and to prevent data loss. Creating solutions that are highly available, and planning to minimize downtime, not only greatly benefits your organization, it allows you to look like a hero when disaster strikes. When considering these solutions, you must also take into account your organization's Recovery Time Objective (RTO) and Recovery Point Objective (RPO).

This chapter prepares you to meet both of these goals. It covers what you should do beyond database backups. Its contents complement the concepts discussed in Chapter 10, "Develop, deploy, and manage data recovery." First, it provides an overview of the high-availability (HA) and disaster-recovery (DR) technologies available for SQL Server, including log shipping, replication, failover clustering, availability groups, and the new Azure SQL Managed Instance link feature. Then, it looks at configuring failover clusters and availability groups on Windows and Linux. Starting in SQL Server 2019, support for Linux extends to availability groups as well as replication, and we provide a guide to your first availability group on Red Hat Linux. Finally, it covers the administration of availability groups, such as monitoring, performance analysis, and alerting.

All code samples for this book are available for download at *https://www.MicrosoftPressStore.com /SQLServer2022InsideOut/downloads*.

> ➤ This chapter deals with SQL Server instances. Disaster recovery technologies provided in Microsoft Azure SQL Database are covered in Chapter 17, "Provision Azure SQL Database." Some concepts for availability groups also apply to Azure SQL Managed Instance, including the new link feature for Azure SQL Managed Instances discussed in this chapter. We discuss Azure SQL Managed Instance in Chapter 18, "Provision Azure SQL Managed Instance."

Overview of high-availability and disaster-recovery technologies

As an enterprise-grade data platform, SQL Server provides features to ensure HA and to prepare for DR. Using these features requires some effort and extra investment, however; you must configure them correctly to provide the desired benefits.

The level of effort and investment to ensure HA and DR should never exceed the value of the data to the organization. In other words, not every database on every server must be configured for HA and DR. Depending on the value of the data and any Service-Level Agreements (SLAs), having backups available off-premises might be sufficient to prepare for disaster. (As always, you should copy your backups off-premises as soon as possible after they are taken, and you should test them regularly.)

For cases in which additional investment is warranted, there are many technologies available. Some are suitable for HA and others for DR, and a few are suitable for both uses. In this first section, we cover the variety of technologies available in SQL Server to build a highly available environment and to prepare for DR.

Inside OUT

What's the difference between HA and DR anyway?

Before covering the different technologies, we should clarify the difference between HA and DR.

HA means your databases automatically remain available in the face of hardware failures, software failures, or any other scenario that causes downtime. HA requires redundant hardware and platforms, as well as automation and planning for how secondary systems can assume the role of the primary system. This chapter discusses HA in the context of the SQL Server layer, but you should also consider the HA of other layers necessary for running applications for end users, such as the network, storage, and application layers.

DR means your data is not lost after a substantial incident (a "disaster"), such as a human error that introduces bad data, a storage failure, a ransomware attack, or a natural disaster like an earthquake or hurricane. Data might be temporarily unavailable until you run your DR plan. A DR plan involves redundant storage of backup files, accomplished by copying backups offsite. You can use other methods for DR, too, such as maintaining online copies of databases in separate datacenters. As discussed in the preceding chapter, a backup shouldn't be considered "taken" until it is copied offsite.

Compare HA and DR technologies

Table 11-1 compares the four major technologies for HA and DR using a variety of attributes. This table is not meant to provide a complete comparison of features; rather, it gathers the details relevant for HA and DR.

Table 11-1 Comparison of four HA and DR technologies in SQL Server 2022

	Log shipping	Failover clustering	Availability groups	Basic availability groups
Capable of automatic failover	No	Yes	Yes	Yes
Instance versions	Should match exactly*	Match exactly**	Match exactly**	Match exactly**
Edition	Web, Standard, Enterprise	Standard, Enterprise	Enterprise	Standard
Readable secondary	Yes, but interrupted by log restores	No	Yes	No
Different indexing on readable secondary	No	No	No	No
Schema changes required to tables	No	No	No	No
Schema changes replicated	Yes	N/A	Yes	Yes
Primary purpose	DR	HA	HA/DR/ Readable secondary	HA/DR
Level	Database	Instance	Databases	Databases
FILESTREAM and FileTable	Yes and yes	Yes with shared disk, yes	Yes and partially‡	Yes and partially‡

* In theory, log shipping to a higher version of SQL Server is possible, in which case there is no path to return to the primary copy after recovering from a disaster.

** Temporarily, these environments can be different versions while applying cumulative updates in a rolling fashion.

‡ FILESTREAM is fully supported. FileTables are supported on the primary replica, but FileTables are not readable on a secondary replica, regardless of replica settings.

Understand log shipping

The log shipping feature in SQL Server enables you to create a copy of a database on a secondary instance, by automatically restoring transaction log backups from the database on a primary instance to one or more secondary instances. You must set up log shipping for each individual database. Therefore, if your application uses multiple databases, you must independently configure each database for log shipping.

NOTE

You can perform transaction log backups only if the database uses the full or bulk-logged recovery model. You cannot configure log shipping on a database in the simple recovery model. For more information on database recovery models, refer to Chapter 10.

The real role of log shipping isn't to provide HA. Unlike other HA features, log shipping does not provide a way to failover to the secondary copy of the database. With log shipping, something resembling failover would involve manual intervention and connection string redirection outside of SQL Server. You can configure the log shipping job to set the secondary database to standby mode, however, allowing for read-only access. This is not as elegant or useful a solution as an availability group's secondary replica. Users concurrently accessing the standby database block the next transaction log restore in the chain.

All the logs are sent to the log shipping secondary database and are restored WITH NORECOVERY, meaning the database maintains "In Recovery" status and prevents you from accessing them. In the event of a disaster, you can restore the last good transaction log backup from the source or, if no more are available, simply bring the destination database online.

In the most common use case, log shipping streams backups to an off-premises DR SQL Server. In this scenario, you could manually bring the remote secondary database online, create a new backup of the secondary database, and restore it to the primary after a disaster that claims the primary database. Another common use for log shipping is to provide a "rewind" copy of the database. That is, you can delay the restoration of the transaction log backups on the secondary instance and provide an uncorrupted backup of the database in the event of a data-related disaster, perhaps caused by an application fault or human error.

Inside OUT

Can you use log shipping to send data from on-premises SQL Server instances to Azure SQL Database or Azure SQL Managed Instance?

You cannot currently configure log shipping with a database in Azure SQL Database or Azure SQL Managed Instance as the destination. However, you can use the Azure Database Migration Service (DMS) to initiate the Log Replay Service (LRS), which is functionally the same as log shipping. If you use LRS, you also have the option to continuously restore differential and log backups to the managed instance. One popular use case for LRS is to migrate databases from on premises to Azure SQL Managed Instance.

SQL Server 2022 introduces a superior alternative with shorter downtime, however: the link feature for Azure SQL Managed Instance. This feature provides near–real time replication via a distributed availability group, and can facilitate a migration, failover, and failback without downtime. We discuss the link feature later in this chapter.

Although log shipping is a time-honored and straightforward way to set up a secondary database, it does have a couple shortcomings:

- You can create no other transaction log backups than those used for log shipping. So, you must find a balance between the replication frequency for DR and the frequency of creating transaction log backups for point-in-time restores—for example, to recover from user error or ransomware attack.

- You can create log-shipped backups quite frequently—every minute, even—but you must plan appropriately for the overhead of creating the transaction log backups and having the files copied over the network to the file share.

Overall, log shipping is considered a rudimentary form of DR—indeed, it was introduced in SQL Server 7.0—that does what it can and does it well. It is capable of continuously shipping a chain of transaction logs to a remote database for months or even years. Let's take a quick look at setting up and configuring log shipping.

Configure log shipping

Log shipping relies on a network share for the folder where transaction log backups will be stored. This folder and share require specific permissions that depend on a few factors. Log shipping uses SQL Server Agent to run scheduled jobs.

Be sure SQL Server Agent is scheduled to start automatically. The account for the transaction log backup job (which runs on the primary server) must have read and write access to the folder (if the folder is located on the primary server) or the network share (if the folder is not located on the primary server). The proxy account for the backup copy job, which runs on the secondary server, must have read access to the file share.

If you are using SQL Server Management Studio (SSMS) to configure log shipping, it will restore a full backup of the database on the secondary server from the network share, using your credentials. If you are using Transact-SQL (T-SQL) scripts to create the log shipping, you must copy and restore this backup manually.

CAUTION

If you let SQL Server create the secondary database(s) during configuration, the data and log files for the secondary database will be placed on the same volume as the data and log file for the destination instance's master database, by default. In SSMS, in the Secondary Database Settings page, you can use the Restore Options button on the Initialize Secondary Database tab to change the destination data and log file directories on the secondary server.

On the primary SQL Server instance, log shipping creates a SQL Server Agent job called LSBackup_<dbname> to back up the transaction logs to the network share. You must schedule the log shipping log backup job to occur on a schedule that meets your RPO, while taking into account the overhead and duration involved with creating, transferring, and restoring the backups.

Log shipping also creates a SQL Server Agent job called LSAlert_<primaryinstancename> that fails if no backup is detected in the desired window. You can monitor the job for failure and also monitor the SQL Server Error Log for severity 16 errors that might be thrown that relate to log shipping not performing (error number 14420) or restoring a backup log operation (error number 14421).

> ➤ To configure SQL alerts, see Chapter 9, "Automate SQL Server administration."

On the secondary SQL Server instance, log shipping creates three SQL Server Agent jobs:

- **LSCopy_<primaryinstancename>.** Copies the backup files from the file share to the secondary server

- **LSRestore_<primaryinstancename>.** Continually restores the transaction log backups

- **LSAlert_<secondaryinstancename>.** Raises an error if no log backup is detected after a certain time

When using SSMS, these steps are mostly automated. Otherwise, you must manually schedule and enable these jobs. Here are a couple recommendations for optimally configuring log shipping:

- Configure the file share on a server other than the primary database server. That way, log files will be copied from the primary server only once. If you configure the file share on the primary server, each secondary will initiate a copy of the backup files. If you have more than one secondary, this will increase the network traffic to your primary server.

- Monitor log shipping activity using the report available in SSMS and configure alerts.

Understand the capabilities of failover clustering

The purpose of failover clustering is to provide a fully automated HA solution that protects against server failures due to hardware or software. Failover cluster instances (FCIs) build on the Windows Server Failover Cluster (WSFC) technology to implement this. In SQL Server on Linux instances, you can use your own cluster manager, such as Pacemaker. Conceptually, when the server hardware or software of an active cluster node fails, the cluster manager detects this and starts the SQL Server instance on another node.

NOTE

Always On is a marketing term to cover two HA technologies: failover cluster instances (FCIs) and availability groups (AGs). Although these two technologies are completely different and accomplish different tasks in different ways, they can also be combined.

An FCI is beneficial because the failover is automated, and because it often takes mere seconds for the failover of the SQL Server instance from one server to another. And even though clients experience connection disruption in the event of a failover, and the SQL Server experiences a restart, no special configuration on the client is required and reconnection is usually prompt. After a failover, the active instance will have the same DNS name and IP address as before. Clients can open a new connection using the same connection string and continue operating.

Failover clustering does not require any form of replication or data duplication. Instead, the SQL Server data and logs are stored on shared storage. Each cluster node has access to the shared storage, and WSFC determines which node is actively connected to shared storage, ensuring that only one node can write to the shared storage at a time. Cluster disks appear only in Windows Explorer on the node that "owns" them.

NOTE

We refer to any form of storage accessible by all nodes in the cluster as *shared storage*. Versions of SQL Server before 2012 required this to be storage that was connected to all cluster nodes. Since SQL Server 2012, however, shared storage can also include file shares. And since SQL Server 2016 and Windows Server 2016, shared storage can include Storage Spaces Direct (S2D) and Cluster Shared Volumes (CSVs). Although all these options can make selecting the appropriate one a little more difficult, they bring SQL Server failover clusters within reach for a much broader set of deployments.

Whichever option you select for storage, be sure it does not become a single point of failure. The entire path from the cluster nodes to the storage should be redundant. With traditional shared storage, this will likely involve configuring Multipath I/O (MPIO) to prevent a single shared drive from being discovered multiple times by each node. Many storage vendors provide the necessary device-specific module (DSMs)—that is, software drivers that work with the Windows MPIO feature. For Fibre Channel and iSCSI storage area networks (SANs), you can also use the generic Microsoft DSM if your vendor does not provide one.

Using WSFC poses additional requirements on the hardware and software configuration of each node as well as on shared storage. As for the hardware, WSFC requires the hardware on each node to be the same, including driver versions. The software on each node must also be the same, including operating system (OS) patches. WSFC provides a validation configuration wizard and the `Test-Cluster` PowerShell cmdlet, which provides detailed analysis and reports on the suitability of the selected servers to become cluster nodes.

➤ For details on the OS and SQL Server configuration necessary to create a failover cluster instance, see the "Configure failover cluster instances" section later in the chapter.

Inside OUT

Are SQL Server Integration Services (SSIS) and SQL Server Reporting Services (SSRS) part of the FCI?

SSIS and SSRS are not part of the FCI and are not cluster-aware services, so they do not follow SQL Server from one server to another during a failover. There are other methods for making those services highly available, however.

In general, SSRS should be configured on a separate Windows Server using the FCI as its database only, or configured on each Windows Server in the WSFC in scale-out deployment. Similarly, SSIS should be installed on each server in the WSFC. It can be manually made into a cluster-aware service, but there are other options. You can review these options here: *https://learn.microsoft.com/sql/integration-services/service/integration-services-ssis-in-a-cluster.*

Understand the capabilities of availability groups

Availability groups (AGs) provide HA and DR capabilities and more. An AG consists of one or more databases—called *availability databases*—that failover together.

Failover can be automatic or manual, and a manual failover can either be planned or forced. Of these three failover methods, when fully synchronized, only forced failover can cause data loss. The secondary replica(s) can optionally be readable in Enterprise edition, allowing some read-only access to be offloaded from the primary read-write databases.

Compared to mirroring or replication, AGs provide a superior set of dynamic management views for monitoring, as well as user interface dialog boxes in SSMS and other tools. AGs offer a formidable and capable feature set of which all DBAs should be aware.

NOTE

Many administrators are familiar with the Microsoft Exchange term *database availability group (DAG)*. DAG is not an acronym used to describe Always On availability groups, however. It is incorrect, and the technologies are very different, though perhaps appear similar at a high level. To prevent miscommunication, you should not use DAG to describe AGs, or to describe distributed availability groups.

Availability groups feature set

The early code name for the AGs project internally at Microsoft was *HADRON*. This wasn't just a cool name. Like the Large Hadron Collider (LHC) beneath the France-Switzerland border, which first collided beams of high-energy particles in 2010, Microsoft was developing HADRON for its initial release in SQL Server in December 2010.

In SQL Server, the acronym HADRON also spells out the three big features of AGs:

- **High availability (HA).** Describes the automatic failover to one or more synchronous secondary replicas, or manual failover to asynchronous secondary replicas.

- **Disaster recovery (DR).** Describes the ability to take valid backups directly on secondary replicas, including integrated backup tools that use customizable replica backup priority.

- **Online (ON).** Refers to the fact that the secondary replicas can be read-only and allowed for the offloading of heavy-duty report workloads. Concurrency with continuous synchronization from the primary replica is achieved via snapshot isolation, to avoid blocking transactions arriving from the primary replica.

Though the science-y HADRON name didn't stick, availability groups also provide some high-tech features: automatic correction of data corruption to repair damaged pages with data from other replicas, and database health detection that can initiate failover in response to database status.

NOTE

Failovers are not initiated when a database becomes suspect due to factors such as transaction log corruption, data file loss, or database deletion. For more on this, read *https://learn.microsoft.com/sql/database-engine/availability-groups/windows /always-on-availability-groups-sql-server.*

You should keep all the features of AGs in mind when developing an architecture to meet your environment's requirements for RPO (data loss tolerance) and RTO (how long before the systems are back online after a disaster).

Availability groups from other HA solutions

AGs operate by transmitting segments of transaction log data from a primary replica to one or more secondary nodes. Like transactional replication, AGs use the transaction log data itself. Blocks of transaction logs are sent to the replicas—a scalable approach, as the primary replica and secondary replica are independent from one another. This minimizes dependencies between replicas, including hardware and networking. There is a limit on the number of replicas in an AG: one primary replica and eight secondary replicas. It is important to test and confirm that the network can handle the level of activity as well as the cost of additional hardware.

Superior to the deprecated database mirroring feature, AGs begin sending blocks of log data as soon as the data is ready to be flushed to a drive, not afterward. So, transaction log data is sent to the secondary AG replica(s) sooner, tightening the gap between replicas.

Unlike a SQL Server instance running on an FCI, AGs require at least two copies of the data—no shared storage in use here—and at least two active instances of SQL Server to accomplish HA. Unlike with FCI, both servers can be of use to the enterprise: one as the primary read/write replica and one as a secondary read-only replica.

The AG listener always provides redirection to the primary node, but can also provide redirection to readable nodes. The listener is an object that works via DNS to maintain the single name for the AG regardless of which instance is primary.

The listener has its own IP address as well as an IP address in each subnet where AG instances exist. Applications use a connection string pointed at the AG listener, and provide a new parameter, `ApplicationIntent`, to declare whether the transactions in the connection will be read-write or read-only. You can route read-write connections to the primary replica, and read-only connections to one of the possible secondary replicas, thus splitting the workloads, even across a WAN.

> ➤ For detailed configuration information, visit *https://learn.microsoft.com/sql/database -engine/availability-groups/windows/configure-read-only-access-on-an-availability -replica-sql-server.*

Configure failover cluster instances

Windows Server Failover Clustering (WSFC) is a Windows Server feature. Each server that will act as a cluster node must have this feature (not a *role*, but a feature) installed. Cluster nodes can join or leave a cluster at any time. However, adding a node to a cluster is not all that is required to run the SQL Server instance(s). We first cover (briefly) some key concepts of WSFC and then move into configuring SQL Server FCIs.

When you create a cluster, Windows sets up an Active Directory (AD) computer account for the cluster's virtual network name (VNN). By default, this VNN is created in the same AD Organizational Unit (OU) as the cluster node. We recommend creating an OU for each cluster you create, because permissions to create additional computer objects are then more easily delegated. Additional computer objects are created for each cluster resource, including each SQL Server instance. The cluster's VNN computer object should be given permission to create new computer objects in the OU. Alternatively, you could pre-stage the computer objects for the new VNNs in the OU. The IP address associated with any VNN should be a static address, not a dynamically assigned address.

SQL Server failover clusters can provide DR options through the configuration of a stretch cluster. In a *stretch cluster*, some of the nodes are geographically located in different datacenters from the others. This provides the ability to failover to another datacenter in the event of a disaster at the primary datacenter. The stretch cluster is configured to work across a wide-area network (WAN) and the outlying nodes do not have access to the same shared storage. This requires the configuration of replication from the cluster nodes in the primary site to the cluster nodes in the remote site(s).

➤ For information on multi-subnet clustering with SQL Server, including considerations for the IP address cluster resource, refer to *https://learn.microsoft.com/sql/sql-server /failover-clusters/windows/sql-server-multi-subnet-clustering-sql-server*.

➤ To read more about multi-subnet cluster configuration for availability groups, see the "Configure RegisterAllProvidersIP and MultiSubnetFailover correctly" section later in the chapter.

NOTE

Instead of configuring a single stretch cluster to provide DR, you should configure two independent clusters, one at each site. Then, to replicate data between sites, set up distributed availability groups, discussed next.

Understand FCI quorum

Creating and operating a WSFC requires an understanding of quorum. Like rules in a governmental meeting, *quorum* establishes that a majority of voting parties are present. The quorum of the cluster determines which nodes in the cluster are operating and how many failed nodes the cluster can sustain. This is tracked in a file called the *quorum log*, stored by default in the \MSCS\ quolog.log file on the quorum resource and continuously accessed by the cluster service.

NOTE

In common Windows-based configurations, AGs use the WSFC as a cluster manager. See the section "Create WSFC for use with availability groups" later in this chapter for more information.

In Windows, this is the WSFC cluster type option. When using WSFC for AGs, the same guidance for quorum in this section applies.

In Linux, there is an external cluster manager: the EXTERNAL cluster type option. A clusterless configuration that does not require a cluster manager is also available with the cluster type option NONE. For more information on these two types, see the section later in this chapter, "Compare different cluster types."

Correctly selecting a quorum configuration is important to avoid a *split-brain* scenario, which occurs when two instances of the cluster are running but are unaware of each other. You can choose from five quorum configurations, each of which accomplishes the basic goal of allowing a majority of the nodes to maintain quorum, often by the use of an extra vote called a *witness* to increase an even number of votes into an odd number:

- **Node majority.** This is the recommended configuration choice for clusters with an *odd* number of nodes. To determine whether the cluster will function—and if so, which nodes will be active cluster members—a majority of nodes must "vote." The number of failures that can be sustained for the cluster to remain operational is $(n / 2) - 1$, where n is the number of cluster nodes, and the result of the division is rounded up. Thus, in a five-node cluster, you can sustain at most two failed nodes, or two nodes that have lost communication with the other nodes, and so on, because $(5 / 2) - 1 = 3 - 1 = 2$.

- **Node and disk majority.** This is the recommended configuration choice for clusters with an *even* number of nodes. Each node gets a vote, and the presence of a shared witness disk, designated as the quorum disk, adds a vote to whichever node owns it. In the case of a four-node cluster, two nodes can fail if the shared disk is online or can be brought online on one of the remaining two nodes. If the shared disk cannot be brought online, the number of nodes that can fail is half minus one, or $(n / 2) - 1$. In the case of a four-node cluster with the witness disk unavailable, only one node can fail for the cluster to remain available.

- **Node and file share majority.** This configuration is used for clusters with an *even* number of nodes but *without* shared drives. The file share witness adds the extra vote only when the number of nodes is even. The witness file share isn't owned by any particular node, but the nodes that cannot reach the file share (due to whatever problem caused them to no longer be able to communicate with their peers) will not be active.

- **Node and cloud witness.** Cloud witness, pointing to an Azure Blob Storage resource as a type of file share witness, is available starting with Windows Server 2016. In this configuration, which is very similar to node and file share majority, the witness is a cloud service—specifically, an Azure storage account. To configure this option, you must provide the name of the storage account and one of its access keys.

- **Disk only.** In the disk-only quorum configuration, node count is never considered. Only the shared witness disk's availability to nodes matters. This means the (single) shared disk becomes a single point of failure; even if all nodes can communicate, if the disk is unavailable, the cluster will not be operational. This mode is largely available for legacy purposes, but it can make it possible for you to start the cluster in case of a significant disaster when there is no other way to achieve quorum.

Because of the intricacies of quorum configuration, we recommend that you use node majority (for a cluster with an odd number of nodes) or node and disk majority (for a cluster with an even number of nodes) as the configuration if shared storage is available. If shared storage is not available, configure node and file share majority for a cluster with an even number of nodes. You should not use the disk-only quorum configuration to operate the cluster; its value lies in recovering a severely broken cluster using only a single node.

Inside OUT

Should you use dynamic quorum management for your AG?

Yes. Starting with Windows Server 2012 R2, dynamic quorum management can remove nodes that drop from a cluster. Dynamic quorum is enabled by default since Windows Server 2012 R2.

Consider a five-node cluster. With dynamic quorum, when three nodes are shut down in a planned manner, their votes are removed, leaving only two votes remaining. This allows the cluster to maintain quorum and continue functioning because those two votes are available on the two remaining nodes.

However, this can be dangerous in the event of a total site failure. Should a site in a cluster that spans two physical locations be left with no way to achieve node majority, no automatic failover is possible without manually "rigging" the node weights to force a failover. Forcing quorum and manually performing a failover is a temporary measure and requires the reestablishment of proper node weights after DR.

As an example, if you have only two nodes at two physical sites, the third vote—for example, a file share witness—should be located at the primary site and moved upon planned failover. This ensures the best chance for the current primary replica to remain online even if there is a network loss between the two sites. If you have three nodes, you should still create a quorum witness, though with dynamic quorum management, it will not be assigned a vote unless needed to make the total quorum vote count an odd number.

Configure a SQL Server FCI

When configuring SQL Server as a cluster resource, you should configure the cluster resources for a single instance in a single cluster resource group. A cluster resource group is the level at which a failover happens—that is, all the resources on a single cluster node that will move together from one node to another during a failover. Cluster resources in a cluster resource group can include the IP address, the SQL Server instance's network name, the shared disks (if any; there aren't any shared disks with Clustered Shared Volumes and Storage Spaces Direct), the SQL Server service itself, the SQL Server Agent, SQL Server Analysis Services (SSAS), and the FILESTREAM file share. If multiple SQL Server instances are configured on a single cluster, each will need a resource group.

CHAPTER 11

If you would like to have multiple servers running active instances of SQL Server simultaneously, you can install additional instances on each FCI. Each SQL Server instance can be active on only one server at a time, but when using multiple instances, each instance can run independently of the others. The following is an example of how these SQL Server instances might be configured on multiple servers:

- **Server 1**

- **SQL Instance A.** Active

- **SQL Instance B.** Passive

- **Server 2**

- **SQL Instance A.** Passive

- **SQL Instance B.** Active

However, we recommend always keeping a passive cluster node—that is, a node that has no active responsibilities. Otherwise, if a failover occurs, one server must run at least one additional instance, increasing the load on the server. If you run each instance on separate hardware, you'll need $n + 1$ cluster nodes, where n is the number of SQL Server instances.

Keep in mind that any cluster configuration of more than two nodes requires SQL Server Enterprise edition.

Inside OUT

How should you configure service accounts for SQL Server in a WSFC?

With a standalone installation, SQL Server will default to virtual service accounts for all services during setup. With a cluster installation, you should specify a domain account for the clustered services: Database Engine, SQL Server Agent, and SSAS if installed. Shared services, such as SSRS, can continue to use a virtual service account.

The domain accounts require no special privileges or rights in advance, so use a domain user account for each SQL Server service that will run on the cluster. SQL Server Setup grants the necessary permissions to each service account, such as access to the data and log folders. The account running the installer will need permissions to make these changes.

You can choose to create a group managed service account (gMSA) for each service. This reduces management overhead because the password for these service accounts is managed by AD and regularly changed. In addition, the security configuration is enhanced because no one knows the password.

Starting with SQL Server 2016 and Windows Server 2016, you can create WSFCs with certificates instead of using AD service accounts, known as *workgroup clusters*. These are based on a concept called an *Active Directory–detached cluster*, which still requires a domain. You can create a domain-independent AG on a workgroup cluster for any mixture of Windows Server nodes that are not joined to the same domain or any domain. For more information, visit *https://learn.microsoft.com/sql/database-engine/availability-groups/windows/domain -independent-availability-groups*.

In the same way that the hardware and OS patch levels should be identical on every cluster node, so too should the SQL Server configuration. The best way to guarantee initial exact configuration is to use configuration scripts to first prepare each cluster node, and then complete the cluster installation with another script. These scripts are valuable because they ensure consistent installation of the SQL Server binaries. They also serve as DR preparation because they document the configuration of each instance, and you can use them to set up a new cluster in case of a disaster.

You can create these scripts by hand. However, this is a tedious and error-prone process. Instead, we recommend starting SQL Server Setup and running the Advanced Cluster Preparation setup from the **Advanced** tab of the **SQL Server Installation Center** window. On the **Ready to Install** step of the installation wizard, the path to the configuration file is displayed. Open the configuration file and save it somewhere. A network share is ideal because it can then be referenced from all cluster nodes that will run the SQL Server instance.

If you prefer to have a completely automated configuration file, you must modify the script as outlined in the following example. You start Setup from the command line by using the /ConfigurationFile=path parameter; then specify the full path to the configuration file:

```
; Add this line
IACCEPTSQLSERVERLICENSETERMS="True"
; Modify the next lines
; Change to True to enable unattended installation to progress
IACCEPTPYTHONLICENSETERMS="True"
; Quiet simple means you'll see the UI auto-progress.
QUIETSIMPLE="True"
; Or, leave QUIETSIMPLE="False" and modify this line for no UI
QUIET="True"
; Delete, or comment out, this line
UIMODE="Normal"
```

> ➤ For more about installing SQL Server from the command line, see Chapter 4, "Install and configure SQL Server instances and features."

To complete the cluster installation, in SQL Server Setup, run the Advanced Cluster Completion setup option. There again, you can choose to save the script for later. The cluster completion phase is where you will do the following (in no particular order):

- Select or create the cluster resource group.

- Set the virtual network name and IP address for the SQL Server instance—how your clients will connect.

- Select the shared storage for the database files.

NOTE

Azure Virtual Machines (VMs) hosting SQL Server FCI used to be limited to one SQL Server instance per cluster. This was a unique limitation to Azure VMs. In recent years, however, Azure VMs were updated to allow for multiple front-end virtual IPs on internal load balancers. You can now have multiple SQL Server FCIs per cluster, just like in an on-premises Windows Server cluster.

Patch a failover cluster

Near-zero downtime is the objective when configuring FCIs. Some events are unexpected, but some regular maintenance tasks such as patching the OS and SQL Server instance are regular activities. You can perform these maintenance tasks with near-zero downtime by using *rolling upgrades*.

To conduct a rolling upgrade, you should have a passive node—that is, a node that, under normal circumstances, does not run any workload. You upgrade the passive node first and, if necessary, reboot it. This reboot does not cause any downtime because the node is not running a workload. When the reboot is complete and the upgrade has been validated, the roles from any active node should be failed over to the passive node.

As indicated, a brief amount of downtime is incurred while this takes place (on the order of seconds). The newly passive node is then upgraded, and so on, until all nodes in the cluster are at the same software version. Although you can choose to return the original passive node to its passive state when all nodes have finished upgrading, this would incur one more interruption and will likely not provide any benefit other than consistency.

First introduced in Windows Server 2012, Cluster-Aware Updating (CAU) automates this process, and you can even schedule rolling upgrades and updates for Windows patches and SQL Server updates. Even though this is not automated, it is a significant benefit with the frequent updates available for modern Windows Server operating systems.

Design availability groups solutions

This section contains information about designing, configuring, and troubleshooting AGs, along with the various features associated with AGs, a core element of SQL Server's HA capabilities. Much of the content applies to SQL Server instances on-premises on Windows, in Azure VMs, in

Azure SQL Managed Instance, and in SQL Server on Linux. Later in this chapter, we talk in detail about configuring an AG in Red Hat Enterprise Linux (RHEL).

➤ For considerations with regard to HA options in containers, see Chapter 3, "Design and implement an on-premises database infrastructure."

You can create AGs using the Availability Groups Wizard in SSMS, T-SQL, or PowerShell. If this is your first time creating an AG, we recommend using the Availability Groups Wizard and scripting out the steps and objects it creates with T-SQL to further your understanding.

In SSMS, creating a copy of a database on a secondary replica SQL Server can be fairly wizard-driven, including the ability to automate the process of taking a full and transaction log backup of the database, copying the data to a file share, and restoring the database to any secondary replica(s). You can script these tasks at the end of the wizard and deploy them to future AGs via T-SQL or PowerShell.

As in many places in this book, although we don't provide a step-by-step walk-through, we do offer pointers and key decisions to make when creating AGs. There is, however, a more in-depth walk-through of AGs in SQL Server on Linux later in this chapter.

Inside OUT

What server principal owns an AG replica?

The server security principal used to create the AG will own the AG replica object by default, creating an immediate follow-up action item for administrators after setup. Each replica object has an owner, listed in the dynamic management view (DMV) `sys.availability_replicas`, where the `owner_sid` is a server-level security principal.

What the `owner_sid` is used for isn't fully documented. However, because it could be used as the authority to make changes to AGs, it should not be an administrator's personal named account. You should either create the AG (and create future replicas) under the security context of a service account that does not expire or immediately change the owner of the AG replica to a service account.

A similar problem occurs when you create an AG with a login that doesn't have an explicit server principal or SQL Server login, but rather has access via a security group. In that case, an AG will be created with the built-in public server role as the `owner_id`. In general, ownership or additional permissions should not be granted to the public role, so you should change this.

Changing the owner of the AG replica to the instance's `sa` login, on instances with mixed mode authentication enabled, is also an acceptable and common practice. For example:
```
ALTER AUTHORIZATION ON AVAILABILITY GROUP::[AG1] to [domain\serviceaccount];
```

Compare different cluster types

While most enterprise implementations of AGs involve Enterprise edition SQL Servers and a WSFC, the instance does not necessarily need to reside on a Windows Server that is a member of a WSFC. You can enable the HA feature and create clusterless AGs starting with SQL Server 2017. The only cluster types available when creating an AG without the presence of a WSFC are External and None. These cluster types are created for non-Windows cluster managers and clusterless AGs, respectively.

Let's compare the three cluster type options—WSFC, External, None—and other possible cluster architectures.

Windows Server Failover Cluster (WSFC)

WSFC is the original supported architecture. It relies on the underlying cluster quorum for failover, discussed earlier in this chapter. Even though SQL Server creates the necessary objects inside the WSFC, manages settings such as preferred/possible resource ownership, and runs any user-initiated failovers, the WSFC quorum is used to detect node outage and trigger automatic failover.

Just because failover isn't automatically prompted by SQL Server, it doesn't mean you can't have HA. There are production enterprise environments with AGs configured for manual failover, but with the failover automated along with other server assets (such as web or application servers) so that the automation isn't piecemeal. PowerShell is a common automation tool for this task, and we provide a sample of such a failover script in Chapter 9.

External

This type of cluster uses an external cluster manager, not the WSFC. SQL Server on Linux supports the use of external cluster managers, with Pacemaker being the most common. Red Hat Enterprise Linux, Ubuntu, and SUSE Linux Enterprise Server are all supported platforms. AGs on Linux clusters require at least *two* synchronous replicas to guarantee HA, but at least *three* replicas for automatic recovery, so we recommend that you set up your AG on at least three nodes.

SQL Server on Linux is not cluster-aware, and AGs on Linux are not tightly bound to the clustering resource manager, as they are on Windows. This means you cannot control failovers from within SQL Server. To manually perform a failover, for example, you must use the pcs command line to manage the Pacemaker cluster manager.

➤ To learn more about setting up AGs in Linux, see the "Configure availability groups in SQL Server on Linux" section later in this chapter.

None

You can implement clusterless AGs that, like the deprecated database mirroring feature, do not require a failover cluster network. Introduced in SQL Server 2017 and available in Standard and

Enterprise editions, this was initially referred to as a *read-scale availability group* in documentation. Now, Microsoft refers to this AG option as *clusterless*. The None option provides a subset of AG features on SQL Servers on Windows and/or Linux replicas.

With the None option, all the machinery of synchronization and failover is within the SQL Server instances. There is no cluster manager. One of the biggest sources of complexity and problems (especially during failover) with AGs based on WSFC is not the SQL Server configuration or behavior, but the configuration or behavior of the quorum and the various forms of quorum witnesses. We discussed these earlier in this chapter, in the section "Understand FCI quorum." Since SQL Server 2012, the causes of AG issues are more likely to be misconfigurations of Windows Server, cluster networks, DNS, or cluster quorum settings, as opposed to SQL Server–based issues.

Although automatic failover is not possible with a read-scale AG, manual planned and forced failover is still possible, as are the usual AG features to which you're accustomed, including both synchronous and asynchronous availability modes, readable secondary nodes, and secondary replica backups. (More on these options later in this chapter.) AGs without a WSFC cluster can still provide readable secondary nodes, load balancing, and read-only routing. Introduced in SQL Server 2019, automatic traffic redirection provides for routing of read/write traffic back to the primary node and does not require a listener. More on this later, in the section "Recent improvements to availability groups."

Failover can be automated with external tools and often is, so that the database, application, and web layers of a multi-tier application failover from one datacenter to another together.

To use this feature, you must select the **Enable Always On Availability Groups** check box in the **SQL Server Properties** dialog box for the SQL Server Database Engine service, accessible from SQL Server Configuration Manager. The Properties page of the SQL Server instance service contains a tab labeled "Always On Availability Groups" (see Figure 11-1).

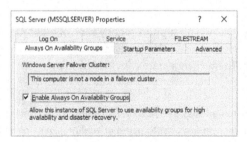

Figure 11-1 In Configuration Manager, you can enable AGs even if the Windows Server is not a member of a WSFC, to use with clusterless, read-scale AGs. This behavior is only possible in SQL Server 2017 and above.

CHAPTER 11

Other possible architectures

You can also consider the following alternate architectures, which might be more appropriate for your environment if you are not running Enterprise edition or if you have geographically separated environment HA requirements.

Basic availability groups

A basic availability group is a limited version of a traditional AG. Basic AGs are supported only on SQL Server Standard edition. This feature wholly replaces the deprecated database mirroring feature but with the modern SSMS dialog box options and monitoring tools.

As with database mirroring, the single secondary replica cannot be readable or backed up. Although each basic AG can support only two replicas, you can create more than one basic AG per server. Basic AGs are supported on SQL Server 2016 and above, mostly to match the features of database mirroring. Otherwise, basic AGs allow for many of the same features as regular AGs, including synchronous and asynchronous replication, manual and automatic failovers, plus management DMVs and commands that are superior to those with database mirroring.

Contained availability groups

SQL Server 2022 introduces a new feature called *contained availability groups*. With contained AGs, DBAs no longer need to create scripts and processes to keep logins and SQL Server Agent jobs synchronized between replicas. Instead, the master and msdb databases are contained within the AG and seeded to all nodes. These system databases are named after the contained AG and appended with the system database name—for example, ContainedAG_msdb.

You use a contained AG listener to interact with the contained system databases, which are referred to internally as *master* and *msdb*. Any changes made to these databases, while connected to the contained AG listener, will be made to the contained system databases themselves.

One limitation of contained AGs is they include no support for any form of replication, distributed AGs, or log shipping to a target database inside the contained AG. There are also considerations with a contained AG if you are using change data capture, log shipping, or transparent data encryption.

> ➤ For more information about contained AGs, see *https://learn.microsoft.com/sql /database-engine/availability-groups/windows/contained-availability-groups-overview.*

Distributed availability groups

With distributed availability groups, you can have an AG treat another AG, typically over a WAN, as a secondary replica. The read-only secondary replicas can be globally dispersed, offloading workloads to regional read-only secondary replicas. Distributed availability groups sound complicated, but they are a proven platform. The new Azure SQL Managed Instance link feature was developed with distributed availability groups as the platform for that PaaS offering.

The two AGs, each with their own listener, do not need to be in the same network or WSFC. This allows for local hardware and geographically remote HA and DR across multi-site deployments. With distributed AGs, you do not need to span a WSFC across the WAN or subnet. There is no risk of accidental failover of the WSFC over the WAN; in fact, there is no automatic failover supported at all between the primary AG and the secondary AG. The AG that is not primary can only serve read-only queries, but it does have a primary replica itself, referred to as the *forwarder*. The primary replica, or forwarder, in the secondary AG is charged with replicating transactions to the other secondary replicas in the secondary AG. Otherwise, distributed AGs operate in much the same way as traditional AGs.

This architecture could be especially useful for future OS and SQL Server version upgrades of instances in an AG because you can have different versions of Windows Server (2012 minimum) and SQL Server (2016 minimum) and perform a fast migration with minimal downtime.

Although each partner AG in a distributed scenario has its own listener, the distributed AG as a whole does not. Applications, perhaps with the aid of DNS aliases, connect to each AG directly after a failover to take advantage of readable secondary replicas.

You can also use distributed AGs to migrate Windows-based AGs to Linux-based AGs, though this is not a permanent, stable, or recommended configuration.

FCIs and availability groups

SQL Server FCIs can themselves be members of AGs, though these AGs do not support automatic failover. The FCI is still capable of automatic failover of the instance hardware, allowing for local HA and hardware availability, but not remote HA.

We do not recommend creating a WSFC that spans a WAN, even if the subnet spans the network. Instead, you should consider AGs without FCIs, or distributed AGs, if you require local hardware HA.

Create WSFC for use with availability groups

We covered WSFCs earlier in this chapter. A failover cluster can be the underlying technology for both FCIs and AGs. If you choose to set up an AG that uses the underlying structure of a WSFC, the first big decision is the same for setting up any WSFC: Quorum votes—specifically, where quorum votes will reside—are key to understanding how the servers will eventually failover. The recommendations remain the same:

- Use the node majority quorum mode when you have an odd number of voting nodes.

- Use the node and file share majority quorum mode when you have an even number of voting nodes.

CHAPTER 11

> ➤ Refer to the section "Understand FCI quorum" earlier in this chapter for more information.

Your quorum strategy might also be different based on two factors:

- Do you intend to mostly run out of one datacenter, with the other datacenter used in disaster operations only?

- Do you intend to have manual failover only, without any automatic failover?

If you answered yes to both, it makes sense to have a quorum vote maintaining uptime in the primary node, including placing a file share witness in the primary node datacenter. If you answered no to either, you should follow best practices for WSFC quorum alignment, including an odd number of quorum votes, with one of the quorum votes in a third location. This can include an Azure Storage Account Cloud Witness, introduced with Windows Server 2016, which is a relatively inexpensive and very reliable witness.

When creating your cluster using the wizard, you do not need to select the **Add All Eligible Storage** check box for the cluster. Similarly, you do not need to run cluster validation wizard checks on your storage. The WSFC for your AG won't have any storage unless you choose to use a shared storage witness as your odd vote. Add that separately. You can view the current quorum votes per member roles in the following DMV: `sys.dm_hadr_cluster_members`.

During cluster validation and after the WSFC is online, you might see warnings in the Failover Cluster Manager that storage is not configured. Because storage is not clustered in AGs, you can ignore these warnings and, in the future, use the Failover Cluster Manager only to view the overall health state of the cluster or to manage quorum.

Do not initiate failovers from the Failover Cluster Manager unless you are forcing quorum in an emergency or recovery scenario. All failovers for the AG should be initiated through SQL Server—for example, via SSMS, T-SQL statements, or PowerShell commands.

> ➤ See the section "Understand failovers in availability groups" later in this chapter for more information.

Inside OUT

What permissions are needed to create AG objects?

When creating the WSFC without domain administrator permissions, you might encounter errors when creating a Cluster Name Object (CNO) or the listener objects in AD. The listener object is created by the CNO, so the CNO must have access to read all properties and to the Create Computer Objects dialog box in the cluster's OU. The user creating the cluster must have rights to grant the CNO these permissions, as well, or grant these permissions to the CNO after it is created. The listener object can also be pre-created by a domain administrator instead of giving the CNO these rights.

Understand the database mirroring endpoint

The endpoint for AG communication, which exists on each SQL Server instance in the AG, is also called the *database mirroring endpoint*. It shares a name, functionality, and port with the endpoint created by the deprecated database mirroring feature.

The endpoint name Hadr_endpoint is given by default to the endpoint. It is used by SQL Server to communicate between instances, not user connections, and is created only for the purposes of AGs (or the deprecated database mirroring feature).

By default, the endpoint communicates on TCP port 5022. This does not need to change unless the port is already in use by another AG. You can view information about the endpoint in the sys.database_mirroring_endpoints (including its current status, role, and encryption settings) and sys.tcp_endpoints (including its port number, IP settings, and listener IP) system reference tables.

If you're creating the AG database_mirroring endpoint manually, you can use the CREATE ENDPOINT T-SQL command or the New-SqlHadrEndpoint PowerShell cmdlet.

> ➤ Network connectivity to the endpoint is a common source of initial problems when configuring AGs. For more information on troubleshooting initial configuration, visit *https://learn .microsoft.com/sql/database-engine/availability-groups/windows/troubleshoot-always-on -availability-groups-configuration-sql-server*.

Recent improvements to availability groups

AGs were first released in SQL Server 2012 and have seen dramatic improvements since then. If you are still the administrator of an AG running on SQL Server 2012, you should consider the advantages of these feature improvements, especially now that SQL Server 2012 has reached the end of extended support.

Replica read-write traffic redirection

SQL Server 2019 introduced the optional ability to redirect read-write connections from a secondary replica back to the primary replica. This behavior is not coordinated by the listener and ensures quick reconnection after a failover for AGs that do not have a listener. Replica read-write redirection is helpful for scenarios where a listener is not available for the AG—for instance, a listener is not supported on the cluster technology, or in a clusterless AG setup where cluster_type = NONE.

Not set by default, the READ_WRITE_ROUTING_URL parameter for the primary replica is required for this behavior. Secondary replicas must also allow all connections, so they must have the ALLOW CONNECTIONS = ALL parameter set, which is also not the default.

When a connection with `Application_Intent=ReadOnly` is sent directly to a secondary replica with `SECONDARY_ROLE (READ_ONLY_ROUTING...)`, the connection continues to the specified server. The same is true when connecting to the primary replica. This feature of routing of read/write traffic back to the primary does not require a listener.

When a connection with `Application_Intent=ReadWrite` arrives at an online secondary replica with `ALLOW CONNECTIONS = ALL`, the connection is routed to the primary replica automatically.

Before SQL Server 2019, a connection with `Application_Intent=ReadWrite` that arrived at a secondary replica with `ALLOW CONNECTIONS = ALL` would communicate with the secondary replica, but a transaction would fail if it attempted to write to the secondary replica, which in all scenarios remains read-only.

> ➤ For more information on the various scenarios of connecting to a secondary replica before and after this feature of SQL Server 2019, see *https://learn.microsoft.com/sql/database -engine/availability-groups/windows/secondary-replica-connection-redirection-always -on-availability-groups*.

To take advantage of this feature, you should:

- Set a `READ_WRITE_ROUTING_URL` on all replicas. This is not set by default.

- Make a habit of declaring `Application_Intent` in all connection strings, including read-write connections.

- Set the secondary replica to ALL to allow all connections.

Cluster types

Improvements introduced in SQL Server 2017 included structural expansion to the very foundation of AGs, including support for replicas to SQL Server on Linux instances and the possibility of cross-platform AGs using an external cluster manager.

Linux servers cannot be part of a WSFC, so the architecture of AGs had to be expanded to operate without a WSFC. As a result, clusterless availability groups, previously referred to as *read-scale availability groups*, have been possible since SQL Server 2017. We discussed the NONE cluster type and its potential advantages for Windows-based SQL Servers without failover clusters earlier in this chapter.

Distributed AGs, where individual clusters treat another cluster as a replica, also became possible beginning with SQL Server 2016. We discussed possible cluster architectures earlier in this chapter.

Replica limits

Since SQL Server 2014, the total number of secondary replicas has been eight, including both synchronous and asynchronous replicas. Starting in SQL Server 2019, the cap on synchronous replicas increased to five, meaning there is one primary replica and up to four synchronous secondary replicas. This was capped at one primary and up to two synchronous replicas in SQL Server 2017.

Before SQL Server 2016, you could only specify two automatic failover replicas: a primary and only one secondary. But since the release of SQL Server 2016, you can specify three: the primary plus up to two secondary replicas.

Distributed transaction support

AGs on Windows now fully support the Microsoft Distributed Transaction Coordinator (MSDTC). Initially, AGs in SQL Server 2012 did not support distributed transactions using MSDTC. This was a deal breaker for migrating some legacy applications to take advantage of AGs.

Since SQL Server 2017 (and including SQL Server 2016 with Service Pack 2), cross-database transactions using MSDTC have been fully supported on the same or different instances. The DTC_SUPPORT setup parameter when creating or altering an AG is provided to enable (DTC_SUPPORT = PER_DB) or disable (DTC_SUPPORT = NONE) distributed transactions.

MSDTC is available in SQL Server on Linux starting with SQL Server 2019 (and SQL Server 2017 CU 16), but MSDTC with AGs is not supported in SQL Server on Linux.

> ### NOTE
> Before SQL Server 2016 with Service Pack 2, it was not possible to modify the DTC_SUPPORT setting of an AG, as cross-database transactions were not supported.

Configure the minimum synchronized required nodes

The REQUIRED_SYNCHRONIZED_SECONDARIES_TO_COMMIT setting establishes a minimum number of synchronized replicas, which you can set to an integer value between 0 and the number of replicas minus 1.

By default, this setting is 0, which mimics the behavior before this feature's introduction in SQL Server 2017. In this case, a synchronous replica that stops responding does not stop the primary replica from committing transactions. Instead, the problematic synchronous replica's state is set to NOT SYNCHRONIZED until it is reachable again and catches up, at which point its state is set back to SYNCHRONIZED. (You can see each replica state in the sys.dm_hadr_database_replica _states DMV on the primary replica or in the Availability Group dashboard for the primary replica in SSMS.)

When greater than zero, this setting guarantees that transactions commit to that number of secondary replicas. At least as many secondary replicas as the value of the setting must be set to SYNCHRONIZED or transactions on the primary replica will not be allowed to commit! This guarantees that the primary database replica cannot introduce new data while there are insufficient secondary synchronous replicas, and therefore automatic failover targets. You should carefully consider the impact of transaction rollbacks on client applications and your data loss tolerance requirements before changing this setting from the default.

Choose the correct secondary replica availability mode

The most important consideration when choosing between the asynchronous-commit availability mode and synchronous-commit availability mode for each secondary replica is the requirement for automatic or manual failover.

Three overall factors guide this decision:

- If your HA goals require automatic failover, you must choose synchronous.

- If your databases are geographically separated, even if they're in the same subnet, you should choose asynchronous-commit availability mode because the performance impact discussed in the following section will be significant. Replicas in asynchronous-commit availability mode do not place as much of a performance burden on the primary replica and are more appropriate for high-latency network environments than synchronous mode, especially over geographically separated datacenters. Performance of the primary replica with only asynchronous-commit availability mode replicas will also be noticeably improved during index maintenance and other bulk data operations. We discuss the performance impact of secondary replicas in the next section.

- If your databases are in the same physical network area, consider whether your performance requirements allow for synchronous commit mode.

This section discusses how synchronous-commit availability mode replicas work and how the commit mode affects their behavior and that of the primary replica. Choosing synchronous-commit availability mode is not without a performance impact on the primary replica. This performance impact has two causes:

- The actual delay of the commit due to the time it takes to receive the acknowledgements from the secondary replica(s)

- The potential for concurrency issues due to the longer lock periods

The commit delay can be measured by using performance counters (if you want to measure the delay for a specific duration) or by querying wait statistics.

➤ Methods for measuring data movement latency are detailed in the Microsoft blog post at *https://techcommunity.microsoft.com/t5/sql-server-support-blog/troubleshooting-data-movement-latency-between-synchronous-commit/ba-p/319141.*

Inside OUT

Does SQL Server compress transaction log data sent to secondary replicas?

By default, asynchronous-commit availability mode compresses transaction logs sent over the network, reducing network bandwidth but increasing CPU load and potentially increasing the amount of time it takes to commit. You can disable this log stream compression with global Trace Flag 1462. This is not generally necessary because of the benefits of the log stream compression over a WAN, but asynchronous replicas within the same datacenter may not benefit from the compression.

The log transport of synchronous commit availability mode is not compressed to make the commit to the secondary replica as fast as possible. You can choose to enable log stream compression with global Trace Flag 9592 if you believe network bandwidth is a bottleneck to the performance of secondary replica synchronization.

In either case, enabling or disabling compression via the global trace flags will affect all AGs on the instance.

Understand the impact of secondary replicas on performance

If you exceed the amount of replica data that your secondary replica hardware can process in a timely fashion, the log redo queue on the secondary replica(s) and the log send queue on the primary replica will begin to grow, as they cannot truncate committed transactional data. These log queues grow under heavy load and must process before the secondary replica can come online. Synchronous commit mode delays commits on the primary replica. In asynchronous commit mode, there are still transaction delay repercussions if the secondary replica(s) cannot match the performance of the primary replica.

A redo backlog on a secondary replica causes the following problematic conditions:

- It delays automatic failover by preventing a failover without data loss, forcing any failover to be a manual failover.

- It delays database recovery at startup after a crash or reboot.

- The data on the secondary replica will be stale, which might reveal itself in queries against read-only secondary nodes.

- It delays data being backed up when using the secondary replica for database or log backups.

- Transactions in the primary replica's transaction log will be delayed, truncating only during transaction log backups because transactions cannot be applied to secondary replicas.

For these reasons, to protect the performance of the primary replica, a secondary synchronous replica might switch to asynchronous because of time-outs when communicating with the primary node. This switch happens automatically and temporarily, and logically blocks the possibility of automatic failover. Favoring the performance of the primary means that synchronous replicas are not guaranteed to provide zero data loss in all workloads, and are best described as *potential* automatic failover partners.

If a synchronous commit secondary replica does not send confirmation before a time-out period, the primary replica marks the secondary replica status as DISCONNECTED, essentially removing it from the AG. The time-out period is 10 seconds by default, but you can change it via the SESSION_TIMEOUT property of the secondary replica. This prevents the primary replica from suffering transaction hardening delays. You can detect when this happens by setting a SQL Agent alert for error numbers like 41416 and 41418, or by monitoring databases for the Availability Replica Role State and Availability Replica Connection State policies.

> ➤ **For more information on SQL Agent alerts and policy-based management (PBM), see Chapter 9.**

A secondary replica that has become DISCONNECTED must be added back to the AG by an administrator. Depending on how far behind it is, it might also need to be reseeded with a new full backup.

You should consider switching the AG's secondary replicas from synchronous to asynchronous if you anticipate a period of heavy, performance-sensitive writes to the system—for example, when performing index maintenance, modifying or moving large tables, or running bulk operations. Afterward, change the replicas back to synchronous. You'll be able to observe their state change from SYNCHRONIZING to SYNCHRONIZED as soon as the secondary replicas have caught up.

Similarly, you must temporarily switch your asynchronous secondary replicas to synchronous mode to perform a manual failover without data loss, and without having to use the FORCE parameter. After the failover, you can switch the replicas back to asynchronous mode. You'll be able to observe their state change from SYNCHRONIZED to SYNCHRONIZING as soon as the secondary replicas have switched to asynchronous.

In SQL Server on Windows, manual failovers of an AG should always be initiated via SQL Server, not by the Failover Cluster Manager. In SQL Server on Linux, all manual and automatic failover actions are initiated by the external cluster manager, such as Pacemaker.

Inside OUT

How many potential synchronous automatic failover partners can a replica have?

Before SQL Server 2016, only one secondary replica could be a potential automatic failover partner with the primary replica. Starting with SQL Server 2016, you can now set up to two synchronous commit secondary replicas in an automatic failover set using the WSFC cluster type, for a total of three (including the current primary) replicas that you can set to be a part of automatic failover.

➤ For more information on failover sets, see *https://learn.microsoft.com/sql/database -engine/availability-groups/windows/failover-and-failover-modes-always-on-availability -groups#failover-sets.*

The preferred owner properties of the AG object in the WSFC determine which of the two secondary replicas is the target of an automatic failover.

SQL Server automatically manages the potential and preferred owners list of AG resources in the WSFC, and there is no method in SQL Server to control this. If you change these settings in the WSFC, they will be overwritten the next time SQL Server performs a failover, and thus we do not recommend doing so.

You can view the current possible and preferred owners in the Failover Cluster Manager. On the **Roles** page, double-click the AG object to open its **Properties** dialog box; you'll find the **Preferred Owners** list on the **General** tab. Then, back in Failover Cluster Manager, under **Other Resources**, double-click the AG object. On the **Advanced Policies** tab, you'll find the **Possible Owners** list.

Understand failovers in availability groups

When an AG fails over, a secondary replica becomes the new primary, and the primary replica (if available) becomes a secondary replica. The properties of replicas after they become primary or secondary should be reviewed and reconfigured after a failover, especially if the failover was unplanned and/or forced. It might not be appropriate given the loss of one or more nodes to support automatic failover, readable secondary nodes, or backup priority settings.

Automatic failover

Automatic failovers provide HA, and rely on properly configured listener and WSFC objects for their success. Only a synchronous-commit availability mode replica can be the destination of an automatic failover.

You can configure the conditions that prompt an automatic failover on a scale of 1 to 5, where 1 indicates that only a total outage of the SQL Server service on the primary replica should initiate a failover, and 5 indicates any number of critical to less-severe SQL Server errors. The default is 3, which prompts an automatic failure in the case of an outage or unresponsive primary replica, but also for some critical server conditions.

> ➤ These flexible failover policy conditions are detailed at *https://learn.microsoft.com/sql/database-engine/availability-groups/windows/flexible-automatic-failover-policy-availability-group#FClevel.*

Automatic failovers will not occur unless they meet the same conditions as a planned failover, which we look at next. Specifically, automatic failovers cannot occur with the possibility of data loss.

Planned failover

A planned failover can occur only if there is no possibility of data loss. Specifically, this means the failover occurs without the use of the FORCE parameter to acknowledge warnings in code or in SSMS dialog boxes. It is therefore only possible to have a planned failover to a secondary replica in synchronous-commit availability mode. That doesn't mean, however, that asynchronous is out of the question. You can move an asynchronous-commit availability mode replica to synchronous, wait for the SYNCHRONIZED state, and then issue a planned failover without data loss.

You should not attempt a planned failover from within the Failover Cluster Manager. Instead, you should use SQL Server commands via SSMS, T-SQL, or PowerShell.

> ➤ For PowerShell code examples of scripted failover, see Chapter 9.

Forced failover

You should attempt a manually initiated, forced failover only in response to adverse cluster conditions such as the loss of the primary node. You should never attempt to force failover from within the Failover Cluster Manager unless adverse cluster conditions have made it impossible to force failover from SQL Server commands via SSMS wizards, T-SQL commands, or PowerShell.

Force failover if WSFC quorum is down

You will not be able to force a failover for AGs based on a WSFC if the WSFC has no quorum. You will first have to force quorum in the Configuration Manager by rigging the vote and modifying node weights. You should consider this step only in emergencies, such as when a disaster has disrupted a majority of cluster nodes. You can accomplish this with a short PowerShell script, to force an online node to assume the primary role without a majority of votes.

```
Import-Module FailoverClusters
$node = 'desired_primary_servername'
Stop-ClusterNode -Name $node
Start-ClusterNode -Name $node -FixQuorum
#FixQuorum forces the cluster to start
# without a valid quorum, which we're about to fix
```

```
(Get-ClusterNode $node).NodeWeight = 1
$nodes = Get-ClusterNode -Cluster $node
#Force this node's weight in the quorum
```

After execution of this temporary fix, you can then address issues with the cluster and nodes to repair long-term stability and/or restore what a partial disaster has wrought. Subsequent nodes or witnesses coming back online could change the vote and cause a quorum failover or failure.

Force failover in other scenarios

If you initiate a forced failover to a synchronous, synchronized secondary replica, the behavior is the same as if you had performed a planned manual failover, as detailed in the previous section. In this way, the behavior of a planned failover in healthy circumstances is no different from the FORCE syntax.

What if the AG isn't healthy, or is in asynchronous commit mode, and a failover must be forced regardless of the risk? The following sample T-SQL command issues a forced failover, allowing for data loss, for execution on the primary replica of the AG named AG1:

```
ALTER AVAILABILITY GROUP [AG1] FORCE_FAILOVER_ALLOW_DATA_LOSS;
```

Again, you should consider this step only if efforts to get the target secondary replica into a synchronized state in synchronous commit mode are unsuccessful. However, just because you're forcing a failover doesn't mean you have to tolerate data loss. (Also, this is the only option for a manual failover for AGs with cluster_type = NONE.) Use the following steps to attempt to prevent data loss:

1. Before any failover, try to get the intended failover target secondary replica into synchronous commit mode. Wait for the synchronization state to indicate Synchronized, not Synchronizing, as is indicated in the Availability Groups dashboard or the sys.dm_hadr _database_replica_states DMV. This is the sample T-SQL code for execution on the primary replica:

    ```
    ALTER AVAILABILITY GROUP [AG1]
        MODIFY REPLICA ON N'secondary_replica_name'
        WITH (AVAILABILITY_MODE = SYNCHRONOUS_COMMIT);
    ```

2. Use the REQUIRED_SYNCHRONIZED_SECONDARIES_TO_COMMIT setting to require a secondary replica to commit any transaction before committing to the primary replica. This is a safety measure to ensure no transactions are lost in failover. By default, this is 0. Execute this on the primary replica:

    ```
    ALTER AVAILABILITY GROUP [AG1]
    SET REQUIRED_SYNCHRONIZED_SECONDARIES_TO_COMMIT = 1;
    ```

3. Demote the primary replica to a secondary replica and ensure it is configured as a readable secondary replica. This means that briefly, the AG will have no writable replica.

CHAPTER 11

This is also a safety measure to ensure no transactions are lost in failover. Execute this on the primary replica:

```
ALTER AVAILABILITY GROUP [AG1] SET (ROLE = SECONDARY);
```

4. Force the failover, now with no chance of data loss, by executing this on the primary replica:

```
ALTER AVAILABILITY GROUP [AG1] FORCE_FAILOVER_ALLOW_DATA_LOSS;
```

5. After a forced failover, you may need to execute the following on all secondary replicas to resume data movement after the interruption.

```
ALTER DATABASE [WideWorldImportersDW]
SET HADR RESUME;
```

6. Because it is a precautionary measure that could affect performance, remember to revert REQUIRED_SYNCHRONIZED_SECONDARIES_TO_COMMIT back to its original state for your environment. By default, this is 0. Execute this on the primary replica:

```
ALTER AVAILABILITY GROUP [AG1]
SET REQUIRED_SYNCHRONIZED_SECONDARIES_TO_COMMIT = 0;
```

NOTE

You should always use SQL Server commands via the SSMS Availability Group dashboard, T-SQL, or PowerShell to initiate failovers, not via the Failover Cluster Manager interface or directly to the WSFC. An exception to this rule is with AGs for which the cluster_type = EXTERNAL. This would be the case for instances on SQL Server on Linux, when using a Linux-based cluster manager such as Pacemaker. In this case, you must use the external cluster manager to initiate all failovers.

Seeding options when adding replicas

Copying the data to the secondary replica to begin synchronization is a prerequisite step for adding a database to an AG. There are a few different ways this can occur, some more automatic than others. The following sections detail the options on the **Add Database to Availability Group** page of the SSMS Availability Groups Wizard—Automatic Seeding, Full, Join Only, and Skip—including explanations of when you should use each one. Each of the four options has a different strategy for moving the data across the network to the secondary replica.

Automatic seeding

Introduced in SQL Server 2016, automatic seeding handles the data copy, performing a backup using the endpoint as a virtual backup device. This is a clever way to automate the backup/restore without using network file shares or requiring the administrator to expend effort backing up, copying, and restoring. This works seamlessly for most cases, given the following caveats:

- In general, you should use the same data and log file paths for all replicas on the same OS (Windows or Linux). Starting with SQL Server 2017, however, this is no longer a requirement for automatic seeding. Keep in mind that the default path to the instance data and log folders includes the named instance names, which could be different from instance to instance. For example, here is the path on this author's named instance on Windows:

```
F:\Program Files\Microsoft SQL Server\MSSQL16.InstanceA\MSSQL\DATA
```

This will not match the path on another server with a different instance name:

```
F:\Program Files\Microsoft SQL Server\MSSQL16.InstanceB\MSSQL\DATA
```

- The only manual intervention required by the administrator is to grant the AG object permissions to create databases on the secondary replicas. This is slightly different from a typical GRANT statement for permissions:

```
ALTER AVAILABILITY GROUP [AG_WWI] GRANT CREATE ANY DATABASE;
```

- After automatic seeding, the AUTHORIZATION (also known as the owner) of the database on the secondary replica might be different from the AUTHORIZATION of the database on the primary. You should check to ensure that they are the same, and alter the database if needed:

```
ALTER AUTHORIZATION ON DATABASE::WideWorldImporters TO [serverprincipal];
```

➤ For more about database authorization, see Chapter 12, "Administer instance and database security and permissions."

- Compression of the log stream sent over the network for the automatic seeding backup transfer is disabled by default. You may choose to enable log stream compression if you suspect that network bandwidth is a bottleneck to the automatic seeding transfer. We do not recommend that you perform automatic seeding during regular production usage anyway, so enabling compression to speed the transfer at the cost of CPU overhead might be worthwhile. You cannot currently enable compression via SSMS dialog boxes; instead, you do it using global Trace Flag 9567. Keep in mind that enabling automatic seeding compression via the global trace flag affects all AGs on the instance.

The automatic seeding backup can take longer than a normal backup, especially if it is over a WAN connection or a distributed AG. During automatic seeding, the source database's transaction log cannot truncate. If automatic seeding takes too long, you can stop it for databases that have yet to complete by using the following code, which changes the replica synchronization preference to MANUAL or Join Only. Use the following T-SQL example on the primary replica:

```
--Stop automatic seeding
ALTER AVAILABILITY GROUP [AG_WWI] --availability group name
    MODIFY REPLICA ON 'SQLSERVER-1\SQL2022' --Replica name
    WITH (SEEDING_MODE = MANUAL); --'Join Only' in SSMS
GO
```

You can view the *progress* of automatic seeding (on all replicas) in the system DMV sys.dm_hadr_physical_seeding_stats, which includes a column that estimates the completion of the automatic seeding, estimate_time_complete_utc. Even though data is displayed for sys.dm_hadr_physical_seeding_stats on both the primary and secondary replica, an estimate might be available only on the primary node. The role_desc column will indicate which end of the automatic seeding the local SQL instance is: source or destination.

You can review the *history* of automatic seeding activity in the DMV sys.dm_hadr _automatic_seeding, on both the primary and the target secondary replica. The current_state field will equal 'SEEDING' for in-progress automatic seeding sessions, as shown in the following T-SQL examples:

```
--Monitor automatic seeding
SELECT s.* FROM sys.dm_hadr_physical_seeding_stats s
ORDER BY start_time_utc desc;
--Automatic seeding history
SELECT TOP 10 ag.name, dc.database_name, s.start_time, s.completion_time,
    s.current_state, s.performed_seeding, s.failure_state_desc, s.error_code,
    s.number_of_attempts
FROM sys.dm_hadr_automatic_seeding s
INNER JOIN sys.availability_databases_cluster dc ON s.ag_db_id =
dc.group_database_id
INNER JOIN sys.availability_groups ag ON s.ag_id = ag.group_id
ORDER BY start_time desc;
```

Troubleshooting automatic seeding

In addition to the guidance in the preceding section, here is a checklist of troubleshooting steps for unsuccessful automatic seeding attempts:

- You must grant permissions to the AG object to create databases on each secondary replica. For example:

```
ALTER AVAILABILITY GROUP [AG_WWI] GRANT CREATE ANY DATABASE;
```

- Check the primary and secondary replica's SQL Server Error Log, which contains error messages related to the attempted automatic seeding backup and restore events.

- Be sure the secondary replica's SQL Server service account has permissions to create and obtain full control over the path where the restore is attempting to place the seeded files. On each replica, you can use different paths, but we do not recommend doing this, because it increases complexity and could be the source of errors in future reconfigurations or restores.

- Check that the same features, including FILESTREAM if applicable, are enabled for the secondary instance before automatic seeding.

- During a lengthy automatic seeding, turn off transaction log backups to the database on the primary replica. Transaction log backups could cause automatic seeding to fail, with the message "The remote copy of database '*databasename*' has not been rolled forward to a point in time that is encompassed in the local copy of the database log."

If automatic seeding fails, drop the unsuccessfully seeded database on the secondary replica, including the database data and log files in the file path. After you have resolved the errors and want to retry automatic seeding, you can do so by using the following sample T-SQL statement. Run this code sample on the primary replica to retry automatic seeding:

```
ALTER AVAILABILITY GROUP [AG_WWI] --availability group name
    MODIFY REPLICA ON 'SQLSERVER-1\SQL2022' --Replica name
    WITH (SEEDING_MODE = AUTOMATIC); --Automatic Seeding
```

Inside OUT

Can you use automatic seeding to add a database with transparent data encryption enabled?

Databases that already have transparent data encryption (TDE) enabled are supported in AGs but require an extra step with automatic seeding. You cannot have a database with TDE enabled for one replica but not enabled for another replica. If you're setting up a new database, enable TDE and then seed it to all secondary replicas. If adding an existing database with TDE enabled to a new replica, distribute the certificate to all secondaries. It is recommended that you test this entire process along with testing failovers before promoting this to your production environment.

Enabling TDE on a database that is already a member of an AG is supported in the SSMS wizard with other seeding modes, starting with SQL Server 2016. (This feature was required to place the SQL Server Integration Services database into an AG.)

Full

This option performs an automatic background backup of the database and log, copies them via a network share (Windows or Linux) that you must set up beforehand, and restores the databases. Configuring the network share and its permissions successfully is the trickiest part of this strategy. The SQL Server service account of the primary replica instance must have read and write permissions to the network share. The SQL Server service account of the secondary replica instance(s) must have read permissions to the network share.

Be sure the secondary replica's SQL Server service account has permissions to create and obtain full control over the path where the restore is attempting to restore the copied backup files. Because you cannot specify REPLACE, the databases and database files should not already exist in place on the secondary replicas. Check also that the same features, including FILESTREAM if applicable, are enabled for the secondary instance before adding the database to the secondary replica.

Join Only (manual backup, copy, and restore)

As a fallback to more automated options, when creating an AG outside of the SSMS dialog boxes, with T-SQL or PowerShell, Join Only is the default and least complicated option. Consider this strategy also when the Full option would take too long within the available maintenance window.

One way to speed up this process is by moving the data before the creation of the AG. Join Only requires the administrator to do the following manually, in this order:

1. Take full and log backups of each database (or use recently taken backups).

2. Copy them to the secondary replica(s).

3. Restore the full backup WITH NORECOVERY.

4. Restore one or more log backups WITH NORECOVERY.

The closer the log chain is to live, the sooner the database will catch up after it is joined to the AG. After the transaction log backup is restored, the database is ready to be joined to the AG on that replica, via SSMS or code.

Skip

Using this option, you can complete setup of the rest of the AG without synchronizing any databases. Choose this if you want to synchronize the replica databases later. This option may be helpful if you are working with very large databases, an extremely slow network, array backups, or on-premises where storage hasn't been attached yet.

Additional actions after creating an availability group

Before SQL Server 2022, AGs could only replicate database-level data, but not server-level data, such as logins. Starting with SQL Server 2022, you now have the option to create a contained AG. As the DBA, your job is to determine whether a standard or contained AG is the best option for your company and to prepare the secondary instances for failover.

Depending on whether you use a contained AG, you either need to create scripts to sync information between replicas or set up the contained AG to create the necessary server-level settings and objects to support normal operations during a failover. We recommend creating these by using a script, which can easily be run on multiple secondaries (including new secondaries that might be added later on) or after a disaster affects the primary or secondary server(s). Using scripts ensures that the server-level configuration is consistently and efficiently applied.

Although database-level settings are populated automatically for a contained AG, including users, user permissions, and database roles, there are server-level objects that the SQL DBA needs to create or update after setting up the AG, performing a failover, or recovering from a disaster.

Before adding a SQL Server instance as a secondary replica of an AG, you should move the server-level objects from the primary replica to the new secondary replica SQL Server instances. Consider the following checklist for all the server-level objects that should exist on all SQL Server replica instances:

- Server-level security, including logins and server roles, can be used to access the replicated databases, plus any explicit server-level permissions or role memberships for logins and roles. The SIDs and passwords of any SQL authenticated logins must match on all replicas.

- The `owner_sid` of the database owner should also exist in the secondary replica instances.

- Create server-level certificates, including certificates used by TDE for databases in the AG.

- Configure Transport Layer Security (TLS) settings and endpoints.

- Create SQL Server Audit configurations.

- Create SQL Server Agent jobs, operators, alerts, retention policies enforced for backup files, log files, various msdb history, and policy-based management.

- Review and match server-level configuration options and surface area configuration options.

- Create backup devices and maintenance plans or backup jobs.

- Configure the Resource Governor. Create the classifier function and any groups and pools.

- Create custom Extended Events sessions for monitoring.

- Create user-defined messages.

- Create server-level triggers, including logon triggers.

- In Azure, configure Azure Network load balancer backend pools (if applicable).

- In your corporate network environment, configure the network firewall to handle all availability group replicas. Test with failover from replica to replica that connectivity is allowed.

NOTE

If you are using a contained AG, some of the items in the preceding list might not need to be scripted and updated manually. This is the primary advantage of the new contained AGs feature. Refer to the section "Contained availability groups" earlier in this chapter for more information.

After the AG is set up, perform the following additional steps:

- Review all settings and document the current configuration. Document the planned settings for each replica in all failover scenarios. When any replica is primary, which should be synchronous/asynchronous, automatic/manual failover, and readable?

- Perform a planned failover to each replica (with replicas in synchronous mode, even if temporarily). Confirm application network connectivity where each replica is primary. A regular failover exercise is recommended.

- Confirm that the cluster network `RegisterAllProvidersIP` setting is configured correctly to work with application connection strings (see the next section). If enabled, confirm that the listener has IPs in each subnet. Confirm that application connection strings are using the proper value for `MultiSubnetFailover`.

- Confirm that application connection strings are using appropriate values for `ApplicationIntent`.

- Configure the read-only secondary replica endpoints and routing URLs for all replicas.

- Add a step to all SQL Server Agent jobs, except those in the Report Server category, to check if the server is primary or secondary.

- Confirm the backup strategy for databases in AGs. If the method for backups is aware of backup priority values, the backup preferences should be configured for each replica. Verify that the Availability Group Properties page for Backup Preferences are configured appropriately on each replica.

Read secondary database copies

This section provides an overview of how the synchronization of secondary replicas works, and then moves into using the secondary replicas to offload heavy read-only workloads from the primary replica. This is the *online* portion of the original HADRON code name acronym for AGs, and it can be integral to the architecture of an enterprise transactional system.

One of the biggest advantages of AGs over the legacy database mirroring feature is the ability to obtain some value out of the secondary database: a live, remote copy of the data. Read-only replicas can be part of your enterprise architecture, providing an easy way to offload heavy workloads to another server, including business intelligence (BI); extract, transform, load (ETL); and integration workloads. Secondary replica databases are not set to read-only using the READ_ONLY option; rather, they are written to by the AG mechanism, and are available to be read by transactions.

How synchronizing secondary replicas works

In synchronous commit mode, transactions must write to the primary server, send to secondary replica(s), commit to secondary replica(s), and then receive an acknowledgement from each secondary replica before it can commit on the primary server.

Log data is written to the drive, or *flushed*, to the primary replica log file, and that data is received by the secondary replicas and applied to the secondary replicas' data files. The log data is then written to the drive to the secondary replica(s) log file(s). The amount of data waiting to be flushed on the secondary replica is known as the *log redo queue*.

In asynchronous commit mode, transactions must write to the primary server and commit; then, transactions are sent to secondary replica(s), commit to secondary replica(s), and the primary replica receives an acknowledgement from each secondary replica.

As a result, asynchronous replicas will never display SYNCHRONIZED with the primary replica, but they can be "caught up" to reflect the same state of all row data. You should expect asynchronous replicas to be shown as SYNCHRONIZING during normal operation. You cannot trust an asynchronous replica to be completely caught up with all transactions from the primary. You can measure the backlog of transactions waiting to be committed to an asynchronous replica by using the sys.dm_hadr_database_replica_states DMV.

> ➤ For a sample of such a query, see the section "Monitor availability group health and status" later in this chapter.

To avoid blocking transactions arriving from the primary replica, secondary replicas use snapshot isolation to return queries using row versioning, stored in the secondary replica's tempdb database. Queries against secondary replicas use the snapshot isolation level, overriding any transaction isolation level settings or table hints.

Readable secondary databases automatically append a 14-byte overhead to each data row to facilitate the row versioning, just as a 14-byte overhead is added to row data on the primary database if snapshot isolation or read committed snapshot isolation (RCSI) is used. The tempdb database also is used to store temporary statistics for indexes in secondary replica databases.

> ➤ For more information about snapshot isolation and RCSI, see Chapter 14, "Performance
> tune SQL Server."

Use the listener for traffic redirection

The AG listener not only forwards traffic to the current primary replica and handles redirection
automatically during failover, but it can also redirect traffic that identifies itself as read-only to
readable secondary replicas. This is especially effective for long-running SELECT statements
coming from reports or other BI systems.

Each replica, when primary, provides a list of endpoints to the listener. You can configure this
routing list on each listener in advance; however, in certain failover scenarios, your desired routing list might change. Updating the read-only routing lists for each replica should be part of
your failover scripting if necessary.

Each replica should have a read-only routing URL, regardless of whether it is currently serving as
a secondary replica. You should also set this in advance, but use it only when the replica is serving as a readable secondary replica. The options to set the READ_ONLY_ROUTING_URL property
and routing list for each replica are available in SSMS in the **Availability Group Properties**
dialog box as of version 19.0. (See Figure 11-2.)

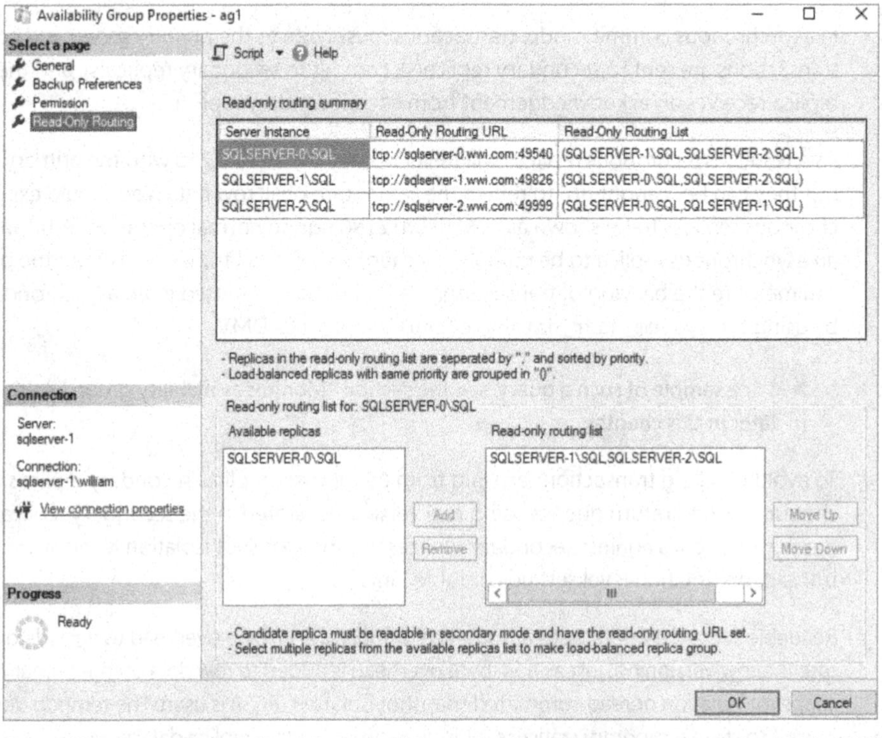

Figure 11-2 The Read-Only Routing page of the Availability Group Properties dialog box in SSMS.

You can configure the read-only routing URLs and routing lists for each replica. Note that each routing list is wrapped in parentheses, indicating that the secondary readable replicas will be load-balanced. Without the parentheses, traffic is directed only to the first replica in the list that is online.

The read-only routing URL is not used for application connection strings. You should always use the listener name for connection strings.

To be routed to a secondary readable replica by the listener, a connection string must specify `ApplicationIntent=ReadOnly`. Otherwise, the listener does not have a way to determine whether the user connection will run only read-only statements. However, starting with SQL Server 2019, the Replica Traffic Redirection feature can prevent errors when accidentally trying to write to a secondary replica via the use of `READ_WRITE_ROUTING_URL`, when `ApplicationIntent=ReadWrite` is specified.

Each replica has a property indicating what types of connections it can receive when it is a secondary replica. Here are the three options for the `ALLOW_CONNECTIONS` parameter for replicas:

- **No.** No user connections are allowed to the secondary replica.

- **Read-intent only.** Only user connections that use the `ApplicationIntent=ReadOnly` parameter in their connection string are allowed, and only read-only statements can be run.

- **Yes.** Any user connections are allowed, though only read-only statements can be run.

NOTE

If application connection strings do not provide a value for `ApplicationIntent`, specifying SECONDARY_ROLE (ALLOW_CONNECTIONS = NO) or SECONDARY_ROLE (ALLOW _CONNECTIONS = READ_ONLY), the databases on a secondary replica will be inaccessible and will block access to your query connections, even in SSMS. This will hide databases on secondary replicas from DMVs and your monitoring tools.

Each replica also has a property indicating the types of connections it can receive when it is a primary replica. Here are the two options:

- **Allow all connections.** This is the default. It allows connections to a secondary replica even if they declare `ApplicationIntent=ReadWrite`. Starting in SQL Server 2019, they are automatically redirected to the primary replica.

- **Allow read/write connections.** Use this when your application connection's strings use `ApplicationIntent`. This setting blocks any user connection that specifies `ApplicationIntent=ReadOnly`. This could be useful if you have report connection strings that use instance names instead of the listener name (not recommended). If you have no secondary replicas set up for read-only access, connections to the replica database via the listener with `ReadOnly` intent will fail.

When connecting to AGs, we recommend that you provide both the `ApplicationIntent` and `MultiSubnetFailover` parameters and appropriate values for each connection string. The default value for `ApplicationIntent` is `ReadWrite`, which is always directed to the primary replica of the AG. `MultiSubnetFailover`, as explained in the next section, is critical for basic connectivity.

Connecting directly to a secondary readable database without using a listener is possible. However, we do not recommend designing connection strings for reporting systems that use a secondary readable SQL Server instance. In future failover scenarios, you would not be able to separate read-write traffic from read-only traffic without reconfiguration. Consider hardcoding a readable secondary replica name only if you're using a connection string that cannot use the `ApplicationIntent` parameter or if using a listener for some reason is not possible.

Configure RegisterAllProvidersIP and MultiSubnetFailover correctly

In a multi-subnet cluster, you should enable the `RegisterAllProvidersIP` setting (1) if your application connection strings will use the listener using `MultiSubnetFailover = Yes`. When `RegisterAllProvidersIP` is enabled in the cluster, the listener has IPs in each subnet.

You can verify that `RegisterAllProvidersIP` is enabled in your cluster and that the listener has an IP in each subnet from the command line, with the following command. In this example, `Listener1` is the name of the AG listener:

```
nslookup Listener1
```

You should see two IP addresses listed, one per subnet, if `RegisterAllProvidersIP` is enabled.

Optimally, you enable the `RegisterAllProvidersIP` setting and specify `MultiSubnetFailover = Yes` when in a multi-subnet cluster. The `MultiSubnetFailover` connection string parameter allows both IPs for the listener to be always registered, and modern connection strings to use a parallel connection attempt to each IP address. The result is a quick connection to the active IP address during normal operation and immediately after failover.

You will notice misconfiguration of the `RegisterAllProvidersIP` and `MultiSubnetFailover` options in the following circumstances:

- If you enable `RegisterAllProvidersIP` with your connection strings using `MultiSubnet Failover = No` or if you do not specify `MultiSubnetFailover`, your application could have very high latency connection times. This is because connection strings attempt to connect to IPs in a non-determinant sequence, based on the DNS query results. As a result, your application may experience network timeouts upon connection to the listener.

- If you disable `RegisterAllProvidersIP`, then `MultiSubnetFailover = Yes` will have no effect, and your applications will not reconnect promptly after AG failovers. Instead, they must wait for DNS to resolve the new primary subnet IP address for the listener. The time-to-live (TTL) could be minutes to hours!

If you are using any connection strings that do not support `MultiSubnetFailover` or do not have the ability to enable that connection string parameter, the `RegisterAllProvidersIP` setting in the cluster should be disabled (0), which is the default.

Inside OUT

Can you use OLE DB to connect to a multi-subnet AG?

There is some confusion about preferred modern data providers due to the temporary deprecation of the popular OLE DB standard.

The older OLE DB–based SQL Native Client (SNAC), appearing as SQLNCLI or SQLNCLI11, has been removed from SQL Server and SSMS starting with SQL Server 2022. Do not use the SNAC for new development, and especially not for connecting to a multi-subnet AG because it cannot specify the needed parameter `MultiSubnetFailover=True`. This could cause long periods of timeouts, as explained in the previous section.

Instead, consider the new MSOLEDBSQL provider, released in 2018 when OLE DB was undeprecated. It is highly recommended that developers convert connection strings from the old providers to MSOLEDBSQL. For more information on the new MSOLEDBSQL provider, visit *https://blogs.msdn.microsoft.com/sqlnativeclient/2017/10/06/announcing-the-new-release-of-ole-db-driver-for-sql-server/*.

To change the `RegisterAllProvidersIP` setting in the cluster network, you can use the following PowerShell script:

```
Import-Module FailoverClusters
# Get cluster network name
Get-ClusterResource -Cluster 'CLUSTER1'
Get-ClusterResource 'AG1_Network' -Cluster 'CLUSTER1' | `
   Get-ClusterParameter RegisterAllProvidersIP -Cluster 'CLUSTER1'
# 1 to enable, 0 to disable
Get-ClusterResource 'AG1_Network' -Cluster 'CLUSTER1' | `
    Set-ClusterParameter RegisterAllProvidersIP 1 -Cluster 'CLUSTER1'
# All changes will take effect once AG1 is taken offline and brought online again.
Stop-ClusterResource AG1_Network' -Cluster 'CLUSTER1'
Start-ClusterResource 'AG1_Network' -Cluster 'CLUSTER1'
# Must bring the AAG Back online
Start-ClusterResource 'AG1' -Cluster 'CLUSTER1'
# Should see the appropriate number of IPs listed now, one in each subnet.
nslookup Listener1
```

NOTE

The `FailoverPartner` connection keyword used with database mirroring does not apply to AGs or the listener. If you're upgrading from database mirroring to AGs, remove the `FailoverPartner` keyword from connection strings. A connection string will fail if both the `MultiSubnetFailover` and `FailoverPartner` keywords are present.

Configure load-balanced read-only routing

Introduced in SQL Server 2016, you can load-balance connections that use `ApplicationIntent=ReadOnly` across multiple read-only replicas in the AG. You can implement this easily by changing the read-only routing list to use parentheses to create load-balanced groups.

For example, the ALTER statement that follows provides a read-only routing list for a three-node AG that is not load-balanced. All read-only queries will be sent to the secondary node SQLSERVER-1, and if it is unavailable, to SQLSERVER-2, and if that is also unavailable, to SQLSERVER-0. This was the behavior before SQL Server 2016. Here is a sample script to configure a read-only routing list for the AG WWI.

```
ALTER AVAILABILITY GROUP [WWI]
MODIFY REPLICA ON 'SQLSERVER-0'
WITH (PRIMARY_ROLE(READ_ONLY_ROUTING_LIST =
('SQLSERVER-1','SQLSERVER-2', 'SQLSERVER-0')));
```

The ALTER statement provides a read-only routing list that is not load-balanced. Note the lack of parentheses around the node names.

With the configuration in the following sample, read-only traffic will be routed to a load-balanced group of SQLSERVER-1 and SQLSERVER-2, and failing those connections, to SQLSERVER-0:

```
ALTER AVAILABILITY GROUP [WWI]
MODIFY REPLICA ON 'SQLSERVER-0'
WITH (PRIMARY_ROLE(READ_ONLY_ROUTING_LIST =
(('SQLSERVER-1','SQLSERVER-2'), 'SQLSERVER-0')));
```

To add load-balanced replica groups in SSMS, access the **Read-Only Routing** page in the **Availability Group Properties** dialog box. Then, in the **Availability Replicas** window, press the Ctrl key while selecting multiple nodes. Finally, select **Add** to add them simultaneously as a load-balanced group.

SQL Server won't stop you from adding the primary replica to its own read-only routing list, so be sure your list is correct before you run the command.

Query Store on replicas

Query Store is an important tool for performance tuning, providing query execution and plan history since SQL Server 2016. Starting in SQL Server 2022, Query Store can collect information from secondary replicas in an AG.

Before you enable Query Store on the secondary replicas, you must update the SQL Server instance to use the global Trace Flag 12606 at startup for all nodes in the AG. After you restart the SQL Server service on each node, you can run the following on the primary node of the AG:

```
ALTER DATABASE CURRENT SET QUERY_STORE = ON;
ALTER DATABASE CURRENT
FOR SECONDARY SET QUERY_STORE = ON
( OPERATION_MODE = READ_WRITE );
```

> ➤ For more information about setting up Query Store on secondary replicas, see *https://learn .microsoft.com/sql/relational-databases/performance/monitoring-performance-by-using -the-query-store#query-store-for-secondary-replicas.*

> ➤ For more on Query Store, see Chapter 14.

Implement a hybrid availability group topology

You can include Azure VMs running SQL Server instances in an AG alongside on-premises SQL Server instances. Azure VMs in multiple regions can be part of the same AG, as well. In terms of SQL Server functionality, the AG feature operates the same, but there are differences in the network setup. Communication is accomplished via a prerequisite site-to-site VPN with Azure to your on-premises subnet.

The Azure VMs that belong to the AG should also be in the same availability set per region so the VMs obtain the benefits of being part of an availability set. (Note that you cannot change a VM from one availability set to another after they are created.) It is possible to put your AGs in different availability zones. This allows you to have your data stored in separate physical locations for additional disaster recovery and business continuity.

The **Add Replica** dialog box in SSMS provides an easy method to add Azure VM replicas, and the **Add Azure Replica** button appears on the **Specify Replicas** page of the Add Replica Wizard when the prerequisites have been met.

The **Add Azure Replica** button does significantly more work than the **Add Replica** button for the new secondary replica, including creating the Azure VM. You can select the Azure VM tenant and the image for the VM, and specify the domain. The Availability Group Wizard handles creating the VM based off the image, configuring the VM's administrator user, and joining the VM to your domain.

CHAPTER 11

NOTE

An important licensing change was introduced in October 2019, allowing customers with Software Assurance as part of their SQL Server license to run free Azure VMs as replicas in their AGs. This dramatically lowers the cost of moving a replica of your existing AG into Azure. For more information, talk to your licensing reseller, and read the announcement blog post at *https://cloudblogs.microsoft.com/sqlserver/2019/10/30/new -high-availability-and-disaster-recovery-benefits-for-sql-server/*.

AG listeners using Azure VMs use an internal Azure load balancer—one per region. You must create the load balancer before you create the listener, so skip this step in your initial AG setup and/or wizard. When creating the load balancer, add all Azure SQL Server VMs in that region to the back-end pool. You can then configure the AG listener to use the Load Balancer IP.

With Azure VMs, creating an AG listener requires an internal load balancer. The load balancer's IP address becomes the listener's IP address.

➤ For a Microsoft-provided walk-through on configuring Azure VM–specific objects such as an internal load balancer, see *https://learn.microsoft.com/azure/azure-sql/virtual-machines /windows/availability-group-manually-configure-tutorial-multi-subnet*.

➤ A detailed walk-through on creating and configuring a new listener between Azure VMs is provided at *https://learn.microsoft.com/azure/azure-sql/virtual-machines/windows /manage-sql-vm-portal*.

CAUTION

Just like any AG, a hybrid on-premises and cloud AG may experience a mismatch of the Bytes per Cluster disk setting, resulting in poor VM performance, transaction logs that are unable to truncate, and the error message "There have been *nnn* misaligned log IOs which required falling back to synchronous IO." See the section "Important SQL Server volume settings" in Chapter 4 for a workaround involving Trace Flag 1800.

➤ For more on Azure VMs, see Chapter 16, "Design and implement hybrid and Azure database infrastructure."

Understand the Azure SQL Managed Instance link feature

An exciting addition to Azure for creating a hybrid environment is the link feature for Azure SQL Managed Instance, which was introduced in preview around the launch of SQL Server 2022. Since this feature is still in preview at the time of this writing, some details and features may have changed by the time you read this. Keep up with the latest on this powerful new feature at *https://learn.microsoft.com/azure/azure-sql/managed-instance/managed-instance-link -feature-overview*.

The new link feature allows for near–real time replication between an on-premises SQL Server instance and an Azure SQL Managed Instance, as if they were in an availability group. (In fact, the link uses distributed availability groups.) However, the link feature does not require you to set up an AG or WSFC in your SQL Server environment (though for SQL Server 2016 instances, setting up a WSFC is required). The link feature enables you to create a connection between a SQL Server instance and a managed instance.

Behind the scenes, this uses a distributed AG that you do not need to manage. The distributed AG spans two separate AGs, but your local on-premises or Azure VM–based instance of SQL Server uses a local availability group created and managed entirely for you. Again, no WSFC is required, except with SQL Server 2016.

There are several use cases where this may come in handy:

- You can use an existing AG with the link feature to add a cloud-based replica to your current AG.

- You can use the link feature to create a read-only node for offloading reporting and analytical workloads to a Managed Instance.

- With SQL Server 2022, you can take advantage of Azure SQL Managed Instance for HA/DR, with the ability to failover and failback. (Failover and failback are not supported in previous versions of SQL Server; more on this in the next section.)

- The link feature offers a superior migration path to Azure SQL Managed Instance than the Log Replay Service (LRS) offered by Azure Database Migration Service (DMS). In general, the link feature provides much faster replication than log shipping. LRS also has an upper limit of 30 days, where the link feature has an unlimited initial seeding duration.

Inside OUT

What versions and editions of SQL Server can use the link feature for Azure SQL Managed Instance?

You can synchronize from SQL Server 2016, SQL Server 2019, or SQL Server 2022. The link feature is supported in Standard, Developer, and Enterprise editions of SQL Server.

Only SQL Server 2022 supports the ability to failover and failback from SQL Server to a SQL managed instance, thanks to the new version compatibility with SQL Server 2022. Prior versions can still use the Azure SQL Managed Instance link for migrations or for read-only workloads.

In SQL Server 2016, at least Service Pack 3 and the Azure Connect Feature Pack are required. Curiously, SQL Server 2017 is not supported at launch, but is expected to be soon thereafter. In SQL Server 2019, at least CU 17 is required.

Failover and failback to Azure SQL Managed Instance with database portability

You can now failover and failback an Azure SQL Managed Instance thanks to a new version compatibility feature being introduced alongside the release of SQL Server 2022. Because of the version-specific nature of the link feature, the ability to failover and failback is limited to SQL Server 2022.

Two new features enable this ability to failover and failback between SQL Server 2022 and Azure SQL Managed Instance:

- Previously, Azure SQL Managed Instance ran at a special version level higher than any public SQL Server release, which meant restoring down was impossible and migration to an Azure SQL managed instance was a one-way ticket. Starting around the SQL Server 2022 release, all managed instances have a new database portability ability. Migrations to Azure SQL Managed Instance are no longer one-way and can be migrated back to SQL Server 2022 if necessary.

- The Azure SQL Managed Instance link feature synchronizes individual databases in your on-premises SQL Server instances to an Azure SQL managed instance. The replication is asynchronous, low latency, and low impact.

New and existing managed instances have database portability. The Azure SQL Managed Instance link feature entered preview with the release of SQL Server 2022. You can now failover and failback from a SQL Server to a managed instance, for example, with a simple wizard-based setup.

With database portability, new Database Engine features that bump the database version will not be delivered to managed instances until they are released in SQL Server CUs. Some Database Engine feature changes with no on-disk metadata changes will also be released at the same time on Azure SQL Managed Instance and for SQL Server.

➤ Additional information on Azure SQL Managed Instance can be found in Chapter 18.

Provision and scale the Azure SQL Managed Instance link feature

To use the link feature for Azure SQL Managed Instance, you must configure your SQL Server 2022 environment, enable availability groups, allow network access, and ensure your databases are in full recovery mode.

➤ Information on how to configure your environment can be found at *https://learn.microsoft .com/azure/azure-sql/managed-instance/managed-instance-link-preparation*.

This section will guide you through provisioning your first Azure SQL Managed Instance link to SQL Server through SSMS. Microsoft has also published a complete walkthrough of automating the setup of an Azure SQL Managed Instance Link via PowerShell here: *https://techcommunity.microsoft .com/t5/modernization-best-practices-and/automating-the-setup-of-azure-sql-managed-instance -link/ba-p/3696961*.

There are different networking requirements if you are using SQL Server in your infrastructure as opposed to SQL Server on an Azure VM. In general, TCP port 5022 is required inbound and outbound for setups outside of Azure. An Azure ExpressRoute virtual private cloud connection between your infrastructure and Azure is recommended because a private connection to Azure for this traffic is required. Other VPN connections from your infrastructure to Azure are supported, such as Azure site-to-site VPN connections and point-to-site VPN connections. In the case of an Azure VM hosting an instance of SQL Server, you can put both the VM and the Azure SQL Managed Instance in the same VNet for the simplest possible networking configuration. From different VNets in Azure, use global VNet peering to connect the two VNets.

When you have completed the setup, you are ready to replicate the databases. Use SSMS 19.0 to select the link feature for Azure SQL Managed Instance and select the **Replicate database** option. At the time of this writing, a similar wizard was not yet developed for Azure Data Studio. You can also programmatically create the link via new PowerShell cmdlets being developed for Az.SQL 3.9.

> ➤ Visit *https://github.com/microsoft/azure-managed-instance-link/* for fully automated migration scripts in PowerShell, including a version leveraging the dbatools.io project.

Always use the latest version of SSMS available. The link feature for the Azure SQL Managed Instance wizard is shown in Figure 11-3.

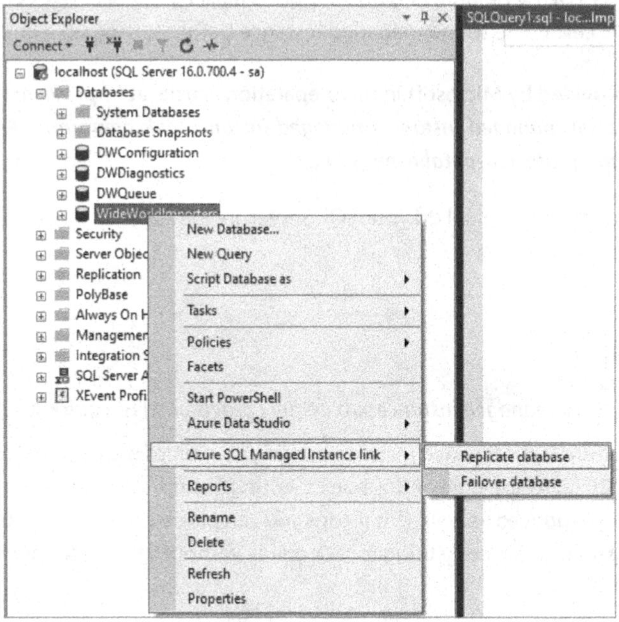

Figure 11-3 The menu path to replicate databases in SSMS using the Azure SQL Managed Instance link.

CHAPTER 11

The link feature wizard pre-populates almost every option for you and creates all necessary Azure objects. Initially the databases report a Restoring... status in the SSMS Object Explorer, and the SEEDING status in the DMV `sys.dm_hadr_physical_seeding_stats`, just as if you were using automatic seeding with an availability group.

Currently, a single link supports a single database, but you can host many databases replicated via the link feature in a single managed instance. Read-write databases not participating in a link can exist in the same managed instance as those synchronized by the link. The link feature itself is free, for as many databases as you want.

The seeding speed of data to the managed instance is primarily limited by the bandwidth between your SQL Server instance and Azure. Setting up a small or empty database should take only seconds.

Once the databases are replicated, you are ready to use the managed instance to offload read-only work, plan for a migration, or failover for HA. As in an AG, the secondary side will be read-only. The link feature does not provide active-active replication where writes are accepted on both sides.

Much like an on-premises AG, the link is tolerant of network failures. In the event of a network outage or service restart on either side, the link will automatically resume without data loss.

The link feature supports TDE by default, and also supports a user-provided TDE certificate. You should upload your TDE certificate to the managed instance before setting up a link.

> ➤ These steps are provided by Microsoft in the preparation article, at *https://learn.microsoft .com/azure/azure-sql/managed-instance/managed-instance-link-preparation#migrate-a -certificate-of-a-tde-protected-database-optional.*

Continue to back up databases as usual on your SQL Server, including your transaction log backups.

Inside OUT

Is something wrong? My managed instance successfully provisioned too quickly.

Nothing's wrong! Azure SQL Managed Instance provisioning times were greatly reduced around November 2022. At the time of this book's writing, a stop/start preview for managed instances was introduced as well. This means you can pause a managed instance you keep around for testing, and quickly bring it back online without waiting for provisioning at all.

Failover and failback tooling and automation

When you are ready to failover to your managed instance, you can use the GUI or wizard in SSMS, or use a combination of PowerShell and T-SQL. Before performing a failover, ensure you have stopped all traffic on the primary node so you do not have data loss.

> ➤ For additional information about how to failover to Azure SQL Managed Instance using SSMS, visit *https://learn.microsoft.com/azure/azure-sql/managed-instance /managed-instance-link-use-ssms-to-failover-database*. If you would like to use Power-Shell and T-SQL, review *https://learn.microsoft.com/azure/azure-sql/managed-instance /managed-instance-link-use-scripts-to-failover-database*.

Configure availability groups in SQL Server on Linux

This section summarizes how to configure AGs with SQL Server on Linux. Red Hat Enterprise Linux (RHEL), Ubuntu, and SUSE Linux Enterprise Server (SLES) are all supported platforms; however, this section focuses specifically on the Microsoft-recommended RHEL, using Pacemaker for the cluster manager, and setting up an AG.

> ➤ You can read how to create a read-scale AG that does not require a cluster manager at *https://learn.microsoft.com/sql/linux/sql-server-linux-availability-group-configure-rs*.

This section assumes you have some limited knowledge of Linux and builds on Linux concepts introduced in Chapter 5, "Install and configure SQL Server on Linux." All commands provided should be run in the bash shell.

Understand the differences between Windows and Linux clustering

There are three main differences between Windows and Linux clustering:

- SQL Server is not cluster-aware when running on Linux. You can configure an AG in SQL Server on Linux to be clustered or clusterless. For an AG with a cluster in SQL Server on Linux, Pacemaker is the cluster provider we use in this chapter, but it is much more limited than WFCS Manager. You can also configure a clusterless or read-scale AG, just as you can with SQL Server on Windows. The rest of this section discusses a cluster-based AG in SQL Server on Linux.

- Because we are not creating an FCI or extending a Windows AG to a Linux replica, VNNs do not exist, so you must manually add the listener name yourself to DNS with the virtual IP you create.

- You must configure a *fencing agent* for your cluster. This ensures misbehaving nodes in the cluster are returned to a known state (which might include forcing it to shut down and restart).

  ➤ To read more on how to configure an appropriate fencing agent in RHEL 8, see *https:// access.redhat.com/documentation/en-us/red_hat_enterprise_linux/8/html/configuring _and_managing_high_availability_clusters/assembly_configuring-fencing-configuring-and -managing-high-availability-clusters.*

Set up an availability group in SQL Server on Linux

To set up an AG on Linux, you must do the following:

1. Create the AG from within SQL Server.

2. Configure the cluster resource manager—in this case, Pacemaker.

3. Add the AG to the cluster.

To reiterate, you must create the AG *before* you create the cluster. This is the opposite order of operations for SQL Server on Windows.

  ➤ A step-by-step walk-through is available at *https://learn.microsoft.com/sql/linux/sql-server -linux-create-availability-group.*

Linux clusters require at least two synchronous replicas to guarantee HA, but at least three replicas for automatic recovery. We recommend you set up your AG on at least three nodes. Each node can be physical or virtual, but Red Hat requires that VMs use the same hypervisor, to keep the platform-specific fencing agents happy. One of these replicas could be in a configuration-only role, running any edition, including SQL Server Express for Linux. We'll discuss this in more detail in a moment.

Configure the server

Each node must have a unique name on the network that is no more than 15 characters in length. (This 15-character limit is a legacy requirement dating back to the old NetBIOS service.) To set the server name, edit the entry in the /etc/hostname file. (Remember to do this on all nodes.)

If you use a DNS server (which we recommend), you do not need to add entries to each node's hosts file. Otherwise, you must add entries for each node that will be in the AG, including the node on which you edit each hosts file. You can find the hosts file at /etc/hosts.

Once you have installed SQL Server and opened TCP port 1433 on the firewall, you can connect to it using Azure Data Studio or SSMS.

Enable availability groups

Now you must enable AGs on each node using `mssql-conf`. The following two commands configure the instance for AGs, and then restart SQL Server:

```
sudo /opt/mssql/bin/mssql-conf set hadr.hadrenabled 1
sudo systemctl restart mssql-server
```

Optionally, you can set up the familiar `AlwaysOn_health` Extended Events session, which will aid with troubleshooting AG issues. We discuss this in more depth later in this chapter, in the section "Analyze Extended Events for availability groups."

To start the session, execute the following command:

```
ALTER EVENT SESSION AvailabilityGroupHealth ON SERVER
WITH (STARTUP_STATE = ON);
```

Create the availability group

To create the AG, you must set up the database mirroring endpoints first (see the upcoming Inside OUT box). This is where things are closer to how Windows works—but remember, the cluster has not been set up yet. You can use the New Availability Group Wizard in SSMS to configure your primary and secondary replicas just as you would on Windows. But because Pacemaker is an external cluster resource manager, you must create the AG with the cluster type and failover mode set to EXTERNAL.

> ## Inside OUT
>
> ### How do you set up the database mirroring endpoints in Linux?
>
> You create a user on each replica, being sure to use a strong password, using CREATE LOGIN, then CREATE USER. Then, you create a certificate to allow the nodes to communicate securely with each other, using CREATE MASTER KEY ENCRYPTION followed by CREATE CERTIFICATE. Copy the certificate and the private key that you generated to the same location on each availability replica, and run the commands again, remembering to use the same password and certificate files. Remember to back up your certificate using BACKUP CERTIFICATE. Finally, create the database mirroring endpoints on all replicas using CREATE ENDPOINT.
>
> ➤ For more information on creating the certificate, visit *https://learn.microsoft.com/sql /linux/sql-server-linux-availability-group-configure-ha#create-a-certificate.*

Add a database

On the primary replica, ensure that the database you want to add to the AG is in the full recovery model and take a full backup of it. When the backup is complete, you can add the database to the AG by using the following T-SQL command:

```
ALTER AVAILABILITY GROUP [LinuxAG1] ADD DATABASE [<dbname>];
```

To check whether the database has been created on the secondary replicas, run the following statements. Note that the second statement is checking the synchronization status; make sure it is SYNCHRONIZING or SYNCHRONIZED.

```
SELECT * FROM sys.databases WHERE name = '<dbname>';
SELECT DB_NAME(database_id) AS 'database', synchronization_state_desc
FROM sys.dm_hadr_database_replica_states;
```

Congratulations! You have created an AG on Linux. The next step is to create the cluster so that your AG is highly available.

Set up the cluster

Each node in the cluster must have an appropriate (paid) subscription for the HA components in RHEL.

> ➤ To read more about subscriptions, visit *https://learn.microsoft.com/sql/linux/sql-server -linux-deploy-pacemaker-cluster*.

After you have registered each replica and configured the subscription, you can configure Pacemaker.

As discussed earlier in this chapter, WSFC uses quorum votes to decide how to manage resources in the cluster. Pacemaker uses a scoring system, which is calculated per resource. We discuss the scoring system and the constraints to control it later in this chapter, in the section "Create colocation constraint and ordering constraint."

Pacemaker does not provide witness functionality like WSFC does. Instead, you have the option to use a third SQL Server as a configuration-only replica. This does not act as a node in the AG, only an extra copy of the AG configuration information. First introduced with SQL Server 2017 CU 1, the configuration-only replica type applies only to AGs that aren't based on WSFC and provides additional coverage for replica loss scenarios for a two-node cluster. The configuration-only replica can be a SQL Server instance of any edition, including SQL Server Express for Linux. As with the various witness types in WSFC, you can have only one configuration-only replica, and it does not contain the synchronized databases, only cluster configuration metadata.

> ➤ Various scenarios and guidance around the use of the configuration-only replica are available at *https://learn.microsoft.com/sql/linux/sql-server-linux-availability-group -ha#two-synchronous-replicas-and-a-configuration-only-replica*.

Configure the cluster resource manager (Pacemaker)

Pacemaker requires the following ports to be opened on the firewall. You can use the same method as described in Chapter 5.

- **TCP.** 2224, 3121, and 21064

- **UDP.** 5405

On each node, install Pacemaker from the command line like so:

```
sudo yum install pacemaker pcs fence-agents-all resource-agents
```

Pacemaker creates a username, hacluster, by default, which requires a proper password. Make sure it is the same one for all nodes:

```
sudo passwd hacluster
```

The pcsd service is required to allow nodes to rejoin the cluster after a restart. You should run this on all nodes for the cluster:

```
sudo systemctl enable pcsd
sudo systemctl start pcsd
sudo systemctl enable pacemaker
```

Create the cluster (Pacemaker)

The commands that follow create the cluster. Note that the nodes must have the correct names, and you must use the hacluster password you set previously. This is where you get to choose the cluster name (not the same as your AG name, but it can be):

```
sudo pcs cluster auth server1 server2 server3 -u hacluster -p <password>
sudo pcs cluster setup --name <clusterName> server1 server2 server3
sudo pcs cluster start -all <PMClusterName> --start -all --enable
```

Now install the SQL Server resource agent:

```
sudo yum install mssql-server-ha
```

Pacemaker is installed; you use the pcs command line tool to manage it. You can run all commands from a single node.

Remember to configure node-level fencing with STONITH, based on your organizational requirements.

➤ For more information about how to set up node fencing, refer to *https://learn.microsoft .com/sql/linux/sql-server-linux-availability-group-cluster-rhel#configure-fencing-stonith*.

CHAPTER 11

Restart nodes after failure

Pacemaker enables you to specify how to handle a failure to restart the cluster. Starting with the Pacemaker package 1.1.18-11.el7, a primary node that fails to restart will continue attempting to restart if `start-failure-is-fatal=false` is set, preventing the entire cluster from coming online. To set this on Linux, use the following code:

```
sudo pcs property set start-failure-is-fatal=true
```

The value should be set to `true` so a secondary node can be promoted and brought online. The `failover-timeout` should also be set to indicate the time between restart attempts.

Create the Pacemaker login in SQL Server

You must create a SQL Server login for Pacemaker on each server so it can manage the AG in the event of a failover. First use CREATE LOGIN, then grant permissions for ALTER, CONTROL, and VIEW DEFINITION of the AG to that login.

For safety, save the credentials on the file system on all servers:

```
echo 'pacemakerLogin' >> ~/pacemaker-passwd
echo 'UseAReallyStrongMasterKeyPassword' >> ~/pacemaker-passwd
sudo mv ~/pacemaker-passwd /var/opt/mssql/secrets/passwd
sudo chown root:root /var/opt/mssql/secrets/passwd
sudo chmod 400 /var/opt/mssql/secrets/passwd
```

These passwords are accessible only by root. You can see the ownership change (chown) and access permission (chmod) commands in the preceding example.

Create an availability group resource and virtual IP resource

The following command (which spans two lines) creates a primary/replica type of availability group resource (the master terminology is unfortunate; it doesn't refer to the master database):

```
sudo pcs resource create ag_cluster ocf:mssql:ag ag_name=LinuxAG1 \
--master meta notify=true
```

In the example of three synchronous replicas, the Pacemaker agent sets REQUIRED_SYNCHRONIZED _SECONDARIES_TO_COMMIT to 1, which ensures that the primary replica will not accept transactions without an online, synchronized secondary replica. By default, this value is 0. We discussed this setting in more detail earlier in this chapter in the section "Configure the minimum synchronized required nodes."

➤ You can read more about data protection for AG configurations specific to SQL Server on Linux at *https://learn.microsoft.com/sql/linux/sql-server-linux-availability-group-ha*.

To create the virtual IP resource, run the following command on one of the nodes (use your own valid IP address here):

```
sudo pcs resource create virtualip ocf:heartbeat:IPaddr2 ip=172.8.0.120
```

Remember that there is no virtual server name equivalent, so ensure that you have DNS configured with the virtual IP resource and virtual server name. Remember to do this in your DR environment, as well.

Create colocation constraint and ordering constraint

As mentioned, Pacemaker uses a scoring system rather than quorum votes to decide on how to manage resources in the cluster. This system is calculated per resource. You can manipulate the scoring system by using constraints. For example, to make sure the virtual IP resource runs on the same host as the primary replica, you can create a constraint with a score of INFINITY. Anything lower than INFINITY is simply taken as a recommendation.

To create a colocation constraint to place the virtual IP and primary replica on the same host, run the following command on one node (note that it again spans two lines):

```
sudo pcs constraint colocation add virtualip ag_cluster-master \
INFINITY with-rsc-role=Master
```

A colocation constraint is implicitly ordered. In the previous example, if a failover occurs, the virtual IP will point to a secondary node before the first node is demoted to secondary, and the second node is promoted to the primary replica. To resolve this, you can create an ordering constraint, which waits for the promotion before pointing the virtual IP resource to the new node. Here's how to do it:

```
sudo pcs constraint order promote ag_cluster-master then start virtualip
```

This concludes the content strictly specific to AGs on SQL Server on Linux. Now we will discuss managing and monitoring AGs across all platforms.

Administer availability groups

Although the built-in Availability Groups dashboards in SSMS provide a base amount of information about overall AG health, they do not provide much in the way of monitoring the performance, current latency, or throughput of the AGs cluster.

This section reviews the insights to be had in monitoring AGs in three main categories: DMVs, wait types, and Extended Events. In all three categories, *most* of the data to be had will be on the primary replicas.

➤ **For more scripts to automate the management of AGs, including failover, see Chapter 9.**

Analyze DMVs for availability groups

This section reviews a few scenarios for which using DMVs to retrieve AG information is useful. You either won't see data or will see incomplete data when viewing availability group DMVs on secondary replicas.

Monitor availability group health and status

You can view dashboards for individual AGs within SSMS or by using the following script, which uses three different DMVs. Both methods provide a complete snapshot of data only when run on a SQL Server instance that serves as the primary replica for an AG, but the script will show information for all replicas, for all AGs in which the instance is the primary replica. This sample is a good foundation script for monitoring.

```
/*Monitor availability group Health
On a secondary replica, this query returns a row for every secondary database on the
server instance. On the primary replica, this query returns a row for each primary data-
base and an additional row for the corresponding secondary database. Recommended execut-
ing on the primary replica. */
IF NOT EXISTS (SELECT @@SERVERNAME
    FROM sys.dm_hadr_availability_replica_states rs
    WHERE rs.is_local = 1
    and rs.role_desc = 'PRIMARY')
SELECT 'Recommend: Run script on Primary, incomplete data on Secondary.';

SELECT AG = ag.name
, Instance = ar.replica_server_name + ' ' +
CASE WHEN is_local = 1 THEN '(local)' ELSE '' END
, DB = db_name(dm.database_id)
, Replica_Role = CASE WHEN last_received_time IS NULL THEN
'PRIMARY (Connections: '+ar.primary_role_allow_connections_desc+')'
ELSE 'SECONDARY (Connections: '+ar.secondary_role_allow_connections_desc+')' END
, dm.synchronization_state_desc, dm.synchronization_health_desc
, ar.availability_mode_desc, ar.failover_mode_desc
, Suspended = CASE is_suspended WHEN 1 THEN suspend_reason_desc ELSE 'NO' END
, last_received_time, last_commit_time, dm.secondary_lag_seconds
, Redo_queue_size_MB = redo_queue_size/1024.
, dm.secondary_lag_seconds
, ar.backup_priority
, ar.endpoint_url, ar.read_only_routing_url, ar.session_timeout
FROM sys.dm_hadr_database_replica_states dm
INNER JOIN sys.availability_replicas ar
on dm.replica_id = ar.replica_id and dm.group_id = ar.group_id
INNER JOIN sys.availability_groups ag on ag.group_id = dm.group_id
ORDER BY AG, Instance, DB, Replica_Role;
```

> ➤ For more information on the data returned in this DMV, read the next code sample and reference *https://learn.microsoft.com/sql/relational-databases/system-dynamic-management -views/sys-dm-hadr-database-replica-cluster-states-transact-sql.*

Monitor for suspect pages and database automatic page repair events

AGs, and the database mirroring feature that came before them, use replicas to automatically repair any corrupted, unreadable data pages on one replica with data from a replica with a readable copy of the data page. This is different from the behavior of DBCC CHECKDB and REPAIR_ALLOW_DATA_LOSS, which could result in lost data when repairing pages.

The automatic page repair is a background process that occurs after the operation that discovered the corrupted page data. Transactions will still fail with an error code 823, 824, or 829 in the SQL Server Error Log.

You should monitor the msdb.dbo.suspect_pages system table and the sys.dm_hadr_auto _page_repair DMV, which will contain entries of these events. For example:

```
--Check for suspect pages (hopefully 0 rows returned)
SELECT * FROM msdb.dbo.suspect_pages WHERE (event_type <= 3);
--Check for autorepair events (hopefully 0 rows returned)
SELECT db = db_name(database_id), * FROM sys.dm_hadr_auto_page_repair;
```

Monitor live availability group performance

Typically, the gap between the primary and an asynchronous replica is mere seconds. You can measure the backlog of transactions waiting to be committed to an asynchronous replica using the sys.dm_hadr_database_replica_states DMV, which provides a wealth of information of interest with respect to tracking how far behind a secondary replica is:

- **log_send_queue_size.** Expressed in kilobytes, this is the amount of log data not yet sent to the secondary replicas.

- **log_send_rate.** Expressed in kilobytes per second, this is the average of data sent to secondary replicas. Values only present for primary replicas.

- **redo_queue_size.** Expressed in kilobytes, this is the amount of log data not yet committed on the secondary replica. This data must be committed before the secondary replica can become primary in a failover, a part of RTO.

- **redo_rate.** Expressed in kilobytes per second, this is the average amount of data committed on the secondary replica.

- **secondary_lag_seconds.** Expressed in seconds, this is a more accurate amount of time the secondary replica is "behind." It does not express how long it would take the secondary replica to catch up.

Dividing log_send_queue_size (KB) by log_send_rate (KB/s) provides a rough estimate for the time it will take to send all data from the primary replica to the secondary replicas. Similarly, dividing redo_queue_size (KB) by redo_rate (KB/s) provides an estimate for the number of seconds it will take a secondary replica to catch up to the primary.

You can combine what we've learned about the `sys.dm_hadr_database_replica_states` and `sys.dm_os_performance_counters` DMVs to create a script, which you can see in the code sample available for download under this chapter's sample scripts.

Analyze wait types for availability groups

You should baseline these wait types and act on increases in these wait types, whether they are sudden or gradual. This section looks at some wait types to note when administering AGs.

> ➤ For more information on wait statistics, such as how to monitor and trend them, see Chapter 8, "Maintain and monitor SQL Server."

There are 60-plus wait types in SQL Server, prefixed with `HADR_*`. Many are background tasks that are expected or will rise when the SQL Server is idle. You should be wary of the following wait types:

- **HADR_SYNC_COMMIT.** This is the transaction delay present when using synchronous mode secondary replicas. This wait type is associated with primary replicas waiting on the acknowledgement of the synchronous replicas when sending log data. An increase in `HADR_SYNC_COMMIT` on the primary replica is caused by performance constraints on the secondary replica. This wait type, and many others, is not present when running only with asynchronous secondary replicas. This wait type does not include the time spent on the secondary replicas processing the redo log data. The secondary replica might be experiencing `WRITELOG`.

- **HADR_SYNCHRONIZING_THROTTLE.** A sudden spike in this wait type indicates that synchronous secondary replicas are trying to get caught up and that transactions are waiting on secondary replicas to commit. Expect to see this wait on synchronous secondary replicas when they are still in the `SYNCRONIZING` state. (Correspondingly, on the primary, you'll see `HADR_SYNC_COMMIT`.)

- **WRITELOG.** This wait type is likely to appear on any SQL Server instance, including AG primary and secondary replicas, when there is heavy write activity. The `WRITELOG` wait is time spent flushing the local SQL Server instance log to the drive and is due to physical I/O subsystem performance.

- **ASYNC_NETWORK_IO.** This wait is not usually associated with network transport speed for AGs; rather, it measures the communication via the network stack to remote clients or storage systems. Misconfigured networks—for example, due to routing problems inside the datacenter or malfunctioning network cards—could explain this wait, but more likely it is not related to AG communication and is caused instead by excessive data sent to remote clients, especially long-running report applications.

You will see some common wait types that are not a cause for concern. For example, the `HADR_WORK_QUEUE` and `WAIT_XTP_OFFLINE_CKPT_NEW_LOG` wait types are an indication of worker

threads waiting; you do not need to worry about them. The HADR_TIMER_TASK and HADR
_CLUSAPI_CALL wait types are also not indicative of a problem, and thus you can ignore them.
If these common wait types are among the top waits, it generally indicates a lack of activity,
not performance problems. Finally, the HADR_GROUP_COMMIT wait indicates that log records are
waiting for a sufficient quantity to be grouped together, and is also not indicative of any performance issue.

Analyze Extended Events for availability groups

SQL Server includes an Extended Event session called AlwaysOn_health. By default, this session
collects Data Definition Language (DDL) events, failover and state changes, and more than 30 SQL
Server errors by number. You can view the details of what the session collected by scripting it.

The AlwaysOn_health session is used by the dashboard, but it can also be queried in aggregate, and by default keeps up to four 5-MB rolling .xel files in the *Instancepath*\MSSQL\Log
folder. This Extended Events session is always present in SQL Server, but not enabled unless you
have configured AGs.

Look for the log_flush_complete event duration in your Extended Events sessions. It includes
the duration (in milliseconds), which indicates the amount of time it took for I/O to complete
the log flush on any replica.

The ucs_connection_send_msg event signals the communication between replicas. This occurs
after the hardening of the block of transaction log data on the secondary replica, and in the
case of synchronous replication, before the hardening of the block on the primary replica.

The hadr_log_block_group_commit and hadr_db_commit_mgr_harden events on the primary
node are the start and end of the log block replication. The hadr_db_commit_mgr_harden event
follows the acknowledgement from any synchronous secondary replicas and the hardening of
the primary transaction log.

You might consider creating an Extended Events session to watch the timing of synchronization
events on your primary and secondary instances. Here is a script to get you started:

```
--Create Extended Events session to monitor availability group synchronization
--Recommended for diagnostic purposes only
--For monitoring events on Primary Replica
CREATE EVENT SESSION [AG_Synchronization_Events_Primary] ON SERVER
ADD EVENT sqlserver.hadr_log_block_group_commit,
ADD EVENT sqlserver.log_flush_start,
ADD EVENT sqlserver.hadr_log_block_send_complete,
ADD EVENT sqlserver.log_flush_complete,
ADD EVENT ucs.ucs_connection_send_msg,
ADD EVENT sqlserver.hadr_receive_harden_lsn_message,
ADD EVENT sqlserver.hadr_db_commit_mgr_harden
ADD TARGET package0.event_file
    (SET filename=N'Synchronization_Events_Primary.xel',
```

CHAPTER 11

```
              max_file_size=(5),max_rollover_files=(2))
WITH (STARTUP_STATE=ON);
GO
--Recommended for diagnostic purposes only
--For monitoring events on a Secondary Replica
CREATE EVENT SESSION [AG_Synchronization_Events_Secondary] ON SERVER
ADD EVENT sqlserver.hadr_transport_receive_log_block_message,
ADD EVENT sqlserver.log_flush_start,
ADD EVENT sqlserver.log_flush_complete,
ADD EVENT sqlserver.hadr_send_harden_lsn_message,
ADD EVENT ucs.ucs_connection_send_msg
ADD TARGET package0.event_file
    (SET filename=N'Synchronization_Events_Secondary.xel',
     max_file_size=(5),max_rollover_files=(2))
WITH (STARTUP_STATE=ON);
GO
ALTER EVENT SESSION [AG_Synchronization_Events_Secondary] ON SERVER STATE=START
ALTER EVENT SESSION [AG_Synchronization_Events_Primary] ON SERVER STATE=START
```

➤ For more information on Extended Events, see Chapter 8.

➤ For more information on the syntax configuring alerts that follow, see Chapter 9.

Alerts for availability groups

Consider placing alerts for a list of errors that are specific to AGs to trigger the sending of non-trivial, actionable emails to your SQL DBA team. If you are not already using SQL Server Agent Alerts for error events to send emails to your SQL DBA team via Database Mail, see Chapter 9. If you are using an external error log–monitoring application, trigger high-priority alarms for the following error messages, each of which is significant:

- **35264.** Database movement for a database has been suspended.

- **35265.** Database movement for a database has resumed; informational only.

- **35273, 35274.** Indicates database failure during recovery at failover.

- **35276.** Synchronization of the database has stopped and cannot be resumed.

- **41418.** A secondary replica has become disconnected from the primary and must be reconnected.

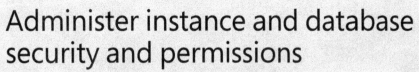

Administer instance and database security and permissions

This chapter covers how to implement security when it comes to accessing the data in your databases, starting with authenticating who you are, what you can access, and what you can do with the data once you have access. Many of these principles apply equally to SQL Server and Azure SQL, but there are some differences due to the fundamental nature of each service.

This chapter begins by covering modes to authenticate who the entity is that is trying to access the database. There are several authentication modes that you can use to access the server, from on-premises Active Directory (AD) on Windows to Azure offerings.

After authenticating to the server where the data is located, the accessing entity is assigned to security principals. A *security principal* is an entity that can be authenticated and then given access to one or more resources on a server or database. Principals are used to obtain access to system activities at the server level, and to database objects at the database level. Once the accessing entity is authenticated and sorted into security principals, those security principals can be given permissions to see and make changes to servers, databases, structures, and data in tables. We cover all this in this chapter.

Lastly, this chapter discusses common security administration tasks that DBAs need to handle, including managing orphaned security identifiers (SIDs), security migration, service account permissions, and more.

All the code for this chapter and the rest of the book is available for download at *https://www .microsoftpressstore.com/SQLServer2022InsideOut/downloads*.

Understand authentication modes

When it comes to security, you should focus on connecting to the database where your data is stored. This section covers an overview of the modes of authentication to a SQL Server instance, database, or one of the Azure SQL database types. You can see the various authentication modes when you first open SQL Server Management Studio (SSMS), as shown in Figure 12-1.

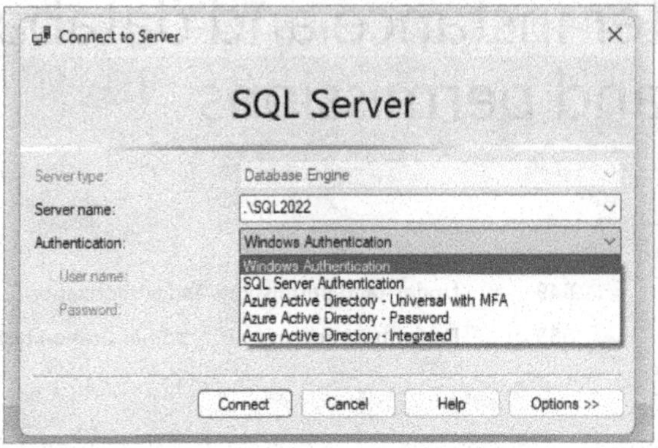

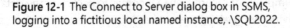

Figure 12-1 The Connect to Server dialog box in SSMS, logging into a fictitious local named instance, .\SQL2022.

Let's start with the authentication methods with which DBAs are most familiar when working with the on-premises versions of SQL Server, because they are still the most commonly used. As Azure continues to become increasingly prevalent both for new and existing applications, it is also important for DBAs to continue to expand their expertise with the new authentication methods.

Windows Authentication

Windows-authenticated logins take advantage of authentication that's built into Windows clients to seamlessly pass credentials in a Windows or domain environment. This is the only authentication method that is turned on by default during installation of SQL Server on-premises, and we strongly recommend it for use in most applications that support it, because it helps alleviate the need to manage multiple logins for most users.

NOTE

Windows Authentication only works with on-premises versions of SQL Server. Azure Active Directory (Azure AD) authentication is covered later in this chapter.

For Windows-authenticated logins, the Windows SID for the account or group is used as the reference value in the SQL Server. For domain accounts, this SID is the same from Windows server to Windows server, making it easy to move security data around.

In a typical business environment, using Windows Authentication means that the existing corporate security administration infrastructure handles account creation/termination, AD security group membership, and password policy. In fact, using AD security groups is a best practice for centrally managed role-based authentication (RBA).

CHAPTER 12

SQL Server Authentication

SQL Server Authentication is an authentication method that stores usernames and passwords of server principals in the master database of the SQL Server instance. SQL DBAs must manage password complexity policy, password resets, locked-out passwords, password expiration, and changing passwords on each instance that uses SQL Server Authentication.

The SID assigned to a newly created SQL Server–authenticated login is generated by the SQL Server instance. Two logins with the same name and password on two SQL Server instances will seem as if they are the same to the DBA, but they will have different SIDs, which will cause some complexities in managing your databases. (This is covered in the "Perform common security administration tasks" section later in this chapter).

You can use SQL Server Authentication to connect to on-premises SQL Server instances, Azure Virtual Machine (VM)–based SQL Server instances, and databases in Azure SQL Database, but other methods of authentication are preferred in all cases when possible.

In the most common usage, SQL Server Authentication authenticates you to the server. However, the same concept can be used for contained databases to authenticate directly to one database. This is covered later in the "Understand authentication modes" section.

Azure Active Directory

The last four authentication types are Azure-based, working in Azure SQL Database, Azure SQL Managed Instance, Azure Synapse, and in SQL Server 2022 on-premises SQL Servers using Azure AD credentials.

To connect to SQL Server 2022 using your Azure credentials, there is more setup than just creating a login. The server needs to be Azure Arc–enabled (covered in Chapter 4, "Install and configure SQL Server instances and features," in the section "Install Azure extension for SQL Server"); as of this writing, this only includes SQL Server 2022 instances on-premises and on Windows.

Azure Active Directory Universal Authentication with MFA

The Authentication drop-down list in the Connect to Server dialog box (refer to Figure 12-1) contains an Azure Active Directory – Universal with MFA option, where MFA stands for *multifactor authentication*. Universal Authentication uses Azure MFA, and when you attempt to connect to your resources with it, SSMS opens an Azure security dialog box that lets you authenticate.

In addition to the password, you are initially prompted to log in with the universal login client, and asked to provide your domain account and whatever extra authentication the AD administrator has configured—for example a PIN, smart card, authenticator app, or even a code that is emailed or texted to you.

As is true for any account on the Internet, it is always better to use MFA whenever possible. It can be more burdensome to use, but someone who gets your password cannot then log in without the second factor in their possession.

Azure Active Directory password authentication

Azure AD accounts can be used for authentication with a username and password for users that have been created in the Azure tenant and granted access. This authentication method makes it possible for you to employ your Azure account to sign into SQL Server via a username and password. This is more secure than SQL Server–based authentication because it is linked to an Azure AD account that is, in theory, managed by an existing Enterprise Security group. You can use this method, for example, to grant an Azure AD account with a Microsoft Office 365 license direct access to a database in Azure SQL Database over the web.

Azure Active Directory integrated authentication

This mode is analogous to Windows Authentication, but using an Azure AD account rather than a Windows Server AD account. Once logged into a Windows machine with your Azure AD account, you can use that Azure AD account to authenticate to the database in a manner very similar to Windows Authentication. No username or password is requested; instead, your profile's local connections are used to connect to the SQL Server. For example, you can use this authentication method when connected via Remote Desktop to an Azure AD–authenticated session on an Azure VM.

This also includes connections from App Services using a managed identity. Managed identities (much like managed service accounts, mentioned in Chapter 4) enable you to eliminate secrets from your app by allowing Azure to manage the principal used by the application to connect to SQL Server. To enable Azure AD authentication in SQL Server, you must register the server in the Azure portal.

➤ For more information about Azure AD authentication in SQL Server 2022, see *https:// cloudblogs.microsoft.com/sqlserver/2022/07/28/azure-active-directory-authentication -for-sql-server-2022/.*

Inside OUT

Can you use Azure managed identities to connect to SQL Server?

Azure App Service managed identities are password-less credentials for connection strings designed for connections through Azure AD to Azure database platforms, including Azure SQL Database, Azure Database for MySQL, and Azure Database for PostgreSQL. (Yes, Azure hosts non–SQL Server relational database platforms!) While you can't use managed identities and Azure AD to connect to SQL Servers on-premises, they are a helpful and simplifying method of securing application access to platform as a service (PaaS) databases.

Azure AD supports two different types of managed identities: system-assigned managed identities (SMIs) and user-assigned managed identities (UMIs). SMIs are managed completely by Azure services, while UMIs are created by tenants and assigned to services as needed.

Databases in Azure SQL Database and Azure SQL Managed Instance are assigned SMIs upon creation but can be configured to use UMIs as well. This allows permissions and access to persist because UMIs are independent of logical servers or managed instances. For example, if you migrate from one Azure SQL Database to another, the original SMI is deleted along with the original Azure SQL Database. However, if the same UMI is assigned to the old and new databases, any permissions needed can be continued (assuming they were all assigned correctly to the UMI).

For more information, see Chapter 17, "Provision Azure SQL Database," and Chapter 18, "Provision Azure SQL Managed Instance."

Azure Active Directory access token

Some command line clients like PowerShell and SQLCMD allow you to authenticate using an Azure AD token created using the Microsoft Authentication Library (MSAL). The documentation for SQLCMD details how to create a token using the -P parameter.

> ➤ For more details, visit *https://learn.microsoft.com/sql/connect/odbc/linux-mac/connecting -with-sqlcmd*.

Advanced types of server principals

Beyond users that map to a set of typical username and passwords, you can create a server principal that is mapped directly to a certificate or to an asymmetric key. Secure access to the SQL Server instance is then possible by any client with the public key of the certificate, using a nondefault endpoint that you create specifically for this type of access.

The SQL Server Service Broker feature, used for asynchronous messaging and queueing, supports Certificate-Based Authentication. As examples, the ##MS_SQLResourceSigning Certificate## and ##MS_SmoExtendedSigningCertificate## login principals, created automatically with SQL Server, are certificate-based.

You can list out the server principals, including the certificate-mapped ones, using the following query:

```
SELECT name, type_desc, is_disabled
FROM    sys.server_principals
ORDER BY type_desc;
```

Authentication to SQL Server on Linux

You can connect to SQL Server instances running on Linux by using Windows Authentication and SQL Server Authentication. Starting with SQL Server 2022, you can also connect to SQL Server on Linux with Azure AD authentication, provided that the computer is Azure Arc–enabled. In the case of SQL Server Authentication, there are no differences when connecting to a SQL Server instance running on Linux with SSMS.

NOTE

There are otherwise very few significant differences between SQL Server on Linux and SQL Server on Windows Server for the purposes of the rest of this chapter, and indeed, for most of the chapters in this book. The biggest differences come with features that rely on Windows constructs, such as the FileTable feature.

It is also possible to join the Linux server to the domain (by using the `realm join` command), using Kerberos, and then connecting to the SQL Server instance on Linux just as you would connect to a SQL Server instance on Windows Server.

➤ The necessary steps are detailed in the SQL Server on Linux documentation at *https://learn .microsoft.com/sql/linux/sql-server-linux-active-directory-authentication*.

Inside OUT

How do you connect to a SQL Server instance on a Linux VM in Azure?

If you are using a Linux VM running in Azure, you need a network security group (NSG) inbound security rule to allow connections to the SQL Server instance. Without it, your authentication attempt will wait and eventually fail with error 1225, "The remote computer refused the network connection."

After allowing network connections to your Azure VM, you must then perform an initial configuration of the SQL Server. Connecting via bash on Ubuntu or PuTTY on Windows (or a similar tool), run the following command:

```
sudo /opt/mssql/bin/mssql-conf setup
```

Bash requires the 64-bit version of Windows and Hyper-V to be enabled.

You can connect to the Linux operating system (OS) itself via the Windows built-in bash shell (a feature introduced with the Windows 10 Creators Update). Since Windows Server 2016 build 1709, the Windows Subsystem for Linux (WSL) feature is included.

For more information, visit *https://msdn.microsoft.com/commandline/wsl/install-on-server*.

Contained database authentication

Contained databases are a partially implemented feature that encourages the database programmer to think of their on-premises database in the same way an independent Azure SQL Database does: as a fully independent container rather than a member of a collection of databases located on an instance. The idea is to shift many server-level concepts to the database level to enable databases to be more mobile between server environments. This has advantages specific to high availability (HA) and cloud-based designs, in that other than connectivity to a server, everything else behaves in the same manner.

We cover containment later in this chapter in the section on "Database principals." Suffice it to say that at this point, you can use this feature to authenticate users to just a single database on the server. This also gives users some access to the tempdb and master databases.

There are two types of contained database authentication: contained users from Windows and contained users with password. Both behave similarly to their instance cousins Windows Authentication and SQL Server Authentication, except in how data is stored for connecting to the server itself.

Grasp security principals

In security terminology, a *security principal* is an entity that can be authenticated, and then be given access to some resource. In SQL Server, a principal is given access through several layers of abstractions, covered in this section.

After you have decided what authentication mode you are going to use to authenticate to your server/database, the next step is to start building your layers of security. For SQL Server and Azure SQL Managed Instance, that means configuring the security context of the entity you are authenticating.

NOTE

There is one concept in database-scoped security that we initially ignore: containment. Contained databases have users that can be accessed directly, without a server login to tie back to. In practice they are rarely used, but it is good to understand the basics, as some of the metadata you will see in SQL Server is affected by containment. Contained database users are discussed later in this chapter.

Given that we're starting on the ground floor of security, let's begin by establishing some important terminology:

- **Scope.** The *scope* of a principal dictates what kinds of access it can be given. SQL Server has two scopes of principals:

  - **Server.** This enables principals to access SQL Server from outside the system and use resources at the instance level. This includes access by people and services.

  - **Database.** Once a principal has accessed the server, each individual database has a security system of its own to determine what can be done with the contents of the database.

- **Login.** The primary server principal used to access resources is commonly called a *login*.

- **User.** The primary database principal used to access database resources is commonly called a *user*.

- **Role.** Another type of principal that is available at either scope is a *role*, which enables you to bundle privileges to grant to another principal (a user or even another role). We cover roles in detail later in this chapter.

In each database, a user can be associated with a maximum of one server login. Logins might not be associated with users in all databases, and it is possible for users to exist without any association to a login. This usually occurs for testing code or accidentally when a login is dropped without dropping the user. (We talk more about this scenario in the "Orphaned SIDs" section later in this chapter.)

Logins and users are given two important identifiers:

- An external surrogate key binary value known as a security identifier (SID) that can link to the external security provider (Windows Authentication or Azure AD). The SID is a binary value.

- A `principal_id` column, which is an integer used in some metadata tables to relate to the principal. For example, role membership is recorded in the sys.server_role_member catalog object and has `role_principal_id` and `member_principal_id` columns.

SIDs are used to link users in a database to server logins, thereby allowing portability if you move/restore the database to a different server where the login has a different `principal_id`. You can view the SID and `principal_id` for a login in the sys.server_principals view:

```
SELECT name, sid, principal_id
FROM   sys.server_principals;
```

Table 12-1 compares the purpose of the database and server principals.

Table 12-1 Comparison of users and logins

Server login	Database user
Authenticates sessions to a SQL Server instance	Identifies the login's context within a database
Can be linked to AD (Windows Authentication mode) or have a password stored in SQL Server's master database	Generally linked to a server login to access data after authentication
	Does not have a password
Assigned to server roles to obtain packaged rights over the server, as well as to all databases if desired	Assigned to database roles to obtain packages of rights to use the database
Not affected by the restore of any user database (restoring the master database will affect logins)	Stored in the user database and brought along with a user database restore
	Used to allow database operations such as SELECT, UPDATE, EXECUTE, CREATE TABLE, and so on
Used to allow server operations such as RESTORE, CONNECT, CREATE DATABASE, DROP DATABASE, or even to view data in any database	

NOTE

It is important to understand this terminology and the differences between the different contexts, not just for interacting with SQL Server, but for communicating with fellow SQL Server and Azure SQL administrators and developers.

The basics of privileges

Moving deeper into the discussion of setting up and configuring server and database principals, it's time to cover the basics of privileges in SQL Server. Most objects in SQL Server have privileges that you can assign to a principal to grant or deny rights to do things. For example, for a table, there are privileges to INSERT, UPDATE, DELETE, and SELECT, which are typically used, as well as REFERENCES that allow you to use a FOREIGN KEY constraint against the table.

Then there are privileges that pertain to the entirety of a server or database, such as ALTER TABLE, CREATE TABLE, BACKUP, and CONTROL. (Some privileges, like SELECT, can be applied to the entire database as well. SELECT rights at the database level give the user the right to read data from all tables, for example.)

➤ **You can see the more complete list of possible permissions at** *https://learn.microsoft.com /sql/relational-databases/security/permissions-database-engine.*

NOTE

We don't cover most of the permission types, nor are you ever likely use a great number of them, but it is important to know they exist in case you have a specific purpose that doesn't match the commonly used permissions discussed here.

There are three statements used to give or take away permissions:

- **GRANT.** Gives a user access to a resource if they have not also been denied access.

- **DENY.** Disallows access to a resource even the user has been granted access in a different way.

- **REVOKE.** Think of this as the DELETE statement for security. REVOKE deletes a GRANT or DENY statement that has been applied.

Here is the basic syntax of each of these security statements:

```
GRANT      permission(s) ON objecttype::Securable TO principal;
DENY       permission(s) ON objecttype::Securable TO principal;
REVOKE     permission(s) ON objecttype::Securable FROM | TO principal;
```

The ON portion of the permission statement may be optional depending on whether you are applying permission to a specific resource or to the entire database or server. For example, you omit the ON portion to grant a permission to a principal for the current database by doing this:

```
GRANT EXECUTE TO [domain\kirby.sql];
```

This statement grants EXECUTE permissions for any stored procedure in the database, including stored procedures that currently exist and any stored procedures created in the future.

Permissions get complex when you start having access to a resource through multiple paths. Roles allow you to group together permissions. (We discuss roles in more depth later in this chapter.) You can be a member of multiple roles, and a role can itself be a member of multiple roles, too. Hence, you might be granted access to read some data—for example, in a schema named Sales—through multiple methods. You might also be denied access via another path.

GRANT and DENY oppose each other, with DENY taking precedence. To demonstrate, consider the following opposing GRANT and DENY statements run from an administrative account on the WideWorldImporters sample database:

```
GRANT SELECT on SCHEMA::Sales to [domain\kirby.sql];
DENY SELECT on OBJECT::Sales.InvoiceLines to [domain\kirby.sql];
```

Or you can grant [domain\kirby.sql] access to insert, update, and delete data using:

```
GRANT INSERT, UPDATE, DELETE on SCHEMA::Sales to [domain\kirby.sql];
```

After applying this GRANT statement, the user [domain\kirby.sql] can query all tables in the Sales schema that exist or are later created, other that the Sales.InvoiceLines table.

It doesn't matter how many times you are granted access to a resource; DENY overrides it. You can delete the DENY using the following:

```
REVOKE SELECT on OBJECT::Sales.Invoices to [domain\kirby.sql];
```

Then you delete the original GRANT using the following statements (which can be condensed into one statement, if desired; they needn't match the GRANT):

```
REVOKE SELECT on SCHEMA::Sales to [domain\kirby.sql];
REVOKE INSERT, UPDATE, DELETE on SCHEMA::Sales to [domain\kirby.sql];
```

Now [domain\kirby.sql] will have no access to the Sales schema, based on the permissions we originally granted, and will not be denied either, because we revoked that on the Sales.Invoice table.

NOTE

You can use the REVOKE *permission* TO or REVOKE *permission* FROM syntax interchangeably. This is to make the syntax a little easier to write and generate code.

Configure login server principals

This section covers some important topics for configuring the logins to your SQL Server instance, including authentication mode, special logins, and server roles (built-in and user-created), and how to best set up a login for your administrative users.

Server authentication mode

When we discuss server authentication mode in this section, we are referring to SQL Server on a Windows or Linux instance. There are two security modes in which your SQL Server can operate: Windows Authentication mode and Mixed mode (or, as the SSMS UI calls it, "SQL Server and Windows Authentication Mode").

The goal is to use Windows Authentication mode for access whenever possible. If the content of this chapter refers to SQL Server Authentication as redundant, often unnecessary, and problematic for administrators, that's intentional; using SQL Server Authentication (in other words, configuring the SQL Server instance in Mixed mode) creates additional administrative overhead and possible security holes of which DBAs must be aware.

If, however, you are in a situation where this is not possible (for example, when it is impossible to use Windows-authenticated accounts due to a certain client API or for network scenarios involving double-hop authentication when Kerberos is not available), it is important to configure your server logins properly. Be sure to enforce password length and password changes, just like you would any login to any service. You don't want users to use PASSWORD1 for their SQL Server login, as it will be one of the first logins attempted in a brute force attack.

CHAPTER 12

This isn't to say that standard logins are insecure. Since SQL Server 2005, usernames and passwords for SQL Server–authenticated logins are no longer transmitted as plain text during the login process. And, unlike with early versions of SQL Server, passwords are not stored in plain text in the database. But because passwords are stored in the database with the server, anyone who gets access to a backup of your master database could rather easily discover the passwords for an instance. For these reasons and more, Windows-authenticated accounts are far more secure.

For the best of both worlds, try using an Azure SQL Managed Instance. That way, you can use the Azure AD authentication modes covered earlier in this chapter and pass in an Azure AD login and password. Azure AD logins are only represented as SID values locally, so this is a far more secure method of managing users, because the instance holds no private user information (and neither do backups and copies of your databases).

Enforcing password policies

As stated, one problem with SQL Server Authentication is that it is a redundant security system within each SQL Server. Included in each server configuration, and in each user, is whether a SQL Server login must adhere to the machine's password policy. It is not required to be enforced.

The policies are applied from the machine's local security policy, inherited from the domain if applicable, including minimum length and complexity requirements.

The Enforce Password Policy check box is selected by default when you open the Login – New dialog box in SSMS (see Figure 12-2), but you can clear the check box to disable this option. So, with SSMS, it is possible to create a login with a noncomplex (or even blank) password.

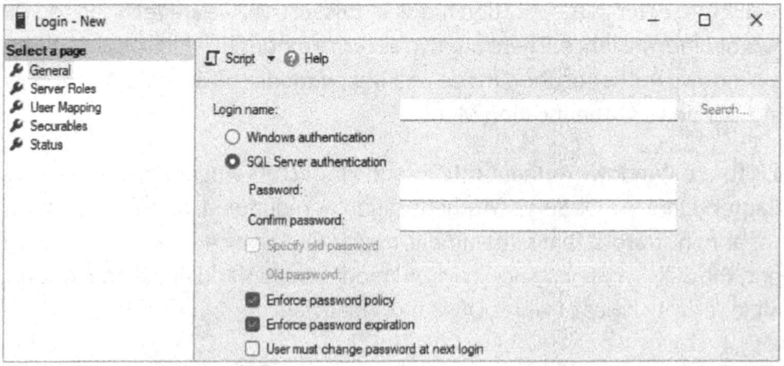

Figure 12-2 The Login – New dialog box in SSMS.

CAUTION

If you try to create a login with a blank password in SSMS, it displays a dialog box that warns you against it and asks you to confirm that you do indeed want to do it. However, it does ultimately allow it if you override the good advice from the user interface.

When you create a login in Transact-SQL (T-SQL) code, the CHECK_POLICY option is not required, but it defaults to ON if not provided. According to Microsoft Docs, there is also no default for the -EnforcePasswordPolicy when using Add-SqlLogin in PowerShell.

➤ For more information, visit *https://learn.microsoft.com/powershell/module/sqlserver /add-sqllogin*.

Inside OUT

Does enabling the CHECK_POLICY option evaluate the current user password?

No. If you enable the CHECK_POLICY option for an existing login that did not already have it enabled, the existing password is not affected. The policy, though, will be enforced the next time the password is changed. So, applications and end users can initially sign into the SQL Server instance by using the existing, potentially noncomplex password, and subsequent DBAs might assume that the password policy is enforced on the existing password. Therefore, you should not enable CHECK_POLICY on a login without then immediately changing the password, or at least setting the MUST_CHANGE option at the same time so that the user must change their password on the next login.

In addition to enforcing password policy, you can enforce a maximum password age by selecting the Enforce Password Expiration check box. You also can force a user to change their password on their next login. Keep in mind, however, that although SSMS has built-in behavior to allow for this password to be changed with a simple dialog box, other applications might not allow users to change their passwords interactively. So, the UI programmer will need to provide this functionality, or the user will be stuck without the ability to access the database.

The bar has been raised by Azure SQL Managed Instance, which does not allow the password policy to be ignored.

Setting the login default database

Each login includes a default database option, which you should set based on how the login principal is to be used. It is convenient to be able to simply log in to a server and be in a desired database without specifying it at login, but it is not without a few concerns.

Authentication of the server principal will fail if its default database is not accessible, including if the database is restoring, is offline, or has been dropped from the instance. Authentication to the server will fail even if it is a member of the sysadmin server role, so you should rarely if ever change the default database of a known administrator login except to one of the system databases that must be there for the server to operate. The sysadmin role has all permissions to the

CHAPTER 12

SQL Server instance. We talk more about the sysadmin role and other server-level roles later in this chapter.

NOTE

Selecting the default database for administrator logins involves an interesting choice between two databases—the master database (the default) or the tempdb database— each of which is always present when the server starts up. In our experience, using tempdb can be a safer choice. Often, when you go to a server to create some code, it is easy to just execute the code without checking the database context. This way, if the USE statement is missed or misspelled, you end up with objects in your tempdb instead of the master database.

This guidance generally follows even for logins that are not a member of the sysadmin server role, unless they should be able to connect to a single database, and connection should be refused otherwise. In this way, the default database setting might be helpful because the login will be denied new connections if that single database is inaccessible, moved to another instance, or dropped from the instance. In each case, the user receives an error if the database is inaccessible.

Server level roles

A *role* in SQL Server is like a group in Windows terminology. It is a grouping to which other principals, referred to as *members* of the role, can be assigned. The role can then have permissions assigned to it, which every member of the role is granted by membership.

Roles are foundational to a solid security scheme and should be used to grant almost all rights on a SQL Server instance. When you grant rights to an individual login or user, over time, permissions can become so complicated, it becomes seemingly impossible to remove them. For example, if you have 10 DBAs on your team, and 100 users, you could end up with thousands of individual permissions to grant, with each user's permissions ending up slightly different from everyone else's over time.

Building a group of roles that match the tasks that your logins and users need to be able to accomplish, and then giving and taking them away as needed, allows for security defined in well-defined chunks of code that can be audited far more easily. If you need a DBA to be able to manage or back up databases, or view three tables in a database, you can create a role, give it a name, and test that it does only what you want it to.

You will work with two kinds of roles: built-in roles, and user-defined roles.

We start by reviewing server roles built into SQL Server, with a focus on when and why they should (and should not) be granted. Several server roles are included in SQL Server, including the one you are likely most familiar with: the all-powerful sysadmin role. We also cover how to create your own user-defined server roles if the ones provided by Microsoft aren't granular enough for you (and they often are not).

Built-in server roles

Server roles bundle together one or more privileges that you want to give to a login. Built-in server roles are groups of broad permissions developed by Microsoft as general roles that people may need. The built-in server roles are generally used to grant administrative logins access to do certain tasks. Most of these are quite powerful in nature and must be given out cautiously, if at all.

In SQL Server 2022, Microsoft has added several new server roles with a naming standard to help them stand out (prefixed with ##MS and suffixed with ##). They were designed to be lighter roles than the previous set were, and should be considered for use before the classic roles where possible. We'll review a few of these new server roles later in this section.

A common concern is that vendor specifications or developers request that inappropriate permissions be given to end users and service accounts via fixed server roles to run their applications. It is essential to understand what you are allowing an application to have access to. While it is not necessarily our assertion that any reputable third-party software is malicious, the bigger concern is whether they can withstand common attacks such as SQL injection.

Server roles are not a feature of Azure SQL Database, though database roles (covered later in this chapter) are provided. This is analogous to how a contained user behaves in SQL Server.

To manage the assignment of server roles to a user, SSMS provides the Membership page in the Login Properties dialog box (see Figure 12-3). By default, only the Public check box is selected, and cannot be cleared. So, new logins are assigned only the public built-in server role.

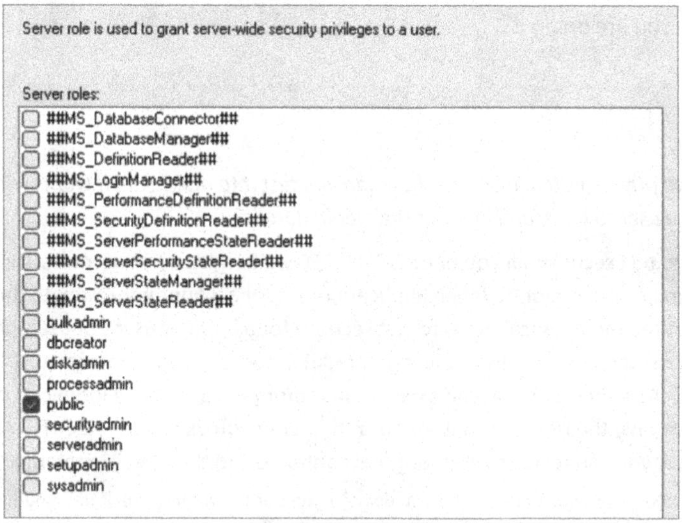

Figure 12-3 The Membership page from the Login Properties dialog box in SSMS. By default, only the public role is selected (and cannot be cleared).

You also can use T-SQL to add and remove members from server roles, as shown in this example:

```
ALTER SERVER ROLE serveradmin ADD MEMBER [domain\kirby.sql]
GO
ALTER SERVER ROLE processadmin DROP MEMBER [domain\kirby.sql]
GO
```

We recommend that whether you initially create your principals using the GUI or by script, you generate scripts for your logins and roles (other than passwords if you are using any SQL Server authenticated logins, though you may wish to include passwords for system accounts, provided that the script is stored in a secure location). This will help you to know what is *supposed* to be on any server. In many organizations, controlling security can be one of the more daunting tasks because getting permissions right in your environments is hard, and when production issues arise, sometimes maintaining scripts is the last thing you think of.

Security sprawl frequently happens when multiple administrators assign rights to users as they ask, but with scripted GRANTs and role assignments, you can add comments and perhaps reference documentation as to who authorized access in the script you have created. Maintaining *idempotent* (re-executable, not making changes unless changes are needed) scripts for adding server-/environment-specific security can help. Recording when that script was last executed in the script along with a check for principals that were modified after the last run is one strategy that can detect unscripted security changes.

Making matters worse, security can get complicated quickly because a role can be a member of a role, and that role the member of another role. The key here is to clearly understand what a role can do, and not just add system roles to user-defined ones without understanding what they do and why you are doing it.

Inside OUT

After you give privileges to a principal, how can you test it to make sure it works without asking for the user to try it, and without their login details?

If you want to test security, all you need is IMPERSONATE rights to an account. This is sometimes done in an application to let an application or user account impersonate the other principal, but the most typical use is to test security for a login or user. For example, say you have a login named Login1, and you just granted it access to a table. You can test this using the EXECUTE AS statement. You can execute this command as either a login or a database user and have only the rights of that user (not the login you executed EXECUTE AS with). Once finished, you can revert to your original context using the REVERT statement.

```
EXECUTE AS LOGIN = 'Login1'; --For a domain account, do not include square brackets
---or the account will not be found
```

```
SELECT * FROM Demo.TableName;
REVERT;
```

For all intents and purposes, you will behave like the security principal you are impersonating. You can also execute the EXECUTE AS statement while already executing as another principal.

This can get confusing, so be careful when doing it, and keep track of how deep you have nested your EXECUTE AS statements. You can see who you *really* are using the ORIGINAL _LOGIN() function.

Let's explore the list of built-in server roles, beginning with the unlimited sysadmin and public roles, then the new roles for SQL Server 2022, followed by the legacy server roles. The new roles are prefixed and suffixed with ##.

- **sysadmin.** This server role has unrestricted access to all operations where there is no code to check for names (for example, row-level security may exclude sysadmin). It is appropriate for properly vetted DBA administrative accounts only. Although software vendors or other accounts can request membership to the sysadmin server role to simplify their security configuration, this is not appropriate. A responsible DBA should push back on granting membership to this role, especially if a user for a single database is requesting sysadmin role membership.

  When granting the sysadmin role, it is unnecessary to grant membership to any other server role (unless needed for row-level security). Granting membership to every server role is redundant because sysadmin doesn't just have rights to do everything; the instance basically ignores security for the members of sysadmin.

  The sysadmin role is also granted certain other permissions, especially in the SSMS code. The privileges of the sysadmin role are nearly equivalent to the GRANT CONTROL SERVER permission, with some slight differences. The most notable of these is the fact that the sysadmin role is unaffected by any DENY permissions; for example:

```
USE master;
GO
--using standard security for simplicity
CREATE LOGIN TestSysadminDeny WITH PASSWORD = '<strong password>'
GO
GRANT CONTROL SERVER TO TestSysadminDeny;
DENY VIEW SERVER STATE TO  TestSysadminDeny;
GO
EXECUTE AS LOGIN = 'TestSysadminDeny';
SELECT * FROM sys.dm_exec_cached_plans;
GO
REVERT;
GO
```

The result is an error:

```
Msg 300, Level 14, State 1, Line 7
VIEW SERVER STATE permission was denied on object 'server', database 'master'.
Msg 297, Level 16, State 1, Line 7
The user does not have permission to perform this action.
```

But if you execute the following code to add the user as a member of the sysadmin role, and then re-execute the statement, it will succeed:

```
ALTER SERVER ROLE sysadmin ADD MEMBER TestSysadminDeny;
```

- **##MS_DatabaseConnector##.** Members of this server role can connect to any database without a user or explicit CONNECT rights assigned. It provides CONNECT ANY DATABASE rights at the server, which gives CONNECT rights in every database. The rights conferred by membership in this role can be overridden by an explicit DENY CONNECT in any database.

- **##MS_DatabaseManager##.** Service accounts for applications that generate databases, such as an on-premises Microsoft SharePoint environment, need permissions to automatically create databases. These service accounts can be granted membership to this server role instead of sysadmin. Members can create new databases directly or by restoring from a backup.

  At the server level, the role has CREATE ANY DATABASE and ALTER ANY DATABASE permissions. At the database, it has the ALTER privilege. ALTER ANY DATABASE not only allows the login to alter databases, but to drop them as well.

  It does not provide rights to access the data inside databases it has created other than running ALTER commands. (If the user creates a database with itself as the owner, then the user has unlimited access to it.)

  In an Azure SQL Database logical server, use **##MS_DatabaseManager##** instead of the dbmanager database level role that exists in the master.

  This is quite a powerful role. For example, consider the following script. It creates a new database owned by sa, then one by a new principal named TestDbManager. The only thing this login cannot do with the database is change the owner, but it can drop the database and make important setting changes.

```
USE master;
GO
--using standard security for simplicity
CREATE LOGIN TestDbManager WITH PASSWORD = '<strong password>';
GO
ALTER SERVER ROLE ##MS_DatabaseManager## ADD MEMBER TestDbManager;
GO
```

Now, still logged in with the sysadmin-enabled login you are using to administer your test instance, create a database and make it owned by the built-in sa login:

```
CREATE DATABASE TestDropSa
ALTER AUTHORIZATION ON DATABASE::TestDropSa TO sa;
GO
```

Next, impersonating the TestDbManager principal, attempt to create, alter, and drop databases:

```
EXECUTE AS LOGIN = 'TestDbManager';
```

You should always make sure you are in the right context when writing test scripts. Too often you think it worked, but in fact you were in the wrong security context.

```
if SUSER_SNAME() <> 'TestDbManager'
        THROW 50000,'You are not in the expected context',1;
```

Then test that you can do what you expect, as follows:

```
CREATE DATABASE TestDrop;
ALTER AUTHORIZATION ON DATABASE::TestDrop TO sa;
```

This command fails with the following error, indicating that it does not have permissions to change the owner. The login will be able to alter authorization to itself or any other account it can impersonate.

```
Msg 15151, Level 16, State 1, Line 17
Cannot find the principal 'sa', because it does not exist or you do not have
permission.
```

You can, however, change very important settings:

```
ALTER DATABASE TestDropSa SET SINGLE_USER;
ALTER DATABASE TestDropSa SET READ_COMMITTED_SNAPSHOT ON;
```

And you can drop the databases:

```
DROP DATABASE TestDrop;
DROP DATABASE TestDropSa;
GO
REVERT; --Go back to original, sysadmin role
```

You must now verify your user context again to make sure you are back out of the previous context. If you change database context—for example, to tempdb—you cannot revert.

Note that the ##MS_DatabaseManager## role does not confer any rights in the databases created. However, if a role member makes themselves the owner of the database, they will have access. You can determine this using the following query:

```
SELECT db.name as databaseName
FROM sys.databases db
JOIN sys.server_principals sp
ON db.owner_sid = sp.sid
WHERE sp.name= 'TestDbManager';
```

- **##MS_DefinitionReader##.** This server role lets you view the code and security information for any object on the SQL Server in any database. It is the same as having the server rights VIEW ANY DATABASE, VIEW ANY DEFINITION, and VIEW ANY SECURITY DEFINITION, which provides VIEW DEFINITION and VIEW SECURITY DEFINITION permissions in each database. It can be overridden by an explicit DENY of the server or database permissions.

- **##MS_LoginManager##.** This allows members to create and delete logins by giving members CREATE LOGIN and ALTER ANY LOGIN rights. This new role is very much like the securityadmin role that has existed for a long time, but with one major difference: It does not come with the power to execute GRANT statements. Members of the securityadmin role can create a new login and grant it CONTROL SERVER, which is almost equivalent to sysadmin. (More on this later in this chapter.)

As an example, the next set of statements shows the basics of what this role can do. It starts with a new login and then adds it to the ##MS_LoginManager## server role.

```
CREATE LOGIN TestLoginManager WITH PASSWORD = '<strong password>';
GO
ALTER SERVER ROLE ##MS_LoginManager## ADD MEMBER TestLoginManager;
GO
```

Change to the security context of the TestLoginManager login:

```
EXECUTE AS LOGIN = 'TestLoginManager';
```

Now, create a new login. (Be careful to test your security context when doing these tests. It is easy to get lost and be confused by something working or not working because you are not actually in the security context you expect.)

```
CREATE LOGIN WhatCanIDo with PASSWORD = '<strong password>';
```

The next question is, what else can you do to the login? You can add it to a role of which it is a member:

```
ALTER SERVER ROLE ##MS_LoginManager## ADD MEMBER WhatCanIDo;
```

However, each of the next three statements will fail. The first two of these will question if the role exists:

```
ALTER SERVER ROLE ##MS_DatabaseConnector## ADD MEMBER WhatCanIDo;
ALTER SERVER ROLE sysadmin ADD MEMBER WhatCanIDo;
```

And the next statement will fail with the error "Grantor does not have GRANT permission":

```
GRANT CONTROL SERVER TO WhatCanIDo;
```

This is an important distinction between the ##MS_LoginManager## role and the security-admin role (covered later in this section). It can only grant new rights for which it explicitly has the GRANT permission or add users to roles it is already a member of itself.

If you want your new login to be able to grant rights, you must give it either the account CONTROL rights over a resource or use the WITH GRANT OPTION on your GRANT statements to allow the account to grant the same rights to other principals.

Now, return to your sysadmin level account:

```
REVERT;
```

Add the login to the ##MS_DatabaseConnector##, and you will see that you can now add your WhatCanIDo account to it, too:

```
ALTER SERVER ROLE ##MS_DatabaseConnector##
        ADD MEMBER TestLoginManager;
EXECUTE AS LOGIN = 'TestLoginManager';
ALTER SERVER ROLE ##MS_DatabaseConnector##
        ADD MEMBER WhatCanIDo;
REVERT;
```

- **##MS_SecurityDefinitionReader##.** This gives the user the VIEW ANY SECURITY DEFINITION right at the server level plus the VIEW SECURITY DEFINITION right in any database to which the user has access. Providing an example of what this gives you access to is a bit trickier than with other permissions. For example, if you do not have access to security definitions, and if you execute SELECT * FROM sys.server_principals; you will get a list that includes sa, all the built in roles, and your login. But if you are a member of this role, you will see every login and role for the server.

➤ For details on the security catalog views, visit *https://learn.microsoft.com/sql /relational-databases/system-catalog-views/security-catalog-views-transact-sql.*

- **##MS_ServerStateReader##.** This role allows member logins access to view the state of the server in all the dynamic management objects (DMOs) and functions, and to view the database state. The role confers VIEW SERVER STATE, VIEW SERVER PERFORMANCE STATE, and VIEW SERVER SECURITY STATE at the server level, and VIEW DATABASE STATE, VIEW DATABASE PERFORMANCE STATE, and VIEW DATABASE SECURITY STATE at the database level.

- **##MS_ServerStateManager##.** This is the same as the role in the previous bullet, with the addition of ALTER SERVER STATE permission. This allows access to some management operations, including certain DBCC commands like those that free cache (FREEPROCACHE and FREESYSTEMCACHE). It also allows the login to show performance details using DBCC SQLPERF, a well-documented command that can view and reset the wait and latch statistics via DMOs, as well as view space utilization data from transaction log files.

NOTE

In Azure SQL Database, resetting wait and latch statistics is not supported.

- **Bulkadmin.** This server role confers permissions to perform BULK INSERT operations from local files. It can be suitable for service accounts for unattended processes that perform automated mass data movement. Only bulk operations from any local folders are allowed; this is the main difference between granting membership to this role and granting the ADMINISTER BULK OPERATIONS permission, which also allows external sources via OPENROWSET.

Principals with this permission can use BCP, SQL Server Integration Services (SSIS), or T-SQL to perform BULK INSERT statements. Note that for BULK INSERT operations, permissions to access the target database and INSERT into the destination tables are also required. ALTER TABLE permissions for the destination table might also be needed, depending on the exact settings used, as it can be set to ignore constraints, which is technically a change to the table.

- **dbcreator.** This role allows members to create and delete databases. It is analogous to the new ##MS_DatabaseManager## role.

- **processadmin.** This role grants admin-level visibility to sessions and requests, and allows users to view and reset server performance information. These permissions can prove useful to non-administrators who monitor activity.

  The role is granted ALTER ANY CONNECTION permissions, allowing members to view and stop (KILL) sessions. The role is also granted VIEW and ALTER SERVER STATE, allowing use of the DMOs.

  Any connection can view its own sessions in the sys.dm_exec_sessions, but with the ALTER ANY CONNECTION permission, a connection can view all sessions and requests active on the server, including system sessions below session_id 50. The ALTER SERVER STATE allows access to DBCC SQLPERF.

- **public.** This role allows you to give access to any authenticated user of your server—which is to say that permissions should be granted to the public server role only in extremely rare occasions. This role should never be used as an easy-button solution to a security issue.

  Every login is a member of the public server role. So, you should not grant additional permissions to this role unless you have considered all the downfalls of doing so, because those permissions will be granted to all current and future logins and users. It is also generally not a good idea to deny access to the public role unless you want to ensure that only sysadmin users can perform some action.

  We don't want to say "never" in either case, because there are use cases for every tool, but most of the time, using the public role is just taking the easy route, much like adding application logins to the sysadmin role.

- **securityadmin.** This role is as close to sysadmin as it gets. The ability to create logins at the server level and users in each database, to grant and revoke permissions at the server and database level, should not be granted lightly. As with the new ##MS_SecurityAdmin## role, members cannot add principals to a role they are not in, but they *can* grant any server permissions, including CONTROL SERVER, which is analogous to sysadmin in most ways (other than it being subject to denies, where sysadmin is not).

Membership in the securityadmin role is required for some service accounts to delegate the management of security to applications, especially those that create databases procedurally and thus must provision security for them—for example, the setup and farm accounts for Microsoft SharePoint on-premises installations.

The securityadmin role possesses the ALTER ANY LOGIN permission and more, including security permissions inside each database, plus management of account status and passwords for SQL Server–authenticated logins.

- **serveradmin.** Membership in the serveradmin server role grants the ability to alter and create endpoints and sp_configure settings, and execute the SHUTDOWN command to shut down the SQL Server instance. The role also grants VIEW and ALTER SERVER STATE permissions allowing for the viewing of a wide array of helpful DMOs.

  ALTER SERVER STATE allows access to DBCC SQLPERF, a well-documented command that can view and reset wait and latch statistics as well as view space-utilization data from transaction log files. As noted, resetting wait and latch statistics is not supported on Azure SQL Database.

  The serveradmin role does not confer access to data or database-level settings or security-related permissions, and so is often combined with other roles to provide a subset of administrative capabilities.

- **diskadmin.** A subset of the serveradmin fixed server role, this role has rights to affect drive resources—for example, to create and drop backup devices.

NOTE

In addition to other permissions, diskadmin has been granted the ALTER RESOURCES permission, which is limited, poorly documented, and not recommended for granting on an individual basis. Instead, grant ALTER RESOURCES only to the diskadmin role.

- **setupadmin.** This role only grants permissions to deal with linked servers using T-SQL statements. To use SSMS to set up linked servers, the sysadmin role is required.

Inside OUT

Should you avoid using any built-in roles?

All the built-in roles have value for certain applications. The legacy roles have existed for more than two decades, and have use cases where they make sense. In many cases, however, they provide more power than desired. So, in SQL Server 2022, Microsoft has added built-in server roles that in some cases are similar to existing roles, but with fewer inherent rights. They also have well-documented rights they confer to members of the role.

When these roles do what you need, and only what you need, they are perfectly acceptable. However, we suggest you scrutinize any security granted via a built-in role to make sure it does what you want. If it doesn't do enough, you might use it and add to it. If it does too much, don't use it, and find individual rights or create a custom role. We cover more about building your own roles and the more common rights you can grant later, but Microsoft provides way more rights that can be granted than we can cover in this book.

Security is difficult, but not taking the time to do it right can lead to much bigger and more difficult problems, like how to explain how confidential information was accessed by everyone inside the company—or worse, everyone *outside* the company.

User-defined server roles

If the built-in server roles don't do exactly what you need them to do—and they rarely will match 1:1 with your needs (other than sysadmin)—it is useful to create your own roles. First available in SQL Server 2012, you can create custom server roles to help you further define the roles that various administrators and non-administrators can be assigned. This can be especially helpful when crafting a package of less-than-sysadmin permissions for deployment managers, security administrators, auditors, developers, integration testers, or for external access.

Inside a DBA team, we might break down duties and grant permissions to suit, for example, junior and senior administrators, or specifically HA administrators, who do not need full sysadmin rights, but do need advanced rights that are not packaged together in any of the built-in roles. The key to creating custom server roles is to have a good understanding of the permissions involved to perform certain tasks and then divvying up permissions.

You also can make custom server roles to be members of any built-in server role except for sysadmin, so if one role has almost everything you need, you can add the custom role as a member of the built-in role and then grant additional rights to the custom role. Similarly, you can create custom database roles in each database. We discuss that later in this chapter.

Following is an example of a potentially useful custom server role. You can create it to allow read-only access to administrators to an instance. In the next section, "Logins for the DBA team," we discuss separating the Windows credentials used by DBAs into an "everyday" account and an administrative account. This custom server role is also useful to provide read-only access to a DBA's "everyday" account.

```
--Create a new custom server role
CREATE SERVER ROLE SupportViewServer;
GO
--Grant permissions to the custom server role
--Run DMOs, see server information
GRANT VIEW SERVER STATE to SupportViewServer;
--See metadata of any database
```

```
GRANT VIEW ANY DATABASE to SupportViewServer;
--Set context to any database
GRANT CONNECT ANY DATABASE to SupportViewServer;
--Permission to SELECT from any data object in any databases
GRANT SELECT ALL USER SECURABLES to SupportViewServer;
GO
--Add the DBA team's accounts
ALTER SERVER ROLE SupportViewServer ADD MEMBER [domain\Kirby];
ALTER SERVER ROLE SupportViewServer ADD MEMBER [domain\Colby];
ALTER SERVER ROLE SupportViewServer ADD MEMBER [domain\David];
```

This doesn't give them complete access to everything, but it does cover many of the things one needs to do day-to-day DBA work in a safe manner and to diagnose problems without accidentally making new problems.

Inside OUT

What level of privileges should database developers have?

This is a very common question when setting up a development instance. Typically, a person may have sysadmin rights on their local machine (this is expected for most of the examples in this book, for example). This is great because they are never encumbered by security issues when trying to write and test code functionality. However, it does mean they will need to be able to impersonate another user to test any security that is created as part of the code.

In all cases, the most important thing is to make sure that any customer data is as safe as possible, and for developers to have as little access as possible, especially so there is somewhere to test that security works in a production environment.

Grant commonly used server privileges

Granting membership to the sysadmin role is appropriate only for administrator accounts that absolutely need complete control. It is inappropriate for developers, power users, and analysts. But what permissions they might need, short of "all of them," is argued over more than you might expect.

As a DBA, you should be aware of permissions that your IT colleagues can be granted. Short of the server sysadmin role or database db_owner roles, give them access to specific activities they need. Avoid handing out superpowers except for DBAs and support personnel who truly need them.

These common securables are server-level and so are not supported (or necessary) in Azure SQL Database. They are not supported even when run in the master database of the Azure SQL Database logical server.

The following subsections present some examples of permissions that you can grant users to do certain tasks, or in one case, all tasks. Hence, it is not only important to know what you can do, but also to understand what privileges mean when you perform an audit of what privileges users have been given on an existing server.

It is not a simple task to determine exactly how a server principal obtained the privileges they have, but it is straightforward to determine what effective rights a user has at the server level with fn_my_permissions, which you can use at the server or database level to see what the current security context has access to. If you run this as a sysadmin, you will see every privilege listed.

```
USE master;
CREATE LOGIN ListEffectivePermissions WITH PASSWORD = '<strong password>';
GRANT CONNECT ANY DATABASE TO ListEffectivePermissions;
```

Next, you can check the login's effective permissions by passing SERVER to the function (the first parameter is for the object to check permissions), which we will use at the database level:

```
EXECUTE AS LOGIN = 'ListEffectivePermissions';
SELECT permissions.permission_name
FROM    fn_my_permissions(NULL, 'SERVER') AS permissions
REVERT;
```

From this you will see the following:

```
permission_name
-------------------------------------------------------------
CONNECT SQL
VIEW ANY DATABASE
CONNECT ANY DATABASE
```

One of these we granted, but there are two others that we did not grant. Every login has one privilege granted on creation: CONNECT SQL (which allows you to connect to the SQL Server). VIEW ANY DATABASE is inherited from the public group, which allows all server principals to see all databases in sys.databases, unless you explicitly DENY this privilege.

VIEW SERVER STATE

```
GRANT VIEW SERVER STATE TO [server_principal]
```

This permission at the server level allows the principal to view several server metadata objects, system views, and DMOs, many of which are essential to a developer who is looking to troubleshoot, analyze, or performance tune. Most of the DMOs need only the VIEW SERVER STATE permission.

This is a relatively safe permission to grant in terms of damage that can be done or data that can be seen. With VIEW SERVER STATE, the principal still has no access to data (other than some values that might show up in a query plan), database objects, logins, or passwords. This is a read-only permission at the server level and provides a lot of diagnostic information for someone doing support without the ability to affect major changes.

CONNECT ANY DATABASE

```
GRANT CONNECT ANY DATABASE TO [server_principal]
```

Introduced in SQL Server 2014, this is a quick way to allow a login to set its context to any current or future database on the server. It grants no other permissions, so while the login can execute USE *DatabaseName*;, it does not indicate that they can execute a SELECT statement and see data in the database. Although it does not create a user in each database for the login, it behaves as if a user had been granted login permission in each database but has been given no other rights (similar to what the CONNECT right confers to a user in a database).

This permission alone doesn't seem very useful, but it is handy for setting up a DBA's "everyday" account or, rather, granting this securable to a Windows-authenticated group to which all DBA "everyday" accounts belong. Consider granting this permission as well as the next, SELECT ALL USER SECURABLES, to grant read-only access to a server, including each database on the server.

SELECT ALL USER SECURABLES

```
GRANT SELECT ALL USER SECURABLES TO [server_principal]
```

Introduced in SQL Server 2014, this permission grants the ability to SELECT from all readable database objects in all user databases. The object types include tables, views, and table-valued functions. It does not give the user access to EXECUTE stored procedures. This is a fast way to give administrators access to read from all current and future databases and their objects, but is not appropriate for non-administrative end users or application logins.

Production data could contain sensitive, personally identifiable, personal information, for instance, so that should not be accessible to even typical support people. In some regulatory environments, granting this permission would not be appropriate and might fail regulatory audit, unless SELECT permission on sensitive tables was denied, masked, or those tables were encrypted, perhaps with the Always Encrypted feature.

Similarly, you could also use this permission to DENY read access to all data on a server by denying this right. This could ensure that administrators (other than those in the sysadmin role) can accomplish a variety of other server-level tasks in production systems with safe assurance that they cannot casually access data using their "everyday" accounts. Members of the sysadmin server role would not be affected by any DENY permission.

> ➤ For more information on the encryption of sensitive data, including Always Encrypted, see Chapter 13, "Protect data through classification, encryption, and auditing."

CONTROL SERVER

```
GRANT CONTROL SERVER TO [server_principal]
```

This permission effectively grants all permissions on a server and all of its databases, and is not appropriate for developers or non-administrators.

While it is similar, granting the CONTROL permission is different from granting membership to the sysadmin server role, but it typically has a very similar effect. Members of the sysadmin role are not affected by DENY permissions, but owners of the CONTROL SERVER permission are.

IMPERSONATE

```
GRANT IMPERSONATE ON LOGIN::[server_principal] TO [server_principal]
```

The IMPERSONATE permission allows the server principal to use the EXECUTE AS statement, the EXECUTE AS clause on a coded object like a stored procedure, or the EXECUTE statement to execute T-SQL code in the security context of another server principal.

This permission can create a complicated administrative environment and should be granted only after you understand the implications and potential inappropriate or malicious use. With this permission, it is possible to configure a login to impersonate a member of the sysadmin role and assume those permissions, so this permission should be granted in controlled scenarios, and perhaps only temporarily.

Other than for developers and support persons doing testing, this permission is commonly granted for applications that use EXECUTE AS to change their connection security context. You can grant the IMPERSONATE permission on logins or users at the database scope.

Logins with the CONTROL SERVER permission already have IMPERSONATE ANY LOGIN permission (unless it has been denied), which should be limited only to administrators who have to occasionally verify what permissions a production user has. It is unlikely that any application that uses EXECUTE AS would need its service account to have permission to IMPERSONATE any login that currently or ever will exist. Instead, service accounts should be granted IMPERSONATE permissions only for known, appropriate, and approved principals that have been created for the explicit purpose of being impersonated temporarily.

ALTER ANY EVENT SESSION

```
GRANT ALTER ANY EVENT SESSION TO [server_principal]
```

A developer might need this permission to trace the SQL Server as part of a troubleshooting expedition after you tell them about Extended Events. This will grant them access to create Extended Events sessions with T-SQL commands but will not give them access to view server metadata in the New Extended Events Session Wizard in SSMS. For that, they will need one further commonly granted developer permission: VIEW SERVER STATE.

Like traces in Profiler (the tool that won't ever fade away), Extended Events sessions can capture events on the server from all databases and processes. You cannot use a trace to capture certain sensitive events—for example, the T-SQL statement CREATE LOGIN for a SQL authenticated login.

NOTE

This is one place where Azure SQL Database differs because for developers to view Extended Events sessions, you must grant them an ownership-level permission, CONTROL DATABASE (discussed later in this chapter in the section "Grant commonly used database level privileges"). In production environments, this isn't recommended for developers or non-administrators.

ALTER TRACE

```
GRANT ALTER TRACE TO [server_principal]
```

A developer might need this permission to trace the SQL Server as part of a troubleshooting expedition into the SQL Server instance (though you should remind them prior to granting this permission that traces are deprecated, and Extended Events are a much better diagnostic tool).

➤ **For more information on monitoring SQL Server, see Chapter 8, "Maintain and monitor SQL Server."**

Because ALTER TRACE is a server-level securable, developers can trace all events on the server, from all databases and processes. Certain sensitive events cannot be traced; the T-SQL statement of CREATE LOGIN for a SQL authenticated login is an example.

Special purpose logins

This section discusses some important special logins to be aware of, including special administrative access, which you should tightly control.

The sa login

The sa login is a special SQL Server–authenticated login that is, simply put, all powerful. It is a known member of the sysadmin server role with a unique SID value of 0x01, and you can (though rarely should) use it for all administrative access. If your instance is in Mixed mode (in which both Windows Authentication and SQL Server Authentication are turned on), and the sa password is known, it can be used to do anything on the server.

Even if you never use the sa account for authentication, it has utility as the *authorization* (in other words, the owner) of databases on a server for many configurations, such as a general corporate server where all the databases are used by the same enterprise. In cases where a server is used for multiple customers, you may wish to have each customer's login own their own database(s). When two databases are owned by the same user, you can enable the DB_CHAINING database setting to allow cross database queries.

> ➤ For more information about cross-database chaining, see *https://learn.microsoft.com /dotnet/framework/data/adonet/sql/enabling-cross-database-access-in-sql-server*.

This known administrator account, however, has obvious potential consequences if used for typical access, much as any sysadmin level login does, with the addition of not being able to tell one user of the account from another. This means it could serve as an anonymous backdoor for malicious or noncompliant activity by current or former employees. In the best case, the sa account should have a wickedly complex password that is locked away for safekeeping.

Applications, application developers, and end users should never use the sa account. This much should be obvious. The sa account, like any SQL Server–authenticated account, can potentially have its password reverse-engineered by a malicious actor who has access to or a copy of the master database .mdf file.

The sa account is a common vector for brute-force attacks to compromise a SQL Server. For this reason, if your SQL Server is exposed to the Internet, we recommend that you rename and/or disable this account.

The BUILTIN\Administrators Windows group

If you have experience administering SQL Server 2005 or older, you probably remember the BUILTIN\Administrators group login, which was created by default to grant access to the sysadmin server role to any account that is also a member of the local Windows Administrator group. This was a convenience that might seem logical. But should anyone who has admin-istrator rights to a server have administrator rights to everything that server has on it? The answer is no.

Beginning with SQL Server 2008, this group was no longer added to SQL Server instances by default, because it is an obvious and serious security back door. Although it was potentially convenient for administrators, it was also targeted by malicious actors. Do not add the BUILTIN\Administrators group to your SQL Server instance—it is no longer there by default for a reason.

Service accounts

Chapter 4 discusses service accounts in greater depth, but it is worth pointing out that service accounts for a server are purely server logins. They are usually given the minimal permissions needed to run the services to which they are assigned by SQL Server Configuration Manager. For this reason, you should not use the Windows Services (services.msc) to change SQL Server feature service accounts.

It is not necessary to grant additional SQL Server permissions to SQL Server service accounts. (You might need to grant additional file-system-level permissions for file locations, however.) The SQL Server Agent service account likely needs to be a member of the sysadmin role in a typical configuration. It is technically not necessary, because you can set credentials that you assign to each job being executed using credentials and proxies.

You also should never grant the NT AUTHORITY\SYSTEM account, which is present by default in a SQL Server instance, any additional permissions. Many Windows applications run under this system account and should not have any nonstandard permissions.

Inside OUT

What about service accounts for instances in an availability group?

For SQL Servers in an availability group, the SQL Server service on each replica instance does not need to have the same domain service account, though this is the simplest approach.

If each replica SQL Server service account is different, you must create a login for each other replica's domain service account on each replica.

Though not recommended, if you choose to use nondomain service accounts for each SQL Server instance, you must create the database mirroring endpoint (not to be confused with the deprecated database mirroring feature) using an encrypted certificate for the instance.

We also recommend that you do not use local or built-in service accounts, including the machine account, though it is also possible to do so by granting each machine's network service account a login on each other's replica. This is not a secure approach.

For more on availability groups, see Chapter 11, "Implement high availability and disaster recovery."

Logins for the DBA team

The first logins you need to create when setting up a new server are for the DBAs so they have access to do everything they need to do. In all but the most rudimentary IT departments, SQL DBAs need access to production SQL Server instances, but need their access governed and constrained to certain uses and privileges—at least most of the time. By this we mean that during your normal duties, it is better if you don't have rights to drop the primary sales database because you "thought you were on your local machine." A day of lost activity (or worse, sales), plus the need to creatively explain to potential employers why you left your previous employer abruptly, is not worth avoiding a few extra steps to make changes and apply upgrades to your production server.

Assuming you are primarily using Windows Authentication for your server access, this means that SQL Server DBAs will sign into a Windows instance using the domain credentials they use to access their email account, timesheet application, and so on. Then, they connect to the SQL Server instance with Windows Authentication on that same account and begin their work. DBAs often use this same method whether they are connecting to a production environment SQL Server or a preproduction (development/testing) environment SQL Server, though we'll talk about using different credentials for each next.

Inside OUT

What is a "production" environment, and how is it different?

The upcoming section talks about "production" versus "preproduction." These terms mean different things to different people (even our authors initially had a different definition of what a preproduction environment was), so let's look at what each environment actually is:

- **Production.** This is the main system of record. It might, for example, connect to actual instruments or machines, control life-critical systems or customer-facing applications, or contain the organization's valuable data. It is subject to disaster recovery plans, needs high availability, and is "the server" to which the CEO of your company refers.

- **Preproduction.** This is a class of systems that may resemble the production environment but isn't visible to the actual machinery (physically or metaphorically speaking) of the business. Preproduction systems go by many names, including development, test, quality assurance (QA), user acceptance testing (UAT), business acceptance testing (BAT), and many others. Very often, this environment will simply be referred to as *dev* or *test*. The key is that we are not talking about user data on which the business relies. Preproduction servers should generally not contain actual customer or patient information, other than a true testing system, such as a UAT or BAT system, where the customer must see their actual data in action; in such cases the system may need to be treated like production with regard to data access and protection.

Developers, report writers, and QA testers should ideally have access only to preproduction systems. If they must troubleshoot a production problem, only trusted developers should be given access, and even then, only temporarily.

DBAs must have access to SQL Server instances in all environments, but, still, we need to discuss how best to arrange for access to production systems.

To illustrate, consider the following scenario: Tasked with backing up and restoring a database from the production environment to the development environment, the DBA uses the connections already open in SSMS, copies the backup to a network share, and then begins the restore. The restore is 50 percent complete when a user calls to ask, "Is the SQL Server down?"

Too often, the problem is exceedingly simple: The DBA is working on the wrong server. In many cases, the development and production servers may look completely alike except for a few letters in the name or DNS entry. A DNS naming standard might just differ by sql.d.company and sql.p.company, and in a query window, it might not be noticed.

At a conference this author once attended, the speaker asked how many SQL Server instances people managed. Well over half of the attendees managed 50+ servers. If one-third of them are production, the other two-thirds look extremely similar to those servers, just in a preproduction configuration. For too many DBAs, it is sadly a rite of passage to muck up a production server, and then repair it with little or no data loss.

If your DBA team isn't already using *two or more* Windows-authenticated accounts each, you should consider segmenting each DBA's production database access from the account they use for the rest of their day-to-day activities, including preproduction systems, but also email, office applications, Office 365, and more. Then consider creating "admin-level" accounts for each DBA that allow no access to preproduction systems, office applications, Office 365, virtual private networks (VPNs)—not even the Internet, except for what is required for the job. The idea is to encourage your DBA team to use its admin accounts only for administrative activities.

For example, suppose Kirby is a DBA. They use Domain\Kirby to access tools for "everyday" activities, such as email, instant messaging, preproduction SQL instances, source control, Office 365, VPN, and more. However, this domain account has limited access to production SQL Servers. For example, they can access server-level DMVs, activity levels, SQL Agent job history, and the SQL Server Error Log, but they cannot create logins, read or update live production data, alter databases, and so on. To perform any of those tasks, Kirby starts SSMS using Run AS *another user* or opens a remote desktop session to another server using Domain\admin-Kirby. This activity is deliberate and requires heightened awareness—the production databases are important! Starting SSMS from within the remote desktop session, Domain\admin-Kirby is a member of the sysadmin server role and can accomplish anything they need to in the production environment. When they're done, they log out. Domain\admin-Kirby also has no VPN access; thus, if it is compromised, it cannot be used to both gain remote access to the corporate network and access SQL Servers.

Of course, since the DBA team are employees just like anyone else, they may have to access the SQL Server as part of their job—for example, to track projects and enter timesheets. However, access to the production servers using their admin account in a way that they have elevated access requires deliberate steps and mental awareness of the task at hand. So, the risk of accidentally running intended-for-development tasks in production is considerably reduced.

After separating the day-to-day from the admin logins for each member of the DBA team, it's time to assign permissions to each as appropriate. If your DBA team has been operating with a single login, this will likely resolve revoking permissions from their existing account and creating a new admin account. Refer to the "User-defined server roles" section, earlier in this chapter, about server roles that you can use to separate duties among a team of DBAs, and a custom server role that you can create to set up read-only access to an entire server.

Database principals

A database security principal is a part of the database and is the anchor in which you can obtain access to data and coded objects in the database. There are two major types of database principals: *users* and *roles*.

Each of these is in some way considered the same, in that you can grant and deny access to database resources using them. Users are the hook to obtain access to a database, whereas a role is a way to group one or more users together to give them a common set of permissions.

Database users

There are four major types of database users: users mapped to logins and groups, users mapped to Windows Authentication principals directly, users who cannot authenticate at all, and contained users.

Users mapped to logins and groups

Users mapped to logins are by far the most common type you will encounter. For example, suppose you created a standard login named Bob and a Windows authenticated login named [Domain\Fred] using the following code:

```
CREATE LOGIN Bob WITH PASSWORD = 'Bob Is A Graat Guy';
--Misspellings in passwords can be helpful!
CREATE LOGIN [Domain\Fred] FROM WINDOWS;
```

Then, you could create users for these logins using:

```
CREATE USER Bob FOR LOGIN Bob;
CREATE USER [Domain\Fred] FOR LOGIN [Domain\Fred];
```

There is nothing stating that the name of the login must match the domain name, but it is a very typical way to create users, and helps to document your database users and where they come from. The following is perfectly legal syntax as well, where you name the user differently from the Windows security principal:

```
CREATE USER fred FOR LOGIN [Domain\Fred];
```

The Windows principal that the login and the database user it references needn't be a Windows-based login. It can be a Windows group, for example, which will allow every member of that group to access the server without being named individually.

You cannot use a \ (backslash) character in a login or database username unless it is a Windows Authentication based login. Trying to execute the two following statements:

```
CREATE LOGIN [Domain\Fred] WITH PASSWORD = '$3cure1';
CREATE USER [Dog\Gone] FOR LOGIN [Domain\Fred];
```

results in two error messages saying Domain\Fred and Dog\Gone are not valid names because they contain invalid characters, and this is true even if Domain\Fred or Dog\Gone is a valid login.

To use the same login name as the user for a Windows Authenticated login, the names must be the same. If you execute:

```
CREATE USER [Dog\Gone] FOR LOGIN [Dog\Gone];
```

Then you will either get an error about Dog\Gone not being a valid Windows user or group, or you have a really cool domain name!

Users mapped to Windows Authentication principals directly

In the previous section, we created the login for [Domain\Fred], so the CREATE USER statement referenced that login. However, a user could be created for that login regardless of the existence of the explicit login principal:

```
CREATE USER [Domain\Sam] FOR LOGIN [Domain\Sam];
```

In a non-contained database, this user can be used by Domain\Sam, if and only if Domain\Sam can authenticate to the server. So, if Sam was a member of Domain\DatabaseUsers, and there was a login mapped to Domain\DatabaseUsers, creating the user Domain\Sam in the database would not only extend Domain\Sam access to the database, but it would give all members of Domain\DatabaseUsers rights to access the server (and as we discussed earlier, rights to see the existence of the database, but not access it).

Users who cannot authenticate at all

A user does not have to have a login at all, even in a non-contained database. This means it cannot be authenticated to, but it can still exist and have rights assigned. In this scenario, the user will not have a SID assigned at all.

> **NOTE**
>
> Another way a user can be in a database and not be authenticated for use at all is from a broken connection to a SID on the server, often from restoring a database on a new server. This scenario, and how to handle it, is covered later in this chapter in the "Orphaned SIDs" section.

While the user principal cannot be authenticated to, it can be impersonated using EXECUTE AS, and is a very useful tool for testing security. It will also be used frequently in the "Understand permissions and authorization" section later in this chapter. The syntax for creating a login-less user is simply:

```
CREATE USER Sally WITHOUT LOGIN;
ALTER RoleYouWantToTest ADD MEMBER Sally;
EXECUTE AS USER = 'Sally';
```

You can then test the role all you want to without connecting to the server with a new login or creating an unneeded login. Database roles are covered in more detail later in this chapter.

Of course, in either case, if you create users and logins for testing, be sure to drop them when you are finished with them. You don't want to leave any test code/data around in your databases when you are finished, even in your preproduction servers.

Users contained in the database

Databases created or altered on a SQL Server instance by using CONTAINMENT = PARTIAL allow the creation of database principals referred to as *contained users*. Contained users are authenticated directly to the database in which they are located. They are not used frequently, but are interesting in how they can show up in the system metadata.

Contained users can be contained users with password or contained Windows Authentication users. Contained users with password behave like SQL Server Authentication principals, and can be used directly, bypassing the server's authentication.

> **NOTE**
>
> Currently, SQL Server 2022 offers only partially contained databases because some objects still cross the database boundary, such as management of the SQL Server instance's endpoints. If fully contained databases were implemented, they would have no external dependencies, even for metadata, temporary objects, configuration, and SQL Agent Jobs. That level of containment is not available in SQL Server 2022.

You can move contained databases from SQL Server instance to instance without the need to re-create server-level objects, such as server-level security (logins). Some features are only partially contained. Use the catalog views sys.dm_db_uncontained_entities and sys.sql _modules to return information about uncontained objects or features. By determining the containment status of the elements of your database, you can discover what objects or features must be replaced or altered to promote containment.

A significant security factor to be aware of with contained databases is that any user with the ALTER ANY USER permission, and of course any user who is a member of the db_owner fixed database role, can grant access to the database and therefore the server's computing and storage resources. Users with this permission can grant access to new users and applications independently of the SQL Server instance's administrators.

Though the concept of creating databases with the specific CONTAINMENT option does not exist in Azure SQL Database, contained databases are specifically developed to assist with the concept of a cloud-based database as a service, to allow databases in Azure SQL Database to be mobile between different cloud hosts and to ensure very high levels of availability.

Table 12-2 compares contained database users to database users and server logins (previously shown in Table 12-1).

Table 12-2   Comparing users, logins, and contained users

Server login	Database user	Contained database user
Authenticates sessions to a SQL Server	Identifies the login's context within a database	Authenticates to a SQL Server and the database they are contained in (plus tempdb)
Can be linked to AD (Windows Authentication) or have a password stored in SQL Server's master database	Generally linked to a server login to access data after authenticated	May have a password or be linked to AD
Assigned to server roles to obtain packaged rights over the server, as well as all databases if desired	Does not have a password	Assigned to database roles to obtain packages of rights to use the database
Not affected by the restore of any user database	Assigned to database roles to obtain packages of rights to use the database	Stored in the user database and brought along with a user database restore
Used to allow server operations such as RESTORE, CONNECT, CREATE DATABASE, DROP DATABASE, or even viewing data in any database	Stored in the user database and brought along with a user database restore	Cannot be given access to external databases directly
	Used to allow database operations such as SELECT, UPDATE, EXECUTE, CREATE TABLE, and so on	

Database roles

Database roles, much like the server roles discussed in the "Server level roles" section earlier in this chapter, allow you to provide packages of permissions to ease the provisioning of database users. You also can create your own user-defined database roles to customize the packages of permissions granted to users.

This section reviews the database roles, both built-in and custom, with a focus on when and why they should be granted. The same list of roles applies to SQL Server and Azure SQL Database.

Built-in database roles

Let's first examine the list of built-in database roles, their permissions, and their appropriate use. These roles have some utility when setting up your security, but in a well-configured database, most users will not be a member of any of these roles. Rather, they will be made a member of a custom role, covered in the next section.

- **db_owner.** This database role's name is a bit misleading because it can have many members. It provides unrestricted access to the database to make any and all changes to that database and contained objects. This is different from being identified as the login that owns the database (represented by the owner_sid in sys.databases). Changing the AUTHORIZATION for the database to a principal confers the same rights as db_owner because the server principal will be mapped to the dbo built-in user when accessing the database, which is a member of the db_owner role.

  The db_owner role does not specifically confer the CONTROL DATABASE permission to its members, but is equivalent in terms of what it is allowed to do. Different from the sysadmin server role, the db_owner role does not bypass DENY permissions. For example:

  ```
  CREATE USER fred WITHOUT LOGIN;
  ALTER ROLE db_owner ADD MEMBER fred;
  DENY SELECT ON dbo.test TO fred;
  GO
  EXECUTE AS USER = 'fred';
  SELECT *
  FROM dbo.test;
  ```

  For a real database, this would return an error message: "The SELECT permission was denied." However, while you can deny members of the db_owner group access to some resource, the actual owner of the database will not be subject to the DENY. Moreover, as a member of the db_owner role, the user will be able to impersonate the dbo user unless you deny them that ability. (While impersonating dbo, the user can easily revoke any denied rights, so it is important to audit users with elevated rights if they have access to any sensitive data.)

  ```
  EXECUTE AS USER = 'dbo'
  SELECT *
  FROM dbo.test;
  GO
  REVERT; REVERT; --Revert twice, once to get back to fred, and another to get back
  to your security context.
  ```

  The only users in the database who can add or remove members from built-in database roles are members of the db_owner role or principals that hold AUTHORIZATION rights for the database. However, a loophole to this is a database role such as:

  ```
  CREATE ROLE ALLPowerful;
  ALTER ROLE db_owner ADD MEMBER allPowerful;
  ```

Unlike the server-level sysadmin role, db_owner can be added to database roles. This is why the general prescription is to avoid adding the db_owner database role to custom roles unless it makes perfect sense for your purposes and you understand the implications.

➤ For more on AUTHORIZATION, the equivalent of "ownership" terminology, see the section "Understand authorization" later in this chapter.

- **db_accessadmin.** This role has the right not only to create and manage database users and custom database roles, but also to create schemas and to grant permissions on all database objects. Among other permissions, db_accessadmin has the ALTER ANY LOGIN and CREATE SCHEMA permissions.

  Members of the db_accessadmin role can create users with or without an association to existing logins. However, members of the db_accessadmin database role cannot fix orphaned users or change the login to which a user is assigned because they do not have the CONTROL DATABASE permission.

  Even though members of the db_accessadmin role can create schemas, they cannot change the authorization for schemas, because they do not have the ALTER ANY SCHEMA permission.

  In a contained database, members of the db_accessadmin role (and the db_owner role) can create users with passwords, allowing new access to the SQL Server instance. Because of the high level of control over permissions and membership in the database, this role should be considered as important as the db_owner role and not given out lightly, especially for contained databases.

- **db_backupoperator.** This role has BACKUP DATABASE (including full and differential backups), BACKUP LOG, and CHECKPOINT permissions for the database. This role does not have rights to restore the database, however, because that requires server-level permissions found in the sysadmin and dbcreator fixed server roles, as well as the owner of the database. So, while this is generally safe in terms of harm that can be done to the server, it does give the user rights to back up the database and do with it what they want to.

NOTE

Remember: Security data in your databases is important, but possibly far more important is making sure someone can't take a copy of your database home with them, either accidentally or on purpose.

- **db_datareader.** This role has rights to execute a SELECT statement using any object in the database, including tables, views, and table-valued functions. Other than utility-based usage, this is a heavy-handed and brute-force way to give access to application accounts, and it ignores the ability for views to abstract the permissions necessary to read from tables. It is preferable to add permissions to individual schemas or specific objects instead of granting SELECT access to the entire database. (Note that there is a database level SELECT privilege that can be granted, which is equivalent to this role in terms of permissions.) There may come a time when you need to add a table, view, or function that you don't want your user to have access to by default, and placing this in a schema that you have not granted rights to typical users is an easy way to accomplish this.

- **db_datawriter.** Members of this role can execute INSERT, UPDATE, and DELETE statements on any table or view in the database. Even more than db_datareader, this role can be dangerous to give to users for it applies to the entire database. You should instead grant write permissions on specific schemas or objects to use stored procedures to accomplish writes. In the same way there was a SELECT database privilege, there are also full database INSERT, UPDATE, and DELETE privileges, which are analogous to this role's offering.

- **db_ddladmin.** This role has the rights to perform DDL statements to alter objects in the database. It has no permission to create or modify permissions, users, roles, or role membership. This role also does not have the permission to EXECUTE objects in the database—even objects that members of this role create.

NOTE

There is no built-in database role that provides EXECUTE permissions, which you should grant more granularly than at the database level. There is an EXECUTE privilege at the database level, however, that will allow you to convey EXECUTE permission to every object at the database level.

- **db_denydatareader.** The inverse of db_datareader, this role denies SELECT on all objects. We discuss this later in this chapter in the "Understand ownership chaining" section, but this is not a complete "no user can read any data" tool because it does not stop certain kinds of access, such as access through a stored procedure.

- **db_denydatawriter.** Like db_denydatareader, this is the opposite of db_datawriter, in that the db_denydatawriter role denies INSERT, UPDATE, and DELETE statements on all objects.

- **db_securityadmin.** Members of this role can manage fixed database roles (but not change the membership of the db_owner role), and create and manage custom roles, role membership, and GRANT, REVOKE, and DENY permissions on database objects in the database. Note that members of the db_accessadmin role can create and manage users, but members of the db_securityadmin cannot.

- **public.** Every database user is a member of the public database role. Under almost all circumstances, you should not grant additional permissions to the public roles in any database, because they will be granted to all current and future users.

Inside OUT

What are some common security antipatterns that you should look out for?

Here are four common worst practices in the wild from software vendors:

- To ensure that all users can execute all stored procedures, grant EXECUTE on all stored procedures.

- To ensure that all users can execute all stored procedures, grant EXECUTE to public.

- To ensure that all users can read data from all views and tables, add users to db_datareader, or grant SELECT permissions to public.

- Add users to the db_owner database role or sysadmin server role.

This full database privilege strategy belies a fundamental arrogance about the relationship between the end user and the vendor application. Software developers should never assume that their application's security apparatus will be the only way to access the database.

In reality, an enterprise's power users, analysts, and developers will access the vendor's database with other applications, including but not limited to Azure Data Studio; SSMS; Microsoft Office applications, including Excel and Access; and ad hoc business intelligence tools such as Microsoft Power BI. Users will have unrestricted access to all data and procedures in the database when connecting to the database with other tools if you must grant them larger access for an application.

In this world of multiplatform devices and data access, it's wise to assume that users can connect to your data outside of the primary application. Database security should be enforced in the database, as well, not solely at the application layer. Instead of ever granting permissions to public roles, grant only appropriate EXECUTE | SELECT | INSERT | UPDATE | DELETE permissions to required objects or schemas to specific principals (ideally linked to domain security groups).

Custom database roles

You can create custom database roles to define the roles that various application users or service accounts need for proper data access. Unlike server roles, custom database roles are not just for administrative purposes. Ideally, you assign collections of data access and database object permissions, assign these permissions only to roles, and then add users to roles. Custom database roles can own schemas and objects, just like database user principals.

As with server roles, the key to creating custom database roles is to have a solid understanding of the tasks you want the members of the role to be able to do and the permission set required to do them. It is unlikely that all users in a database will need the same data access, and not all read-only access will be the same.

```
--Create a new custom database role
USE WideWorldImporters;
GO
-- Create the database role
CREATE ROLE WebsiteExecute AUTHORIZATION dbo;
GO
-- Grant access rights to a specific schema in the database
GRANT EXECUTE ON Schema::Website TO WebsiteExecute;
GO
```

Like users, custom database roles can themselves be made members of other database roles. Be careful putting built-in database roles as members of custom roles, however, as you may end up giving users more rights than you intend. It is a very good practice to use proper naming of roles so you don't have a role like:

```
CREATE ROLE ReadOneTable AUTHORIZATION dbo;
```

That ends up with the rights of the db_owner role because someone later runs the following:

```
ALTER ROLE db_owner ADD MEMBER ReadOneTable;
```

It's even worse because while members of the db_securityadmin built-in role cannot change membership in db_owner, they can change membership in the ReadOneTable role, which then conveys db_owner level rights.

In an ideal configuration, you should create security groups for access roles based around job function, levels of oversight, and zones of control. So, if you have people who can report on data in the Warehouse schema, you could create a WarehouseReporting role and give it all the necessary rights in the database to do that task. DatabaseManagers might then have their own role. One method that you may find useful is to create domain groups to match the job function, for example, Domain\WarehouseReporting, Domain\WarehouseManagement, and Domain\DatabaseManagers.

Your AD environment might already have different groups for different job functions, including SQL Server DBAs (for both their "everyday" and administrative accounts). These existing groups can be assigned to database roles, so all security is managed outside of database but still allows for the level of control desired. Security can certainly be difficult to configure properly, but a well-thought-out list of groups and database roles can help manage ongoing security in your SQL Server database and application.

Use role membership to handle environment differences

Security is one of the most complicated parts of the DBA's job. Most code and objects in a database are of the sort where you strive to ensure that your preproduction servers (development, testing, QA, and so on) and production servers have the same structures and security for the same purposes. There is obviously a lifecycle involved, and the development environment will have changes in progress, QA will have changes you believe are ready to release, and production will have the least up-to-date code, because this is the environment for well-tested code. But over time, version by version, the code will be the same.

In security, no two environments will look even somewhat alike when it comes to who uses them. You will not want a salesclerk to have the same access on your development server as the production server where they are taking point-of-sale actions (which is likely done in another security context).

This is where roles come into play. If you only ever grant and deny privileges to roles, you will be able to put that security code into your source control system, test it in development and QA, and then apply it to production. For example, you might create the following role:

```
CREATE ROLE SalesSchemaRead;
```

And grant it rights:

```
GRANT SELECT ON SCHEMA::Sales TO SalesSchemaRead;
```

Because you will have tested that the role works, you will be certain that it works in every environment. In the development environment, you can test this schema with user [Domain\TestUser], and it will have the same access as the [Domain\RealUser] does in production if you make them a member of the SalesSchemaRead group. Then the only thing you need to manage outside of your code source control is which users are members of which roles in the different environments. Of course, it is a good idea to have your environmental scripts, like security, in source control as well.

Grant commonly used database level privileges

Much like at the server level, it is rare that we want to just give a user complete db_owner level access to a database. Typically, if you are being careful not to give users too much access to a database, you will find that none of the database roles match your desires well enough. This section discusses several permissions that are commonly useful to grant to users and programmers at the database level.

VIEW DEFINITION

```
GRANT VIEW DEFINITION ON schema.objectname TO [database_principal];
```

This provides permission to the developer to view the T-SQL code of database objects, without the rights to read or change the objects. This is known as the *metadata* of the objects.

Developers might need access to verify that code changes have deployed to production—for example, to compare the code of a stored procedure in production to what is in source control. This is also a safe permission to grant developers because it does not confer any SELECT or any modification permissions.

Instead of going through each object in a database, you might instead want to GRANT VIEW ANY DEFINITION TO [*principal*]. This applies the permission to all objects in the current database context—for example, to be able to compare the code and structures in the production environment to prepare a release, without being able to see what data is stored in the objects.

SHOWPLAN

```
GRANT SHOWPLAN TO [server_principal]
```

As part of performance tuning, developers almost certainly need access to view a specific query's runtime plan for queries against any database on the server. Seeing the execution plan is not possible even if the developer has the appropriate SELECT or EXECUTE permissions on the database objects in the query. This applies to both estimated and actual runtime plans.

The SHOWPLAN permission, however, is not enough: Developers must also have the appropriate read or read/write permissions to run the query that generates the plan.

Non-administrators and developers can still view *aggregate* cached runtime plan statistics via several DMVs, such as sys.dm_exec_cached_plans without the SHOWPLAN permission, if they have the VIEW SERVER STATE permission.

IMPERSONATE

```
GRANT IMPERSONATE ON USER::[database_principal] TO [database_principal]
```

The IMPERSONATE permission allows the user of the EXECUTE AS statement and the EXECUTE AS clause on a coded object like a stored procedure to impersonate another user temporarily. This permission can create a complicated administrative environment and should be granted only after you understand the implications and potential inappropriate or malicious use. With this permission, it is even possible to impersonate a member of the sysadmin role and assume those permissions temporarily, so it should be granted only in controlled scenarios, and perhaps only on a temporary basis.

This permission is often granted for applications that use EXECUTE AS to change their connection security context. You can grant the IMPERSONATE permission on logins or users.

Logins with the CONTROL SERVER permission already have IMPERSONATE ANY LOGIN permission, which should be limited to administrators only. It is unlikely that any application that uses EXECUTE AS needs its service account to have permission to IMPERSONATE any login that currently exists or ever will exist. Instead, service accounts should be granted IMPERSONATE permissions only for known, appropriate, and approved principals that have been created for the explicit purpose of being impersonated temporarily.

CONTROL DATABASE

```
GRANT CONTROL ON DATABASE::[Database_Name] TO [database_principal]
```

This effectively grants all permissions on database and is not appropriate for most developers or pretty much any non-administrators.

Granting the CONTROL permission is different from granting membership to the db_owner database role, but it has a very similar effect. Members of the sysadmin role or logins mapped to the dbo database user are not affected by DENY permissions, but members of a database role (even db_owner) or users who have been granted CONTROL will still be affected by a DENY.

➤ For more information about monitoring SQL Server activity, see Chapter 8.

Understand permissions and authorization

Let's examine the basics of SQL Server permissions as they pertain to creating objects in a database and then giving access to users. Previously, we covered the basics of using GRANT, REVOKE, and DENY, as well as setting up database roles. Now we want to discuss giving users access to do things with database objects.

Permissions for controlling Data Definition Language and Data Manipulation Language

T-SQL statements, and the permissions that can be applied to them, can be sorted into two basic categories of actions:

- **Data Definition Language (DDL).** DDL statements are used to define structures in the database, such as tables, stored procedures, or functions.

- **Data Manipulation Language (DML).** DML statements are used to fetch data from a table or to modify the contents of a table.

Each type of statement has a very different purpose. DDL is typically used by an administrator or developer in preproduction environments, and by a select few or automated processes in production (such as a change management system). It is also not unusual to allow a user to store results and data permanently in a database, with very tight control as to where they can create new objects. DML, in contrast, is used to determine what users can do with the data and code within the databases.

The goal of a proper security plan is to allow users access to do what you want them to (create and drop their own tables), but not what they should not (drop tables of other users, or worse perhaps, the application).

DDL

Sample DDL statements include things like CREATE TABLE, ALTER TABLE, UPDATE STATISTICS, CREATE PROCEDURE, CREATE OR ALTER PROCEDURE, and so on. Pretty much any statement that is used to modify the code or settings of the database applies.

CHAPTER 12

The security needed to execute these statements include the following base categories:

- **ALTER.** Grants the ability to change the properties of a specific named object, or of all objects if used without referencing a specific object. It is also the permission required to execute the TRUNCATE statement on a table.

- **ALTER ANY.** Gives a user the right to change any database securable.

- **CREATE <securable type>.** Gives a user the right to create a given type of securable.

- **VIEW DEFINITION.** Grants the database principal the right to look at the code of any object in the database.

As you can tell from this list, you must be careful with these permissions. Most security concerns will not be programmers doing things incompetently or perhaps maliciously; rather, they are more likely to be edge cases that somehow get missed during testing—for example, an application generating code that drops a different object than expected, like dbo.Sales instead of temp. Sales, because the schema was accidentally left off.

DML

DML statements manipulate data in tables. The following statements access and modify data in tables and are commonly used: DELETE, INSERT, BULK INSERT, MERGE, SELECT, UPDATE, TRUNCATE TABLE, EXECUTE PROCEDURE.

The rights given to perform DML include the following:

- **SELECT, INSERT, UPDATE, DELETE.** These four permissions are the foundational ones. They give the user the right to either view, change, create, or delete data from a certain securable, or, if no securable is included in the call, the entire database.

- **EXECUTE.** Used to let a user execute a stored procedure or scalar function.

Inside OUT

Is TRUNCATE *really a DDL command?*

To remove all rows from a table, the TRUNCATE TABLE command accomplishes the task faster than a DELETE statement without a WHERE clause—if the TRUNCATE TABLE command is allowed. You cannot use TRUNCATE TABLE if you have FOREIGN KEY constraints that reference your table or with a temporal table.

This is because TRUNCATE is a deallocation of data pages, as opposed to a DELETE, which removes rows from a table. Individual *rows* are not logged as deleted; rather, the *data pages* are deallocated. The TRUNCATE operation is written to the transaction log. When inside an

explicit transaction, TRUNCATE can be rolled back because the pages are not fully deallocated until the transaction commits.

If this sounds like something closer to a DROP than a DELETE, you're right! You will find that
TRUNCATE TABLE requires rights to modify the structure of the table.

As of the previous edition of this book, Microsoft had classified TRUNCATE as a DML statement, but with SQL Server 2022, TRUNCATE TABLE is listed as DDL. (For more information,
see *https://learn.microsoft.com/sql/t-sql/statements/statements*.) Unlike most discussions
of semantics, this one really doesn't matter that much. Understand that TRUNCATE TABLE is
DDL, which gives it an importance that calling it DML does not.

Three more DML statements are deprecated, but are needed to modify permissions for the deprecated text, ntext, and image data types. Do not use them except for legacy support.

- READTEXT

- UPDATETEXT

- WRITETEXT

How permissions accumulate

As discussed, when building a complete security solution, it is best to use roles to provide a
security interface that you can keep the same in all of your environments. Each of these roles
should be distinct in purpose, but in general be able to work together. It is not at all unreasonable to say you might have two roles: one that allows a user to view sales data and another to
view warehouse data. The purpose of each of these may overlap slightly—for example, both
might need access to the Sales.Customer table.

Giving two roles similar but different permissions generally makes perfect sense for a proper
security configuration. A database principal's access is based on the summation of all the roles
of which they are members and any privileges they are directly given. Order doesn't matter, but
as noted earlier in this chapter, GRANT and DENY oppose each other, and even one DENY wins out
over any number of GRANTs.

To demonstrate, consider the following opposing GRANT and DENY statements run from an
administrative account on the WideWorldImporters sample database, which you can find at
https://learn.microsoft.com/sql/samples/wide-world-importers-oltp-install-configure.

```
CREATE ROLE SalesSchemaRead GRANT SELECT on SCHEMA::sales to SalesSchemaRead;
DENY SELECT on OBJECT::sales.InvoiceLines to SalesSchemaRead;
```

Next, create a login-less user to test with.

```
CREATE USER TestPermissions WITHOUT LOGIN;
ALTER ROLE SalesSchemaRead ADD MEMBER TestPermissions;
```

Assuming the database user TestPermissions is only a member of this single role, SalesSchemaRead, they would have permission to execute SELECT statements on every object in the Sales schema except for the Sales.SalesInvoice table.

If the following code is run as the user TestPermissions:

```
USE WideWorldImporters;
GO
EXECUTE AS USER = 'TestPermissions';
SELECT TOP 100 * FROM Sales.Invoices;
SELECT TOP 100 * FROM Sales.InvoiceLines;
REVERT;
```

The result is this:

```
Msg 229, Level 14, State 5, Line 4
The SELECT permission was denied on the object 'InvoiceLines',
database 'WideWorldImporters', schema 'sales'.
```

And 100 rows are returned from the Invoices table. The Sales.Invoices table was still accessible to TestPermissions because it was in the Sales schema, even though the user was denied access to Sales.InvoiceLines.

Now, let's add another role that has the specific purpose of *not* allowing access to the Sales schema:

```
CREATE ROLE SalesSchemaDeny;
DENY SELECT on SCHEMA::sales to SalesSchemaDeny;
ALTER ROLE SalesSchemaDeny ADD MEMBER TestPermissions;
```

This results in the following when TestPermissions runs the same pair of SELECT statements as before:

```
Msg 229, Level 14, State 5, Line 4
The SELECT permission was denied on the object 'Invoices',
database 'WideWorldImporters', schema 'sales'.
Msg 229, Level 14, State 5, Line 5
The SELECT permission was denied on the object 'InvoiceLines',
database 'WideWorldImporters', schema 'sales'.
```

The DENY on the entire sales schema overlapped and overruled the GRANT.

Now, execute the following:

```
REVOKE SELECT on SCHEMA::sales to SalesSchemaDeny;
```

The REVOKE removed the effective DENY permission on the same scope. Now, the only thing that will be denied to TestPermissions is access to InvoiceLines.

NOTE

In the previous sample code snippets, for simplicity, we're granting access to an individual named user, TestPermissions. As we've already said, but is worth repeating, you should avoid granting rights to individual (users and logins) as a best practice. As mentioned earlier in the "Use role membership to handle environment differences" section, you should make roles for job responsibilities, and keep them the same in preproduction and production environments. Then, you can even test with a login-less user like TestPermissions and it will be no different from using any other user in the system in terms of their database access.

Understand authorization

This section covers the topic of database ownership and its impact on the overall security of a database. Beginning with SQL Server 2008, *ownership* is redefined as *authorization*. *Ownership* is now a casual term, whereas *authorization* is the concept that establishes this relationship between an object and a principal that has primary responsibility for it.

Changing the AUTHORIZATION for any object, including a database, is the preferred, unified approach, rather than describing and maintaining object ownership with a variety of syntax and management objects. In the case of a database, however, although authorization over a database does not imply membership in the db_owner role, it does grant the equivalent highest level of permissions to the server principal that owns it. For this reason, named individual accounts (for example, your own [domain*bookreader*]) should generally not be the AUTHORIZATION on a database. (This may vary for certain types of community/shared servers with many databases, but for most enterprise servers, it is not going to be desirable.)

The problem—which many developers and administrators do not realize—is that when a user creates a database, that user is the default owner of the database, and that user principal's SID is listed as the owner_sid in sys.databases.

First, this gives this user access to everything in this database—including the ability to drop the database—even if they have no other server rights. Second, if the database's owner_sid principal account were ever to expire or be removed in AD, or you were to move the database to another server without that principal, you would encounter problems with IMPERSONATION and AUTHORIZATION of child objects, which could surface as a wide variety of errors or application failures. This is because the owner_sid is the account used as the root for authorization for the database. It must exist and be a valid principal.

For this reason, DBAs should change the AUTHORIZATION databases to either a known high-level, noninteractive service account or to the built-in sa principal (SID 0x01), which likely doesn't actually get used as a login to the server. Proper database authorization is a standard item on any good SQL Server health check.

If there are databases with sensitive data that should not allow any access from other databases, they should not have the same owner_sid as less-secure databases, and/or you should not enable cross database ownership chaining at the server level. (It is not enabled by default.)

Change database authorization

When ownership was redefined as authorization, the stored procedure sp_changedbowner was deprecated in favor of the ALTER AUTHORIZATION syntax. For example:

```
ALTER AUTHORIZATION ON DATABASE::[databasename] TO [server_principal];
```

In SQL Server databases, the new owner can be a SQL Server–authenticated login or a Windows-authenticated login. To change the ownership of a database by running the ALTER AUTHORIZATION statement, the principal that's running needs the TAKE OWNERSHIP permission and the IMPERSONATE permission for the new owner.

The new owner of the database must not already exist as a user in the database. If it does, the ALTER statement will fail with the error message, "The proposed new database owner is already a user or aliased in the database." You will need to drop the user before you can run the ALTER AUTHORIZATION statement. The login, when they access the database, will have db_owner rights, because they are the owner of the database.

For Azure SQL Database, the new owner can be a SQL Server–authenticated login or a user object federated or managed in Azure AD, though groups are not supported.

To change the ownership of a database in Azure SQL Database, there is no sysadmin role of which to be a member. The principal that alters the owner must either be the current database owner, the administrator account specified upon creation, or the Azure AD account associated as the administrator of the database. As with any permission in Azure SQL Database, only Azure AD accounts can manage other Azure AD accounts. You can manage SQL Server–authenticated accounts by SQL Server–authenticated or Azure AD accounts.

Understand ownership chaining

Views, stored procedures, triggers, and functions abstract the permissions necessary to read and write from tables and other views. They do this using a concept called *ownership chaining*. Ownership chaining is a name that pre-dates the concept of authorization and has remained the common term used. Ownership chaining says that if the owner of a coded object is the same as the owner of all referenced objects, all a caller needs is access to the coded object. This section explores how coded objects can simplify the minimum permissions you must assign.

This is an important concept to understand, so that you, as a DBA, can follow the principle of least privilege (PoLP) and grant only the minimum rights necessary for an application or end user to access data. We could even go as far as to DENY SELECT access on base table objects to application users and still provide them with data access via the stored procedures, view, and functions we have designed for appropriate data access.

Users accessing the database with minimal rights would only need EXECUTE permissions on stored procedures and scalar functions, and SELECT permissions on views and table valued functions.

There are several important caveats that can break this ownership chaining abstraction and require that whoever is accessing data via a coded object also has permissions for the underlying database objects:

- The procedure cannot perform any ALTER operations, which are not abstracted by the stored procedure. This includes IDENTITY_INSERT.

- The procedure does not perform any dynamic SQL command such as sp_executesql or EXEC ('SQL statements') to access objects. This is one of the built-in safeguards against abuse like SQL injection attacks. Dynamic SQL doesn't rule out chaining for other objects, but it does for any statement executed dynamically.

- The underlying database objects referenced by the coded object must have the same authorization. User A cannot confer rights to user B based on what it has access to via privileges, only rights that have been obtained by being the authorization principal on the objects.

- If the referenced objects are in different databases, the databases must have the same authorization, and cross database chaining must be turned on at the server level with EXEC sp_configure 'cross db ownership chaining'; or at the database level using ALTER DATABASE <databaseName> SET DB_CHAINING ON;.

Not violating any of those conditions, thanks to the intact database permission chain, you can GRANT EXECUTE permission to a principal and *no other permissions,* and you can run a stored procedure successfully that accesses many objects, owned by the same principal that owns the procedure. Now, the database principal has no way to access the database objects outside of your stored procedure.

A demonstration of permissions with views, stored procedures, and functions

The following code demonstrates how to create a testing user and a testing table in the tempdb database. (You can use any database where you have rights to create objects.) Run this code while logged in as a member of the sysadmin role:

```
USE tempdb;
GO
CREATE USER TestOwnershipChaining WITHOUT LOGIN;
```

```
GO
CREATE SCHEMA Demo;
GO
CREATE TABLE Demo.Sample (
SampleId INT IDENTITY (1,1) NOT NULL CONSTRAINT PKOwnershipChain PRIMARY KEY,
Value NVARCHAR(10) );
GO
INSERT INTO Demo.Sample (Value) VALUES ('Value');
GO 2 --runs this batch 2 times so we get two rows
```

We've inserted two rows into the `Demo.SampleTable`. Now let's test various ways to access this table, without granting any permissions to it.

Inside OUT

When testing with EXECUTE AS, *how can you determine what your current security context is?*

The following section uses the EXECUTE AS statement, which enables you to simulate the permissions of another principal. If you are using SSMS, this will affect only the current query window.

You must always follow EXECUTE AS with a REVERT, which stops the impersonation and restores your own permissions. Each execution of REVERT affects only one EXECUTE AS.

If you run into issues, you can always find out what principal you are running by using this statement:

`SELECT ORIGINAL_LOGIN(), SUSUER_SNAME(), CURRENT_USER;`

It will provide you with two values:

- **ORIGINAL_LOGIN().** The name of the login with which you connected to the instance. This will not change even after you use EXECUTE AS USER or EXECUTE AS LOGIN.

- **SUSER_SNAME().** The login you are executing as. It could be the name from EXE-CUTE AS LOGIN or it could be the login of the user if you executed EXECUTE AS USER.

- **CURRENT_USER.** The name of the user whose security content you have assumed. This is the equivalent of USER_NAME(). It can be either the user you have executed as or the username in the database for a login you are impersonating.

Test permissions using a view

In this section, we will create a view on the Demo.Sample table and try to access it. Note that we just created the TestOwnershipChaining database principal and have not granted it any other permissions. Outside of what is granted to the public role, TestOwnershipChaining has no permissions. Execute this and all the following code in this section while logged in as a member of the db_owner database role (or with your administrator login that is a member of the sysadmin role):

```
CREATE VIEW Demo.SampleView
AS
        SELECT Value AS ValueFromView
        FROM Demo.Sample;
GO
GRANT SELECT ON Demo.SampleView TO TestOwnershipChaining;
GO
```

The TestOwnershipChaining principal now has access to the view Demo.SampleView, but not to the Demo.Sample table.

Now, attempt to read data from the table:

```
EXECUTE AS USER = 'TestOwnershipChaining';
SELECT * FROM Demo.Sample;
REVERT;
```

This results in the following error:

```
Msg 229, Level 14, State 5, Line 26
The SELECT permission was denied on the object 'Sample', database 'tempdb', schema
'Demo'.
```

Why? Remember that we have granted no permissions to the table Demo.Sample. This is as intended. However, the user TestOwnershipChaining can still access the data in Demo.Sample via the view:

```
EXECUTE AS USER = 'TestOwnershipChaining';
SELECT * FROM Demo.SampleView;
REVERT;
```

Here are the results:

```
ValueFromView
---------------------------
Value
Value
```

Note also that database principal TestOwnershipChaining has access only to the columns that the view Demo.SampleView provides (and rows if desired by using a WHERE clause). Applications can use view and stored procedure objects to provide appropriate SELECT, INSERT, UPDATE, and DELETE access to underlying table data by blocking access to specific rows and columns and not granting SELECT access (or other rights) directly to the table.

> ➤ For more information on techniques to allow appropriate data access, including Always Encrypted, see Chapter 13.

NOTE

Single statement table-valued functions (TVFs) behave essentially like views, and identically when it comes to security.

Test permissions using a stored procedure

Let's demonstrate the same abstraction of permissions by using a stored procedure, and then also demonstrate a case when it fails. Start by creating the stored procedure object:

```
CREATE PROCEDURE Demo.SampleProcedure AS
BEGIN
SELECT Value AS ValueFromProcedure
FROM Demo.Sample;
END
GO
GRANT EXECUTE ON Demo.SampleProcedure to TestOwnershipChaining;
```

Now try to run as the TestOwnershipChaining principal:

```
EXECUTE AS USER = 'TestOwnershipChaining';
EXEC Demo.SampleProcedure;
REVERT;
```

The output from the procedure shows the rows of the table:

```
ValueFromProcedure
-----------------------------
Value
Value
```

Just like the view object, this works without any access to the Demo.Sample table. The user TestOwnershipChaining was able to access the data in the table due to ownership chaining.

Now, let's break a stored procedure's ability to abstract the permissions using dynamic SQL:

```
CREATE OR ALTER PROCEDURE Demo.SampleProcedure_Dynamic AS
BEGIN
DECLARE @sql nvarchar(max)
SELECT @sql = 'SELECT Value as ValueFromProcedureDynamic FROM Demo.Sample;';
EXEC sp_executesql @sql;
END
GO
GRANT EXECUTE ON Demo.SampleProcedure_Dynamic to TestOwnershipChaining;
```

When you execute this version of the procedure:

```
EXECUTE AS USER = 'TestOwnershipChaining';
EXEC Demo.SampleProcedure_Dynamic;
REVERT;
```

Here are the results:

```
Msg 229, Level 14, State 5, Line 63
The SELECT permission was denied on the object 'Sample', database 'tempdb', schema
'Demo'.
```

We used the dynamic SQL command sp_executesql, passing in a string of T-SQL, which as a security feature automatically breaks the permission abstraction.

> ### NOTE
>
> It's generally not a big issue, but this could be a security risk, because although running an object might not allow you to access the data in the table, it does tell the user of the existence of a table named Demo.Sample in the tempdb database. To stop this in a procedure, use proper error handling with a THROW … CATCH block. You cannot use dynamic SQL in a VIEW object, but if the ownership chain is broken (for example, the authorization is different on the schemas that you are using in the query), it would have the same behavior.

It is possible to get around this built-in safety feature by using the EXECUTE AS setting on the stored procedure. With EXECUTE AS, you can have the code in the procedure behave as a different principal. The same can be said of using the AS clause of the EXECUTE statement:

```
EXECUTE ('<Statements>') AS USER = '<UserName>';
```

The most common mistake that people make with EXECUTE AS is they default to the all-powerful dbo user, and then they write a procedure to let the user pass in any string to execute to a dynamic SQL statement. It seems fine; it uses stored procedures for access, and the application can do pretty much what it needs. Then the user finds it and realizes they can do anything. Or worse, the application doesn't deal with SQL injection issues and a hacker exploits this risk to steal your data.

If you absolutely must use sp_executesql in a stored procedure, a far safer way is to create a user principal without a login, for which you can grant access to the specific resource in the specific manner that they need. So, if the stored procedure should be able to query the sales table for sales figures, you might grant that user SELECT rights on the sales object only. Note that this does require the user to be in all environments with the same rights, so it may require extra scripts for your general deployment processes, because you want this user to be checked into your source control with the code and not the environmental users. If you use a source control tool with decent filtering capabilities, you could check in only database users that have no related logins.

In this case, we create a database principal named ElevatedRights, grant it select rights to Demo.Sample, and then execute the code as that user:

```
CREATE USER ElevatedRights WITHOUT LOGIN;
GRANT SELECT ON OBJECT::Demo.Sample TO ElevatedRights;
GO
```

```
CREATE OR ALTER PROCEDURE Demo.SampleProcedure_Dynamic
WITH EXECUTE AS 'ElevatedRights'
AS
BEGIN
DECLARE @sql nvarchar(1000)
SELECT @sql = 'SELECT Value as ValueFromProcedureDynamic FROM Demo.Sample;';
EXEC sp_executesql @SQL;
END;
GO
GRANT EXECUTE ON OBJECT::Demo.SampleProcedure_Dynamic to TestOwnershipChaining;
```

Now, executing the procedure, access to the data is possible and data is returned.

```
EXECUTE AS USER = 'TestOwnershipChaining';
EXEC Demo.SampleProcedure_Dynamic;
REVERT;
```

The ElevatedRights user will not even be able to execute the procedure, just the SELECT statement. And because the user has no login, if you don't grant any user IMPERSONATE permissions on it, it will be completely benign, security-wise.

Let us reiterate: Security is difficult to do well because there is so much to it. Not only that, getting it *really* right means asking, "What can my system users do?" Too often, though, we think, "Only lock down the valuables," and put the key under the mat in the front of the house. It is going to take a great deal more work for you as an administrator to make sure security is done right, but keeping information away from the wrong eyes both inside and outside of your organization is completely worth all of it.

NOTE

Multi-statement and scalar table–valued functions behave like stored procedures when it comes to ownership chaining security.

Access a table even when SELECT is denied

Let's take these examples one final step further and DENY SELECT permissions to TestOwnership Chaining. Will we still be able to access the underlying table data via a view and stored procedure?

```
DENY SELECT ON Demo.Sample TO TestOwnershipChaining;
GO
EXECUTE AS USER = 'TestOwnershipChaining';
SELECT *
FROM   Demo.Sample; --show that the user in fact cannot access the table
GO
SELECT * FROM Demo.SampleView --test the view
GO
EXEC Demo.SampleProcedure; --test the stored procedure
GO
```

```
EXEC Demo.SampleProcedure_Dynamic; --test the stored procedure
GO
REVERT;
GO
```

Executing this code, you will see four blocks of output: one error message stating SELECT permission was denied and three more with column headings ValueFromView, ValueFromProcedure, and ValueFromProcedureDynamic and two rows of output each. We should note that this is both a good thing and a bad thing at times. It is, however, very important to realize that only the dynamic stored procedure could be affected by a DENY, and only if you deny the user that is impersonated.

NOTE

If you want to fully limit access to an object, even being accessed in a coded object, even by the system administrators (at least without them changing code), you will need to use row-level security (RLS). This feature allows you to limit access to rows in a table by defining a predicate that is like a WHERE clause added to your query on each execution. Chapter 13 covers RLS.

Perform common security administration tasks

Beyond the tasks we have covered so far—namely, creating server and database security principals such as logins, users, and roles—there are several other common security tasks that a DBA will need to handle when something isn't right. This section covers several such tasks.

Orphaned SIDs

An *orphaned SID* is a user who is no longer associated with its intended login. The user's SID no longer matches, even if the username and login name do.

Any time you restore a non-contained database from one SQL Server to another, the database users transfer, but the server logins in the master database do not. This causes SQL Server–authenticated logins and Windows accounts that are local to the host computer to break. However, Windows-authenticated logins (the ones that have access to the server, at least) will still work (assuming the login has CONNECT permissions at the server level).

The most common way a user is orphaned is as follows:

1. A database is restored from one SQL Server instance to another.

2. Even if there is a login that matches previously existing SQL Server–authenticated logins by name, the SIDs will be different on each server (unless you prepare for this ahead of time, covered in the section "Create login with known SID" later in this chapter). When restoring the database from one server to another, the SIDs for the server logins and

database users no longer match. Their *names* will still match, but data access cannot be granted to end users. Windows-authenticated logins and their associated users in the restored database will not be different, so Windows-authenticated logins will continue to authenticate successfully and grant data access to end users via the database users in each database, assuming the login has access to the servers.

3. The SID must be rematched before SQL Server–authenticated logins will be allowed access to the restored database.

NOTE

By default, Windows-authenticated logins have an equal but opposite issue: If you restore a copy of a database from a production environment to a development environment, you might not want the production database principals to have access. For this, you will need to go in and remove the logins after restoring the database.

Problem scenario

Suppose a database exists on server1 but does not exist on server2.

Original state

server1

SQL Login = Kirby

SID = 0x5931F5B9C157464EA244B9D381DC5CCC

Database User = Kirby

SID = 0x5931F5B9C157464EA244B9D381DC5CCC

server2

SQL Login = Kirby

SID = 0x08BE0F16AFA7A24DA6473C99E1DAADDC

Then, the database is restored from server1 to server2. Now, we find ourselves in this problem scenario:

Orphaned SID

server1

SQL Login = Kirby

SID = 0x5931F5B9C157464EA244B9D381DC5CCC

Database User = Kirby

SID = 0x5931F5B9C157464EA244B9D381DC5CCC

server2

SQL Login = Kirby

SID = 0x08BE0F16AFA7A24DA6473C99E1DAADDC

Database User = Kirby

SID = 0x5931F5B9C157464EA244B9D381DC5CCC ← Orphaned SID

The resolution

The resolution for this problem scenario is to use the following command to alter the user and tell SQL Server the existing login to match with:

```
ALTER USER Kirby WITH LOGIN = Kirby;
```

This changes the SID of the user to match the SID of the login on server2—in this case, 0x08B E0F16AFA7A24DA6473C99E1DAADDC. Again, the relationship between the server login and the database user has nothing to do with the name, so it could be user Bob matched to login Kirby with the same resolution.

Assuming you are using the same name for user and login, you can use the following script in the restored database to generate an ALTER USER script for your SQL Server login–based database principals to map them to server logins.

If you are accustomed to using sp_change_users_login to fix orphaned SIDs, that stored procedure has been deprecated, and replaced by the ALTER USER … WITH LOGIN statement:

```
DECLARE @IncludeUsersWithoutLogin bit = 0;
SELECT   'ALTER USER ' + QUOTENAME(dp.name COLLATE DATABASE_DEFAULT) +
            CASE WHEN sp.sid IS NOT NULL THEN
         ' WITH LOGIN = ' + QUOTENAME(dp.name) + '; '
            ELSE ' WITHOUT LOGIN;' END AS SQLText,
            *
FROM     sys.database_principals AS dp
         LEFT OUTER JOIN sys.server_principals AS sp
            ON dp.sid = sp.sid
WHERE    dp.is_fixed_role = 0
   AND dp.sid NOT IN ( 0x00 ) --guest
   AND (sp.name IS NOT NULL or @IncludeUsersWithoutLogin = 1)
   AND dp.type_desc = 'SQL_USER'
   AND dp.name <> 'dbo'
ORDER BY dp.name;
```

It is a good practice to run this type of script to handle orphaned SIDs every time you finish a restore that brings a database from one server to another.

Create login with known SID

In the case of transferring all the logins for a server, you can prevent orphaned SIDs by re-creating SQL Server–authenticated logins on multiple servers, each with the same SID. This is not possible using the SSMS user interface; instead, you must accomplish this by using the CREATE LOGIN command, as shown here (or using tools discussed later in this chapter):

```
CREATE LOGIN [Kirby] WITH PASSWORD=N'<strongpassword>', SID =
0x5931F5B9C157464EA244B9D381DC5CCC;
```

Using the SID option, you can manually create a SQL Server login with a known SID so your SQL Server–authenticated logins on multiple servers share the same SID. Obviously, the SID must be unique from other logins' SID values on each instance.

The previous code example used sys.server_principals to identify orphaned SIDs. You can also use sys.server_principals to identify the SID for any SQL Server–authenticated login. Creating SQL Server–authenticated logins with a known SID is not only helpful to prevent orphaned SIDs, but it can also save time for migrations involving large numbers of databases, each with many users linked to SQL Server–authenticated logins, without unnecessary outage or administrative effort.

We'll look more closely at this topic later in this chapter when we examine SQL Server security migrations.

Migrate SQL Server logins and permissions

Moving SQL Server logins from one SQL Server instance to another is a common task that a DBA will do when setting up new instances or migrating instances. It is a very good idea to maintain scripts in case a server crashes. Or, perhaps more importantly, you must audit permissions on a server to see if they have changed without authorization—something that frequently occurs when you have too many people with sysadmin rights, particularly when a DBA is on call and must fix a problem at 3 a.m.

Moving logins and all server-level permissions involves multiple steps. Ideally, as a DBA, you will use SSMS's dialog boxes as little as possible for tasks that must be repeated. GUI-driven solutions to most problems are the most time-consuming and could result in a disagreeable amount of button-clicking and inconsistencies. Well-built and tested T-SQL or PowerShell scripts are superior in terms of manageability, repeatability, and deepening your understanding of the underlying security objects.

NOTE

In a server migration, all database-level permissions, database roles, and users, will be moved with the backup/restore of each database.

This section discusses various methods of migrating security, some of which apply to either SQL Server instances or Azure SQL Database logical servers.

Inside OUT

Should you have scripts of principals and passwords?

It is always good to have scripts available to re-create special system objects, users, and so on. This is certainly true for system accounts where you need to be able to re-create the account with its password.

However, be extra careful to store such data in a *very* safe location, ideally itself encrypted with a secure password. What if, for example, you have a server for which you use a standard login that has sysadmin rights, and you have a file on a DBA's computer with the account name and password in clear text? If this gets in the wrong hands, it could be the key to a lot more access than you probably want.

We strongly suggest maintaining login scripts in an encrypted manner, where only people authorized to use the script can access it. Consider using Azure Key Vault to store these and other organization secrets.

Move logins using SQL Server Integration Services (SQL Server only)

Since SQL Server 2008 R2, SSIS has shipped with a Transfer Logins task that you can use to move logins from one server to another, including between different versions of SQL Server.

You use SQL Server Data Tools (SSDT) to create a new SSIS project. As Figure 12-4 shows, this provides an in-the-box, do-it-yourself alternative to the steps that follow, which involve custom scripts to migrate permissions from one server to another. The task is highly configurable, allowing for the creation of both Windows-authenticated and SQL Server–authenticated logins on the target instance, with their original SIDs if desired. A Fail/Replace/Skip option is provided for login names that already exist on the destination.

Logins created by the Transfer Logins task arrive at the destination disabled. You must enable them again before you can use them.

This SSIS task does not move any of the role memberships or server permissions that these logins might have been granted on the source instance. Ideally these should be scripted and stored in source control to be able to quickly re-create a server (unlike standard accounts, where you need passwords).

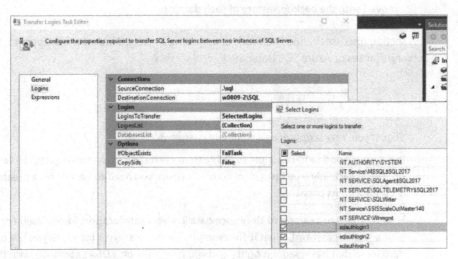

Figure 12-4 The Transfer Logins Task Editor dialog box in SSIS.

> ➤ To read more about moving permissions and roles, see the sections "Move server role membership using T-SQL (SQL Server only)" and "Move server permissions using T-SQL (SQL Server only)" later in this chapter.

Move Windows-authenticated logins using T-SQL (SQL Server only)

This is the easiest of the steps, assuming the source and target SQL Server instance are in the same domain. Moving Windows-authenticated logins is as easy as scripting out the CREATE LOGIN statements for each login.

You do not necessarily need to use Object Explorer in SSMS for this operation. The system catalog view sys.server_principals contains the list of Windows-authenticated logins. (The type is 'U' for Windows user and 'G' for Windows group.) The default_database_name and default_language_name columns are also provided, and you can script them with the login.

Here's a sample script:

```
--Create windows logins
SELECT CONCAT('CREATE LOGIN ', QUOTENAME(name) +
     ' FROM WINDOWS WITH DEFAULT_DATABASE =' + QUOTENAME(default_database_name)+
     ', DEFAULT_LANGUAGE = '+ QUOTENAME(default_language_name))  + ';'AS
CreateTSQL_Source
FROM sys.server_principals
WHERE type_desc in ('WINDOWS_LOGIN','WINDOWS_GROUP')
AND name NOT LIKE 'NT SERVICE\%'
AND is_disabled = 0
ORDER BY name, type_desc;
```

As in the previous section, this script does not generate T-SQL for any of the role memberships or server permissions that these logins might have been granted on the source instance.

NOTE

Anywhere you build a script and output names, you can use the QUOTENAME system function to put square brackets around the name. Most people don't like square brackets around names in their code, but generated scripts should handle any name thrown at them, including spaces, or even embedded square brackets.

Move SQL Server–authenticated logins using T-SQL (SQL Server only)

A time-honored reference for this task has been made available by Microsoft for years, yet was never implemented with the SQL Server product itself. Since 2000, DBAs have referenced Microsoft support article 918992, "Transfer logins and passwords between instances of SQL Server" (*https://support.microsoft.com/help/918992/*), which provides scripts to move standard logins and their hashed passwords to a different server (which can be a different version or edition of SQL Server). Doing this requires you to create a pair of stored procedures on your server as part of the process: sp_hexadecimal and sp_help_revlogin.

With the aid of these stored procedures, you can generate a hash of a SQL Server–authenticated password with its login, and then re-create the SQL Server–authenticated login on another server with the same password. It is not possible in the strictest terms to reverse-engineer the SQL Server–authenticated login password, but given enough time, a hacker can find a password that will hash to that value—called a *hash collision*—that will more than likely be the original password (such is the nature of hash values). Since you have the hash values, the same password that the user knows will match the hash that you re-create on the new server.

Once again, these stored procedures only re-create the SQL Server–authenticated logins; they do not re-create any of the role memberships or server permissions that those logins might have been granted on the source instance. The next two sections discuss moving server roles and server permissions.

Move server role membership using T-SQL (SQL Server only)

If you do not manage your server role memberships in a script, you ought to. And if you need to build that script or to move accounts to a new server, you can use the following script instead of working through the dialog boxes in SSMS for each role. This script retrieves server role membership via SQL Server catalog views and includes options to add logins to server roles.

```
--server level roles
SELECT DISTINCT
       CONCAT('ALTER SERVER ROLE ', QUOTENAME([r].[name]), ' ADD MEMBER ',
QUOTENAME([m].[name])) AS [createtsql]
FROM [sys].[server_role_members] AS [rm]
    INNER JOIN [sys].[server_principals] AS [r]
```

```
             ON [rm].[role_principal_id] = [r].[principal_id]
         INNER JOIN [sys].[server_principals] AS [m]
             ON [rm].[member_principal_id] = [m].[principal_id]
    WHERE [r].[is_disabled] = 0
        AND [m].[is_disabled] = 0 -- ignore disabled accounts
        AND [m].[name] NOT IN ( 'dbo', 'sa' ); -- ignore built-in accounts
```

Move server permissions using T-SQL (SQL Server only)

Moving server permissions can be extremely time-consuming if you choose to do it by identifying them on the Securables page of each SQL Server Login Properties dialog box. Instead, we
advise you to script the permissions to re-create them on the destination server by using catalog views. Ideally, the output of this script should be placed in source control. Security should
not be given out without some minimal review process to make sure that security matches what
the agreed-upon security says it should be.

Here is a script that will output a script of your permissions to groups:

```
--SERVER LEVEL SECURITY
SELECT   RM.state_desc + N' ' + RM.permission_name
         + CASE WHEN E.name IS NOT NULL THEN
             'ON ENDPOINT::[' + E.name + '] '
             ELSE ''
             END + N' TO '
         + CAST(QUOTENAME(U.name COLLATE DATABASE_DEFAULT) AS nvarchar(256))
         + ';' AS CREATETSQL
FROM     sys.server_permissions AS RM
         INNER JOIN sys.server_principals AS U
             ON RM.grantee_principal_id = U.principal_id
         LEFT OUTER JOIN sys.endpoints AS E
             ON E.endpoint_id = RM.major_id
                AND RM.class_desc = 'ENDPOINT'
WHERE  u.is_fixed_role = 0
--Note, public is not considered a fixed role because you
--can grant it permissions
--NOTE: this ignores many of the built in accounts,
--but if you have made changes to these
--accounts you may need to make changes to the WHERE clause
AND U.name NOT LIKE '##%' -- IGNORE SYSTEM ACCOUNTS
AND U.name NOT IN ( 'DBO', 'SA', ) -- IGNORE BUILT-IN ACCOUNTS
AND U.name NOT LIKE 'NT SERVICE%'
AND U.name NOT LIKE 'NT AUTHORITY%'
ORDER BY RM.permission_name, U.name;
```

Move Azure SQL Database logins

It is not possible to use sp_hexadecimal and sp_help_revlogin on an Azure SQL Database
server for SQL Server–authenticated logins. Scripting an Azure SQL Database login from SSMS
obfuscates any password information, just as it does on a SQL Server instance. And, because you
do not have access to sys.server_principals, sys.server_role_members, or sys.server

_permissions, scripting these server-level permissions in Azure SQL Database isn't possible. (The system catalog view sys.server_principals is a dependency of sp_help_revlogin.) Further, creating a login with a password hash is not supported in Azure SQL Database.

The solution for migrating Azure SQL Database password-based logins from one server to another is to have a script for your special logins, to re-create other logins on the destination server with a new secure password, and to have the users change the password when they use them.

The three types of Azure-authenticated principals are stored in the Azure SQL database, not at the Azure SQL logical server level, and are administered via the Azure portal. Like other database users and permissions, you can move these principals to a destination server along with the database itself.

Move other security objects

Do not forget to move other server-level objects to the destination server, as appropriate. These objects include linked server connections and SQL Server Audits, for which you can generate scripts (albeit without passwords in the case of linked servers). Given this, it is definitely advantageous to securely store your linked server-creation scripts with their passwords.

You also should re-create SQL Server credentials and any corresponding proxies in use by SQL Server Agent on the destination server, although you cannot script credentials. (Thankfully, in terms of security, you must re-create them manually.) You can script proxies in SQL Server Agent by using SSMS, and you should re-create them, including their assigned subsystems.

Alternative migration approaches

There is no easy way to accomplish this goal within the SSMS dialog boxes or to "generate scripts" of all SQL Server server–level security.

Some third-party products are available to accomplish the task. There is also a free package of Windows PowerShell cmdlets, including some designed to assist with security migrations. You can find these in the dbatools.io free open source GPL-licensed Windows PowerShell project, which is available at *http://www.dbatools.io*.

If your SQL Server resides on a VM, cloning the instance at the VM level might provide some transportability for the VM from one environment to another, to bypass the process of rebuilding a SQL Server instance altogether. For version upgrades, hardware changes, or partial migrations, however, a VM-level clone is obviously not a solution.

As has been said, and can't be repeated enough, the number-one way of preparing for a migration is to have idempotent (repeatable) scripts to re-create most of your security at the server level, rather than trying to re-create a server from the thousands of independent changes that were made over time. This, along with checks to make sure no new, unscripted security has been added without being added to the main script, will save you tons of time.

There is one more potential SQL Server–based method of server login information migration that is no less complex or troublesome. If you are moving from one SQL Server to another of the exact same version, backing up and restoring the master database from one SQL Server instance to another is a potential, albeit not particularly recommended, solution. (This obviously does not apply to Azure SQL Database.) Restoring a master database from one server to another involves myriad potential configuration changes to server-specific encryption keys, service accounts, user permissions, and server identification information, which might not be supported. The process is not outlined in any support documentation, and we do not recommend it.

A migration of the master database is advisable only when the destination server of the restored database has the identical volume letters and NTFS permissions and access to the same service accounts, in addition to the same SQL Server version and edition.

Dedicated administrator connection

The dedicated administrator connection (DAC) is an admin-only reserved connection into the SQL Server instance or Azure SQL Database for use as an emergency method to authenticate to the server when some problematic condition otherwise prevents it. Examples include miscon-figuration of security, misconfiguration of the Resource Governor, misconfiguration of prompts created FOR LOGON, or other interesting conditions that block even members of the sysadmin server role.

Only one member of the server sysadmin role at a time can connect using the DAC, much like a database in single-user mode. Do not attempt to connect to the DAC via Object Explorer in SSMS. (Object Explorer cannot connect to the DAC, by design.)

The DAC has resource limitations to curb the impact of DAC commands. You cannot perform all administrative tasks through the DAC. For example, you cannot issue BACKUP or RESTORE commands from the DAC. You should use the DAC only to diagnose and remediate issues that prevent normal access, and then return to a normal connection. Do not use the DAC to carry out long-running queries against user data, DBCC CHECKDB, or to query the dm_db_index _physical_stats DMV.

When using the DAC to connect to an Azure SQL Database, you must specify the database name in your connection string or connection dialog box. Because you cannot change data-base contexts with the USE syntax in Azure SQL Database, you should always make connections directly to the desired database via the database or initial catalog parameters of the con-nection string.

There are several ways to sign into a SQL Server instance or Azure SQL Database using the DAC via a login that is a member of the sysadmin role:

- In SSMS, open a new query or change the connection of a query by providing the server name as usual, but preceded by ADMIN. For example:

  ADMIN:servername

Or, for a named instance (ensure that the SQL browser is running):

```
ADMIN:servername\instancename
```

- From a command prompt, you can connect to the DAC via SQLCMD with the parameter -A; for example:

```
C:\Users\Kirby>sqlcmd -S servername -A
```

Or, for a named instance (ensure the SQL Browser service is running):

```
C:\Users\Kirby>sqlcmd -S servername\instancename -A
```

- In SSMS, change a query window to SQLCMD mode. Then use the following query:

```
:CONNECT ADMIN:servername
```

Or, for a named instance (ensure the SQL Browser service is running):

```
:CONNECT ADMIN:servername\instancename
```

- In Windows PowerShell, use the DedicatedAdministratorConnection parameter of the Invoke-SqlCmd cmdlet to provide a connection to the DAC. For example:

```
Invoke-SqlCmd -ServerInstance servername -Database master`
-Query "SELECT @@SERVERNAME" -DedicatedAdministratorConnection
```

Or, for a named instance (ensure the SQL browser is running):

```
Invoke- SqlCmd -ServerInstance servername\instancename`
-Database master -Query "SELECT @@SERVERNAME" -DedicatedAdministratorConnection
```

Allowing remote DAC connections

By default, DAC connections are only allowed locally. You can use the Surface Area Configuration dialog box in the Facets section of SSMS (refer to Chapter 1, "Get started with SQL Server tools") to allow remote DAC connections via the RemoteDacEnabled setting. You also can use sp_configure to enable the Remote Admin Connections option.

We recommend that you do so because it is invaluable to gaining access to a SQL Server when Remote Desktop Protocol (RDP) or similar technologies are unable to connect to the Windows host of the SQL Server instance. Enabling remote DAC does not require a service restart.

The endpoint port that SQL Server uses to listen to DACs is announced in the SQL Server Error Log upon startup. For example, you will see this shortly after the SQL Server service starts: "Dedicated admin connection support was established for listening locally on port 1434." This is the default port for default instances, whereas named instances use a randomly assigned port that changes each time the service is started.

Remotely connecting to the DAC with SSMS is also possible by addressing the port number of the DAC instead of the ADMIN: syntax. For example, providing a connection string in SSMS to *servername\instancename*,49902 connects to the DAC endpoint.

CHAPTER 13

Protect data through classification, encryption, and auditing

Security is incredibly important to private industry and the public sector. The number of leaks and hacks of sensitive information continues to increase, and data professionals are at the forefront of securing this information. Along with the technical features built into SQL Server, Azure SQL Database, and Azure SQL Managed Instance, organizations should embrace the guidelines in privacy laws worldwide for handling and managing customer information.

Continuing from Chapter 12, "Administer instance and database security and permissions," which focuses on authorization, this chapter covers features in the Database Engine and the underlying operating system (OS) that help you to secure your server and the databases that reside on it.

It begins with privacy and how it guides the responsibilities of the data professional. Then it gets into the technical details of what it means to encrypt data and looks at the SQL Server and Azure SQL Database features that help you achieve and maintain a more secure environment. It also looks at securing the network, the OS, and the database itself, right down to the column and row level.

Throughout the chapter, you should be thinking about *defense in depth*—that is, combining different features and strategies to protect your data and minimize the fallout if your data is stolen.

Sample scripts in this chapter, and all scripts for this book, are all available for download at *https://www.MicrosoftPressStore.com/SQLServer2022InsideOut/downloads*.

Privacy in the modern era

A chapter about protecting your data estate is incomplete without a discussion of external policies and procedures to ensure that protection. This section is provided as a reminder to keep abreast of current local and international legislation, using one particular regulation as a reference.

CAUTION

This section does not constitute legal advice. Consult your own legal counsel for more information.

General Data Protection Regulation (GDPR)

On May 25, 2018, the General Data Protection Regulation (GDPR) came into effect in the European Union (EU). It provides for the protection of any *personal data* associated with *data subjects* (EU residents) located in the EU. Organizations across the world may be affected if they process personal data belonging to EU residents.

Whenever your organization deals with an EU resident's personal data, you are responsible for ensuring it is managed according to that legislation. The good news is, this is a business problem, not a technical one. Your organization must develop policies and procedures to enforce the requirements of the GDPR; you as a data professional then create technical solutions to satisfy those procedures. These requirements include the following:

- Pseudonymization

- Right of access

- Right to erasure

The following subsections list problem statements and proposed solutions to achieve these requirements as they might apply to data professionals. (Note that this is not an exhaustive list.)

Pseudonymization

- **Problem statement.** Personal data must be transformed in a way that the resulting data cannot be attributed to a data subject without additional information.

- **Proposed solution.** This can be implemented through encryption. We cover this in detail later in this chapter in the section "Introduction to security principles and protocols," including various methods to ensure that sensitive data is not made available to privileged users and administrators.

  ## NOTE

  Anonymizing data is different from encrypting or masking data.

Right of access

- **Problem statement.** A data subject may request access to their personal data.

- **Proposed solution.** This can be achieved through standard Transact-SQL (T-SQL) queries, assuming you have taken measures to appropriately handle encryption of the data and authentication of the data subject. Chapter 2, "Introduction to database server components," covers authentication and authorization.

Right to erasure

- **Problem statement.** A data subject may request erasure of their personal data.

- **Proposed solution.** To erase personal data, you must identify it. This can become arduous with more than a few databases. Organizations may not appreciate the numerous environments in which they store personal data, including scaled-out applications, data warehouses, data marts, data lakes, and email. Fortunately, you can catalog and tag sensitive data in SQL Server and Azure SQL Database.

Inside OUT

Is there an easy way to identify sensitive data?

You can use the Data Discovery and Classification feature in SQL Server Management Studio (SSMS) to identify columns that should be encrypted. After the classification engine scans your database, you can then apply these classifications using Always Encrypted or dynamic data masking, as well as give columns persistent labels (such as Confidential).

➤ Read more about data and classification for SQL Server at *https://learn.microsoft.com /sql/relational-databases/security/sql-data-discovery-and-classification*. For Azure SQL Database, Azure SQL Managed Instance and Azure Synapse Analytics, you can read more at *https://learn.microsoft.com/azure/sql-database/sql-database-data -discovery-and-classification*.

For a much broader and richer set of classification tools and features, consider Microsoft Purview for your organization (discussed next).

Microsoft Purview overview

Microsoft has combined several security and compliance products and services under the name *Microsoft Purview*.

➤ You can read more about this change at *https://azure.microsoft.com/blog/azure-purview -is-now-microsoft-purview/*.

Microsoft Purview provides your organization with a unified overview of its governance and compliance portfolio, including its data estate. You can register, scan, map, and catalog your data estate, which includes sources such as SQL Server and Azure SQL, from within the Microsoft Purview governance portal. While your databases stay where they are, their metadata is copied into Microsoft Purview.

➤ For an in-depth look at how Microsoft Purview can help your organization, see *https:// learn.microsoft.com/microsoft-365/compliance/purview-compliance*.

Microsoft Purview provides a set of deep categorization and classification tools for governing your data estate. This means that your SQL Server or Azure SQL environments might fall under a much broader management scope. Therefore, you must work with your data governance partners to register, classify, and manage data assets.

CAUTION

When dropping and re-creating a table, you may lose any data classifications associated with that table. This is a similar problem with setting granular permissions, so it is good practice to store and maintain your Data Definition Language (DDL) scripts in a source control system.

Inside OUT

What's included in Azure SQL?

As a reminder, when you see the phrase *SQL Server* alone, it is assumed to be the user-installed, year-versioned product. It may also be used in the context of the Database Engine, the common Query Optimizer and storage engine that all Microsoft SQL products use. SQL Server can run on-premises or in Azure VMs and can even be installed as part of a VM image from the Azure Marketplace.

The phrase *Azure SQL* refers to a product that includes Azure SQL Database and Azure SQL Managed Instance. Just because you see "applies to SQL Server" doesn't mean it applies to Azure SQL Database or Azure SQL Managed Instance, but it could. Various features, like the intelligent query processing (IQP) features discussed in Chapter 14, "Performance tune SQL Server," sometimes arrive in Azure SQL Database and Azure SQL Managed Instance before appearing in the next version of SQL Server, or vice versa. For various marketing and technological reasons, these products are still often grouped together because the products themselves are still extremely similar.

Introduction to security principles and protocols

Information security is about finding a balance between the value of your data and the cost of protecting it. Ultimately the business and technical decision makers in your organization make this call, but at least you have the technical tools available to undertake these measures to protect yourself. In other words, you should not leave security solely to the IT department.

SQL Server implements several security principles through cryptography and other means, which you can use to build up layers of security to protect your environment.

Computer cryptography is implemented through some intense mathematics that use very large prime numbers; we won't delve deeply into specifics here. Instead, this section explains various security principles and goes into some detail about encryption. It also covers network protocols and how cryptography works. This will aid your understanding of how SQL Server and network security protect your data. Keep in mind that encryption is *not* the only way to protect data.

Secure your environment with defense in depth

Securing a SQL Server or Azure SQL environment requires several protections that work together to make it difficult for an attacker to get in, snoop around, steal or modify data, and then get out.

Defense in depth is about building layers of protection around your data and environment. These measures might not be completely effective on their own, but work well as part of an overall strategy because each layer helps weaken and isolate an attack long enough to allow you to respond.

Layers involved in defense in depth typically include the following:

- **Perimeter security.** You should install perimeter security in the form of a firewall and other network defenses to protect against external network attacks. From a physical aspect, don't let just anyone plug a laptop into an unattended network point, or allow them to connect to your corporate wireless network and have access to the production environment. Logical and physical *segmentation* involves keeping sensitive servers and applications on a separate part of the network, perhaps off-premises in a separate datacenter or in the Azure cloud. You then protect these connections—for example, by using a virtual private network (VPN).

- **Authentication and authorization.** From within the network, you must implement authentication (who you are) and authorization (what you can do), preferably through Active Directory (AD), which is available on both Windows and Linux.

- **Policies.** On the servers themselves, you should ensure that the file system is locked down with a policy that does at least the following:

  - Enforces permissions and modern protocols for files, folders, and network shares

  > SMB 1.0 (also known as CIFS) is a deprecated file-sharing protocol that Microsoft recommends removing from your environment. For more information about disabling SMB 1.0, see *https://techcommunity.microsoft.com/t5/Storage-at-Microsoft/Stop-using-SMB1/ba-p/425858*. SMB 2.0 and higher are still supported.

  - Denies access to unauthorized users

  - Denies access to untrusted storage devices

  - Ensures service accounts do not have system administrator privileges

  - Encrypts the file system (optional but recommended)

- **Permissions.** SQL Server permissions should be set correctly so that the service account does not have administrative privileges on the server, and database files, transaction logs, and backups cannot be accessed by unauthorized users.

- **Application security.** On the application side, you can implement coding practices that protect against things like SQL injection attacks, and you can implement encryption in your database (and backup files).

➤ The SQL Vulnerability Assessment tool in SSMS can help identify possible security vulnerabilities. Read more about it at *https://learn.microsoft.com/sql/relational-databases/security /sql-vulnerability-assessment*.

Inside OUT

What is SQL injection?

One of the most prevalent attack vectors for a database is to manipulate the software application or website to attack the underlying database.

SQL injection is a technique that exploits applications that do not *sanitize* input data. A carefully crafted Uniform Resource Identifier (URI) in a web application, for example, can manipulate the database in ways that a naïve application developer might not expect.

If a web application exposes database keys in the Uniform Resource Locator (URL), for example, an industrious person can craft a URL to read protected information from a table by changing the key value. An attacker might be also able to access sensitive data or modify the database itself by appending T-SQL commands to the end of a string to perform malicious actions on a table or database.

In a worst-case scenario, in just a few seconds, a SQL injection attack could exfiltrate the entire database (that is, the data removed without your knowledge), and you might hear about it only when your organization is blackmailed or sensitive data is leaked.

You can avoid SQL injection by ensuring that all data input is escaped, sanitized, and validated. To be very safe, all SQL Server queries should use parameterization.

➤ You can read more about defending against SQL injection attacks at *https://learn .microsoft.com/sql/relational-databases/security/sql-injection*. The Open Web Application Security Project (OWASP) is also an excellent resource to identify and defend against potential vulnerabilities, including SQL injection. You can visit the OWASP website at *https://www.owasp.org*.

The difference between hashing and encryption

In a security context, data that is converted in a repeatable manner to an unreadable, fixed-length format using a cryptographic algorithm and that *cannot* be converted back to its original form is said to be *hashed*. In contrast, data that is converted to an unreadable form that *can* be converted back to its original form using a cryptographic key is said to be *encrypted*.

Cryptographic algorithms can be defeated in certain ways, the most common being brute-force and dictionary attacks. Let's take a quick look at each of these:

- **Brute-force attack.** In a brute-force attack, the attacking code checks every possible combination of a password, passphrase, or encryption key against the hashing or encryption service until it finally arrives at the correct value. Depending on the type of algorithm and the length of the password, passphrase, or key, this can take anywhere from a few milliseconds to many years.

- **Dictionary attack.** A dictionary attack takes a list of words from a dictionary (which can include common words, passwords, and phrases) and uses these against the hashing or encryption service. Dictionary attacks take advantage of the fact that we are bad at remembering passwords and tend to use common words. A dictionary attack is a lot faster to perform, so attackers typically attempt this first.

As computers become more powerful and parallelized, the length of time to run a brute-force attack continues to decrease. Countermeasures do exist to protect against some of these attacks, and some encryption systems cannot be defeated by a brute-force attack. These countermeasures are beyond the scope of this book, but it is safe to say that sufficiently complex algorithms and long encryption keys take several years to compromise.

> ➤ Security expert Bruce Schneier suggests that an algorithm with a 512-bit block and key size and 128 rounds (meaning the encryption algorithm is applied 128 times with a slightly different change in each pass) will be sufficiently complex for the foreseeable future. Schneier's essay "Cryptography after the Aliens Land" is available at *https://www.schneier.com/essays/archives/2018/09/cryptography_after_t.html*.

Hashing

A *cryptographic hash function* (algorithm) takes variable-length data (usually a password) and applies a mathematical formula to convert it to a fixed size, or *hash value*.

This is the recommended method of securing passwords. When a password has been hashed correctly, it cannot be decrypted into its original form. When used with a random *salt* (a random string applied along with the hash function), the result is a password that is impossible to reconstruct—even if the same password is used by different people.

To validate a password, it must be hashed using the same hash function again, with the same salt, and compared against the stored hash value.

Because hash values have a fixed size (the length depends on the algorithm used), there is a chance that two sets of data (two different passwords) can result in the same hash value. This is called a *hash collision*, and it is more likely to occur with shorter hash value lengths. This is why longer hashes are better.

NOTE

Use passwords that are at least 15 characters in length and, preferably, more than 20 characters. You should also employ a password manager so you don't have to memorize multiple passwords. Brute-force attacks take exponentially longer for each additional character you choose, so don't be shy about using phrases or sentences (with spaces), either. Password length matters more than complexity.

Inside OUT

Why should you use a salt, and what is a rainbow table?

If you don't use a random salt, the same hash value will be created each time the hash function is applied against a particular password. Additionally, if more than one person uses the same password, the same hash value will be repeated.

Imagine an attacker has a list of commonly used passwords and knows which hash function you used to hash the passwords in your database. This person could build a catalog of possible hash values for each password in that list. This catalog is called a *rainbow table*.

It becomes very easy to compare the hash values in your database against the rainbow table to deduce which password was used. Thus, you should always use a random salt when hashing passwords in your database. Rainbow tables become all but useless in this case.

Encryption

Data encryption is the process of converting human-readable data, or *plain text*, into an encrypted form by applying a cryptographic algorithm called a key (*cipher*) to the data. This process makes the encrypted data (*ciphertext*) unreadable without the appropriate key to unlock it. Encryption facilitates both the secure *transmission* and *storage* of data.

Over the years, many ciphers have been created and subsequently defeated (*cracked*). In many cases, this is because both central processing units (CPUs) and graphics processing units (GPUs) have become faster and more powerful, reducing the length of time it takes to perform brute-force and other attacks. In other cases, the implementation of the cryptographic function was flawed, and attacks on the implementation itself have been successful.

Inside OUT

Why are GPUs used for cracking passwords?

A GPU is designed to process identical instructions (but not necessarily the same data) in parallel across hundreds or thousands of cores, ostensibly for rendering images on a display many times per second.

This coincides with the type of work required to crack passwords through brute force, because those thousands of cores can each perform a single arithmetic operation per clock cycle through a method called *pipelining*.

Because GPUs can operate at billions of cycles per second (GHz), this results in hundreds of millions of hashes per second. Without a salt, many password hashes can be cracked in a few milliseconds, regardless of the algorithm used.

A primer on protocols and transmitting data

Accessing a database involves the transmission of data over a network interface, which must occur in a secure manner. A *protocol* is a set of instructions for transmitting that information over a specific network port. A *port* is one of 65,535 possible connections per protocol that can be made to a networked device. The most common protocol for SQL Server is *Transmission Control Protocol* (*TCP*). It is always associated with an IP address and a port number.

Inside OUT

What's with all these protocols and ports?

Over the years, the development of official and unofficial standards has resulted in a set of commonly used protocols and ports. Along with TCP, another common protocol is User Datagram Protocol (UDP). Most network traffic uses these two protocols. For example:

- **TCP ports 1433 and 1434.** SQL Server
- **TCP ports 2382 and 2383.** SQL Server Analysis Services
- **TCP port 80.** HTTP
- **TCP port 443.** HTTPS
- **TCP port 22.** Secure Shell (SSH)
- **UDP port 53.** Domain Name System (DNS)

The Internet Protocol suite

To discuss security on a network, you must understand cryptographic protocols. To discuss the network itself, you must discuss the biggest network of them all: the Internet.

The Internet is a network of networks (it literally means "between networks") that transmits data using a suite of protocols. These include TCP, which sits on top of another protocol, called Internet Protocol (IP). Together, they are called TCP/IP. TCP/IP is the most common network protocol stack in use today. Most of the services on the Internet, as well as local networks, rely on TCP/IP.

NOTE

The full IP suite comprises TCP, IP, Address Resolution Protocol (ARP), Internet Control Message Protocol (ICMP), UDP, and Internet Group Management Protocol (IGMP). All these are required to implement the full TCP/IP stack.

IP is a connectionless protocol, meaning each individual unit of transfer, also known as a *network packet* or *datagram*, contains a *payload* (the data itself) and a *header* that indicates where it came from and where it needs to go (the routing information).

IP network packets might be delivered out of order, with no delivery guarantee at all. This low overhead makes the protocol fast and allows packets to be sent to several recipients at once (*multicast* or *broadcast*). TCP, however, provides the necessary instructions for reliability, sequencing (the order of packets), and data integrity. If a packet is not received by the recipient, or a packet is received out of order, TCP can resubmit the data again using IP as its delivery mechanism.

Versions of IP in use today

Internet Protocol Version 4 (IPv4) has a 32-bit address space, which provides nearly 4.3 billion addresses (2^{32}, or approximately 4.3×10^9). Unfortunately, when this version was first proposed in September 1981, very few people could have imagined the Internet would be as large and important as it is today. With billions of humans online, and billions of devices connected, the available IPv4 address space is all but depleted.

> ➤ You can read the IPV4 specification, known as Internet Engineering Task Force Request For Comments #791, at *https://tools.ietf.org/html/rfc791*.

Techniques like Network Address Translation (NAT), which uses private IP addresses behind a router with a single valid public IP address representing that entire network, have held off the depletion over the years, but time and address space have run out.

Internet Protocol Version 6 (IPv6) has an address space of 128 bits, which provides more than 340 undecillion (340 trillion trillion) addresses (2^{128}, or approximately 3.4×10^{38}). This number is so staggeringly huge that, even with networks and devices being added every minute, including the upward trend in the use of the Internet of Things (IoT), each of these devices can have its own unique address on the Internet without ever running out of addresses.

➤ You can read the IPV6 Specification, known as Internet Engineering Task Force Request For Comments #8200, at *https://tools.ietf.org/html/rfc8200*.

Inside OUT

What is the Internet of Things?

Until a few years ago, computing devices such as servers, desktop computers, laptops, and mobile devices were the only devices connected to the Internet. Today, millions of objects embedded with electronics have found their way online, including coffee machines, security cameras, home automation systems, vehicle trackers, heart monitors, industrial measurement devices, and many, many more. Together, all these devices comprise the IoT.

Ignoring the fact that many of these devices should not have publicly accessible Internet addresses in the first place, the growth trend is exponential, with IPv6 making this massive growth possible. Hybrid cloud platforms such as Azure have services dedicated to managing the communication and data requirements of these devices, including Azure SQL Database and Azure SQL Managed Instance. In fact, SQL Server itself can also run on IoT edge devices.

➤ For more information about Azure SQL Edge, visit *https://azure.microsoft.com/products /azure-sql/edge/*.

Deconstruct an IP address

An IP address is displayed in a human-readable notation but is binary under the hood:

- **IPv4.** The address is broken into four subclasses of decimal numbers, each ranging from 0 to 255, and separated by a decimal point. For example, 52.178.167.109 is a valid IPv4 address.

- **IPv6.** The address is broken into eight subclasses of hexadecimal numerals, each being four digits wide, and separated by a colon. If a subclass contains all zeros, it can be omitted. For example, 2001:d74f:e211:9840:0000:0000:0000:0000 is a valid IPv6 address that can be simplified to 2001:d74f:e211:9840:: with the zeros omitted (note the double-colon at the end to indicate the omission).

➤ You can read more about IPv6 address representation at *http://www.ciscopress.com/articles /article.asp?p=2803866*.

NOTE

Hexadecimal is a counting system that uses all the decimal numbers plus the first six letters of the Latin alphabet to represent the 16 values between 0 and 15 (10 = A, 11 = B, 12 = C, 13 = D, 14 = E, 15 = F). Using hex is a convenient way to describe binary values that would otherwise take up a lot of space to display.

Adoption of IPv6 across the Internet is taking decades, so a hybrid solution is currently in place, by which IPv4 and IPv6 traffic is shared across compatible devices. If that doesn't sound like enough of a headache, let's add routing into the mix.

Find your way around the Internet

Routing between networks on the Internet is performed by the Border Gateway Protocol (BGP), which sits on top of TCP/IP. BGP is necessary because there is no map of the Internet. Devices and entire networks appear and disappear all the time.

BGP routes billions of network packets through millions of routers based on a best-guess scenario. Packets are routed based on trust: routers provide information to one another about the networks they control, and BGP implicitly trusts that information.

BGP is therefore not secure, because it was designed solely to address the scalability of the Internet, which was (and still is) growing exponentially. It was a "quick fix" that became part of the fabric of the infrastructure long before security was a concern.

Efforts to secure BGP have been slow. It is therefore critical to assume that your own Internet traffic will be hijacked at some point. When this happens, proper cryptography can prevent third parties from reading your data.

A brief overview of the World Wide Web

The World Wide Web (the web) is a single component of the greater Internet, along with email and other services that are still very much in use today, such as File Transfer Protocol (FTP) and Voice over IP (VoIP).

The web uses the Hypertext Transfer Protocol (HTTP), which sits on top of TCP/IP. A web server provides mixed media content (text, graphics, video, and other media) in Hypertext Markup Language (HTML) format, which is transmitted using HTTP and then interpreted and rendered by a web browser. Modern web browsers include Microsoft Edge, Google Chrome, Mozilla Firefox, and Apple Safari.

NOTE

The modern web browser is hugely complex, doing a lot more than rendering HTML, but for the purposes of this discussion and in the interest of brevity, we gloss over those extras.

How does protocol encryption fit into this?

The explosive adoption of the web in the 1990s prompted public-facing organizations to start moving their sales online for electronic commerce (e-commerce) ventures, which created the need for secure transactions. Consumers wanted to use their credit cards safely and securely so they could shop and purchase goods online.

Remember that the Internet is built on IP, which is stateless and has routing information in the header of every single packet. This means anyone can place a hardware device (or software) in the packet stream, do something with the packet, and then pass it on (modified or not) to the destination without the sender or recipient having any knowledge of this interaction. Because this is a fundamental building block of a packet-switching network, it's very difficult to secure properly.

As discussed, encryption transforms your data into an unreadable format. Now, if someone connected to the same network were to intercept encrypted packets, that person couldn't see what you're doing. The payload of each packet would appear garbled and unreadable unless this person had the key to decrypt it.

Netscape Communications created a secure version of HTTP in 1994 called HTTPS, which stands for HTTP Secure or HTTP over Secure Sockets Layer (SSL). Over the years, the moniker of HTTPS has remained, but as standards improved, it came to be known as HTTP over Transport Layer Security (TLS).

Understand symmetric and asymmetric encryption

When we talk about data moving over the network, that usually means TCP/IP is involved, and we must transmit that data securely, through encryption. You can encrypt data in two ways: symmetric and asymmetric. Each has its advantages and disadvantages.

Symmetric encryption (shared secret)

A secret key—usually a password, passphrase, or random string of characters—is used to encrypt data with a particular cryptographic algorithm. This secret key is shared between the sender and the recipient, and both parties can encrypt and decrypt all content using this secret key.

If the key is accidentally leaked to a third party, the encrypted data could be intercepted, decrypted, modified, and re-encrypted—again, without either the sender or recipient being aware of this. This type of attack is known as a *man-in-the-middle* attack.

Asymmetric encryption (public key)

Also known as *public key encryption* (*PKE*), asymmetric encryption generates a key-pair composed of a *public key* (used to encrypt data) and a *private key* (used to decrypt that data). The public key can be widely distributed.

The private key never needs to be shared. Therefore, this method is far more secure, because only you can use your private key to decrypt the data. Unfortunately, however, asymmetric encryption requires a lot more processing power, and both parties need their own key-pairs.

Inside OUT

What encryption method should you use for SQL Server?

For practical purposes, SQL Server manages the keys internally for both symmetric and asymmetric encryption. Owing to the much larger overhead of asymmetric encryption, however, you should use symmetric encryption to encrypt any data at rest in SQL Server that you want to protect. Using the encryption hierarchy, layers above the data can be protected using passwords or asymmetric keys. (We discuss this shortly).

Digital certificates

Public keys require discoverability, which means that they must be made publicly available. If a sending party wants to sign a message for the receiving party, the burden is on the sender to locate the recipient's public key to sign a message. For small-scale communications between two private entities, this might be done by sharing their public keys with each other.

For larger-scale communications with many senders and one recipient (such as a web or database server, for example), a *certificate authority* (CA) can provide the public key through a *digital certificate*, which the recipient (the website or database administrator) can install directly on the server. This certificate serves as an electronic signature for the recipient, which includes its public key. The CA is trusted by both the sender and the recipient, and the sender can verify that the recipient is indeed who it claims to be.

Digital certificates, also known as *public key certificates*, are defined by the X.509 standard. Many protocols use this standard, including TLS and its predecessor, SSL.

> ➤ You can read more about how digital certificates and TLS relate to SQL Server and Azure SQL Database later in this chapter. The X.509 standard is available at *https://www.itu.int /rec/T-REC-X.509*.

Inside OUT

What is a certification authority?

A certification authority (CA) is an organization or entity that issues digital certificates, which include the name of the owner, the owner's public key, and start and expiration dates. The certificate is automatically revoked after it expires, and the CA can revoke any certificate before then.

For the certificate to be trusted, the CA itself must be trustworthy. It is the responsibility of the CA to verify the owner's identity so that any certificates issued in that owner's name can be trusted.

In recent years, several CAs have lost their trustworthy status, either because their verification process was flawed or their signing algorithms were weak. Take care when choosing a CA for your digital certificates.

Protect the data platform

You use multiple layers of defense as you go down the stack of your data environment. Even if you use virtual machines (VMs) and containers in a cloud environment, the same principles apply.

Each layer protects the layer below it using a combination of encryption keys (asymmetric and symmetric), certificates, and other obfuscation techniques. SQL Server provides features that protect sensitive data from unauthorized users, even if they manage the data. Azure SQL services share a lot in common with SQL Server, and have unique protections, which we call out where applicable.

This section breaks down each layer into network, OS, the SQL Server instance, and finally the database itself, including columns and rows. Much of this hierarchy is encrypted by SQL Server, starting at the OS layer and working all the way down to individual cells in a table. Figure 13-1 shows this hierarchy.

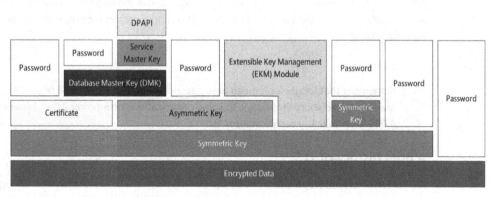

Figure 13-1 The SQL Server encryption hierarchy.

Secure the network with TLS

Data is in motion from the moment it is read from, or written to, the buffer pool in SQL Server, Azure SQL Database, and Azure SQL Managed Instance. *Data in motion* is data that the Database Engine provides over a network interface. Protecting data in motion requires several considerations, from perimeter security to cryptographic protocols for the communication itself, and the authorization of the application or process accessing the data.

SQL Server 2022 protects data by default during transmission over a network connection, using Transport Layer Security (TLS). Any network protocols and APIs involved must support encrypting and decrypting the data as it moves in and out of the buffer pool.

NOTE

You may have a network storage device connected to the underlying OS and encrypted using TLS. However, SQL Server is not aware of this encryption. See Chapter 2 for more information.

As mentioned, TLS is a security layer on top of a transport layer, or *cryptographic protocol*. Most networks use the TCP/IP stack and TLS is designed to secure traffic on TCP/IP-based networks.

How TLS works

With TLS protection, before two parties can exchange information, they must mutually agree on which encryption key and cryptographic algorithm to use. This is called a *key exchange* or *handshake*. TLS works with both symmetric and asymmetric encryption, which means the encryption key could be a shared secret or a public key (usually with a certificate).

After the key exchange, the handshake is complete, and a secured communication channel allows traffic between the two parties to flow. This is how data in motion is protected from external attacks.

NOTE

Remember that longer keys mean better security. Public keys of 1,024 bits (128 bytes) are considered short these days, so some organizations now prefer 2,048-bit or even 4,096-bit public key certificates for TLS.

A brief history of TLS

Just as earlier cryptographic protocols have been defeated or considered weak enough that they will eventually be defeated, so too have SSL and TLS had their challenges:

- The prohibition of SSL 2.0 is covered at *https://tools.ietf.org/html/rfc6176*.

- Known attacks on TLS are available at *https://tools.ietf.org/html/rfc7457*.

TLS 1.2 was defined in 2008 and is the most widely available public version.

NOTE

TLS 1.3 is supported for SQL Server 2022 on Windows, but is not supported in all client libraries at the time of this writing. TLS 1.3 is not yet supported for SQL Server on Linux.

Like its predecessors, TLS 1.2 is vulnerable to certain attacks, but as long as you don't use older encryption algorithms (for instance 3DES, RC4, and IDEA), it is good enough while we wait for TLS 1.3 to propagate. You should use TLS 1.2 or TLS 1.3 wherever possible. Once support is available in client libraries, however, you should switch to TLS 1.3. SQL Server ships with older versions of TLS, so you must disable 1.0 and 1.1 at the OS level to ensure you use at least TLS 1.2.

➤ You can see how to disable older versions of TLS in the Microsoft Knowledge Base article at *https://support.microsoft.com/help/3135244.*

Inside OUT

How does TLS 1.3 work with the TDS protocol?

Client libraries use the Tabular Data Stream (TDS) protocol to connect to SQL Server. In previous versions of SQL Server, the initial portion of the TDS connection was not secure by default. With SQL Server 2022, TDS has been updated to version 8.0, and the connection negotiation process can now be secured using TLS. If you are using updated versions of the ODBC and OLE DB client libraries, your client connection string needs `Encrypt=strict` to take advantage of this improved security. All TDS traffic will then be protected by TLS encryption. TDS 8.0 is fully compatible with both TLS 1.2 and TLS 1.3.

➤ You can read more about how TDS and TLS interact at *https://learn.microsoft.com/sql /relational-databases/security/networking/tds-8-and-tls-1-3.*

Data protection from the OS

At the top of a server's encryption hierarchy, protecting everything below it, is the OS. Windows Server provides an application programming interface (API) for system-level and user-level processes to take advantage of data protection (encryption) on the file system. SQL Server and other applications can use this data protection API to configure Windows to automatically encrypt data on the drive without having to encrypt data through other means. SQL Server uses the Data Protection API (DPAPI) for transparent data encryption (TDE).

Inside OUT

How does data protection work for SQL Server on Linux?

The mechanism that Microsoft created to enable SQL Server to run on Linux and inside containers is called the Platform Abstraction Layer (PAL). It aligns all code specific to the OS in one place, forming a bridge with the underlying platform. The PAL includes all APIs, including file system and DPAPIs. This makes SQL Server 2022 platform-agnostic.

➤ To read more about the PAL, visit the official SQL Server Blog at *https://cloudblogs.microsoft .com/sqlserver/2016/12/16/sql-server-on-linux-how-introduction*.

The encryption hierarchy in detail

As mentioned, each layer of the hierarchy protects the layer below it using a combination of keys (asymmetric and symmetric) and certificates. (Refer to Figure 13-1.) Individual layers in the hierarchy can be accessed by a password at the very least unless an extensible key management (EKM) module is being used. The EKM module is a standalone device that holds symmetric and asymmetric keys outside of SQL Server.

The database master key (DMK) is protected by the service master key (SMK), and both are symmetric keys. The SMK is created when you install SQL Server and is protected by the DPAPI.

If you want to use TDE on your database (see the "Configure TDE on a user database" section later in this chapter), it requires a symmetric key called the database encryption key (DEK), which is protected by an asymmetric key in the EKM module or by a certificate through the DMK. This layered approach helps to prevent your data from falling into the wrong hands.

NOTE

Although we do not recommend 3DES for TLS, you can still use 3DES lower in the SQL Server security hierarchy to secure DEKs because these are protected by the SMK, the DMK, and a certificate, or entirely by an HSM/EKM module like Azure Key Vault. (See the next section, "Use EKM modules with SQL Server," for more information.)

There are two considerations when deciding how to secure a SQL Server environment, which you can implement independently:

- **Data at rest.** In the case of TDE, data is encrypted as it is persisted to the storage layer from the buffer pool and decrypted as it is read into memory. You can also encrypt your storage layer independently from SQL Server, but this does not form part of the encryption hierarchy.

- **Data in motion.** This refers to data being transmitted over a network connection. Any network protocols and APIs involved must support encrypting and decrypting the data as it moves in and out of the buffer pool.

As mentioned, data is in motion from the moment it is read from or written to the buffer pool. Between the buffer pool and the underlying storage, data is at rest.

NOTE

TDE encrypts database backup files along with the data and transaction log files. TDE is available with SQL Server Enterprise and Standard editions, and is enabled by default in Azure SQL.

Inside OUT

How do you import certificates into SQL Server?

Since SQL Server 2019, you can import your TLS certificates using SQL Server Configuration Manager.

To do so, open Configuration Manager and expand the SQL Server Network Configuration branch for your instance. Then right-click **Protocols for <InstanceName>** and select **Properties**. Next, select **Import** to open the Certificate Import Wizard. Follow the prompts and enter the appropriate credentials, confirm the addition of the certificate, and restart the instance.

After the restart, reopen the **Properties** dialog box to see your imported certificate. To view the certificate details, select **View**. To force all traffic to use this certificate, select the **Force Encryption** option on the **Flags** tab. Remember that changing the flag requires another SQL Server restart.

➤ For more information about installing certificates in an availability group, including a step-by-step guide, see *https://learn.microsoft.com/sql/database-engine/configure-windows/manage-certificates*.

Use EKM modules with SQL Server

Organizations might choose to take advantage of a separate security appliance called a hardware security module (HSM) or extensible key management (EKM) device to generate, manage, and store encryption keys for the network infrastructure outside a SQL Server environment. The HSM/EKM device can be a hardware appliance, a USB device, a smart card, or even software, as long as it implements the Microsoft Cryptographic Application Programming Interface (MCAPI) provider. SQL Server can use these keys for internal use.

EKM is an advanced SQL Server setting and is disabled by default. To use the key or keys from an HSM/EKM device, you must enable EKM by using the `sp_execute 'EKM provider enabled' 1;` command. Then, the device must be registered as an EKM module for use by SQL Server. After the HSM/EKM device creates a key for use by SQL Server (for TDE, for instance), the device exports it securely into SQL Server via the MCAPI provider.

The module might support different types of authentication (Basic or Other), but only one of these types can be registered with SQL Server for that provider. If the module supports Basic authentication (a username and password combination), SQL Server uses a credential to provide transparent authentication to the module.

The extensible key management feature of SQL Server is only supported in Standard and Enterprise editions, and is not available for SQL Server on Linux.

Inside OUT

What is a credential?

In SQL Server, a credential is a record of authentication information that the Database Engine uses to connect to external resources. Credentials provide security details for processes to impersonate Windows users on a network, though they can also be used to connect to other services like Azure Storage and, of course, an HSM/EKM device.

You can create credentials for use by all databases in the master database using the CREATE CREDENTIAL command, or per individual database using the CREATE DATABASE SCOPED CREDENTIAL command. Chapter 12 contains more information on logins. Chapter 8, "Maintain and monitor SQL Server," goes into more detail about credentials.

> ➤ To read more about EKM in SQL Server, visit *https://learn.microsoft.com/sql/relational-databases/security/encryption/extensible-key-management-ekm*.

Cloud security with Azure Key Vault

You can use Azure Key Vault in addition to, or as a drop-in replacement for, a traditional HSM/EKM device. For this to work, your SQL Server instance (whether on-premises or on a VM in the cloud) requires Internet access to the Key Vault.

Key Vault is implemented as an EKM provider inside SQL Server, using the SQL Server Connector (a standalone Windows application) as a bridge between Key Vault and the SQL Server instance. To use Key Vault, you must create the vault and associate it with a valid Azure Active Directory (Azure AD).

Begin by registering the SQL Server service principal name in Azure AD. Then you install the SQL Server Connector and enable EKM in SQL Server.

➤ You can read more about service principal names and Kerberos in Chapter 2.

You must then create a login for SQL Server to use to access Key Vault, and map that login to a new credential that contains the Key Vault authentication information.

➤ A step-by-step guide for this process is available at *https://learn.microsoft.com/sql /relational-databases/security/encryption/setup-steps-for-extensible-key-management -using-the-azure-key-vault.*

Master keys in the encryption hierarchy

Since SQL Server 2012, both the SMK and DMK are symmetric keys encrypted using the Advanced Encryption Standard (AES) cryptographic algorithm. AES is faster and more secure than Triple Data Encryption Standard (3DES), which was used in SQL Server before 2012. Starting with SQL Server 2022, you can back up and restore your master key using Azure Blob Storage instead of the local file system, by using the URL argument and pointing it to an Azure Blob Storage location.

➤ For more information on using Azure Blob Storage to back up and restore your master key, see *https://learn.microsoft.com/sql/t-sql/statements/backup-master-key-transact-sql.*

NOTE

When you upgrade from an older version of SQL Server that was encrypted using 3DES, you must regenerate both the SMK and DMK to upgrade them to AES.

Inside OUT

What is the difference between DES, 3DES, and AES?

Data Encryption Standard (DES) is a symmetric key algorithm developed in the 1970s, with a key length of 56 bits. It has been considered cryptographically broken since 1998. In 2012 it was possible to recover a DES key in less than 24 hours if both a plain-text and cipher-text pair were known.

Its successor, the Triple Data Encryption Standard (3DES), applies the DES algorithm three times (each time with a different DES key) to each block of data being encrypted. However, with current consumer hardware, the entire 3DES key space can be searched, making it cryptographically weak.

Advanced Encryption Standard (AES) uses keys that are 128, 192, or 256 bits in length. Longer keys are much more difficult to crack using brute-force methods, so AES is considered safe for the foreseeable future. It also happens to be much faster than 3DES.

The SMK

In SQL Server, the SMK is at the top of the encryption hierarchy. It is automatically generated the first time the SQL Server instance starts, and it is encrypted by the DPAPI in combination with the local machine key (which itself is created when Windows Server is installed). The key is based on the Windows credentials of the SQL Server service account and the computer credentials. (On Linux, the local machine key is part of the PAL used by SQL Server.)

NOTE

You will get a new SMK if you change the service account that runs SQL Server, but it is considered "self-healing"—meaning you don't have to do anything else once it has changed.

If you need to restore or regenerate an SMK, you first must decrypt the entire SQL Server encryption hierarchy, which is a resource-intensive operation. You should perform this activity only in a scheduled maintenance window. If the key has been compromised, however, you shouldn't wait for the maintenance window.

CAUTION

It is essential that you back up the SMK to a file and then copy it securely to an off-premises location. Losing this key will result in total data loss if you need to recover a database or environment.

To back up the SMK, you can use the following T-SQL script, but be sure to choose a randomly generated password. The password will be required for restoring or regenerating the key at a later stage. Keep the password separate from the SMK backup file so they cannot be used together if your secure backup location is compromised. Ensure that the folder on the drive is adequately secured. You can also use an Azure Blob Storage URL instead of a local file path. After you back up the key, transfer and store it securely in an off-premises location.

```
BACKUP SERVICE MASTER KEY TO FILE = 'c:\SecureLocation\service_master_key'
    ENCRYPTION BY PASSWORD = '<UseAReallyStrongPassword>';
GO
```

The DMK

The DMK is used to protect asymmetric keys and private keys for digital certificates stored in the database. A copy of the DMK is stored in the database for which it is used as well as in the master database. The copy is automatically updated by default if the DMK changes. This allows SQL Server to automatically decrypt information as required. A DMK is required for each user database that will use TDE. Refer to Figure 13-1 to see how the DMK is protected by the SMK.

CAUTION

Remember to back up the DMK to a file, as well, and copy it securely to an off-premises location.

It is considered a security best practice to periodically regenerate the DMK to protect the server from brute-force attacks. The idea is to ensure that it takes longer for a brute-force attack to break the key than the length of time for which the key is in use. For example, suppose you encrypt your database with a DMK in January and regenerate it in July, causing all keys for digital certificates to be re-encrypted with the new key. If anyone has begun a brute-force attack on data encrypted with the previous DMK, all results from that attack will be rendered useless by the new DMK.

You can back up the DMK using the following T-SQL script. The same rules apply as with backing up the SMK (choose a random password, store the file off-premises, and keep the password and backup file separately). You can also use an Azure Blob Storage URL instead of a local file path. This script assumes the master key exists.

```
USE WideWorldImporters;
GO
BACKUP MASTER KEY TO FILE = 'c:\SecureLocation\wwi_database_master_key'
    ENCRYPTION BY PASSWORD = '<UseAReallyStrongPassword>';
GO
```

➤ You can read more about the SMK and DMK at *https://learn.microsoft.com/sql/relational -databases/security/encryption/sql-server-and-database-encryption-keys-database -engine.*

Encrypt data with TDE

Continuing with our defense-in-depth discussion, an additional way to protect your environment is to encrypt data at rest—namely the database files and, when TDE is enabled, all backups of that database.

Third-party providers, including storage vendors, provide excellent on-disk encryption for your direct-attached storage (DAS) or storage area network (SAN) as a file-system solution or at the physical storage layer. Provided your data and backups are localized to this solution, and no files are copied to machines that are not encrypted at the file-system level, this might be an acceptable solution for you.

NOTE

If files in this scenario are copied to another device, they may not be encrypted. Consult with your storage vendor to discuss options for broader protection.

If you have either the Enterprise or Standard edition of SQL Server, you can use TDE, which encrypts data, transaction log, and backup files at the file-system level by using a DEK. Should someone manage to acquire these files via a backup server or Azure Storage archive, or by gaining access to your production environment, that person will not be able to attach the files or restore the database without the DEK.

The DEK is a symmetric key (shared secret) that is secured by a certificate stored in the master database. If using HSM/EKM or Azure Key Vault, the DEK is protected by an asymmetric key in the EKM module, instead. The DEK is stored in the boot record of the protected database (page 0 of file 1) so that it is easily available during the recovery process.

NOTE

Because it is implemented within the Database Engine, TDE is invisible to any applications that access TDE-encrypted data. No application changes are required to take advantage of TDE for the database.

In the data file, TDE operates at the page level, because all data files are stored as 8-KB pages. Before being flushed from the buffer pool, the contents of the page are encrypted, the checksum is calculated, and then the page is written to the drive. When reading data, the 8-KB page is read from the drive, decrypted, and then the contents are placed into the buffer pool.

NOTE

Even though encryption might to some degree increase the physical size of the data it is protecting, the size and structure of data pages is not affected. Instead, the number of pages in the data file might increase.

For log files, the contents of the log cache are also encrypted before writing to and reading from the drive.

> ➤ **To read more about checkpoint operations and active virtual log files (VLFs) in the transaction log, refer to Chapter 3, "Design and implement an on-premises database infrastructure."**

Backup files constitute the contents of the data file, plus enough transaction log records to ensure that the database restore is consistent (redo and undo records of active transactions when the backup is taken). Practically speaking, this means the contents of new backup files are encrypted by default after TDE is enabled.

NOTE

Files associated with the buffer pool extension are not encrypted if you use TDE. To encrypt buffer pool extension files, you should use a file-system encryption method such as BitLocker or EFS. To read more about BitLocker, visit *https://learn.microsoft.com /windows/security/information-protection/bitlocker/bitlocker-overview*.

Configure TDE on a user database

To use TDE on SQL Server, you must create a DMK if you don't have one already. Verify that it is safely backed up and securely stored off-premises. If you have never backed up the DMK, the Database Engine will warn you after you use it that the DMK has not yet been backed up. If you don't know where that backup is, back it up again. This is a crucial detail to using TDE (or any encryption technology).

Next, you create a digital certificate or use one that you have acquired from a CA. In the next example, the certificate is created on the server directly. Then, you create the DEK, which is signed by the certificate and encrypted using a cryptographic algorithm of your choice.

> ➤ To read more about managing database encryption keys in SQL Server, visit *https://learn
> .microsoft.com/sql/relational-databases/security/encryption/sql-server-and-database
> -encryption-keys-database-engine*.

Although you do have a choice of algorithm, we recommend AES over 3DES for performance and security reasons. Additionally, you can choose from three AES key sizes: 128, 192, or 256 bits. Remember that larger keys are more secure, but will add additional CPU overhead when encrypting data. If you plan to rotate your keys every few months, you can safely use 128-bit AES encryption because no brute-force attack (using current computing power) can compromise a 128-bit key in the months between key rotations.

After you create the DEK, you enable encryption on the database. The command completes immediately, but the process takes place in the background because each page in the database must be read into the buffer pool, encrypted, and persisted to the drive.

Inside OUT

How does TDE affect tempdb?

Enabling TDE on a user database automatically enables TDE for the tempdb system database as well (if it is not already enabled). This can add overhead that adversely affects performance for unencrypted databases that use tempdb. If you want to disable TDE on tempdb, all user databases must have it disabled first.

The following script provides a summary of the steps to enable TDE:

```
USE master;
GO
-- Remember to back up this database master key once it is created
CREATE MASTER KEY ENCRYPTION BY PASSWORD = '<UseAReallyStrongPassword>';
GO
```

```
CREATE CERTIFICATE WideWorldServerCert WITH SUBJECT = 'WWI DEK Certificate';
GO
USE WideWorldImporters;
GO
CREATE DATABASE ENCRYPTION KEY
    WITH ALGORITHM = AES_128
    ENCRYPTION BY SERVER CERTIFICATE WideWorldServerCert;
GO
ALTER DATABASE WideWorldImporters SET ENCRYPTION ON;
GO
```

Verify whether TDE is enabled for a database

To determine which databases are encrypted with TDE, issue the following T-SQL query:

```
SELECT name, is_encrypted FROM sys.databases;
```

If a user database is encrypted, the is_encrypted column value for that database is set to 1. tempdb will also show a value of 1 in this column.

Manage and monitor the TDE scan

Enabling TDE on a database requires each data page to be read into the buffer pool before being encrypted and written back out to the drive. If the database instance is under a heavy workload, you can pause the scan and resume it at a later stage.

To pause the scan on the WideWorldImporters sample database, issue the following T-SQL command:

```
ALTER DATABASE WideWorldImporters SET ENCRYPTION SUSPEND;
```

To resume the scan on the same database, issue the following T-SQL command:

```
ALTER DATABASE WideWorldImporters SET ENCRYPTION RESUME;
```

You can also check the progress of the TDE scan using the encryption_scan_state column in the sys.dm_database_encryption_keys DMV. To see when the state was last modified, refer to the encryption_scan_modify_date column in the same DMV.

Protect sensitive columns with Always Encrypted

Although TDE is useful for encrypting the entire database at the file-system level, it doesn't prevent database administrators and other users from having access to sensitive information within the database.

The first rule of storing sensitive data is that you should avoid storing it altogether when possible. For example, credit-card information makes sense in a banking system, but not in a sales database, so it should not be stored in one.

NOTE

Many third-party systems can encrypt your data securely but are beyond the scope of this chapter. Keep in mind that there is a small but inherent risk in storing encryption keys with data, as SQL Server does. Your organization must balance that risk against the ease of managing and maintaining those keys.

If you must store sensitive data, Always Encrypted protects how data is *viewed* at the column level. It works with applications that use specific connection types (*client drivers*; see the next section) to interact with SQL Server. These client drivers are protected by a digital certificate so that only specific applications can view the protected data.

> ➤ To learn about column-level encryption, which uses a symmetric key, see *https://learn .microsoft.com/sql/relational-databases/security/encryption/encrypt-a-column-of-data*.

Always Encrypted was introduced in SQL Server 2016 and has been available on all editions since SQL Server 2016 with Service Pack 1. Since SQL Server 2019, Always Encrypted can also be combined with hardware-level secure enclaves to provide additional functionality. Secure enclaves leverage virtualization-based security (VBS) to isolate a region of memory inside the SQL Server process. SQL Server 2022 improves performance in the secure enclave with multithreading and key caching.

To use Always Encrypted, the database employs two types of keys: *column encryption keys* and *column master keys* (discussed shortly).

The encryption used by Always Encrypted is one of two types.

- **Deterministic.** This is the same as generating a hash value without a salt. The same encrypted value will always be generated for a given plain-text value. Without secure enclaves, this is useful for joins, indexes, searching, and grouping, but makes it possible for people to guess what the hash values represent.

- **Randomized.** This is the same as generating a hash value with a salt. No two of the same plain-text values will generate the same encrypted value. Without secure enclaves, this does not permit joins, indexes, searching, and grouping for those encrypted columns. SQL Server 2022 supports nested loop, hash, and merge joins, as well as GROUP BY and ORDER BY clauses.

As you can see in Table 13-1, secure enclaves provide a much richer experience when protecting data with Always Encrypted.

Table 13-1 Functionality available with Always Encrypted encryption

Operation	Without enclave		With enclave	
	Randomized	Deterministic	Randomized	Deterministic
In-place encryption	No	No	Yes	Yes
Equality comparison	No	Yes (external)	Yes (internal)	Yes (external)
Beyond equality	No	No	Yes	No
LIKE predicate	No	No	Yes	No
Joins	No	No	Yes	No
GROUP BY clause	No	No	Yes	No
ORDER BY clause	No	No	Yes	No

Without secure enclaves, you can use randomized encryption for values that are not expected to participate in joins or searches, while deterministic encryption is useful for values like social security numbers and other government-issued values because it helps for searching and grouping. With secure enclaves, randomized encryption is useful for both scenarios.

Inside OUT

What is a secure enclave?

Before SQL Server 2019, operations on Always Encrypted data were limited to certain equality operations inside the Database Engine, and only with data protected by deterministic encryption. Any other operations required that the data be moved out of the database and operated on at the client side.

A secure enclave, which requires SQL Server to be installed on physical hardware, is a trusted region of memory inside the SQL Server process. It is not possible to view the data inside the enclave, even with a debugger. Now operations can be performed on encrypted data without moving the data outside of the Database Engine.

➤ To read more about the virtualization-based security underlying secure enclaves, visit *https://www.microsoft.com/security/blog/2018/06/05/virtualization-based-security-vbs -memory-enclaves-data-protection-through-isolation*.

Because Always Encrypted is meant to prevent unauthorized persons from viewing data (including database administrators), you should generate the keys elsewhere and store them in a trusted key store (in the operating system's key store for the database server and the application

CHAPTER 13

server, or an EKM module such as Azure Key Vault), away from the database server. To maintain the chain of trust, the person who generates the keys should not be the same person who administers the database server.

Client application providers that support Always Encrypted

The following providers currently support Always Encrypted:

- Microsoft .NET Data Provider for SQL Server

- Microsoft JDBC Driver 6.0 or higher

- ODBC Driver 13.1 for SQL Server or higher

- Microsoft Drivers 5.2 for PHP for SQL Server or higher

The connection between the Database Engine and application is made using a client-side encrypted connection. Each provider has its own appropriate method to control this setting:

- **.NET.** Set `ColumnEncryptionSetting` in the connection string to `Enabled` or configure the `SqlConnectionStringBuilder.ColumnEncryptionSetting` property as `SqlConnectionColumnEncryptionSetting.Enabled`.

- **JDBC.** Set `columnEncryptionSetting` to `Enabled` in the connection string or configure the `SQLServerDataSource()` object with the `setColumnEncryptionSetting("Enabled")` property.

- **ODBC.** Set the `ColumnEncryption` connection string keyword to `Enabled` and use the `SQL_COPT_SS_COLUMN_ENCRYPTION` pre-connection attribute or set it using the Data Source Name (DSN) with the `SQL_COLUMN_ENCRYPTION_ENABLE` setting.

- **PHP.** Set the `ColumnEncryption` connection string keyword to `Enabled`. Note that PHP drivers use ODBC drivers for encryption.

Additionally, the application must have the `VIEW ANY COLUMN MASTER KEY DEFINITION` and `VIEW ANY COLUMN ENCRYPTION KEY DEFINITION` database permissions to view the column master key and column encryption key (see next section).

The column master key and column encryption key

The column master key (CMK) protects one or more column encryption keys (CEKs). The CEK is encrypted using AES encryption and is used to encrypt the actual column data. You can use the same CEK to encrypt multiple columns, or you can create a CEK for each column that needs to be encrypted.

Inside OUT

Can you add indexes to columns protected by a secure enclave?

Indexes are permitted on enclave-enabled columns protected with randomized encryption. The enclave needs access to the CEK for all operations involving the index.

Microsoft recommends that your database has accelerated database recovery (ADR) enabled before creating your first index on an enclave-enabled column using randomized encryption. This ensures that your encrypted data is immediately available after a database is restored.

➤ You can read more about ADR in Chapter 3.

Metadata about the keys (but not the keys themselves) is stored in the database's system catalog views:

- `sys.column_master_keys`

- `sys.column_encryption_keys`

This metadata includes the type of encryption and location of the keys, plus their encrypted values. Even if a database is compromised, the data in the protected columns cannot be read without access to the secure key store.

➤ To read more about considerations for key management, visit *https://learn.microsoft.com /sql/relational-databases/security/encryption/overview-of-key-management-for-always -encrypted*.

Use the Always Encrypted Wizard

The easiest way to configure Always Encrypted is to use the Always Encrypted Wizard in SSMS. As noted, you must have the following permissions before you begin:

- `VIEW ANY COLUMN MASTER KEY DEFINITION`

- `VIEW ANY COLUMN ENCRYPTION KEY`

If you plan to create new keys, you also need the following permissions:

- `ALTER ANY COLUMN MASTER KEY`

- `ALTER ANY COLUMN ENCRYPTION KEY`

CHAPTER 13

In SSMS, in **Object Explorer**, right-click the name of the database that you want to configure, select **Tasks**, and choose **Encrypt Columns**. This opens the Always Encrypted wizard.

On the **Column Selection** page, choose the column you want to encrypt, and then select the encryption type (deterministic or randomized). If you want to decrypt a previously encrypted column, you can choose **Plaintext**.

On the **Master Key Configuration** page, you can create a new key using the local OS certificate store or using a centralized store like Azure Key Vault or an HSM/EKM device. If you already have a CMK in your database, you can use it instead. Also choose the master key source—either **Current User** or **Local Machine**.

NOTE

Memory-optimized and temporal tables are not supported by this wizard, but you can still encrypt them using Always Encrypted.

Limitations in Always Encrypted

Certain column types are not supported by Always Encrypted, including:

- image, (n)text, xml, sql_variant, timestamp or rowversion data types

- string columns with non-BIN2 collations (reduced features are available with non-BIN2 collations, but for best results, use a BIN2 collation)

- FILESTREAM columns

- Columns with IDENTITY or ROWGUIDCOL properties

- Columns with default constraints or referenced by check constraints

> ➤ **You can read the full list of limitations and find out more about Always Encrypted at** *https:// learn.microsoft.com/sql/relational-databases/security/encryption/always-encrypted -database-engine.*

Configure Always Encrypted with secure enclaves

Always Encrypted with secure enclaves requires a complex environment to guarantee the security it offers. This includes the following:

- **Host Guardian Service (HGS).** Install HGS in a Windows Server 2022 failover cluster with three computers in its own AD forest. These computers must not be connected to an existing AD, and none of them can be used for the SQL Server installation. Microsoft suggests that this cluster be isolated from the rest of your network, and that different administrators manage this environment. The only access to HGS will be through HTTP (TCP port 80) and HTTPS (TCP port 443).

- **SQL Server 2022.** Install SQL Server 2022 on Windows Server 2022, on its own physical hardware. VMs do not support the recommended Trusted Platform Module (TPM) enclave attestation, which is hardware-based.

  ➤ You can read more about TPM attestation at *https://learn.microsoft.com/windows-server /identity/ad-ds/manage/component-updates/tpm-key-attestation*.

- **Tools for client and development.** Install the requisite tools on your client machine:

  - Microsoft .NET Data Provider for SQL Server 2.1.0 or later

  - SSMS (SSMS) 19.0 or later

  - SQL Server PowerShell module version 21.1 or later

  - Visual Studio 2017 or later

  - Developer pack (SDK) for .NET Standard 2.1 or later

  - `Microsoft.SqlServer.Management.AlwaysEncrypted.EnclaveProviders` NuGet package

  - `Microsoft.SqlServer.Management.AlwaysEncrypted.AzureKeyVaultProvider` NuGet package version 2.2.0 or later, if you plan to use Azure Key Vault for storing your column master keys

- **Configured enclave.** From the client/development machine, you use SSMS to enable the enclave. Rich computations are disabled by default for performance reasons. If you want to use this feature, you must enable it after every SQL Server instance restart using Trace Flag 127. Make sure you test the performance impact on your environment before enabling this feature in production.

- **Enclave-enabled keys.** This works in a similar way to regular Always Encrypted keys, except the CMKs provisioned through HGS are marked as enclave-enabled. You can use SSMS or PowerShell to provision these keys, and store them either in the Windows Certificate Store or Azure Key Vault.

- **Encrypted sensitive columns.** You use the same methods to encrypt data as before.

  ➤ A step-by-step walkthrough of this process is available at *https://learn.microsoft.com/sql /relational-databases/security/encryption/configure-always-encrypted-enclaves*.

Row-level security

Protecting the network and database instance is good and proper. However, this does not protect assets within the environment from, say, curious people snooping on salaries in the human resources database. Or perhaps you have a customer database, and you want to restrict the data those customers can access.

Row-level security, which does not use encryption, operates at the database level to restrict access to a table through a security policy, based on group membership or execution context. Access to the rows in a table is protected by an inline table-valued function, which is invoked and enforced by the security policy. It is functionally equivalent to a WHERE clause.

The function checks whether the user is allowed to access a particular row, while the security policy attaches this function to the table. So, when you run a query against a table, the security policy applies the predicate function.

Row-level security supports two types of security policies, both of which you can apply simultaneously:

- Filter predicates, which limit the data that can be seen

- Block predicates, which limit the actions a user can take on data

Hence, a user might be able to see rows, but will not be able to insert, update, or delete rows that look like rows they can see. This concept is covered in more detail in the next section.

CAUTION

There is a risk of information leakage if an attacker writes a query with a specially crafted WHERE clause and, for example, a divide-by-zero error, to force an exception if the WHERE condition is true. This is known as a *side-channel attack*. It is wise to limit the ability of users to run ad hoc queries when using row-level security.

Filter predicates for read operations

You can silently filter rows that are available through read operations. The application then has no knowledge of the other data that is filtered out.

Filter predicates affect all read operations. This list is taken directly from the official documentation at *https://learn.microsoft.com/sql/relational-databases/security/row-level-security*:

- **SELECT.** Cannot view rows that are filtered.

- **DELETE.** Cannot delete rows that are filtered.

- **UPDATE.** Cannot update rows that are filtered. It is possible to update rows that will be subsequently filtered. (The next section covers ways to prevent this.)

- **INSERT.** No effect (inserting is not a read operation). Note, however, that a trigger could cause unexpected side effects in this case.

Block predicates for write operations

These predicates block access to write (or *modification*) operations that violate the predicate. Block predicates affect all write operations:

- **AFTER INSERT.** Prevents the insertion of rows with values that violate the predicate. Also applies to bulk insert operations.

- **AFTER UPDATE.** Prevents the updating of rows to values that violate the predicate. Does not run if no columns in the predicate were changed.

- **BEFORE UPDATE.** Prevents the updating of rows that currently violate the predicate.

- **BEFORE DELETE.** Blocks DELETE operations if the row violates the predicate.

Dynamic data masking

Data masking works on the principle of limiting exposure to data by obfuscation. It does not use encryption. Without requiring too many changes to the application or database, you can mask *portions* of columns to prevent lower-privilege users from seeing them, such as with full credit-card numbers and other sensitive information.

You define the mask in the column definition of the table using the MASKED WITH (FUNCTION = [type]) syntax. You can add masking after table creation using the ALTER COLUMN syntax.

NOTE

One of the limitations for dynamic data masking before SQL Server 2022 was the lack of granular security. In SQL Server 2019 and earlier, the UNMASK privilege was available only at the database level. In SQL Server 2022, UNMASK can be granted at the database, schema, table, and even the column level to a database principal, as well as conferred via ownership chaining.

Four types of masks are available:

- **Default.** The column is masked according to the data type (not its default value). Strings use XXXX (fewer if the length is less than four characters); numeric values use a zero value; dates use midnight on January 1, 1900; and binary uses a single byte binary equivalent of zero. If a string is too short to complete the entire mask, part of the prefix or suffix will not be exposed.

- **Email.** Only the first letter and the trailing domain suffix is not masked—for example, aXXX@XXXXXXX.com.

- **Random.** This replaces a numeric data type with a random value within a range you specify.

- **Custom string.** Only the first and last letters are not masked. There is a custom padding string in the middle, which you specify.

➤ You can read more about dynamic data masking, including samples of how to set it up, at *https://learn.microsoft.com/sql/relational-databases/security/dynamic-data-masking.*

Limitations with masking data

Dynamic data masking has some limitations. It does not work on Always Encrypted columns, nor on FILESTREAM or COLUMN_SET column types. Computed columns are also excluded, but if the computed column depends on a masked column, the computed column inherits that mask and returns masked data.

If a column has dependencies, you cannot perform dynamic data masking on it without removing the dependency first, adding the dynamic data mask, and then re-creating the dependency. Finally, a masked column cannot be a used as a FULLTEXT index key.

CAUTION

It is possible to expose masked data with carefully crafted queries. This can be done using a brute-force attack or using inferences based on the results. If you are using data masking, you should also remove the ability of the user to run ad hoc queries and ensure their permissions are sound. For more on permissions, see Chapter 12.

Protect Azure SQL Database with Microsoft Defender for SQL

All security features discussed thus far work equally on SQL Server, Azure SQL Database, and Azure SQL Managed Instance. These include TDE, Always Encrypted, row-level security, and dynamic data masking.

That's great if you're just comparing SQL Server to its Azure SQL siblings. But there are some features unique to Azure SQL under the Microsoft Defender for SQL offering that are worth looking at. We cover these in the subsections that follow. Keep in mind that because Azure features and products are always evolving, this is only a brief overview, and is subject to change.

Inside OUT

How do you protect an Azure SQL Managed Instance?

In Azure SQL Managed Instance, each managed instance is isolated on their own independent virtual network (VNet), so they can only be accessed through Azure AD, and not Windows Authentication. Aside from that, Azure SQL Managed Instance shares all the same protections and security features as SQL Server and Azure SQL Database.

Vulnerability assessment

You can enable vulnerability assessments on your Azure SQL Database and Azure SQL Managed Instance subscriptions for a monthly fee. This provides a basic monthly overview of your Azure SQL environment and includes steps to mitigate any vulnerabilities it finds.

➤ **For more information about vulnerability assessments and how to subscribe to the service,** visit *https://learn.microsoft.com/azure/azure-sql/database/sql-vulnerability-assessment*.

Azure SQL Advanced Threat Protection (ATP)

The risks of having a publicly accessible database in the cloud are numerous. To help protect against attacks, you can activate SQL Advanced Threat Protection (ATP), which runs 24 hours a day on each of your Azure SQL databases, for a monthly fee. This service notifies you by email whenever it detects atypical behavior.

NOTE

ATP includes protection for Azure SQL Database, Azure SQL Managed Instance, Azure Synapse Analytics, SQL Server on Azure VMs, and Azure Arc–enabled SQL Server instances.

Some interesting threats include SQL injection attacks, potential vulnerabilities, and unfamiliar database access patterns, including unfamiliar logins or access from unusual locations. Each notification includes possible causes and recommendations to deal with the event. ATP ties into the Azure SQL audit log (discussed later in this chapter); thus, you can review events in a single place and decide whether each one was expected or malicious.

Although this does not prevent malicious attacks (over and above your existing protections), you are given the necessary tools to mitigate and defend against future events. Given how prevalent attacks like SQL injection are, this feature is very useful in letting you know if that type of event has been detected. You can enable ATP using the Azure portal, PowerShell, or the Azure CLI.

➤ **To read an overview on Azure SQL ATP,** visit *https://learn.microsoft.com/azure/azure-sql /database/threat-detection-overview*.

Built-in firewall protection

Azure SQL is secure by default. All connections to your database environment pass through a firewall. No connections to the database are possible until you add a rule to the firewall to allow access.

To provide access to all databases on an Azure SQL Database server, you must add a server-level firewall rule through the Azure portal (or PowerShell or Azure CLI) with your IP address as a range. This does not apply to Azure SQL Managed Instance, because you access the instance through a private IP address inside the VNet.

> ➤ To read more about protecting your Azure SQL Database, see Chapter 17, "Provision Azure SQL Database."

Ledger overview

The ledger feature, introduced in Azure SQL Database and now available in SQL Server 2022, provides an additional layer of auditing in your database. Ledger is based on the same underlying technology as temporal tables, along with an offsite cryptographic attestation feature, which gives you a transparent layer of tamper evidence for sensitive data without requiring changes to your applications.

Ledger does not *prevent* database tampering; rather, it provides *evidence* that tampering has occurred. You should use the ledger feature in combination with other security and auditing features as part of your defense-in-depth strategy.

Ledger generates a SHA-256 hash of modified rows for each transaction, and these hashes are combined with previous hashes to form a chain of dependent hashes known as a *blockchain*. A block of these hashes is called a *database digest*, which is a cryptographic hash that represents the state of the database at the time hash was computed. Database digests combine to form a *database ledger*.

Immutable storage

Although these hashes are stored internally, they must also be copied and stored outside the database in tamper-proof storage so you can compare the state of the database at a point in time with a known external hash value. The ledger feature pushes database digests to immutable storage when a block is closed, and these digests can be sent offsite to Azure Blob Storage or on-premises to an Azure confidential ledger or third-party immutable storage device. You choose the external storage when setting up the ledger feature.

A block is closed after 30 seconds, or when 100,000 transactions have occurred, whichever happens sooner. You can also manually trigger this event using the sys.sp_generate_database_ledger_digest stored procedure.

Ledger verification

To verify whether tampering has occurred, the external database digest can be compared against the hashes stored in the database. During the ledger verification process, all hashes are recalculated using the sys.sp_verify_database_ledger_from_digest_storage stored procedure. Depending on the size of the database and the number of transactions, this can take a significant amount of time.

If any data has been tampered with, these recomputed hashes will not match the database digests stored in the external database ledger. This proves that tampering has occurred. You can then use additional auditing methods to identify when and how the tampering occurred.

Inside OUT

What does "tampering" mean?

SQL Server uses transactions to ensure consistency in a database, meaning that every modification is atomic, consistent, isolated, and durable (the ACID compliance model). An attacker might tamper with the database files—for example, by directly modifying the underlying pages with a hex editor or re-creating a table or even an entire database with an entirely new history to replace the original. This type of tampering would not be evident unless an external digest is kept separate from the attacker.

Ledger considerations and limitations

The external database ledger must be placed in secure, tamper-proof storage, with different permissions and access levels than your database administrators. An attacker with access to both the SQL Server instance and the external database ledger can bypass any system checks and render the protections useless.

Updateable ledger tables are fully compatible with system-generated temporal tables.

➤ You can read more about temporal tables in Chapter 7, "Understand table features," in the section "Special table types."

NOTE

You cannot use an existing history table when enabling the ledger feature on an updateable ledger table.

Data storage requirements

Ledger is based on the same underlying technology as temporal tables. Depending on the type of ledger table used, you might need to monitor your database storage usage closely. An append-only ledger table will not permit the deletion of rows, while an updateable ledger table must maintain a full history of database modifications. In both these types of ledger tables, the metadata columns require storage as well.

Once you enable the ledger feature for a table, you cannot disable it. For practical reasons, this means you can't delete data from your database while the ledger feature is enabled. Enabling the ledger feature for an entire database is not recommended. You should restrict usage to sensitive data only.

You can define a custom history table when creating an updateable ledger table as long as it mirrors the schema of the ledger table. You can create the history table in its own schema, which means it can be stored in a separate filegroup. You can also enable data compression on this history table. Keep in mind, though, that not all data types compress well.

➤ **For more information about the types of data compression, see Chapter 3.**

Types of ledger tables

There are two types of ledger tables:

- Append-only tables

- Updateable ledger tables

A history table is also created for updateable ledger tables. You cannot modify the schema of a ledger table.

As with temporal tables, a ledger table needs two GENERATED ALWAYS columns to represent when data was created and the sequence in which it occurred. However, because the ledger feature operates at the transactional level, these columns store *transaction* information instead of dates and times. You can choose your own names for the GENERATED ALWAYS columns when creating a new ledger table or when altering an existing table to enable the ledger feature. For updateable ledger tables, there are two additional columns that store when a row version was deleted and the sequence in which it occurred.

Append-only ledger table

As the name implies, you cannot delete rows from append-only ledger tables. This type of table is useful for security event information and system logs. Because it only allows INSERT operations, an append-only ledger table doesn't have a history table.

The system-generated names for the GENERATED ALWAYS columns are as follows, and are used for transaction information about when the row version was generated:

- `ledger_start_transaction_id (bigint)`

- `ledger_start_sequence_number (bigint)`

Updateable ledger table

Updateable ledger tables work in much the same way as temporal tables, providing a history of changes to the table, and have the same schema as the ledger table. As noted in the "Data storage requirements" section, you can store the history in a different filegroup with its own storage if you choose to define the history table yourself.

The system-generated names for the GENERATED ALWAYS columns are as follows, and are used for transaction information about when the row version was generated or modified.

- ledger_start_transaction_id (bigint)

- ledger_end_transaction_id (bigint)

- ledger_start_sequence_number (bigint)

- ledger_end_sequence_number (bigint)

Although similar in some respects, temporal tables and ledger tables provide different querying features, so you can create an updateable ledger table that is also a temporal table. Take care with your storage requirements if you choose this combination, however, because the history must be retained in two separate history tables.

➤ For more information about updateable ledger tables, see *https://learn.microsoft.com/sql /relational-databases/security/ledger/ledger-updatable-ledger-tables*.

The following CREATE TABLE script demonstrates the creation of an updateable ledger table with an anonymous (system-generated) history table. The use of LEDGER = ON is for illustration purposes because each table in a ledger table is updateable by default.

```
CREATE TABLE dbo.Products (
    ProductId INT NOT NULL PRIMARY KEY CLUSTERED
    , ProductName VARCHAR(50) NOT NULL
    , CategoryId INT NOT NULL
    , SalesPrice MONEY NOT NULL
)
    WITH (
    SYSTEM_VERSIONING = ON,
    LEDGER = ON
);
```

Ledger view

For every table on which you enable the ledger feature, the database creates a ledger view, which shows all the rows that were created and/or modified and the sequence in which these changes took place. You can customize the names of the columns in the ledger view if you want, but if you don't, these are the system-generated names.

- **ledger_transaction_id (bigint).** This column displays the ID of the transaction for the creation or modification of a row in the ledger table, and references the ledger_start_ transaction_id and ledger_end_transaction_id values.

- **ledger_sequence_number (bigint).** This column displays the sequence number in which the creation and/or modification took place. This references the ledger_start_ sequence_number and ledger_end_sequence_number values in the ledger table.

- **ledger_operation_type (tinyint).** This column displays 1 for insert operations or 2 for delete operations. Modifying a row in the ledger table generates a delete operation followed by an insert operation.

- **ledger_operation_type_desc (nvarchar(128)).** This column displays a text value for the ledger_operation_type, which will either be INSERT or DELETE.

The ledger_operation_type and ledger_operation_type_desc columns have limited use in append-only ledger tables, and are there for consistency with updateable ledger table views.

Find the names of system-generated ledger objects

If you don't choose custom values for the names of the ledger history table and ledger view, you can use the following query to return the names of the system-generated objects:

```
SELECT ts.[name] + '.' + t.[name] AS [ledger_table]
    , hs.[name] + '.' + h.[name] AS [history_table]
    , vs.[name] + '.' + v.[name] AS [ledger_view]
FROM sys.tables AS t
INNER JOIN sys.tables AS h ON h.object_id = t.history_table_id
INNER JOIN sys.views v ON v.object_id = t.ledger_view_id
INNER JOIN sys.schemas ts ON ts.schema_id = t.schema_id
INNER JOIN sys.schemas hs ON hs.schema_id = h.schema_id
INNER JOIN sys.schemas vs ON vs.schema_id = v.schema_id;
GO
```

Audit with SQL Server and Azure SQL Database

Auditing is the act of tracking and recording events that occur in the Database Engine. Since SQL Server 2016 with Service Pack 1, the SQL Server Audit feature is available in all editions, as well as in Azure SQL Database.

➤ Chapter 17 covers configuring auditing in Azure SQL Database in depth.

SQL Server Audit

There is a lot going on in the Database Engine. SQL Server Audit uses Extended Events to give you the ability to track and record those actions at both the instance and database level.

NOTE

Although Extended Events carry minimal overhead, it is important that you carefully balance auditing against performance impact. Use targeted auditing by capturing only those events that are necessary to fulfill your audit requirements.

➤ You can read more about Extended Events in Chapter 8.

Audits are logged to event logs or audit files. An event is initiated and logged every time the audit action is encountered, but for performance reasons, the audit target is written to asynchronously. The permissions required for SQL Server auditing are complex and varied because of the different requirements for reading from and writing to the Windows event log, the file system, and SQL Server itself.

Requirements for creating an audit

To keep track of events (called *actions*), you must define a collection, or *audit*. The actions you want to track are collected according to an *audit specification*. Recording those actions is done by the *target* (destination). The following list explains these terms in more depth:

- **Audit.** The SQL Server audit object is a collection of server or database actions (which might also be grouped together). Defining an audit creates it in the *off* state. After it is enabled, the destination receives the data from the audit.

- **Server audit specification.** This audit object defines the actions to collect at the instance level or database level (for all databases on the instance). You can have multiple server audits per instance.

- **Database audit specification.** You can monitor audit events and audit action groups. Only one database audit can be created per database per audit. Server-scoped objects must not be monitored in a database audit specification.

- **Target.** You can send audit results to the Windows Security event log, the Windows Application event log, or an audit file on the file system. You must ensure there is always sufficient space for the target. If you are using the Windows Application event log, keep in mind that the permissions required to read the Windows Application event log are lower than those required to read the Windows Security event log.

An audit specification can be created only if an audit already exists.

➤ To read more about audit action groups and audit actions, visit *https://learn.microsoft.com/sql /relational-databases/security/auditing/sql-server-audit-action-groups-and-actions*.

Inside OUT

What if an audit shuts down the instance or prevents SQL Server from starting?

SQL Server can be shut down by a failure in the audit. If it does, you will find an entry in the log saying MSG_AUDIT_FORCED_SHUTDOWN. You can start SQL Server in single-user mode using the -m option at the command line, which writes an entry to the log saying MSG_AUDIT_SHUTDOWN_BYPASSED.

An audit initiation failure also can prevent SQL Server from starting. In this case, you can use the -f command line option to start SQL Server with minimal configuration (which is also single-user mode). In minimal configuration or single-user mode, you can then remove the offending audit that caused the failure.

Creating a server audit in SQL Server Management Studio (SSMS)

Verify that you are connected to the correct instance in SSMS. Then, in **Object Explorer**, expand the **Security** folder. Next, right-click the **Audits** folder and select **New Audit** on the shortcut menu that opens.

The **Create Audit** dialog box opens. (See Figure 13-2.) You can configure the settings to your requirements or leave the defaults as is. Just be sure to enter a valid file path if you select **File** in the **Audit Destination** list box. We also recommend that you choose an appropriate name to enter into the **Audit Name** box (the default name is based on the current date and time).

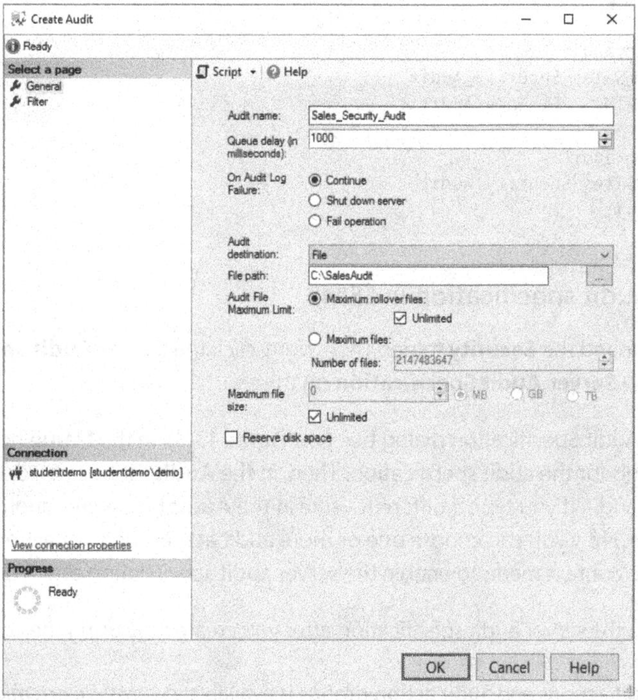

Figure 13-2 Creating an audit in SSMS.

Remember to enable the audit after it is created. It will appear in the **Audit** folder, which is inside the **Security** folder in Object Explorer. To do so, right-click the newly created audit and select **Enable Audit** on the shortcut menu.

Create a server audit using T-SQL

The server audit creation process can be quite complex, depending on the destination, file options, audit options, and predicates. As demonstrated in the preceding section, you can use SSMS to configure a new audit and create a script of the settings before selecting **OK** to produce a T-SQL script. You can also do this manually.

> ➤ To read more about creating a server audit in T-SQL, visit *https://learn.microsoft.com/sql/t-sql /statements/create-server-audit-transact-sql*.

To create a server audit in T-SQL, verify that you are connected to the appropriate instance. Then run the following code sample, changing the audit name and file path as needed. Note that this code also sets the audit state to ON; it is created in the OFF state by default. Also, this audit will not have any effect until an audit specification and target are also created.

```
USE master;
GO
-- Create the server audit.
CREATE SERVER AUDIT Sales_Security_Audit
    TO FILE (FILEPATH = 'C:\SalesAudit');
GO
-- Enable the server audit.
ALTER SERVER AUDIT Sales_Security_Audit
    WITH (STATE = ON);
GO
```

Create a server audit specification in SSMS

In Object Explorer, expand the **Security** folder. Then, right-click the **Server Audit Specification** folder and select **New Server Audit Specification** on the shortcut menu.

In the Create Server Audit Specification dialog box (see Figure 13-3), in the **Name** box, type a name of your choosing for the audit specification. Then, in the **Audit** list box, select the previously created server audit. If you type a different value in the **Audit** box, a new audit will be created by that name. Now you can choose one or more audit actions or audit action groups. Remember to use the context menu to enable the server audit specification after you create it.

Remember to turn on the server audit specification after you create it by using the context menu.

> ➤ A full list of audit actions and audit action groups is available at *https://learn.microsoft.com /sql/relational-databases/security/auditing/sql-server-audit-action-groups-and-actions*.

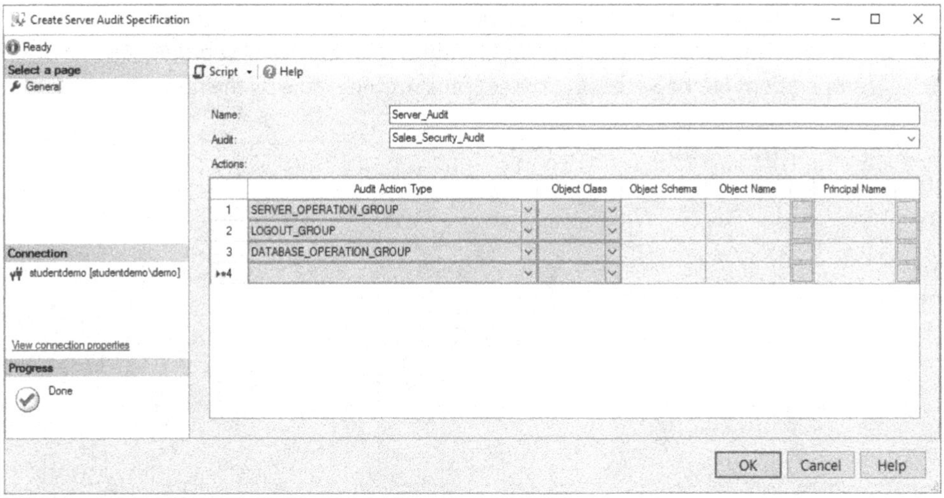

Figure 13-3 Creating a server audit specification in SSMS.

NOTE

If you have selected an audit group action, you cannot select Object Class, Object Schema, Object Name, or Principal Name, because the group represents multiple actions.

Create a server audit specification using T-SQL

In much the same way you create the audit itself, you can create a script of the configuration from a dialog box in SSMS or you can do it manually, as shown in the following script. Note that the server audit specification refers to a previously created audit.

```
USE [master];
GO
-- Create the server audit specification.
CREATE SERVER AUDIT SPECIFICATION Server_Audit
FOR SERVER AUDIT Sales_Security_Audit
    ADD (SERVER_OPERATION_GROUP),
    ADD (LOGOUT_GROUP),
    ADD (DATABASE_OPERATION_GROUP)
WITH (STATE = ON);
GO
```

Creating a database audit specification with SSMS

As you would expect, the location of the database audit specification is under the database security context.

In Object Explorer, expand the database on which you want to perform auditing, and then expand the **Security** folder. Then right-click the **Database Audit Specifications** folder and select **New Database Audit Specification** in the shortcut menu. Remember again to use the context menu to turn it on. Figure 13-4 shows an example of capturing SELECT and INSERT operations on the Sales.CustomerTransactions table by the dbo user.

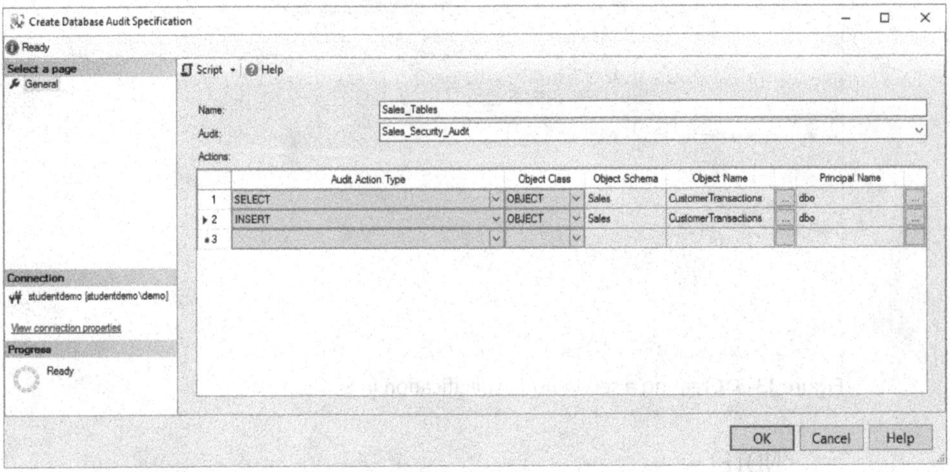

Figure 13-4 Creating a database audit specification in SSMS.

Creating a database audit specification with T-SQL

Again, verify that you are in the correct database context. Then create the database audit specification by referring to the server audit that was previously created. Next, specify which database actions you want to monitor, as demonstrated in the following code. The destination is already specified in the server audit, so as soon as this is enabled, the destination will begin logging the events as expected.

```
USE WideWorldImporters;
GO
-- Create the database audit specification.
CREATE DATABASE AUDIT SPECIFICATION Sales_Tables
    FOR SERVER AUDIT Sales_Security_Audit
    ADD (SELECT, INSERT ON Sales.CustomerTransactions BY dbo)
    WITH (STATE = ON);
GO
```

Viewing an audit log

You can view audit logs in SSMS or in the Security Log in the Windows Event Viewer. This section describes how to do it using SSMS.

> **NOTE**
>
> To view audit logs, you must have CONTROL SERVER permission.

In Object Explorer, expand the **Security** folder, and then expand the **Audits** folder. Then, right-click the audit log you want to view and select **View Audit Logs** on the shortcut menu.

Figure 13-5 shows two audit events that have been logged, with the Event Time showing the most recent events first. In the first event (second row), the audit itself has been changed (it was enabled). The second event is a SELECT statement that was run against the table specified in the database audit specification example presented earlier. Note that the Event Time is in UTC format. This is to avoid issues regarding time zones and daylight saving time.

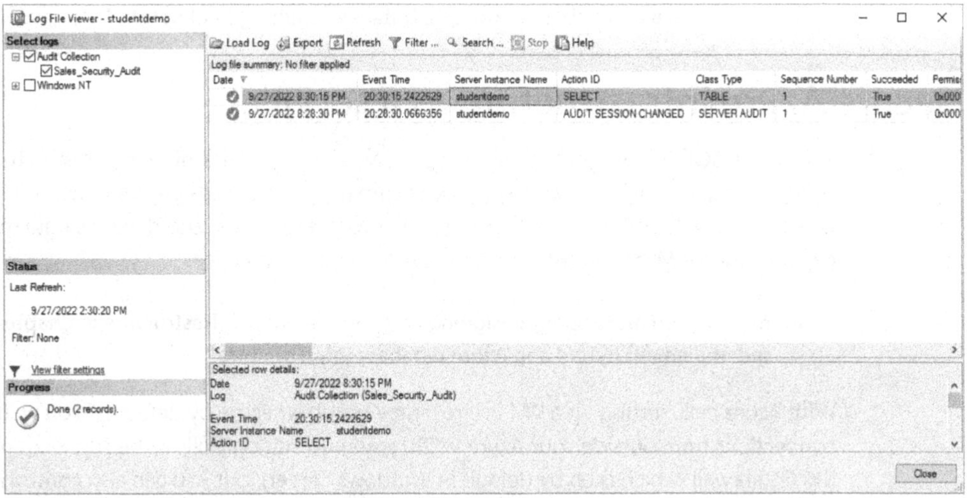

Figure 13-5 File Viewer dialog box for viewing a SQL Server audit.

There are many columns in the audit that you cannot see in Figure 13-5. Notable among them are Server Principal ID (SPID), Session Server Principal Name (the logged-in user), and Statement (the command that was run). The point here is that you can capture a wealth of information.

> **NOTE**
>
> You can also view the audit log in an automated manner using the built-in T-SQL system function sys.fn_get_audit_file, though the data is not formatted the same way as it is through the File Viewer in SSMS. For more information, see *https://learn.microsoft.com /sql/relational-databases/system-functions/sys-fn-get-audit-file-transact-sql.*

Auditing with Azure SQL

With Azure SQL Database and Azure SQL Managed Instance auditing, you can track database activity and write it to an audit log in a storage container in your Azure Storage account. (You are charged for storage accordingly.) This helps you to remain compliant with auditing regulations as well as to see anomalies to gain greater insight into your Azure SQL environment, as discussed earlier in the section "Protect Azure SQL Database with Microsoft Defender for SQL."

Auditing enables you to retain an audit trail, report on activity in each database, and analyze reports, which include trend analysis and security-related events. You can also define server-level and database-level policies. Server policies automatically cover new and existing databases.

If you enable server auditing, that policy applies to any databases on the server. Thus, if you also enable database auditing for a particular database, that database will be audited by both policies. You should avoid this unless retention periods are different or you want to audit for different event types.

> ➤ You can read more about Azure SQL Database auditing in Chapter 17.

Secure Azure infrastructure as a service

You secure SQL Server running on an Azure VM, which is an example of infrastructure as a service (IaaS), in much the same way you secure the on-premises product. Depending on the edition, you can use TDE, Always Encrypted, row-level security, and dynamic data masking. You can also enable Microsoft Defender for SQL for an additional fee.

> ➤ You can read more about designing an Azure database infrastructure in Chapter 16, "Design and implement hybrid and Azure database infrastructure."

With Azure IaaS, setting up a VM in a resource group is secure by default. If you want to allow connections from outside your Azure VNet, you must not only allow the connection through the OS firewall (which is on by default in Windows Server), but you can also control connections through a network security group (NSG). In addition, you can control access through a network appliance such as a firewall or NAT device. This provides finer-grained control over the flow of network traffic in your VNet, which is needed to set up Azure ExpressRoute, for example.

Network security groups

A network security group (NSG) controls the flow of traffic in and out of the entirety (or part) of an Azure VNet subnet.

Inside OUT

What is a subnet?

A subnet, short for *subnetwork*, is a logical separation of a larger network into smaller sections, making the network easier to manage and secure. Subnetting can be complex and is beyond the scope of this book. If you are subnetting yourself, there are subnet calculators online to which you should refer. Because Azure VNets use subnets, this is a high-level overview.

Subnets are identified by a *network ID*, which is rendered in *network prefix notation* (also known as *Classless Inter-Domain Routing*, or *CIDR*). You will recognize this as a network address in IPv4 format followed by a slash and a decimal value—for example /8, /16, /24, and so on. This suffix is confusingly known as the network *prefix*. The lower (shorter) the prefix, the more addresses are available.

This is a shorthand for the IP addresses that are available in that subnet, with the network address as the starting value. For example, 192.168.1.0/24 means there are 256 possible addresses, starting at 192.168.1.1, up to and including 192.168.1.254. All subnets reserve the first address (in this case, 192.168.1.0) for the network identifier, and the last address (in this case, 192.168.1.255) for the broadcast address.

An NSG provides security for an entire subnet by default, which affects all the resources in that subnet (see Figure 13-6). If you require more control, you can associate the NSG with an individual network interface card (NIC), thus further restricting traffic.

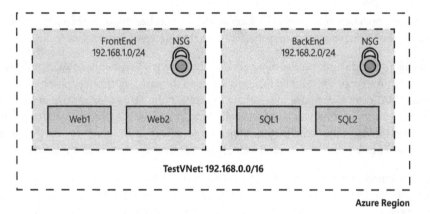

Figure 13-6 A typical VNet, with each subnet secured by an NSG.

NOTE

When you create a VM using Azure Resource Manager, it comes with at least one virtual NIC, which you manage through an NSG. This is important, because individual NICs can belong to different NSGs, which provides finer control over the flow of network traffic on individual VMs.

As with typical firewalls, the NSG has rules for incoming and outgoing traffic. When a packet hits a port on the VNet or subnet, the NSG intercepts the packet and checks whether it matches one of the rules. If the packet does not qualify for processing, it is discarded (dropped).

Rules are classified according to source address (or range) and destination address (or range). Depending on the direction of traffic, the source address can refer to inside the network or outside, on the public Internet.

This becomes cumbersome with more complex networks, so to simplify administration and provide flexibility, you can use service tags to define rules by service name instead of IP address. You can also use default categories—namely `VirtualNetwork` (the IP range of all addresses in the network), `AzureLoadBalancer` (the Azure infrastructure load balancer), and `Internet` (the IP addresses outside the range of the Azure VNet).

> ➤ You can read more about Azure VNet security and get a full list of service tags at *https:// learn.microsoft.com/azure/virtual-network/security-overview*.

User-defined routes and IP forwarding

As a convenience for Azure customers, all VMs in an Azure VNet can communicate with one another by default, irrespective of the subnet in which they reside. This also holds true for VNets connected to your on-premises network by a VPN and for Azure VMs communicating with the public Internet (including those running SQL Server).

In a traditional network, communication across subnets like this requires a gateway to control (route) the traffic. Azure provides these system routes for you automatically.

You might decide that this free-for-all communication is against your network policy and that all traffic from your VMs should first be channeled through a network appliance such as a firewall or NAT device. Virtual appliances are available in the Azure Marketplace at an additional cost, or you could configure a VM yourself to run as a firewall. A user-defined route with IP forwarding facilitates this. With a user-defined route, you create a subnet for the virtual appliance and force traffic from your existing subnets or VMs through the virtual appliance.

You must enable IP forwarding for the VM for that VM to receive traffic addressed to other destinations. This is an Azure setting, not a setting in the guest OS. (See *https://learn.microsoft.com /azure/virtual-network/virtual-network-scenario-udr-gw-nva*.) You might also need to enable IP forwarding in the VM itself in certain circumstances.

CAUTION

With user-defined routes, you cannot control how traffic *enters* the network from the public Internet. User-defined routes only control how traffic *leaves* a subnet. This means that your virtual appliance must be in its own subnet. If you want to control traffic flow from the public Internet as it enters a subnet, use an NSG.

Until you create a routing table (by user-defined route), subnets in your VNet rely on system routes. A user-defined route adds another entry in the routing table, so a technique called *longest prefix match* (*LPM*) kicks in to decide which is the better route to take by selecting the most specific route (the one with the longest prefix). As you saw in Figure 13-6, a /24 prefix is longer than a /16 prefix, and a route entry with a higher prefix takes precedence.

If two entries have the same LPM match, the order of precedence is as follows:

- User-defined route

- BGP route

- System route

Remember BGP? It's used for ExpressRoute. ExpressRoute is a VPN service by which you can connect your Azure VNet to your on-premises network, without going over the public Internet. You can specify BGP routes to direct traffic between your network and the Azure VNet.

Additional Azure networking security features

There are additional features worth discussing here to improve the management and security of an Azure VNet as it relates to SQL Server or Azure SQL Database.

VNet service endpoints

Service endpoints make it possible for you to restrict access to certain Azure services that were traditionally open to the public Internet so they are available only to your Azure VNet. (See Figure 13-7.)

Configurable through the Azure portal, PowerShell, or the Azure CLI, you can block public Internet access to your Azure Storage and Azure SQL Database resources. Additional service endpoints are available, and more will be introduced in the future.

> ➤ To read more about VNet service endpoints, visit *https://learn.microsoft.com/azure/virtual -network/virtual-network-service-endpoints-overview.*

Distributed-denial-of-service protection

Azure provides protection against distributed-denial-of-service (DDoS) attacks for VNets. This is helpful, given that attacks against publicly accessible resources are increasing in number and complexity.

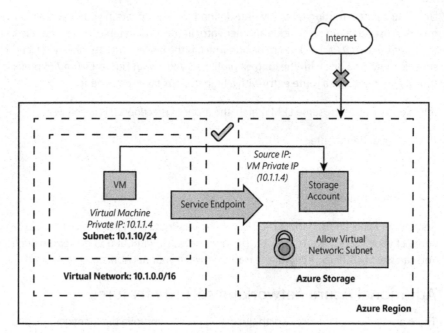

Figure 13-7 A service endpoint protecting an Azure Storage account.

The basic service included in your subscription provides real-time protection using the scale and capacity of the Azure infrastructure to mitigate attacks (see Figure 13-8). For an additional cost, you can take advantage of built-in machine learning algorithms to protect against targeted attacks, with added configuration, alerting, and telemetry.

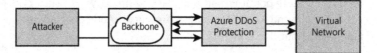

Figure 13-8 Azure DDoS protection defending a VNet against attacks.

You can also use the Azure Application Gateway web application firewall to protect against more sophisticated attacks. Combined with Azure SQL Database auditing and NSGs, these features provide a comprehensive suite of protection from the latest threats.

> ➤ To read more about Azure DDoS protection, see *https://azure.microsoft.com/services /ddos-protection*.

Performance tune SQL Server

This chapter reviews the database concepts and objects most associated with tuning the performance of queries and coded objects within the Database Engine for SQL Server, Azure SQL Database, and Azure SQL Managed Instance. Much of this content also applies to dedicated SQL pools in Azure Synapse Analytics, though that product is not a focus of this book.

The first two sections of this chapter look at isolation levels and durability, including the ACID properties of a relational database management system (RDBMS). These correspond to settings and configurations that affect performance.

As you might have learned in an introductory database class, ACID properties are as follows:

- **Atomicity.** A transaction is committed as an all or nothing operation and cannot leave the database in an incomplete state.

- **Consistency.** A transaction brings the entire database from one state to another—not just a shard of a database.

- **Isolation.** Transactions, though handled concurrently, are processed sequentially and independently. Incomplete transactions should not be visible to other transactions.

- **Durability.** In the event of hardware failure, committed data survives. The data must exist in non-volatile memory.

It's important to understand the principals of ACID not just from an academic or theoretical standpoint. Various features of modern database systems violate ACID principles in creative and advantageous ways to increase performance. You should be aware of the tradeoffs. For example:

- Globally scalable databases like Azure Cosmos DB violate *consistency* in important, controlled, and well-documented ways. The database systems behind many global websites rely on *eventual* consistency. This is typically a design decision related to the application architecture from inception. For more about consistency, refer to Chapter 7, "Understand table features."

- If you want a data layer without *isolation*, try designing a multiuser application to write data to a flat file, where there is no serialization of concurrent writers. Similarly, the READ UNCOMMITTED isolation level in SQL Server violates isolation, allowing the changes of an uncommitted transaction to be read.

- SQL Server's in-memory OLTP functionality, introduced in SQL Server 2014, can be configured to violate *durability*. Similarly, data changes cached by applications in memory, but not immediately committed to the database, violate Durability.

This chapter covers various features that tweak SQL Server defaults to improve performance for certain scenarios. It is important to understand both your application performance needs and how SQL Server features and configuration options can meet them.

It also explores the process of how SQL Server executes queries, including the execution plans that the query processor creates to execute your query. It discusses how execution plans are captured, analyzed, reported on, and manipulated by the Query Store feature. It covers execution plans in some detail, what to look for when performance tuning, and how to control when query execution plans go parallel, meaning SQL Server can use multiple processors to execute your query without the code changing at all.

Inside OUT

Is this all there is to performance tuning?

Entire books have been written on this topic! We can't go into that degree of detail in a single chapter, but we do provide a deep-enough discussion to jumpstart and accelerate your learning on SQL Server performance tuning, especially in the role of an administrator. This includes the newest features added in SQL Server 2022, of which some are quite amazing, and many of which leverage the rich query history data collected by the Query Store.

Optimizing queries is not the ultimate solution to every performance issue. Look for opportunities to make changes in tables (better data types, indexes, partitions) as well as data architectures. Consider the use of PolyBase to read data in place, in its native source, as opposed to ETL solutions that copy data into SQL Server.

The Query Store in particular has a powerful payload of new features in SQL Server 2022. Both Microsoft and the authors of this book recommend enabling and configuring Query Store on all databases. In fact, Query Store will be enabled by default on new databases in SQL Server 2022, and this change has come to Azure SQL Database as well.

Some of SQL Server 2022's best new performance features require Query Store to be enabled in each database. Look into new passive features like degree of parallelism (DOP) feedback, cardinality estimation (CE) feedback, and new interactive features like Query Store hints.

One of the best new features of SQL Server 2022 is Parameter Sensitive Plan (PSP) optimization, which attempts to all but solve the problem of bad execution plans due to parameter sniffing. PSP optimization doesn't require Query Store to be enabled, only that you are in database compatibility level 160.

Performance tuning can be a daunting task as organizations want to process more and more data, but Microsoft is adding new features to the product in every version.

The examples in this chapter behave identically in SQL Server instances and databases in Azure SQL Managed Instance and Azure SQL Database unless otherwise noted. All sample scripts in this book are available for download at *https://MicrosoftPressStore.com/SQLServer2022InsideOut/downloads*.

Understand isolation levels and concurrency

When working on a multiuser system, the fundamental problem is how to handle scenarios in which users need to read and write the same data, concurrently. So, if there is a row—say row X—and user 1 and user 2 both want to do something with this row, what are the rules of engagement? If both users want to read the row, one set of concerns exists. If one user wants to read the row and the other wants to write to it, this is another set of issues. Finally, if both users want to write to the row, still another set of concerns arises. This is where the concept of isolation comes in, including how to isolate one connection from the other.

This is all related to the concept of atomicity, and as such, to transactions containing one or more statements, because we need to isolate logical atomic operations from one another. Even a single statement in a declarative programming system like Transact-SQL (T-SQL) can result in hundreds and thousands of steps behind the scenes.

Isolation isn't only a matter of physical access to resources (a disk drive is fetching data from a row, so the next reader must wait for that to complete). This is a different problem for the hardware. Instead, while one transaction is doing its operations, other transactions need to be just as isolated from the data the user has affected. The performance implications are large, because the more isolated the operations need to be, the slower processing must be. However, the freer and less isolated transactions are, the greater the chance for loss of data.

Here are some the phenomena that can occur between two transactions:

- **Dirty read.** Reading data that another connection is in the process of changing. The problem is much like trying to read a paper note that someone else is scribbling on. You might see an incomplete message, or even see words that the writer will scratch out in the future.

- **Non-repeatable read.** Reading the same data over again that has changed or gone away. This problem is like when you open a box of doughnuts and see there is one left. While you are standing there, in control of the box, no one can take that last doughnut. But step away to get coffee, and when you come back, that doughnut might have a bite taken out of it. A repeatable read always gives you back rows with the same content as you first read (but might include more rows that did not exist when you first read them).

- **Phantom read.** When you read a set of data, but then come back and read it again and get new rows that did not previously exist. In the previous doughnut example, this is the happiest day of your life, because there are now more doughnuts. However, this can be bad if your query needs to get back the same answer every time you ask the same question.

- **Reading a previously committed version of data.** In some cases, you might be able to eliminate blocking by allowing connections to read a previously committed version of data that another connection is in the process of changing after your transaction started. A real-world example of this regularly happens in personal banking. You and your partner see you have $50 in your account, and you both attempt to withdraw $50, not realizing the intentions of the other. Without transaction serialization and a fresh version of the row containing your balance, your ATM might even say you have $0 after both transactions, using stale information. This does not change the cruel overdraft fees you will be receiving, of course.

Where this gets complicated is that many operations in a database system are bundled into multistep operations that need to be treated as one atomic operation. Reading data and getting back different results when executing the same query again, during what you expect to be an atomic operation, greatly increases the likelihood of returning incorrect results.

These phenomena can be understood by how they are bundled by the *isolation levels* that allow them to occur. For example, the default isolation level, READ COMMITTED, is subject to nonrepeatable reads and phantom rows, but not dirty reads. This provides adequate protection and performance in most situations, but not all.

You need a fundamental understanding of these effects. These aren't just arcane keywords you study only when it is certification time; they can have a profound effect on application performance, stability, and—absolutely the most important thing for any RDBMS—data integrity.

For example, suppose you are writing software to control trains using track A. Two trains traveling in opposite directions need to use track A, so both conductors ask if the track is vacant, and are assured that it is. So, both put their trains on the track heading toward each other. Not good.

Understanding the differing impact of isolation levels on locking and blocking, and therefore on concurrency, is the key to understanding when you should use an isolation level different from the default of READ COMMITTED. Table 14-1 presents the isolation levels available in the Database Engine along with the phenomena that are possible in each.

Table 14-1 Isolation levels and phenomena that can be incurred

Isolation level	Dirty reads	Nonrepeatable reads	Phantom rows	Reading a previously committed version of data
READ UNCOMMITTED	X	X	X	
READ COMMITTED		X	X	
REPEATABLE READ			X	
SERIALIZABLE				
READ COMMITTED SNAPSHOT (RCSI)		X	X	X
SNAPSHOT				X

Inside OUT

Should you always just use SERIALIZABLE *to be safe?*

At this point in the process, it probably seems like you should protect your data with the SERIALIZABLE isolation level in every case. Safety first, right? However, this approach hinders performance. It's a bit like wearing a full-body enclosure explosive ordnance disposal suit to mow your lawn.

Most real-world scenarios you deal with will not require strict isolation between connections. In fact, the SQL Server default READ COMMITTED isolation level will suffice for many applications.

However, software development frameworks do take a "safety first" approach, including using SERIALIZABLE by default. For example, the .NET System.Transactions infrastructure creates Serializable isolation level transactions by *default*. While safe, as we detail in this chapter, in many application scenarios you can understandably achieve far greater scalability and performance with virtually no danger by stepping IsolationLevel to RepeatableRead or ReadCommitted.

➤ For more information, see *https://learn.microsoft.com/dotnet/api/system.transactions .isolationlevel*.

When you choose an isolation level for a transaction in an application, you should consider primarily the transactional safety and business requirements of the transaction in a highly concurrent multiuser environment. The performance of the transaction should be a distant second priority (yet still a priority) when choosing an isolation level.

Locking, which SQL Server uses for the normal isolation of processes, is not the issue. It is the way that every transaction in SQL Server cooperates with others when dealing with disk-based tables.

The default isolation level of READ COMMITTED is generally safe because it only allows connection to access data that has been committed by other transactions. Dirty reads are generally the only modification phenomenon that is almost universally bad. With READ COMMITTED, modifications to a row will block reads from other connections to that same row. This is especially important during multi-statement transactions, such as when parent and child rows in a foreign key relationship must be created in the same transaction. In that scenario, reads should not access either row in either table until both changes are updated.

Since the READ COMMITTED isolation level allows non-repeatable reads and phantom rows, it does not ensure that row data and row count won't change between two SELECT queries on the same data in a transaction. READ COMMITTED isolation levels allow SQL Server to release locks from objects it has read and lets other users have any access, holding only locks on resources that it has changed.

For some application scenarios, this might be acceptable or even desired, but not for others. To avoid these two problematic scenarios (which we talk more about soon), you need to choose the proper, more stringent isolation level for the transaction.

For scenarios in which transactions must have a higher degree of isolation from other transactions, escalating the isolation level of a transaction is appropriate. For example, if a transaction must write multiple rows, even in multiple tables and statements, it cannot allow other transactions to change data it has read during the transaction, where escalating the isolation level of a transaction is appropriate.

For example, the REPEATABLE READ isolation level blocks other transactions from changing or deleting rows needed during a multistep transaction. Unlike READ COMMITTED, REPEATABLE READ has the effect of holding locks on resources and preventing any other readers from changing them until it has completed, thus avoiding non-repeatable reads.

If the transaction in this example needs to ensure that the same exact rows in a result set are returned throughout a multistep transaction, the SERIALIZABLE isolation is necessary. It is the only isolation level that prevents other transactions from inserting new rows inside of a range of rows. It prevents other connections from adding new rows by not only locking rows it has accessed, but also ranges of rows that it would have accessed had they existed. For example, say you queried for rows LIKE 'A%' in a SERIALIZABLE transaction and got back Apple and Annie. If another user tries to insert Aardvark, it is prevented until the LIKE 'A%' transaction is completed.

Lastly, it is essential to understand that every statement is a transaction. UPDATE TableName SET column = 1; operates in a transaction, as does a statement like SELECT 1;. When you do not manually start a transaction, it is referred to as an *implicit* transaction. An *explicit* transaction is one where you start with BEGIN TRANSACTION and end with COMMIT TRANSACTION or

ROLLBACK TRANSACTION. The REPEATABLE READ and SERIALIZABLE isolation levels can gather a lot of locks, more so with explicit transactions of multiple statements, if they are not quickly closed. The more locks are present, the more likely your connection might be stuck indefinitely waiting or participate in a deadlock where one session must be terminated.

➤ For more on monitoring database locking and blocking, see Chapter 8, "Maintain and monitor SQL Server."

Inside OUT

When blocked, do your connections wait indefinitely? Can you control this?

By default, the timeout for a request being blocked in SQL Server is indefinite, and it is rarely set to anything different. This is not to be confused with an application connection provider that implements a timeout limitation. Applications that time out are receiving an application-layer timeout, not a timeout from the Database Engine.

You can determine the current setting of the lock timeout using the global variable @@LOCK _TIMEOUT. The default is -1, indicating there is no limit to the time a request will wait if blocked by another request's locks. When the value is positive, and a connection waits on a lock longer than the timeout, error 1222 is raised, with the following message: "Lock request time out period exceeded. The statement has been terminated." This is different from the timeout error generated by an application connection provider, which is just a duration of execution.

You can change the SQL Server timeout from the default *for the current session* by using the following statement,

```
SET LOCK_TIMEOUT n;
```

where n is the number of milliseconds before a request is cancelled by SQL Server. This might be handy in niche scenarios—perhaps when queries execute in a loop and regularly poll a table for reporting, or for first-in, first out (FIFO) or last-in, first-out (LIFO) purposes. Many business processes use FIFO queues. For example, fast food restaurants process tickets more or less sequentially, or FIFO, as food orders arrive.

Take caution in implementing this change to SQL Server's default lock timeout. Try to first understand the cause of the blocking. If you change the lock timeout in code, ensure that any applications creating the sessions are prepared to handle the errors gracefully. Similar to deadlock detection, applications should detect these errors and automatically retry.

SQL Server does have a configuration setting for a timeout for outgoing remote connections called Remote Query Timeout, which defaults to 600 seconds. This timeout applies only to connections to remote data providers, not to requests run on the SQL Server instance. It specifies the number of seconds that the query can execute, not how long it can be blocked, before it is terminated.

The most complex of the phenomena concerns reading data that is not the committed version that was initially accessed. There are two main places where this becomes an issue.

- **Reading previous versions of data.** When you use SNAPSHOT or READ COMMITTED SNAPSHOT (RCSI), your query will see how data looked when first accessed within the transaction. This means the data later in the transaction might not match the current state of the database.

  A side effect of this is that in SNAPSHOT isolation level, if two transactions try to modify or delete the same row, you will get an update conflict, requiring you to restart the transaction.

- **Reading new versions of data.** In any isolation level that allows phantoms and non-repeatable reads, running the same statement twice can return entirely different results. This becomes important in multistep transactions with multiple SELECT statements that access the same data. This might be desirable or problematic; the application developer should understand the difference.

Isolation levels are important to understand. It can be tricky to test your code to see what happens when two connections simultaneously try to make incompatible reads and modifications to data. Mature application performance testing always incorporates simulated concurrent users' sessions accessing the same data.

Understand how concurrent sessions become blocked

This section reviews a series of examples of how concurrency works in a multiuser application interacting with SQL Server tables. First, it discusses how to diagnose whether a request is being blocked or if it is blocking another request. Note that these initial examples assume that SQL Server has been configured in the default manner for concurrency. We will adjust that later in this chapter to give you more ways to tune performance.

What causes blocking?

We have alluded to it already, and the answer is that when you use resources, they are locked. These locks can be on several different levels and types of resources, as seen in Table 14-2.

Table 14-2   Lockable resources (not every type of resource)

Type of Lock	Granularity
Row or row identifier (RID)	A single row in a heap (a table without a clustered index).
Key	A single value in an index. (A table with a clustered index is represented as an index in all physical structures.)
Key range	A range of key values (for example, to lock rows with values from A–M, even if no rows currently exist). Used for SERIALIZABLE isolation level.

Type of Lock	Granularity
Extent	A contiguous group of eight 8-KB pages.
Page	An 8-KB index or data page.
HoBT	An entire heap or B-tree structure.
Object	An entire table (including all rows and indexes), view, function, stored procedure, and so on.
Application	A special type of lock that is user-defined.
Metadata	Metadata about the schema, such as catalog objects.
Database	An entire database.
Allocation unit	A set of related pages that are used as a unit.
File	A data or log file in the database.

Locks on a given resource are of a mode. Table 14-3 lists the modes that a data object might be in. Two of the most important ones are shared (indicating a row is being read only) and exclusive (indicating a row should not be accessible by any other connection.)

Table 14-3 Lock modes

Lock Mode	Definition
Shared	Grants access for reads only. This mode is generally used when users are looking at but not editing data. It's called "shared" because multiple processes can have a shared lock on the same resource, allowing read-only access. However, sharing resources prevents other processes from modifying the resource.
Exclusive	Gives exclusive access to a resource and is also used during data modification. Only one process might have an active exclusive lock on a resource.
Update	Used to inform other processes that you're planning to modify the data. Other connections might also issue shared locks, but not update or exclusive locks, while you're still preparing to do the modification. Update locks are used to prevent deadlocks (covered later in this section) by marking rows that a statement will possibly update rather than upgrading directly from a shared lock to an exclusive one.
Intent	Communicates to other processes that taking one of the previously listed modes might be necessary. It establishes a lock hierarchy with existing locks. You might see this mode as intent shared, intent exclusive, or shared with intent exclusive.
Schema	Used to lock the structure of a resource when it's in use so you cannot alter a structure (like a table) when a user is reading data from it. (Schema locks show up as part of the mode in many views.)

As queries are performing different operations, such as querying data, modifying data, or changing objects, resources are locked in a given mode. Blocking comes when one connection has a resource locked in a certain mode, and another connection needs to lock a resource in an incompatible mode. You can see the compatibility of different modes in Table 14-4.

NOTE

To read this table, pick the lock mode in one axis; an X will be displayed in any compatible column in the other axis. For example, an update lock is compatible with an intent shared and a shared lock, but not with another update lock, or any of the exclusive variants.

Table 14-4   Lock modes and compatibility

Mode	IS	S	U	IX	SIX	X
Intent shared (IS)	X	X	X	X	X	
Shared (S)	X	X	X			
Update (U)	X	X				
Intent exclusive (IX)	X					
Shared intent exclusive (SIX)		X				
Exclusive (X)						

If a connection is reading data, it will take a shared lock, allowing other readers to also take a shared lock, which will not cause a blocked situation. However, if another connection is modifying data, it will get an exclusive lock, which will prevent the connection (and any other connections) from accessing the exclusively locked resources in any manner (other than ignoring the locks, discussed later in this section).

How to observe locks and blocking

You can find out in real time whether a request is being blocked. The dynamic management object (DMO) sys.dm_db_requests, when combined with sys.dm_db_sessions on the session_id column, provides data about blocking and the state of sessions on the server. This provides much more information than the legacy sp_who or sp_who2 commands, as you can see in this query:

```
--This query will return a plethora of information
--in addition to just the session that is blocked
SELECT r.session_id, r.blocking_session_id, *
FROM sys.dm_exec_sessions s
LEFT OUTER JOIN sys.dm_exec_requests r ON r.session_id = s.session_id;
--note: requests represent actions that are executing, sessions are connections,
--hence LEFT OUTER JOIN
```

You can see details of what objects are locked by using the sys.dm_tran_locks DMO, or what locks are involved in blocking by using this query:

```
SELECT
        t1.resource_type,
        t1.resource_database_id,
        t1.resource_associated_entity_id,
        t1.request_mode,
        t1.request_session_id,
```

```
        t2.blocking_session_id
FROM sys.dm_tran_locks as t1
INNER JOIN sys.dm_os_waiting_tasks as t2
    ON t1.lock_owner_address = t2.resource_address;
```

The output of this query reveals the type of resource that is locked (listed in Table 14-3) and the mode listed in Table 14-4, with a few exceptions.

➤ **You can find more details about locks and** `sys.dm_tran_locks` **at** *https://learn.microsoft .com/sql/relational-databases/system-dynamic-management-views/sys-dm-tran-locks -transact-sql.*

Now, let's review some scenarios to detail exactly why and how requests can block one another in the real world when using disk-based tables. This is the foundation of concurrency in SQL Server and helps you understand why the NOLOCK query hint appears to make queries perform faster.

Change the isolation level

As mentioned, by default, connections use the READ COMMITTED isolation level. If you need to change that for a session, there are two methods: using the SET TRANSACTION ISOLATION LEVEL statement and using hints. In this manner, the isolation level can be changed for an entire transaction, one statement, or one object in a statement.

Use the SET TRANSACTION ISOLATION LEVEL statement

You can change the isolation level of a connection any time, even when already executing in the context of a transaction that is uncommitted. You are not allowed to swap to and from the SNAPSHOT isolation level because, as we'll discuss later in this chapter, this isolation level works very differently.

For example, the following code snippet is technically valid to change from READ COMMITTED to SERIALIZABLE isolation levels. If one statement in your batch required the protection of SERIALIZABLE, but not others, you can execute:

```
SET TRANSACTION ISOLATION LEVEL READ COMMITTED;
BEGIN TRAN;
SET TRANSACTION ISOLATION LEVEL SERIALIZABLE;
SELECT...;
SET TRANSACTION ISOLATION LEVEL READ COMMITTED;
COMMIT TRAN;
```

This code snippet is trying to change from the READ COMMITTED isolation level to the SNAPSHOT isolation level:

```
SET TRANSACTION ISOLATION LEVEL READ COMMITTED;
BEGIN TRAN;
SET TRANSACTION ISOLATION LEVEL SNAPSHOT;
SELECT...
```

CHAPTER 14

Attempting this results in the following error:

```
Msg 3951, Level 16, State 1, Line 4
Transaction failed in database 'databasename' because the statement was run under
snapshot isolation but the transaction did not start in snapshot isolation. You cannot
change the isolation level of the transaction after the transaction has started.
```

In .NET applications, you should change the isolation level of each transaction when it is created, as it might not be in READ COMMITTED by default, which offers far better performance.

Use table hints to change isolation

You also can use isolation level hints to change the isolation level at the individual object level. This is an advanced type of coding that you shouldn't use frequently, because it generally increases the complexity of maintenance and muddies architectural decisions with respect to concurrency. Just as in the previous session, however, you might want to hold locks at a SERIALIZABLE level for one table but not others in the query. For example, you might have seen developers use NOLOCK at the end of a table, effectively (and dangerously) dropping access to that table into the READ UNCOMMITTED isolation level:

```
SELECT col1 FROM dbo.Table (NOLOCK);
```

> ### NOTE
> Aside from the inadvisable use of NOLOCK in the preceding example, using a table hint without WITH is deprecated syntax (since SQL Server 2008). It should be written like this, if you need to ignore locks:
>
> ```
> SELECT col1 FROM dbo.TableName WITH (READUNCOMMITTED);
> ```

In addition to the (generally undesirable) NOLOCK query hint, there are 20-plus other table hints that can be useful, including the ability for a query to use a certain index, to force a seek or scan on an index, or to override the Query Optimizer's locking strategy. We discuss how to use UPDLOCK later in this chapter—for example, to force the use of the SERIALIZABLE isolation level.

In almost every case, table hints should be considered for temporary and/or highly situational purposes. Table hints can make maintenance of these queries problematic, and could even cause surprise errors in the future. For example, using the INDEX or FORCESEEK table hint could result in poor query performance or even cause the query to fail if the table's indexes are changed.

> ➤ For detailed information on all possible table hints, see *https://learn.microsoft.com/sql/t-sql/queries/hints-transact-sql-table*.

Inside OUT

What value is the READPAST *table hint for concurrency?*

Isolation is generally a matter of keeping one connection from corrupting or seeing another connection's changes. Sometimes though, you might want to just get any row (or rows) that no other user has a hold on. READPAST is a table hint, not an isolation level, that will allow you to return only the rows that meet a filter condition without becoming blocked.

READPAST can be useful in very specific circumstances, limited to when there are SQL Server tables used as a stack or queue, with a loose FIFO architecture. READPAST allows a query to ignore rows that are currently being locked—it skips them. User transactions can fetch the first row in the stack that isn't locked in an incompatible lock mode.

The process typically works like this: Each process looks for rows that need attention, and updates one row that it will work on, claiming and locking it from other processes. Now, other READPAST processes can't read that row, but they can claim and update the next row. When they are complete with the task, they update the row with a status of done, so the next user doesn't see that row when reading from the stack. In this way, a multithreaded process that is regularly selecting rows from a table can afford to skip the rows currently being worked on, and read them on the next pass.

Outside these limited scenarios, READPAST is not appropriate because it will likely return *incomplete* data.

Understand and handle common concurrency scenarios

Here we look at some common concurrency scenarios and discuss and demonstrate how SQL Server processes the rows affected by the scenario.

NOTE

Chapter 7 covers memory-optimized tables. Their concurrency model is very different from disk-based tables, though similar to how row-versioned concurrency is implemented, particularly the SNAPSHOT isolation level. The differences for memory-optimized tables are discussed later in this chapter.

Understand two requests updating the same rows

Two users attempting to modify the same resource is possibly the most obvious concurrency issue. As an example, suppose one user wants to add $100 to a total, and another wants to add

$50. If both processes happen simultaneously, only one row may be modified—or if we take it to the absurd extreme, data corruption could occur to the physical structures holding the data if pointers are mixed up by multiple modifications.

Consider the following steps involving two writes, with each transaction coming from a different session. The transactions are explicitly declared using the BEGIN/COMMIT TRANSACTION syntax. In this example, the transactions use the default isolation level READ COMMITTED.

All examples have these two rows, simply so it isn't just a single row—though we do only manipulate the row where Type = 1. When testing more complex concurrency scenarios, it is best to have large quantities of data to work with, as indexing, server resources, and so on do come into play. These examples illustrate fundamental concurrency examples.

1. A table contains only two rows with a column Type containing values of 0 and 1.

```
CREATE SCHEMA Demo;
GO
CREATE TABLE Demo.RC_Test (Type int);
INSERT INTO Demo.RC_Test VALUES (0),(1);
```

2. Transaction 1 begins and updates all rows from Type = 1 to Type = 2.

```
--Transaction 1
SET TRANSACTION ISOLATION LEVEL READ COMMITTED;
BEGIN TRANSACTION;
UPDATE Demo.RC_Test SET Type = 2
WHERE  Type = 1;
```

3. Before transaction 1 commits, transaction 2 begins, and issues a statement to update Type = 2 to Type = 3. Transaction 2 is blocked and waits for transaction 1 to commit.

```
--Transaction 2
SET TRANSACTION ISOLATION LEVEL READ COMMITTED;
UPDATE Demo.RC_Test SET Type = 3
WHERE  Type = 2;
```

4. Transaction 1 commits.

```
--Transaction 1
COMMIT;
```

5. Transaction 2 is no longer blocked and processes its update statement. Transaction 2 then commits.

The resulting table will contain a row of Type = 3, and one of Type = 0, as the second transaction will have updated the row after the block was ended. This is because when transaction 2 started, it waited for the exclusive lock to be removed after transaction 1 committed.

Inside OUT

When two users try to update the same data, which connection's changes are actually saved?

Consider the case where two SQL Server sessions start transactions, read in the same row, then try to update the same row simultaneously. The reads can be done simultaneously, but one update is blocked until the other completes. Then the second update executes and completes, potentially overwriting the changes from the first update (assuming they are updating the same columns).

This is what is known as a *lost update* problem. In the default isolation level of READ COMMITTED, the rows would be overwritten. Using REPEATABLE READ, the second transactions would be unable to change the data the other connection had read in, preventing lost data but causing a deadlock.

To avoid this, consider making UPDATE statements *idempotent*. This is a rather academic term that nonetheless is important to know. Idempotent describes functions that only take effect once, and are harmless if executed more than once. For example:

```
UPDATE dbo.Employee
SET Salary = Salary * 1.05
WHERE EmployeeID = 5;
```

The previous query is not idempotent. Execution of the previous UPDATE statement would increase salary by 5 percent each time it is executed. The following statement *is* idempotent, and is safer to execute because it changes data only once, and only for the intended original state of the row. If executed again, the UPDATE statement would safely affect 0 rows.

```
UPDATE dbo.Employee
SET Salary = Salary * 1.05
WHERE EmployeeID = 5 and Salary = 100000;
```

The previous query is idempotent, and safer to execute.

CHAPTER 14

Understand how a write blocks a read

One of the most painful parts of blocking comes when users are trying to write data that other users are blocked from reading. What can even be more problematic is that some modification statements actually lock rows in the table even if they don't make any changes (typically due to poorly written WHERE clauses or a lack of indexing causing full table scans).

Consider the following steps involving a write and a read, with each transaction coming from a different session. In this scenario, an uncommitted write in transaction 1 blocks a read in transaction 2. The transactions are explicitly started using the BEGIN/COMMIT TRANSACTION syntax. In this example, the transactions do not override the default isolation level of READ COMMITTED:

1. A table with a column Type contains only two rows, with values of 0 and 1.

    ```
    CREATE SCHEMA Demo AUTHORIZATION dbo;
    CREATE TABLE Demo.RC_Test_Write_V_Read (Type int);
    INSERT INTO Demo.RC_Test_Write_V_Read VALUES (0),(1);
    ```

2. Transaction 1 begins and updates rows with Type = 1 to Type = 2.

    ```
    --Transaction 1
    SET TRANSACTION ISOLATION LEVEL READ COMMITTED;
    BEGIN TRANSACTION;
    UPDATE Demo.RC_Test_Write_V_Read SET Type = 2
    WHERE  Type = 1;
    ```

    Note that transaction 1 has not committed or rolled back.

3. Before transaction 1 commits, in another session, transaction 2 begins and issues a SELECT statement for rows WHERE Type = 2. Transaction 2 is blocked and waits for transaction 1 to commit.

    ```
    --Transaction 2
    SET TRANSACTION ISOLATION LEVEL READ COMMITTED;
    SELECT Type
    FROM   Demo.RC_Test_Write_V_Read
    WHERE  Type = 2;
    ```

4. Transaction 1 commits.

    ```
    --Transaction 1
    COMMIT;
    ```

5. Transaction 2 is no longer blocked and processes its SELECT statement.

6. Transaction 2 returns one row where Type = 2. This is because when transaction 2 started, it saw only one row where Type = 2, but still waited for committed data until after transaction 1 committed.

Understand nonrepeatable reads

There are certain scenarios where you need to have the same row values returned every time you issue a SELECT statement, or read data in any data manipulation language (DML). A prime example is the case where you look for the existence of some data before allowing some other action to occur. For example: Insert an order row, but only if a payment exists. If that payment is changed or deleted while you are creating the order, free products might be shipped!

Consider the following steps involving a read and a write. In this example, the transactions do not override the default isolation level of READ COMMITTED, and each transaction is started from a different session. The transactions are explicitly declared using the BEGIN/COMMIT TRANSACTION syntax. In this scenario, transaction 1 will suffer a nonrepeatable read when it reads rows that are changed by a different connection because the default READ COMMITTED does not offer any protection against phantom or nonrepeatable reads.

1. A table contains only two rows with a column Type value of 0 and 1.

```
CREATE TABLE Demo.RR_Test (Type int);
INSERT INTO Demo.RR_Test VALUES (0),(1);
```

2. Transaction 1 starts and retrieves rows where Type = 1. One row is returned for Type = 1.

```
--Transaction 1
SET TRANSACTION ISOLATION LEVEL READ COMMITTED
BEGIN TRANSACTION
SELECT Type
FROM   Demo.RR_Test
WHERE  Type = 1;
```

3. Before transaction 1 commits, transaction 2 starts and issues an UPDATE statement, setting rows of Type = 1 to Type = 2. Transaction 2 is not blocked and is immediately processed.

```
--Transaction 2
BEGIN TRANSACTION;
SET TRANSACTION ISOLATION LEVEL READ COMMITTED
UPDATE Demo.RR_Test
SET  Type = 2
WHERE Type = 1;
```

4. Transaction 1 again selects rows where Type = 1 and is blocked.

```
--Transaction 1
SELECT Type
FROM   Demo.RR_Test
WHERE  Type = 1;
```

5. Transaction 2 commits.

```
--Transaction 2
COMMIT;
```

6. Transaction 1 is immediately unblocked. No rows are returned, because no committed rows now exist where Type = 1. Transaction 1 commits.

```
--Transaction 1
COMMIT;
```

The result set from transaction 1 contains a row where Type = 2, because the second transaction has modified the row. When transaction 2 started, transaction 1 had not placed any locks on the data, allowing for writes to happen. Because it is doing only reads, transaction 1 does not place exclusive locks on the data. Transaction 1 suffered from a nonrepeatable read: The same SELECT statement returned different data during the same multistep transaction.

Inside OUT

Can the application efficiently verify data hasn't changed during a transaction?

For some scenarios, you might want to consider an additional application-based verification of data on top of the database's isolation protection. To ensure data hasn't changed during a transaction, add a column of type rowversion, which changes each time the row is changed.

When the application fetches data and eventually updates a row, the application should remember the initial value of the rowversion column, and later include the rowversion column value in the filter of the eventual update. If it doesn't match, the row must have changed during your transaction, so the update will affect zero rows. (See the Inside OUT earlier in this chapter about idempotency.) When the application detects zero row updates, it should prompt the user with the latest data.

Prevent a nonrepeatable read

Consider the following steps involving a read and a write, with each transaction coming from a different session. This time, we protect transaction 1 from dirty reads and nonrepeatable reads by using the REPEATABLE READ isolation level. A read in the REPEATABLE READ isolation level will block a write. The transactions are explicitly declared using the BEGIN/COMMIT TRANSACTION syntax:

1. A table contains only rows with a column Type value of 0 and 1.

   ```
   CREATE TABLE Demo.RR_Test_Prevent (Type int);
   INSERT INTO Demo.RR_Test_Prevent VALUES (0),(1);
   ```

2. Transaction 1 starts and selects rows where Type = 1 in the REPEATABLE READ isolation level. One row with Type = 1 is returned.

   ```
   --Transaction 1
   SET TRANSACTION ISOLATION LEVEL REPEATABLE READ;
   BEGIN TRANSACTION;
   SELECT Type
   FROM   Demo.RR_Test_Prevent
   WHERE  TYPE = 1;
   ```

3. Before transaction 1 commits, transaction 2 starts and issues an UPDATE statement, setting rows of Type = 1 to Type = 2. Transaction 2 is blocked by transaction 1.

```
--Transaction 2
BEGIN TRANSACTION;
SET TRANSACTION ISOLATION LEVEL READ COMMITTED;
UPDATE Demo.RR_Test_Prevent
SET  Type = 2
WHERE Type = 1;
```

4. Transaction 1 again selects rows where Type = 1. The same rows are returned as in step 2.

5. Transaction 1 commits.

```
--Transaction 1
COMMIT TRANSACTION;
```

6. Transaction 2 is immediately unblocked and processes its update. Transaction 2 commits.

```
--Transaction 2
COMMIT TRANSACTION;
```

Transaction 1 returned the same rows each time and did not suffer a nonrepeatable read. The resulting table contains two rows, one where Type = 2, and the original row where Type = 0. This is because when transaction 2 started, transaction 1 had placed read locks on the data it was selecting, blocking writes until it committed. Transaction 2 processed its updates only when it could place exclusive locks on the rows it needed.

Understand phantom rows

Phantom rows cause issues for transactions when you expect the exact same result back from a query. Say you're writing a value to a table that sums up 100 other values (flaunting the fundamentals of database design's normalization rules!)—for example, a financial transactions ledger table that calculates the current balance. You sum the 100 rows, then write the value. If it is important that the total of the 100 rows matches perfectly, you cannot allow nonrepeatable reads or phantom rows.

Consider the following steps involving a read and a write, with each transaction coming from a different session. In this scenario, we describe a phantom read:

1. A table contains only two rows, with Type values 0 and 1.

```
CREATE TABLE Demo.PR_Test (Type int);
INSERT INTO Demo.PR_Test VALUES (0),(1);
```

2. Transaction 1 starts and selects rows where Type = 1 in the REPEATABLE READ isolation level. Rows are returned.

```
--Transaction 1
SET TRANSACTION ISOLATION LEVEL REPEATABLE READ;
```

```
BEGIN TRANSACTION;
SELECT Type
FROM    Demo.PR_Test
WHERE   Type = 1;
```

3. Before transaction 1 commits, transaction 2 starts and issues an INSERT statement, adding another row where Type = 1. Transaction 2 is not blocked by transaction 1.

```
--Transaction 2
SET TRANSACTION ISOLATION LEVEL READ COMMITTED;
INSERT INTO Demo.PR_Test(Type)
VALUES(1);
```

4. Transaction 1 again selects rows where Type = 1. An additional row is returned compared to the first time transaction 1 ran the SELECT.

```
--Transaction 1
SELECT Type
FROM    Demo.PR_Test
WHERE   Type = 1;
```

5. Transaction 1 commits.

```
--Transaction 1
COMMIT TRANSACTION;
```

Transaction 1 experienced a phantom read when it returned a different number of rows the second time it selected from the table inside the same transaction. Transaction 1 had not placed any locks on the range of data it needed, allowing for writes in another transaction to happen within the same dataset. The phantom read would have occurred to transaction 1 in any isolation level, except for SERIALIZABLE. Let's look at that next.

Prevent phantom reads

Consider the following steps involving a read and a write, with each transaction coming from a different session. In this scenario, we protect transaction 1 from a phantom read.

1. A table contains two rows with Type values of 0 and 1.

```
CREATE TABLE Demo.PR_Test_Prevent (Type int);
INSERT INTO Demo.PR_Test_Prevent VALUES (0),(1);
```

2. Transaction 1 starts and selects rows where Type = 1 in the SERIALIZABLE isolation level. The one row where Type = 1 is returned.

```
--Transaction 1
SET TRANSACTION ISOLATION LEVEL SERIALIZABLE;
BEGIN TRANSACTION;
SELECT Type
FROM    Demo.PR_Test_Prevent
WHERE   Type = 1;
```

3. Before transaction 1 commits, transaction 2 starts and issues an INSERT statement, adding a row of Type = 1. Transaction 2 is blocked by transaction 1.

    ```
    --Transaction 2
    SET TRANSACTION ISOLATION LEVEL READ COMMITTED;
    INSERT INTO Demo.PR_Test_Prevent(Type)
    VALUES(1);
    ```

4. Transaction 1 again selects rows where Type = 1. The same result set is returned as it was in step 2—the one row where Type = 1.

    ```
    --Transaction 1
    SELECT Type
    FROM   Demo.PR_Test_Prevent
    WHERE  Type = 1;
    ```

5. Transaction 1 executes COMMIT TRANSACTION.

    ```
    --Transaction 1
    COMMIT TRANSACTION;
    ```

6. Transaction 2 is immediately unblocked and processes its insert. Transaction 2 commits.

If you query the table again, you will see there are now two rows where Type = 1.

Transaction 1 did not suffer from a phantom read the second time it selected from the table because it had placed a lock on the range of rows it needed. The table now contains additional rows where Type = 1, but they were not inserted until after transaction 1 had committed.

The case against the READ UNCOMMITTED isolation level

If locks take time, ignoring those locks will make things go faster. While this is true, the tradeoffs are often not worth it.

NOTE

This section also pertains to using the NOLOCK hint on your queries.

Locks coordinate our access to resources, allowing multiple users to do multiple things in the database without crushing the other users' changes. The READ COMMITTED isolation level (and an extension we will discuss in the section on the SNAPSHOT isolation level called READ COMMITTED SNAPSHOT) does the best to balance locks with performance. Locks are still held for dirty resources (exclusively locked data that has been changed by the user). But they are held only long enough to perform reads on a row and are then released after resources are read. The process is as follows:

1. Grab a lock on a resource.

2. Read that resource.

3. Release the lock on the resource.

4. Repeat until you are out of resources to read.

No one else can dirty (modify) the row we are reading because of the lock, but when we are done, we release the lock and move on. Locks on modifications to on-disk tables work the same way in all isolation levels, even READ UNCOMMITTED, and are held until the transaction is committed.

The effect of the NOLOCK table hint and the READ UNCOMMITTED isolation level is that no locks are taken inside the database for reads, save for schema stability locks. Though, a query using NOLOCK could still be blocked by data definition language (DDL) commands, such as an offline indexing operation. Put another way, if you enable the READ UNCOMMITTED isolation level for your connection, things will go faster.

This is a strategy that many DBA programmers have tried before: "We had performance problems, but we've been putting NOLOCK in all our stored procedures to fix it." It will improve performance, but it can easily be detrimental to the integrity of your data.

The biggest issue is that a query might be reading a set of data and see data that doesn't even meet the constraints of the system. So, if a transaction for $1,000,000 is in a query, and the transaction is later rolled back (perhaps because the payment details failed), who knows what celebratory alarms might have gone off, thinking we had $1,000,000 in sales today!

The case against using the READ UNCOMMITTED isolation level is deeper than performance and more than simply reading dirty data. A developer might argue that data is rarely ever rolled back, or that the data is for reporting only. In production environments, however, these are not enough to justify the potential problems.

A query in the READ UNCOMMITTED isolation level could return invalid data in the following real-world, provable ways:

●   Read uncommitted data (dirty reads).

●   Read committed data twice.

●   Skip committed data.

●   Return corrupted data.

●   The query could fail with the error "Could not continue scan with NOLOCK due to data movement." In this scenario, where you ignored locks, the data structure that was to be scanned now no longer exists because of other changes to data pages. The solution to this problem is the solution to a lot of concurrency issues: Be prepared to re-execute your batch on this failure.

One final caveat: In SQL Server, you cannot apply NOLOCK to tables when used in modification statements, and it ignores the declaration of the READ UNCOMMITTED isolation level in a batch that includes modification statements. For example:

```
INSERT INTO dbo.testnolock1 WITH (NOLOCK)
SELECT * FROM dbo.testnolock2;
```

SQL Server knows that it will use locks for the INSERT, and makes it clear by way of the following error being thrown:

```
Msg 1065, Level 15, State 1, Line 17
The NOLOCK and READUNCOMMITTED lock hints are not allowed for target tables of INSERT,
UPDATE, DELETE or MERGE statements.
```

However, this protection doesn't apply to the *source* of any writes, hence yet another danger. This following code *is allowed* and *is very dangerous* because it could write invalid, uncommitted data!

```
INSERT INTO testnolock1
SELECT * FROM testnolock2 WITH (NOLOCK);
```

In summary, don't use READ COMMITTED isolation level or NOLOCK unless you really understand the implications of reading dirty data and have an ironclad reason for doing so. For example, it is an invaluable tool as a DBA to be able to see the changes to data being made in another connection. For example,

```
SELECT COUNT(*) FROM dbo.TableName WITH (NOLOCK);
```

allows you to see the count of rows in dbo.TableName. However, using NOLOCK for performance gains is short-sighted.

Continue reading for the recommended ways to increase performance without the chance of seeing dirty data, as we introduce version-based concurrency in the next section.

Inside OUT

Which isolation level does your .NET application use?

By default, if the programmer has not changed any settings, the .NET System.Transaction infrastructure uses the SERIALIZABLE isolation level—the safest but least practical choice. SERIALIZABLE provides the most isolation for transactions, so by default .NET transactions do not suffer from dirty reads, nonrepeatable reads, or phantom rows.

You might find, however, that queries from your application using the SERIALIZABLE isolation level are frequently blocked or are the source of blocking, and that reducing the isolation of certain transactions results in better performance. Evaluate the potential risk of nonrepeatable reads and phantom rows for each new .NET transaction, and reduce the isolation level to REPEATABLE READ or READ COMMITTED only where appropriate. And, following guidance throughout this chapter, avoid the READ UNCOMMITTED isolation level in any production code unless you have a full understanding of why you are doing this.

For applications with high transactional volume, consider also using the SNAPSHOT isolation level to increase concurrency.

You can set the isolation level of any transaction when it is begun by setting the Isolation Level property of the TransactionScope class. You can also default a new database connection's isolation level upon creation. Remember, however, that you cannot change the isolation level of a transaction after it has begun.

Understand row version-based concurrency

In the interest of performance, application developers too often seek to solve concurrency concerns (reduce blocking, limit access to locked objects) by trying to avoid the problem with the tantalizingly named NOLOCK. The performance gains appear too large to consider other alternatives, since the problems we have mentioned only happen "occasionally," even if it takes 30 hours of meetings, coding, or testing to try to figure out the issues, because they seem random and non-repeatable.

A far safer option, without the significant drawbacks and potential for invalid data and errors, allows you to read a previously committed version of data using row-versioning techniques that give the user a view of a version of the data that was properly committed. This gives you tremendous gains, and never lets the user see dirty data.

Version-based concurrency is available in the SNAPSHOT isolation level or by altering the implementation of READ COMMITTED. This is often referred to as RCSI as a shortcut, even in this book, but it is not an isolation level. Rather, it is a setting at the database level.

Row versioning allows queries to read from rows locked by other queries by storing previous versions of a row, then reading those versions instead. The SQL Server instance's tempdb keeps a copy of committed data, which can be served up to concurrent requests. In this way, row versioning allows access only to committed data, without blocking access to data locked by writes. By increasing the workload of tempdb for disk-based tables, performance is dramatically improved. Row versioning increases concurrency without the dangers of accessing uncommitted data.

The SNAPSHOT isolation level works at the transaction level. Once you start a transaction and access any data in the transaction, such as the third statement in the following snippet,

```
ALTER DATABASE dbname SET ALLOW_SNAPSHOT_ISOLATION ON; -- required once
SET TRANSACTION ISOLATION LEVEL SNAPSHOT;
BEGIN TRANSACTION;
SELECT * FROM dbo.Table1;
--Don't forget to COMMIT or ROLLBACK this transaction
--if you execute this code with a real table
```

your queries will see a transactionally consistent view of the database. No matter what someone does to the data in dbo.Table1 (or any other table in the same database), you will always see how the data looked as of the start of the first statement executed in that database in your transaction (in this case the SELECT statement). This is great for some things, such as reporting. SNAPSHOT gives you the same level of consistency to the data you are reading as SERIALIZABLE, except that work can continue even while things are changing. It is not susceptible to nonrepeatable reads and phantom rows.

The SNAPSHOT isolation level can be problematic for certain types of code because if you need to check if a row exists to do some action, you can't see if the row was created or deleted after you started your transaction context. And as discussed, you can't switch out of SNAPSHOT temporarily, then apply locks to prevent non-repeatable reads, and go back to seeing a consistent, yet possibly expired, view of the database.

Access data in SNAPSHOT isolation level

The beauty of the SNAPSHOT isolation level is its effect on readers of the data. If you want to query the database, you generally want to see it in a consistent state, and you don't want to block others. A typical example is when you are writing an operational report. Suppose you query a child table and you get back 100 rows with distinct parentId values. But querying the parent table indicates there are only 50 parentId values (because between queries, another process deleted the other 50).

Consider the following steps involving a read and a write, with each transaction coming from a different session. In this scenario, we see that transaction 2 has access to previously committed row data, even though those rows are being updated concurrently.

1. A table contains only rows with a column Type value of 0 or 1.

    ```
    CREATE TABLE Demo.SS_Test (Type int);
    INSERT INTO Demo.SS_Test VALUES (0),(1);
    ```

2. Transaction 1 starts and updates rows where Type = 1 to Type = 2.

    ```
    --Transaction 1
    BEGIN TRANSACTION;
    SET TRANSACTION ISOLATION READ COMMITTED;
    ```

```
UPDATE Demo.SS_Test
SET  Type = 2
WHERE Type = 1;
```

3. Before transaction 1 commits, transaction 2 sets its session isolation level to SNAPSHOT and executes BEGIN TRANSACTION.

```
--Transaction 2
SET TRANSACTION ISOLATION LEVEL SNAPSHOT;
BEGIN TRANSACTION;
```

4. Transaction 2 issues a SELECT statement WHERE Type = 1. Transaction 2 is not blocked by transaction 1, a row where Type = 1 is returned.

```
--Transaction 2
SELECT Type
FROM  Demo.SS_Test
WHERE  Type = 1;
```

5. Transaction 1 executes a COMMIT TRANSACTION.

6. Transaction 2 again issues a SELECT statement WHERE Type = 1. The same rows from step 3 are returned. Even if the table has all its data deleted, the results will always be the same for the same query while in the SNAPSHOT level transaction. When transaction 2 is committed or rolled back, queries on that connection will see the changes that have occurred since the transaction started.

Transaction 2 was not blocked when it attempted to query rows that transaction 1 was updating. It had access to previously committed data, thanks to row versioning.

Implement row-versioned concurrency

You can implement row-versioned isolation levels in a database in two different ways:

- **Enabling SNAPSHOT isolation.** This simply allows for the use of SNAPSHOT isolation and begins the background process of row versioning.

- **Enabling RCSI.** This changes the default isolation level to READ COMMITTED SNAPSHOT.

You can implement both or either.

It's important now to introduce another fundamental database concept: pessimistic versus optimistic concurrency. Pessimistic concurrency uses locks to prevent write conflict errors. This is the approach SQL Server takes by default with the READ COMMITTED isolation level. Optimistic concurrency uses row versions with a tolerance for write conflict errors and requires sometimes sophisticated conflict resolution.

It's important to understand the differences between these two settings, because they are not the same:

- READ COMMITTED SNAPSHOT configures optimistic concurrency for reads by overriding the default isolation level of the database. When enabled, all queries will use RCSI unless overridden, not READ COMMITTED.

- SNAPSHOT isolation mode configures optimistic concurrency for reads and writes. You must then specify the SNAPSHOT isolation level for any transaction to use SNAPSHOT isolation level. It is possible to have update conflicts with SNAPSHOT isolation mode that will not occur with READ COMMITTED SNAPSHOT. Update conflicts are covered in the next section.

The statements to implement SNAPSHOT isolation in the database are not without consequence. Even if no transactions or statements use the SNAPSHOT isolation level, behind the scenes, tempdb begins storing row version data for disk-based tables, minimally for the length of the transaction that modifies the row. This way, if a row-versioned transaction starts while rows are being modified, the previous versions are available.

NOTE

Memory-optimized tables share properties with SNAPSHOT **isolation level but are implemented in an extremely different manner. They are based completely on row-versioning and do not use tempdb. Memory-optimized tables are further discussed in Chapter 15, "Understand and design indexes."**

The following code snippet allows all transactions in a database to start in the SNAPSHOT isolation level:

```
ALTER DATABASE databasename SET ALLOW_SNAPSHOT_ISOLATION ON;
```

After you execute only the preceding statement, all transactions will continue to use the default READ COMMITTED isolation level, but you now can specify the use of the SNAPSHOT isolation level at the session level or in table hints, as shown in the following example:

```
SET TRANSACTION ISOLATION LEVEL SNAPSHOT;
```

Using SNAPSHOT isolation level on an existing database can be a lot of work, and, as we discuss in the next section, it changes how we handle executing queries in some very important ways. Because of the optimistic locking approach, what once was write blocking becomes an error message for you to try again. Alternatively, if you want to apply the "go faster" solution that mostly works with existing code, you need to alter the meaning of READ COMMITTED to read row versions instead of waiting for locks to clear.

While SNAPSHOT isolation works at the transaction level, READ COMMITTED SNAPSHOT works at the statement level. You can use READ_COMMITTED_SNAPSHOT independently of

ALLOW_SNAPSHOT_ISOLATION. Similarly, these settings are not tied to the MEMORY_OPTIMIZED
_ELEVATE_TO_SNAPSHOT database setting to promote memory-optimized table access to
SNAPSHOT isolation.

Here's how to enable RCSI:

```
ALTER DATABASE databasename SET READ_COMMITTED_SNAPSHOT ON;
```

CAUTION

Changing the READ_COMMITTED_SNAPSHOT database option on a live database where
you have memory-optimized tables set to DURABILITY = SCHEMA_ONLY will empty
those tables. You need to move the contents of the table to a more durable table before
changing the state of READ_COMMITTED_SNAPSHOT.

➤ Chapter 7 discusses memory-optimized tables in greater detail.

For either of the previous ALTER DATABASE statements to succeed, no other transactions can
be open in the database. It might be necessary to close other connections manually or to put
the database in SINGLE_USER mode. Either way, we do not recommend that you perform this
change during production activity.

Inside OUT

If changing to RCSI is so much faster, why is this not the default?

Good question. READ COMMITTED remains the default in SQL Server and Azure SQL Managed
Instance. This has to do with historical precedent and stability of migrated workloads more
than anything.

However, in Azure SQL Database, read committed snapshot isolation (RCSI) *is* the default. It
can be reverted to READ COMMITTED, of course.

Designing new applications around a scalability boost like RCSI as an underlying assump-
tion can be smart. Be aware that enabling RCSI on a legacy application can be complex,
even if it is beneficial in the long run. The workload of tempdb will increase in RCSI compared to READ COMMITTED, potentially dramatically. You should test your full production
workload at scale with RCSI enabled before applying it to production.

It is essential to be aware and prepared for the increased activity in the tempdb database, both
in activity and space requirements. To avoid autogrowth events when enabling RCSI, increase
the size of the tempdb data and log files and monitor their size. Although you should try
to avoid autogrowth events by growing the tempdb data file(s) yourself, you should also

verify that your tempdb file autogrowth settings are appropriate in case things grow larger than expected.

➤ **For more information on file autogrowth settings, see Chapter 8.**

If tempdb exhausts all available space on its volume, SQL Server will be unable to row-version rows for transactions and will terminate them with SQL Server error 3958. You can find these in the SQL Server Error Log. (Refer to Chapter 1, "Get started with SQL Server tools.") SQL Server will also issue errors 3967 and 3966 as the oldest row versions are removed from tempdb to make room for new row versions needed by newer transactions.

NOTE

Before SQL Server 2016, the READ COMMITTED SNAPSHOT **and** SNAPSHOT **isolation levels were not supported with columnstore indexes. Beginning with SQL Server 2016,** SNAPSHOT **isolation and columnstore indexes are fully compatible.**

Understand update operations in the SNAPSHOT isolation level

Transactions that read data in SNAPSHOT isolation or RCSI have access to previously committed data—instead of being blocked—when data needed is being changed. This is important to understand and could result in an UPDATE statement experiencing a concurrency error when you start to change data. Update conflicts change how systems behave; you need to understand this concept before deciding to implement your code in the SNAPSHOT isolation level.

When modifying data in the SNAPSHOT isolation level, you can only have one dirty version of a physical resource. So, if another connection modifies a row and you only read the row, you see previous versions. But if you change a row that another connection has also modified, your update was based on out of data information and will be rolled back.

For example, consider the following steps, with each transaction coming from a different session. In this example, transaction 2 fails due to a concurrency conflict, or *write-write error*.

1. A table contains multiple rows, each with a unique Type value.

    ```
    CREATE TABLE Demo.SS_Update_Test
    (Type int CONSTRAINT PKSS_Update_Test PRIMARY KEY,
     Value nvarchar(10));
    INSERT INTO Demo.SS_Update_Test VALUES (0,'Zero'),(1,'One'),(2,'Two'),(3,'Three');
    ```

2. Transaction 1 begins a transaction in the READ COMMITTED isolation level and performs an update on the row where ID = 1.

    ```
    --Transaction 1
    BEGIN TRANSACTION ;
    UPDATE Demo.SS_Update_Test
    SET  Value = 'Won'
    WHERE Type = 1;
    ```

3. Transaction 2 sets its session isolation level to SNAPSHOT and issues a statement to update the row where ID = 1. This connection is blocked, waiting for the modification locks to clear.

```
--Transaction 2
SET TRANSACTION ISOLATION LEVEL SNAPSHOT;
BEGIN TRANSACTION
UPDATE Demo.SS_Update_Test
SET Value = 'Wun'
WHERE Type = 1;
```

4. Transaction 1 commits using a COMMIT TRANSACTION statement. Transaction 1's update succeeds.

5. Transaction 2 immediately fails with error 3960:

```
Msg 3960, Level 16, State 2, Line 8
Snapshot isolation transaction aborted due to update conflict. You cannot use
snapshot isolation to access table 'dbo.AnyTable' directly or indirectly in
database 'DatabaseName' to update, delete, or insert the row that has been
modified or deleted by another transaction. Retry the transaction or change
the isolation level for the update/delete statement.
```

Transaction 2 was rolled back. Let's try to understand why this error occurred, what to do about it, and how to prevent it.

NOTE

The SNAPSHOT isolation level with disk-based tables in SQL Server is not pure row-versioned concurrency, which is why in the previous example, transaction 2 was blocked by transaction 1. Using memory-optimized tables, which are based on pure row-versioned concurrency, the transaction would have failed immediately rather than being blocked. In either case, your application must have automated retry logic to gracefully handle update conflict errors.

In SQL Server, SNAPSHOT isolation uses locks to create blocking, but it doesn't prevent updates from colliding for disk-based tables. It is possible for a statement to fail when committing changes from an UPDATE statement if another transaction has changed the data needed for an update during a transaction in SNAPSHOT isolation level.

For disk-based tables, the update conflict error will look like error 3960, which we saw a moment ago. For queries on memory-optimized tables, the update conflict error will look like this:

```
Msg 41302, Level 16, State 110, Line 8
The current transaction attempted to update a record that has been updated since this
transaction started. The transaction was aborted.
```

If you decide to use SNAPSHOT as your modification query's isolation level, you must be ready to handle an error that isn't really an error; rather, it's just warning to re-execute your statements after checking to see if anything has changed since you started your query. This is the same when handling deadlock conditions, and will be the same for handling all modification conflicts using memory-optimized tables.

Inside OUT

How can developers implement application retry logic?

There are many options available to handle retry patterns and transient faults, especially important in SNAPSHOT isolation environments, but also in Azure and cloud distributed environments where transient network errors must be anticipated.

One way developers might implement this is via `Microsoft.Data.SqlClient`, which introduced configurable retry logic in version 3. The retry logic can be configured through code or app configs.

➤ For more information, see *https://learn.microsoft.com/sql/connect/ado-net/configurable-retry-logic* and *https://learn.microsoft.com/azure/azure-sql/database/troubleshoot-common-connectivity-issues.*

Even though optimistic concurrency of the SNAPSHOT isolation level increases the potential for update conflicts, you can mitigate these by doing the following to specifically attempt to avoid update conflicts:

- Minimize the length of transactions that modify data. While it seems like this would be less of an issue because readers aren't blocked, long-running transactions increase the likelihood of modification conflicts. Also, tempdb needs to keep track of more row versions.

- When running a modification in SNAPSHOT isolation level, avoid using statements that place update locks on disk-based tables inside multistep explicit transactions.

- Specify the UPDLOCK table hint to prevent update conflict errors for long-running SELECT statements. UPDLOCK places locks on rows needed for the multistep transaction to complete. The use of UPDLOCK on SELECT statements with SNAPSHOT isolation level is not a panacea for update conflicts, however, and it could in fact create them. For example, frequent SELECT statements with UPDLOCK could increase the number of update conflicts. Regardless, your application must handle errors and initiate retries when appropriate.

NOTE

If two concurrent statements use UPDLOCK, with one updating and one reading the same data, even in implicit transactions, an update conflict failure is possible if not likely.

- Consider avoiding writes altogether while in SNAPSHOT isolation mode. Use it only to do reads where you do not plan to write the data in the same transaction you have fetched it in.

Specifying table granularity hints such as ROWLOCK or TABLOCK can prevent update conflicts, although at the cost of concurrency. The second update transaction must be blocked while

CHAPTER 14

the first update transaction is running—essentially bypassing SNAPSHOT isolation for the write. If two concurrent statements are both updating the same data in SNAPSHOT isolation level, an update conflict failure is likely for the statement that started second.

Understand on-disk versus memory-optimized concurrency

Queries using memory-optimized tables (also referred to as in-memory OLTP tables) can perform significantly faster than queries based on the same data in disk-based tables. Memory-optimized tables can improve the performance of frequently written-to tables by up to 40 times over disk-based tables.

However, this almost magical performance improvement comes at a price—not just in the need for extra memory, but also, the way memory-optimized tables implement concurrency controls is different from disk-based tables. In the concurrency scenarios previously introduced, all the concurrency protections provided were based on locking—in other words, waiting until the other connection completed, and then applying the changes. However, locking applies only to on-disk tables, not memory-optimized tables.

With memory-optimized tables, locking isn't the mechanism that ensures isolation. Instead, the in-memory engine uses pure row versioning to provide row content to each transaction. In pure row versioning, an UPDATE statement inserts a new row and updates the effective ending time-stamp on the previous row. A DELETE statement only updates the effective ending timestamp on the current row. If you are familiar with the data warehousing concept of a *slowly changing dimension* (SCD), this is similar to an SCD type 2. It is equally similar to how temporal tables work, though both the current and historical data are in the same physical structure.

> ➤ For more explanation of temporal tables, see Chapter 7.

Previous versions hang around as long as they are needed by transactions and are then cleaned up. Data is also hardened to what is referred to as the *delta file* for durability purposes, as well as the transaction log.

If two transactions attempt to modify the same physical data resource at the same time, one transaction will immediately fail due to a concurrency error rather than being blocked and wait-ing. Only one transaction can be in the process of modifying or removing simultaneously. The other will fail with a concurrency conflict (SQL error 41302). However, if two transactions insert the same value for the primary key, an error will not be returned until the transaction is commit-ted, as it is not the same physical resource.

This is the key difference between the behavior of pessimistic and optimistic concurrency. Pes-simistic concurrency uses locks to prevent write conflict errors, whereas optimistic concurrency uses row versions with acceptable risk of write conflict errors. On-disk tables offer isolation levels that use pessimistic concurrency to block conflicting transactions, forcing them to wait. Memory-optimized tables offer optimistic concurrency that will cause a conflicting transaction to fail.

Memory-optimized tables allow you to use SNAPSHOT, REPEATABLE READ, and SERIALIZABLE isolation levels, and provide the same types of protections. In the case of a nonrepeatable read, SQL error 41305 is raised. In the case of a phantom read, a SQL error 41325 is raised. Because of these errors, applications that write to memory-optimized tables must include logic that gracefully handles and automatically retries transactions. They should already handle and retry in the case of deadlocks or other fatal database errors.

Understand memory-optimized data and isolation

All data read by a statement in memory-optimized tables behaves like the SNAPSHOT isolation level. Once your transaction starts and you access memory-optimized data in the database, further reads from memory-optimized tables will be from a consistent view of those objects. (The memory-optimized and on-disk tables are in different "containers," so your consistent view of the memory-optimized data doesn't start if you read on-disk tables only.)

However, what makes your work more interesting is that when in the REPEATABLE READ or SERIALIZABLE isolation level, the scan for phantom and non-repeatable read rows is done during commit rather than as they occur.

For example, consider the following steps, with each transaction coming from a different session. A typical scenario might be running a report of some data. You read a set of data, perform some operation on it, and then read another set of rows, and your process requires the data to all stay the same.

1.   A table contains many rows, each with a unique ID. Transaction 1 begins a transaction in the SERIALIZABLE isolation level and reads all the rows in the table.

2.   Transaction 2 updates the row where ID = 1. This transaction commits successfully.

3.   Transaction 1 again reads rows in this same table. No error is raised, and rows are returned as normal.

4.   Transaction 1 commits. An error is raised (41305), alerting you to a non-repeatable read. Even though this was in the SERIALIZABLE isolation level, the check for a non-repeatable read is done first, since this is a reasonably easy operation, whereas the scan for phantom rows requires the engine to run a query on the data to see if extra rows are returned.

Most uses of isolation levels other than SNAPSHOT with memory-optimized data should be limited to operations like data-integrity checks, where you want to make sure that one row exists before you insert the next row.

> ➤ For more details on conflict detection and retry logic with memory-optimized tables, see *https://learn.microsoft.com/sql/relational-databases/in-memory-oltp/transactions-with -memory-optimized-tables#conflict-detection-and-retry-logic.*

CHAPTER 14

Specify the isolation level for memory-optimized tables in queries

The isolation level is specified in a few mildly confusing ways for memory-optimized tables. The first method is in an ad hoc query, not in an existing transaction context, where you can query the table as you always have and it will be accessed in the SNAPSHOT isolation level.

If you are in the context of a transaction, it will not automatically default to the SNAPSHOT isolation level. Rather you need to specify the isolation level as a hint, such as:

```
BEGIN TRANSACTION;
SELECT *
FROM   dbo.MemoryOptimizedTable WITH (SNAPSHOT);
```

You can make it default to SNAPSHOT isolation level by enabling the MEMORY_OPTIMIZED _ELEVATE_TO_SNAPSHOT database option. This promotes access to all memory-optimized tables in the database up to the SNAPSHOT isolation level if the current isolation level is not REPEATABLE READ or SERIALIZABLE. It also promotes the isolation level to SNAPSHOT from isolation levels such as READ UNCOMMITTED and READ COMMITTED. This option is disabled by default, but you should consider enabling it; otherwise, you cannot use the READ UNCOMMITTED or SNAPSHOT isolation levels for a session including memory-optimized tables.

If you need to use REPEATABLE READ or SERIALIZABLE, or your scenario does not meet the criteria for automatically choosing the SNAPSHOT isolation level, you can specify the isolation level using table concurrency hints. (See the section "Use table hints to change isolation" earlier in this chapter.) Only memory-optimized tables can use this SNAPSHOT table hint, not disk-based tables.

Finally, you cannot mix the disk-based SNAPSHOT isolation level with the memory-optimized SNAPSHOT isolation level. For example, you cannot include memory-optimized tables in a session that begins with SET TRANSACTION ISOLATION LEVEL SNAPSHOT, even if MEMORY_OPTIMIZED _ELEVATE_TO_SNAPSHOT = ON or you specify the SNAPSHOT table hint.

> ➤ For more information on configuring memory-optimized tables, see Chapter 7. We discuss more about indexes for memory-optimized tables in Chapter 15.

Understand durability settings for performance

As discussed at the beginning of this chapter, the last of the four basic requirements for an RDBMS, ACID, is that data saved is durable. Once you believe it is saved in the database, it is written to non-volatile memory, and it is assumed that if the server restarts the data cannot be lost. This is a very important requirement of relational databases. It is also detrimental to performance because non-volatile memory is slower than volatile memory.

For performance's sake, there are two configurations to increase performance, at the detriment of durability:

- **Use memory-optimized tables and set the durability property on the table to SCHEMA_ONLY.** This creates a logless, memory-based object that will be emptied when the service is restarted, with only the schema remaining. This can be useful in certain scenarios and provides amazing performance—even hundreds of times faster than on-disk tables. It is not, however, a universally applicable tool to increase application performance, because it makes the table completely non-durable.

- **Use delayed durability.** This alters the durability of your data slightly, but possibly enough to make a difference in how long it takes to return control to your server's clients when it makes sense.

NOTE

The process of writing data to disk and memory is changing as powerful new technologies arrive. SQL Server 2019 introduced the hybrid buffer pool to use persistent memory modules (PMEM) that write data to non-volatile memory storage instead. Chapter 2, "Introduction to database server components," provides more details on the hybrid buffer pool, as does the Microsoft Docs article located here: *https://learn.microsoft.com/sql/database-engine/configure-windows/hybrid-buffer-pool*.

This section looks at a way to alter how durability is handled in SQL Server in a manner that can be useful on very small departmental servers as well as enterprise servers.

Delayed durability database options

Delayed durability allows transactions to avoid synchronously committing to a disk. Instead they synchronously commit only to memory, but asynchronously commit to storage. This opens the possibility of losing data in the event of a server shutdown before the log has been written, so it does have dangers. This engine feature was introduced in SQL Server 2014 and works the same today.

Databases in Azure SQL Database also support delayed durability transactions, with the same caveat and expectations for data recovery. Some data loss is possible, so you should use this feature only if you can re-create important transactions in the event of a server crash.

NOTE

Distributed and cross-database transactions are always durable.

At the database level, you can set the DELAYED_DURABILITY option to DISABLED (default), ALLOWED, or FORCED. ALLOWED allows any explicit transaction to be coded to be optionally set to delayed durability, using the following statement:

```
COMMIT TRANSACTION WITH ( DELAYED_DURABILITY = ON );
```

Setting the DELAYED_DURABILITY option to FORCED means that every transaction, regardless of what the person writing the COMMIT statement wishes, will have asynchronous log writes. This obviously has implications on all database activity, and you should consider it carefully with existing applications.

Additionally, for natively compiled procedures, you can specify DELAYED_DURABILITY in the BEGIN ATOMIC block. Take, for example, this header of a procedure in the WideWorldImporters sample database:

```
CREATE PROCEDURE [Website].[RecordColdRoomTemperatures_DD]
@SensorReadings Website.SensorDataList READONLY
WITH NATIVE_COMPILATION, SCHEMABINDING, EXECUTE AS OWNER
AS
BEGIN ATOMIC WITH
(
    TRANSACTION ISOLATION LEVEL = SNAPSHOT,
    LANGUAGE = N'English',
    DELAYED_DURABILITY = ON
)
    BEGIN TRY
    ...
```

The delayed durability options, implemented at either the database level or the transaction level, have use in very-high-performance workloads for which the bottleneck to write performance is the transaction log itself. This is accomplished by writing new rows only to memory, then asynchronously and eventually committing to disk. Transactions could therefore be lost in the event of a SQL Server service shutdown; however, you can gain a significant performance increase, especially with write-heavy workloads. As Microsoft Docs advise, "If you cannot tolerate any data loss, do not use delayed transaction durability."

Even if you cannot employ delayed durability in your normal day-to-day operations, it can be a very useful setting when loading a database, particularly for test data. Because log writes are written asynchronously, instead of every transaction waiting for small log writes to complete, log writes are batched together in an efficient manner.

NOTE

While delayed durability does apply to memory-optimized tables, the DELAYED_DURABILITY **database option is not related to the** DURABILITY **option when creating optimized tables.**

A transaction that changes data under delayed durability will be flushed to the disk as soon as possible, whenever any other durable transaction commits in the same database, or whenever a threshold of delayed durability transactions builds up.

You can also force a flush of the transaction log with the system stored procedure sys.sp _flush_log. Otherwise, the transactions are written to a buffer in memory and await a log flush event to become durable on disk. SQL Server manages the buffer but makes no guarantees as to the amount of time a transaction can remain in buffer.

It's important to note that delayed durability is simply about reducing the I/O bottleneck involved with committing a massive quantity of writes to the transaction log. This has no effect on isolation (locking, blocking) or access to any data in the database that must be read to perform the write. Otherwise, delayed durability transactions follow the same rules as other transactions.

NOTE

Any SQL Server instance service shutdown, whether it be a planned restart or sudden failure, could result in delayed durability transactions being lost. This also applies when a failover cluster instance (FCI), availability group, or database mirror fails over. Transaction log backups and log shipping will similarly contain only transactions made durable. You must be aware of this potential when implementing delayed durability. For more information, see *https://learn.microsoft.com/sql/relational-databases/logs/control-transaction-durability*.

How SQL Server executes a query

This section dives into the *execution plan*, which is the operational map provided by SQL Server for each query. It mentions key features, especially database scoped configurations, that are important to being proactive and reactive to query performance.

Inside OUT

How much has the Query Optimizer changed recently?

The internal Query Optimizer to develop a query plan in SQL Server is very complex, and increasingly so with recent improvements in the intelligent query processing (IQP) family of features. Specifically, new feedback features in SQL Server 2022 such as cardinality estimation (CE), degree of parallelism (DOP), and the existing memory grant feedback features are powerful adaptive processes that allow the Query Optimizer to learn from its mistakes. The Query Store is becoming increasingly valuable to built-in query improvement features, and you should consider enabling it for every database. (Query Store is enabled by default for all new databases on SQL Server 2022.)

➤ You can find out much more about the latest advanced features for query performance later in this chapter. To read more about the IQP features, see *https://learn.microsoft.com/sql/relational-databases/performance/intelligent-query-processing*.

Understand the query execution process

When a user writes a query, that query could be one line of code like `SELECT * FROM dbo.TableName;` or it could be a statement that contains 1,000 lines. This query could be a batch of multiple statements, use temporary objects, or employ other coded objects such as user-defined functions, not to mention table variables, and perhaps a cursor thrown in for good measure.

After writing a query, the user tries to execute it.

First, the code is parsed and translated to structures in the native language of the query processor. If the query is a technically correct T-SQL syntax, it will pass this phase. For example, if there are syntax errors like `SLECT * FROM dbo.TableName;` then the query will fail with a syntax error.

After the code is parsed and prepared for execution, the Query Optimizer tries to calculate the best way to run your code. It then runs it again using the same process, by saving what is referred to as the *query plan*, *execution plan*, or *explain plan*, depending on which tool you are using.

If the query plan has already been compiled, it might be in cache. This is complex. The Query Optimizer might choose to use the cached query plan, saving valuable CPU time. A new feature in SQL Server 2022, Parameter Sensitive Plan (PSP) optimization, also beneficially affects decisions regarding plan reuse. (More on that later.)

Getting the right query plan for different parameters, or server load, is where the real rocket science comes in for software engineers. That engine work is why a person with no understanding of how computers work can write a query in less than 30 seconds that will access 100 million rows, aggregate the values of one or more columns, filter out values they don't want to see, and obtain results in just a few seconds.

You will deal with three kinds of execution plans:

- **Estimated.** Something you can ask for, to show you what the execution plan will probably look like.

- **Actual.** Provides details about what actually occurred, which can vary from the estimated plan for multiple reasons, including SQL Server's IQP features, which we will discuss more later in this chapter.

- **Live.** Shows you the rows of data flowing through during execution.

The execution plan that is created is a detailed blueprint of the Query Optimizer's plan for processing any statement. Each time you run a statement, including batches with multiple statements, an execution plan is generated. Query plans share with you the strategy of execution for queries; inform you of the steps the Database Engine will take to retrieve data; detail the various transformation steps to sort, join, and filter data; and finally return or affect data. All statements you execute will create an execution plan, including DML and DDL statements.

The plan contains the estimated costs and other metadata of each piece required to process a query, and finally the DML or DDL operation itself. This data can be invaluable to developers and DBAs for tuning query performance. When you look at the query plan, you can see some of the estimates made, compared to the actual values.

Variances between the actual versus estimated values sometimes stack up to become real problems, and that's why significant engineering effort was put into new features in SQL Server 2022 such as CE feedback, DOP feedback, and memory feedback. These powerful feedback features allow the Query Optimizer to notice actual versus estimate variance and adjust the plan on the next execution.

Execution plans are placed in the procedure cache, which is stored in active memory, that SQL Server uses when a statement is executed again. The procedure cache can be cleared manually, and is reset when you restart the Database Engine. Plans from the procedure cache are reused for a query when that exact same query text is called again.

Queries reuse the same plan only if every character of the query statement matches, including capitalization, whitespace, line breaks, and text in comments. There are a few exceptions to this rule, however:

- SQL Server will parameterize a query or stored procedure statement, allowing some values, like literals or variables, to be treated as having a different value on each execution. For example, these two queries will share a single execution plan:

```
SELECT column_a, column_b FROM table WHERE column_a = 123;
SELECT column_a, column_b FROM table WHERE column_a = 456;
```

  This automatic parameterization is extraordinarily valuable to performance, but is also sometimes frustrating. More on this in the section "Understand parameterization and parameter sniffing" later in this chapter.

- A new feature of SQL Server 2022, PSP optimization, comes into play to help solve a classical problem with *parameter sniffing*. Again, more on that later in this chapter, but in short: Now SQL Server can keep multiple cached plans for a single query.

➤ For more information about PSP optimization, see *https://learn.microsoft.com/sql /relational-databases/performance/parameter-sensitivity-plan-optimization.*

View execution plans

Let's now look at how you can see the different types of execution plans in SQL Server Management Studio (SSMS) and Azure Data Studio and view them in some detail. The differences between the two tools, for the purposes of this section, are minimal.

Display the estimated execution plan

You can generate the estimated execution plan quickly and view it graphically from within SSMS or Azure Data Studio by choosing the **Display Estimated Execution Plan** option in the **Query** menu or by pressing **Ctrl+L**. An estimated execution plan will return for the highlighted region or for the entire file if no text is selected.

You can also retrieve an estimated execution plan in T-SQL code by running the following statement. It will be presented in an XML format:

```
SET SHOWPLAN_XML ON;
```

> ### NOTE
> When changing a SET SHOWPLAN option, it must be the only statement in a batch, as it changes the returned output.

In SSMS, in Grid mode, the results are displayed as a link as for any XML output. SSMS knows this is a plan, however, so you can select the link to view the plan graphically in SSMS. You can then save the execution plan as a .sqlplan file by right-clicking the neutral space of the plan window and selecting **Save Execution Plan As**.

You can also configure the estimated text execution plan in code by running one of the following statements, which return the execution plan in one result set or two, respectively:

```
SET SHOWPLAN_ALL ON;
SET SHOWPLAN_TEXT ON;
```

The text plan of the query using one of these two statements can be useful if you want to send the plan to someone in an email in a compact manner.

> ### NOTE
> When any of the aforementioned SET options are enabled for a connection, SQL Server does not run statements, it only returns estimated execution plans. Remember to disable the SET SHOWPLAN_* option before you reuse the same session for other queries.

As expected, the estimated execution plan is not guaranteed to match the actual plan used when you run the statement, but it is usually a very reliable approximation that you can use to see if a query looks like it will execute well enough. The Query Optimizer uses the same information for the estimate as it does for the actual plan when you run it.

To display information for individual steps, hover over a step in the execution plan. In SSMS or Azure Data Studio, select an object, right-click on it, and select **Properties**. After you have a bit of experience with plans, you'll notice the estimated execution plan is missing some information that the actual plan returns. The missing fields are generally self-explanatory in that they are values you would not have until the query has actually executed—for example, **Actual Number of Rows for All Executions**, **Actual Number of Batches**, and **Estimated Number of Rows for All Executions**.

Display the actual execution plan

You can view the actual execution plan used to execute the query along with the statement's result set from within SSMS by choosing the **Include Actual Execution Plan** option in the **Query** menu or by pressing **Ctrl+M** to enable the setting. After enabling this setting, when you run a statement, you will see an additional tab appear along with the execution results after the results of the statements have completed.

> ### NOTE
> Turning on the actual execution plan feature will add extra time to the execution of your query. If you are comparing runs of a query, this could skew the results.

You can also return the actual execution plan as a result set using T-SQL code, returning XML that can be viewed graphically in SSMS, by running the following statement:

```
SET STATISTICS XML ON;
```

The actual execution plan is returned as an XML string. In SSMS, in Grid mode, the results display as a link, which you can view graphically by selecting the link. Remember to disable the SET STATISTICS option before you reuse the same session if you don't want to get back the actual plan for every query you run on this connection.

You can save both estimated and actual execution plans as a .sqlplan file by right-clicking the neutral space of the plan window and selecting **Save Execution Plan As**.

You might see that the total rows to be processed does not match the total estimated number of rows for that step—or rather, the multiple of that step's estimated number of rows and a preceding step's estimated number of rows.

For an example of an execution plan, consider the following query in the WideWorldImporters sample database:

```
SELECT * FROM Sales.Invoices
JOIN Sales.Customers
on Customers.CustomerId = Invoices.CustomerId
WHERE Invoices.InvoiceID like '1%';
```

Figure 14-1 shows part of the actual execution plan for this query.

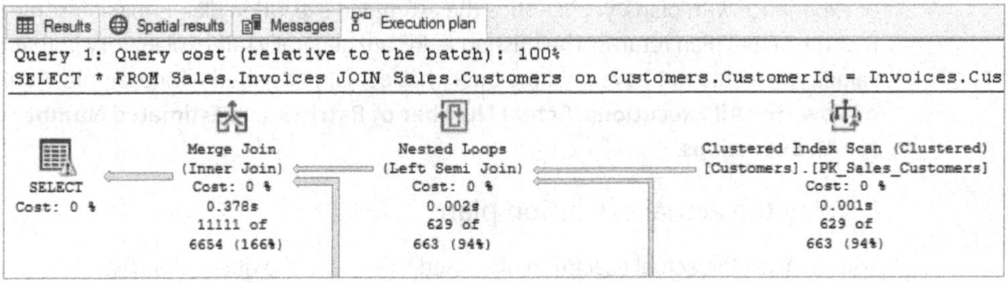

Figure 14-1 Sample query plan, showing a portion of the actual execution plan.

In Figure 14-1, on the Merge Join (Inner Join) operator, you can see that 11111 of 6654 rows were processed. The 6654 was the estimate, and 11111 was the actual number of rows.

Inside OUT

What's the difference between Number of Rows Read and Actual Number of Rows?

This is an important distinction, and it can tip you off to a significant performance issue. Both are "actual" values. However, Actual Number of Rows contains the number of values in the range of rows we expect to retrieve, whereas Number of Rows Read contains the number of rows that were actually read based on the number of rows that needed to be accessed to filter the rows for a predicate you have included.

The difference could significantly affect performance, and the solution is likely to change the query so that the predicate is narrower and/or better aligned with indexes on the table. Alternatively, you can add indexes to better fit the query predicates and make for more efficient searches.

One of the easiest ways to reproduce this behavior is with a wildcard search—for example in the WideWorldImporters sample database:

```
SELECT Invoices.InvoiceID
FROM Sales.Invoices
WHERE Invoices.InvoiceID like '1%';
In the XML, in the node for the Index Scan, you see:
<RunTimeInformation>
<RunTimeCountersPerThread Thread="0" ActualRows="11111" ActualRowsRead="70510"
...
```

Defined as ActualRowsRead in the XML of the plan, this value is displayed as Number of Rows Read in SQL Server Management Studio. Similarly, ActualRows is displayed as Actual Number of Rows.

Displaying live query statistics

Live query statistics, introduced in SSMS v16, are an excellent feature. With this feature, you can generate and display a "live" version of the execution plan using SSMS. It allows you to access live statistics on versions of SQL Server starting with SQL Server 2014. To use it, enable the **Live Execution Statistics** option for a connection via the **Query** menu in SSMS.

If you execute the query from the previous section with live query statistics enabled, you will see something like what's shown in Figure 14-2. Notice that 1,684 of the estimated 6,654 rows have been processed by the Merge Join operator, and 93 rows have been processed by the Nested Loops (Left Semi Join) operator.

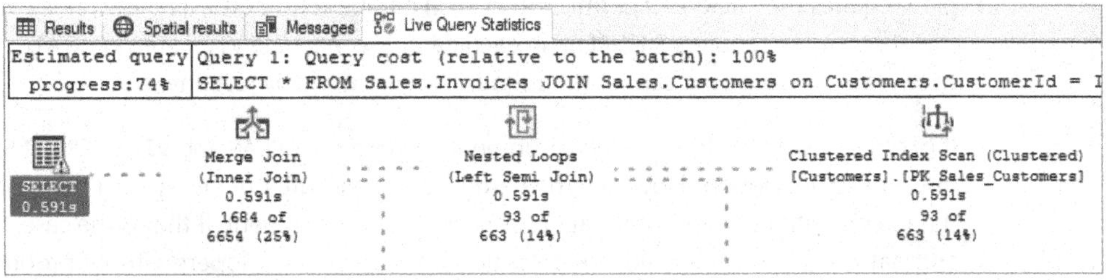

Figure 14-2 Sample live query statistics.

The Live Query Statistics window initially displays the execution plan more or less like the estimated plan, but fills out the details of how the query is being executed as it is processing it. If your query runs quickly, you'll miss the dotted, moving lines and the various progress metrics, including the duration for each step and overall percentage completion. The percentage is based on the actual rows processed currently incurred versus a total number of rows processed for that step.

The Live Query Statistics window contains more information than the estimated query plan, such as the actual number of rows and number of executions, but less than the actual query plan. The Live Query Statistics window does not display some data from the actual execution plan such as actual execution mode, number of rows read, and actual rebinds.

Returning a live execution plan will noticeably slow down query processing, so be aware that the individual and overall execution durations measured will often be longer than when the query is run without the option to display live query statistics. However, it can be worth it to see where a query is hung up in processing.

If your server is configured correctly to do so, you can see the live query plan of executing queries in action by using the Activity Monitor in SSMS. In the Activity Monitor you can access the live execution plan by right-clicking any query in the **Processes** or **Active Expensive Queries** panes and selecting **Show Live Execution Plan**.

NOTE

Capturing live query execution statistics has some overhead, so use when it is valuable and not by default.

Permissions necessary to view execution plans

Not just anyone can view a query's execution plans. There are two ways you can view plans, and they require different kinds of permissions.

If you want to generate and view a query plan, you will first need permissions to execute the query, even to get the estimated plan. Additionally, retrieving the estimated or actual execution plan requires the SHOWPLAN permission in each database referenced by the query. The live query statistics feature requires SHOWPLAN in each database, plus the VIEW SERVER STATE permission to see live statistics, so it cannot (and should not) be done by just any user.

It might be appropriate in your environment to grant SHOWPLAN and VIEW SERVER STATE permissions to developers. However, the permission to execute queries against the production database might not be appropriate in your regular environment. If that is the case, there are alternatives to providing valuable execution plan data to developers without production access. For example:

- Providing database developers with saved execution plan (.sqlplan) files for offline analysis.

- Configuring dynamic data masking, which might already be appropriate in your environment for hiding sensitive or personally identifying information for users who are not sysadmins on the server. Do not provide UNMASK permission to developers, however; assign that only to application users.

- Sometimes, an administrator may need to execute queries on a production server due to differences in environment or hardware, but be cautioned on all of what that means in terms of security, privacy, and so on.

➤ For more information on dynamic data masking, see Chapter 13, "Protect data through classification, encryption, and auditing."

There are several tools that provide the ability to see existing execution plans. For example, Extended Events and Profiler can capture execution plans. Query reports in Activity Monitor, such as Recent Expensive Queries, also allow you to see the plan (if it is still available in cache). Dynamic management views (DMVs) that provide access to queries that executed (such as sys.dm_exec_cached_plans) or requests (sys.dm_exec_requests) will have a column named `plan_handle` that you can pass to the `sys.dm_exec_query_plan` DMV to retrieve the plan. To access plans in this manner, the server principal needs the `VIEW SERVER STATE` permission or must be a member of the sysadmin server role.

Finally, and perhaps the best way to view execution plans, is the Query Store, which is covered later in this chapter. For this, you need `VIEW DATABASE STATE` permissions or to be a member of the db_owner fixed role.

Understand execution plans

At this point, we have established the basics of what an execution plan is, where to find it, and what permissions you need to see it. After you have a graphical execution plan in front of you, you need a basic understanding of reading how the T-SQL statement was processed and how future queries that use this same plan will operate. The next several sections outline this process.

Read graphical execution plans

This section steps you through reviewing execution plans in SSMS and covers some of the most common things to look for.

Start an execution plan

First, start an execution plan. For our purposes, run a simple one, like for the following query:

```
SELECT Invoices.InvoiceID
FROM Sales.Invoices
WHERE Invoices.InvoiceID like '1%';
```

Figure 14-3 shows the resulting estimated query plan.

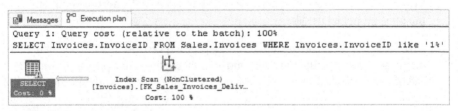

Figure 14-3 Simple query plan.

To display details for individual steps, position your pointer over a step in the execution plan to open a detailed tooltip-style window, much like the one shown in Figure 14-4. An interesting detail immediately should come to you when you look at the plan. It doesn't say it is scanning the `Sales.Invoices` table, but rather an index. If an index has all the data needed to execute the query, the index "covers" the needs of the query, and the table's other data structures are not touched.

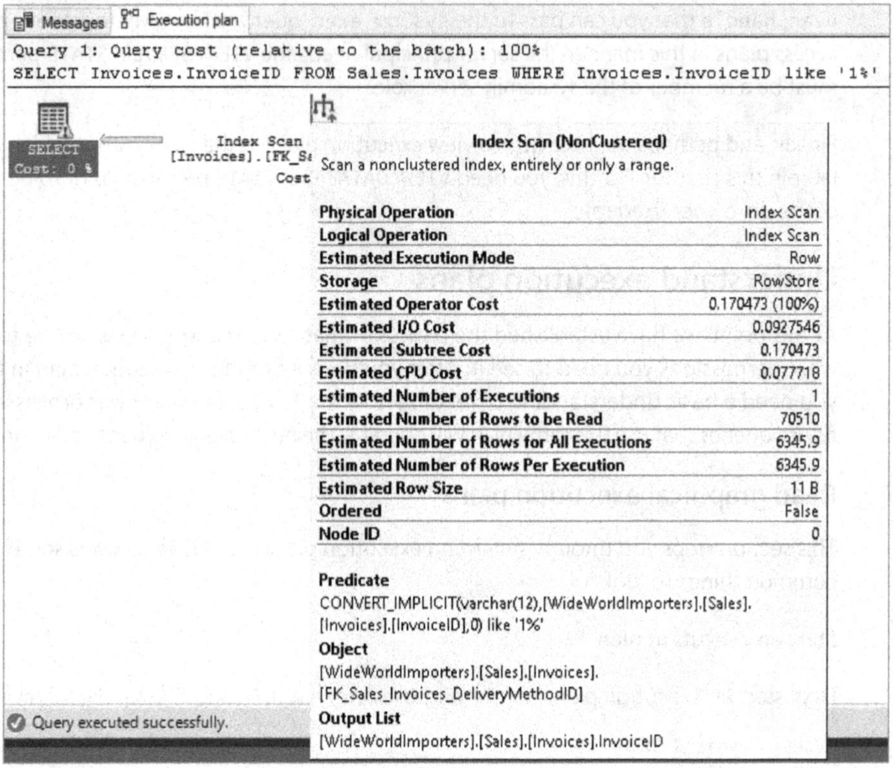

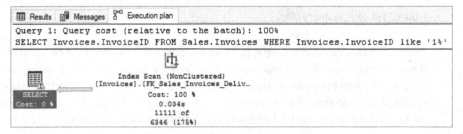

Figure 14-4 Simple query plan with statistics.

In SSMS, you can also select an operator in the execution plan and then press **F4** or open the **View** menu and choose **Properties Window** to open its **Properties** window, where you will see the same estimated details.

Now, let's get the actual execution plan, by pressing **Ctrl+M** or using one of the other methods discussed earlier. Execute the query and you will see the actual plan, as shown in Figure 14-5. It will be *nearly* identical to the estimate plan in Figure 14-3, but with more information.

Figure 14-5 Actual execution plan for the sample query.

The first thing you should notice is that the query plan has a few more details. In particular, 11,111 of 6,346 rows were processed, where 6,346 is the estimated number of rows that would be returned by the query. This guess was based on statistics, which do not give perfect answers. When you are tuning larger queries, very large disparities between such guesses and the actual number require investigation.

Open the **Properties** pane and you'll notice the returned estimate and actual values for some metrics, including Number of Rows, Executions, IO Statistics, and more. Look for differences in estimates and actual numbers here; they can indicate an inefficient execution plan and the source of a poor performing query. Your query might be suffering from a poorly chosen plan because of the impact of parameter sniffing or due to stale, inaccurate index statistics.

> ➤ We discuss parameter sniffing later in this chapter, including a new feature in SQL Server 2022 intended to avoid this classic problem, PSP optimization. Chapter 15 discusses index statistics.

Notice that some values, like Cost Information, contain only estimated values, even when you are viewing the actual execution plan. This is because the operator costs aren't sourced separately; rather, they are generated the same way for both the estimated and actual plans and do not change based on statement execution. Furthermore, cost is not just comprised entirely of duration. You might find that some statements far exceed others in terms of duration, but not in cost.

NOTE

You can also review execution plans with a well-known third-party tool called Plan Explorer, a free download from *https://www.sentryone.com/plan-explorer*. It provides several additional ways to sort plan operators that are often helpful when working with very large query plans.

Start with the upper-left operator

The upper-left operator reflects the basic operation the statement performed—for example, SELECT, DELETE, UPDATE, INSERT, or any of the DML statements. (If your query created an index, you could also see CREATE INDEX.) This operator might contain warnings or other items that require your immediate attention. These typically appear with a small yellow triangle warning icon, over which you can position your mouse pointer to obtain additional details.

This was an intentional teaching opportunity! For example, in our sample plan, the SELECT operator is at the far left, and it has a triangle over it. You can see in the ToolTip that this is due to the following:

```
Type conversion in expression (CONVERT_IMPLICIT(varchar(12),[WideWorldImporters].
[Sales].[Invoices].[InvoiceID],0)) may affect "CardinalityEstimate" in query plan
choice, Type conversion in expression (CONVERT_IMPLICIT(varchar(12),[WideWorldImport
ers].[Sales].[Invoices].[InvoiceID],0)>='1') may affect "SeekPlan" in query plan choice.
```

In other words, we used a LIKE on an integer value, so the query plan is warning us that it cannot estimate the number of rows as well as it can if our WHERE clause employed integer comparisons to integers.

Select the upper-left operator and press **F4** or open the **View** menu in SSMS and choose **Properties Window**. It lists some other things to look for. You'll see warnings repeated in here, along with additional aggregate information.

NOTE

Yellow triangles on an operator indicate something that should grab your attention. The alert could tip you off to an implicit conversion—for example, a data-type mismatch that could be costly. Investigate any warnings reported before moving on.

Also look for the **Optimization Level** entry. This typically says **Full**. If the **Optimization Level** is **Trivial**, it means the Query Optimizer bypassed optimization of the query altogether because it was straightforward enough—for example, if the plan for the query only needed to contain a simple Scan or Seek operation along with the operation operator, like SELECT. If the **Optimization Level** is not **Full** or **Trivial**, this is something to investigate.

Look next for the presence of a value for **Reason For Early Termination**. This indicates the Query Optimizer did not spend as much time as it could have selecting the best plan. Here are a few possible reasons:

- **Good Enough Plan.** This is returned if the Query Optimizer determined that the plan it picked was good enough to not need to keep optimizing.

- **Time Out.** This indicates the Query Optimizer tried as many times as it could to find the best plan before taking the best plan available, which might not be good enough. If you see this, consider simplifying the query—in particular, by reducing the use of functions and potentially modifying the underlying indexes.

- **Memory Limit Exceeded.** This is a rare and critical error indicating severe memory pressure on the SQL Server instance.

Look right, then read from right to left

Graphical execution plans build from sources (rightmost objects) and apply operators to join, sort, and filter data from right to left, eventually arriving at the leftmost operator. Among the rightmost objects, you'll see scans, seeks, and lookups of different types. You might find some quick, straightforward insight into how the query is using indexes.

Each of the items in the query plan are referred to as *operators*. Each operator is a module of code that does a certain task to process data.

Two of the main types of operators for fetching data from a table or index are seeks and scans.

A *seek* operator finds a portion of a set of data through the index structure, similar to how you would use the index of a book to locate coverage of a specific topic. Seek operators are generally the most efficient operators and can rarely be improved by additional indexes. The seek operation finds the leaf page in the index, which contains the keys of the index, plus any included column data (which in the case of a clustered table will be all the data for the row).

If the leaf data contains everything you need, it means the operation was covered by the index. However, if you need more data than the index contains, a lookup operator will join with the seek operator using a join operator. This means that although the Query Optimizer used a seek, it needed a second pass at the table in the form of a lookup on another object, typically the clustered index, using a second seek operator.

Key lookups (on clustered indexes) and RID lookups (on heaps) are expensive and inefficient, particularly when many rows are being accessed. These lookups can add up to a very large percentage of the cost of a query.

If key lookup operators are needed frequently, they can usually be eliminated by modifying the index that is being scanned. For instance, you could modify an existing nonclustered index to include additional columns. For an example, see the section "Design rowstore nonclustered indexes" in Chapter 15.

The other typical data source operator is a *scan*. Scan operations aren't great unless your query is intentionally returning a large number of rows out of a table or index. Scans read all rows from the table or index, which can be very inefficient when you need to return only a few rows, but more efficient when you need many rows. Without a nonclustered index with a well-designed key (if one can be found) to enable a seek for the query, a scan might be the Query Optimizer's only option. Scans can be ordered if the source data is sorted, which is useful for some joins and aggregation options.

Scans on nonclustered indexes are often better than scans on clustered indexes, in part due to what is likely a smaller leaf page size, because a nonclustered index doesn't *usually* have all the columns on the leaf page. Nonclustered indexes suffer from the same issues with key lookups.

NOTE

Very few queries are important enough to deserve their own indexes. Think "big picture" when creating indexes. If you create a new index for every slow query, the accumulated weight of nonclustered indexes will begin to slow writes to the table. As a guiding principle, more than one query should benefit from any new nonclustered index. Avoid redundant or overlapping nonclustered indexes. See Chapter 15 for more information on creating nonclustered indexes, including "missing" indexes.

Other types of scans include the following:

- **Table scan.** This indicates that the table has no clustered index. Chapter 15 discusses why this is probably not a good idea.

- **Index scan.** This scans the rows of an index, even the included columns of the index, for values.

- **Remote scan.** This includes any object that is preceded by "remote," which is the same operation but over a linked server connection. You troubleshoot these the same way, but potentially by making changes to the remote server instead. An alternative to linked server connections that might be superior in many cases is PolyBase. PolyBase can use T-SQL to query a variety of external data sources, including nonrelational and other relational data sources. Like a linked server, PolyBase accomplishes this by reading the data in place without data movement, or "virtualizing" the data.

> ➤ For more details on PolyBase, see Chapter 7.

- **Constant scan.** These appear when the Query Optimizer deals with scalar values, repeated numbers, and other constants. These are necessary operators for certain tasks and generally not actionable from a performance standpoint.

- **Columnstore index.** This is an incredibly efficient operator when you are working with lots of rows but relatively few columns, and likely will outperform a clustered index scan or index seek where millions of rows, for example, must be aggregated. There is no need to create a nonclustered index to replace this operator unless your query is searching for a few rows.

Inside OUT

More about columnstore indexes

Since SQL Server 2016, columnstore indexes have been a viable option for read-write tables in a transactional system. In previous versions of SQL Server, nonclustered columnstore indexes did not allow writes to the table, and so couldn't easily be adopted in transactional databases. If you aren't using them already to optimize large row count queries, consider adding them to your toolbelt.

Furthermore, since SQL Server 2016 with Service Pack 1, columnstore indexes have been available to all editions of SQL Server, even Express edition, though editions below Enterprise edition have limits to the amount of columnstore cache in memory.

In Azure SQL Database, clustered and nonclustered columnstore indexes are supported on Standard tier DTU databases (S3 and above), 100 eDTU and larger elastic pools, and all vCore-based databases (both General Purpose and Business Critical).

The weight of the lines connecting operators tells part of the story, but isn't the full story

SQL Server dynamically changes the thickness of the gray lines to reflect the actual number of rows. You can get a visual idea of where the bulk of data is coming from by observing the pipes (they look like arrows pointing to the left), which draw your attention to the places where performance tuning could have the biggest impact. If you hover over the line in your query plan, you can see the rows transmitted in each step. (See Figure 14-6.)

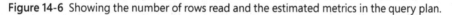

```
☐ Results  ☐ Messages  ☐ Execution plan

Query 1: Query cost (relative to the batch): 100%
SELECT Invoices.InvoiceID FROM Sales.Invoices WHERE Invoices.InvoiceID like '1%'
```

Index Scan (NonClustered)
[Invoices].[FK_Sales_Invoices_Deliv...
Cost: 100 %

SELECT
Cost: 0 %

Actual Number of Rows for All Executions	11111
Number of Rows Read	70510
Estimated Number of Rows Per Execution	6345.9
Estimated Number of Rows for All Executions	6345.9
Estimated Row Size	11 B
Estimated Data Size	68 KB

Figure 14-6 Showing the number of rows read and the estimated metrics in the query plan.

The visual weight and the sheer number of rows does not, however, directly translate to cost. Look for where the pipe weight changes from light to heavy, or vice versa. Be aware of when bolder pipes are joined or sorted.

Operator cost share isn't the full story, either

When you run multiple queries, the cost of a query relative to the batch is displayed in the query execution plan header. The batch cost relative to the rest of the operators in the statement is displayed within each plan. SQL Server uses a cost-based process to decide which query plan to use.

When optimizing a query, it is usually useful to start with the costliest operators. But deciding to address only the highest-cost single operator in the execution plan might be a dead end.

Look for join operators and understand the different algorithms

As you read from right to left in a query of any complexity, you'll likely see the paths meet at a join operator. Two tables, indexes, or the output from another operator can be joined together. There are three types of join operators to be aware of, particularly because they represent where a large percentage of the cost of an execution plan stems from: merge join, hash match, and nested loop. Any one of these can be the fastest way to join two sets of data, depending on the size of the sets, whether they are indexed, and whether they are sorted already (and if not, whether it would be too costly to sort them with a sort operator).

NOTE

There is also an adaptive join operator, first introduced in SQL Server 2017, which allows the Query Optimizer to situationally choose between the hash match and nested loop operators. This is mentioned again in the "Intelligent query processing" section later in this chapter.

A merge join operator merges two large, sorted sets of data. The query processor can scan each set, in order, matching rows from each table with a single pass through the sets. This can be quite fast, but the requirement for ordered sets is where the cost comes in. If you are joining two sets that are keyed on the same column, they are then sorted, so two ordered scans can be merged. The Query Optimizer can choose to sort one or both inputs to the merge join, but this is often costly.

Hash match is the join operator used to join two large sets, generally when there is no easily usable index and sorting is too costly. As such, it has the most overhead, because it creates a temporary index based on an internal hashing algorithm to bucketize values to make it easier to match one row to another. This hash structure is in memory if possible, but might spill onto disk (using tempdb). The presence of a hash join is not necessarily a bad thing; just know that it is the least efficient algorithm to join two data set, precisely because they are not suited for the other two operators.

NOTE

When the Query Optimizer does something that seems weird, like sort sets of data for an internal operation like a join, it is usually because it has calculated that for the design of your database, this is the best way to do it. As discussed, with complex queries, it sometimes take too long to find the absolute best way to process the query. And sometimes, the plans are suboptimal—for example, where statistics are not up to date. This is one reason to make sure plans have full optimization.

The most efficient join algorithm is the one that sounds the least optimized: nested loops. This join algorithm is the basic row-by-row processing that people preach about you as a programmer never doing. It takes one row in one input and searches the other input for values that meet the join criteria. When joining two sets together, one is indexed on the join key, and doesn't need to fetch additional data using a key lookup. Nested loops are very fast. The additional operators were implemented to support larger, ideally reporting-style, workloads.

Each of the following options could reduce the cost of a join operator.

- There might be an opportunity to improve the indexing on the columns being joined, or perhaps, you have a join on a compound key that is incompletely defined. Look for common joins in queries—can an index be crafted to match?

- In the case of a merge join, you might see a preceding sort operator. This can be an opportunity for you to sort the data already sorted according to how the merge join requires the data to be sorted. If this is a composite key, perhaps change the ASC/DESC property of an index key column, or create a new nonclustered index with columns sorted differently. The result could result in a new execution plan without the cost of the sort operator.

- Filter at the lowest level possible. Perhaps a WHERE clause could exist in a subquery instead of at the top level of the query, or in the definition of a derived table or common table expression (CTE) instead of in the subsequent query.

- Hash operators are the most expensive. Reducing the row counts going into a hash match or hash join could allow the Query Optimizer to use a less memory-intensive and less costly join operator.

- Nested loops are often necessitated by key lookups and are sometimes quite costly. Address them with a new or modified nonclustered index to eliminate the nearby key lookup, or to make an accompanying index seek more capable.

Inside OUT

If it is bad to write looping code, why is this usually the best way for SQL Server to perform the task?

This really comes down to the type of code that is executing the different code elements. T-SQL is an interpreted, declarative language. There can be a significant cost to executing a statement. This cost does not show up when you are running a few statements, but when you run hundreds of statements, it becomes obvious.

The query processor runs in very efficient machine code and is highly optimized to process joins in just three ways. While you may write FROM Table1 JOIN Table2 ON…, the resulting amount of code that is executed to pull data from disk to memory, and then do the comparisons, is astonishing. As such, the architects of the Database Engine did not optimize for you to go row by row with a cursor, but to leave it to the engine.

Look for parallel icons

The left-pointing pair of arrows in a yellow circle shown in Figure 14-7 indicate that this operator has been run with a parallel-processing execution plan. We talk more about parallelism later in this chapter; the important thing here is to be aware that your query has gone parallel.

CHAPTER 14

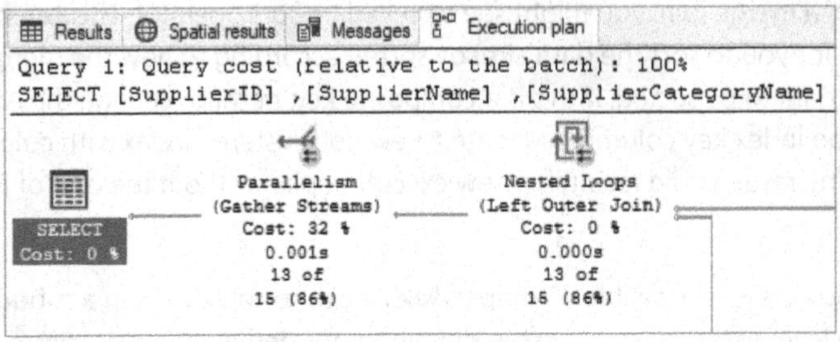

Figure 14-7 The parallel indicator on a clustered index scan operator.

This doesn't mean multiple sources or pipes are being read in parallel; rather, it means the work for individual tasks has been broken up behind the scenes. The Query Optimizer decided it was faster if your workload was split up and run into multiple parallel streams of rows. Typically, this is a good thing, but at scale, excessive parallelism can lower overall performance.

> ➤ We discuss parallelism in more detail later in this chapter in the section "Understand parallelism."

You might also see one of the three different parallelism operators—distribute streams, gather streams, and repartition streams—each of which appear only for parallel execution plans.

Understand cardinality estimation

When a query plan is being generated, one of the most important factors you will deal with is the cardinality estimation (CE). *Cardinality* is defined as the number of items in a set (hence, a cardinal number is a non-negative integer). The importance of cardinality estimation cannot be overstated and is analogous to how you might do a task. If you own an e-commerce store and ship three products a week, you might be able to walk two miles with your stack of packages to the post office at the end of the week and be efficient enough. If you must ship 300,000 products a day, however, the net effect of each product being shipped needs to be the same, but the way you achieve this must be far more optimized and include more than just one person.

SQL Server makes the same choices. You join table X with table Y on column ID. If X has 1,000 rows, and Y has 10, the solution is easy. If they each have a billion rows, and you are looking for a specific value in table X—say, value = 'Test'—there are many choices to make. How may rows in X have a value of 'Test'? And once you know that value, how many values of ID in X will match ID values in Y?

This estimation is done in two ways. The first is with guesses based on histograms of the data. The table is scanned when creating statistics. Statistics are created by executing UPDATE STATISTICS or through the automatic gathering of statistics that occurs as data changes, based on the AUTO _UPDATE_STATISTICS database setting.

Take the first case, where the tables are small. The engine stores a histogram that has something like what's shown in Table 14-5.

Table 14-5 Sample histogram of a small table

RANGE_HI_KEY	RANGE_ROWS	EQ_ROWS	DISTINCT_RANGE_ROWS	AVERAGE_RANGE_ROWS...
Smith	400	200	20	10
Tests	200	120	23	5

From this, the number of rows equal to 'Test' can be guessed to be less than 400 because Test is between Smith and Tests; less than 200, because approximately 200 rows matched Smith; and approximately 10 matches because there are approximately 20 distinct values. Exactly how this estimation is done is proprietary, but it is important to keep your statistics up to date using maintenance methods. (See Chapter 8 for more details on proper upkeep of SQL Server.)

From SQL Server 7.0 to SQL Server 2012, the same CE algorithms were used. However, since SQL Server 2014, Microsoft has been significantly tweaking the cardinality estimator with each release. And now, in SQL Server 2022, the new CE feedback feature allows SQL Server to automatically adapt query plans based on the estimate and actual number of rows processed, enhancing performance stability and automating an otherwise complex troubleshooting exercise.

> ➤ CE feedback is discussed later in this chapter. You can find out more at *https://learn.microsoft .com/sql/relational-databases/performance/intelligent-query-processing-feedback#cardinality -estimation-ce-feedback.*

The problem with cardinality estimation is that it is an inexact science. The guesses made are usually close enough, but sometimes can be off just enough to affect performance. Outdated statistics can lead to this, but that's not the only explanation. Estimating filtered rowcounts in query plans is complex. That's why it's important that the new SQL Server 2022 "feedback" features allow SQL Server to quickly learn from mistakes.

There are a few methods to control which cardinality estimator is used. The first is to use the database's compatibility level, like with this command to use the SQL Server 2022 cardinality estimator:

```
ALTER DATABASE [db_name] SET COMPATIBILITY_LEVEL = 160;
```

Or you can elect to go backward and use the legacy SQL Server 2012 compatibility level:

```
ALTER DATABASE [db_name] SET COMPATIBILITY_LEVEL = 110;
```

Changing the database's compatibility level is often an unnecessary or drastic change. In your testing, consider keeping your modern compatibility level and reverting only to the legacy cardinality estimator (which pre-dated SQL Server 2014):

```
ALTER DATABASE SCOPED CONFIGURATION SET LEGACY_CARDINALITY_ESTIMATION = ON;
```

Here also, reverting to the legacy cardinality estimator can be too drastic a change for the entire database. In compatibility level 130 (SQL Server 2016) and higher, there is a query hint you can use to modify an individual query to use legacy cardinality estimation (CE version 70):

```
SELECT …
FROM …
OPTION (USE HINT ('FORCE_LEGACY_CARDINALITY_ESTIMATION'));
```

What if you cannot modify the query to use the OPTION syntax because it resides deep within a business intelligence suite, an ETL tool, or third-party software? SQL Server 2022 has a solution for you: Identify the query in Query Store metadata and then provide a Query Store hint, shaping the query without altering any code. For example:

```
EXEC sys.sp_query_store_set_hints @query_id= 555,
@query_hints = N'OPTION(USE HINT(''FORCE_LEGACY_CARDINALITY_ESTIMATION''))';
```

In this example, the Query Store is used to identify a specific problematic query, which had been assigned query_id 555. This new SQL Server 2022 feature is only available when Query Store is enabled for the database, which we recommend.

NOTE

Query Store is enabled by default for all new databases on SQL Server 2022.

➤ For more information about Query Store hints, see the "Query Store hints" section later in this chapter.

For the most part, we suggest using the latest cardinality estimator possible, and addressing issues in your queries, but realize this is not always a feasible solution.

➤ For more information, including how to tell which version of cardinality estimation was used, see *https://learn.microsoft.com/sql/relational-databases/performance/cardinality -estimation-sql-server*.

Inside OUT

Are there tools to help predict the performance impact of upgrading the database compatibility level?

The Query Tuning Assistant (QTA) can help you find queries that might be affected by a compatibility level upgrade. It is primarily created to handle upgrade tasks (you launch the tool in SSMS by right-clicking the database and choosing **Tasks > Database Upgrade > New Database Upgrade Session**), but can be used for any database that is not in the max compatibility level for a server.

Starting in an earlier compatibility level, QTA benchmarks Query Store data for the number of days that represent a full business cycle of activity. Then, you set your database to a later compatibility level and capture more activity. QTA will compare before and after the compatibility level upgrade and point out regressed query plans. This analysis comes with advice on how to make things work better in the new target compatibility level. For obvious reasons, this should be done on hardware and data load similar to production, but not on your production SQL Server instance.

➤ For more details, see Chapter 19, "Migrate to SQL Server solutions in Azure," where we discuss using QTA for migrations. Also check out this lab that Microsoft created: *https://github .com/microsoft/tigertoolbox/blob/master/Sessions/Winter-Ready-2019/Lab-QTA.md.*

Understand parameterization and parameter sniffing

SQL Server parameterization occurs when the Query Optimizer detects values (such as the search criteria of a WHERE clause statement) that can be parameterized. For instance, the statements in a stored procedure are parameterized from the definition.

A query can be parameterized when it meets certain conditions. For example, a query might have values that could take on multiple values. A query such as

```
SELECT Value From TableName WHERE Value = 'X';
```

can be parameterized, and the literal 'X' replaced by a parameter, much like if you were writing a stored procedure. This type of automatic parameterization is the default, referred to as *simple parameterization*. (Prior to SQL Server 2005, this was named *auto-parameterization*.)

The criteria for a query to qualify for simple parameterization are complex and lengthy. For example, a query where you reference more than one table will not be parameterized. If you change the PARAMETERIZATION database setting to FORCED, more complex queries will be parameterized. Object-Relational Mapping (ORM) frameworks like Entity Framework (EF) are likely to generate many queries that are too sophisticated for simple parameterization. With load testing, you could determine that your EF application could benefit from forced parameterization.

You can also rewrite a query to ensure it will get a parameterized plan by using a variable:

```
DECLARE @Value varchar(10) = 'X';
SELECT Value From TableName WHERE Value = @Value;
```

This query will be parameterized no matter how complex it is. There are additional ways a query will be parameterized through client APIs, but the best way to parameterize your queries is with stored procedures.

NOTE

Instead of complex procedurally developed queries coming out of object-relational mappers (ORMs) like Entity Framework in ADO.NET, consider stored procedures for application create, read, update, and delete (CRUD) operations. Stored procedures provide superior parameterization for security and cached execution plan reusability.

Simple parameterization is extraordinarily valuable, but also sometimes frustrating. With parameterization, it's possible for two potentially helpful or potentially problematic conditions to occur:

- You can reuse a query plan for multiple queries for which the query text is exactly the same, except for parameterized values. That's helpful!

- The same query could use the same execution plan for two different values of a parameter, resulting in vastly different performance. That's problematic for one of the two values.

For example, you might create the following stored procedure to fetch orders placed for goods from a certain supplier:

```
CREATE OR ALTER PROCEDURE Purchasing.PurchaseOrders_BySupplierId
    @SupplierId int
AS
SELECT PurchaseOrders.PurchaseOrderID,
       PurchaseOrders.SupplierID,
       PurchaseOrders.OrderDate
 FROM   Purchasing.PurchaseOrders
WHERE  PurchaseOrders.SupplierID = @SupplierId;
```

The plan cached for this procedure will depend on the value that is passed in on the *first* compilation. For example, if the larger rowcount query (@SupplierID = 5) is used first and has its query plan cached, the query plan will choose to scan the clustered index of the table, because the value of 5 has a relatively high cardinality in the table. If the smaller rowcount query (@SupplierID = 1) is run first, its version of the plan will be cached, which will use an index seek and a key lookup. In this case, the plan with a seek and key lookup is far less efficient for very large row counts, but will be used for all values of the parameterized statement.

Here are a few advanced troubleshooting avenues to alleviate this scenario:

- In SQL Server 2022, a new IQP feature, PSP optimization, actively adapts query plans to avoid this exact scenario. (More on this new feature at the end of this chapter, in the section "Intelligent query processing.") Between PSP optimization and Query Store hints, SQL Server 2022 provides multiple superior options to deal with this classic problem.

- Query Store hints, also new to SQL Server 2022, further allow administrators to tweak existing query plans with powerful hints, shaping query performance without the need for code changes. For example, even if you set simple parameterization at the database level, you could apply the query hint PARAMETERIZATION FORCED to individual complex queries. Query Store hints can specify this and many other query hints without changing the application code. With SQL Server 2022, you can even specify different Query Store hints on primary and secondary replicas of an availability group.

- You can use the OPTIMIZE FOR query hint to demand that the query analyzer use a cached execution plan that substitutes a provided value for the parameters. You can also use OPTIMIZE FOR UNKNOWN to instruct the query analyzer to optimize for the most common value, based on statistics of the underlying data object. You can modify the code to use OPTIMIZE FOR hints, or use the Query Store hints feature to apply a desired OPTIMIZE FOR hint without the need for code changes.

- The RECOMPILE query hint or procedure option does not allow the reuse of a cached plan, forcing a fresh query plan to be generated each time the query is run. Similarly, you can modify the code to use RECOMPILE hints, or use the Query Store hints feature to apply a desired RECOMPILE hint without the need for code changes.

- You can use the Query Store feature (implemented with a GUI in SSMS and via stored procedures behind the scenes) to visually look at plan performance and force a query to use a specific plan currently in cache, using an easy graphical interface or T-SQL stored procedures. For more information, see the section "Leverage the Query Store feature" later in this chapter.

- You can use the legacy plan guide feature (implemented via stored procedures) to guide the query analyzer to a plan currently in cache. You identify the plan via its plan_handle setting. Plan guides have been mostly replaced by the Query Store and Query Store hints feature, which provide a more granular and far easier way to tune query plans without code changes.

- Use the USE PLAN query hint to provide the entire XML query plan for SELECT statements. This is the least convenient option to override the query analyzer. Consider using the Query Store instead.

- An extreme solution is to disable parameter sniffing at the database level using the PARAMETER_SNIFFING = OFF database-scoped configuration option. This will cause all plans in the database to act like the OPTIMIZE FOR UNKNOWN hint has been provided.

Inside OUT

What if you use both plan guides and Query Store forced plans?

Danger! It is possible to create competing plan guides or Query Store forced plans. This is certainly not recommended and could become confusing. If you create competing plan guides or Query Store forced plans, you'll generally see the Query Store forced plan "win," but this is not guaranteed or documented as far as we can determine.

In case you are troubleshooting competing plan guides and Query Store forced plans, you can view any existing plan guides and forced query plans with the following queries of the system catalog:

```
SELECT * FROM sys.plan_guides;
SELECT *
FROM sys.query_store_query AS qsq
INNER JOIN sys.query_store_plan AS qsp
    ON qsp.query_id = qsq.query_id
WHERE qsp.is_forced_plan = 1;
```

Explore the procedure cache

The *procedure cache* is a portion of memory that contains query plans for statements that have been executed. New execution plans enter the procedure cache only when a statement is run. If the procedure cache already contains a plan matching a previous run of the current statement, the execution plan is reused, saving valuable time and resources. This is one reason complex statements can appear to run faster the second time they are run, in addition to the fact that data may be cached on a second execution.

The procedure cache is empty when the SQL Server service starts and grows from there. SQL Server manages plans in the cache, removing them as necessary under memory pressure. The size of the procedure cache is managed by SQL Server and is inside the memory space configured for the server in the Max Server Memory configuration setting. Plans are removed based on their cost and how recently they have been used. Smaller, older plans and single-use plans are the first to be cleared, though this formula of automatic plan cache maintenance is complex.

NOTE

If you are using SQL Server on Azure VMs, Azure SQL Database, or Azure SQL Managed Instance, look for the availability of newer memory optimized series of hardware. These are available for Azure VMs and in preview for various tiers and compute generations and offer a higher ratio of system memory to vCPUs.

Plans are compiled based on the state of the database and its objects when the plan is generated. Dramatic changes to underlying data might not cause an automatic plan recompilation, so recompiling a plan manually might help by creating a more optimized plan. Many data definition changes to tables referenced in the stored procedure will cause an automatic recompilation.

Inside OUT

If you run a statement only once, does SQL Server need to remember its plan?

By default, SQL Server adds an execution plan to the procedure cache the first time it is generated, because it expects that it might be executed again. You can view the number and size of cached execution plans with the `sys.dm_exec_cached_plans` DMV.

You might find that a large amount of space in the procedure cache is dedicated to storing execution plans that have been used only once. These single use plans can be referred to as *ad hoc* execution plans, from the Latin, meaning "for this situation." This should not be confused with the other way that this term is used in SQL Server circles to mean "all queries not contained in a stored procedure, trigger, or function."

The guidance on whether to enable the related server configuration option `optimize for ad hoc workloads` is complex.

If you find that a SQL Server instance is storing many single-use plans, as many do, enabling the **Optimize For Ad Hoc Workloads** server configuration option might benefit performance. This option does not optimize ad hoc queries; rather, it optimizes SQL Server memory by storing an execution plan stub for single-use queries. A full plan cache will appear in memory only after the same query has been detected twice. Queries might then benefit from the cached plan only upon their third execution.

However, **Optimize For Ad Hoc Workloads** also hides single-use queries, especially the plans for very expensive single-use queries that commonly come from an object-relational mapper (ORM) like Entity Framework. This could hide these resource-hogging queries from Query Store.

Clear the procedure cache

You might find that manually clearing the procedure cache is useful when performance testing or troubleshooting. Typically, you want to reserve this activity for preproduction systems.

There are a few common reasons to clear out cached plans in SQL Server. One is to compare two versions of a query or the performance of a query with different indexes; you can clear the cached plan for the statement to allow for proper comparison.

NOTE

While this can be a good thing to try, what you are testing is not only your query, but your hardware's ability to fetch data from the disk. When you look at the output of SET STATISTICS IO ON, the Logical Reads measurement gives you an accurate comparison for two or more queries. The presence of Physical Reads tells you that data the query needed was not in cache. Higher amounts of physical reads indicate that the server's ability to hold everything needed in RAM might not be sufficient.

You can manually flush the entire procedure cache, or individual plans in cache, with the following database-scoped configuration command, which affects only the current database context, as opposed to the entire instance's procedure cache:

```
ALTER DATABASE SCOPED CONFIGURATION CLEAR PROCEDURE_CACHE;
```

This command was introduced in SQL Server 2016 and is effectively the same as the DBCC FREEPROCCACHE command within the current database context. It works in both SQL Server and Azure SQL Database. DBCC FREEPROCCACHE is not supported in Azure SQL Database, and should be deprecated from your use going forward in favor of ALTER DATABASE.

CAUTION

We strongly recommend against clearing the procedure cache in a live production environment during normal business hours. Doing so will cause all new statements to have their execution plans compiled, dramatically increasing processor utilization, and potentially dramatically slowing performance.

You can also remove a single plan from cache by identifying its plan_handle and then providing it as the parameter to the ALTER DATABASE statement. Perhaps this is a plan you would like to remove for testing or troubleshooting purposes that you have identified with the script in the previous section:

```
ALTER DATABASE SCOPED CONFIGURATION CLEAR PROCEDURE_CACHE 0x06000700CA920912307B86
7DB70100000100000000000000000000000000000000000000000000000000000000;
```

You can alternatively flush the cache by object type. This command clears cached execution plans that are the result of ad hoc statements and prepared statements (from applications, using sp_prepare, typically through an API):

```
DBCC FREESYSTEMCACHE ('SQL Plans');
```

The advantage of this statement is that it does not wipe the cached plans from "programmability" database objects such as stored procedures, multi-statement table-valued functions, scalar user-defined functions, and triggers. The following command clears the cached plans from these types of objects:

```
DBCC FREESYSTEMCACHE ('Object Plans');
```

NOTE

DBCC FREESYSTEMCACHE **is not supported in Azure SQL Database.**

You can also use DBCC FREESYSTEMCACHE to clear cached plans associated with a specific Resource Governor Pool, as follows:

```
DBCC FREESYSTEMCACHE ('SQL Plans', 'poolname');
```

Analyze cached execution plans

You can analyze execution plans in aggregate starting with the sys.dm_exec_cached_plans DMV, which contains a column named plan_handle. The plan_handle column contains a system-generated varbinary(64) string that can be used with a number of other DMVs. As seen in the code example that follows, you can use the plan_handle to gather information about aggregate plan usage, obtain plan statement text, and retrieve the graphical execution plan itself.

You might be used to viewing the graphical execution plan only after a statement is run in SSMS, but you can also analyze and retrieve plans for queries executed in the past by using the following query against a handful of dynamic management objects (DMOs). These DMOs return data for all databases in SQL Server instances, and for the current database in Azure SQL Database. The following query can be used to analyze different aspects of cached execution plans. Note that this query might take a considerable amount of time as written, so you might want to pare down what is being output for your normal usage.

```
SELECT
    p.usecounts AS UseCount,
    p.size_in_bytes / 1024 AS PlanSize_KB,
    qs.total_worker_time/1000 AS CPU_ms,
    qs.total_elapsed_time/1000 AS Duration_ms,
    p.cacheobjtype + ' (' + p.objtype + ')' as ObjectType,
    db_name(convert(int, txt.dbid )) as DatabaseName,
    txt.ObjectID,
    qs.total_physical_reads,
    qs.total_logical_writes,
    qs.total_logical_reads,
    qs.last_execution_time,
    qs.statement_start_offset as StatementStartInObject,
      SUBSTRING (txt.[text], qs.statement_start_offset/2 + 1 ,
      CASE
          WHEN qs.statement_end_offset = -1
          THEN LEN (CONVERT(nvarchar(max), txt.[text]))
          ELSE qs.statement_end_offset/2 - qs.statement_start_offset/2 + 1 END)
      AS StatementText,
      qp.query_plan as QueryPlan,
      aqp.query_plan as ActualQueryPlan
FROM sys.dm_exec_query_stats AS qs
INNER JOIN sys.dm_exec_cached_plans p ON p.plan_handle = qs.plan_handle
OUTER APPLY sys.dm_exec_sql_text (p.plan_handle) AS txt
```

```
OUTER APPLY sys.dm_exec_query_plan (p.plan_handle) AS qp
OUTER APPLY sys.dm_exec_query_plan_stats (p.plan_handle) AS aqp
--tqp is used for filtering on the text version of the query plan
CROSS APPLY sys.dm_exec_text_query_plan(p.plan_handle, qs.statement_start_offset,
qs.statement_end_offset) AS tqp
WHERE txt.dbid = db_id()
ORDER BY qs.total_worker_time + qs.total_elapsed_time DESC;
```

The preceding code sorts queries by a sum of the CPU time and duration, descending, returning the longest running queries first. You can adjust the ORDER BY and WHERE clauses in this query to find, for example, the most CPU-intensive or most busy execution plans. Keep in mind that the Query Store feature, as detailed later in this chapter, will help you visualize the process of identifying the most expensive and longest running queries in cache.

As you will see after running in the previous query, you can retrieve a wealth of information from these DMOs, including statistics for a statement within an object that generated the query plan. The query plan appears as a blue hyperlink in SSMS's Results to Grid mode, opening the plan as a new .sqlplan file. You can save and store the .sqlplan file for later analysis. Note too that this query might take quite a long time to execute as it will include a line for every statement in each query.

For more detailed queries, you can add code to search only for queries that have certain details in the plan—for example, looking for plans that have a reason for early termination value. In the execution plan XML, the reason for early termination will show in a node StatementOptmEarly AbortReason. You can add the search conditions before the ORDER BY in the script, using the following logic:

```
and tqp.query_plan LIKE '%StatementOptmEarlyAbortReason%'
```

Included in the query is sys.dm_exec_query_plan_stats, which provides the actual plan XML for a given plan_handle.

> ➤ **More details on** sys.dm_exec_query_plan_stats **are available at** *https://learn.microsoft*
> *.com/sql/relational-databases/system-dynamic-management-views/sys-dm-exec-query*
> *-plan-stats-transact-sql.*

Permissions required to access cached plan metadata

The only permission needed to run the previous query in SQL Server is the server-level VIEW SERVER STATE permission, which might be appropriate for developers to have access to in a production environment because it does not give them access to any data in user databases.

In Azure SQL Database, because of the differences between the Basic/Standard and Premium tiers, different permissions are needed. In the Basic/Standard tier, you must be the server admin or Azure Active Directory Admin to access objects that would usually require VIEW SERVER STATE. In the Premium tier, you can grant VIEW DATABASE STATE in the intended database in Azure SQL Database to a user who needs permission to view the preceding DMVs.

Understand parallelism

Parallelism in query processing, and computing in general, is a very complex topic. Luckily, much of the complexity of parallelism in SQL Server is generally encapsulated from the DBA and programmer.

A query that uses parallelism, and one that doesn't, can be the same query with the same plan (other than allowing one or more operators to work in parallel.) When SQL Server decides to split and stream data needed for requests into multiple threads, it uses more than one logical processor to get the job done. The number of different parallel threads used for the query is called the *degree of parallelism* (DOP). Because parallelism can never exceed the number of logical processors, naturally the maximum degree of parallelism (MAXDOP) is capped.

The main job of the DBA is to tune the MAXDOP for the server, database, and individual queries when the defaults don't behave well. On a server with a mixed load of OLTP and analytics workloads, some larger analytics queries can overpower other active users.

MAXDOP is set at the server level using the server UI in SSMS, or more commonly using the sp_configure system stored procedure. Starting in SQL Server 2019, there is a **MaxDOP** tab in SQL Setup, which proposes an initial MAXDOP for your server configuration. In previous versions, the system default was **0** (allowing all processors to be used in a single statement).

Parallelism is a seemingly magical way to make queries run faster (most of the time), but even *seeming* like magic comes at a price. While queries might perform fastest in a vacuum going massively parallel, the overuse of parallelism creates a multithreading bottleneck at scale with multiple users. Split into too many different parts, queries slow down *en masse* as CPU utilization rises and SQL Server records increasing values in the CXPACKET wait type.

> ➤ We talk about CXPACKET **here, but for more about wait type statistics, see Chapter 8.**

Until SQL Server 2016, MAXDOP was only a server-level setting, a setting enforced at the query level, or a setting enforced for sessions selectively via the Resource Governor, an Enterprise edition feature. Since SQL Server 2016, the MAXDOP setting is also available as a database-scoped configuration. You can also use the MAXDOP query hint in any statement to override the database or server level MAXDOP setting.

> ➤ For more details on Resource Governor, see Chapter 3: "Design and implement an on-premises database infrastructure," and Chapter 8.

Setting a reasonable value for MAXDOP will determine how many CPUs will be used to execute a query, but there is another setting to determine what queries are allowed to use parallelism: cost threshold for parallelism (CTFP). This enforces a minimum bar for query cost before a query can use a parallel execution plan. The higher the threshold, the fewer queries go parallel. This setting is low by default, but its proper setting in your environment depends on the workload and processor count. More expensive queries usually benefit from parallelism more than simpler queries, so limiting the use of parallelism to the worst queries in your workload can help. Similarly, setting the CTFP too high could have an opportunity impact, as performance is limited, queries are executed serially, and CPU cores go underutilized. Note that CTFP is a server-level setting only.

If large queries are already a problem for performance and multiple large queries regularly run simultaneously, raising the CTFP might not solve the problem. In addition to the obvious solutions of query tuning and index changes, it might be worth it to include the use of columnstore indexes for analytic queries and use MAXDOP as a hint instead to limit some very large queries from taking over your server.

A possible indication of parallelism being an issue is when the CXPACKET wait is a dominant wait type experienced over time by your SQL Server. You might need to adjust both MAXDOP and CTFP when performance tuning. You can also view the live and last wait types for a request using `sys.dm_exec_requests`. Make these changes in small, measured gestures, and don't overreact to performance problems with a small number of queries. Use Query Store to benchmark and trend the performance of high-value and high-cost queries as you change configuration settings.

Another flavor of CPU pressure, and in some ways the opposite of the CXPACKET wait type, is the SOS_SCHEDULER_YIELD wait type. The SOS_SCHEDULER_YIELD is an indicator of CPU pressure, indicating that SQL Server was forced to share time, or "yield" to other CPU tasks, which might be normal and expected on busy servers. Whereas CXPACKET is the SQL Server complaining about too many threads in parallel, SOS_SCHEDULER_YIELD is the acknowledgement that there were more runnable tasks than available threads. In either case, you should adopt a strategy of reducing CPU-intensive queries and rescheduling or optimizing CPU-intensive maintenance operations. This is more economical than simply adding CPU capacity.

Inside OUT

How can you reduce processor utilization during maintenance operations?

If processor utilization spikes during maintenance operations such as index maintenance or integrity checks, you can force them to run serially. Although this can increase the duration of maintenance, other queries should be less negatively affected.

You can use the MAXDOP query hint at the end of index maintenance to force index rebuild steps to run serially. Combined with the ONLINE hint, an Enterprise edition feature, your scripted index maintenance might run longer but have a minimal impact on concurrent queries. You can also specify MAXDOP when creating indexes. You cannot specify a MAXDOP for the reorganize step.

```
ALTER INDEX ALL ON WideWorldImporters.Sales.Invoices REBUILD
WITH (MAXDOP = 1, ONLINE = ON);
```

You can also enable Trace Flag 2528 to disable parallelism server-wide for DBCC CHECKDB, DBCC CHECKFILEGROUP, and DBCC CHECKTABLE operations. Keep in mind these operations can take hours to complete on large databases and might run longer if single-threaded.

Force a parallel execution plan

You know how to specify MAXDOP = 1 to force a query *not* to use parallelism. What about forcing parallelism? You can use a query hint to force a statement to compile with a parallel execution plan. This can be valuable in troubleshooting, or to force a behavior in the Query Optimizer for experimentation, but is not usually a necessary or recommended option for live code.

Appending the following hint to a query will force a parallel execution plan, which you can see using the estimate or actual execution plan output options:

```
... OPTION(USE HINT('ENABLE_PARALLEL_PLAN_PREFERENCE'));
```

> ### NOTE
>
> The presence of certain system variables or functions can force a statement to compile to be serial—that is, without any parallelism. This behavior will override the new ENABLE_PARALLEL_PLAN_PREFERENCE option.
>
> The @@TRANCOUNT system variable forces a serial plan, as do any of the built-in error reporting functions, including ERROR_LINE(), ERROR_MESSAGE(), ERROR_NUMBER(), ERROR_PROCEDURE(), ERROR_SEVERITY(), and ERROR_STATE(). This pertains only to using these objects in a query. Using them in the same batch, such as in a TRY ... CATCH handler, will not affect the execution plans of other queries in the batch.

Use advanced engine features to tune queries

In the past few versions of SQL Server and Azure SQL Database, the programmers building the Database Engine have started to add especially advanced features to go from the same cost-based optimizations we have had for many years, to tools that can sense when plans need to be adjusted before a DBA does. Not that any of these features will replace well-written code and a DBA who understands the architecture of how queries work, but as data needs explode, the more the engine can do for you, the better.

Internal improvements in SQL Server 2022

Microsoft has published a few details on some internal performance improvements that were introduced deep inside the Database Engine. Here is a summary of these advanced changes. None require an opt-in or deep understanding of the tech involved in order for you to benefit from them in SQL Server 2022.

- **Reduced buffer pool I/O promotions.** There is a documented phenomenon involving the read-ahead mechanism that pulls data from storage into the buffer pool. To read more about this complex topic, see this old Microsoft blog post at *https://learn.microsoft.com /archive/blogs/ialonso/the-read-ahead-that-doesnt-count-as-read-ahead*. New to SQL Server 2022, the number of incidents where a single page would be promoted to an extent has been reduced. This makes SQL Server's access of the physical I/O subsystem to populate memory more efficient. This change was delivered with SQL Server 2022 and pushed to Azure SQL Database and Azure SQL Managed Instance at the time of this writing.

- **Enhanced spinlock algorithms.** Another complex topic from deep within the Database Engine improves the performance of SQL Server when multiple threads generate spinlocks. This is an oversimplification of a complex topic, of course, but the details on this performance tune are limited. This change was delivered with SQL Server 2022 and pushed to Azure SQL Database and Azure SQL Managed Instance at the time of this writing.

- **Virtual Log File (VLF) allocation improvements.** In certain growth scenarios, the number of VLFs allocated to the transaction log was less efficient than it could have been. For small growth increments in small transaction log files, a single 64 MB VLF is created, instead of multiple VLFs. Over time, these VLF growth patterns make for a more efficient transaction log internal structure that benefits recovery and log truncation. For more details on the formulas involved here, visit *https://learn.microsoft.com/sql/relational-databases/sql-server -transaction-log-architecture-and-management-guide#virtual-log-files-vlfs*. This change was delivered with SQL Server 2022 and pushed to Azure SQL Database at the time of this writing.

Recent improvements to tempdb

Each of the past versions of SQL Server versions has introduced significant new features to improve the performance of the tempdb database. SQL Server 2022 introduces some key improvements to how tempdb works internally that do not require any configuration. You benefit from them immediately.

CHAPTER 14

In SQL Server 2022, system page latches in tempdb have received concurrency enhancements. Both Global Allocation Map (GAM) and Shared Global Allocation Map (SGAM) pages received updates to improve concurrency, an extension of the concurrency improvements to Page Free Space (PFS) pages in tempdb that were introduced with SQL Server 2019. Also in SQL Server 2019, memory-optimized metadata in tempdb cure some specific bottlenecks at high scale having to do with how temporary objects can be created, modified, and destroyed.

➤ For more information, see Chapter 3.

Leverage the Query Store feature

The Query Store provides a practical history of execution plan performance for a single database, which persists even when the server has been restarted (unlike the plan cache itself, which is cleared, eliminating all the interesting data that one needs for tuning queries over time). It can be invaluable for the purposes of investigating and troubleshooting sudden negative changes in performance, allowing the administrator or developer to identify both high-cost queries and the quality of their execution plans, and especially when the same query has multiple plans, where one performs poorly and the other well.

Starting with SQL Server 2022, and likely to be a default in Azure SQL Database and Azure SQL Managed Instance in the near future, the Query Store is enabled and in read/write mode by default for new databases. Databases migrated to SQL Server 2022 retain their Query Store settings.

The Query Store is most useful for looking back in time toward the history of statement execution. It can also assist in identifying and overriding execution plans by using a feature similar to, but different from, the plan guides or Query Store hints feature. As discussed in the previous section, plan guides are used to override a query's plan. Instead of plan guides, consider instead the Query Store's ability to force plans, or the Query Store hints feature (introduced in SQL Server 2022 and Azure SQL Database) to shape query plans without code changes.

The Query Store allows you to find plans that are not working well, but only gives you the ability to force an entire plan that worked better from the history it has stored. The Query Store has a major benefit over legacy plan guides in that there is an SSMS user interface to access it, see the benefits, and find places where you might need to apply a new plan.

You see live Query Store data as it happens from a combination of both memory-optimized and on-disk sources. Query Store minimizes overhead and performance impact by capturing cached plan information to in-memory data structure. The data is *flushed* (persisted) to disk at an interval defined by Query Store, by a default of 15 minutes. The **Disk Flush Interval** setting defines how much Query Store data can be lost in the event of an unexpected system shutdown.

NOTE

Queries are captured in the context of the database where the query is executed. In the following cross-database query example, the query's execution is captured in the Query Store of the WideWorldImporters sample database.

```
USE WideWorldImporters;
GO
SELECT * FROM
AdventureWorks.[Purchasing].[PurchaseOrders];
```

Microsoft delivered the Query Store to the Azure SQL Database platform *first*, and then to the SQL Server product. In fact, Query Store is at the heart of the Azure SQL Database Advisor feature that provides automatic query tuning. The Query Store feature's overhead is quite manageable, tuned to avoid performance hits, and is already in place on millions of customer databases in Azure SQL Database.

The VIEW DATABASE STATE permission is all that is needed to view the Query Store data.

Initial configuration of Query Store

Query Store is identical between the Azure SQL Database and SQL Server in operation, but not in how you activate it. Query Store is enabled automatically on Azure SQL Database and all new databases starting with SQL Server 2022, but it is not automatically on for existing databases that you migrate to SQL Server 2022.

When should you enable Query Store? Enabling Query Store on all databases you have in your environment is a generally acceptable practice, as it will be useful in discovering performance issues in the future when they arise. You can enable Query Store via the database's **Properties** dialog box, in which a **Query Store** page is accessible from the menu on the left, or you can turn it on via T-SQL by using the following command:

```
ALTER DATABASE [DatabaseOne] SET QUERY_STORE = ON;
```

This will enable Query Store with the defaults; you can adjust them using the UI.

NOTE

As with almost any configuration task, while it is acceptable to use the UI the first few times, it will always be better to have a script in T-SQL or PowerShell to capture settings in a repeatable manner. Use the **Script** button in most SSMS UIs to output a script of what has changed when you are setting new values.

Query Store begins collecting data when you activate it. You will not have any historical data when you first enable the feature on an existing database, but you will begin to immediately see data for live database activity. You can then view plans and statistics about the plan in the Query Store reports.

In versions before SQL Server 2019, the default Query Store capture mode setting was ALL, which included all queries that were executed. In SQL Server 2019, this default has been changed to AUTO, which is recommended. The AUTO Query Store capture mode forgets queries that are insignificant in terms of execution duration or frequency. Further, the CUSTOM Query Store capture mode allows for more fine tuning that may become necessary on large and busy databases. While AUTO works fine for most servers, you can use custom capture policies to configure the tradeoff: the amount of history remembered by Query Store versus the amount of storage the Query Store consumes inside the user database.

The Query Store retains data up to two limits: a max size (1,000 MB by default), and a Stale Query Threshold time limit in days (30 by default). If Query Store reaches its max size, it cleans up the oldest data. Because Query Store data is saved in the database, its historical data is not affected by the commands we looked at earlier in this chapter to clear the procedure cache, such as DBCC FREEPROCACHE.

You should almost always keep the size-based cleanup mode set to the default, Auto. If not, when the max size is reached, Query Store will stop collecting data and enter read-only mode, which does not collect new data. If you find that the Query Store is not storing more historical days of data than your stale query threshold setting in days, increase the max size setting.

Troubleshoot with Query Store data

Query Store has several built-in dashboards, shown in Figure 14-8, to help you examine query performance and overall performance over recent history.

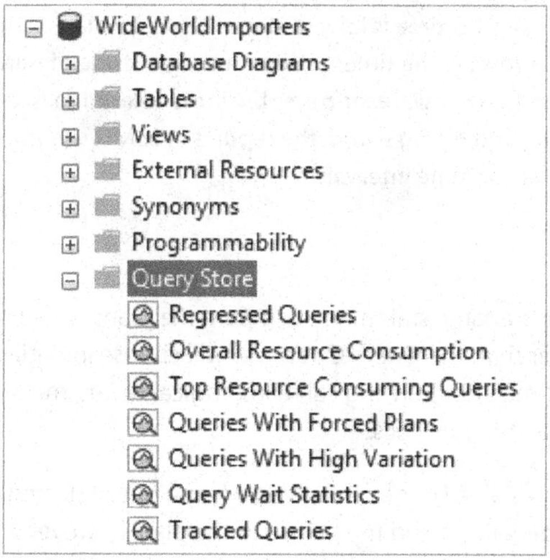

Figure 14-8 The SQL Server Object Explorer list of built-in dashboards available for Query Store in SSMS.

You can also write your own reports against the collection of system DMOs that present Query Store data to administrators and developers by using the VIEW DATABASE STATE permission.

➤ You can view the schema of the well-documented views and their relationships at *https:// learn.microsoft.com/sql/relational-databases/performance/how-query-store-collects-data*.

On many of the dashboards, there is a button with a crosshairs symbol, as shown in Figure 14-9. If a query seems interesting, expensive, or is of high value to the business, you can select this button to view a new window that tracks the query when it's running as well as various plans identified for that query.

Figure 14-9 The Query Store toolbar at the top of the screen on many of the dashboards—in this example, the toolbar for the Regressed Queries report.

Inside OUT

When should you force a statement to use a certain execution plan?

Assess the statement's execution plans using a variety of factors before choosing to force a plan. Just because the duration or CPU time is lowest, doesn't mean a plan is superior. It could be that the table had fewer rows at the time, or was running outside of normal operating hours with no competition for hardware, or other business-related reasons. Query Store allows for a variety of slicing and dicing within the reports in SSMS; use the **Configure** button to examine various criteria and time intervals.

You can review the various plans for the same statement, compare the plans, and if necessary, force a plan that you believe is better than the Query Optimizer will choose into place. Compare the execution of each plan by CPU time, duration, logical reads, logical writes, memory consumption, physical reads, and several other metrics.

Most of all, the Query Store can be valuable by informing you when a query started using a new plan. You can see when a plan was generated and the nature of the plan; however, the cause of the plan's creation and replacement is not easily deduced, especially when you cannot correlate to a specific DDL operation or system change. Query plans can become invalidated automatically due to large changes in statistics resulting from data inserts or deletes, changes made to other statements in the stored procedure, changes to any of the indexes used by the plan, or manual recompilation due to the RECOMPILE option.

As discussed in the upcoming "Query Store hints" section, forcing a statement (see Figure 14-10) to use a specific execution plan should not be a common activity. If you have access to the source code, work on a code change, only using a forced plan temporarily. For systems where you have no code access, you can use a Query Store hint for specific performance cases, problematic queries demanding unusual plans, and so on. Note that if the forced plan is invalid, such as an index changing or being dropped, SQL Server will move on without the forced plan and without a warning or error, although Query Store will still show that the plan is being forced for that statement. Note that once a plan has been forced for this statement (using the **Force Plan** button), the plan is displayed with a check mark.

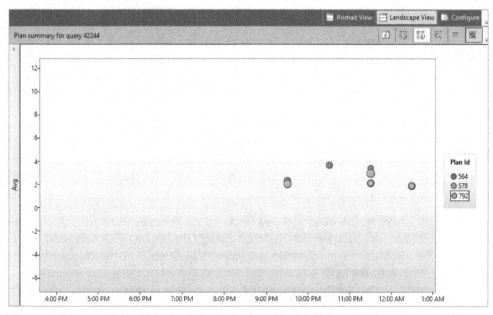

Figure 14-10 The Query Store records the query's execution results.

Inside OUT

How should you force a statement to use a certain execution plan?

Your options for forcing a statement to follow a certain execution plan are using plan guides, stored procedures (which also allow you to make slight changes to the plan by adding a hint to the plan, rather than replacing the entire plan), the USE PLAN hint, or the Query Store interface (and its underlying stored procedures) to force an execution plan. Of these options, the Query Store makes the business of forcing query plans easiest to implement and evaluate.

These are advanced options for limited, temporary, and/or diagnostic use only. Overriding the Query Optimizer's execution plan choice is an advanced performance tuning technique. It is most often necessitated by query parameter sniffing, which can be addressed in a variety of ways, detailed in this chapter.

Consider instead using Query Store hints to provide a variety of powerful query-shaping hints without code changes, and let the Query Optimizer make good choices from there.

Finally, without using Query Store or plan guides, you can use the USE PLAN query hint to provide the entire XML query plan for any statement execution. This is the least convenient option, and like other approaches that override the query analyzer, should be considered an advanced and temporary performance tuning technique.

Query Store hints

In past editions of this book, in this space, we'd discuss plan guides—an aging and well-documented feature that was inconvenient if not downright painful to implement. The new Query Store hints feature is a superior alternative to plan guides. Query Store hints provide powerful tools to shape queries without making code changes, giving administrators and developers options to modify query plans substantially and easily.

Query Store hints were in preview for Azure SQL Database and Azure SQL Managed Instance starting mid-2021, and later Microsoft brought the feature to SQL Server 2022. Like many of the new IQP features introduced in SQL Server 2022, Query Store hints require the Query Store to be enabled on the database. For this reason, you should strongly consider enabling, monitoring, and customizing the Query Store feature on every performance-sensitive database.

Query Store hints give administrators an easy replacement to the older plan guides feature, which was introduced in SQL Server 2005. You can use Query Store to force replacement plans into action. You can use Query Store hints to force hints into query plans. All require no code changes, giving administrators and developers options to modify query plans coming from third-party software, SSIS packages, and business intelligence tools.

With both plan guides and Query Store hints, you can influence a plan by simply adding a hint (a common example would be WITH RECOMPILE). This can be very useful if you have a plan that is being chosen by SQL Server that doesn't work for you and you have no way to change the query code in question. Combined with new improvements around parameter sniffing thanks to PSP optimization, it is easy to achieve performance gains in SQL Server 2022.

Query Store is a more complete tuning solution than plan guides, capturing plans from the plan cache and tracking query performance with different plans over time. A suite of reports and graphical tools make it easy to investigate query performance. Like with plan guides, you can manually override the query plan chosen with a previously observed plan. Further, the automatic plan correction feature can automatically override a query plan with a previously observed plan that performed better. Automatic plan correction was introduced with SQL Server 2017.

This section reviews aspects of both tools to help guide you as to which tool to choose. Note, however, that tools that force a plan to override what the Query Optimizer has chosen are not considered the best approach to query tuning. If you have an application where you own the source code, forcing a plan might be good to do until you can make a change to code, but should not be your primary tuning tool. If it is a third-party application, you should work with your vendor on a proper solution, but these features will help you to get past a serious issue.

Inside OUT

Can you apply Query Store hints on secondary replicas?

Yes. When the Query Store for secondary replicas feature is enabled, hints can be applied to primary and secondary replicas independently.

For safety, when an availability group fails over, hints aren't applied from the old primary to the new primary, in case the capabilities of the replica aren't the same.

At the time of this book's writing, Query Store for secondary replicas is a nascent public preview feature behind a trace flag, so look for more development in this area by Microsoft in future cumulative updates for SQL Server 2022 and in Azure SQL platforms.

Use Query Store hints

Currently, like plan guides, Query Store hints are driven by T-SQL stored procedures and not accessible from within any GUI (yet). But the identification of queries can occur through the Query Store interface, through a unique key for all queries captured by the Query Store, query_id.

CAUTION

Query Store hints—like plan guides or forcing plans using USE PLAN or the Query Store—are an advanced troubleshooting technique and are not without some risk.

The following steps will detail how to back out of a Query Store hint quickly. Be prepared to observe and rollback any hints.

1. Identify a useful hint for the query, ideally by using a non-production performance testing environment with similar hardware and data scale.

2. Identify the Query Store–assigned `query_id` for the query. Note that the `query_id` will be different on different instances of SQL Server.

3. Use `sys.sp_query_store_set_hints` to apply a hint. Most query hints are supported. For example, to apply the `MAXDOP 1` hint to `query_id` 1234, use the following:

```
EXEC sys.sp_query_store_set_hints @query_id= 1234,
@query_hints = N'OPTION(MAXDOP 1)';
```

> ➤ **For a complete list of supported query hints, review the Microsoft Docs article for** `sys.sp` `_query_store_set_hints` **at** *https://learn.microsoft.com/sql/relational-databases/system* *-stored-procedures/sys-sp-query-store-set-hints-transact-sql#supported-query-hints.*

You can specify more than one query hint in a Query Store hint, just as you would in the `OPTION` clause of any T-SQL query. For example, to specify `MAXDOP 1` and the pre-SQL Server 2014 cardinality estimator, use this:

```
EXEC sys.sp_query_store_set_hints @query_id= 1234,
@query_hints = N'OPTION(MAXDOP 1,
USE HINT(''FORCE_LEGACY_CARDINALITY_ESTIMATION''))';
```

The Query Store hint takes effect immediately and adds three attributes to the execution plan XML: `QueryStoreStatementHintId`, `QueryStoreStatementHintText`, and `QueryStoreStatementHintSource`. If you're curious, you can review these to see the Query Store hint in action, and prove the hint altered the query without code changes.

4. Observe and confirm that your hint is helping the query's execution. Confirm the Query Store hint(s) currently in place for your query as follows:

```
SELECT * FROM sys.query_store_query_hints
WHERE query_id = 1234;
```

5. Remove the Query Store hint when necessary with `sys.sp_query_store_clear_hints`. (You want to prepare for this ahead of time.)

```
EXEC sys.sp_query_store_clear_hints @query_id = 1234;
```

6. Set yourself a reminder to reevaluate any Query Store hints on a regular basis. Data distributions change and the winds of fate blow. Changes to underlying data and concurrent server workloads might cause Query Store hints to generate suboptimal execution plans in the future.

If you set a Query Store hint, it will overwrite any existing hint for that `query_id`. Query Store hints will override other hard-coded statement level hints and plan guides, but you should avoid conflicting instructions as they could be confusing for others in your environment.

Inside OUT

Does the Query Store work on readable secondary replicas in an availability group?

Yes! A new feature of SQL Server 2022 includes a complex mechanism to capture Query Store data asynchronously on secondary, read-only replicas and harden the Query Store to the primary replica of an availability group.

This means that some intelligent query processing features can now be replica aware, including memory grant feedback. Memory grant feedback can aid primary and secondary replicas differently, which is good, because primary and secondary replicas should have different workloads.

As of the writing of this book, this feature was in public preview. Look for more development and announcements around this feature.

Automatic plan correction

Automatic plan correction is a feature that relies on the Query Store to detect and revert query duration regression. For example, suppose a commonly executed query normally runs in 100 milliseconds, but then changes execution plans and starts finishing in 2 minutes. Instead of waiting for complaints of slow performance, the engine can notice this regression and deal with it. SQL Server 2017 introduced this feature to the on-premises versions of the Database Engine, and was originally released for Azure SQL Database.

A typical use case is to view the regressed queries report in Query Store, identify a query that has regressed in duration, and then force a better past execution plan into use. With automatic plan correction enabled, the database can detect plan regression and take action to force the previous plan back into action, automatically. The sample syntax for enabling automatic plan correction is below:

```
ALTER DATABASE WideWorldImporters SET AUTOMATIC_TUNING (FORCE_LAST_GOOD_PLAN = ON );
```

The `sys.dm_db_tuning_recommendations` DMO captures plan recommendations based on query performance regression. This doesn't happen immediately—the feature has an algorithm that requires several executions before regression is identified. When a recommendation appears in `sys.dm_db_tuning_recommendations`, it includes a large amount of diagnostic data, including a plain-language explanation for the recommendation to be generated, and a block of JSON data containing diagnostic information.

➤ A sample query to parse this data is available at *https://learn.microsoft.com/sql/relational-databases/automatic-tuning/automatic-tuning*.

Intelligent query processing

Intelligent query processing (IQP) is not a tool or a GUI option, but rather a suite of behind-the-scenes features that make the processing of queries more efficient. Many are specific to the database compatibility version; you don't benefit from them in an older version compatibility. Some features help to pick or adapt a query plan to current conditions. Others are just straight up changes to how the Database Engine uses long existing query constructs. In every case, the goal of IQP features is to improve the way queries are processed without code changes.

The remainder of this chapter covers the new IQP features in SQL Server 2022 and some of the most significant features in recent versions, though a review of the complete list of the IQP suite of performance features is worthwhile.

➤ For more information, see *https://learn.microsoft.com/sql/relational-databases/performance /intelligent-query-processing*.

Inside OUT

Do you need to enable Query Store for the latest query tuning performance features to work?

Yes, many of the newest IQP features in SQL Server 2022 depend on Query Store data—specifically the three new feedback features that help SQL Server perform better on successive execution of a query. Memory grant feedback, cardinality estimation (CE) feedback, and degree of parallelism (DOP) feedback all require the Query Store to be active in that database.

Batch mode on rowstore

One of the features added, along with columnstore indexes, in SQL Server 2012 was a type of processing known as *batch mode*. Columnstore indexes were built to process compressed row-groups containing millions of rows. A new processing mode was needed when the heuristics told the query processor it would be worthwhile to work on batches of rows at a time.

➤ For more details on batch and row mode processing, see *https://learn.microsoft.com/sql /relational-databases/query-processing-architecture-guide*.

Starting with SQL Server 2019 and included in Azure SQL Database, this feature was extended to work for certain types of queries with row store tables and indexes as well as columnstore tables and indexes. A few examples:

● Queries that use large quantities of rows in a table, often in analytical queries touching hundreds of thousands of rows.

● Systems that are CPU bound in nature. (I/O bottlenecks are best handled with a column-store index.)

The feature is enabled when the compatibility level is at least 150. Though unusual, if you find it is harming performance, you can turn it off using ALTER DATABASE without lowering the compatibility level:

```
ALTER DATABASE SCOPED CONFIGURATION SET BATCH_MODE_ON_ROWSTORE = OFF;
```

Instead of changing this setting for the database, you could disallow this feature for a specific query, perhaps one that touches large number of rows. You can use the query hint ALLOW _BATCH_MODE. For example:

```
SELECT …
FROM …
OPTION(USE HINT('ALLOW_BATCH_MODE'));
```

NOTE

Columnstore and rowstore indexes continue to exchange advantageous features. In SQL Server 2022, ordered clustered columnstore indexes arrived, a feature first introduced for Azure Synapse Analytics. We cover this more in the next chapter.

Cardinality estimation (CE) feedback

Similar to other feedback features, CE feedback allows the Query Optimizer to adapt to changes in query performance based on suboptimal CE. CE estimates the total number of rows in the various stages of a query plan. (Constraints and key relationships between tables can help inform and shortcut estimation, another good reason to put them in place.)

CE feedback is a process by which the Query Optimizer learns by modeling query behavior over time. This feature requires both compatibility level 160 (for SQL Server 2022) and the Query Store to be enabled for the database.

In the past, the cardinality estimator and the database's compatibility level were closely linked. (Changes in SQL Server 2014 improved the cardinality estimator in most but not all cases, with severe impacts when it missed.) CE feedback does not change the database compatibility level for the query, but makes incremental corrections via the Query Store hint feature.

➤ **For more about Query Store hints, see the "Understand cardinality estimation" section earlier in this chapter.**

At the time of this writing, CE feedback is not yet available in Azure SQL Database or Azure SQL Managed Instance, but should be available in the near future.

SQL Server 2022 also added a persistence feature for CE feedback. Persistence helps CE feedback avoid poor adjustment decisions by remembering query information, even if a plan is evicted from cache. Using the Query Store, estimates can be considered over multiple query executions.

Degree of parallelism (DOP) feedback

DOP feedback has perhaps the biggest impact of all the feedback features introduced to make SQL Server more adaptive to observed performance. The ability for the Query Optimizer to analyze and adapt to observed query performance and make changes to parallelism with each query execution is a powerful self-tuning feature.

DOP feedback is introduced with SQL Server 2022, and requires the Query Store feature to be enabled. Further, the DOP_FEEDBACK database scoped configuration can be enabled or disabled if necessary.

Instead of worrying about optimizing the database's MAXDOP for the most important parts of a workload, DOP feedback automatically adjusts parallelism for repeating queries with the goal of increasing overall concurrency and reducing wait times. Smartly, DOP feedback excludes some wait types that are not relevant to this part of query performance, such as buffer latch, buffer IO, and network IO waits.

DOP feedback adjusts queries automatically by adding the MAXDOP query hint, but never at a value exceeding the database's MAXDOP setting. You might consider exploring the performance gains with DOP feedback in a different (higher) MAXDOP setting for your server or database in SQL Server 2022.

At the time of this writing, DOP feedback is not yet available in Azure SQL Database or Azure SQL Managed Instance, but should be available in the near future.

SQL Server 2022 also added a persistence feature for DOP feedback. Persistence helps the DOP feedback feature avoid poor adjustment decisions by remembering query information, even if a plan is evicted from cache. Using the Query Store, optimal parallelism can be considered over multiple executions.

Memory grant feedback

When a query executes, it uses some amount of memory. Memory grant feedback lets future executions of the same query know if the memory granted for the execution was too much or too little, so it can adjust future executions. Memory grant feedback was introduced in SQL Server 2017 for batch mode executions, and in SQL Server 2019 for row mode executions.

If for some reason you want to disable this feature in a database, you can do so without lowering the database compatibility level using the following statements:

```
-- SQL Server 2017
ALTER DATABASE SCOPED CONFIGURATION SET DISABLE_BATCH_MODE_MEMORY_GRANT_FEEDBACK = OFF;
-- Azure SQL Database, SQL Server 2019 or later
ALTER DATABASE SCOPED CONFIGURATION SET BATCH_MODE_MEMORY_GRANT_FEEDBACK = OFF;
For row mode queries, this feature is controlled using:
ALTER DATABASE SCOPED CONFIGURATION SET ROW_MODE_MEMORY_GRANT_FEEDBACK = OFF;
```

SQL Server 2022 further enhances memory grant feedback with two additional features: persistence and percentile improvement. Both are intended to help the Query Optimizer avoid expensive memory spills by accurately estimating (or at worst, overestimating) the amount of memory needed for crucial parts of an execution plan.

Memory grant feedback persistence allows SQL Server to remember query memory grant information even if a plan is evicted from cache. Using the Query Store, feedback can be considered over multiple executions. Persistence also applies to CE feedback and DOP feedback, as stated.

Memory grant feedback percentile adjustment allows the memory grant adjustment to examine the recent history of query execution, not just the most recent execution. The complex calculation now includes the 90th percentile of past memory grants over time. The percentile adjustment only applies to memory grant feedback.

When the new Query Store for secondary replicas feature is enabled, memory grant feedback is replica aware and can help primary and secondary replica workloads differently.

Parameter Sensitive Plan optimization

Parameter Sensitive Plan (PSP) optimization, new in SQL Server 2022, addresses the age-old problem of queries getting a suboptimal execution plan when the value of a filter wildly changes the result sets. PSP solves the problem in an intuitive way: by allowing *more than one* cached execution plan to be saved for a single query.

Imagine a search query for sales, filtered on customer, where `customer_id = @customer_id`. Customer 1 has been purchasing goods for decades, and has millions of invoice line items. Customer 2 is a new customer with a single invoice. In previous versions of SQL Server, should the execution plan for customer 2 become *the* execution plan for this search query, performance of the query on customer 1 would be poor. This is because the operators chosen for the execution plan would be unlikely to scale from one row to millions of rows in the result set.

Previous solutions required an understanding of query parameterization and the application of a variety of strategies, including cache preparation, synthetically calling queries with their largest filter parameters using the `OPTIMIZE FOR` query hint, or using plan guides. Between PSP optimization and Query Store hints, SQL Server 2022 provides multiple superior options to deal with this classic problem. PSP optimization uses a complex set of instructions that require a significant amount of performance data to act and cache a different plan, in an effort to minimize memory utilization associated with unnecessary plan retention.

PSP optimization is part of the database compatibility level 160 feature set, so be sure to update the compatibility level for any databases migrated up to SQL Server 2022. Query Store is not required for PSP optimization, but it is recommended.

If for some reason you need to disable PSP optimization, you can do so without lowering the database compatibility level with the PARAMETER_SENSITIVE_PLAN_OPTIMIZATION database-scoped configuration option.

➤ For a deep dive on the internals of PSP optimization, see *https://learn.microsoft.com/sql /relational-databases/performance/parameter-sensitivity-plan-optimization.*

CAUTION

A known bug in an early public preview of PSP optimization in SQL Server 2022 raised an error when you did not specify two part names (schemaname.objectname) in stored procedures that were not in the dbo schema. While this bug has been fixed, it's just another reminder that a good best practice is to always specify two-part names in your T-SQL code, even for objects in the dbo schema.

Table variable deferred compilation

Table variable deferred compilation was introduced in SQL Server 2019 to deal with the glaring lack of statistics for a table variable at compile time. Previously, SQL Server defaulted to a guess of one (1) row for the number of rows in the table variable. This provided poorly performing plans if the programmer had stored any significant number of rows in the table variable.

Similarly, an IQP feature introduced in SQL Server 2017 called *interleaved execution* improved the performance of multi-statement table-valued functions. Interleaved execution let the Query Optimizer execute parts of the query during optimization to get better estimates, because if your multi-statement table-valued function is going to output 100,000 rows, the plan needs to be considerably different.

Instead of using the guess of 1 to define the query plan, table variable deferred compilation waits to complete the actual plan until the table variable has been loaded the first time, and then the rest of the plan is generated.

NOTE

Table variable optimizations do not make table variables the best choice for large numbers of rows. Table variables still lack column statistics, a key difference between them and temp tables (prefixed with # or ##) that can make temp tables far superior for large rowsets.

T-SQL scalar user-defined function (UDF) inlining

A common culprit of poor performance in custom applications is user-defined functions (UDFs). Every programmer who has taken any class in object-oriented programming (OOP) instinctively desires to modularize or de-duplicate their code. So, if you have a scenario in which you want to classify some data (say, something simple like CASE WHEN 1 THEN 'True' ELSE 'False' END), it makes sense from a programmer's perspective to bundle this up into a coded module (code reuse). However, UDFs can become a bear trap at scale for application performance.

Introduced in SQL Server 2019, scalar UDF inlining alleviates some of the performance hit introduced by UDFs at scale; it's an automatic, no-code-change-necessary, performance boost. This is a complex fix that substitutes scalar expressions or subqueries in the query during query optimization. Throughout the post-RTM life of SQL Server 2019, cumulative updates added complexity, issue fixes, and restrictions to UDF inlining.

> ➤ For details, see *https://learn.microsoft.com/sql/relational-databases/user-defined-functions /scalar-udf-inlining*.

Example of scalar UDF inlining

To demonstrate UDF inlining, we created the following overly simple UDF in the WideWorld Importers sample database:

```
USE WideWorldImporters;
GO
CREATE SCHEMA Tools;
GO
CREATE FUNCTION Tools.Bit_Translate
(@value bit)
RETURNS varchar(5)
AS
BEGIN
    RETURN (CASE WHEN @value = 1 THEN 'True' ELSE 'False' END);
END;
```

To demonstrate, execute the function in the same query twice: once in SQL Server 2017 (14.0) database compatibility level, before scalar UDF inlining was introduced, and again with SQL Server 2022 (16.0) database compatibility level behavior.

```
SET STATISTICS TIME ON;
ALTER DATABASE WideWorldImporters SET COMPATIBILITY_LEVEL = 140; --SQL Server 2017
GO
SELECT Tools.Bit_Translate(IsCompressed) AS CompressedFlag,
CASE WHEN IsCompressed = 1 THEN 'True' ELSE 'False' END AS CompressedFlag_Desc
FROM  Warehouse.VehicleTemperatures;
GO
ALTER DATABASE WideWorldImporters SET COMPATIBILITY_LEVEL = 160; -- SQL Server 2022
GO
SELECT Tools.Bit_Translate(IsCompressed) AS CompressedFlag,
CASE WHEN IsCompressed = 1 THEN 'True' ELSE 'False' END
FROM  Warehouse.VehicleTemperatures;
```

On the 65,998 rows returned in each result set, you will likely not notice a difference in performance. Checking the output from SET STATISTICS TIME ON on this author's machine, the execution in COMPATIBILITY LEVEL = 160 was only about 75 milliseconds faster on average.

Looking at the actual plan CPU used for the two executions in Figure 14-11, you can see an interesting difference.

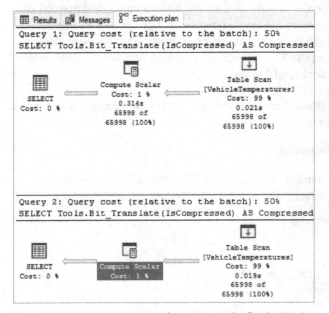

Figure 14-11 Query plan output for two runs, the first in SQL Server 2017 (14.0) compatibility level, and the second in SQL Server 2022 (16.0) benefitting from scalar UDF inlining.

The big thing to notice between these two executions is that the compute scalar in query 2 appears as a typical compute scalar operator, for any scalar expression not including a UDF. In query 1, it shows rows passing through, and an amount of time as it calculates the scalar for each row that passes through. Even in this extremely simple case, we saved time because we avoided running the function in a cursor-like loop for every row.

There are limitations to scalar UDF inlining, such as not working when time dependent intrinsic functions like SYSDATETIME() are present. You cannot change security context using EXECUTE AS (only EXECUTE AS CALLER, the default, is allowed). You also cannot benefit from scalar UDF inlining when referencing table variables or table-valued parameters.

> ➤ For more details and the complete list of requirements see *https://learn.microsoft.com/sql /relational-databases/user-defined-functions/scalar-udf-inlining.*

Scalar UDF inlining has immediate value for databases whose programmers have overused scalar UDFs. For many, scalar UDF inlining removes the problematic performance stigma associated with scalar UDFs, opening up more use cases. Formatting functions and translation functions where it might be easier than creating a table are now possible and will perform very well, as opposed to destroying your performance.

Understand and design indexes

This chapter dives into indexing of all kinds—not just clustered and nonclustered indexes—including practical development techniques for designing indexes. It mentions memory-optimized tables throughout, including hash indexes for extreme writes and columnstore indexes for extreme reads. The chapter reviews missing indexes and index usage, and then introduces statistics—how they are created and updated. There are important performance-related options for statistics objects. Finally, it explains special types of indexes for niche uses.

In SQL Server you have access to a variety of indexing tools in your toolbox.

We've had clustered and nonclustered indexes in all 21st-century versions of SQL Server—those two rowstore index types that are the bread and butter of SQL Server. We cover those in the first half of this chapter, including important new options for SQL Server 2022.

Introduced in SQL Server 2012, columnstore indexes presented a new and exciting way to perform analytical queries on massive amounts of compressed data. They became an essential tool for database developers, and this chapter discusses them in detail. SQL Server 2014 brought memory-optimized tables and their uniquely powerful hash indexes for latchless querying on rapidly changing data. You can even combine the power of these two new concepts now, with columnstore index concepts on memory-optimized tables, allowing for live analytical-scale queries on streamed data. First, though, we're going to dive into the index design concepts.

Inside OUT

What's the difference between rowstore and columnstore?

If these terms are new to you, *rowstore indexes* describe the only type of clustered indexes (and nonclustered indexes) that existed before SQL Server 2012. These indexes are traditional B+ tree indexes that have always existed in SQL Server and continue to be foundational to OLTP workloads. Rowstore structures also include tables without a clustered index (known as *heaps*), as well as memory-optimized tables.

> *Columnstore indexes* were introduced in SQL Server 2012 and serve a different purpose. They are superior to rowstore data storage for performance only in appropriate situations—specifically, in scans of millions of rows or more in large tables. Highly compressed, columnstore indexes take up less storage (and therefore, need less I/O) to serve queries typical in enterprise reporting, data warehousing, and OLAP scenarios. Columnstore indexes have important new performance enhancements in SQL Server 2022 that we'll discuss in this chapter.
>
> Both rowstore and columnstore indexes are important tools for database designers in modern applications. In some database designs, rowstore, columnstore, and hash-based indexes on memory-optimized tables all play a role. We discuss all these at length in this chapter.

All scripts for this book are all available for download at *https://www.MicrosoftPressStore.com /SQLServer2022InsideOut/downloads*.

Design clustered indexes

Let's be clear about what a clustered index is, and then state the case for why every table in a relational database should have one, with very few exceptions.

First, we will discuss rowstore clustered indexes. It is also possible to create a clustered columnstore index. We discuss that later in this chapter.

Whether you are inheriting and maintaining a database or designing the objects within it, there are important facts to know about clustered indexes. In the case of both rowstore and columnstore indexes, the clustered index stores the data rows for all columns in the table. In the case of rowstore indexes, the table data is logically sorted by the clustered index key; in the case of clustered columnstore indexes, there is no key. Memory-optimized tables don't have a clustered index structure inherent to their design but could have a clustered columnstore index created for them.

Choose a proper rowstore clustered index key

There are four marks of a good clustered index key for most OLTP applications, or in the case of a compound clustered index key, the first column listed. The column order matters. Let's review four key factors that will help you understand what role the clustered index key serves, and how best to design one:

- **Increasing sequential value.** A value that increases with every row inserted (such as 1,2,3..., or an increasing point in time, or an increasing alphanumeric) is useful in efficient page organization. This means the insert pattern of the data as it comes in from the business will match the loading of rows onto the physical structures of the table.

A column with the `identity` property, or populated by a value from a sequence object, matches this perfectly. Use date and time data only if it is highly unlikely to repeat, and then strongly consider using the `datetimeoffset` data type to avoid repeated data once annually during daylight saving time changes.

- **Unique.** A clustered index key does not need to be unique, but in most cases it should be. (The clustered key also does not need to be the primary key of the table, or the only uniqueness enforced in the table.) A unique (or near-unique) clustered index means efficient seeks. If your application will be searching for individual rows out of this table regularly, you and the business should know what makes those searches unique.

  Unique constraints, whether nonclustered or clustered, can improve performance on the same data and create a more efficient structure. A unique constraint is the same as a unique rowstore nonclustered index.

  If a clustered index is declared without the UNIQUE property, a second key value is added in the background: a four-byte integer *uniquifier* column. SQL Server must have some way to uniquely identify each row. The key from the rowstore clustered index is used as the row locator for nonclustered indexes, which leads to the next factor.

- **Nonchanging.** Choose a key that doesn't change, and is a system-generated key that shouldn't be visible to end-user applications or reports. In general, when end users can see data, they will eventually see fit to *change* that data. You do not want clustered index keys to ever change (much less PRIMARY KEY values). A system-generated or surrogate key of sequential values (like an IDENTITY column) is ideal. A field that combines system or application-generated fields such as dates and times or numbers would work too.

  The negative impact of changing the clustering key includes the possibility that the first two aforementioned guidelines would be broken. If the clustered key is also a primary key, updating the key's values could also require cascading updates to enforce referential integrity. It is much easier for everyone involved if only columns with business value are exposed to end users and, therefore, can be changed by end users. In normalized database design, we would call these *natural keys* as opposed to *surrogate keys*.

- **Narrow data type.** The decision with respect to data type for your clustered index key can have a large impact on table size, the cost of index maintenance, and the efficiency of queries at scale. The clustered index key value is also stored with every nonclustered index key value, meaning that an unnecessarily wide clustered index key will also cause unnecessarily wide nonclustered indexes on the table. This can have a very large impact on storage on drives and in memory at scale.

  The narrow data type guidance should also steer you away from using the `unique identifier` field, which is 16 bytes per row, or four times the size of an integer column per row, and twice as large as a `bigint`. It also steers away from using wide strings, such as names, addresses, or URLs.

Inside OUT

Why might unique identifiers be a poor choice for the clustered index key, even for the "oil rig problem"?

There is a common design challenge to store rows from multiple (perhaps disconnected) data sources in the same table—for example, oil rigs, medical devices, or a supervisory control and data acquisition (SCADA) system. Each data source must create unique values for itself, but those values must then be combined into a single table. The `uniqueidentifier` data type and `newid()` function can be an option because they generate values uniquely across multiple servers.

This is not a good design for scale, however, because unique identifiers are random, meaning inserts will fragment a table with each new row. This will cause page splits (an expensive I/O operation) as the rows naturally merge into the rest with each insert in the "middle" rather than at the end, inserting sequentially. (You can mitigate this, though not significantly, by altering the fill factor of each index that uses the unique identifier as a key. However, this is also not desirable, because it will further increase the space to store the same data.)

Even the `newsequentialid()` function, which can only be used as a column default, has fatal flaws. Used to create sequential unique identifier values, after a server restart, the sequence might start at a new point, meaning that eventually you will be back to writing new rows in the middle of existing rows, causing page splits again.

Numerous events could trigger a reset to the starting point of the `newsequentialid()` function, which is based on the MAC address of the network interface card (NIC) on the server. Therefore, any failover of a failover cluster instance (FCI) or availability group (AG) will result in a new starting point, as well as any future upgrade or migration to new hardware. Similarly, changing the tier of Azure SQL Database, reimaging an Azure Virtual Machine (VM) with an ephemeral OS, or starting a new container without an explicit MAC will reset the starting point. Finally, and most importantly, the MAC of any NIC could change on startup of a VM in VMWare or HyperV. Obviously, given this list, `newsequentialid()` is fatally flawed and shouldn't be relied on for sequential values long-term.

This design problem usually involves these devices merging their data periodically—not continuously. A pair of `INT`s should be a good replacement for a unique identifier field in those cases. Consider instead a solution using multiple integers—one that autoincrements and one that identifies the data source, if you are considering the `uniqueidentifier` data type. Even two four-byte integers are half the size of a unique identifier, and they compress better.

In the case of continuous connected application integration into a single table, consider using the SEQUENCE feature of SQL Server, introduced in SQL Server 2012, instead of a unique identifier. Using the SEQUENCE object will allow multiple database connections to write rows using a unique, autoincrementing, ascending, procedurally generated integer.

It is ironic that a number of Microsoft-developed platforms use unique identifiers heavily, and sometimes with very public failures—for example, the Windows 7 RC download page. (Read Paul Randal's blog, "Why did the Windows 7 RC download failure happen?" at *https://www.sqlskills.com/blogs/paul/why-did-the-windows-7-rc-download-failure-happen/*.)

But systems like Microsoft SharePoint and even SQL Server's own merge replication needed to be developed for utility and versatility across unlimited client environments and a wide array of user expertise. When designing your own systems, take advantage of your knowledge of the business environment to design better clustered index keys that escape the inefficiencies of the uniqueidentifier data type.

If you must use the uniqueidentifier data type for your clustered index, exclude those tables from automated index reorganization plans, and rebuild your indexes fully at regular intervals. This will avoid additional and unnecessary overhead during maintenance periods by reorganizing indexes that will become fragmented almost immediately. We discuss maintenance plans in Chapter 8, "Maintain and monitor SQL Server."

CHAPTER 15

The clustered index is an important decision in the structure of a new table. For the vast majority of tables designed for relational database systems, however, the decision is fairly easy. An identity column with an INT or BIGINT data type is the ideal key for a clustered index because it satisfies the aforementioned four recommended qualities of an ideal clustered index. A procedurally generated timestamp or other incrementing time-related value, combined with a unique, autoincrementing number, also provides for a common, albeit less-narrow, clustered index key design.

When a table is created with a primary key constraint and no other mention of a clustered index, the primary key's columns become the clustered index's key. This is typically safe, but a table with a compound primary key or a primary key that does not begin with a sequential column could result in a suboptimal clustered index. It is important to note that the primary key does not need to be the clustered index key, but often should be. It is possible to create nonunique clustered indexes or to have multiple unique columns or column combinations in a table.

When combining multiple columns into the clustered index key, keep in mind that the column order of an index, clustered or nonclustered, does matter. If you decide to use multiple columns to create a clustered index key, the first column should still align as closely to the other three rules, even if it alone is not unique.

In the sys.indexes catalog view, the clustered index is always identified as `index_id = 1`. If the table is a heap, there will instead be a row with `index_id = 0`. This row represents the heap data.

The case against intentionally designing heaps

Without a clustered index, a table is known as a *heap*. In a heap, the Database Engine uses a structure known as row identifier (RID), which uniquely identifies every row for internal purposes. The structure of the heap has no order when it is stored. RIDs do not change, so when a record is updated, a forwarding pointer is created in the old location to point to the new. Also, if the row that has the forwarding pointer is moved to another page, it gets another forwarding pointer. Even deleted rows can have forwarding pointers! If that sounds like it is complicated or would increase the amount of I/O activity needed to store and retrieve the data, you're right.

Furthering the performance problems associated with heaps are that table scans are the only method of access to read from a heap structure, unless a nonclustered index is created on the heap. It is not possible to perform a seek against a heap; however, it is possible to perform a seek against a nonclustered index that has been added to a heap. In this way, a nonclustered index can provide an ordered copy for some of the table data in a separate structure.

One edge case for designing a table purposely without a clustered index is if you would only ever insert into a table. Without any order to the data, you might reap some benefits from rapid, massive data inserts into a heap. Other types of writes to the table (deletes and updates) will likely require table scans to complete and likely be far less efficient than the same writes against a table with a clustered index.

Deletes and updates typically leave wasted space within the heap's structure, which cannot be reclaimed even with an index rebuild operation. To reclaim wasted space inside a heap without re-creating it, you must, ironically, create a clustered index on the table, then drop the clustered index. You can also use the `ALTER TABLE ... REBUILD` Transact-SQL (T-SQL) command to rebuild the heap.

The perceived advantage of heaps for workloads exclusively involving inserts can be easily outweighed by the significant disadvantages whenever accessing that data—when query performance would necessitate the creation of a clustered and/or nonclustered index. Table scans and RID lookups for any significant number of rows are likely to dominate the cost of any execution plan accessing the heap. Without a clustered index, queries reading from a table large enough to gain significant advantage from its inserts would perform poorly.

Microsoft's expansion into modern unstructured data platforms, including integration with Azure Data Lake Storage Gen2, S3-compatible storage, Apache Spark, and other architectures, is likely to be more appropriate when rapid, massive data inserts are required. This is especially true for when you will continuously collect massive amounts of data and then only ever analyze the data in aggregate. These alternatives, integrated with the Database Engine starting with SQL Server 2016, or a focus of new Azure development such as Azure Synapse, would be superior to intentionally designing a heap.

Further, adding a clustered index to optimize the eventual retrieval of data from a heap is non-trivial. Behind the scenes, the Database Engine must write the entire contents of the heap into the new clustered index structure. If any nonclustered indexes exist on the heap, they also will be re-created, using the clustered key instead of the RID. This will likely result in a large amount of transaction log activity and tempdb space being consumed.

Understand the OPTIMIZE_FOR_SEQUENTIAL_KEY feature

Earlier in this chapter, we sang the praises of a clustered index key with an increasing sequential value, such as an integer based on an identity or sequence. For very frequent, multithreaded inserts into a table with an identity or sequence, the "hot spot" of the page in memory with the "next" value can provide some I/O bottleneck. (Long term, this is still likely preferable to frag-mentation-upon-insertion, as explained in the previous section, and only surfaces at scale.)

A useful feature introduced in SQL Server 2019 is the OPTIMIZE_FOR_SEQUENTIAL_KEY index option, which improves the concurrency of the page needing rapid inserts for rowstore indexes from multiple threads.

You might observe a high amount of the PAGELATCH_EX wait type on sessions performing inserts into the same table. You can observe this with the dynamic management view (DMV) sys.dm _exec_session_wait_stats, or at an instance aggregate level with sys.dm_os_wait_stats. You should see this wait type drop when the new OPTIMIZE_FOR_SEQUENTIAL_KEY index option is enabled on indexes in tables that are written to by multiple requests simultaneously. Note that this isn't the PAGEIOLATCH_EX wait type, more associated with physical page conten-tion, but PAGELATCH_EX, associated with memory page contention.

> ➤ For more information on observing wait types with DMVs, including the differences
>   between the PAGEIOLATCH_EX and PAGELATCH_EX wait types, see Chapter 8.

Let's take a look at implementing OPTIMIZE_FOR_SEQUENTIAL_KEY. In our contrived example, multiple T-SQL threads frequently executing single-row inserting statements mean that the top two predominant wait types accrued via the DMV sys.dm_os_wait_stats are WRITELOG and PAGELATCH_EX. As Chapter 8 explained, the WRITELOG wait type is fairly self-explanatory— sending data to the transaction log—while PAGELATCH_EX is an indication of a "hot spot" page, symptomatic of rapid concurrent inserts into a sequential key.

By enabling OPTIMIZE_FOR_SEQUENTIAL_KEY on your rowstore indexes—both clustered and nonclustered—you should see some reduction in PAGELATCH_EX and the introduction of a small amount of a new wait type, BTREE_INSERT_FLOW_CONTROL, which is associated with the new OPTIMIZE_FOR_SEQUENTIAL_KEY setting.

NOTE

The new OPTIMIZE_FOR_SEQUENTIAL_KEY option is not available when creating columnstore indexes or for any indexes on memory-optimized tables.

CHAPTER 15

You can query the value of the OPTIMIZE_FOR_SEQUENTIAL_KEY option with a new column added to sys.indexes of the same name. Note that this new option is not enabled by default, so it must be enabled manually on each index. The option is retained after an index is disabled and then rebuilt. For existing rowstore indexes, you can change the new OPTIMIZE_FOR _SEQUENTIAL_KEY option without a rebuild operation, with the following syntax:

```
ALTER INDEX PK_table1 on dbo.table1
SET (OPTIMIZE_FOR_SEQUENTIAL_KEY = ON);
```

NOTE

There are only a handful of index settings that can be set like this without a rebuild operation, so the syntax might look a little unusual. The index options ALLOW_PAGE_LOCKS, ALLOW_ROW_LOCKS, OPTIMIZE_FOR_SEQUENTIAL_KEY, IGNORE_DUP_KEY, **and** STATISTICS _NORECOMPUTE **can be set without a rebuild.**

Design rowstore nonclustered indexes

Each table almost always should have a clustered index that both defines the order and becomes the data structure of the data in the table. Nonclustered indexes provide additional copies of the data in vertically filtered sets, sorted by nonprimary columns.

You should approach the design of nonclustered indexes in response to application query usage, and then verify over time that you are benefitting from indexes. (You can read more about index usage statistics later in this chapter.) You might also choose to design a unique rowstore nonclustered index to enforce a business constraint. A unique constraint is implemented in the same way as a unique rowstore nonclustered index. This might be a valuable part of the table's behavior even if the resulting unique rowstore nonclustered index is never queried.

Here are the properties of ideal nonclustered indexes:

- Broad enough to serve multiple queries, not just designed to suit one query.

- Well-ordered keys eliminate unnecessary sorting in high-value queries.

- Well-stocked INCLUDE sections prevent lookups in high-value queries, but can become out of control if too much value without investigation is given to the missing index DMVs.

- Proven beneficial usage over time in the sys.dm_db_index_usage_stats DMV.

- Unique when possible (keep in mind a table can have multiple uniqueness criteria).

- Key column order matters, so in a compound index, it is likely best for the most selective (with the most distinct values) columns to be listed first.

Nonclustered indexes on disk-based tables are subset copies of a rowstore table that take up space on storage and in memory. (On memory-optimized tables, indexes interact with the disk much differently. More on that later in this chapter.) You must spend time maintaining all nonclustered indexes. They are kept transactionally consistent with the data in the table, serving a limited, reordered set of the data in a table. All writes (including deletes) to the table data must also be written to the nonclustered index (in the case of updates, when any indexed column is modified) to keep it up to date. (On columnstore optimized tables, this happens a little differently, with a delta store of change records.)

The positive benefit rowstore nonclustered indexes can have on SELECT, UPDATE, and DELETE queries that don't use the clustered index, however, is potentially very significant. Keep in mind that some write queries might appear to perform more quickly because accessing the data that is being changed can be optimized, as with accessing the data in a SELECT query. Your applications' writes will slow with the addition of nonclustered indexes, and adding many nonclustered indexes will certainly contribute to poor write performance. You can be confident that creating any one well-designed nonclustered index will contribute to reads greatly, and not have a perceivable impact on writes.

You should not create nonclustered indexes haphazardly or clumsily; you should plan, modify, combine them when appropriate, and review them regularly to make sure they are still useful. (See the section "Understand and provide index usage" later in this chapter.) However, nonclustered indexes represent a significant source of potential performance tuning that every developer and database administration should be aware of, especially in transactional databases. Remember: Always look at the "big picture" when creating indexes. Very rarely does a single query rise to the level of importance of justifying its own indexes.

NOTE

Starting with SQL Server 2019, the RESUMEABLE syntax can be used when creating an index with the ONLINE syntax. An ALTER INDEX and CREATE INDEX statement can be similarly paused and resumed. For more on RESUMABLE index maintenance, see Chapter 8.

Understand nonclustered index design

Let's talk about what we meant a moment ago when we said, "You should not create nonclustered indexes haphazardly or clumsily." When should you create a nonclustered index, and how should you design them? How many should you add to a table?

Even though adding nonclustered indexes on foreign key columns can be beneficial if those referencing columns will frequently be used in queries, it's rare that a useful nonclustered index will be properly designed with a single column in mind. This is because outside of joins on foreign keys, it is rare that queries will be designed to both seek and return a single column from a table. Starting a database design with indexes on foreign key columns is useful; that doesn't mean, however, that they can't be changed to have more columns at the end of the key list or in the include list.

Further, nonclustered rowstore index design should always be aware of all the indexes on a table and looking for opportunities to combine indexes with overlapping keys. In the next section, we'll talk about index keys and overlapping index keys.

Choose a proper index

When creating new nonclustered indexes for a table, you must always compare the new index to existing indexes. The order of the key of the index matters. In T-SQL, it looks like this:

```
CREATE NONCLUSTERED INDEX IDX_NC_InvoiceLines_InvoiceID_StockItemID
ON [Sales].[InvoiceLines] (InvoiceID, StockItemID);
```

In this index, `InvoiceID` and `InvoiceLineID` are defined as the key. Using Object Explorer in SQL Server Management Studio (SSMS), you can view the index properties to see the same information. This nonclustered index represents a copy of two of the columns of data in the `InvoiceLines` table, sorted by the column `InvoiceID` first, and then the `StockItemID`. Neither of these columns are the primary key or the first key of the clustered index, which we can assume is `InvoiceLineID`.

To emphasize that the order of key columns in a nonclustered index matters, the two indexes that follow are completely different structures, and will best serve different queries. It's unlikely that a single query would have much use for both nonclustered indexes, though SQL Server can still choose to use an index with less-than-optimal key order rather than scan a clustered index:

```
CREATE INDEX IDX_NC_InvoiceLines_InvoiceID_StockItemID
ON [Sales].[InvoiceLines] (InvoiceID, StockItemID);
CREATE INDEX IDX_NC_InvoiceLines_StockItemID_InvoiceID
ON [Sales].[InvoiceLines] (StockItemID, InvoiceID);
```

The columns with the most distinct values are more selective and will usually best serve queries if they are listed before less-selective columns in the index order. Note, though, that the order of columns in the `INCLUDE` portion of a nonclustered index (more on that later) does not matter.

Remember also from the previous section on clustered indexes that the clustered index key is already inside the key of the nonclustered index. There might be scenarios when the missing indexes feature (more on this later) suggests adding a clustered key column to your nonclustered index. It does not change the size of a nonclustered index to do this; the clustered key is already in a nonclustered index. The only caveat is that the order of the nonclustered index keys still determines the sort order of the index. So, having the clustered index key column(s) in your nonclustered index key won't change the index's size, but could change the sort order of the keys, creating what is essentially a different index when compared to an index that doesn't include the clustered index key column(s).

The default sort order for index column values is ascending. If you want to sort in descending order, you must be explicit in that as in the query that follows. If queries frequently call for data to be sorted by a column in descending order, which might be common for queries looking for the most recent data, you could provide that key value like this:

```
CREATE INDEX IDX_NC_InvoiceLines_InvoiceID_StockItemID
ON [Sales].[InvoiceLines] (InvoiceID DESC, StockItemID);
```

Creating the key's sort order incorrectly might not matter to some queries. For example, the nested loop operator does not require data to be sorted in a particular order, so different sort orders in the keys of a nonclustered index might not make a significant impact to the execution plan. On the other hand, a merge join operator requires data in both inputs to the operator to be sorted in the same order, so changing the sort order of the keys of an index—especially the first key—could simplify an execution plan by eliminating unnecessary sort operators. This is among the strategies of index tuning to consider. Remember to review the query plan performance data that the Query Store collects to observe the impact of index changes on multiple queries.

> ➤ For more on performance tuning, see Chapter 14, "Performance tune SQL Server."

Understand redundant indexes

Nonclustered index keys shouldn't overlap with other indexes in the same table. Because index key order matters, you must be aware of what is and what isn't an overlapping index. Consider the following two nonclustered indexes on the same table:

```
CREATE INDEX IDX_NC_InvoiceLines_InvoiceID_StockItemID_UnitPrice_Quantity
ON [Sales].[InvoiceLines] (InvoiceID, StockItemID, UnitPrice, Quantity);
CREATE INDEX IDX_NC_InvoiceLines_InvoiceID_StockItemID
ON [Sales].[InvoiceLines] (InvoiceID, StockItemID);
```

Both indexes lead with `InvoiceID` and `StockItemID`. The first index includes additional data. The second index is completely overlapped. Queries may still use the second index, but because the leading key columns match the other index, the larger index will provide very similar performance gains. If you drop `IDX_NC_InvoiceLines_InvoiceID_StockItemID`, you'll have fewer indexes to maintain, and fewer indexes to take up space in memory and on disk. The space it requires, the space in memory it consumes when used, and the effort it takes to keep the index up to date and maintained could all be considered redundant. The index `IDX_NC_InvoiceLines_InvoiceID_StockItemID` isn't needed and should be dropped, and queries that used it will use `IDX_NC_InvoiceLines_InvoiceID_StockItemID_UnitPrice_Quantity`.

> ### NOTE
> Before dropping an index entirely, you can disable it. This keeps the index definition metadata so you can re-create it later if needed. While disabled, the index does not consume any resources.

Consider, then, the following two indexes:

```
CREATE INDEX IDX_NC_InvoiceLines_InvoiceID_StockItemID_UnitPrice_Quantity
ON [Sales].[InvoiceLines] (InvoiceID, StockItemID, UnitPrice, Quantity);
CREATE INDEX IDX_NC_InvoiceLines _StockItemID_InvoiceID
ON [Sales].[InvoiceLines] (StockItemID, InvoiceID);
```

Note that the second index's keys are in a different order. This is physically and logically a different structure than the first index.

Does this mean both of these indexes are needed? Probably. Some queries might perform best using keys in the second index's order. The Query Optimizer can still use an index with columns in a suboptimal order—for example, to scan the smaller structure rather than the entire table. The Query Optimizer might instead find that an index seek and a key lookup on a different index is faster than using an index with the columns in the wrong order.

You can verify whether or not each index has been used in the `sys.dm_db_index_usage_stats` DMV, which we discuss later in this chapter, in the section "Understand and provide index usage."

The Query Store can be an invaluable tool to discover queries that have regressed because of changes to indexes that have been dropped, reordered, or resorted.

Understand the INCLUDE list of an index

In the B+ tree structure of a rowstore nonclustered index, key columns are stored through the two major sections of the index object:

- **Branch levels.** These are where the logic of seeks happens, starting at a narrow "top" where key data is stored so it can be traversed by SQL Server using binary decisions. A seek moves "down" the B+ tree structure via binary decisions.

- **Leaf levels.** These are where the seek ends and data is retrieved. Adding a column to the INCLUDE list of a rowstore nonclustered index adds that data only to the leaf level.

Inside OUT

How can you see the properties and storage for each level of the index's B+ tree?

You can view the `page_count`, `record_count`, `space_used` statistics, and more for each level of a B+ tree by using the DETAILED mode of the `sys.dm_db_index_physical_stats` dynamic management function. Only the leaf level (`index_level = 0`) is visible in other modes. The mode parameter is the fifth parameter passed in, as demonstrated in the following code:

```
SELECT * FROM sys.dm_db_index_physical_stats
(DB_ID(), object_id('Sales.Invoices'), null , null, 'DETAILED');
```

An index's INCLUDE statement allows for data to be retrievable in the leaf level only, but not stored in the branch level. This reduces the overall size and complexity needed to cover a query's need. Consider the following query and execution plan (see Figure 15-1) from the WideWorldImporters sample database. (Figure 15-2 shows the properties of the index seek in the following script.)

```
SELECT CustomerID, AccountsPersonID
FROM [Sales].[Invoices]
WHERE CustomerID = 832;
```

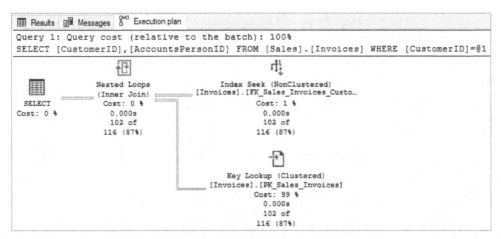

Figure 15-1 This execution plan shows an index seek and a key lookup on the same table. The Key Lookup represents 99 percent of the cost of the query.

Object
[WideWorldImporters].[Sales].[Invoices].
[FK_Sales_Invoices_CustomerID]
Output List
[WideWorldImporters].[Sales].[Invoices].InvoiceID,
[WideWorldImporters].[Sales].[Invoices].CustomerID
Seek Predicates
Seek Keys[1]: Prefix: [WideWorldImporters].[Sales].
[Invoices].CustomerID = Scalar Operator((832))

Figure 15-2 The properties of the Index Seek in the previous sample script. Note that `CustomerID` is in the seek predicate and also in the output list, but that `AccountsPersonID` is not listed in the output list.

Note in Figure 15-2 that `CustomerID` is in the seek predicate and also in the output list, but that `AccountsPersonID` is not listed in the output list. Our query is searching for and returning `CustomerID` (it appears in both the SELECT and WHERE clauses), but our query also returns `AccountsPersonID`, which is not contained in the index `FK_Sales_Invoices_CustomerID`. (It searches the indexes then joins that result with the clustered index.)

Here is the code of the nonclustered index `FK_Sales_Invoices_CustomerID`, named because it is for `CustomerID`, a foreign key reference:

```
CREATE NONCLUSTERED INDEX [FK_Sales_Invoices_CustomerID]
ON [Sales].[Invoices]
( CustomerID ASC );
```

To remove the key lookup, add an included column to the nonclustered index so the query can retrieve all the data it needs from a single object:

```
CREATE NONCLUSTERED INDEX [FK_Sales_Invoices_CustomerID]
ON [Sales].[Invoices]
( CustomerID ASC )
INCLUDE ( AccountsPersonID )
WITH (DROP_EXISTING = ON);
GO
```

Let's run our sample query again (see Figure 15-3):

```
SELECT CustomerID, AccountsPersonID
FROM [Sales].[Invoices]
WHERE CustomerID = 832;
```

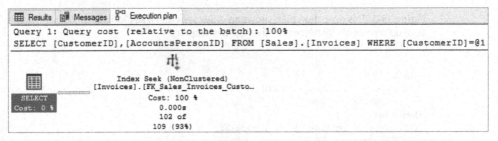

Figure 15-3 The execution plan now shows only an index seek. The key lookup that appeared in Figure 15-1 has been eliminated from the execution plan.

Note in Figure 15-3 that the key lookup has been eliminated. The query was able to retrieve both CustomerID and AccountsPersonID from the same index and required no second probe of the table for AccountsPersonID. The estimated subtree cost, in the properties of the SELECT operator, is now 0.0034015, compared to 0.355919 when the key lookup was present. Although this query was a small example for demonstration purposes, eliminating the key lookup represents a cost reduction by two orders of magnitude, without changing the query.

Just as you do not want to add too many nonclustered indexes, you also do not want to add too many columns unnecessarily to the INCLUDE list of nonclustered indexes. Columns in the INCLUDE list, as you saw in the previous code example, still require storage space. For infrequent queries that return small sets of data, the key lookup operator is probably not worth the cost of storing additional columns in the INCLUDE list of an index. Every time you include a column, you increase the overhead of the index.

In summary, you should craft nonclustered indexes to serve many queries intelligently, you should always try to avoid creating overlapping or redundant indexes, and you should regularly review to verify that indexes are still being used as applications or report queries change. Keep this guidance in mind as you move into the next section!

Create filtered nonclustered indexes

Nonclustered indexes are a sort of vertical partition of a table, but you can also create a horizontal filter of an index. A filtered index has powerful potential uses to serve up prefiltered data. Obviously, filtered indexes are only then suited to serve data to queries with matching WHERE clauses.

Filtered indexes could have particular use in table designs that include a soft delete flag, a processed/unprocessed status flag, or a current/archived flag. Work with developers to identify this sort of table design usage.

Imagine a scenario where a table has millions of rows, with a few rows marked as "unprocessed" and the rest marked as "processed." An application might regularly query this table using WHERE processed = 0, looking for rows to process. A nonclustered index on the processed column, resulting in a seek operation in the execution plan, would be much faster than scanning the entire table. But a filtered index with the same WHERE clause would only contain the few rows marked "unprocessed," resulting in a performance gain for the same query with no code changes.

You can easily add a filter to an index. For example:

```
CREATE INDEX [IX_Application_People_IsEmployee]
ON [Application].[People]([IsEmployee]) WHERE IsEmployee = 1
WITH (DROP_EXISTING = ON);
```

In your database, look for potential uses of new filtered indexes in columns that are of the bit data type, use a prefix like "Is" or a suffix like "Flag," or perhaps, when a query only ever looks for data of a certain type, or data that is NULL or NOT NULL. Work with developers to identify potential uses when the majority of data in the table is not needed for many queries.

Adding a filter to an existing index might make it unusable to queries that do not use the same query. Avoid adding a filter to an existing nonclustered index marked unique, as this will change the enforcement of the constraint and the intent of the unique index. Filtered nonclustered indexes can be created with the unique property to enforce filtered uniqueness. For example, this could have potential uses in employee IDs that are allowed to be reused, or in a data warehouse scenario where a table needs to enforce uniqueness on only the active records of a dimension.

Understand the missing indexes feature

The concept of intelligently combining many similar indexes into one super-index is crucial to understanding the utility of using SQL Server's built-in missing indexes feature. First introduced in SQL Server 2005, the missing indexes feature revolutionized the ability to see the big picture when crafting nonclustered indexes. The missing indexes feature has been passively gathering information on every database since SQL Server 2005 as well as in Azure SQL Database.

CHAPTER 15

The missing indexes feature collects information from actual query usage. SQL Server passively records when it would have been better to have a nonclustered index—for example, to replace a scan for a seek, or to eliminate a lookup from a query's execution plan. The missing indexes feature then aggregates these requests, counts how many times they have occurred, calculates the cost of the statement operations that could be improved, and estimates the percentage of that cost that would be eliminated (this percentage is labeled the *impact*). Think of the missing indexes feature as the database wish list of nonclustered indexes.

There are, however, some caveats and limitations with regard to the missing indexes feature. The recommendations in the output of the missing index dynamic management objects (DMOs) will likely include overlapping (but not duplicate) suggestions. Also, only rowstore nonclustered indexes can be suggested—remember this feature was introduced in SQL Server 2005—so clustered columnstore and other types of indexes won't be recommended. Finally, recommendations are lost when any data definition language (DDL) changes to the table occur and when the SQL Server instance restarts.

You can look at missing indexes any time, with no performance overhead to the server, by querying a set of DMOs dedicated to this feature. You can find the following query, which concatenates the CREATE INDEX statement for you according to a simple, self-explanatory naming convention. As you can see from the use of system views, this query is intended to be run in a single database:

```
SELECT mid.[statement], create_index_statement =
      CONCAT('CREATE NONCLUSTERED INDEX IDX_NC_'
    , TRANSLATE(replace(mid.equality_columns, ' ',''), '],[ ','___')
    , TRANSLATE(replace(mid.inequality_columns, ' ',''), '],[ ','___')
    , ' ON ' , mid.[statement] , ' (' , mid.equality_columns
    , CASE WHEN mid.equality_columns IS NOT NULL
      AND mid.inequality_columns IS NOT NULL THEN ',' ELSE '' END
    , mid.inequality_columns , ')'
    , ' INCLUDE ('+ , mid.included_columns ,+ ')' )
, migs.unique_compiles, migs.user_seeks, migs.user_scans
, migs.last_user_seek, migs.avg_total_user_cost
, migs.avg_user_impact, mid.equality_columns
, mid.inequality_columns, mid.included_columns
FROM sys.dm_db_missing_index_groups mig
INNER JOIN sys.dm_db_missing_index_group_stats migs
ON migs.group_handle = mig.index_group_handle
INNER JOIN sys.dm_db_missing_index_details mid
ON mig.index_handle = mid.index_handle
INNER JOIN sys.tables t ON t.object_id = mid.object_id
INNER JOIN sys.schemas s ON s.schema_id = t.schema_id
WHERE mid.database_id = DB_ID()
-- count of query compilations that needed this proposed index
--AND      migs.unique_compiles > 10
-- count of query seeks that needed this proposed index
--AND      migs.user_seeks > 10
-- average percentage of cost that could be alleviated with this proposed index
```

```
--AND        migs.avg_user_impact > 75
-- Sort by indexes that will have the most impact to the costliest queries
ORDER BY migs.avg_user_impact * migs.avg_total_user_cost desc;
```

At the bottom of this query is a series of filters that you can use to find only the most-used, highest-value index suggestions. If this query returns hundreds or thousands of rows, consider spending an afternoon crafting together indexes to improve the performance of the actual user activity that generated this data.

Some indexes returned by the missing indexes queries might not be worth creating because they have a very low impact or have been part of only one query compilation. Others might overlap each other. For example, you might see these three index suggestions:

```
CREATE NONCLUSTERED INDEX IDX_NC_Gamelog_Team1 ON dbo.gamelog (Team1) INCLUDE (GameYear,
GameWeek, Team1Score, Team2Score);
CREATE NONCLUSTERED INDEX IDX_NC_Gamelog_Team1_GameWeek_GameYear ON dbo.gamelog (Team1,
GameWeek, GameYear) INCLUDE (Team1Score);
CREATE NONCLUSTERED INDEX IDX_NC_Gamelog_Team1_GameWeek_GameYear_Team2 ON dbo.gamelog
(Team1, GameWeek, GameYear, Team2);
```

You should not create all three of these indexes. Instead, you should combine the indexes you deem useful and worthwhile into a single index that matches the order of the needed key columns and covers all the included columns, as well. Here is the properly combined index suggestion:

```
CREATE NONCLUSTERED INDEX IDX_NC_Gamelog_Team1_GameWeek_GameYear_Team2
ON dbo.gamelog (Team1, GameWeek, GameYear, Team2)
INCLUDE (Team1Score, Team2Score);
```

This last index is a good combination of the previous suggestions. It delivers maximum positive benefit to the most queries and minimizes the negative impact to writes, storage, and maintenance. Note that the key columns list overlaps and is in the correct order for each of the previous index suggestions, and that the INCLUDE columns list also covers all the columns needed in the index suggestions. If a column is in the key of the index, it does not need to exist in the INCLUDE of the index.

However, don't create this index yet. You should still review existing indexes on the table before creating any missing indexes. Perhaps you can combine a new missing index and an existing index, in the key column list or the INCLUDE column list, further increasing the value of a single index.

After combining missing index suggestions with each other and with existing indexes, you are ready to create the index and see it in action. Remember: Always look at the big picture when creating indexes. Rarely does a single query rise to the level of importance of justifying its own indexes. For example, in SSMS, you will sometimes see text suggesting a missing index for this query, as illustrated in Figure 15-4. (This text will be green on your screen, but appears gray in this book.)

CHAPTER 15

```
⊞ Results  ⚑ Messages  ⚏ Execution plan
Query 1: Query cost (relative to the batch): 100%
SELECT il.InvoiceID, il.InvoiceLineID, StockItemID, CustomerID FROM [Sale
Missing Index (Impact 99.2851): CREATE NONCLUSTERED INDEX [<Name of Missi
```

Figure 15-4 In the Execution plan tab, in the header of each execution plan. Text starting with "Missing Index" will alert you to the possible impact. Do not create this index on the spot!

This is somewhat valuable, but do not create this index on the spot! Always refer to the complete set of index suggestions and other existing indexes on the table, combining overlapping indexes when possible. Consider the green missing index alert in SSMS as only a flag that indicates you should spend time investigating new missing indexes.

To recap, when creating nonclustered indexes for performance tuning, you should do the following:

1. Use the missing index DMVs to identify new big-picture nonclustered indexes:

   - Don't create indexes that will likely only help out a single query; few queries are important enough to deserve their own indexes.

   - Consider nonclustered columnstore indexes for very large rowcount tables where queries often have to scan millions of rows for aggregates. (You can read more on columnstore indexes later in this chapter.)

2. Combine missing index suggestions, being aware of key order and INCLUDE lists.

3. Compare new index suggestions with existing indexes; perhaps you can combine them.

4. Review index usage statistics to verify whether indexes are helping you. (More on the index usage statistics DMV in a moment.)

Inside OUT

Does the missing indexes feature suggest only rowstore nonclustered index?

Yes. The missing indexes feature can't help you with proper clustered index design; that's up to you, the informed database designer. It can provide some insight into usage after a time, but that would mean running a typical production workload against a heap and suffering the performance issues likely to arise.

Here's another limitation to the missing indexes feature: It is not aware of clustered or nonclustered columnstore indexes, which are incredibly powerful structures to add for massive row count queries on large tables. The missing indexes feature (introduced in SQL Server 2005) cannot suggest columnstore indexes (introduced in SQL Server 2012). The missing indexes feature will even suggest an index to replace a useful columnstore index. Be aware of all indexes in your table, including columnstore indexes, when considering new indexes.

When you have created a columnstore index on a table, you might need to ignore index suggestions that look like the same workloads that are currently benefitting from the columnstore. For a query that requires a scan on many rows in the table, the Query Optimizer is unlikely to pick a nonclustered index over a nonclustered columnstore index. The columnstore index will typically vastly outperform a nonclustered index for massive row count queries, though the missing index feature might still count this as a new nonclustered index suggestion.

Understand when missing index suggestions are removed

Missing index suggestions are cleared out for any change to the tables—for example, if you add or remove columns or indexes. Missing index suggestions are also cleared out when the SQL Server service is started and cannot be manually cleared easily. (You can take the database offline and back online, which would clear out the missing index suggestions, but this seems like overkill.)

Logically, make sure the missing index data that you have collected is also based on a significant sample of actual production user activity over time spanning at least one business cycle. Missing index suggestions based on development activity might not be a useful representation of intended application activity, though suggestions based on end-user testing or training could be.

Understand and provide index usage

You've added indexes to your tables, and they are used over time, but meanwhile the query patterns of applications and reports change. Columns are added to the database, new tables are added, and although you add new indexes to suit new functionality, how does a database administrator ensure that existing indexes are still worth keeping?

SQL Server tracks this information for you automatically with yet another valuable DMV: `sys .dm_db_index_usage_stats`. Following is a script that measures index usage within a database, combining `sys.dm_db_index_usage_stats` with other system views and DMVs to return valuable information. Note that the `ORDER BY` clause places indexes with the fewest read operations (seeks, scans, lookups) and the most write operations (updates) at the top of the list.

```
SELECT TableName = sc.name + '.' + o.name, IndexName = i.name
    , s.user_seeks, s.user_scans, s.user_lookups
    , s.user_updates
    , ps.row_count, SizeMb = (ps.in_row_reserved_page_count*8.)/1024.
```

CHAPTER 15

```
      , s.last_user_lookup, s.last_user_scan, s.last_user_seek
      , s.last_user_update
FROM sys.dm_db_index_usage_stats AS s
  INNER JOIN sys.indexes AS i
ON i.object_id = s.object_id AND i.index_id = s.index_id
    INNER JOIN sys.objects AS o ON o.object_id=i.object_id
    INNER JOIN sys.schemas AS sc ON sc.schema_id = o.schema_id
    INNER JOIN sys.partitions AS pr
ON pr.object_id = i.object_id AND pr.index_id = i.index_id
      INNER JOIN sys.dm_db_partition_stats AS ps
ON ps.object_id = i.object_id AND ps.partition_id = pr.partition_id
WHERE o.is_ms_shipped = 0
--Don't consider dropping any constraints
AND i.is_unique = 0 AND i.is_primary_key = 0 AND i.is_unique_constraint = 0
--Order by table reads asc, table writes desc
ORDER BY user_seeks + user_scans + user_lookups asc, s.user_updates desc;
```

Any indexes that rise to the top of the preceding query should be considered for removal or redesign, given the following caveats:

- Before dropping any indexes, you should ensure you have collected data from the index usage stats DMV that spans at least one complete business cycle. The index usage stats DMV is cleared when the SQL Server service is restarted. You cannot manually clear it. If your applications have week-end and month-end reporting, you might have indexes present and tuned specifically for those critical performance periods.

- Logically, verify that the index usage data that you have collected is based on actual production user activity. Index usage data based on testing or development activity would not be a useful representation of intended application activity.

- Note the final WHERE clause that ignores unique constraints and primary keys. Even if a nonclustered index exists and isn't used, if it is part of the uniqueness of the table, it should not be dropped.

Again, the Query Store can be an invaluable tool to monitor for query regression after indexing changes.

➤ **For more info on the Query Store, see Chapter 14.**

Like many DMVs that are cleared when the SQL Server service restarts, consider a strategy of capturing data and storing index usage history periodically in persistent tables.

Server-scoped dynamic management views and functions require VIEW SERVER STATE permission on the server. Database-scoped dynamic management views and functions require VIEW DATABASE STATE permission on the database.

➤ **For more information, see** *https://learn.microsoft.com/sql/relational-databases/system -dynamic-management-views/system-dynamic-management-views.*

Understand columnstore indexes

Columnstore indexes were first introduced in SQL Server 2012, making a splash in their ability to far outperform clustered and nonclustered indexes for aggregations. They were typically used in the scenario of nightly refreshed data warehouses, but now they have beneficial applications on transactional systems, including on memory-optimized tables.

Since their introduction, the evolution of columnstore indexes has greatly expanded their usefulness:

- Before SQL Server 2016, the presence of a nonclustered columnstore index made the table read-only. This drawback was removed in SQL Server 2016; now nonclustered columnstore indexes are fully featured and quite useful in a variety of applications aside from nightly refresh databases.

- Starting with SQL Server 2016 with Service Pack 1, columnstore indexes became available below Enterprise edition licenses of SQL Server (though with a limitation on columnstore memory utilization).

- Snapshot isolation and columnstore indexes are fully compatible. Before SQL Server 2016, using read-committed snapshots and snapshot isolation levels was not supported with columnstore indexes.

- You can place a clustered columnstore index on a memory-optimized table, providing the ability to do analytics on millions of rows of live real-time online transactional processing (OLTP) data.

- Starting with SQL Server 2017, a variety of batch mode features grouped under the intelligent query processing (IQP) label increased performance of queries with columnstore indexes.

  ➤ For more about the suite of features under IQP, see Chapter 14.

- Starting with SQL Server 2019, using the WITH (ONLINE = ON) syntax is supported for creating and rebuilding columnstore indexes.

These key improvements opened columnstore indexes to be used in transactional systems, when tables with millions of rows are read, resulting in million-row result sets.

Columnstore indexes have two compression levels. In addition to the eponymous default COLUMNSTORE compression level, there is also a COLUMNSTORE_ARCHIVE compression option, which further compresses the data at the cost of more CPU when needing to read or write the data.

As with rowstore indexes, you can compress each partition of a table's columnstore index differently. Consider applying COLUMNSTORE_ARCHIVE compression to partitions of data that are old

CHAPTER 15

and rarely accessed. You can change the data compression option for rowstore and columnstore indexes by using the index rebuild operation via the DATA_COMPRESSION option. For columnstore indexes, you can specify the COLUMNSTORE or COLUMNSTORE_ARCHIVE options, whereas for rowstore indexes, you can use the NONE, ROW, and PAGE compression options.

➤ **For more detail on data compression, see Chapter 3, "Design and implement an on-premises database infrastructure."**

You cannot change the compression option of a rowstore index to either of the columnstore options, or vice versa. Instead, you must build a new index of the desired type.

The sp_estimate_data_compression_savings system stored procedure can be used to estimate the size differences between the compression options. Starting with SQL Server 2019, this stored procedure includes estimates for the two columnstore compression options. In SQL Server 2022, sp_estimate_data_compression_savings can be used to estimate savings for XML compression as well.

➤ **See the "XML compression" section at the end of the chapter for more information.**

NOTE

There is currently a three-way incompatibility between the sp_estimate_data _compression_savings **system stored procedure, columnstore indexes, and the memory-optimized tempdb metadata feature introduced in SQL Server 2019. You cannot use** sp_estimate_data_compression_savings **with columnstore indexes if the memory-optimized tempdb metadata feature is enabled. For more information visit** *https://learn .microsoft.com/sql/relational-databases/system-stored-procedures/sp-estimate-data -compression-savings-transact-sql.*

Design columnstore indexes

Columnstore indexes don't use a B+ tree; instead, they contain highly compressed data (on disk and in memory), stored in a different architecture from the traditional clustered and non-clustered indexes. They are the standard for storing and querying large data warehouse fact tables. Unlike rowstore indexes, there is no "key" or "include" of a columnstore index, only a set of columns that are part of the index. For non-ordered columnstore indexes, the order of the columns in the definition of index does not matter. This is the default index. You can create "clustered" or "nonclustered" columnstore indexes, though this terminology is used more to indicate what role the columnstore index is serving, not what it resembles behind the scenes.

Clustered columnstore indexes do not change the physical structure of the table like rowstore clustered indexes. Ordered clustered columnstore indexes sort the existing data in memory by the order key(s) before the index builder compresses them into index segments. Any sorted data overlap is reduced, which allows for better data elimination when querying, and therefore faster performance because the amount of data read from disk is smaller. If all data can be sorted in memory at once, then data overlap can be avoided. Owing to the size of tables in data warehouses, this scenario doesn't happen often.

➤ **For more information, visit** *https://learn.microsoft.com/azure/synapse-analytics/sql-data -warehouse/performance-tuning-ordered-cci.*

You can also create nonclustered rowstore indexes on tables with a clustered columnstore index, which is potentially useful to enforce uniqueness, and support single row fetching, deleting, and updating. Columnstore indexes cannot be unique, and so cannot replace the table's unique constraint or primary key. Clustered columnstore indexes might also perform poorly when a table receives updates, so consider the workload for a table before adding a clustered columnstore. Tables that are only ever inserted into, but never updated or deleted from, would be an ideal candidate for a clustered columnstore index.

You can combine nonclustered rowstore and nonclustered columnstore indexes on the same table, but you can have only one columnstore index on a table, including clustered and nonclustered columnstore indexes. You can even create nonclustered rowstore and nonclustered columnstore indexes on the same columns. Perhaps you create both because you want to filter on the column value in one set of queries, and aggregate in another. Or perhaps you create both only temporarily, for comparison.

You can also create nonclustered columnstore indexes on indexed views—another avenue to quick-updating analytical data. The stipulations and limitations regarding indexed views apply, but you would create a unique rowstore clustered index on the view, then a nonclustered columnstore view.

You can add columns in any order to satisfy many different queries, greatly increasing the versatility of the columnstore index in your table. This is because the order of the data is not important to how columnstore indexes work.

The size of the key for columnstore indexes, however, could make a big difference in performance. The columns in a columnstore index should each be limited to 8,000 bytes for best performance. Data larger than 8,000 bytes in a row is compressed separately outside of the columnstore compressed row group, requiring more decompression to access the complete row.

While the large object data types `varchar(max)`, `nvarchar(max)`, and `varbinary(max)` are supported in the key of a columnstore index, they are not stored in-line with the rest of the compressed data, but rather outside the columnstore structure. These data types are not recommended in columnstore indexes. Starting with SQL Server 2017, they are supported, but still not recommended.

➤ **For more on data type restrictions and limitations for columnstore indexes, visit** *https://learn .microsoft.com/sql/t-sql/statements/create-columnstore-index-transact-sql#LimitRest.*

CHAPTER 15

The most optimal data types for columns in a columnstore index are data types that can be stored in an 8-byte integer value, such as integers and some date- and time-based data types. They allow you to use what is known as *segment elimination*. If your query includes a filter on such values, SQL Server can issue reads to only those segments in row groups that contain data within a range, eliminating ranges of data outside of the request. The data is not sorted, so segment elimination might not help all filtering queries, but the more selective the value, the more likely it will be useful. Other data types with a size less than 8,000 bytes will still compress and be useful for aggregations, but should generally not appear as a filter, because the entire table will always need to be scanned unless you add a nonclustered index.

Understand batch mode

Batch mode is one of the existing features lumped into the intelligent query processing (IQP) umbrella—a collection of performance improvements. Batch mode has actually been around since SQL Server 2014. Like many other features listed under IQP, batch mode can benefit workloads automatically and without requiring code changes.

Batch mode is useful in the following scenarios:

- **Analytical queries.** Usually, these queries use operators like joins or aggregates that process hundreds of thousands of rows or more.

- **Your workload is CPU bound.** However, you should consider a columnstore index even if your workload is I/O bound.

- **Heavy OLTP workload.** You may decide that creating a columnstore index adds too much overhead to your heavy transactional workload, and your analytical workload is not as important.

- **Support.** Your application depends on a feature that columnstore indexes don't yet support.

Batch mode uses heuristics to determine whether it can move data into memory to be processed in a batch rather than row by row. Columnstore indexes reduce I/O and batch processing reduces CPU usage, ultimately speeding up the query.

You'll see *Batch* (instead of the default *Row*) in the Actual Execution Mode of an execution plan operator when this faster method is in use. Batch mode processing appears in the form of batch mode operators in execution plans, and benefits queries that process millions of rows or more.

➤ **For more information on IQP features, see Chapter 14.**

Initially, only queries on columnstore indexes could benefit from batch mode operators. Starting with compatibility level 150 (SQL Server 2019), however, batch mode for analytic workloads became available outside of columnstore indexes. The query processor might decide to use batch mode operators for queries on heaps and rowstore indexes. No changes are needed for your code to benefit from batch mode on rowstore objects, as long as you are in compatibility level 150 or higher.

> ➤ For more information on which operators can use batch mode execution, go to *https:// learn.microsoft.com/sql/relational-databases/indexes/columnstore-indexes-query -performance.*

NOTE

Batch mode has not yet been extended to in-memory OLTP tables or other types of indexes like full-text, spatial, or XML indexes. Batch mode will also not occur on sparse and XML columns.

Understand the deltastore of columnstore indexes

The *columnstore deltastore* is an ephemeral location where changed data is stored in a clustered B+ tree rowstore format. When certain thresholds of inserted rows are reached, typically 1,048,576 rows, or when a columnstore index is rebuilt or reorganized, a group of deltastore data is "closed." Then, via a background thread called the *tuple mover*, the deltastore rowgroup is compressed into the columnstore. The number of rows SQL Server compresses into a rowgroup might be smaller under memory pressure, which happens dynamically.

The COMPRESSION_DELAY option for both nonclustered and clustered columnstore indexes has to do with how long it takes changed data to be written from the deltastore to the highly compressed columnstore.

The COMPRESSION_DELAY option does not affect the 1,048,576 number, but rather how long it takes SQL Server to move the data into the columnstore. If you set the COMPRESSION_DELAY option to 10 minutes, data will remain in the deltastore for at least an extra 10 minutes before SQL Server compresses it. The advantage of data remaining in the deltastore, delaying its eventual compression, could be noticeable on tables that continue to be updated and deleted. Updates and deletes are typically very resource intensive on columnstore indexes. Delete operations in the columnstore are "soft" deleted, marked as removed, and then eventually cleaned out during index maintenance. Updates are actually processed as deletes and inserts into the deltastore.

The advantage of COMPRESSION_DELAY is noticeable for some write workloads, but not all. If the table is only ever inserted into, COMPRESSION_DELAY doesn't really help. But if a block of recent data is updated and deleted for a period before finally settling in after a time, implementing COMPRESSION_DELAY can speed up the write transactions to the data and reduce the maintenance and storage footprint of the columnstore index.

CHAPTER 15

Changing the COMPRESSION_DELAY setting of the index, unlike many other index settings, does not require a rebuild of the index, and you can change it at any time. For example:

```
ALTER INDEX [NCCX_Sales_InvoiceLines]
    ON [Sales].[InvoiceLines]
    SET (COMPRESSION_DELAY = 10 MINUTES);
```

SQL Server can ignore the deltastore for inserts when you insert data in large amounts. This is called *bulk loading* in Microsoft documentation, but is not related to the BULK INSERT command. When you want to insert large amounts of data into a table with a columnstore index, SQL Server bypasses the deltastore. This increases the speed of the insert and the immediate availability for the data for analytical queries, and reduces the amount of logged activity in the user database transaction log.

Under ideal circumstances, the best number of rows to insert in a single statement is 1,048,576, which creates a complete, compressed columnstore row group. The number of rows to trigger a bulk load is between 102,400 rows and 1,047,576 rows, depending on memory. If you specify TABLOCK in the INSERT statement, bulk loading data into the columnstore occurs in parallel. The typical caveat about TABLOCK is applicable here, as the table might block other operations at the time of the insert in parallel.

Demonstrate the power of columnstore indexes

To demonstrate the power of this fully operational columnstore index, let's review a scenario in which more than 14 million rows are added to the WideWorldImporters.Sales.InvoiceLines table. About half of the rows in the table now contain InvoiceID = 69776.

To demonstrate, start by restoring a fresh copy of the sample WideWorldImporters database from *https://learn.microsoft.com/sql/samples/wide-world-importers-oltp-install-configure*.

The following sample script drops the existing WideWorldImporters-provided nonclustered columnstore index and adds a new nonclustered index we've created here. This performs an index scan to return the data. Remember that InvoiceID = 69776 is roughly half the table, so this isn't a "needle in a haystack" situation; it isn't a seek. If the query can use a seek operator, the nonclustered rowstore index would likely be better. When the query must scan, columnstore is king.

```
USE WideWorldImporters;
GO
-- Fill haystack with 3+ million rows
INSERT INTO Sales.InvoiceLines (InvoiceLineID, InvoiceID
, StockItemID, Description, PackageTypeID, Quantity
, UnitPrice, TaxRate, TaxAmount, LineProfit, ExtendedPrice
, LastEditedBy, LastEditedWhen)
SELECT InvoiceLineID = NEXT VALUE FOR [Sequences].[InvoiceLineID]
, InvoiceID, StockItemID, Description, PackageTypeID, Quantity
, UnitPrice, TaxRate, TaxAmount, LineProfit
, ExtendedPrice, LastEditedBy, LastEditedWhen
FROM Sales.InvoiceLines;
GO 3 --Runs the above three times
```

```
-- Insert millions of records for InvoiceID 69776
INSERT INTO Sales.InvoiceLines (InvoiceLineID, InvoiceID
, StockItemID, Description, PackageTypeID, Quantity
, UnitPrice, TaxRate, TaxAmount, LineProfit, ExtendedPrice
, LastEditedBy, LastEditedWhen)
SELECT InvoiceLineID = NEXT VALUE FOR [Sequences].[InvoiceLineID]
, 69776, StockItemID, Description, PackageTypeID, Quantity
, UnitPrice, TaxRate, TaxAmount, LineProfit
, ExtendedPrice, LastEditedBy, LastEditedWhen
FROM Sales.InvoiceLines;
GO
--Clear cache, drop other indexes to only test our comparison scenario
DBCC FREEPROCCACHE
DROP INDEX IF EXISTS [NCCX_Sales_InvoiceLines]
ON [Sales].[InvoiceLines];
DROP INDEX IF EXISTS IDX_NC_InvoiceLines_InvoiceID_StockItemID_Quantity
ON [Sales].[InvoiceLines];
DROP INDEX IF EXISTS IDX_CS_InvoiceLines_InvoiceID_StockItemID_Quantity
ON [Sales].[InvoiceLines];
GO
--Create a rowstore nonclustered index for comparison
CREATE INDEX IDX_NC_InvoiceLines_InvoiceID_StockItemID_Quantity
     ON [Sales].[InvoiceLines] (InvoiceID, StockItemID, Quantity);
GO
```

Now that the data is loaded, you can perform the query again for testing. (See Figure 15-5.) Note we are using the STATISTICS TIME option to measure both CPU and total duration. (Remember to enable the actual query plan before executing the query.)

```
SET STATISTICS TIME ON;
SELECT il.StockItemID, AvgQuantity = AVG(il.quantity)
FROM [Sales].[InvoiceLines] AS il
WHERE il.InvoiceID = 69776 --1.8 million records
GROUP BY il.StockItemID;
SET STATISTICS TIME OFF;
```

Figure 15-5 The execution plan of our sample query starts with an Index Seek (NonClustered) on the rowstore nonclustered index. Note the large amount of parallelism operators along the way.

The sample query on 69776 had to work through 1.8 million records and returned 227 rows. With the rowstore nonclustered index, the cost of the query is 4.52 and completes in 844 ms of CPU time (due to parallelism), 194 ms of total time. (These durations will vary from system to system; the lab environment was a four-core Intel processor with Hyper-Threading enabled.)

Now, let's create a columnstore index, and watch our analytical-scale query benefit.

CHAPTER 15

NOTE

Starting with SQL Server 2019, using the `WITH (ONLINE = ON)` **syntax is supported for creating and rebuilding columnstore indexes.**

```
--Create a columnstore nonclustered index for comparison
CREATE COLUMNSTORE INDEX IDX_CS_InvoiceLines_InvoiceID_StockItemID_quantity
    ON [Sales].[InvoiceLines] (InvoiceID, StockItemID, Quantity) WITH (ONLINE = ON);
GO
```

Perform the query again for testing. Note again we are using the `STATISTICS TIME` option to measure both CPU and total duration. (See Figure 15-6.)

```
SET STATISTICS TIME ON;
--Run the same query as above, but now it will use the columnstore
SELECT il.StockItemID, AvgQuantity = AVG(il.quantity)
FROM [Sales].[InvoiceLines] AS il
WHERE il.InvoiceID = 69776 --1.8 million records
GROUP BY il.StockItemID;
SET STATISTICS TIME OFF;
```

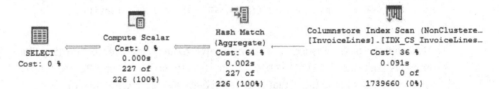

Figure 15-6 The execution plan of our sample query, now starting with a Columnstore Index Scan (NonClustered).

The sample query on 69776 still returns 227 rows. With the benefit of the columnstore non-clustered index, however, the cost of the query is 1.54 and completes in 47 ms of CPU time, 160 ms of total time. This is a significant but relatively small sample of the power of a columnstore index on analytical scale queries.

Understand indexes in memory-optimized tables

Memory-optimized tables support table performance less bound by I/O constraints, providing high-performance, latchless writes. Memory-optimized tables don't use the locking mechanics of pessimistic concurrency, as discussed in Chapter 14. Data rows for memory-optimized tables are not stored in data pages, and so do not use the concepts of disk-based tables.

Memory-optimized tables can have two types of indexes: hash and nonclustered. Nonclustered indexes for memory-optimized tables behave similarly on memory-optimized tables as they do for disk-based tables, whereas hash indexes are better suited for high-performance seeks for individual records. You must create at least one index on a memory-optimized table. Either of the two types of indexes can be the structure behind the primary key of the table, if you want both the data and the schema to be durable.

Indexes on in-memory tables are never durable and will be rebuilt whenever the database comes online. The schema of the memory-optimized table is always durable; however, you can choose to have only the schema of the table be durable, not the data. This has utility in certain scenarios as a staging table to receive data that will be moved to a durable disk-based or memory-optimized table. You should be aware of the potential for data loss. If only the schema of the memory-optimized table is durable, you do not need to declare a primary key. However, in the CREATE TABLE statement, you must still define at least one index or a primary key for a table by using DURABILITY = SCHEMA_ONLY. Our suggestion is that only in very rare situations should a table not have a primary key constraint, no matter the durability.

Adding indexes to memory-optimized tables increases the amount of server memory needed. There is otherwise no limit to the size of memory-optimized tables in Enterprise edition; however, in Standard edition, you are limited to 32 GB of memory-optimized tables per database.

Earlier versions of SQL Server put a cap on the number of indexes on a memory-optimized table. That cap was raised from 8 to 999 in SQL Server 2017.

Although there is no concept of a rowstore clustered index in memory-optimized tables, you can add a clustered columnstore index to a memory-optimized table, dramatically improving your ability to perform analytical scale queries on the data even as it is rapidly inserted. Because columnstore indexes cannot be unique, they cannot serve as the primary key for a memory-optimized table.

Let's go over the basics of using hash and nonclustered indexes on memory-optimized tables.

Understand hash indexes for memory-optimized tables

Memory-optimized hash indexes are an alternative to the typical B+ tree internal architecture for index data storage. Hash indexes are best for queries that look for the needle in the haystack, and are especially effective when matching exact values, but they are not effective at range lookups or queries with an ORDER BY.

One other limitation of the hash index is that if you don't query all the columns in a hash index, they are generally not useful. The WHERE clause must try to seek each column in the hash index's key. When there are multiple columns in the key of the indexes but not all columns—or even just the first column—are queried, hash indexes do not perform well. This is different from B+ tree-based nonclustered indexes, which perform fine if only the first column of the index's key is queried.

Hash indexes are currently available only for memory-optimized tables, not disk-based tables. You can declare them by using the UNIQUE keyword, but they default to a non-unique key. You can create more than one hash index.

There is an additional unique consideration for creating hash indexes. Estimating the best number for the BUCKET_COUNT parameter can have a significant impact. The number should be as close as possible to the number of unique key values that are expected. BUCKET_COUNT should be between 1 and 2 times this number.

Hash indexes always use the same amount of space for the same-sized bucket count, regardless of the rowcount within. For example, if you expect the table to have 100,000 unique values in it, the ideal BUCKET_COUNT value would be between 100,000 and 200,000.

Having too many or too few buckets in a hash index can result in poor performance. More buckets will increase the amount of memory needed and the number of those buckets that are empty. Too few buckets will result in queries needing to access more, larger buckets in a chain to access the same information.

Ideally, a hash index is declared unique. Hash indexes work best when the key values are unique or at least highly distinct. If the ratio of total rows to unique key values is too high, a hash index is not recommended and will perform poorly. Microsoft recommends a threshold of less than 10 rows per unique value for an effective hash index. If you have data with many duplicate values, consider a nonclustered index instead.

You should periodically and proactively compare the number of unique key values to the total number of rows in the table. It is better to overestimate the number of buckets. You can change the number of buckets in a memory-optimized hash index by using the ALTER TABLE/ALTER INDEX/REBUILD commands. For example:

```
ALTER TABLE [dbo].[Transactions]
ALTER INDEX [IDX_NC_H Transactions_1]
REBUILD WITH (BUCKET_COUNT = 524288);
--will always round up to the nearest power of two
```

Understand nonclustered indexes for memory-optimized tables

Nonclustered indexes for memory-optimized tables behave similarly on memory-optimized tables to how they behave on disk-based tables. Instead of a B+ tree like a rowstore, disk-based nonclustered index, they are in fact a variant of the B-tree structure called the Bw-tree, which does not use locks or latches. They outperform hash indexes for queries that perform sorting on the key value(s) of the index, or when the index must be range scanned. Further, if you don't query all the columns in a hash index, they are generally not as useful as a nonclustered index.

You can declare nonclustered indexes on memory-optimized tables unique. However, the CREATE INDEX syntax is not supported. You must use the ALTER TABLE/ADD INDEX commands or include them in the CREATE TABLE script.

Neither hash indexes nor nonclustered indexes can serve queries on memory-optimized tables for which the keys are sorted in the reverse order from how they are defined in the index. These types of queries simply can't currently be serviced efficiently from memory-optimized indexes. If you need another sort order, you need to add the same B-tree index with a different sort order.

Remember: You can also add a clustered columnstore index to a memory-optimized table, dramatically improving your ability to analyze fast-changing data.

Understand index statistics

When we talk about statistics in SQL Server, we do not mean the term generically. Statistics on one or more columns in tables and views are created as needed by the Query Optimizer to describe the distribution of data within indexes and heaps.

Statistics are important to the Query Optimizer to help it make query plan decisions, and they are heavily involved in the concept of cardinality estimation. The SQL Server cardinality estimator (CE) provides accurate estimations of the number of rows that queries will return—a big part of producing query plans.

> ➤ For more on the performance impact of statistics on cardinality estimation, see Chapter 14.

Making sure statistics are available and up to date is essential for choosing a well-performing query plan. Stale statistics that have evaded updates for too long contain information that is quite different from the current state of the table and will likely cause poor execution plans.

There are several options in each database regarding statistics maintenance. Chapter 4, "Install and configure SQL Server instances and features," reviews some of these, but we present them again here in the context of understanding how indexes are used for performance tuning.

Automatically create and update statistics

Most statistics needed for describing data to the SQL Server are created automatically, because the AUTO_CREATE_STATISTICS database option is enabled by default. This results in automatically created indexes with the _WA_Sys_<column_name>_<object_id_hex> naming convention.

When the AUTO_CREATE_STATISTICS database option is enabled, SQL Server can create single-column statistics objects based on query need. These can make a big difference in performance. You can determine that a statistics object was created by the AUTO_CREATE_STATISTICS = ON behavior because it will have the name prefix _WA. You can also use the following query:

```
SELECT *
FROM sys.stats
WHERE auto_created = 1;
```

The behavior that creates statistics for indexes (with a matching name) happens automatically, regardless of the AUTO_CREATE_STATISTICS database option.

Statistics are not automatically created for columnstore indexes. Instead, statistics objects that exist on the heap or the clustered index of the table are used. As with any index, a statistics object of the same name is created; however, for columnstore indexes it is blank, and in place for logistical reasons only. This statistics object is actually populated on the fly and not persisted in storage.

As you can imagine, statistics must also be kept up to date with the data in the table. SQL Server has an option in each database for AUTO_UPDATE_STATISTICS, which is ON by default and should almost always remain on.

You should only ever disable both AUTO_CREATE_STATISTICS and AUTO_UPDATE_STATISTICS when requested by highly complex application designs, with variable schema usage, and a separate regular process that creates and maintains statistics, such as Microsoft SharePoint. On-premises SharePoint installations include a set of stored procedures that periodically run to create and update the statistics objects for the wide, dynamically assigned table structures within. If you have not designed your application to intelligently create and update statistics using a separate process from that of the SQL Server engine, we recommend that you never disable these options.

Inside OUT

Should you enable the AUTO_UPDATE_STATISTICS *and* AUTO_UPDATE_STATISTICS _ASYNCHRONOUSLY *database settings?*

Yes! (Again, unless an application specifically recommends that you do not, such as SharePoint.)

Starting with compatibility level 130, the ratio of data modifications to rows in the table that helps identify out-of-date statistics has been aggressively lowered, causing statistics to be automatically updated more frequently. This is especially evident in large tables in which many rows are regularly updated. In SQL Server 2014 and before, this more aggressive behavior was not enabled by default, but could be enabled via Trace Flag 2371 starting with SQL Server 2008 R2 with Service Pack 1.

It is more important now than ever to enable AUTO_UPDATE_STATISTICS_ASYNCHRONOUSLY, which can dramatically reduce the overhead involved in automatic statistics maintenance.

Manually create statistics for on-disk tables

You can also create statistics manually during troubleshooting or performance tuning by using the CREATE STATISTICS statement.

Consider manually creating statistics for large tables, and with design principles similar to how nonclustered indexes should be created. The order of the keys in statistics does matter, and you should choose columns that are regularly queried together to provide the most value to queries.

When venturing into creating your own statistics objects, consider using filtered statistics, which can also be helpful if you are trying to carry out advanced performance tuning on queries with a static filter or specific range of data. Like filtered indexes (covered earlier in this chapter) or even filtered views and queries, you can create statistics with a similar WHERE clause. Filtered statistics are never automatically created.

➤ For more information on maintaining index statistics, see Chapter 8.

Understand statistics on memory-optimized tables

Statistics are created and updated automatically on memory-optimized tables, and serve the same role as they do for on-disk structures. Memory-optimized tables require at least one index to be created, and a matching statistics object is created for that index object.

It is recommended to always create memory-optimized tables in databases with the highest compatibility level. If a memory-optimized table was created with a SQL Server 2014 (12.0) compatibility level, you must manually update the statistics object using the UPDATE STATISTICS command. Then, if the AUTO_UPDATE_STATISTICS database option is enabled, statistics will update as normal. Statistics for new memory-optimized tables are not automatically updated if the database compatibility level was below compatibility level 130 when the tables were created.

➤ For more on memory-optimized tables, see Chapter 7, "Understand table features."

Understand statistics on external tables

You can also create statistics on external tables—that is, tables that do not exist in the SQL Server database but instead are transparent references to data stored in Azure Blob Storage via PolyBase.

You can create statistics on external tables, but currently, you cannot update them. Creating the statistics object involves copying the external data into the SQL Server database only temporarily, and then calculating statistics. To update statistics for these datasets, you must drop them and re-create the statistics. Because of the data sizes typically involved with external tables, using the FULLSCAN method to update statistics is not recommended.

➤ For more on external tables, see Chapter 7.

CHAPTER 15

Understand other types of indexes

There are other types of indexes that you should be aware of, each with specific, limited uses for certain SQL Server features—for example, the Full-Text Search engine, spatial data types, and the xml data type. Though not nearly as common as other types of indexes mentioned in this chapter, they have powerful specific uses.

Understand full-text indexes

If you have chosen to install the SQL Server Full-Text Search feature, you can take advantage of the full-text service (fdhost.exe) to query vast amounts of data using special full-text syntax, looking for word forms, phrases, thesaurus lookups, word proximity, and more. (You can of course choose to add the feature via SQL Server Setup if it is not already installed.)

Because they have specific uses for particular architectures and applications, we won't spend much time on them here. Developers might take advantage of powerful full-text functions CONTAINS or FREETEXT.

By design, full-text indexes require a unique nonclustered or clustered rowstore index on the table in which they are created, with a single column in the key. We recommend that you give this index an integer key for performance reasons, such as an identity column. Full-text indexes are usually placed on varchar or nvarchar columns, often with large lengths, but you can also place them on xml and varbinary columns.

It is important to understand the two viable options to updating the full-text index. A full population of the full-text index is effective but will consume more resources than an incremental load strategy. If the table receives writes frequently, you should consider the two possible incremental load strategies. By default, the CHANGE_TRACKING AUTO option enables the change tracking feature on the table that hosts the full-text index, which makes it possible for changes to propagate into the full-text index. This asynchronously keeps the full-text data synchronized with minimal overhead. If enabling change tracking is not an option for the table, you can instead add or use an existing column with the timestamp data type in the table and then periodically update the full-text index by starting an incremental population. Consider both strategies, along with your requirements for frequency of updates to the full-text index. Both are superior to frequent full populations.

Understand spatial indexes

A spatial index is a special B-tree index that uses a suite of special code and geometry methods to assist in performing spatial and geometry calculations. Developers can use these data structures for non-Euclidean geometry calculations, distance and area calculations on spheres, and more. Spatial indexes can improve the performance of queries with spatial operations.

You can create these indexes only on columns that use the spatial data types `geometry` or `geography`, and you can create different types of indexes on the same spatial column to serve different calculations. To create a spatial index, the table must already have a primary key.

You create spatial indexes by using bounding boxes or tessellation schemes for `geometry` and `geography` data types. Consult the documentation and the developers' intended use of spatial data when creating these indexes here: *https://learn.microsoft.com/sql/relational-databases /spatial/spatial-indexes-overview.*

Understand XML indexes

XML indexes are created for much the same benefit as nonclustered indexes. You use them to prevent the runtime *shredding* of XML files each time they are accessed, and to instead provide a persistent row set of the XML data's tags, values, and paths.

Because the `xml` data type is stored as a BLOB and has an upper limit of 2 GB of data per row, XML data can be massive, and XML indexes can be extremely beneficial to reads. Like nonclustered indexes, they also incur an overhead to writes.

Primary XML indexes prevent the on-demand shredding of the data by providing a reference to the tags, values, and paths. On large XML documents, this can be a major performance improvement.

Secondary XML indexes enhance the performance of primary XML indexes. They are created on either path, value, or property data in the primary XML index and benefit a read workload that heavily uses one of those three methods of querying XML data.

> ➤ Consult the documentation and the developers' intended use of XML data when creating XML indexes at *https://learn.microsoft.com/sql/relational-databases/xml/xml-indexes -sql-server.*

XML compression

SQL Server 2022 introduces XML compression, which can compress off-row XML data for both XML columns and XML indexes, providing a much-needed improvement when storing XML data in SQL Server.

When you enable XML compression, the underlying storage is changed to a compressed binary format, but this doesn't change how you query the data, and it doesn't require any application changes.

Although XML compression works in a similar way to data compression, it only affects the `xml` data type and associated XML indexes. You can run data compression and XML compression side by side on the same tables, but it must be enabled explicitly on primary and secondary XML indexes.

CHAPTER 15

Space saving with XML compression

The similarity with data compression extends to two system objects: the `sp_estimate_data_compression_savings` system stored procedure and the `sys.dm_db_index_physical_stats` dynamic management function.

You can use `sp_estimate_data_compression_savings` to estimate how much space you will save by compressing XML columns and indexes. In SQL Server 2022, this stored procedure takes a new parameter, `@xml_compression`, which is a Boolean value. You can assign it a `bit` value of 1, 0, or NULL (the default).

To find out how much space you have saved once you have compressed your XML data, use `sys.dm_db_index-physical_stats`. The following query returns the average row size in bytes, number of records, and number of data pages occupied to show you the benefits of compression:

```
SELECT o.name,
    ips.partition_number,
    ips.index_type_desc,
    ips.record_count, ips.avg_record_size_in_bytes,
    ips.min_record_size_in_bytes,
    ips.max_record_size_in_bytes,
    ips.page_count, ips.compressed_page_count
FROM sys.dm_db_index_physical_stats ( DB_ID(), NULL, NULL, NULL, 'DETAILED') ips
JOIN sys.objects o on o.object_id = ips.object_id
ORDER BY record_count DESC;
```

Design and implement hybrid and Azure database infrastructure

This chapter examines options for designing a database infrastructure in which some or all your data is hosted in a public cloud—specifically, the Microsoft Azure cloud. It begins with an overview of cloud and Azure concepts. It then discusses considerations for deploying SQL Server–based infrastructure using infrastructure as a service (IaaS), platform as a service (PaaS), or a hybrid approach. The chapter ends with a cursory listing of some non–SQL Server data platform services in Azure, exploring the flexibility the cloud has to offer.

All scripts for this book are available for download at *https://www.MicrosoftPressStore.com /SQLServer2022InsideOut/downloads*.

> ➤ Detailed coverage of several PaaS offerings—specifically, Azure SQL Database and Azure SQL Managed Instance—is found in Chapter 17, "Provision Azure SQL Database," and Chapter 18, "Provision Azure SQL Managed Instance," respectively. Migrating to Azure is covered in Chapter 19, "Migrate to SQL Server solutions in Azure."

NOTE

Microsoft Azure consists of multiple "clouds," including the public cloud as well as Azure Government and sovereign clouds in China and Germany. The content of this chapter applies to the public cloud. Service and feature availability may vary in the other cloud environments.

Cloud computing and Microsoft Azure

You have likely already encountered many different definitions of cloud computing. Rather than present you with yet another one, we will briefly discuss some key features of cloud computing and how they apply to SQL Server offerings in Azure:

- **Financial accounting.** With traditional on-premises environments, there is usually a significant initial outlay of capital. This is called *capital expenditure*, or "CapEx." Expenses in Azure, on the other hand, generally fall under the category of *operational expenditure*, or "OpEx." With OpEx, there is no initial monetary outlay and little long-term financial commitment. The fees you pay are pay-per-use charges and are all-inclusive: hardware, licensing, electricity, monitoring, and more.

Some Azure subscription models incentivize you to commit to a minimum annual spend in return for a reduced service cost.

OpEx might not be cheaper than CapEx overall, depending on how efficiently you provision cloud services. These considerations are beyond the scope of this text, but we strongly encourage you to plan early to optimize your resource allocation.

- **Elasticity.** This means the resources you provision are not fixed in terms of capacity. In on-premises environments, you provision hardware and software (licensing) sufficient to accommodate peak demand. In Azure, elasticity gives you the ability to scale up and down or out and in as needed to accommodate demand at any given moment.

- **Control.** With on-premises deployments of SQL Server, the DBA team decides which hardware to select, when to apply patches, and when to upgrade to a major new release. If you select an Azure PaaS offering, it's the team at Microsoft that makes these decisions. They announce changes and updates using a variety of channels; as a cloud DBA, one of your tasks will include regularly reviewing these announcements. You must thoroughly understand your Azure environment to determine which changes or updates will affect your application(s).

Database as a service

Azure provides many types of services, including virtual machines (VMs), web applications, and, of course, Azure SQL Database. Cloud services are often categorized in one of three types: infrastructure as a service (IaaS), platform as a service (PaaS), and software as a service (SaaS). In this book, we may refer to Azure SQL Database as database as a service (DBaaS), which is a specialized type of PaaS.

You might also choose to host SQL Server databases in the cloud using Azure Virtual Machine (VM) images, which can come with a SQL Server version pre-installed. In that case, you are using IaaS. With IaaS, you gain increased control and complete feature parity with on-premises deployments. IaaS also introduces more responsibility for sizing VM specifications appropriately and managing software updates for both the operating system (OS) and SQL Server.

Azure SQL Managed Instance is a more recent addition to the SQL Server offerings in Azure. Azure SQL Managed Instance strikes a better balance between feature parity and control than IaaS, especially with the backup portability feature introduced in November 2022 that allows backups and failover with on-premises SQL Server 2022 instances. We discuss Azure SQL Managed Instance and the link feature for Azure SQL Managed Instance in Chapter 18.

Managing Azure with the Azure portal and PowerShell 7

When you are ready to begin using Azure, you must deploy, manage, and eventually tear down resources when applications are retired or upgraded. To manage on-premises Microsoft environments, you might use various GUI tools (often based on the Microsoft Management Console) or PowerShell.

The primary GUI in Azure is the Azure portal. It helps if you also become comfortable managing resources using PowerShell.

The latest version of PowerShell 7, based on .NET 3.1 Core, was introduced in 2020 as a unified platform. There is no more distinction between PowerShell Core and PowerShell. PowerShell 7 allows you to execute the same PowerShell scripts on a variety of platforms: a half dozen Linux distributions, macOS 10.13+, Windows 7 and later versions, and Windows Server 2008 R2 and later versions. A third option for managing Azure is the Azure Command-Line Interface (CLI). You can use the Azure CLI across platforms (Windows, macOS, and Linux) and within the Azure portal using Azure Cloud Shell.

PowerShell 5.1 remains the default version of PowerShell installed on current and recent Windows operating systems, and it should handle many tasks. The dbatools open source library of PowerShell modules, for example, requires PowerShell 3 for Windows operating systems, or PowerShell 6.1 for Linux and macOS.

If you intend to use PowerShell scripting as a core part of your enterprise's automation, auditing, or provisioning, manually installing PowerShell 7 is recommended.

To install PowerShell 7, see *https://learn.microsoft.com/powershell/scripting/install/installing -powershell*. The GitHub releases page at *https://github.com/PowerShell/PowerShell/releases* lists stable, pre-release, and Long Term Support (LTS) releases. The releases shown first might be preview releases, so scroll down to find the release marked *latest*. The LTS releases contain only security updates and other fixes, minimizing the impact of any new features or changes to sensitive, stable code. For most use cases, you should use the current stable release. For more information about the PowerShell Support Lifecycle and these releases, visit *https://aka.ms /pslifecycle*.

For managing Azure and Azure SQL Database using PowerShell 7, you should always use the latest Azure PowerShell module, Az. The module is updated frequently, so be sure to regularly check for updates. To check the version of PowerShell currently installed, use `$psversiontable` and look at the value of `PSVersion`.

You can install the PowerShell module using the following PowerShell command, run with administrator privileges:

```
Install-Module -Name Az -AllowClobber
```

NOTE

The `-AllowClobber` parameter is generally only necessary if you also have the older AzureRM module installed in Windows PowerShell. The AzureRM PowerShell module is deprecated, will be retired in February 2024, and hasn't received feature updates since December 2018. You should plan to migrate any scripts that use the AzureRM module to the Az module. For more information, see *https://learn.microsoft.com/powershell/azure /new-azureps-module-az.*

Be patient while the module downloads all its child modules; there are quite a few of them to manage most Azure services.

To update the module in place, use the following:

```
Update-Module Az
```

Before you can manage your Azure resources with PowerShell, you must log in to Azure. Use the `Connect-AzAccount` to use the device login mechanism. A popup window with multifactor authentication will launch to confirm your Azure credentials.

After logging in, the `Get-AzContext` cmdlet outputs information about the active subscription. If you need to switch the subscription, use the `Get-AzSubscription` cmdlet to see a list of all subscriptions your account can manage. You can then use the `Select-AzSubscription` cmdlet to change the active subscription to another one. This is illustrated using the following commands, which assume you have a subscription with the name `'Pay-As-You-Go'`.

```
Get-AzSubscription
# A list of subscriptions is displayed.
# You can copy and paste a subscription name on the next line.
Select-AzSubscription -SubscriptionName 'Pay-As-You-Go'
```

NOTE

Managing SQL resources in Azure is discussed in Chapters 17 and 18.

Azure exposes a complete REST API that third-party tools or in-house developed tools can use to perform virtually any action in the Azure environment. Developers might not even need to call the APIs directly because for many platforms, official client libraries are available. The use of the REST API is not covered in this book.

➤ For a discussion on the use of the REST API, see *https://learn.microsoft.com/rest/api/azure/.*

Azure governance

Even relatively modest on-premises environments require governance—organizational processes and procedures by which the environment is managed and responsibilities are delineated. Governance is also a necessity in cloud environments. This chapter can't delve into all of the governance issues related to cloud operations. It does, however, discuss some Azure features that allow governance to be formalized.

Azure resources are organized in a hierarchy of containers. The container at the top level is the subscription. The subscription is primarily a billing boundary; all resources in a single subscription appear on a single invoice and have the same billing cycle. There are also life cycle consequences: If a subscription is discontinued, all resources within the subscription stop. (Eventually, the subscription and resources are deleted.)

Security configuration is also associated with the subscription; a subscription trusts a single Azure Active Directory (Azure AD) instance. This means all user accounts used to manage resources within a subscription must exist within the trusted Azure AD instance. Microsoft accounts, or user accounts from other Azure AD instances, can be added as external users to the trusted instance. An organization can choose to have multiple Azure subscriptions that trust the same Azure AD instance.

➤ **For more information on Azure AD, see Chapter 12, "Administer instance and database security and permissions."**

As illustrated in Figure 16-1, a single subscription can have many resources of several types, and Azure SQL Database is just one. *Resource groups* allow you to organize these resources by life cycle and to provide a security boundary. Resource groups are logical containers that have a name and a bit of metadata. The resources in a resource group are deleted if the resource group itself is deleted, hence the life cycle relationship between the resources and the resource group.

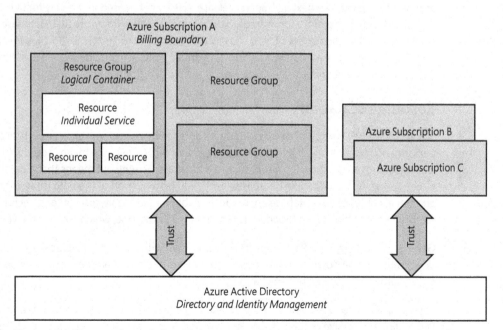

Figure 16-1 The container relationship between an Azure subscription, resource groups, and resources.

Using role-based access control (RBAC), permissions can be granted on a resource group, and those permissions apply to the resources within the group. Configuring permissions this way can be a huge timesaver and increase visibility into permission assignments. This is discussed in more detail in the "Security in Azure SQL Database" section in Chapter 17. Up front, you must know that the permissions assigned to the Azure SQL Database resource don't grant permissions to sign into the database itself.

NOTE

You can move resources between resource groups and subscriptions. When moving resources, the Azure region in which they are located does not change, even if the target resource group's location is different. The location of a resource group determines only where that resource group's metadata is stored, not where the actual resources are hosted.

Cloud-first

If you've been working with SQL Server for more than a few years, you've likely noticed the increased release cadence. This is a direct result of the *cloud-first* approach in SQL Server product development that Microsoft adopted a few years ago. Cloud-first in this context means that new features are generally first made available in Azure SQL Database as a preview feature. Those preview features are usually opt-in and are closely monitored by the product team. The close monitoring allows the team to quickly identify usage patterns and issues. These features are then included in the next SQL Server release. A feature released in this way for SQL Server 2022 was Query Store hints, for example, which was in preview for Azure SQL Database for more than a year before the release of SQL Server 2022. Features like SHORTEST_PATH, UTF-8 support, Always Encrypted, dynamic data masking, and graph tables were made available in Azure SQL Database before their release in SQL Server.

Resource scalability

Scalability is a key feature of cloud computing, and can be considered along a vertical axis of performance (scaling up) or a horizontal axis (scaling out). *Scaling up* means additional hardware resources are assigned to a server or to a database. *Scaling out* means that a database is either broken up into multiple databases, each holding a portion of the data (sharding), or that additional copies of the database are made available for read-only connections, such that those read-only connections are offloaded from the primary database, which handles the writes.

Generally, scalability with PaaS resources is easier than with IaaS resources. Scaling a VM up or down causes some downtime, but is considerably less onerous than moving a database to different hardware as the workload changes.

You can scale up or scale down an Azure SQL Database with minimal impact to applications. Depending on the size of the database and the nature of the scale operation, the operation can take several hours to complete. This scaling activity is completed while the database is online, though at the end of the scale operation, existing connections are dropped.

This benefit, and many others, of PaaS might encourage you to look first at PaaS for your cloud database needs. That is a valid strategy: Choose PaaS unless it is unable to meet your requirements, in which case fall back to IaaS.

When managing many databases, each with potentially many different scaling needs, you should also consider running these databases in an elastic pool. An *elastic pool* is a group of databases on a single logical server that share the resources available within the pool. We discuss elastic pools in depth in the "Elastic pools" section later in this chapter.

Scaling out in Azure SQL Database (recall that is the PaaS offering) can be accomplished using read-only replicas in service tiers that support them. Read-scale replicas are discussed later in this chapter, along with elastic pools, which are ideally suited for sharding databases.

Networking in Azure

Networking in Azure is an extensive topic that cannot be fully covered in a single section of this chapter. Therefore, we focus on the aspects of Azure networking that are critical to the successful operation of the various types of SQL Server deployments.

An Azure *Virtual Network* (*VNet*) is a resource type that defines an IP range, subnets, and more, as discussed later in this section. In some Azure deployments, you might not find a VNet; many PaaS resources don't require it and some deployments wouldn't benefit from it. However, many IaaS and some PaaS resources require or automatically configure their own VNet, such as Azure VM and Azure SQL Managed Instance.

You might not be too excited about exposing services to the public Internet. To secure your VNet, you can use network security groups (NSGs), which are discussed a little later, or Azure Firewall. Azure Firewall is a fully managed service that provides granular control over connections to and from the VNet.

A VNet can be divided into multiple subnets. Each subnet might then have its own route table, NSG, and service endpoints. Brief definitions of some of these networking features follow:

- **Network security group (NSG).** An NSG combines security rules that define the inbound and outbound traffic that is allowed or denied. An NSG can be applied to a subnet or a single VM network interface. NSGs can define source and target IP ranges and ports, service tags, or application security groups (ASGs).

- **Service tag.** A service tag allows you to define a rule in an NSG without knowing the details about source or target IP addresses. An example of a service tag relevant for this book is Sql.KoreaCentral. This service tag defines the IP addresses of the Azure SQL Database service in the Korea Central region of Azure.

- **Application security group (ASG).** An ASG is essentially just a name. It can be assigned to multiple network interfaces, and a network interface can have multiple ASGs assigned. The ASGs can then be used instead of a source or destination IP or IP range, simplifying the maintenance of security rules as VMs are added or removed from your Azure infrastructure.

  ➤ An example of how ASGs can simplify rules is available at *https://learn.microsoft.com/azure /virtual-network/network-security-groups-overview#application-security-groups*.

- **Service endpoint.** A service endpoint is a connection between the VNet and Azure services. Using service endpoints increases security because Azure services deployed to the VNet using a service endpoint are accessible only from the VNet. Service endpoints also provide routing benefits because the traffic between the resources in the VNet and the Azure services does not take the same route as Internet traffic. Not all Azure services support service endpoints, but Azure SQL Database does.

Private Link is a technique that allows you to assign a private IP address from a VNet to a PaaS service. With a Private Link enabled, public endpoints traditionally assigned to PaaS services can be completely ignored. Connections to the service can be established only from the same VNet, a peered VNet, a cross-region VNet-to-VNet connection, Express Route, or a virtual private network (VPN). Like service endpoints, only select PaaS services support Private Link. Azure SQL DB supports it, but Azure SQL Managed Instance does not (perhaps, yet). A Private Link for Azure SQL Database handles inbound connections only and has no effect on outbound traffic.

  ➤ Private networking between on-premises and Azure is discussed in the "Hybrid cloud with Azure" section later in this chapter.

Azure Private Link for Azure SQL Database and Azure Synapse Analytics allows you to connect to various PaaS resources in Azure via a private endpoint.

  ➤ Learn more about Private Link for Azure SQL Database at *https://learn.microsoft.com/azure /sql-database/sql-database-private-endpoint-overview*.

NOTE

At the time of this writing, Private Link availability depends on the service in use.

Cloud models and SQL Server

Azure offers several ways to manage and query data in a SQL Server or an Azure SQL platform:

- **Infrastructure as a service (IaaS).** SQL Server running on an Azure VM.

- **Platform as a service (PaaS).** Azure SQL Database, Azure SQL Managed Instance, and Azure Synapse Analytics. These services might also be referred to as database as a service (DBaaS).

- **Hybrid cloud.** Combines the best features of on-premises SQL Server with Azure—specifically, a SQL Server feature that supports Backup to URL, or the link feature for Azure SQL Managed Instance.

Azure SQL resources, whether IaaS or PaaS, can be managed in a centralized management hub. You can use this centralized view of SQL Server VMs, Azure SQL Database logical servers and databases, and Azure SQL Managed Instance to efficiently manage SQL resources at scale. The experience of creating new SQL resources is also streamlined.

Each of the following sections discusses specific terminology and configuration considerations for running an optimal SQL Server deployment in Azure. Specifics for deploying Azure SQL Database and Azure SQL Managed Instance are covered in the next two chapters.

> ➤ Configuring availability groups for SQL Server instance on Azure VMs is simpler thanks to a new preview feature to configure multiple subnets in the same Azure virtual network, removing the requirement to use Azure load balancers. For more information, see *https:// learn.microsoft.com/azure/azure-sql/virtual-machines/windows/availability-group-azure -portal-configure.*

Infrastructure as a service

Take what you've learned in the first three chapters of the book about VMs, and that's IaaS in a nutshell, optimized for a SQL Server environment.

As detailed in Chapter 2, "Introduction to database server components," a VM shares physical resources with other VMs. In the case of Azure VMs, there are some configurations and optimizations that can make your SQL Server implementation perform well, without requiring insight into the other guest VMs.

When creating a SQL Server VM in Azure, you can choose from different templates, which provide a wide range of options for different virtual hardware configurations, operating systems, and, of course, versions and editions of SQL Server.

Azure VMs are priced using a time-based usage model, which makes it easier to get started. You pay per minute or per hour, depending on the resources you need, so you can start small and scale upward. In many cases, if performance is not acceptable, moving to better virtual hardware is very easy and requires only a few minutes of downtime.

Azure VM performance optimization

Many of the same rules for physical hardware and VMs outlined in Chapter 3, "Design and implement an on-premises database infrastructure," apply to Azure VMs used for SQL Server. These include changing power-saving settings to High Performance, correctly configuring max server memory usage, spreading tempdb over several files, and so on.

When you deploy a VM using one of the Microsoft-provided SQL Server templates, some of these tasks are done for you. For instance, power-saving settings are set to High Performance already, and tempdb files are configured properly when you configure a new Azure VM running SQL Server 2016 or higher.

There are a variety of options for storage on Azure VMs, but you'd follow some of the same best practices there as well. The OS should be on its own volume, but database and log files should be separated on other volumes, just as in an on-premises server hosting a SQL Server instance. There is one particularly useful exception: the ultra-fast, local SSD on the temporary disk (volume letter D:), which can host the tempdb data and log files. More on that later in this chapter, in the section "Locate tempdb files on the VM."

Inside OUT

What is Azure Blob Storage?

Coming from a database background, you probably think of a BLOB as a large object in binary format stored using the `varbinary(max)` data type.

In a similar vein, Azure Blob Storage is a service for storing unstructured text or binary data as objects (binary large objects or BLOBs), accessible using HTTP or HTTPS. You can think of these BLOBs conceptually as files. The BLOBs can contain any type of data, including SQL Server files, but the service doesn't know, care, or provide any functionality to handle structured data.

As a storage service, Azure Storage focuses on high availability (HA), performance, and disaster recovery (DR) functions. These highly desirable attributes make Azure Storage attractive for many scenarios. You'll find later in this chapter that many services take advantage of this service.

➤ To read more about using Azure Blob Storage with SQL Server backups, visit *https://learn .microsoft.com/sql/relational-databases/backup-restore/sql-server-backup-and-restore -with-microsoft-azure-blob-storage-service*.

Azure Disk Storage

The storage disks for Azure VMs are provided through several storage offerings. These options are listed in order of increasing ranges of input/output per second (IOPS).

- **Standard HDD.** Designed for backups and low-cost, latency-insensitive workloads.

- **Standard SSD.** Suited for low-use enterprise workloads, including web servers and development and test environments.

- **Premium SSD.** Recommended for production workloads and other performance-sensitive environments.

- **Premium SSD v2.** Introduced in October 2022 and is recommended when available for production enterprise workloads. Unlike Premium SSD, Premium SSD v2 has independently configurable size and IOPS, meaning that you do not need to overprovision or stripe storage to get a desired level of IOPS. You may save money and get more performance by reconfiguring to use Premium SSD v2. For more information, see *https://aka.ms/premiumv2doc*.

- **Ultra SSD.** Ideal for transaction-heavy workloads, including large-scale database and analytics environments.

- ➤ The exact max throughput measured in IOPS is regularly updating in Azure Storage, so we'll avoid printing them here. Consult the Azure portal for the latest figures. You can see the disk comparison chart at *https://learn.microsoft.com/azure/virtual-machines/disks-types*.

As mentioned, SQL Server's main performance bottleneck is tempdb, followed closely by transaction log files, all of which are I/O-bound. Consider these when making your price-performance decisions around Azure VM storage for SQL Server instances.

Inside OUT

Can you use Standard HDD storage for SQL Server?

Yes, you can choose Standard HDD or SSD storage instead of Premium storage for your SQL Server VM, but we do not recommend it unless you have a large number of Standard drives in a striped configuration.

With solid-state storage, you pay for the entire drive, even if you use only a portion of it. With Standard storage, you pay only for what you are using. Although this is an attractive cost-saving opportunity, and might be useful for a development environment, the storage is not dedicated and is much slower.

Standard storage's relatively low maximum of IOPS and throughput will likely negatively affect your SQL Server's performance.

You have the choice between unmanaged and managed disks, but managed disks are the clear option for provisioning new VMs.

- **Unmanaged disks.** VM disks are managed by you, from creating the storage account and the container, to attaching the virtual hard disks (VHDs) to a VM and configuring redundancy and scalability. Unmanaged disks are now a deprecated technology and not recommended for new development. Unmanaged disks will be retired, requiring migration, by September 30, 2025. For more information, visit *https://learn.microsoft.com /azure/virtual-machines/unmanaged-disks-deprecation*.

- **Managed disks.** You specify the size and type of drive you need (Premium or Standard), and Azure handles the creation, management, and scaling for you.

➤ **For more information about performance best practices, visit** *https://learn.microsoft.com /azure/azure-sql/virtual-machines/windows/performance-guidelines-best-practices-checklist*.

NOTE

Maximum throughput can be limited by Azure VM bandwidth. Each Azure VM also has a maximum uncached disk throughput. You might not be able to address disk performance issues in SQL Server Azure VMs by adding disks or selecting disks with higher throughput numbers. Instead, you might need to select a larger VM. In many cases, you can select a higher size VM to get more system memory while keeping the vCore count the same.

We recommend a minimum of two P30 drives for SQL Server data files. The first drive is for transaction logs, and the second is for data files and tempdb.

Disk striping options

To achieve better performance (and larger drive volumes) out of your SQL Server VM, you can combine multiple drives into various RAID configurations by using Storage Spaces on Windows-based VMs or mdadm on Linux-based VMs. Depending on the Azure VM size, you can stripe up to 64 Premium storage drives together in an array.

An important consideration with RAID is the stripe (block) size. As noted, a 64-KB block size is most appropriate for an online transactional processing (OLTP) SQL Server environment. However, large data warehouses can benefit from a 256-KB stripe size, due to the larger sequential reads from that type of workload.

➤ **To read more about the different types of RAID, see Chapter 2.**

Storage account bandwidth considerations

Azure Storage costs are dictated by three factors: bandwidth, transactions, and capacity. Bandwidth is defined as the amount of data egress from the storage account. For Azure VMs running SQL Server, if the storage account is in the same region as the VM, there is no additional bandwidth cost. If there is any external access on the data, however, such as log shipping to a different location or using the AzCopy tool to synchronize data to another region (for example), there is a cost associated with that.

➤ **For more information on the latest version of** AzCopy, **visit** *https://learn.microsoft.com/azure /storage/common/storage-use-azcopy-v10*.

Drive caching

For SQL Server workloads on Azure VMs, you should enable ReadOnly caching on the Premium storage drive when attaching it to the VM, but only for data files and tempdb data files. This increases the IOPS and reduces latency for your environment, and avoids the risk of data loss that might occur due to ReadWrite caching. For drives hosting transaction logs, do not enable caching: Set caching to NONE.

➤ You can read more about drive caching and performance best practices for SQL Server on Azure VMs at *https://learn.microsoft.com/azure/azure-sql/virtual-machines/windows /performance-guidelines-best-practices-storage*.

SQL Server data files in Azure Storage

Instead of attaching a data drive to your machine running SQL Server, you can use Azure Storage to store your user database files directly, as blobs. This provides migration benefits (data movement is unnecessary), high availability (HA), snapshot backups, and cost savings with storage. For system databases, this feature is neither recommended nor supported.

CAUTION

Because performance is critical, especially when accessing storage over a network, you must test this offering, especially for heavy workloads.

To get this to work, you need a storage account and container on Azure Storage, a shared access signature (SAS), and a SQL Server credential for each container.

There are some limitations that might affect your decision:

- FILESTREAM data is not supported, which affects memory-optimized objects, as well. If you want to use FILESTREAM or memory-optimized objects, you must use locally attached storage.

- Only .mdf, .ndf, and .ldf extensions are supported.

- Geo-replication is not supported.

➤ You can read more (including additional limitations) at *https://learn.microsoft.com/sql /relational-databases/databases/sql-server-data-files-in-microsoft-azure*.

Virtual machine sizing

Microsoft recommends certain types, or *series*, of Azure VMs for SQL Server workloads. Each of these series of VMs comes with different size options.

CHAPTER 16

> ➤ You can read more about performance best practices for SQL Server in Azure VMs at *https://learn.microsoft.com/azure/azure-sql/virtual-machines/windows/performance-guidelines-best-practices-vm-size*.

It is possible to resize your VM within the same series (going larger is as simple as choosing a bigger size in the Azure portal), and in many cases you can even move across series as the need arises.

You can also downgrade your VM to a smaller size to scale down after running a resource-intensive process or if you accidentally overprovision your server. Provided the smaller VM can handle additional options you might have selected (data drives and network interfaces tend to be the deciding factor here), it is equally simple to downgrade a VM to a smaller size by choosing the VM in the Azure portal.

Both growing and shrinking the VM size requires downtime, but it usually takes just a few minutes at most.

> ➤ At the time of this writing, the Edsv5 series, M-series, and Mv2 series are best suited to OLTP workloads, with the M-series providing the highest RAM to vCore ratio. For more information, visit *https://learn.microsoft.com/azure/azure-sql/virtual-machines/windows/performance-guidelines-best-practices-vm-size#checklist*.

Choosing the right series can be confusing, especially with new sizes and series coming out all the time. The ability to resize VMs makes this decision less stressful.

NOTE

You pay separately for solid-state drives attached to Azure VMs. Keep this in mind when identifying the right VM for your workload.

Locate tempdb files on the VM

Many Azure VMs come with a temporary drive, which is provisioned automatically for the Windows page file and scratch storage space. The drive is not guaranteed to survive VM restarts and does not survive a VM deallocation.

A fairly common practice with Azure VMs is to place the SQL Server tempdb on this temporary drive because it uses solid-state storage and is theoretically faster than a Standard storage drive. However, this temporary drive is thinly provisioned. Recall in Chapter 2 how thin provisioned storage for VMs is shared among all the VMs on that host.

Placing the tempdb on this drive might require preparation, because it can result in high latency—especially if other guests using that underlying physical storage have done the same thing. Whether this issue will affect you is determined in part by the series of VM. If you created the VM using a SQL Server template from Microsoft, then no preparation is necessary. If you created a VM image yourself or used a generic VM image, then you must register the VM with the SQL VM resource provider (recommended and covered in the next section) or perform the steps in the blog post at *https://cloudblogs.microsoft.com/sqlserver/2014/09/25/using-ssds-in -azure-vms-to-store-sql-server-tempdb-and-buffer-pool-extensions/*.

Manage SQL Server virtual machines in the Azure portal

The Azure portal provides support for managing VMs with SQL Server installed. When you create a VM from an image that includes SQL Server, the VM is registered with the SQL VM resource provider. If you create a VM without SQL Server pre-installed and install SQL Server yourself, you can register the VM with the resource provider.

CAUTION

If you are using Azure Hybrid Benefit licensing (discussed later in this chapter), you must register the VM with this resource provider. As of this writing, you no longer need to restart the SQL Server service, which is an appreciated improvement. The steps to regis- ter a VM where you installed SQL Server yourself are found at *https://learn.microsoft.com /azure/azure-sql/virtual-machines/windows/sql-agent-extension-manually-register -single-vm*.

Beyond this compliance requirement, the SQL VM resource provider extends the default VM management options to include automated patching, automated backup, and additional moni- toring capabilities. You can take advantage of automated backup and patching, but you are not required to. Both automated management features are discussed in additional detail below. The automated features depend on the SQL Server IaaS Agent extension, which is installed in the VM when the SQL VM resource provider is installed in Full mode.

Inside OUT

What about the SQL Server configuration tab?

Before the availability of the SQL VM resource provider, a SQL Server configuration tab was available for managing SQL Server from the VM resource. With the advent of the SQL VM resource provider, this tab is now deprecated. It is the only method, however, that can be used to manage SQL Server versions that have reached end of support—namely SQL Server 2008, SQL Server 2008 R2, and SQL Server 2012. You must still register those VMs with the SQL VM resource provider if you are taking advantage of the Azure Hybrid Benefit.

Automated backup

There are a few requirements for the automated backup feature. Chief among them is that only specific versions of SQL Server running on specific Windows Server versions are supported.

Additionally, the user databases selected for automated backup must be running in the full recovery model.

> ➤ Read more about recovery models in Chapter 10, "Develop, deploy, and manage data recovery."

You can configure automated backup to retain backups between 1 and 30 days in an Azure storage account of your choice. Optionally, backups can be encrypted. When encryption is enabled, a certificate is generated that is protected by a password. The certificate is stored in the same storage account where the backups are kept.

Starting with SQL Server 2016, Automated Backup v2 is available. This offers additional control, including the ability to include the system databases in the backups. The system databases are not required to run in the full recovery model.

In v2 as in v1, the backup schedule can be determined automatically by Azure, in which case the log growth is used to determine the frequency of backups. In addition, v2 allows the administrator to set the frequency of the full and log backups.

This service can be particularly advantageous to enterprises short on staff, particularly in the DBA skill set.

> ➤ For more information about the automated backup service for SQL Server, visit *https:// learn.microsoft.com/azure/azure-sql/virtual-machines/windows/automated-backup*.

NOTE

In addition to this automated backup feature, which is convenient but somewhat limited, Azure also supports backing up SQL Server using Azure Backup for SQL VMs. For more information, visit *https://learn.microsoft.com/azure/azure-sql/virtual-machines /windows/backup-restore#azbackup*.

Automated patching

If you want the Azure infrastructure to patch Windows and SQL Server, you can enable automated patching for SQL Server VMs. You choose a day of the week, a start hour (which is in the server's time zone), and a maximum duration for the maintenance.

Every week at that time, Windows Updates marked as *Important* will be downloaded and installed while the maintenance window is active. If the maintenance window is too short for all patches to be applied, the remaining patches will be installed during the next scheduled maintenance period. After installing patches, the system might be rebooted, thus incurring downtime.

NOTE

SQL Server cumulative updates are not included in the automated patching; you are still responsible for installing those.

Because of the possibility of multiple periods of performance impact and downtime each month, automated patching might not be appropriate for production systems that must be highly available. On the other hand, configuring automated patching for development and test VMs can reduce the burden on administrators, allowing them to focus on the health of the production systems.

➤ More information about the automated patching service is available at *https://learn.microsoft .com/azure/azure-sql/virtual-machines/windows/automated-patching*.

Confidential VMs

Introduced in 2022, Azure confidential VMs ensure that the data storage, memory, OS, and processor activity are strongly protected against host access inside the datacenter. These boundaries are hardware-enforced and provide an extra layer of protection for the most sensitive of data and adherence to strict compliance requirements. In October 2022, Microsoft announced the first SQL Server images available for provisioning on confidential VMs.

The use case for confidential VMs is for extremely sensitive data and/or to achieve special privacy certification for Azure VMs. Azure confidential VMs use AMD Secure Encrypted Virtualization-Secure Nested Paging (SEV-SNP) technology, which is a fancy way of securing the hypervisor and other host management access. The processor's state and memory are encrypted by keys generated by the processor itself. Confidential VMs also feature new UEFI boot features and a dedicated virtual Trusted Platform Module (TPM). No further adaption of the operating system, code, or database platforms on the VM are necessary to achieve this level of protection. In the future, we may see these enhanced security features become mainstream on modern operating systems and virtual hosting platforms.

At the time of this book's writing, Azure offers four generations of scalable hardware in both general purpose and memory optimized sizing, each with a C in the second letter of their name: DCasv5, ECasv5, DCadsv5, ECadsv5. For more information, see *https://learn.microsoft.com/azure /confidential-computing/confidential-vm-faq-amd*.

Platform as a service

With PaaS resources, you can focus on a task without having to worry about the administration and maintenance surrounding that task. This makes it a lot easier to get up and running. You can use DBaaS resources—including Azure SQL Database, Azure Synapse Analytics, and Azure SQL Managed Instance—to complement or replace your organization's data platform requirements. This section introduces the currently available PaaS SQL Server offerings in the Azure cloud.

CHAPTER 16

➤ Complete coverage of Azure SQL Database is found in Chapter 17. Complete coverage of Azure SQL Managed Instance is found in Chapter 18.

Azure SQL Database provides a single database or set of databases logically grouped in an elastic pool and the freedom to not concern yourself with resource allocation (CPU, RAM, storage, licensing, OS), installation, and configuration of that database. You also don't need to worry about patching or upgrades at the OS or instance level, tempdb, backups, corruption, or redundancy. In fact, the built-in support for database recovery is excellent (including point-in-time restores). You can even add long-term backup retention to keep your backups for up to 10 years. Microsoft's Data Platform is about choosing the right component to solve a particular problem, as opposed to one offering being all things to all people.

Azure SQL services (including Azure SQL Database, Azure SQL Managed Instance, and Azure Synapse Analytics) are part of a larger vision, combining the strengths of the Database Engine with other Azure components, breaking the mold of a self-contained or standalone system. A change in mindset is necessary to appreciate it for what it offers, instead of criticizing it for its perceived shortcomings.

Azure SQL Database purchase models

Azure SQL Database charges are calculated based on one of two purchasing models: by database transaction units (DTUs) or by vCores. In general, Microsoft recommends the vCore purchasing model for most production workloads, but DTU offers a lower end of performance that is simpler and cheaper. You may find databases in the DTU purchasing model easier to manage for pre-production environments and the vCore purchasing model better for high-performance production environments. If you are migrating legacy applications to Azure SQL Database, you may find better parallels to on-premises performance in the vCore purchasing model.

In this section, you'll learn what DTUs and vCores are and how to choose the right purchasing model for your needs.

NOTE

It is possible to convert from the DTU-based purchasing model to the vCore model, and vice versa, without incurring downtime.

Database transaction units (DTUs)

DTUs are likely the Azure SQL Database concept that new adopters struggle with the most. DBAs must comprehend what it means and come to terms with the fact that this single measure is how you determine the level of performance to expect for your database.

A DTU is a blended measure of hardware resources provided for the database, including CPU, memory, and data and transaction log I/O. An increase in DTU results in a linear increase in each of the hardware resources. Thus, when doubling the DTUs for a database, you effectively double how much CPU, memory, and I/O is assigned to your database. Microsoft determined the relative mix of these hardware measures using a benchmark developed for this purpose. This benchmark, called the DTU benchmark, is designed to be representative of common OLTP workloads.

➤ To read a detailed description of the benchmark, visit *https://learn.microsoft.com/azure /azure-sql/database/service-tiers-dtu#dtu-benchmark*.

As you'll learn in Chapter 17, when creating a database using the DTU purchasing model, you specify the number of DTUs for that database by specifying the pricing tier and service objective. Additional differences between the pricing tiers are also discussed in that chapter.

Inside OUT

How do you know how many DTUs to provision?

Accurately provisioning DTUs for your database workload prevents slow response times or excessive charges. Aside from the workload monitoring you should do anyway to right-size workloads in the cloud, Microsoft does provide a tool to perform initial SKU estimations for cloud services. This tool helps to estimate the DTUs for Azure SQL Database, but also the compute and storage tiers to choose for Azure SQL Managed Instance or SQL Server on Azure VMs. The Database Migration Assistant (DMA) plays a helpful role in this exercise, which is currently provided in a .NET Core console application. For more information on the SqlAssessment.exe utility, see *https://learn.microsoft.com/sql/dma/dma-sku-recommend-sql-db*.

➤ For more information on QPI, see *https://learn.microsoft.com/azure/azure-sql/database /query-performance-insight-use*.

Selecting a DTU pricing tier and service objective

The DTU model offers three service tiers: Basic, Standard, and Premium. Because Azure SQL Database is billed by the hour, the selection of a service tier and service objective determines how much you will be charged for your database. However, there are additional considerations. Specific pricing and other details might change by the time the ink on this page has dried; thus, we focus more on general concepts that you should be aware of and how they will influence your selection of a tier.

NOTE

You can find current pricing for Azure SQL Database at *https://azure.microsoft.com/pricing /details/azure-sql-database/*.

The Basic tier provides the lowest available DTUs. You pay significantly less, but sacrifice performance and some availability guarantees. This tier is suitable for development purposes and perhaps very small-scale applications.

The Standard and Premium tiers are the two main choices for production databases. At first glance, you will notice that the Premium tier provides considerably more DTUs and does so at a higher cost per DTU compared to Standard. This is because of architectural differences between these tiers. The database files in Standard tier databases are stored in Azure Storage. This means the files are not local to the Database Engine. In the Premium tier, they are stored on local SSDs. This difference in the locality of the database files has performance implications, as you might expect. Further, there is also a difference in how intra-region high availability (HA) is handled. HA for Standard tier databases is ensured through the replication of the back end storage. In the Premium tier, HA is achieved by using availability group technology.

vCore

For some workloads, the DTU purchasing model might not be appropriate. Or, your workload may not fit into the pre-selected DTU balance of resources. For example, Microsoft recommends using the vCore purchasing model for most production Azure SQL Database deployments, especially for migrations from on-premises SQL Server applications. The vCore model allows the administrator to select a combination of hardware generation, number of CPU cores, and memory that is assigned to a single database or elastic pool. This makes it easier to compare the capacity you pay for with on-premises capacity.

Be careful about comparing cloud or hybrid performance with on-premises performance. There are a lot of factors that affect the performance of the Database Engine that won't be evident when comparing CPU and memory capacity.

NOTE

The lowest end of the vCore purchasing model is significantly more powerful, and therefore more expensive, than the lowest service objective with the DTU purchasing model. For comparison purposes, a single vCore is roughly equivalent to 100 DTUs in the standard tier and 125 DTUs in the premium tier.

Another difference is that the vCore model includes no storage. You will be billed for the actual storage consumed at the rate of Azure premium storage in the region where your database is hosted.

Like the DTU model, the vCore model offers service tiers: General Purpose, Business Critical, and Hyperscale. The main differences between the General Purpose and Business Critical tiers are found in the use of remote Azure Blob Storage versus local solid-state storage (resulting in 10 times higher IOPS at the lowest end and about 28 times higher at the highest end) and support for in-memory objects. Both differences are much like the difference between the Standard and Premium service tiers in the DTU purchasing model. The Business Critical tier also offers the option to provision additional replicas for HA.

➤ The architecture of the Hyperscale service tier is so different, it is covered in the "Hyperscale service tier" subsection below.

➤ Read-scale replicas are discussed in the "Read scale-out" section later in this chapter.

NOTE

vCore is your only option when considering Azure SQL Managed Instance. This is also the case for the Hyperscale service tier and serverless compute tier offerings. The serverless compute tier is discussed later in this section.

Reserved capacity

For scenarios where you can determine a minimum amount of Azure SQL Database resources you will use, you can reduce your total cost by prepaying for capacity. Capacity is reserved for a specific region, deployment type, performance tier (confusingly, another name for service tier that is used in this context), and a term of one or three years. When you reserve capacity, any database resources that meet those criteria are billed at the reserved capacity rate, which is prepaid. Bear in mind that the prepaid rate does not include charges that aren't ordinarily included in the normal billing rates—notably software, networking, and storage charges.

NOTE

You do not need to reserve capacity for all your Azure SQL Database needs if you're uncertain of your requirements for certain instances, such as dev/test. You can purchase reserved capacity for those instances that you are confident you will need, and additional capacity will be invoiced at your normal billing rate.

NOTE

Reserved capacity is available only with the vCore purchasing model and with Azure SQL Managed Instance.

➤ Discussing the entire process of reserving capacity for licensing benefits is outside the scope of this book. For guidance, visit *https://learn.microsoft.com/azure/sql-database /sql-database-reserved-capacity*.

Serverless compute tier

Consider the serverless compute tier for "spiky" workloads requiring heavy, unpredictable resource utilization followed by periods of relatively low utilization, or even no utilization, when the service can auto-pause and auto-resume itself.

The serverless compute tier affords the DBA the ability to select a minimum and maximum number of vCores to assign to a single database. Based on workload, the Azure service fabric will automatically scale up and down how many cores are assigned.

Combined with the auto-scaling of vCores comes an automatic calculation of a minimum and maximum amount of memory that will be assigned. The maximum storage size is determined by the DBA and billed separately. vCores are charged on a per vCore-per-second basis, taking minimum RAM and storage into account.

> ### NOTE
>
> **Compute tier is another level of differentiation in Azure SQL Database and is different from the service tier or the purchasing model. Beyond the auto-scaling of CPU and RAM, the entire database can be paused after a configurable number of hours of inactivity. This brings Azure SQL Database even closer to the ideal of cloud computing: Pay exactly for what you need, when you need it.**

There is a downside to the serverless tier, especially when auto-pausing is enabled. When database activity resumes, there is a delay due to the warm-up period required. Even when auto-pausing is not enabled, frequent memory trimming and the occasional need for the Azure fabric to load-balance databases between servers might cause delays and dropped connections. The good news is that if serverless turns out to be a poor choice for your database, you can move it to the provisioned compute tier without downtime.

> ➤ Additional details on the serverless compute tier can be found at *https://learn.microsoft.com /azure/azure-sql/database/serverless-tier-overview*.

Hyperscale service tier

The Hyperscale service tier offers significantly larger database sizes combined with other benefits to ensure that managing these very large databases (VLDBs) doesn't affect availability.

Architecturally, the Hyperscale tier is quite different from the General Purpose and Business Critical tiers. Hyperscale introduces a very different deployment style for the SQL Server Database Engine: The query processing engine is separated from the storage engine and the log service, and these components run on different systems. This radical departure from how SQL Server is deployed allows storage and compute resources to scale completely independently from each other. Figure 16-2 illustrates the architecture of the Hyperscale tier.

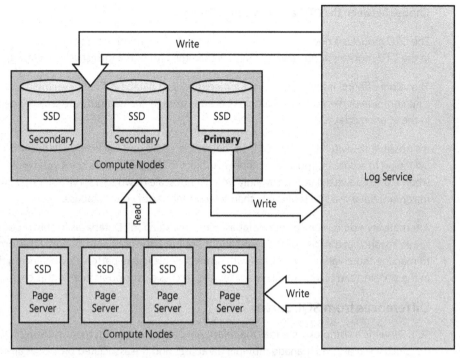

Figure 16-2 High-level overview of the Hyperscale architecture.

More than just greater maximum size, the Hyperscale architecture allows for several other impressive feats:

- Instantaneous backups that require no CPU or storage operations on the compute nodes (by leveraging Azure Storage snapshots).

- Warm buffer pools after startup, thanks to persisting the buffer pool using an in-memory table that is stored on fast local solid-state storage, a concept known as Resilient Buffer Pool Extensions (RBPEX).

- A recovery point objective (RPO) of 0 minutes with a recovery time objective (RTO) of less than 10 minutes; moreover, RTO is not affected by database size.

- The ability to migrate databases to the Hyperscale tier and back, or to "reverse migrate" from the Hyperscale tier, was made generally available in September 2022.

➤ For a technical deep dive into the Hyperscale architecture, read the paper presented by the Microsoft Azure and Microsoft Research teams at SIGMOD '19 at *https://www.microsoft.com /research/uploads/prod/2019/05/socrates.pdf*.

Choose between the DTU and vCore purchasing model

The DTU model is a good choice for low-end needs. The monthly cost of the lowest service tier in the DTU model is about seven times less than the cost of the lowest vCore offering.

The vCore offering is more attractive for medium-sized databases that nevertheless have significant compute or memory requirements because storage and compute are scaled independently in the vCore model.

It's possible to switch from the DTU model to the vCore and back again without downtime. Switching to a different purchase model is subject to the same restrictions you would encounter when scaling down a database. Mainly, you cannot scale down to a service tier that allows a maximum database size that is less than the current size of your database.

Alternatively, you can place your databases in an elastic pool. Databases in elastic pools use a single instance of the Database Engine and share the same pool of resources. It becomes easier to manage those varying workloads with unpredictable usage patterns by balancing the group in the pool instead of individual databases. We discuss elastic pools later in this chapter.

Differences from SQL Server

SQL Server is a complete, standalone relational database management system (RDBMS) designed to create and manage multiple databases and the associated processes around them. It includes a great many tools and features, including a comprehensive job scheduler.

Think of Azure SQL Database, then, as an offering at the database level. Because of this, only database-specific features are available. You can create objects such as tables, views, user-defined functions, and stored procedures, as well as memory-optimized objects. You can write queries, and you can connect an application to it.

What you *can't* do with Azure SQL Database is run scheduled tasks directly via Windows Task Scheduler or SQL Agent, though other cloud-based automation solutions are available, detailed later in this section.

Querying other databases within Azure SQL Database is limited, though elastic database queries are a preview feature. Azure SQL Managed Instance allows cross-database queries just like a SQL Server instance.

You can't restore an Azure SQL database from a SQL Server backup, but with new features introduced in Azure SQL Managed Instance, version parity does allow for backups to be restored into and out of a SQL managed instance.

In Azure SQL Database and Azure SQL Managed Instance, you don't have access to a file system, so importing data is more complicated. You can't manage system databases, and in particular, you can't manage tempdb, though Azure SQL Managed Instance does allow for some tempdb configuration.

There is currently no support for user-defined SQL Server common language runtime (CLR) procedures (instead, consider Azure SQL Managed Instance). However, the native SQL CLR functions, like those necessary to support the hierarchyid and geospatial data types, are available.

On-premises environments typically use only integrated authentication to provide single sign-on (SSO) and simplified login administration. In such environments, SQL Server Authentication is often disabled. Disabling SQL Server Authentication is not supported in Azure SQL Database. Instead of integrated authentication, there are several Azure AD authentication scenarios supported. These are discussed in more detail in Chapter 17.

Azure SQL Database does not support multiple filegroups or files. By extension, several other Database Engine features that use filegroups are unavailable, including FILESTREAM and FileTable.

➤ You can read more about FILESTREAM and FileTable in Chapter 7, "Understand table features."

Database limitations

Azure SQL Database is subject to certain size limitations, such as the maximum database size. The maximum database size varies based on the purchase model and the pricing tier. In the DTU purchase model, the database size includes only the size of the data; the size of transaction logs is not counted. In the vCore purchase model, you are billed for the actual amount of storage consumed by your database, including the transaction log and backups.

If you are designing an application for the cloud, size limitations are less of a restriction when deciding whether to adopt Azure SQL Database. This is because an application designed to operate at cloud-scale should shard its data across several database instances. In addition to overcoming database size limitations, the benefits of sharding also include faster DR and the ability to locate the data closer to the application if the application runs in different Azure regions.

To provide predictable performance for Azure SQL Database, there are limits to the number of concurrent requests, concurrent logins, and concurrent sessions. These limits differ by service tier and service objective. If any limit is reached, the next connection or query attempt will fail with error code 10928.

➤ You can find an exhaustive list of these operational limits online at *https://learn.microsoft.com /azure/azure-sql/database/resource-limits-logical-server*.

One final limitation to be aware of is that a single server has an upper limit on the total DTUs it can host as well as on the total number of databases. For a large deployment, this might require distributing databases across servers. We recommend against operating at or near this limit because overall performance can become suboptimal. As of this writing, you should limit the number of databases per server to around 5,000.

NOTE

Any limitations discussed in this chapter are subject to change frequently, so be sure to review current limitations before deciding whether Azure SQL Database is right for you. You can do so here: *https://learn.microsoft.com/azure/azure-sql/database/resource-limits-logical-server.*

The resource limits—whether DTUs or vCores—force us to rethink how we best use the service. It is easy to waste a lot of money on Azure SQL Database because it requires a certain DTU service level at certain periods during the day or week, but at other times it is idle. It is possible to scale an Azure SQL database up and down as needed, but if this happens regularly, it makes the usage, and therefore the cost, unpredictable. Elastic pools (see the upcoming section on this) are a great way to get around this problem by averaging out resource usage over multiple databases with elastic DTUs or vCores.

Other SQL Server services

In addition to the Database Engine, an on-premises deployment of SQL Server might include the following:

- **SQL Server Agent.** To schedule maintenance tasks or other activities

- **SQL Server Integration Services (SSIS).** To load or extract data

- **SQL Server Reporting Services (SSRS).** To provide report functionality

- **SQL Server Analysis Services (SSAS).** To support analytical workloads

These services are not included in Azure SQL Database. Instead, comparable functionality is often available through separate Azure services. A complete discussion of the available alternatives in Azure is beyond the scope of this book. The descriptions that follow are intended to merely name some of the alternatives and their high-level uses and direct you to an online starting point to learn more:

- **SQL Server Agent alternatives.** To schedule recurring tasks for Azure SQL Database instances, DBAs should consider using Azure Automation. This service makes it possible to reliably execute potentially long-running PowerShell scripts. You can use Azure Automation to automate management of any Azure or third-party cloud service, including Azure SQL Database. In addition, there is a gallery of reusable scripts available.

  If you only require execution of T-SQL statements in your recurring tasks and you don't need complex job branching logic between steps, elastic database jobs might also be a suitable replacement. These are covered in the upcoming "Elastic database jobs" section.

➤ For more information on using Azure Automation with Azure SQL Database, see *https://learn.microsoft.com/azure/azure-sql/database/automation-manage.*

➤ Find an introduction to Azure Automation at *https://learn.microsoft.com/azure/automation /overview*.

● **SSIS alternatives.** Instead of SSIS, use Azure Data Factory to perform tasks such as extracting data from various sources, transforming it by using a range of services, and finally publishing it to data stores for consumption by business intelligence (BI) tools or applications. Azure Data Factory includes an SSIS-compatible integration runtime, which allows you to run SSIS packages in Azure.

You can use SSIS to extract data from and load data to Azure SQL Database, and you can use Data Factory to extract data from and load data to on-premises data stores. The decision about which service to use depends largely on where most of your data resides, which services you plan to use to transform the data, whether you allow a cloud service to connect to your on-premises environment using a gateway service, and the cost of data egress if you are bringing your data back on-premises.

➤ You can learn more about Data Factory at *https://learn.microsoft.com/azure/data-factory/*.

● **SSRS alternatives.** Microsoft Power BI is a recommended cloud-native replacement for SSRS. Power BI is a powerful tool to create interactive visualizations using data from various sources. You can embed Power BI dashboards and reports in applications. You can also access them directly using a web browser or mobile app. Power BI Premium supports paginated reports, the type of reports you would develop with SSRS in the past. If you must have SSRS, you can run it in a VM on Azure, but you must pay for or provide a SQL Server license.

➤ You can learn more about Power BI at *https://aka.ms/powerbidocs*.

● **SSAS alternatives.** There are several alternative Azure services to replace SSAS. Foremost, there is Azure Analysis Services. It is built on SSAS; as such, existing tabular models can be migrated from on-premises SSAS deployments to the cloud. Alternatively, Power BI also includes tabular model functionality that might replace SSAS and has significant investment from Microsoft as the path forward for analytical workloads. For new development of enterprise data warehousing and analytical solutions, you should consider Azure Synapse Analytics, an enterprise analytical solution to unify non-relational and relational data in dedicated SQL and serverless SQL pools. Power BI, SQL data warehousing, Spark compute pools, machine learning, and easy low-code, web-based development are all included in the broad Azure Synapse platform.

➤ **In addition to these replacements, we include a brief overview of other data services in Azure in the last section of this chapter, "Other data services in Azure."**

CHAPTER 16

> **NOTE**
>
> Some of the limitations described in this section can be addressed by using Azure SQL Managed Instance. We cover Azure SQL Managed Instance in detail in Chapter 18.

That said, Azure SQL Database is not going to completely replace SQL Server. Some systems are not designed to be moved into this type of environment, and there's nothing wrong with that. Microsoft will continue to release a standalone SQL Server product. On the other hand, Azure SQL Database is perfect for supporting web applications that can scale up as the user base grows. For new development, you can enjoy all the benefits of not having to maintain a database server at a predictable cost.

Read scale-out

If you're thinking a read scale-out replica is a secondary database instance that provides read-only access to your data, you are correct. Provisioning these replicas in Azure SQL Database is supported in the Premium, Business Critical, and Hyperscale service tiers. In the Premium and Business Critical tiers, it is also enabled by default when you create a new database.

> **NOTE**
>
> Some features are not available on the replica database. These features are the Query Store, Extended Events, SQL Profiler, and, crucially perhaps in regulated environments, Audit. It is possible to disable the read scale-out feature. However, database-scoped Extended Events can collect data.

An application indicates its intent for a read-only or read-write connection using the `ApplicationIntent` property in the connection string. Specifically, a value of `ReadOnly` causes the connection gateway to direct the connection to a read-only replica, if available. Not specifying `ApplicationIntent` or specifying a value of `ReadWrite` directs the connection to the primary replica.

> **Inside OUT**
>
> *What's the difference between a read-scale replica and a readable secondary?*
>
> A readable secondary database is a feature of geo-replication, which is discussed in detail in Chapter 17. As a feature of geo-replication, secondary databases are created by the DBA and generally located in a different region from the primary. Read scale-out is configured by the Azure infrastructure and the replicas live in the same region as the primary. Read scale-out comes with no extra cost, unlike geo-replication.

Microsoft recommends that if read scale-out is enabled on geo-replicated databases, it should also be enabled on the secondary database(s).

Although there is some overlap in the functionality between these two features, read-scale replicas are primarily designed for load balancing, while readable secondaries are designed for HA and DR.

Elastic pools

As noted, Azure SQL Database has limits on its size and resources. Like Azure VMs, Azure SQL Database is pay-per-usage. Depending on what you need, you can spend a lot or a little on your databases.

Elastic pools increase the scalability and efficiency of your Azure SQL Database deployment by providing the ability to pool several databases to share resources, whether priced according to DTUs or vCores.

Without elastic pools, each database might be provisioned with enough resources to handle its peak load. This can be inefficient. If you group databases with different peak load times in an elastic pool, the Azure fabric automatically balances the resources assigned to each database depending on their load. You can set limits to ensure that a single database does not starve the other databases in the pool of resources.

The best use case for elastic pools is one in which databases in the pool have low average resource utilization with spikes that occur from time to time. This might be due to a reporting-type query that runs once a day, or a help desk system that experiences a lot of traffic at certain times of the day, for instance. The elastic pool evens out these spikes over the full billing period, giving you a more predictable cost for an unpredictable workload across multiple databases.

NOTE

An elastic pool is tied to a single logical server. It's not possible to pool databases hosted on various logical servers in a single overarching pool. This has been in preview for a few years and there is no date for general availability.

Multitenant architecture

Azure SQL databases in an elastic pool enable you to provision new databases with predictable growth and associated costs. Managing these databases is much easier in this environment because the administrative burden is lowered. Performance is also predictable because the pool is based on the combined resource utilization.

CHAPTER 16

However, not all scenarios benefit from the use of elastic pools. The most beneficial are those in which databases experience their peak load at separate times. Imagine a software company with clients around the world, with each using a different Azure SQL Database in the elastic database pool. Each "tenant" database peaks at different times of day, using the majority of the pool's resources at peak operating hours. You must monitor the usage patterns of each customer and balance the elastic database pools according to your expected business model.

> ➤ For more information on multitenancy in Azure SQL Database, visit *https://learn.microsoft* *.com/azure/architecture/guide/multitenant/service/sql-database.*

Database consolidation

In an on-premises environment, database consolidation means finding a powerful enough server to handle the workload of many databases, each with its own workload pattern. Similarly, with elastic database pools, the number of databases is limited by the pool's size. For example, in the DTU purchasing model, the current maximum elastic pool size is 4,000 elastic DTUs (eDTUs) in a premium pool. This means you can operate up to 160 databases (at 25 DTUs each) in that single pool, sharing their resources.

In the vCore purchasing model, the maximum elastic pool size on the Business Critical tier gives you as many as 128 virtual cores along with 3,767 GB of RAM and 4 TB of data storage.

Combined with autoscale settings, depending on resource boundaries, consolidation makes a lot of sense for an organization with many small databases, just as it does with an on-premises SQL Server instance.

Elastic database tools

Scale-out in Azure SQL Database is also achieved using the elastic database tools client library, which is available for .NET and Java applications. Applications developed using this library can save their data in different Azure SQL databases based on data-dependent routing rules while retaining the ability to run SELECT queries across all shards. This is a popular model for SaaS applications because you can assign each SaaS customer its own database.

> ➤ You can find more information on the elastic database tools at *https://learn.microsoft.com* */azure/azure-sql/database/elastic-scale-get-started.*

Azure SQL Database elastic query

Perhaps the most surprising limitation in Azure SQL Database is that support for cross-database queries is very limited. This means it is not possible to write a query that uses a three- or four-part object name to reference a database object in another database or on another server. Consequently, semantic search is not available.

Azure SQL Database elastic query, which is still in preview at the time of writing, aims to provide a solution. For both vertically and horizontally partitioned databases, this feature can provide a way to write T-SQL statements that are executed across databases by leveraging the external data sources and external tables feature.

CAUTION

Azure SQL Database elastic query is not recommended for extract, transform, load (ETL) operations. When multiple sources are involved in a query, if a source is unavailable, the entire query will fail. You must include retry logic in your application as a best practice.

There are some limitations, however. On the Standard tier, the first query can take several minutes to run because the functionality to run the query needs to be loaded first. Additionally, access is currently read-only for external data. Performance does improve on the higher tiers as costs increase, but this is not meant to replicate home-grown systems that have many databases tightly bound together.

➤ Read more about Azure SQL Database elastic query, and horizontal and vertical database partition scenarios, at *https://learn.microsoft.com/azure/azure-sql/database/elastic-query -overview*.

Elastic database jobs

A SQL Server instance can run the same query against multiple databases from a list of registered servers or a central management server. In a similar manner, the elastic database jobs feature enables you to run a script written in T-SQL against multiple databases in Azure SQL Database. For example, if your organization offers its customers a SaaS solution, each customer might receive their own database instance, and the schemas of all databases must be kept synchronized.

Elastic jobs remain in public preview as of the writing of this book, but a generally available (GA) announcement is expected. Let's discuss what elastic database jobs can do for your Azure SQL environment.

An elastic database job can target the databases that are part of a custom group of databases. A job is inserted into a job database, which is a standalone Azure SQL Database on a logical server referred to as the *agent server*. An Azure resource called an *elastic job agent* is created, pointed at the agent server and job database. Job credentials, which allow the agent to connect to the target databases, are stored in the job database, as is the list of target databases itself. Elastic database jobs can consist of multiple steps and can have a rudimentary schedule with simple recurrence rules. (See Figure 16-3.) Finally, the results can be stored in the job database, and diagnostics are available from the Elastic Job Agent pane in the Azure portal. This flow is very similar to a SQL Server Agent job.

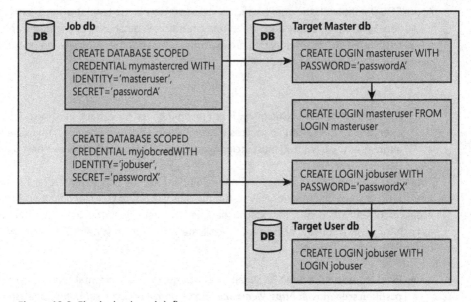

Figure 16-3 Elastic database job flow.

➤ You can read about elastic scale in Chapter 17 and find out more about elastic database jobs, such as their architecture and setup, at *https://learn.microsoft.com/azure/azure-sql /database/elastic-jobs-overview*.

NOTE

Some on-premises use cases for the SQL Server Agent might be addressed with elastic database jobs. For other use cases, you must use other Azure functions to automate tasks. Refer to the "Other SQL Server services" section earlier in this chapter for a brief intro to Azure Automation.

Shard databases with split-merge

Azure SQL Database is designed for SaaS scenarios because you can start small and grow your system as your customer base grows. This introduces several interesting challenges, however, including, for example, what happens when a database reaches its maximum resource limit and size.

Sharding is a technique by which data is partitioned horizontally across multiple nodes to improve either the performance or the resiliency of an application. In the context of Azure SQL Database, sharding refers to distributing data across more than one database when it grows too large. (If this sounds like table partitioning, you're mostly right.)

It is all very well to add more databases (shards) to support your application, but how do you distribute your data evenly across those new databases? The split-merge tool can move data from constrained databases to new ones while maintaining data integrity. It runs as an Azure web service, which means there is an associated cost. The tool uses shard map management to decide what data segments (shardlets) go into which database (shard) using a metadata store (an additional standalone Azure SQL Database) and is completely customizable.

➤ To read about how this process works in detail, visit *https://learn.microsoft.com/azure /azure-sql/database/elastic-scale-overview-split-and-merge.*

Hybrid cloud with Azure

Azure SQL Database is not designed to completely replace SQL Server. Many thousands of organizations all over the world are quite happy with the security, performance, and low latency offered by hosting their environment on-premises, but would like to use certain components in the cloud.

The most common implementation of a hybrid cloud is with Azure AD. Instead of having to manage user accounts in two places (on-premises and in Azure, for Microsoft 365, for example), you can synchronize your Active Directory Domain Service (AD DS) with Azure AD and manage it all in one place.

Mixing your on-premises and Azure environments, in whichever way you do it, falls under the definition of a *hybrid cloud*. Microsoft has some interesting ways of helping you achieve this, especially around the data platform and SQL Server.

Azure Hybrid Benefit

Users can obtain significant savings on SQL Server VM or Azure SQL Database list prices if they have active Windows or SQL Server core licenses with Software Assurance. This is called the Azure Hybrid Benefit. Exactly which type of licenses can be converted or reused, and how they map to Azure offerings, is covered in detail in the Azure Hybrid Benefit FAQ found at *https:// azure.microsoft.com/pricing/hybrid-benefit/faq/.*

➤ You can calculate the expected savings using the Azure Hybrid Benefit Savings Calculator at *https://azure.microsoft.com/pricing/hybrid-benefit/.*

Azure Hybrid Benefit is available for SQL Server VMs, Azure SQL Database using the vCore pur-chase model, and Azure SQL Managed Instance. In other words, Azure SQL Database in the DTU purchase model is not eligible for discounted rates using Azure Hybrid Benefit.

NOTE

Azure Hybrid Benefit is a feature unique to Azure. It is different from the Software Assur-ance license mobility benefit, which might be used to reassign SQL Server core licenses to third-party providers offering unmanaged services, such as VMs or hosted SQL Server.

CHAPTER 16

Automate backups with SQL Server managed backups

With SQL Server on Azure VMs, you can automate SQL Server native backups that write directly to Azure Blob Storage. (This works with an on-premises version of SQL Server, as well, but latency can be an issue.)

By default, the schedule depends on the transaction workload, so a server that is idle will have fewer transaction log backups than a busy server. This reduces the total number of backup files required to restore a SQL Server database in a DR scenario.

You can also use advanced options to define a schedule. However, you must set this up before enabling managed backups to avoid unwanted backup operations. Additionally, the retention period is customizable, with the maximum being 30 days.

You can configure these backups at the instance or database level, providing much-needed flexibility for smaller database environments that would not ordinarily have a full-time database administrator on hand.

You can fully encrypt backups through SQL Server backup encryption, and Azure Blob Storage is encrypted by default (for data at rest).

> ➤ You can read more about encryption in Chapter 13, "Protect data through classification, encryption, and auditing."

There is an associated cost with the Azure Storage container required to store these database backups, but when the retention period is reached, older files are cleared out, keeping the costs consistent. If you were building your own custom backup solution, you would incur similar costs anyway, and there is a good chance the managed backup storage costs will be lower.

> ➤ To read more about SQL Server managed backup to Microsoft Azure, visit *https://learn .microsoft.com/sql/relational-databases/backup-restore/sql-server-managed-backup-to -microsoft-azure*.

Azure SQL Edge

For the Internet of Things (IoT), a lot of effort is expended in getting sensors and other devices to report their data to a SQL Server instance or Azure SQL Database in the cloud. Azure SQL Edge is a repackaged SQL Server instance that can run on low-power and IoT edge computing devices, with either 64-bit ARM or Intel x64 CPUs—for example, a Raspberry Pi computer. Edge includes the full SQL Server Database Engine running on Linux, along with some analytics features, including data streaming and time-series support.

Typical use cases for Azure SQL Edge include sitting on the factory floor, in supervisory control and data acquisition (SCADA) settings, or other continuously streamed, lightweight processing applications where low-voltage processes win on convenience, durability, and/or survivability.

➤ You can read more about Azure SQL Edge at *https://azure.microsoft.com/products /azure-sql/edge/.*

Azure Stack

This is Microsoft's version of an edge and hybrid cloud in which you can install certain Azure services on-premises on Microsoft-approved hardware. This brings the power of Azure to your own datacenter.

➤ Hardware requirements can be found on Microsoft Docs, at *https://learn.microsoft.com /azure-stack/hci/concepts/system-requirements.*

After you have developed the solutions that best suit your organization, you can deploy your applications and solutions to the Azure region that makes the most sense, or just keep them on-premises, hosted on Azure Stack.

You can use the Azure Stack Hub to expose Azure SQL databases as a service; or, use the SQL resource provider for virtual machines hosting SQL Server instances. This enables your users to create databases without having to provision a VM every time. Think of it as an on-premises version of Azure SQL Database.

Keep in mind that certain features like elastic pools, and scaling databases, are not available at this time.

➤ You can read more about SQL databases on Azure Stack at *https://learn.microsoft.com /azure-stack/operator/azure-stack-sql-resource-provider-deploy.*

Azure Arc–enabled data services

Azure Arc–enabled data services provide the ability to run data services on-premises, on the edge, in the cloud, or multi-cloud using an underlying Kubernetes infrastructure.

At the time of this writing, this option is available for Azure SQL Managed Instance and Azure Database for PostgreSQL Hyperscale (Citus). Hyperscale (Citus) is a new Azure platform offering horizontally scaled PostgreSQL clusters.

With Azure Arc–enabled data services, you can run cloud services close to the workload for improved performance, services such as patching, new features and frequent updates, and the Microsoft Defender security module.

You can run services such as self-service provisioning, automated backup and restore, and monitoring locally with or without a network connection to Azure, ensuring continued functionality if connectivity is lost.

➤ You can read more about Azure Arc–enabled data services at *https://azure.microsoft.com /products/azure-arc/hybrid-data-services/.*

Private networking between on-premises and Azure

Many organizations want to ensure a secure channel between their environments, whether that is using Azure VNets or their on-premises network and Azure. You can achieve this using a VPN.

A VPN encrypts traffic over any network (including the Internet) through a tunnel that it creates. All traffic that travels through the tunnel is secure, which means no attackers can monitor the traffic. However, there is a performance overhead with encrypting that traffic, which makes the connection slightly slower.

There are two main ways that Azure implements connections between your on-premises environment and Azure itself. One of these is through a traditional VPN service over the Internet (site-to-site), and the other is through a dedicated connection that does not use the public Internet (Azure ExpressRoute).

Site-to-site VPN

There are two scenarios when connecting systems to an Azure VNet: connecting two Azure VNets together and connecting an external network to an Azure VNet.

To connect two Azure VNets together in the same region, you can create a peering network—in other words, no part of the VNet goes out to the Internet—which is priced per gigabyte transferred.

If you want a VPN gateway instead, which creates a connection between your on-premises network and an Azure VNet, those are priced according to the maximum bandwidth you would require (100 Mbps, 650 Mbps, 1 Gbps, and 1.25 Gbps) and charged at an hourly rate (which, depending on what you need, is also reasonably priced).

Azure ExpressRoute

If the speeds of site-to-site VPNs are not satisfactory, and you want to connect your on-premises network to your Azure VNet, you can use ExpressRoute. With its low latency, ExpressRoute expands your existing network to the virtually limitless services available in Azure, depending on your budget, of course. Microsoft recommends ExpressRoute for data migration, replication, and other HA and DR strategies.

> ➤ *For more information about ExpressRoute, see https://azure.microsoft.com/services /expressroute.*

This type of bandwidth gives you the flexibility to move entire VMs from on-premises to Azure for test environments and migrations. Your customers can use Azure web services that take data from your on-premises environment without ever going over the public Internet.

You can also use it to create a DR site, using SQL Server log shipping. Perhaps you want to extend your availability group to the cloud, which you can do by using a distributed availability group (see Chapter 2). Using ExpressRoute, you can treat Azure as an extension of your own network, as illustrated in Figure 16-4.

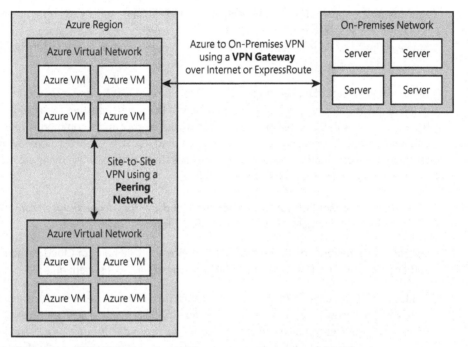

Figure 16-4 Azure VNets can connect to an on-premises network in various ways.

Inside OUT

How fast can data be transferred over a VPN connection?

Network speed is measured in bits per second (bps). Because there are 8 bits in a byte, a single byte would take 8 seconds to be transmitted at 1 bps, at the theoretical maximum throughput (perfect network conditions).

For speeds in the gigabit-per-second (Gbps) range, it takes at least 8 seconds to transfer 1 GB at a speed of 1 Gbps. It will take slightly longer due to latency and other overhead, like encryption.

Transferring data over large distances incurs latency due to the universal speed limit known as the speed of light. A network packet will take approximately 65 milliseconds to move across the continental United States and back again. You must consider both network speed and latency when planning migrations, as well as DR and HA scenarios.

Cloud security

Although we didn't include a comprehensive discussion of cloud security in this book, this section does provide a few considerations for DBAs considering a cloud migration.

First, many SQL Server offerings in the cloud support the same security features as on-premises. This is true for SQL Server in Azure VMs, and largely true for Azure SQL Database and Azure SQL Managed Instance. Specific security considerations for the PaaS offerings are discussed in Chapters 17 and 18, respectively.

An important aspect of managing security in Azure is Microsoft Defender for Cloud. Found in the Azure portal, it provides an integrated view of the security posture for all your Azure resources. Microsoft Defender for Cloud also provides metrics and recommendations to help you improve the security of your resources, including the SQL resources. Some Microsoft Defender for Cloud features are available in the paid Standard tier, while many are included with the cost of your existing resources.

➤ Learn more about Microsoft Defender for Cloud at *https://learn.microsoft.com/azure /defender-for-cloud/defender-for-cloud-introduction.*

SQL recommendations you might receive from Microsoft Defender for Cloud include enabling auditing on Azure SQL Databases and enabling vulnerability assessment on a SQL Server VM.

Deploying SQL resources in Azure means you must understand security in Azure in general. As a DBA, you must know who has access to view and especially manage SQL resources. Permissions to manage resources can be given at the account, subscription, resource group, and individual resource level. You must know how to monitor changes to Azure resources. Further, you must learn about networking in Azure.

NOTE

If you work in any sort of government or military setting, you're likely familiar with the acronym Security Technical Implementation Guide (STIG). The United States Department of Defense's Defense Information Systems Agency (DISA) released the first STIG for Microsoft Azure SQL Database in November 2022. A STIG may go a long way to helping certify Azure SQL-based applications for high security clearance. For more information, visit *https://public.cyber.mil/announcement/disa-releases-the-microsoft-azure-sql-database-security-technical-implementation-guide/.*

Other data services in Azure

Azure offers more data services than we cover in this book. We mention these here briefly because in today's multi-platform environments, there is more to our world than SQL Server. Each of these different offerings have their strengths and weaknesses. Deploying a modern application might involve mixing these different services to create a single solution to serve a business need.

Azure Synapse Analytics

The most closely related offering is Azure Synapse Analytics, which includes the Azure platform formerly known as Azure SQL Data Warehouse, Power BI, Azure Data Factory, the open-source SynapseML library of machine learning pipelines, and much more. Built on Apache Spark compute and Azure Data Lake Storage, Azure Synapse Analytics (not to be confused with Synapse Analytics, a different company) is a broad PaaS service optimized for parallel query processing and large data volumes.

Azure Synapse can scale a variety of different relational and non-relational storage and compute independently by leveraging Azure Storage and a massively parallel processing engine. This makes it suitable for storing enormous amounts of disparate data that arrive in the cloud in different ways.

> ➤ Learn more about Azure Synapse Analytics at *https://learn.microsoft.com/azure/synapse -analytics/*.

Azure Synapse Link

New for SQL Server 2022 is Azure Synapse Link. It provides a direct connection between Azure Synapse and SQL Server 2022, allowing on-premises data to be sent in a bulk upload—and then at regular intervals—using change data capture (CDC)—to Azure Synapse. From there, Azure Synapse can consume your relational data from an on-premises SQL Server side-by-side with streamed, IoT, delta store, non-relational, and other data.

> ➤ You can learn more about connecting Azure Synapse Link to SQL Server 2022 at *https:// learn.microsoft.com/azure/synapse-analytics/synapse-link/connect-synapse-link-sql -server-2022*.

Non-relational Azure data offerings

Azure provides several services and features for non-relational data management. These services enable you to work with data in a variety of formats outside of relational data. This would include graph, spatial data, key-value pairs, JSON, and XML documents.

Multi-model capabilities in Azure SQL

A recent addition to Azure SQL Database and Azure SQL Managed Instance is multi-model capabilities. This is valuable for when you have small amounts of unstructured data that you must incorporate into a typically relational database architecture. It can be useful for in-memory technologies to improve the performance of analytics. Or you can create copies of your data and offload some analytic workloads from the primary database for performance or convenience when using transactional replication or readable replicas.

You don't need specialized APIs for access. You can use JSON Path expressions, XQuery/XPath expressions, spatial functions, and graph query expressions in the same T-SQL query—in your preferred tool or programming language—to access the data in the database.

> ➤ Read more about multi-model data capabilities at *https://learn.microsoft.com/azure /azure-sql/multi-model-features.*

Cosmos DB

Outside the realm of relational database management systems, Azure Cosmos DB is noteworthy. This is a globally distributed database service that supports multiple data models, including key-value, document, graph, and relational. Azure Cosmos DB provides multiple distinct APIs atop a single global database service.

Various APIs include the API for NoSQL, Apache Gremlin, Apache Cassandra, MongoDB, Azure Table storage, and PostgreSQL.

> ➤ Learn more about Azure Cosmos DB at *https://learn.microsoft.com/azure/cosmos-db/.*

Third-party fully managed data platforms

Azure also offers third-party fully managed database platforms—namely Azure Database for MariaDB, Azure Database for MySQL, and Azure Database for PostgreSQL. These are all relational databases offered as PaaS, with similar scaling and flexibility options to Azure SQL Database.

> ➤ You can learn more about these services at *https://azure.microsoft.com/products/category /databases/.*

Provision Azure SQL Database

This chapter delves into Azure SQL Database, a cloud database service that provides SQL Server relational Database Engine. Azure SQL Database is a platform as a service (PaaS) offering designed for cloud applications to take advantage of relational database services, without most of the overhead of managing the Database Engine. Azure SQL Database is also designed to meet various requirements, from hosting a single database associated with an organization's line-of-business application to hosting thousands of databases for a global software as a service (SaaS) offering. This chapter looks at Azure SQL Database concepts and how to provision and manage databases.

➤ For an overview of cloud concepts and an introduction to the different SQL Server offerings in Microsoft Azure, see Chapter 16, "Design and implement hybrid and Azure database infrastructure." Azure SQL Managed Instance is covered in Chapter 18, "Provision Azure SQL Managed Instance."

In this chapter, you'll learn how to create your first server and database, with thorough coverage of the available options and why each one matters. Next, this chapter explains how to create and manage elastic pools.

Security must be on your checklist when deploying any database, and perhaps even more so in the cloud. This chapter includes coverage of the security features specific only to Azure SQL Database. Finally, this chapter reviews features designed to prepare your cloud-hosted database for disaster recovery.

➤ For security features common to SQL Server, refer to Chapter 12, "Administer instance and database security and permissions," and Chapter 13, "Protect data through classification, encryption, and auditing."

Throughout this chapter, you will find many PowerShell samples to complete tasks. This is important because the flexibility of cloud computing offers quick setup and teardown of resources. Automation through scripting becomes a must-have skill—unless you prefer to work overtime in the web GUI.

CHAPTER 17

➤ If you need an introduction to PowerShell 7, we discussed it in the previous chapter. Also refer to *https://github.com/PowerShell/PowerShell/tree/master/docs/learning-powershell*.

The scripts for this book are all available for download at *https://www.MicrosoftPressStore.com /SQLServer2022InsideOut/downloads*.

> ## Inside OUT
>
> *How do I keep up with new Azure SQL Database features?*
>
> Database as a service (DBaaS) platforms move faster than releases of SQL Server. Many new Database Engine features arrive on Azure SQL Database first, then show up in the next release of SQL Server. Azure SQL Database and Azure SQL Managed Instance likely have had new features announced since this book was published. It's also true that some features arrive in SQL Server first, then are later introduced to Azure SQL platforms.
>
> New features often move from "(preview)" to "generally available (GA)" in a few months, but sometimes they stay in preview for longer as Microsoft continues to gather feedback and telemetry on adoption.
>
> Keep up with the latest new features in Azure SQL Database on the "What's new" page: *https://learn.microsoft.com/azure/azure-sql/database/doc-changes-updates-release -notes-whats-new*.

Provision an Azure SQL Database logical server

The Azure SQL Database service introduces a concept called an *Azure SQL logical server* (note the lowercase *server*). This server is quite different from what you might be used to on-premises. A logical server is best described as a connection endpoint rather than an instance. For example, the Azure SQL logical server (just called *logical server* or just *server* from here on) does not provide compute or storage resources. It does not provide much configuration. And although there is a virtual master database, there is no model, tempdb, or msdb database—those are abstracted away. In addition to missing several features of an on-premises SQL Server, there are also features that are unique to logical SQL servers: firewall configuration and elastic pools to name just two.

➤ You can find more information about firewall configuration later in this chapter. We covered elastic pools in Chapter 16.

You should consider that your server determines the geographic region where your data will be stored. When a single logical server hosts multiple databases, these databases are collocated in the same Azure region, but they might not be hosted on the same hardware. That is of no consequence to you when using the databases, but the point serves to illustrate the purely *logical* nature of logical servers.

Creating a logical server is the first step in the process of deploying a database. The logical server determines the region that will host the database(s), provides the basis for access control and security configuration (more on that later), and provides the fully qualified domain name (FQDN) of the endpoint.

NOTE

Using the Azure portal, it is possible to provision a new logical server while creating a new database. All other methods require two separate steps or commands, so for consistency, we will discuss each separately in this chapter. This will allow the focus to remain on each distinct element (server and database) of your provisioning process.

You might be interested to know that provisioning a logical server does not incur usage charges. Azure SQL Database is billed based on the resources assigned to each database or elastic pool. The logical server acts only as a logical container for databases and provides the connection endpoint. This is also why there are no performance or sizing specifications attached to a logical server.

Inside OUT

When should you create a new logical server?

The logical server determines the region where the databases are located. Your databases should be in the same region as the applications or users that access them, both to avoid cross-region traffic charges and to have the lowest possible latency when running queries.

Security considerations can also dictate how many logical servers you operate. Because the server admin login and Azure Active Directory (Azure AD) principal assigned as server admins have complete control and access to all databases on a logical server, you might set up different logical servers for different applications or different environments, such as development, test, and production. On the other hand, the threat detection feature (discussed in detail in the section "Security in Azure SQL Database" later in this chapter) is charged per logical server. Therefore, you'll likely want to strike a balance between manageability, cost, and security.

The final factors when considering creating a new logical server or reusing an existing one are the database life cycle and billing aggregation. The database life cycle is tied directly to the logical server, so if you operate databases with very different life cycles, you could benefit from improved manageability by hosting those on different logical servers.

As it relates to billing, because your usage is charged per database, you might find benefits in aggregating charges for specific databases. You can aggregate charges by using a resource group or by using tags. Recall that all databases are tied to the resource group of the logical server where they are hosted. If you want to aggregate charges for several databases, these databases could be deployed to the same logical server, or you could assign the same tag and value to each database even if they are hosted on different servers in different resource groups.

CHAPTER 17

Create an Azure SQL Database server using the Azure portal

To provision a server using the Azure portal, use the search feature to find **SQL Database** and then use the **Create SQL Database Server** page. You must provide the following information to create a server:

- **Subscription.** The subscription in which you create the server determines which Azure account will be associated with databases on this server. Database usage charges are billed to the subscription.

- **Resource group.** The resource group where this server will reside. Review the section "Azure governance" in Chapter 16 to learn about the importance of resource groups.

- **Server name.** The logical server name becomes the DNS name of the server. The domain name is fixed to *database.windows.net*. This means your logical server name must be globally unique and lowercase. There are also restrictions as to which characters are allowed, though these restrictions are comparable to on-premises server names.

- **Location.** The Azure region where any databases are physically located. Azure SQL Database is available in most regions worldwide. You should carefully consider the placement of your servers and, by consequence, your databases. Your data should be in the same region as the compute resources (Azure Web Apps, for example) that will read and write the data. When you locate the applications that connect to the server in the same region, you can expect latency in the order of single-digit milliseconds. Another consequence of locating resources in other regions is that you might end up paying per gigabyte for the egress from the region where the data is located. Not all services incur these charges, but you must be aware before going this route.

- **Authentication method.** You have the option to use only SQL Authentication, only Azure AD Authentication, or both SQL and Azure AD Authentication.

- **Server admin login.** This username is best compared to the sa account in a SQL Server. However, you cannot use sa or other common SQL Server identifiers for this username; they are reserved for internal purposes. You should choose a generic name rather than one derived from your name because you cannot change the server admin login later.

- **Password.** The password associated with the server admin login. It is required only when you choose to use SQL Authentication. The admin password should be very strong and carefully guarded—ideally stored in Microsoft Azure Key Vault. Unlike the login itself, Azure users with specific roles can change it.

- **Azure AD Admin.** If you choose to use Azure AD Authentication on the logical server, you must specify an Azure AD user or group as the Azure AD Admin.

➤ You can read more about applying role-based access control (RBAC) to your Azure SQL Database resources later in this chapter.

When you create a new SQL Database logical server using the Azure portal, you can enable the new server's firewall to accept connections from all Azure resources. Before deploying any databases, we recommend that you either use a virtual network (VNet) service endpoint or configure the firewall to only allow connections from known IP addresses, as described in Chapter 16.

➤ You can read more about the firewall in the section "Server- and database-level firewall" later in this chapter.

Another decision you'll make at the server level is whether to enable Microsoft Defender for SQL, which is covered later in this chapter.

As with all Azure resources, you can add tags to the Azure SQL logical server resource, as well as the databases, SQL elastic pools, storage accounts, and so on. Tags are name-value pairs that enable you to categorize and view resources for billing or administrative purposes. Tags are highly recommended for your own enterprise organization, and they can also be used in reporting. Most commonly, you'll want to add a "Created By" tag, so that others in your environment know who created the resource.

There are other settings you might want to configure when you create a server, but they are found on the resource page after the server has been provisioned. For example, you can choose to use a service-managed key or a customer-managed key for transparent data encryption (TDE). You might also want to enable the system-assigned managed identity (SMI), which is useful for allowing the server to access other resources such as an Azure Key Vault. You can also create user-assigned managed identities (UMIs). These options are all covered later in this chapter.

Create a server using PowerShell

To provision a server using PowerShell, use the `New-AzSqlServer` cmdlet, as demonstrated in the following code example. You must modify the values of the variables in lines 1 through 6 to fit your needs. These commands assume the following objects already exist:

- A resource group with the name SSIO2022

- An Azure Key Vault with a secret named SQLAdminPwd

The server will be created in the active Azure tenant and subscription, so be sure to set your context appropriately before creating your server.

```
$resourceGroupName = "SSIO2022"
$location = "southcentralus"
$serverName = "ssio2022"
$adminSqlLogin = "SQLAdmin"
```

```
$adminSqlSecret = Get-AzKeyVaultSecret -VaultName 'SSIO-KV' -Name 'SQLAdminPwd'
$cred = $(New-Object -TypeName System.Management.Automation.PSCredential -ArgumentList
$adminSqlLogin, $($adminSqlSecret.SecretValue) )
$tags = @{"CreatedBy"="Kirby"; "Environment"="Dev"}
New-AzSqlServer -ResourceGroupName $resourceGroupName `
  -ServerName $serverName `
  -Location $location `
  -SqlAdministratorCredentials $cred `
  -AssignIdentity `
  -IdentityType "SystemAssigned" `
  -Tags $tags
```

The `New-AzSqlServer` PowerShell cmdlet allows you to create managed identities, specify the key to be used for TDE, specify the minimum TLS version, and disable public network access while provisioning the server.

The preceding script creates a server with the (SQL Authentication) server administrator specified. You might also want to specify the Azure AD admin as well.

In this script, the `Get-AzKeyVaultSecret` cmdlet is used to obtain the password for the `SQLAdmin` server administrator. This cmdlet retrieves the secret object from the key vault. Then the secret value is used to create a PowerShell credential object. The secret value is a secure string, so the plain text password is never exposed by the script. All values needed to create a server are provided as parameters to the `New-AzSqlServer` cmdlet. The script also creates a system-assigned managed identity for the server.

NOTE

All the sample Azure PowerShell scripts throughout this chapter build on the existence of an Azure SQL Database logical server named ssio2022 in a resource group named SSIO2022. You must choose your own server name because it must be globally unique. The sample scripts available for download are all cumulative and define the value just once, which makes it easy to make a single modification and run all the sample scripts.

Establish a connection to your server

With a server created, you can establish a connection. Azure SQL Database supports only one protocol for connections: TCP. In addition, you have no control over the TCP port number; it is always 1433.

NOTE

Some corporate networks might block connections to Internet IP addresses with a destination port of 1433. If you have trouble connecting, check with your network administrators.

Figure 17-1 shows the different values entered in the **Connect to Server** dialog box after you use SQL Server Management Studio (SSMS) to connect to the newly created server. When you first establish the connection, SSMS prompts you to create a firewall rule to allow this connection (see Figure 17-2). You must sign in with your Azure account to create the firewall rule.

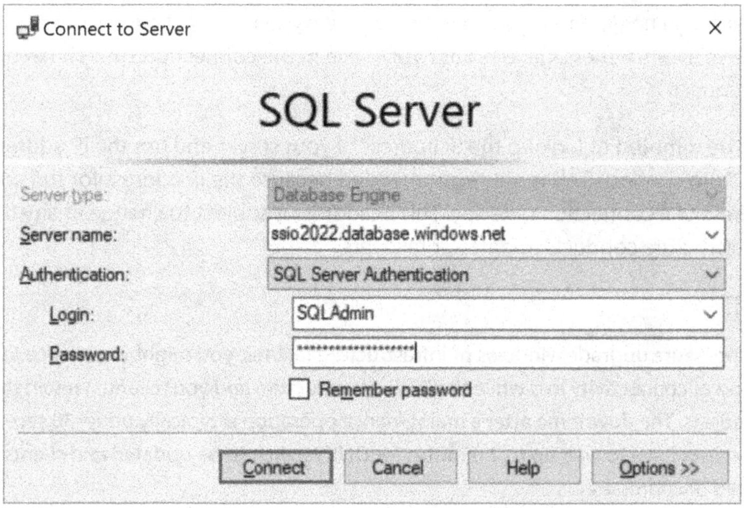

Figure 17-1 The Connect to Server dialog box, showing values to connect to the newly created Azure SQL Database logical server.

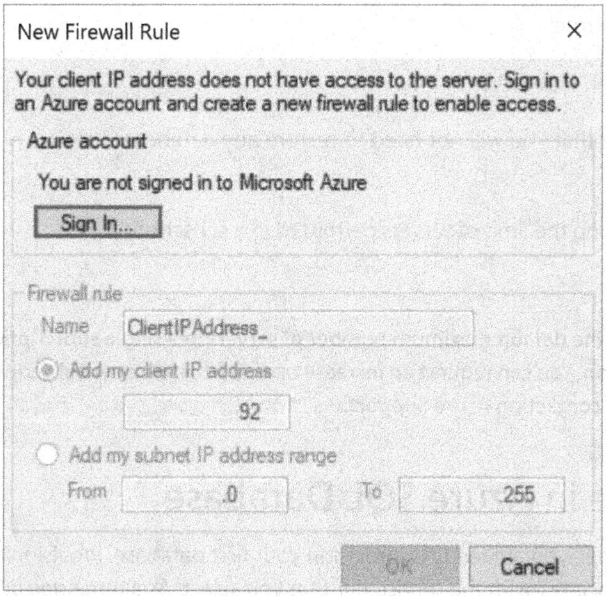

Figure 17-2 The New Firewall Rule dialog box that opens if the IP address attempting to connect is not included in any existing firewall rule.

CHAPTER 17

Connections to Azure SQL Database are always encrypted, even if this is not specified in the connection string. For older client libraries, you might need to specify encryption explicitly in the connection string because these libraries might not support the automatic upgrade of the connection. If you neglect to specify it explicitly when using these older client libraries, you might receive an error message. Use `Encrypt=True` in the connection string if needed to successfully connect.

You might be tempted to look up the IP address of your server and use the IP address instead of the FQDN to connect. This is not recommended because the IP address for the server is really the IP address of a connection gateway. This IP address is subject to change at any time as the Azure infrastructure conducts updates or failovers.

NOTE

During Azure upgrade windows or infrastructure failures, you might experience a brief period of connectivity loss while the DNS infrastructure and your client(s) retain the cached IP address. The downtime after a maintenance operation is typically under 10 seconds, but you might have to wait up to 2 minutes for DNS records to be updated and clients to clear cached IP addresses.

Delete a server

Deleting a server is a permanent, irreversible operation. You should delete a server only if the following conditions are true:

- You no longer need that server's name.

- You are confident that you will not need to restore any databases that are or were hosted on it.

- You are approaching the limit of servers permitted in a subscription.

NOTE

As of this writing, the default maximum number of servers in a single subscription is 20 in a single region. You can request an increase up to 250 servers per subscription in a single region by contacting Azure Support.

Provision a database in Azure SQL Database

After provisioning a server, you are ready to provision your first database. Provisioning a database incurs charges associated with the service tier that you select. As a reminder, pricing for Azure SQL Database is per database or elastic pool, not per logical server.

The sections that follow discuss the process of provisioning a database using the Azure portal, PowerShell, Azure CLI, and Transact-SQL (T-SQL).

NOTE

You can provision a new Azure SQL Database logical server while provisioning a new database only by using the Azure portal. All other methods require two separate steps or commands.

Create a database using the Azure portal

There are several ways to create a new database in Azure SQL Database using the Azure portal. One is to start from the **Overview** pane of an existing server. You can also start from the **Create New Service** pane. The method you choose determines which values you must provide:

- **Subscription.** Select the subscription that will be used to bill the charges for this database. The subscription you select here will narrow down the list of server choices later. This parameter is not shown when the process is started from a server.

- **Resource Group.** Choose to create a new resource group or use an existing one. If you choose to create a new resource group, you must also create a new server. Choosing an existing resource group does not narrow the list of server choices later.

- **Database Name.** The database name must be unique within the server and meet all requirements for a database name in SQL Server.

- **Server.** You can select an existing logical server in the selected subscription or create a new one. If you select a server in a different resource group from the one you selected, the resource group value will be updated automatically to reflect the correct selection. This is because the life cycle of a database is tied to the life cycle of the server, and the life cycle of the server is tied to the resource group. Therefore, a database cannot exist in a different resource group than its server. This server value is locked when the process is started from a logical server.

- **Elastic Database Pool.** We discuss elastic pools in detail in the "Provision an elastic pool" section later in this chapter. From the **Create SQL Database** pane, you can select an existing elastic pool or create a new one.

- **Backup Storage Redundancy.** This affects how your point-in-time restore and long-term retention backups are replicated. As of this writing, you can choose locally redundant, zone-redundant, or geo-redundant backup storage.

- **Data Source.** You select one of three values that match the previously mentioned options: Blank Database, Sample, or Backup. You can create a database from one of three sources:

  - **Blank.** A blank database is just that: There are no user database objects.

  - **Sample.** The new database will have the lightweight Adventure Works schema and data.

  - **Backup.** You can restore the most recent daily backup of another Azure SQL Database in the subscription.

- **Collation.** The collation selected here becomes the database's default collation. Unlike on-premises, there is no GUI to set the new database's collation name. You can type the collation name from memory or use a basic UI to search the list of valid SQL Server collation names.

- **Backup.** You are prompted to provide this only if you select Backup as the data source. The database you select will be restored to its most recent daily backup, which means it might be up to 24 hours old.

➤ You can read more about options for restoring database backups in the "Understand default disaster recovery features" section later in this chapter.

- **Service and Compute Tier.** When creating a standalone database, you must select a service tier and a compute tier. The service tier determines the hourly usage charges and several architectural aspects of your database. (Chapter 16 discusses service tiers and compute tiers.) It is possible to mix service tiers of databases within a logical server, underscoring the fact that the server is merely a logical container for databases and has no relationship to any performance aspects. The compute tier specifies whether you want a serverless or provisioned database. When selecting the service and compute tier, you can also set a maximum database size. Your database will not be able to run INSERT or UPDATE T-SQL statements when the maximum size is reached.

- **Maintenance Window.** When creating a standalone database, you might have the option to change the maintenance window while creating the database. Although the drop-down is always present in the Azure portal, the maintenance windows available depend on the region in which you are provisioning your database, which itself depends on your logical server's region.

Inside OUT

How do you choose the right hardware?

At the time of this book's writing, standard-series (Gen5) hardware is recommended for a balance of memory and compute that suits most workloads. Other hardware configurations become available over time, and some are being retired.

Gen4 hardware is being retired. At the time of this writing, it is still possible to create an Azure SQL Database on Gen4 hardware, but it is not recommended. As of the time of this book's writing, in March 2023, remaining Gen4 hardware will be automatically upgraded to Gen5. Hardware generation options for Azure SQL change periodically.

M-series hardware has also been retired and is no longer available, and existing M-series hardware will be migrated to comparable standard-series (Gen5) hardware by September 2023.

Create a database using PowerShell

The following script illustrates how to create a new general purpose standalone database with two vCores on an existing server named ssio2022. The database collation is set to `Latin1_General_CI_AS`. The `-Vcore`, `-ComputeGeneration`, `-ComputeMode`, `-CollationName`, and `-Edition` parameters are optional. We show them here as an example of a commonly specified configuration. The default collation for Azure SQL Database is `SQL_Latin1_General_CP1_CI_AS`, which might not be desirable.

➤ Collation is discussed in detail in Chapter 4, "Install and configure SQL Server instances and features."

Pay attention to the server name. It is lowercase because the parameter value must match exactly. Logical server names cannot contain uppercase characters.

```
$resourceGroupName = "SQL2022"
$serverName = "ssio2022"
$databaseName = "Contoso4"
$tags = @{"CreatedBy"="Kirby"; "Environment"="Dev"}
New-AzSqlDatabase -ResourceGroupName $resourceGroupName `
    -ServerName $serverName `
    -Edition "GeneralPurpose" `
    -Vcore 2 `
    -ComputeGeneration "Gen5" `
    -ComputeMode "Provisioned" `
    -CollationName "Latin1_General_CI_AS" `
    -DatabaseName $databaseName `
    -Tags $tags
```

CHAPTER 17

Other optional parameters include the following:

- **CollationName.** Similar to the database collation in SQL Server, this is the collation for the SQL database user data.

- **CatalogCollation.** This parameter determines the collation of character data in the database's metadata catalog. Note that you cannot set this database property in the GUI. This value defaults to SQL_Latin1_General_CP1_CI_AS. The catalog collation, used for system metadata, cannot be changed. This is a concept specific to Azure SQL Database and not SQL Server. This is a multitenancy feature, allowing you to have a consistent collation for schema but client-specific collations for user data.

- **ElasticPoolName.** When specified, this database will be added to the existing elastic pool on the server. Elastic pools are covered later in this chapter.

- **MaxSizeBytes.** Sets the maximum database size in bytes. You cannot set just any value here; there is a list of supported maximum sizes. The available maximum sizes depend on the selected service tier.

- **SampleName.** Specify AdventureWorksLT if you want the database to have the available sample schema and data.

- **LicenseType.** Use this parameter to take advantage of Azure Hybrid Benefit discounted pricing.

- **Tags.** This parameter is common to many Azure cmdlets. You can use it to specify an arbitrary number of name-value pairs. Tags are used to add custom metadata to Azure resources. You can use both the Azure portal and PowerShell to filter resources based on tag values. You can also obtain a consolidated billing view for resources with the same tag values. An example is –Tags @{"Tag1"="Value 1";"Tag 2"="Value 2"}, which associates two name-value pairs with the database. The name of the first tag is Tag1 with Value 1, and the name of the second tag is Tag 2 with Value 2.

After creating the database, you can retrieve information about it by using the Get-AzSqlDatabase cmdlet, as shown here:

```
$resourceGroupName = "SSIO2022"
$serverName = "ssio2022"
$databaseName = "Contoso"
Get-AzSqlDatabase -ResourceGroupName $resourceGroupName `
-ServerName $serverName `
-DatabaseName $databaseName
```

Create a database using Azure CLI

The Azure CLI enables you to use the same set of commands to manage Azure resources regardless of the platform of your workstation: Windows, macOS, Linux, and even using the Azure portal's Cloud Shell.

NOTE

Installing the Azure CLI on different operating systems is not covered in this text. Guidance for each OS is available at *https://learn.microsoft.com/cli/azure/install-azure-cli*.

The following Azure CLI command creates a database with the same parameters as those found in the preceding PowerShell script. After creating the database, the new database's properties are retrieved.

> ➤ You can find the full list of supported CLI commands for Azure SQL Database at *https://learn .microsoft.com/cli/azure/sql/db*.

```
az sql db create \
  --resource-group SSIO2022 \
  --server ssio2022 \
  --name Contoso \
  --collation Latin1_General_CI_AS \
  --edition GeneralPurpose \
  --capacity 2 \
  --family Gen5 \
  --compute-model Provisioned \
  --tags Environment=Dev CreatedBy=Kirby
az sql db show --resource-groupSIO2022 --server ssio2022 --name Contoso
```

NOTE

For clarity, long parameter names are used in the preceding example. Many parameters for the az command also have a shorthand version. For example, instead of using `--resource-group`, you can use `-g`. The `--help` (shorthand: `-h`) parameter shows both the long and shorthand parameter names, if a shorthand version is available. As with PowerShell, we recommend using the long parameter names to aid maintenance and understanding.

Create a database using T-SQL

The following T-SQL script creates a new Azure SQL database with the same properties as in both previous examples. To create a new database, connect to the server on which the new database will reside—for example, using SSMS or Azure Data Studio:

```
CREATE DATABASE Contoso COLLATE Latin1_General_CI_AS
(EDITION = 'GeneralPurpose', SERVICE_OBJECTIVE = 'GP_Gen5_2');
```

Because the T-SQL command is run in the context of a server, you do not need to, nor can you, provide a server name or resource group name. You cannot use T-SQL to create a database based on the AdventureWorksLT sample, but you can use it to restore a database backup from a database on the same or a different server using the AS COPY OF clause, as shown here:

```
CREATE DATABASE Contoso_copy AS COPY OF Server1.Contoso;
```

Inside OUT

How do you copy an Azure SQL database from another server?

It is possible to create a database as a copy of another database on a different server, but there are some additional conditions that must be met. You must sign into the master database on the target server using a login that is either the server administrator or a member of the dbmanager role. The login must have the same name and password as the database owner of the source database on the source server.

It is possible to copy a database from another server in a different subscription, or even a different tenant. This must be done using a SQL Authentication login. Copying a database in another tenant is not supported when either the source or target server has Azure AD Authentication enabled.

Remember, this uses the last available backup of the source database. The operation might take some time to complete. The `state_desc` column in sys.databases will show the value `'COPYING'` while the copy operation is in progress. To monitor the copying progress, you can query the sys.dm_operation_status catalog view. The `percent_complete` column in sys.dm_operation_status will provide a progress report of the restore operation.

You do not have to use the same service objective for the new copy of the database, but you must choose a service objective within the same tier. Be careful to make it large enough to provide sufficient resources to complete the copy operation.

Scale up or down

Azure SQL Database scale operations are conducted with minimal disruption to the availability of the database. A scale operation is performed by the service using a replica of the original database at the new service level. When the replica is ready, connections are switched over to the replica. Although this does not cause data loss and is completed in a time frame measured in seconds, active transactions might be rolled back. The application should be designed to handle such events and to retry the operation.

Scaling down might not be possible if the database size exceeds the maximum allowed size for the lower service objective or service tier. If you know you will likely scale down your database, you should set the current maximum database size to a value equal to or less than the future maximum database size for the service objective to which you might scale down.

In most tiers, scaling is initiated by an administrator. Only the serverless tier supports autoscaling. If the serverless tier does not meet your needs, you can consider deploying databases to an elastic pool (discussed shortly) to automatically balance resource demands for a group of databases. Another option to scale without administrator intervention is to use Azure Automation to monitor resource usage and initiate scaling when a threshold has been reached. You can use the

PowerShell `Set-AzSqlDatabase` cmdlet to set a new service tier with the `-Edition` parameter, and a new service objective with the `-RequestedServiceObjectiveName` parameter.

Provision a named replica for a Hyperscale database

In June 2022, the named replica feature for Azure SQL Database Hyperscale became generally available. Named replicas enable you to scale out read-only workloads to up to 30 replicas. Named replicas share the same storage, but not compute. Each replica can have a different service-level objective (compute size). Named replicas allow isolated access, where a user can be granted read-only access to a specific replica without being granted access to the primary or other replicas.

➤ **See Chapter 16 for more information on the Hyperscale tier of Azure SQL Database.**

➤ **For more information on use cases for Azure SQL Database Hyperscale named replicas, see this post on the Azure SQL blog:** *https://techcommunity.microsoft.com/t5/azure-sql-blog /azure-sql-database-hyperscale-named-replicas-feature-is/ba-p/3455674.*

Named replicas allow for several differences from the primary replica that are not supported in normal high availability replicas, including the following:

- They can have a different database name from the primary replica.

- They can be located on a different logical server from the primary replica, as long as they are in the same region.

- You can configure different authentication for each named replica by creating different logins on logical servers hosting named replicas.

Unlike high availability (HA) replicas, named replicas appear as regular databases in the Azure portal and REST API. They cannot be used as a failover target.

To create a named replica using the Azure portal, locate the existing Hyperscale database. Then, in the **Data Management** section in the left menu, choose **Replicas**. Next, on the **Replicas** page, choose **Create Replica**. (See Figure 17-3.) Be sure to select **Named Replica** for the replica type on the **Basics** page of the wizard that starts.

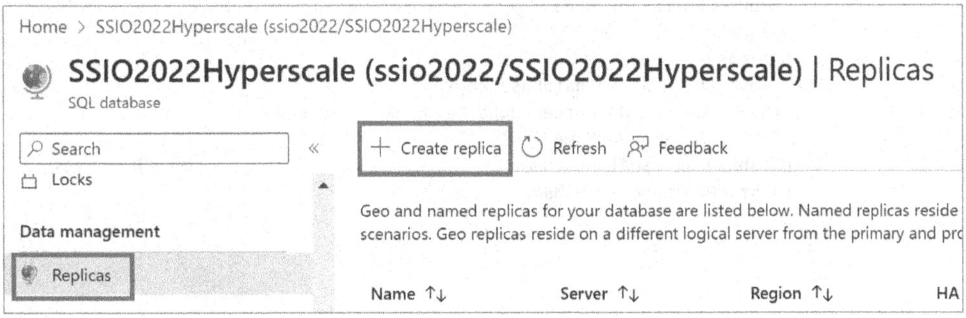

Figure 17-3 Selections in the Azure portal to create a named replica for a Hyperscale database.

CHAPTER 17

➤ For detailed instructions to create a named replica in the Azure portal, T-SQL, PowerShell, or Azure CLI, review *https://learn.microsoft.com/azure/azure-sql/database/service-tier -hyperscale-replicas*.

Provision an elastic pool

Chapter 16 discussed the benefits and use cases of elastic database pools. Elastic pools are created per server, and a single server can have more than one elastic pool. The number of eDTUs or vCores available depends upon the service tier, as is the case with standalone databases.

Beyond the differences between tiers described in Chapter 16, which also apply to elastic pools, the relationship between the maximum pool size, and the selected eDTU or vCore and the maximum number of databases per pool, are also different per tier.

You can create elastic pools with the Azure portal, PowerShell, the Azure CLI, or the REST API. After an elastic pool is created, you can create new databases directly in the pool. You also can add existing single databases to a pool and move databases out of pools.

In most of the following sections, no distinction is made between standalone databases and elastic pool databases. Managing standalone databases is similar to managing databases in elastic pools. Also, whether a database is in an elastic pool or standalone makes no difference for establishing a connection.

Use the following PowerShell script to create a new elastic pool on the ssio2022 server and move the existing Contoso database to the pool:

```
$resourceGroupName = "SIO2022"
$serverName = "ssio2022"
$databaseName = "Contoso"
$poolName = "Contoso-Pool"
# Create a new elastic pool
New-AzSqlElasticPool -ResourceGroupName $resourceGroupName `
    -ServerName $serverName `
    -ElasticPoolName $poolName `
    -Edition "GeneralPurpose" `
    -Vcore 4 `
    -ComputeGeneration Gen5 `
    -DatabaseVCoreMin 0 `
    -DatabaseVCoreMax 2
# Now move the Contoso database to the pool
Set-AzSqlDatabase -ResourceGroupName $resourceGroupName `
    -ServerName $serverName `
    -DatabaseName $databaseName `
    -ElasticPoolName $poolName
```

This script creates a new pool named `Contoso-Pool` in the general purpose service tier and provides four total vCores. A single database will be assigned no more than two vCores. The parameters `-Vcore`, `-DatabaseVCoreMin`, and `-DatabaseVCoreMax` have a list of valid values depending on the selected tier and each other.

➤ For more information on the vCore-related PowerShell parameters, see *https://learn.microsoft .com/powershell/module/az.sql/set-azsqlelasticpool*.

➤ To understand the possible values for vCore-related PowerShell parameters, refer to *https:// learn.microsoft.com/azure/azure-sql/database/resource-limits-vcore-elastic-pools*.

Manage database space

The Azure SQL Database service manages the growth of data and log files. For log files, the service also manages shrinking the log file. Data files are not automatically shrunk because of the potential impact on performance. Each service tier has an included maximum database size. When your database size approaches that maximum, you can choose to pay for extra storage space (up to a certain limit, again determined by the service tier) or scale your database up.

In some cases, the database data space might be allocated for your database but no longer in use. This effect can be especially significant in elastic pools. If many databases in a single pool have a significant amount of unused space, the pool maximum size might be reached sooner than expected.

➤ For a discussion on how to determine the amount of unused allocated space for all databases in a pool, visit *https://learn.microsoft.com/azure/sql-database/sql-database-file-space -management#understanding-types-of-storage-space-for-an-elastic-pool*.

If you don't expect your databases to need the unused space, you might consider reclaiming that space. Beware of the need to rebuild indexes after shrinking and the fact that rebuilding indexes will cause the data file to grow again to some extent. All other caveats related to shrinking database files and rebuilding indexes apply. If you decide to shrink the database file, use the standard T-SQL statement:

```
DBCC SHRINKDATABASE ('Contoso');
-- Rebuild all indexes after shrink!
```

➤ See Chapter 8, "Maintain and monitor SQL Server," for information on rebuilding indexes.

NOTE

As with on-premises SQL Server databases, Azure SQL Database supports auto-shrink. There are no valid reasons to enable auto-shrink.

CHAPTER 17

Security in Azure SQL Database

As with many PaaS cloud services, certain security operations are handled for you by the cloud provider. As it relates to security in Azure SQL Database, this includes patching the OS and the database service.

Other aspects of security must be managed by you, the cloud DBA. Some Azure SQL Database security features, such as transparent data encryption (TDE), are shared with on-premises SQL Server. Others are specific to Azure SQL Database and include firewall configuration, access control, and auditing and threat detection. We discuss these features of Azure SQL Database in the upcoming sections. Microsoft's commitment regarding Azure SQL Database is to not differentiate the service tiers with security features. All the features discussed in this section are available in all service tiers, though some features incur additional charges.

Security features shared with SQL Server 2022

An important security consideration is access control. Azure SQL Database implements the same permission infrastructure that's available in SQL Server 2022. This means database and application roles are supported, and you can set very granular permissions on database objects and operations using the data control language (DCL) statements GRANT and REVOKE. Refer to Chapter 12 for more information.

TDE is enabled by default for any new database. This hasn't always been the case, so if your database has been around for a long time, you should verify whether it is enabled. When TDE is enabled for a database, not only are the database files encrypted, but the geo-replicated backups are, too. You will learn more about backups in the "Prepare Azure SQL Database for disaster recovery" section later in this chapter. TDE is covered in Chapter 13.

Other security features shared with SQL Server 2022 are dynamic data masking, row-level security, and Always Encrypted. Chapter 13 looks at these features in detail.

Server- and database-level firewall

A server is accessed using an FQDN, which maps to a public IP address. To maintain a secure environment, you must manage firewall entries to control which IP addresses can connect to the logical server or database.

NOTE

You can associate a server with a VNet, offering enhanced network security when connecting to other Azure resources in the same VNet. VNets can be used to communicate with on-premises resources as well as other Azure resources. They can be peered with other VNets to allow traffic to flow through. VNets offer a more secure way to connect to databases. However, there might still be times when you must add IP addresses in a firewall rule. This might be because a resource doesn't have service endpoints or private endpoints, or the rare case when you have a truly customer-facing database. But whenever possible, consider connecting to your database through VNets.

When creating a new server using the Azure portal, you might choose to allow any Azure resource through the server-level firewall. This is convenient, but it leaves the server open to unauthorized connection attempts from an attacker who merely needs to create an Azure service such as a web app. Servers created using other methods—for example, PowerShell—do not have any default firewall rules, which means any connection attempt is refused until at least one firewall rule is created.

Database-level firewall rules take precedence over server firewall rules. After you have created database firewall rules, you can remove the server firewall rule(s) and still connect to the database. However, if one server will be hosting several databases that each need to accept connections from the same IP addresses, keeping the firewall rules at the server level might be more sensible. It is also convenient to keep server-level firewall rules in place for administrative access.

You can find server-level firewall rules in the virtual master database in the sys.firewall_rules catalog view. Database-level firewall rules are in the user database in the sys.database_firewall_rules catalog view. This makes the database more portable, which can be advantageous in combination with contained users. Especially when using geo-replication, discussed in the "Prepare Azure SQL Database for disaster recovery" section later in this chapter, having portable databases avoids unexpected connection issues when failing-over databases to another server.

> Learn more about contained databases in Chapter 12.

Configure the server-level firewall

You can create server-level firewall rules using the Azure portal, PowerShell, Azure CLI, or T-SQL. As seen earlier, SSMS might prompt you to create a firewall rule when establishing a connection, though you would not use this method to create firewall rules for your application's infrastructure. To create a firewall rule, you provide the following:

- **Rule Name.** This has no impact on the operation of the firewall; it exists only to create a human-friendly reminder about the rule. The rule name is limited to 128 characters. The name must be unique in the server.

- **Start IP Address.** This is the first IPv4 address of the range of allowed addresses.

- **End IP Address.** This can be the same as the start IP address to create a rule that allows connections from exactly one address. The end IP address cannot be lower than the start IP address.

NOTE

When configuring server-level IP firewall rules, the maximum number allowed is 128. There can be up to 256 database-level IP firewall rules.

Managing firewall rules in a dynamic environment can quickly become error prone and resource intensive. For example, when databases on a server are accessed from numerous Azure Web App instances, which often scale up and down and out and in, the rules must be updated frequently. Rather than resorting to allowing any Azure resource to pass through the server-level firewall, you should consider automating firewall rule management.

The first step in such an endeavor is to create a list of allowed IP addresses. This list could include static IP addresses, such as from your on-premises environment for management purposes, and dynamic IP addresses, such as from Azure Web Apps or Azure virtual machines (VMs). In the case of dynamic IP addresses, you can use the Az PowerShell module to obtain the current IP addresses of Azure resources.

After you build the list of allowed IP addresses, you can apply it by looping through each address, attempting to locate that IP address in the current firewall rule list, and adding it if necessary. In addition, you can remove any IP addresses in the current rule list that are not on your allowed list.

This is not always an option. There are Azure services whose IP addresses are impossible to obtain. In this scenario, you should review if those services can be joined to a VNet where your server has an endpoint. If not available, you must allow access from all Azure services or re-architect your solution to avoid using those services.

In PowerShell, the `New-AzSqlServerFirewallRule` cmdlet provides the `-AllowAllAzureIPs` parameter as a shortcut to create a rule to allow all Azure services. You do not need to provide a rule name, start, or end IP address. Using the CLI to achieve the same outcome, you create a rule with `0.0.0.0` as both the start and end IP address. You must provide a rule name for the command to work, but you'll find that in the Azure portal, the rule is not shown. Instead, the toggle switch is in the on position.

NOTE

When SSMS offers to create a server-level firewall rule, you must sign in with an Azure AD user account whose default directory matches the directory associated with the subscription where the logical server exists. Otherwise, the creation of the firewall rule will fail with an HTTP status code 401 error.

Inside OUT

How do you set a firewall rule with an Azure AD B2B user?

Azure AD supports business-to-business (B2B) or guest users. A B2B user is a user created in one tenant and added to another tenant as a guest. That user accesses Azure resources using the same Azure AD credentials as in their default directory (home tenant) but has access to resources in both their home tenant and the external tenant to which they have been added. B2B users can be granted access to the Azure SQL Database logical server resource in Azure, in the control plane. B2B users can also be granted access to the server for data plane purposes, such as connecting to the server with SSMS.

A member user in their home tenant can use the SSMS **New Firewall Rule** dialog box to add their IP address to the allowed list. SSMS doesn't support a B2B user adding a firewall rule through the dialog box. But B2B users with proper permissions can still add firewall rules through the Azure portal, PowerShell, Azure CLI, or REST API.

Once the firewall rule is added, a B2B user who authenticates to the server using Azure AD Authentication will be able to connect. Even if a B2B user has access on the data plane with a SQL Authentication user, they would still have to use the Azure AD credentials to access the control plane to add a server-level firewall rule.

Configure the database-level firewall

To configure database-level firewall rules, you must have already established a connection to the database. This means you must at least temporarily create a server-level firewall rule to create database-level firewall rules. You can create and manage database-level firewall rules only using T-SQL. Azure SQL Database provides the following stored procedures to manage the rules:

- **sp_set_database_firewall_rule.** Creates a new database-level firewall rule or updates an existing firewall rule.

- **sp_delete_database_firewall_rule.** Deletes an existing database-level firewall rule using the name of the rule.

The following T-SQL script creates a new database-level firewall rule allowing a single (fictitious) IP address, updates the rule by expanding the single IP address to a range of addresses, and finally deletes the rule:

```
EXEC sp_set_database_firewall_rule N'Headquarters', '1.2.3.4', '1.2.3.4';
EXEC sp_set_database_firewall_rule N'Headquarters', '1.2.3.4', '1.2.3.6';
SELECT * FROM sys.database_firewall_rules;
EXEC sp_delete_database_firewall_rule N'Headquarters';
```

Integrate with virtual networks

Azure SQL Database can be integrated with one or more VNet subnets. By integrating a logical server with a VNet subnet, other resources in that subnet can connect to the server without requiring a firewall rule.

In addition to removing the need to create firewall rules, the traffic between these resources stays within the Azure backbone and does not go across public Internet connections at all, thereby providing further security and latency benefits.

CHAPTER 17

VNet integration and the public endpoint of the Azure SQL server can be used simultaneously.

➤ **Chapter 16 discusses VNets in more detail.**

Azure Private Link for Azure SQL Database

Azure SQL Database now supports the Azure Private Link feature, which creates a private endpoint for use by various Azure services. This private endpoint becomes an IP address that can only be used by certain services within Azure, including a VNet.

By using Private Link endpoints, you can further reduce the network surface area of an Azure SQL Database. You should make an effort to eliminate all public access to your Azure SQL Database that is secured by only a username and password. A Private Link's network traffic uses only the Microsoft infrastructure network and not the public Internet.

Azure SQL Database integration with Private Link continues. For more on the features and capabilities possible, visit *https://learn.microsoft.com/azure/azure-sql/database/private -endpoint-overview*.

➤ **For more information, see the "Networking in Azure" section in Chapter 16.**

Control access using Azure AD

To set up single sign-on (SSO) scenarios, easier login administration, and secure authentication for application identities, you can enable Azure AD Authentication. When Azure AD Authentication is enabled for a server, an Azure AD user or group is given the same permissions as the server admin login. In addition, you can create contained users referencing Azure AD principals. So, user accounts and groups in an Azure AD domain can authenticate to the databases without needing a SQL Authentication login.

For cases in which the Azure AD domain is federated with an Active Directory Domain Services (AD DS) domain, you can achieve true SSO comparable to an on-premises experience. The latter case excludes any external users or Microsoft accounts that have been added to the directory; only federated identities can take advantage of this. Furthermore, it also requires a client that supports it.

> ### NOTE
> The principal you set as the Azure AD admin for the server must reside in the directory associated with the subscription where the server resides. The directory associated with a subscription can be changed, but this might have effects on other configuration aspects, such as role-based access control (RBAC), which we describe in the next section.

If users from other directories need to access your SQL Server, add them as guest users in the Azure AD domain backing the subscription.

To set an Azure AD admin for a server, you can use the Azure portal, PowerShell, or Azure CLI. You use the PowerShell `Set-AzSqlServerActiveDirectoryAdministrator` cmdlet to provision the Azure AD admin. The `-DisplayName` parameter references the Azure AD principal. When you use this parameter to set a user account as the administrator, the value can be the user's display name or user principal name (UPN). When setting a group as the administrator, only the group's display name is supported.

If the group you want to designate as administrator has a display name that is not unique in the directory, the `-ObjectID` parameter is required. You can retrieve the `ObjectID` value from the group's properties in the Azure portal or via PowerShell using the `Get-AzADGroup` cmdlet.

NOTE

If you decide to configure an Azure AD principal as server administrator, it's always preferable to designate a group instead of a single user account.

After you set an Azure AD principal as the Azure AD admin for the server, you can create contained users in the server's databases. Contained users for Azure AD principals must be created by other Azure AD principals. Users authenticated with SQL Authentication cannot validate the Azure AD principal names, and, as such, even the server administrator login cannot create contained users for Azure AD principals.

Contained users are created by using the T-SQL CREATE USER statement with the FROM EXTERNAL PROVIDER clause. The following sample statements create an external user for an Azure AD user account with UPN 1.penor@contoso.com and for an Azure AD group Sales Managers:

```
CREATE USER [1.penor@contoso.com] FROM EXTERNAL PROVIDER;
CREATE USER [Sales Managers] FROM EXTERNAL PROVIDER;
```

By default, these newly created contained users will be members of the `public` database role and will be granted CONNECT permission. You can add these users to additional roles or grant them additional permissions directly like any other database user. Azure B2B users can be added as contained users with the same CREATE statement used for users whose default directory is the same directory tied to the Azure subscription containing the database and server. For guest users, use their UPN in their default tenant as the username. For example, suppose Earl is a user in the ProseWare, Inc. tenant with UPN earl@proseware.com. To grant access to the Contoso database, first make sure the user has been added as a guest user in the Contoso tenant, then create the user earl@proseware.com in the Contoso database. Chapter 12 has further coverage of permissions and roles.

CHAPTER 17

Inside OUT

What happens if users are unable to connect using Azure AD credentials?

The workstation from which users connect must have .NET Framework 4.6 or later and the Microsoft Active Directory Authentication Library for Microsoft SQL Server installed. These prerequisites are installed with certain developer and DBA tools, but they might not be available on end-user workstations. If not, you can obtain them from the Microsoft Download Center.

Grant access to Azure AD managed identities

Most Azure resources have a system-assigned managed identity (SMI or SAMI) and can also be assigned a user-assigned managed identity (UMI or UAMI). A *managed identity* is a special type of service principal that can only be used with a specific Azure resource. When the managed identity is deleted, the corresponding service principal is automatically removed. With a managed identity, there is no need to manage credentials—you have no access to the password. Managed identities can be used to access other Azure resources. By default, a new SMI is created and enabled, but you can additionally configure one or more UMIs.

UMIs can serve as service identity for one or more Azure SQL databases or SQL managed instances. When you create a UMI, you can choose to disable the SMI.

A user interface update in September 2022 to the Azure portal displays the SMI for the Azure SQL logical server in the **Properties** page.

> ➤ For more on SMIs vs UMIs, including how to get and set them, see *https://learn.microsoft .com/azure/azure-sql/database/authentication-azure-ad-user-assigned-managed-identity*.

Services such as Azure Data Factory, Azure Machine Learning Services, Azure Synapse Link for Azure SQL Database, and Azure Automation support authentication via managed identities. Contained users can be created in an Azure SQL database for these managed identities. From there, you can add these users to built-in or custom roles or directly grant permissions, just as you would any other user account.

To create a user in a database for a managed identity, you need the display name of the managed identity. For system-assigned managed identities, this is the name of the resource to which it belongs. The following example creates an external user for the system-assigned managed identity that is associated with an Azure Data Factory named MyFactory.

```
CREATE USER [MyFactory] FROM EXTERNAL PROVIDER;
```

CAUTION

Different resource types have different scopes within which the resource name is required to be unique. For example, data factories must be globally unique across all of Azure, but logic apps only have to be unique within the resource group. Be careful when granting access to managed identities when there are multiple service principals with the same display name. If you have three logic apps with the same name in the same tenant as your database, you will encounter problems when trying to grant database access to the managed identity for one of the logic apps.

➤ For recommendations for Azure resource naming conventions in Microsoft's Cloud Adoption Framework for Azure, visit *https://learn.microsoft.com/azure/cloud-adoption -framework/ready/azure-best-practices/naming-and-tagging.*

Use Azure role-based access control

All operations discussed thus far have assumed that your user account has permission to create servers, databases, and pools, and can then manage these resources. If your account is the service administrator or subscription owner, no restrictions are placed on your ability to add, manage, and delete resources. Most enterprise deployments, however, require more fine-grained control over permissions to create and manage resources. Using Azure role-based access control (RBAC), administrators can assign permissions to Azure AD users, groups, or service principals at the subscription, resource group, or resource level.

RBAC includes several built-in roles to which you can add Azure AD principals. The built-in roles have a fixed set of permissions. You also can create custom roles if the built-in roles do not meet your needs.

➤ For a comprehensive list of built-in roles and their permissions, visit *https://learn.microsoft .com/azure/active-directory/role-based-access-built-in-roles.*

Three built-in roles relate specifically to Azure SQL Database:

- **SQL DB Contributor.** This role can primarily create and manage Azure SQL databases, but not change security-related settings. For example, this role can create a new database on an existing server and create alert rules.

- **SQL Security Manager.** This role can primarily manage security settings of databases and servers. For example, it can create auditing policies on an existing database but cannot create a new database.

- **SQL Server Contributor.** This role can primarily create and manage servers, but not databases or security-related settings.

Permissions do not relate to server or database access; instead, they relate to managing Azure resources. Indeed, users assigned to these RBAC roles are not granted any permissions in the database—not even the CONNECT permission.

NOTE

An Azure AD user in the **SQL Server Contributor** role can create a server and thus define the server administrator login's username and password. Yet, the user's Azure AD account does not obtain any permissions in the database at all. If you want the same Azure AD user to have permissions in the database, including creating new users and roles, you must use the steps in this section to set up Azure AD integration and create an external database user for that Azure AD account.

Audit database activity

Microsoft Defender for SQL provides auditing and threat-detection for Azure SQL Database, allowing you to monitor database activity using Azure tools. In on-premises deployments, *Extended Events* are often used for monitoring. SQL Server builds on Extended Events for its SQL Server Audit feature (discussed in Chapter 13). This feature is not present in Azure SQL Database in the same form, but a large subset of Extended Events is supported in Azure SQL Database.

➤ You can find more details about support for Extended Events at *https://learn.microsoft.com /azure/sql-database/sql-database-xevent-db-diff-from-svr*.

Azure SQL Database auditing creates a record of activities that have taken place in the database. The types of activities that can be audited include permission changes, T-SQL batch execution, and auditing changes themselves.

➤ Audit actions are grouped in audit action groups. A list of audit action groups is available in the PowerShell reference for the Set-AzSqlDatabaseAudit cmdlet at *https://learn.microsoft .com/powershell/module/az.sql/set-azsqldatabaseaudit#parameters*.

NOTE

By default, all actions are audited. The Azure portal does not provide a user interface for selecting which audit action groups are included. Customizing audited events requires the use of the PowerShell cmdlet or the REST API.

Auditing and advanced threat protection are separate but related features. Investigating alerts generated by advanced threat protection is easier if auditing is enabled. Auditing is available at no initial charge, but there is a monthly fee per server for activating Microsoft Defender for SQL, which contains the Advanced Threat Protection functionality. There are also charges for writing and storing logs in a storage account or a Log Analytics workspace.

You can enable auditing at the server and database level. When auditing is enabled at the server level, all databases hosted on that server are audited. After you enable auditing on the server, you can still turn it on at the database level as well. This does not override any server-level settings; rather, it creates two separate audits. This is not usually desired, though in environments with specific compliance requirements that only apply to one or a few databases on a single server, it can make sense. These compliance requirements might include longer retention periods or additional action groups that must be audited.

In addition to auditing normal operations on the databases and server, you can also enable auditing of Microsoft Support operations for Azure SQL Server. This allows you to audit Microsoft support engineers' operations when they need to access your server during a support request.

Auditing events are stored in an Azure Storage account or sent to a Log Analytics workspace or Event Hub. The configuration of Event Hubs is beyond the scope of this book. The other two options are covered later in this chapter.

Configure auditing to a storage account

When configuring auditing in the Azure portal, the target storage account must be in the same region as the server. This limitation does not exist when configuring auditing using PowerShell, Azure CLI, or the REST API. Be aware that you might incur data transfer charges for audit data or deal with latency if you choose a storage account in a different region from the server. Many types of storage accounts are supported, but Premium page blobs are not.

You can configure the storage account to require storage account keys or managed identity for access. If you choose to use managed identity, the **Allow trusted Microsoft services to access this storage account** setting will be enabled, and the server's managed identity will be assigned the Storage Blob Data Contributor RBAC role.

To configure auditing, you must create or select an Azure Storage account. We recommend that you aggregate logging for all databases in a single storage account. When all auditing is done in a single storage account, you will benefit from having an integrated view of audit events.

You also must decide on an audit log retention period. You can choose to keep audit logs indefinitely or you can select a retention period. The retention period can be at most 3,285 days, or about 9 years.

The following PowerShell script sets up auditing for the Contoso database on the ssio2022 server:

```
$resourceGroupName = "SSIO2022"
$location = "southcentralus"
$serverName = "ssio2022"
$databaseName = "Contoso"
# Create your own globally unique name here
$storageAccountName = "azuresqldbaudit"
# Create a new storage account
$storageAccount = New-AzStorageAccount -ResourceGroupName $resourceGroupName `
```

```
    -Name $storageAccountName -Location $location -Kind Storage `
    -SkuName Standard_LRS -EnableHttpsTrafficOnly $true
# Use the new storage account to configure auditing
$auditSettings = Set-AzSqlDatabaseAudit `
    -ResourceGroupName $resourceGroupName `
    -ServerName $serverName -DatabaseName $databaseName `
    -StorageAccountResourceId $storageAccount.Id -StorageKeyType Primary `
    -RetentionInDays 365 -BlobStorageTargetState Enabled
```

The first cmdlet in the script creates a new storage account with the name azuresqldbaudit. Note that this name must be globally unique, so you must update the script with a name of your choosing before running the script. Storage account names can contain only lowercase letters and digits.

➤ For more details on the New-AzStorageAccount cmdlet, see *https://learn.microsoft.com /powershell/module/az.storage/new-azstorageaccount.*

The second cmdlet, Set-AzSqlDatabaseAudit, configures and enables auditing on the database using the newly created storage account. The audit log retention period is set to 365 days.

NOTE

To set auditing at the server level, use the Set-AzSqlServerAudit cmdlet. This cmdlet uses the same parameters, except you'll omit the -DatabaseName parameter.

View audit logs from a storage account

There are several methods you can use to access the audit logs. Which method you use largely depends on your preferences and the tools you have available on your workstation. This section discusses some of these methods in no particular order.

If your goal is to quickly review recent audit events, you can see the audit logs in the Azure portal. In the **Auditing** pane for a database, select **View Audit Logs** to open the **Audit records** pane. This pane shows the most recent audit logs, which you can filter to restrict the events shown by, say, the latest event time or to only show suspect SQL injection audit records, for example. This approach is rather limited because you cannot aggregate audit logs from different databases, and the filtering capabilities are minimal.

A more advanced approach is to use SQL Server Management Studio (SSMS). SSMS 17 introduced support for opening audit logs directly from Azure Storage. Alternatively, you can use Azure Storage Explorer to download audit logs and open them using older versions of SSMS or third-party tools.

Audit logs are stored in the sqldbauditlogs blob container in the selected storage account. The container follows a hierarchical folder structure: logicalservername\DatabaseName\SqlDbAuditing _AuditName\yyyymmdd. The blobs within the date folder are the audit logs for that date, in Coordinated Universal Time (UTC). The blobs are binary Extended Event files (.xel).

NOTE

Azure Storage Explorer is a free and supported tool from Microsoft. You can download it from *https://azure.microsoft.com/features/storage-explorer/.*

After you obtain the audit files, you can open them in SSMS. On the **File** menu, select **Open**, and select **Merge Audit Files** to open the **Add Audit Files** dialog box, shown in Figure 17-4.

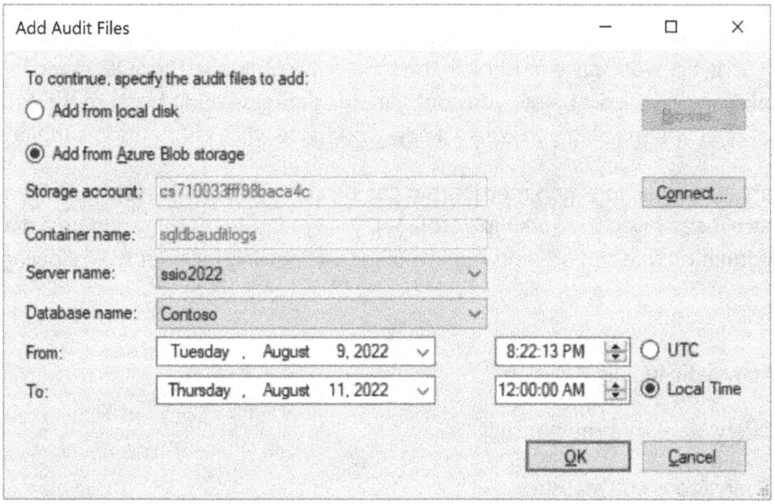

Figure 17-4 SSMS 17 introduced support for opening and merging multiple Azure SQL Database audit files directly from an Azure Storage account.

A third way of examining audit logs is by querying the sys.fn_get_audit_file system function with T-SQL. You can use this to perform programmatic evaluation of the audit logs. The function works with locally downloaded files or you can obtain files directly from the Azure Storage account. To obtain logs directly from the Azure Storage account, you run the query using a connection to the database whose logs are being accessed. The following T-SQL script example queries all audit events logged to the azuresqldbaudit storage account from October 16, 2022, for the Contoso database on the ssio2022 server:

```
SELECT * FROM sys.fn_get_audit_file ('https://azuresqldbaudit.blob.core.windows.net/
sqldbauditlogs/ssio2022/Contoso/SqlDbAuditing_Audit/2022-10-16/', default, default);
```

➤ Find more information on sys.fn_get_audit_file at *https://learn.microsoft.com/sql /relational-databases/system-functions/sys-fn-get-audit-file-transact-sql.*

The output from the system function can be visualized and analyzed using Power BI. To get started, a sample Power BI dashboard template is available for download from the Microsoft Tech Community. Using the template, you only need to provide the server name, storage account name, and credentials. You can use the template as is or customize it. The template can

CHAPTER 17

be used directly in the free Power BI Desktop tool. You might also choose to publish it to your organization's Power BI service.

➤ The template and a walkthrough on using it are available from the Microsoft Tech Community at *https://techcommunity.microsoft.com/t5/Azure-Database-Support-Blog /SQL-Azure-Blob-Auditing-Basic-Power-BI-Dashboard/ba-p/368895*.

Configure auditing to a Log Analytics workspace

When configuring audit events to be sent to a Log Analytics workspace using the Azure portal, the Log Analytics workspace must be in the same subscription as the SQL server and database. The workspace must exist before you configure the database audit because the Azure portal does not offer you the ability to create a new workspace while configuring auditing.

There are additional logs and metrics that can be configured to be sent to the Log Analytics workspace (or archived in Azure Blob Storage). You configure these by adding a diagnostic setting. Information that can be captured in a diagnostic setting includes the following:

- SQL insights

- Automatic tuning

- Query Store runtime statistics

- Query Store wait statistics

- Database wait statistics

- Timeouts

- Blocks

- Deadlocks

- SQL security audit events

- Metrics

View audit logs in a Log Analytics workspace

There are several ways to access audit logs stored in a Log Analytics workspace. You can access the logs for a single database or server in the Azure portal on the **Logs** pane for the resource. You can also go to the **Logs** pane for the Log Analytics workspace in the Azure portal. Or you can go to the **Auditing** pane for the resource and select **View Audit Logs**.

One advantage of using a Log Analytics workspace is that you can send the logs for many SQL servers and databases to one workspace to spot trends and outliers across resources. You can also send logs from many different types of resources to the same workspace and track an issue or security event across your tech stack. Log Analytics also allows you to create dashboards from data stored in a workspace.

To query a Log Analytics workspace, you must use a Kusto query. Kusto Query Language (KQL) uses schema entities organized in a hierarchy similar to SQL: databases, tables, and columns. The following sample Kusto query requests the count of database authentication failures grouped by client IP address.

```
AzureDiagnostics
|where action_name_s == 'DATABASE AUTHENTICATION FAILED'
|summarize count() by client_ip_s
```

> ➤ For a KQL quick start guide, visit *https://learn.microsoft.com/azure/data-explorer/kql-quick -reference*.

Microsoft Defender for SQL

As discussed in Chapter 13, Microsoft Defender for SQL is the collective name for two services that are enabled at the logical server level and apply to all databases on that server. These services are:

- **Vulnerability assessment.** Assesses your database against security best practices

- **Advanced Threat Protection.** Provides alerts when potentially malicious activity is detected in the database

Understand vulnerability assessment

Vulnerability assessment consists of a set of rules that are evaluated against one or more databases on the server. Optionally, you can schedule weekly automatic scans of all databases on the server. Unfortunately, at the time of this writing, the schedule for these weekly scans is not customizable. This means the vulnerability scan might run at a time when your database is under heavy load. Fortunately, though the impact on compute utilization is measurable, the scan completes quickly.

Because one size does not fit all when it comes to best practices, many rules can be configured with a custom baseline. If your environment uses user-defined roles, you must review the current configuration and approve it as a baseline. Then, during the next scan, the rule will fail only if the membership is different from the baseline.

The value of vulnerability assessment is further enhanced by the actionable steps and, when appropriate, T-SQL scripts provided to remediate the failure. A scan itself will not modify the database or server automatically; the scan is read-only. However, with a single tap, the suggested remediation script can be opened in the Azure portal's online query editor.

CHAPTER 17

Inside OUT

Should you use SSMS or the Azure portal to conduct the vulnerability assessment?

Although SSMS has a built-in vulnerability assessment scanner, and the rule sets between SSMS and the Azure portal are the same, this section discusses configuring vulnerability assessment using the Azure portal as part of Advanced Data Security.

There is a difference in the evaluation that is conducted between both. In addition to examining the user databases, the periodic recurring scans that can be configured in the Azure portal also include the virtual master system database. Further, when configuring custom baselines for rules using SSMS, the baselines are stored in a folder local to the computer where SSMS is installed. Custom baselines approved in the Azure portal are stored in the portal with the database metadata and are thus available to any user who runs or reviews vulnerability assessment scans.

Our recommendation is to take advantage of the periodic recurring scans in the Azure portal and examine the weekly reports. Customize the baselines as needed. In addition, administrators in highly regulated environments should consider running the vulnerability analysis also from SSMS, where the baselines can be stored locally or potentially in a source control system, for enhanced control.

➤ For directions on how to use SSMS to run a vulnerability assessment scan, see *https://learn .microsoft.com/sql/relational-databases/security/sql-vulnerability-assessment*.

Configure Advanced Threat Protection

Advanced Threat Protection examines the database activity for anomalies. If an anomaly is detected, it then alerts Azure service administrators and co-administrators or a list of configured email addresses. As of this writing, there are more than a dozen different alerts for SQL Database, including:

- A possible vulnerability to SQL injection

- Attempted logon by a potentially harmful application

- Login from a principal user not seen in 60 days

- Login from a suspicious IP

- Potentially unsafe action

- Potential SQL brute force attempt

- Unusual export location

➤ Additional information about these threats is at *https://learn.microsoft.com/azure/sql -database/sql-database-threat-detection-overview#advanced-threat-protection-alerts*.

You can disable each threat type individually if you do not want to detect it.

The configuration of Advanced Threat Protection allows the DBA to specify one or more email addresses that should receive alerts. Optionally, subscription administrators and owners can also receive alerts via email. DBAs should consider including the enterprise security team's alert address in the list for rapid triage and response.

➤ For elementary guidance on using the Azure Security Center for incident response, visit *https://learn.microsoft.com/azure/security-center/security-center-incident-response*.

Advanced Threat Protection does not require auditing to be enabled for the database or server, but auditing records will provide for a better experiencing investigating detected threats. Audit records are used to provide context when Advanced Threat Protection raises an alert.

To effectively analyze detected threats, the following audit action groups are recommended:

- `BATCH_COMPLETED_GROUP`

- `SUCCESSFUL_DATABASE_AUTHENTICATION_GROUP`

- `FAILED_DATABASE_AUTHENTICATION_GROUP`

Enabling these groups will provide details about the events that triggered the threat detection alert.

Prepare Azure SQL Database for disaster recovery

Hosting your data on Microsoft's infrastructure does not excuse you from preparing for disasters. Even though Azure has high levels of availability, your data can still be at risk due to human error and significant adverse events. Azure SQL Database provides default and optional features that will ensure high availability (HA) for your databases when properly configured.

Understand default disaster recovery features

Without taking any further action after provisioning a database, the Azure infrastructure takes care of several basic disaster recovery (DR) preparations. First among these is the replication of data files across fault and upgrade domains within the regional datacenters. This replication is not something you see or control, but it is there. This is comparable to the on-premises use of availability groups or storage tier replication. The exact method of replication of the database files within a datacenter depends on the chosen tier. As Azure SQL Database evolves, the methods Microsoft employs to achieve local HA are of course subject to change.

Regularly scheduled backups are also configured by default. A full backup is scheduled weekly, differential backups take place every few hours, and transaction log backups every 5 to 10 minutes. The exact timing of backups is managed by the Azure fabric based on overall system workload and the database's activity levels. These backups are retained for a period of 7 days (by default, and the maximum for the Basic service tier) to 35 days (maximum).

You can use backups to restore the database to a point-in-time within the retention period. You also can restore a database that was accidentally deleted to the same server from which it was deleted. Remember: Deleting a server irreversibly deletes all databases and backups. You should generally not delete a server until the backup-retention period has expired, just in case. After all, if Microsoft Defender for SQL is disabled, there is no cost associated with a server without databases.

You also can restore databases to another Azure region. This is referred to as a *geo-restore*. This restores databases from backups that are geo-replicated to other regions using Azure Storage replication. If your database has TDE enabled, the backups are also encrypted.

Although these default features provide valuable DR options, they are likely not adequate for production workloads. For example, the estimated recovery time (ERT) for a geo-restore is less than 12 hours, with a recovery point objective (RPO) of less than 1 hour. Further, the maximum backup retention period is 35 days for the Standard and Premium tiers, and only 7 days for the Basic tier. Some of these values are likely unsuitable for mission-critical databases, so you should review the optional DR features covered in the next sections and configure them as needed to achieve an acceptable level of risk for your environment.

Manually export database contents

In addition to the automatic, built-in backup discussed in the preceding section, you might need to export a database. This could be necessary if you need to restore a database in an on-premises or infrastructure as a service (IaaS) environment. You might also need to keep database backups for longer than the automatic backups' retention period, though we encourage you to read the "Use Azure Backup for long-term backup retention" section later in this chapter to understand all options for long-term archival.

The term *backup* is inappropriate when referring to a BACPAC file. (You can read more about BACPAC files in Chapter 6, "Provision and configure SQL Server databases.") A significant difference between a database backup and an export is that the export is not transactionally consistent. During the data export, data manipulation language (DML) statements in a single transaction might have completed before and after the data in different tables that were extracted. This can have unintended consequences and can even prevent you from restoring the export without dropping foreign key constraints.

Databases can be exported via the Azure portal, PowerShell, Azure CLI, the SQLPackage utility, SSMS, or Azure Data Studio. The SQLPackage utility might complete and export more quickly, as it allows you to run multiple sqlpackage.exe comments in parallel for subsets of tables to speed up export operations.

Inside OUT

Do BACPAC exports require a firewall rule to allow all Azure services?

The Azure SQL Database Export Service, which is used to export to a BACPAC file, can run anywhere in the Azure region of the source database server. Because the IP address of the host running the service is not known in advance, you must open the server firewall to allow all Azure IP addresses to access the server. For more information, review the "Server- and database-level firewall" section earlier in this chapter.

Enable zone-redundant configuration

Applicable only to the general purpose, premium, and business critical (with Gen5 or newer hardware) service tiers, zone-redundant configuration is an optional setting that distributes the default HA nodes between different datacenters in the same region. Zone-redundant configuration provides fault tolerance for several classes of failures that would otherwise require handling by geo-replication. Zone redundancy places multiple replicas within an Azure datacenter but in different availability zones within the physical infrastructure. Availability zones are physically discrete from each other and more tolerant to localized disasters affecting the datacenter. They're a low cost and fast way to increase survivability without geo-replication.

Unlike geo-replication, which is discussed in the next section, there is no change to the connection string required if a single datacenter suffers an outage.

There is no additional cost associated with this feature, so your decision to enable it is entirely based on the workload's ability to accept a few extra milliseconds of latency before transactions commit.

➤ For additional information about zone-redundant configuration, visit *https://learn.microsoft .com/azure/sql-database/sql-database-high-availability#zone-redundant-configuration*.

Zone-redundant deployments increase the service-level agreement's (SLA's) availability guarantee from the normal 99.99 percent to at least 99.995 percent.

Configure geo-replication

If your DR needs are such that your data cannot be unavailable for a period of up to 12 hours, you will likely need to configure geo-replication. When you geo-replicate a database, all transactions are replicated to one or more active secondary databases. Geo-replication takes advantage of the availability groups feature also found in on-premises SQL Server.

You can configure geo-replication in any service tier and any region. To configure geo-replication, you must provision a server in another region, though you can do this as part of the configuration process if you are using the Azure portal.

CHAPTER 17

In the event of a disaster, you are alerted via the Azure portal of reliability issues in the datacenter hosting your primary database. You then need to manually fail over to a secondary database. Using geo-replication only, there is no automatic failover (but keep reading to learn about failover groups, which do provide automatic failover capability). Failover is accomplished by selecting (one of) the secondary database(s) to be the primary.

Because the replication from primary to secondary is asynchronous, an unplanned failover can lead to data loss. The RPO for geo-replication, which is an indicator of the maximum amount of data loss expressed as a unit of time, is 5 seconds. Although no more than 5 seconds of data loss during an actual disaster is a sound objective, when conducting DR drills, no data loss is acceptable. A planned change to another region, such as during a DR drill or to migrate to another region permanently, can be initiated as a planned failover. A planned failover will not lead to data loss because the selected secondary will not become primary until replication is completed.

Unfortunately, a planned failover cannot be initiated from the Azure portal. However, the Set-AzSqlDatabaseSecondary PowerShell cmdlet with the -Failover parameter and without the -AllowDataLoss parameter will initiate a planned failover. If the primary is not available due to an incident, you can use the portal or PowerShell to initiate a failover with the potential for some data loss, as just described. If you have multiple secondaries, after a failover, the new primary will begin replicating to the remaining available secondaries without a need for further manual configuration.

NOTE

When you first configure geo-replication using the Azure portal, it informs you of the recommended region for the geo-replicated database. You are not required to configure the secondary in the recommended region, but doing so will provide optimal perfor-mance for the replication between regions. The recommendation is based on Microsoft's knowledge of connectivity between its datacenters in different regions.

For each secondary database, you are charged the same hourly rate as for a primary database, with the same service tier and service objective. A secondary database must have the same ser-vice tier as its primary, but it does not need to have the same service objective or performance level. For example, a primary database in the Standard tier with service objective S2 can be geo-replicated to a secondary database in the Standard tier with service objective S1 or S3, but it cannot be geo-replicated to a secondary in the Basic or Premium tier.

To decide whether your service objective for secondaries can be lower than that of the pri-mary, you must consider the read-write activity ratio. If the primary is write-heavy—that is, most database operations are writes—the secondary will likely need the same service objective to be able to keep up with the primary. However, if the primary's utilization is mostly toward read operations, you could consider lowering the service objective for the secondary. You can monitor the replication status in the Azure portal or use the PowerShell

`Get-AzSqlDatabaseReplicationLink` cmdlet to ensure that the secondary can keep up with the primary.

CAUTION

If one or more secondary databases cannot keep up with the rate of change at the primary database, the primary database will be throttled to allow all secondaries to catch up.

As of this writing, geo-replication introduces a limitation on the scalability of databases. When a primary database is in a geo-replication relationship, its service tier cannot be upgraded (for example, from Standard to Premium) without first upgrading all secondaries. To downgrade, you must downgrade the primary before any secondaries can be downgraded. As a best practice, when scaling up or down, you should ensure that the secondary database has the higher service objective longer than the primary. In other words, when scaling up, scale up secondary databases first; when scaling down, scale down secondary databases second.

Inside OUT

What are other uses for geo-replication?

The judicious configuration of geo-replication and application programming can enable you to downgrade your primary Azure SQL database to a lower service objective. Because secondaries are readable, you can use them to run read-only queries. If you direct some of the read queries, such as for reporting or data integration purposes, to secondary databases, the primary might be able to consume fewer resources.

In addition to potentially lowering service objective requirements, you also can use active geo-replication during application upgrades to move a database to another region with minimal downtime.

Set up failover groups

As discussed in the previous section, geo-replication represents a very capable option for DR planning. Geographically distributing relational data with an RPO of 5 seconds or less is a goal that few on-premises environments can achieve. However, the lack of automatic failover and the need to configure failover on each database individually creates overhead in any deployment, whether it has a single database in an organization with a single DBA or many hundreds or thousands of databases. Further, because a failover causes the writable database to be hosted on a different logical server with a different DNS name, connection strings must be updated, or the application must be modified to try a different connection.

Failover groups build on geo-replication to address these shortcomings. Configured at the server level, a failover group can include one, multiple, or all databases hosted on that server.

All databases in a group are recovered simultaneously. By default, failover groups are set to automatically recover the databases in case of an outage, though you can disable this. With automatic recovery enabled, you must configure a grace period. This grace period offers a way to direct the Azure infrastructure to emphasize either availability or data guarantees. By increasing the grace period, you emphasize data guarantees, because the automatic failover does not occur if it will result in data loss until the outage has lasted as long as the grace period. By decreasing the grace period, you emphasize availability. In practical terms, this means that if the secondary database in the failover group is not up to date after the grace period expires, the failover will occur, resulting in data loss.

When you configure a failover group, two new DNS CNAME records are created:

- The first CNAME record refers to the read-write listener and it points to the primary server. During a failover, this record is updated automatically so it always points to the writable replica. The read-write listener's FQDN is the name of the failover group prepended to database.windows.net. This means your failover group name must be globally unique.

- The second CNAME record points to the read-only listener, which is the secondary server. The read-only listener's DNS name is the name of the failover group prepended to secondary.database.windows.net. If the failover group name is ssio2022, the FQDN of the read-write listener will be ssio2022.database.windows.net and the FQDN of the secondary will be ssio2022.secondary.database.windows.net.

NOTE

As of this writing, a failover group can have only one secondary. For high-value databases, you should still configure additional secondaries to ensure HA isn't lost in case of a failover.

You can create failover groups with existing geo-replication already in place. If the failover group's secondary server is in the same region as an existing geo-replication secondary, the existing secondary will be used for the failover group. If you select a region for the failover secondary server where no replica is configured yet, a new secondary server and database will be created during the deployment process. If a new secondary database is created, it will be created in the same tier and with the same service objective as the primary. (Recall that these replicas incur service charges.)

Unlike with geo-replication, the Azure portal supports the initiation of a planned failover for failover groups. You can also initiate a planned failover by using PowerShell. Planned failovers do not cause data loss. Both interfaces also support the initiation of a forced failover, which, as with geo-replication's unplanned failover, can lead to data loss within the 5-second RPO window.

Inside OUT

How can you effectively provision auditing and Microsoft Defender for SQL with geo-replication?

When configuring auditing for geo-replicated databases, you should configure auditing at the server level on both the primary and secondary server. You should not enable auditing at the database level. By configuring auditing at the server level, the audit logs will be stored in the same region as the server, thereby avoiding cross-region traffic.

As a side effect of configuring auditing on the secondary databases' server, you can set a different retention period, though we do not recommend this configuration because valuable correlations between events on the primary and secondary can be lost. As described in the security section, you can use SSMS to merge audit files from different servers and databases to analyze them together. You should apply the same configuration for Microsoft Defender for SQL.

NOTE

DR and business-continuity planning should not just consider Azure SQL Database resources, but also other Azure services your application uses. These might include Azure Web Apps, VMs, DNS, storage accounts, and more. For more information on designing HA services that include Azure SQL Database, see *https://learn.microsoft.com /azure/sql-database/sql-database-designing-cloud-solutions-for-disaster-recovery*.

Use Azure Backup for long-term backup retention

To meet compliance and regulatory requirements, you might need to maintain a series of long-term database backups. Azure SQL Database can provide a solution using long-term retention (LTR). You can elect to retain full backups for a maximum of 10 years. Retained backups are stored in Azure Blob Storage, which is created for you; you don't need to provide a storage account.

Long-term backup retention is configured at the server level, but databases on the server can be selectively included or excluded. To begin, you create a retention policy. As its name indicates, the retention policy determines how long the backups are retained. After you configure retention, the next full backups that meet the criteria for weekly, monthly, or yearly will be retained. In other words, existing backups are not included in the long-term retention. A different retention period can be specified for weekly, monthly, and yearly full backups. You can also choose a simpler configuration, to keep only some of the backups.

➤ For more information on creating a vault as well as step-by-step guidance, see *https://learn .microsoft.com/azure/sql-database/sql-database-long-term-backup-retention-configure*.

When a database is deleted, you will continue to be charged for the backup's contents; however, the charges will decrease over time as backup files older than the retention period are deleted.

You can configure long-term backup retention by using the Azure portal or PowerShell. Although only primary or standalone databases are backed up and will therefore be the only databases that have backups added to storage, you should also configure long-term backup retention on geo-replicated secondaries. This ensures that in case of a failover, backups from the new primary database will be added to its vault, without further intervention. After a failover, a full backup is immediately taken, and that backup is added to long-term storage. Until a failover takes place, no additional costs are incurred for configuring retention on the secondary server.

NOTE

When the server hosting a database is deleted, the database backups are immediately and irrevocably lost. This does not apply to long-term backup retention. If you configured LTR for a database, the LTR backups can be used to restore databases to a different server in the same subscription.

Provision Azure SQL Managed Instance

Azure SQL Managed Instance is a fully managed, always up-to-date instance of SQL Server running in Azure. It was designed with almost full compatibility with the latest SQL Server Database Engine. With the release of SQL Server 2022, it also includes a new compatibility feature to allow for failover and failback from SQL Server 2022 instances to managed instances.

There are many new features currently in preview for Azure SQL Managed Instance at the time of this book's writing. Like many platform as a service offerings, Azure SQL Managed Instance is actively developed and in a state of constant improvement. The Azure SQL Managed Instance platform is a focus of considerable engineering investment for Microsoft. This chapter highlights as many new preview features as possible, given the time of this book's writing.

Several new features were added to Azure SQL Managed Instance in the "November 2022 feature wave," an opt-in program for rolling out new features first to dev/test subscriptions, then to production subscriptions. Depending on where you're reading this, your SQL managed instance may have access to some features covered in this chapter. For more information on the November 2022 feature wave, visit *https://learn.microsoft.com/azure/azure-sql/managed-instance /november-2022-feature-wave-enroll.*

Inside OUT

How do I keep up with all the new Azure SQL Managed Instance features?

New features often move from "(preview)" to "generally available (GA)" in a few months, but sometimes they stay in preview for longer as Microsoft continues to gather feedback and telemetry on adoption. A lot has been introduced to Azure SQL Managed Instance since it was first announced in 2017. As it is on its own development cycle, much has changed in this chapter over the past three editions of this book.

> Keep up with the latest new features in Azure SQL Managed Instance on the "What's new" page: *https://learn.microsoft.com/azure/azure-sql/managed-instance/doc-changes-updates-release-notes-whats-new*. Also pay attention to the various items in the November 2022 feature wave as they progress to being generally available to all SQL managed instances.

With Azure SQL Managed Instance, database administrators don't have access to the underlying virtual operating system (OS)—there is no Remote Desktop connection, for example. Otherwise, an Azure SQL managed instance is a SQL Server instance.

Azure SQL Managed Instance significantly simplifies administrator effort in the following ways:

- Hardware and infrastructure is completely managed and easily upgradeable over time. (The latest premium series and memory-optimized premium series hardware offerings were introduced in mid-2022.)

- Backups are automated, and user-initiated backups are also available.

- Point-in-time restores are possible with retention limits, initiated through the Azure portal, Azure CLI, and PowerShell. Even restores of deleted databases are possible.

- Geo-restores of SQL Managed Instance databases to another region are easily accomplished thanks to geo-redundant backup storage.

- High availability (HA) is automated (and user-customizable), and auto-failover groups are easily created via the Azure portal or PowerShell. A listener endpoint allows for both read/write and read-only application access to the cluster.

- Unlike Azure SQL Database, SQL Managed Instance provides an isolated environment with dedicated compute, storage, and virtual networks (VNets). The same security and authentication features, like transparent data encryption (TDE), Azure Active Directory (Azure AD) integration, SQL Audit, and Advanced Threat Protection are available.

- With the new link feature for Azure SQL Managed Instance and SQL Server 2022, you can synchronize a database from your infrastructure to a managed instance, and failover and failback from SQL Server 2022 to SQL Managed Instance. We discuss this exciting new feature throughout this chapter. For even more information, see Chapter 11, "Implement high availability and disaster recovery."

- Azure SQL Managed Instance offers easy migration from on-premises installations via the new link feature for Azure SQL Managed Instance (more on this later). Designed specifically to offer 99.99 percent or better availability with minimal management, a SQL managed instance is ideal for migrating existing enterprise on-premises SQL Server instances. In comparison, migrating legacy on-premises applications to Azure SQL Database can be more difficult.

Inside OUT

What's actually included in Azure SQL?

It can be confusing in documentation, and even in this book, to keep track of which marketing names cover which products.

When you see *SQL Server* alone, it is assumed to be the user-installed, year-versioned product like SQL Server 2022, sometimes referred to anachronistically as the *box product*. SQL Server may also be used in the context of the SQL Server Database Engine, or just Database Engine, the common query optimizer and storage engine that all Microsoft SQL products use.

SQL Server can run on-premises or in Azure Virtual Machines (VMs); it can even be installed for you as part of a VM image from the Azure Marketplace.

Azure SQL includes Azure SQL Database and Azure SQL Managed Instance. Early Microsoft marketing used phrasing like *Azure SQL Database managed instance* but that was shortened to *Azure SQL Managed Instance*. You might, however, see *managed instance* when we're talking in proper context about your managed instance—that is, a specific managed instance.

Just because you see "Applies to SQL Server" in Microsoft Learn docs doesn't mean it applies to Azure SQL Database or Azure SQL Managed Instance as well. Recently, a vast internal team at Microsoft has been reviewing the tens of thousands of documentation articles for SQL Server, adding "Applies to Azure SQL Managed Instance" where appropriate.

Various features, like the intelligent query processing (IQP) features discussed in Chapter 14, "Performance tune SQL Server," sometimes arrive on Azure SQL Database or Azure SQL Managed Instance *before* arriving in SQL Server, and vice versa. For various marketing and technological reasons, these products are still often grouped together because the products themselves are still extremely similar.

SQL Server, Azure SQL Database, and Azure SQL Managed Instance orbit each other, increasingly independently. For example, you've likely seen many Microsoft Learn docs shared by Azure SQL Database and Azure SQL Manage Instance split up. This is especially important as the vCore tier hardware becomes more distinct, for example.

CHAPTER 18

What is Azure SQL Managed Instance?

Azure SQL Managed Instance is a platform as a service (PaaS) offering for SQL Server. It has nearly 100 percent compatibility with the current Enterprise edition of the Database Engine and automatically upgrades its versions. A managed instance never requires a prolonged outage for patching or even major version upgrades.

Azure SQL Managed Instance has its own internal database version number, which, until the release of SQL Server 2022, was higher than any version of SQL Server. Starting around the SQL Server 2022 release, Azure SQL managed instances run with a new compatibility level setting. New managed instances receive the compatibility setting by default, and existing managed instances will see it enabled automatically. More on this new compatibility level later.

Azure SQL Managed Instance features allow for an easy lift and shift from on-premises to the cloud with minimal to no application or database changes. The isolation and security of your SQL managed instance is protected with its own VNet and private IP addresses.

It is also important when choosing a SQL managed instance to understand what it is *not*. A SQL managed instance is not an alternative for many secondary SQL Server features. A SQL managed instance is intended for a traditional OLTP workload, but not to replace the other SQL Server services.

A quick rundown of feature differences:

- SQL Server Integration Services (SSIS) is not also hosted inside the SQL managed instance. Instead, you should migrate existing SSIS packages with an Azure Integration Runtime (IR) inside Azure Data Factory, another PaaS offering. Your SQL managed instance can host the SSISDB catalog for the SSIS IR, however.

- SQL Server Analysis Services (SSAS) is not provided by Azure SQL Managed Instance. You can host it in a separate SQL Server instance in an Azure VM or as a PaaS offering with Azure Analysis Services, but the modern direction is to move this workload to Power BI Premium services.

- You must replace SQL Server Reporting Services (SSRS) with either Power BI paginated reports or a SQL Server instance with SSRS in an Azure VM. A SQL managed instance can host your SSRS catalog databases for that Azure VM, however.

- Availability groups are built in and pre-configured for SQL managed instances, and are also configurable through the Azure portal, to dramatically simplify your SQL HA solution.

- Other features that aren't supported in Azure SQL Database are supported in Azure SQL Managed Instance, such as SQL Agent, Database Mail, a fully configurable Query Store, change data capture (CDC), linked servers, and transactional replication.

- Service Broker was not initially supported in Azure SQL Managed Instance, but support was later introduced in 2021. For specific limitations, see *https://learn.microsoft.com/sql/database-engine/configure-windows/sql-server-service-broker#service-broker-and-azure-sql-managed-instance*.

- Security features like Always Encrypted, dynamic data masking, row-level security, SQL Audit, and TDE are all supported.

- Like Azure SQL Database, Azure SQL Managed Instance provides support for Azure AD integration, with the `CREATE LOGIN … FROM EXTERNAL PROVIDER` syntax.

Although many items that comprise a SQL managed instance are similar to the latest version of SQL Server, there are a few things that make it different as well.

Differences between SQL Server and Azure SQL Managed Instance

When assessing the benefits of a SQL managed instance, it is important to compare like servers and services. The SQL managed instance benefits from always being up to date in the cloud, which means that some features in on-premises SQL Server may be either unnecessary or have alternatives. There are also specific cases when a particular feature works in a slightly different way.

High availability

High availability (HA) is built in and pre-configured using technology similar to availability groups (AGs). If you currently use AGs, you will find there are several operations that are not supported, including:

- Creating AGs

- Altering AGs

- Dropping AGs

- Creating endpoints for database mirroring

- The SET HADR clause of the alter database statement

There are a few HA features used in SQL managed instances that are different from on-premises:

- **INSTANCE_LOG_GOVERNOR wait.** This is a Resource Governor constraint that slows down logging to ensure replicas do not get out of sync. Index rebuilds, for example, are an activity that can be affected by this governor.

- **HADR_DATABASE_FLOW_CONTROL and HADR_THROTTLE_LOG_RATE_SEND_RECV waits.** You will see these waits if the secondary replicas get behind. They slow the primary to prevent data loss.

Azure SQL Managed Instance can also be a part of your hybrid HA and disaster recovery (DR) solution with the addition of the link feature for Azure SQL Managed Instance, introduced around the same time as SQL Server 2022. More on this later in this chapter and in Chapter 11.

Differences

Azure SQL Managed Instance and an on-premises SQL Server have a few general differences that you should consider. These are behavior changes that can affect your decision as to whether and how to use Azure SQL Managed Instance.

- All Azure SQL Managed Instance databases use the full recovery model to guarantee HA and no data loss. If your on-premises database uses the simple or bulk-logged model, you may find SQL Managed Instance slower for bulk-logged operations.

- With SQL Managed Instance, TDE is enabled by default. This can be disabled, but if any of the databases in an instance are encrypted, tempdb will still be encrypted.

Version compatibility with SQL Server 2022

Before the time of the release of SQL Server 2022, Azure SQL Managed Instance ran at a special version level higher than any public SQL Server release, which meant restoring to SQL Server was impossible. Migration to a managed instance used to be a one-way ticket.

Starting around the SQL Server 2022 release, SQL managed instances began running with compatibility to the latest SQL Server 2022 build. New SQL managed instances have SQL Server 2022 version compatibility by default and existing SQL managed instances receive it automatically. Existing SQL managed instances actually began receiving the rollout of the new compatibility level in the months before the release of SQL Server 2022.

This means you can failover and failback from an on-premises SQL Server version using the new link feature for Azure SQL Managed Instance. Failing over and failing back from a SQL managed instance is not supported for previous versions of SQL Server.

Thanks to the new compatibility option, migrations to Azure SQL Managed Instance are no longer a one-way ticket, and can be reversed if necessary. Multi-cloud SQL Server solutions involving Azure SQL Managed Instance are possible. Including an Azure SQL Managed Instance in an on-premises availability group is possible.

The new version compatibility feature for Azure SQL Managed Instance cannot be disabled or opted out of at this time. New Database Engine features that bump the database version are not delivered to SQL managed instances until they are released in SQL Server cumulative updates. Some Database Engine feature changes with no on-disk metadata changes will also be released at the same time on Azure SQL Managed Instance and SQL Server.

Microsoft has acknowledged that in the future, it's possible that Azure SQL Managed Instance may introduce functionality that requires changes to the database format, making backups incompatible with SQL Server 2022. At that point, customers would be offered a choice between version compatibility and the new SQL managed instance–only features.

Time to provision and start/stop

One limitation of Azure SQL Managed Instance was the delay in provisioning. It could take many hours to provision a managed instance, but this time has been reduced with recent announcements. Provisioning Azure SQL Managed Instance has been faster with recent changes behind the scenes.

There is also less reason to provision/de-provision SQL managed instances now that there is a start/stop feature. The start/stop feature allows SQL managed instances to be stopped to save money and resumed quickly. This is especially useful for testing or proof-of-concept (POC) environments. When stopped, all compute and license costs are paused. Storage and backup storage for the SQL managed instance remain billed. As of the time of this book's writing, the new stop/start feature for Azure SQL Managed Instance is in preview as part of the November 2022 feature wave. For details, visit *https://learn.microsoft.com/azure/azure-sql/managed-instance /instance-stop-start-how-to*.

Azure SQL Managed Instance is not an inexpensive cloud product to consume, but now its costs can be mostly paused. This feature is in preview at the time of this writing.

Maintenance window and advance maintenance alerts

A feature introduced in 2022 enables administrators to choose from a few different pre-determined schedules for maintenance. This allows you to schedule planned Azure maintenance windows around the business.

Advance maintenance notifications 24 hours before each planned maintenance window are also available, though for Azure SQL Managed Instance, they are in preview at the time of this book's writing.

By default, Azure SQL Managed Instance can perform planned maintenance and upgrades from 5 p.m. to 8 a.m., any day of the week, in the time zone local to the Azure datacenter.

Two alternate maintenance windows are also available:

- **Weekdays.** 10 p.m. to 6 a.m. Monday through Thursday, local to the Azure datacenter.

- **Weekends.** 10 p.m. to 6 a.m. Friday through Sunday, local to the Azure datacenter.

CHAPTER 18

Azure planned maintenance should typically complete well within a single maintenance window, but sometimes it can span multiple windows. On rare occasions, critical security patches might be applied in the default maintenance window.

Backup and restore

Managed instances automatically handle backups for you. Much like on-premises backups, a SQL managed instance takes full backups every week, differential backups every 12 to 24 hours, and transaction log backups about every 10 minutes, based on compute size and database activity.

Backups are stored as Azure Storage blobs and replicated to another datacenter for protection against datacenter outages or disasters. Restores are automatically handled as well, as the system determines which restore path to take.

Inside OUT

Can you restore an Azure SQL Managed Instance database to your own SQL Server instance for testing?

Yes, but only for restores to SQL Server 2022.

This answer used to be a flat "no," but as of November 2022, the new version compatibility provides a way to back up and restore from SQL Server 2022. You cannot restore from a SQL Managed Instance database to older versions of SQL Server, or to Azure SQL Database.

You can also synchronize to a SQL Server 2022 instance with the link feature for Azure SQL Managed Instance. This allows for bidirectional failover to SQL Server 2022.

You can upload a SQL Server backup to restore to a SQL managed instance. You can also export the data from a SQL managed instance to on-premises or testing environments. Consider the scalable Azure Data Factory Copy activity or other data movement strategies.

Backup storage

Azure SQL Managed Instance backups are written to geo-redundant Azure Blob Storage by default, so your backups are immediately off site. In order of ascending safety, backup redundancy can be set to local-only, zone-redundant, geo-redundant (default), or geo-zone-redundant storage (GZRS). GZRS takes advantage of availability zones within Azure regions and zones in a geo-redundant paired Azure region.

Inside OUT

Can you change your backup redundancy setting any time?

When changing to a more broadly distributed redundancy for your backup storage, like from local to geo-redundant storage, there may be a 10+ minute delay for keys, storage, and other automation to be created in the additional geographies. Then, a full backup is immediately taken. If you don't want to affect your production systems during normal operating hours, don't change your backup storage redundancy setting until after hours.

> ### NOTE
>
> For concerns about data residency or other regulations, you can configure backup redundancy to local-only or zone-redundant storage.

You cannot geo-restore backups to the paired Azure region if you choose locally redundant storage (LRS) or zone-redundant storage backups. The cheapest option is LRS, which replicates data three times within a single datacenter in the primary region and provides 99.999999999 percent storage uptime. Of course, uptime isn't the entire story on data safety. LRS is safe, but not the safest in terms of disaster survivability.

Manual backups in Azure SQL Managed Instance

The only type of backups you can manually initiate are copy-only full backups, written to a registered Azure Blob Storage location using BACKUP TO URL. You can then restore from that backup as desired to SQL managed instances, including geo-restores in other Azure datacenters in the event of a disaster. There are some hurdles to using the backups elsewhere, however.

By default, you cannot restore this backup externally because of the TDE key, which is service managed and itself cannot be exported. This is a by-default security measure. There are two workarounds:

- Create a customer-managed TDE key (a bring-your-own-key, or BYOK) setup. Then you can manage the same TDE key in a SQL Server instance outside the SQL managed instance. This is a required preparation step for the link feature for Azure SQL Managed Instance.

  ➤ For more information on providing your own key, see *https://learn.microsoft.com/azure/azure-sql/database/transparent-data-encryption-byok-overview*.

- Choose reduced safety by disabling TDE for the database. This may violate safety and privacy regulations in your industry. Not recommended.

CHAPTER 18

There is a limitation of 32 stripes for the SQL managed instance backup and a stripe size of 195 GB, which is the maximum blob object size, enough for 4 TB of compressed data storage.

Restores to a SQL managed instance

Azure SQL Managed Instance does not allow you to specify full physical paths, so all corresponding scenarios are logically supported differently. For example, RESTORE does not support WITH MOVE, and CREATE DATABASE doesn't allow physical paths.

The options to restore are:

- **Restore to a point in time.** This option restores a copy in the same SQL managed instance or a different SQL managed instance under the same subscription.

- **Restore a deleted database.** This option restores a deleted database to the SQL managed instance from which the backup was taken.

- **Restore to a new region.** This option creates a new database in any existing server anywhere in the world and is used in case of a geographic disaster.

- **Restore from a specific long-term backup.** This option only works if a long-term policy has been set. Long-term retention can be configured for up to 10 years.

Backup retention policies

Short-term retention policies for backups include policies needed for point-in-time restores, while long-term retention policies involve the full backups commonly needed for regulatory compliance. These policies can be configured per database.

NOTE

Review your short- and long-term backup retention policies when creating a new SQL managed instance to comply with your own regulatory or policy requirements.

By default, short-term retention is 7 days for the general purpose tier and up to 35 days for business critical. By default, long-term retention is not enabled. You can configure individual retention of:

- Weekly backups

- The first backup of each month

- The nth week of each year, up to 10 years

The long-term policy does not apply until the *next* backup of that type occurs.

CAUTION

If you reduce your retention period by changing tiers or modifying retention policies, then all backups older than the new retention period are no longer available.

Security

Azure SQL Managed Instance provides most of the same security features as the latest SQL Server on-premises Enterprise edition.

> ➤ **Additional information about managing instances and database security can be found in Chapter 12, "Administer instance and database security and permissions."**

A SQL managed instance can be created with SQL Authentication, Azure AD Authentication, or both:

- If SQL Authentication is enabled with a single SQL-authenticated server administrator account, that account is the administrator of the SQL managed instance. This is specified during or after provisioning. It is a member of the sysadmin server role and is separate from the built-in sa account, which also exists in Azure SQL Managed Instance but is disabled by default.

- If Azure AD Authentication is enabled, the Azure AD admin account must be linked to a user or group in Azure AD. This account has sysadmin permissions and creates Azure AD and SQL logins in the master database for the SQL managed instance.

- As of August 2022, Windows Authentication for Azure AD principals is supported. You can now enable the use of Windows Authentication for Azure SQL Managed Instance, allowing for a more seamless experience for users in a hybrid infrastructure environment. This is particularly useful for legacy applications where Azure AD options don't work. It allows enterprises to lift and shift to Azure while leveraging existing and familiar authentication methods. Windows Authentication for Azure AD principals to SQL managed instances is available for servers joined to an Active Directory (AD) in your own infrastructure, to Azure AD, or to hybrid Azure AD. This is made possible in Azure using Kerberos.

> ➤ **For more information, visit *https://learn.microsoft.com/azure/azure-sql/managed-instance /winauth-azuread-overview*.**

Azure AD Authentication

A SQL managed instance needs permissions to read Azure AD to perform tasks such as authenticate users in security groups and create new users.

> ➤ **For detailed information on how to create Azure AD server principal logins for SQL managed instances, visit *https://learn.microsoft.com/azure/azure-sql/managed-instance/aad -security-configure-tutorial#create-an-azure-ad-server-principal-login-for-a-managed -instance-using-ssms*.**

NOTE

Some features in this space rely on recent versions of SQL Server Management Studio (SSMS). Always use the latest version of SSMS when dealing with Azure SQL platforms. SSMS 19 was introduced and previewed alongside SQL Server 2022. Get the latest version at *https://aka.ms/ssms.*

Azure AD database principals are created at the database level. This account can be either a user or a group. It does not have to be an administrator, but it must be configured to use Azure AD to connect to the database. Both server principals and admin accounts can overlap in permissions. The server principal takes precedence in the event of a conflict.

Certificates

SQL managed instances do not access file shares or folders. You cannot create from or back up to a file share for certificates, nor can you back up or create from a file or assembly.

➤ **Find details on how to handle certificates at** *https://learn.microsoft.com/sql/t-sql/statements /create-certificate-transact-sql.*

Contained database users

Like SQL Server and Azure SQL Database, Azure SQL Managed Instance supports partially contained databases and contained database users. You can map a user in a partially contained database directly to an Azure AD account.

You should avoid logins (in the master database) and contained users (in a user database) with the same name. This can cause confusion because the contained user connection takes precedence over the login when connecting to the user database.

Configuration differences

There are several configurations to note with SQL managed instances that are different from SQL Server:

- Buffer pool extensions are not supported.

- The deprecated database mirroring feature is not supported.

- Multiple log files are not supported.

- In-memory tables are a business critical tier–only feature.

- SQL Server Agent is always running.

- FILESTREAM and FileTable are not supported.

- DBCC undocumented statements that are enabled in SQL Server do not function.

- Session-level trace flags are not supported.

- R and Python external libraries and tables are not supported.

NOTE

Machine Learning Services in Azure SQL Managed Instance are a different topic. R and Python scripts for in-database machine learning are supported. For more information, see *https://learn.microsoft.com/azure/azure-sql/managed-instance/machine-learning -services-overview.*

- Linked servers are supported for other managed instances, SQL Server instances, and Azure SQL Database targets, and support both SQL Authentication and Azure AD Authentication. In 2020, support for linked servers to Azure Synapse serverless SQL pools and dedicated SQL pools was added.

- Cross-instance Service Broker message exchange is supported only between SQL managed instances. Service Broker is enabled by default and cannot be disabled.

- Extended stored procedures (including `xp_cmdshell`) are not supported.

- Azure SQL Managed Instance automatically manages XTP filegroup and files for databases containing in-memory OLTP objects.

- The tempdb database is split into 12 data files by default. Starting in September 2022, you can configure the number of tempdb data files the same way you can in SQL Server. Changes to add or remove tempdb data files take effect immediately without the need to restart, although the Database Engine will use the new, empty tempdb data files first until all the tempdb data files level out over time.

- By default, tempdb data files have a growth rate of 254 MB, and transaction log files have a growth rate of 64 MB. Starting in September 2022, these growth rates can be reconfigured, just like in SQL Server. The growth rate and current size of all tempdb data files should always be the same.

- Prior to SQL Server 2022, transaction log files could not benefit from instant file initialization (IFI). Now, transaction log file growth events less than or equal to 64 MB can benefit from IFI. You should leave your transaction log file autogrowth rate set to the default of 64 MB. Also, consider proactive growing data and log files to avoid autogrowth events altogether. For more on IFI, see Chapter 3, "Design and implement an on-premises database infrastructure."

NOTE

Data virtualization for Azure SQL Managed Instance became generally available in September 2022 for external data sources to Azure Data Lake Storage (ADLS) Gen2 and Azure Blob Storage. This includes support for using a managed identity authentication that automatically provides a managed instance with authentication to Azure Storage. Though it is data virtualization, it is not called PolyBase in Azure SQL Managed Instance. PolyBase remains the name for the SQL Server feature set for data virtualization. For more information, see *https://techcommunity.microsoft.com/t5/azure-sql-blog/data-virtualization-now-generally-available-in-azure-sql-managed/ba-p/3624292*.

There are several features and syntax that cannot be used in a SQL managed instance. This is because the instance automatically handles these features and therefore they are not relevant and can't be changed. A list of these features can be found at the following Microsoft Docs locations:

- *https://learn.microsoft.com/azure/azure-sql/database/features-comparison*

- *https://learn.microsoft.com/azure/azure-sql/managed-instance/transact-sql-tsql-differences-sql-server*

➤ You can keep track of known issues at *https://learn.microsoft.com/azure/azure-sql/managed-instance/doc-changes-updates-known-issues*, and follow what's new in Azure SQL Managed Instance here: *https://learn.microsoft.com/azure/azure-sql/managed-instance/doc-changes-updates-release-notes-whats-new*.

Inside OUT

Does Azure SQL Managed Instance support distributed transactions?

In short, yes. There is a feature to execute distributed transactions between multiple databases on different SQL managed instances. However, there's some terminology to sort out here.

Support for distributed database transactions across multiple SQL managed instances is provided via ADO.NET and the `System.Transaction` class, where the ability to perform distributed transactions is native to Azure SQL Database and Azure SQL Managed Instance. Distributed transactions that write data are currently limited to other SQL managed instances. This requires setting up a server trust group (STG) containing the SQL managed instances needed for the distributed transactions. For more information, see *https://learn.microsoft.com/azure/azure-sql/database/elastic-transactions-overview*.

The distributed database transactions don't involve or require the Microsoft Distributed Transaction Coordinator (MSDTC), which isn't generally available in Azure SQL Managed Instance. However, distributed transactions using a cloud-managed MSDTC are coming soon. A product group blog post in July 2022 announced a private preview for an Azure cloud–managed DTC that allows for distributed transactions between Azure SQL Managed Instance databases, SQL Server instances hosted anywhere, and even non-Microsoft database platforms. For more information, see *https://techcommunity.microsoft.com/t5/azure-sql-blog/ms-dtc-for-azure-sql-managed-instance-extending-distributed/ba-p/3576839*.

If you need support for queries using the same MSDTC functionality as you have with SQL Server, and they don't work in the limited scenarios supported by the cloud-managed DTC preview, consider SQL Server on Azure VMs. This distributed transaction capability is different from Azure SQL Database *elastic queries*, a useful feature only for Azure SQL Database that has been in preview status for years.

Create a SQL managed instance

You can create a SQL managed instance using the Azure portal (recommended for your first time), PowerShell, the Azure CLI, ARM and Bicep templates, or the REST API.

When creating a SQL managed instance for the first time, plan to have a few hours to spare. Fortunately, the time it takes to provision a managed instance has decreased recently. The Azure portal directs you in which VNets to use, ensuring you have all the necessary items before starting the deployment.

➤ A list of those regions can be found at *https://azure.microsoft.com/explore/global-infrastructure/products-by-region/?products=azure-sql&regions=all*.

A SQL managed instance is supported for the following subscription types.

- Enterprise Agreement (EA)

- Pay-As-You-Go

- Cloud Service Provider (CSP)

- Enterprise Dev/Test

- Pay-As-You-Go Dev/Test

- Subscriptions with monthly Azure credit for Visual Studio subscribers

Select a service tier and service objective

Azure SQL Managed Instance is based on the vCore purchasing model. The intent is to make it easier to transition from SQL Server on-premises so you can independently choose to scale out compute and storage. Maximum instance storage scales up by the number of vCores.

There are two different service tiers for SQL managed instances:

- **General purpose.** Balances usage with scalable compute and storage options. HA is built-in based on Azure Blob Storage and the Azure Service Fabric. This is a technical distinction only—HA replicas in the general purpose tier are "cold" as opposed to "hot" because replication occurs at the storage level, not at the database level.

  Geo-replicated read-only replicas inside failover groups are available at additional cost. The general purpose tier allows for storage up to 16 TB with 5–10 ms latency. The tempdb system database files are stored on SSDs local to the SQL managed instance (including in failover groups). The tempdb is allocated 24 GB per vCore.

- **Business critical.** Typically used for applications with high I/O requirements that can suffer only minimal impact due to maintenance operations. It offers the highest resilience to failures by using isolated replicas. HA is built-in based on a technology similar to AGs and Azure Service Fabric. Failover groups offer asynchronously replicated, read-only replicas that can be used for reporting or other read-only workloads.

  The business critical tier allows for storage up to 5.5 TB on faster premium-series hardware (1–2 ms latency) than general purpose. In memory-optimized premium series hardware, business critical supports up to 16 TB of storage. All data and log files, including tempdb files, are stored on solid-state drives (SSDs) local to the SQL managed instance (including in failover groups). They are limited only by the maximum available size of storage.

> ➤ For more information about solid-state storage, see Chapter 2, "Introduction to database server components."

These resource limits are regularly increased and may have changed since the time of this book's writing. For current details, visit *https://learn.microsoft.com/azure/azure-sql/managed -instance/resource-limits*.

All Azure SQL Server Managed Instance service tiers guarantee at least 99.99 percent availability, and independently scale storage size and compute, with up to 100 percent service credit for uptime violations.

> ➤ See the service-level agreement (SLA) for more information, at *https://azure.microsoft.com /support/legal/sla/azure-sql-sql-managed-instance*.

Inside OUT

What if you need better than 99.99 percent availability?

If you need guaranteed HA higher than 99.99 percent (roughly 52 minutes per year of down-time), with no impact on maintenance operations and outages, there are options to consider.

First, selectable maintenance windows and maintenance window alerts help you plan for and avoid planned impact to business-critical time windows, as mentioned earlier in this chapter.

In the business critical tier, the zone redundant configuration offers an SLA to 99.995 percent (roughly 26 minutes per year). Zone redundancy, as discussed in other places in this book, is a way to increase data redundancy and survivability without geo-replication, and could be particularly useful for concerns over data residency. Zone redundancy rep-licates data between the multiple physically isolated infrastructure zones within a single Azure datacenter.

If the ability to handle critical servicing tasks, planned events, and unplanned events is mis-sion or life critical, consider the general purpose, business critical, or Premium tiers of the Azure SQL Database configured for zone redundant deployments, which offer 99.995 per-cent uptime (roughly 26 minutes per year of downtime).

If 99.995 percent is still unacceptable for mission- or life-critical operational needs, for the safety of those involved you should consider investing in on-premises infrastructure and other redundancies.

The service tier and compute hardware options are independent of each other. Compute hard-ware options as of the writing of this book are as follows:

- **Standard-series.** Up to 80 logical CPUs based on Intel E5-2673 v4 (Broadwell) 2.3-GHz processors, vCore = 1 LP (hyper-thread), 5.1 GB per vCore.

- **Premium-series.** Up to 80 logical CPUs based on Intel Ice Lake 8370C 2.8-GHz proces-sors, 7 GB RAM per vCore.

- **Premium-series memory optimized.** Up to 64 logical CPUs based on Intel Ice Lake 8370C 2.8-GHz processors. Almost double the RAM per core at 13.6 GB RAM per vCore.

- **Gen4.** Deprecated and unavailable for new instances. As of the time of this book's writ-ing, in March 2023 remaining Gen4 hardware will be automatically upgraded to Gen5.

Previously, *standard-series* was known as Gen5. To reduce confusion, Microsoft has moved away from numerically incrementing these hardware generations, but still provides the base platform hardware. Gen5, Gen6, and Gen7 hardware is all considered in the standard-series label, has the same resource limits, and is not user-selectable. In the future, Microsoft will simply upgrade the hardware underneath standard-series and premium-series labels.

You can derive specific hardware information about your instance of Azure SQL Managed Instance from the sys.dm_user_db_resource_governance dynamic management view (DMV). This information is not hidden and is documented at *https://learn.microsoft.com/azure/azure-sql /managed-instance/service-tiers-managed-instance-vcore*.

There are some differences between the internal reporting and marketing names. Hardware for standard-series is labeled as *standard-series (Gen5)* but could use Broadwell, Skylake, or Cascade Lake Intel processors. Hardware for instances reported as Gen7 uses Intel 8272CL (Cascade Lake) processors, for example. Premium-series hardware generations are reported in the DMV as Gen8.

> ➤ For up-to-date details on the different service tiers and hardware options, and their resource limits, visit *https://learn.microsoft.com/azure/azure-sql/managed-instance/resource-limits*. These limits regularly increase as Microsoft continuously evolves the hardware.

With Software Assurance from your on-premises offering, you can exchange existing licenses for discounted rates on a SQL managed instance using Azure Hybrid Benefit for SQL Server at *https://azure.microsoft.com/pricing/hybrid-benefit*.

Use the Azure portal to provision a SQL managed instance

It is highly recommended that you use the Azure portal to provision SQL managed instances until you fully understand the experience—particularly the networking aspects. The Azure portal automates much of this for you and limits the number of issues that can arise.

The following instructions can help you complete the task of creating a SQL managed instance through the Azure portal:

1. Choose +**Create A Resource**.

2. In the search box, type **managed instance**, and choose **Azure SQL Managed Instance** from options that appear. Select **Create**.

    The **Basics** tab contains the minimum required information.

3. In the **Subscriptions** drop-down list, choose the subscription. (See the note earlier in "Create a SQL managed instance" about available subscriptions.)

4. In the **Resource group** drop-down list, choose the resource group. Alternatively, select **Create New** and follow the prompts to create a new resource group.

5. In the **Managed Instance Name** box, type a name for the SQL managed instance.

6. In the **Region** drop-down list, choose a region.

7. Select the **Configure Managed Instance** link in the **Compute + Storage** section of the **Basics** tab.

8. Choose the **General Purpose** or **Business Critical** tier, and an option in the **Hardware Generation** section. See the previous section for more information.

9. Use the **vCores** slider to specify a number of vCores. Use the **Storage in GB** slider to choose a maximum storage amount. These settings can be adjusted in the future, but at the cost of a brief service interruption.

10. If it's available, select the **Azure Hybrid Benefit** check box. This can save you money, as the SQL Server license is automatically included in the cost of the SQL managed instance.

11. Choose a **Backup** option (discussed earlier in this chapter):

    ▪ **Geo-Redundant.** The default.

    ▪ **Zone-Redundant.** This might be useful to avoid data residency concerns.

    ▪ **Locally Redundant.** This can lower costs for pre-production systems.

12. Select **Apply**.

13. At the bottom of the **Basics** tab, choose to allow **Azure AD Authentication**, **SQL Authentication**, or both.

    While fundamentally different in the integration with AD, this is similar to deciding whether to enable Windows Authentication, SQL Authentication, or Mixed mode when installing a SQL Server.

    If Azure AD Authentication is enabled, select an Azure AD administrator account.

    If SQL Authentication is enabled, provide a **Managed Instance admin login** and **Password**. Then, select **Next : Networking**.

14. This is where you define the level of access, connection type, VNet, and public endpoints (if desired). If you have a compliant VNet, choose it from the **Virtual Network/Subnet** drop-down list. Otherwise, it is recommended that you allow the Azure portal to create a new one for you. Reusing the VNet from an existing SQL managed instance can reduce the provisioning time.

CHAPTER 18

15.   Open the **Connection Type** drop-down list and choose a connection type for the private endpoint. The default value is **Proxy**; however, we recommend you choose **Redirect**.

If you choose **Proxy**, all connections are proxied via Azure SQL Managed Instance gateways. So, to enable connectivity, the client must have outbound firewall rules that allow only the IP address of the Azure SQL Managed Instance gateway port 1433.

With the **Redirect** option, clients establish connections directly to the node hosting the database. So, you need outbound firewall rules to allow all Azure IP addresses in the region using network security groups (NSGs) with service tags for ports 11000–11999, not just the Azure SQL Managed Instance gateway. This allows packets to go directly to the database, reducing latency.

➤ For more information, see *https://learn.microsoft.com/azure/azure-sql/managed-instance/connection-types-overview*.

16.   Optionally, enable the **Public Endpoint** setting.

For security reasons, **Public Endpoint** is disabled by default because it allows access to the SQL managed instance without a VPN and can be a security risk.

When **Public Endpoint** is enabled, you're given the option to **Allow access from: Azure Services**, **Internet**, or **No Access**. Ideally, you should choose **No Access** and enable only specific endpoints later as needed.

➤ For information on using Azure SQL Managed Instance securely with public endpoints, visit *https://learn.microsoft.com/azure/azure-sql/managed-instance/public-endpoint-overview*.

NOTE

Connections for the link feature for Azure SQL Managed Instance must be made via private endpoints. An Azure ExpressRoute virtual private cloud connection between your infrastructure and Azure is recommended. Other VPN connections from your infrastructure to Azure are supported, such as Azure site-to-site VPN and point-to-site VPN.

17.   For the **Minimum TLS Version** setting, select the highest value possible based on existing applications. Some legacy connection drivers do not support the latest versions of Transport Layer Security (TLS), so you might have to allow less secure TLS versions until those issues can be resolved and the drivers upgraded. TLS 1.3 support is introduced in SQL Server 2022 and Window Server 2022 and will likely be introduced for Azure SQL Managed Instance after this book is published. Select **Next : Security**.

18.   You have the option to begin a free trial of an add-on Azure service, the **Microsoft Defender for SQL**. Microsoft Defender for SQL is an analytics-driven threat-detection service that continuously identifies and mitigates potential database vulnerabilities. For more information, see Chapter 16, "Design and implement hybrid and Azure database infrastructure."

19. For the **Identity** setting, choose one of the following options:

- **System-Assigned Identity (SMI).** This is the default. A new system-assigned identity (SMI) will be created.

- **User-Defined Managed Identity (UMI).** A UMI can serve as service identity for one or more Azure SQL databases or managed instances. UMIs have been generally available for Azure SQL Database and Azure SQL Managed Instance since June 2022.

You can create an SMI and choose one or more UMIs. This is necessary to eventually allow Azure AD Authentication for your managed instance. If you choose to use more than one UMI, you also must specify which UMI is the primary and default UMI.

➤ For more information, see *https://learn.microsoft.com/azure/azure-sql/managed-instance /winauth-azuread-kerberos-managed-instance*.

Using UMI offers certain advantages. For example, you can reuse a UMI for multiple instances. UMIs can also be created to serve different features. For example, you might have one UMI that serves up Azure AD Authentication and another UMI that serves up TDE. You must also choose a UMI if you intend to bring your own customer-managed key for TDE.

If you delete an Azure SQL Database logical server or a SQL managed instance, the SMI is deleted as well. A UMI, however, is independent of any servers or instances to which it is assigned, and is not deleted automatically.

➤ For more on SMIs versus UMIs, see *https://learn.microsoft.com/azure/azure-sql/database /authentication-azure-ad-user-assigned-managed-identity*.

20. Choose a **Service Principal** setting. The *service principal* is a relatively new feature with a specific goal in mind: to enable Windows Authenticated logins, via Kerberos, for Azure SQL Managed Instance. This allows an even smoother lift-and-shift migration to Azure for existing applications with significant investment in Windows Authenticated principals for authentication.

21. Choose a **Transparent Data Encryption (TDE)** key. As stated, TDE is enabled by default. You can disable it later, but this is not recommended.

TDE prevents databases from being restored to another instance without a certificate present. "Encryption of data at rest" is a common regulatory requirement, so security policies often require TDE. Specify whether you want to use a service-managed key for TDE or bring your own *user-managed* key. You use your own key if you want your backups to have more portability between your managed instances. Select **Apply**, then select **Next : Additional Settings**.

➤ For more information on providing your own key, see *https://learn.microsoft.com/azure/azure -sql/database/transparent-data-encryption-byok-overview*.

CHAPTER 18

22. If you don't want to use the default collation, select the **Find a Collation** button and choose a collation.

23. Open the **Time Zone** drop-down list and choose a time-zone setting.

24. Under Geo-Replication, choose **Yes** to specify that this SQL managed instance should be the secondary to another SQL managed instance in a geo-replicated Failover Group.

   If you choose **Yes**, the primary SQL managed instance must already exist, and you must take additional steps to create a VPN gateway between the primary and secondary.

   ➤ For more on creating a SQL managed instance as a secondary replica, see *https://learn .microsoft.com/azure/azure-sql/managed-instance/failover-group-add-instance-tutorial*.

25. Choose a **Maintenance window** schedule, as discussed earlier in this chapter in the section "Maintenance window and advance maintenance alerts." Then select **Next : Tags**.

26. Add as many tags as you want to the SQL managed instance. At the very least, add a tag that indicates you are the person who created the SQL managed instance, and what role the resource plays (dev, test, production, etc.). Then select **Next : Review + create**.

27. Review your settings and the cost.

28. Select the **Download a template for automation** link at the bottom of the tab to see how your current selections will look in ARM JSON.

   ➤ For more on deploying via ARM templates programmatically, see the next section.

29. Select **Create** to deploy, and monitor the progress in Azure portal Notifications.

Inside OUT

Why is this taking so long?

Creating a SQL managed instance may take a full business day, though the provisioning process has improved recently. The first managed instance will take the longest; subsequent instances in the same pool are quicker. The VNet setup is usually what takes the most time.

Don't cancel the provisioning operation. Regardless of how long the process takes, it is best to let it fail on its own (if it is going to fail), because it will make the subsequent steps simpler.

If provisioning takes longer than 36 hours, it is likely because the process failed and is rolling back. Allowing the process to roll back will save you many hours of fixing, troubleshooting, and determining how to get back to a clean start.

Use PowerShell to provision a SQL managed instance

Creating a SQL managed instance using PowerShell and the Azure Resource Manager (ARM) template requires an existing valid VNet and subnet where you can deploy your SQL managed instance. It is beneficial to use PowerShell or ARM JSON templates if you are deploying more than one SQL managed instance, but it's only recommended once you have some experience with it.

> **NOTE**
>
> If you plan to deploy a lot of Azure resources programmatically, consider diving into Bicep, a relatively new declarative language that builds on ARM templates. (Bicep? ARM? Get it?) Bicep files are more concise and easier to read than ARM JSON. For more information, see *https://learn.microsoft.com/azure/azure-resource-manager/bicep/overview*.

It can take a long time for the provisioning process to complete—and for you to find out if you have missed a step or made a mistake. At minimum, it is highly recommended that you complete at least one SQL managed instance deployment in a test environment before attempting this in production to ensure you understand all the steps and pieces needed for the deployment.

VNet and subnet creation

Networking—specifically the VNet and subnet configuration—is the most likely configuration component to cause a SQL managed instance provision failure. To remedy this, Azure SQL Managed Instance has transitioned from manual to service-aided subnet configuration. This means subnet configuration is now automated and SQL Managed Instance can control the management traffic while data traffic (TDS) is still under your control.

It is still possible to create your own subnet inside the VNet. If you choose to do this, use a dedicated subnet. This subnet:

- Cannot have any other cloud services associated with it

- Cannot be a gateway subnet

- Cannot contain any resource other than the SQL managed instance

- Must be delegated to the Microsoft.SQL/managedInstance resource provider

> ➤ **For additional details about VNets, see** *https://learn.microsoft.com/azure/azure-sql/managed-instance/virtual-network-subnet-create-arm-template*.

Delegating a subnet to an Azure service allows that service to establish basic network configuration rules for that subnet. It provides the customer with full control over managing the integration of the Azure service into its VNet.

An NSG must be associated with the SQL managed instance's subnet. You can use an NSG to control access to the SQL managed instance's data endpoint by filtering traffic on port 1433, and

CHAPTER 18

ports 11000–11999 when Azure SQL Managed Instance is configured for redirect connections. Services automatically add the rules required to allow uninterrupted flow of management traffic.

A route table is associated with the SQL managed instance's subnet and is automatically created. You can add entries to the route table to route traffic that has on-premises private IP ranges as a destination through the VNet gateway or network virtual appliance (NVA). The November 2022 feature wave further simplified this once-manual task, reducing the number of mandatory routes from 13 to 5.

> ➤ **For more about the route table, see** *https://learn.microsoft.com/azure/azure-sql/managed -instance/connectivity-architecture-overview# #network-requirements.*

Service endpoints can be used to configure VNet rules and storage accounts that keep backups and audit logs.

Pre-creating the VNet requires you to properly size the subnet for the SQL managed instance because it cannot be resized after you put resources inside it. However, you can move your SQL managed instance to a different subnet after provisioning.

> ➤ **For more information, see** *https://learn.microsoft.com/azure/azure-sql/managed-instance /vnet-subnet-move-instance.*

Once the VNet is installed, you can complete the provisioning using the Azure CLI locally. (Using the cloud shell is discouraged, as this process can be quite lengthy.)

> ➤ **The step-by-step guide is available at** *https://learn.microsoft.com/azure/azure-sql/managed -instance/scripts/create-configure-managed-instance-cli.*

Once you have the prerequisites and networking set up, you can create a SQL managed instance either with PowerShell or an ARM template.

> ➤ **For PowerShell, see** *https://learn.microsoft.com/azure/azure-sql/managed-instance/scripts /create-configure-managed-instance-powershell.*

> ➤ **To create the SQL managed instance using ARM templates, visit** *https://learn.microsoft.com /azure/azure-sql/managed-instance/create-template-quickstart.*

> ➤ **Both Bicep and ARM JSON templates are available at** *https://learn.microsoft.com/azure /templates/microsoft.sql/managedinstances.*

Delete a SQL managed instance

Just as provisioning a SQL managed instance is a lengthy and complicated process, with many objects created in the background, deleting a managed instance can take hours to properly remove the objects.

In the REST API, deleting a SQL managed instance is a single command:

```
DELETE https://management.azure.com/subscriptions/{subscriptionId}/resourceGroups
/{resourceGroupName}/providers/Microsoft.Sql/managedInstances/
{managedInstanceName}?api-version=2015-05-01-preview.
```

The API call is DELETE, followed by a space, and then the URL (as shown), with all the items in the curly braces resolved with the names of your SQL managed instance's items.

This is relatively simple when the SQL managed instance is working correctly. Issues arise when a SQL managed instance is not correctly created and you want to start over. To avoid issues with deleting the instance, do not cancel a deployment in progress. Complex challenges arise when deployments are only partially complete, and they are far more difficult to fix after the fact.

If the preceding API call does not resolve your issue, review your networking settings. Check the "Network requirements for SQL managed instances" section later in this chapter to confirm you have the requirements set up correctly. Then try again. Do not try to delete a subnet before the SQL managed instance has been deleted.

Establish a connection to a SQL managed instance

After you have created your SQL managed instance, consider how you will connect to it. The most secure and common way to connect to a SQL managed instance is via a subnet, whether that is a gateway subnet for your on-premises solutions, a Web App front-end subnet, or an IaaS apps sub-net. Figure 18-1 provides an overview of the more common communication architectures.

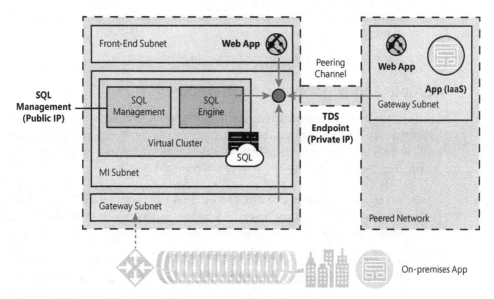

Figure 18-1 Azure SQL Managed Instance connections diagram.

Create the endpoints via the Azure portal

The recommended way to create the public and private endpoints shown in Figure 18-1 is to do so during the creation of the SQL managed instance itself. It was briefly mentioned earlier in the section "Use the Azure portal to provision a SQL managed instance" that you can define your public and private endpoints in the **Connection Type** section of the **Networking** tab of the Create Azure SQL Managed Instance wizard.

As discussed, Proxy mode is the default. This mode is simpler from a networking standpoint because you only need port 1433 for private network connections or port 3342 for public network connections. However, it is recommended that you instead use Redirect mode and configure your firewall accordingly. Redirect mode enables direct connectivity to the SQL managed instance, without an Azure proxy gateway component, resulting in reduced latency and improved throughput. You must configure firewalls in your infrastructure and network NSGs in your Azure resources to allow port 1433 and ports 11000–11999.

Redirect mode is ideal for peer-to-peer networking and for use with other Azure services. Enabling a public endpoint gives you the ability to connect to your managed instance from the Internet without using a VPN; it uses TDS only.

> ➤ If you did not choose these when you provisioned your SQL managed instance, you can still do so manually following the directions at *https://learn.microsoft.com/azure/azure-sql /managed-instance/public-endpoint-configure.*

NOTE

Connections via the public endpoint have the word *public* in the connection string. For example:

```
instance_name.public.host_name.database.windows.net
```

Create a VPN gateway via PowerShell

Native VNet implementation and connectivity to your on-premises environment will need a VPN gateway. An Azure ExpressRoute virtual private cloud connection between your infrastructure and Azure is recommended. Other VPN connections from your infrastructure to Azure are supported, such as Azure site-to-site VPN and point-to-site VPN.

> ➤ To configure a point-to-site VPN, Microsoft has provided a handy PowerShell script: *https:// learn.microsoft.com/azure/azure-sql/managed-instance/point-to-site-p2s-configure#attach -a-vpn-gateway-to-your-managed-instance-virtual-network.*

Creating a VPN gateway to the SQL managed instance VNet is best done from your client machine. Install PowerShell 7.1.3 and Azure PowerShell 1.4.0 or newer on your on-premises client.

➤ Instructions for how to install the Azure PowerShell module can be found at *https://learn .microsoft.com/powershell/azure/install-az-ps#install-the-azure-powershell-module.*

Install or update your local Az PowerShell module with the following commands:

```
Install-Module -Name Az
Update-Module -Name Az
```

To create the VPN gateway, you need the subscription ID, the resource group, and the name of the VNet name you used to create your managed instance. You will also need to create a certificate name prefix of your choosing. These items are used in the following PowerShell script:

```
$scriptUrlBase = 'https://github.com/microsoft/sql-server-samples/tree/master/samples/
manage/azure-sql-db-managed-instance/attach-vpn-gateway'
$parameters = @{
  subscriptionId = '<subscriptionId>'
  resourceGroupName = '<resourceGroupName>'
  virtualNetworkName = '<virtualNetworkName>'
  certificateNamePrefix = '<certificateNamePrefix>'
  }
Invoke-Command -ScriptBlock ([Scriptblock]::Create((iwr ($scriptUrlBase+
'/attachVPNGateway.ps1?t='+ [DateTime]::Now.Ticks)).Content)) -ArgumentList
$parameters, $scriptUrlBase
```

The deployment initiated by the preceding script could take up to an hour to complete.

This code creates and installs the required certificates on the client machine. It then calculates the IP subnet range needed for the gateway and then creates the gateway. Finally, it deploys the ARM template that attaches the VPN gateway to the VPN subnet.

➤ Steps to create a point-to-site VPN connection to your SQL managed instance from an on-premises server, requiring both PowerShell and the Azure portal, are available at *https:// learn.microsoft.com/azure/azure-sql/managed-instance/point-to-site-p2s-configure#create -a-vpn-connection-to-your-managed-instance.*

After you have completed the VPN connection and your TDS endpoints are ready to use, there are three main ways to connect.

- Connect from an on-premises computer.

- Connect from a VM.

- Connect applications from any location.

Connect from an on-premises computer

A connection from an on-premises computer is sometimes called a *point-to-site connection*. To connect using SSMS (the most recent version), start by creating a connection to the VPN from your on-premises machine. On Windows 10 or later, or Windows Server 2016 or later, from the **Network and Internet** option, go to **VPN**, then choose your managed instance VNet to select the connection. If prompted for an elevated privilege, choose to elevate and continue to make the connection. When connecting using SSMS, remember to enter the fully qualified host name of the SQL managed instance in the **Server Name** box.

Connect from a virtual machine

When connecting to a SQL managed instance from a VM, the process is different if your VM is an Azure VM or an on-premises VM.

Azure VM connections

For an Azure VM, the connection is over a private IP to TDS using a VM in a subnet separate from the one created for the SQL managed instance. The VNet employed to create the SQL managed instance cannot be used because it is dedicated to the SQL managed instance.

To connect to the VM, you can use a Remote Desktop connection or Azure Bastion, a more secure type of remote desktop connection from within the browser. Azure Bastion does not require opening up the same RDP/SSH ports to the public Internet.

➤ To create and connect to a SQL managed instance from an Azure VM, refer to *https://learn .microsoft.com/azure/azure-sql/managed-instance/connect-vm-instance-configure*. For more information on RDP via Azure Bastion, visit *https://learn.microsoft.com/azure/bastion /bastion-connect-vm-rdp-windows*.

VM from on-premises

For a VM on-premises, the connection method is a bit different because you need to attach a VPN gateway to the managed instance. This is easily done with the script in the previous section, "Create a VPN gateway via PowerShell." This script creates and installs the certificates on the client machine, calculates the VPN gateway subnet range, creates the subnet for the gateway, and deploys the ARM template that attaches the VPN gateway to the VPN subnet that you need for access.

➤ You can also find the instructions at *https://learn.microsoft.com/azure/azure-sql/managed -instance/point-to-site-p2s-configure#attach-a-vpn-gateway-to-your-managed-instance -virtual-network*.

Connect to applications

Applications can connect to SQL managed instances regardless of where they are hosted: in the cloud, on-premises, or a hybrid option. With Azure SQL Managed Instance, you can choose what is best for your application. There are many options to choose from to connect.

Applications in the cloud

Consider the following for a cloud-hosted application:

- An application inside the same VNet is the simplest, because even if they exist in separate subnets, they can connect with the correct connection string.

- An application inside a different VNet is useful if you have VNets in different subscriptions because this method works for that scenario. You have two options with this approach:

  - **Azure Virtual network peering.** This is the preferable method because it uses the Azure backbone network, so there are no latency issues between the peered VNets. With this method, the VNets have to be in the same region.

  - **VNet-to-VNet, using a VPN gateway.** If Azure Virtual network peering is not an option, use a VPN gateway.

Applications on-premises

Consider the following for hybrid infrastructure with application on-premises and the database platform in Azure SQL Managed Instance:

- An on-premises application can connect through a private IP using either a site-to-site VPN connection or Azure ExpressRoute. Azure ExpressRoute is a service that lets you create a private connection to your on-premises location and is recommended over VPN connections. ExpressRoute avoids moving data over the public Internet.

➤ For more information on Azure ExpressRoute, visit *https://learn.microsoft.com/azure /expressroute/expressroute-introduction.*

- An application on a developer's machine is the same as the point-to-site connection covered earlier in the "Create a VPN gateway via PowerShell" and "Connect from an on-premises computer" sections.

- On-premises with VNet peering can work when the VPN gateway is installed in a separate VNet and subscription from the SQL managed instance where the networks are peered.

➤ This should be used only in special cases, details for which can be found at *https://learn .microsoft.com/azure/azure-sql/managed-instance/connect-application-instance#connect -from-on-premises-with-vnet-peering.*

- An Azure App Service–hosted application is accessed using a private IP. If using your App Service requires a gateway, that gateway subnet must be created outside the SQL managed instance VNet. This is different from the classic setup for on-premises gateways. In this situation, the gateway must go through the peering channel.

➤ Review the most suitable networking and connections options for your organization at *https://learn.microsoft.com/azure/azure-sql/managed-instance/connect-application -instance*.

Network requirements for SQL managed instances

The dedicated subnet is important enough to mention separately in this section, as it is a subject that commonly causes issues—especially if you are provisioning the Azure SQL managed instance outside of the Azure portal.

CAUTION

Subnets can take a long time to create or configure. It is common for this process to take 24 hours or more if an issue arises, as it needs to roll back the process before you are notified. To prevent issues when creating managed instances, do not cancel a creation. Let the creation fail on its own if there is an issue.

The most common challenges with a managed instance have to do with networking. You can prevent many of these issues by meeting the requirements laid out in this section *before* you begin provisioning any instances.

Subnet

Managed instances need a dedicated subnet that is not a gateway subnet. The subnet can only house managed instances. The subnet cannot be shared with other resources.

NOTE

A SQL managed instance must be inside a subnet that is dedicated to that SQL managed instance.

Network security group

The NSG associated with the SQL managed instance must define the inbound and outbound security rules before any other rules. If you are doing transactional replication in your managed instance and have a publisher or distributor, you will need to open port 445 (outbound) to allow access to the Azure file share.

CAUTION

There should be only one *inbound* rule for ports 9000, 9003, 1438, 1440, 1452, and one *outbound* rule for ports 80, 443, and 12000. These are TCP management endpoint ports. SQL managed instance provisioned through Azure Resource Manager (ARM) deployments will fail if inbound and outbound rules are configured separately for each port. If these ports are in separate rules, the deployment will fail with a VnetSubnetConflict WithIntendedPolicy **error.**

User-defined route table

A user-defined or static route table associated with the VNet must include specific entries. These can be found at *https://learn.microsoft.com/azure/azure-sql/managed-instance/connectivity -architecture-overview#mandatory-user-defined-routes-with-service-aided-subnet-configuration*.

Service endpoints

By default, SQL managed instances do not have service endpoints, and we recommend you disable this option when you create the VNet. Service endpoints allow trusted traffic through the Azure backbone network and allow the Azure service to recognize the traffic.

A feature to allow service endpoint policies has been introduced to improve data egress protection to Azure Storage. This allows granular control over which storage accounts can be accessed and closes a potential data egress door from bad actors inside.

Service endpoint policies are free and may be valuable tools for administrators looking to expose Azure Storage access for BULK INSERT, or storage accounts for transactional replication synchronization or the Azure Database Migration Service. This feature was introduced in preview in November 2021.

> ➤ For more information, visit *https://techcommunity.microsoft.com/t5/azure-sql-blog/harden -your-azure-sql-managed-instance-workloads-against-data/ba-p/2893145*.

IP addresses

SQL managed instances require 16 IP addresses, and a minimum (that does not allow for scale out) of 32 are recommended. Since a SQL managed instance VNet can use up to 256 IP addresses, the number of SQL managed instances that can be deployed in a single subnet depends on the subnet range. A subnet with the prefix /27 or below is recommended.

Inside OUT

Why do SQL managed instances need so many IP addresses?

When a SQL managed instance is created, several virtual resources and networking devices are created in addition to your primary instance. How many depends on the tier you choose. They are used to ensure HA during regular operations as well as service maintenance. This is all done behind the scenes for you and is mostly invisible to you but for the IP addresses they require.

Migrate data to Azure SQL Managed Instance

Azure SQL Managed Instance targets the migration scenario from IaaS or from on-premises. In both cases, you will want to bulk move your data. There are four options for you to choose from:

- Link feature for Azure SQL Managed Instance

- Azure Data Migration Service

- Backup and restore

- Managed instance pools

Each has their own benefits, as outlined in this section.

Link feature for Azure SQL Managed Instance

The new link feature for Azure SQL Managed Instance, introduced in preview with SQL Server 2022, provides the fastest migration to Azure SQL Managed Instance with the least downtime. It is the recommended approach for migrating SQL Server 2022 workloads to Azure SQL Managed Instance.

It allows for near–real time replication via a distributed availability group and can facilitate migration without downtime as well as failover and failback to SQL Server 2022.

Because the link feature uses the underlying technology of distributed availability groups (without requiring the source SQL Server to be in an AG), the initial seeding occurs without downtime or interruption during normal database activity. Just as an AG would be, the initial seeding is limited only by the bandwidth of the connection to Azure.

Previously, Azure SQL Managed Instance ran at a special version level higher than any public SQL Server release, which meant restoring down was impossible and migration to a managed instance was a one-way ticket. Migrations to Azure SQL Managed Instance are no longer one-way, and can be migrated back to SQL Server 2022 if necessary by performing a failover.

The link feature for Azure SQL Managed Instance is a faster migration path to Azure SQL Managed Instance than the Log Replay Service (LRS) offered by Azure Database Migration Service (DMS), discussed next. Migration via LRS is actually still a preview feature, while the link feature is receiving active attention and development from Microsoft engineers.

The link feature for Azure SQL Managed Instance is for one SQL Server database at a time. However, multiple links can be created to a single SQL managed instance. This may allow you to design a cloud-based consolidated infrastructure, or, to migrate multiple SQL Server databases to a single SQL managed instance.

In general, the link feature provides much faster replication than log shipping, with no downtime.

➤ For more information on the link feature for Azure SQL Managed Instance, see Chapter 11.

Azure Data Migration Service

The Azure Database Migration Service (DMS) is a managed service designed to enable migrations to Azure SQL platforms with minimal downtime. You can use DMS for migrations to Azure SQL Managed Instance as well as a variety of other migration sources and destinations—even migrations from AWS RDS and Oracle to Azure SQL platforms.

There are online and offline migrations, depending on your organization's tolerance for downtime. It is recommended you do a trial run with the offline migration to determine what your downtime will be before you decide which method to use. Using DMS for online migrations requires the Premium pricing tier.

Whether you use online or offline migration, create your Azure Database Migration Service in the same region as your target SQL managed instance. This prevents errors, cuts down on the downtime and migration time, and limits any movement of data across regions or geographies.

➤ There are several prerequisites that you should review before you begin. They can be found at *https://learn.microsoft.com/azure/dms/tutorial-sql-server-managed-instance-online #prerequisites*.

➤ Chapter 19, "Migrate to SQL Server solutions in Azure" has a section on Data Migration Service.

NOTE

For online migrations using Azure Database Migration Service, do not append multiple backups into a single backup media. Ensure instead that each backup is a separate backup file. You will need both a backup and a subsequent log backup on the share that is used.

Migrate with backup and restore

The backup and restore migration method leverages the simplicity of moving SQL backups to Azure Blob Storage, or backing up directly to it. Backups in Azure Blob Storage can be directly restored into a SQL managed instance using the traditional Transact-SQL (T-SQL) RESTORE command. It's recommended and cheaper to use block storage, not page storage, for SQL Server backup files.

The backup file in Azure Blob Storage must be secured with a shared access signature (SAS) key, and the credential using the SAS token must be created with CREATE CREDENTIAL. (It is possible, but not recommended, to use page blobs and a storage access key if desired.) Chapter 10, "Develop, deploy, and manage data recovery," details how to do this.

CHAPTER 18

You can begin the migration by restoring your database with the standard T-SQL RESTORE syntax. Consider backing up to multiple files for faster backup and restore performance, with a limit of 64 backup files.

> ➤ For a complete walkthrough with T-SQL, see *https://learn.microsoft.com/sql/relational-databases/backup-restore/sql-server-backup-to-url#Examples.*

Restores to SQL managed instance are asynchronous. Should the connection to your SQL managed instance be lost, the RESTORE continues. You can check the status of the operation with sys.dm_operation_status. Replace 'mydb' with your database name in the following T-SQL script:

```
SELECT * FROM sys.dm_operation_status
WHERE major_resource_id = 'mydb'
ORDER BY start_time DESC;
```

The version of SQL Server you take your backup from is important. Backups starting from SQL Server 2012 with Service Pack 1 CU2 can be directly uploaded as .bak files to Azure Blob Storage with the BACKUP TO URL syntax. For versions before SQL Server 2016, you cannot use a SAS, so you need to perform the backup using the deprecated WITH CREDENTIAL syntax.

If you are restoring a database with TDE enabled using a native restore, migrate the certificate to the target SQL managed instance before you perform the restore. This is no different from how you would move your TDE certificate for a SQL Server instance.

Your backup will not be restored when you use the restore method for SQL Managed Instance if your .bak file has any features that are not supported. Backups containing databases that have active in-memory objects, for example, cannot be restored to the general purpose tier.

Inside OUT

Can you use backup and restore to get the settings from the system databases?

System database restores are not supported with a SQL managed instance. It is recommended that you script out the system databases and run them on the destination instance independently of your backup and restore processes if needed.

Managed instance pools

You can create pools of SQL managed instances, allowing you to migrate multiple smaller instances for the price of a single larger instance. Similar to Azure SQL Database elastic pools, you can host multiple SQL managed instances that share the total vCore allocation.

Azure SQL Managed Instance pools allow SQL managed instances to reserve as few as two vCores. For example, you could host eight lightweight 2-vCore instances inside a single general purpose 16-vCore managed instance pool, within the same VNet. The 2-vCore instances are not available as standalone managed instances. For simplified networking, you can deploy multiple managed instance pools and multiple non-pooled managed instances in the same VNet subnet.

This feature is currently in preview and only available for the general purpose tier. Additionally, it is currently only possible via PowerShell cmdlets, not the Azure portal.

➤ For more information, visit *https://learn.microsoft.com/azure/azure-sql/managed-instance /instance-pools-overview*.

Azure SQL Managed Instance administration features

It is the Azure SQL Managed Instance services that enable a DBA to spend less time on administrative tasks that make a SQL managed instance such an attractive option. The following services are either simplified for the administrator or handled completely, saving time and the need for the expertise.

High availability

Azure SQL Managed Instance offers 99.99 percent uptime without concern for maintenance and upgrade outages. To ensure high availability (HA), Azure SQL Managed Instance employs two models and price options based on your tolerance for degradation during maintenance. We'll break down the HA features of each service tier.

General purpose

The general purpose service tier leverages the separation of compute and storage. This tier contains two layers:

- **Stateless compute.** This layer runs the Database Engine process and contains the cached data on SSD for things like tempdb, plan cache, and the buffer pool. This is operated by the Azure Service Fabric, controls the health of the node, and performs any failovers.

- **Stateful.** This layer contains the database files stored in Azure Blob Storage with built-in redundancy.

When a failure or upgrade occurs, the Azure Service Fabric moves the stateless process to a different node. The Blob Storage in the stateful layer is not affected. The data and log files are attached to the newly initialized SQL Server. This tier can experience degradation as this transition occurs and the instance starts with an initialized cache. As mentioned, Azure SQL Managed Instance

CHAPTER 18

does not use instant file initialization, so it is important to understand all aspects that can affect degradation.

Business critical

The business critical service tier uses a quorum of engine nodes to guarantee minimal impact during maintenance. This tier integrates the Database Engine and the storage layer into a single node, and uses replication to additional nodes to create a three-node or four-node cluster. The database files are on SSD storage to improve I/O, and HA is achieved by using technology similar to the AGs seen on-premises.

Instead of an underlying Windows Server Failover Cluster (WSFC), the Azure Service Fabric manages the cluster and node health detection. To avoid dreaded "split-brain" scenarios, Azure maintains special witness nodes called *seed nodes* that determine quorum within a ring of cluster objects. This complex global cluster management is mostly invisible to you and completely configured for you.

The cluster includes a single primary replica and as many as three secondary replicas. To ensure durability, the primary replica writes each transaction to at least one secondary replica before committing the transaction. This durability guarantees there is always a node to fail over to, in case of a crash on the primary replica. Should a crash occur, the failover is initiated by the Azure Service Fabric. When a new primary is created, an additional replica is also created to ensure quorum, and the connections are redirected to the new primary.

Forced versus unforced failovers

Similar to forced versus unforced failovers in a SQL Server AG, unforced failovers occur regularly during maintenance processes.

Forced failovers are user initiated, but don't necessarily mean there is data loss. A forced failover might occur because of a service tier change, such as changing the SKU or count of vCores. Manual failovers to a replica in a failover group are also forced failovers.

Regardless of whether a failover is forced or unforced, the SLA is honored.

Inside OUT

How do you see the last time your SQL managed instance failed over?

Even though you and your applications may not have noticed, you can see the last manual or Azure-initiated failover time by looking at the `sqlserver_start_time` column from the `sys.dm_os_sys_info` DMV. The time zone is the local system date in the replica where the instance started.

Retry logic for transient connectivity issues

All applications connecting to cloud-hosted services should gracefully handle transient connectivity issues with automatic retry logic. This is not novel to Azure SQL platforms. Retry logic in your apps—even for on-premises solutions—should be in place for automatic retrying of sessions that are the victims of deadlocks, for example.

Retry logic is code that can retry a call when a transient connectivity fault occurs. A transient fault can occur, for example, when Azure dynamically reconfigures servers for a heavy workload and causes clients to lose their connection. It is recommended that the client program has retry logic so it can reestablish the connection after increasingly escalating, randomized delay intervals. This exponential backoff logic ensures the database does not get overwhelmed in a retry situation with many connections trying to reconnect all at once, spreading out the reconnections so that applications don't essentially launch a distributed denial-of-service (DDoS) attack on their own database platform! Exponential delays with a randomized delay buffer are common guidance for any application connecting to any cloud asset.

> **NOTE**
>
> **Exponential backoff is included as a feature in the Microsoft.Data.SqlClient .NET library.**

➤ **For a list of common transient error codes for Azure SQL, visit** *https://learn.microsoft.com /azure/azure-sql/database/troubleshoot-common-errors-issues#list-of-transient-fault -error-codes.*

Replication

Azure SQL Managed Instance can use transactional replication to replicate data to another SQL managed instance database, a single SQL Server database, or a pooled database in an Azure SQL Database elastic pool. A SQL managed instance can host a publisher, distributor, and subscriber database, just like SQL Server.

➤ **Common configurations can be found at** *https://learn.microsoft.com/azure/azure-sql /managed-instance/replication-transactional-overview#common-configurations.*

For the SQL managed instance to be a publisher and/or distributor, there are a few requirements.

- The instance cannot participate in geo-replication.

- The publisher, distributor, and subscriber must all be on the same VNet or have VNet peering set up between all three networks.

- The authentication used between all parties must be SQL Authentication and the replication working directory must be an Azure Storage Account share, set up using TCP outbound port 445 in the security rules of the NSG.

- Bidirectional and one-way replication are both supported; however, updatable subscriptions are not.

Scale up or down

SQL manage instances use vCores that allow you to define the CPU cores and configure the storage capacity you need for your instance within each tier. All databases in the SQL managed instance share these resources. The storage and CPU can be scaled up or down as needed within the limits of the service tier; however, changing these resources does cause downtime.

Different service tiers have different limitations. For example, if you downgrade from business critical to general purpose, the backup retention period is different. If a database exceeds the threshold database size, then extra storage costs will apply. If you are upgrading to a higher tier, you must explicitly increase the size.

Monitor SQL managed instances

In general, monitoring and tuning a SQL managed instance can involve many of the same tools as a SQL Server instance, as detailed in other places in this book. This section talks about some monitoring topics specific to Azure SQL Managed Instance.

sys.server_resource_stats

Many of the same DMVs mentioned elsewhere work the same on a SQL managed instance. One DMV was created specifically for SQL managed instances: `sys.server_resource_stats`. It provides 14 days of past telemetry, including CPU and storage utilization, and is sampled every 15 seconds. CPU is expressed as a percentage of the utilization of the vCores currently allocated to the instance. This DMV is roughly the equivalent to `sys.resource_stats`, a DMV specifically created to provide utilization telemetry for Azure SQL Database only.

Azure Monitor

Integrated into the Azure portal are metrics, alerts, and diagnostic logs (formerly called *resource logs*) for many different Azure resources—Azure SQL Managed Instance included.

In the Azure portal screen for a SQL managed instance, you can use the **Metrics** page, under **Monitoring**, to query a variety of live and historical utilization statistics. The **Alerts** page provides for the configuration of alert rules to send notifications to action groups, such as the email address of a distribution group of Azure administrators. Alerts in recent years were overhauled and provide much more customizability; older alerts are now called *classic*. You could, for example, configure an alert to be emailed out when CPU utilization for the SQL managed instance averages above 90 percent.

Diagnostic Logs is the Azure standard name for a variety of metrics collected that aren't sent anywhere by default. Creating diagnostic settings for an Azure resource, including a SQL managed instance, defines a data pipeline between emitted, streamed data logs such as resource usage statistics or SQL security audit events, and an endpoint. The endpoints include a Log Analytics workspace (ideal for consuming and analyzing streamed data), Azure Storage, an Azure Event Hub, or third-party partner solutions. Sending this diagnostic settings data to Log Analytics is the recommended and most straightforward solution.

You can then review the output of the diagnostic settings data in Azure portal, on the **Logs** page under **Monitoring**. The Azure Monitor Log Analytics browser uses a browser-based Kusto Query Language (KQL) querying tool with graphical output.

Azure SQL Analytics

Azure SQL Managed Instance is among the services that access Azure SQL Analytics. Azure SQL Analytics is a monitoring tool for performance that is in long-term public preview and is not actively developed by Microsoft at this time. Azure SQL Analytics collects and visualizes performance metrics and has built-in intelligence for troubleshooting. The metrics help you customize monitoring rules, alerts, and identify issues.

> ➤ For more information, see *https://learn.microsoft.com/azure/azure-monitor/insights/azure-sql*.

Link feature for Azure SQL Managed Instance

The new link feature for Azure SQL Managed Instance promises to synchronize SQL Servers hosted anywhere, including on-premises, to a SQL managed instance. Not specifically tied to the development life cycle of SQL Server 2022, this feature remains in preview at the time of this book's writing.

Here are a few things to keep in mind about the link feature:

- The link feature doesn't require SQL Server 2022; it can be configured for SQL Server versions going back to SQL Server 2016 (but for some reason, not SQL Server 2017 at the time of this writing).

- Some features of the SQL managed instance link require SQL Server 2022—specifically, the holy grail of hybrid HA, which is the ability to fail over *and fail back* from an on-premises or Azure VM–hosted SQL Server to a managed instance.

- The link feature provides a path for a seamless, no-downtime migration from an on-premises SQL Server to Azure SQL Managed Instance. This is faster and more useful than Log Replay Service via DMS.

- The link feature promises fast asynchronous replication so it can provide a cloud-based, read-only replica for reporting and further integration, including with Azure Synapse Analytics, Power BI, and more.

- The link feature for Azure SQL Managed Instance is supported in SQL Server 2022 Standard and Enterprise editions.

- The link feature for Azure SQL Managed Instance is for one SQL Server database at a time. However, you can create multiple links to a single SQL managed instance, consolidating workloads from different SQL Servers.

- There is no built-in listener or other application redirection technology specifically created for the link feature at the time of this writing. There are two options:

  - You can create a CNAME in your DNS and point applications to the CNAME. Then, at the time of failover, change the CNAME and wait for DNS TTL to expire.

  - If you have an existing AG with a listener, you can use that listener for failovers via the link feature for Azure SQL Managed Instance. You would essentially add the listener, not an individual SQL Server instance, to the link feature. After a failover, the listener would redirect read/write traffic to the SQL managed instance automatically.

NOTE

Keep in mind this book was written with the link feature for Azure SQL Managed Instance in preview. A more sophisticated hybrid listener alternative may be introduced in the future.

➤ **For more information on the public preview of this feature, visit the announcement blog at** *https://aka.ms/mi-link-preview*, **or visit Microsoft Docs at** *https://aka.ms/mi-link*.

➤ **The link feature for Azure SQL Managed Instance is discussed further in Chapter 11.**

Azure SQL Managed Instance security features

Security for Azure SQL Managed Instance is provided by several different features, including Azure AD, multifactor authentication, and authorization.

Azure Active Directory

Azure AD enables Microsoft services to integrate with centrally managed identities and permissions to enhance security. Combined with multifactor authentication (MFA), Azure AD increases data security while still supporting single sign-on (SSO).

> For details on how to set up MFA, visit *https://learn.microsoft.com/azure/sql-database/sql-database-ssms-mfa-authentication-configure*.

If you are using a hybrid option, or you need to connect to legacy or on-premises applications, you can also use Azure AD with an on-premises Active Directory Domain Service (AD DS) that is federated with the Azure AD. This centralized authentication:

- Provides an alternative to native SQL Server Authentication.

- Discourages the creation of multiple user identities across database servers.

- Allows centralized and simple password changes.

- Allows for external (Azure AD) groups.

- Enables integrated Windows Authentication and other forms of authentication supported by Azure AD.

In addition, Azure AD:

- Uses contained database users to authenticate identities at the database level.

- Supports token-based authentication for applications connecting to Azure SQL Managed Instance.

- Supports ADFS (domain federation) or native user/password authentication for a local Azure AD without domain synchronization.

- Supports MFA when using SSMS.

- Supports Active Directory Interactive Authentication when using SQL Server Data Tools (SSDT). Active Directory Integrated Authentication connects to the SQL managed instance by using identities. This is similar to the connection from a federated domain.

Access control using Azure AD

Azure AD is slightly different for SQL managed instances compared to dedicated SQL pools in Azure Synapse or Azure SQL Database.

The Azure AD must be associated with the same subscription as the SQL managed instance. (A directory can be associated with multiple subscriptions.) Once you have provisioned an Azure AD admin for your SQL managed instance, you can create Azure AD server logins.

> Detailed steps to complete this can be found at *https://learn.microsoft.com/azure/sql-database/sql-database-aad-authentication-configure#provision-azure-ad-admin-sql-managed-instance*.

You can create logins and users in Azure SQL Managed Instance based on Azure AD users (managed, federated, and guest), Azure AD groups (managed and federated), and Azure AD applications via service principals.

Modern interactive flow

A recommended step is to enable the *modern interactive flow*, a trust-based improvement to authentication for the latest operating systems (Windows 10 20H1, Windows Server 2022, or higher) and either Azure AD or hybrid Azure AD.

At the time of this writing, this modern authentication alternative using Azure AD and Kerberos is in preview. It is compatible with other organizational settings to enforce MFA for tools like SSMS and web applications when they authenticate to Azure SQL Managed Instance.

The modern interactive flow is a newer alternative to the *trust-based authentication flow*, which is used for AD-joined clients running at least Windows 10 or Windows Server 2012. Determining which is right for you involves assessing all the clients and applications connecting to your managed instance. To start, ask yourself, do all administrators, app developers, and business intelligence developers have a supported OS? If so, consider enabling the modern interactive flow when it is out of preview.

➤ For more information, visit *https://learn.microsoft.com/azure/azure-sql/managed-instance /winauth-azuread-setup.*

Set up Azure Active Directory

Azure SQL Managed Instance is most often used to replace a traditional SQL Server installation, so it is natural that it supports the traditional SQL-authenticated logins and integration with Azure AD.

Azure AD server principals are the Azure version of on-premises database logins in your SQL Server. These let you specify users and groups from your Azure AD tenant (think AD groups on-premises).

Inside OUT

How do you know which logins in your managed instance are Azure AD users?

Azure AD logins are signified with a value of EXTERNAL_LOGIN or EXTERNAL_GROUP in the type_desc column of sys.server_principals, with the type column set to E for login or X for groups.

To create the login for these specific server-level principals in conjunction with the Azure AD, use the CREATE LOGIN syntax with the FROM EXTERNAL PROVIDER option. When FROM

EXTERNAL PROVIDER is specified, the login name must represent an existing Azure AD account that is accessible in Azure AD by the current SQL managed instance.

Azure AD-authenticated logins can be created for:

- Azure AD cloud-only identities

- SSO Azure AD hybrid identities with password authentication or pass-through authentication

- Federated authentication

➤ For more information, see *https://learn.microsoft.com/azure/azure-sql/database /authentication-aad-configure.*

Enable Windows Authentication via Kerberos for Azure AD

You can add a service principal to a SQL managed instance to enable authentication of Windows Authenticated logins via Kerberos. This allows an even smoother lift-and-shift migration to Azure for existing applications that have significant investment in Windows Authenticated principals for authentication.

This feature was announced in August 2022 and is currently in preview at the time of this book's writing. The SQL managed instance service principal allows for Windows Authentication on SQL managed instances for devices or VMs joined to Active Directory, Azure AD, or hybrid Azure AD.

➤ For more information on this developing feature, visit *https://learn.microsoft.com/azure /azure-sql/managed-instance/winauth-azuread-overview.*

Azure SQL Managed Instance data protection features

Managed instances secure your data by providing built-in security features to make administering it easier. This section discusses some of the features you should be familiar with.

➤ Many of these security and data protection features are discussed in more detail in Chapter 13.

Prevent data exfiltration

A variety of strategies and technologies are needed to ensure that data is not exfiltrated from your enterprise, even by inside actors. Some regulations and audit compliance might require you to report on various strategies. In August 2022, the Azure SQL Managed Instance program group published a lengthy blog post on a variety of permissions and restrictions to consider inside and outside of the database engine, located here: *https://techcommunity.microsoft.com /t5/azure-sql-blog/prevent-data-exfiltration-in-azure-sql-managed-instance/ba-p/3590381.*

CHAPTER 18

One aspect of this is the ability to configure custom service policies, a feature in preview at the time of this book's writing.

Isolation

Security isolation is achieved in Azure SQL Managed Instance with VNet implementations and using VPNs or ExpressRoute to connect to your on-premises machines. The only endpoints exposed are through private IP addresses. The underlying infrastructure is always dedicated, ensuring a single-tenant infrastructure completes the trifecta of isolation security.

Auditing

Azure SQL Managed Instance tracks events in the audit log file of the Azure Storage account. The audit file is used to maintain regulatory compliance, gain insight into discrepancies, and uncover suspected security violations using threat detection. Threat detection is built-in and used to expose unusual attempts to access databases. There are alerts regarding suspicious activities, potential vulnerabilities, SQL injection attacks, and anomalous database access patterns. These alerts, which you can view from the Azure Security Center, provide details of suspicious activity, offering recommendations on how to resolve the issues.

Data encryption

Azure SQL Managed Instance has a similar suite of data protection features as SQL Server. For example:

- Data encryption in motion is provided using TLS.

- Always Encrypted is offered to protect data in flight, at rest, and during query processing.

- As discussed, encryption of data at rest is achieved via TDE. TDE encrypts the data and log files, using real-time I/O encryption and decryption when it is accessed. Azure SQL Managed Instance supports a user-provided, or *bring your own key* (*BYOK*) TDE certificate.

  ➤ **For more information on providing your own key, see** *https://learn.microsoft.com/azure /azure-sql/database/transparent-data-encryption-byok-overview*.

When configuring the link feature for Azure SQL Managed Instance, you upload your TDE certificate from your SQL Server first, before beginning the synchronization.

Automated key rotation is a security feature to prevent keys from becoming compromised or expired. Automated key rotation is an important security feature and a big time saver. Automated key rotation for BYOK TDE certificates became generally available for Azure SQL Database and Azure SQL Managed Instance in October 2022.

➤ **Look for more information on this feature soon, and check out the preview announcement here:** *https://techcommunity.microsoft.com/t5/azure-sql-blog/automated-key-rotation-for-tde-byok-now-available-in-preview-for/ba-p/3607932*.

Row-level security

Row-level security controls access to specific rows of data in a table based on the user executing a query. Row-level security simplifies design and coding by enabling you to implement restrictions on the user and not on other factors. Combined with Azure AD, this can be a powerful security feature to tie data access to an individual's domain security groups.

Dynamic data masking

Although not encryption, dynamic data masking is a data-filtering technique used to limit exposure by masking data. This provides an added layer of protection as well as the ability to determine what roles can select sensitive data, and what roles see obfuscated, or *masked*, data. This allows the data to look different to specific users without actually changing the underlaying data.

Support for granular permissions for dynamic data masking was added to Azure SQL Managed Instance in 2021. These granular permissions were first introduced for Azure SQL Database and Azure Synapse Analytics. Dynamic data masking limits sensitive data by masking—not modifying—that data for certain database roles. These same capabilities were added in SQL Server 2022.

CHAPTER 18

Migrate to SQL Server solutions in Azure

SQL Server 2022 is the most cloud-connected SQL Server version ever. There are several new and interesting sections in this chapter to look forward to.

This chapter starts with migration options for SQL Server and for Azure infrastructure as a service (IaaS) and platform as a service (PaaS) offerings. It then investigates common migration failures when using Azure Database Migration Service (DMS). Next, it covers Azure Data Factory (ADF), and wraps up—along with the book—with best practices to achieve a successful migration to Azure.

All scripts for this book are available for download at *https://www.MicrosoftPressStore.com /SQLServer2022InsideOut/downloads*.

Migration services options

Microsoft offers several ways to help you migrate to newer versions of SQL Server or to an Azure IaaS or PaaS offering. In this chapter we hope to make it clear which will be most useful to you, and in what scenarios.

These tools have evolved over the last few years to specialize in certain use cases. Let's begin with an introduction to the Microsoft players in this realm; then we can identify the best uses for each one.

- **Microsoft Assessment and Planning (MAP) toolkit.** A starting point for many projects, the MAP toolkit is an agentless multi-product planning and assessment tool used to inventory an entire information technology infrastructure, including SQL Server, by scanning IP addresses, Active Directory (AD), and network assets. The MAP toolkit gathers information to a SQL Server database and has a lightweight reporting suite built in.

- **Total Cost of Ownership (TCO) calculator.** This Azure-provided website defines and calculates the TCO for migrations to Azure, including cost savings from Azure migrations: *https://azure.microsoft.com/pricing/tco/calculator*.

- **Database Experimentation Assistant (DEA).** This experimentation solution for SQL Server upgrades provides feedback on potential upgrade issues.

- **Azure Data Migration Assistant (DMA).** This tool helps you upgrade to a modern data platform. The DMA detects compatibility issues that could affect database functionality in a new version of SQL Server or Azure SQL Database.

- **Azure Database Migration Service (DMS).** This entirely managed service is used to perform online and offline migrations to Azure SQL platforms. A legacy, soon-to-be deprecated version is managed within the Azure portal, and a newer version is run as an extension in Azure Data Studio (ADS).

- **SQL Server Migration Assistant (SSMA).** This tool is designed to automate database migration to SQL Server from Microsoft Access, DB2, MySQL, Oracle, and SAP ASE.

- **Data Access Migration Toolkit (DAMT).** This ADS extension supports the migration of application source code from one database platform to another.

- **Azure SQL Managed Instance Link to SQL Server.** This new SQL Server 2022 and SQL Managed Instance feature can provide hybrid high availability (HA), disaster recovery (DR), and cloud-based readable secondary replicas. Because it synchronizes data and can failover to a SQL managed instance, it is also effectively an easy, no-downtime migration from SQL Server instances in your infrastructure up to Azure SQL Managed Instance. The underlying distributed availability group is configured for you.

➤ For more information, see Chapter 11, "Implement high availability and disaster recovery," and Chapter 18, "Provision Azure SQL Managed Instance."

Microsoft has a table that outlines the different uses for each of these tools and includes a few third-party options as well—ones that are outside the scope of this book. You can find them all at *https://learn.microsoft.com/azure/dms/dms-tools-matrix*.

The primary use of these tools is to support your migration journey. From the business-justification phase to implementation, let's focus on some of these tools individually to see how they can support migrations.

Microsoft Assessment Planning toolkit

The MAP toolkit is an automated, agentless, multi-product planning and assessment tool used to speed up migrations.

The purpose of this tool is to accelerate and automate the overall assessment process. It gathers details by discovering the current hardware and software environment, and it returns detailed readiness assessment reports with recommendations to support enterprises as they determine their future business needs. MAP is an extensive tool for planning the entire IT department.

From one single networked computer, MAP enables you to inventory and assess many Windows technologies and account for their licenses, assets, disk space, versions, and so on.

➤ You can download the MAP toolkit from *https://www.microsoft.com/download/details .aspx?&id=7826*.

➤ For a guided walkthrough of the MAP tool, see *https://learn.microsoft.com/training/modules /sql-server-discovery-using-map/*.

Inside OUT

How often can you run the MAP toolkit?

The free MAP toolkit can be run as often as needed. In fact, the tool is handy for not just migrations, but for other IT management tasks, like assessing volume licensing compliance and storage requirements. It might just become a part of your regular workflow routine.

Consider a quarterly business review or audit requirement for licensing. The MAP toolkit can help with discovering which servers and desktops are running SQL Server, and it can create reports to show to both technical and management audiences.

Total Cost of Ownership calculator

The TCO calculator helps with migrations to Azure. Using the TCO calculator, you can enter data for workloads individually, categorized by server, database, storage, and networking. You can also add information about Azure options, existing licensing via Software Assurance, and more costs—even your local price per kilowatt-hour of electricity.

➤ You can find this tool online at *https://azure.microsoft.com/pricing/tco/calculator/*.

If you sign in, there is also an option to download and upload these workloads in an Excel worksheet; each workload has its own tab. The Excel worksheet contains comments to help you understand how to fill it out.

To make this task easier and comparable, the calculator uses industry standard averages provided by Nucleus Research as a starting point. These can be adjusted; however, the industry standards make decisions easier when a value is not clear to you. Like with any TCO calculator, the more accurate the input, the more accurate the output.

The final report contains your estimated cost savings over the years. It includes categories such as compute, datacenter, networking, labor, storage savings, and detailed breakdowns on these values.

You can run this tool repeatedly to compare versions. The TCO calculator can be a powerful and standardized way to quantify the long-term impact of a cloud migration when used along with other available options in this list.

Database Experimentation Assistant

The DEA is a tool for evaluating upgrades of SQL Server with specific workloads. The foundation of the DEA is Distributed Replay, a feature that has been deprecated in SQL Server 2022.

> ➤ For more information about DEA, and a link to download it, visit *https://learn.microsoft.com /sql/dea/database-experimentation-assistant-overview*.

The DEA can test workloads coming from SQL Server versions as early as 2005. The purpose of the DEA is to give you confidence in a successful upgrade. This is a first step in your analysis to determine the types of issues, if any, you might encounter in an upgrade scenario with on-premises servers.

This tool can be instrumental in creating a baseline for testing upgrades and comparing workloads. The DEA looks for:

- SQL code that has compatibility issues

- SQL code that might run slower

- Query plans that might run slower

- Workload comparisons between the different versions

These issues and comparisons are found using Distributed Replay, first introduced in SQL Server 2012 and originally only a command line tool. It has since been expanded to provide a graphical user interface (GUI) and simpler setup.

The tool collects data via system traces. You run a workload on a machine and collect the workload; then you can "replay" that workload on other SQL Server versions, configurations, or setups. The data collection can be run for a single database or multiple databases, including all the databases on an instance, which could include linked servers.

After the analysis is run, the tool provides a report showing the performance implications based on a threshold you choose. For example, if you deem a 7 percent improvement to be a notable amount, set the threshold to **7%**, and the report will reflect any improvement as better than 7 percent and any degradation as worse. These are shown in a pie chart; you can drill into each section for further details. Summary statistics and graphs for individual queries display how many queries have degraded, errored, improved, stayed the same, or did not have enough information.

This tool can be run multiple times. Once it has been set up with a workload, it is relatively easy to use that workload to compare many different setups, configurations, and versions.

You can capture and replay the workload on Azure SQL Database and Azure SQL Managed Instance, with the additional requirement of using an Azure Blob Storage account to store the captured trace data.

> ## Inside OUT
>
> **Can the Data Experimentation Assistant (DEA) be used only for version comparison?**
>
> The DEA can be used for hardware changes, configuration changes, and feature comparisons between different versions of SQL Server. You can also use this feature to test other changes. For example, you can test the performance a different index would have on your workload by not changing anything other than the index.

Azure Data Migration Assistant

You can use the DMA to find compatibility issues and other migration challenges when targeting SQL Server on a variety of platforms. DMA can recommend performance improvements and allows you to move a schema, data, and uncontained objects from a source to a target server. This is a first step in your analysis to determine the types of issues you might encounter in an upgrade scenario or migration to Azure SQL Database.

When targeting an Azure PaaS database, DMA:

- Finds compatibility issues with the Azure version

- Finds partially supported or unsupported features

- Identifies new features in the target that are recommended for performance, security, and storage enhancements

- Provides recommendations on how to resolve issues

When targeting SQL Server on-premises or in an Azure virtual machine (VM), the DMA:

- Detects compatibility issues for upgrades

- Identifies feature recommendations and potential benefits for performance, security, and storage enhancements

In migrations to Azure or to an on-premises SQL Server, DMA can help migrate:

- Database schemas

- Data and users

- Server roles

- Logins (Windows and SQL Server)

➤ You can download DMA from the download center, at *https://www.microsoft.com/download /details.aspx?id=53595.*

NOTE

The DMA does not support migration to Azure SQL Managed Instance. For more on this, see the section at the end of this chapter on the Azure SQL Migration extension for ADS.

If you intend to use DMA on a production database, it is recommended that you run it during non-peak workload times, and run each piece for the assessment separately. For example, run the compatibility issues and new features recommendations at different times to avoid consuming too many resources. To reduce performance impact, it is best to run DMA on a machine other than the SQL Server host.

If you are migrating logins or data across networks, use Transport Layer Security (TLS) encryption. This will slow your migration but is worth the added overhead. Be sure your test run is encrypted so your estimates are accurate.

DMA can be run multiple times without issue. It is recommended to run it as often as needed to resolve all issues before migration. It is also useful for informational purposes when running upgrades. Even if you are not migrating to another server or the cloud, this tool can make you aware of potential issues in performing an in-place upgrade.

Inside OUT

How do you handle agent jobs when using DMA?

DMA does not copy linked servers, SQL Server Agent jobs, or Service Broker endpoints. Check out the open-source tools at the end of this section for options to re-create what is needed after migration.

Specifics for Linux migrations

While the overall migration workflow for Windows and Linux is the same, the move from Windows to Linux requires a couple of additional considerations.

Linux and Windows use different path formats and path separator characters. As a result, to migrate to SQL Server on Linux, the user must provide both the Windows and Linux versions of the path to the location of the physical file. You can provide both versions of the path in different ways depending on the location of the physical file. Use Samba to share the file with other computers on the network. Use the mount command to mount the share onto the computer running Linux.

Although the migration of AD logins is officially supported by SQL Server on Linux, it requires additional configuration to work successfully. The details are outside the scope of this chapter, but can be found at *https://learn.microsoft.com/sql/linux/sql-server-linux-active-directory -authentication*.

After performing the required configuration, you can migrate AD logins as usual. Standard SQL authentication works as expected without any additional setup.

Azure Database Migration Service

The Azure DMS is a managed service designed specifically for the migration of multiple databases. SQL Server sources and Azure SQL targets are naturally supported, but DMS can also facilitate migrations from PostgreSQL, MySQL, AWS RDS, and MongoDB. DMS migration targets include Azure SQL Managed Instance, Azure SQL Database, Azure Database for PostgreSQL, Azure Database for MySQL, and Azure Cosmos DB.

DMS is actually two different versions of a service developed by Microsoft to facilitate migrations to Azure database platforms using a fully managed Azure infrastructure. The original version of DMS is driven entirely by the Azure portal, and a newer version is driven by the Azure SQL Migration extension for Azure Data Studio (ADS). This is an important distinction as DMS continues to evolve. The original version is currently labeled as "Legacy – to be deprecated," and by the time you read this book, might already have been replaced. We recommend using DMS solutions provided by ADS when possible. Not all combinations of sources and targets have been developed for the newer, ADS-driven experience at the time of this writing.

Microsoft Docs provides tutorials for migrations of SQL Servers using the Azure portal or ADS. As this product continues to be actively developed with the ADS solution, use the documentation for the latest steps and features.

DMS is a combination of DMA that generates assessments and a migration service that performs the steps needed to migrate the data to the cloud.

The DMS Standard compute tier for offline migrations is completely free. The premium tier, which allows for both online and offline migration, is free for 183 days from the creation of the service, after which it charges hourly.

Inside OUT

Is DMS available everywhere?

At the time of this writing DMS is available in most regions, with a few exceptions. Availability might have changed since, though, so always check the up-to-date list here: *https://azure.microsoft.com/global-infrastructure/services/?products=database-migration*.

Using DMS to perform an online migration requires creating an instance based on the premium pricing tier. DMS can perform both online (continuous sync) and offline migrations. It is recommended that if you are migrating only SQL Server databases, you should access your existing database(s) with DMA. For other SQL offering source migrations, access your existing database with SSMA.

With an offline migration, the downtime begins at the time the migration begins. To limit your downtime, you should use the online migration options to keep things in sync for the time between migration completion and application reconfiguration to cut over to the migration target. The online option allows for minimal downtime.

Inside OUT

How do you know how long a migration will take?

Regardless of the migration method used for the live cutover, it is recommended that an offline migration be done during testing to determine the approximate length of time for the migration. This rough estimate will also help you determine if an offline migration is possible for your scenario.

To improve performance, also consider using the multi-CPU general purpose pricing tier when you create your service instance. This will enable the service to take advantage of multiple vCPUs for parallelization and faster data transfer during the migration period and change tiers when complete. Alternatively, you can temporarily scale up your Azure SQL Database target instance to the premium tier during the data migration operation to minimize Azure SQL Database throttling that might affect data transfer activities when using lower-level SKUs.

Azure SQL Migration extension for Azure Data Studio

When you choose the newer Azure Database Migration Service in the Azure portal, you are prompted to install ADS and the Azure SQL Migration extension for ADS. The extension assists with DMS migrations, including for multiple databases to Azure collectively. This is particularly useful when you have multiple dependent databases that need to be migrated at once.

At the time of this book's writing, the Azure SQL Migration extension for ADS can perform migrations to SQL Server on Azure VM or Azure SQL Managed Instance. More targets could be introduced after this book is published. For other platforms not yet supported by the extension, use the legacy DMS wizard in the Azure portal.

➤ The extension is available in the Extensions Marketplace, at *https://marketplace.visualstudio .com/items?itemName=ms-databasemigration.data-access-migration-toolkit*.

Once installed, the Migration extension is a global extension made available in any of your database context menus. Right-click the instance under **Servers**, and choose **Manage**. Then, under **General**, choose **Azure SQL Migration**. (See Figure 19-1.)

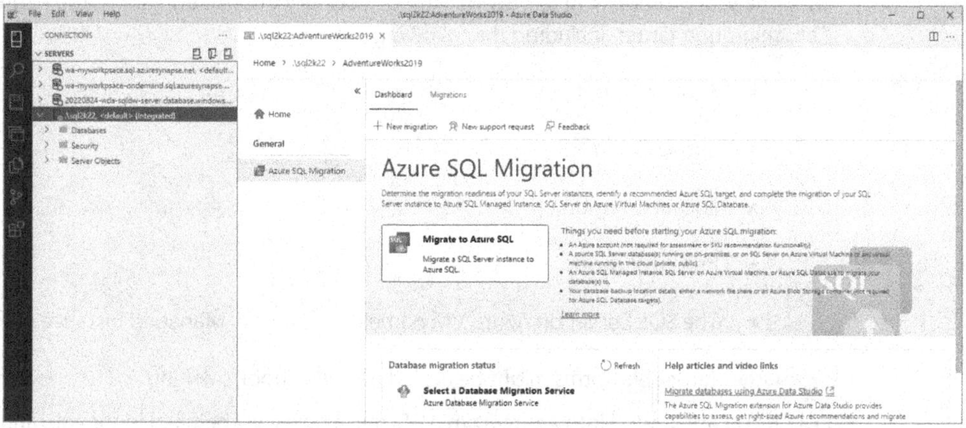

Figure 19-1 Azure SQL Migration extension in ADS.

When you select the large **Migrate to Azure SQL** button on the Azure SQL Migration page (refer to Figure 19-1), you see two options: **Start a new session** and **Resume a saved session**. Remember: The DMS is a fully managed cloud service, and this ADS-based wizard will guide you all the way to a completed migration.

Let's review what happens next:

1. The tool detects every database you are currently connected to in ADS. Assess any online database on the instance.

2. The tool assess the viability of the database for migration. Depending on the outcome of that assessment, it lists options in the **Choose your Azure SQL Target** section. Each option comes with a recommended configuration once performance data has been collected.

    If you choose to have ADS collect performance data now, it is important to collect that data at peak workload to accurately reflect the database's workload. So, do this step during a busy workday.

The minimum amount of time for a performance reading is 10 minutes, but the longer you let it run, the more accurate it becomes. If you've collected performance data using this tool before, select it from its stored location.

After you have collected a representative sample of performance data on the databases to be migrated, stop the collection. A procedural recommendation will be displayed; you can choose to scale up or down Azure resources based on the observed data. By default, only up to the 95th percentile of observed activity will be considered. This can also be customized.

You can take advantage of any preview service tiers of hardware. For example, the Azure SQL Managed Instance Memory Optimized – Premium series tier is in preview at the time of this writing.

3. The tool prompts you to provide all the necessary information about the Azure SQL migration target, including the following:

    -   Azure account

    -   Subscription

    -   Location region

    -   Resource group

    -   The SQL Server on Azure VM name or Azure SQL Managed Instance of your target

    Other target platforms might be added after this book's writing.

    If you are logged into Azure from ADS, these fields will be filled in for you, and you can adjust selections with the drop-down menus.

4. The tool prompts you to choose whether you want to migrate online or offline. For an offline migration, the application downtime begins when the migration starts. With an online migration, the downtime is limited to the cutover at the end of migration. (Note that the premium DMS service is required for an online migration; again, this is free for 183 days).

5. Now you designate where you previously placed the backup you want to migrate. You must choose a recent backup or create a new backup and use the WITH CHECKSUM option. The backup can be in your infrastructure in a network share or you can upload it to an Azure Blob Storage container.

6. The Migration service orchestrates the migration activities and tracks progress. The option is to create a new migration project or use one that was previously created if available.

7. The final step is to review all the details and ensure nothing has been missed or is incorrect. Once you have verified the details, the migration is ready to start.

While the migration is running you will see a window on the Azure SQL Migration screen that updates you on the status of the migration. (See Figure 19-2.) In the top-right corner of the window is a **Refresh** button to allow for manual refreshes of the window. When the migration is complete, you can expand each bar in the window to see more details.

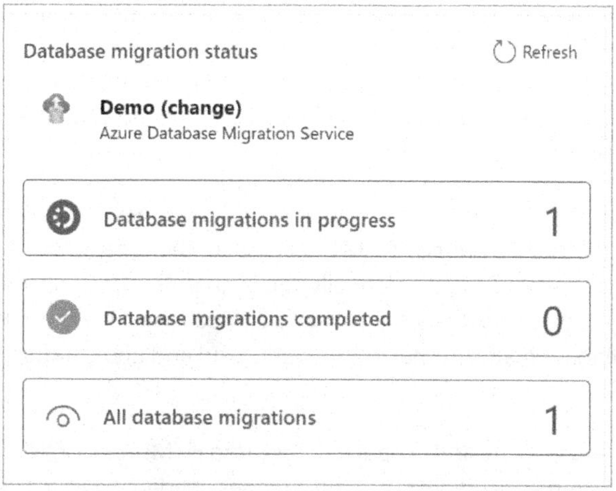

Figure 19-2 Database migration status.

SQL Server Migration Assistant

The SSMA was designed specifically for migration of non-SQL Server workloads to a SQL Server machine. This includes Microsoft Access, DB2, MySQL, Oracle, and SAP ASE. Each of these sources has very different requirements and processes for migration.

Despite its age, the SSMA remains actively developed, and a new version was released in August 2022. Support for migrations to Azure Synapse Analytics (from Oracle only) was recently introduced.

For the most current information, it is recommended that you review the documentation directly for each solution:

- **Microsoft Access.** *https://learn.microsoft.com/sql/ssma/access/sql-server-migration -assistant-for-access-accesstosql.*

- **DB2.** *https://learn.microsoft.com/sql/ssma/db2/migrating-db2-data-into-sql-server-db2tosql.*

- **MySQL.** *https://learn.microsoft.com/sql/ssma/mysql/sql-server-migration-assistant-for -mysql-mysqltosql.*

- **Oracle.** *https://learn.microsoft.com/sql/ssma/oracle/sql-server-migration-assistant-for -oracle-oracletosql.*

- **SAP Adaptive Server Enterprise (ASE) (formerly SAP Sybase ASE).** *https://learn .microsoft.com/sql/ssma/sybase/sql-server-migration-assistant-for-sybase-sybasetosql.*

Data Access Migration Toolkit

The DAMT is a new Visual Studio Code extension developed by Microsoft, currently in preview. It is designed to scan your code solutions and identify actions needed for migration to SQL Server.

> ➤ You can download and install the DAMT to your local installation of Visual Studio Code here: *https://marketplace.visualstudio.com/items?itemName=ms-databasemigration.data-access-migration-toolkit.*

DAMT can help identify compatibility issues as well as extract SQL queries and data access APIs (in Java only, at the time of this book's writing). DAMT helps cover the other important part of a database platform migration: the application. Manually checking potentially billions of lines of nested code for deprecated code and for functionality and compatibility issues can be impractical. Often, this aspect of database platform changes is overlooked and understaffed, and often many issues are missed.

DAMT scans Java and .NET source code and produces a report in HTML and JSON of its findings. This report provides a summary and details of the changes needed. You can use the HTML report to plan your pre-migration application development efforts. You can use the JSON version as an input for DMA to obtain additional information before you attempt your migration.

Inside OUT

Can you run the toolkit against test files?

Yes. An excellent way to verify that all the updates and changes have been made to the file, stored procedures, and SQL statements is to branch off your Git repository. Then, as you make changes to the new branch, continually check it to make sure you are not missing something as your migration project progresses.

Resolve common migration failures using Database Migration Service

The following list outlines the most common issues with SQL Server migrations to Azure SQL. Other database platforms might have other nuances and migration blockers to SQL Server. The majority of migration failures occur with online migrations.

> ➤ For known migration issues with third party database vendors, visit *https://learn.microsoft.com/azure/dms/known-issues-troubleshooting-dms.*

- Support for online migrations to Azure SQL Database using DMS extends only to Enterprise, Standard, and Developer editions, so ensure you are using a supported edition before beginning.

- *Certain data types* are not supported. The SQL server `sql_variant` data type is not currently supported by DMS for online migrations to Azure SQL Database. To check your tables for this data type, run the following query:

```
SELECT DISTINCT c.TABLE_NAME,c.COLUMN_NAME,c.DATA_TYPE
FROM INFORMATION_SCHEMA.columns AS c
WHERE c.data_type in ('sql_variant');
```

- Timestamp columns are not migrated as the source timestamp value. Azure generates a new timestamp value in the target table. If you need the source value migrated instead, contact the engineering team at *AskAzureDatabaseMigrations@service.microsoft.com*.

- DMS only supports SQL Server backups created with a checksum. Verify the SQL Server backups you choose for the migration have been taken WITH CHECKSUM. (This is usually a good idea anyway.) If you choose to let DMS take the backup, it will be taken with checksum.

- DMS also does not support SQL Server backups that are appended to a single backup. Ensure each full and log backup are written to separate files.

- DMS does not support migrating SQL Server databases with more than one transaction log file. This is usually a bad idea anyway. Resolve this problem before migrating.

- The SQL Server FILESTREAM and FileTable features are not supported for Azure SQL Managed Instance. The source database can't contain a FILESTREAM filegroup. For workloads that depend on these features, migrate to Azure VMs instead.

- In-memory OLTP is not available in the DTU Standard or vCore general purpose tier for Azure SQL Database. If your source SQL Server uses in-memory objects, choose either the premium or business critical tier of Azure SQL Database *as the migration target.*

- SQL Server *temporal tables* might present challenges for online migration. Be cautious when using these tables. You can use the following code to determine which, if any, of your tables are temporal:

```
SELECT name, temporal_type, temporal_type_desc
FROM sys.tables
WHERE temporal_type <> 0;
```

- Active *triggers* could create challenges for online migration because they might fire during the migration. Use the following code to determine if you have any active triggers. DMS disables and enables triggers for some database sources, but for others, it might be necessary to manually disable all triggers in the database before taking the backup that will be used for the migration. Enable triggers after the database migration is complete, and before application activity is restored.

```
SELECT s.name 'Schema', T.name 'Table Name', G.name 'Trigger'
FROM sys.tables AS T
INNER JOIN sys.triggers AS G ON G.parent_id = T.object_id
INNER JOIN sys.schemas AS S ON s.schema_id = t.schema_id
WHERE is_disabled = 0;
```

Large object columns with data larger than 32 KB

Large object data types might require special handling. In this context, these are data types that exceed the maximum row size of 8,000 bytes. Columns larger than 32 KB might get truncated at the target. You can use the following code to determine which, if any, of your columns will be affected. This script might take a while to run on databases with many tables and columns.

```
DROP TABLE IF EXISTS #results;
CREATE TABLE #results (tablename nvarchar(256), columnname sysname, [datalength_bytes]
bigint, INDEX cl_results CLUSTERED (tablename, columnname) );
DECLARE @tablename nvarchar(256), @columnname sysname;
DECLARE cur_columns CURSOR LOCAL FAST_FORWARD FOR
SELECT schema_name(o.schema_id)+'.['+o.name+']', c.name
FROM sys.columns AS c
INNER JOIN sys.objects AS o ON c.object_id = o.object_id
WHERE o.type_desc = 'user_table';
OPEN cur_columns;
FETCH NEXT FROM cur_columns INTO @tablename, @columnname;
WHILE @@FETCH_STATUS=0
BEGIN
    INSERT INTO #results (tablename, columnname, [datalength_bytes])
    EXEC ('SELECT '''
        +@tablename+''', '''
        +@columnname+''', MAX(datalength(['+@columnname+']))'
        +  ' FROM ' +@tablename);
    FETCH NEXT FROM cur_columns INTO @tablename, @columnname;
END
CLOSE cur_columns;
DEALLOCATE cur_columns;
SELECT tablename, columnname, [datalength_bytes] FROM #results
WHERE [datalength_bytes] > 32765;
```

Final notes for migration

When the migration of your data is complete, there are a few more items you want to include in your migration plan. These relate to connectivity error handling, security, and the application.

Once your data has migrated, the most important thing is being able to connect to it. To find your connection string, locate the resource in the Azure portal, whether it is an Azure SQL Database or an Azure SQL Managed Instance. Then, in the pane on the left side of the screen, select **Settings** and then **Connection Strings** to find the details you need based on the connection type you want. Options include ADO.NET (SQL Authentication), JDBC (SQL Authentication), ODBC (includes Node.js and SQL Authentication), PHP (SQL Authentication), and Go (SQL Authentication). Each of these options provides a link to download the associated driver for SQL Server as well.

Open source PowerShell migration with dbatools

There is a well-developed, community-driven open source option to automate many SQL Server administrative tasks, including migration, available at *https://dbatools.io*. This open source PowerShell library was created by Chrissy LeMaire, a Data Platform and PowerShell MVP; a host of DBAs worldwide help to expand and improve the library.

> ➤ To perform an offline migration of an on-premises SQL Server to Azure SQL Managed Instance with dbatools, review this Microsoft blog post by a member of the Microsoft SQL Server product team at *https://techcommunity.microsoft.com/t5/Azure-SQL-Database /Automate-migration-to-SQL-Managed-Instance-using-Azure/ba-p/830801*.

For this offline migration process, Azure PowerShell controls and manages the Azure resources and dbatools initiates the migration of the logins and agent jobs. This process requires that you have version 150.18147.0 or higher of Microsoft.SqlServer.SqlManagementObjects, the SQL Server Management Objects (SMO) library.

If you want to perform an online migration, use DMS.

Offline migration with dbatools

Some prerequisites before getting started:

- It's recommended to use dbatools with at least PowerShell 5.1, the version installed in Windows 10 and Windows Server 2019. Newer versions are supported, such as PowerShell 7 (recommended).

- The location you are executing the PowerShell commands from needs access to both the source SQL Server and the target managed instance.

- You can install dbatools from the online PowerShell Gallery with the command `Install -Module -Name dbatools`. If the PowerShell Gallery isn't accessible from your workstation, offline installation alternatives are provided at *https://dbatools.io/offline*.

- You might have your favorite PowerShell terminal or scripting environment, but Visual Studio Code with the official PowerShell extension is as good as any. The Windows Power-Shell Integrated Scripting Environment (ISE), which was the standard host for PowerShell scripting for a long time, is no longer actively developed.

- To use this open-source solution, you need the `Az.Resources`, `Az.Storage`, and `dbatools` modules. If you have access to the PowerShell Gallery, you can use the following PowerShell commands to obtain them:

```
Install-Module -Name Az.Resources
Install-Module -Name Az.Storage
Install-Module -Name dbatools
```

Migration code

Each of the following sample scripts initializes the variables needed for each step. You can update each one for your environment names (your resource group name, for example). Create a new storage account for temporary use to hold the migrated data. You can remove this temporary storage account at the end; there is an example that shows you how to do just that at the end of this section.

The scripts in this section's examples use the Azure public endpoint to connect to Azure SQL Managed Instance. For more transport security when it comes time to migrate your production data, set up a point-to-site virtual private network (VPN) or Azure ExpressRoute. Alternatively, run the script from a VM that is placed in the same subnet as your managed instance.

Storage setup

To move your databases, you need a temporary Azure Blob Storage account. If you already have one you'd like to use, you can skip this step.

If you choose to create a new Azure Blob Storage account for this purpose, note that names are limited to a maximum of 24 characters, can contain only numbers and lowercase letters, and must be globally unique within Azure.

Choose or create a storage account in the same region as your Azure SQL managed instance. This makes a significant difference in the speed of the database restore process. If you load your data in a different region, there could be delays and extra cost incurred to move it to the region of the SQL managed instance.

The following PowerShell script creates an Azure Blob Storage account that will be used in this example:

```
$resourceGroup = "YourResourceGroupName"
$location = "northeurope" # Refer to Get-AzLocation
$containerName = "mycontainername"
$blobStorageAccountName = "newstorageaccountname" # must be unique in Azure
New-AzResourceGroup -Name $resourceGroup -Location $location
$storageAccount = New-AzStorageAccount -ResourceGroupName $resourceGroup `
-Name $blobStorageAccountName `
-Location $location `
-SkuName "Standard_LRS" `
-Kind "StorageV2"
$ctx = $storageAccount.Context
New-AzStorageContainer -Name $containerName -Context $ctx -Permission Container
```

Execute this script to create the temporary Azure Blob Storage account to use for migrating your data into Azure.

Source instance setup

Generate the shared access signature (SAS) key, which enables your SQL Server instance to access the Azure Blob Storage account and puts the database backups in that location. This SAS key should be stored in the credential object on the source SQL Server instance. For example, the following sample script using the dbatools cmdlet New-DbaCredential:

```
$sourceInstance = "servername" # or servername/instancename
$sas = (New-AzStorageAccountSASToken -Service Blob -ResourceType Object `
-Permission "rw" -Context $ctx).TrimStart("?")
$sourceCred = New-DbaCredential -SqlInstance $sourceInstance `
-Name "https://$blobStorageAccount.blob.core.windows.net/$containerName" `
-Identity "SHARED ACCESS SIGNATURE" `
-SecurePassword (ConvertTo-SecureString $sas -AsPlainText -Force)
```

Database migration

Place backups of your SQL Server database(s) in Azure Blob Storage. The simplest way is to back up directly to a URL. Here is where dbatools comes in:

```
$sourceInstance = "servername" # or servername/instancename
$sourcedatabase = "databasename"
Backup-DbaDatabase -SqlInstance $sourceInstance -Database $sourceDatabase `
-AzureBaseUrl "https://$blobStorageAccount.blob.core.windows.net/$containerName" `
-BackupFileName "WideWorldImporters.bak" `
-Type Full -Checksum -CopyOnly
```

To migrate multiple databases, place them in the Database parameter value, in a comma-separated list.

If you are taking a backup of a large database, you might also want to create backups on multiple files (striped backups) and set some of the following parameters: COMPRESSION, MAXTRANSFERSIZE = 4194304, BLOCKSIZE = 65536.

➤ For more information on striped backups, see Chapter 10, "Develop, deploy, and manage data recovery."

Migrating databases to target instance

The migration stage takes place on your SQL managed instance. This requires you to create a SAS token that will enable Azure SQL Managed Instance to read a .bak file from Azure Blob Storage, create a credential with this SAS token, and restore the databases:

```
## Generate new SAS token that will read .bak file
$sas = (New-AzStorageAccountSASToken -Service Blob -ResourceType Object `
-Permission "r" -Context $ctx).TrimStart('?')
# -ResourceType Container,Object
$targetLogin = Get-Credential -Message "Login to target Managed Instance as:"
$target = Connect-DbaInstance -SqlInstance $targetInstance -SqlCredential $targetLogin
```

```
$targetCred = New-DbaCredential -SqlInstance $target `
-Name "https://$blobStorageAccount.blob.core.windows.net/$containerName" `
-Identity "SHARED ACCESS SIGNATURE" `
-SecurePassword (ConvertTo-SecureString $sas -AsPlainText -Force) `
-Force

Restore-DbaDatabase -SqlInstance $target -Database $targetDatabase `
-Path "https://$blobStorageAccount.blob.core.windows.net/$containerName/WideWorld
Importers.bak"
```

This script prompts for the SQL login details that should be used to access the managed instance. It results in the selected database backup being restored on the target managed instance, completing your database migration.

Server-level objects migration

After you migrate your database objects, you might still need to migrate server-level objects such as SQL Agent jobs and operators or logins. The dbatools Copy-Dba* commands provide a set of useful scripts that you can apply to migrate these objects.

Of the set of commands that follow, use and customize only those relevant to your environment. As mentioned, this is where you can migrate SQL Server Agent jobs, linked servers, and endpoints.

➤ If you do not see the command you need here, review the documentation at *https://docs .dbatools.io.*

```
$sourceInstance = "servername" # or servername/instancename
$targetInstance = "myserver.public.instancename.database.windows.net,3342"
# Azure SQL Managed Instance name with port
$targetLogin = Get-Credential
# provide sign in credential for the target SQL Server instance,
# for example, a SQL Authenticated username and password
Copy-DbaSysDbUserObject -Source $sourceInstance -Destination $targetInstance `
-DestinationSqlCredential $targetLogin
Copy-DbaDbMail -Source $sourceInstance -Destination $targetInstance `
-DestinationSqlCredential $targetLogin
Copy-DbaAgentOperator -Source $sourceInstance -Destination $targetInstance `
-DestinationSqlCredential $targetLogin
Copy-DbaAgentJobCategory -Source $sourceInstance -Destination $targetInstance `
-DestinationSqlCredential $targetLogin
Copy-DbaAgentJob -Source $sourceInstance -Destination $.targetInstance `
-DestinationSqlCredential $targetLogin
Copy-DbaAgentSchedule -Source $sourceInstance -Destination $targetInstance `
-DestinationSqlCredential $targetLogin
Copy-DbaLogin -Source $sourceInstance -Destination $targetInstance `
-DestinationSqlCredential $targetLogin -ExcludeSystemLogins
Copy-DbaLinkedServer -Source $sourceInstance -Destination $targetInstance `
-DestinationSqlCredential $targetLogin
Copy-DbaEndpoint -Source $sourceInstance -Destination $targetInstance `
-DestinationSqlCredential $targetLogin
```

Cleanup process for PowerShell migration

If the Azure Blob Storage account you used for the migration is meant to be temporary, you can remove it using the following PowerShell command. It is good practice to always clean up resources you no longer need.

```
$resourceGroupName = "YourResourceGroupName"
$blobStorageAccountName = "newstorageaccountname"
Remove-AzStorageAccount -ResourceGroupName $resourceGroupName -Name `
$blobStorageAccountName -Force
```

Migrate with Azure Data Factory

ADF contains tools that can be used to integrate and migrate data. ADF integration runtime (IR) is a service that allows integration of data across different network environments. IRs are also used for data migration; however, they are typically not used for full migrations, but rather as a part of an ongoing process of migrating data.

An ADF IR can also be used to read and write data between on-premises and cloud data sources. An IR provides the compute environment where the activity either runs from or gets dispatched from.

ADF *pipelines* define the IR that dispatches an activity. ADF stores the JSON of the data movement and metadata of the database where the dispatching is initiated. This is not only important for compliance, security, and performance, but also for egress costs. ADF has been optimized for a global service reach by allowing the IR to exist in a different location from the ADF it belongs to.

> ➤ A list of regions in which ADF is available can be found at *https://azure.microsoft.com/global -infrastructure/services/?products=data-factory*.

ADF has three different types of integration runtimes: Azure IR, self-hosted IR, and the Azure-SSIS IR. Let's look at each in the next three sections.

Azure integration runtime

The Azure IR dispatches activities, usually between Azure resources. There is no infrastructure or patching, and you only pay for the actual utilization.

You might find there is a point where more data integration units (DIUs) cost more money, but because the IR is running more quickly, they might be less expensive overall. (DIUs are a measure that represents the power of a single unit in ADF—a combination of CPU, memory, and network resource allocation.) A different default number of DIUs is used for various scenarios. You can override the default by specifying a (usually higher) value in the dataIntegrationUnits property. DIUs only apply to Azure IRs.

Data flows versus the copy data activity

In ADF, data flows perform data transformations. Behind the scenes, they use scaled-out Spark clusters. These activities can be operationalized using existing ADF scheduling, control, flow, and monitoring capabilities. Low-code and GUI based, they are very user friendly and require no writing of code. Data flows can only be executed by Azure IRs, not by self-hosted IRs or Azure SSIS runtimes.

The Copy activity can be executed by Azure IRs or self-hosted IRs. The Copy activity has built-in connectors for a huge variety of Azure services, databases, NoSQL platforms, file storage plat-forms, HTTP, OData, ODBC, REST, and even external services and applications.

> ➤ For a complete list of supported Copy activity data stores and formats, see *https://learn .microsoft.com/azure/data-factory/copy-activity-overview#supported-data-stores-and -formats.*

Azure integration runtime location

It is considered best practice to choose the same region as the destination data store. This might require you to create a new Azure IR in a particular region.

When an ADF instance is created, an Azure IR named AutoResolveIntegrationRuntime is auto-matically deployed. This IR cannot be removed. This does not automatically mean it is a good idea to use it, however, for two reasons:

- The location of the ADF instance could cause a compliance issue—for example, if the data needs to stay in a particular region. This is a typical need for governments, finance, and other institutions. To work around this, you can create the runtime in the needed region and use the connectVia property in your linked services definition to force the use of that runtime. Linked services are JSON-defined connections between a data store and the IR. The connectVia property is specified in JSON and refers to the name of the Azure IR or self-hosted IR.

> ➤ For more information, see *https://learn.microsoft.com/azure/data-factory/concepts-linked -services.*

- Queue times for activity startup can be longer in the AutoResolveIntegrationRuntime, which is assigned resources from the Azure region. This works fine in most cases. The service-level agreement (SLA) for startup time is 4 minutes, so this is not the instant execution you might be used to with SQL Server Agent jobs and SSIS packages. You can reduce queueing time by choosing your own IR and/or increasing the time to live (TTL) value in your IR configuration. This will keep hold of resources longer before releasing them. This is especially helpful when you have a series of activities to execute in a limited span of time, but there are delays or pauses between each. You cannot change the TTL of the AutoResolveIntegrationRuntime.

Self-hosted integration runtime

You can use the self-hosted IR both in the cloud and on a private network. This is a common method for moving data from on-premises to a cloud VM. An Azure IR is used to dispatch transform activities, such as a Stored Procedure activity.

We wouldn't use the self-hosted IR for a Databricks Notebook activity. This illustrates how these runtimes can be used collectively. The self-hosted IR can be used to move data to the cloud and then the Azure IR can be used to dispatch the transform activities from a Databricks notebook. Another typical use case for the self-hosted IR is to provide support for datastores that require you to bring your own driver.

➤ The full list of supported data stores for copy activities can be found at *https://learn.microsoft .com/azure/data-factory/copy-activity-overview#supported-data-stores-and-formats*.

The self-hosted IR runs only on Windows servers and must be installed on a machine inside the private network in which the source or target is located.

NOTE

For the purposes of ADF and because of the networking involved, an Azure VM is the equivalent of an on-premises server. If your data is stored in either, you will still need to use the self-hosted IR rather than the Azure IR.

You can share a self-hosted IR across multiple Azure data factories, but they must be in the same tenant. If you need to work across multiple tenants, you will need one self-hosted IR per tenant containing a data factory.

Self-hosted IR servers and nodes

There is a limit of only one self-hosted IR on a server. If you do not want to use a second server, share the self-hosted IR for two different data factories.

Shared data factories must be in the same Azure AD tenant and have a managed identity. Self-hosted IRs can be associated with multiple on-premises servers or Azure VMs, a sort of IR cluster. Each associated server is called a *node*. Each self-hosted IR can have up to four nodes, benefitting both HA and scalability. The additional nodes can improve performance and throughput during data movement between on-premises and cloud data stores. This scale-out lends itself to HA and multi-node self-hosted IR use cases.

➤ For more information, see *https://learn.microsoft.com/azure/data-factory/create-self -hosted-integration-runtime?tabs=data-factory#high-availability-and-scalability*.

Inside OUT

Should the self-hosted IR be on the same server as the data source?

It is recommended that the self-hosted IR be on a different server, but close to the data source. Being on a different server prevents it from competing with the data source for resources. Having the server that hosts the self-hosted IR nearby reduces as much network latency as possible. It is recommended that you do not co-locate an ADF self-hosted IR and a Power BI on-premises in a data gateway on the same machine.

➤ Step-by-step instructions for creating a self-hosted IR using PowerShell can be found at *https://learn.microsoft.com/azure/data-factory/self-hosted-integration-runtime -automation-scripts*.

Potential issues with self-hosted integration runtimes

There are tasks that might fail in a self-hosted IR. The many steps that go into setting up the integrations and systems vary based on workload and use case. For this reason, Microsoft maintains up-to-date documentation on common issues and their solutions at *https://learn.microsoft .com/azure/data-factory/self-hosted-integration-runtime-troubleshoot-guide*. This link includes information on how to view the error logs if you are unfamiliar, and is updated regularly with common issues people encounter.

Azure-SSIS integration runtime

The Azure-SSIS IR can be used both in the cloud and on-premises. This IR is installed in Azure and joined to a private network to support data access.

The Azure-SSIS IR is made up of a cluster of Azure VMs that you can scale manually by specifying the number of nodes in the cluster. You regulate runtime costs by ensuring you stop the runtime when it is not being used.

This runtime supports packages deployed to an SSIS Catalog (SSISDB) running on Azure SQL Database. You can deploy your existing SSIS packages to the Azure-SSIS IR with minimal modification. When your SSIS project's deployment target is an Azure SQL Database, it uses the project deployment model (recommended). When the deployment target is a file system, it deploys with a package deployment model.

After the runtime is provisioned, you can use either SQL Server Data Tools, SQL Server Management Studio, or the command line tools (`dtinstall`/`dtutil`/`dtexec`) to deploy and run SSIS packages in Azure.

Azure-SSIS integration runtime location

The location of the Azure-SSIS IR is important to ensure the best performance of any data integration processes. Although the location of the Azure-SSIS IR does not need to be the same as the ADF, it should be in the same region where the Azure SQL Database hosting the SSISDB is located to limit the traffic between two regions.

When possible, it is best if the Azure-SSIS IR and the Azure SQL Database are in the same virtual network (VNet) to minimize data movement.

> ➤ For step-by-step directions on how to set up an Azure-SSIS IR, see *https://learn.microsoft* *.com/azure/data-factory/tutorial-deploy-ssis-packages-azure#create-an-azure-ssis* *-integration-runtime/.*

Best practices for security and resilience during migration

Finally, let's review some strategic and tactical best practices for your data migration.

Network security

During database migration, provide a single file share location when possible. This shared folder should be accessible by the source server and the target server to avoid a copy operation. A copy operation might introduce a delay based on the size of the backup file, and the added step increases the chances of failure.

You must provide the correct, minimal permissions to the shared folder to avoid migration failures or, conversely, to avoid accidentally exposing data. The shared folder should also be temporary in nature to avoid unnecessarily storing a large amount of sensitive data. The permissions can be specified in DMA, for example. If the SQL Server instance runs under network service credentials, temporarily give the correct permissions on the network share to the machine account for the SQL Server instance.

For a secure migration, if connecting to the source and target servers over the public Internet, encrypt the connection. Using TLS encryption increases the security of data transmitted across the networks between DMA and the SQL Server instance. (TLS 1.3 is supported by SQL Server 2022 on Windows and its updated ODBC and OLEDB data providers.) This is particularly important when migrating SQL logins. TLS encryption prevents the SQL logins being migrated from being intercepted and/or modified on-the-fly by an attacker.

If all application access is transmitted across a secure internal network or private external network, encryption might not be required. Consider your application security and regulatory requirements. Enabling network transport encryption might slow performance due to the extra overhead involved in encrypting and decrypting packets.

Cloud requirements for application resilience

Cloud application architecture must be designed to gracefully handle intermittent network hiccups for more than a few seconds, for any reason. Similarly, once migrated from on-premises to Azure, it is important for legacy applications to be modified to gracefully handle and recover from transient network connectivity failures.

Transient connectivity issues can occur for a variety of expected reasons in any cloud platform. For example, when a PaaS database is moved or reconfigured, the application might momentarily lose connection to the database. These issues can be planned by the cloud provider (for example, load balancing or patching) or unplanned (for example, a failover). It is not a matter of if, but when, so all applications must be designed to be resilient when these failures occur in their error handling and connectivity retry components.

When reconnecting after a transient network connectivity issue, applications should not attempt to immediately reconnect and continue trying until they succeed. Instead, cloud-based applications should use an exponentially increasing wait with a randomized delay. This gradually connects each of the many clients to the cloud resources, reducing network congestion and avoiding a sudden resource overload. Retry delays are not typically present in many legacy applications designed to be on-premises. If these retry delays are not introduced after a cloud migration, they can create a ripple effect, unwittingly causing a denial of service (DoS) attack on your own cloud services!

There are many approaches to implementing retry logic with exponential back off. One of the ways developers might implement this is via the Microsoft.Data.SqlClient, which introduced a new configurable retry logic with version 3 in 2021. The retry logic can be configured through code or application configuration files.

➤ **For more information, see** *https://learn.microsoft.com/sql/connect/ado-net/configurable -retry-logic* and *https://learn.microsoft.com/azure/azure-sql/database/troubleshoot -common-connectivity-issues.*

Index

A

accelerated database recovery (ADR), 103, 107, 239–240, 335

access and authentication
  anonymous, 397–398
  Azure AD, 850–853, 909
  backup, 467
  database migration and, 226–227
  integrated authentication, 82–87
  Mixed Mode, 143
  modes of, 549–555
  permissions and authorization, 593–605
  right of access, 618
  role-based access control, 155, 794, 850, 853–854
  Shared Access Signature (SAS), 313–315, 468–469
  security principals, 555–593, 621
  security tasks, 605–615
  SMTP server, 399
  SQL Server via Linux, 206

access token, 553

ACID properties, 669

Active Expensive Queries, 35–36

active log, 106

Activity Monitor, 32–36

actual execution plans, 706, 709–710

ad hoc queries, 122, 172

addresses, TCP/IP, 627

administration/administrator
  availability group, 543–548
  Azure AD, 850–851
  Azure SQL Managed Instance, 903–908
  dedicated connections, 614–615
  footprint, 2
  foundations of automated, 394–412
  logins, 579–582
  Maintenance Plans, 414–425
  multiple-server, 428–434
  passwords, 209

PowerShell, 434–444
privileges, 199, 573–577
security tasks, xxix, 605–615
tools for, xxxi, 1

Advanced Data Security, 860

Advanced Encryption Standard (AES), 463, 637, 641, 645

affinity masks, 122–124

agent servers, 819, 920

alert notifications
  administrator, 38–39
  availability group, 548
  Azure SQL Managed Instance, 875
  SQL Server Agent, 407–410

alphanumeric data types, 250

Always Encrypted, 12, 642–648

Always On, 74

analytics, 309, 827, 906–907

antivirus exclusions, 171

append-only ledger tables, 655

application security groups (ASGs), 795, 796

applications, 675, 698, 701, 896–898, 905, 928, 938

architecture, Linux vs. Windows, 197

architecture, on-premises database
  configuration settings, 115–127
  data compression, 109–112
  data files and filegroups, 93–98
  file types, 93
  partition tables, 108–109
  temporary database management, 113–114
  transaction log, 99–108

assessment, upgrade, 4, 5

atomicity, 669, 671

attacks
  brute-force and dictionary, 623
  DDoS, 667–668
  ransomware, 451–453
  SQL injection, 599, 622, 652, 860, 912

auditing, 657–664, 854–859, 912

authentication. *See* access and authentication

authorization and permissions, 593–605, 621

auto close, 233

auto_create_stats, 420

auto_update_stats, 341, 784

autogrowth events, 344–345, 369

automatic failovers, 515–516

automatic plan correction, 745

automatic seeding, 518–521

automating scripts, 10

availability groups (AGs)
  administration, 543–548
  Always On, 74
  asynchronous commits, 79, 512–517, 546
  Azure SQL Database, 797
  backing up, 426–428
  capabilities of, 494–496
  designing, 502–532
  failovers in, 515–518
  hybrid topology, 531–532
  Linux, 81–82, 537–543
  multiserver administration in, 430
  PowerShell with, 442–444
  read-scale, 80, 510
  recent improvements, 509–512
  resource creation, 542
  seeding options, 518–522
  server-level options, 522–523
  service accounts, 579
  SQL Server Agent, 411–412
  synchronizing database replicas, 525
  synchronous commits, 79, 512–517, 546
  types of, 80–81
  WSFC with, 507–508

Average Disk seconds per Read or Write, 375–376

Plug into learning at

MicrosoftPressStore.com

The Microsoft Press Store by Pearson offers:

- Free U.S. shipping

- Buy an eBook, get three formats – Includes PDF, EPUB, and MOBI to use with your computer, tablet, and mobile devices

- Print & eBook Best Value Packs

- eBook Deal of the Week – Save up to 50% on featured title

- Newsletter – Be the first to hear about new releases, announcements, special offers, and more

- Register your book – Find companion files, errata, and product updates, plus receive a special coupon* to save on your next purchase

 Pearson